Great Lives from History

The 18th Century

1701-1800

Great Lives from History

The 18th Century

1701-1800

Volume 1
Fanny Abington - Little Turtle

Editor
John Powell
Oklahoma Baptist University

Editor, First Edition
Frank N. Magill

SALEM PRESS
Pasadena, California   Hackensack, New Jersey

Editor in Chief: Dawn P. Dawson

Editorial Director: Christina J. Moose

Acquisitions Editor: Mark Rehn

Research Supervisor: Jeffry Jensen

Research Assistant: Rebecca Kuzins

Manuscript Editors: Desiree Dreeuws, Andy Perry

Production Editor: Andrea E. Miller

Graphics and Design: James Hutson

Layout: Eddie Murillo

Photo Editor: Cynthia Breslin Beres

Editorial Assistant: Dana Garey

Cover photos: Pictured left to right, top to bottom: Alessandro Volta (The Granger Collection, New York), Toussaint Louverture (The Granger Collection, New York), Fanny Burney (The Granger Collection, New York), Catherine the Great (The Granger Collection, New York), Johann Sebastian Bach (The Granger Collection, New York), Mustafa III (Hulton Archive/Getty Images), Junípero Serra (The Granger Collection, New York), Betsy Ross (Library of Congress), Daniel Boone (The Granger Collection, New York)

∞ The paper used in these volumes conforms to the American National Standard for Permanence of Paper for Printed Library Materials, Z39.48-1992 (R1997).

Some of the essays in this work originally appeared in the following Salem Press sets: *Dictionary of World Biography* (© 1998-1999, edited by Frank N. Magill) and *Great Lives from History* (© 1987-1995, edited by Frank N. Magill). New material has been added.

Library of Congress Cataloging-in-Publication Data

Great lives from history. The 18th century, 1701-1800 / editor, John Powell ; editor, first edition, Frank N. Magill.
    p. cm.
   Some of the essays in this work were originally published in Dictionary of world biography and the series of works collectively titled, Great lives from history, both edited by Frank N. Magill.
   Includes bibliographical references and index.
   ISBN-13: 978-1-58765-276-9 (set : alk. paper)
   ISBN-10: 1-58765-276-5 (set : alk. paper)
   ISBN-13: 978-1-58765-277-6 (v. 1 : alk. paper)
   ISBN-10: 1-58765-277-3 (v. 1 : alk. paper)
   [etc.]
  1. Biography—18th century. I. Title: 18th century, 1701-1800. II. Title: Eighteenth century, 1701-1800.
III. Powell, John, 1954- IV. Magill, Frank Northen, 1907-1997. V. Dictionary of world biography. VI. Great lives from history.
  D285.G74 2006
  909.7092′2—dc22

          2006005336

First Printing

PRINTED IN THE UNITED STATES OF AMERICA

CONTENTS

CONTENTS

PUBLISHER'S NOTE

Great Lives from History: The Eighteenth Century, 1701-1800 is the fifth installment in the revised and expanded *Great Lives* series, initiated in 2004 with *The Ancient World, Prehistory-476 C.E.* (2 vols.) and followed in 2005 by *The Middle Ages, 477-1453* (2 vols.) and *The Renaissance and Early Modern Era, 1454-1600* (2 vols.) and in 2006 by *The Seventeenth Century, 1601-1700* (2 vols.). It will be joined by *Great Lives from History: The Nineteenth Century* and *The Twentieth Century*. The entire series, when complete, will cover more than 3,300 lives in essays ranging from 6 to 10 columns in length.

EXPANDED COVERAGE

This ongoing series is a revision of the 10-volume *Dictionary of World Biography* (*DWB*) series (1998-1999), which in turn was a revision and reordering of Salem Press's 30-volume *Great Lives from History* series (1987-1995). The expanded *Great Lives* differs in substantial ways from *DWB*:

- The coverage of each set has been increased significantly. In the current two volumes, for example, 221 original essays from *Dictionary of World Biography: 17th & 18th Centuries* (1999) are enhanced by 132 new entries for a total of 353 essays covering 355 major figures, including 48 women.

- Fifty sidebars, quotations from primary source documents, have been added to enhance and supplement the text throughout.

- A section of maps has been added to the front matter of each volume to allow students and other users of this reference work to locate personages geographically.

- Essays from the original *DWB* on all personages falling into the time frame are reprinted in this new series with updated and annotated bibliographies.

SCOPE OF COVERAGE

Both the geographic and the occupational scope of the individuals covered in *Great Lives from History: The Eighteenth Century, 1701-1800* is intentionally broad, with a view to including influential individuals worldwide. The figures covered in these volumes are identified with one or more of the following countries or regions: Africa (4 essays), American Colonies (60), Arabia (1), Austria (12), Brazil (1), Burma (1), Canada (11), Caribbean (2), China (5), Denmark (1), England (120), Ethiopia (1), France (61), Germany (29), Haiti (1), Hungary (1), India (5), Iran (3), Iraq (1), Ireland (17), Italy (16), Jamaica (1), Japan (6), Korea (1), Lithuania (1), Mali (1), Mexico (1), Netherlands (1), Nigeria (2), Ottoman Empire (4), Peru (1), Poland (3), Portugal (1), Prussia (9), Russia (12), Scotland (27), Southeast Asia (2), Spain (7), Sweden (3), Switzerland (4), Thailand (1), Turkey (4), Ukraine (1), United States (53), and Vietnam (1).

The editors have sought to provide coverage that is broad in areas of achievement as well as geography, while at the same time including the recognized shapers of history essential in any liberal arts curriculum. Major world leaders appear here, as well as the giants of religious faith who were central to the century: monarchs, presidents, popes, philosophers, writers, social reformers, educators, and military leaders who left their imprint on political as well as spiritual institutions. Also, however, the set includes figures who have received little attention in the past, from Alaungpaya to Peg Woffington to Yongzheng.

By category, the contents include figures whose achievements fall into one or more of the following areas: archaeology (2 essays), architecture (10), art (30), astronomy (6), biology (5), business (19), cartography (4), chemistry (12), church reform (2), dance (1), diplomacy (23), economics (9), education (15), engineering (6), exploration (10), geography (4), government and politics (147), historiography (13), landscape architecture (1), law (19), literature (63), mathematics (14), medicine (7), military (48), music (21), patronage of the arts (11), philosophy (39), physics (9), religion and theology (39), scholarship (17), science and technology (45), social reform (30), sociology (2), theater (19), warfare and conquest (52), and women's rights (10).

ESSAY LENGTH AND FORMAT

Each essay ranges from 1,500 to 3,000 words in length (roughly 3 to 5 pages) and displays standard ready-reference top matter offering easy access to biographical information:

- The essay title is the name of the individual; editors have chosen the name as it is most commonly found in Western English-language sources.

- The individual's nationality or ethnicity and occupation or historical role follow on the second line, including reign dates for rulers.

- A summary paragraph highlighting the individual's historical importance indicates why the person is studied today.

- The "Born" and "Died" lines list the most complete dates of birth and death available, followed by the most precise locations available, as well as an indication of when these are unknown, only probable, or only approximate; both contemporary and modern place-names (where different) are listed. A question mark (?) is appended to a date or place if the information is considered likely to be the precise date or place but remains in question. A "c." denotes circa and indicates that historians have only enough information to place the date of birth or death in a more general period. When a range of dates is provided for birth or death, historians are relatively certain that it could not have occurred prior to or after the range.

- "Also known as" lists all known versions of the individual's name, including full names, given names, alternative spellings, pseudonyms, and common epithets.

- "Area(s) of achievement" lists all categories of contribution, from Architecture and Art through Social Reform and Theater.

The body of each essay is divided into three parts:

- "Early Life" provides facts about the individual's upbringing and the environment in which he or she was reared, as well as the pronunciation of his or her name, if unfamiliar to English speakers. Where little is known about the individual's early life, historical context is provided.

- "Life's Work," the heart of the essay, consists of a straightforward, generally chronological, account of the period during which the individual's most significant achievements were accomplished.

- "Significance" is an overview of the individual's place in history.

- "Further Reading" is an annotated bibliography, a starting point for further research.

- "See also" lists of cross-references to essays in the set covering related personages.

- "Related articles" lists essays of interest in Salem's companion publication, *Great Events from History: The Eighteenth Century, 1701-1800* (2 vols., 2006).

SPECIAL FEATURES

Several features distinguish this series as a whole from other biographical reference works. The front matter includes the following aids:

- Complete List of Contents: This alphabetical list of contents appears in both volumes.

- Key to Pronunciation: A key to in-text pronunciation appears in both volumes.

- List of Maps and Sidebars.

- Maps: The front matter of each volume contains a section of maps displaying major regions of the world during the eighteenth century.

The back matter to Volume 2 includes several appendixes and indexes:

- Rulers and Heads of State, a geographically arranged set of tables listing major world rulers and leaders, including their regnal dates or terms of office.

- Chronological List of Entries: individuals covered, arranged by birth year.

- Category Index: entries by area of achievement, from Architecture to Women's Rights.

- Geographical Index: entries by country or region, from Africa and Albania to the Ukraine and Wales.

- Personages Index: an index of all persons, both those covered in the essays and those discussed within the text.

- Subject Index: a comprehensive index including personages, concepts, books, artworks, terms, battles, civilizations, and other topics of discussion, with full cross-references from alternative spellings and to the Category and Geographical Indexes.

USAGE NOTES

The worldwide scope of *Great Lives from History* resulted in the inclusion of names and words transliterated from languages that do not use the Roman alphabet. In some cases, there is more than one transliterated form in use. In many cases, transliterated words in this set follow the American Library Association and Library of Congress (ALA-LC) transliteration format for that language. However, if another form of a name or word has been judged to be more familiar to the general audience, it is used instead. The variants for names of essay subjects are listed in ready-reference top matter and are cross-referenced in the subject and personages indexes. The Pinyin transliteration was used for Chinese topics, with Wade-Giles variants provided for major names and dynasties. In a few cases, a common name that is not Pinyin has been used. Sanskrit and other South Asian names generally follow the ALA-LC transliteration rules, although again, the more familiar form of a word is used when deemed appropriate for the general reader.

Titles of books and other literature appear, upon first mention in the essay, with their full publication and translation data as known: an indication of the first date of publication or appearance, followed by the English title in translation and its first date of appearance in English; if no translation has been published in English, and if the context of the discussion does not make the meaning of the title obvious, a "literal translation" appears in roman type.

Throughout, readers will find a limited number of abbreviations used in both top matter and text, including "r." for "reigned," "b." for "born," "d." for "died," and "fl." for flourished. Where a date range appears appended to a name without one of these designators, the reader may assume it signifies birth and death dates.

CONTRIBUTORS

Salem Press would like to extend its appreciation to all who have been involved in the development and production of this work. Special thanks go to John Powell, Associate Professor of History at Oklahoma Baptist University, who developed the contents list and coverage notes for contributing writers to ensure the set's relevance to the high school and undergraduate curricula. The essays were written and signed by historians, political scientists, and scholars of regional studies as well as independent scholars. Without their expert contributions, a project of this nature would not be possible. A full list of their names and affiliations appears in the front matter of this volume.

CONTRIBUTORS

Douglas Carl Abrams
Bob Jones University

Elizabeth C. Adams
Frostburg State University

Michael Adams
*City University New York,
    Graduate Center*

Patrick Adcock
Henderson State University

Jacob H. Adler
Independent Scholar

C. D. Akerley
United States Naval Academy

William H. Alexander
Norfolk State University

J. Stewart Alverson
*University of Tennessee at
    Chattanooga*

Emily Alward
Independent Scholar

Majid Amini
Virginia State University

Richard J. Amundson
Independent Scholar

Deborah Elwell Arfken
*University of Tennessee at
    Chattanooga*

Bryan Aubrey
Independent Scholar

Theodore P. Aufdemberge
Concordia College

Tom L. Auffenberg
Ouachita Baptist University

Ehrhard Bahr
*University of California, Los
    Angeles*

Christopher Baker
*Armstrong Atlantic State
    University*

Anita Baker-Blocker
Independent Scholar

Thomas F. Barry
Himeji Dokkyo University

Maryanne Barsotti
Independent Scholar

Robert A. Becker
Louisiana State University

Alice H. R. H. Beckwith
Providence College

Graydon Beeks
Pomona College

S. Carol Berg
College of St. Benedict

Donna Berliner
Southern Methodist University

Milton Berman
University of Rochester

Terry D. Bilhartz
Sam Houston State University

Louis R. Bisceglia
San Jose State University

Carol Blessing
Point Loma Nazarene University

John Braeman
University of Nebraska

Gerhard Brand
*California State University, Los
    Angeles*

John R. Breihan
Independent Scholar

Celeste Williams Brockington
Independent Scholar

Alan Brown
Independent Scholar

William H. Burnside
John Brown University

D. Burrill
Independent Scholar

Stephen Burwood
*State University of New York,
    Binghamton*

Andrew J. Butrica
Rutgers University

Joseph P. Byrne
Belmont University

Byron D. Cannon
University of Utah

John Carpenter
University of Michigan

James A. Casada
Independent Scholar

Gilbert T. Cave
Independent Scholar

David F. Channell
University of Texas at Dallas

Nan K. Chase
Appalachian State University

Victor W. Chen
Chabot College

Patricia Cook
Emory University

Richard A. Cosgrove
University of Arizona—Tucson

Frederic M. Crawford
Independent Scholar

LouAnn Faris Culley
Kansas State University

Light Townsend Cummins
Austin College

Frank Day
Clemson University

Bruce J. DeHart
University of North Carolina at Pembroke

Andria Derstine
Detroit Institute of Arts

M. Casey Diana
University of Illinois, Urbana-Champaign

Charles A. Dranguet, Jr.
Independent Scholar

Margaret Duggan
South Dakota State University

Charles Duncan
Clark-Atlanta University

Joyce Duncan
East Tennessee State University

William E. Eagan
Moorhead State University

Lester Eckman
Independent Scholar

James W. Endersby
University of Missouri

Thomas L. Erskine
Salisbury University

Paul F. Erwin
University of Cincinnati

Robert D. Fiala
Concordia College

Paul Finkelman
Brooklyn Law School

Edward Fiorelli
St. John's University

Michael S. Fitzgerald
Pikeville College

Robert J. Frail
Centenary College

Margot K. Frank
Randolph-Macon Women's College

Shirley F. Fredricks
Independent Scholar

Sheldon Goldfarb
University of British Columbia

Margaret Bozenna Goscilo
University of Pittsburgh

Norbert Gossman
University of Detroit

Sidney Gottlieb
Sacred Heart University

Ronald Gray
Beijing Language and Culture University

Johnpeter Horst Grill
Mississippi State University

Jimmie F. Gross
Armstrong State College

Surendra K. Gupta
Pittsburg State University

Michael Haas
Independent Scholar

Irwin Halfond
McKendree College

Gavin R. G. Hambly
University of Texas at Dallas

Lowell H. Harrison
Western Kentucky University

Peter B. Heller
Manhattan College

Carlanna Hendrick
Independent Scholar

Joyce E. Henry
Ursinus College

Mark C. Herman
Edison College

Nina Hibbin
Independent Scholar

Richard L. Hillard
University of Arkansas at Pine Bluff

John R. Holmes
Franciscan University of Steubenville

Ronald Howard
Mississippi College

Caralee Hutchinson
Independent Scholar

CONTRIBUTORS

Raymond Pierre Hylton
Virginia Union University

Robert Jacobs
Central Washington University

Bruce E. Johansen
University of Nebraska at Omaha

David Kasserman
Independent Scholar

Leigh Husband Kimmel
Independent Scholar

Kenneth F. Kiple
Independent Scholar

Phillip E. Koerper
Independent Scholar

Grove Koger
Boise Public Library

Carl E. Kramer
Independent Scholar

Abraham D. Kriegel
Memphis State University

Paul E. Kuhl
Winston-Salem State University

Lyndall Baker Landauer
Lake Tahoe Community College

Eugene Larson
Los Angeles Pierce College

Harry S. Laver
University of Kentucky

Roland V. Layton, Jr.
Hiram College

Douglas A. Lee
Vanderbilt University

Steven Lehman
John Abbott College

Denyse Lemaire
Rowan University

Thomas Tandy Lewis
*Anoka-Ramsey Community
   College*

James Livingston
Northern Michigan University

Roger D. Long
Eastern Michigan University

Michael Loudon
Eastern Illinois University

William C. Lowe
Mount St. Clare College

Eric v.d. Luft
*State University of New York,
   Upstate Medical University*

Maxine N. Lurie
Independent Scholar

R. C. Lutz
CII

Michael McCaskey
Georgetown University

Sandra C. McClain
James Madison University

Robert McColley
University of Illinois

Barry McGill
Oberlin College

James Edward McGoldrick
*Greenville Presbyterian
   Theological Seminary*

William C. Marceau
St. John Fisher College

Marsha Kass Marks
Independent Scholar

Laurence W. Mazzeno
Alvernia College

Patrick Meanor
*State University of New York,
   College at Oneonta*

Richard D. Miles
Wayne State University

Sara Joan Miles
Wheaton College

Mary-Emily Miller
Independent Scholar

Randall M. Miller
St. Joseph's University

Peter Monaghan
Independent Scholar

Ronald O. Moore
Independent Scholar

Robert A. Morace
Daemen College

Terry R. Morris
Shorter College

Katharine M. Morsberger
Independent Scholar

Robert E. Morsberger
*California State Polytechnic
   University, Pomona*

Raymond Lee Muncy
Independent Scholar

Alice Myers
Simon's Rock College of Bard

Bryan D. Ness
Pacific Union College

Roger L. Nichols
Independent Scholar

Richard L. Niswonger
Independent Scholar

Charles H. O'Brien
Western Illinois University

Robert H. O'Connor
North Dakota State University

James H. O'Donnell III
Independent Scholar

Robert M. Otten
Marymount University

Lisa Paddock
Independent Scholar

Robert J. Paradowski
Rochester Institute of Technology

Jan Pendergrass
University of Georgia

Mark Pestana
Grand Valley State University

R. Craig Philips
Michigan State University

Susan L. Piepke
Bridgewater College

Clifton W. Potter, Jr.
Lynchburg College

William S. Pretzer
Henry Ford Museum

Jonathan L. Price
Independent Scholar

Charles H. Pullen
Queen's University

Steven J. Ramold
Eastern Michigan University

Rose Reifsnyder
Independent Scholar

Dennis Reinhartz
University of Texas at Arlington

Rosemary M. Canfield Reisman
Charleston Southern University

Earl A. Reitan
Illinois State University

Edward A. Riedinger
Ohio State University Libraries

Joseph F. Rishel
Duquesne University

Deborah D. Rogers
University of Maine

Carl Rollyson
*Baruch College, City University
New York*

Joseph Rosenblum
Independent Scholar

Robert Ross
Independent Scholar

Irving N. Rothman
University of Houston

Vicki A. Sanders
Riverside Military Academy

Stephen P. Sayles
University of La Verne

Elizabeth D. Schafer
Independent Scholar

William J. Scheick
University of Texas at Austin

Helmut J. Schmeller
Fort Hays State University

Beverly Schneller
Millersville University

Thomas C. Schunk
Independent Scholar

Martha A. Sherwood
University of Oregon

J. Lee Shneidman
Adelphi University

R. Baird Shuman
*University of Illinois, Urbana-
Champaign*

Shumet Sishagne
Christopher Newport University

David Curtis Skaggs
Bowling Green State University

C. Edward Skeen
Memphis State University

Andrew C. Skinner
Brigham Young University

Anna Sloan
Amherst College

Richard L. Smith
Ferrum College

Norbert C. Soldon
Independent Scholar

James E. Southerland
Brenau College

Robert M. Spector
Worcester State College

Joseph L. Spradley
Wheaton College

William R. Stacy
Oberlin College

Diane Prenatt Stevens
Indiana University

Leslie A. Stricker
Park University

Fred Strickert
Wartburg College

Taylor Stults
Muskingum College

Charles R. Sullivan
University of Dallas

James Sullivan
California State University, Los Angeles

Patricia E. Sweeney
Derby Neck Library

Glenn L. Swygart
Tennessee Temple University

Roy Talbert, Jr.
Coastal Carolina College

Alice Taylor
Shorter College

Cassandra Lee Tellier
Capital University

Phyllis Ann Thompson
Appalachian State University

Carole Watterson Troxler
Elon College

Lisa Urkevich
American University of Kuwait

Paul Varner
Oklahoma Christian University

Mary E. Virginia
Independent Scholar

Paul R. Waibel
Belhaven College

John R. Wallace
University of California, Berkeley

Miriam Wallraven
University of Tuebingen, Germany

Harry M. Ward
University of Richmond

Donald V. Weatherman
Lyon College

Martha Ellen Webb
University of Nebraska—Lincoln

Shawncey Webb
Independent Scholar

Leigh Wetherall
Sheffield Hallam University

Mary B. Wickwire
University of Massachusetts

Lance Williams
Independent Scholar

John F. Wilson
University of Hawaii—Manoa

John D. Windhausen
Saint Anselm College

Michael Witkoski
University of South Carolina

Byron A. Wolverton
Southwest Texas State University

William Ross Woofenden
Swedenborg School of Religion

Clifton K. Yearley
State University of New York, Buffalo

Kristen L. Zacharias
Albright College

Robert Zaller
Drexel University

Philip B. Zaring
Independent Scholar

Yunqiu Zhang
North Carolina A&T State University

KEY TO PRONUNCIATION

Many of the names of personages covered in *Great Lives from History: The Eighteenth Century, 1701-1800* may be unfamiliar to students and general readers. For these unfamiliar names, guides to pronunciation have been provided upon first mention of the names in the text. These guidelines do not purport to achieve the subtleties of the languages in question but will offer readers a rough equivalent of how English speakers may approximate the proper pronunciation.

Vowel Sounds

Symbol	Spelled (Pronounced)
a	answer (AN-suhr), laugh (laf), sample (SAM-puhl), that (that)
ah	father (FAH-thur), hospital (HAHS-pih-tuhl)
aw	awful (AW-fuhl), caught (kawt)
ay	blaze (blayz), fade (fayd), waiter (WAYT-ur), weigh (way)
eh	bed (behd), head (hehd), said (sehd)
ee	believe (bee-LEEV), cedar (SEE-dur), leader (LEED-ur), liter (LEE-tur)
ew	boot (bewt), lose (lewz)
i	buy (bi), height (hit), lie (li), surprise (sur-PRIZ)
ih	bitter (BIH-tur), pill (pihl)
o	cotton (KO-tuhn), hot (hot)
oh	below (bee-LOH), coat (koht), note (noht), wholesome (HOHL-suhm)
oo	good (good), look (look)
ow	couch (kowch), how (how)
oy	boy (boy), coin (koyn)
uh	about (uh-BOWT), butter (BUH-tuhr), enough (ee-NUHF), other (UH-thur)

Consonant Sounds

Symbol	Spelled (Pronounced)
ch	beach (beech), chimp (chihmp)
g	beg (behg), disguise (dihs-GIZ), get (geht)
j	digit (DIH-juht), edge (ehj), jet (jeht)
k	cat (kat), kitten (KIH-tuhn), hex (hehks)
s	cellar (SEHL-ur), save (sayv), scent (sehnt)
sh	champagne (sham-PAYN), issue (IH-shew), shop (shop)
ur	birth (burth), disturb (dihs-TURB), earth (urth), letter (LEH-tur)
y	useful (YEWS-fuhl), young (yuhng)
z	business (BIHZ-nehs), zest (zehst)
zh	vision (VIH-zhuhn)

COMPLETE LIST OF CONTENTS

VOLUME 1

VOLUME 2

LIST OF MAPS AND SIDEBARS

Volume 1

Volume 2

ASIA IN THE EIGHTEENTH CENTURY

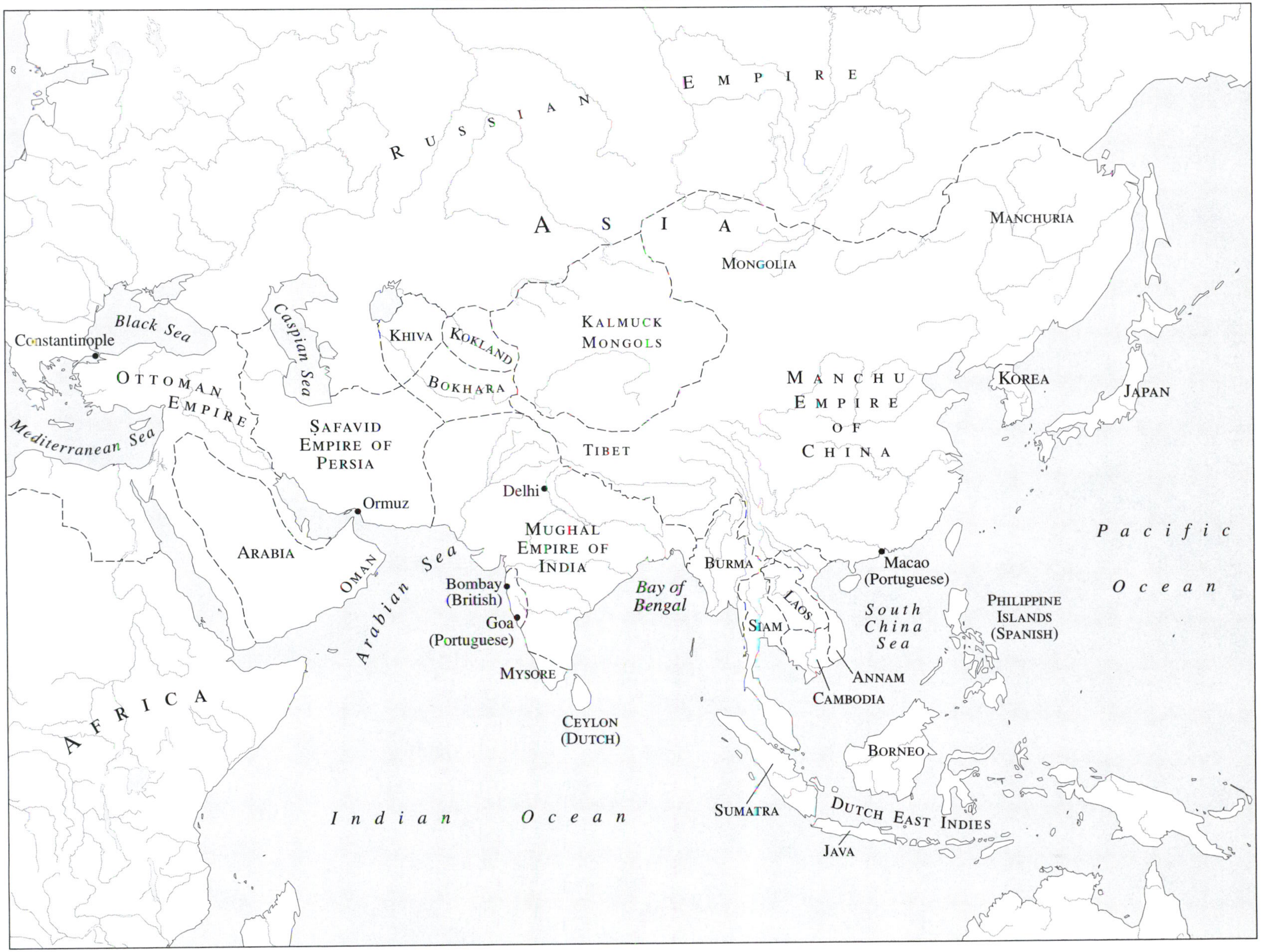

Pacific Ocean

JAPAN

MANCHURIA

KOREA

MANCHU EMPIRE OF CHINA

MONGOLIA

PHILIPPINE ISLANDS (SPANISH)

Macao (Portuguese)

South China Sea

BORNEO

ANNAM

CAMBODIA

DUTCH EAST INDIES

EMPIRE

Laos

SIAM

JAVA

KALMUCK MONGOLS

BURMA

SUMATRA

RUSSIAN

ASIA

TIBET

Bay of Bengal

CEYLON (DUTCH)

KOKAND

MUGHAL EMPIRE OF INDIA

Delhi

KHIVA

BOKHARA

MYSORE

Bombay (British)

Goa (Portuguese)

Indian Ocean

SAFAVID EMPIRE OF PERSIA

Ormuz

Arabian Sea

Caspian Sea

OMAN

ARABIA

OTTOMAN EMPIRE

Black Sea

Constantinople

Mediterranean Sea

AFRICA

xxix

AFRICA IN THE EIGHTEENTH CENTURY

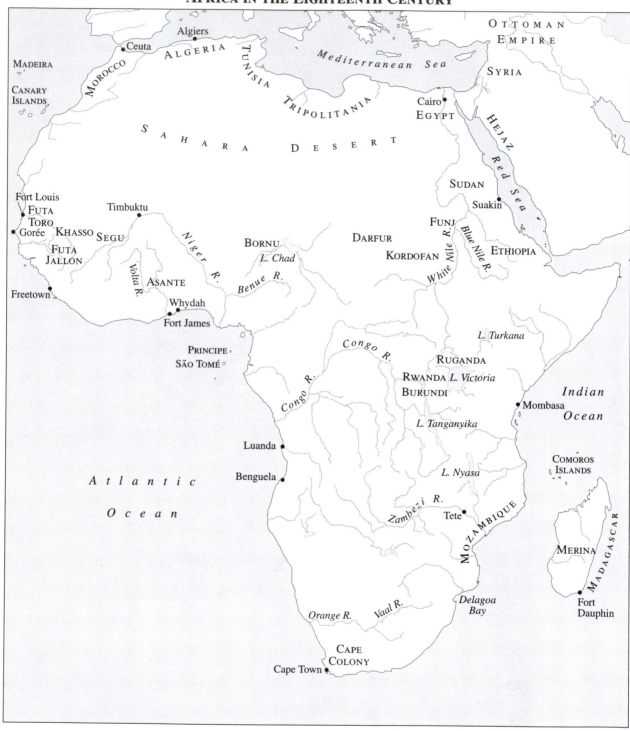

OTTOMAN EMPIRE

Algiers

Ceuta

MADEIRA

MOROCCO

ALGERIA

TUNISIA

TRIPOLITANIA

Mediterranean Sea

SYRIA

CANARY ISLANDS

SAHARA DESERT

Cairo

EGYPT

HEJAZ

Red Sea

Fort Louis

FUTA TORO

KHASSO

Gorée

SEGU

Timbuktu

Niger R.

Volta R.

FUTA JALLON

Freetown

ASANTE

Whydah

Fort James

BORNU

L. Chad

Benue R.

DARFUR

KORDOFAN

SUDAN

Suakin

FUNJ

White Nile R.

Blue Nile R.

ETHIOPIA

PRINCIPE

SÃO TOMÉ

Congo R.

Congo R.

Congo R.

L. Turkana

RUGANDA

RWANDA

L. Victoria

BURUNDI

L. Tanganyika

Mombasa

Indian Ocean

A t l a n t i c

O c e a n

Luanda

Benguela

L. Nyasa

COMOROS ISLANDS

Zambezi R.

Tete

MOZAMBIQUE

MERINA

MADAGASCAR

Orange R.

Vaal R.

Delagoa Bay

Fort Dauphin

CAPE COLONY

Cape Town

SOUTH AMERICA IN THE EIGHTEENTH CENTURY

Porto Bello

Caracas

DUTCH
GUIANA

Paramaribo
Cayenne

Santa Fé de Bogota

FRENCH
GUIANA

= Portuguese South America

= Spanish South America

NEW
GRANADA

Quito

Japurá R.

Negro R.

Amazon   *R.*

A m a z o n   *Basin*

Manaus

Purus R.

Madeira R.

A m a z o n

B   R   A   Z   I   L

Lima

Cuzco

Bahia (Salvador)

Andes

Arequipa

Santa Cruz

MINAS
GERAIS

La Plata

Paraná R.

Minas Novas

Mountains

Rio de Janeiro

Asunción

B   R

Pacific

Porto Alegre

Colonia do
Sacramento

Santiago

Buenos Aires

Montevideo

Atlantic

Negro R.

Patagonia

Ocean

Ocean

Malvinas
(Falkland Islands)

NORTH AMERICA, 1775

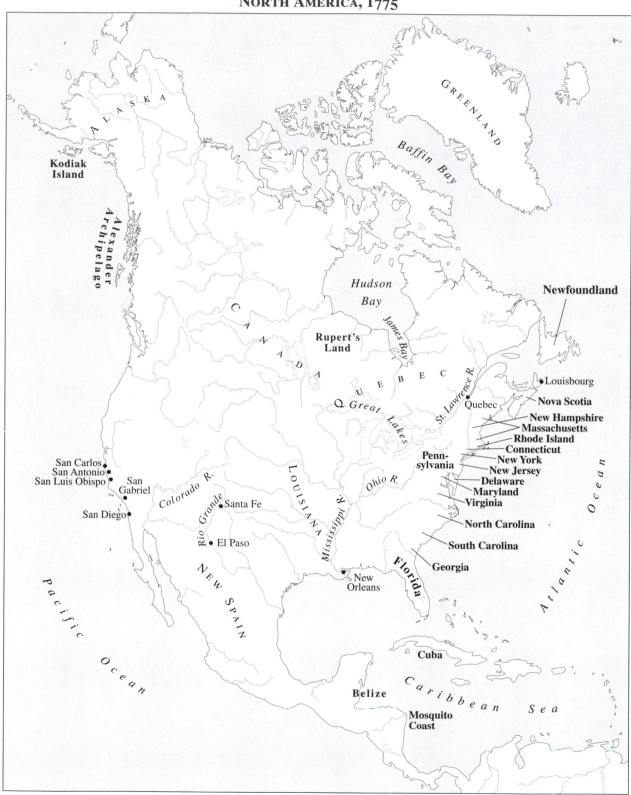

ALASKA

Kodiak Island

Alexander Archipelago

GREENLAND

Baffin Bay

C A N A D A

Hudson Bay

Rupert's Land

James Bay

Newfoundland

Louisbourg

Nova Scotia

Q U E B E C

St. Lawrence R.

Quebec

Q Great Lakes

New Hampshire
Massachusetts
Rhode Island
Connecticut
New York
New Jersey
Delaware
Maryland
Virginia

Penn-sylvania

Ohio R.

San Carlos
San Antonio
San Luis Obispo
San Gabriel

Colorado R.

L O U I S I A N A

Mississippi R.

North Carolina

South Carolina

San Diego

Rio Grande

Santa Fe

El Paso

N E W   S P A I N

New Orleans

Georgia

Florida

Atlantic Ocean

Pacific Ocean

Cuba

Belize

Mosquito Coast

C a r i b b e a n   S e a

EUROPE IN THE EIGHTEENTH CENTURY

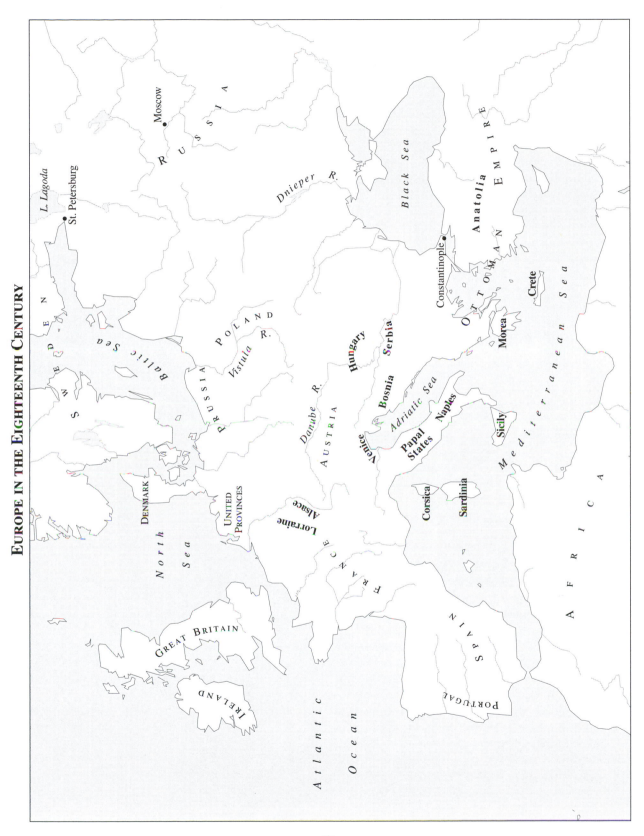

Moscow

RUSSIA

L. Lagoda

St. Petersburg

Dnieper R.

Black Sea

Anatolia

OTTOMAN EMPIRE

Constantinople

Crete

Morea

Mediterranean Sea

SWEDEN

Baltic Sea

POLAND

Vistula R.

PRUSSIA

Hungary

Serbia

Bosnia

Adriatic Sea

Naples

Sicily

Danube R.

AUSTRIA

Venice

Papal States

DENMARK

North Sea

UNITED PROVINCES

Lorraine Alsace

FRANCE

Corsica

Sardinia

SPAIN

AFRICA

GREAT BRITAIN

IRELAND

Atlantic Ocean

PORTUGAL

Great Lives from History

The 18th Century

1701-1800

FANNY ABINGTON
English actor

A star of the English and Irish stage, Abington dazzled theater audiences with vivacious acting and a well-modulated voice. She was also a leading fashion icon, with women of wealth and social rank following the trends she set in clothing, hairstyle, and decor.

Born: 1737; London, England
Died: March 4, 1815; London, England
Also known as: Frances Barton (birth name); Frances Barton Abington (full name)
Areas of achievement: Theater, music, art, patronage of the arts

EARLY LIFE

Fanny Abington, who was given the name Frances Barton at birth, grew up in a squalid part of London called Vinegar Yard. Her father, a former solider, ran a cobbler's stall, and her brother worked as a stable boy at Hanway Yard. When Fanny was just fourteen years old, her mother died. The motherless Fanny sold flowers and sang songs around Covent Garden, winning her the nickname "Nosegay Fan." Tales of the impoverished maiden standing on tavern tables and reciting poetry are probably false, as are allegations she engaged in prostitution. She held jobs as a ballad singer, a hatmaker's assistant, and a kitchen maid. In the latter role she worked under Robert Baddeley, a comedic actor, who cooked for the renowned actor and playwright Samuel Foote.

In 1775, Theophilus Cibber, who may have been a friend of Fanny, formed a troupe of new actors and put on a series of ten shows at the Haymarket. Fanny made her acting debut as Miranda in Mrs. Centlivre's *The Busy Body* (pr., pb. 1709) on August 21. She received no formal credit for her appearances until September 1, when her name appeared on the bill for her role as Kitty Pry in Colley Cibber's *The Provok'd Husband* (pr., pb. 1728).

Fanny was a natural on stage. Her contemporaries described her as tall and pale, with blue eyes, a snub nose, and an alluring figure. A certain vivacity in her acting and a well-modulated voice also warranted mention by her early admirers. After the Haymarket show she performed in Bath and then Richmond. Her work in these venues caught the attention of several important men connected with the Drury Lane Theatre, one of the best theaters in the world. In the fall of 1756, she accepted an invitation to join this venerable company.

LIFE'S WORK

Fanny Abington performed three seasons with Drury Lane. At first, competing for parts against such admired actors as Kitty Clive, she won acclaim for her portrayal of secondary characters and appearances in pantomimes. On June 19, 1757, she ended the season as Lucy in John Gay's *The Beggar's Opera* (pr., pb. 1728). Fanny's contract paid only 30 shillings per week. Still, she may have spent some of the money on music lessons with James Abington, a king's trumpeter. Fanny married James Abington on September 27, 1759.

In her third season at Drury Lane, Fanny quarreled with actor and stage manager David Garrick. She fancied herself a superior actor, and it is possible he did not share this opinion. In November, 1759, Fanny and her husband moved to Dublin, where she became an immediate sensation both on and off the stage. She performed many roles in Ireland, beginning with Mrs. Sullen in George Farquhar's *The Beaux' Stratagem* (pr., pb. 1707) at the Smock Alley Theatre on December 11, 1759. She also gained fame as an arbiter of style when the cap she wore as Kitty in James Townley's *High Life Below Stairs* (pr., pb. 1759) became a fashion craze known simply as the "Abington." From that time forward, women of rank shamelessly emulated her dress and hairstyles. It has been suggested that by the end of her career, Fanny's acting salary plus fees for fashion and wedding decoration advice annually totaled some £1,500. Fanny moved to the Crow Street Theater on May 22, 1760, then alternated between it and Smock Alley for the next several years.

Not long after arriving in Ireland, Fanny began an affair with a wealthy member of the Irish parliament. He died in 1765 and left her a tidy sum. Later, another affair did nothing to tarnish her public reputation. At some point, Fanny freed herself from her husband by paying him a pension.

At Garrick's invitation, Fanny returned to Drury Lane in 1765. She played the Widow Belmour in Arthur Murphy's *The Way to Keep Him* (pb. 1760) in November and, when Kitty Clive retired in 1769, Fanny took over her roles. For the next twenty years, Fanny was London's leading comic actress, generating high box-office returns. However, she became increasingly egocentric and disagreeable. Garrick was a primary target of her ire, and many unfriendly letters dating from 1774 confirm a contentious relationship. Fanny alleged that he gave away

1

parts promised to her and one night refused to play a familiar role that had been assigned on short notice, forcing him to scramble for another actress. She also accused Garrick of favoring Jane Pope, the only actress paid more than Fanny in 1773.

In 1776, Garrick announced his retirement. Fanny claimed she too was leaving the stage and entreated the ailing manager to appear at her farewell benefit. Proceeds from benefit shows went to the performer for whom it was given. Garrick agreed and played Archer in *The Beaux' Stratagem*. The next season, Fanny signed on with his replacement, Richard Brinsley Sheridan, and continued acting for nearly fifteen more years.

In 1777, Sheridan put on his own play, *The School for Scandal* (pr. 1777, pb. 1780), at Drury Lane. The role of Lady Teazle, a country girl transformed into a fine lady, was written expressly for Fanny and became her greatest success. Nonetheless, in 1782, she battled with Sheridan and moved to Covent Garden. She played Lady Flutter in Frances Sheridan's *The Discovery* and was exceptionally well received. Fanny also enjoyed considerable success as a comedian. However, against the counsel of friends and advisers, she portrayed Scrub in *The Beaux' Stratagem* on February 10, 1786, and failed miserably. Her only other major flop was an ill-fated turn as Ophelia played opposite Garrick's Hamlet in 1776.

Fanny retired suddenly in 1790, but she returned to the London stage in 1797 and reprised her role as Beatrice in William Shakespeare's *Much Ado About Nothing* (pr. c. 1598-1599). The critics wrote polite but unfavorable reviews, making references to her diminished voice and portly figure. Her last part was as Lady Racket in Murphy's *Three Weeks After Marriage* (pb. 1776) on April 12, 1799.

She died on March 4, 1815. Although rumors suggested she was in financial straits, her will bequeathed a generous estate.

Significance

Fanny Abington's rise from poverty to fame and fortune shows that eighteenth century London theater welcomed aspirants of all economic backgrounds. It also suggests that Fanny possessed a great deal of talent, as performers generally ascended to the stage through family connections, high-level sponsorships, or, as in Fanny's case, upon discovery by a theater scout. Despite her humble beginnings, Fanny charmed members of the highest ranks of society. She spoke French and Italian fluently and is said to have held her intellectual own with generals, philosophers, and royalty.

The dozen or more theatrical portraits painted of Fanny provide visual proof of her importance and status as a much-loved actor. Among the many artists that captured her image, Sir Joshua Reynolds, reputedly an ardent admirer, is perhaps the most famous. His *Mrs. Abington as the Comic Muse* (c. 1768) complements another of his paintings, *Mrs. Siddons as the Tragic Muse* (1784), and equates Fanny with Sarah Siddons, the most acclaimed tragic actress of the time. Reynolds's depiction of Fanny as Miss Prue in William Congreve's *Love for Love* (1695) is often cited as the best portrait he ever made of her.

—*Rose Reifsnyder*

Further Reading

Highfill, Philip H., Kalman A. Burnim, and Edward A. Langhans, eds. *A Biographical Dictionary of Actors, Actresses, Musicians, Dancers, Managers, and Other Stage Personnel in London, 1660-1800*. Carbondale: Southern Illinois University Press, 1973. One of the most comprehensive accounts of Abington's life and stage career available.

Hume, Robert D., ed. *The London Theatre World, 1660-1800*. Carbondale: Southern Illinois University Press, 1980. An excellent compilation of essays by the leading authorities of English drama. The book includes a well-researched chapter on the social status of actors and the conventions of English theater life.

McIntyre, Ian. *Garrick*. London: Penguin Books, 1999. Provides insight into Abington's acrimonious relationship with the actor and stage manager David Garrick. Includes two illustrations of Abington and an extensive bibliography.

Mann, David D., Susan Garland, and Camille Garnier. *Women Playwrights in England, Ireland, and Scotland, 1660-1823*. Bloomington: Indiana University Press, 1996. Includes a brief summary of the major milestones in Abington's life and career.

Morwood, James, and David Crane, eds. *Sheridan Studies*. New York: Cambridge University Press, 1995. Includes several references to Abington's relationship with playwright and stage manager Richard Brinsley Sheridan. The first chapter provides background information about London theater.

Robins, Edward. *Twelve Great Actresses*. New York: G. P. Putnam's Sons, 1900. Robins provides a colorful, if sometimes fanciful, account of Abington's life and work, including descriptive passages concerning several notable men with whom she worked and associated. Includes one illustration of Abington.

Solkin, David H., ed. *Art on the Line: The Royal Academy Exhibitions at Somerset House*. New Haven, Conn.: Yale University Press, 2001. Includes a chapter discussing the portraits made of actresses in late eighteenth century London, with an emphasis on the images of Abington, Sarah Siddons, and writer Mary Robinson.

See also: Hannah Cowley; David Garrick; Anne Oldfield; Sir Joshua Reynolds; Mary Robinson; Richard Brinsley Sheridan; Sarah Siddons; Peg Woffington.

Related articles in *Great Events from History: The Eighteenth Century, 1701-1800:* December 7, 1732: Covent Garden Theatre Opens in London; 1742: Fielding's *Joseph Andrews* Satirizes English Society; August, 1763-April, 1765: David Garrick's European Tour.

ROBERT AND JAMES ADAM
British architects

Robert Adam, one of the greatest British architects, created a new approach to building design in the eighteenth century, which linked the architecture and the interior design of his buildings into a single design scheme, now called the neoclassical style. His new style of decorative design was named for him. His brother James contributed to the Adam enterprise as a close family associate and business partner, and to a lesser degree as an architect and designer on his own merit.

ROBERT ADAM

Born: July 3, 1728; Kirkcaldy, Fifeshire, Scotland
Died: March 3, 1792; London, England

JAMES ADAM

Born: July 21, 1732; Edinburgh, Scotland
Died: October 20, 1794; London, England
Areas of achievement: Architecture, business

EARLY LIVES

Robert and James Adam grew up as members of a close-knit family of four boys and six girls in Edinburgh, and as part of a large, accomplished, and distinguished extended family. Their father, William Adam, was Scotland's leading architect by 1730, known particularly for his grand design and construction of Hopetoun House, one of Scotland's largest and finest eighteenth century houses. Along with their early education at Edinburgh High School, the boys received an in-house apprenticeship in building from their father, a man of great energy and skill. Some of the boys' friends included Adam Smith, David Hume, and James Hutton, who, with Robert and others, were the core of the brilliant Scottish Enlightenment.

The brothers attended the University of Edinburgh. The Stuart rebellion led by Charles Edward (Bonnie Prince Charlie) in 1745 disrupted their formal education; after these troubles, Robert began to work for his father full-time, and James eventually joined them. Robert, together with his older brother John, also an architect, learned much of his basic building craft from work, especially at Fort George, to improve Scottish military defenses. Consequently, when William Adam died in 1748, John, Robert, and later James were well prepared to take over his thriving architectural firm.

Robert had extraordinary talent and ambition, and as he worked and learned, he also saved for a Grand Tour of Europe, a virtual necessity, he had decided. The opportunity came in 1754 at the invitation of Charles Hope, younger brother of the earl of Hopetoun. Robert had saved £5,000 by then, and, with family urging, he agreed.

Robert exuded great energy and seriousness of purpose, particularly about antiquities and architecture, yet he was a charming, delightful young Scotsman. He loved to sing and dance, although as a canny Scot, he assiduously avoided the opportunities to gamble available on the Continent. He was assertive, was hard-headed, loved comfort, and was a social climber. His few portraits show him to be fair, with a long and rather prominent nose, a slightly recessive mouth and strong chin, and dominant, lively eyes; he was a handsome man with a well-proportioned body.

James's portraits show him perhaps taller, slim, with long hands and fingers, a long nose, a prominent mouth, and a somewhat receding chin. He, too, presented a pleasing countenance. James, however, was not ambitious, seldom completing plans or fulfilling his intentions, and he could be expensively self-indulgent. To some he was arrogant, highly critical, and flippant. He loved hobnobbing with the wealthy. Generally, James

A medallion portraying Robert Adam, architect. (Library of Congress)

way and expecting the same treatment as the aristocrat. As a result, he was invited to social affairs that he might not otherwise have had the opportunity to attend. Aside from his genuine enjoyment on these occasions, he learned how to make himself and his ideas attractive to the aristocracy. In Rome he met many of the British nobility; when he returned to London to open a firm, he had no shortage of affluent clients.

Robert had the good luck to meet in Florence Charles-Louis Clérisseau, a teacher of architecture and an artist skilled at drawing and sketching Roman ruins. Immediately, Robert hired the Frenchman to teach him those skills that he lacked and knew he must have. Through Clérisseau, he met another teacher, Laurent Pêcheux, a painter and skilled draftsman. Ultimately, he became friends with the greatest Italian draftsman and engraver of the century, Giovanni Battista Piranesi. Piranesi recognized Adam's talent and his enthrallment with all aspects of classical Roman art. With Clérisseau and occasionally Pêcheux, and sometimes alone with Piranesi, Robert devoted more than three years to sketching, studying, and measuring—learning all that he might about antique Roman art. Impelled by his will to be the best, the young student perfected his artistry, acquired a comfortable familiarity with the French and Italian languages, gathered precise measurements of ancient Rome's great buildings, and fixed his mastery of Rome's decorative arts. He returned to London armed with hundreds of sketches, which he later used as sources for his work there. He also carried home drawings of Roman emperor Diocletian's palace, which he published in 1764 with great success.

James, too, went on a Grand Tour, from 1760 to 1763, and although it had less effect on him, he nevertheless returned to England with extensive experience in the fine arts, which made him an important partner in the London firm and a creditable architect himself. While abroad, James had also employed Clérisseau as a guide and teacher and had also received a warm reception from Piranesi. James's shallowness, however, and his penchant for enjoying himself above all else, foredoomed him to a less distinguished career than that of his brother: He never achieved Robert's command of the history of Roman art although he made many visits to churches, great houses, and palaces to see their paintings and objects of art and, along with Robert, returned to England with many artifacts and artworks.

Until Robert Adam changed it, the dominant architectural style in Great Britain had been Palladian, a style named for the sixteenth century Italian architect Andrea

was a charming, likable fellow with enough art and building experience to give him an air of authority.

Neither Adam married. In Robert's case, his work dominated all, leaving little time for family life. After the father died, the Adam family remained a close, devoted unit: After Robert set up his office in London, James, their younger brother William, and their sisters Janet and Elizabeth joined him. The sisters managed their brothers' household affairs. John, as heir to his father's property, remained in Edinburgh.

LIVES' WORK

The Grand Tour upon which Robert Adam embarked in the autumn of 1754 profoundly changed his life. His four years abroad gave him confidence as well as the expertise that would serve his ambitious nature. The moneyed circles in Great Britain traditionally looked upon those in the arts as rather lowly craftsmen, not as professionals of independent standing. Robert, however, insisted upon going with Charles Hope as an equal, paying his own

Palladio and based upon his study of ancient Roman architecture. His rural villas inspired the English with their strict symmetry, dramatized by a central block, perhaps domed, a portico front set high on a rusticated base, and wide steps sweeping up to the entry. If the building had wings, they were a matching pair. Above the base the stone was smooth. Aside from the columns and pediment of the entry porch, plain, evenly balanced windows gave the facade its decoration. Inside, the rooms were harmoniously proportioned and placed.

Early eighteenth century British architects revived Palladio's style and applied it with sometimes stunning success to the spate of country houses then being built with Great Britain's new wealth. By the 1760's, however, the clear simplicity and drama of Palladianism were overburdened with elaborations and decorative mistakes. Enter Robert Adam, with his knowledge and determination to design according to the purest standards of ancient Rome, alone.

Once installed in London in 1758, Robert got important commissions, particularly a highly visible and successful gate and screen before the Admiralty in London. A major work followed with Kedleston House in Derbyshire. There, his modifications to plans and construction already in progress produced an Adam tour de force. On the exterior he adapted a Roman triumphal arch for the design of the garden front. Inside, his plan presented visitors with dramatic surprises, as they progressively moved up steps to the entry, the vestibule, the hall, the saloon—surprises achieved principally by altering shapes of the rooms and also through the Roman character of his interior design.

At Syon House, near London, the owners asked Adam to design a suite of rooms in an old nunnery. Under severe constraint from the old construction, he became architect of the interior and produced a series of variously shaped and decorated rooms. Robert also received commissions to build two major houses, Lansdowne House in London and Luton Hoo in Bedfordshire. Their grand design magnified the Adam renown. Meanwhile, at Osterly Park near London, Robert remade an Elizabethan house into a stunning eighteenth century country house with interiors showing the extraordinary talent of the Adam firm. By late 1763, James had returned from Italy to join him on these projects.

The Adam style was now apparent. The exteriors of Adam houses, with variations, were simple and balanced, the art of the design coming from repetition of light, flowing detail. Exterior columns were smooth, freestanding, and structurally necessary, and windows

plain or with unaffected ornament. The Adams set their houses low, when possible, frequently with the foundation only slightly evident, giving the entrance approach a welcome openness and quiet dignity. Ancient Rome was the source for the design.

The opulence was inside, in the beauty and richness of the materials used and in their bold and unexpected design. The Adams restrained the opulence with a relatively simple, repetitive, and increasingly light pattern of decoration. In place of ubiquitous Palladian white, they returned color to the rooms, but within limits: very pale green and sage green, oyster white, cream, warm pink, and frequently green and pink in the same design. They used gilt, but not lavishly, and strong colors such as cerulean and ultramarine blue, purple, deep red, and burnt sienna, but sparingly and principally for contrast. Accents such as ceramic plaques and painted genre scenes set in ovals, squares, and rounds were strong but quiet. The rooms themselves varied from square to circular, rectangular, oval, cubed, some with niches, others without, many with semicircular apses, perhaps half-domed, perhaps set off by a screen of paired columns. The Adams were endlessly inventive. The results were graceful, charming, a new style.

In London, the brothers also designed important town houses, complete with stables and coaches but within narrow property restrictions. Here the challenge was to squeeze in sizable, interesting rooms without apparent strain. Robert's brilliant grasp of space and proportion and his willingness to tamper with architectural verities showed themselves especially—with the Williams-Wynn House, the Derby House, and the Home House. Later he designed terraces of town houses for Fitzroy Square in London and Charlotte Square in Edinburgh.

The brothers nearly met their financial nemesis with the novel and ambitious Adelphi scheme, which boldly projected a long row of town houses atop wharves and storage halls on the banks of the Thames River. The Adelphi was built but was a financial disaster, perhaps as a result of poor financial management by James and William that not even brother John could restore.

Commissions continued to flow, however, especially castles in northern England. Robert explained the anomaly of a Roman purist building a medieval castle by pointing out that the refined classical designs of southern England would be overwhelmed by the wild nature of the northern landscape. The interiors of his assertive castles, at Wedderburn, Mellerstain, and Culzean, however, were pure Adam. James, on his own, designed a Riding

School building in Edinburgh and a judicial court building in Hertford.

The Adams participated in Edinburgh's booming expansion of the 1760's, particularly with their imposing Register House, a huge government building, though not completed to their plans. Robert was asked to design a new building for the University of Edinburgh. His plan was a masterpiece of controlled surprise and restrained elegance, but only the entry wing was built as planned, and it, too, was spoiled by nineteenth century modifications. He and James died before the enterprise was fully established. Indeed, in Scotland, John died only months after Robert, and sadly the firm collapsed in bankruptcy in 1801.

SIGNIFICANCE

Robert and James Adam published their three-volume *The Works in Architecture* starting in 1773. Its plates showed the facades, floor plans, and detailed ornament of their style. Although, in the preface, the Adams overstate their claim to "a kind of revolution" in architecture, within the context of the eighteenth century they did not exaggerate by much. Whether it be in the fine details of their design or in the architecture—particularly the room arrangement of their buildings—they produced startling new designs and a new conception of what an architect should do.

Their architecture relied upon a pleasing arrangement of volumes of mostly unadorned structural blocks held together by harmonious proportions and the design motifs of ancient Rome. The Adams were propagators of what is now called the neoclassical style, a style based on the simple purity and beauty of ancient Greek and Roman art, and about Rome the Adams were experts. The brothers are also significant in that they stressed movement in their architectural facades. Using a number of slight variations on the surface plane of their structures, they made those surfaces livelier and more variable to the eye. They extended their architecture to the interiors of their buildings, creating ingeniously shaped rooms while maintaining ideal geometrical proportion.

The Adams went further, insisting they be responsible for the entire room design. Their firm employed renowned plasterers, such as Joseph Rose, and the excellent painter Antonio Zucchi; they designed the furniture and employed craftsmen to make it, among them Thomas Chippendale and Matthew Boulton. The fabric, drapery, chandeliers, wine-coolers, inkstands, keyhole covers—they oversaw all. To this integrity they brought their own remarkable sense of style, so that nearly all of their designs were aesthetically successful. Their new Etruscan-style rooms (Greek, in fact) were immensely popular, and their tapestry rooms, with tapestries from ceiling to floor designed for that room alone, received similar praise.

The Adams brought elegance to architecture and design, the mark of neoclassical art. The simple, flowing quality of their designs, their inventiveness, and their refusal to allow decoration to obscure basic design were characteristics that set their work apart from that of their British and continental contemporaries.

—Philip B. Zaring

FURTHER READING

Beard, Geoffrey. *The Work of Robert Adam*. Edinburgh: John Bartholomew and Son, 1978. A good general overview of Robert's life and work, from architecture to door furniture. Extensive illustrations, many in color, of what survives.

Fleming, John. *Robert Adam and His Circle in Edinburgh and Rome*. Cambridge, Mass.: Harvard University Press, 1962. An excellent study, beautifully written, of Robert's early life in Scotland, his Grand Tour, and his first two years in London (to 1760). Fleming's impressive scholarship embraces young James as well. Illustrated in part with Robert's drawings and based upon extensive correspondence between Robert and his family.

Harris, Eileen. *The Genius of Robert Adam: His Interiors*. New Haven, Conn.: Yale University Press, 2001. Each chapter describes Adam's interior designs for a specific project.

King, David N. *The Complete Works of Robert and James Adam: Built and Unbuilt*. 2d ed. New York: Architectural Press, 2001. A comprehensive overview of the works of both architects, including plans for unbuilt structures. Many illustrations, maps, and indices of people and places.

Rowan, Alistair. *Designs for Castles and Country Villas by Robert and James Adam*. Oxford, England: Phaidon Press, 1985. Rowan has assembled forty-seven architectural designs, of which sixteen were built, for a book he believes the Adams had intended to publish.

Rykwert, Joseph, and Anne Rykwert. *The Brothers Adam: The Men and the Style*. London: Collins, 1985. The Rykwerts analyze the brothers, their architecture, and their interior design with authority. The book is fresh, scholarly, and essential for study of the Adams. Includes an excellent bibliography.

Stillman, Damie. *The Decorative Work of Robert Adam.* New York: Transatlantic Arts, 1966. A close study with 173 illustrations, each accompanied by authoritative commentary. (For an excellent background on the decorative art of plasterwork, see Geoffrey Beard, *Decorative Plasterwork in Great Britain*, 1975.)

Summerson, Sir John N. *Architecture in Britain, 1530 to 1830.* Harmondsworth, England: Penguin Books, 1977. This great architectural historian analyzes the Adam style and the Adam achievement with authority.

Yarwood, Doreen. *Robert Adam.* New York: Charles Scribner's Sons, 1970. An enjoyable appreciation of Robert and his successes, written for the general reader.

See also: Matthew Boulton; Lancelot Brown; David Garrick; Nicholas Hawksmoor; David Hume; Adam Smith; Sir John Vanbrugh; Johann Joachim Winckelmann.

Related articles in *Great Events from History: The Eighteenth Century, 1701-1800:* 1715-1737: Building of the Karlskirche; 1726-1729: Voltaire Advances Enlightenment Thought in Europe; 1748: Excavation of Pompeii; 1748-1755: Construction of Istanbul's Nur-u Osmaniye Complex; 1759-1766: Construction of the Bridgewater Canal; 1762: *The Antiquities of Athens* Prompts Architectural Neoclassicism; November, 1777-January 1, 1781: Construction of the First Iron Bridge.

ABIGAIL ADAMS
American educator, writer, and feminist

An early proponent of humane treatment and equal education for women, Abigail Adams wrote eloquent, insightful letters that provide a detailed social history of her era and her life with John Adams.

Born: November 22, 1744; Weymouth, Massachusetts
Died: October 28, 1818; Quincy, Massachusetts
Also known as: Abigail Smith (birth name)
Areas of achievement: Women's rights, education, literature, government and politics, business

EARLY LIFE
Abigail Adams, born Abigail Smith, was one of four children of William Smith, minister of North Parish Congregational Church of Weymouth, and Elizabeth (Quincy) Smith from nearby Braintree, Massachusetts. Both parents were members of prominent New England families of merchants, statesmen, and ministers. From her parents, Abigail learned a conservative, rational Puritanism. She retained throughout her life a solid Christian faith and shared with her Puritan forebears a belief in the fundamental depravity of humankind. These religious convictions influenced her political opinions.

Observing her mother's example, Abigail learned her future roles as wife and mother, duties instilled in girls from an early age during this time in American history. As a minister's wife, Elizabeth Smith provided relief for the town's poor, nursed the town's sick, and presented herself as a model wife. She was nurturing and kind to her children.

In eighteenth century Massachusetts, education was prized. In government-supported schools, boys studied Latin, Greek, French, mathematics, and literary arts in preparation for higher education either at Harvard College or abroad. Girls, however, were educated almost exclusively at home, receiving only rudimentary training in reading and writing; some remained illiterate. They learned domestic skills such as sewing, fine needlework, and cooking, which were considered vital preparation for marriage. Abigail received only informal home instruction yet shared with her sisters the advantage of a keen intellect and unlimited access to her father's extensive library.

In her early adolescence, Abigail was encouraged in her studies by a young watchmaker and scholar, Richard Cranch. Although self-educated, Cranch conveyed his passion for scholarship to Abigail and to her sisters Mary and Elizabeth. It was through Cranch, who wedded Mary, that Abigail met her future husband.

Abigail proved a shrewd judge of character when at the age of nineteen she married Harvard-educated lawyer John Adams. Although they were not social equals—he was from a markedly less prominent family and practiced a profession that was poorly regarded—the match proved exceedingly profitable and satisfying for both parties. In John, Abigail found a man who appreciated and even encouraged her forthrightness and her intellectual ability, while John in turn received emotional, financial, and intellectual support from Abigail.

LIFE'S WORK

Abigail Adams is best known for her remarkably detailed, eloquent letters. Although many creative outlets were considered unsuitable for women to pursue, letter writing was a socially sanctioned literary art for women in the eighteenth century. Abigail, who felt compelled to write, naturally selected that medium.

During her first ten years of marriage, however, Abigail's letter writing was not prolific as she was kept extraordinarily busy with domestic affairs. Enduring five pregnancies in seven years, she also suffered the death of an infant daughter. In addition, she was plagued by several physical afflictions including frequent colds, rheumatism that caused acute swelling of her joints, and insomnia.

During these early years, she moved her household several times to remain with John in his work. The turmoil of their lives as they uprooted their family paralleled the contemporary political events in which John played a leading role. This was a pattern they would repeat throughout his working life and would include residences in Boston, Philadelphia, New York, Paris, and London. Abigail demonstrated repeatedly that she was extraordinarily adaptable and found pleasure in observing foreign customs. She always, however, longed for the idealized pastoral life in Braintree that she had shared with John during their first few years of marriage.

In 1775, John embarked for Congress on the first of frequent extended absences from Abigail. With her husband away, Abigail weathered several personal tragedies, including a difficult pregnancy in 1777, during which she apparently suffered from toxemia and finally eclampsia, a condition that is usually fatal to the infant and often to the mother. A remarkable series of letters were written between John and Abigail during this period; in them, Abigail expressed loneliness and fear for her unborn child. The child, a girl, was indeed stillborn. John and Abigail's letters provide invaluable information on the social history of parent-and-child relationships.

The pattern of intimate and frequent letters continued over the next twenty-five years as John, an extraordinarily ambitious man, accepted political positions that removed him from home for periods often extending to years. While Abigail considered their separation as a patriotic sacrifice, she nevertheless frequently expressed her loneliness to John, imploring him to return home.

Because she was a married woman, Abigail was legally prevented from owning property in her own name. Notwithstanding, she repeatedly demonstrated her ingenuity and self-sufficiency. During their first ten years together, John's legal fees and the income from their farm supported the family. As events took him farther from home, his legal practice was largely abandoned and Abigail assumed most financial duties. She never welcomed the addition to her already burdensome domestic responsibilities, yet she consistently proved herself a competent manager. Abigail deplored debt and worked to ensure that her family avoided it. She successfully ran the farm for four years during which she was responsible for the odious chore of collecting rents from several tenants as well as supervising agricultural production. Scarcity of labor and acute inflation made the task a difficult one. After four years, she lessened her burden by renting the farm.

In 1778, Abigail began requesting luxury goods from John, who was then serving as a diplomat in

---

REMEMBERING THE LADIES

Abigail Adams wrote a letter to Congress in 1776, demanding that women not only have a voice in the new nation but also have freedom from cruelty and abuse at the hands of men. She warned that without representation and legal protection, women would be positioned to rebel and to follow no laws.

Remember the ladies, and be more generous and favorable to them than your ancestors. Do not put such unlimited power into the hands of the Husbands. Remember all Men would be tyrants if they could. If particular care and attention is not paid to the Ladies we are determined to foment a Rebellion, and will not hold ourselves bound by any laws in which we have no voice, or Representation.

That your Sex are Naturally Tyrannical is a Truth so thoroughly established as to admit of no dispute, but such of you as wish to be happy willingly give up the harsh title of Master for the more tender and endearing one of Friend. Why, then, not put it out of the power of the vicious and the Lawless to use us with cruelty and indignity without impunity. Men of Sense in all Ages abhor those customs which treat us only as the vassals of your Sex.

Source: Abigail Adams, "Remember the Ladies," in *Living History America*, edited by Erik Bruun and Jay Crosby (New York: Tess Press, 1999), pp. 150-151.

France. She then profitably sold these items, which, because of war shortages and inflation, were scarce in Massachusetts. At the same time, Abigail also purchased land and speculated in currency. Through these endeavors, she kept her family solvent.

During the ten years in which she saw her husband only sporadically, Abigail expanded her literary interests, exploring, partly through John's guidance, political theory, biography, and history. She also wrote voluminously, to John, to other family members, and to friends. It was during this period that Abigail wrote to John of her political views regarding women's roles in the new nation. Her famous letter of March 31, 1776, in which she requested John to "Remember the Ladies," has established Abigail's reputation as an early proponent of women's rights. In context, however, it is clear that Abigail wrote not of political rights per se but of women's legal rights, specifically those that guaranteed them protection from physical abuse. At the time, divorce, although allowed in a few extreme instances, was generally unavailable. In addition, women abrogated all rights to property ownership upon marriage, which in turn made them ineligible to vote because property ownership was a key qualification for voting.

Abigail Adams. (Library of Congress)

Abigail also advocated equal education for women. She argued for equal education within the context of her perception of women's traditional domestic roles. The concept of "Republican motherhood" held that because women taught the sons who were destined to become leaders, women had an important role in maintaining the existence of an informed citizenry capable of supporting a republican government. To teach their sons successfully, these women required an education equal to that of boys and men, which Abigail hoped would be supported by law.

Although she is now considered an early advocate of women's rights, Abigail saw her own life as highly traditional. An adept manager of her family's resources, she nevertheless viewed her role as currency speculator, land purchaser, and farmer as aberrant and a patriotic sacrifice. She was comfortable only, it seems, in her domestic role, and in that, as in all else, she excelled. Abigail lived to see her son John Quincy establish a successful diplomatic and political career. Several personal tragedies marred her happiness, including the death of her son Charles from alcoholism when he was thirty years old and her daughter Nabby's brutally painful mastectomy and subsequent death from breast cancer.

Until 1800, when John retired from government office, Abigail functioned at times as host during his several years as a diplomat, first in England, then in France. She also served two terms as the vice president's wife during the George Washington administration and finally as First Lady during her husband's presidency from 1797 to 1801.

During the last eighteen years of her life she retired with her husband to Quincy (formerly Braintree) and lived in relative domestic peace surrounded by children, grandchildren, sisters, nieces, and nephews. At the family's Quincy farm, Abigail pursued her lifelong hobby of gardening. Dying of typhoid fever in 1818, she was mourned by John, who, lamenting the loss of his "dearest friend," survived his wife by eight years.

SIGNIFICANCE

Abigail Adams always functioned within the prescribed social roles for women of her time. She was an affectionate, protective mother who cared for her children physically and emotionally her entire life. She provided intellectual and emotional companionship as well as financial support for her brilliant but irascible husband John Adams. Although Abigail for a time functioned as merchant, farmer, and speculator, she viewed these roles as a patriotic sacrifice to support the political career of her husband.

While her own marriage provided her intellectual and emotional satisfaction, she condemned the tyranny of men over women and longed for legal protection for women. Women's education she hoped would one day rival that of men. She also yearned for the day when women would be able to limit the number of children they had. Nevertheless, her life must be viewed within the context of her eighteenth century world, where she functioned primarily within the domestic sphere. She was not a public advocate for women's rights; the term "women's rights" was not even used in her time. Yet, she did not view her role within her marriage as less valuable than that of her husband. To Abigail and to John, marriage was a true partnership.

She was a supremely shrewd, able woman who took every advantage available to her to expand her intellectual horizons, and she enjoyed a wide correspondence through her letters. In addition to providing an idea of this remarkable woman's psyche, Abigail Adams's copious letters give a detailed social history of her era and details into the character of her husband and of several other political leaders, including her close friend Thomas Jefferson.

—Mary E. Virginia

FURTHER READING

Adams, Abigail. *The Book of Abigail and John: Selected Letters of the Adams Family, 1762-1784.* Edited by L. H. Butterfield, Marc Friedlaender, and Mary-Jo Kline. Boston: Northeastern University Press, 2002. This revised text includes a foreword by David McCullogh, author of a best-selling biography of John Adams. Abigail's letters are her literary achievement—eloquent, informative, and illuminating.

Akers, Charles W. *Abigail Adams: An American Woman.* Boston: Little, Brown, 1980. Written specifically for the college undergraduate and high school student, Akers's work is admirably detailed and readable. Abigail's life is well grounded in historical context.

Gelles, Edith B. *Portia: The World of Abigail Adams.* Bloomington: Indiana University Press, 1992. An insightful biography of Adams, viewing her not only as John's wife and John Quincy's mother but also within the context of her domestic and predominantly female world. This work requires a knowledge of fundamental historical events, so it should be read in conjunction with a broader history, such as that of Akers. Includes an instructive introductory chapter, footnotes, a bibliography, and a chronology.

Levin, Phyllis Lee. *Abigail Adams: A Biography.* New York: St. Martin's Press, 1987. By far the most detailed biography of Adams, making extensive use of research sources. Unlike other biographers, Levin provides ample discussion of Abigail's life during the years after John Adams's retirement, although Levin does so against the backdrop of John Quincy's career. Similarly, Abigail's earlier life is viewed against John's career. Just shy of five hundred pages, the work contains footnotes, a bibliography, and a family tree.

Nagel, Paul C. *The Adams Women: Abigail and Louisa Adams, Their Sisters, and Daughters.* New York: Oxford University Press, 1987. While not exclusively about Abigail, Nagel's work is useful for placing Abigail's life within the context of her close female relations, including her sisters Mary and Elizabeth. Despite his admiration of her intellect, Nagel provides a portrait of Adams that is largely unsympathetic, making her appear domineering.

Withey, Lynne. *Dearest Friend: A Life of Abigail Adams.* New York: Simon & Schuster, 2001. Withey judges Adams by twentieth century standards rather than understanding her within her historical context. The author focuses extensively on Abigail's political views while paying scant attention to her more notable successes in her domestic roles, viewing Abigail as a "prisoner" in her world.

See also: John Adams; Mary Astell; Georgiana Cavendish; Thomas Jefferson; Sophie von La Roche; Catherine Macaulay; Mary Wortley Montagu; Betsy Ross; Jean-Jacques Rousseau; George Washington; Mary Wollstonecraft.

Related articles in *Great Events from History: The Eighteenth Century, 1701-1800:* April, 1762: Rousseau Publishes *The Social Contract*; December 16, 1773: Boston Tea Party; April 19, 1775: Battle of Lexington and Concord; January 10, 1776: Paine Publishes *Common Sense*; July 4, 1776: Declaration of Independence; October 27, 1787-May, 1788: Publication of *The Federalist*; April 30, 1789: Washington's Inauguration; 1790's: First U.S. Political Parties; February 22, 1791-February 16, 1792: Thomas Paine Publishes *Rights of Man*; 1792: Wollstonecraft Publishes *A Vindication of the Rights of Woman*; September 19, 1796: Washington's Farewell Address.

JOHN ADAMS
President of the United States (1797-1801)

As a member of the Continental Congress, Adams helped bring the American colonies to the point of independence in 1776. As one of the new nation's first diplomats, he helped negotiate the treaty that ended the American War of Independence. As the second president of the United States, he kept the young nation out of war.

Born: October 30, 1735; Braintree (now Quincy), Massachusetts
Died: July 4, 1826; Quincy, Massachusetts
Areas of achievement: Government and politics, diplomacy, law

EARLY LIFE

John Adams was born in Braintree, Massachusetts, where his family had lived for nearly a century. His father was a farmer and a town constable who expected his eldest son, John, to become a Congregational minister. The young Adams attended the Free Latin School in Braintree and then enrolled at Harvard College in 1751. On graduation in 1755, he taught school for a while at Worcester before deciding to abandon the ministry to take up law instead. In 1758, the intelligent, studious Adams returned to Braintree to practice law in what was still a country town only 10 miles from Boston.

Six years later, he married Abigail Smith, a woman who matched him in intelligence and ambition and perhaps exceeded him in practicality. Short and already stocky (colleagues later called him rotund), Adams seemed to be settling into the life of a successful country courthouse lawyer who might, in time, aspire to a seat in the legislature when, in 1765, the English parliament altered American colonial politics forever by passing the Stamp Act. The ensuing Stamp Act crisis offered to the ambitious Adams a quick route to popularity, influence, and public office. He did not miss his chance.

LIFE'S WORK

In 1765, John Adams denounced the stamp tax in resolutions written for the Braintree town meeting. When they were reprinted around the colony, his reputation as an opponent of English arrogance began to grow. Those in Boston who led the opposition to English taxes (including John Adams's distant relative, Samuel Adams) began to bring him more actively into their campaigns. He moved to Boston and won a seat in the Massachusetts General Court. He became, in effect, the local antigovernment party's lawyer, writing some of its more important public papers for the Boston town meeting and defending its members in court against charges brought by the Crown.

When Parliament answered the 1773 Boston Tea Party with the Coercive (or Intolerable) Acts in 1774, the general court chose Adams as a delegate to the intercolonial congress scheduled to meet in Philadelphia that fall, to discuss what the colonies should do. He wrote a "Declaration of Rights," which the First Continental Congress adopted, which based colonial rights to self-government not only on their charters and on the inherent rights of Englishmen but also on "the immutable laws of nature." Those were the grounds on which many colonists would soon challenge not merely England's right to tax them but also England's right to govern them at all. In good part, those were the grounds that underlay the Declaration of Independence.

Before the Congress met again, war began at Lexington in April, 1775. When Adams arrived at the Second Continental Congress in the spring of 1775, he already believed that the only true constitutional connection between the colonies and England was through the king—a position he set out in newspaper essays signed "Novanglus." He had not yet, however, openly called for a severing of all ties to the mother country. He had seen the colonists' rage run out of bounds in the Stamp Act ri-

John Adams. (Library of Congress)

liberties, not to establish new ones, and that the new Constitution ought to conserve as much of England's admirable constitutional heritage as possible. The constitution he drafted included relatively high property qualifications for voting and holding office (to ensure stability); it left the structure of Massachusetts's government much as it had been before independence, except for replacing English officials with elected American ones.

For more than a year after independence, Adams served on a variety of committees in Congress and in Massachusetts, doing work that was as exhausting as it was important. In October, 1777, he withdrew from Congress and returned to Massachusetts, but in November, Congress named him one of its emissaries to France, charged with raising loans for the republic across Europe and with negotiating treaties of friendship, trade, and alliance, especially with the French nation.

That alliance was concluded before Adams arrived in Paris, but he stayed on and was immediately caught up in the roiling jealousies that were endemic at the American mission there. Adams especially disliked and distrusted Benjamin Franklin, whose demeanor, integrity, honesty, and morals he judged inferior to his own.

ots of 1765. He had been disturbed and angered by the joy with which some colonists greeted the closing of civil and criminal courts in Massachusetts when English authority collapsed in the colony. He was worried that a revolution might get out of hand and establish not liberty, but mob rule. Although such worries stayed very much in his mind, by the time the Second Continental Congress met, Adams realized that there were no practical alternatives left but armed resistance or submission to Parliament. At the Congress, therefore, he worked both openly and by guile to bring reluctant and sometimes timid delegates to accept the inevitability of independence. When the Congress finally agreed to act, after more than one year of war, it was Adams who wrestled Thomas Jefferson's declaration through to adoption on July 4, 1776.

Adams had applauded Thomas Paine's *Common Sense* when it appeared in January, 1776, but he disliked the very democratic plan of government advocated by Paine. The kind of government Adams favored can be seen most clearly in the plan he drew up for Massachusetts's revolutionary constitution. Adams thought the purpose of the American Revolution was to preserve old

Adams returned to Massachusetts in August, 1779, but by December, he was back in France to help negotiate a peace treaty with England. He feuded with Franklin almost constantly over which of them was responsible for what in conducting the republic's diplomacy, but ultimately, all three peace commissioners (Adams, Franklin, and John Jay) agreed to negotiate a separate treaty between the United States and England, a treaty that did not directly involve France.

Though Franklin was responsible for the broad outlines of the agreement, Adams worked out some crucial compromises, without which the treaty may well have failed. Adams persuaded the English, for example, to concede to American fishing rights off the Newfoundland and Nova Scotia coasts in return for the new nation agreeing to open its courts to Loyalists. Adams stayed on for a year in France after the war ended in 1783, and then moved to London as the United States' first minister to the Court of St. James in 1785. He spent three years there, trying with little success to iron out problems between the United States and England (mostly involving noncompliance with the peace treaty).

While in London, he wrote the three-volume *A Defense of the Constitutions of the United States of America* (1787-1788), in which he explained his conservative and primarily English approach to the proper constitution of civil governments. The work was frank in its praise of the basic principles of the English constitution and earnest in its cautions about the risks of letting government rely too heavily on popular majorities to determine policy and law. Indeed, some Americans began to consider Adams soft on aristocracy and even monarchy. The first volume of *A Defense of the Constitutions of the United States of America* appeared in time to influence the thinking of delegates at the Constitutional Convention.

Adams returned home in 1788, and he was chosen as George Washington's vice president under the new Constitution of 1787. He did not like the job. "My country," he wrote to his wife, "has in its wisdom contrived for me the most insignificant office that ever the invention of man contrived or his imagination conceived." For the next eight years, nevertheless, he served Washington loyally, presiding over the senate and breaking tie votes in favor of Federalist policies. His reward came in 1797, when, as Washington's chosen successor, Adams defeated Jefferson and became the second president of the United States.

Adams's presidency was at best only a partial success. He had hoped, as Washington had in 1789, to become president of a united people. By the time he took office, however, the people had already divided themselves into two rival political parties: the Federalists (ostensibly led by Adams) and the National (or Jeffersonian) Republicans, led by Adams's vice president and old friend, Thomas Jefferson.

Furthermore, world affairs all but guaranteed that his presidency would be troubled. As Adams took office, for example, the United States was already dangerously close to war with France. The French, who had already fought their own revolution and created a republic of sorts, were at war with England and were angry that the United States had refused to aid France, a conflict called the XYZ affair. By 1797, the French were beginning to seize American ships on the high seas. When American peace commissioners, whom Adams had sent to France to try to work things out short of war, reported that the French had demanded bribes to begin serious negotiations, Americans reacted angrily. Adams asked Congress to prepare for a war that seemed inevitable, but, at the same time, he refused to abandon his efforts to avoid it if possible. For the remainder of his presidency, Adams stuck to the same policy—prepare for war, but work for peace—until (just as he left office) it yielded a new treaty of amity between the United States and France.

In the meanwhile, the Federalist Party, influenced by Alexander Hamilton more than by Adams, forced through Congress very high (and very unpopular) taxes to pay for the war they confidently expected to begin at any moment. Moreover, Federalist congressmen passed, and Adams signed, the unpopular Alien and Sedition Acts in 1798. The first act raised to fourteen the number of years an immigrant had to live in the country before becoming a citizen and was evidently designed to prevent recent Irish immigrants from voting against Federalists, whom they rightly believed to be pro-English. The second, the Sedition Act, made the publication of virtually all criticism of federal officials a crime. Both laws lost whatever legitimacy they may have had in the eyes of the

---

ON THE FOURTH OF JULY

John Adams, in a letter to his wife, Abigail Adams, celebrates the long-term historical significance of the July 2, 1776, vote for the Declaration of Independence and its official adoption two days later. John Adams, a major figure in the fight for American independence, got the date for the holiday wrong, but his belief that independence would be celebrated for many, many years was right on target.

The second day of July 1776, will be the most memorable Epocha, in the history of America. I am apt to believe that it will be celebrated by succeeding generations as the great anniversary festival. It ought to be commemorated as the day of deliverance, by solemn acts of devotion to God Almighty. It ought to be solemnized with pomp and parade, with shows, games, sports, guns, bells, bonfires and illuminations, from one end of the continent to the other, from this time forward, forevermore.

You will think me transported with enthusiasm, but I am not. I am well aware of the toil, and blood, and treasure, that it will cost us to maintain this declaration, and support and defend these States. Yet, through all the gloom, I can see the rays of ravishing light and glory.

Source: John Adams, in *Living History America*, edited by Erik Bruun and Jay Crosby (New York: Tess Press, 1999), p. 150.

public when the supposedly imminent war, which might have justified them as national defense measures, failed to come.

Federalist judges and prosecutors enforced the laws anyway, jailing, for example, several prominent Republican newspaper editors for violating the Sedition Act by criticizing Adams (though no Federalist editor ever went to jail for vilifying Jefferson). The partisan application of the law left Adams and the Federalists saddled with a reputation as opponents of free speech as the election of 1800 approached. Adams was further crippled by growing divisions in his own party (Hamilton actually campaigned against him) and by the slow pace at which his diplomacy worked. Most voters did not know, for example, until after they had voted, that Adams's policy had succeeded and that a lasting peace with France had been arranged.

In the election of 1800, Adams lost to Jefferson by eight electoral votes. Exhausted, bitterly disappointed, and tired as well of the constant bickering and criticism, public and private, of the last four years, Adams retired from public life on the day Jefferson was inaugurated. He returned to his home in Quincy to spend his time farming, reading, and writing an occasional essay on law or history. He died on July 4, 1826, a few hours after his great antagonist and greater friend, Jefferson, died in Virginia.

SIGNIFICANCE

Throughout his life, John Adams never got the praise he thought was his due. He was an important writer in the years preceding independence, but none of his writings had the broad impact of John Dickinson's *Letters from a Farmer in Pennsylvania, to the Inhabitants of the British Colonies* (1767-1768) or the great popular appeal of Thomas Paine's *Common Sense*. In the long run, however, through his writings on government and constitutions, Adams contributed as much or more to the development of republican constitutional thought than all but two or three of the founders.

His work in Europe negotiating the Treaty of Paris (1783) was at times brilliant, but it was the colorful and cunningly rustic Benjamin Franklin who caught the public's eye. Adams was president of the United States, but he immediately followed Washington in that office and inevitably Americans compared the two and found Adams the weaker president. Adams claimed that he did not seek the people's praises, but all of his life he watched men who were no more intelligent than he, no more dedicated to the republic, and no more successful in serving it

win the kind of warm public applause that seemed beyond his grasp. He was respected but not revered, and he knew it.

Broadly speaking, Adams made three major contributions to the revolution and the new republic. First, he worked in Massachusetts and in Congress to keep the revolution from running amok and destroying what was good in the English political tradition. He demonstrated to skeptical Tories and doubtful rebels, by both his words and his work, that independence need not be an invitation to anarchy, despotism, or mob rule, and so he helped make independence an acceptable alternative to submission. Second, with Jay and Franklin, he protected American interests in the double-dealing diplomatic atmosphere of Paris and London during the war, and he won for the republic a treaty that secured its independence as well as the vast undeveloped territories and other economic resources it needed to survive and develop. Third, as president, he kept the new republic out of what would have been a bitter, divisive war fought under a new, untested Constitution; thanks to Adams's skillful foreign policy, the republic did not have to face its first war under the Constitution for another twelve years.

Yet Adams never completely accepted the more democratic implications of the revolution, and so, by the end of his career, he was both one of the most important of the republic's founders and one of the least appreciated.

—Robert A. Becker

FURTHER READING

Adams, Abigail. *The Book of Abigail and John: Selected Letters of the Adams Family, 1762-1784*. Edited by L. H. Butterfield, Marc Friedlaender, and Mary-Jo Kline. Boston: Northeastern University Press, 2002. This revised text includes a foreword by David McCullogh, author of a best-selling biography of John Adams. John and Abigail's letters illustrate their remarkable relationship and the private and public worlds in which they lived.

Adams, John. *The Portable John Adams*. Edited by John Patrick Diggins. New York: Penguin Books, 2004. A collection of Adams's writings containing portions of his diary and autobiography as well as some of his political works, including "A Dissertation on Canon and Feudal Law" and "Thoughts on Government."

Cappon, Lester J., ed. *The Adams-Jefferson Letters: The Complete Correspondence Between Thomas Jefferson and Abigail and John Adams*. 2 vols. Chapel Hill: University of North Carolina Press, 1959. Covers the years 1777 to 1826. Excellent in conveying the revolutionary and early national periods through Adams's eyes. The letters following 1812 are remarkable, with the two aging rebels reminiscing about the revolution and their presidencies and speculating about the nation's future.

Ferling, John E. *Adams vs. Jefferson: The Tumultuous Election of 1800*. New York: Oxford University Press, 2004. Ferling describes how this "contest of titans" marked a turning point in American history, with Adams's Federalists and Jefferson's Republicans battling over two different ideas of how the new nation should be governed.

Grant, James. *John Adams: Party of One*. New York: Farrar, Straus, and Giroux, 2005. A compact, well-written biography, examining Adams's early life and public career. Grant bases his biography on Adams's diaries, letters, and unfinished autobiography.

Jensen, Merrill. *The Founding of a Nation: A History of the American Revolution, 1763-1776*. New York: Oxford University Press, 1968. One of the best accounts of the origins and events of the revolution from the Grenville Program of 1763 to the Declaration of Independence. Narrative in form, scholarly, and nicely written.

McCullogh, David. *John Adams*. New York: Simon & Schuster, 2001. A highly praised, best-selling biography. Offers a clearly written, comprehensive, and balanced account of Adams's life, with detailed descriptions of events and prominent personalities of the time.

Morris, Richard B. *The Peacemakers: The Great Powers and American Independence*. New York: Harper & Row, 1965. Still the best account of the negotiations leading to peace in 1783. An extremely detailed work.

Shaw, Peter. *The Character of John Adams*. Chapel Hill: University of North Carolina Press, 1976. Examines Adams's ideas in the light of his (especially Puritan) background and his personal experiences at each stage of his life and career. Controversial but interesting and insightful.

Smith, Page. *John Adams*. 2 vols. Garden City, N.Y.: Doubleday, 1962. One of the most complete and detailed accounts of Adams's life. Especially helpful on particular incidents or periods of Adams's life.

See also: Abigail Adams; Samuel Adams; John Dickinson; Benjamin Franklin; George III; Alexander Hamilton; John Hancock; Richard Howe; Thomas Hutchinson; John Jay; Thomas Jefferson; Robert Morris; Thomas Paine.

Related articles in *Great Events from History: The Eighteenth Century, 1701-1800:* March 22, 1765-March 18, 1766: Stamp Act Crisis; December 16, 1773: Boston Tea Party; April 19, 1775: Battle of Lexington and Concord; May 10-August 2, 1775: Second Continental Congress; January 10, 1776: Paine Publishes *Common Sense*; May, 1776-September 3, 1783: France Supports the American Revolution; July 4, 1776: Declaration of Independence; February 6, 1778: Franco-American Treaties; March 1, 1781: Ratification of the Articles of Confederation; 1783: Loyalists Migrate to Nova Scotia; September 3, 1783: Treaty of Paris; October 27, 1787-May, 1788: Publication of *The Federalist*; April 30, 1789: Washington's Inauguration; 1790's: First U.S. Political Parties; September 19, 1796: Washington's Farewell Address; June 25-July 14, 1798: Alien and Sedition Acts.

SAMUEL ADAMS
American politician

Strategically placed in Boston, the center of resistance to English colonial policies, Adams was one of the most significant organizers of the American Revolution.

Born: September 27, 1722; Boston, Massachusetts
Died: October 2, 1803; Boston, Massachusetts
Areas of achievement: Government and politics, military

EARLY LIFE

Samuel Adams's American ancestry began with Henry Adams, who emigrated from Devonshire, England, to Quincy, Massachusetts, in the early seventeenth century. One branch of the family included John Adams, who became second president of the United States. Samuel Adams's grandfather was a sailor, Captain John Adams. His father, Samuel Adams, Sr., lived his entire life in Boston, operating a malt house, or brewery, and was an active member of the old South Church. He was also active in local politics, establishing the first of the Boston Caucus Clubs, which played a vital role in the early upheavals of the revolutionary period.

Samuel Adams, then, was born into an active and influential civic-minded Boston family. He grew up familiar with and keenly interested in local politics and knew most Boston political leaders through their friendship with his father. Many of those leaders were prominent in Massachusetts colonial politics as well. Samuel absorbed the traditional independent-mindedness of Boston and thought of Massachusetts as autonomous and largely self-governing within the broader parameters of the British Empire.

Educated in the small wooden schoolhouse in the rear of King's Chapel, Samuel received a traditional grounding in Latin and Greek grammar, preparatory to entering Harvard College. When he received the A.B. degree in 1740 and the master of arts in 1743, his interest in politics was already clear. He titled his thesis, "Whether It Be Lawful to Resist the Supreme Magistrate, If the Commonwealth Cannot Otherwise Be Preserved."

LIFE'S WORK

Samuel Adams thus embarked upon his life's work in colonial politics, but he also had to make a living for his family. To that end, his father gave him £1,000 to help him get started in business. He promptly lent £500 to a friend (who never repaid the loan) and lost the other £500 through poor management. His father then took him into partnership in his malt house, from which the family made a modest living.

Adams lived an austere, simple life and throughout his life had little interest in making money. At a time of crisis just before the war, General Thomas Gage governed Massachusetts under martial law and offered Adams an annuity of £2,000 for life. Adams promptly rejected the offer; "a guinea never glistened in my eyes," he said. A man of integrity, he would not be bribed to refrain from doing what he believed to be right. His threadbare clothing was his trademark, reflecting his austerity and lack of interest in material things.

In 1748 his father died, leaving him one-third of his modest estate. Adams gradually sold most of it during the busy years of his life and was rescued from abject poverty in his retirement years only by a small inheritance from his son. During most of his life, his only income was a small salary as a clerk of the Massachusetts General Assembly.

Adams married Elizabeth Checkley, the daughter of the minister of New South Congregational Church, in 1749. She died eight years later, survived by only two of their five children, a boy and a girl. Adams reared the children and managed alone for seven years but remarried in 1764 to Elizabeth Wells. He was then forty-two years old, and she was twenty-four.

Adams was of average height and muscular build. He carried himself straight in spite of an involuntary palsied movement of his hands and had light blue eyes and a serious, dignified manner. He was very fond of sacred music and sang in the choir of New South Church. Personable, he maintained a close relationship with his neighbors and was constantly chatting with those he met along the street. He had a gift for smoothing over disputes among his friends and acquaintances and was often asked to mediate a disagreement. Adams was a hard worker, and through the years his candle burned late at night as he kept up his extensive correspondence, much of which does not survive today. His second cousin, John Adams, likened him to John Calvin, partly because of his deep piety but also because of his personality: He was "cool . . . polished, and refined," somewhat inflexible, but consistent, a man of "steadfast integrity, exquisite humanity, genteel erudition, obliging, engaging manners, real as well as professed piety, and a universal good character. . . ."

Samuel Adams was very interested in political philosophy and believed strongly in liberty and Christian virtue and frugality. He helped organize discussion clubs and the *Public Advertiser*, a newspaper to promote understanding of political philosophy. He served in political offices large and small, as fire ward, as moderator, and as tax collector. An orthodox Christian, he warned of the political implications of the "fallen" nature of humans, susceptible as most individuals were to self-aggrandizement, if not corruption. Colonial Americans believed that power had the tendency to corrupt, and Adams was no exception. Speaking for the Boston town meeting, Adams said,

> [Such is] the depravity of mankind that ambition and lust of power above the law are . . . predominant passions in the breasts of most men. [Power] converts a good man in private life to a tyrant in office.

Despite mythology to the contrary, Adams was not a mob leader, though he was popular with the common workers of Boston. He was opposed to violence and sought to achieve his aims by political means. No evidence has ever been found placing Adams at any of the scenes in Boston involving mob violence such as the Boston Massacre, the wrecking of Lieutenant Governor Thomas Hutchinson's house, or the physical harassment of merchants. He has often been charged with "masterminding" these events, but only by conjecture, not on the basis of historical evidence.

In his early forties, Adams was well known in Boston politics when the Stamp Act crisis occurred in 1765-1766, the beginning of the revolutionary period. Along with his friend James Otis, Adams spoke out strongly and wrote much against the dangers of the Stamp Act. Before the Boston town meeting, Adams denied the right of the British parliament to tax the colonists. The Massachusetts charter gave Americans the right "to govern and tax ourselves." If Parliament could tax the colonies, then the English living in America would become "tributary slaves" without representation. Adams called for a unified resistance to this "tyranny" throughout the colonies. The Boston town meeting then elected Adams to a seat in the Massachusetts General Assembly, where he was soon elected to the position of clerk, a position he held for ten years.

This principle of opposing taxation without representation became one of the most significant rallying points for resisting British control of the colonies. Adams nevertheless stressed that he had no desire for colonial representation in the British parliament. Since the colonists would be considerably outnumbered and since travel to England was so slow, it would be "impracticable for the subjects in America" to have a tiny voice in Parliament. Instead, Adams and most of his fellow American strategists wanted to be able to make their own laws in their own American "parliaments." "All acts," wrote Adams,

> made by any power whatever other than the General Assembly of this province, imposing taxes on the inhabitants, are infringements of our inherent and unalienable rights as men and British subjects. . . .

On November 1, 1765, the day the Stamp Act was to go into effect, Boston buildings were draped in mourning black and the church bells tolled slowly. Governor Francis Bernard ordered the Boston militia to muster as a pre-

Samuel Adams. (Library of Congress)

cautionary peacekeeping measure. Yet the men would not respond; one drummer sounded the call only to have his drum promptly broken. The rest of the drummers preserved their instruments by not using them. In direct violation of the Stamp Act, the Massachusetts General Assembly voted 81 to 5 to open the law courts of the province without using stamped papers, as required by the act.

In 1772, Adams sought and received the authorization of the Boston town meeting to create a Committee of Correspondence to inform and consult with other towns in the province, with a view to concerted and coordinated action. This was not a new idea. It had been customary for many years in Europe and in America for legislative bodies to use committees to handle official correspondence with other such governing authorities. As early as 1768, Richard Henry Lee had suggested to the Virginia House of Burgesses the formation of an intercolonial system of correspondence among the provincial assemblies. It was in Boston, however, that the idea was finally implemented.

As clerk of the Massachusetts General Assembly, Adams expanded the circular-letter type of correspondence to include all the colonies. In time, those letters contributed significantly to the unified action of the colonies. Realizing the potential strength in such an arrangement, the British secretary of state for the colonies, Lord Hillsborough, instructed the governor of Massachusetts to order the General Assembly to rescind a circular letter sent to other colonies. Instead, the General Assembly, in a heated debate, voted 92 to 17 to refuse to rescind the letter. The governor dissolved the legislature, but Adams—a pioneer in realizing the enormous importance of communication and information in sustaining any cause—published the names of the seventeen who had voted against the measure, impairing their political future. Britain now sought to obtain evidence to arrest and deport to England for prosecution those who resisted British law. Adams also published that letter, and the effect was electrifying, because it showed the clear intention of the British government to bypass the cherished English right of trial by jury of one's peers.

The political year of 1773 began with now-governor Hutchinson's opening speech to the Massachusetts General Assembly on the issue of parliamentary supremacy. Did the British parliament have authority over the elected assembly of Massachusetts, and, if so, to what extent? Adams headed the committee of the assembly designated to reply to the governor. He simply and cleverly took Hutchinson's own famous book, *History of*

Massachusetts Bay (1760), and compared what he had written earlier with the current message. Adams found many inconsistencies and contradictions. The governor's book, for example, acknowledged that the founders of Massachusetts Bay Colony had been assured by the Crown that "they were to be governed by laws made by themselves" and not by Parliament.

Adams also had a hand in the Boston Tea Party later that same year. The British East India Company was partially owned by the British government but, because of mismanagement, had stockpiled a great quantity of tea that needed to be sold before it spoiled. The Tea Act of spring, 1773, gave the company a monopoly on tea sales in America but sharply cut the price of tea. The controversial tea tax (set by the Townshend Acts of 1767) would continue to be levied, but the actual price, including the tax, paid in America for tea would only be about one-half that paid by a Londoner.

This monopoly on the tea trade was potentially seriously damaging to American free enterprise. Without competition, merchant trade could not prosper, and the Americans would eventually pay unnecessarily high prices for imports. Moreover, a precedent would be set regulating trade excessively instead of following more of a free market system. Adams, however, chose to focus on the taxation issue rather than the monopoly issue, because the former could be defended more emotionally and symbolically. When American patriots refused to allow the tea to be landed, the governor refused to allow the merchant ships to return with their cargoes of tea. The standoff ended when colonists destroyed thousands of pounds of tea by dumping it into the bay.

The response of the British government inflamed the angry Americans. The Boston Port Act closed the port of Boston and threatened to ruin the city as a commercial center. Salem and Marblehead merchants responded by inviting the merchants of Boston to use their docks and warehouses free of charge. Contributions of food and supplies came from many colonies. Adams asked the people of Massachusetts to support a "Solemn League and Covenant" not to buy British goods. (The wording of the boycott was significant, reminiscent to American colonists of the English Civil War and of the heroism of the later Scottish Covenanters.)

General Gage in effect established martial law in Boston and even dissolved the General Assembly. The assembly, however, was in the process of selecting delegates to the First Continental Congress in Philadelphia. When General Gage's messenger arrived to order the assembly to disband, Adams, who was the clerk, locked the doors to keep the messenger out until the delegation process was completed. The elected delegates included both Samuel Adams and John Adams. General Gage considered arresting Samuel Adams but did not want to provoke a violent reaction, which such a measure would assuredly incite.

The 300-mile trip to Philadelphia was the longest of Adams's life. Even there, however, he found himself influential politically, becoming the key member of the newly organized Committee of Safety, a coordinating group. Adams was also the chairman of the Donation Committee, which distributed gifts of food and supplies collected along the Atlantic seaboard for the aid of the unfortunate people of the Boston area. The Committee of Safety began collecting weapons and supplies, and it even stored cannon at Concord.

An active member of the Continental Congress, Adams played a significant political role throughout the Revolutionary War. After the war, he approved of the new U.S. Constitution, but only after assurances were given him that a bill of rights was to be added. Adams became lieutenant governor of Massachusetts in 1789 and governor in 1793, retiring from that office in 1797. He died on October 2, 1803, at the age of eighty-one, having devoted his life to the cause of liberty and independence in a new nation, the United States of America.

SIGNIFICANCE

It would be difficult to overestimate the importance of Samuel Adams to the American Revolution. Along with Virginia, New York, and Pennsylvania, Massachusetts led the way to independence. There was no center of power quite so volatile, however, as Massachusetts. It was there that the events that sparked the revolution occurred, events that included resistance to the Stamp Act, the Boston Massacre, the *Liberty* incident, and organized boycotts, as well as letters of protest.

Adams was involved in all these events. His importance, moreover, was recognized in the very highest echelons of the British government. When King George III ordered Governor Hutchinson to London for consultation, one of the questions he asked him was what accounted for the importance of Adams in the colonies. Hutchinson's reply reflected his frustration with Adams: "A great pretended zeal for liberty and a most inflexible natural temper. He was the first that publicly asserted the independency of the colonies upon the kingdom."

It is true that Adams was a principal advocate of complete independence from the British, but not until 1775. All that he had advocated for years following the Stamp Act crisis was self-government within the British system. He did not push for independence until it became obvious to him that the king was a "tyrant [with] an unalterable determination to compel the colonies to absolute obedience."

—*William H. Burnside*

FURTHER READING

Adams, Samuel. *The Writings of Samuel Adams*. Edited by H. A. Cushing. 4 vols. New York: G. P. Putnam's Sons, 1904-1908. Indispensable primary material, including letters, newspaper articles, and official correspondence of the Massachusetts General Assembly.

Alexander, John K. *Samuel Adams: America's Revolutionary Politician*. Lanham, Md.: Rowman & Littlefield, 2002. In this biography, Alexander argues that Adams was America's first professional, modern politician, who fought to protect constitutional liberties.

Bailyn, Bernard. *The Ideological Origins of the American Revolution*. Cambridge, Mass.: Belknap Press, 1967. Not much on Adams directly, but essential for understanding his ideological milieu. Bailyn finds, as did Adams, that the war was fought over constitutional issues.

Chidsey, Donald Barr. *The Great Separation: The Story of the Boston Tea Party and the Beginning of the American Revolution*. New York: Crown, 1965. Written in a popular novelist's style, this book brings to life the issues and actions surrounding the Boston Tea Party, including Adams's role.

Fowler, William M., Jr. *Samuel Adams: Radical Puritan*. Edited by Oscar Handlin. New York: Longman, 1997. A brief biography that places Adams's life within the context of Boston politics. Fowler argues that Adams was the revolutionary leader most concerned with upholding the Puritan values of Massachusetts.

Galvin, John R. *Three Men of Boston*. New York: Thomas Y. Crowell, 1976. Recounts the events leading up to the revolution in Boston by focusing on Samuel Adams, Thomas Hutchinson, and James Otis. Galvin captures the complexity of the period and shows how the issues and events were interrelated.

Hosmer, James K. *Samuel Adams*. Boston: Houghton Mifflin, 1885. A standard nineteenth century biography of Adams.

Maier, Pauline. *The Old Revolutionaries: Political Lives in the Age of Samuel Adams*. New York: Alfred A. Knopf, 1980. The chapter "A New Englander as Revolutionary: Samuel Adams" brilliantly analyzes Adams's historical significance. Maier analyzes the interpretive data on Adams and introduces many fresh insights.

Montross, Lynn. *The Reluctant Rebels: The Story of the Continental Congress, 1774-1789.* New York: Harper and Brothers, 1950. This work examines the critical role of the Continental Congress in the American Revolution, discussing Adams's contributions to the Congress.

See also: Abigail Adams; John Adams; John Singleton Copley; Benjamin Franklin; Thomas Gage; George

III; John Hancock; Thomas Hutchinson; Thomas Jefferson; Paul Revere; George Washington.

Related articles in *Great Events from History: The Eighteenth Century, 1701-1800:* 1712: Stamp Act; March 22, 1765-March 18, 1766: Stamp Act Crisis; June 29, 1767-April 12, 1770: Townshend Crisis; March 5, 1770: Boston Massacre; December 16, 1773: Boston Tea Party; September 5-October 26, 1774: First Continental Congress; April 19, 1775: Battle of Lexington and Concord; May 10-August 2, 1775: Second Continental Congress; July 4, 1776: Declaration of Independence; September 17, 1787: U.S. Constitution Is Adopted.

JOSEPH ADDISON
British writer and journalist

With Richard Steele, Addison published The Tatler *and* The Spectator, *which combined literature and journalism to establish the magazine as an important medium of cultural expression. Addison's literary criticism led to a Romantic sensibility in English literature, and his prose, which was literate but not inaccessible or difficult, revolutionized English prose style.*

Born: May 1, 1672; Milston, Wiltshire, England
Died: June 17, 1719; London, England
Also known as: Marmaduke Myrtle (pseudonym)
Area of achievement: Literature

EARLY LIFE
Joseph Addison was born to Jane Gulston and to Lancelot Addison, rector of the local Anglican parish. Little is known about Joseph Addison's youth except that his father's promotion to the deanery at Lichfield Cathedral moved the family in 1683. Addison, probably intending to enter Holy Orders, enrolled in Lancelot's alma mater, Queen's College at Oxford, in 1687.

A year later, Addison, like England itself, headed in a more secular direction. The Glorious Revolution of 1688 ended the line of Stuart kings who ruled by Divine Right and began a line of monarchs who ruled by parliamentary invitation. Addison, who enthusiastically welcomed the revolution, transferred to Magdalen College in 1689 on the strength of his reputation as a Latin scholar. Addison's interests in ancient and modern literature brought him into contact with writers and publishers anxious to bring classical texts to English readers through easy

translations. In 1693 and 1694, Addison published several original English poems as well as translations.

This modest literary success brought Addison to the notice of important Whig politicians such as John Somers and Charles Montagu. In the highly partisan world of postrevolutionary London, successful politicians needed skillful writers who could defend party policies with intelligence and wit. In the mid-1690's, Addison seems to have decided on a career in politics rather than in religion. In 1699, he accepted a government grant to make the Grand Tour of the Continent and study rival European cultures. Addison was abroad for four years, keeping in regular touch with his political patrons by writing witty letters of commentary on his travels. He peppered his account with clever metaphors and humorous turns of phrase: "The French," he wrote in a typical passage, "sing, laugh and starve." His patrons wanted protégés who could be entertaining as well as useful.

A portrait of Addison painted before he left Oxford shows a handsome young man with a broad forehead, alert eyes, and a fine, aquiline nose. He is dressed like a stylish young gentleman in a long wig of cascading curls, and over a plain dark coat is a long scarf, knotted and tossed rakishly to the side.

Addison soon proved useful to Somers and Montagu. The Whig Party needed a poet to celebrate in serious verse the victory of their general, the first duke of Marlborough, at Blenheim. Addison's mini-epic *The Campaign* (1705) fit their needs exactly. The poem was widely read, and Addison was handsomely rewarded with a political appointment. For the next five years Addison held a series of increasingly important posts, even as he kept busy with literature, writing a book of his travels, a comic opera, and several pamphlets on topical issues.

LIFE'S WORK

On April 12, 1709, the first issue of *The Tatler* appeared, the product of Richard Steele, another writer allied with the Whig Party. Steele planned to shape the political opinions and influence the social manners of London's middle and upper classes by a thrice-weekly broadsheet that dispensed news about foreign affairs, city happenings, and theatrical or literary trends. The job proved to be more than Steele could handle alone; by issue 24, Steele was incorporating material supplied by Addison, an acquaintance from Charter School (which both had attended before the university) and the Kit-Kat Club (a clique of Whig politicians, poets, and publishers).

During its successful run, Addison authored about one-fifth of the 271 issues of *The Tatler*. Steele noted the distinctive contributions of his friend in his farewell to his readers, praising Addison for "noble discourses" on learned topics such as the immortality of the soul and for the "finest strokes of wit and humour." Addison's contributions were limited because of his duties as chief secretary to the lord lieutenant of Ireland. *The Tatler* ceased publication when the Whigs lost control of the government to their rivals, the Tories.

Joseph Addison. (Library of Congress)

With their party out of power, Addison and Steele tried to repeat *The Tatler*'s success. On March 1, 1711, they published the first issue of *The Spectator*. More ambitious than *The Tatler*, *The Spectator* appeared daily except Sunday, eschewed explicit political propagandizing, and sought to interest its readers in high culture. *The Spectator* was spectacularly popular for its time, with a daily readership estimated at twenty thousand. It lasted for 555 issues, until December 6, 1712. Addison and Steele contributed equally—251 issues apiece—and used contributions from friends for the remaining 53 issues.

Addison and Steele's contemporary John Gay remarked how different *The Spectator* was from any daily paper before it. He praised its "prodigious run of wit and learning." Skillfully, Addison and Steele varied the paper's tone and content: one day a humorous account of the latest fad, the next day a discourse on the appeal of epic poetry, on the third day a rational argument for belief in a supreme being. Addison and Steele's purpose, to delight their readers even as they instructed them, was expressed in an early issue: "It was said of Socrates, that he brought Philosophy down from Heaven, to inhabit among men; and I shall be ambitious to have it said of me, that I have brought Philosophy . . . to dwell in Clubs and Assemblies, at Tea-Tables, and in Coffee-Houses." To give unity to the varied topics, they created the editorial persona of Mr. Spectator, an eccentric, friendly gentleman insatiably curious about London life.

THE SPECTATOR

In the first pages of the first issue of The Spectator, *Joseph Addison describes the periodical's title character, the Spectator, from whose point of view its articles are written. In the passage below, the Spectator tells of the London coffeehouses, smoking houses, chocolate houses, and general meeting places that he frequents. Gossip about these sorts of locales would form the basis for published essays.*

There is no place of general resort wherein I do not often make my appearance; sometimes I am seen thrusting my head into a round of politicians at Will's, and listening with great attention to the narratives that are made in those little circular audiences. Sometimes I smoke a pipe at Child's; and, while I seem attentive to nothing but the *Postman*, overhear the conversation of every table in the room. I appear on Sunday nights at Saint James's Coffee House, and sometimes join the little committee of politics in the inner room, as one who comes there to hear and improve. My face is likewise very well known at the Grecian, the Cocoa Tree, and in the theaters both of Drury Lane and the Haymarket. I have been taken for a merchant upon the Exchange for above these ten years, and sometimes pass for a Jew in the assembly of stock-jobbers at Jonathan's.

Source: Joseph Addison, in *The Spectator*, no. 1 (March 1, 1711). The Spectator Text Project. http://tabula.rutgers.edu/spectator/index.html. Accessed September, 2005. Orthography modernized by the editors.

Three months after *The Spectator*'s cessation, Steele began the *Guardian* (1713), a paper directed at the domestic household rather than London society. Addison took over the editorship after ninety-six issues and continued the project until October, 1713. Within a year, Addison revived *The Spectator* but after two months had to give up writing to attend to another crisis. After Queen Anne's death, the British parliament invited George, the elector of Hanover, to sit upon the English throne. Addison participated in the transition government that supervised George I's accession.

A year later, Addison found occasion for a new periodical. He began *The Freeholder* on December 23, 1715, in support of George I, whose rule was then being challenged by a rebellion in Scotland on behalf of the Stuart line exiled in 1688. All the persuasive skills and good humor Addison had developed in previous journals were employed in the effort to keep the English happy with their German-born king. *The Freeholder* offered itself as the thinking person's guide to sensible, civilized, conservative politics amid the excesses of rebellion.

The Hanover monarchy survived, and Addison tasted the rewards of both political success and literary eminence. In 1715, he was appointed a commissioner of trade and two years later a secretary of state. He married

the widowed countess of Warwick in 1716. He wrote a comedy, *The Drummer: Or, The Haunted House* (1716), which had a mildly successful run. His last venture in periodical journalism occurred under ironic circumstances. Addison once more called upon his learning and wit in *The Old Whig* (1719) to defend his party's Peerage Bill before Parliament; sadly, his opponent in this pamphlet war was his former ally, Richard Steele. Two months later Addison died peacefully in his bed.

SIGNIFICANCE

Joseph Addison and Richard Steele's *Tatler, Spectator*, and *Guardian* are literary achievements of the first rank. They are verbal mosaics of literary criticism, lighthearted social commentary, short fiction, and advice about manners. They used the resources of art on topics previously regarded as too ephemeral or practical for literature. Their mixture of journalism and art immortalized an age. The pages of these journals provide an unparalleled insight into the life of London's leisured classes at the start of the eighteenth century.

The literary consequences of Addison and Steele's journalism were profound. They established periodical journals and magazines as artifacts in literary culture, as mediums of both criticism and imaginative, often experimental, writing. For more than two centuries the conventions of their periodicals have reappeared in publication after publication: the use of departments, the creation of a persona, and the mix of informative and entertaining articles in the same issue.

Addison's special contributions to these periodicals were his learning, his wit, and his prose style. His knowledge of classical and contemporary literature enabled him to write accessible, intelligent literary criticism. His *Spectator* papers on the "pleasures of the imaginations," for example, are a landmark in criticism, often regarded as the starting point of a Romantic sensibility in English literature. Addison's wit is gentle in comparison to the slashing repartee of Restoration writers; its subtlety and good-naturedness became synonymous with the British sense of humor.

Most important, Addison revolutionized English prose style. By cultivating a middle style that combined the self-conscious artistry of the high style with the conversational immediacy of the low style, Addison perfected a prose that was literate yet easy to read. His style invites the reader's participation in the writer's imaginative act. It was the style that underlay the explosion of literature (the novel, the familiar essay, the travel book) in the later eighteenth century. Samuel Johnson, the most knowledgeable critic of the time, summed up Addison's import thus: "Whoever wishes to attain an English style, familiar but not coarse, and elegant but not ostentatious, must give his days and nights to the volumes of Addison."

—Robert M. Otten

FURTHER READING

Bloom, Edward A., and Lillian D. Bloom. *Addison and Steele: The Critical Heritage*. Boston: Routledge and Kegan Paul, 1980. This invaluable collection reprints critical estimates of the authors and their journals beginning in the early 1700's. It contains many of the famous, as well as hard-to-find, evaluations by eighteenth century commentators.

_____. *Joseph Addison's Sociable Animal: In the Market Place, on the Hustings, in the Pulpit*. Providence, R.I.: Brown University Press, 1971. The lengthiest study of Addison's contribution to the worldview of the emerging British middle class. By connecting ideas scattered throughout the periodical essays, the Blooms systematize Addison's economic, political, and religious thinking.

Bond, Richmond P. *The "Tatler": The Making of a Journal*. Cambridge, Mass.: Harvard University Press, 1971. Bond investigates the day-to-day problems involved with writing, composing, printing, and selling a journal in early eighteenth century London. The book is a salutary reminder of the pressures that literary enterprises face in a commercial era.

Dammers, Richard H. *Richard Steele*. Boston: Twayne, 1981. Dammers takes seriously Steele's efforts to reform manners through literature and to promote a general philosophy of benevolence. In his discussion of the journals, Dammers pays special attention to Steele's attitudes toward men and women in their married state.

Evans, James E., and John N. Wall, Jr. *A Guide to Prose Fiction in "The Tatler" and "The Spectator."* New York: Garland, 1977. The authors provide a number-by-number summary of both journals. The general reader will find the guide useful for tracing themes or topics among the 826 issues. The literary student will discover how much these periodical essays relied upon fictional devices and conventions.

Goldgar, Bertrand. *The Curse of Party: Swift's Relations with Addison and Steele*. Lincoln: University of Nebraska Press, 1961. This book focuses on the complications caused by the political affiliations of writers in Augustan London. In the case of Jonathan Swift, Addison, and Steele, political differences created personal as well as professional enmity among writers who shared important cultural ideals, a vision of literature's importance, and a willingness to experiment with traditional genres.

Johnson, Samuel. *Johnson's Chief Lives of the Poets*. Preface by Matthew Arnold. New York: H. Holt, 1879. Includes Johnson's life of Addison, in which he examines Addison's importance to subsequent periodical literature. Johnson, whose *Idler* and *Rambler* papers imitated Addison and Steele's journals, realized the problems of achieving commercial success while maintaining quality in content and presentation.

Ketcham, Michael G. *Transparent Designs: Reading, Performance, and Form in "The Spectator" Papers*. Athens: University of Georgia Press, 1985. The author argues that *The Spectator* reshaped the eighteenth century vision of society—in which public activity and private life were radically separated—into a social vision that blended the public and private spheres. He concludes that this new vision shaped not only the explosion of periodical journalism in the century but also the rise of the novel.

Otten, Robert M. *Joseph Addison*. Boston: Twayne, 1982. This study appreciates Addison's achievement as a writer who constantly adapted to the changing demands of audience and circumstance. It discusses his inventiveness in approaching familiar topics or repeated themes through a variety of techniques and perspectives.

Smithers, Peter. *The Life of Joseph Addison*. 2d ed. Oxford, England: Clarendon Press, 1968. Smithers is Addison's most comprehensive, sympathetic, and judicious biographer. He appreciates that Addison's vision of citizenship underlies both his own career and his effort to bring "Philosophy into Clubs and Assemblies." The book is especially good at placing Addison's literary works in their historical context.

See also: Fanny Abington; Queen Anne; John Baskerville; George Berkeley; William Blake; Georgiana

Cavendish; Daniel Defoe; George I; William Godwin; Samuel Johnson; First Duke of Marlborough; Mary Wortley Montagu; John Newbery; Alexander Pope; Richard Brinsley Sheridan; Richard Steele; Jonathan Swift; John Peter Zenger.

Related articles in *Great Events from History: The Eighteenth Century, 1701-1800:* March 1, 1711: Addison and Steele Establish *The Spectator*; January 7, 1714: Mill Patents the Typewriter; March 20, 1750-March 14, 1752: Johnson Issues *The Rambler*.

MARIA GAETANA AGNESI
Italian mathematician and charity worker

In her youth, Maria Agnesi advocated education for young women, in part by demonstrating her own impressive intellectual abilities. Her two-volume textbook on the calculus provided a complete synthesis of the mathematical methods developed during the Scientific Revolution. In her later years, she devoted herself to charitable work for the sick, poor, and aged.

Born: May 16, 1718; Milan (now in Italy)
Died: January 9, 1799; Milan
Areas of achievement: Mathematics, social reform, education, religion and theology

EARLY LIFE
Maria Gaetana Agnesi (mah-REE-ah gah-ay-TAHN-ah ahn-YAY-zee) was born to a wealthy and literate Italian family, the oldest of twenty-one children. According to most accounts, her father, Pietro Agnesi Mariami, became a mathematics professor at the University of Bologna, but there is no record of this. He and her mother, Anna Brivia, recognized Maria's abilities early and encouraged her to develop her intellect. Her special gift for languages was evident, as she could speak French fluently by the age of five. Impressively, at age nine she wrote a lengthy discourse in Latin on the importance of higher education for women entitled *Oratio qua ostenditur artium liberalium studia femineo sexu neutiquam abhorreri* (1727; an oration by which it is shown that the study of the liberal arts should not at all be abhorred by the female sex), which was printed at Milan. By the age of eleven, Maria was known as the Walking Polyglot and the Seven-Tongued Orator for her competence in Italian, French, German, Spanish, Latin, Greek, and Hebrew.

Maria's father engaged leading university professors to be her tutors. Their home became a gathering place for the most distinguished intellectuals of the time, both Italian and foreign. Maria participated in most of these meetings, engaging the guests in abstract academic discussions. Her younger sister, Maria Teresa (b. 1720), was a composer, singer, and harpsichordist who often performed her music at these meetings while Maria Gaetana presented theses in Latin on a wide variety of scientific and philosophical topics and defended them in the native language of her questioners. By the age of fourteen, Agnesi was solving difficult problems in ballistics and geometry. At seventeen, she circulated a critical commentary on the *Traité analytique des sections coniques* (1696; analytical treatise on conic sections) by the French mathematician Guillaume de L'Hôpital.

LIFE'S WORK
Although Agnesi had an attractive and agreeable manner, she was not eager to continue the public displays of her extraordinary learning. At the age of twenty, she expressed a desire to enter a convent. However, the death of Pietro Agnesi's second wife gave her another opportunity to retire from public life by assuming responsibility for her father's household and care for her twenty younger siblings. For the next two decades, she devoted herself to these duties along with the study of mathematics and the education of her younger brothers.

After her father's meetings were discontinued, Maria published a collection in Latin of 190 of the theses she had defended as a girl in a book called *Propositiones philosophicae* (pb. 1738; philosophical propositions). The topics covered in this book indicate the breadth of her knowledge in the sciences and philosophy of her day, including mechanics, hydromechanics, elasticity, celestial mechanics, universal gravitation, chemistry, mineralogy, botany, zoology, logic, and ontology. The theses on these topics appear together with a plea for the education of women.

For the next decade, Maria concentrated on mathematics, culminating in the publication of her most important mathematical work as a text for her younger brothers. *Instituzioni analitiche ad uso della gioventù italiana* (1748; *Analytical Institutions*, 1801) consisted of two volumes of 1,020 pages plus 59 pages of figures engraved by Marc' Antonio Dal Rè. Agnesi wrote the book in Italian rather than Latin to make it more accessible to young students. Her facility with languages enabled her to draw from a wide range of authors, producing the most complete synthesis of eighteenth century mathematics for at least the next fifty years. The second volume was later translated into French by Pierre d'Antelmy as *Traités élémentaires de calculus* (1775; elementary treatise on calculus), and the entire book was translated into English by the Cambridge mathematics professor John Colson and published in London in 1801 as *Analytical Institutions*.

The first volume of *Analytical Institutions* deals with the analysis of finite quantities, using algebra and geometry to construct and analyze geometric curves. The second volume develops differential and integral calculus and gives an introduction to the emerging topic of differential equations. It was the first text to give a systematic presentation of both differential and integral calculus, es-

tablishing the modern differential notation of Gottfried Wilhelm Leibniz over the more archaic "fluxions" of Isaac Newton. The English translation of 1801 introduced England to modern calculus notation.

One geometric curve discussed by Agnesi in *Analytical Institutions* has come to be uniquely associated with her name in an unusual but confusing way. She called this bell-shaped curve a versed sine or "versiera" (from the Latin *vertere*, meaning "to turn"). John Colson in his 1801 English translation confused this term with the Italian word *avversiera*, which means "witch." Hence, this curve came to be known as the "Witch of Agnesi" in the English-speaking world.

Agnesi dedicated *Analytical Institutions* to Empress Maria Theresa of Austria, who rewarded her with a diamond ring and a letter in a diamond-encrusted crystal case. Pope Benedict XIV sent her a congratulatory letter with a gold medal and a wreath made of gold and precious stones. She was elected to the Bologna Academy of Sciences and commended by the French Academy of Sciences for producing the best book of its kind. Pope Benedict named Agnesi an honorary professor of mathematics at the University of Bologna in 1750, although there is no record of her teaching there.

After her father's death in 1752, Agnesi turned increasingly to religious studies and charitable work. For the rest of her life, she devoted herself to the needs of the poor, starting with a small hospital in her home. During nearly forty years of charitable work, Agnesi gave away her inheritance to the poor, beginning with her diamond ring and crystal box from Maria Theresa, and even begged for money from others to provide for those in need. In 1771, she founded a charitable home for the aged with the Blue Nuns in Milan called Pio Albergo Trivulzio, acting as director of this hospice for several years. According to some sources, she took the blue habit of the Augustinian nuns before she died at the age of eighty.

SIGNIFICANCE

Maria Gaetana Agnesi was the first woman to publish a book on mathematics in modern Europe. Her most important contribution was the publication of *Analytical Institutions* in 1748. This was the first comprehensive and systematic textbook covering both differential and integral calculus with a unified notation. It is the first surviving mathematical work written by a woman

Maria Gaetana Agnesi. (Library of Congress)

and the most valuable work in establishing the calculus for at least the next fifty years. It unified the ideas and methods of the greatest mathematicians of the Scientific Revolution, including the analytic geometry of René Descartes and the newly developed calculus of Newton and Leibniz, establishing the superior notation of Leibniz. She also led the way in applying the calculus to many original problems in geometry and physics.

In addition to her mathematical work, Agnesi lived an exemplary life of service. Although science had faltered to some extent after the condemnation of Galileo a century earlier, Agnesi contributed to the revival of scientific work in Italy and the associated Catholic Enlightenment. She was an early advocate of education for women and a champion of this cause in several publications. Her devotion to duty and her lifelong service to the poor and needy set a worthy example of Christian charity.

—*Joseph L. Spradley*

FURTHER READING

Alic, Margaret. *Hypatia's Heritage*. Boston: Beacon Press, 1986. Focuses on the historical contributions of women in science, including a discussion of the work of Maria Agnesi.

Gray, S. I. B., and Tagui Malakyan. "The Witch of Agnesi: A Lasting Contribution from the First Surviving Mathematical Work Written by a Woman." *College Mathematical Journal* 30, no. 4 (September, 1999): 258-268. This commemorative article on the two hundredth anniversary of Agnesi's death discusses her life and the geometric curve named for her.

Mazzotti, Massimo. "Maria Gaetana Agnesi: Mathematics and the Making of the Catholic Enlightenment." *Isis* 92, no. 4 (December, 2001): 657-683. Places Agnesi's work in the context of the Italian enlightenment of the mid-eighteenth century.

Osen, Lynn M. *Women in Mathematics*. Cambridge, Mass.: MIT Press, 1974, 1995. Includes a chapter on Agnesi and her mathematical contributions.

Smith, Sanderson. *Agnesi to Zeno: Over One Hundred Vignettes from the History of Math*. Emeryville, Calif.: Key Curriculum Press, 1996. This book on historical developments in mathematics includes a one-page introduction to the life and work of Agnesi followed by questions and projects for math students.

See also: Jean le Rond d'Alembert; Benjamin Banneker; Benedict XIV; Leonhard Euler; Joseph-Louis Lagrange; Colin Maclaurin; Maria Theresa.

Related articles in *Great Events from History: The Eighteenth Century, 1701-1800*: 1718: Bernoulli Publishes His Calculus of Variations; 1733: De Moivre Describes the Bell-Shaped Curve; 1740: Maclaurin's Gravitational Theory; 1743-1744: D'Alembert Develops His Axioms of Motion; 1748: Agnesi Publishes *Analytical Institutions*; 1748: Euler Develops the Concept of Function; 1763: Bayes Advances Probability Theory; 1784: Legendre Introduces Polynomials.

AHMED III
Ottoman sultan (r. 1703-1730)

Ahmed III reigned during a transitional period in which costly foreign wars were balanced by notable cultural achievements and the first stirrings of Westernization.

Born: December 30, 1673; Edirne, Ottoman Empire (now in Turkey)
Died: July 1, 1736; Constantinople, Ottoman Empire (now Istanbul, Turkey)
Area of achievement: Government and politics

EARLY LIFE

Ahmed (ahkh-MEHD) III's father was Mehmed IV Avci (r. 1648-1687). His mother was a Cretan concubine (*haseki*), Rabia Gülnüsh Emetullah, a native of Rethymnon enslaved at the time of the Ottoman conquest. She had already given birth to another son, the future Mustafa II (r. 1695-1703), in 1664. Although Mehmed would have a number of favorite slave women in his harem, his passion for Gülnüsh seems never to have waned. Long outliving her husband, she was to play an important role during the reigns of both her sons.

Despite the vagaries of his eccentric father, Ahmed and his older brother enjoyed a more normal childhood than most Ottoman princes. Because Mehmed IV Avci detested Constantinople and Topkapi Sarayi (the imperial palace), the boys grew up in the palaces and gardens around Edirne, where they enjoyed much greater freedom than they would have done in Topkapi Sarayi, and Ahmed seems to have been exposed to influences and impressions denied most sultans' sons, including some contact with Europeans, the legacy of which would manifest itself during his reign.

Mehmed was deposed in 1687 and taken to the Kafes, the "cage" within Topkapi Sarayi where Ottoman princes were traditionally confined. Because those who deposed him preferred that his brother, Süleyman İbrahim II (r. 1687-1691), and then his second brother, Ahmed II (r. 1691-1695), succeed him, Mehmed's two sons joined him in the Kafes. Both brothers proved childless, however, so Mustafa succeeded to the throne in 1695. It was thus fortunate for Ahmed that the Ottoman dynastic law of fratricide had fallen into abeyance. Mustafa's reign ended when a Janissary mutiny led to his deposition. He was returned to the Kafes, and Ahmed replaced him on August 22, 1703.

LIFE'S WORK

During the first seven years of his reign, Ahmed III consolidated his hold over the institutions of government. The memory of the circumstances in which he had come to the throne seemed to produce a paranoia in which he felt safe only when surrounded by a small clique of advisers whom he could trust: his mother, now *valide sultan*; the *kizlar aghasi* (the Agha of the Black Eunuchs, responsible for the women's quarters of the palace); and his favourite, Silahdar Ali Paşa, soon to become his son-in-law.

Back in Constantinople, Ahmed hunted down all those he believed took part in the uprising against his brother. Also, he reduced the Janissary corps and transferred the corps of *bostancis* (guards responsible for the palaces and gardens) into the Janissary corps en masse. He replaced the guards with the last known *devshirme* recruits, young Balkan Christian males levied to serve as *kapikulus* (slaves of the Porte). Deeply suspicious of those around him, Ahmed found it difficult to give his confidence to any grand vizier not drawn from his immediate entourage, and during his early reign, viziers came and went with extraordinary rapidity. At last, in 1706, he appointed a man of real ability, Chorlulu Ali Paşa. Chorlulu had entered the palace service and been rapidly promoted during the reigns of Ahmed II and Mustafa II, reaching the rank of *silahdar* (custodian of the sultan's weapons), a post in which he made himself indispensable. Between 1706 and 1710, he initiated major reforms, redressed grievances, and reduced waste in state expenditure, being rewarded in 1708 by marriage to a daughter of Mustafa II.

Chorlulu sought desperately to avoid military adventures, making bitter enemies in the process. Ahmed be-

Ahmed III. (Hulton Archive/Getty Images)

came alienated by his policy of noninvolvement and dismissed him in June, 1710. After Chorlulu's fall, the sultan appointed another able man, Köprülü Noman Paşa, but he also proved too independent and within two months was sacked. He was replaced in September, 1710, by the time-serving Baltaci Mehmed Paşa (whose wife was said to be the sultan's mistress).

Meanwhile, Czar Peter the Great had made an ill-judged attack on Moldavia with insufficient troops and inadequate supplies. Ambushed by the grand vizier with an Ottoman army twice the size of the Russian force, Peter capitulated (July 20, 1711), and the Treaty of the Pruth (July 23, 1711) enabled him to extricate himself with considerable humiliation. A final peace was not concluded with Russia until the Treaty of Adrianople (June 5, 1713).

Silahdar Ali Paşa, appointed grand vizier on April 27, 1713, commanded a formidable force that quickly overran the Morea (summer, 1715), but Ottoman aggression in Dalmatia, which threatened Croatia, was too much for Charles VI, who renewed his old alliance with Venice (April 13, 1716). The Holy Roman Emperor's field commander, Prince Eugene of Savoy, prosecuted the war with great vigor, and when the grand vizier marched against the fortress of Peterwardein, he was defeated, losing his life on the battlefield (August 5, 1716). Belgrade, linchpin of the Ottoman line of defense on the Danube frontier, capitulated on August 20, 1717. Peace was signed at Passarowitz (July 21, 1718), where the sultan's negotiators were compelled to recognize the loss of Belgrade, much of Serbia, and the Banat of Temesvar and Oltenia (then known as Little Wallachia), as well as granting extensive commercial privileges to the emperor's subjects. Venice made a separate peace but failed to regain the Morea.

As for the sultan, he had had enough of war in the west, although the collapse of the Persian Ṣafavid Dynasty in 1722 compelled him to look to his eastern frontiers. In May, 1718, Ahmed appointed as grand vizier a companion from his early years of gilded captivity in Edirne, Nevshehirli İbrahim Paşa, who remained his right hand and close collaborator until the end of his reign. These twelve years saw the sultan and grand vizier presiding over a kind of golden age, which some historians have called an Ottoman renaissance (nicknamed *lale devri*, the Tulip Age, from the sultan's passion for tulips). During these years, the court, a hive of literary and artistic patronage, became the center of a luxuriant ceremonial life, which at least one historian has suggested consciously mirrored Louis XIV's Versailles in its goals of enhancing the sultan's prestige and leading the elite into lavish consumption. Contemporary European observers waxed exuberant in describing the extravagance and hedonism of a capital that now included a considerable Western presence, as well as increasing contacts with foreign parts. However tenuous the process, Westernization had begun.

Exemplifying the Westernization of Ahmed's court was the career of İbrahīm Mūteferrika (1674-1745), a statesman, diplomat, and ardent advocate of Ottoman reform. Born in Kolosvár (Transylvania) of Christian parents and raised a Unitarian, he fled Transylvania to avoid Catholic persecution and became an aide to the Ottoman-backed Transylvanian leader, Imre Tököly. İbrahim, now a convert to Islam, joined the Ottoman service, rising high in the bureaucracy. His linguistic skills and knowledge of Europeans made him especially valuable to the Porte for roving diplomatic missions, activities that spanned the reigns of both Ahmed III and Mahmud I (r. 1730-1754). Supported by İbrahim Paşa, the grand vizier, and even, surprisingly, by the şheyhülislām, c. 1724 İbrahim Mūteferrika set up the first Ottoman printing press with equipment and workers imported from the West. He was careful, however, not to involve himself with theological material. Although only a few books were printed and the press was closed down in 1742, its very existence indicated that the winds of change were blowing through the heart of the Ottoman Empire.

Ahmed III's golden age ended abruptly in one of the worst outbursts of the mob violence and civic disorder so endemic to Ottoman history. This was the uprising of September-November, 1730, led by Patrona Halil, a former Albanian Janissary turned clothes seller, which exposed the capital to unparalleled bloodshed, rapine, and mayhem. The affair combined the traditional simmering violence of a great metropolis, impoverished and overtaxed to meet the sultan's extravagances, with a visceral fury against innovation, Western influences, and the court's decadent lifestyle, which ran counter to traditional Islamic values. In vain, the sultan, to appease the mob, had İbrahim Paşa, the deputy grand vizier, and the Kapudan Paşa (high admiral) strangled, but the rebels remained implacable: They had wanted the culprits delivered to them alive. On October 1, 1730, Ahmed resigned and was replaced by his nephew, Mahmud I, whose place he took as a captive in the Kafes.

SIGNIFICANCE

Ahmed III's reign was of great significance in the history of the Ottoman Empire. After the disturbed reign of his brother, Mustafa II, Ahmed introduced a semblance of order to the realm before being drawn into conflict with Russia and subsequently the Venetian Republic and Habsburg Austria. In the period of peace after 1718, he inaugurated a remarkable cultural flourishing, a kind of Ottoman renaissance, which also saw significant moves toward Westernization.

—*Gavin R. G. Hambly*

FURTHER READING

Freely, John. *Inside the Seraglio*. London: Penguin Books, 1999. A highly readable account of the sultan and his times.

Kurat, Akdes Nimat. *The Despatches of Sir Robert Sutton: Ambassador in Constantinople, 1710-1714*. London: Royal Historical Society, 1953. Penetrating contemporary observations on the war years.

Kurat, A. N., and J. S. Bromley. "The Retreat of the Turks, 1683-1730." In *A History of the Ottoman Empire to 1730*, edited by V. J. Parry et al. New York: Cambridge University Press, 1976. Excellent narrative of the reign.

Quataert, Donald. *The Ottoman Empire, 1700-1922*. New York: Cambridge University Press, 2000. Sophisticated analysis of a changing empire under stress.

Shaw, Stanford J. *History of the Ottoman Empire and Modern Turkey*. 2 vols. New York: Cambridge University Press, 1976. Dependable narrative and excellent insights.

Shay, Mary Lucille. *The Ottoman Empire from 1720 to 1734 as Revealed in Despatches of the Venetian Bailo*. Urbana: University of Illinois Press, 1944. An observer's vivid account of the last years of the reign.

See also: Charles VI; Levni; Mahmud I; Peter the Great.
Related articles in *Great Events from History: The Eighteenth Century, 1701-1800*: 1702 or 1706: First Arabic Printing Press; November 20, 1710-July 21, 1718: Ottoman Wars with Russia, Venice, and Austria; 1718-1730: Tulip Age; 1736-1739: Russo-Austrian War Against the Ottoman Empire.

ALAUNGPAYA
King of Burma (r. 1752-1760)

Alaungpaya established a central Burmese kingdom by conquering and unifying areas ruled by warlords and ethnic leaders, founding the Alaungpaya Dynasty. He implemented religious, social, civic, and legal reforms domestically while reinforcing his political authority and seeking diplomatic relations with foreign representatives.

Born: c. 1714; Moksobomyo, Shwebo (now in Myanmar)
Died: April 13, 1760?; Kinyua, Thaton district, Burma (now in Myanmar)
Also known as: Alaung Phra; Alompra; Aungzeya
Areas of achievement: Warfare and conquest, government and politics

EARLY LIFE
Because Alaungpaya (ah-lah-oong-PI-ah) invented much of his biography to validate his power, historians cannot confirm, or deny, the biography's claims. Contemporary sources agree on some basics. He was born around 1714 in Moksobomyo, north of Burma's capital at Ava, and named Aungzeya. His father, like many of his ancestors, was a community leader. His parents called him Aungzeya. Eighteenth century Burmese used personal names only and did not have surnames.

Burmese kings usually were not hereditary rulers. Instead, they acquired power by courage demonstrated through military performance and by winning public support. They chose officials based on ability, bravery, and loyalty, and laws were based on customs. A variety of ethnic groups, including the Shan, Manipuri, and Mon, lived independently in Burma and also nearby.

As an adult, Aungzeya served as an official in Moksobomyo after his father retired. When the Burmese king died in 1733, his son became ruler but was unable to control the chaos that occurred during this transition of power. Manipuri horsemen raided villages and overwhelmed the inept Burmese military. Disgusted by the weak king, terrorized residents talked about having more effective leaders who would defend them, and the name Aungzeya circulated as a possibility. Infuriated, the king demanded Aungzeya arrested as a potential traitor. Aungzeya stated he was uninterested in ruling and resumed his normal activities for almost twenty years.

LIFE'S WORK
Aungzeya's ambitions changed in 1752. Pegu, a Mon kingdom, was the catalyst for Aungzeya's rise to power as Alaungpaya. Pegu king Binnya Dala seized Ava in April of 1752. That victory secured political control for the Mon, who usurped the Burmese Toungoo Dynasty's power, which had been in place since 1486. Binnya Dala underestimated the people's support. He dispersed delegates to secure headmen's and officials' allegiance in the western and northern provinces. Two men refused, each stating he was king and demanding villages declare allegiance to him.

Now in his late thirties, Aungzeya realized that the situation could become volatile. He resented this power shift and schemed how to overthrow Binnya Dala to avoid serving him. He also worried that the two self-declared kings would endanger Burma. Because of his arrest in 1733, Aungzeya's name was known in surrounding villages, where people respected him. He began reinforcing Moksobomyo's defenses and recruited an army, encouraging men to join him in a revolution to oust the Mon. People from forty-six nearby towns relocated to Moksobomyo. After securing headmen's permission, Aungzeya ordered all those villages razed and water sources, woods, and plants near Moksobomyo destroyed to hinder attackers. He demanded a new council that represented all villagers.

While Moksobomyo was being prepared for an attack, scouts patrolled the surrounding area and warned that Mon warriors were approaching. Aungzeya convinced the council to fight the Mon instead of swearing allegiance, emphasizing that honorable men only make oaths they will never betray. He told his parents that he was prepared to fight because he had to protect Burma, vowing he would triumph and become king. His mother tried to dissuade him, stressing that the people inside Moksobomyo's walls were outnumbered. Aungzeya replied that his supporters' desire to defeat the Mon would prevail. The defensive forces repulsed initial attacks and gained additional soldiers as well as cannon and weapons. After five days of fighting, the Mon forces retreated and built fortifications by the river. Aungzeya's troops razed those structures and forced the Mon to flee to Ava.

Aungzeya declared himself Burma's king and adopted the name Alaungpaya, suggesting he was a future Buddha. He said his ancestors had belonged to the dynasty that ruled Ava's first kingdom. Wanting to establish a separate identity from prior kings and capitals, Alaungpaya renamed his hometown Shwebo, derived from the Burmese word *shwe*, representing gold, in honor of his victories, and he designated it his dynasty's capital. He designed his royal city to include a palace, moat, spirit shrine, watchtower, and the Shwe Dagon Pagoda built at the place of his birth. That pagoda later became his tomb.

In 1753, Alaungpaya's army attacked and conquered Ava. They then traveled through the Irrawaddy River valley to rout the Mon in southern Burma and unify Upper and Lower Burma. Alaungpaya's victories included seizing Dagon in 1755 and renaming it Yangon (now called Rangoon) for use as a port. Within two years, Alaungpaya's forces controlled Pegu, captured Binnya Dala, and also subdued Shan and Manipur rivals. Alaungpaya changed names of places to assert his dominance and legitimacy as a ruler. He expected former leaders to pay homage and recognize his authority.

Alaungpaya sought diplomatic relations with Great Britain to counter the Mon-France alliance striving to control Burmese territory. He wrote a letter to King George II and became enraged when George failed to respond directly to him. Instead, Alaungpaya contemptuously dealt with envoys, quizzing them about English protocol and customs. A 1757 treaty, the first that Burma achieved with a European interest, outlined ample trading benefits for the British East India Company, which disappointed Alaungpaya when England did not reciprocate with sufficient promised military support. Tensions were further strained when a customs agent told Alaung-paya that the English at Negrais assisted Mon rebels on that island. As a result, Alaungpaya's soldiers killed alleged traitors and destroyed their factory in 1759. This incident disrupted Burma's diplomatic involvement with Great Britain until the late nineteenth century.

Although he wanted to focus on domestic concerns, Alaungpaya relentlessly followed the Mon into Siam (now called Thailand), considering them a threat to Burmese interests. The Burmese army moved through Martaban and Tavoy, then through the Tenasserim region and towns by the Gulf of Siam before going northward and circling the Siamese capital Ayutthaya (also called Ayuthia) by early April, 1760. Arriving during the rainy season, Alaungpaya suffered dysentery, according to Burmese sources, although other accounts indicate he was wounded. His troops transported him home to Burma. Alaungpaya died en route (sources cite two possible death dates), and his cremated ashes were buried in his tomb at Shwebo.

SIGNIFICANCE

Expanding Burma's territory, Alaungpaya initiated what became the final Burmese dynasty, which endured until 1885. His reign was notable because it was the third time Burma had been unified. Alaungpaya's achievement followed the successful unifications by Pagan ruler Anawrahta from 1044 to 1077 and Toungoo king Bayinnaung from 1551 to 1581. When he was king, Alaungpaya prevented foreign powers, particularly France and England, from conquering Burma or interfering with domestic policies.

Alaungpaya often enslaved or executed his enemies, yet he created an environment that pleased his followers. The Burmese optimistically embraced Alaungpaya as a leader after previous leaders had been disappointing and ineffective. Alaungpaya introduced reforms to resolve a religious schism. He forbade animal sacrifices for religious purposes, especially slaughtering cows that were crucial for pulling equipment for planting rice, a crop he encouraged people to cultivate. He promoted the arts, appointing court poets. Interested in the creation of law codes, Alaungpaya helped prepare the law treatise *Manugye*. Rules included the prohibition of alcohol consumption because that drink could weaken military forces. He exempted everyone aged sixty and older from required service to leaders and paid their expenses if they participated in religious activities and made pilgrimages.

Alaungpaya tried to improve water resources and transportation with the creation of a dam, canals, and reservoirs. Indicating Alaungpaya's enduring influence on

Burmese culture, generations of officials have traveled to Shwebo to obtain soil for ceremonial usages because they associate it with victory and Alaungpaya's transformation of Burma.

—Elizabeth D. Schafer

FURTHER READING

Aung, Maung Htin. *A History of Burma*. New York: Columbia University Press, 1967. The first English-language history of Burma written by a Burma native. Thorough account of Alaungpaya's dynasty based on primary sources. Includes a chronology, appendices with dynastic charts, and an annotated bibliography.

Cady, John F. *A History of Modern Burma*. Ithaca, N.Y.: Cornell University Press, 1958. A scholar who taught in Rangoon describes political and military organization in eighteenth century Burma, explaining Burmese viewpoints and the use of symbols and personnel to assert royal authority.

Harvey, Godfrey E. *History of Burma: From the Earliest Times to 10 March 1824, the Beginning of the English Conquest*. Reprint. New Delhi, India: Asian Educational Services, 2000. An Indian Civil Service employee's detailed account of Alaungpaya's rise to power and his conquests, containing some inaccuracies and biased comments because of misunderstandings of Burmese language and culture.

Okudaira, Ryuji, and Andrew Huxley. "A Burmese Tract on Kingship: Political Theory in the 1782 Manuscript of *Manugye*." *Bulletin of the School of Oriental and African Studies* 64 (2001): 248-259. Analyzes a legal volume that originated when Alaungpaya was king and was supplemented when his son Bodawpaya became king, revealing aspects of eighteenth century Burmese culture, society, and politics.

Trager, Frank N. *Burma: From Kingdom to Republic: A Historical and Political Analysis*. New York: Praeger, 1966. A lengthy discussion of Alaungpaya's interests in diplomatic agreements with England based on primary Burmese and English sources, describing treaty negotiations in detail. Includes extensive endnotes.

See also: George II; Nguyen Hue; Taksin.

Related articles in *Great Events from History: The Eighteenth Century, 1701-1800:* 1752-1760: Alaungpaya Unites Burma; September, 1769-1778: Siamese-Vietnamese War.

JEAN LE ROND D'ALEMBERT
French mathematician and philosopher

A pioneer in the use of differential calculus, d'Alembert applied his mathematical genius to solving problems in mechanics. He provided valuable assistance with Denis Diderot's Encyclopedia *and wrote a number of treatises on musical theory.*

Born: November 17, 1717; Paris, France
Died: October 29, 1783; Paris, France
Also known as: Jean-Baptiste Daremberg
Areas of achievement: Mathematics, physics, science and technology, philosophy, music

EARLY LIFE

On the night of November 17, 1717, Mme Claudine-Alexandrine Guérin, marquise de Tencin, gave birth to a son whom she promptly abandoned on the steps of the Church of Saint-Jean-Le-Rond. There, he was baptized with the name of the church, Jean le Rond d'Alembert (zhah luh-roh dah-lahm-behr); he was then sent to the Maison de la Coucher, from which he went to a foster home in Picardy. When his father, Louis-Camus Destouches, a military officer, returned to Paris, he sought his son and arranged for the child to be cared for by Mme Rousseau, the wife of a glazier. D'Alembert would always regard Mme Rousseau as his real mother and would continue to live with her until 1765, when illness compelled him to seek new quarters in the home of Julie de Lespinasse.

Destouches continued to watch over his illegitimate child, sending him to private schools; when Destouches died in 1726, he left the boy a legacy of twelve hundred livres a year. The sum, though not luxurious, guaranteed him an independence he cherished throughout his life. Through the interest of the Destouches family, the young man entered the Jansenist Collège des Quatre-Nations, where he took the name Jean-Baptiste Daremberg, later changing it, perhaps for euphony, to d'Alembert. Although he, like many other Enlightenment figures, abandoned the religious training he received there, he never shed the Cartesian influence that dominated the school.

After receiving his *baccalauréat* in 1735, he spent two years studying law, receiving a license to practice in 1738. Neither jurisprudence nor medicine, to which he devoted a year, held his interest. He turned to mathematics, for which he had a natural talent. At the age of twenty-two, he submitted his first paper to the Academy of Sciences. In that piece, he corrected a number of errors in Father Charles Reyneau's *Analyse demontrée* (1714). A second paper, on refraction and fluid mechanics, followed the next year, and in May, 1741, he was made an adjunct member of the Academy of Sciences.

LIFE'S WORK

Two years later, d'Alembert published a major contribution to mechanics, *Traité de dynamique* (1743), which includes his famous principle stating that the force that acts on a body in a system is the sum of the forces within the system restraining it and the external forces acting on that system. Although Sir Isaac Newton and Johann Bernoulli had already offered similar observations, neither had expressed the matter so simply. The effect of d'Alembert's principle was to convert a problem of dynamics to one of statics, making it easier to solve. The treatise is characteristic of d'Alembert's work in several ways: It illustrates his exceptional facility with mathematics, it reveals a desire to find universal laws in a discipline, and it indicates his ability to reduce complex matters to simple components. Over the next several years, he wrote a number of other innovative works in both mathematics and fluid mechanics.

At the same time that d'Alembert was establishing himself as one of Europe's leading mathematicians—in 1752, Frederick the Great offered him the presidency of the Berlin Academy—he emerged as a leading figure of the Parisian salons. In 1743, he was introduced to the influential Mme du Deffand, who would secure his election to the French Academy in 1754. He remained a fixture of her assemblies until Julie de Lespinasse, whom he met there, established her own salon following a quarrel with the older woman. Later in the 1740's, he also joined the gatherings at the homes of Mme Marie-Thérèse Rodet Geoffrin and Anne-Louise Bénédicte de Bourbon, duchesse du Maine. Not striking in appearance—he was short and, according to a contemporary, "of rather undistinguished features, with a fresh complexion that tends to ruddiness," his eyes small and his mouth large—he compensated for his looks with his excellent ability with mimicry and his lively conversation.

While enjoying the female-dominated world of the salons, d'Alembert was also meeting a number of important male intellectuals, with whom he dined weekly at the Hôtel du Panier Fleuri—Denis Diderot, Jean-Jacques Rousseau (no relation to his stepmother), and Étienne Bonnot de Condillac. He probably also knew Gua de Malves, a fellow mathematician and member of the Academy of Sciences, who was chosen as the first editor of the *Encyclopédie: Ou, Dictionnaire raisonné des sciences, des arts, et des métiers* (1751-1772; *Encyclopedia*, 1965), and Malves may have been the one who introduced d'Alembert to the project; after Malves resigned, d'Alembert was named coeditor with Diderot.

D'Alembert did not plan to assume as much responsibility for the work as his coeditor. He wrote to Samuel Formey in September, 1749:

> I never intended to have a hand in [the *Encyclopedia*] except for what has to do with mathematics and physical astronomy. I am in a position to do only that, and besides, I do not intend to condemn myself for ten years to the tedium of seven or eight folios.

It was Diderot who conceived of the work as a summation of human knowledge, but d'Alembert's involvement extended well beyond the mathematical articles that the title page credits to him.

His contributions took many forms. He used his scientific contacts to solicit articles, and his connection with

Jean le Rond d'Alembert. (Library of Congress)

the world of the salons, which Diderot did not frequent, permitted him to enlist support among the aristocracy and upper middle class. Not only was such backing politically important, given the controversial nature of the enterprise, but also the financial assistance d'Alembert secured may well have prevented its collapse. Mme Geoffrin alone is reported to have donated more than 100,000 livres.

Also significant are the fifteen hundred articles that d'Alembert wrote, including the important *Discours préliminaire* (1751; *Preliminary Discourse to the Encyclopedia of Diderot*, 1963). Praised by all the great French intellectuals as well as Frederick the Great, it seeks to explain the purpose and plan of the *Encyclopedia* by showing the links between disciplines and tracing the progress of knowledge from the Renaissance to 1750. In its view of the Enlightenment as the culmination of progress in thought, it reflects the philosophes' optimistic, humanistic attitude. D'Alembert's own understanding of the role of the philosopher and the nature of learning also emerges clearly in this essay. For him, "The universe is but a vast ocean, on the surface of which we perceive certain islands more or less large, whose link with the continent is hidden from us." The goal of the scientist is to discover, not invent, these concealed links, and mathematics would provide the means for establishing these connections. Just as physicists of the twenty-first century seek the one force that impels all nature, so d'Alembert sought the single principle that underlies all knowledge.

In 1756, d'Alembert went to Geneva to visit Voltaire, his closest friend among the philosophes, and to gather information for an article on this center of Calvinism. In an earlier work, d'Alembert had antagonized the Church by criticizing ecclesiastical control of education. "Genève," with its intended praise of Protestant ministers, provoked sharp protests from the Catholic establishment in France, and Calvinists were upset as well by d'Alembert's portrait of them as virtual agnostics.

Opposition to the *Encyclopedia* was growing in court circles; in March, 1759, permission to publish would be withdrawn. Never as daring as Voltaire or Diderot, d'Alembert resigned as coeditor in 1758, despite protests from his friends and associates. He did, however, continue to write articles on mathematics and science.

While the controversy surrounding the enterprise, especially "Genève," was the primary reason for d'Alembert's distancing himself from the *Encyclopedia,* another important factor was his growing disagreement with Diderot over the direction the work had been taking. By 1758, Diderot, who had published a treatise on mathe-

matics, *Mémoires sur différens sujets de mathématiques* (1748), had come to believe that no further progress was possible in that field, so he rejected his coeditor's emphasis on mathematics as the key to knowledge, stating that "the reign of mathematics is over." D'Alembert's Cartesian theories also troubled Diderot. Like René Descartes, d'Alembert believed that matter is inert; Diderot disagreed. While d'Alembert maintained that the most precise sciences were those such as geometry that relied on abstract principles derived from reason, Diderot regarded experimentation and observation—empiricism—as the best guarantees of reliability. For d'Alembert, the more abstruse the science the better, for he sought to solve problems. Diderot preferred knowledge that directly affected life. In later years, Diderot continued to praise d'Alembert's mathematical abilities, and d'Alembert unsuccessfully tried to secure Diderot's election to the French Academy, but the two remained only distant friends.

Withdrawing from the *Encyclopedia* did not signal d'Alembert's rejection of the Enlightenment. Instead, he sought to use the French Academy as a forum to promulgate the views of the philosophes. His first speech before the French Academy urged toleration and freedom of expression, and in 1769 he nearly succeeded in having the body offer a prize for the best poem on the subject of "The Progress of Reason Under Louis X," the notion of such progress being a fundamental tenet of the Enlightenment. In 1768, when the king of Denmark, Christian VII, visited the French Academy, and again in March, 1771, when Gustavus III of Sweden attended a session, d'Alembert spoke of the benefits of enlightened policies. Through his influence in the salons, he arranged for the election of nine philosophes to the French Academy between 1760 and 1770, and a number of others sympathetic to their cause also entered because of d'Alembert. Elected permanent secretary of the body in 1772, he threafter used his official eulogies to attack the enemies of the Enlightenment and to encourage advanced ideas.

D'Alembert also continued to publish. The first three volumes of *Opuscules mathématiques* (1761-1780) contain much original work on hydrodynamics, lenses, and astronomy. His anonymous *Sur la destruction des Jésuites en France* (1765; *An Account of the Destruction of the Jesuits in France,* 1766), occasioned by the suppression of the order, discusses the danger of linking civil and ecclesiastical power because theological disputes then disturb domestic peace. In addition to attacking the Jesuits, d'Alembert urged the suppression of their rivals, the Jansenists.

Active as he was in the French Academy, d'Alembert's last years were marked by physical and emotional pain. Devoted to Julie de Lespinasse, he was doubly distressed by her death in 1776 and the discovery of love letters to her from the comte de Guibert and the marquis de Mora. As permanent secretary of the French Academy, d'Alembert was entitled to a small apartment in the Louvre, and there he spent the final seven years of his life, which ended on October 29, 1783. Although he produced little original work of his own during this period, he remained an important correspondent of Voltaire and Frederick the Great, urging the monarch to grant asylum to those persecuted for their views. He also encouraged young mathematicians such as Joseph-Louis Lagrange, Pierre-Simon Laplace, and the marquis de Condorcet.

SIGNIFICANCE

Voltaire sometimes doubted Jean le Rond d'Alembert's zeal for the cause of Enlightenment, and d'Alembert's distancing himself from the *encyclopédistes* reveals that he was not one to take great risks. He observed that "honest men can no longer fight except by hiding behind the hedges, but from that position they can fire some good shots at the wild beasts infesting the country." From his post in the salons and the French Academy, he worked, as he told Voltaire, "to gain esteem for the little flock" of philosophes.

If Voltaire could accuse d'Alembert of excessive caution, d'Alembert could in turn charge Voltaire with toadying to the powerful. In his 1753 *Essai sur les gens de lettres*, d'Alembert urged writers to rely solely on their talents, and he reminded the nobility that intellectuals were their equals. "I am determined never to put myself in the service of anyone and to die as free as I have lived," he wrote Voltaire. Neither Frederick the Great's repeated invitations to assume the presidency of the Berlin Academy nor Catherine the Great's offer of 100,000 livres a year to tutor her son Grand Duke Paul could lure him away from France and independence.

In both his life and thought he was loyal to the ideals of the philosophes, so it is fitting that early twentieth century scholar Ernst Cassirer should choose him as the representative of the Enlightenment and call him "one of the most important scholars of the age and one of its intellectual spokesmen." His belief in the ability of reason to solve any problem epitomizes the view of eighteenth century intellectuals, but he also recognized the role of experimentation and imagination. In his *Eléméns de musique théorique et practique suivant les principes de M. Rameau* (1752), d'Alembert dissented from Jean-Philippe Rameau's view that one can devise mathematical rules for composition. As in his article on elocution in the *Encyclopedia,* he argued that rules are necessary, but only genius can elevate a work beyond mediocrity. Excellent scientist though he was, he ranked the artist above the philosopher.

—*Joseph Rosenblum*

FURTHER READING

Cassirer, Ernst. *The Philosophy of the Enlightenment.* Translated by Fritz A. C. Koelln and James P. Pettegrove. Princeton, N.J.: Princeton University Press, 1951. Explores how Enlightenment thinkers looked at nature, psychology, religion, history, society, and aesthetics. Includes a great deal of information about d'Alembert.

Essar, Dennis F. *The Language Theory, Epistemology, and Aesthetics of Jean Lerond d'Alembert.* Oxford, England: Voltaire Foundation at the Taylor Institution, 1976. A study of d'Alembert's philosophy. Argues that d'Alembert's "position in the Enlightenment remains of central, pivotal importance." Also treats d'Alembert's mathematical and scientific contributions.

Grimsley, Ronald. *Jean d'Alembert, 1717-83.* Oxford, England: Clarendon Press, 1963. A topical study of d'Alembert's contributions to the *Encyclopedia,* his relations with other philosophers, and his own views. Largely ignores the scientific and mathematical aspects of d'Alembert's career.

Hankins, Thomas L. *Jean d'Alembert: Science and the Enlightenment.* Oxford, England: Clarendon Press, 1970. An ideal complement to Grimsley's book, for it concentrates on d'Alembert's contributions to science and mathematics. Relates d'Alembert's achievements to those of other scientists and the role of science to that of philosophy in the eighteenth century.

James, Ioan. *Remarkable Mathematicians: From Euler to von Neumann.* Washington, D.C.: Mathematical Association of America, 2002. Includes a chapter on d'Alembert's contributions to mathematics.

Kafker, Frank A. *The Encyclopedists as a Group: A Collective Biography of the Authors of the "Encyclopédie."* Oxford, England: Voltaire Foundation, 1996. Examines the life and thought of d'Alembert and the other authors who created the *Encyclopedia.*

Pappas, John Nicholas. *Voltaire and d'Alembert.* Bloomington: Indiana University Press, 1962. Drawing heavily on the correspondence between the two, this study seeks to rectify the view, fostered in large part by Voltaire, that d'Alembert was a hesitant follower of the older intellectual. Notes that the influence was mutual and shows where the two differed.

Van Treese, Glen Joseph. *D'Alembert and Frederick the Great: A Study of Their Relationship*. New York: Learned Publications, 1974. Treats the origin, nature, and consequences of the friendship between d'Alembert and the Prussian ruler. Offers a portrait of the two men and their age.

See also: Catherine the Great; Étienne Bonnot de Condillac; Marquis de Condorcet; Denis Diderot; Frederick the Great; Joseph-Louis Lagrange; Jean-Philippe Rameau; Jean-Jacques Rousseau; Voltaire.

Related articles in *Great Events from History: The Eighteenth Century, 1701-1800*: 1704: Newton Publishes *Optics*; 1718: Bernoulli Publishes His Calculus of Variations; 1733: De Moivre Describes the Bell-Shaped Curve; 1738: Bernoulli Proposes the Kinetic Theory of Gases; 1740: Maclaurin's Gravitational Theory; 1743-1744: D'Alembert Develops His Axioms of Motion; 1748: Agnesi Publishes *Analytical Institutions*; 1748: Euler Develops the Concept of Function; 1751-1772: Diderot Publishes the *Encyclopedia*; 1754: Condillac Defends Sensationalist Theory; January, 1759: Voltaire Satirizes Optimism in *Candide*; April, 1762: Rousseau Publishes *The Social Contract*; July, 1764: Voltaire Publishes *A Philosophical Dictionary for the Pocket*; 1782-1798: Publication of Rousseau's *Confessions*; 1784: Legendre Introduces Polynomials; c. 1794-1799: Proust Establishes the Law of Definite Proportions.

ETHAN ALLEN
American military leader and political philosopher

Allen led Vermont settlers in their fight for land rights and secured the first military victory of the American Revolution at Fort Ticonderoga.

Born: January 21, 1738; Litchfield, Connecticut
Died: February 12, 1789; Burlington, Vermont
Areas of achievement: Military, warfare and conquest, government and politics

EARLY LIFE

The eldest of eight children born to Joseph Allen and Mary Baker, Ethan Allen was named for firmness and strength. The family moved to Cornwall, Connecticut, when Ethan was two years old. Joseph, a literate farmer, recognized his son's keen mental abilities and sent him from the frontier community to Salisbury to prepare for entry into Yale College under the tutelage of a Congregational minister, the Reverend Jonathan Lee. As a young child, Ethan had become a prodigious reader and serious thinker who delighted in scribbling his thoughts on paper, so he made excellent progress in his studies.

When his father died suddenly in April, 1755, however, the strapping seventeen-year-old Ethan returned home to help his mother run the extensive family farm. Joseph Allen had been a town leader—a selectman and church member, respected for his hard work, his accumulation of land, and his belief in the dignity of others. However, he had also been regarded as a free spirit and a heretic, qualities Ethan was to exhibit.

In 1757, when he was nineteen, Allen joined the armed services under Colonel Ebenezer Marsh to defend Fort William Henry in the French and Indian War. Although the fort fell to the French within two weeks and Allen did not see any action during the short period of his muster, he did discover the next frontier of land, the New Hampshire Grants (what is now southern Vermont).

After his service, Allen used his energy as an entrepreneur, first starting a blast furnace to smelt ore in 1762 and later opening a lead mine. In the same year, he married Mary Brownson. They had three children, Lucy, Pamela, and Mary Ann. During this time, Allen became fast friends with Thomas Young, a Salisbury physician and Deist, with whom he enjoyed free-ranging discussions about the philosophies of Plutarch, Sir Isaac Newton, and John Locke, men whose ideas would preoccupy him all his life; this interest was later reflected in Allen's book *Reason the Only Oracle of Man* (1785). Often the discussions took place in local taverns, where he earned a reputation as a hard drinker and roaring brawler.

Tiring of his life as a businessman and family man, Allen moved to the frontier country of the Grants during 1766 and 1767 to live for months by his knowledge of the wilderness. There he noted the peaceful relations between the Native Americans and the few white settlers.

LIFE'S WORK

After the French and Indian War (1754-1763), migration to land north of Massachusetts and Connecticut, bounded by the Connecticut River and Lake Champlain, increased significantly. Former soldiers had seen the new frontier and had chosen to move their families where they could have more land, form their own settlements, and escape the chafing requirements of landlords. As they moved to the new town of Bennington, chartered in 1750, and the New Hampshire Grants, they bought their lots from land speculators who had received grants from Governor Benning Wentworth of New Hampshire. Unfortunately, because land charters were often vague and contradictory, title to the land was controversial. Finally, King George III settled the matter and gave the land to New York.

From his days in Salisbury, Connecticut, Ethan Allen was familiar with boundary disputes. He had observed the economic and social struggles among those who lived on the land "at will" and those who owned it legally. When New York landlords attempted to regrant the already occupied Bennington land at stiff prices, men from the Grants met in 1770 at the Catamount Tavern in Bennington to form a military association, with Allen as their colonel commander. This rowdy group of three hundred young woodsmen, called the Green Mountain Boys because they stuck green sprigs in their hats, vowed to tackle the problem with force and terror but never loss of life. To assist the cause, Allen wrote bombastic articles for the *Connecticut Courant* about the unfair power the landowners exerted over the struggling young settlers. A showdown occurred in 1771 when three hundred New Yorkers attempted to evict James Breakenridge from his Bennington farm and reclaim the property. Because the Green Mountain Boys stood firmly armed in their belief that they were upholding the law of New Hampshire, the New Yorkers retreated, both then and later.

Settlers flowed into the Grants, and Allen sold his Connecticut land and became a major landowner by 1772, particularly because of his Onion River holdings near what is now Burlington, Vermont. However, strife between the wealthy New Yorkers and the poor Grantsmen intensified when the New Yorkers forbade gatherings of three or more settlers. The Green Mountain Boys held public meetings and prepared to fight New York.

Ethan Allen in prison. (Library of Congress)

Allen already had gained a reputation as a fiery patriot because of his defense of settlers' rights, but he enhanced his reputation and secured his position in history when, accompanied by Benedict Arnold, he led eighty-three Green Mountain Boys in a surprise attack on Fort Ticonderoga on May 10, 1775. Coming after the battles at Lexington and Concord, the conquest of the strategic Fort Ticonderoga on Lake Champlain was important. Allen and his troops captured a generous supply of artillery pieces that would later serve the Continental army.

Exhilarated by the easy capture of Fort Ticonderoga, Allen proposed to attack Canada while the British were vulnerable. His superior, General Montgomery, was not convinced, and he assigned Allen the task of persuading the Canadians to aid the American cause. When a restless military colleague, Major John Brown, proposed a combined attack on Montreal instead, Allen enthusiastically agreed. When Brown's forces failed to meet the Green Mountain Boys, however, Allen was forced to surrender to British officers, who considered him a rowdy and shameful enemy. He and his men were imprisoned on board various small, dank ships and taken first to Ireland, then England, and finally back to the colonies. This sorry situation is recounted in Allen's *A Narrative of Colonel Ethan Allen's Captivity* (1779).

While their rowdy leader was imprisoned for thirty-two months, from September, 1775, to May, 1778, Grants settlers from twenty-two towns held a convention and voted to form a new state, New Connecticut. Spurned by Congress in its attempts to join the Union, on June 4, 1777, the new state became Vermont, an independent republic boasting a liberal constitution developed with guidance from Allen's longtime friend Thomas Young.

Vermont sent a constant flow of requests to Congress in its effort to become a member of the Union, but Governor Clinton of New York was adamant against admission of the rebels. The situation became fragile when New Hampshire towns decided they wanted to join the new republic of Vermont.

In 1779, Congress ordered Vermont to cease its existence as an independent republic. Allen was incensed, and he persuaded the Vermont Assembly to be equally upset and defiant. To emphasize its restraining order, Congress next forbade the distribution of supplies by the Continental Commissary at Bennington. While this hostile stalemate continued, Allen began discussions with the British, through Lieutenant General Frederick Haldimand, concerning the return of Vermont to the British Empire. Whether Allen was toying with treason or merely manipulating the Union's suspicion of the British is difficult for historians to determine. Nevertheless, in November, 1780, some Vermont assemblymen acted upon their suspicions and introduced resolutions that would lead to Allen's impeachment. Although the resolutions were never issued, Allen resigned his command and left the British negotiations in the hands of his brother Ira, who continued to bargain for more than two years. With the defeat of the British army at Saratoga and at Yorktown and the end of the American Revolution in 1783, the possibility of bringing Vermont into the British Empire was not realistic.

Allen slipped into a quieter life after the death in 1783 of his first wife from tuberculosis, and in 1785 he married Fanny Montresor Buchanan—who was, ironically, the daughter of a New York landowner. This new marriage brought him great pleasure, and they had three children, Fanny, Hannibal, and Ethan Alphonso.

Two other important events happened in Allen's life in 1785: one last military effort and the publication of an important book. The Connecticut settlers of the Wyo-ming Valley of Pennsylvania, experiencing a threat to their land claims by Pennsylvania, asked Allen to lead the charge to vindicate their rights. In return, the settlers promised to deed Wyoming Valley land to him. Allen warmed to the prospect, but Pennsylvania resolved the argument by ceding the land rights to the settlers.

Also in that year, Allen published his long, controversial attack on conventional religion, *Reason the Only Oracle of Man*. In this treatise, begun many years earlier with Young, Allen mocked clergymen and prayer and proclaimed that men and women were their own sources of happiness or wickedness. People could know God best, he maintained, through harmony with nature. Allen then moved to Burlington, where he farmed his considerable acres, wrote *An Essay on the Universal Plenitude of Being* (1788), and discussed philosophy whenever possible.

In February, 1789, on the way home from a blustery trip to seek hay for his farm animals, Allen became sick and never recovered. Wild tales abound about the cause of his death, but he probably suffered a stroke. As a brigadier general, the fifty-one-year-old Allen received a military funeral that was hugely attended by Green Mountain Boys and Vermont settlers.

For years, Allen had been the energy behind the republic of Vermont. With his death, the New York land-grant claim was settled, and the settlers of the independent republic resolutely voted to join the United States, an event that took place on March 4, 1791.

SIGNIFICANCE

Ethan Allen once described himself as "a conjurer by profession." Others have described him as a bandit, manipulator, renegade, and agitator, but to Vermont settlers, he was a tough, courageous hero. He led their efforts to honor their land rights, voiced their concerns to authorities, and with the Green Mountain Boys enforced their principles.

A passionately democratic man, Allen was one of few who recorded the events and issues of the day, publishing them for others to debate. According to his brother Ira, Allen often decided what course Vermont should take and persuaded others to follow. Clearly, without Allen the settlement would not have become a resourceful republic, nor would the conquest of Fort Ticonderoga have become the first important victory of the Revolutionary War.

Always a towering presence, after his death Allen became legendary in his military prowess, personal invincibility, and loyalty to Vermont's principles.

—Deborah Elwell Arfken

FURTHER READING

Bellesiles, Michael. *Revolutionary Outlaws: Ethan Allen and the Struggle for Independence on the Early American Frontier.* Charlottesville: University Press of Virginia, 1993. A lengthy scholarly examination of Allen's role in frontier democracy and the social history of Vermont.

Fisher, Dorothy Canfield. *Vermont Tradition.* Boston: Little, Brown, 1953. Contains a chapter on Allen and argues that the unorthodox rustic fit Vermont's culture well. Explains why Allen is the only person who could have led Vermonters at this important time in American history.

Hahn, Michael T. *Ethan Allen: A Life of Adventure.* Shelburne, Vt.: New England Press, 1994. For young adult readers, shows the complexities of Allen's life. Includes a helpful chronology and a short bibliography.

Holbrook, Stewart H. *Ethan Allen.* New York: Macmillan, 1940. Gives a full and admiring biography, but sources are undocumented. Bibliography.

Jellison, Charles A. *Ethan Allen: Frontier Rebel.* Syracuse, N.Y.: Syracuse University Press, 1969. Provides important reasons for Allen's controversial behavior and reinterprets his life in the light of its folklore. Examines Allen's writings and has extensive notes about sources.

Sherman, Michael, Gene Sessions, and P. Jeffrey Potash. *Freedom and Unity: A History of Vermont.* Barre: Vermont Historical Society, 2004. This 730-page book provides a comprehensive account of Vermont history, from prehistoric times to the beginning of the twenty-first century. Includes information about Ethan Allen and the other rebels and outlaws who helped separate Vermont politically and culturally.

See also: John André; Benedict Arnold; Daniel Boone; Joseph Brant; George III; Daniel Shays.

Related articles in *Great Events from History: The Eighteenth Century, 1701-1800:* May 28, 1754-February 10, 1763: French and Indian War; April 19, 1775: Battle of Lexington and Concord; September 19-October 17, 1777: Battles of Saratoga.

LORD AMHERST
British military commander and governor

One of the greatest heroes of the Seven Years' War, Amherst commanded the British and colonial forces that seized Canada from the French.

Born: January 29, 1717; Sevenoaks, Kent, England
Died: August 3, 1797; Montreal, Kent, England
Also known as: Jeffrey Amherst (full name)
Areas of achievement: Military, warfare and conquest, government and politics

EARLY LIFE

Lord Amherst was born Jeffrey Amherst at his family's country house. The second son of a prominent barrister, Amherst attracted the favorable attention of the neighboring Sackville family, whose head was the duke of Dorset. (One of Amherst's boyhood friends was Lord George Sackville, who, as Lord George Germain, would be a cabinet colleague during the American Revolution.)

In 1731, Dorset helped to launch Amherst's military career by obtaining a commission for him in the First Foot Guards. The regiment's commander, General John Ligonier, recognized Amherst's abilities and fostered his career. When, in 1743, Ligonier went to Germany to command British forces during the War of the Austrian Succession, he took Amherst with him as a staff officer. As such, Amherst was present at Dettingen and a number of other major battles. In the later years of the war, Amherst served on the staff of the duke of Cumberland, the younger son of George II. With both Ligonier and Cumberland as patrons, Amherst advanced rapidly and was a lieutenant colonel by the time the war ended in 1748.

A tall, spare man with a prominent nose, Amherst had a hawkish appearance. Cool and reserved in manner, he was nevertheless adept at dealing with troublesome colleagues and subordinates. He tended to be methodical in his approach to his duties; some thought him too much so, while others praised his thoroughness and administrative ability.

LIFE'S WORK

The Seven Years' War (1756-1763) marked the emergence of Lord Amherst as a major figure in the army. At the beginning of the war, he was sent to Germany to take charge of the commissariat that supplied the mercenaries hired to protect King George II's native territory of Hanover. In 1757, Cumberland arrived to take command of the Hanoverian army, and Amherst rejoined his staff.

The French inflicted a major defeat on Cumberland at Hastenback (July, 1757), and he was subsequently forced into signing an embarrassing truce that George II later repudiated. Cumberland returned to England in disgrace. Amherst, however, escaped the misfortunes of his patron. In fact, his prospects improved because General Ligonier replaced Cumberland as commander in chief.

Though the German phase of the war continued to preoccupy the king, his ministers were more interested in eliminating France as a colonial rival, especially in North America. There the war had opened, as elsewhere, with a series of British defeats. Amherst was a key figure in the government's plans to turn the direction of the war in America. He was recalled from Germany, promoted to major general, and named to command an expedition that was being outfitted for an assault on Louisbourg. (Credit for Amherst's appointment is often given to William Pitt the Elder. It was, however, Ligonier who was primarily responsible.) Located on Cape Breton Island, Louisbourg was the largest French fortress in North America, safeguarding communications with Canada by sea.

Lord Amherst. (Library of Congress)

The Louisbourg expedition was Amherst's first major command, and he made the most of the opportunity. He had under him an army of about fourteen thousand soldiers and a sizable fleet under Admiral Edward Boscawen. Aided by a group of able young subordinates that included James Wolfe and William Howe, Amherst carefully cut off all avenues of escape from Louisbourg. After a siege of almost two months, the French surrendered on July 27, 1759. It was Great Britain's first major victory on land and opened one of the major routes into Canada.

Elsewhere, things had not gone as well. Sir James Abercromby, attempting to invade Canada from New York by way of Lake Champlain, had been defeated by the French at Fort Ticonderoga. At the end of 1758, Amherst replaced Abercromby as commander in chief of British forces in North America. The conquest of Canada became the British government's priority for 1759. Amherst was to command, though the overall strategy was decided in London. This called for a three-pronged approach. An amphibious expedition under Wolfe and Admiral Sir Charles Saunders would sail up the St. Lawrence River with Quebec as its objective. Amherst, with a large force of regulars and colonial troops, would move north from Albany along the Lake Champlain route, then link up with Wolfe on the St. Lawrence. Finally, a smaller force under Colonel John Prideaux would take Fort Niagara, cross Lake Ontario from the west, and then move down the St. Lawrence. Amherst preferred the command given to Wolfe. Ligonier, however, believed that Amherst should be with the largest force, where his prestige as commander in chief would promote greater cooperation from the colonists.

The overall strategy proved successful, though Amherst had to adapt it to fit changing circumstances. In September, 1759, Wolfe won his famous victory at Quebec, though he was killed in action. Encountering much greater logistical difficulties, Amherst moved more slowly. He captured Fort Ticonderoga and Fort Crown Point and secured control of Lake Champlain, but he was unable to break through to the St. Lawrence before winter arrived. In the west, Niagara fell to the British, and the victors proceeded to extend their control over Lake Ontario. The next year, Amherst moved to complete the task that had been so well begun. Moving east from Lake Ontario, north from Lake Champlain, and west from Quebec, his forces converged on the St. Lawrence Valley. Amherst maneuvered his men skillfully, and on September 8, 1760, Montreal fell with little bloodshed. Canada was now British, a state of affairs formally confirmed by the Treaty of Paris in 1763.

Success in Canada secured Amherst's military reputation and made him one of the war's greatest heroes in the English-speaking world. He collected a variety of rewards. In 1759, he was named royal governor of Virginia. (This was largely a sinecure worth £1,500 per year; the governor's duties were carried out by the lieutenant governor.) Amherst also received a vote of thanks from Parliament, and, in 1761, George III made him a Knight of the Bath. In America, New England towns and a Virginia county were named for him.

Amherst remained in America as commander in chief until the end of the war. With the French defeated, his main worry became relations with the American Indian tribes, many of which had been French allies. Especially uncertain was the state of things in the vast trans-Appalachian region now passing under British control. Amherst had a decidedly negative opinion of American Indians in general, and his conduct of relations with them was the least successful episode of his career. Seeing his own policy as one based on honesty and economy, Amherst ignored the advice of knowledgeable colonists, such as Sir William Johnson, and stopped a number of practices that had worked in the past, particularly the custom of giving gifts to tribes that remained peaceful. Amherst also stopped supplying the American Indians with ammunition, on which many of them had come to depend for hunting. Amherst thus did little to convince many of the tribes that their interests were secure under British rule. The result was to foster discontent, which led to Pontiac's War, a large-scale indigenous peoples' uprising named after the famous Ottawa chief. Spreading over much of the back country and lasting into 1766, the rebellion frustrated Amherst's attempts to put it down quickly. (At one point, he seriously considered trying to deal with unfriendly tribes by sending them blankets infected with smallpox.)

Amherst returned to England before the final suppression of the uprising. During the next decade, he enjoyed a relatively quiet life, though in 1768, he became involved in a dispute with the Chatham administration over its decision to send a resident governor to Virginia. Amherst did not want to go out to the colony but was offended when he was asked to resign so that someone else could be appointed. In anger, he resigned his military appointments as well. George III eventually soothed the general's wounded pride by promising him a peerage and giving him a new regiment. In 1772, Amherst returned to a more active role in military affairs when he was appointed Lieutenant General of the Ordnance.

The American Revolution marked the next major phase of Amherst's career. While generally supporting the British policies that provoked the American colonists, Amherst had no desire to return to America in a military capacity. In early 1775, he turned down a request that he return as commander in chief in America. After the war broke out, Amherst gave Lord North's government the benefit of his advice. In 1776, the king kept his promise and made Amherst a peer, creating him Baron Amherst of Holmesdale. As Lord Amherst, he proved a regular attender in the House of Lords, where he continued to support the war. In 1778, however, he refused the American command for a second time.

After France entered the war in 1778, Amherst became more active. He was promoted to general and named commander in chief of the army. The position was roughly analogous to a modern chief of staff, with direct command over the forces within the British Isles. It did not, however, carry great influence over the direction of the war in America. This was largely in the hands of Lord George Germain, the secretary of state for the colonies. Amherst devoted himself to administrative matters and to preparations for home defense, for there was a real threat of a French invasion. He also took the lead in suppressing the Gordon Riots, which shook London for a week in June, 1780. With the fall of Lord North's government in 1782, Amherst's term as commander in chief came to an end.

Amherst then retired to his country house (named Montreal) in Kent. With the outbreak of war with revolutionary France in 1793, however, he returned to active duty and once again held the position of commander in chief. By this time, Amherst was seventy-six years old and in failing health. His return was not successful, and two years later, he resigned in favor of the king's son, Frederick, duke of York. Amherst was compensated with promotion to field marshal, the highest rank in the British army. Amherst's last retirement was relatively brief: He died on August 3, 1797.

SIGNIFICANCE

Apart from his subordinate, James Wolfe, Lord Amherst was the best-known British general of the Seven Years'

War and arguably the most successful. The conquest of Canada was his most notable achievement, and he has traditionally been regarded as one of the founding fathers of English Canada. The campaign may have taken longer than originally intended, but Amherst's careful and professional approach minimized the risks in a situation where defeat would have had disastrous consequences. Amherst also, by his development of light infantry tactics, did much to adapt the British army to North American conditions.

Subsequent phases of Amherst's career were less dramatic, though not without importance. His insensitive approach to American Indian relations helped to bring on Pontiac's War, an event that contributed to the British resolve to maintain an army in America after 1763. This policy was, in turn, a factor in promoting the British to look for new sources of revenue in the colonies. The measures that resulted eventually led to the American Revolution. During the period of growing strife with the Americans, Amherst was often sought out by the king and cabinet because of his knowledge of American conditions. He gave advice, joined the cabinet (as commander in chief), and did much to prepare Great Britain for a threatened invasion. After the British defeat at Saratoga in 1777, Amherst was one of the first to realize that Great Britain lacked the military resources to continue an offensive war in America. His advice in favor of a more defensive, naval-oriented strategy, however, was not taken. In the end, Amherst witnessed, as commander in chief, the reduction of an American empire he had done much to expand.

—William C. Lowe

FURTHER READING

Amherst, Jeffrey Lord. *The Journal of Jeffrey Amherst.* Edited by John Clarence Webster. Chicago: University of Chicago Press, 1931. Amherst's detailed account of his North American command, describing events from 1758 through 1763. A basic source, useful for showing Amherst's perception of events.

Flexner, James Thomas. *Mohawk Baronet.* Boston: Little, Brown, 1959. Rev. ed. *Lord of the Mohawks: A Biography of Sir William Johnson.* A well-researched and well-written biography of a colonist who had great influence with the Iroquois. Johnson participated in Amherst's campaigns but differed sharply with him over American Indian policy. Flexner saw Amherst as primarily responsible for Pontiac's War.

Gipson, Lawrence Henry. *The Great War for Empire: The Victorious Years, 1758-1760.* Vol. 7 in *The British Empire Before the American Revolution.* New York: Alfred A. Knopf, 1957. A sound account of the phase of the Seven Years' War that included Amherst's major victories. Useful for placing the Canadian campaign in the overall context of the war.

Long, J. C. *Lord Jeffery Amherst: A Soldier of the King.* New York: Macmillan, 1933. The best biography of Amherst, though not definitive. It emphasizes his Seven Years' War experience and tends to be uncritical. As a side note, the book's title misspells Amherst's first name and purposely transposes it with his title; properly used, "lord" before a name indicates the younger son of a duke or marquess.

Mackesy, Piers. *The War for America, 1775-1783.* Cambridge, Mass.: Harvard University Press, 1964. The best account of the Revolutionary War from the British perspective. Provides a well-rounded picture of Amherst's role as military adviser and commander in chief.

Nester, William R. *"Haughty Conquerors": Amherst and the Great Indian Uprising of 1763.* Westport, Conn.: Praeger, 2000. A history of Pontiac's War and Amherst's role in the rebellion.

Parkman, Francis. *France and England in North America.* 9 vols. 1865-1892. Reprint. 2 vols. Edited by David Levin. New York: Library of America, 1983. Volume 2 contains the classic and still valuable account of the Seven Years' War in North America. Very influential in establishing the traditional view of its subject. While James Wolfe is Parkman's hero on the British side, Amherst's campaigns are covered in highly readable fashion.

Peckham, Howard H. *Pontiac and the Indian Uprising.* Princeton, N.J.: Princeton University Press, 1947. The standard work on Pontiac's War that is critical of Amherst's insensitive approach to dealing with the American Indians. The work shows, however, that there were other factors at work as well.

Rogers, H. C. B. *The British Army of the Eighteenth Century.* New York: Hippocrene Books, 1977. Contains a chapter on Amherst's campaigns during the Seven Years' War. Argues that his efforts were more important in winning Canada than was Wolfe's more famous victory at Quebec.

See also: Sir Guy Carleton; Thomas Gage; George II; George III; William Howe; Lord North; William Pitt the Elder; Pontiac; George Rodney; John Graves Simcoe; James Wolfe.

Related articles in *Great Events from History: The Eighteenth Century, 1701-1800:* December 16, 1740-November 7, 1748: War of the Austrian Succession; January, 1756-February 15, 1763: Seven Years' War; June 8-July 27, 1758: Siege of Louisbourg; April 19, 1775: Battle of Lexington and Concord; September 19-October 17, 1777: Battles of Saratoga; February 6, 1778: Franco-American Treaties; June 2-10, 1780: Gordon Riots; September 3, 1783: Treaty of Paris; April 20, 1792-October, 1797: Early Wars of the French Revolution.

JOHN ANDRÉ
English military officer

As an intelligence officer for the British during the American Revolution, André convinced American general Benedict Arnold to turn over the fortress of West Point to secure British victory in the war. However, André was captured while returning to British lines, and the conspiracy was discovered.

Born: May 2, 1750; London, England
Died: October 2, 1780; Tappan, New York
Areas of achievement: Military, warfare and conquest

EARLY LIFE

Unlike most British officers of his era, John André came from humble origins. Although he was born in London, both of his parents had emigrated to England from the Continent. His Swiss father and French mother were Protestant Huguenots who left Europe in search of religious freedom. As a child, André was tutored near London. Later, he attended the University of Geneva, where he achieved a reputation as an excellent student specializing in mathematics and military drawing. As a young man, his aspirations were to be an artist and a poet. In 1769, his father, a successful merchant, died and left him a substantial sum of money. André took over his father's business for a few months but soon tired of it. In 1771, he bought a commission as a second lieutenant in the British army and embarked on a military career.

André was tall, slender, and handsome; he looked younger than his years. Military life suited him, and he quickly rose through the ranks. As an officer, he continued to write and to sketch. These talents, in addition to being a creative outlet for André, endeared him to senior military officers who needed a reliable aide to monitor intelligence operations and provide effective reports. Bored with military drilling in England, André traveled to Germany. Within a few months, however, his regiment was ordered to Canada. André delayed making the trip, and when he did go, he took the long way, visiting Philadelphia and New York, eventually traveling up the Hudson River to his new station in Quebec. His arrival in the American colonies coincided with the onset of the Revolutionary War in April, 1775.

André was stationed at St. Johns on the Richelieu River north of Lake Champlain. Soon the Continental army, commanded jointly by Ethan Allen and Benedict Arnold, began an invasion of Canada. On November 3, after a series of skirmishes, the British garrison at St. Johns surrendered to Continental army general Richard Montgomery. André was now a prisoner of war. The British prisoners were taken from Quebec to Pennsylvania. André was interned first in Lancaster and then in Carlisle. Eventually, he was returned to the British as part of a prisoner exchange and was reassigned to British headquarters in New York, under the command of General William Howe.

LIFE'S WORK

In June, 1777, John André was promoted to major and named aide-de-camp for General Charles Grey. The military campaign took the army around New York, New Jersey, and Pennsylvania. André participated in battles at Brandywine, Germantown, Monmouth, and Tappan, serving as Grey's aide until November, 1778. During this time, he recorded the movements and operations of the British army. In 1777 and 1778, British troops occupied Philadelphia and spent the winter there. André lived in Benjamin Franklin's house and soon became a figure in (Loyalist) Philadelphia society. He attended grand balls where his own plays and poetry were presented.

While in Philadelphia, André developed friendly relationships with several women, including a close one with the young and beautiful Margaret "Peggy" Shippen. André continued to correspond with Shippen after the British abandoned Philadelphia and returned to safety in New York. Following the Continental army's reoccupation of the city, Shippen met and fell in love with the city's new military commandant, Major General Benedict Arnold. She married Arnold in Philadelphia, and after George Washington gave Arnold the command of the defensive garrison at West Point on the Hudson River, the couple moved to upstate New York.

Back in the city of New York, Major André was promoted to the post of adjutant general of the British army now commanded by General Henry Clinton. Among André's responsibilities was military intelligence. André would gather information on the American forces and seek out any American informers willing to sell information to the British. One of the Americans with whom André maintained contact was Arnold.

Early in the war, Arnold was a leader in important American campaigns, including the invasion of Canada and the decisive victory over the British at Saratoga. Arnold, however, was disappointed by promotion of junior officers and lived well above his means. With his salary as a Continental army officer, Arnold could not afford to keep himself and his wife in the luxurious lifestyle to which they had become accustomed. He had been accused of several crimes earlier in his career but was ac-

quitted of all serious charges. André believed that Arnold would be willing to give the British important information even though this action would constitute treason. The two men maintained a lengthy correspondence from shortly after Arnold's marriage to Shippen in 1779 to 1780. The two officers exchanged coded messages across enemy lines. Eventually, Arnold agreed to provide tactical information to the British.

For British protection and a military commission, Arnold needed to offer André and the British something valuable. The American fortress at West Point defended the Hudson River in New York and prevented the British from isolating New England from the rest of the American colonies. If the British could capture and hold West Point, the American rebellion could be suppressed quickly. Arnold would defect and surrender the garrison to André in exchange for British money and protection. Arnold gave André safe passage through the American lines using a false identity; André would pretend to be a New York merchant named John Anderson.

The capture of John André in Tarrytown, New York. (Library of Congress)

André sailed up the Hudson River on the British warship *Vulture* and planned for Arnold to meet him just south of the defenses at West Point. Arnold, however, sent a message that they should meet in a farmhouse a few miles from the river. This violated their earlier agreement; André did not wish to cross enemy lines or to be out of uniform. However, having come so far already, André agreed to the request. André and Arnold met alone late on the evening of September 21, 1780, talking through the night and over breakfast the next morning. André obtained maps of the fortress at West Point and the surrounding defenses, and Arnold explained how he had intentionally weakened its defenses to permit quick capture by a British assault. Their morning discussions, however, were interrupted by artillery barrage. The *Vulture* had come under attack and retreated down the river.

André and Arnold, who were both known for their resolve, panicked. Arnold returned immediately to West Point. André wore a civilian greatcoat to cover his British uniform, hid the plans for West Point in one of his boots, and traveled overland back to New York rather than returning to the *Vulture* as originally planned. Traveling alone as he neared the British lines, André encountered three Continental army irregulars at Tarrytown. Although he showed them a letter of safe passage signed by General Arnold, the three men became suspicious and subdued André. Searching his possessions, they found the plans to West Point and turned him over to army forces at nearby North Castle. The commanding officer sent messages both to West Point and to General Washington that a man called John Anderson had been captured holding secret plans for the fortress. Initially, André was sent back toward West Point, but he was recalled as Major Benjamin Tallmadge and other officers in the Washington camp realized that André was a British spy and Arnold was a traitor.

By coincidence, General Washington returned to West Point for an inspection the day after André was captured. Arnold received the message from North Castle during discussions with members of Washington's personal staff. Realizing the plot would soon be uncovered, he made excuses and left. He immediately fled to the *Vulture* to escape capture. André, however, was not so lucky; he was again a prisoner of war. Washington reinforced West Point and issued orders to hold André as a spy.

An investigation followed André's arrest, and he was taken to Mabie's Tavern in Tappan, New York, for trial. André admitted his role in the conspiracy but refused to concede that he was anything other than a soldier performing his duty. The facts of the case—he wore civilian clothes, used a false identity, and held secret meetings with an American traitor—did not mesh with his statement that he was not a spy. André, adjutant general of the British army, was convicted of espionage. He had a number of supporters among the Continental army, including Tallmadge and Washington's aide-de-camp, Alexander Hamilton. However, Washington rejected their pleas for clemency. The British had imposed capital punishment on Continental army soldiers accused as spies, including Nathan Hale. Justice in the new American republic would be dispensed in the same manner.

André received the death penalty for his crime. He wrote to Washington requesting that he be shot by a firing squad as an enemy soldier rather than taken to the gallows as a spy, but he received no reply from Washington. At noon on October 2, 1780, André was hanged. Continental army officers later admired the courage and composure that André maintained throughout his trial, his imprisonment, and his execution.

SIGNIFICANCE

Major John André, adjutant general of the British army, failed in his plot to take control of West Point when he was captured and the plans he had received from General Benedict Arnold were discovered. After this incident, the British never seriously challenged the Continental army in the northern colonies. A year after André's execution for espionage, the British would surrender. Americans would soon characterize Arnold as the terrible traitor and André as the honorable but unwitting victim in this tragedy. As George Washington later said of André, "He was more unfortunate than criminal: an accomplished man and a gallant officer." A memorial to André was erected in Westminster Abbey in London, to which his remains were removed in 1821.

—*James W. Endersby*

FURTHER READING

André, John. *Major André's Journal*. 1904. Reprint. New York: Arno Press, 1968. André's journal presents an eyewitness account of British military operations from June, 1777, to November, 1778. The manuscript was unknown for many years and discovered in a sealed box in England in 1902.

Brandt, Claire. *The Man in the Mirror: A Life of Benedict Arnold*. New York: Random House, 1994. A fine biography of the American conspirator that contains several chapters on his relationship with André. Includes a chronology, maps, and a comprehensive bibliography.

Decker, Malcolm. *Ten Days of Infamy: An Illustrated Memoir of the Arnold-André Conspiracy.* New York: Arno Press, 1969. A brief but informative history of André's last days. Includes photographs, illustrations, foldout maps, a chronology, and a bibliography.

Flexner, James Thomas. *The Traitor and the Spy: Benedict Arnold and John André.* 1953. Reprint. Boston: Little, Brown, 1975. A readable and well-researched history that effectively contrasts the two major characters in the conspiracy. Includes illustrations, a comprehensive bibliography, and an index.

Hatch, Robert McConnell. *Major John André: A Gallant in Spy's Clothing.* Boston: Houghton Mifflin, 1986. A fine biography of André that emphasizes the perspective of Benjamin Tallmadge. Includes a map, illustrations, an extensive bibliography, and an index.

Morpugo, J. E. *Treason at West Point: The Arnold-André Conspiracy.* New York: Mason/Charter, 1975. This sympathetic portrayal of the key players in the plot to surrender West Point speculates about their psychological motivations. Includes illustrations.

Randall, Willard Sterne. *Benedict Arnold: Patriot and Traitor.* New York: William Morrow, 1990. A lengthy biography of Arnold that contains several chapters on his relationship with André. Includes numerous illustrations and an extensive bibliography.

Smith, Joshua Hett. *Narrative of the Causes Which Led to the Death of Major John André.* 1808. Reprint. New York: Arno Press, 1969. The saga as told by the man who escorted André to the rendezvous with Arnold and part of the way back to British lines. Smith was later court-martialed as a spy but acquitted.

Walsh, John Evangelist. *The Execution of Major André.* New York: Palgrave, 2001. Recounts in narrative style the events leading to André's capture and execution. In Walsh's opinion, André was badly cast as a spy but agreed to help Arnold because of greed and a desire for prestige.

See also: Ethan Allen; Benedict Arnold; Sir Guy Carleton; Sir Henry Clinton; Benjamin Franklin; Nathanael Greene; Alexander Hamilton; William Howe; George Washington.

Related articles in *Great Events from History: The Eighteenth Century, 1701-1800:* April 19, 1775: Battle of Lexington and Concord; September 19-October 17, 1777: Battles of Saratoga.

QUEEN ANNE
Queen of Great Britain and Ireland (r. 1702-1714)

Through her devotion to the Church of England, Anne maintained the provisions of the Act of Settlement of 1701, thereby fostering the cause of constitutional government while preventing another civil war.

Born: February 6, 1665; London, England
Died: August 1, 1714; London, England
Area of achievement: Government and politics

EARLY LIFE

Of the seven children born to James, duke of York, and his first wife, Anne Hyde, only two survived infancy: Anne and Mary, who was three years Anne's senior and the future Queen Mary I. Concerned by his younger daughter's poor eyesight, James sent Anne to Paris to be treated by a noted oculist. While in France, Anne lived first with her paternal grandmother, Dowager Queen Henrietta Maria, who died in 1669, and then with her father's youngest sister, Henrietta Annie, duchess of Orleans. At the age of five, Anne returned to England, but she continued to be troubled by poor eyesight all of her life.

When Anne was six her mother died of cancer, and rather than leave his nieces under the sole supervision of their father, King Charles II sent them to live with Colonel Edward Villiers, a devout Protestant. Both the duke and the duchess of York had made the politically unwise decision to accept the Roman Catholic faith, but the king would not allow Mary and Anne, who stood next in line for the throne, to make the same choice. While under the care of Colonel Villiers, Anne met and fell under the spell of Sarah Jennings, who, as the duchess of Marlborough (later Sarah Churchill), would dominate the early years of Anne's reign. In 1673, the duke of York married an Italian princess, Mary of Modena, and Sarah Jennings entered her service as a maid of honor.

Neither pretty like her sister Mary nor clever like her friend Sarah, Anne was soon forgotten amid the glitter of the Restoration court. Then Charles II discovered that his shy niece possessed one gift worth developing, her voice. Under the supervision of Elizabeth Barry, a leading actor of the day, Anne mastered elocution, a skill that would later earn for her the reputation of being perhaps the finest public speaker to occupy the British throne.

In November, 1677, Anne's life was changed by the marriage of her sister to their first cousin, William of Orange. Ill with smallpox, Anne was unable to attend the wedding, and Mary, on the eve of her departure for her new home in the Netherlands, was forbidden to visit her sister lest she risk infection. A year later Sarah Jennings married John Churchill, leaving thirteen-year-old Anne alone. During the next five years she grew into an unassuming young woman who longed to imitate the private bliss of her sister and her best friend. In 1683, she married Prince George of Denmark, a man twelve years her senior. Dull-witted and troubled by chronic asthma, he was nevertheless a loving and understanding husband who sustained his wife through her various illnesses and the loss of their seventeen children. On her twentieth birthday, February 6, 1685, Charles II died, and Anne was thrust into the midst of national affairs by the accession of her father as James II.

LIFE'S WORK

During his brief reign of almost four years, James II managed to forfeit the goodwill of his subjects by offending most of them, including his younger daughter; but these affronts still lay in the future. Anne was now permitted to choose the members of her own household, and predictably Sarah Jennings, now Sarah Churchill, was appointed first lady of the bedchamber. "Mrs. Freeman," Sarah's pet name, provided "Mrs. Morley," Anne's pet name, with the intellectual companionship not found in her marriage, as well as sage advice in times of trouble. Although James II treated his daughter with love and deference, he would not permit her to visit her sister in June, 1687, fueling speculation that pressure would soon be put upon her to change her religion. Mary was the wife of the champion of the Protestant cause, but Anne, always so eager to please, might prove a better choice as sovereign if she were to become a Roman Catholic. With Sarah's support, Anne prepared to defend her devotion to the Church of England, but this crisis of conscience never materialized.

Rumors began to circulate during November, 1687, that the queen was pregnant. Princess Anne had her doubts, about both the pregnancy, because of her stepmother's age, and the legitimacy of the healthy prince, born the following June, which was a month ahead of schedule. Anne was not alone in her doubts, and the prospect of an unending dynasty of Roman Catholic monarchs rallied opposition to James II and his policies. By November, 1688, when William of Orange landed at Torbay at the invitation of a group of prominent noblemen, England was on the verge of another civil war. Luckily, the crisis passed with the flight of James II, his

Queen Anne. (Hulton Archive/Getty Images)

queen, and their son to France the following month. Through the tense weeks, Anne supported her sister and brother-in-law, despite her deep love for her father.

The years of separation had changed the sisters, and Anne soon learned to her dismay that Queen Mary did not approve of Sarah Churchill. Anne refused to dismiss her dearest friend, and so a breach developed between the royal sisters that was widened when John Churchill was arrested for treason in 1691. Although he was acquitted, relations between Mary and Anne never really improved before the queen's death from smallpox in December, 1694. William (now King William III) and his sister-in-law were never friends, and after the death of Mary they became almost open enemies. William III would reign alone until his death. He was followed by Anne, and then the duke of Gloucester, Anne's only surviving child. The boy was delicate, but he was England's hope of a continuing Protestant line.

In July, 1700, the eleven-year-old duke of Gloucester died of scarlet fever; Anne acquiesced with reluctance, the following year, to the Act of Settlement. After William's death she would become queen, and if she died without issue the Crown would pass to her cousin, the Protestant electress Sophia of Hanover and her heirs. James II died in France on September 6, 1701, and King Louis XIV publicly recognized his son as James III. Anne's father had forgiven her for her rebellion before his death, and with his blessing she calmly waited for the inevitable. Six months later William III was dead, and Anne was queen.

Anne's coronation on April 23, 1702, was a triumph for her and the Churchills. Sarah was made Mistress of the Robes, and John was created duke of Marlborough. The power to reward was pleasant, but the reality of governing an imperial state was almost overwhelming. Queen Anne, who had received no training for the task she had to perform, wisely relied on her ministers for advice, and in the first eight years of her reign, that meant Marlborough and the Whigs. In May, 1702, England was drawn into the War of the Spanish Succession, and although the government was supposedly bipartisan, the Whig policy of total commitment to a land war prevailed over the Tory preference for a purely naval war with economic sanctions. Anne might have been inclined to the Tory position, but she was too dependent on Marlborough and his close friend, the first earl of Godolphin, to oppose their policies. Hoping to dislodge the queen, the Tories appealed to her special interest, the Church of England, with the Occasional Conformity Bill, which would restrict the activities of the Dissenters (non-Anglican Protestants),

who were active supporters of the Whigs. The measure passed the Tory-dominated House of Commons only to be defeated in the Whig-controlled House of Lords.

The Tories then concentrated their attack on Marlborough, but he countered their criticism with the brilliant victory at Blenheim in August, 1704. Once again the Tories tried to punish the Dissenters, only to fail. The nation and the queen supported the ministry, a fact that was demonstrated by a resounding Whig victory in the election of 1705. As more Tories left the government, Queen Anne began to lose confidence in her advisers. The key to this change was the duchess of Marlborough. Always a woman of strong opinions, Sarah now became tyrannical and overbearing. While her husband was winning the war, Sarah was losing the affection and support of the queen with her constant badgering.

The duchess of Marlborough introduced a poor relation, Abigail Masham, into the queen's service in 1707, an event that went unnoticed by most. One person who saw Masham's potential was Robert Harley, a moderate Tory who had held various positions in the ministry. Quietly he began to work through her to undermine Sarah's influence. Even his removal from office at Marlborough's insistence in 1708 did not retard the erosion of the power once enjoyed by "Mrs. Freeman." The election of 1708 proved another Whig victory, and the war-weary queen was forced to replace more Tories with politicians who now arrogantly refused to make peace with King Louis XIV on any terms but their own.

Dr. Henry Sacheverell delivered his famous sermon at St. Paul's Cathedral on November 5, 1709, the anniversary of William III's landing at Torbay in 1688. Queen Anne, who was in mourning for her husband, seemed cheered by the Tory divine's attack on the government and the Glorious Revolution, but she, like many others, was shocked when the Whig leaders dragged him into court. The move to impeach Sacheverell proved a fatal mistake. The trial was a sensation, and every day the courtroom was packed. Even the queen attended incognito. Sacheverell was found guilty, but his punishment was minor, and when his three years' suspension from preaching was done, Queen Anne rewarded him with a handsome living. It was really the Whigs who were convicted in March, 1710, and at the polls they were sentenced by the voters to defeat.

As her Whig ministers began to depart, Queen Anne turned on the duchess of Marlborough, whom she dismissed in April, 1710. By September only Marlborough remained; his public dismissal and humiliation were postponed until December 31, 1711. Queen Anne was served for the last four years of her reign by politicians who fully shared her views on church and state. At the head of the Tory ministry was Robert Harley, who was raised to the peerage as earl of Oxford in 1711. His most able colleague, indeed his chief rival, was Henry St. John, to whom fell the task of making a secret peace with the French. For his masterful negotiating of the Treaty of Utrecht, St. John was made First Viscount Bolingbroke, a reward he resented because it placed him below Oxford in the peerage.

The signing of the treaty in 1713 did little to enhance Great Britain's prestige abroad; its allies felt betrayed and not inclined to trust the British again. Among those former friends was the elector of Hanover, who, after his mother Sophia, was heir to the throne of Great Britain. Firmly in league with the Whigs, he was determined to punish Oxford, Bolingbroke, and their political friends for their perfidy. For their part, the Tories now feverishly began to work for a restoration of the son of James II and Mary of Modena, and at first they had the halfhearted support of the queen.

As the war came to a close, Anne's health seemed to deteriorate. Everyone she had loved was gone, and her only consolation was alcohol, which relieved both pain and loneliness. Few were completely aware of the queen's condition until July 24, 1714, when she collapsed during a cabinet meeting. All during her reign she had faithfully attended those weekly sessions, but the bitter altercation between Oxford and Bolingbroke on that occasion was too much for her nerves. Two days later she dismissed the earl of Oxford from her government, but it was the moderate Whigs, not Bolingbroke, to whom she turned in her last hours. The queen who had refused to discuss the succession during her lifetime, now, on her deathbed, chose her cousin, the elector of Hanover, to follow her. Sophia was dead, but the elector, now King George I, would preserve the church that Anne had loved and served. On Sunday, August 1, 1714, Anne died, with only her personal physician in attendance.

SIGNIFICANCE

Queen Anne was a woman of average intelligence who governed an exceptional generation. Her education was at best superficial, but she recognized her inadequacies and relied on her ministers for their advice. Her personal life was tragic, but she was sustained by the Church of England in every adversity. At the end of her reign she accepted a distant cousin as her heir because he would preserve that church.

—*Clifton W. Potter, Jr.*

FURTHER READING

Bucholz, R. O. *The Augustan Court: Queen Anne and the Decline of Court Culture*. Stanford, Calif.: Stanford University Press, 1993. Bucholz examines how and why court culture declined in importance by the early eighteenth century despite Anne's efforts to restore it to its former glory. Maintains that Anne was not dependent upon her female favorites but was able to exert independence over Sarah Churchill and Abigail Mesham.

Butler, Iris. *Rule of Three*. London: Hodder and Stoughton, 1967. This work provides valuable psychological insight into the characters of Anne, Sarah Churchill, and Abigail Masham. It is rich with many previously unpublished items.

Feiling, Sir Keith. *A History of the Tory Party, 1640-1714*. Oxford, England: Oxford University Press, 1924. Although dated in its analysis of events, this is nevertheless a work of remarkable scholarship, providing a very valuable overview of the period.

Green, David. *Queen Anne*. New York: Charles Scribner's Sons, 1970. A well-written and easily read biography, but lacking the sympathy and understanding that must be part of any study of Anne.

Gregg, Edward. *Queen Anne*. London: Routledge and Kegan Paul, 1980. More scholarly than earlier biographies, this work presents a sympathetic portrait of Anne in a forthright and lively way. Until a complete revisionist study appears, this is the best work available.

Hamilton, Elizabeth. *The Backstairs Dragon: A Life of Robert Harley, Earl of Oxford*. London: Hamish Hamilton, 1969. Harley's character is restored by this study, one that will also enhance the reader's understanding of the politics of the early eighteenth century.

Holmes, Geoffrey. *British Politics in the Age of Anne*. London: Macmillan, 1967. This work contains a wealth of information, and it carefully unravels the tangled knot of politics in the early eighteenth century. It is perhaps the best book on the subject.

Trevelyan, George Macaulay. *England Under Queen Anne*. 3 vols. London: Longmans, Green, 1930-1934. Long the standard work on the period. Trevelyan's conclusions may find detractors, but none can fault his style or scholarship.

Waller, Maureen. *Ungrateful Daughters: The Stuart Princesses Who Stole Their Father's Crown*. New York: St. Martin's Press, 2003. Describes the Glorious Revolution of 1688 as a family feud, in which Anne and her sister Mary betrayed their father, King James II, by supporting William of Orange's bid for the throne.

See also: Second Duke of Argyll; Mary Astell; First Viscount Bolingbroke; Sarah Churchill; George I; First Earl of Godolphin; First Duke of Marlborough.

Related articles in *Great Events from History: The Eighteenth Century, 1701-1800:* May 26, 1701-September 7, 1714: War of the Spanish Succession; June 12, 1701: Act of Settlement; May 15, 1702-April 11, 1713: Queen Anne's War; February, 1706-April 28, 1707: Act of Union Unites England and Scotland; March 23-26, 1708: Defeat of the "Old Pretender"; April 11, 1713: Treaty of Utrecht; 1721-1742: Development of Great Britain's Office of Prime Minister.

LORD ANSON
English admiral and administrator

Through his great achievements during active service at sea and at the Admiralty ashore, Anson was instrumental in making British naval predominance one of the major legacies of the wars of the mid-eighteenth century.

Born: April 23, 1697; Shugborough, Staffordshire, England
Died: June 6, 1762; Moor Park, Hertfordshire, England
Also known as: George Anson (birth name)
Areas of achievement: Military, warfare and conquest, government and politics

EARLY LIFE

Lord Anson was born George Anson in his family's country house, the second son of a gentry family with strong legal connections. Little is known of his boyhood or early education. In 1712, at the age of fifteen, he entered the Royal Navy as a volunteer in time to see action in the closing stages of the War of the Spanish Succession. In 1716, after further service as a midshipman, he was commissioned a lieutenant. Thereafter, Anson's advancement was rapid. In 1722, he was given his first command, the sloop *Weasel*. Two years later, after only twelve years of service, he was promoted to captain and took command of HMS *Scarborough*, a frigate. Anson spent much time during the next fifteen years in American waters, patrolling the southern coast and the Bahamas for pirates, smugglers, and Spanish cruisers. He also took advantage of his time ashore to make a number of successful real estate investments in South Carolina.

Anson's rapid progress as a young naval officer was a result of a combination of family ties and ability. It was certainly to his advantage that an uncle (Thomas Lord Parker, later earl of Macclesfield) was an eminent judge who eventually became lord chancellor. Aristocratic patronage was by itself not enough to propel one to the top in the eighteenth century navy, and Anson impressed his superiors from the beginning with his ability to master the intricacies of seamanship and with the potential he displayed for leadership. Contemporary accounts of his personality stress his intelligence and his devotion to his profession, as well as a certain reserve or shyness that was especially evident in social situations. (Anson did not marry until he was fifty-one.) Taller than average, with a round, open face, Anson had penetrating eyes, his most striking physical feature.

LIFE'S WORK

When war with Spain broke out in 1739 (the War of Jenkins's Ear), which subsequently was absorbed into the larger War of the Austrian Succession), Lord Anson was captain of the sixty-gun *Centurion*. Recalled from the West Indies to England, he was promoted to commodore and given command of a small squadron of six ships intended to harass Spanish colonies on the western coast of South America and interrupt Spanish shipping in the Pacific. This set the stage for the most famous episode in Anson's career.

Anson's Pacific command turned into a four-year voyage around the world that is justly regarded as one of the greatest feats of eighteenth century seamanship. Delays in fitting out his squadron prevented Anson's departure until the fall of 1740, with the result that weather conditions were at their worst when the expedition reached Cape Horn. The squadron experienced tremendous hardships in rounding the cape. When he was finally able to regroup in the Pacific, Anson found that almost two-thirds of his nine hundred men had died and that most of the rest (including himself) had scurvy. The squadron was also down to three ships. After recuperating for three months on the island of Juan Fernandez, Anson began to prey with some success on Spanish shipping, and he captured the port of Paita, Peru.

He barely missed, however, a greater prize, the fabled "Manila Galleon" (which annually carried rich cargoes

49

Lord Anson. (Library of Congress)

from Manila to Acapulco and back). In May, 1742, Anson turned westward to cross the Pacific. Once again, hardships multiplied, and the men were devastated by scurvy. By the time another place for recuperation was found (the island of Tinian), Anson was down to his flagship, the *Centurion*, and about two hundred of his original force. Some new recruits were found at Macao, and Anson then began to cruise off the Philippines. In June, 1743, he found his object, the treasure galleon *Nuestra Señora de Cabadonga*, inbound from Acapulco. Though greatly outnumbered, the crew of the *Centurion* was better drilled and within hours forced the Spanish to surrender. The prize was one of the richest ever taken by the Royal Navy, worth between £400,000 and £500,000. Anson then deposited his prisoners at Canton and headed home, this time by way of the Indian Ocean and Africa. The rest of the voyage was relatively uneventful, and in June, 1744, after almost four years, *Centurion* returned to England.

Anson was only the seventh Englishman to circumnavigate the globe and quickly became the newest hero in a war that had not produced many. Though the expedition had suffered horrendous difficulties and great loss of life, there was general agreement that Anson's leader-

ship had made the difference between triumph and disaster. The officers who survived the ordeal certainly appear to have learned their craft: Eight of them subsequently became admirals.

Anson's voyage brought him wealth, glory, and a much larger role in naval affairs. In short order, he was promoted to rear admiral, elected to Parliament and—at the very end of 1744—made a lord of the Admiralty, the board that administered the navy's affairs. By this time, France had joined Spain as an enemy. In 1746, Anson was promoted to vice admiral and given command of the Channel fleet. In May, 1747, he led it into a major battle off Cape Finisterre against a French fleet escorting a convoy bound for Canada. Anson's fleet sank or captured all the French ships-of-the-line, while taking more than £300,000 in prize money. As a further reward for his victory in what became known as the First Battle of Finisterre, George II granted Anson a peerage: In June, 1747, he was created Baron Anson of Soperton.

After the victory off Finisterre, Lord Anson spent relatively little time at sea. Peace returned in 1748. The remainder of Anson's career was dominated by service at the Admiralty. A member of the board since 1744, in 1751 Anson became first lord of the Admiralty, a position he retained with but one brief interruption (from November, 1756, to July, 1757) until his death. The appointment owed something to the powerful political connections Anson had acquired, especially through his marriage in 1748 to Lady Elizabeth Yorke. Lady Anson was the daughter of the earl of Hardwicke, lord chancellor and close associate of the duke of Newcastle. The first lord of the Admiralty was usually considered to be one of the cabinet, so Anson now found himself to be at the center of British politics, in addition to carrying the primary responsibility for the Royal Navy's well-being. Though never comfortable in politics (and inclined to resist the tendency of politicians to meddle in naval affairs), Anson proved a diligent and cooperative colleague to his fellow ministers.

During his years at the Admiralty (including those preceding his appointment as first lord), Anson won a justified reputation as an energetic and extremely effective naval administrator and reformer. Improvements taking place during Anson's tenure included the organization of the Royal Marines on a permanent footing, annual inspections of dockyards, maintenance of a large reserve of out-of-service ships that could be mobilized in the event of war, the drafting of a new set of the Articles of War (the legal code under which the navy operated), standardization of officers' uniforms into the blue and white familiar in eighteenth century paintings, a more rational system of classifying (by rate) the navy's ships, and a building program to prepare the fleet for the likely resumption of warfare with France.

Though the navy was chronically underfunded during the early 1750's, it was largely because of Anson's management that it was in sound shape when the Seven Years' War broke out in 1756. The war, however, began badly for Great Britain, and the navy was especially embarrassed by the fall of Minorca in May, 1756. Anson had dispatched an expedition under Admiral John Byng to relieve the British garrison of the beleaguered island, but it failed to achieve its mission. (Byng was subsequently executed for dereliction of duty.) Though Anson cannot be held wholly responsible for the disaster, he did appoint Byng to command the expedition, and he later refused it additional reinforcement (for fear of weakening the home fleet, which was Great Britain's main line of defense). The episode was one of the few failures with which he was ever associated. The loss of Minorca also contributed to the political confusion that led to the fall of the duke of Newcastle's ministry, to which Anson belonged.

By July, 1757, a new ministry (a coalition formed by William Pitt the Elder and the duke of Newcastle) had taken office, and Anson was back at the Admiralty. As first lord, Anson played a major role in turning the direction of the war around. His contributions were many. One was a stepped-up building program that steadily increased the size of the fleet until in 1760, for the first time in British history, there were more than three hundred ships in commission. As part of this, Anson introduced a number of seventy-four-gun ships-of-the-line, smaller but more maneuverable than older models. He also increased substantially the number of frigates. Anson also appointed the men who put this force to effective use, displaying considerable skill in selecting commanders. Some of those he chose were protégés, such as Sir Charles Saunders, Richard Lord Howe, and Augustus Keppel, all of whom had been with Anson on his famous voyage. Others, such as Sir Edward Hawke, Edward Boscawen, and George Brydges Romney, gained prominence on their own before catching Anson's eye.

At one point in 1758, Anson himself returned to sea, settling a squabble among his admirals by assuming command of the fleet blockading the French coast. He eventually returned the fleet to Hawke's command and with it the task of preventing assistance being sent to French forces overseas. The necessity of periodic returns to England to refit and resupply had weakened past efforts at blockading. Anson solved the problem, at least for 1759, by organizing a system of resupply by sea that enabled Hawke's fleet to remain on station for almost a year. It was in no small measure because of this that Hawke was able to engage and shatter a French fleet at the Battle of Quiberon Bay in November, 1759.

After Quiberon Bay, the naval war was well in hand, and the Admiralty's operations continued to bear the stamp of Anson's professionalism. In 1761, Anson's achievements were further recognized when he was given the honor of transporting George III's new bride, Charlotte of Mecklenburg, the future Queen Charlotte, to England. It was, in fact, while escorting the new queen's brother on a tour of the naval base at Portsmouth that Anson caught a cold that developed into pneumonia. He died on June 6, 1762, at Moor Park, Hertfordshire, a large country house north of London that Anson had bought with some of his Spanish prize money.

SIGNIFICANCE

More than any other single person, it was Lord Anson who made Great Britain the world's dominant naval power in the mid-eighteenth century. His celebrated voyage around the world demonstrated the superiority of British seamanship and greatly increased British knowledge of and interest in the Pacific. Furthermore, Anson was the first British naval officer to deal with the Chinese government. His victory at Finisterre helped to secure British dominance in European waters and contributed to changes in the navy's fighting instructions that would be employed by a succession of eighteenth century admirals.

As important as Anson's service at sea was, however, his greatest service to his country was given at the Admiralty. There, Anson proved to be the greatest naval administrator of his era. By keeping the fleet up to strength, making a host of wise appointments, and supporting the ships at sea to an unprecedented extent, Anson played a central role in making the Seven Years' War the decisive conflict in the long-standing colonial and maritime rivalry between Great Britain and France. British predominance at sea and overseas was no small legacy.

—*William C. Lowe*

FURTHER READING

Anson, George. *A Voyage Round the World in the Years MDCCXL, I, II, III, IV*. Compiled by Richard Walter. 1748. Rev. ed. Edited by Glyndwr Williams. New York: Oxford University Press, 1974. A firsthand account of the famous voyage from notes made by Anson. The collection is traditionally attributed to Richard Walter, Anson's chaplain, under whose name it was first published in 1748.

Barrow, Sir John. *The Life of George, Lord Anson.* London: J. Murray, 1839. The first full biography of Anson. It is still useful though it is marred by some inaccuracies. Valuable for the range of its coverage and for its inclusion of primary sources.

Corbett, Sir Julian. *England in the Seven Years' War: A Study in Combined Strategy.* 2 vols. London: Longmans, 1907. Reprint. New York: AMS Press, 1973. The standard account of the Seven Years' War from the British perspective. Particularly strong in its treatment of naval affairs.

Marcus, Geoffrey J. *Heard of Oak: A Survey of British Seapower in the Georgian Era.* New York: Oxford University Press, 1975. Overall survey of the eighteenth century navy by a prominent naval historian. Useful for putting Anson's career into context.

Middleton, Richard. *The Bells of Victory: The Pitt-Newcastle Ministry and the Conduct of the Seven Years' War, 1757-1762.* New York: Cambridge University Press, 1985. By far the best account of the British government at war during this crucial conflict. Downplays the traditional view of Pitt as the architect of victory. Anson emerges as an important contributor to what was, in effect, a highly successful team effort.

Pack, S. W. C. *Admiral Lord Anson.* London: Cassell, 1960. Still the best modern biography of Anson. Written by a naval officer, it devotes more attention to Anson's achievements at sea than to his work at the Admiralty.

Richmond, Sir Herbert. *The Navy in the War of 1739-48.* 3 vols. Cambridge, England: Cambridge University Press, 1920. A standard account of the Royal Navy in the Wars of Jenkins's Ear and the Austrian Succession. Useful for putting Anson's circumnavigation and victory at Finisterre into context.

Stokes, G. P. "Defying Storm, Scurvy, and Spain." *Military History* 20, no. 2 (June, 2003). Recounts Anson's expedition aimed at intercepting the Spanish treasure galleon, as well as describing the battle between Anson's ship, the *Centurion*, and the Spanish treasure ship *Nuestra Señora de Cabadonga*.

Williams, Glyndwr. *The Prize of All the Oceans: The Dramatic True Story of Commodore Anson's Voyage Round the World and How He Seized the Spanish Treasure Galleon.* New York: Viking Press, 2000. A detailed account of Anson's four-year voyage by a retired professor who specializes in the history of exploration.

See also: William Bligh; Louis-Antoine de Bougainville; Queen Charlotte; George II; George III; Richard Howe; Arthur Phillip; William Pitt the Elder.

Related articles in *Great Events from History: The Eighteenth Century, 1701-1800:* May 26, 1701-September 7, 1714: War of the Spanish Succession; 1739-1741: War of Jenkins's Ear; December 16, 1740-November 7, 1748: War of the Austrian Succession; January, 1756-February 15, 1763: Seven Years' War.

SECOND DUKE OF ARGYLL
English-born Scottish general and politician

Thoroughly pro-English, Argyll used his political status as the most powerful Scottish lord and his military generalship to advance the cause of union between Scotland and England despite various Jacobite uprisings.

Born: October 10, 1680; Ham House, Petersham, Surrey, England
Died: October 4, 1743; Sudbrook, Surrey, England
Also known as: John Campbell (birth name); Duke of Greenwich; Marquess of Kintyre and Lorne; Earl of Greenwich; Earl of Campbell and Cowall; Viscount of Lochow and Glenyla; Baron of Chatham; Lord of Inverary, Mull, Morvern, and Tirie
Areas of achievement: Warfare and conquest, military, government and politics, diplomacy

EARLY LIFE

The second duke of Argyll, given the name John Campbell at birth, was the elder of the two sons of Archibald Campbell, tenth earl and first duke of Argyll, and Elizabeth Tollmash. As head of Clan Campbell, the largest clan in Scotland, the ruler of Argyll occupied a unique position to influence Scottish politics and Anglo-Scottish relations. When the ninth earl, Archibald's father, was beheaded in Edinburgh on June 30, 1685, under orders of English king James II on trumped-up charges of treason dating from 1681, Archibald took refuge in the Netherlands and actively supported the Glorious Revolution of 1688 that replaced James with William of Orange (who became King William III). John grew up immersed in this atmosphere of strong affinity to English Protestant politics and was in many ways more English than Scottish.

King William III and Mary II commissioned fourteen-year-old John Campbell as colonel of the earl of Argyll's Regiment of Foot in 1694. This regiment had been created in 1689 as the first Scots Highland regiment in the army of Great Britain. Accompanied by his tutor, Alexander Cunningham, the boy traveled with the regiment until it was disbanded in 1697. Cunningham then took Campbell on a tour of Europe from 1699 to 1700. Campbell preferred the military life and returned to armed service in 1702 under the command of John Churchill, duke of Marlborough, in the War of the Spanish Succession. He saw action that summer as colonel of the Tenth Regiment of Foot.

Among the many favors that William gave Archibald in return for his service was the newly created dukedom of Argyll, which superseded the earldom, on June 21, 1701. Campbell succeeded as duke when his father died on September 25, 1703.

LIFE'S WORK

Appointed as high commissioner of the Scottish parliament in April, 1705, John Campbell (now the second duke of Argyll) immediately used this position to promote union with England, mostly by threats and intimidation. Queen Anne of England rewarded him for these efforts by creating him earl of Greenwich in November, 1705, and promoting him to major general in 1706.

Argyll soon wearied of civilian political machinations, and so he returned to Marlborough's service in the War of the Spanish Succession. He distinguished himself in the Flanders campaign of 1706, saving Marlborough's life at Ramillies. He played key roles at Menin and Ostend in 1706, Oudenarde in 1708, and Ghent in 1708-1709. These exploits earned him the nickname Red John of the Battles. Promoted to lieutenant general in 1709, he participated in the Siege of Tournai and fought with extraordinary courage at Malplaquet, also in 1709. Upon returning to England in 1710 he was knighted for his military accomplishments. Meanwhile, however, the former mentor-protégé relationship between Marlborough and Argyll had deteriorated to the extent that the two generals actively hated each other. Mainly to keep Argyll away from Marlborough, the queen promoted Argyll to general and gave him the command of British forces in Spain in 1711.

Argyll and his younger brother Archibald grew increasingly upset with the English handling of Scottish affairs, particularly regarding the malt tax. Although loyal to the English crown, Argyll never was afraid to speak his opinion, especially in defense of Scotland against English aspirations or chauvinism. In 1713, Argyll went so far as to advocate revoking the Act of Union of 1707. Anne perceived this as disloyalty and stripped him of several of his most important offices in March of 1714.

Queen Anne's death on August 1, 1714, opened the door to Argyll's restoration to favor. The succession to the British throne was in doubt, with Jacobite Scots supporting the claim of James Edward Stuart, the Roman Catholic son of James II, and nearly everyone else supporting George Louis, elector of Hanover, Anne's German Protestant second cousin. Hanover peacefully ascended as King George I in accordance with the 1701 Act of Settlement. Since Argyll was well known as an anti-Jacobite, George immediately restored all his offices.

Argyll's former ally in the Scottish parliament, John Erskine, the sixth earl of Mar, rallied Jacobite sentiment throughout Scotland and started the first Jacobite Rebellion on September 6, 1715. Argyll's small army of infantry and dragoons defeated Mar's superior force at Sheriffmuir on October 13, 1715. Mar retreated north, James Stuart arrived in Scotland to find an already defeated cause, and the two went into permanent exile. English and Dutch reinforcements under General William Cadogan mopped up. Even though Argyll was honored for the victory at Sherrifmuir, Cadogan, a close friend of Marlborough, reported that Argyll had not pursued the enemy with sufficient zeal. George reacted by stripping Argyll of his offices once again.

Various intrigues soon reinstated Argyll as a powerful member of the British court. George I made him duke of Greenwich in 1719, and George II elevated him to field marshal in 1736. From the mid-1720's until the abrupt end of his public career in 1742, Argyll was at odds with the prime minister, Robert Walpole, especially in the aftermath of the Porteous riots in Edinburgh in 1736. Throughout the 1730's, Argyll defended Scotland against what he perceived was unwarranted English intrusion into Scottish affairs. In these efforts he was opposed as much by his own brother Archibald as by Walpole, for Argyll ran his dukedom as an absolute monarchy and wanted no interference. After the Scots, encouraged by Argyll, defeated Walpole in the election of 1741, matters came to a head. The king sided with Walpole and forced Argyll to retire from all his public offices in March, 1742.

Argyll is buried in Westminster Abbey. Since he had five daughters but no male heir, his English titles ended with him and the Scottish titles—and the dukedom of Argyll—passed to his brother Archibald.

SIGNIFICANCE

The second duke of Argyll's greatest legacy was his help in cementing the union among Scotland, England, and Wales to create the United Kingdom of Great Britain in 1707. His military accomplishments against the Jacobites and, especially, his political maneuvers, contributed to this end. He was typically more interested in his personal advancement than in the cause of either Scotland or England, but usually this meant siding with England.

He always expected and nearly always received royal favors for his services. He was an obnoxious man and made enemies easily, but his skill at both diplomacy and war persuaded Queen Anne, the first duke of Marlborough, and others who intensely disliked and even distrusted him to swallow their antipathy and use him to their advantage.

—*Eric v.d. Luft*

FURTHER READING

Campbell of Airds, Alastair. *From the Restoration to the Present Day.* Vol. 3 in *A History of Clan Campbell.* Edinburgh: Edinburgh University Press, 2004. The definitive work on its subject, commissioned by the Clan Campbell Education Foundation. Much of Chapter 5, "Sheriffmuir and After," concerns Argyll.

Dickson, Patricia. *Red John of the Battles: John, Second Duke of Argyll and First Duke of Greenwich, 1680-1743.* London: Sidgwick & Jackson, 1973. The only full-length biography of Argyll.

Ferguson, William. *Scotland: 1689 to the Present.* Edinburgh: Mercat Press, 1987. A standard history of Scotland, with a strong focus on the eighteenth century.

_____. *Scotland's Relations with England: A Survey to 1707.* Edinburgh: Saltire Society, 1994. An authoritative work by a professor of history at the University of Edinburgh.

Phillipson, Nicholas T., and Rosalind Mitchison, eds. *Scotland in the Age of Improvement: Essays in Scottish History in the Eighteenth Century.* Edinburgh: Edinburgh University Press, 1996. Two articles, "The Changing Role of the House of Argyll in the Scottish Highlands," by Eric Cregeen, and "Who Steered the Gravy Train, 1707-1766?," by J. M. Simpson, explore Argyll's life.

Shaw, J. Stuart. *The Political History of Eighteenth-Century Scotland.* New York: St. Martin's Press, 1999. A well-reviewed and rich interpretation of the achievements of the second and third dukes of Argyll—the period of Scottish history from 1703 to 1761.

See also: Queen Anne; George I; George II; First Duke of Marlborough; Robert Walpole.

Related articles in *Great Events from History: The Eighteenth Century, 1701-1800:* May 26, 1701-September 7, 1714: War of the Spanish Succession; June 12, 1701: Act of Settlement; February, 1706-April 28, 1707: Act of Union Unites England and Scotland; March 23-26, 1708: Defeat of the "Old Pretender"; September 11, 1709: Battle of Malplaquet; September 6, 1715-February 4, 1716: Jacobite Rising in Scotland.

SIR RICHARD ARKWRIGHT
English inventor and industrialist

Through exceptional drive, organizational ability, and unbounded confidence, Arkwright synthesized cotton spinning by machine into a continuous process under one roof and thereby established a factory system that was modeled during the Industrial Revolution.

Born: December 23, 1732; Preston, Lancashire, England
Died: August 3, 1792; Cromford, Derbyshire, England
Areas of achievement: Science and technology, business

EARLY LIFE

Richard Arkwright was the youngest of thirteen children. Only the barest details of his early life are known, an ignorance the older, successful Arkwright did nothing to dispel. His formal education was slight: His Uncle Richard taught him to read and write. While apprenticed to a barber at Kirkham, a village to the west of Preston, he is said to have attempted to improve on his meager educational skills and even attended a school in the winter months.

His apprenticeship completed, Arkwright moved the few miles to Bolton. There, he worked for a wig maker. His early career was marked by attempts to succeed in business for himself. He kept a public house that, after initial success, failed. It is said that at this time he exhibited a genius for mechanics, bleeding (a standard medical therapy of the time), and tooth drawing; both these latter two talents were taught as part of the traditional barber's trade.

In 1755, Arkwright was married and a son, Richard, was born. What happened to his first wife is unclear. He was remarried in 1761. Following his second marriage, Arkwright was able to use his wife's money to set himself up as a traveling merchant. Buying human hair at country fairs from impoverished young women, Arkwright dyed the hair with a process of his own and sold it to commercial wig makers. In this business he achieved quite a measure of success.

At that time, Lancashire was full of spinners and weavers working in their own homes. The demand for spun cotton was increasing and, despite certain improvements in the spinning process, the problem of mechanizing spinning remained unresolved. On his travels through the villages and towns, Arkwright heard discussions and speculations surrounding the solution to this pressing problem. So involved in the spinning question did Arkwright become that, by the late 1760's, he was devoting all of his efforts to overcoming the technical difficulties of mechanizing the spinning process.

LIFE'S WORK

By January, 1768, Arkwright and his paid assistant, the clock maker John Kay, set up a working model of a spinning machine in Preston. The machine, later known as the water frame, was not a profoundly original breakthrough, but it was a dramatic development. Like many inventors of this period, Arkwright drew heavily on the work of others. He lived at a time and in a place of great technological ferment. He reworked the ideas of others and came up with a new synthesis of existing ideas that led to a successful machine, in terms of both the quantity of production and the quality of the product.

Arkwright's character was commented upon by many people. The futile attempts of his own son and of William Nicholson, secretary of the Chamber of Manufacturers, to compile materials for a biography of him a few years after his death demonstrate Arkwright's secrecy and his determination to erase all records of the means by which he acquired such wealth. What is clear is that Arkwright prompted suspicion in his rivals, was generally feared for his aims, and was self-sufficient, domineering, and vulgar. His whole life seemed to be driven by the desire to make money. He generally began work at five in the morning and finished at nine in the evening. He often conducted his business in a coach driven by four powerful, swift horses while traveling between his various factories.

Upon viewing Joshua Wright's famous portrait of Arkwright, Thomas Carlyle, the great nineteenth century English literary critic and liberal, described the industrialist as "a plain, almost gross, bag-cheeked, pot bellied Lancashire man, with an air of painful reflection, yet also of copious free digestion." A close student of Arkwright's career and a near contemporary, Edward Baines, was more substantial in his assessment: "His natural disposition was ardent, enterprising, and stubbornly persevering: His mind was as coarse as it was bold and active, and his manners were rough and unpleasing." In this description, one can see a type—the self-made industrialist—that was to become more familiar as machine production spread to other industries and to other countries.

In April, 1768, mindful of the trouble suffered by James Hargreaves, who had been attacked by angry

Lancashire cotton spinners afraid of unemployment, Arkwright decided to set up production in Nottingham in the English Midlands, where Hargreaves had found a more tranquil home. There, Arkwright needed increased financial backing and eventually found it in two successful stocking manufacturers, Samuel Need and Jedediah Strutt.

The following year, 1769, a patent was granted for Arkwright's new spinning machine, and a small factory was set up in Nottingham to produce cotton thread by means of the machine, powered by horses. Horsepower proved to be too expensive for Arkwright's taste and so, in 1771, with Strutt's backing, Arkwright could begin to develop his invention on a large scale by building a factory at Cromford, near Derby. The site was somewhat unusual. It was in the middle of nowhere, with no roads or other communications to the outside world and no nearby settlement. Its greatest asset was that it was located on the River Derwent, whose rushing waters could drive Arkwright's machines, henceforth known as water frames. It was from the use of water power that early factories were often known as mills. In addition, hot springs running into the river above the mill ensured that the waters would not freeze in winter.

Sir Richard Arkwright. (Library of Congress)

Over the years, Arkwright built up a community around his factory, the first of the cotton villages; he built houses and dormitories, a school, and a church. Roads were built to connect Cromford with Derby and Nottingham.

Armed with his patent for the water frame, Arkwright sought to expand his business. In 1773, he and his partners set up weaving workshops in Derby. There, for the first time in England, pure cotton cloth, or calico, was produced. The water frame made it possible. Previously, cotton had been combined with linen, since the method of hand spinning cotton produced a thread of uneven quality and strength. Linen thread was necessary as warp in weaving so as to avoid the problem of constant breakage of cotton thread when put under stress. Arkwright's machine, through its use of pairs of rollers, was able to spin cotton to a uniform fineness and then twist the thread on spindles or flyers to give it strength. The quality of cotton thread was thus greatly improved, strengthened, and made more uniform.

Demand for the new calico cloth was immediate. At this point, Arkwright faced a serious problem. England's wealth had been built originally upon wool and woolen textiles. The acquisition of India by England had led to competition at home with lighter imported cotton goods. To protect domestic woolen manufactures, Parliament passed an act in 1736 ordering a double duty to be paid on all cotton goods. If Arkwright were to succeed, he would have to secure a change in the law. Despite the opposition of the Lancashire manufacturers, Arkwright's petition to Parliament resulted in a new law, the Calico Act of 1774, which acknowledged the fledgling pure cotton textile industry and swept away all impediments to its development.

Arkwright's overwhelming competitive position in cotton spinning, protected as it was by his patent of 1769, was supplemented in 1775 by the grant of a second patent covering all parts of the spinning process. It caused a furor among other cotton manufacturers, who maintained that Arkwright claimed originality for machinery already in use: a carding machine, crank and comb, roving frame, feeder, and other, minor features. The only originality, it was claimed, lay in Arkwright's arrangement of them into an integrated, powered system operating under one roof. In taking out this patent, Arkwright aimed to obtain a monopoly on spinning machinery and an overwhelming place in spinning output. His monopolistic tendencies were supplemented by plans at various times to buy up the entire world output of cotton; to apply his machinery, acquire new patents, and consequently acquire a monopoly for woolen and worsted spinning; and even, as he boasted, to pay the national debt.

The 1775 patent was, in effect, a declaration of war against the rest of the cotton industry. The Lancashire manufacturers in particular resented the very principle of patents and combined against Arkwright. In an action in the courts in 1781 for patent infringement, Arkwright's case against a Lancashire cotton-mill owner, Colonel Mordaunt, was thrown out, his patent for the carding machine invalidated. Until this time, for a period of six years, Arkwright was able to expand his interests with Strutt, enter partnerships with several others to build more factories in the Midlands and Lancashire, collect royalties from licenses given under his patents, supply the machinery himself to licensees, and buy into their industrial activities. Thus, despite his failure to secure an extension of the water-frame patent beyond 1783 and the loss of his carding patent in 1781, Arkwright was still the richest cotton spinner in England, with the most, and the best-run, factories and the ability to set cotton-thread prices for the industry.

Further troubles came from cotton spinners themselves. Machinery threatened the livelihoods of thousands of them. The American Revolution led to a trade depression; many were impoverished and unemployed. The jenny, water frame, carding machine, and other new machines cut drastically the number of workers needed. The result was that factories, especially in Lancashire, the center of cotton production, were physically attacked and the machines were broken. Among the factories destroyed was Arkwright's at Birkacre, then the largest in Great Britain. Fortunately, trade resumed and the cotton industry surged after 1779.

The campaign to resecure his cotton-spinning patents led Arkwright back into court in 1785. Initially, he was successful. His success so alarmed cotton manufacturers in Lancashire that, led by Sir Robert Peel, father of the future prime minister, they obtained a writ for a new trial. The case against Arkwright, as identified for the jury by Justice Buller, rested on three points: the originality of his invention, his claim to have developed it himself, and the sufficiency of his official specification of the invention. The two chief prosecution witnesses were John

Kay, Arkwright's paid assistant at the time the water frame was developed, and Thomas Highs, who Kay asserted was the original inventor. Kay said that he had made models for Highs and later duplicated them when asked by Arkwright. The claims of other inventors for aspects of Arkwright's 1775 patent were also promoted. The special jury found against Arkwright on all three points. Arkwright lost all patent rights. Any other person would have been crushed by the four years of patent fights, but Arkwright was undaunted.

At the end of 1783, Arkwright financed Samuel Oldknow, who was to become the foremost muslin manufacturer in England. From 1784, Arkwright's Scottish interests were firmly established: He helped finance the cotton mills of David Dale at New Lanark (whose son-in-law and successor was Robert Owen, the famous industrial reformer and Socialist) and mills in Perthshire and Ayrshire. In addition, Arkwright continued to build new mills of his own, expand existing ones, and replenish machinery in the light of the latest improvements. In 1790, Arkwright began to apply steam power to his works with a Boulton and Watt engine at his Nottingham factory. Thereafter, the water frame driven by steam power came to be called a throstle.

In 1786, Arkwright was knighted after he delivered a loyal address to George III upon the king's escape from assassination. The following year, he was made High Sheriff of Derbyshire, an unusual honor for a person in trade. He apparently carried out his duties with flamboyance. His elegant coach was accompanied by thirty javelin men in sumptuous livery, and he provided great banquets during the period of the assize (a major regional law court). Like many successful merchants and later manufacturers, Arkwright invested in personal loans and land. In 1789, he purchased the manor of Cromford, beginning the construction of a church for his workers and a castle for himself. He died of complications related to his lifelong subjection to asthma, leaving his castle unfinished.

SIGNIFICANCE

Much speculation has surrounded Sir Richard Arkwright's development of the water frame. The language used to describe it and his other inventions in both patent descriptions was deliberately vague and misleading. Other persons have been put forward as the true originators of the various spinning machines claimed by Arkwright. The patent trials of 1781 and 1785 brought forth accusations taken up by later writers. Whatever the truth may be, and there is considerable doubt concerning Arkwright's claims to originality, he is a seminal figure in the history of the Industrial Revolution. After the patent trials in which he had testified on Arkwright's behalf, James Watt commented,

> As to Mr. Arkwright, he is, to say no worse, one of the most self-sufficient, ignorant men I have ever met with, yet, by all I can learn, he is certainly a man of merit in his way, and one to whom Britain is much indebted, and whom she [Britain] should honour and reward, for whoever invented the spinning machine, Arkwright certainly had the merit of performing the most difficult part, which was the making it useful.

From the late 1770's until his death, despite his clashes with the Manchester Committee of Trade over patent rights, Arkwright led the cotton industry. Indeed, in 1788, Arkwright's name headed the trade's fight against its most serious rival, the powerful British East India Company. Arkwright's factory communities, with their twenty-four-hour production schedules, twelve-hour work shifts, massive employment of children, poor ventilation, paternalism, and work incentives (which included bonuses, distinctive clothing for prize workers, and annual celebrations) had been copied by numerous others by the end of the eighteenth century. His factory organization served as a model well into the nineteenth century. To Sir Edward Baines, Arkwright

> possessed very high inventive talent, as well as an unrivalled sagacity in estimating at their true value the mechanical contrivances of others, in combining them together, perfecting them, arranging a complete series of machinery, and constructing the factory system—itself a vast and admirable machine, which has been the source of great wealth, both to individuals and to the nation.

Finally, according to Paul Mantoux, the great historian of the Industrial Revolution, Arkwright

> personified the new type of the great manufacturer, neither an engineer nor a merchant, but adding to the main characteristics of both, qualifications peculiar to himself: those of a founder of great concerns, an organizer of production and a leader of men. Arkwright's career heralded a new social class and a new economic era.

—*Stephen Burwood*

FURTHER READING

Baines, Sir Edward. *History of the Cotton Manufacture in Great Britain*. New York: Augustus M. Kelley, 1966. Originally published in 1835 and a major source for subsequent works, this book's frontispiece is the famous portrait that inspired Thomas Carlyle. Very informative about inventions, Arkwright (chapter 9), and the development of the industry.

Berg, Maxine. *The Age of Manufactures: Industry, Innovation, and Work in Britain, 1700-1820*. 2d ed. New York: Routledge, 1994. An excellent survey of eighteenth century British industry, featuring two chapters on the textile industry, with information on Arkwright.

Daniels, George W. *The Early English Cotton Industry*. Manchester, England: Manchester University Press, 1920. Good background treatment, especially concerned with breakthroughs in weaving. Chapters 3 and 4 deal substantially with Arkwright.

Deane, Phyllis. *The First Industrial Revolution*. 2d ed. New York: Cambridge University Press, 1979. One of the standard works on the causes, course, and consequences of the Industrial Revolution. Chapter 6 deals with the cotton industry and Arkwright's part in it.

Fitton, R. S. *The Arkwrights: Spinners of Fortune*. Manchester, England: Manchester University Press, 1989. A biography of the Arkwright family by an author who has written a previous book on the subject.

Fitton, R. S., and A. B. Wadsworth. *The Strutts and the Arkwrights, 1758-1830*. Manchester, England: Manchester University Press, 1973. Reconstructed largely from Strutt family letters and the business records of the Strutt company. Full of valuable insight and direct quotation concerning this important partnership, which dissolved in 1783. Contains the best account of Arkwright's life and valuable insight into Arkwright's business behavior.

Guest, Richard. *A Compendious History of the Cotton Manufacture: With a Disproval of the Claim of Sir Richard Arkwright to the Invention of Its Ingenious Machinery*. 1823. Reprint. New York: Augustus M. Kelley, 1968. Advances the claim of Thomas Highs to authorship both of the water frame and of the spinning jenny. Excellent quotations from the 1785 patent trial and wonderful sketches of the various mechanical inventions. Arkwright was successful, the author claims, only because he made the clock maker John Kay drunk and stole the invention.

Mantoux, Paul. *The Industrial Revolution in the Eighteenth Century: An Outline of the Beginnings of the Modern Factory System in England*. Translated by Marjorie Vernon. 1927. Reprint. Chicago: University of Chicago Press, 1983. Published originally in French (1906), this work is, in many ways, unsurpassed as an account of the Industrial Revolution.

Unwin, George. *Samuel Oldknow and the Arkwrights: The Industrial Revolution in Stockport and Marple.* Manchester, England: Manchester University Press, 1924. A model business history drawn mainly from voluminous records discovered by chance in Oldknow's factory, long abandoned following a fire. Very good for the business correspondence of Arkwright and his market position. Arkwright financed Oldknow, who became England's foremost muslin manufacturer. In the complete absence of any business records of Arkwright himself, this and Fitton and Wadsworth's work on the Strutts are the best sources for information about Arkwright's business methods.

See also: John Fitch; George III; James Hargreaves; John Kay; Thomas Newcomen; James Watt; Eli Whitney.

Related articles in *Great Events from History: The Eighteenth Century, 1701-1800:* 1701: Plumier Publishes *L'Art de tourner*; 1705-1712: Newcomen Develops the Steam Engine; 1733: Kay Invents the Flying Shuttle; 1764: Invention of the Spinning Jenny; 1765-1769: Watt Develops a More Effective Steam Engine; 1767-1771: Invention of the Water Frame; 1779: Crompton Invents the Spinning Mule; April, 1785: Cartwright Patents the Steam-Powered Loom; February 14, 1788: Meikle Demonstrates His Drum Thresher; 1790: First Steam Rolling Mill; December 20, 1790: Slater's Spinning Mill; 1793: Whitney Invents the Cotton Gin; 1795: Invention of the Flax Spinner.

BENEDICT ARNOLD
American military leader

Despite his skillful leadership of the colonial forces in the American Revolution, Arnold's betrayal of his country has made his name a synonym for treason.

Born: January 14, 1741; Norwich, Connecticut
Died: June 14, 1801; London, England
Area of achievement: Military

EARLY LIFE

Benedict Arnold was born in Norwich, Connecticut. His mother had been a wealthy widow and a member of one of the first families to settle in Norwich. Her family name was Hannah Waterman, but she became Hannah King and inherited her husband's estate before marrying Benedict Arnold III, the father of the famous general and later traitor. The first Benedict Arnold had served three times as governor of Rhode Island. Benedict Arnold III had been a cooper of limited means but later became involved in the West Indies trade.

Benedict Arnold (the IV) attended local schools, including one directed by the Reverend James Cogswell, a relative of his mother, at Canterbury, Connecticut. He was a fair student, and he earned a reputation for being boisterous, a daredevil, and a prankster. Shortly after he entered his teens, he was apprenticed to an apothecary, but the humdrum routine bored him, and he soon enlisted as a young recruit in the French and Indian War. Almost as quickly as he arrived in New York for training, he deserted the cause and returned home to Norwich. One description of his appearance at the time portrayed him as having dark hair, a dark complexion, and light gray eyes. As he matured, he developed a strong, stocky frame. He was energetic and possessed unusual endurance.

Hannah Arnold died when Benedict was eighteen years old, and without her restraining influence, Benedict's father became a drunkard. After his father's death in 1761, the young Benedict left Norwich for the larger town of New Haven, where he became a druggist and a bookseller. He later became a successful merchant and expanded his trade connections with the West Indies and Canada. On February 22, 1767, he married Margaret Mansfield, the daughter of a prominent New Haven government official. Margaret and Benedict had three children: Benedict, Richard, and Henry. Arnold labored to provide his family with the luxuries that wealthy families then enjoyed. In pursuing this goal, he traveled often to the West Indies and Quebec. On trips to the West Indies, his ships carried lumber and horses. On the return voyages, he brought to New England molasses, sugar, and rum. It is likely that part of his wealth came from smuggling.

One incident in Honduras during one of his voyages revealed his hot temper as well as his early affinity for using weapons. When a drunken British sea captain cursed him, Arnold challenged him to a duel. At the first shot,

Arnold wounded his opponent, who then decided to apologize rather than face a second round. The aggressive Arnold became a captain in the Connecticut militia in December, 1774. When the conservative New Haven town fathers faced the issue of war, upon news of the battles at Lexington and Concord, they decided to remain neutral. Arnold, however, favored war and led his patriots into the streets of New Haven. He demanded and received the keys to the powder house. Arnold was ready and eager for action.

LIFE'S WORK

Taking his militia company to Cambridge, Benedict Arnold asked the Massachusetts Committee of Safety to sponsor him in an expedition against Ticonderoga. The committee gave him a colonel's commission and authorized him to recruit troops and to seize the eighty cannon at the fort. Unfortunately for Arnold, Ethan Allen, of Vermont, set out on the same mission. Arnold, without his own troops, joined with Allen's forces, but the two disagreed on who should have command. They issued joint orders but continued to disagree on who was the

Benedict Arnold. (Library of Congress)

rightful superior. They took Fort Ticonderoga in May, 1775, and the cannon were later carried across New England to Boston, where they would be the major factor in forcing the British to evacuate that city. Meanwhile, Arnold's own troops arrived, and he sailed north on Lake Champlain and conquered the fort at St. John's in Quebec. When the Massachusetts government began to question his conduct in the Lake Champlain area, Arnold resigned his commission and returned to New Haven. The Massachusetts congress refused to pay Arnold for supplies he had purchased for his troops in the Lake Champlain struggle. To add to his woes, his wife had died on June 19, 1775, before his return home.

Despite discouragements, Arnold went to Cambridge and discussed with George Washington a plan to lead a force against Quebec City by way of Maine. The typical approach for armies had been by way of Lake Champlain and the St. Lawrence River. A force led by Philip Schuyler would indeed follow this traditional route, but Arnold's men would set out across the Maine woods to meet Schuyler's force before reaching Quebec. Arnold eagerly accepted leadership of the Maine expedition and set out in September, 1775. The journey was an arduous and heroic adventure. Many of the seven hundred men he took with him turned back rather than face the hardships of ice, snow, and short provisions. When Schuyler became ill, General Richard Montgomery assumed command and met with Arnold before the assault on Quebec. During a blinding snowstorm on New Year's Eve, 1775, the two armies attacked Quebec City. Despite their heroism, the venture failed, leaving Montgomery dead and Arnold wounded. Arnold now laid siege to the city until spring, when British reinforcements arrived. He then began a skillful retreat that inflicted heavy losses on the British. After his retreat, charges of misconduct in Canada were brought against him, but after much delay the U.S. Congress finally cleared his name in May, 1777.

Arnold began to get the clear impression that his heroic efforts for the revolutionary cause were going unappreciated. After a brilliant campaign on Lake Champlain, in which he defeated a large fleet of British vessels in October, 1776, Congress created five new major generals, all of whom had been ranked below Brigadier General Arnold. Washington scarcely restrained Arnold from resigning his commission. Arnold returned to Connecticut and while there held off a British attack on Danbury. In recognition of this service, Congress gave him the major generalship he had coveted.

During 1777, Arnold had a major role in preventing the British from severing New England from the rest of the colonies. The British plan—which, if successful, would have been a fatal blow to the colonial cause—called for an assault from Canada, in the north, by way of the Lake Champlain route, to be led by John Burgoyne. At the same time, William Howe was to lead his army from New York up the Hudson River to join with Burgoyne. A third force would come in from the west, via the Mohawk Valley. In August, 1777, Arnold foiled the movement from the west by capturing Fort Stanwix in the Mohawk Valley, barely firing a shot.

By this time, General Horatio Gates commanded the American forces along the Hudson River. After Arnold returned from Fort Stanwix to link his forces with those of Gates, he quarreled with General Gates and was relieved of his leadership position. Although he was technically not in command, he led his forces into battle at the Second Battle of Saratoga and helped win one of the most strategic victories of the American Revolution. In the battle he suffered a wound to the same leg that had been injured at Quebec. Congress restored to him the seniority that he had lost when the five major generals were moved ahead of him.

In June of 1778, he took command of the city of Philadelphia and began living there a lifestyle that demanded more than his trifling salary as an officer could support. In April of 1779, he married a Philadelphia socialite, Peggy Shippen. Her associations with leading Loyalists may have been a factor in Arnold's treason. Arnold was again distressed by renewed charges against him by enemies in Congress. He demanded a court-martial, which vindicated him of all the significant charges. He was infuriated, however, by Washington's gentle rebuke of him for minor offenses. Meanwhile, he began corresponding with the British commander in chief Henry Clinton and offered to provide military secrets in exchange for money.

In July, 1780, Arnold became commander of the fort at West Point. He arranged to betray that vital fort to Clinton for £20,000. Clinton sent Major John André to discuss plans for seizure of the fort. After the meeting with Arnold, André, returning to the British ship the *Vulture* on the Hudson River, was captured by American soldiers, and his papers were found in a stocking. Because he had donned civilian clothes for his mission he was executed as a spy. News of the capture led Arnold to flee to the waiting British vessel. He then entered the British army as a brigadier general and led forces in both Virginia and his native Connecticut. He spent his remaining ten years in England and Canada. He died an embittered and maligned man on June 14, 1801.

SIGNIFICANCE

Benedict Arnold's life is a study in contrast. Through two-thirds of his life he received adoration and admiration from American patriots. He was one of the bravest and most skilled of American military leaders. His military genius may have surpassed that of Washington. His character lacked, however, one of the most important virtues of his commander in chief: the patience and the willingness to endure in a noble cause even when appreciation and respect are at low ebb. Although Arnold's name has become a byword for treachery, one should not forget his years of valiant service in the struggle for independence. At the same time, none of his heroic acts can erase the memory of his treachery in the West Point conspiracy. Even the British people refused him the respect he sought in his later years.

Arnold hoped that the British would give him a proper command for a general of his abilities, but they used him in only two minor ventures in the American Revolution. He led a force in Virginia that burned Richmond, and he later made a foray into Connecticut, dismaying his former neighbors by an assault on New London. Back in England, he hoped to be given a position in the struggle on the Continent against the French Revolution. The British were suspicious of the former traitor, however, and the earl of Louderdale warned the House of Lords, in a speech, that Arnold was the very symbol of treachery. Arnold thereby had one last opportunity for battle. He challenged the earl to a duel. In the contest, Arnold missed and the earl refused to fire. Arnold's business ventures followed the same unfortunate pattern as his military career, and in death he left behind an impoverished wife and family.

—*Richard L. Niswonger*

FURTHER READING

Arnold, Isaac N. *The Life of Benedict Arnold: His Patriotism and His Treason.* Chicago: A. C. McClurg, 1880. The author, a distant relative of Arnold, requests "one drop of pity" for the man who would have been canonized in American history if he had fallen on the battlefield at Saratoga. Although an older biography, it remains one of the better ones.

Flexner, James Thomas. *The Traitor and the Spy: Benedict Arnold and John André.* Boston: Little, Brown, 1975. Literary style and scholarly research are both present in this exciting account of Arnold and John André, his comrade in the West Point plot. Contains illustrations, footnotes, and a useful bibliography.

Martin, James Kirby. *Benedict Arnold, Revolutionary Hero: An American Warrior Reconsidered.* New York:

New York University Press, 1997. A biography focusing on Arnold's military career through 1778. Martin bases his research upon accounts by Arnold's soldiers, papers by other war commanders, and official congressional records. He views Arnold not as a traitor but as a victim of the American Revolution and its politics.

Randall, Wallace Sterne. *Benedict Arnold: Patriot and Traitor*. New York: Morrow, 1990. Focuses on the complex character of Arnold to explain why he offered his services to the British in 1779. Provides new information on the role of Arnold's wife, Peggy Shippen, in the betrayal.

Van Doren, Carl. *Secret History of the American Revolution*. New York: Viking Press, 1941. A general history of treason during the revolution. Van Doren does not view Arnold as a disillusioned hero who was sincerely converted to the Loyalist cause, but as an unscrupulous traitor. The most valuable part of the book is an appendix that reproduces sixty-eight letters dealing with the affairs of Arnold and André.

Wallace, Willard M. *Traitorous Hero: The Life and Fortunes of Benedict Arnold*. New York: Harper and Brothers, 1954. An objective biography, in which Wallace concludes that Arnold was the most talented battlefield commander to fight in the revolution.

Wilson, Barry K. *Benedict Arnold: A Traitor in Our Midst*. Montreal: McGill-Queen's University Press, 2001. Explores Arnold's role in Canadian history. Includes his tour of rural Quebec as a Yankee trader in the 1760's and 1770's, his business enterprises in New Brunswick, and his military maneuvers in Quebec during the revolution.

See also: Ethan Allen; John André; Sir Guy Carleton; Sir Henry Clinton; George III; William Howe; Roger Sherman; John Graves Simcoe; George Washington.

Related articles in *Great Events from History: The Eighteenth Century, 1701-1800:* May 28, 1754-February 10, 1763: French and Indian War; April 19, 1775: Battle of Lexington and Concord; September 19-October 17, 1777: Battles of Saratoga.

FRANCIS ASBURY
English-born American preacher

Asbury led the dramatic growth of Methodism in the United States from 1771 until his death in 1816. He was to American Methodism what John Wesley was to English Methodism.

Born: August 20, 1745; Hamstead Bridge, Handsworth, Staffordshire, England
Died: March 31, 1816; Spottsylvania, Virginia
Area of achievement: Religion and theology

EARLY LIFE

Francis Asbury's birthplace was located near Birmingham, which had been the site of religious controversy and conflict. As in most industrial centers, where the workers were exploited, Methodism spoke to the masses more than did Anglicanism. From the first, Asbury's intellectual gifts were apparent and, as is often the case, made him the object of ridicule and abuse by his schoolmates. He left school and became a servant in the home of a wealthy but irreverent family, and then he became an apprentice, though the nature of his trade remains in doubt.

His mother, a dominant influence in his life, had a vision before his birth concerning his religious future as a spreader of the Gospel among the heathens; she read the Bible to him and prayed with him when he was young. Although Asbury's mother attended Wesleyan meetings, she wanted her son to have a career as an Anglican. It was not until he was fifteen years old, however, that he was converted to Methodism, though he did not leave the Church of England until he went to America. Still in England, within a year he was preaching, and he joined the Methodist ministry before he was twenty and made preaching his sole vocation. He preached in the Staffordshire, Gloucestershire, Bedfordshire, Sussex, and Northamptonshire circuits, and in 1770 was in Wiltshire. During these years he demonstrated his tendency to take charge and to "ramble," that is, to go outside his own circuit, for which he was reprimanded by William Orp, one of his superiors.

LIFE'S WORK

When he was twenty-six years old, Francis Asbury, along with Richard Wright, responded to John Wesley's call for volunteers to spread Methodism in America. Wright's work was undistinguished, but Asbury would become America's most outstanding Methodist. Asbury arrived in Philadelphia on October 27, 1771, but he preferred to preach in the country rather than in the city. In 1772, Wesley appointed him to be his assistant in America, but Thomas Rankin soon superseded him as assistant.

Asbury was assigned to New York City, but he also traveled widely through Westchester County on horseback. His so-called rambling, which had brought him some criticism in England, now served him in good stead. The villages he served became what was called a circuit, and he and his fellow ramblers were known as "circuit riders." When he was transferred to Maryland, he tripled the number of circuits and doubled the Methodist membership in the course of one year by riding on horseback through the different circuits. Even while riding, he was busy praying, singing hymns, and learning languages, and often in foul weather. The bad weather—and overwork—made him almost always ill. Sometimes he had to be lifted onto his horse and tied to the saddle, and his swollen feet would often not fit into the stirrups.

He also preached during the American Revolution, when the official Methodist position, as proclaimed by Rankin, his supervisor, was opposed to the rebellion against England. In fact, Asbury was the only English Methodist minister to remain in the colonies. When Rankin returned to England, Asbury carried on in his stead, although he did not receive Rankin's title. Because he refused to sign Maryland's oath of allegiance (he considered all oaths wrong), he was in danger during the war and was even fired upon and forced to flee to Delaware, where he continued to preach. In 1784, in recognition of Asbury's work, Wesley sent Thomas Coke (a bishop who later worked with Asbury on the Methodist Book of Discipline) to America to consecrate him as a superintendent, but he would not assume any title until the other ministers approved. Since a superintendent was similar to a bishop, he assumed the latter title, despite Wesley's protests. By creating additional bishops, Asbury kept his power, illustrating his political prowess; his rivals considered him a dictator.

The first Methodist conference, which was held in 1785, was followed by several other conferences, and the first council met in 1789, at which time he successfully urged the Methodists to congratulate George Washington on winning the presidency. Since the Methodist Church was the first church to do so, the Methodists got favorable press. Asbury extended the Methodist mission to New England in 1791 but had troubles with James O'Kelly, who withdrew from the church after a leadership squabble. The 1790's saw a general membership de-

cline, which was reversed after 1800, at which time membership numbers rose to more than 100,000. During the first decade of the 1800's, Methodism expanded, despite Asbury's antislavery stance and his declining health. Although he lost some of his power to William McKendree in 1808, his travels resembled triumphal processions, and he was one of the best-known Americans of his day.

He had his critics, partly because he insisted, like Wesley, that ministers study five hours a day, and because he held Methodist ministers to a high standard. No other minister could travel as far on horseback or preach as many sermons, and this was accomplished while he was sick. He rode 5,000 miles per year on horseback. He traveled south to Georgia, twice crossed the Alleghenies, and went north to New York State and New England. He preached thousands of sermons (reportedly more than sixteen thousand), his last occurring in Richmond, Virginia, just a week before his death. Since many of the other Methodist ministers had other jobs, none could even approach his commitment to the church. In addition, he never received more than $85 per year in salary, and he gave away money and clothes to the needy.

SIGNIFICANCE

In addition to his preaching and administering, Francis Asbury was a great recruiter of other preachers and a tireless reader and writer. His journal and letters, edited in 1958, are compiled in three volumes. It is for his preaching and evangelism, however, that he is best known. By example, sheer force of will, and political savvy Asbury brought John Wesley's Methodism to the United States, where at the time of his death it was the second largest Protestant denomination, second only to the Baptists. If it had not been for the defections of William Hammett, who broke away to establish the Primitive Methodists, and William O'Kelly (James O'Kelly's son), who had clashed with Asbury over what he considered Asbury's Anglicanism, the Methodists would have even been more numerous.

The 214,000 Methodists in 1816 were scattered throughout the country east of the Mississippi River and even beyond the Mississippi in Missouri and Arkansas. On October 15, 1924, President Calvin Coolidge dedicated a statue of Asbury in Washington, D.C., where he attributed America's freedom to the work of preachers such as Asbury. As a testament to his importance, countless Methodist churches are called Asbury United Methodist Churches. His legacy—the American Methodist

Church—has itself been divided into many other Protestant denominations with Wesleyan ties.

—*Thomas L. Erskine*

FURTHER READING

Asbury, Herbert. *A Methodist Saint: The Life of Francis Asbury.* New York: Knopf, 1927. A largely sympathetic account of Asbury's life plus some relevant letters and documents.

Baker, Frank. *From Wesley to Asbury: Studies in Early American Methodism.* Durham, N.C.: Duke University Press, 1976. Baker devotes two chapters to Asbury, one examining Asbury as an apprentice and the other as a master craftsman.

Collins, John Smiley. *Man of Devotion: Francis Asbury.* Nashville, Tenn.: Upper Room, 1971. A short biography with an interesting chapter on Asbury's establishment of colleges.

Duren, William Larkin. *Francis Asbury: Founder of American Methodism and Unofficial Minister of State.* New York: Macmillan, 1928. A biography, with an interesting account of Asbury's personality and his problems with his rivals.

Ludwig, Charles. *Francis Asbury: God's Circuit Rider.* Milford, Mich.: Mott Media, 1984. A biographical account that focuses on Asbury's preaching.

Salter, Darius. *America's Bishop: The Life of Francis Asbury.* Nashville, Tenn.: Abington, 1966. A comprehensive, definitive biography with an exhaustive bibliography.

Smeltzer, Guy. *Bishop Francis Asbury: Field Marshal of the Lord.* Denver, Colo.: Eastwood, 1982. A biography with chapters on Asbury's political and economic philosophy and a thorough discussion of the context within which Methodism flourished.

See also: Charles Wesley; John Wesley.

Related articles in *Great Events from History: The Eighteenth Century, 1701-1800:* 1739-1742: First Great Awakening; October 30, 1768: Methodist Church Is Established in Colonial America; 1773-1788: African American Baptist Church Is Founded; January 16, 1786: Virginia Statute of Religious Liberty; July 28-October 16, 1789: Episcopal Church Is Established; 1790's-1830's: Second Great Awakening.

MARY ASTELL
English philosopher, writer, and educator

The first English female philosopher, Astell created a rationale for women's education, questioning and rejecting the role of "wife" as a woman's lot and asserting equality between women's and men's souls. She was an early critic of the political writings of John Locke, and she helped to influence contemporary ideas on the liberal democratic state.

Born: November 12, 1666; Newcastle-on-Tyne, England
Died: May 9, 1731; London, England
Areas of achievement: Philosophy, education, women's rights, literature, government and politics

EARLY LIFE

Mary Astell was the eldest child of Peter and Mary (née Errington) Astell, from northeast England. Mary's father, a coal merchant in this important coal-producing region, came from a line of barristers, clergy, and members of the powerful coal-merchants guild. They had received a coat of arms but no land through a distant uncle as a boon for fighting against the Spanish during the Middle Ages. Mary's mother was from a wealthy Catholic family, whose nominal gentry status led its members to be Royalists, a conservative political stance Mary Astell retained throughout her life and writings.

Astell was a bright child who loved to read a wide range of literature, including classical authors and seventeenth century writers John Milton and Abraham Cowley. She also read the works of Aphra Behn, the first Englishwoman to be a professional writer. Astell's uncle, Ralph Astell, a bachelor church curate and poet, might have nurtured her intellectual curiosity. Ralph was well versed, through his Cambridge education, in the Cambridge Platonists, a group of seventeenth century philosophers. It is likely that he introduced his niece to the debate between the material philosophy of Thomas Hobbes and the spiritual focus of these Platonic philosophers. Astell's early lessons helped form the basis of her later achievements, as her writings combined logic and religion, expressed her love of learning, and strove to extend that opportunity to other women.

Astell's father died when she was twelve; his financial legacy was not enough to sustain his family for long, however. The next year, her uncle Ralph died. She lived with her mother, aunt, and grandmother in debt and economic insecurity, revealing to Astell how difficult it was for women to support themselves without a husband, a societal problem she would address in her writings.

When she was twenty years old, Astell left for London to try to earn money as a writer and to seek support from wealthy relatives. She resided in the neighborhood of Chelsea. Unsuccessful at gaining patronage from her relations, she solicited William Sancroft, archbishop of Canterbury, for support and showed him a collection of her poems. He responded generously with gifts and contacts, helping her meet a publisher, Rich Wilkin, to show her writings. Astell's subsequent time in Chelsea was a period of exploring her ideas in rela-

---

REFLECTIONS UPON MARRIAGE

Mary Astell argued that women—as rational beings created by God—are not bound to men but are in service to God, making women answerable to God alone. Any service a woman provides to a man is merely business.

That the Custom of the World has put Women, generally speaking, into a State of Subjection, is not deny'd; but the Right can no more be prov'd from the Fact, than the Predominancy of Vice can justifie it. A certain great Man has endeavour'd to prove by Reasons not contemptible, that in the Original State of things the Woman was the Superior, and that her Subjection to the Man is an Effect of the Fall, and the Punishment of her Sin. And that Ingenious Theorist Mr. Whiston [likely Thomas Whiston] asserts, That before the Fall there was a greater equality between the two Sexes. However this be 'tis certainly no Arrogance in a Woman to conclude, that she was made for the Service of GOD, and that this is her End. Because GOD made all Things for Himself, and a Rational Mind is too noble a Being to be Made for the Sake and Service of any Creature. The Service she at any time becomes oblig'd to pay to a Man, is only a Business by the Bye. Just as it may be any Man's Business and Duty to keep Hogs; he was not Made for this, but if he hires himself out to such an Employment, he ought conscientiously to perform it.

Source: Mary Astell, *Reflections upon Marriage*, in *Astell: Political Writings*, edited by Patricia Springborg (New York: Cambridge University Press, 1996), pp. 10-11.

---

tion to other thinkers. She developed friendships with female aristocrats, who also financially supported her work, and she continued to write and publish. She also helped open a school for girls.

LIFE'S WORK

Mary Astell was both a product of and a departure from the late seventeenth and eighteenth century age of Enlightenment. Her writings reflect the ideas of universal truths and natural law. Considering that few women of her time were educated, it is remarkable that she was able to continue reading and to engage with leading philosophical and political ideas of the era. She studied leading philosophers such as Francis Bacon, René Descartes, and John Locke, and critiqued and adapted their ideas to argue for women's inherent abilities to reason.

In 1693, Astell initiated her most important correspondence, influential in refining her philosophy, with John Norris of Bemerton, England, a preeminent Cambridge Platonist. Shortly afterward, in 1694, Astell's best-known work, *A Serious Proposal to the Ladies*, was published anonymously—she signed the work "A Lover of Her Sex." The proposal calls for a reli-

gious and educational community for women, in essence, a women's college in the Anglican tradition, which would be the first college for women anywhere. Always mindful that she did not have a formal education, Astell argued that women deserve to have their God-given reason cultivated, which in turn would benefit society.

Astell continued to correspond with Norris, who functioned as a mentor. Their letters, published in 1695, are documents of their discussions about the nature of the soul and its ability to love God through the intellect. Their discussion of the need to place love for God above human relationships was a substantial part of Astell's rationale for developing a women's religious community in her *A Serious Proposal to the Ladies*; she adapted to Anglican use the Catholic convent's pattern of advocating singleness for women so that they could focus on improving their minds and souls, free from male authority or other distractions.

Her proposal was popular enough to warrant reprinting. In 1695 and 1696, she published a corrected second and third version, then a second part—"Wherein a Method Is Offer'd for the Improvement of Their Minds"—in 1697. This second part, dedicated to the future queen of England, Princess Anne, who supported women's causes, lays out more specific instructions for the proposed religious and educational community. Arguing vehemently that Christianity is the ultimate way of right reason, Astell asserts that, to attain truth, one needs to rein in passions and emotions, long considered the primary attributes of the female personality.

Astell published another important work, *Reflections upon Marriage*, in 1700. This volume, a critical examination of the marriage customs of the day, argues against female servitude in the form of marriage. Astell condemns the scant education women receive, which prepares them to be wives only. She also condemns a particular double standard of marriage, which allows husbands but not wives to have extramarital affairs. Urging her female readers to value themselves more highly than does society, Astell admonishes women to think before entering into marriage. She radically questions the value of marriage and the desire to have a husband to attain social status, saying that many women would be happier unmarried so that they could develop themselves and their relationship with God rather than be decorative household "objects." She herself provided a role model by remaining single.

From 1704 until 1709, Astell published a series of pamphlets, largely responding to the works of male writers (including Daniel Defoe and Lord Shaftesbury). She strongly supported the unified Anglican Church against those who would allow toleration for other religions, argued for the necessity of a central authority in church and state, defended Charles I, and countered the notion that humans were naturally good and, therefore, not in need of salvation. Her views were sometimes satirized in newspapers and other writings, but she was also admired by those within the church; by her friend Mary Wortley Montagu, a feminist writer; and by her circle of wealthy, intellectual Chelsea friends, including Lady Catherine Jones, Lady Elizabeth Hastings, Lady Ann Coventry, and Elizabeth Hutcheson.

Astell stopped writing in 1709 to open a charity school for girls in Chelsea, assisted by her friends. The school was primarily practical in focus, teaching the basics of literacy rather than philosophical and religious contemplations discussed in *A Serious Proposal to the Ladies*. Astell ran the school, living alone in an age when living alone was not for "respectable" women. At the age of sixty, she moved into the lodgings of Lady Jones. Astell died of breast cancer five years later, in 1731.

SIGNIFICANCE

In the 1980's, feminist historians and literary critics rediscovered and began publishing Mary Astell's work, helping to promote a renaissance of her thought. Her writings influenced other female thinkers from her own day, including Mary Wollstonecraft in her 1792 work, *A Vindication of the Rights of Woman*. Samuel Johnson's fictional work *Rasselas* featured a princess who—based on Astell's ideas—founded a women's college. Astell forged the way for future female philosophers and apologists for female education. Although some contemporary critics fault her for her conservative Tory views, which refused to recognize equality among the classes, she worked within the political system of her time to show that women could do far more for society than previously thought. Some question exists about whether she was a lesbian, yet her achievements extend beyond sexual identity to seeking a life free from male domination and the suppression of women's abilities.

—*Carol Blessing*

FURTHER READING

Astell, Mary. *Astell: Political Writings*. Edited by Patricia Springborg. New York: Cambridge University Press, 1996. Part of the Cambridge Texts in the History of Political Thought series, this is the first complete modern edition of Astell's *Reflections upon Marriage, A Fair Way with Dissenters*, and *An Impartial Enquiry into the Origins of Rebellion*. The text introduces overlooked aspects of Astell's thought: She was a major critic of Locke's writings, and her work was part of the intellectual movement that introduced the modern idea of liberal democracy.

_____. *A Serious Proposal to the Ladies, Parts I and II*. Edited by Patricia Springborg. Peterborough, Ont.: Broadview Press, 2002. Springborg's introduction to Astell's work provides a strong overview of her era and philosophical antecedents.

Broad, Jaqueline. *Women Philosophers of the Seventeenth Century*. New York: Cambridge University Press, 2002. The chapter on Astell places her among her female contemporaries, analyzes her works in relation to seventeenth century male philosophers, and discusses her correspondence with John Norris.

Bryson, Cynthia B. "Mary Astell: Defender of the 'Disembodied Mind.'" *Hypatia* 13, no. 4 (Fall, 1998): 40-62. Bryson argues that Astell was the first English feminist and that she relied on Cartesian dualistic concepts for her cultural critique.

Donawerth, Jane. *Rhetorical Theory by Women Before 1900*. Lanham, Md.: Rowman & Littlefield, 2002. Provides a brief biography and discussion of Astell's rhetorical style, as linked to her use of logic.

Duran, Jane. "Mary Astell: A Pre-Humean Christian Empiricist and Feminist." In *Representing Women Philosophers*, edited by Cecile T. Tougas and Sara Ebenreck. Philadelphia: Temple University Press, 2000. Hypothesizes that Astell's writings on marriage anticipate those of David Hume.

Perry, Ruth. *The Celebrated Mary Astell*. Chicago: University of Chicago Press, 1986. This scrupulously researched and detailed work, the only full-length biography of Astell, contains illustrations, a manuscript of her poetry, and her extent correspondence.

Weiss, Penny A. "Mary Astell: Including Women's Voices in Political Theory." *Hypatia* 19, no. 3 (Summer, 2004): 63-84. Weiss discusses Astell's response to Thomas Hobbes's ideas, arguing that Astell provided an early feminist critique of his works.

See also: Abigail Adams; Queen Anne; Joseph Butler; Daniel Defoe; David Hume; Samuel Johnson; Mary Wortley Montagu; Mary Wollstonecraft.

Related articles in *Great Events from History: The Eighteenth Century, 1701-1800:* 1726-1729: Voltaire Advances Enlightenment Thought in Europe; 1739-1740: Hume Publishes *A Treatise of Human Nature*; April, 1762: Rousseau Publishes *The Social Contract*; July, 1764: Voltaire Publishes *A Philosophical Dictionary for the Pocket*; 1781: Kant Publishes *Critique of Pure Reason*; February 22, 1791-February 16, 1792: Thomas Paine Publishes *Rights of Man*; 1792: Wollstonecraft Publishes *A Vindication of the Rights of Woman*.

BA'AL SHEM TOV
Polish religious leader

Ba'al Shem Tov brought Eastern European Jewry out of a long period of decay and spread a rejuvenated religious outlook through society. He founded the modern Hasidic branch of Judaism.

Born: August 27, 1698; Okup, Podolia (now in Ukraine)
Died: May 23, 1760; probably near Medzhibozh, Podolia (now in Ukraine)
Also known as: Israel ben Eliezer (birth name)
Areas of achievement: Religion and theology, medicine

EARLY LIFE

Ba'al Shem Tov (BAY-uhl shehm tawv), which means "master of the good name," was born Israel ben Eliezer in the village of Okup in Polish Ukraine. One of the strongholds of Judaism from the Middle Ages, the region was filled with Jewish schools, community organizations, and businesses. Israel's parents were poor and elderly, and they died when he was a young child. Some sources report that Eliezer was an infant when his parents died, but at least one scholar believes he was old enough to be influenced by his father's dying words: "Fear nothing, because God will take care of all."

The boy had a strikingly exuberant spirit, and even though he was taken under the wing of community leaders, he made his own way from an early age. Eliezer sporadically attended elementary school and spent many hours wandering in the nearby forests and studying nature; by night, he studied the mystical texts of the Kabbala. At age twelve, Eliezer was made an assistant to the schoolmaster, and later he became a synagogue attendant. Even as a boy, he was known for his warm, magnetic personality and for his study of Judaism.

Although Eliezer was married at eighteen, his bride died almost immediately after the ceremony, and the young widower commenced a life of wandering. He worked in Halicz as a school assistant before settling in the Ukrainian village of Blust, near Brody, as a teacher. In his personal habits, Israel showed the utmost simplicity.

His second marriage was fraught with conflict before it began. Eliezer was betrothed to Hannah, the daughter of a leading citizen in a nearby town, but her father died before the wedding. Hannah's brother, who disliked Israel's rough appearance and seemingly limited prospects, opposed the marriage. By now, however, Hannah had fallen in love with her fiancé, and the couple were married and left Brody, taking only a few belongings. Later, when Hannah's brother became aware of Ba'al Shem Tov's powers of healing and spirituality, he repented of his harsh treatment and helped the couple financially.

In their early married life, Eliezer and his wife settled in the Carpathian Mountains, where she helped support him as he performed menial labor and returned to the forest to learn everything he could about plants, the themes of nature, and the relationship between God and the mind.

LIFE'S WORK

The work of Ba'al Shem Tov evolved from his study of nature and what he perceived as God's relationship to the natural world and to humans. The troubled times in which he lived, moreover, directed his studies toward helping peasants. Ultimately, Ba'al Shem Tov sparked a popular revival of Judaism.

During the sixteenth and seventeenth centuries, Judaism flourished in Eastern Europe, especially in Poland. The Jewish population in the region grew tenfold, from fifty thousand to one-half million, between 1500 and 1650. Jews enjoyed vibrant educational and social institutions and were accorded some measure of self-government. In the mid-1600's, however, anti-Jewish violence killed 100,000 people and destroyed seven hundred communities.

After this devastating blow, Jewish institutions were crippled, and mystical strains of the religion gained popularity over the more formal and structured Talmudic study. The asceticism of the earlier scholar Isaac Luria, which emphasized self-mortification as the way to know God, took hold. There was little in formal Talmudic Judaism to appeal to the needs of the dispirited masses. This was a time of deep pessimism and superstition for the Jews of Eastern Europe.

During this period, amulets came into widespread use as talismans to ward off evil spirits and to invite beneficent ones. A person who produced these amulets was called a *ba'al shem*, meaning that he manipulated the letters of God's name to produce potent phrases. Eliezer became a *ba'al shem* of such renown that the adjective *tov*, or "good," was added to his name, and he became popularly known as Ba'al Shem Tov. Yet he was more than merely a *ba'al shem*.

As Ba'al Shem Tov took to the forests in his twenties, he became a skilled herbalist and was known throughout the area as a sort of homeopathic doctor. His wit and charm combined with his healing skills drew throngs of people to him for help. Not only could he cure their physical ailments, but he also offered psychological counseling. His followers included Jewish and gentile peasants, members of the nobility, and some religious leaders.

While wandering by himself in the Carpathian Mountains, Ba'al Shem Tov had formulated a pantheistic outlook: He believed that God was present in all living things and that even the struggle with Satan could be found within the godliness of the natural world. From this belief, he discerned that it was possible for a true communion with God to spring from the close relation between God's creations and the actions of everyday human life. This kind of communion, in observing the minutiae of Jewish law and in performing necessary tasks, was the basis of modern Hasidism. It constituted a valuable and sincere form of prayer.

Ba'al Shem Tov wanted this kind of modest yet constant religious observance to be joyful, which meant an end to asceticism and unhealthy self-denial as ways to know God and the beginning of dancing and singing in prayerful practice. He wanted Jews' spiritual ardor to be buttressed with good health habits. A sound body and a rested soul would be ready to begin again each day a new cycle of observance and communion with God. Since he wanted those who had gone astray to have an easy path to repentance, he was considerably more lenient than many Jewish leaders in treating human frailties.

At age thirty-six, Ba'al Shem Tov emerged from his long period of solitary study to share his wisdom. By 1740, he had established his home and spiritual community in Medzhibozh, a town in the frontier region of Poland, Ukraine, and Lithuania, where he was to live the rest of his life. Ba'al Shem Tov made a good living providing amulets and advice, and his inspirational stories and parables were the treasured source of a rich oral legacy. His voluminous correspondence required the help of two secretaries. Among the adherents who came to his new spiritual community were some of the rabbis who were to spread Hasidism, including Rabbi Jacob Joseph, Rabbi Dov Baer of Merzeritz, and Rabbi Pinchas.

Hasidism, by definition, were pious disciples, and Ba'al Shem Tov was the *zaddik*, their master. Through his ordination of visiting cantors, prayer leaders, rabbis, and lay followers, Hasidism spread like a wave through Jewish society. The religion was now accessible to everyone, unlike the rigid and rationalist system of Talmudic study that heretofore had been held up as the pinnacle of Jewish observance. Ba'al Shem Tov did not oppose formal Talmudic study himself but said that he had no time for such a luxury. These teachings of Ba'al Shem Tov were not met with universal approval: The Hasidic communities that spread through the region were opposed by some orthodox scholars.

During a journey to a theological debate in 1759, Ba'al Shem Tov fell ill, and he died a short time later. The Hasidic movement, however, gained strength after his death, and by 1780, Hasidism so threatened the orthodox leaders that the movement was excommunicated by Jewish civil authority.

Ba'al Shem Tov left little written record, no more than a few letters, and his legacy was based on oral tales passed down among his disciples. It was not until 1814-1815 that *Shivhei ha-Besht* (*In Praise of the Ba'al Shem Tov*, 1970) was published by his followers. After this came a wider body of literature that further propelled the growth of Hasidism.

SIGNIFICANCE

Ba'al Shem Tov began a populist movement that revitalized Polish Jewry, a movement that would last two hundred years, until the Holocaust forced its remnants to the New World. The large, vibrant Hasidic community in Brooklyn, New York, for example, is a sign that the underlying theme of joyful daily observance still holds great appeal among Jews. Despite the brutal dislocation of the Polish Jews in the twentieth century, the oral legacy begun by Ba'al Shem Tov's first disciples has remained unbroken to the present. The pattern of early Hasidism, with a local spiritual leader surrounded by a community of disciples, has endured.

Some of the herbal remedies discovered by Ba'al Shem Tov have survived in modern medicine. His treatments of insanity and melancholy relied on influencing the mind rather than inflicting punishment, anticipating modern psychiatric practices. The patterns of song and dance that formed in Hasidism may be discerned in contemporary popular culture, although some of the earlier gesticulation and conjuring have faded.

Although he lived simply, Ba'al Shem Tov did not despise riches. In one of his tales, he takes into account the sad family history of a rich man for whom eating was a form of revenge against anti-Semitic violence. Ba'al Shem Tov explains that sincere prayers from such a person may be more pleasing to God than the supplications of a person prideful of his or her own poverty and asceticism. In the same vein, Baʿal Shem Tov was not reluctant to proclaim the importance of a *zaddik*, or righteous master, in spreading his message. He was mindful of his critics and supplied ample justification to protect his appeal.

—*Nan K. Chase*

FURTHER READING

Blumenthal, David R. *Understanding Jewish Mysticism.* Vol. 2. New York: Ktav, 1982. Explores the evolution of Hasidism in its daily rituals, stories, prayers, community relations, and modern Hasidic lore. Contains unusual instructions for mystic spells. The text of a short tale about Baʿal Shem Tov is included with comments.

Etkes, Immanuel. *The Besht: Magician, Mystic, and Leader.* Translated by Saadya Sternberg. Hanover, N.H.: University Press of New England, 2004. English translation of a Hebrew biography. Etkes attempts to refute claims that Baʿal Shem Tov was a childlike mystic, wandering the fields in prayer and engaging in acts of piety. Instead, he maintains that Baʿal Shem Tov did not intend to found a religious movement.

Heschel, Abraham J. *The Circle of the Baal Shem Tov: Studies in Hasidism.* Chicago: University of Chicago Press, 1985. A testament to the growth of Hasidic studies, this historical work explores the beginnings of Hasidism through the lives of Baʿal Shem Tov's philosophical circle.

Klepfisz, Herszel. *Culture and Compassion: The Spirit of Polish Jewry from Hasidism to the Holocaust.* New York: Ktav, 1983. Written by one of the foremost scholars of Hasidism. Klepfisz traces his own descent from the original disciples of the Hasidic movement. A warm, personal look at the spiritual life of the Polish Jews.

Noveck, Simon. *Creators of the Jewish Experience.* Washington, D.C.: B'nai B'rith Books, 1985. The chapter on seminal Jewish theologians places the life of Baʿal Shem Tov in the relatively modern role of guiding the religion in new directions. Succinct biographical selections.

Rosman, Murray Jay. *Founder of Hasidism: A Quest for the Historical Baʿal Shem Tov.* Berkeley: University of California Press, 1996. Rosman bases his biography upon the accounts of Baʿal Shem Tov or contemporary eyewitnesses to separate the truth about the origins of Hasidism from the legends.

Seltzer, Robert M. *Jewish People, Jewish Thought: The Jewish Experience in History.* New York: Macmillan, 1980. A major reference work on the roots of Judaism from earliest times. Contains a concise definition of Hasidism and is valuable in explaining the early fractures in the movement. Contains illustrations, numerous clear maps, and a detailed bibliography.

Weiss, Joseph. *Studies in Eastern European Jewish Mysticism.* Edited by David Goldstein. New York: Oxford University Press, 1985. Detailed analysis of Hasidic teachings and the lives of the early followers. A tightly woven vessel for some of the historical riches of Hasidism.

See also: Elijah ben Solomon; Moses Mendelssohn.

Related article in *Great Events from History: The Eighteenth Century, 1701-1800*: August 5, 1772-October 24, 1795: Partitioning of Poland.

JOHANN SEBASTIAN BACH
German composer

Bach pioneered modern classical music, setting the parameters of composition that have remained largely unchanged to the present. So significant was his contribution to musical composition that some historians divide the history of music into the periods "before Bach" and "after Bach."

Born: March 21, 1685; Eisenach, Thuringia, Ernestine Saxon Duchies (now in Germany)
Died: July 28, 1750; Leipzig, Saxony (now in Germany)
Area of achievement: Music

EARLY LIFE

Johann Sebastian Bach (yoh-HAHN zay-BAHS-tyahn BAHKH) was born in the shadow of Wartburg Castle, in the spring of 1685, in Eisenach, a few miles from where his fellow composer, George Frideric Handel, was born in the same year. Bach came from seven generations of talented musicians. His father was a court musician for the duke of Eisenach, and several of his close relatives were organists in the larger nearby churches. His eldest brother was apprenticed to the famous Johann Pachelbel.

Bach was only nine years old when his mother died, and his father died the following year. Consequently, in 1695, he moved thirty miles to Ohrdruf to live with his brother, the organist at St. Michael's Church. He continued his musical education and also began studying New Testament Greek and other basic subjects at the cloister school. His brother, an excellent musician, taught him keyboard techniques and worked with him on the construction of a new organ. Very early, Bach became interested in the harmonic structure underlying the melodies he copied from manuscripts.

In March of 1700, Bach, at the age of fifteen, walked 200 miles with a fellow student to the ancient northern German city of Lüneburg to attend the Knights' Academy, a school of practical education for young noblemen. The curriculum included courtly dancing, fencing, and riding, as well as the study of feudal law, politics, and history. Young Bach had the ability to read music at first sight and supported himself largely by singing and playing the organ.

Bach broadened his experiences while at Lüneburg. More than once, he walked the thirty miles to Hamburg to hear two of the largest organs in the world. The great organist Johann Reincken was in Hamburg, and Dietrich Buxtehude lived in Lübeck. Bach also observed a French community of Huguenot exiles; music was a focal point of their lives, and Bach heard French instrumental music performed by French orchestras, which enhanced his understanding of German and Italian musical forms.

LIFE'S WORK

In 1703, Bach was ready for his first career appointment; he found it with the installation of a new organ in the old church at Arnstadt, a small city of lovely, tree-lined streets some twenty-five miles from Eisenach. His salary was substantial enough to enable him to purchase a harpsichord, several books, and clothing that befitted his new position. His duties as church organist were light, but his choir, he said, consisted of "a band of ruffians."

Bach's early compositions, as might be expected, were marked by immaturity. Perhaps his best organ work of this period was the serene Pastorale in F Major, characterized by its "free flow and logical unfolding of melody." At Arnstadt, Bach also wrote his first cantata, later revised, *For Thou Wilt Not Leave My Soul in Hell*, whose continuous melody creates the musical equivalent of a soliloquy.

Needing greater depth to his musical experience, Bach, in the autumn of 1705, received what was supposed to be a one-month leave of absence to observe and listen to the great Dietrich Buxtehude in Lübeck. Bach was impressed with Buxtehude's arrangement of cantatas in his Vesper Concerts, sung as dialogues between soloists and the chorus. When, after four months, Bach finally returned to Arnstadt, he brought fresh ideas with him and began ornamenting his organ playing with coloratura and countermelodies.

In 1707, Bach left Arnstadt to become organist at St. Blaise Church in Mühlhausen. That same year, at twenty-three years of age, he married his second cousin, Maria Barbara. At Mühlhausen, Bach gained valuable technical experience in overseeing the repair of the aged organ in the church. He was also called upon to write music for various civic occasions, such as the cantata *God Is My King*, calling for a brass ensemble, two woodwind ensembles, a string section, and two separate choirs.

The duke of Saxe-Weimar, Wilhelm Ernst, appointed Bach chamber musician and court organist in 1708 and, later, his concertmaster. The duke doubled Bach's salary, as the composer entered a completely different social world. Bach loved the melodic warmth and intensity of Italian music, and his compositions began to resemble

Johann Sebastian Bach. (The Granger Collection, New York)

fortunately, most of Bach's work from the Köthen years is lost, but he captured the vitality of that pleasant place in the Brandenburg Concertos and in *The Well-Tempered Clavier*, both written in Köthen.

Bach's relaxed, joyful lifestyle was marred by two tragedies. In 1719, his one-year-old son Leopold Augustus died, and the next year, while he was traveling with the prince in northern Germany, his wife suddenly died. In December, 1721, Bach, age thirty-six, married Anna Magdalena Wilcken, who was twenty years old. Anna had a lovely soprano voice, and Bach often wrote music for her to sing. They were devoted to each other and often worked together, since they both earned their living as musicians at the Köthen court. Of the thirteen children whom Anna bore, seven died as infants. Altogether, Bach had twenty children, ten of whom survived to adulthood.

Bach spent the last twenty-seven years of his life in Leipzig, Germany, writing church music of such quality that it continues to be performed. He had not wanted to leave Köthen, but his main purpose in life was not yet fulfilled. Years before, he had written that his chief goal in life was to write "well-conceived and well-regulated church music to the glory of God." To realize his creative ideas for church music and to provide a better education for his sons at St. Thomas School, Bach took a 75 percent reduction in salary and relinquished his post of court musician to take up one of the most famous cantorships in Germany.

Bach's principal responsibilities in his cantorship revolved around St. Thomas Church and the St. Thomas School. Leipzig was an imperial free city, so it had no princely court and, thus, no court orchestra. The town musicians were employed at both church and civic events. Since the Lutheran Church was the established church, the government officials on the city council of Leipzig had the responsibility of securing a music director for all musical activities in the four churches of Leipzig. Bach had to compose or select, plan, and arrange the music for each liturgy. He personally directed his music on alternate Sundays at St. Thomas Church and at St. Nicholas Church.

As director of music, Bach also composed cantatas for festive civic occasions such, as visits by royalty or the

that style. His cousin, Johann Gottfried Walther (1684-1748), was his close companion, and he and Bach developed musical theory together. Both men were particularly interested in the philosophical values underlying music, believing music to be a gift from God and of great spiritual importance. Bach wrote many dances and loved joyful music.

During his Weimar years, Bach composed some of the greatest organ music ever written. He perfected his technique of counterpoint, mastering the relation between melody and harmony. The Bachs had six children born to them at Weimar, two of whom (twins) died at birth.

Bach's fame spread throughout Germany, albeit more as a performing musician than as a composer. In 1717, Prince Leopold of Köthen appointed Bach his court conductor and chapel master, and Bach entered a creative, relaxed period of his life. As chapel master, Bach was left alone to create as he saw fit. The twenty-three-year-old Prince Leopold loved music and understood it well. Un-birthdays of leading citizens of the town. His office also made him cantor of St. Thomas School, in charge of teenage boys. He called the boys for the opening of classes at 6:00 A.M., taught several classes, and had prayers with them at 8:00 P.M. He also visited the sick in the school hospital next to the church.

Weak-sighted for years, partly because of overwork and poor lighting, Bach was almost blind by 1749. The next year, after two strokes, Bach died in Leipzig at the age of sixty-five. In a most fitting culmination of his life and calling, his final work was the chorale *Before Thy Throne I Now Appear*.

Bach's joyful legacy continues to inspire and refresh countless thousands. His wives and children loved him, and he helped them develop their varied musical talents. All of his children, he believed, were born musicians, and he could put on a vocal and instrumental concert with his own family alone. He wrote many songs of love for his wives. Bach was "temperate, industrious, devout, a home lover, and a family man; genuine, hospitable, and jovial. Frugality and discipline ruled in the Bach home, also unity, laughter, loyalty, and love."

Portraits of Johann Sebastian Bach from young man to old all reveal the same serious demeanor, intelligent eyes, cheerful disposition, determined lips, and kindly face. He loved life, his family, his music, and his God, as his works demonstrate. He wrote cheerful dances as well as joyful church music, because he separated neither his life nor his music into sacred and secular categories but saw the purpose of all music as "the glory of God and the re-creation of the human spirit."

SIGNIFICANCE

Three categories of musical performance were common in the early eighteenth century: church music, theatrical music, and chamber music. Johann Sebastian Bach's eleven hundred compositions fall into the first and last categories. His instrumental concertos, suites, and overtures were mostly intended for drawing-room performance. His three hundred church cantatas were his "musical sermons," consciously designed to complement the spoken word and illumine the liturgy. Bach composed five entire yearly sets of cantatas. His passions and orato-

---

BACH'S MUSIC AND PEDAGOGY

Bach, in addition to composing music that was designed solely for performance, created many compositions that, while undeniably beautiful, were also intended as learning tools for students and amateur musicians. Bach's delight in combining aesthetic and pedagogical qualities in his work may be seen in the following inscription, taken from the title page of his own fair copy of a collection of his piano studies.

HONEST METHOD, by which the amateurs of the clavichord—especially, however, those desirous of learning—are shown a clear way not only (1) to learn to play cleanly in two parts, but also, after further progress, (2) to handle three obligate parts correctly and well; and along with this not only to obtain good inventions but to develop the same well; above all, however, to achieve a cantabile style in playing and at the same time acquire a strong foretaste of composition.

Source: Johann Sebastian Bach, *Inventionen Sinfonien* (Munich, Germany: G. Henle Verlag, n.d.), p. 4.

---

rios are musical dramas full of action and events, more dramatic than much that was written for the theater.

Bach's compositions were true masterpieces, in the sense that they broke the established rules governing music and created new rules in their place. His personal, subjective understanding of melody, countermelody, harmony, counterpoint, and other basic components of a musical composition came to constitute the objective standards by which classical music was created and judged. In many ways, Bach's greatest works still stand as the aesthetic ideal for serious Western music, and his basic harmonic and chord progressions have found their way, in altered form, into the pop music repertoire as well.

Although Bach lived his entire life in Germany, he quickly learned other national styles of music and incorporated them into his compositions: From France, he acquired delicate dance suites and restrained instrumental music. From his native Germany, he particularly loved and employed fugal techniques. From Italy, melodic and dramatic operatic music and the vocal motets of the Renaissance found their way into his compositions.

Bach's library reveals something of his thinking and attitude toward life. The eighty-one volumes that Bach owned all dealt with theological and religious subjects, and Bach used them to find the precise wording he wanted for his lyrics. He personally selected the 141 verses of Scripture in *The Saint Matthew Passion* and took equal care in planning its musical composition.

Many appreciate and love as great art *Jesu, Joy of Man's Desiring*, *Sheep May Safely Graze*, and Bach's glorious *Christmas* Oratorio, but to understand them fully, one must realize the spiritual view of life that motivated Bach. His belief in the reality of eternity caused his music to be timeless.

—William H. Burnside

FURTHER READING

Chiapusso, Jan. *Bach's World*. Bloomington: Indiana University Press, 1968. A thorough biography that gives attention to the cultural and historical setting in which Bach composed his music. The author understands the musical philosophy underlying composition, and he applies his knowledge to Bach's work.

David, Hans T., and Arthur Mendel, eds. *The New Bach Reader: A Life of Johann Sebastian Bach in Letters and Documents*. Revised and enlarged by Christoph Wolff. New York: W. W. Norton, 1998. Includes many of the letters and other documents written by Bach. Also contains a twenty-eight-page "Portrait in Outline" and a lengthy section entitled "Bach as Viewed by His Contemporaries."

Dowley, Tim. *Bach: His Life and Times*. Neptune City, N.J.: Paganiniana, 1981. A brief and profusely illustrated book that recounts Bach's life in a succinct, interesting manner. A fascinating introduction to the subject.

Heckscher, Martin A., et al. *The Universal Bach: Lectures Celebrating the Tercentenary of Bach's Birthday*. Philadelphia: American Philosophical Society, 1986. An interesting collection of essays written for the three hundredth birthday of Bach under the auspices of the Basically Bach Festival of Philadelphia. The five essays examine Bach's musical symbolism and Bach as a musical scholar and biblical interpreter.

Schweitzer, Albert. *J. S. Bach*. 2 vols. New York: Macmillan, 1950. A profoundly intellectual but sensitive biography by an eminent Bach scholar. Bach's techniques of composition are examined in an erudite fashion.

Terry, Charles Sanford. *Bach: A Biography*. 2d ed. London: Oxford University Press, 1933. One of the oldest "modern" biographies of Bach. Tends to be dry and somewhat wordy, but carefully accurate. Includes seventy-six photographs of places where Bach lived and worked; the photos, taken in the early twentieth century, are themselves an important historical record.

Williams, Peter. *The Life of Bach*. New York: Cambridge University Press, 2004. An examination of Bach the man and the composer. Williams questions whether the centuries of acclaim for Bach's music have made it impossible objectively to evaluate the composer's work.

Wolff, Christoph. *Johann Sebastian Bach: The Learned Musician*. New York: W. W. Norton, 2000. Biography focusing on Bach's performing and composing by a noted Bach scholar. Wolff analyzes Bach's innovations in harmony and counterpoint within the context of European musical and social history.

See also: George Frideric Handel; Joseph Haydn; Wolfgang Amadeus Mozart.

Related articles in *Great Events from History: The Eighteenth Century, 1701-1800*: c. 1701-1750: Bach Pioneers Modern Music; April 13, 1742: First Performance of Handel's *Messiah*; January, 1762-November, 1766: Mozart Tours Europe as a Child Prodigy.

ISAAC BACKUS
American religious leader

Backus led opposition to the Congregational state church in the Puritan colonies and helped modify the rigid Puritan view of predestination. He strongly supported the American Revolution, became a major leader in the struggle to guarantee complete religious liberty and separation of church and state in the new United States, recorded much of the history of New England—especially of the Baptists—and was a founder of Rhode Island College, now Brown University.

Born: January 9, 1724; Norwich, Connecticut
Died: November 20, 1806; Middleborough, Massachusetts
Areas of achievement: Religion and theology, government and politics, historiography, education

EARLY LIFE

Isaac Backus was born just before the First Great Awakening broke out in the American colonies. His parents were Samuel and Elizabeth Tracy Backus. The Backus family enjoyed more than average wealth and had been active politically since the founding of Norwich in 1660. Samuel's father, Joseph Backus, had been a member of the Connecticut assembly, to which Samuel also was elected. Samuel died when Isaac was sixteen years old, leaving a widow with eleven children, including a six-week-old infant. However, Elizabeth Backus was a strong and godly woman, having had a religious conversion experience in 1721. Elizabeth did experience a short period of depression following the death of Samuel, but her faith and spirit were soon renewed. Elizabeth then exerted a strong spiritual influence on all of her children. She later shared both the trials and the successes of Isaac's early work.

Shortly before the death of Samuel Backus, English Evangelist George Whitefield and Jonathan Edwards, from Northampton, Massachusetts, brought the Great Awakening to Connecticut. Several other Evangelists then took up the cause. One Evangelist was James Davenport, who brought the revival to Norwich and whose preaching led to the conversion of Samuel and Isaac. Davenport later helped end Elizabeth's depression. Isaac's conversion, on August 24, 1741, came while he was mowing, alone in a field; he felt a deep conviction to repent his sins and follow Jesus Christ. Several months later, he joined his mother's First Congregational Church of Norwich.

LIFE'S WORK

At the time of Isaac Backus's conversion, the Connecticut Congregational Church, established as the state church by the Puritans of the seventeenth century, was undergoing much controversy. The extreme Calvinistic doctrine of predestination, the role of a state church, and the concept of complete religious liberty were the major issues. The Old Lights in the church, who upheld the rigid views on predestination, did not give much support to the Great Awakening, and they advocated punishment for those who deviated from the state church. The New Lights, however, developed an Evangelical Calvinism, supported the revivals, and opposed the persecution of those who did not support the state church. The New Lights included Elizabeth Backus and her son Isaac Backus.

In early 1745, a large group of New Lights withdrew for the church in Norwich and founded a separatist church close by. Among the approximately thirty men was Isaac Backus, and his mother was part of a larger number of women. When the group refused orders to disband, they were suspended from the Norwich church. Elizabeth Backus and several of her other sons were jailed several times, once for thirteen days, for not paying state church taxes.

With his stand against the established state church of Connecticut, the course of Isaac Backus's life was set. It was inevitable that he would soon feel the call to preach and to become embroiled, along with his mother, in the controversies of the day and in the revivals of the Great Awakening. He preached his first sermon on September 27, 1746, exhibiting great power and effectiveness. Following his preaching and teaching throughout the Norwich area, the members of a separatist church in Titicut, Massachusetts, asked him, in December of 1747, to become their pastor. He was ordained on March 31, 1748, and he married Susanna Mason on November 29, 1749.

By 1749, Backus's problems with the state church led him to evaluate the entire concept of an established church. He was also questioning the doctrine of baptism. Both ideas led him to the Baptists, founded in America by Roger Williams in Rhode Island in 1639. The question of baptism involved infant baptism as opposed to adult, or believers', baptism and immersion as opposed to other modes of baptism. Backus hesitated to join them because they were a persecuted group: He feared that some secret mischief lurked in their beliefs. In spite of his misgivings, Backus was baptized by immersion on August 22, 1751, but continued as pastor the Titicut church for the next five years. In June, 1756, a Baptist church was established in Middleborough, Massachusetts, with Backus called as its first pastor.

Backus soon became a leader of the Baptists in Massachusetts, a denomination that also had an established Congregational Church. After helping organize more than twenty new Baptist churches in the colony, he was among the creators of the Warren Association in 1767. The association's mandate was to give Baptists a united voice in fighting for complete religious liberty in the colony, which would mean the disestablishment of the state church. The association was the first of its kind in Massachusetts. The group formed several committees in 1769 to petition the Massachusetts courts concerning the persecution of Baptists and others who paid taxes to support the state church. In effect, Baptists were being punished for conducting their own separate activities. An advertisement placed by the association in the Boston *Evening Globe* in 1770 included a veiled threat that, if the courts did not address their concerns, they would appeal to the British crown. Coming less than six months after the Boston Massacre, this threat greatly disturbed the Massachusetts authorities.

Three years later Backus led the Baptists in publishing an "Appeal to the Public for Religious Liberty, Against the Oppressions of the Present Day." They realized that the American conflict with Great Britain afforded the Baptists an excellent opportunity to establish complete freedom of religion in independence-seeking America. Backus joined others on a trip to Philadelphia in September, 1774, for the opening of the First Continental Congress, and they secured an audience with several national leaders at that meeting, including John Adams and Samuel Adams from Massachusetts. They reminded the delegates that only two things are worth fighting for: religion and liberty. Because they were supporting the struggle for political liberty, they expected the Continental Congress to support their desire for religious liberty. Although they did not get a firm guarantee, they did get a promise from the Massachusetts delegation to help improve the lot of Baptists in that colony.

Backus continued his efforts during the American Revolution. His desire for religious freedom would become a national campaign, reminding people that no denomination had been more unanimous in its support of the revolution than the Baptists. After the U.S. Constitution was written in 1787, Backus joined others in urging an amendment be added to guarantee complete freedom

of religion. With the aid of leaders such as James Madison, the First Amendment was ratified as part of the Bill of Rights in 1791. The amendment begins with the declaration that there could be no national established church and includes the right to practice—or not practice—a religion of one's choice.

SIGNIFICANCE

Isaac Backus died in Middleborough on November 20, 1806. Although he lived to see the national guarantees of the First Amendment, he could not fully enjoy those in his adopted state of Massachusetts. John Adams had reportedly told Backus at the First Continental Congress in 1774 that Backus could expect a change in the solar system before Massachusetts would give up its state church. Indeed, the state did not disestablish the Congregational Church until 1833. Only then was Backus's goal of separation of church and state fully realized.

Backus was a delegate at the Massachusetts Convention in 1788 that ratified the U.S. Constitution. He wrote *A History of New England, with Particular Reference to the Denomination of Christians Called Baptists* and more than thirty other pamphlets and tracts. He contributed to theological development by reconciling the rigid Calvinistic idea of human depravity with the Enlightenment concepts of free will and self-determination. He also was a founder of Rhode Island College, now Brown University, in 1764, and was a trustee there from 1765 to 1799.

—*Glenn L. Swygart*

FURTHER READING

Bush, L. Russ, and Tom J. Nettles. *Baptists and the Bible*. Rev. ed. Nashville, Tenn.: Broadman and Holman, 1999. Chapter 4 includes a section entitled "Isaac Backus and the Great Cloud of Witnesses," which details his work as a revivalist, as a defender of biblical inspiration, and as an advocate of religious liberty.

Cairns, Earle E. *Christianity Through the Centuries*. Grand Rapids, Mich.: Zondervan, 1996. Chapter 32 includes a discussion of New England Congregationalism and the role played by Backus and other Baptists in opposing the state church.

Grenz, Stanley. *Isaac Backus: Puritan and Baptist*. Macon, Ga.: Mercer University Press, 1983. Grenz details the life and work of Backus, beginning within the context of the Puritan movement and concentrating on his social and theological work. Includes a summary of Backus's writings and an excellent bibliography.

McBeth, H. Leon. *The Baptist Heritage*. Nashville, Tenn.: Broadman Press, 1987. Chapters 7 and 8 cover in detail Backus's life, his role in the Great Awakening, and his impact on the struggle for religious liberty. Includes an excerpt of a letter from Elizabeth Backus to Isaac concerning her imprisonment.

McLoughlin, William G. *Isaac Backus and the American Pietistic Tradition*. Boston: Little, Brown, 1967. The standard biography of Backus, which details the conflict between the Old Light and New Light Congregationalists, and discusses Backus's contributions to religious liberty and separation of church and state in America.

See also: John Adams; Samuel Adams; Francis Asbury; Jonathan Edwards; Ann Lee; James Madison; John Wesley; George Whitefield.

Related articles in *Great Events from History: The Eighteenth Century, 1701-1800:* 1739-1742: First Great Awakening; October 30, 1768: Methodist Church Is Established in Colonial America; March 5, 1770: Boston Massacre; 1773-1788: African American Baptist Church Is Founded; September 5-October 26, 1774: First Continental Congress; April 19, 1775: Battle of Lexington and Concord; May 10-August 2, 1775: Second Continental Congress; July 4, 1776: Declaration of Independence; January 16, 1786: Virginia Statute of Religious Liberty; September 17, 1787: U.S. Constitution Is Adopted; July 28-October 16, 1789: Episcopal Church Is Established; 1790's-1830's: Second Great Awakening; December 15, 1791: U.S. Bill of Rights Is Ratified.

JEAN-SYLVAIN BAILLY
French astronomer and politician

Bailly, a renowned astronomer and historian of science, was elected president of the Third Estate in 1789. In the same year, he became the first mayor of Paris under the New Republic. He soon fell out of favor, however, and was later guillotined by the Revolutionary Tribunal of Paris.

Born: September 15, 1736; Paris, France
Died: November 12, 1793; Paris, France
Areas of achievement: Science and technology, astronomy, historiography, government and politics

EARLY LIFE

Jean-Sylvain Bailly (zhahn-seel-va bah-yee) was born into a family of painters to the royal court in Versailles. His father was court painter and custodian of the royal art collection at Versailles. Although it was originally understood that Jean-Sylvain would apprentice under his father and inherit his post, he showed little interest in art. Instead, he showed a strong aptitude for mathematics, and through a special arrangement he was tutored in calculus by Monsieur de Moncarville, whose son was in turn tutored in art by Jean-Sylvain's father.

Bailly also had literary aspirations and as a teen penned two plays. The playwright Lanoue, after being shown the plays, told Bailly they were so poor he should burn them. From this point forward, Bailly focused most of his attention on the sciences and was soon drawn especially to astronomy by Abbé Nicolas Louis de Lacaille.

LIFE'S WORK

Bailly made his first mark in astronomy by calculating the orbit of Halley's comet when it appeared in 1759, a clear sign of his fascination for the mathematical side of astronomy. He calculated the orbits of several lesser comets as well. As a result of these and other astronomical observations and calculations, he was elected to the French Academy of Sciences in 1763.

Bailly continued his astronomical work, studying the orbits of the moons of Jupiter. It was well known that, despite careful observation, there were inconsistencies in their orbital paths. A number of astronomers had tried mathematical solutions. Bailly's solution was elegant, considering the knowledge of the time (Laplace later found a better solution). He published two books dealing with the moons of Jupiter: *Essai sur la théorie des des satellites de Jupiter* (1766; essay on the theory of the satellites of Jupiter) and *Mémoires sur les inégalités de la lumière des satelites de Jupiter* (1771; memoirs on the uneven illumination of the satellites of Jupiter).

Bailly's interests also strayed into questions concerning the ultimate fate of the Earth and the other planets. He postulated that each planet has an inner heat that is at some stage of cooling. Jupiter he considered too hot for life, and the Moon was too cold. Because the cooling was a continuing process, he believed that all the planets would eventually cool to the point where all matter would cease movement.

As his renown grew, Bailly was admitted to the French Academy and the Academy of Humanities. He developed a long-term relationship with Voltaire, later publishing many of the letters they exchanged. He also met Benjamin Franklin, a fellow scientist and politician.

During the 1770's and 1780's, Bailly published a number of books, including his most famous work, a three-volume history of modern astronomy, *Histoire de l'astronomie moderne* (1779-1782). This work followed his earlier *Histoire de l'astronomie ancienne* (1775; history of ancient astronomy). In a book on Indian and Oriental astronomy, he showed that the ancient Vedic astronomical tables not only were very accurate but also were probably of ancient origin. He was also fascinated with Plato's writings on Atlantis in the *Critias* (360-347 B.C.E.; English translation 1793), and he wrote a book resurrecting Plato's theories about the origin of Atlantis, *Lettres sur l'Atalantide de Platon et sur l'ancienne histoire de l'Asie* (1779; letters on Plato's Atlantis and the ancient history of Asia). Bailly also speculated that the ancient Eden of the Bible was polar and claimed evidence from ancient Egyptian and Syrian manuscripts as support.

In 1789, the French Revolution exploded, bringing an

Jean-Sylvain Bailly. (Library of Congress)

abrupt change to Bailly's life. Because of his fame as a scientist and his high level of integrity, he was catapulted into politics. On May 5, 1789, Bailly was elected president of the Third Estate, the assembly (somewhat like the British parliament) that represented the larger part of the French population. As a member of the bourgeoisie, the upper-class citizenry that often served on the Third Estate, he served as a political link between the working classes and the First and Second Estates (the clergy and the nobility, respectively). On July 15, Bailly was again elevated, this time to mayor of Paris, the city's first mayor of the New Republic.

With no experience as a politician, Bailly was now thrust into one of the most difficult political situations imaginable. Because of the new humanistic ideas of the Enlightenment, the expansion of the middle class leading to clashes with the aristocracy, and the serious governmental financial crisis, Paris was thrown into anarchy. The only advantage Bailly had entering office was that he was on relatively good terms with most of the political players from the French monarchy on down.

Conditions in Paris were unmanageable. The peasants and middle class had overthrown the city's police powers by storming the Bastille, Paris's notorious prison-fortress. With no police protection, many merchants' shops were looted. Commerce came to a standstill. To make matters worse, the grain harvest had been very poor, and the city was short on bread. With the shortage, bakers raised bread prices to exorbitant heights, reflecting their increased costs but further enraging the populace.

At first, Bailly felt honored to serve as mayor, but reality soon set in. The first order of business was to secure the food supply, the most inflammatory source of unrest. To do this, Bailly and his administration enacted price caps on bread so the working classes could afford to eat. Then he began to troll far and wide for grain sources, even to the point of buying from other countries. At any given time, there was often only about a day's supply of grain in the city. Bailly managed to keep the precarious nature of the situation from the people, hoping it would prevent further rioting.

The other pressing need was to restore order through reforming the municipal government of Paris. The previous administration was so bureaucratically complex that no progress could be made, so a completely new constitution had to be enacted. Even this process was fraught with difficulty, as each of the districts of the city wanted to retain autonomy. Bailly was a strong proponent of a centralized government with the mayor having broad powers, whereas the elected assembly he had to work with wanted a much-less-centralized power structure. Eventually, Bailly had to compromise, with the result that his office as mayor had very little power: The right to enact laws was retained by each of the city's departments.

In spite of Bailly's initial success, the instability of Paris grew worse. Establishment of a national guard was helpful, but when "royal troops" were sent to Paris with orders to kill civilians and then fall back, Bailly saw no choice but to respond more forcefully to the unrest. On July 17, 1791, Bailly imposed martial law. Rioting broke out everywhere, and it was on this fateful day that General Lafayette ordered his militia to fire on an unruly mob at the Champs de Mars. Twenty-four civilians were killed in the attack. Lafayette went into exile two days later, and Bailly's reputation was irreparably damaged.

On September 19, Bailly was forced to resign as mayor. Refusing to exile himself, he left Paris and moved to Nantes, where he spent the next couple of years writing his memoirs. Late in 1793, he was arrested while visiting Laplace in Melun. He was tried on November 10 by the Revolutionary Tribunal. Two days later, on November 12, 1793, Bailly was led to the Champs de Mars so he could be executed on the spot where his crime was committed. He was marched before a jeering, rock-throwing mob for several hours and was later led to a place near the Seine, where he was guillotined.

SIGNIFICANCE

Jean-Sylvain Bailly's place in history has been nearly forgotten. His accomplishments in astronomy, although notable at the time, have lost much of their importance. His accomplishments in the history of astronomy have been more lasting, however, and his book on the subject remains a classic. His astronomical achievements are permanently commemorated by Bailly Crater, the largest crater on the near side of the moon.

Bailly's greater significance was certainly the role he played in the French Revolution. Although a man of science, he was also a man of deep moral convictions. This trait was recognized by those who helped propel him into politics. His inexperience was both an advantage and a disadvantage. Not having ever served in office before, he was unsullied by the political machinations so common in politics, thus gaining the trust of the populace. On the other hand, his lack of experience made him an easy target for those who were more experienced at the game. In some ways, it is surprising that he survived in his role as mayor as long as he did.

Bailly's lasting legacy lies in the fact that he stood by the people of Paris in one of their darkest hours. He was a voice of reason between the extremes of anarchy and monarchy. He helped shape the constitution that lay at the foundation of the New Republic. He also paid the ultimate price for his role. He could have gone into exile to Great Britain or elsewhere, but he chose to remain in France, where, at the age of fifty-seven, he was executed in the city he loved.

—*Bryan D. Ness*

FURTHER READING

Brucker, Gene A. *Jean-Sylvain Bailly: Revolutionary Mayor of Paris*. Urbana: University of Illinois Press, 1950. A short overview of Bailly's life during his political career from his election to the presidency of the Third Estate to his resignation as mayor of Paris.

Brush, Stephen G. *A History of Modern Planetary Physics*. 2 vols. New York: Cambridge University Press, 1996. Contains a few brief sections discussing some of Bailly's astronomical research and theories.

Pulet, Ann L. *Jean-Antoine Houdon: Sculptor of the Enlightenment*. Chicago: University of Chicago Press, 2005. Contains pictures and discusses the bust sculpted in honor of Bailly's election as mayor of Paris.

See also: Georges Danton; Benjamin Franklin; Louis XVI; Robespierre; Voltaire.

Related articles in *Great Events from History: The Eighteenth Century, 1701-1800*: 1704-1712: Astronomy Wars in England; 1705: Halley Predicts the Return of a Comet; 1725: Flamsteed's Star Catalog Marks the Transition to Modern Astronomy; June, 1752: Franklin Demonstrates the Electrical Nature of Lightning; May 5, 1789: Louis XVI Calls the Estates-General; July 14, 1789: Fall of the Bastille; October, 1789-April 25, 1792: France Adopts the Guillotine; April 20, 1792-October, 1797: Early Wars of the French Revolution.

SIR JOSEPH BANKS
English scientist and explorer

Combining his knowledge of botany and an inherited fortune, Banks led the scientific group on Captain James Cook's expedition in the Endeavour *and, for forty-one years, as president of the Royal Society, supported and encouraged various scientific activities.*

Born: February 13, 1743; London, England
Died: June 19, 1820; Spring Grove, Heston Parish, Isleworth, England
Areas of achievement: Science and technology, exploration

EARLY LIFE

Joseph Banks was the only son of William Banks, of Revesby Abbey, and of the daughter of William Bate of Derbyshire, who is referred to as Sarah, Sophia, or Marianne by various writers. The Banks family was landed gentry, represented in Parliament and associated with all the great families in England. William Banks was strongly religious, but Joseph did not seem to follow any formal religion. He had a private tutor for some time; then, in April, 1752, he was sent to Harrow, and in September, 1756, to Eton. He was cheerful, with a generous disposition, but no student. At fourteen, he discovered the beauty of flowers and plants, embarking on a lifetime study. He was entered a gentleman commoner at Christ Church, Oxford, in December, 1760.

His father died in 1761, and his mother moved to Turret House, Paradise Walk, Chelsea, with her daughter, Sarah Sophia. This was near the Chelsea Physic Garden. In Chelsea, Banks could pursue his botany and natural history interests while vacationing from Oxford.

Oxford's botany professor gave Banks permission to go to Cambridge to find a teacher. There, he met Israel Lyons, who was proficient in botany and mathematics. Lyons became a reader or lecturer in botany at Oxford, giving his series of lectures in July, 1764, paid for by pupil subscriptions organized by Banks. Banks's regular residence at Oxford ended in December, 1763, with irregular attendance in 1764 and 1765. In February, 1764, he had taken control of his inheritance, making him a wealthy young man. He made good progress under Lyons's teaching and attracted attention for his knowledge of natural history. In May, 1766, when he was elected a fellow of the Royal Society at age twenty-three, Banks already had left on his first scientific exploration.

LIFE'S WORK

Joseph Banks joined an Oxford friend, Lieutenant Constantine Phipps, serving on HMS *Niger* on April 7, 1766. The ship was being sent to Labrador and Newfoundland on fishery protection duty under Sir Thomas Adams. Banks was its naturalist, and the two made observations and collections in Newfoundland, Labrador, and Portugal. Banks's journal was not published for almost two hundred years, nor was any formal report made to the Royal Society, where he attended his first meeting on February 15, 1767. His dried specimens became the basis for his herbarium, a center for the study of natural history. In 1767 and 1768, he toured parts of England and Wales, but nothing was published until 1899.

Banks abandoned his plans to visit Carolus Linnaeus in Sweden and Lapland in the spring of 1768 to concentrate on a Pacific expedition to observe the transit of Venus in 1769. The Admiralty agreed to fit out vessels and appointed Lieutenant James Cook commander of the *Endeavour* on May 25, 1768. Banks applied to the council of the Royal Society to join in with ten others and, with the support of Lord Sandwich, the Admiralty gave approval on July 22, 1768.

The group included Dr. Daniel Carl Solander, a Swede and pupil of Linnaeus, who arrived in England in July, 1760, making an impact on English science and natural history. In 1764, Solander finally obtained an assistantship in the British Museum and was elected to the Royal Society. Banks met him in 1767. The principal artist was Sydney Parkinson, along with John Reynolds, Alexander Buchan, and Henry Spöring. Banks expended about £10,000 of his own money outfitting himself and his staff. This was to be the first British voyage of discovery equipped with a scientific staff that was officially recognized.

The *Endeavour* sailed from Plymouth on August 25, 1768. Banks and Cook began journals, which complement each other, as did the ship's crew. They sailed around the globe in three years, returning on July 12, 1771. Banks examined the specimens collected, Solander described them, and Parkinson drew them. In Tahiti, Banks studied the indigenous peoples and showed his ability to connect and communicate well by getting back a stolen astronomical quadrant, which was needed to observe the transit of Venus. He lost his two black servants, Richmond and Dollin, who died at Tierra del Fuego. Buchan, the landscape artist, died at Tahiti, while the other three artists died before returning to England. Hundreds of new species were collected, new peoples and new lands were discovered, charting was done, and dangers were overcome. Solander continued to work with Banks as associate and secretary until he died. Cook and Banks were hailed as heroes. Oxford granted Banks an honorary doctor in civil law degree on November 21, 1771. A tradition of scientific work on British voyages of discovery had begun.

The travelers were summoned to Windsor to be received by King George III, and Banks began a friendship that lasted his lifetime. Banks, Solander, and Cook also visited with Lord Sandwich to report on the voyage. John Hawkesworth, official recorder of this Cook voyage, worked with various journals, including Banks's, preparing three volumes, published in 1773. This, however, represented only a small part of the information gathered by the expedition.

Preparations were begun for a second voyage by Cook in the *Resolution*. Banks and Solander planned to take part, but with a larger group of assistants, so extra quarters had to be constructed on deck. This made the ship too cumbersome, however, and Cook was concerned. Lord Sandwich and the Admiralty objected, and Banks withdrew. The scientists who finally sailed with Cook, in 1772, were Dr. Johann Reinhold Forster and his son Georg.

Banks then decided to go to Iceland. He chartered the brig *Sir Lawrence* for five months. Collections were made in Iceland, with stops at the Orkney Islands and Scotland. The printed material and manuscripts formed the British Museum's Icelandic Collection. Descriptions of the natural pillars of Staffa and some drawings were published in *Tour in Scotland* by Thomas Pennant in 1774, but Solander's work on the flora of Iceland and most of the drawings were never published.

Banks took an active role working on the natural history collections of Cook's second and final voyages. He then took on the role of promoter of science when George III selected Banks as his unofficial scientific adviser.

Banks began to work on an open-air herbarium for exotic plants from all over the world at Royal Kew Gardens. This encouraged botanical exploration, the study of economic uses of various plants, and the development of botanical gardens in other British settlements, the first in Jamaica around 1775.

Banks first served on the council of the Royal Society in 1774, and, in 1778, was elected president. He also became an ex officio trustee of the British Museum, and he held both posts for more than forty years. This placed him in the forefront of all scientific activity. His London center was 32 Soho Square, the home of his growing library and botanical collections. His sister, Sarah Sophia, presided over the house. When he married Dorothea Hugessen, daughter of William Weston Hugessen of Norton of Kent, on March 23, 1779, Sarah continued to live with them. He also bought Spring Grove, in Heston, developing the gardens there with the help of his wife and sister. In 1781, he was made a baronet.

Solander's death in 1782 deprived Banks of an excellent secretary and associate and prevented the publication of Solander's manuscript. Many species in Australia and New Zealand had to be rediscovered later. Dr. Jonas Dryander, another Swede, became

Sir Joseph Banks. (Library of Congress)

Banks's librarian and curator. Late in the summer of 1783, Banks had a carriage accident, after which he developed gout, troubling him for the rest of his life.

Early in 1784, there was renewed interest in settlement in Australia, an idea presented by Banks in 1779. By 1786, he called for establishing a colony at New South Wales and continued to be active in the affairs of the new colony in Australia. He had many other interests: transplanting breadfruit from the Pacific to the West Indies for food; improving English wool quality by importing the first merino sheep from Spain; founding the African Society, which became the Royal Geographic Society; advising the British East India Company on transplanting tea from China to India; supporting James Edward Smith in forming the Linnaean Society of London; getting Francis Bauer appointed at Kew Gardens in 1790; and selecting Archibald Menzies as naturalist for the Vancouver expedition to the northwest Pacific coast in North America, from 1791 to 1795.

Banks was invested with the Order of the Bath on July 1, 1795, taking the lizard as his device. He was sworn into the Privy Council in 1797. France honored him in 1802 with membership in the National Institute of France. When the Royal Horticultural Society was formed in 1804, Banks was present and became a vice president. He was also a member of the Society of Arts, the Engineers' Society, the Dilettanti Society, and the Society for the Improvement of Naval Architecture. He was active on the Council of the Society of Antiquaries, the Board of Longitude, and the Royal Institute.

In 1810, Robert Brown published his work on the plant collection from the Flinders expedition and became Banks's secretary when Dryander died. Banks continued his vast correspondence, even during wartimes. In fact, he was responsible for saving the collections and helping foreign scientists on no fewer than ten occasions. He attended meetings and club dinners, even though he had to be carried or wheeled in a chair by his servants during the last fifteen years of his life. He continued to be active mentally, attending his last meeting in March, 1820. He died June 19, 1820, at Spring Grove and was buried in Heston Church with simple services and no headstone.

His will provided that Robert Brown was to have the use of his library and herbarium, and at Brown's death they were to go to the British Museum. Brown turned over the library and collections in 1827 and became keeper at the British Museum. The later scattering of Banks's papers and manuscripts through sales at Sotheby's has hindered efforts to produce a full biogra-

phy, although his library and collections are still available and used in the British Library.

SIGNIFICANCE

Sir Joseph Banks had an outstanding part in the celebrated first voyage of Cook (1768-1771). Along with his activities in Labrador and Newfoundland, Banks had established a pattern of collection and scientific exploration that enriched the British Museum and the rest of the world. He made his collections available to all, but it was unfortunate that he did not publish so that more people might have had easier access to his work.

In his role as president of the Royal Society he supported individuals and a variety of scientific activities. In both botany and settlement support he is truly the "father of Australia" and the first European to lead botanical investigation of New Zealand. He made the Royal Kew Gardens a world-renowned institution and helped develop numerous other botanical gardens throughout the world. He was a friend to king and commoner, a prodigious correspondent, a promoter of scientific societies and organizations in a wide range of fields, a promoter of scientific exploration, and an important link between the amateur tradition in British science and the modern scientific community.

—*Mary-Emily Miller*

FURTHER READING

Banks, Joseph. *The Endeavour Journal of Joseph Banks, 1768-1771*. Edited by J. C. Beaglehole. 2 vols. Sydney: Angus and Robertson, 1962. A carefully researched and faithfully presented version of Banks's journal and a fitting companion to Beaglehole's *The Life of Captain James Cook* (1974). Here is the tale of the scattering of Banks's work around the globe. Beaglehole suggests that Banks did not publish because he was an amateur who lost interest in the work when completed.

_____. *Journal of the Right Hon. Sir Joseph Banks, Bart., K.B., P.R.S. During Captain Cook's First Voyage in H.M.S. Endeavour in 1768-71 to Terra del Fuego, Tahite, New Zealand, Australia, the Dutch East Indies, etc.* Edited by Sir Joseph D. Hooker. New York: Macmillan, 1896. A one-volume version of Banks's journal, very much abridged. Contains information on the people mentioned in the journal and a biographical sketch of Banks, which Beaglehole considers full of errors.

Cameron, Hector Charles. *Sir Joseph Banks, K.B., P.R.S.: The Autocrat of the Philosophers*. London: Batchworth Press, 1952. A very readable account of

Banks's wide range of activities, with sections on Kew Gardens, Banks's correspondents, his role as president of the Royal Society, the founding of Australia, his promotion of science, his life at home, and his detractors.

Captain Cook's Florilegium. London: Lion and Unicorn Press, 1973. Thirty engravings from the drawings of plants collected by Banks and Daniel Solander on Captain Cook's first voyage to the islands of the Pacific. Features accounts of the voyage and descriptions of the botanical explorations and prints. Exquisite engravings based on the drawings and sketches of Sydney Parkinson with Solander's descriptions and collection data, and new names given by other botanists.

Fara, Patricia. *Sex, Botany, and Empire: The Story of Carl Linnaeus and Joseph Banks*. New York: Columbia University Press, 2004. Despite its title, the book focuses more on Banks and Linnaeus than on sex and botany, describing how Carolus Linnaeus developed a system to classify organisms and how Banks, who never met Linnaeus, popularized the classification system.

Gascoigne, John. *Science in the Service of Empire: Joseph Banks, the British State, and the Uses of Science in the Age of Revolution*. New York: Cambridge University Press, 1998. Examines how Banks promoted the scientific discoveries of his age to advance the economic and political interest of British society. The illustrations enhance the text.

Maiden, J. H. *Sir Joseph Banks: The "Father of Australia."* London: Kegan Paul, Trench, Trübner, 1909. Contains a brief personal sketch and comments on Banks, extensively quoting from journals, letters, and other sources. There are also brief sketches of men who worked with Banks, numerous illustrations, charts, and works written, edited by, or concerning Banks.

O'Brian, Patrick. *Joseph Banks: A Life*. Chicago: University of Chicago Press, 1997. O'Brian, who specializes in maritime history, has written a narrative biography of Banks. The book is particularly strong in describing Banks's voyage with Cook.

Smith, Edward. *The Life of Sir Joseph Banks, President of the Royal Society, with Some Notices of His Friends and Contemporaries*. London: John Lane, 1911. Started as a detailed life of Banks but forced into abbreviation by the publisher, this work is a reference for most later comments on Banks. It contains seventeen illustrations, while the bulk of the work covers the period of Banks's life beginning with his election as president of the Royal Society.

See also: Comte de Buffon; James Cook; George III; Carolus Linnaeus.

Related articles in *Great Events from History: The Eighteenth Century, 1701-1800:* c. 1732: Society of Dilettanti Is Established; Beginning 1735: Linnaeus Creates the Binomial System of Classification; 1749-1789: First Comprehensive Examination of the Natural World; 1751: Maupertuis Provides Evidence of "Hereditary Particles"; August 25, 1768-February 14, 1779: Voyages of Captain Cook; 1770: Publication of Holbach's *The System of Nature*; 1779: Ingenhousz Discovers Photosynthesis; January 26, 1788: Britain Establishes Penal Colony in Australia.

BENJAMIN BANNEKER
American mathematician and astronomer

Banneker's calculations provided the essential data for almanacs published from 1792 through 1797. A free black in a slave state, Banneker overcame obstacles of rural isolation, little formal education, and racial prejudice to establish himself as a respected scientist, earn a place on the crew that surveyed the District of Columbia, and become a symbol of racial equality in the abolitionist movement. He is also known for his letter to Thomas Jefferson calling on him to end slavery in America.

Born: November 9, 1731; Baltimore County, Maryland
Died: October 9, 1806; Baltimore, Maryland
Areas of achievement: Mathematics, astronomy, science and technology

EARLY LIFE

Benjamin Banneker's American antecedents came in bonds to colonial Maryland. His grandmother, Molly Welsh, was a convict transported from England to Maryland in about 1683. After completing a period of servitude, she became a free landowner in the western part of Baltimore County near the Patapsco River. In 1692, Molly bought two Africans and in a few years restored freedom to both. One of the men, named Bannka, claimed to be the kidnapped son of an African king. In defiance of laws that forbade miscegenation, Molly married the prince and took Banneky as her surname.

The Bannekys had four daughters. The oldest, Mary, born in about 1700, married an African who had been given freedom as a baptismal gift. He had chosen Robert as his Christian name and, when married, took Banneky as his surname. The name's spelling varied until the mid-eighteenth century, when it settled at Banneker. Three of the four children born to Robert and Mary grew to maturity. The oldest, and the only son, was Benjamin, born in 1731.

In about 1729, Robert bought 25 acres of land close to Molly's farm. On March 10, 1737, when Benjamin was five years old, Robert purchased 100 acres from the nearby Stout plantation. The title was in Robert's and Benjamin's names to ensure that the family could protect its freedom should Robert die suddenly. Maryland laws were not sympathetic to free blacks and authorized reenslavement of those who did not own property.

Banneker's education was rudimentary. His grandmother taught him to read from the Bible. For a few months, he attended a country school where the schoolteacher, probably a Quaker, taught black and white children. Benjamin learned to write a very clear, even beautiful, script and mastered the fundamentals of mathematics through basic algebra. At some point, he also learned to play the flute and the violin. Though meager, this education powerfully shaped the course of Banneker's life. He purchased his own Bible in 1763, read it diligently, and sprinkled his writings with scriptural quotations. He never formally joined a Christian denomination, but he often attended Quaker, and sometimes Methodist, services. His reading interests went beyond the Bible to literature in general. He painstakingly compiled a small library, composed essays in his own commonplace book, and wrote poetry.

Mathematics, though, was the subject that most stimulated his intellectual curiosity. He had unusual abilities with numbers. As a young man, he became locally famous for being able to solve fairly complex computations in his head. He had a special fondness for mathematical puzzles and liked to trade tricky problems with his neighbors.

It was probably during such an exchange with a neighbor that Banneker first saw and then borrowed a watch. The timepiece fascinated him, and he dismantled it to observe its moving parts. Using the watch as a model, Banneker produced a clock made entirely of hand-carved hardwoods. The clock kept accurate time, struck the hours, and was the wonder of the Patapsco valley.

Banneker completed the clock in 1753, when he was twenty-two. His father died six years later, leaving Benjamin the sole owner of the Stout acreage. The rest of the property was divided among Benjamin and his two married sisters. Banneker lived with his mother until she died in 1775. He never married and lived the rest of his life on his well-kept, productive farm. He might have died in obscurity had not the Ellicott brothers bought land adjoining the Banneker farm.

LIFE'S WORK

Joseph, Andrew, and John Ellicott brought their large families and the families of several workers to the Patapsco valley in 1771, when Benjamin Banneker was about forty years old. Before they were fully settled, the Ellicotts and their workers bought food from the existing farms. Andrew Ellicott's young son George developed a special friendship with Banneker. At age fifteen in 1775,

George was recognized as a mathematical prodigy, an accomplished surveyor, and a gifted astronomer. With George's encouragement and assistance, Banneker rapidly mastered advanced mathematics and became fascinated with astronomy. In the fall of 1788, George loaned Banneker books on mathematics and astronomy, a telescope, a set of drafting instruments, a lamp, and a large, oval drop-leaf table.

Banneker soon spent clear nights in open fields observing the heavens. When recording his observations in cold weather he dressed heavily and wrapped himself in blankets. At dawn he returned to his cabin and slept for a few hours. He spent most of the rest of the day at the oval table studying the borrowed books and plotting the movements of the stars. The calculation of a star's location for a particular date could involve as many as ten different algebraic and logarithmic operations.

Benjamin Banneker, 1980 U.S. commemorative postage stamp. (Arkent Archive)

As he gained a sure grasp of astronomy, Banneker began the ambitious project of calculating an ephemeris—a table showing the positions of the Earth, Moon, planets, and stars throughout the year. The ephemeris was the basis for projecting eclipses and predicting weather conditions. It was, therefore, the major component of an almanac, a compilation of astronomical and weather-related data for a given year. He was encouraged in this project by his mentor George and by George's cousin, Major Andrew Ellicott. Major Ellicott had prepared ephemerides for publication from 1781 through 1786, but the demands of his work as surveyor forced him to abandon the time-consuming calculations. In the summer of 1790, Banneker submitted completed ephemerides for 1791 to three publishers, but none of the editors bought his work. Although discouraged, Banneker began an ephemeris for 1792.

In January of 1791, President George Washington instructed Secretary of State Thomas Jefferson to have the District of Columbia surveyed. On February 2, 1791, Jefferson named Major Ellicott the chief surveyor. Ellicott was to find the true meridian and longitude of the future capital and to prepare a topographical map of the ten-square-mile tract of land. Because he was shorthanded, Ellicott turned to Banneker for help. Banneker had no practical experience as a surveyor, but he had mastered the mathematics involved and knew how to work with most of the astronomical instruments.

On February 7, 1791, Banneker, at age fifty-nine, made his first trip outside Baltimore County. During his three-month stay at the site of the future capital, he gained valuable experience as assistant to Ellicott. He learned to use the astronomical clock and other instruments new to him. He also kept a resolution to abstain from drinking wine and hard liquor while working with the surveying crew.

Upon his return home, he finished the ephemeris for 1792. Meanwhile, Joseph and George Ellicott had interested members of the Society of Friends and the antislavery societies in Baltimore and Philadelphia in Banneker. Through their assistance, Banneker's 1792 ephemeris was published by the Baltimore firm of Goddard and Angell. The almanac, *Benjamin Banneker's Pennsylvania, Delaware, Maryland and Virginia Almanack and Ephemeris for the Year of Our Lord, 1792* was sold in Baltimore, Philadelphia, and Alexandria beginning in December, 1791. The editors of the almanac included a note in the work's front matter, stating that the almanac was "an extraordinary Effort of Genius—a COMPLETE and ACCURATE EPHEMERIS . . . calculated by a sable Descendant of Africa. . . ." The editors argued that the almanac was proof that skin color had no relationship to mental or intellectual capacity, that all people were alike, and that slavery should be ended. The first four thousand copies quickly sold out, as did a second printing by Goddard and Angell and a condensed edition printed by William Young in Philadelphia.

Banneker prepared an ephemeris that was published in an almanac each year through 1797. The almanacs were extremely popular and sold well. At least twenty-eight editions of these almanacs appeared in those six years. Starting in 1794, Banneker computed tide tables for Chesapeake Bay, a feature that competing almanacs did not contain.

The elderly astronomer was of average height and had a full head of thick, white hair. Though portly, his posture, gentlemanly behavior, and staff gave him a dignified air. Banneker continued to calculate ephemerides through the 1802, the year he turned seventy-one. His capacity for work had diminished, and he was unable to complete the rigorous computations. He died quietly in his home four years later on October 9, 1806.

SIGNIFICANCE

Benjamin Banneker's abilities as a mathematician and astronomer made him famous in his lifetime. There was, however, much more to his fame than his scientific accomplishments themselves. Banneker was the son and grandson of Africans. He was a free black in a predominantly white society that almost universally regarded black people as being mentally inferior to whites. Banneker's best-known activity—in his lifetime and since—was his correspondence with Thomas Jefferson.

On August 19, 1791, Banneker sent the author of the Declaration of Independence a handwritten copy of his ephemeris and a long letter. He introduced himself as a black man and then eloquently pleaded with Jefferson to use his influence to end the slavery that still kept some of the children of humankind's one Father from enjoying their "inalienable rights." Jefferson responded by expressing the hope that people would soon recognize that circumstances, not natural endowments, kept blacks in a condition that suggested inferiority, but he made no pledge to do anything more than to send Banneker's almanac to abolitionists in France.

Those two letters were printed in the 1793 almanac and reprinted frequently in abolitionist literature in the nineteenth century. Benjamin Banneker had become a symbol of racial equality because he was an example of black achievement. His name has been invoked over the

years in black educational efforts, such as Benjamin Banneker College of Prairie View A&M University at Prairie View, Texas.

—Paul E. Kuhl

FURTHER READING

Allen, Will W., comp. *Banneker: The Afro-American Astronomer*. Washington, D.C.: Black Heritage Library, 1921. Reprint. Freeport, N.Y.: Books for Libraries Press, 1971. This work is based largely on primary sources. However, the book contains a paper by Daniel Murray that advances the oft-repeated, undocumented claim that Banneker worked with Major Pierre Charles L'Enfant and had a copy of the city's plans for use after L'Enfant left the capital site in a rage.

Allen, William G. *Wheatley, Banneker, and Horton*. Boston: D. Laing, 1849. Reprint. Freeport, N.Y.: Books for Libraries Press, 1970. A condensation of an earlier work on records held by the Ellicott family.

Armistead, Wilson. *A Tribute for the Negro: Being a Vindication of the Moral, Intellectual, and Religious Capabilities of the Colored Portion of Mankind, with Particular Reference to the African Race*. 1848. Reprint. Miami, Fla.: Mnemosyne, 1969. A collection of abolitionist literature. The material on Banneker consists of a brief biographical sketch and a reprint of the Jefferson correspondence.

Baker, Henry E. "Benjamin Banneker, the Negro Mathematician and Astronomer." *Journal of Negro History* 3 (April, 1918): 99-118. A fine sketch based upon a rare work prepared by George Ellicott's daughter Martha Ellicott Tyson.

Bedini, Silvio A. *The Life of Benjamin Banneker: The First African-American Man of Science*. 2d rev. ed. Baltimore: Maryland Historical Society, 1999. An excellent study of Banneker, based on careful review of secondary materials, previously unused material from private archives, and Banneker's commonplace book and journal. Originally published in 1971, this expanded edition includes new photographs and information on Banneker's African roots.

Cerami, Charles. *Benjamin Bannecker: Surveyor, Astronomer, Publisher, Patriot*. New York: J. Wiley, 2002. A clearly and simply written biography that examines Banneker's life and the breadth of his career.

Miller, John Chester. *The Wolf by the Ears: Thomas Jefferson and Slavery*. New York: Free Press, 1977. Miller treats the correspondence between Banneker and Jefferson in the context of Jefferson's life and slavery in the United States.

ANNA BARBAULD
English writer

Barbauld, a Unitarian dissenter, was one of the most respected and well-known literary figures of eighteenth century England. Although she is renowned for her poetry, which addresses topics ranging from domestic issues to political propaganda, she also was an influential writer of educational and children's literature and was a literary critic and an editor.

Born: June 20, 1743; Kibworth Harcourt, Leicestershire, England
Died: March 9, 1825; Stoke Newington, England
Also known as: Anna Aikin (birth name); Anna Letitia Barbauld; Anna Lætitia Barbauld
Areas of achievement: Literature, education, religion and theology, government and politics

EARLY LIFE

Anna Barbauld (BAHR-boh) was the eldest child and only daughter of Jane Jennings Aikin and John Aikin, a Presbyterian dissenter and distinguished minister and schoolteacher. Anna received a conventional domestic education from her mother, customary for girls at that time, and later convinced her father to teach her Latin and Greek. At an early age (she was able to read by the age of three) she began to read extensively in her father's library and learned French, German, and Italian.

When she was fifteen years old, her father became a tutor at Warrington, the leading dissenting academy established to provide an education for nonconformist clergymen who were excluded from the universities of Oxford and Cambridge. Although as a girl she was not allowed to study at Warrington academy, she nevertheless was able to profit from the congenial intellectual environment. She remained aware, however, of the differences between her limited educational opportunities and those of her younger brother John, with whom she maintained a close relationship until his death in 1822. She published her first volume of poetry in 1773, which proved to be a great success and paved the way for her prolific writing and career. She encountered the same success with her *Miscellaneous Pieces in Prose* (co-authored with her brother) in 1773.

In 1775, she married Rochemont Barbauld, a clergyman of French descent and a former pupil at Warrington, and moved with him to Palgrave in Suffolk, where the couple set up a boarding school for boys. The years in which Barbauld spent educating children also established her career as a writer of educational literature. Her marriage seems to have been a happy one, and many of Barbauld's poems, including "To Mr. Barbauld, with a Map of the Land of Matrimony," celebrate her relationship with her husband.

LIFE'S WORK

Anna Barbauld's writing life was long and varied, but she is best known for her poetry. While some of her poems focus on topics traditionally considered to be feminine—such as love, domestic life, nature, and religion—she was also the author of satires and political poems. Her first collection, *Poems* (1773), already introduced her different voices. The collection includes personal poems for friends and family, such as "On Mrs. P[riestley]'s Leaving Warrington"; Romantic poems, such as "A Summer Evening's Meditation"; and political poems, such as "Corsica."

Barbauld acquired her reputation as an educational writer for children mainly because of *Lessons for Children* (1778, 1779, 1787, 1788), devised for her adopted son, her nephew Charles Aikin—the Barbaulds had no children of their own—and *Hymns in Prose for Children* (1781). After the Barbaulds' resignation from the school, they toured France and Switzerland. When they returned to England, they settled in Hampstead and Anna Barbauld continued teaching small numbers of both girls and boys.

She resumed her friendship with bluestockings Hannah More and Elizabeth Montagu, and she wrote several political pamphlets. As a Unitarian dissenter, she was a spokeswoman for liberal causes and for peace, but the times were difficult for dissenters. The Barbaulds were publicly criticized and threatened because of her husband Rochemont's refusal to sign loyalty oaths to the government. Consequently, Barbauld advocated equal rights for all citizens with her pamphlet *Address to the Opposers of the Repeal of the Corporation and Test Acts* (1790). In another pamphlet, entitled *Sins of Government, Sins of the Nation* (1793), she denounced England's declaration of war against France. In addition to her pamphlets, her poems testify to her politics and courage. She announced that she was strongly in favor of abolition with the poem *Epistle to William Wilberforce, Esq. on the Rejection of the Bill for Abolishing the Slave Trade* (1791). However, she was more conservative in other works. For instance, with "The Rights of Woman" (wr. 1793, pb. 1825), she entered into a debate with Mary Wollstonecraft on the role of women in society. Women's sphere, Barbauld argued, was the domestic one, even though her position here stood opposed to her own public voice.

In 1802, the Barbaulds moved to Stoke Newington to care for Anna's brother, John Aikin, whose health had declined. Here she began her editorial work with *The Correspondence of Samuel Richardson* (1804). In the following years, Barbauld's private life deteriorated, as Rochemont was increasingly affected by a mental illness that led him to attack Anna with a knife in 1808; the attack led to the couple's separation. Later that same year, Rochemont committed suicide. Anna's grief led her to seek comfort in religion and to concentrate even more of her energy on writing; in 1809, she began contributing to the *Monthly Review* and later edited fifty volumes of the series *The British Novelists* (1810), each prefaced by a biographical and critical sketch and introduced by her essay "On the Origin and Progress of Novel-Writing," which made her one of the leading literary critics of the day.

In 1812, her most famous poem, *Eighteen Hundred and Eleven*, was published, in which she criticized the long-lasting war between England and France and prophesied that England as a nation would be surpassed like other powers in world history. The poem is a culmination of her lifelong political views—consequently, she attacks England severely for sacrificing its democratic principles. This provoked aggressive criticism and the accusation of treason, so that Barbauld, although she continued writing, did not publish further texts independently. Ultimately, it was John Wilson Croker's harsh

critique in the *Quarterly Review* that seemed to have effectively silenced her at the height of her powers as a poet—an incident that underscored the reality that social criticism and political criticism were not only dangerous but often also forbidden discourses, especially for women.

After Barbauld's death in 1825, her niece Lucy Aikin published *The Works of Anna Lætitia Barbauld, with a Memoir by Lucy Aikin* (1825) and *A Legacy for Young Ladies* (1826). Her still unpublished manuscripts and papers were destroyed in the bombing of London in September, 1940, the early days of World War II.

SIGNIFICANCE

Anna Barbauld was acclaimed for her genius and talent. Contemporaries such as Oliver Goldsmith, William Wordsworth, and the young Samuel Taylor Coleridge praised and admired her poetry in particular. However, resentment against dissent and the general, negative reactions to Enlightenment radicalism in the early nineteenth century contributed to Barbauld's professional demise. Her poetry was revalued, but not until the 1980's, and she has yet to receive adequate credit for her work as an educator and critic.

Barbauld's work has received less attention than it deserves, likely because it defies simple categorization. Although she held strong views on liberty and equality, she cannot be classified exclusively as a feminist writer. While much of her work is influenced by political discussion, her poetry also uses homely and playful subjects and has a tone that has been regarded as "feminine." Furthermore, although she is received as a political author today, her religious works are often ignored as well. Her independence of thought and her intellectual versatility have made it a challenge to classify and define her work and her political positions.

—*Miriam Wallraven*

FURTHER READING
Bradshaw, Penny. "Gendering the Enlightenment: Conflicting Images of Progress in the Poetry of Anna Lætitia Barbauld." *Women's Writing* 5, no. 3 (1998): 353-372. Analyzes the conflict between a feminine set of ideal Enlightenment values in Barbauld's poetry and an opposing set of masculine concepts, including exploitation and repression, particularly visible in slavery, colonialism, and the exploitation of nature.

Keach, William. "Barbauld, Romanticism, and the Survival of Dissent." *Essays and Studies* (*Romanticism and Gender*) 1998: 44-61. Disproves Barbauld's image as "pretty poetess" by retracing the dissenting culture in Romanticism, which is central to much of her poetry up to the 1790's and beyond.

McCarthy, William. "'We Hoped the Woman Was Going to Appear': Repression, Desire, and Gender in Anna Letitia Barbauld's Early Poems." In *Romantic Women Writers: Voices and Countervoices*, edited by Paula R. Feldman and Theresa M. Kelley. Hanover, Md.: University Press of New England, 1995. Argues for a biographical reading of Barbauld's poems, which uncovers her concern with gender, female desire, the construction of "woman," and her own subjectivity.

McCarthy, William, and Elizabeth Kraft, eds. *The Poems of Anna Letitia Barbauld*. Athens: University of Georgia Press, 1994. Accompanied by an accessible introduction to Barbauld's poetry, a chronology, and extensive notes on each poem.

Ross, Marlon B. "The Birth of a Tradition: Making Cultural Space for Feminine Poetry." In *The Contours of Masculine Desire: Romanticism and the Rise of Women's Poetry*, edited by Marlon B. Ross. New York: Oxford University Press, 1989. Situates Barbauld in a transitional phase in which sociohistorical conditions transformed the "bluestocking" into the "feminine poetess." Analyzes Barbauld's place among her contemporaries by interpreting her political, polemical, and more "feminine" poems.

See also: Mary Astell; William Blake; Fanny Burney; Oliver Goldsmith; Sophie von La Roche; Mary Wortley Montagu; Hannah More; Joseph Priestley; William Wilberforce; Mary Wollstonecraft.

Related article in *Great Events from History: The Eighteenth Century, 1701-1800:* 1792: Wollstonecraft Publishes *A Vindication of the Rights of Woman.*

JOHANN BERNHARD BASEDOW
German educator

Basedow, believing that children should be permitted their childhood, taught them accordingly, encouraging them to learn through observation and experience more than through books. He insisted on a secular approach to an education that included nature study, physical education, and manual training.

Born: September 11, 1723; Hamburg (now in Germany)

Died: July 25, 1790; Magdeburg, Brandenburg (now in Germany)

Area of achievement: Education

EARLY LIFE

Johann Bernhard Basedow (yoh-HAHN BURN-hahrt BAHZ-uh-doh) was born in the northeastern German seaport of Hamburg, the son of an unhappy, alcoholic wig maker, a man of dark moods, whose wife lapsed into madness and died shortly after the birth of her son. As a youth, Basedow exhibited erratic behavior. He was given to practical jokes, which annoyed his father. The boy, who learned Latin from his father by the time he was eight, ran away from home but soon returned and applied himself to his studies.

By the time he was twenty, Basedow had entered the University of Leipzig as a student in theology. His unconventional, though brilliant, thinking and his extreme egotism soon put him at odds with important faculty members, and he decided not to prepare for the priesthood. Rather, in 1749, he became a tutor in Holstein, and during his three years of tutoring he discovered that teaching was his real vocation. His views were unique for his time in that he eschewed book learning and was convinced that people learn best from observation and experience. Basedow taught Latin as though he were a Roman citizen, chatting informally in Latin with his students, who began to learn by what modern theorists have termed the audiolingual approach. By 1752, Basedow had taken a doctorate in foreign languages at the University of Kiel, where his dissertation explored some of the new methods of teaching he had developed as a tutor.

Soon afterward, Basedow accepted his first regular teaching job, in a Danish academy attended by the children of affluent, influential Danes. A gifted teacher, Basedow drew attention to himself by his unorthodox religious views and by his heterodox teaching methods. He advocated nonsectarian teaching, a shocking idea in his day. By 1761, he was no longer welcome among the Danes and moved to a classical *Gymnasium* (a German secondary school) in Altona, near his birthplace. Long a philosophical rationalist, Basedow issued broadsides so shocking to the people of Altona that the Church barred him and his family from taking Holy Communion and they were placed under an ecclesiastical ban. Anyone who read his work was threatened with exile, but these restraints did not stifle Basedow, who issued vituperation after vituperation.

LIFE'S WORK

Basedow was forty-five and had lost several teaching jobs when he published his *Vorstellung an Menschenfreunde und vermögende Männer über Schulen, Studien, und ihren Enfluss in die öffentliche Wohlfahrt* (1768). His tract, in part a direct appeal for funds from the affluent readers at whom the book was directed, called for nonsectarian schools, noninvolvement of the clergy in schools, the establishment of a state school board, and educational reform based on the philosophies and methodologies expounded by John Amos Comenius in *Orbis sensualium pictus* (1658; *The Visible World in Pictures*, 1659), by John Locke in *Some Thoughts Concerning Education* (1693), and by Jean-Jacques Rousseau in *Émile: Ou, De l'éducation* (1762; *Emilius and Sophia: Or, A New System of Education,* 1762-1763). Basedow's book received wide attention and, remarkably, brought to its author a flood of contributions sufficient to ensure his family's future for some years and to allow him the leisure to work on two other books he had promised his supporters. Contributions came to him from every sector—from Catholics, Protestants, Jews, and, quite particularly, Freemasons, to whom the secularization of education was especially appealing.

Two years afterward, Basedow published the books he had promised, *Des Methodenbuchs für Väter und Mütter der Familien und Völker* (1770; *Book of Methods for Fathers and Mothers of Families and Nations*, 1913) and *Des Elementarbuchs für die Jugend und für ihre Lehrer und Freunde in gesitteten Ständen* (1770), both of which were reissued later as the multivolume *Elementarwerke* (1774), as richly illustrated for pedagogical purposes as Comenius's *The Visible World in Pictures* had been. The aim of *Elementarwerke* was to entice children to read while keeping them completely captivated by what they were doing. The volumes covered much of what was then known about the world, including commerce, manners, virtue, science, and how to adapt to situations.

The work was received enthusiastically, and its publication encouraged Prince Leopold of Anhalt-Dessau to subsidize a school in which Basedow could practice his unique teaching methods. The prince offered Basedow a considerable yearly sum for his efforts. In December, 1774, Basedow, aided by three assistants, opened his quite expensive boarding school, the Philanthropinum (later named the Institute), to which the affluent, many of them daunted by the novelty of the operation, sent their children only in small numbers and often reluctantly, attracted usually because Basedow was eager to work with children who experienced difficulties in more conventional schools. At no time did the school's total enrollment exceed fifty students, including Basedow's two children.

Basedow expected to enroll three kinds of students: those who planned to attend a university, those preparing to become teachers themselves, and those who would enter service occupations after they left school. He encouraged impoverished students to enroll by offering them subventions, but attracting students to a school of this kind was a continuing problem, as were the financial struggles that continued to plague Basedow.

The school, which distributed a twenty-item list of rules and regulations, forbade its students to powder their hair and to rouge their cheeks, as was then the custom among many upper-class children. The school day was divided into segments for studying (five hours), for manual work and play (six hours), and for physical activities such as fencing, dancing, or singing (three hours). Although a religious attitude was encouraged among students, no time was devoted to the discussion of minor points of theological disagreement, as was the custom in many religiously oriented schools of that period.

Among its other departures from conventional educational practices, Basedow's school was coeducational. It emphasized play over study, consistent with the theory that real learning takes place from informal activities. Even the foreign languages the school offered, Latin and French, were approached by emphasizing the spoken languages rather than by the rote learning of vocabulary and of paradigms for the conjugation of verbs or the declension of nouns. Perhaps the most controversial element in Basedow's education new pedagogy, however, was its insistence that students receive sex education and that this education be provided in a straightforward and honest manner. Simple anatomical terms were to be used, along with charts and drawings that would amplify the instruction.

Basedow aimed to prepare students for the real world. So far did his means of achieving this end depart from expected norms that the public became indignant. Basedow, a tall person, unprepossessing in appearance, had a monumental ego that stood in the way of his communicating meaningfully with those who questioned his educational procedures. When challenged, he became defensive, so that his opponents usually wanted to defeat him rather than understand him.

Perhaps the greatest influence upon Basedow's educational philosophy, greater even than his reading of Rousseau's *Emilius and Sophia,* was John Locke's concept of the tabula rasa, the blank slate that Locke considered constituted the mind of every newborn infant, and his strident calls in *Some Thoughts Concerning Education* for an emphasis on physical education. Locke's conception of the human mind joined with his recognition of the need to develop a sound body justified Basedow's notion that observation, experience, and play are quintessential ingredients of any effective education.

Not surprisingly, Basedow lasted for only two years as director of his school before he turned to regular teaching. He continued teaching for eight more years, and in 1784 he resigned from the school altogether. The institution continued until 1793, when, burdened by debt and low enrollments, it was forced to close. The closing of the school did not mark the end of Basedow's educational influence. Joachim Heinrich Campe, who succeeded Basedow as director, opened a school of his own, based on Basedow's principles, in Hamburg and ran it for several years until he became director of education for the state of Brunswick. In his later years, in collaboration with others who admired Basedow's ideas, Campe published a sixteen-volume work that called for school reform of the kind Basedow had earlier promulgated.

Another educator who taught under Basedow's influence, Christian Saltzmann, founded his own school in Schnepfenthal in Coxe-Saxony in 1784 and ran it until his death, following Basedow's general pedagogical theories but adapting them wisely to his immediate situation. Saltzmann's school, on falling into the hands of his assistants, prospered and continued to flourish for more than one hundred years after its founding.

SIGNIFICANCE

Johann Bernhard Basedow is a striking example of a man far ahead of his time. Educational ideas that sounded extreme at the beginning of the eighteenth century are taken quite for granted by twentieth century Western society. Basedow, flourishing in a time of educational reform marked by such eminent thinkers as Rousseau, Johann Heinrich Pestalozzi, Johann Friedrich Herbart, and Friedrich Froebel, has not received the celebrity they commanded. Nevertheless, his educational writings and practices directly affected the history of Western education.

His idea of secularizing schools is widely accepted in most Western countries today. Basedow's support of co-education, at a time when such an idea was virtually unthinkable and when the education of women was severely limited, was courageous. That notion not only came of age in the twentieth century but also has finally been generally accepted, as has the establishment of central governing bodies for education as suggested by Basedow.

As Western society has grown more open, frank, and honest, sex education has pervaded the schools. As society has grown increasingly diverse and as the age for leaving school has increased in most countries, manual training, now extended to include sophisticated levels of vocational education, has become a significant element of education, having exceeded by far anything Basedow could have envisioned. Even though such an eminent figure as Immanuel Kant lauded Basedow's Philanthropinum publicly, most people were not yet ready for Basedow's proposals during his lifetime. His cause was undoubtedly damaged by his unattractive demeanor and by his enormous ego, both of which stood in the way of many who could not separate the man from his farsighted pedagogy.

—*R. Baird Shuman*

FURTHER READING

Good, Harry, and James D. Teller. *A History of American Education*. 3d ed. New York: Macmillan, 1973. This brief profile of Basedow relates his pedagogical theories to the development of education in the United States and comments on Kant's admiration of the Philanthropinum. The section sometimes tends to be irritatingly didactic.

_____. *A History of Western Education*. 3d ed. New York: Macmillan, 1969. This treatment, although brief, is fuller than that in the authors' *A History of American Education*. Offers good commentary on Basedow's most important books and considers contemporary criticism of those books.

Graves, Frank Pierrepont. *Great Educators of Three Centuries: Their Work and Its Influence on Modern Education*. New York: AMS Press, 1971. Reprint of a collection of lectures on education originally published in 1912. Includes a lecture on Basedow and the Philanthropinum.

Lucas, Christopher J. *Our Western Educational Heritage*. New York: Macmillan, 1971. Although brief, Lucas's treatment relates Basedow well to those who influenced him most substantially—Comenius, Locke, Rousseau—and presents a clear exposition on the establishment of the Philanthropinum.

Meyer, Adolphe E. *An Educational History of the Western World*. 2d ed. New York: McGraw-Hill, 1972. Meyer's presentation of Basedow, although limited, is in many ways the most complete one available. Overwritten but well researched and accurate, it gives valuable insights into the early influences that shaped Basedow's personality.

Randall, John Herman. *The Making of the Modern Mind*. 50th anniversary ed. New York: Columbia University Press, 1976. A brilliant overall cultural history that relates Basedow to the philosophical movement of rationalism. Badly dated, but the book's shrewd observations make it worthwhile for modern readers.

See also: Immanuel Kant; Jean-Jacques Rousseau.
Related articles in *Great Events from History: The Eighteenth Century, 1701-1800*: August 3, 1713: Foundation of the Spanish Academy; 1741: Leadhills Reading Society Promotes Literacy; 1782-1798: Publication of Rousseau's *Confessions*; 1785: First State Universities Are Established.

JOHN BASKERVILLE
English printer and designer

Baskerville designed and produced printing type, or fonts, and crafted and printed meticulously designed books that set new standards for fine printing.

Born: January 28, 1706 (baptized); Wolverly, Worcestershire, England
Died: January 8, 1775; Birmingham, England
Area of achievement: Science and technology

EARLY LIFE

John Baskerville was born in a rural district in England. Very little is known about his parents, family, and early life. He evidently was the last of many children, most of whom died young. The first notice of his activities comes in 1723, when he was taken on as a footman in the rectory of King's Norton, near Birmingham. The clergyman noticed that his young servant had some education, talent, and interest in writing and made him the writing master for the parish.

In 1726, Baskerville moved into Birmingham proper and established himself as a writing master. At about the same time, his interest in writing and letters led him to learn the trade of stone carving, with special attention to gravestone engraving. The one surviving example of his work, a small slab used as a shop-window display, illustrates his considerable talent as a designer of letters. Nevertheless, Baskerville seems to have barely eked out a living as writing master and stone engraver.

Eighteenth century Birmingham was a flourishing town, a magnet for many industrious individuals eager to exploit the town's location and resources to participate in England's expanding economy. One such person was John Taylor. In the mid-1730's, Taylor established a japanning business in Birmingham. Japanning, a technique for painting metal or wood surfaces, had been introduced into England from Asia. The procedure involved applying several layers of a special varnish to produce a deep, luxurious appearance. A variety of colors and ornamental figures and scenes could be painted on the more expensive items. Japanned goods were in great demand by England's style-conscious middle class. Taylor, and others, became wealthy supplying this growing demand for attractive domestic goods.

Baskerville followed in his footsteps, possibly literally. One story about Baskerville, probably apocryphal but nevertheless interesting, has it that he followed Taylor from shop to shop buying identical amounts of the same ingredients for the varnish. In this manner, he supposedly learned both the contents and their proportions in the varnish. Whether the story is true, Baskerville managed to set up a successful japanning business by 1740, employing many workers in his shop. In 1742, he obtained a patent for a process for grinding and shaping thin metal plates before japanning.

LIFE'S WORK

John Baskerville continued with his japanning enterprise for the rest of his life. In the 1740's, he rose rapidly to a position of wealth and looked the part of the eighteenth century English bourgeois: full-faced and jowly, with a prominent nose and slightly bushy eyebrows. He was notorious for his fondness for rich, bright clothing and was pictured wearing a powdered wig, green coat, scarlet waistcoat, and gold lace. He had a specially made chariot with lavishly japanned door panels and in 1748 built a fine house just outside town. He was considered vain, highly sensitive, and pedantic. Also, he endured a certain amount of antipathy because he lived for years with a woman who remained married to her exiled husband, although Baskerville eventually married her, after her first husband died.

Nevertheless, Baskerville became a man of substance in the community: He was a member of the Lunar Society, a famous Birmingham society of men interested in science and Enlightenment thought. His reputation as a writing master and connoisseur of fine penmanship coincided with his position as an entrepreneur and maker of fine metalwares. At about this time, he became interested in combining his interest in letters and metalworking by producing a printing type of his own design. Convinced that his letters would appear favorably only if he controlled their use, he set up a print shop along with his typefoundry. Designing and casting type and printing books was almost a hobby for him, and never his primary source of income. Still, his influence on the book trades was substantial.

Producing type first required a design for the typeface, and it was here that Baskerville made his real contribution. He developed a style of type in various sizes that drew upon his experiences as a writing master. His typefaces had a particular cant and a strong delineation between thick and thin strokes, much like handwriting. After drawing the individual letters, each one had to be cut in relief onto the end of a steel shank. This shank, or punch, was hardened and then driven into a piece of copper, creating a mold, or matrix, for the letter. The matrix was fitted into a wooden mold and molten metal was poured into it. Type was cast by skilled workers in Baskerville's own foundry. Baskerville was primarily assisted by John Handy, who was evidently responsible for cutting the punches and ensuring that the individually cast type was flawless.

Creating font types of his own design and manufacture was only the beginning for Baskerville. His goal was to produce books of great typographical art and distinction. He carefully laid out the margins and spacing of each page. He acquired a knowledge of printing presses and made some minor adjustments to his. Baskerville paid special attention to the quality of ink and paper used. Indeed, he developed his own procedure for making ink and experimented with making small quantities of paper. He was the first book printer to use "wove" paper, that is, paper made from molds in which the wire is interlaced to produce a strong, fine paper. Perhaps what gave each page its distinctive sheen was that each sheet passed through heated copper rollers or plates immediately after printing. This process, akin to calendaring paper and also to the process Baskerville had developed for metal

John Baskerville. (Hulton Archive/Getty Images)

plates, set the ink as well as compressing the paper fibers themselves. His attention to these details and his innovations produced books that had a look unlike any others of the eighteenth century.

Baskerville chose to publish books on the basis of their stature in literature rather than their money-making potential. His goal was to provide models of fine typography and printing. He printed his first book, Vergil's *Bucolica, Georgica et Aeneis,* in 1757, some eight or nine years after beginning his typographical efforts. Over the next eighteen years, he printed only about fifty-four more books, but they included some of the most innovative, aesthetically pleasing, and talked-about volumes of his own and subsequent times. He produced notable volumes of John Milton, Horace, Joseph Addison, William Congreve, and the earl of Shaftesbury. In 1758, he was appointed printer at Cambridge. There he produced an edition of the Book of Common Prayer and, in 1763, a folio edition of the Bible. Soon afterward he ended his association with the university.

Baskerville's type design and printed works were controversial. Many people believed that his highly contrasting typefaces and bright pages were difficult and tiring to read. In fact, his aesthetic was more influential in

Europe, especially France, than in his homeland. After his death, in 1775, his widow—to whom, in the absence of progeny, he had left his estate—sold most of his foundry equipment, including the punches, to Pierre-Augustin Caron de Beaumarchais in France. For the next twenty years, his type designs were more common there than in his homeland. In 1953, however, the remaining punches and matrices were presented to Cambridge University as a gift from the French printing firm of Deberny Peignot.

SIGNIFICANCE

John Baskerville exemplifies an important social trend in eighteenth century England: the opening of society to persons of talent and ambition. From humble beginnings, he managed to become a wealthy, influential, and respectable member of an international community, counting Matthew Boulton, Benjamin Franklin, and Pierre-Augustin Caron de Beaumarchais among his admirers.

His contributions to the book trades include some of the most distinguished examples of fine printing ever produced. He provided a model of type and book design that altered the standards of typography during the last half of the eighteenth century. He demonstrated that typeface, layout, presswork, and material all played a significant role in the art of the book. Baskerville's typefaces, which were revived in the early twentieth century, found a popular reception and have been adapted to machine typesetting.

—*William S. Pretzer*

FURTHER READING

Benton, Josiah H. *John Baskerville: Type-founder and Printer, 1706-1775.* 1914. Reprint. New York: Burt Franklin, 1968. An early and important biography full of opinions about Baskerville's works.

Dreyfus, John. *The Survival of Baskerville's Punches.* Cambridge, England: Private printing, 1949. A careful history of the uses and fate of the punches for Baskerville types.

Gaskell, Philip. *John Baskerville: A Bibliography.* 2d ed. New York: Cambridge University Press, 1973. A short introduction to Baskerville's work and a full bibliographic description of his publications.

Legros, Lucien A., and J. C. Grant. *Typographical Printing-Surfaces: The Technology and Mechanism of Their Production.* London: Longmans, Green, 1916. A magisterial work covering nearly all aspects of typefounding.

Pardoe, Frank E. *John Baskerville of Birmingham: Letter-Founder and Printer.* London: Frederick Muller, 1975. A modern biography that exceeds all previous Baskerville biographies in scholarship and objectivity.

Reed, Talbot B. *A History of the Old English Letter Foundries.* Edited by A. F. Johnson. London: Faber and Faber, 1952. A seminal work on the history of typefounding in England with a substantial section on Baskerville, placing his types in the context of English typography.

Straus, Ralph, and Robert K. Dent. *John Baskerville: A Memoir.* Cambridge, England: Cambridge University Press, 1907. A biography that made use of local research materials and personal items and is the source of much personal information about Baskerville. A standard source.

Uglow, Jenny. *The Lunar Men: Five Friends Whose Curiosity Changed the World.* New York: Farrar, Straus and Giroux, 2002. The book focuses on five Birmingham scientists and inventors who organized a society to share their knowledge. One of the five, Matthew Boulton, was a friend of Baskerville, and the book describes the friendship. It also discusses Baskerville's work and personality.

Updike, Daniel B. *Printing Types: Their History, Forms, and Use.* 4th ed. New Castle, Del.: Oak Knoll Press, 2001. A seminal work on every aspect of typography, with some special attention to the aesthetic properties of Baskerville's type. Expanded edition.

See also: Joseph Addison; Pierre-Augustin Caron de Beaumarchais; Matthew Boulton; Benjamin Franklin; John Newbery.

Related articles in *Great Events from History: The Eighteenth Century, 1701-1800:* 1702 or 1706: First Arabic Printing Press; Beginning April, 1763: The *North Briton* Controversy.

Hester Bateman
English silversmith and businesswoman

Bateman expanded a small workshop into one of the most important silver manufacturing houses in England and produced a prodigious amount of domestic silver objects remarkable for their elegance and innovative design. The Bateman family's works are highly prized collectibles.

Born: October 7, 1708 (baptized); London, England
Died: September 16, 1794; St. Andrew, Holborn, England
Also known as: Hester Needham (birth name); Hester Neden
Areas of achievement: Art, patronage of the arts, business

Early Life
The birth of Hester Bateman, the third child of Thomas Needham and Ann Needham née Booth, was never formally registered. Ann wed Thomas, who had at least two children from previous marriages, in May 1703. She was his third wife. Hester received no formal education, and as an adult she signed legal documents with an "X."

Around 1725, Hester Needham married John Bateman at "The Fleet," a debtors' prison where jailed parsons performed weddings in exchange for gin or tobacco. The couple held a formal church ceremony on May 20, 1732. John earned a living as a wire drawer and chain maker, which means he finished or made small pieces for master goldsmiths and silversmiths, who then branded the work as their own. Although he had some formal schooling, he never completed an apprenticeship, and thus could not legally work within London's city limits. As was common practice at the time, Hester Bateman worked alongside her husband in his shop.

Hester and John Bateman had six children. Their first, John, was born in 1730, followed by Letticia and Ann by 1736. Peter arrived in 1740, William in 1745, and Jonathan in 1747. Around 1740, the Batemans lived in Cripplegate, a middle-class neighborhood popular with silver and gold workers. In 1747, they moved to Bunhill Row, a street in an upscale neighborhood just outside London, and employed at least one maid but probably more. They eventually purchased the houses directly next to their own, and subsequent generations of Bateman's occupied these properties for more than one hundred years.

In 1760, Hester Bateman's husband died of consumption. His will stipulated that she was to receive all of his silversmithing tools, which clearly indicated that he expected she would carry on his business.

Life's Work
As anticipated, and like many widowed silversmiths and other tradespersons of the time, Hester Bateman took over her husband's workshop after his death. She was fifty-one years old. She registered her first silversmith's mark, an "HB" composed in scroll letters, in 1761 at Goldsmith's Hall in London. She initially continued her husband's practice of filling contracts for master silversmiths who stamped the work as their own. In 1774, however, she sharply curtailed the amount of outwork done in her shop and began creating the now sought-after pieces stamped with the "HB" mark.

Bateman specialized in useful domestic products, and her silver is most widely appreciated for its elegance and simplicity. Among the some eleven thousand pieces thought to bear the "HB" mark are spoons, forks, dinner plates, goblets, creamers, wine labels, sugar bowls, and teapots. Unlike most silversmiths of the time, however, Bateman did not limit the variety of products she made. Because she received commissions from wealthy individuals, city guilds, government offices, businesses, and churches in England and Wales, her oeuvre extends to medals, trophies, spurs, and ecclesiastical items, including a pair of verger's wands still being used at St. Paul's Cathedral in London.

The great majority of Bateman's work nonetheless catered to the growing middle class. She utilized time-saving production methods and took full advantage of new technologies to keep prices within their financial reach. While some of her more famous contemporaries continued to create flamboyant pieces, she capitalized on the trend for classic design that began in the mid-eighteenth century, when archaeological discoveries were made at Herculaneum and Pompeii. Her work thus favored simple decorative elements such as beaded edging, piercing, and bright-cut engraving. As the name suggests, beaded edging creates a pattern that recalls a row of dots or beads. Piercing involves cutting away pieces of silver with a steel blade. Bright-cut engraving, a technique popularized in the mid-eighteenth century, is achieved with a special tool that makes faceted, light-reflecting chips in the silver. Bateman's sons are most likely responsible for the bright-cut engraving adorning her work.

Some scholars argue Bateman lacked the training and

skill to have ever made or designed a piece of silver herself. Given that "maker's marks" are better termed "sponsor's marks," and that the masters designated by the stamps often had little or no physical contact with the objects, this viewpoint—true or not—does nothing to diminish Bateman's reputation for superior marketing skills and business acumen. She ran a highly productive silversmith house.

Under her leadership, the small shop grew into a manufacturing enterprise that ranked among the top silver producers from about 1770 to 1810. Robust economic conditions enabled many women silversmiths to gain prominence in the eighteenth century, but Bateman's large-scale success warrants special commendation given that women-owned businesses were generally not accepted as legitimate. Furthermore, silver was a risky industry. Highly skilled French Huguenot (Protestant) silversmiths seeking religious freedom in England provided stiff competition for customers, and the growing popularity of Sheffield plate (low-cost sheets of copper and silver hammered together) was driving many silversmiths out of business.

Despite the challenges, Bateman prospered. One of her sons had completed his apprenticeship and another nearly finished when she assumed control of the family business, and they ultimately worked in the shop alongside Bateman and their siblings, their sibling's spouses, and apprentices. Bateman quite likely employed outworkers, too. For most of the period of her management, at least seven people worked exclusively on the silver items sold with the "HB" mark.

Bateman retired in 1790, after thirty-one years at the helm of the family business. Her sons, Peter and Jonathan, immediately took over the shop and acquired a joint mark in December, but Jonathan died about four months later, in 1791. Peter then teamed with Ann Bateman née Dowling, his late brother's wife and an accomplished silversmith with blood ties to the silversmiths of the French court. Peter and Ann successfully continued the business into the first years of the nineteenth century. Ann's son, William, gained partner status in 1815, and his son, also named William, took over operations in 1839. The last Bateman piece dates to about 1877.

Nothing is known of Hester Bateman's life after retirement, other than that she lived in Holbrook with her daughter and died in 1794.

SIGNIFICANCE

The large number of dealers, collectors, and museums with an interest in Hester Bateman's silver pieces provides incontrovertible evidence of her importance in the world of antiques. In the 1970's, her work commanded double and triple the price of similar pieces by her contemporaries—female or male—and a large number of Bateman fakes now troubles the market. Her influence extends beyond the showroom, too, as there are references to Bateman silver in novels such as Jonathan Gash's *The Ten Word Game* (2004) and Jonathan Kellerman's *Billy Straight: A Novel* (1998). Bateman herself is the subject of Rosalind Laker's historical romance novel *The Silver Touch* (1987).

At a time when women were not encouraged to compete on equal footing with men, Bateman's shrewd management skills grew a small family business into a thriving enterprise. The compelling story of a middle-aged widow left to support a large family, however, often overshadows her considerable achievements in business and marketing. Bateman's entrepreneurial successes, and that of several of her notable female contemporaries, has yet to receive the level of study and recognition it deserves.

—Rose Reifsnyder

FURTHER READING

Ewald, Elin Lake. "Hester Bateman: Eighteenth-Century Silversmith." *Ms.* 4 (March, 1976): 40-46. Provides a solid contextual background for eighteenth century women silversmiths and the silversmith trade, along with a discussion of the business and artistic decisions that ensured Bateman's success in her lifetime and into the present day. Includes a sidebar explaining how silver objects were made.

Glanville, Philippa, and Jennifer Faulds Goldsborough. *Women Silversmiths, 1685-1845: Works from the Collection of the National Museum of Women in the Arts.* New York: Thames and Hudson, 1990. Provides an excellent discussion of women's roles in and contributions to the business of making and selling silver objects. Includes a social and artistic context for specific pieces (shown in full-color photographs) created by Bateman and more than thirty-five other prominent women silversmiths.

Robinson, Jane. *Women Out of Bounds.* New York: Carroll & Graf, 2002. Robinson provides a very short synopsis of Bateman's life and work.

Scott, Deborah. "The Cult of Hester Bateman." *Antique Collector* (April, 1984): 74-79. While recognizing Bateman's importance as a business leader, the article argues that Bateman herself probably never made or designed a piece of silver.

Shure, David S. *Hester Bateman, Queen of English Sil-versmiths.* Garden City, N.Y.: Doubleday, 1959. A comprehensive, if uncritical, account of Bateman, her family, and her silversmith business. Incorporates extensive research of parish records and includes a family tree. Black-and-white plates illustrate silver pieces made in Bateman's workshop.

Wees, Beth Carver. *English, Irish, and Scottish Silver at the Sterling and Francine Clark Art Museum.* New York: Hudson Hills Press, 1997. Includes numerous references to and illustrations of silver pieces by Bateman and many members of her family.

See also: Matthew Boulton; Paul Revere; Josiah Wedgwood.

Related articles in *Great Events from History: The Eighteenth Century, 1701-1800:* 1701: Plumier Publishes *L'Art de tourner*; 1797: Wollaston Begins His Work on Metallurgy.

PIERRE-AUGUSTIN CARON DE BEAUMARCHAIS
French dramatist

Beaumarchais was an inventor, political agent, musician, and writer whose place in history was most firmly established by two dramatic works, The Barber of Seville *and* The Marriage of Figaro. *The plays highlight central issues of the French political climate in the late 1700's by poking fun at the aristocracy and enunciating a middle-class point of view.*

Born: January 24, 1732; Paris, France
Died: May 18, 1799; Paris, France
Also known as: Pierre-Augustin Caron (birth name)
Areas of achievement: Literature, government and politics, music

EARLY LIFE

Pierre-Augustin Caron de Beaumarchais (pee-ehr-aw-goo-sta kah-rohn duh boh-mahr-shay) was one of ten children of André-Charles Caron and the former Louise-Nichole Pichon. An artistic child, Pierre exhibited his creativity early and in a number of ways. He learned to play the flute, violin, and harp. Having learned the clock maker trade from his father, at twenty-one years of age, Pierre invented a new watch escapement mechanism, for which he was awarded a patent in 1754 from the French Academy of Sciences. He was known at court for having made a watch for Mme Pompadour and was subsequently contracted to make a watch for King Louis XV. He was also appointed music teacher to the king's daughters. In 1756, he married a wealthy widow, Madeleine Francquet. She died only a year later, leaving Pierre her property, from which he then took the name "Beaumarchais."

Beaumarchais was a handsome, shrewd individual with strong social ambitions. Unable to resist the temptation of politics and its intrigues, he was sent on a mission to England by Joseph Pâris-Duverney, the financial adviser to Mme Pompadour, to negotiate for a monopoly of the slave trade. Although unsuccessful in his efforts, he accumulated business skills and began amassing a fortune of his own as Pâris-Duverney's associate. In 1761, he purchased the office of secretary to the king.

LIFE'S WORK

In 1764, Beaumarchais traveled to Spain for commercial ventures and to seek revenge for his family on José Clavijo y Farjardo, keeper of the Spanish royal archives, who had twice pledged to marry Beaumarchais's sister Marie but had broken his promises. Although not a tragic encounter, the German romantic writer Johann Wolfgang von Goethe later used Beaumarchais's account of the event in his *Mémoires* (1773-1774) as inspiration for his tragic drama, *Clavigo* (pr., pb. 1774; English translation, 1798, 1897). Beaumarchais himself used the incident as the basis for *Eugénie* (pr., pb. 1767; *The School of Rakes*, 1795), his first drama. The play had only modest success, as did *Les Deux Amis: Ou, Le Négotiant de Lyon* (pr., pb. 1770; *The Two Friends: Or, The Liverpool Merchant*, 1800), but these two works and his experiences in Spain marked the beginning of one of the most distinguished careers in French dramatic history.

In 1768, Beaumarchais married Geneviève-Madeleine Wetterbled Lévêque. Mme de Beaumarchais died in 1770 amid unfounded rumors that her husband had poisoned her. In this period, he continued to write short, witty stage works called *parades*. He also wrote pamphlets and memoirs concerning legal cases in which he was involved as an agent for the king and to defend himself from problems arising from sexual liaisons. His

Pierre-Augustin Caron de Beaumarchais. (Library of Congress)

Mémoires were a product of these essays, and with them he began to gain true acclaim as a writer. Unsurpassed for their humorous satirical style, they were said to have been the envy of Voltaire, whose books had been banned from publication. After Voltaire's death, Beaumarchais opened a printing business in Kehl to escape French censors and made available the first complete set of Voltaire's works, in seventy volumes (1784-1790). Unfortunately, the edition was a financial disaster.

Beaumarchais was preoccupied by the plight of the social classes and their treatment by the court. He addressed these issues in his writing. Paradoxically, he was pleading the case for the lower classes against the nobility of which he had become a member; however, his status informed him of the issues from the viewpoints of both the court and the public. In 1772, Beaumarchais wrote the first of the two dramatic works (part of a trilogy) that were to bring him lasting literary fame. *Le Barbier de Séville: Ou, La Précaution inutile* (pr., pb. 1775; *The Barber of Seville: Or, The Useless Precaution,* 1776) was rejected by the Théâtre Italien. Although in 1773 and 1774 the Comédie-Française accepted the play for production, Beaumarchais's questionable political involvements brought recriminations from the court, and

the play was prohibited from opening. In 1775, after he was finally granted royal permission to premier *The Barber of Seville*, the opening was a complete failure. In three days, Beaumarchais cut the play from five acts to four, and it was produced the second time to great applause.

The story is of a clever servant (Figaro, the barber) who impertinently spoils the marriage plans of Dr. Bartholo, Rosine's elderly guardian, in order to advance a love affair between Rosine and a Spanish nobleman, Count Almaviva. Clear glimpses of the growing revolutionary sentiment among the middle class in France are revealed, as the servant is cast as superior in wit and cunning to the nobility whom he serves. In 1778, Beaumarchais continued his crafty assault on the upper classes in *La Folle Journée: Ou, Le Mariage de Figaro* (wr. 1775-1778, pr. 1784, pb. 1785; *The Marriage of Figaro*, 1784), in which the barber himself seeks permission to marry the countess's maidservant. Unfortunately, the philandering count also has designs on Susanna, and it is up to the servants again to outwit the nobility. Beaumarchais's less than subtle attacks on French nobility did not escape the notice of King Louis XVI, and the play was banned for a number of years. It was performed in a private home in 1783, and, finally, in 1784, it received its first public performance. The third play in the trilogy, *L'Autre Tartuffe: Ou, La Mère Coupable* (pr. 1792, pb. 1797; *Frailty and Hypocrisy*, 1804) was not as strong a work as its earlier counterparts and has never been widely acclaimed.

American independence was another major issue that occupied Beaumarchais. In 1776, as France was struggling with the disruption of its class system, the American colonies were fighting England. Beaumarchais began correspondence in 1775 with Charles Gravier, comte de Vergennes, the French foreign minister. Vergennes gave Beaumarchais one million livres in 1776 to finance ships and munitions for the American colonies. Beaumarchais remained a main director of France's activity in support of the American Revolution. In 1779, a letter from the American Congress declared their debt to him, which, despite reminders, was never repaid. His revolutionary activities extended to his being a secret agent and gunrunner for France during the French Revolution. In 1792, a deal to purchase guns from Holland for

France won him prison time and inclusion on a list of émigrés.

In 1786, Beaumarchais had married Marie-Thérèse Willermanulas, and he moved his family to Hamburg until 1796, when they were finally allowed to reenter Paris. The government continued to investigate him for his political involvements and his financial situation deteriorated. In 1799, he died of apoplexy in Paris.

SIGNIFICANCE

Pierre-Augustin Caron de Beaumarchais was a multifaceted human being with many professional accomplishments. A man of the Enlightenment, he was an inventor, musician, politician, secret agent, revolutionary, and literary figure. The human social values promoted in his stage works represent the cornerstone of Beaumarchais's beliefs. They reflect the changing times in which he lived, when the Western world was experiencing revolution and significant turbulence within the established social classes. Although he bought himself membership in the nobility, he believed strongly in each person's right to make the choices that brought happiness. That same spirit provoked his involvement in American and French politics when, at great personal risk, he aggressively assisted the cause of independence.

It was his two major dramatic masterpieces–*The Barber of Seville* and *The Marriage of Figaro*—however, that left his mark on the world. In these works, Beaumarchais expressed his love of freedom and passion for the liberated human soul. The plays were influential beyond France and became the basis for opera librettos for two famous composers. In 1786, Wolfgang Amadeus Mozart used the *The Marriage of Figaro* as the basis for his opera of the same title, produced in Vienna. In 1816, Gioacchino Rossini (1792-1868) wrote his operatic version of *The Barber of Seville*, which was produced in Rome. The operatic stories are somewhat altered and have lives of their own, but they have done much to help keep the spirit of Beaumarchais's writing alive.

—*Sandra C. McClain*

FURTHER READING

Beaumarchais, Pierre-Augustin Caron de. *The Figaro Trilogy*. New York: Oxford University Press, 2003. Includes all three plays in a new English translation by David Coward, whose introduction gives helpful historical context and chronology of Beaumarchais's life and work.

Frischauer, Paul. *Beaumarchais: Adventurer in the Century of Women*. New York: Viking Press, 1935. Interesting account of Beaumarchais's life as it was affected by the important women of his time: Countess du Barry, Mme Pompadour, and Marie-Antoinette. Good for historical perspective.

Howarth, W. D. *Beaumarchais and the Theatre*. New York: Routledge, 1995. Provides an excellent discussion of prevailing scholarship on Beaumarchais and French theater, some of which was not previously available in English translation.

Morton, Brian N., and Donald C. Spinelli. *Beaumarchais and the American Revolution*. Lanham, Md.: Rowman and Littlefield, 2003. Detailed historical account of Beaumarchais's revolutionary activities in France and America.

Ratermanis, J. B., and W. R. Irwin. *The Comic Style of Beaumarchais*. Seattle: University of Washington Press, 1961. Analyzes Beaumarchais's style in the context of eighteenth century French theater and his use of literary comic conventions to make aesthetic points. Figaro and Barber are discussed in detail, but introduction and conclusion chapters provide succinct point summaries.

Tallentyre, S. G. *The Friends of Voltaire*. New York: G. P. Putnam's Sons, 1907. Chapter on Beaumarchais is an easily readable account of his life with attention to the literary works as well as the author's political and revolutionary activity.

See also: Louis XV; Louis XVI; Wolfgang Amadeus Mozart; Madame de Pompadour; Charles Gravier de Vergennes.

Related articles in *Great Events from History: The Eighteenth Century, 1701-1800*: May, 1776-September 3, 1783: France Supports the American Revolution; April 27, 1784: First Performance of *The Marriage of Figaro*; July 14, 1789: Fall of the Bastille; April 20, 1792-October, 1797: Early Wars of the French Revolution; January 21, 1793: Execution of Louis XVI.

CESARE BECCARIA
Italian economist and criminologist

Beccaria's An Essay on Crimes and Punishments *became one of the major works of the Enlightenment, leading to prison reform, judicial reform, and the abolition of cruel and inhumane punishment. Translated into almost every European language, it remains the single most important work on criminology.*

Born: March 15, 1738; Milan (now in Italy)
Died: November 28, 1794; Milan
Also known as: Cesare Bonesana Beccaria (full name); Marchese di Beccaria
Areas of achievement: Law, social reform

EARLY LIFE

Cesare Beccaria (CHAY-zahr-ay bayk-kah-REE-ah) was the eldest child of an aristocratic Milanese family. At the age of eight, he started his formal education at a Jesuit school in Parma. He found this education to be wedded to fanaticism and antithetical to the spirit of humanism. He attended the University of Parva, where he received a law degree in 1758. There was little about Cesare during his early years that marked him as particularly exceptional.

Cesare's first life crisis came in 1760, when his parents objected to his engagement to the sixteen-year-old Teresa di Blasco. Cesare married her anyway in 1761, and his parents relented in their objections once the first of three children was born in 1762. At the time of his marriage, Cesare formed a close friendship with two brothers, Pietro Verri and Alessandro Verri, who were leading Milanese supporters of the Enlightenment. The three formed an intellectual society called the Academy of Fists. The group focused on the political writings of such philosophers as Thomas Hobbes, David Hume, Denis Diderot, and Montesquieu. Reform of the prison system became a topic of intense discussion, as did economics and the general reform of public policy. Pietro was interested in writing a history of torture, while Alessandro, who was a Milanese prison official, related the horrors he had witnessed in day-to-day prison life. From 1764 to 1766, the three friends published the Enlightenment journal *Il Caffé*, which contained both their own work and that of others.

Beccaria's first published writing had been a 1762 article on monetary disorders in Milan. In it, he examined the value of goods and the relationship of value to quantity, transportability, tax policies, and the number of sellers in relation to buyers. His second economic piece, written in 1764, studied the relationship of high tariffs to smuggling. Beccaria found that high tariffs led to increased smuggling, which in turn led to decreased tariff revenues. He therefore concluded that raising tariffs was a self-defeating policy. However, it was another treatise *Dei delitti e delle penne* (1764; *An Essay on Crimes and Punishments*, 1767) that transformed a virtually unknown twenty-six-year-old into a famous Enlightenment intellectual and writer.

LIFE'S WORK

The idea of writing an essay on crime and punishment originated with the Verri brothers, and they seem to have provided Beccaria with information as well as editorial help. The essay was first published anonymously. Beccaria put his name to future editions of *An Essay on Crimes and Punishments* only after the work received official praise instead of condemnation.

Beccaria's landmark work begins by declaring that criminal laws, which have never been given proper study, are in great need of reform. For Beccaria, justice should be rational rather than emotional and based on the utilitarian principle of providing the greatest happiness to the greatest number of individuals in society. The end goal of justice is not punishment or vengeance but rather bringing security and order to society, protecting the social contract, and promoting the public good. Punishments should fit crimes and be geared toward stopping individuals from committing crimes. Beccaria found certainty and swiftness of punishment to be a far greater deterrence to future crime than cruelty or severity of punishment. He also asserted that punishment should be based on clearly stated rational laws passed by a legislature and widely known by society. Laws should be clear enough to allow judges and juries to decide questions of fact, such as guilt or innocence, rather than becoming bogged down interpreting the law itself.

Beccaria found that the degree of virtue and education in society, as well as the rewards given for good behavior, were powerful deterrents to crime. Capital punishment, on the other hand, did not serve as a deterrent. Instead, it provided a nonvirtuous example for people that it is proper to take lives. He found the use of torture to be one of the worst of barbarities continued from the primitive past, because the practice condemned both the guilty and the innocent and favored the strong over the weak. Prisons, for Beccaria, became institutions where punishment was designed to reform the criminal and resocialize individuals so they could later contribute to the public good.

Beccaria's work was an instant success. It was translated into French in 1766 by André Morellet (who also edited the structure to make it more logically cohesive) and underwent seven editions in six months. It was translated into most major European languages and was printed in the United States in 1777. Beccaria visited Paris in 1766 as an Enlightenment hero. However, something happened during the visit. Some historians refer to personality quirks that soon made Beccaria a subject of ridicule by fellow intellectuals. Others refer to his homesickness, which caused him to race back to Milan after a short three-week visit. Still others refer to a manic-depressive (bipolar) personality, which shifted after a few years of frenetic intellectual activity into incapacitating depression. Suffice it to say that Beccaria ended his friendship with the Verri brothers and other members of his intellectual circle. He stopped writing and did not produce a single essay again.

In 1768, Beccaria received a chair in public economy at the Palantine School in Milan, where he lectured for two years. In 1771, he was appointed to the supreme Economic Council of Milan, where he drew a salary as a public official until his death. On the council, he discussed many issues pertaining to economic and educational reform but did not choose to write about them. Beccaria remarried in 1774, three months after the death of his first wife. He then became involved in many depressing years of legal squabbling with his brothers and sisters over family inheritance. The coming of the French Revolution in 1789 filled Beccaria with joyful optimism that the French could build a rational society based on serving the public good. However, with the advent of the Reign of Terror in 1794, optimism turned into despair. He died in Milan on November 28, 1794, before the Reign of Terror reached its apex.

SIGNIFICANCE

At the height of the Enlightenment, in a single essay, Cesare Beccaria introduced modern ethical and intellectual principles to criminal law and the penal system. *An Essay on Crimes and Punishments* found instant receptivity throughout Europe and was embraced by the so-called Enlightened Despots. Indeed, as his influence spread, if one wished to cast one's national image as "modern" or "progressive," Beccaria's re-

forms simply could not be ignored. Beccaria's ideas also found great acceptance in the United States, where they influenced the framers of the U.S. Constitution and the writing of the Bill of Rights, and became part of the basic principles of the U.S. judicial system. *An Essay on Crimes and Punishments* also was incorporated into the judicial reform movement in England: Reformers such as Samuel Romilly used Beccaria's arguments to reduce the number of capital crimes in the nation.

In the twentieth century, Beccaria's lucid arguments became the basis for renewed prison reform, for the termination of the death penalty in many European nations, and even for more humane means of execution in those nations that retained it. The fact that his treatise remains a "must read" in most classes in criminology through the early twenty-first century is ample testimony to both the power and progressive nature of his ideas. Since no individual system has completely enacted Beccaria's proposed reforms, his influence is still felt in all efforts to further reform criminal law.

Beccaria's utilitarian arguments advocating the greatest good for the greatest number influenced the formation of the British Utilitarian movement under Jeremy Benthem. Beccaria's economic ideas, while having little lasting impact, are interesting in that they predated the writings of other tariff reformers and in their similarity to some of the major conclusions of the economist Adam Smith.

—Irwin Halfond

FURTHER READING

Akers, Ronald L., and Christine S. Sellers. *Criminological Theories: Introduction, Evaluation, and Application*. Los Angeles: Roxbury, 2000. A textbook study of Beccaria's ideas and their influence on criminology to contemporary times.

Maestro, Marcello T. *Cesare Beccaria and the Origins of Penal Reform*. Philadelphia: Temple University Press, 1973. Still the best of the few studies on Beccaria. Index and bibliography.

Phillipson, Coleman. *Three Criminal Law Reformers: Beccaria, Bentham, Romilly*. Montclair, N.J.: Patterson Smith, 1970. An interesting study of Beccaria and the influence of his ideas on later judicial reformers. Bibliography and index.

Young, David, ed. *On Crimes and Punishments*. Indianapolis, Ind.: Hackett, 1997. A textbook paperback translation of Beccaria's famous essay containing a lengthy and informative introduction.

See also: Jeremy Bentham; Denis Diderot; David Hume; Montesquieu; Adam Smith.
Related articles in *Great Events from History: The Eighteenth Century, 1701-1800*: 1748: Montesquieu Pub-

lishes *The Spirit of the Laws*; September 17, 1787: U.S. Constitution Is Adopted; December 15, 1791: U.S. Bill of Rights Is Ratified; April 20, 1792-October, 1797: Early Wars of the French Revolution.

BENEDICT XIV
Roman Catholic pope (1740-1758)

Benedict XIV is best known for his extensive scholarship and writing on a broad range of ecclesiastical, historical, and legal matters. As pope, he deftly directed Church affairs at a time when European powers and the Enlightenment directly threatened the central role that Catholicism had traditionally played in Western culture.

Born: March 31, 1675; Bologna, Papal States (now in Italy)
Died: May 3, 1758; Rome, Papal States
Also known as: Prospero Lorenzo Lambertini (birth name)
Areas of achievement: Religion and theology, government and politics

EARLY LIFE

The future Benedict XIV was born into the patrician family of Marcello Lambertini and Lucretia Lambertini of Bologna. He was christened Prospero Lorenzo. The young Lambertini's early education came from tutors, and when he was thirteen years old he went to Rome to study at the Collegium Clementianum. There he developed strong interests in history, literature, and theology and directed his studies toward law and theology. He graduated from the University of Rome with doctoral degrees in both civil and canon law and in theology at the age of nineteen.

A hard-working rather than brilliant scholar, Lambertini went on to hold numerous offices in the Church hierarchy, beginning with assistant lawyer in the Curia. In 1701, Pope Clement XI appointed him consistorial advocate for two canonization procedures (that is, procedures for raising people to the status of sainthood), and in 1708 he was raised to the office of promoter of the faith, overseeing all canonization activities. As he would do so often, Lambertini used his experience as overseer of canonization to produce an important study of the process titled *De servorum Dei beatificatione et beatorum canonizatione* (1734-1738; on the beatification of the servants of God and the canonization of the beatified), which remains a significant manual.

In 1712, Lambertini became canon theologian at the Vatican and assessor of the Congregation of Rites; in 1718, he was made secretary of the Congregation of the Council. In 1725, he was appointed titular bishop of Theodosia, and two years later he became bishop of Ancona in Italy. On April 30, 1728, Pope Benedict XIII raised Lambertini to the cardinalate, and three years later he replaced the archbishop of Bologna, who had become Pope Clement XII. During his time in Rome, Lambertini became fast friends with many of the city's intellectuals and developed deep interests in the city's history and antiquities.

LIFE'S WORK

Lambertini rapidly gained a reputation for his diligent pastoral work as archbishop of Bologna. He reformed clerical education and held a diocesan synod following the recommendation of the Council of Trent. He wanted his priests to be firmly grounded in Scripture and theology but also familiar with the scientific currents of the day. He fostered parish life and personally visited every parish in his diocese. After the death of Clement XII, the conclave for electing his successor opened on February 17, 1740. It was a difficult election, beset by factionalism among the fifty-four cardinals, that lasted more than six months and resulted in more than 250 votes before Lambertini was elected as a compromise candidate. He took the name Benedict in recognition of his patron, Benedict XIII.

Benedict XIV's early papacy was dominated by the hostilities of the War of the Austrian Succession and continuing demands by Europe's monarchs for greater control over the Church in their respective nations. Benedict's reputation for secular as well as theological scholarship and his clear interests in the cultural currents of the day recommended him to Europe's powerful as a person with whom they could do business. He proved to be a political realist and quickly reached concordats with the king of Portugal in 1740 and the rulers of Savoy and Naples in 1741; negotiations with Spain stretched over a dozen years.

In each of these agreements, Benedict permitted greater secular interference in Church affairs, from taxing the clergy to allowing laymen to sit on Church tribunals. With the French, Benedict had to sort out the problems caused by Clement XI's condemnation of Jansenist teachings in the bull *Unigenitus* (1713). French authorities asked for direction in the form of a less-authoritative document called an encyclical rather than a bull, and they received *Ex omnibus christiani orbis* (1756), in which Benedict counseled withholding the sacraments only from the most publicly vociferous Jansenists. Though he was criticized by some for his concessions to secular authority, others have seen them as necessary to prevent the outright nationalization of the Catholic Church. Benedict enjoyed good relations with Frederick the Great, despite—or perhaps because of—the Protestant ruler's seizure of Catholic Silesia in 1740.

As ruler of the Papal States, Benedict had to be careful to retain his realism, even as Habsburg and Bourbon troops marched across his neutral territory, violating its sovereignty. He provided for the needs of his people by building roads and granaries throughout the Papal States, fostering agriculture and commerce (which had sunk to new lows under his predecessors), and attacking usurious lending in the encyclical *Vix pervenit* (1745). He also sought to rationalize the financial administration of the Papal States without drastically altering the existing bureaucratic framework: Melioration rather than real reform seems to have been at the heart of his papacy.

As leader of the Roman Catholic Church, Benedict XIV faced numerous issues and challenges presented by the radical social changes throughout Europe. Regarding marriages of Catholics and Protestants, he ruled in the bull *Magnae nobis admirationis* (June 29, 1748) that such mixed couples could not be permitted full wedding ceremonies and that in order to be blessed at all, the couple must pledge to raise their children to be Catholics. In parts of Asia, Jesuit missionaries had been allowing a good deal of local culture to infuse Catholic rituals, a practice that drew much conservative criticism. In his bull *Ex quo singulari* (July 11, 1742), Benedict condemned such practices in China, and in *Omnium sollectitudinum* (September 12, 1744) he extended the condemnation to missionaries in Malabar.

At the end of his reign, Benedict came under pressure from the Portuguese first minister to investigate perceived abuses of the Jesuits in Portugal. His appointment of Cardinal Saldanha as chief inspector in 1758 set in motion the events that led to the suppression of the order

by Pope Clement XIV in 1773. Benedict reached accords with several of the Eastern Orthodox churches, but old disagreements over the wording of creeds prevented fuller reunification.

Although Benedict was in tune with much of the new thinking of the Enlightenment, he supported the condemnation of Freemasonry by Clement XII in his own bull *Providas Romanorum Pontificum* (March 18, 1751), which called unsuccessfully for the suppression of the Masons by Catholic rulers. He also oversaw the placement of the works of Voltaire and *The Spirit of the Laws* by Montesquieu on the Index of Forbidden Books. Finally, he encouraged the practice of holding diocesan synods, which he as bishop had found so rewarding, through dissemination of his book *De synodo dioecesana* (1748; on diocesan synods), which he wrote while archbishop of Bologna. He signaled his concern for episcopal soundness early on by establishing a commission to aid in the choosing of bishops. On the other hand, he discouraged the proliferation of religious holidays in European countries and the use of secular music in Catholic services.

Benedict found many outlets for his secular interests in Rome. His intense interest in history and Rome's heritage led him to found academies for the study of Roman and Christian antiquities, Church history, and the history of canon law and liturgy. He established a museum of Christian history and expanded the Vatican library by some thirty-three hundred precious manuscripts. He also had the library's entire collection cataloged. Benedict's early writings were published in Rome and filled twelve folio volumes; a later, complete edition consists of seventeen volumes and includes 760 letters to one French cardinal alone.

SIGNIFICANCE

By the mid-eighteenth century, the Papal States and the Catholic Church had long been dominated by sophisticated aristocratic rulers who managed to retain the Papacy's integrity and authority in a rapidly changing world. Benedict XIV represented not the ruling class but rather the deeper traditions of sound Church pastoral leadership combined with a liberal realism. He was willing to compromise with the more powerful secular authorities when it meant that Church prerogatives would be preserved. His stances on matters of Church discipline and administration, while reformist, were nevertheless firm and unyielding and served to bolster support for the Church from important quarters. Benedict's own broad intellectual interests and inviting personality recommended him to Europe's ruling class in a way that family or even extensive experience could not.

—*Joseph P. Byrne*

FURTHER READING

Chadwick, Owen. *The Popes and European Revolution.* New York: Oxford University Press, 1981. Studies Benedict's pontificate in relation to the social, intellectual, and political movements of his day.

Haynes, Renée. *Philosopher King: The Humanist Pope Benedict XIV.* London: Weidenfeld and Nicolson, 1970. This remains the only monographic biography on Benedict in English.

Pastor, Ludwig. *History of the Popes from the Close of the Middle Ages.* Vols. 35 and 36. Translated by Ernest Graff. St. Louis, Mo.: Herder, 1923-1969. Pre-sents a full biography of Benedict and a detailed discussion of his pontificate.

Wright, A. D. *The Early Modern Papacy: From the Council of Trent to the French Revolution, 1564-1789.* New York: Longman, 2000. Examines Benedict in the context of his many roles as pope and the challenges of the mid-eighteenth century.

See also: Frederick the Great; Montesquieu; Pius VI; Voltaire.

Related articles in *Great Events from History: The Eighteenth Century, 1701-1800*: September 8, 1713: Papal Bull *Unigenitus*; May, 1727-1733: Jansenist "Convulsionnaires" Gather at Saint-Médard; December 16, 1740-November 7, 1748: War of the Austrian Succession.

JEREMY BENTHAM
English legal scholar and social reformer

Bentham's lifelong critical analysis of English law and society laid the foundations for the early nineteenth century political reforms that saved England from violent social revolution. He is best known for his utilitarian ideas and for extending legal thought beyond questions of law. Also, with his brother, he conceptualized a structure of confinement and surveillance called a Panopticon.

Born: February 15, 1748; London, England
Died: June 6, 1832; London, England
Areas of achievement: Philosophy, social reform, law

EARLY LIFE

Jeremy Bentham was the son of a prosperous English lawyer named Jeremiah Bentham. The elder Bentham wanted his son to have advantages that he had missed, so the father was delighted at his precocious son's ability to read at the age of three. Young Bentham accordingly was packed off to the Westminster School and then on to Oxford by the time he was twelve. Because of his youth and small stature, this "dwarfish phenomenon," as Bentham called himself, never engaged in the usual activities of the boys his age. While his peers may have played cricket, he contented himself with badminton. His world was contained within the boundaries of books and ideas.

At Westminster School, Bentham encountered his first acknowledged intellectual battle with English law.

All students at the school were required to sign an oath supporting the Thirty-nine Articles of Religion of the Church of England. Already an advocate of logical thinking, the young prodigy privately believed that the articles were so irrational and contrary to the Scriptures that the Church was forcing perjury on those required to sign them. In this instance, and throughout his entire life, however, Bentham obeyed the law and did the expected but privately agonized over what he had done, vowing silently to battle for the reform of the English legal system, not to mention the Church of England.

Perhaps no other scholar in English history spent so much time studying and writing about the law and the legal system but practically no time practicing it. Once the brilliant youngster finished his course of study at Westminster, he entered Oxford. Toward the middle of his third year at Oxford, he attended a lecture by the most famous English legal scholar of his day, William Blackstone, the first of whose *Commentaries on the Laws of England* would be published beginning in 1765. The fifteen-year-old student eagerly attended the presentation given by the forty-year-old jurist, the first professor of English law at Oxford.

Diligently, Bentham attempted to follow the lecture by recording its essentials in notes, but he could not. There were so many internal fallacies and illogical premises in what Blackstone pronounced that Bentham gave up his attempts at note taking.

This incident likely marked the beginning of Bentham's lifelong battle against English law and the legal system that supported it. While Blackstone might marvel at the "glorious inconsistency" of English law, Bentham denounced English law as an abhorrent mass of confusion, designed to be manipulated by those with the money and patience sufficient to retain the proper attorneys.

Most repugnant to Bentham throughout his lifetime of intellectual jousting was falsehood. At Westminster School, he had despised being forced to sign the Thirty-nine Articles of Religion; he believed not only that the statements were lies but also that his signature compounded the prevarication. Subsequently, in his attendance at Blackstone's lecture, he encountered English law as an even greater fabric of falsification. Especially frustrating to him was the notion of fiction in law, a method by which legal entities might be created or destroyed at the whim of the court and its attorneys. Appalled at this practice, Bentham declared that "in English law, fiction is a syphilis, which runs in every vein, and carries into every part of the system the principle of rottenness."

Jeremy Bentham. (Library of Congress)

LIFE'S WORK

Although Jeremy Bentham read law at Lincoln's Inn after he took his master's degree from Oxford in 1766 and was called to the bar the following year, he was never a successful practicing lawyer. Instead, he spent each day in his rooms reading and writing about the law or conversing with the other law students who came to call. He set himself the daily task of writing more than fifteen folio practice pages of commentary on English law or society. These trial pages, or drafts, dealt with numerous subjects of interest to him. The dedication and intensity with which Bentham labored were so consuming that he suffered bouts of psychosomatic blindness. Only the loving attendance of his friends brought him through these extremely depressing periods.

In the course of his long life, many thousands of pages were written, many on subjects he never fully developed and many of which were never published. His first publication was a critique of Blackstone, printed anonymously in 1776 under the title *A Fragment on Government*. So brilliant and masterful was this work that it was attributed to many great minds of the time. Ironically, when his proud father accidentally revealed the true authorship of the essay, the headline-hungry public no longer was interested.

Bentham's accomplishment did, however, bring him to the attention of William Petty, Lord Shelburne, who introduced him to the world of the nobility by extending his patronage to the young intellectual. Perhaps most important, Shelburne helped broaden Bentham's criticisms of English law to include constitutional law along with his ongoing considerations of civil and penal law. Although Shelburne could never provide Bentham an office of political power, he did afford him an insight into the functions of the enlightened minority within the English political establishment.

In what Bentham thought, said, and wrote for the next seventy years, he did what few Englishmen had ever dared, and did so successfully. As his intellectual godson, John Stuart Mill, explained, "Bentham broke the spell. . . . Who, before Bentham, dared to speak disrespectfully in express terms, of the British Constitution, or the English Law?" He was not, however, merely a "negative philosopher," wrote Mill, but a person of questioning spirit who demanded the "why" of everything and then applied his "essentially practical mind" toward a system of solutions for the problems which he saw.

Fourteen years after his first published work, Bentham introduced his proposition commonly known as the principle of utility, or the utilitarian idea. In *An Introduction to the Principles of Morals and Legislation* (1789), Bentham proclaimed that through legislation the government could achieve the greatest good for the greatest number of individuals in society. Whether Bentham realized it or not, he had in effect launched a major reform crusade in English politics, the ultimate results of which would not be realized until the various social changes undertaken by English reformers had passed through Parliament after the Reform Bill of 1832.

Despite the implicit radicalism of his ideas, Bentham continued to live his rather ordinary existence as legal scholar and budding political philosopher. Two events that influenced his thinking in major ways were his trip to Russia for a visit with his brother Sam in the 1780's and his correspondence with the political leaders of the French Revolution in the 1790's.

From his travels abroad and his lengthy correspondence in response to the queries from his friends in France about reorganizing government and society there, Bentham drew new inspiration for his critiques of his own society. He became convinced that the very framework of English society needed a thoroughgoing revision based on his utilitarian principles. Made independently wealthy by his father's death in 1792, Bentham could thereafter use the family home at Queen Square Place and the income from the estate to support himself, his ideas, and any social experiments he might choose to undertake.

Bentham and his brother Sam did attempt to implement one philanthropic scheme, a model prison that was grandly named the Panopticon. From Sam's architectural knowledge was drawn the plan for the building laid out in the shape of a wheel. In the model prison, the keeper resided in the center of the wheel, where he could see all the prisoners. By a clever structural arrangement of floors and walls, the inmates could not see one another or the keeper but were imprisoned in isolation, away from the corrupting influences of one another. Although many applauded the theories of the Benthams, lack of government support forced them to abandon their plans. Not until 1813 did the British government attempt to repay them for the money they had spent trying to persuade Parliament to adopt their plan.

However intellectually and emotionally democratized Bentham may have become, he did not take up his role as inspiration for a political movement until after 1808, when he met James Mill. Mill's writing and activism helped turn Bentham's political teachings into practice. Out of this background developed those politicians known as the Benthamites, who sometimes were called the Philosophical Radicals or the Utilitarians. Within a little more than a decade, the publications of James Mill, coupled with the activities of his son, John Stuart Mill, brought the Utilitarians into public prominence. Convinced that nothing positive would be written about them either by the Whig *Edinburgh Review* or the *Tory Quarterly Review*, the Utilitarians used their mentor's financial backing to launch the *Westminster Review*.

In the twilight years between 1820 and Bentham's death in 1832, the elderly sage still drew a circle of admirers, disciples, and curiosity seekers to his home in London. By this time, Bentham's hearing had failed so badly that within an hour visitors often found themselves exhausted from raising their voices to be heard. His voice continued to be heard, however, even after his death. To further the goal of spreading Bentham's ideas, his followers were responsible for the establishment of University College, London. There his bones rest, dressed in his usual clothing, a wax model of his head atop the auto-icon, and his skull at his feet.

SIGNIFICANCE

The emergence of the Benthamites into political activism was by no means the first occasion on which Jeremy Bentham's ideas aroused controversy and criticism. No one could engage in a lifelong critique of English law and society without awakening the wrath of powerful individuals determined to protect the establishment. Bentham's responses to criticism were sometimes regarded as petty and perhaps uninformed. As John Stuart Mill explained, however, Bentham's reactions were peculiar because the great philosopher was

> essentially a boy. He had the freshness, the simplicity, the confidingness, the liveliness and activity, all the delightful qualities of boyhood, and the weaknesses which are the reverse side of those qualities—the undue importance attached to trifles, the habitual mismeasurement of the practical bearing and the value of things, the readiness to be either delighted or offended on inadequate cause.

Despite this criticism, which some scholars regard as unfounded, Mill praised Bentham as one of the two men (Samuel Taylor Coleridge was the other) to whom England was "indebted not only for the greater part of the important ideas which have been thrown into circulation among its thinking men in their time, but for a revolution in its general modes of thought and investigation." For more than fifty years, Bentham had labored to bring order out of chaos of the English legal system by providing a logical basis for codification that would render the law at once comprehensible and just.

Bentham's investigation into the legal system, moreover, was so fundamental that his conclusions reached far beyond simple matters of law. The critical scholar saw how the entire fabric of society was interwoven with the law. Hence, he attacked not only laws, courts, and attorneys, but also prisons, poor relief, municipal organizations, rotten boroughs, Parliament, the established clergy, the titled nobility, and the idle landed gentry. Some of his followers would even go so far as advocating the abolition of the monarch; others fought for the principle of a vote for every Englishman.

Even as age overtook Bentham physically, the ideas he had so long espoused were finally becoming accepted by new English political leaders. Reform did not mean revolution, as the emerging politicians understood, so Great Britain in the next decades could carry out change without the turbulence of the French Revolution of 1789. Thanks for this accomplishment, in large measure, should go to a mild little man whose life testified to the notion that the pen and the written word, indeed, were mightier than the sword and its conquests.

—James H. O'Donnell III

FURTHER READING

Bentham, Jeremy. *The Works of Jeremy Bentham*. Edited by John Bowring. 11 vols. Edinburgh: William Tait, 1838-1843. These eleven volumes totaling more than sixty-five hundred pages indicate the prodigious output from Bentham's pen—perhaps in excess of six million words. Including memoirs and selected correspondence, this is the repository where all research on Bentham must start.

Crimmins, James E. *On Bentham*. Belmont, Calif.: Thomson/Wadsworth Learning, 2004. A brief introduction to Bentham's philosophy by an author who has written several books on utilitarianism.

Englemann, Stephen G. *Imagining Interest in Political Thought: Origins of Economic Rationality*. Durham, N.C.: Duke University Press, 2003. Examines Bentham's ideas about self-interest and public interest to demonstrate how his philosophy forms the basis of contemporary liberalism.

Foucault, Michel. *Discipline and Punish: The Birth of the Prison*. Translated by Alan Sheridan. New York: Vintage Books, 1978. A classic work that includes a renowned chapter on Bentham and "Panopticism," the system whereby a prisoner or person otherwise confined "is seen, but he does not see." Includes notes and a bibliography.

Halevy, Elie. *The Growth of Philosophic Radicalism*. New York: A. M. Kelley, 1949. Originally published in French in 1901, this is the classic analysis of the emergence of the Benthamites. Halevy remains the acknowledged master of the political history of early Victorian England.

Long, Douglas G. *Bentham on Liberty: Jeremy Bentham's Idea of Liberty in Relation to His Utilitarianism*. Toronto: University of Toronto Press, 1977. The author's involvement in the Bentham Research Project at University College, London, led him to the mass of unpublished manuscripts held there. From them, Long has concluded that Bentham, in searching for a science of humanity and society, believed that liberty was secondary to security in establishing a plan for social action.

Mack, Mary Peter. *Jeremy Bentham: An Odyssey of Ideas*. New York: Columbia University Press, 1963. In preparing this magisterial biography of Bentham's first forty-four years, the author examined not only the published sources but also unpublished manuscripts. This is the standard modern study of Bentham but ends with his father's death and Bentham's subsequent inheritance. Reference will have to be made to Elie Halevy and John Stuart Mill for insight into the later years.

Mazlish, Bruce. *James and John Stuart Mill: Father and Son in the Nineteenth Century*. New York: Basic Books, 1975. This is an important study for understanding the three-way intellectual relationship among Bentham and the two Mills. It offers insights into the personalities as well as the philosophies of the forces behind utilitarianism.

Mill, John Stuart. *On Bentham and Coleridge*. Edited by F. R. Leavis. New York: G. W. Stewart, 1951. The classic account of Bentham by his intellectual godson and heir, who was himself a leader of the utilitarians. While useful in placing Bentham in his proper perspective as one of England's premier thinkers, it unfortunately contributes to the notion that he was at times petty. Whatever its shortcomings, it should be consulted by anyone who wants to study Bentham.

Postema, Gerald J. *Bentham: Moral, Political, and Legal Philosophy*. 2 vols. Burlington, Vt.: Ashgate/Dartmouth, 2002. A collection that offers wide-ranging interpretations of Bentham's philosophy. The first volume investigates Bentham's psychology and theories of social welfare, liberty, and democracy. The second volume examines his ideas about the legal system.

Semple, Janet. *Bentham's Prison: A Study of the Panopticon Penitentiary*. New York: Oxford University Press, 1993. Semple examines and discusses Bentham's prison reform plan and his political dealings to make the plan a reality.

See also: Cesare Beccaria; Sir William Blackstone; Edmund Burke; First Baron Erskine; Johann Gottlieb Fichte; Thomas Paine; Jean-Jacques Rousseau; Mary Wollstonecraft.

Related articles in *Great Events from History: The Eighteenth Century, 1701-1800:* April, 1762: Rousseau Publishes *The Social Contract*; 1790: Burke Lays the Foundations of Modern Conservatism; February 22, 1791-February 16, 1792: Thomas Paine Publishes *Rights of Man*; 1792: Wollstonecraft Publishes *A Vindication of the Rights of Woman*; 1792-1793: Fichte Advocates Free Speech; April 20, 1792-October, 1797: Early Wars of the French Revolution.

VITUS JONASSEN BERING
Danish-born explorer

A sailor in the service of Russia, Bering confirmed the existence of a strait between Asia and North America, led the first European expedition to cross from Siberia to the northwest coast of America, and commanded the Great Northern Expedition of 1733-1742 in its exploration of Siberia.

Born: August 12, 1681; Horsens, Denmark
Died: December 19, 1741; Bering Island, Russia
Area of achievement: Exploration

EARLY LIFE

Vitus Jonassen Bering (VEE-toos YOH-nahs-suhn BAY-rihng) was born in Denmark, but he spent most of his adult life in the service of other countries. He sailed to the East Indies—then the object of exploitation by a number of European countries—on a Dutch expedition, returning to Europe in 1703. That same year, at the age of twenty-three, Bering entered the service of Russia as a sublieutenant in the Russian navy as one of a great number of non-Russians recruited by Czar Peter the Great in his attempt to modernize and "Europeanize" the Russian Empire. Serving in the Black Sea, the Sea of Azov (an arm of the Black Sea), and the Baltic Sea during the Great Northern War with Sweden (1701-1721), he received his first command in 1710. He was made captain second class in 1720 but was passed over for further promotion.

Bering was apparently the victim of bureaucratic infighting but may also have drawn criticism for his sometimes unimaginative and obstinate adherence to orders. In any case, he resigned his commission in disappointment in 1724 and withdrew to his estate at Vyborg, on the Gulf of Finland. Within weeks he had been recalled to service and appointed captain first class—but with a specific mission. He was then forty-four years old.

LIFE'S WORK

Ostensibly concerned with the hypothetical Northwest Passage between Asia and North America but perhaps more preoccupied with identifying further sources of wealth for his rapidly expanding empire, the dying Czar Peter the Great had left somewhat vague instructions for the exploration of the frigid seas east of Siberia. Acting on the czar's orders, Russian admiral Fyodor Apraksin appointed Bering to head the expedition Peter had envisioned, making fellow Dane Martin Spanberg (sometimes spelled Spangberg) and Russian Aleksei Chirikov his seconds-in-command.

The difficulty of the czar's orders was compounded by the enormous extent of the Russian Empire. Okhotsk, the tiny Siberian port from which Bering was to mount his expedition, lay almost 3,500 miles east of the new Russian capital of St. Petersburg. Although Bering was able to follow Russia's system of rivers for much of the way, merely guiding the expedition as far as its nominal point of departure was nevertheless already an extraordinary undertaking. The explorer departed St. Petersburg on February 5, 1725, several days behind the main body of his expedition, and reached Okhotsk on October 1, 1726—some twenty months later.

Bering's party transported the tools, iron fittings, canvas, and rope necessary to build and outfit a ship on Siberia's eastern seaboard, and they recruited hundreds of workers and artisans along the way. Expecting to cut the lumber necessary for the ship's hull once he reached the coast, Bering was appalled to discover that only the most stunted trees and bushes grew in the region. He had no choice but to winter in Okhotsk, and in the spring he supervised the building of the *Fortuna*, a small ship whose timbers were secured with twigs and leather thongs. The *Fortuna* then carried men and supplies (in two trips) to the settlement of Bolsheretsk, on the southwestern shore of the Kamchatka Peninsula. After spending several more harrowing months crossing the peninsula's mountainous spine to the Pacific coast fort of Nizhnekamchatsk, Bering found forests substantial enough to supply the timber for another, hardier ship, the *St. Gabriel*, which he launched in mid-July, 1728.

The rest of Bering's voyage proved simple, if tantalizingly inconclusive. The *St. Gabriel* reached an island Bering christened St. Lawrence (now part of Alaska) and sailed as far north as 67° 18′. It is clear in retrospect that Bering had indeed passed between the westernmost tip of North America and the easternmost tip of Asia through what is now known as the Bering Strait, but poor weather conditions prevented him from sighting the American continent. Fearful of the approaching winter, he returned to Kamchatka, on whose eastern coast he and his crew spent the winter of 1728.

The following spring, the *St. Gabriel* rounded the southern cape of Kamchatka—a first for Europeans in these little-known waters—and returned to Okhotsk. Bering eventually returned to St. Petersburg on March 1, 1730, bringing to an end what would be known as the First Kamchatka Expedition. In recognition of his accomplishment, he was appointed captain commander, although officials unhappy with what seemed to be the inconclusive nature of his discoveries delayed his pay for several years.

Bering went on to propose a second expedition designed to facilitate Russian exploitation of the Far East. The Russian government commissioned him to lead such an expedition, but by the time he set off in 1733, the scale and scope of his already ambitious suggestions had been vastly expanded. As a result, the Second Kamchatka Expedition that Bering had envisioned subsequently became known as the Great Northern Expedition. Involving extensive exploration of both the interior of Siberia and its seacoasts, this project was to occupy Bering for the rest of his life.

The Great Northern Expedition was a logistical nightmare, yet its geographical importance proved to be unequaled in the annals of discovery. As envisioned by officials comfortably ensconced in St. Petersburg, several contingents of the expedition would explore the great expanse of Siberia's northern seacoast from the port of Archangel (which lies only 10° east of St. Petersburg) all

the way to the eastern tip of Asia. Another contingent was to follow the eastern coast of Siberia, chart the course of the Kurile Islands (which stretch southward from the tip of Kamchatka), and open trade with Japan (which lies even farther south).

The third component of the expedition, which Bering was to undertake personally but which he was not able to begin until 1740, involved confirming the existence of a strait between Asia and North America and exploring the nearer shores of the latter continent. In the meantime Bering had grown exhausted from crossing the breadth of Asia once again and overseeing the work of the thousands of men—scientists, artists, surveyors, craftsmen, and laborers—who were directly or indirectly under his command. Complicating the situation was the attitude of the Russian government itself, which had unrealistically high expectations of what Bering and his men might accomplish but unrealistically low expectations of what the grandiose scheme might cost. Thus, eight years passed before Bering could turn his attention to North America.

Bering was finally able to sail from Okhotsk on the ship *St. Peter* in September of 1740, taking with him as surgeon and naturalist Georg Wilhelm Steller. Bering's lieutenant

Vitus Jonassen Bering. (The Granger Collection, New York)

from the previous expedition, Aleksei Chirikov, had departed a few days before on the sister ship *St. Paul*. The crews wintered on the eastern coast of Kamchatka and set out on the final leg of their outward journey in early June, 1741. The two ships were almost immediately driven apart during a storm. On this expedition, however, the weather permitted Bering, in mid-July, to sight the mainland of North America in the shape of a volcano he named Mount St. Elias and to land a few days later on an island he named Kayak in order to take on fresh water.

By this time, Bering was suffering, like most of his men, from scurvy, a disease brought on by a lack of vitamin C, which is contained in fresh fruits and vegetables, and so he had little interest in these momentous discoveries. On its return trip, the *St. Peter* followed the chain of the Aleutian Islands back to Asia but ran aground on a desolate island off the coast of Kamchatka. Bering died on this island, subsequently named after him, on December 19, 1741.

SIGNIFICANCE

Vitus Jonassen Bering's status as an explorer is ambiguous, and the nature of his accomplishment—although of key importance to Russia's movement into Asia—is a triumph of logistics rather than exploration. Reports of what is now known as the Bering Strait date from as early as 1566, and a Cossack named Semyon Ivanovich Dezhnyov sailed from the Arctic Ocean into the Pacific in 1648, but neither he nor anyone else realized the significance of his feat at the time. Surgeon and naturalist Steller complained bitterly that Bering showed no interest in the Alaskan lands he discovered in 1741, although by then he was fatally ill. Bering believed correctly that he had confirmed on his first expedition that Asia and North America were separate continents, but he seems to have been reluctant even then to seize the opportunity he had been given.

Bering's most enduring accomplishment remains his management of the Great Northern Expedition, possibly the most involved undertaking in the history of exploration. Given the loftiest instructions but little in the way of practical support, Bering managed to lay the groundwork for the Russian exploitation of Siberia and Alaska, usually under the most appalling conditions of weather and terrain imaginable. That the many men under his command accomplished so much—and often went to their death—in the face of bureaucratic indifference and antagonism is a testament to Bering's considerable organizational skills and moral character.

—*Grove Koger*

FURTHER READING

Bobrick, Benson. *East of the Sun: The Epic Conquest and Tragic History of Siberia*. New York: Poseidon Press, 1992. A popular but substantial history of Siberia, placing Bering's expeditions in the context of Russian expansion across northern Asia and into North America. Map, chronology, illustrations, notes, extensive bibliography. A natural complement to W. Bruce Lincoln.

Fisher, Raymond H. *Bering's Voyages: Whither and Why*. Seattle: University of Washington Press, 1977. Examines the underlying reasons for the voyages undertaken by Bering at the behest of Peter the Great, concluding that Peter's ultimate goal was territorial aggrandizement. Maps, bibliography.

Ford, Corey. *Where the Sea Breaks Its Back: The Epic Story of a Pioneer Naturalist and the Discovery of Alaska*. Boston: Little, Brown, 1966. A popular account of Steller's contribution to natural history and his expedition with Bering. Ford creates a sympathetic portrait of a figure often criticized for his abrasiveness and impatience. Maps, short bibliography.

Frost, O. W. *Bering: The Russian Discovery of America*. New Haven, Conn.: Yale University Press, 2003. Frost uses newly discovered materials, including personal letters and evidence derived from the discovery of Bering's grave, to examine the personality, life, and voyages of Bering and his uneasy relationship with naturalist Georg Steller.

Golder, F. A., ed. *Bering's Voyages: An Account of the Efforts of the Russians to Determine the Relation of Asia and America*. 2 vols. New York: American Geographical Society, 1922-1925. The best compilation of primary sources on Bering's expeditions. The first volume translates the log books and official reports of the expeditions, while the second translates Steller's journal. Extensive editorial material, illustrations, bibliography, and notes.

Hunt, William R. *Arctic Passage: The Turbulent History of the Land and People of the Bering Sea, 1697-1975*. New York: Charles Scribner's Sons, 1975. Hunt discusses Bering's voyages and Steller's discoveries in the book's opening chapters. Illustrations, bibliography.

Lincoln, W. Bruce. *The Conquest of a Continent: Siberia and the Russians*. New York: Random House, 1994. A comprehensive history of Russian expansion through Siberia. Unlike Bobrick, Lincoln finds Bering an unimaginative and limited commander. Maps, illustrations, notes, bibliography.

Møller, Peter Ulf, and Natasha Okhotina Lind. *Under Vitus Bering's Command: New Perspectives on the Russian Kamchatka Expeditions*. Aarhus, Denmark: Aarhus University Press, 2002. Using evidence from newly discovered Russian documents, the authors recount the history of the two expeditions, the participants' daily life, the beginnings of scientific ethnology, and other aspects of the voyages.

Neatby, L. H. *Discovery in Russian and Siberian Waters*. Athens: Ohio University Press, 1973. Several chapters are devoted to Bering, Chirikov, and the Great Northern Expedition. A sympathetic account that emphasizes the often heroic characteristics of the key figures. Brief bibliography.

Steller, Georg Wilhelm. *Journal of a Voyage with Bering, 1741-1742*. Stanford, Calif.: Stanford University Press, 1988. A complete and modernized translation of Steller's account, rendered even more useful by an introduction, chronology, maps, extensive notes, and bibliography. An important supplement to Golder.

See also: Peter the Great.

Related articles in *Great Events from History: The Eighteenth Century, 1701-1800*: c. 1701-1721: Great Northern War; May 27, 1703: Founding of St. Petersburg; November 20, 1710-July 21, 1718: Ottoman Wars with Russia, Venice, and Austria.

GEORGE BERKELEY
Irish philosopher

Berkeley developed a novel theory of sense perception that led to the denial of the existence of physical—or material—objects. Serving as the link between John Locke's commonsense materialism and David Hume's skepticism, Berkeley's ideas spanned the philosophical gap between classical traditionalism and the emergence of modern science.

Born: March 12, 1685; Dysert Castle, near Thomastown, Kilkenny, Ireland
Died: January 14, 1753; Oxford, England
Areas of achievement: Philosophy, religion and theology, science and technology

EARLY LIFE

George Berkeley was the eldest son of William Berkeley. Little is known of his boyhood, but there is evidence that he was a precocious child. In 1696, he attended the Kilkenny School, and in 1700, Trinity College, Dublin, where he studied mathematics, logic, languages, and philosophy. He was graduated in 1704 and received his master's degree in 1707, becoming a fellow of Trinity College. During this period, the principal influences upon his thought were the ideas of English philosopher John Locke and the continental thinkers Nicolas Malebranche and Pierre Bayle.

Berkeley had begun the line of thought that he was to pursue in his later major works, that is, his argument for the immateriality of objects, based on the subjectivity of sense perceptions. Before the age of thirty, he had published three of the most important philosophical works in eighteenth century England—books that have become classics in English philosophy. All three were published within a four-year period: in 1709, *An Essay Towards a New Theory of Vision*; in 1710, *A Treatise Concerning the Principles of Human Knowledge*; and, in 1713, *Three Dialogues Between Hylas and Philonous*.

LIFE'S WORK

In the first work, George Berkeley's design is to show how human sight conceptualizes distance, magnitude, and the location of objects, and whether ideas of sight and touch are similar or different. His goal in the second work is to demonstrate that an uncritical acceptance of materialism inevitably leads to skepticism and atheism. The last work is a fascinating refinement and extension of *A Treatise Concerning the Principles of Human Knowledge,* in which Berkeley argues in dialogue form that the notion of a "material substratum" is a meaningless verbal abstraction.

Even though these books, as an example of English prose, are superb in style and clarity, they were, when they appeared, either dismissed, ridiculed, or ignored. Common sense convinced most people that "matter" was real enough, and Samuel Johnson's declaration, "I refute him thus," upon kicking a large stone, was refutation enough.

In 1709, Berkeley was made a deacon in the Church of England, and he was ordained a priest in 1710. In 1713, Berkeley traveled to London, where he met Joseph Addison, Richard Steele, Alexander Pope, and Jonathan Swift. Berkeley was present at the first night of Addi-

George Berkeley. (Library of Congress)

son's play *Cato* (1713) and wrote a lively description of the evening. He wrote essays for Steele's *Guardian* against the ideas of the freethinkers. Pope praised Berkeley, and Swift presented him at court.

In 1713-1714, Berkeley traveled on the Continent, where he probably met and conversed with Malebranche. He returned there in 1716-1720, serving as tutor to George Ashe, son of the bishop of Clogher. On his return, he published *De motu* (1721), in which he argued against Sir Isaac Newton's notion of absolute space, time, and motion and made reference to his ideas on immaterialism. This work also earned for Berkeley the title "precursor of Mach and Einstein." He retained his fellowship at Trinity College until 1724, when he became dean of Derry.

Disappointed in having failed to attract the interest of educated English society in his philosophical theories, Berkeley turned his attention toward propagating the Christian Gospel and educating American Indians, even settling on a scheme to build a college in Bermuda for this purpose. He was granted a charter, with the archbishop of Canterbury acting as trustee and Parliament allotting a grant of £20,000 for the project. There was,

however, some opposition to the plan, and the project was eventually abandoned.

In 1728, Berkeley was married to Anne Forster, an intelligent and well-educated woman, and they moved to Newport, Rhode Island. The marriage was a happy one, and six children—four sons and two daughters—would be born to the couple. Returning to Ireland in 1731, Berkeley was appointed bishop of Cloyne. There he administered his diocese with skill and grace for eighteen years. At the time of his leaving America he had donated generously of his books and money to Yale University, and it is interesting to note that America honored his largess 150 years later when the university town of Berkeley, California, was given his name.

In Ireland, Berkeley's writing continued. He produced works on religious apologetics, optics, and mathematics. In his later work, he attacked Deism, analyzed geometrical optics, and raised questions concerning the theory of physical fluxions. (On this latter issue, he was a constant opponent of Newton.) These topics appear in *Alciphron: Or, The Minute Philosopher* (1732); *The Theory of Vision: Or, Visual Language, Showing the Immediate Presence and Providence of a Deity, Vindicated and Explained* (1733), a revised and expanded version of *An Essay Towards a New Theory of Vision*; *The Analyst: Or, A Discourse Addressed to an Infidel Mathematician* (1734); *A Defense of Free-Thinking in Mathematics* (1735); *The Querist* (1735-1737); and *Siris: A Chain of Philosophical Reflextions and Inquiries Concerning the Virtues of Tar Water and Divers Other Subjects* (1744).

Alciphron, *The Theory of Vision*, *The Analyst*, and *A Defense of Free-Thinking in Mathematics* all reflect the same general objective: to mount a critical attack against materialism, religious freethinking, and atheism. Berkeley's position, although not an idiosyncratic view of matter, perception, and mathematics, is essentially negative. It is an attempt to destroy what had become the generally accepted eighteenth century viewpoint on these issues. His opponents, he argued, find the entities of religious belief mysterious and difficult to understand, but they are no more mysterious or difficult to believe, he concluded, than the scientific picture of the world offered by Galileo and Newton. Any person who can digest, he writes, the notions of force, gravity, fluxions, and infinitesimals should not be squeamish about accepting the hidden points of divinity.

The Querist, in contrast, is a treatise on economics and an analysis of the relations among work, production, and wealth. *Siris* is a curious piece written toward the end of his life, in which he maintains that tar water (resinous residue of pine and fir trees) is an efficacious medical treatment against famine and dysentery. *Siris* is a pious book pervaded with mysticism, yet, at the same time, it contains Berkeley's most systematic and penetrating account of the philosophical assumptions of science. In *Siris,* Berkeley achieved what he had sought in all of his other books—a large, sympathetic readership. The book was an instant success, going through six editions in the first year.

After 1745, Berkeley continued to be active in public affairs, speaking out often on political events. In 1752, the Berkeleys moved to Oxford, where Berkeley entered Christ Church College. He died suddenly on January 14, 1753, and was buried in Christ Church Chapel.

Significance

As a man whose life was ideas, George Berkeley's life must be evaluated in terms of the contribution he made to empiricist philosophy. Berkeley's works serve as the philosophical bridge between John Locke's notions of common sense and the skepticism of David Hume. Yet in a fundamental way, Berkeley stands alone. He was a more tenacious empiricist than Locke, for he insisted that the senses are the avenue of knowledge. Moreover, while Berkeley rejected every noetic intuitive device as an access to knowledge, as did Hume, his conclusions do not end in skepticism. Berkeley's method of direct sensory experience leads neither to Locke's contradictions nor to Hume's doubt and agnosticism, but to an irresistible vision of God.

Berkeley argued that the source of intellectual confusion can be traced to Galileo's, Newton's, and Locke's hypothesis that something called "matter" exists independent of the mind and sensory experience. It is, Berkeley declares, quite the other way around. Sensory experiences do not lead to doubt and an abstracted notion of "substratum" called matter but, rather, to a direct manifestation of the reality of mind or spirit. As a human entity, mind or spirit is finite and temporal; as a divine entity it is infinite and eternal. It is, on one hand, "inner," the private sensation that induces thought, memory, dreams, and imagination; on the other hand, it is "outer," the public sensory entities that reveal the nature of the external world of objects. In Berkeley's view, experience never provides an account of materiality standing apart from the reality of mind.

Berkeley further argued that the empirical method offers no sensory distinction between objective and subjective qualities; in fact, primary qualities are as subjective as the senses of color, taste, and sound. Berkeley's point is that experience is a complex of visual, factual, and locomotor sen-

---

THINGS EXIST THROUGH PERCEPTION ALONE

George Berkeley argued that things do not exist if not perceived, that there are no material beings in and of themselves—that is, there are no things that exist unperceived. He asks, rhetorically, Can one consider that a thing exists without considering that a thing must first be perceived? Again, if a thing is not perceived, it does not exist, for one cannot conceive of a thing without at least thinking about it—perceiving it in one's mind.

It is indeed an opinion strangely prevailing amongst men, that houses, mountains, rivers, and in a word all sensible objects, have an existence, natural or real, distinct from their being perceived by the understanding. But, with how great an assurance and acquiescence soever this principle may be entertained in the world, yet whoever shall find in his heart to call it in question may, if I mistake not, perceive it to involve a manifest contradiction. For, what are the forementioned objects but the things we perceive by sense? and what do we perceive besides our own ideas of sensations? and is it not plainly repugnant that any one of these, or any combination of them, should exist unperceived?

Some truths there are so near and obvious to the mind that a man need only open his eyes to see them. Such I take this important one to be, viz., that all the choir of heaven and furniture of the earth, in a word all those bodies which compose the mighty frame of the world, have not any subsistence without a mind, that their *being* is to be perceived or known; that consequently so long as they are not actually perceived by me, or do not exist in my mind or that of any other created spirit, they must either have no existence at all, or else subsist in the mind of some Eternal Spirit—[It] is being perfectly unintelligible, and involving all the absurdity of abstraction, to attribute to any single part of them an existence independent of a spirit. To be convinced of which the reader need only reflect, and try to separate in his own thoughts the *being* of a sensible thing from its *being perceived.*

Source: George Berkeley, "Objects of Human Knowledge," excerpted in *A Treasury of Philosophy*, edited by Dagobert D. Runes, vol. 1 (New York: Grolier, 1955), items 4 and 6, pp. 146-148.

sations, a product of the mind. All that is known is comprehended as immediacy; in Berkeley's most famous phrase, *esse es percipi*, meaning, to be is that, and only that, which is perceived.

Berkeley started with the lofty goal of solving the philosophical problems of his time and ended with a book for curing bodily ills. Sadly, no clear assessment of his great philosophical contribution was available during his lifetime. It took the next great British empiricist, David Hume, to demonstrate the significance of Berkeley's philosophical skepticism and its systematic doctrine of immaterialism.

Berkeley's influence on contemporary philosophy is significant. He taught the Anglo-American philosophers who followed him that there is a conceptual difference between the subjective, inchoate impressions spun within imagination and memory, and objective reality that requires cognitive order, vividness, and repetition. Berkeley insisted unequivocally that claims about the external world, if they are to have meaning, must be verbal declarations about undiluted sensory experience. For this reason, contemporary philosophical phenomenalism owes him much. "The table I write on," he wrote, "I say, exists, that is, I see and feel it, and were I out of my study I should say it existed, meaning thereby that if I was in my study I might perceive it, or that some other spirit does perceive." In the language of contemporary phenomenology, meaningful utterances about sense data require sensate experience, and the meaningfulness of unsensed assertions requires, at least conditionally, an accounting of what sensory experience must occur if the utterance is going to be more than empty nonsense. Contemporary theories of knowledge learned this lesson well from Berkeley's unrelenting view of empiricism.

—D. Burrill

FURTHER READING

Berkeley, George. *Alciphron.* 2 vols. London: Printed for J. Tonson, 1732. A defense of the Christian religion written in the form of a dialogue between Alciphron, the speaker of truth, and all "free-thinkers, fatalists, skeptics, enthusiasts, and libertines."

_____. *A New Theory of Vision and Other Select Philosophical Writings.* London: J. M. Dent and Sons, 1910. Berkeley's analysis of the perception of space. He assumes that visual space is a quality of the mind, reducible to visual signs of tangible space.

_____. *Three Dialogues Between Hylas and Philonous.* Chicago: Open Court, 1947. A charming dialogue between Hylas (the materialist) and Philonous

(the person of wisdom). Philonous eventually persuades Hylas to give up his belief in the existence of matter, thus allowing him to hold consistent views about the real world of the spirit. This is a book of the highest literary quality written in a century noted for its great literary achievements.

_____. *A Treatise Concerning the Principles of Human Knowledge.* Edited by C. M. Turbayne. New York: Library of Liberal Arts, 1965. Berkeley's systematic attack on the materialism of the new science, and the attending result of skepticism, irreligion, and atheism.

_____. *The Works of George Berkeley, Bishop of Cloyne.* Edited by A. A. Luce and T. E. Jessop. 9 vols. Edinburgh: Thomas Nelson, 1948-1957. The exhaustive collection of Berkeley's work, including private manuscripts and letters.

Fraser, Alexander Campbell. *Life and Letters of George Berkeley, D.D.* Oxford, England: Clarendon Press, 1871. The most definitive single volume about Berkeley's philosophy. Traces his life from his family roots in Kilkenny to his last days in Oxford. Included are some rare documents, including a memoir of Berkeley's travels in Italy and sermons preached in Trinity College, Dublin, and Rhode Island.

Pappas, George S. *Berkeley's Thought.* Ithaca, N.Y.: Cornell University Press, 2000. An overview of Berkeley's philosophy, including his ideas on abstraction, perception, common sense, and skepticism.

Richie, A. D. *George Berkeley: A Reappraisal.* Manchester, England: Manchester University Press, 1967. Richie argues that the key to understanding Berkeley can be found in his theory of vision.

Stoneham, Tom. *Berkeley's World: An Examination of the Three Dialogues.* New York: Oxford University Press, 2002. A clear, detailed study of *Three Dialogues Between Hylas and Philonous.* Provides an overview of the work and examines its ideas, including Berkeley's thoughts on substance, causation, action, and free will.

Umbaugh, Bruce. *On Berkeley.* Belmont, Calif.: Wadsworth/Thomson Learning, 2000. A concise, understandable 96-page introduction to Berkeley's philosophy.

Warnock, G. J. *Berkeley.* London: Penguin Books, 1953. Warnock's volume is a good modern introduction, particularly useful in its account of Berkeley's views of science, mathematics, and language. Also examines Berkeley's continued influence on modern philosophy.

See also: Joseph Addison; Mary Astell; Marquise du Châtelet; Étienne Bonnot de Condillac; Denis Diderot; Adam Ferguson; David Hume; Samuel Johnson; Immanuel Kant; Alexander Pope; Friedrich Schiller; Richard Steele; Jonathan Swift; Giambattista Vico.

Related articles in *Great Events from History: The Eighteenth Century, 1701-1800:* October, 1725: Vico Publishes *The New Science*; 1726-1729: Voltaire Advances Enlightenment Thought in Europe; 1739-1740: Hume Publishes *A Treatise of Human Nature*; 1751-1772: Diderot Publishes the *Encyclopedia*; 1754: Condillac Defends Sensationalist Theory; July, 1764: Voltaire Publishes *A Philosophical Dictionary for the Pocket*; 1770: Publication of Holbach's *The System of Nature*; 1781: Kant Publishes *Critique of Pure Reason*.

JOSEPH BLACK
Scottish chemist

A pioneer of quantitative experimental chemistry, Black discovered carbon dioxide, the first gas to be isolated and have its properties systematically identified. He also proposed the theories of latent and specific heats and, as a gifted lecturer, raised the profile of chemistry to a philosophical and public science.

Born: April 16, 1728; Bordeaux, France
Died: December, 6, 1799; Edinburgh, Scotland
Areas of achievement: Chemistry, science and technology

EARLY LIFE

Joseph Black's father, John Black, came from a family of Scottish-Irish merchants. During the first half of the eighteenth century, John Black prospered as a factor in the wine trade. With success came prominence in Bordeaux society, and among the family's closest friends was Montesquieu, president of the Sovereign Court of Bordeaux and author of *The Spirit of the Laws* (1748). Joseph's mother, Mary, also was from a family of merchants. She had descended from the Gordons of Aberdeenshire, Scotland, and her lineage, like her husband's, connected the world of eighteenth century trade to the world of the eighteenth century Enlightenment. Among Black's cousins on his mother's side was the Scottish social philosopher Adam Ferguson, author of *An Essay on the History of Civil Society* (1767). Joseph Black would later be best man at Ferguson's wedding, and Ferguson an early biographer of Black.

Joseph Black was the ninth of fifteen children. Protestant outsiders in Catholic France, the large family compensated with close ties of mutual support. Both John Black and Mary Gordon generously provided for their children's advancement, and an extensive family correspondence reveals that the children amply returned their affection. In 1740, Joseph Black was enrolled in a private school in Belfast, where he learned sufficient Latin and Greek to enter the University of Glasgow in the fall of 1744.

By the spring of 1748, Black had completed the undergraduate arts curriculum. The following fall he began the study of medicine. Black's choice of medicine satisfied his father's concern that his son get a professional education. It also satisfied Black's own developing interests in natural philosophy. The choice proved fortunate. The previous year William Cullen had become professor of medicine at the University of Glasgow. At Glasgow, Cullen introduced a chemistry that was less subordinate to the pharmaceutical needs of medicine and more an autonomous science posing its own distinct questions—a chemistry, in short, that was more "philosophical." The young Black quickly attracted the attention of the new professor of medicine. By 1749, Black had become Cullen's laboratory assistant.

LIFE'S WORK

In 1752, Joseph Black left Glasgow to do his medical thesis at the more prestigious University of Edinburgh. Published in June, 1754, the thesis was a milestone in Scottish philosophical chemistry. In June of 1755, Black presented his results to the Philosophical Society of Edinburgh. In the now classic paper, "Experiments upon Magnesia Alba, Quicklime, and Some Other Alcaline Substances" (pb. 1756), Black demonstrated that when heated, alkaline substances such as magnesium carbonate emitted a gas that Black called "fixed air." This demonstration meant that "air" was not itself an element but instead made up of chemically distinct gases. It also meant that, contrary to previous understanding, a gas could combine with a solid. Furthermore, Black established that the gas he had discovered, fixed air, or carbon dioxide, was a by-product of fermentation and respiration, and that among its properties were mild acidity, a greater density than common air, and its not supporting life or combustion.

Black's paper secured his scientific reputation and future career. When in 1755 Cullen became professor of chemistry at the University of Edinburgh, Black succeeded him at Glasgow as a professor of medicine and a lecturer in chemistry. Black now followed Cullen's suggestions and turned to the study of heat. Black's experiments on alkalis had been distinguished by their elegant design and quantitative rigor. So, too, were his observations on heat. Furthermore, historians of science sometimes credit him with the development of the ice calorimeter. Black's observations soon led him to discover both latent heats and specific heats. The amount of heat absorbed or released by substances—say, water in freezing or water in vaporizing—without a change in temperature is a latent heat, and the different amounts of heat required to raise equal masses of different substances an equal interval in temperature are called specific heats.

Black never published his work on heat, but he did publicize it. As the rich collection of student notes makes clear, Black began his course on chemistry with a detailed presentation of his research on the effects of heat. Indeed, from the early 1760's, Black largely abandoned the laboratory for the lecture hall. In 1766, with Cullen's appointment as a professor of medicine, Black took up the chair of chemistry at Edinburgh. In his new position, Black increasingly focused on applied chemistry.

Already at Glasgow, Black had forged a close professional and, eventually, personal and business relationship with James Watt, who had been appointed instrument maker to the university. In 1769, Black loaned Watt the money needed to obtain a patent on his steam engine. As Watt himself affirmed, the methodological and theoretical background for his invention was laid by Black's meticulous program of experimentation and his investigation of latent and specific heats. Now, in the 1770's and 1780's, Scottish agricultural improvers such as Henry Home, Lord Kames, sought Black's chemical imprimatur for their proposals even as entrepreneurs sought Black's advice on the metallurgy of coal and iron, the bleaching of textiles, and the manufacture of glass. Black also maintained a medical practice and in 1776 was the attending physician at the death of philosopher David Hume.

Black's dedication to bringing together university and industry as well as philosophy and improvement was a trait he shared with the profusion of clubs in eighteenth century Scotland. He was a member not only of the Philosophical Society (later Royal Society) of Edinburgh but also of less formal civic groups, such as the Select Society or the Poker Club. Dearest to Black was the Oyster Club, weekly dinners with his closest friends William Cullen, the geologist James Hutton, and Adam Smith, the author of *The Wealth of Nations* (1776). Black's friendship with Smith went back to their days as students and then new faculty members at the University of Glasgow. When Smith died in 1790, Black and Hutton served as his executors. In the mid-1790's, Black's own health, which had never been robust, began to fail. On December 6, 1799, just three days after he had managed to complete yet another course of lectures, Black died peacefully at his home in Edinburgh.

SIGNIFICANCE

Joseph Black was an important precursor of the chemical revolution of the late eighteenth century. Britain's preeminent professor of chemistry, Black was uniquely influential. Across his career, he introduced Scottish philosophical chemistry to as many as five thousand students. From the last decade of the eighteenth century until well into the nineteenth century, these students would edit chemical journals in Germany and hold chairs in chemistry at universities such as Cambridge, Oxford, Columbia, Princeton, and Yale.

During the 1790's, Black was among the first to bring Antoine-Laurent Lavoisier's reform of chemical nomenclature to an English-speaking audience. However, in 1789, the very year in which Lavoisier's *Traité élémentaire de chimie* (*Elements of Chemistry, in a New Systematic Order, Containing All the Modern Discoveries*, 1790) was published, Lavoisier wrote Black acknowledging "the important revolutions which your discoveries have caused in the Sciences." Black's discovery of carbon dioxide opened the way for Joseph Priestley's discovery of oxygen and Lavoisier's own demonstration of oxygen's role in calcination and combustion. To be sure, Black's measurement of latent and specific heats still worked within a framework of a chemical theory that imagined heat as a caloric fluid that was lost when a body was cooled and gained when a body was heated. His measurements, however, also turned on a distinction between heat and temperature that laid the groundwork for nineteenth century thermodynamics and a conception of heat as kinetic energy.

From his earliest years in Bordeaux, Black stood at the crossroads between the great economic transformation that was the Industrial Revolution and the great cultural transformation that was the European Enlightenment. His life work balanced a calling to make the study of chemistry "philosophical" with a civic commitment to the "improvement" of Scotland. The balance that Black achieved was a model for chemistry's continuing career in Britain as a public science—a career that culminated in Sir Humphry Davy's lectures to the Royal Institution in the early nineteenth century. The balance that Black achieved also marked a critical moment in European cultural history, a moment before specialization would estrange the "two cultures" of the sciences and the humanities, a moment when chemistry remained a liberal vocation.

—Charles R. Sullivan

FURTHER READING

Black, Joseph. *Experiments upon Magnesia Alba, Quicklime, and Some Other Alcaline Substances*. Edinburgh: E. & S. Livingstone, 1966. A modern reprint of the 1756 publication of Black's classic work. A brief, 46-page text.

Donovan, A. L. *Philosophical Chemistry in the Scottish Enlightenment: The Doctrines and Discoveries of William Cullen and Joseph Black*. Edinburgh: Edinburgh University Press, 1975. In the absence of a modern biography of Black, this work is the most authoritative account of Black's life and contributions to chemistry.

Golinski, Jan. *Science as Public Culture: Chemistry and Enlightenment in Britain, 1760-1820*. New York: Cambridge University Press, 1992. Argues that Cullen and Black successfully established chemistry as an integral part of the civic culture of the Scottish Enlightenment.

Greenberg, Arthur. *A Chemical History Tour*. Hoboken, N.J.: John Wiley and Sons, 2000.

_____. *The Art of Chemistry*. Hoboken, N.J.: John Wiley and Sons, 2003. These two lavishly illustrated companion volumes situate Black within the development of chemical ideas in the eighteenth century.

Simpson, A. D. C., ed. *Joseph Black, 1728-1799: A Commemorative Symposium*. Edinburgh: Royal Scottish Museum, 1982. Includes short essays on Black's life, medical practice, contributions to the study of heat, and the natural philosophical and institutional background to Black's philosophical chemistry.

See also: Henry Cavendish; Adam Ferguson; David Hume; Antoine-Laurent Lavoisier; Montesquieu; Joseph Priestley; John Roebuck; Adam Smith; Georg Ernst Stahl; James Watt.

Related articles in *Great Events from History: The Eighteenth Century, 1701-1800:* 1714: Fahrenheit Develops the Mercury Thermometer; 1723: Stahl Postulates the Phlogiston Theory; 1738: Bernoulli Proposes the Kinetic Theory of Gases; 1742: Celsius Proposes an International Fixed Temperature Scale; 1745: Lomonosov Issues the First Catalog of Minerals; 1748: Montesquieu Publishes *The Spirit of the Laws*; June 5, 1755: Black Identifies Carbon Dioxide; 1765-1769: Watt Develops a More Effective Steam Engine; 1771: Woulfe Discovers Picric Acid; August 1, 1774: Priestley Discovers Oxygen; 1781-1784: Cavendish Discovers the Composition of Water; 1789: Leblanc Develops Soda Production.

SIR WILLIAM BLACKSTONE
English legal scholar and jurist

Blackstone has remained the most famous jurist in the history of English law. His Commentaries on the Laws of England *has endured as the most influential work in English legal literature. He was the last jurist to synthesize the common law of his own age and present it cohesively to his contemporaries. He succeeded so well that his* Commentaries *retains its place among the masterpieces of legal writing.*

Born: July 10, 1723; Cheapside, London, England
Died: February 14, 1780; Wallingford, Berkshire, England
Areas of achievement: Law, scholarship

EARLY LIFE

William Blackstone was born amid tragic circumstances, for his father had died prior to his birth. Orphaned at age twelve, Blackstone was reared by a maternal uncle who supervised his education. Blackstone attended Charterhouse School in 1735 and soon demonstrated an inclination toward academic work in a variety of fields. In 1738, Blackstone entered Pembroke College, Oxford. The young man combined a strong intellectual bent with an industry rare at Oxford in the eighteenth century.

He was a large individual who had a positive aversion to exercise in all forms. His size helped to project a commanding presence in all circumstances. In 1741, he went to the Middle Temple, one of the four Inns of Court that monopolized the training of barristers. He was elected a fellow of All Souls College in 1743, and two years later he earned the bachelor of civil law degree.

In this period, Blackstone performed many tasks for All Souls, including the post of librarian, wherein he helped in the foundation of the Codrington Library. He recognized that he did not possess the qualities required for success at the bar, and therefore he concentrated increasingly on his Oxford prospects. He took the doctorate in civil law in 1750. His reputation for legal learning grew to the extent that he was mentioned prominently for the Regius Chair of Civil Law that fell vacant in 1753. Blackstone did not receive the appointment, but this failure marked a turning point in his life. Because the study of Roman or civil law appeared a dead end for his plans, he turned his attention to another area for his endeavors.

Blackstone was not a collegial person. He had a difficult personality that did not win affection for him easily. His marriage, however, was happy and produced seven children. He had sincere religious convictions within the Anglican Church. In addition to his academic work, Blackstone had a public career in the House of Commons from 1761 to 1770. He did not play a major role in the Commons, for his speeches lacked the vitality necessary for greater impact.

LIFE'S WORK

In 1753, William Blackstone advertised a series of lectures he would offer on the laws of England. The novelty of this announcement lay in the fact that the academic study of law at Oxford and Cambridge had always focused on Roman law. To propose the formal study of the laws and constitution of England represented a revolutionary departure. These lectures enjoyed a great success and eventually formed the nucleus of Blackstone's greatest contribution to English law, *Commentaries on the Laws of England* (1765-1769).

In 1756, he published an outline of the lectures that made him a prime candidate for the newly founded chair of English law at Oxford, a position made possible by a bequest from Charles Viner. Viner had acquired a substantial reputation as a legal scholar, and he left a sum of £12,000 for this initial professorship. In 1758, Blackstone became the inaugural holder of the Vinerian chair, which was to become the oldest and most prestigious professorship of English law.

Between 1765 and 1769, Blackstone published the four volumes of *Commentaries* that established his reputation forever after as a major jurist of common law. In the tradition of Ranulf de Glanville in the twelfth century, Henry de Bracton in the thirteenth, Thomas Littleton in the fifteenth, and Sir Edward Coke in the seventeenth, Blackstone attempted to state the fundamental principles (with examples) of major divisions of common law. The publication history of the *Commentaries* testified to the extraordinary influence that the work obtained. Between 1769 and Blackstone's death in 1780, eight editions appeared. Over the next seventy years, an additional fifteen editions strengthened the legacy. Numerous American editions placed Blackstone firmly in the midst of American constitutional development.

In the area of constitutional law, Blackstone contributed significantly to the evolving doctrine of the sovereignty of Parliament expressed in the formula of king in

Parliament. Though this doctrine did not originate with Blackstone, his explanation of it in the context of the 1760's brought a new dimension to the consequences of the Glorious Revolution in 1688. John Locke had usually served as the justifier for the events of 1688 and afterward. He had advanced a theory of vested rights for each citizen that no authority could transgress, especially a tyrannical monarch.

Blackstone was equally as anxious to vindicate the Glorious Revolution. The gradual lessening of the king's active political role removed the fear of executive authority. Blackstone emphasized the great truth of the modern British constitution: In matters of fundamental importance, Parliament must prevail. Parliament possessed by 1765 the right to legislate on any matter in any manner. Later glosses would qualify the Blackstonian dicta by adding that the only limitation on parliamentary sovereignty was that Parliament could not bind its successors.

Sir William Blackstone. (Library of Congress)

His enunciation of parliamentary sovereignty had a special relevance to the contemporary debate between Great Britain and its American colonies. His statement of the doctrine accentuated the constitutional gap that intensified the disaffection prior to the American Revolution. Blackstone specifically rejected the claims of the American colonists based on Lockean grounds and asserted the right of Parliament to legislate on their behalf. Parliamentary sovereignty, despite changes in its application, has remained the foundation of the modern British constitution.

In the evolution of common law from the twelfth century to Blackstone's era, there had occurred a significant degree of overlapping jurisdictions and technicalities. From this morass, Blackstone rescued common law by dividing it into four areas that might easily be understood by the educated layperson. Prior to 1765, the literature of common law had consisted primarily of unreadable, obscure abridgments, incomplete collections of cases, and various confusing attempts at scholarship. Out of this amorphous mass of legal material, Blackstone sought to identify basic principles that would act as guides to the law as a whole.

He expressed the existing state of the law in terms of the rights of the individual, primarily property law, and he discussed private wrongs, or the law of torts. He divided public law into that governing the individual's relation to the state and the area of public wrongs, or criminal law. The purpose in each case was to make sense of the law, whose needless complexities had already become legendary. Blackstone realized this goal admirably. The *Commentaries* owed its popularity as much to literary merit as to command of legal issues. It was the first work of modern legal literature that looked to an audience wider than that of lawyers only.

Perhaps the most frequent criticism of Blackstone has concentrated on the extent to which he presented an overly optimistic view of common law as it existed in 1765 and thereby retarded reform for a legal system that did possess many defects. In this role, as many critics have charged, Blackstone acted as an apologist for the existing social, legal, and political structure. That Blackstone rarely censured the existing order may be conceded. In some areas, however, such as the ferocity of the criminal law, he never hesitated to express his misgivings about its efficacy. Blackstone is best understood as a practical lawyer who wrote his account of common law in institutional terms that were part of a general European trend, not as a crass defender of the Whig oligarchy. He took a chaotic mass of legal rules and turned them into a legal system consistent with the national consciousness of an emerging imperial power. In the process, Blackstone naturally extolled the virtues of common law.

In view of his towering reputation as a jurist, it was ironic that Blackstone enjoyed little success on the bench, where he served as a justice of the Court of Common Pleas from 1770 until his death, on February 14, 1780. His decisions have not won the same praise from posterity as his legal writings. Blackstone rarely came to a firm decision, and new trials were granted after his decisions more frequently than for any other judge of his time. Even his best opinions rarely pointed to new directions for common law.

SIGNIFICANCE

Sir William Blackstone has retained his fame as the most illustrious jurist in the history of common law. The *Commentaries on the Laws of England* represents the most influential law book in British history. It introduced a new form of legal literature, expanded the audience for legal scholarship, and provided a new norm for legal education. Common law was presented as a practical guide to life, not an arcane series of rules important to a few. Blackstone made the study of common law a university pursuit, an intellectual effort worthy of serious students.

Blackstone's influence in the United States was as great as in his home country. The *Commentaries* provided the basic education for lawyers and judges for generations. His account of common law proved the primary vehicle for the resilience of English law in the United States after 1783. Legal education in America followed the university model pioneered by Blackstone as Vinerian professor. His greatest legacy remains in the minds of countless lawyers and laypersons who regard the law as an object of veneration, a pursuit that demands sustained intellectual effort.

—*Richard A. Cosgrove*

FURTHER READING

Blackstone, Sir William. *Commentaries on the Laws of England.* 9th ed. 4 vols. Edited and introduced by Wayne Morrison. London: Cavendish, 2001. This edition of Blackstone's commentaries has been rewritten in modernized English.

Boorstin, Daniel J. *The Mysterious Science of the Law: An Essay on Blackstone's "Commentaries," Showing How Blackstone, Employing Eighteenth Century Ideas of Science, Religion, History, Aesthetics, and Philosophy, Made of the Law at Once a Conservative and a Mysterious Science.* Chicago: University of Chicago Press, 1996. An updated edition of the original 1941 book, with a new foreword by the author. Boorstin provides an intellectual history of the eighteenth century, showing how Blackstone interpreted the ideas of his age to establish principles of common law.

Cairns, John W. "Blackstone, an English Institutist: Legal Literature and the Rise of the Modern State." *Oxford Journal of Legal Studies* 4 (Winter, 1984): 318-360. An excellent article that emphasizes the European background to the writing of the *Commentaries*. It stresses that Blackstone was not merely an apologist for the status quo.

Cosgrove, Richard A. *Scholars of the Law: English Jurisprudence from Blackstone to Hart.* New York: New York University Press, 1996. This work includes a chapter about Blackstone and the "intersection of positivism and natural law theory."

Doolittle, I. G. "Sir William Blackstone and His *Commentaries on the Laws of England* (1765-69): A Biographical Approach." *Oxford Journal of Legal Studies* 3 (Spring, 1983): 99-112. Doolittle argues for the varied achievements of Blackstone, not only in jurisprudence. Provides an excellent contrast for the interpretation of Blackstone's contributions.

Hanbury, Harold G. *The Vinerian Chair and Legal Education.* Oxford, England: Basil Blackwell, 1958. One Vinerian professor writes a sympathetic account of his predecessor. The treatment of the *Commentaries* is especially enlightening.

Harman, Charles E. *The Men Who Made the Law: During the Time of Justinian's Compilation and Blackstone's "Commentaries."* Brookings, Oreg.: Old Court Press, 2002. Harman traces the sources of the law from the Roman Empire through Blackstone's age.

Kennedy, Duncan. "The Structure of Blackstone's *Commentaries.*" *Buffalo Law Review* 28 (Fall, 1979): 205-382. Kennedy indicts Blackstone for his legitimizing of the socioeconomic world of 1765. This article presents the most important argument for Blackstone acting as an apologist for the established order.

Landau, Norma, ed. *Law, Crime, and English Society, 1660-1830.* New York: Cambridge University Press, 2002. This work includes an essay by David Lieberman called "Mapping Criminal Law: Blackstone and the Categories of English Jurisprudence."

Lockmiller, David A. *Sir William Blackstone.* Chapel Hill: University of North Carolina Press, 1938. Still the best available biography of Blackstone; however, it contains a number of defects and should be consulted with care. It has won qualified approval from subsequent scholars.

Milsom, S. F. C. "The Nature of Blackstone's Achievement." *Oxford Journal of Legal Studies* 1 (Spring, 1981): 1-12. An important summation of the work of Blackstone by a leading legal historian. It emphasizes the role that Blackstone played in making law a practical account of life.

See also: Jeremy Bentham; First Baron Erskine; First Earl of Mansfield; Thomas Paine; Jean-Jacques Rousseau; Mary Wollstonecraft.

Related articles in *Great Events from History: The Eighteenth Century, 1701-1800:* April, 1762: Rousseau Publishes *The Social Contract*; February 22, 1791-February 16, 1792: Thomas Paine Publishes *Rights of Man*; 1792: Wollstonecraft Publishes *A Vindication of the Rights of Woman*; 1792-1793: Fichte Advocates Free Speech.

WILLIAM BLAKE
English poet and artist

Blake was a gifted and highly original poet, painter, engraver, and draftsman, and is regarded as one of the great English Romantic poets.

Born: November 28, 1757; London, England
Died: August 12, 1827; London, England
Areas of achievement: Literature, art

EARLY LIFE
At the time of William Blake's birth in 1757, London was a city of contraries. Blake's birthplace, 28 Broad Street, was near fashionable Bond Street and Golden Square, an elegant oasis of a park, but also, as has been observed, within sight of almost every sort of evil in eighteenth century London. Within walking distance of the crowded city were miles of green fields and hedgerows, hills and heaths, and quiet villages. Innocence and experience were, so to speak, almost on Blake's doorstep from his earliest years. Here, too, were the sites of his early visions. At age four, he said he was frightened by God peering at him through a window. Later, he reported seeing a tree full of angels and angels with the hay makers in the fields.

Though his father, James Blake, a respectable hosier, came close to thrashing him for falsehood when he spoke of the tree full of angels, he was sensitive enough to listen to the boy's request not to be sent to school. In 1768, at the age of ten, Blake was sent to Henry Pars, the best drawing teacher in London, and the senior Blake was not only able to afford the tuition but also to purchase casts for study at home and to give his son pocket money to purchase prints and drawings. Amused and impressed by his serious young customer, whose preference for Michelangelo, Raphael, Giulio Romano, Albrecht Dürer, and Martin Helmskerk, among others, ran counter to the

taste of the time, the print seller often gave young Blake a special bargain.

In 1772, at age fourteen, Blake was apprenticed to James Basire, a somewhat old-fashioned but highly reputable engraver. Blake was thereby provided with a trade by which he could earn his living while pursuing his art. Engravers were much in demand for book illustrations; making plates from drawings, paintings, and sculpture was excellent training in draftsmanship. In 1774, Basire sent Blake to Westminster Abbey to make drawings for Richard Gough's *Sepulchral Monuments in Great Britain* (1786, 1796). There, Blake developed a love of the Gothic and of linear drawing. He also had several visions in the Abbey. After completing his apprenticeship, Blake began to study at the Royal Academy (1769), where he first exhibited some of his work in 1780. In 1782, he married Catherine Boucher, whom he taught not only to read and write but also to assist him in making prints and to help illuminate his books.

Blake's education was not confined to the visual arts. He read George Champman's translations of the works of Homer, Thomas Percy's *Reliques of Ancient English Poetry* (1765) and *Northern Antiquities* (1770), and the works of Edmund Spenser, William Shakespeare, Alexander Pope, John Dryden, Thomas Gray, Edward Young, Francis Bacon, Sir Isaac Newton, John Locke, Voltaire, and Samuel Johnson, studying them with care and vigorous disagreement. He also read works by his contemporaries Thomas Paine, William Godwin, William Cowper, William Wordsworth, George Gordon, Lord Byron, and a number of mystical writers, especially Emanuel Swedenborg, Philippus Aurcolus Paracelsus, and Jakob Böhme. John Milton and, above all, the Bible were major influences, and Blake taught himself Greek,

Latin, Hebrew, French, and Italian. He had been drawing since earliest childhood; at age twelve, he began to write verses. In 1783, poems he wrote between the ages of twelve and twenty were published in *Poetical Sketches*. In them, there are occasional glimpses of the mature Blake.

LIFE'S WORK

In July, 1784, William Blake's father died, and in October of that year Blake opened a print shop in partnership with James Parker. In 1785, the business failed, and the Blakes moved to less-expensive lodgings. Blake's beloved younger brother Robert lived with them, dying of consumption in 1787, at age nineteen. Blake nursed him, without sleep, for two weeks, and as his brother died, Blake saw his spirit ascend. From then on, Blake claimed to communicate regularly with Robert, on one occasion receiving from him a highly complex and original method of engraving the plates for his illuminated books. Continuing with engraving to support himself and Catherine (they never had children), he also began to experiment with illuminated printing.

In 1789, Blake published *Songs of Innocence*, but it was not published in the modern sense of the word. Blake

William Blake. (Library of Congress)

and Catherine produced the books from start to finish. Following Robert's advice, Blake wrote the text and outlines on the plate with acid-impervious material and then had acid eat away the plate so that the material to be printed was in high relief. A plate to be engraved had to be polished and cleaned with great care so that it would not scratch the copper. For the printing, the Blakes ground the colors and mixed the ink. Then, the sheets were printed, one at a time, laid to dry, and carefully hand-colored, with almost no two alike. For most of his regular engraving commissions, Blake did fine etching on copper by hand. Sometimes he used acid, but the finest effect required all handwork. This exacting and arduous process was Blake's major source of income, requiring an amount of persistence and hard labor rather contrary to the outlook of a visionary, which he would "curse and bless" at once for its difficulty and for the beauty and perfection of the results.

Another of the contraries in Blake's life was his involvement in the world about him. Although he was a solitary man, given to visions, he became acquainted, largely through his work for the publisher Joseph Johnson, with many of his more famous contemporaries, including Paine, Joel Barlow, Godwin, and Mary Wollstonecraft. He illustrated Wollstonecraft's *Original Stories from Real Life* (1788). Blake also became acquainted with many current works of literature, philosophy, and science. He illustrated, among others, Erasmus Darwin's *The Botanic Garden* (1791).

In 1791, Johnson set Blake's prose work *The French Revolution* in type, but the work was never printed and survives only in a set of proof sheets. In many quarters, the French Revolution and its sympathizers were looked upon with suspicion and, after the Reign of Terror in 1793, were looked upon with horror. Living, as he did, in the heart of London, Blake was very aware of the realities of political and economic injustice. There were many trials for sedition, and the atmosphere of political unrest and suspicion was to continue at least until the English defeat of France, its traditional enemy, at Waterloo in 1815. Even in 1791, it was not surprising that Johnson should have had second thoughts about publishing Blake's work.

Blake's output as a writer and artist was extensive. He left more than thirty major works, many of them lengthy, among the most outstanding of which are *The Marriage of Heaven and Hell* (1790), *America: A Prophecy* (1793), *Visions of the Daughters of Albion* (1793), *Songs of Innocence and Songs of Experience* (1794), *The First Book of Urizen* (1794), *Europe: A Prophecy* (1794), *The Song of*

Los (1795), *Milton: A Poem* (1804-1808), *Jerusalem: The Emanation of the Giant Albion* (1804-1820), and the unfinished *The Four Zoas* (1797-1807). He made well over eight hundred engravings, including those for his masterpiece, *The Book of Job* (1826); paintings illustrating Milton's *Paradise Lost* (1667) and John Bunyan's *The Pilgrim's Progress* (1678); and individual paintings and drawings, some of which he exhibited at the Royal Academy between 1780 and 1808. Much of his artwork survives, thanks to the efforts of Thomas Butts, who early saw the value of Blake's art, becoming his patron and purchasing a number of works. The first major modern exhibitions of his work began in the late nineteenth century.

By 1795, Blake was having difficulty finding engraving commissions; his style was out of fashion. William Hayley, a minor poet, seemed to offer a solution, inviting the Blakes to come to Felpham, on the English Channel; commissioning him to illustrate his own work, *A Series of Ballads* (1802); and undertaking to find other commissions for him. Blake remained there for three years. Though he found time for his own work, he became more and more unhappy with Hayley's lack of sensitivity to his work and his increasingly patronizing attitude. *A Series of Ballads* did not sell well.

In 1803, after the war with France was resumed, Blake evicted a drunken soldier, Scofield, from his garden. Scofield accused him of seditious remarks, and Blake was brought to trial. Blake's relations with Hayley were already stressful, and this was a final blow. After Blake was acquitted in January of 1804, the Blakes returned to London, where they were to remain.

The years 1805 to 1810 brought a series of frustrations. In 1805, Blake's designs for Robert Blair's *The Grave* (1743), a popular poem, were purchased for a small sum by the publisher Robert Cromek, who then gave the much more lucrative commission for the engraving to a fashionable engraver. In 1806, Blake outlined a plan for a large engraving of Geoffrey Chaucer's Canterbury pilgrims, a most original idea at the time.

Cromek gave the idea to Thomas Stothard, a prominent artist, who, though presumably a friend of Blake, used it himself. In 1808, the edition of *The Grave* illustrated by Blake was published, to receive only one review, and that a devastating one. Blake continued to exhibit works at the Royal Academy, but his only one-man show, in 1809-1810, was a failure, reviewed scathingly by the same critic. The exhibit's *A Descriptive Catalogue*, one of the few works by Blake printed in his lifetime, contains his theories on art. Henry Crabb Robinson, an influential writer and critic, saw and liked the exhibition, but his review appeared only in a German publication.

By 1821, Blake was forced to sell his print collection and move into smaller quarters, where he was to remain until his death. There, with only one dimly lighted room for sleeping, eating, engraving, and writing, he continued, undaunted, to work. He was discovered by and influenced a group of young painters, among them Samuel Palmer and John Linnell, who respected and visited the artist.

A ROMANTIC VISION OF LONDON

In "London," William Blake expresses a nightmarish vision of London as an oppressive city, choking the life from its inhabitants. Perhaps more than any other of his poems, this reaction against the beginnings of modern industrialism and late eighteenth century politics marks Blake as one of the first and most distinctive voices in the British Romantic movement.

> I wander thro' each charter'd street,
> Near where the charter'd Thames does flow,
> And mark in every face I meet
> Marks of weakness, marks of woe.
> In every cry of every Man,
> In every Infant's cry of fear,
> In every voice, in every ban,
> The mind-forg'd manacles I hear.
> How the Chimney-sweeper's cry
> Every black'ning Church appals;
> And the hapless Soldier's sigh
> Runs in blood down Palace walls.
> But most thro' midnight streets I hear
> How the youthful Harlot's curse
> Blasts the new born Infant's tear,
> And blights with plagues the Marriage hearse.

Source: William Blake, *Songs of Experience*, excerpted in Representative Poetry Online. http://eir.library.utoronto.ca/rpo/display/poem184.html. Accessed September, 2005.

Despite illness, Blake during his final years engraved his masterpiece, *The Book of Job,* and began his illustrations for Dante's *The Divine Comedy* (1320), which he left unfinished at his death on August 12, 1827. Catherine Blake died four years later. Some of Blake's manuscripts were destroyed by Frederick Tatham, his executor, and of his plates for engraving only a fragment of one for *America* has survived.

It is not surprising that Blake was so little appreciated in his own time. In his lifetime, he was known almost solely for his painting and engraving. Only one of his three obituaries even mentions his writing. His poetry, prose, and illuminated books were available only in manuscript and in very limited editions, and his complex system of thought was difficult to comprehend, particularly without the entire body of his work upon which to draw.

In interpreting Blake's work, one must keep in mind that he was fully convinced of the reality of his visions. He perceived the images he received, whether verbal or visual, as coming from a source beyond himself. Interpretations of his ideas should be prefaced by the observation that as his poetry is rich in symbolism and layers of meaning, it has given rise to a great variety of interpretations and descriptive terminology.

In religion, Blake was certainly no more eccentric than many of his contemporaries, such as Joanna Southcott, John Wesley, and George Whitefield, who had brought evangelical fervor to the mainstream of English religious life. In his writings, however, Blake's dominant concern was for the spiritual state created by adverse political conditions, which he saw as but one level of reality, though a significant one, relating spiritual and temporal realities by vivid images.

"Visionary" applies to Blake's art as well, paintings and drawings reflecting and reinforcing his ideas and images; indeed, Blake saw them as a unit. The dominant sense a series of pages gives is one of motion observed and caught by the artist: figures in action, swirling and definite lines, often vivid colors. Though Blake's illuminated books are strikingly original in their artistic fusion of word and image, Blake was influenced by the masses of illustrated books popular in the eighteenth century and earlier, including children's books. Blake, in one sense, simply carried to its logical conclusion both the doctrine of *ut pictura poesis* (as painting, so is poetry), current since the Renaissance, and the eighteenth century use of personification. As a known painter and engraver, he shared ideas and friendship with his artist contemporaries, Henry Fuseli, James Barry, John Flaxman, George Romney, and Thomas Stothard.

Blake's language was actually further from that of his poetic contemporaries than his art was from that of his fellow painters. *Poetical Sketches* gives evidence of both his knowledge of and his discomfort with traditional and current English prosody. *Songs of Innocence* and *Songs of Experience*, many of the poems deceptively simple on first reading, depart from the conventions upon which they are based and are more complex than Wordsworth and Samuel Taylor Coleridge's *Lyrical Ballads* (1798-1800), with which they have been compared. They are a good introduction to Blake's thought, with innocence and experience portrayed as contraries, which must be absorbed into a state of higher innocence that incorporates both visions and adds a new dimension. The prophetic books, a bold experiment in free verse well ahead of their time, require more effort; *America* is one of the more accessible works.

SIGNIFICANCE

William Blake's reputation was obscured until 1863. In that year, Alexander Gilchrist's full biography was published, completed by his widow, Anne Gilchrist, with Dante Gabriel Rossetti and William Michael Rossetti. Gilchrist had been able to draw upon the reminiscences of those who knew Blake, and to describe Blake's London with some accuracy. Blake sources, however, are full of legend and misinformation, and it is advisable to check them against modern authorities. In 1893, Edwin J. Ellis and William Butler Yeats undertook an edition of the poetry, with a long introduction by Yeats, who, influenced by Blake, created a mythology of his own. It was not until 1927, with Mona Wilson's biography and Geoffrey Keynes's edition of the poetry, that accurate Blake texts and scholarly biography became available.

Blake has been called "the first modern poet." He anticipated by almost a century the *fin de siècle* and modern movement in the depiction of inner rather than outer states and the use of symbols and abstraction in the arts. In the twentieth century, Blake has been increasingly valued as a gifted and highly original poet, whose influence has been more indirect than direct. He has been considered an ancestor of or a precursor to a number of modern and contemporary cultural phenomena and ideas: Hegelianism, Marxism, evolution, Freudian and Jungian psychology, psychedelic drugs and resulting experiences, and even theories of relativity.

Blake's enduring value, however, may well lie in his intense awareness of both the preeminence of spiritual values and the difficult and humble lives people led in the actual world, and his ability to fuse these areas of awareness in images ranging from the most simple and earthly to the most abstract and apocalyptic.

—*Katharine M. Morsberger*

FURTHER READING

Ackroyd, Peter, Robin Hamlyn, Marilyn Butler, and Michael Phillips. *William Blake*. New York: Harry N. Abrams, 2001. Reproductions of 250 works exhibited in 2001 at the Tate Museum in London and the Metropolitan Museum of Art in New York. The collection has four essays, with one that examines the Gothic and spiritual influences on Blake's art and another about his life in South London in the 1790's.

Bentley, G. E., Jr. *Blake Records: Documents (1714-1841) Concerning the Life of William Blake (1757-1827) and His Family*. 2d ed. New Haven, Conn.: Yale University Press, 2004. This updated edition brings together all known documentary records on Blake, including writing by his contemporaries.

_____. *The Stranger from Paradise: A Biography of William Blake*. New Haven, Conn.: Yale University Press, 2001. Bentley, a noted Blake scholar, presents a comprehensive, detailed portrait of an eccentric genius who saw the world as a product of his personal imagination. Includes 50 color and 120 black-and-white illustrations.

_____. *William Blake: The Critical Heritage*. Boston: Routledge and Kegan Paul, 1975. A collection of criticism by Blake's contemporaries, arranged topically.

Blake, William. *Blake's Poetry and Designs*. Edited by Mary Lynn Johnson and John E. Grant. New York: W. W. Norton, 1979. A good introductory selection of Blake's poetry and prose, with commentary by nineteenth and twentieth century critics. Illustrations, several in color.

_____. *The Complete Poetry and Prose of William Blake*. Edited by David V. Erdman. Berkeley: University of California Press, 1982. A thoroughly annotated collection, with commentary by Harold Bloom. For variant readings, see Geoffrey Keynes's (1927) and G. E. Bentley's (1978) editions of Blake's writings.

Bronowski, Jacob. *William Blake and the Age of Revolution*. New York: Harper & Row, 1965. Bronowski relates Blake's writings to the Industrial Revolution in this brief and readable work.

Erdman, David V. *Blake, Prophet Against Empire: A Poet's Interpretation of the History of His Own Times*. 1954. Rev. ed. Princeton, N.J.: Princeton University Press, 1969. A detailed analysis of Blake's works in the context of the political and social history of his times.

Essick, Robert N. *William Blake, Printmaker*. Princeton, N.J.: Princeton University Press, 1980. A biographical study of Blake's development as an artist, with detailed commentary on etching and printmaking techniques. Illustrated.

Frye, Northrop, et al. *Blake: A Collection of Critical Essays*. Englewood Cliffs, N.J.: Prentice-Hall, 1966. A useful collection of critical views on various aspects of Blake's work.

Hagstrum, Jean. *William Blake, Poet and Painter*. Chicago: University of Chicago Press, 1964. Excellent study of the interrelationships between Blake's poetry and designs, including historical and philosophical background.

Wilson, Mona. *The Life of William Blake*. 1927. 2d ed. New York: Oxford University Press, 1971. Wilson's was considered the most authoritative biography of Blake until Bentley's biography was published in 2001.

See also: Joseph Addison; Anna Barbauld; Robert Burns; Hannah Cowley; Thomas Gainsborough; William Godwin; Thomas Paine; Alexander Pope; Sir Joshua Reynolds; George Romney; Suzuki Harunobu; Emanuel Swedenborg; Charles Wesley; John Wesley; George Whitefield; Mary Wollstonecraft.

Related articles in *Great Events from History: The Eighteenth Century, 1701-1800:* March 1, 1711: Addison and Steele Establish *The Spectator*; December 10, 1768: Britain's Royal Academy of Arts Is Founded.

WILLIAM BLIGH
English naval officer

Notorious for having lost the Bounty *to mutineers in the South Pacific in 1789, Bligh had a long and distinguished but controversial career in the British navy.*

Born: September 9, 1754; Plymouth, Devonshire, England
Died: December 7, 1817; London, England
Areas of achievement: Exploration, military, cartography

EARLY LIFE

William Bligh was the only child of Francis Bligh (1721-1780) and Jane Pearce Bligh (1713-1769). His mother, a widow when she married Francis in 1753, had a daughter Catherine who was nineteen when William was born. His father, who would remarry twice following Jane's death, was customs officer at Plymouth. The Bligh line was well established and quite distinguished in the English West Country.

William's half sister Catherine married John Bond, a surgeon serving on HMS *Monmouth* in 1762. Through this connection and perhaps those of his father, just before his eighth birthday, William was made a captain's servant on this sixty-four-gun ship as part of the traditional preparation for a career as a naval officer. For the next eight years, Bligh was educated, mostly ashore, in mathematics, astronomy, and the various aspects of navigation and seamanship. His subsequent achievements suggest that he was an outstanding, even brilliant, student.

From 1770 until 1776, Bligh served aboard three ships, mostly as a midshipman. He then passed separate examinations qualifying him both as a naval lieutenant and as a sailing master. It was in the latter capacity, as a warrant officer rather than a commissioned officer, that Bligh was selected by the explorer Captain James Cook for his third voyage to the Pacific. For a young man of twenty-one, this appointment as master of HMS *Resolution* was a conspicuous honor, and Bligh performed very well. However, it was also the first subtle indication that his talents were more as a nautical technician than as a naval leader. The long voyage, from 1776 through 1780, bore this out. Bligh's navigation, seamanship, and chartwork were outstanding, but he was quite critical of his fellow officers, including Cook. He felt, with considerable justification, that others were given credit for his work. He was open in expressing his opinions, which re-

sulted in his not being promoted to lieutenant at the end of the voyage.

Bligh's next several years were busy and successful. He served on four naval vessels, in the process securing promotion. He married Elizabeth Betham, his beloved "Betsy," with whom he eventually had six daughters. On temporary half pay from naval service, he captained three merchant vessels on the West Indian run. On the last of these, the *Britannia*, Bligh sailed with Fletcher Christian, first his protégé, then the leader of those who deposed Bligh and seized the *Bounty*.

LIFE'S WORK

In August, 1787, William Bligh was appointed commander of HMS *Bounty* and ordered to transport breadfruit trees from Tahiti for transplantation in the West Indies. The breadfruit were intended to serve as cheap homegrown food for slaves on West Indian plantations. Bligh accepted the appointment eagerly. Although he would command a small (ninety-foot), inadequately crewed (forty-seven-man) ship as a poorly paid lieutenant, captaincy of the *Bounty* offered a return to naval service on a voyage with Cook-like undertones of exploration and discovery in the South Seas.

Before the *Bounty* sailed in December, 1787, Bligh lobbied unsuccessfully for promotion. Status and money aside, promotion (to commander or even captain) would have enabled him to carry other commissioned officers and marines to provide discipline and security. However, Lieutenant Bligh was assisted only by warrant officers and midshipmen. Two of the former, John Fryer the master and William Peckover the gunner, commanded watches. The third watch was commanded by Christian, whose status was ambiguous. Officially a midshipman, Christian joined the ship as master's mate but early in the voyage was promoted to acting lieutenant. Given that Christian was relatively young and inexperienced, promotion to a position that was effectively second in command was a clear sign of Bligh's trust in and esteem for him.

Bligh's orders were to proceed to Tahiti via Cape Horn, the southern tip of South America. He sailed into headwinds and storms at the cape for a month and was forced to turn back and proceed by way of the Indian Ocean and a route south of Australia. This delayed arrival in Tahiti until October, 1788. Weighing the various accounts available, the voyage was a mixed bag. Bligh's account emphasizes his prudent handling of the ship and its supplies, his constant concern with the crew's health, and the relative harmony of the outbound voyage. Other accounts, some well after the fact, stress Bligh's strained relations with his warrant officers and petty officers, his inconstant temperament and tendency toward verbal abuse, and his stinginess with food. However, Bligh's relationship with Christian before reaching Tahiti appears to have been quite good.

The *Bounty* expedition remained in Tahiti from late October, 1788, until early April, 1789, procuring, potting, and nurturing the young breadfruit trees. Christian spent this time ashore in overall command of the party gathering the breadfruit. Because the *Bounty* carried two botanists, this was very light duty. Christian's other activities are not completely known, especially whether he formed a relationship with a particular Tahitian woman. Certainly he, like most of the crew, was active sexually: Christian was among the many treated for sexually transmitted diseases.

When the *Bounty* left Tahiti, it was a different ship in several important aspects. It now carried 1,015 small breadfruit trees, as well as a variety of other plants, with the entire collection contained in 774 pots, 39 tubs, and 24 boxes. For twenty-three weeks, discipline had been slack if not nonexistent. Food and sex, the delights of sailors, had been readily available. Three men, including the master-at-arms, had deserted but been recaptured. Abruptly, the freedom and spaciousness of an island paradise were exchanged for a long, dangerous voyage in a tiny ship that was made even smaller because of the space needed for the floating garden. In addition, the ambitious, accomplished commander's protégé, Christian, had shown himself to be human—all too human.

On April 28, 1789, between five and six in the morning, Christian, supported by roughly one-quarter of the crew, seized control of the *Bounty*. Before casting Bligh and eighteen "loyalists" adrift in *Bounty*'s twenty-three-foot launch, Christian famously uttered, "I am in hell." His meaning will never be certain, but a reasonable interpretation is that Bligh's tongue-lashings after the ship left Tahiti had placed Christian in a hell suspended between naval idealism and South Seas sensuality. Christian's action makes psychological sense: Break the tension and escape hell by "running away with" the *Bounty*, the formal naval charge against the mutineers.

If Christian was torn between duty and freedom, Bligh was not. Once in the launch, his duty was clear: Save the men, sail to a port, return to England, recover

the *Bounty*, and prosecute the mutineers. Bligh, always strong-willed, now became the most determined of men. With almost no provisions, in hazardous waters with a half-hearted crew, he sailed the launch about 3,800 miles in forty-eight days to Kupang on Timor in the Dutch East Indies, arriving on June 14, 1789. This is generally regarded as the most remarkable instance of small-boat navigation known.

Upon returning to England, Bligh was court-martialed, the usual procedure when a naval ship was lost. He was honorably acquitted, rapidly promoted to commander and then captain, and placed in command of a second breadfruit expedition. (Wisely, the Admiralty decided not to send Bligh in pursuit of the mutineers.) This time, Bligh sailed as a captain, with two ships and a full complement of officers and marines. The *Providence* and the *Assistant* reached Tahiti on April 9, 1792. Wasting no time, Bligh secured and loaded more than two thousand breadfruit trees and departed on July 20, 1792. Many trees died en route, but the bulk of them were delivered safely to the West Indies in January and February, 1793. For his accomplishment, Bligh was awarded one thousand guineas by the Jamaican house of assembly and the gold medal by the Royal Society of Arts.

William Bligh. (Library of Congress)

For the next ten years, Bligh captained successively larger Royal Navy ships, culminating in command of seventy-four-gun ships. He served bravely and effectively in the Battles of Camperdown (1797) and Copenhagen (1801). Following the latter engagement, Bligh was commended publicly by Vice Admiral Horatio Nelson, of Trafalgar fame, for his conduct of his ship *Glatton*. In the periods between his naval commands, he continued his nautical surveying and charting and was elected a fellow of the Royal Society in 1801 for his cumulative work in navigation and botany.

Mingled with these achievements were three significant controversies. In 1797, Bligh, though relatively blameless, was one of a number of officers temporarily removed from their ships during the general mutiny at the Nore. In 1804-1805, Bligh and his second lieutenant on the *Warrior* took turns court-martialing one another. The lieutenant was acquitted, but the charges against Bligh were "partially proved," and he was reprimanded for his abusive language. Finally, during his governorship of New South Wales, Australia (1806-1810), Bligh was again deposed by one of his subordinates. No formal guilt was attached to Bligh, but he obviously had not been an effective governor. Despite these difficulties, Bligh was promoted to rear admiral, then vice admiral, but never sailed as such.

SIGNIFICANCE

William Bligh was a near genius in the areas of navigation, nautical surveying, and chart making. He is substantially credited with discovery of the Fiji Islands and of an important passage in the Torres Strait between Australia and New Guinea. He was instrumental in the introduction of breadfruit into the West Indies. He advanced to the higher ranks of the Royal Navy at a time when the best officers might be a blend of skilled seaman, fighting commander, practical scientist, daring explorer, and observant ethnographer. His precise, graceful writing continues to be read. Individuals such as Bligh (and they were relatively few) were the backbone of English sea domination and thus of the British Empire.

Bligh, however, had failings related to his genius that made him unsuitable for higher command. Much has been made of his difficult temperament and especially of his abusive language. However, these are only symptoms of his deeper character. The evidence indicates that Bligh was a man of extraordinary focus and concentration. He ignored all but the immediate task at hand and moved relentlessly toward its comple-

tion. In surveying an uncharted coast, this worked well; in attempting to lead much less dedicated men in ambiguous circumstances—the *Bounty* expedition, the chaotic situation in New South Wales—Bligh's tunnel vision and his consequent irritable, impatient behavior were sometimes a disaster. It is unfair, but not hard to understand, that he is remembered largely for disasters.

—John F. Wilson

FURTHER READING

Alexander, Caroline. *The Bounty: The True Story of the Mutiny on the Bounty*. New York: Viking Press, 2003. Alexander reconstructs the mutiny and its aftermath, portraying Bligh as a brilliant navigator who was not the brutal taskmaster of legend.

Bligh, William. *A Book of the Bounty*. Edited by George Mackaness. London: Dent, 1938. This Everyman's Library edition includes selected writings by Bligh on the *Bounty* voyage and mutiny and minutes of the court-martial of the mutineers.

Christian, Glynn. *Fragile Paradise*. Boston: Little, Brown, 1982. Beautifully illustrated, this search for Fletcher Christian by a descendant uncovers new information about Christian and his relationship with Bligh.

Dening, Greg. *Mr. Bligh's Bad Language*. New York: Cambridge University Press, 1994. Scholarly yet provocative, this postmodern treatment does a good job of setting the scenes in both the Pacific Islands and London. Illustrated, with a bibliography.

Hough, Richard. *Captain Bligh and Mr. Christian*. New York: Dutton, 1973. A well-written narrative that develops the theme of a broken affection between Bligh and Christian. The 1984 film *The Bounty* is based on this book.

Kennedy, Gavin. *Captain Bligh*. London: Duckworth, 1989. A full, pro-Bligh biography that contains a discussion of Christian's activities after the mutiny.

Mackaness, George. *The Life of Vice-Admiral William Bligh*. 1931. Rev. ed. Sydney: Angus and Robertson, 1951. Written by an Australian, this standard biography develops Bligh's governorship in considerable detail.

Nordhoff, Charles, and James Norman Hall. *Mutiny on the Bounty*. Boston: Little, Brown, 1932. Widely available in paperback, this historical novel is splendid reading. With its companion volumes *Men Against the Sea* and *Pitcairn's Island*, it formed the basis for the 1935 and 1962 *Bounty* films.

Toohey, John. *Captain Bligh's Portable Nightmare.* London: Fourth Estate, 1999. Recounts the *Bounty*'s voyage to Java. Reevaluates Bligh's reputation, concluding he was a man of his time misunderstood by later generations.

Wahlroos, Sven. *Mutiny and Romance in the South Seas.* Topsfield, Mass.: Salem House, 1989. This useful work is part month-by-month chronicle and part encyclopedia of persons, places, and ships. Extensive bibliography included.

See also: Lord Anson; Louis-Antoine de Bougainville; James Bruce; James Cook; Richard Howe; Sir Alexander Mackenzie; Arthur Phillip; George Vancouver.

Related articles in *Great Events from History: The Eighteenth Century, 1701-1800:* December 5, 1766-March, 16, 1769: Bougainville Circumnavigates the Globe; August 25, 1768-February 14, 1779: Voyages of Captain Cook; July 22, 1793: Mackenzie Reaches the Arctic Ocean.

LUIGI BOCCHERINI
Italian composer

Boccherini was one of the most prolific composers of all time, creating almost five hundred instrumental compositions, from trios to symphonies. With Joseph Haydn and Wolfgang Amadeus Mozart, he helped to establish the style and structure of the classic string quartet and concerto.

Born: February 19, 1743; Lucca (now in Italy)
Died: May 28, 1805; Madrid, Spain
Also known as: Ridolfo Luigi Boccherini (full name)
Area of achievement: Music

EARLY LIFE

Luigi Boccherini (lew-EE-jee bohk-kay-REE-nee) was the third of five children of Leopoldo Boccherini and Maria Santa Boccherini. His father, one of the first musicians to play solos on the double bass, noticed that Luigi displayed a remarkably sensitive ear at an early age. Leopoldo therefore hoped that his son would develop musical talent and began giving him cello lessons when he was five. After a few months, Luigi's father sent him to Abbate Domenico Francesco Vanucci, maestro di cappella at Lucca's cathedral. This composer, cellist, singer, and choirmaster taught the young Boccherini cello, harmony, and composition, as well as Latin and Italian, at the seminary of San Martino. When Boccherini was thirteen years of age, Vanucci realized that his pupil knew at least as much about music as he did.

After Boccherini gave his first public performance during the Festival of the Holy Cross in September, 1756, his father sent him to Rome. He auditioned for the celebrated cellist and composer Giovanni Battista Costanzi and was immediately accepted. Boccherini and his father were appointed cellist and double-bass player in the orchestra of the Imperial Theater in Vienna in December, 1757. In 1760, Boccherini wrote six trios for two violins and cello obligato, his First Opus, and its admirers in Vienna included Christoph Gluck. Other family members also found success in Vienna, as one brother and two sisters danced in the ballet. His other brother, Giovanni-Gastone, after failing as a dancer, a singer, and a violinist, became a librettist, eventually collaborating with Joseph Haydn.

Despite the advances he made in Vienna as cellist and composer, Boccherini wanted to spend the rest of his life in his native town and, in August, 1760, petitioned the Grand Council of Lucca for a position as cellist in the council's chapel; he received no reply. After a major success with a 1764 concert of his works in Vienna, he finally won his Lucca appointment, but the inexperienced Boccherini had expected too much and was disappointed to discover that the council would not pay for his compositions except for the expenses of getting the music copied. On December 9, 1764, attracted by the renown of Giovanni Battista Sammartini, he left for Milan.

In Milan, Boccherini wanted to exchange views with other talented composers and musicians. Such contacts led in 1765 to what historians of classical music consider to be the first formation of a string quartet for regular public performances. This quartet, which consisted of Boccherini (apparently the originator of the idea), Filippo Manfredi, Pietro Nardini, and Giovanni Giuseppe Cambini, played compositions by Haydn and Boccherini.

In the spring of 1765, Boccherini returned to Lucca and to his official duties. Later that year, Boccherini missed two performances, the first sign of an incurable condition that may have been tuberculosis and that grew steadily worse, forcing him eventually to abandon his ambitions as a virtuoso concert cellist. When his father died in 1766, the young composer became anxious over assuming sole responsibility for his career. Needing an experienced adviser, he went to the violinist Manfredi, fourteen years his senior, who invited Boccherini to tour with him.

LIFE'S WORK

Early in 1767, Boccherini and Manfredi arrived in Paris, where Boccherini's music had already been published. Boccherini was soon befriended by the baron de Bagge, an influential patron of the arts, as well as the music publisher Jean-Baptiste Vénier and Madame Brillon de Jouy, a prominent harpsichordist, for whom he composed his Op. 5 (opus 5). Through the baron de Bagge, Boccherini met the intellectual elite of France and became aware of the musical avant-garde.

In 1768, the Spanish ambassador to France invited Boccherini and Manfredi to Madrid, where they hoped for the patronage of the prince of the Asturias, the heir to the Spanish throne, and were lured by the legend of the favorable treatment of artists in the court of Charles III and by the illusion of wealth possible in a country enamored of Italian music. The king and the prince, however, had little musical judgment and were guided entirely by the Italian violinist and composer Gaetano Brunetti. After receiving helpful advice about composition from Boccherini, Brunetti became jealous of this potential rival and decided to prejudice the court against him.

At the end of 1769, Boccherini received a major boost to his career when he met the Infante Don Luis, brother of the king, and composed six quartets (Op. 8) in his honor. Luis was much more sophisticated about music than were his brother and nephew and delighted in supporting musicians slighted at court. Impressed by Boccherini's talent and his personal charm, Luis appointed him cellist and composer of his chamber on November 8, 1770. Boccherini was to be paid thirty thousand reals annually, more than Luis's confessor and his personal physician, and the composer's art flourished for the next fifteen years.

Sometime after entering the service of Luis, Boccherini married Clementina Pelicho—sources do not provide a date—and their first child, a daughter, was born in 1776. When Luis also married and moved to Las Arenas, Boccherini and his family followed. The composer settled down for the next nine years to work on chamber music almost exclusively, since only a small number of musicians were available in Las Arenas.

By 1783, the Boccherinis had three daughters and two sons, but Clementina died suddenly in 1785. After Luis

Luigi Boccherini. (Library of Congress)

died later that year, Charles III continued the composer's salary, appointing him cellist of the Chapel Royal. Boccherini never actually performed this duty, however, because of his illness. The death of Don Luis left Boccherini free to dedicate his works to any patron, and Frederick William II, king of Prussia, appointed him composer of his chamber, although Boccherini continued to live in Madrid. Frederick William, also patron to Haydn and Wolfgang Amadeus Mozart, was fond of the Italian's works, since he himself was an amateur cellist. Among the many pieces Boccherini presented to the Prussian monarch was *La Tirana* (1792), his most famous quartet.

Boccherini's most important Madrid patrons during this time were the countess-duchess of Benavente-Osuna and her husband, the marquis. The countess-duchess made him director of a sixteen-piece orchestra that performed in her palace. Because the marquis was an ardent guitarist, Boccherini transcribed several of his piano pieces for his benefactor's instrument. At the request of the mother of the marquis, he composed *La Clementina* (1786), his only opera, with a libretto by Ramón de la Cruz.

In 1787, Boccherini married Maria del Pilar Joaquina Porreti, daughter of his late friend the cellist Domingo

Porreti. He then ceased composing and performing for the countess-duchess of Benavente-Osuna and withdrew into isolation. He may have decided to devote himself entirely to composition, since his productivity increased, despite ill health, between 1787 and 1796. Almost no documentation exists for the events of Boccherini's private life during this period. While some sources place him at the court of Frederick William, there is no substantial evidence that he ever left Madrid.

Boccherini's fortunes began to take a bad turn in 1798. After Frederick William died, his son halted the composer's pension. Boccherini was then forced to accede to the instructions of his Paris publisher, Ignaz Joseph Pleyel, also a composer. The correspondence between the two reveals that Boccherini had many problems with this demanding, perhaps envious, publisher. When Pleyel advertised himself as the sole proprietor of Boccherini's works, the composer demanded to know if he was still alive. Pleyel's published Boccherini scores were full of errors, and many pieces languished in drawers until the publisher deemed the time right for his own financial benefit.

Boccherini was nevertheless highly regarded in France, and in 1799 he dedicated six quintets, Op. 57, to that nation. As a result, he was invited to become one of the five directors of the Conservatoire in Paris, but he did not want to leave Spain, which he had come to regard as his native country. When Lucien Bonaparte arrived in Madrid as France's ambassador in 1800, he became Boccherini's final patron. The composer was paid richly for organizing the music for the ambassador's parties in the palace of San Bernardino.

After Lucien Bonaparte left Madrid in 1801, Boccherini had nothing on which to live except what he earned from the sale of his works. The pension continued by Charles IV was meager. Despite increasingly bad health, he composed as much as before. Two of his daughters died during an 1802 epidemic, and his wife and another daughter died in 1804. Boccherini began a set of six quartets around this time but was too weak to continue after writing the first movement of the second. He died, apparently of pulmonary suffocation, on May 28, 1805. A century later, Lucca asked Madrid for the composer's ashes, and they were transferred to his birthplace in 1927 and interred in the Basilica of San Francesco.

SIGNIFICANCE

Luigi Boccherini was considered second only to Haydn as a composer for cello and violin in the late eighteenth century, but, as tastes shifted from classical to Romantic music, he became, despite proponents such as Frédéric Chopin and Aleksandr Borodin, somewhat passé. Boccherini's rococo style was thought too delicate and ornate, too superficial and monotonous. Because his music is charming, gentle, and even effeminate, he was called "Haydn's wife" by the violinist Giuseppe Puppo. Still, Mozart is thought to have been influenced by Boccherini, and Ludwig van Beethoven adapted many of his methods and idioms.

Boccherini was all but forgotten when what is still his best-known work, the minuet from the String Quartet in E Major, Op. 13, No. 5, was rediscovered in the 1870's as a jewel of the rococo art. In 1895, the Dresden cellist Friedrich Grützmacher published his free arrangement of the Cello Concerto in B-flat. Boccherini was known primarily for these two works, partly because most of his music was available only in flawed editions, until after World War II, when he began to be reevaluated. The Quintetto Boccherini, formed in Rome in 1949, helped renew interest in the composer, touring throughout the world as well as making many recordings.

As a result, Boccherini has finally been recognized as a significant pioneer in the development of chamber music. He helped the technique of string instruments to progress from an almost primitive simplicity to a subtle sophistication. With Haydn and Mozart, he clarified and solidified the sonata form. He contributed to the maturity of the string quartet by writing as if for four blended soloists rather than for a small orchestra, and he virtually invented the quintet and sextet. He has most often been praised by critics for the balance, symmetry, and lyricism of his compositions. Of Boccherini, Sir William Henry Hadow, an English critic and composer, wrote,

> So long as men take delight in pure melody, in transparent style, and in a fancy alert, sensitive and sincere, so long is his place in the history of music assured.

—Michael Adams

FURTHER READING

Cowling, Elizabeth. *The Cello*. New York: Charles Scribner's Sons, 1975. History of the instrument and its composers and players from the sixteenth century to 1960. Includes an excellent brief biography of Boccherini combined with analysis of his contribution to the literature of the cello.

Gérard, Yves, ed. *Thematic, Bibliographical, and Critical Catalogue of the Works of Luigi Boccherini.*

Translated by Andreas Mayor. New York: Oxford University Press, 1969. Compiled to supplement Germaine de Rothschild's biography, and corrects errors in earlier catalogs of Boccherini's compositions.

Griffiths, Paul. *The String Quartet*. New York: Thames and Hudson, 1983. Traces the development of the string quartet from 1759 to 1913. Evaluates Boccherini's contribution to this development and compares his chamber music to that of Haydn and Mozart.

Heartz, Daniel. "The Young Boccherini: Lucca, Vienna, and the Electoral Courts." *Journal of Musicology* 13, no. 1 (Winter, 1995): 103. Profile of Boccherini, describing his personality, musical education and development, and public performances.

Le Guin, Elisabeth. "'One Says That One Weeps, but One Does Not Weep': Sensible, Grotesque, and Mechanical Embodiments in Boccherini's Chamber Music." *Journal of the American Musicological Society* 55, no. 2 (Summer, 2002): 207. Examines the characteristics and performance of Boccherini's chamber music.

Newman, William S. *The Sonata in the Classic Era*. Chapel Hill: University of North Carolina Press, 1963. History of the sonata from 1740 to 1820. Provides an overview of Boccherini's life combined with a brief but detailed analysis of his contribution to the sonata form.

Rothschild, Germaine de. *Luigi Boccherini: His Life and Work*. Translated by Andreas Mayor. New York: Oxford University Press, 1965. The only biography in English is very brief but contains all the relevant information known to exist. Emphasis is on Boccherini's life, with little analysis of his work. Includes a bibliography and an appendix with all extant Boccherini letters, all to his publishers.

Sadie, Stanley, and John Tyrell, eds. *The New Grove Dictionary of Music and Musicians*. 2d ed. Vol. 3. New York: Grove Press, 2001. Biography and descriptions of Boccherini's compositions. Also available online.

See also: Johann Sebastian Bach; Charles III; Christoph Gluck; George Frideric Handel; Joseph Haydn; Wolfgang Amadeus Mozart.

Related articles in *Great Events from History: The Eighteenth Century, 1701-1800*: c. 1701-1750: Bach Pioneers Modern Music; January 29, 1728: Gay Produces the First Ballad Opera; April 13, 1742: First Performance of Handel's *Messiah*; January, 1762-November, 1766: Mozart Tours Europe as a Child Prodigy; October 5, 1762: First Performance of Gluck's *Orfeo and Euridice*; August 3, 1778: Opening of Milan's La Scala; 1795-1797: Paganini's Early Violin Performances.

GERMAIN BOFFRAND
French architect

Boffrand developed an approach to interior design resulting in rooms where architecture, sculpture, paintings, and furnishings all interacted to convey a unified mood. His concern with the interrelationship between each room, the building plan, and the overall site resulted in works of visual, intellectual, and emotional harmony.

Born: May 16, 1667; Nantes, France
Died: March 19, 1754; Paris, France
Area of achievement: Architecture

EARLY LIFE

Germain Boffrand (zhehr-ma boh-frahnd) conceived of architecture as environmental sculpture, in part as a result of his early training. His father was a provincial sculptor who apprenticed his son in 1681 to François Girardon, the most honored official sculptor during the second half of the seventeenth century in France. Boffrand never denied his training in sculpture. Indeed, toward the end of his career in 1745, he published a treatise on the casting of Girardon's monumental bronze equestrian statue of Louis XIV.

Girardon had worked with architect Jules Hardouin-Mansart at Versailles, which may have been the means by which Boffrand became an apprentice at the Royal Office of Architecture, Service des Bâtiments du Roi, under Hardouin-Mansart in 1685. Boffrand was only nineteen when he began work on the early drawings for the Place Vendôme. The experience Boffrand gained in this project would be useful for him after 1732, when he joined the federal department of bridges and roads, of which he eventually became the director.

Boffrand's connection with the theater during his youth perhaps had an impact on his ability to produce an architecture that conveyed a particular mood and idea. Boffrand's theatrical architectural space is not surprising for an eighteenth century French architect trained in the Royal Office of Architecture, since the major architectural patron of the seventeenth century in France was Louis XIV. Louis's palace, Versailles, was the stage upon which this king's play of absolute monarchy and controlled court life was enacted, and Versailles was, in part, the travail of Hardouin-Mansart, Boffrand's teacher.

LIFE'S WORK

Contemporary information about Boffrand's career comes from official documents in the French archives of state and from his buildings. There also exist accounts of his works and character from French and other European architects, including the letters of Johann Balthasar Neumann, written on a study trip to Paris in 1724, and from Boffrand's own book *Livre d'architecture* (1745; English translation, 1950's).

Between about 1702 and 1719, Boffrand worked under conditions that allowed him a certain amount of freedom of design. His patrons were non-French nobility, including the duke of Lorraine and Maximilian II Emanuel, elector of Bavaria. Being French gave Boffrand an elevated status distinct from that of the local architects. In addition, he maintained his contacts in Paris and erected speculative buildings in the districts of Saint Germain and Saint Honoré. These new areas of the city, developed on the left bank of the Seine River, became the most fashionable addresses in Paris.

Yet Boffrand's freedom probably was one of necessity, since there were few government commissions between the death of Louis XIV and the coming of age of Louis XV. While he was often experimental, he was also literate, exhibiting a knowledge of architectural theory written by his contemporaries as well as the books of earlier architects, particularly the late Renaissance Italian Andrea Palladio.

From 1702 to 1722, Boffrand worked for the duke of Lorraine on many projects, including the palace Château Lunéville. Beginning at Lunéville as the representative of his architectural mentor Hardouin-Mansart, Boffrand eventually became first architect to the duke in 1711, three years after Hardouin-Mansart's death. Two aspects of Lunéville are experimental, while also revealing an interest in the literature of architecture—the chapel and the design of the *corps-logis,* or main body, of the palace. Like the chapel at Versailles, which Hardouin-Mansart initiated but which was completed by his brother-in-law,

the chapel at Lunéville consisted of a tall, open nave ringed by aisles and galleries that stood on load-bearing, free-standing columns. Such a design takes its origin from the Greco-Gothic ideal described by the Abbé de Cordemoy in his *Nouveau Traité de toute l'architecture* (1706). R. D. Middleton singled out the chapel at Lunéville as the first work to put Cordemoy's ideas into practice. Using load-bearing columns at Lunéville, Boffrand focused the weight of the building on slender supports, allowing the walls and interior space to be more open, as was the case in Gothic interiors. Rather than use complex Gothic colonettes, Boffrand employed classical columns for support. The understanding of structural engineering revealed in the chapel at Lunéville is similar to the thinking followed by nineteenth and early twentieth century architects in creating the curtained, walled skyscraper.

Palladio's influence is obvious in the hunting lodge Boffrand built for the elector of Bavaria in 1705. This structure, Bouchefort, was an octagon with four porticoes set in the center of a circular courtyard, which was the terminus of seven avenues leading into the forest of Soignies, near Brussels. The plan of the central pavilion was inspired by Palladio's Villa Almerico, called Rotonda, which was a square with four identical porticoes.

Other innovative plans by Boffrand were the x-shaped Malgrange II, never built but perhaps related to the Althan Palace in Vienna of around 1693, by Johann Bernhard Fischer von Erlach, and the Hôtel Amêlot de Gournay, one of the speculative structures Boffrand erected in Paris in 1712. At Amêlot de Gournay, Boffrand took a rectangular lot and organized the structure around an enclosed oval courtyard, articulating the space with ovals and polygons into a convenient, rhythmically organic design.

Received directly into first-class membership in the Academy of Architects in 1709, Boffrand also rejoined the royal building service in that year. His primary contributions to the development of the rococo-style interior began with a French royal commission in 1710—the salon of the Petit Luxembourg Palace. At Luxembourg, he used a continuous band of molding, the impost, in a new way. The impost, set below the ceiling, curved up over the doors, windows, and mirrors, visually uniting the room and giving no indication of the corners where one wall joined another. With this innovation, Boffrand eliminated the box-shaped room. At Malgrange I, he continued this process of unification in the oval salon of 1711, linking the walls and the ceiling as well through the use of decorative floral-relief sculpture. Although the design elements were complex, Boffrand maintained unity through the use of symmetry and repetition. Boffrand's masterpiece in rococo design was the salon of the princess of Soubise, where all the design elements work together, projecting a remarkable sense of light and harmony.

During the economic crisis of 1719-1720, known as the Mississippi Bubble, Boffrand lost his fortune. In addition, his affiliation with the court of Lorraine ended. Although he did continue some activities in the private realm, most of the second half of his career was devoted to public projects and consultancies. He served as architect and member of the board of the general hospital system in Paris from 1724, worked on the restoration at Nôtre Dame de Paris between 1725 and 1727, and joined the central administration of the French bridges and highway department in 1732. He consulted with Austrian architect Neumann over the design of the Würzburg Residenz in 1724. François Cuvilliés consulted with Boffrand in the 1730's and took the salon of the princess of Soubise as his inspiration for the salon of the Amalienburg hunting lodge in Munich.

SIGNIFICANCE

Germain Boffrand's *Livre d'architecture* encapsulates his career and sheds light on his interests as well as those of his contemporaries. Dedicated to the king of France, the chapters reveal Boffrand as an architect and an intellectual. The first chapter, a dissertation on good taste, is followed by a statement of principles of architecture extracted from Horace, an ancient Roman poet and critic. An essay on the shape and use of Doric, Ionic, and Corinthian forms and decorative systems is followed by comments on interior furnishings and plans, on elevations, and on his own buildings.

Defining good taste as the ability to distinguish between the good and the excellent, Boffrand praised the ancient Greeks, crediting them with developing enduring principles of architecture based on observation of nature and thoughtful reflection. The Greeks, he believed, began with utilitarian rustic huts, which they developed into convenient, efficient, well-proportioned structures. These principles were absorbed into Roman culture and were lost, according to Boffrand, with the fall of Rome.

Boffrand's ideas about classical architecture were not original, but his perceptions of Gothic architecture put him in the avant-garde of his time. In his *Livre d'architecture,* Boffrand suggested that the Goths used branches, vines, and leaves as the inspiration for their high, decorated vaults. He pictured Gothic vaults as a forest where the tree branches joined overhead. With this image, Boffrand likened the origin of Gothic architecture to the origin of ancient Greek architecture as explained by the ancient Roman architect Vitruvius, since both began with the natural, rude hut. Boffrand's text may have been an influence upon Marc-Antoine Laugier, who proposed the primitive hut as the source of all good design.

Boffrand concluded his introductory chapter with remarks on his interests in building sites and the importance of expressing the spirit of the owner of a house in architectural terms. These concerns bring to mind Boffrand's readings of Palladio's four books on architecture and Boffrand's applications of these ideas in his buildings. Boffrand's thoughtful, humane understanding of how climate, setting, and ornamentation of a building could affect the mood and spirit of its inhabitants is his legacy to later generations of architects and builders.

—*Alice H. R. H. Beckwith*

FURTHER READING

Blomfield, Reginald. *A History of French Architecture: From the Death of Mazarin Until the Death of Louis XV, 1661-1774.* Reprint. New York: Hacker Art Books, 1973. This two-volume set is very accessible to English readers, but much of the information is out of date and inaccurate. It should be read in conjunction with Wend von Kalnein's work.

Blunt, Anthony, ed. *Baroque and Rococo Architecture and Decoration.* London: Elek, 1978. The chapter on France by Christopher Tadgell is concise and insightful. The other chapters set Boffrand in the context of German and Austrian rococo architecture.

Boffrand, Germaine. *Book of Architecture Containing the General Principles of the Art and the Plans, Elevations, and Section of Some of the Edifices Built in France and in Foreign Countries.* Translated by David Britt, edited by Caroline van Eck. Burlington, Vt.: Ashgate, 2002. An English translation of Boffrand's *Livre d'architecture,* in which Boffrand presents his aesthetics of architecture. Includes an introduction and notes by Eck, placing Boffard within the context of eighteenth century architectural theory. Illustrations, including all of the illustrations published in the original edition of the book.

Garms, Jörg. "Projects for the Pont Neuf and Place Dauphine in the First Half of the Eighteenth Century." *Journal of the Society of Architectural Historians* 26 (1967): 102-113. This essay on two of the major city-planning projects in eighteenth century Paris reveals the context in which Boffrand's design project for the Place Louis XV can be understood.

Kalnein, Wend von. *Architecture in France in the Eighteenth Century*. Translated by David Britt. New Haven, Conn.: Yale University Press, 1995. A new edition of the book originally published in 1972. The treatment of Boffrand is evenhanded and quite complete, including illustrations of floor plans as well as photographs of buildings.

Kimball, Sidney Fiske. *The Creation of the Rococo Decorative Style*. New York: Dover, 1980. By focusing on establishing which French architect was the first to begin the development of the rococo style, Kimball tends to diminish the importance of Boffrand's work. Yet there is much information on rococo architects quoted verbatim from the French state archives that can be found only in France or in this book.

Middleton, R. D. "The Abbé de Cordemoy and the Graeco-Gothic Ideal: A Prelude to Romantic Classicism." *Journal of the Warburg and Courtauld Institutes* 25, nos. 1/2 (1962): 278-320. An exhaustive and excellent account of the interest in medieval architecture in France from the sixteenth to the eighteenth century. Traces Boffrand's interest in Gothic architecture and explains the relationship between his chapel at Lunéville and eighteenth century architectural theory.

Thoenes, Christof, and Bernd Evers, eds. *Architectural Theory from the Renaissance to the Present*. Los Angeles: Taschen, 2002. An essay about Boffrand is included in this illustrated collection of important and influential essays about architecture published since the Renaissance.

See also: Johann Bernhard Fischer von Erlach; Jean-Honoré Fragonard; Louis XV; Giovanni Battista Tiepolo; Antoine Watteau.

Related articles in *Great Events from History: The Eighteenth Century, 1701-1800*: 1785: Construction of El Prado Museum Begins; 1787: David Paints *The Death of Socrates*.

First Viscount Bolingbroke
English politician, diplomat, and writer

As a Tory politician in Parliament during Queen Anne's reign, Bolingbroke served as secretary of war and later as northern secretary of state. He defended the Church of England and the aristocracy and played a major role in the negotiation of the Treaty of Utrecht. His political writings were both a part of his opposition and an exposition of his political ideas.

Born: September 16, 1678; Wiltshire, England
Died: December 12, 1751; London, England
Also known as: Henry St. John (birth name); Baron St. John
Areas of achievement: Government and politics, diplomacy, philosophy

Early Life
First Viscount Bolingbroke was born Henry St. John, the only son of Sir Henry St. John and Lady Mary Rich, daughter of the second earl of Warwick. Of Presbyterian and gentry background, his father inherited the manors of Battersea and Wandsworth. The young Bolingbroke was educated at Eton; his attendance at Christ Church College, Oxford, is unconfirmed, but Oxford did confer an honorary degree upon him in 1702. At an early age, Bolingbroke was conspicuous for his public debauchery. Following a tour of the Continent, after the fashion of gentlemen of the age, he married Frances Winchcombe in 1700.

In 1701, Bolingbroke was elected to Parliament for the family borough of Wootton-Bassett in Wiltshire. He prepared the bill to secure the Protestant succession, the Act of Settlement of 1701. As a commissioner of public accounts, he investigated the charges against William's ministers in the War of the League of Augsburg. Twice he supported bills against occasional conformity, a practice whereby casual performance of Anglican obligation met the requirement of the Test Act for office. From the beginning Bolingbroke distinguished himself as a speaker of ability in Commons, associated with Robert Harley, a moderate of the Tory Party.

Life's Work
When Harley joined the ministry of the earl of Godolphin and the duke of Marlborough in 1704, Bolingbroke was made secretary of war. At the time, he had confidence in Marlborough's conduct of the War of the Spanish Succession. That confidence was misplaced, however, in that Marlborough pursued a continental strategy in the

war, and Bolingbroke, who conceded the necessity of war with France, favored "more vigorous action at sea, urging that England could humble the enemy most effectively by striking at her colonies and overseas trade." If the exigencies of war were of principal benefit to the moneyed interest, the Bank of England and the great trading companies, and at the expense of the aristocratic-landed order of the realm, especially the country gentlemen, only Bolingbroke's concession of the necessity of war with France explains the pursuit of policy (at least as determined by Marlborough) contradictory to both his politics and his principles. Increasingly, it would become the wrong kind of war of benefit to the wrong interest, especially after the French defeat at Ramillies.

Despite earlier support, Bolingbroke contributed substantially to the defeat of a third Occasional Conformity Bill in 1704. The election of 1705, hardly supportive of his kind of Toryism, and the discrepancy in the troop count following the British defeat at Almanza (29,295 authorized; 8,660 counted) both weakened his position in the ministry. He left office with Harley on February 11, 1708, following the revelation of the treason of William Grey, a clerk in Harley's office. Bolingbroke's father claimed the family seat in Parliament, and as no other seat could be found, Bolingbroke retired to his wife's property, Bucklebury, to devote himself to philosophy, reflection, and the reading of history.

The prosecution of the Reverend Henry Sacheverell, the general economic discontent at home, and the continuation of the war with the collapse of peace negotiations at The Hague restored Harley to office in August, 1710. In September, Bolingbroke was appointed northern secretary of state. Peace was the priority of the new ministry. All were convinced, Bolingbroke wrote,

> of the unreasonableness and even of the impossibility of continuing the war on the same disproportionate foot. Their universal sense was that we had taken, except the part of the States General, the whole burden of the war upon us . . . while the entire advantage was to accrue to others . . . the first favorable occasion ought to be seized of making peace . . . [to] the interest of our country . . . as well as . . . of our party.

The new initiative, however, was not inaugurated by Bolingbroke. He was not informed of the preliminaries until they were presented to the entire ministry in April, 1711. He reassured the Dutch that any negotiation would be carried out in concert with the States General and publicly stated that there would be no separate peace. In May, he issued to the duke of Ormonde the order prohibiting

any military action against the French without informing the Allies. British duplicity, the ministry's willingness to parley with the French without including the Allies, became the basis for the Allied identification of England as "Perfidious Albion"—an onus for which Harley and Bolingbroke are both particularly responsible.

In March, 1711, the marquis de Guiscard, charged with supplying British intelligence secrets to the French, attacked and seriously wounded Harley with a penknife. The attack may have been intended for Bolingbroke, but no proof of his culpability in the marquis's treasonous behavior was established, and in fact Bolingbroke broke his sword in defending Harley. During Harley's convalescence, Bolingbroke secured the queen's permission for a military expedition against Quebec, commanded by Jack Hill, brother of the queen's favorite, Lady Abigail Masham. The expedition failed miserably, though Bolingbroke may have profited personally. As the negotiations continued, Bolingbroke extracted commercial advantage for England from France in exchange for recognition of the claims of Philip Anjou (Philip V) to the Spanish throne. Territorial demands would include Gibraltar and portions of New France in North America; the South Sea Company would receive a monopoly of the Spanish-American slave trade, known as *asiento*.

The peace preliminaries were signed on September 27, 1711. While peace was popular, a peace that obviously betrayed the Allies was not—at least not with the Whigs. They had demanded that the French be driven from Spain as the price for ending the war: "No peace without Spain." To discredit the Whigs at home and the Allies abroad, Bolingbroke began a propaganda campaign, using newspapers and pamphlets, including *The Examiner,* to cultivate public opinion on behalf of the peace. Jonathan Swift would also write his famous *The Conduct of the Allies* (1711). Marlborough was charged with financial malfeasance, as £35 million was unaccounted for; he would be censured as gently as possible, according to Swift, but Robert Walpole would be expelled and sent to the Tower of London. Finally, to overcome Whig opposition in the Lords, the queen was forced to create twelve new Tory peers. Bolingbroke confessed that the action was "an unprecedented and invidious measure, to be excused by nothing but necessity, and hardly by that." The trade provisions with the French, however, would be defeated by nine votes in the Commons. The Treaty of Utrecht was concluded on March 31, 1713, but not before Bolingbroke warned the French that if they did not sign, the queen would ask for new supplies to renew the war.

In support of Tory churchmen, the ministry passed an act in 1711 to build fifty new churches in London and thereabout. Bolingbroke led the Commons in support of the Landed Qualifications Act, which required income of £600 from landed property for shire members of Parliament and £300 for borough members of Parliament. The assault on the Whigs continued with the creation of the South Sea Company, a Tory financial institution, which assumed £9 million of the unsecured national debt. Harley served as its governor, and Bolingbroke was a director. In 1711, Bolingbroke founded the Brothers Club, men of wit, learning, and breeding, which included Swift, Alexander Pope, Dr. John Arbuthnot (the queen's physician), and, later, John Gay. For thirty years they exposed the folly of humankind, particularly the corruption and venality of the new order of money.

It was in July, 1712, that Bolingbroke was elevated to the peerage as a viscount and as Baron St. John. (He had desired an earldom; the third earl of Bolingbroke, the elder branch of the St. John line, had died without heir in 1711.) He considered the title of viscount less a reward than a punishment. In October, he was passed over in a

First Viscount Bolingbroke. (Library of Congress)

distribution of the Order of the Garter. He blamed Oxford (Harley had been elevated to earl of Oxford in 1711). The inconstancy of their relationship had long existed and, as Queen Anne's reign came to a close, Bolingbroke plotted openly against the earl.

Bolingbroke convinced the dying queen to dismiss Oxford on July 27, 1714. His design may have been to achieve control over the ministry to secure his political fortune with a Stuart restoration. Tories of his ilk could not hope for favor with the Hanoverian succession, for, after all, he had betrayed them in the war. If he hoped to alter the Act of Settlement, he was denied; moreover, James III, the Old Pretender, refused to abandon his Roman Catholicism for the Church of England. The duke of Shrewsbury, who replaced Oxford, proceeded to arrange for the Hanoverian succession upon Anne's death on August 1, 1714.

With the convocation of Parliament in March, 1715, Bolingbroke fled London for France under cover of night. Walpole moved, with unanimous consent, an act of attainder against him. In France, Bolingbroke told the English ambassador that he intended to retire, that he had no Jacobite intention, but by July he had accepted office as secretary of state. He prepared the necessary documents for the 1715 invasion of Scotland and England, making allowance for the security of the Church of England. Apparently, he had little confidence in its prospect for success, or for that matter in the Pretender and his advisers. Within the year, he was dismissed on charges of treachery. He explained his behavior in *A Letter to Sir William Wyndham* (wr. 1717, pb. 1753), writing that he had acted not out of loyalty to the Stuarts but rather in the belief that a Stuart rule would better serve the interest of the Tory Party. For party, not England, he had sacrificed himself and in so doing had tainted Tories with the odious label of Jacobite. Bolingbroke's political career was ended.

Confessed loyalty to King George I, however, would not restore him; for ten years Bolingbroke would remain in France. He joined French courtiers at fashionable Parisian salons, attended by the company of Voltaire and Montesquieu and other distinguished and learned men. Even before Lady Bolingbroke died in 1718 (his neglect and infidelity certainly influenced her decision to leave her property to the heirs of her sister), Bolingbroke began an affair with Marie Claire Deschamps de Marcilly, whom he married in May, 1720. He bought a small estate near Orleans, where he renewed his philosophical studies, including an examination of the chronology of the Bible.

Through Lord John Carteret, Bolingbroke secured a pardon from the king in 1723, and two years later Parliament restored his property. Walpole had opposed any restoration, and only George I's threat of dismissal forced him to compromise: Inherit property Bolingbroke might, but he would not be permitted to sit in the Lords. The result was the renewal of the old animosity between the two, defined by one historian as the source of energy in English political life from 1725 to 1740.

Settled at Dawley, near Uxbridge on what he called a farm, Bolingbroke found politics irresistible. Articles bitterly assaulting Walpole and his policies began appearing in *The Craftsman* in December, 1726. Bolingbroke hoped to join together opposition Whigs under Sir William Pulteney, earl of Bath, and Tories under Sir William Wyndham. Defections brought on by the Excise Crisis in 1733 raised his hopes that Walpole might be ousted. Bolingbroke used an attack upon the Septennial Act as the vehicle to that end and Wyndham as his mouthpiece. Walpole responded with a virulent counterattack, calling Bolingbroke an "anti-minister" and asking, "Can there be imagined a greater disgrace to human nature than such a wretch as this?" Dismayed and discouraged, Bolingbroke returned to France. There, in 1736, he wrote *Letter on the Spirit of Patriotism* (1749), which defined and defended opposition politics.

During a brief return to England in 1738, Bolingbroke met Frederick, the prince of Wales, now center of the opposition. The result was *The Idea of a Patriot King* (1740), which was trusted to Alexander Pope and was not to be published. (His wishes were not honored, as Pope had it printed in 1744.) He inherited Battersea upon his father's death in 1742. Walpole also resigned his office in 1742, but his departure did not open the door for a belated resumption of Bolingbroke's political career. His wife died on March 18, 1750, and Bolingbroke followed on December 12, 1751, of cancer, to be buried in the family vault at Battersea. His estate was inherited by the heirs of his father's second marriage.

Bolingbroke's most important writings were composed and published during the heat of political battle; other works were not published, at his instructions, until after his death. *Fragments: Or, Minutes of Essays* (1754) was written in France from 1726 to 1734. The work is primarily concerned with religion and philosophy, which reflect Bolingbroke's rationalism. He wrote:

It may be truly said, that God, when he gave us reason, left us to our free-will, to make a proper or improper use of it; so that we are obligated to our Creator, for a certain rule, and sufficient means of arriving at happiness, and have none to blame but ourselves when we fail of it. It is not reason, but perverse will, that makes men fall short of attainable happiness. And we are self condemned when we deviate from that rule.

The "philosophical fragments" also included criticism of the social contract theory of Thomas Hobbes and John Locke, one of the early significant critiques of Locke. Political society had its origins in paternal authority, he maintained; therefore, the purpose of government was not the protection of individual rights. The purpose was the same as in natural society, namely, the maintenance of peace and order, the disposition of justice according to natural law, and a paternal pursuit of the good of the people. His hierarchy and duty would be juxtaposed to Locke's individualism and rights. He defined Locke's natural order as a "speculative whimsy."

Bolingbroke defined the king in Parliament and the English constitution as of a mixed nature, that the executive and legislative powers were not rigidly separated. Both, he argued, are constitutionally dependent, in that they share legislative powers; yet at the same time both are constitutionally independent in that each is prevented from the subjugation of the other. A patriot king would achieve that constitutional balance, so that the king would no longer be held in bondage by his minister, or the legislature in bondage to the executive. The patriot king would exemplify honor and virtue. He would of necessity be a great and good man, whose status would enable him to rise above all factions and parties. He would purge his court of self-serving men and would appoint in their places men committed to the general good of the commonwealth. Historian Isaac Kramnick wrote:

Politics for Bolingbroke's circle was played out in an elaborate theater, where the style of performance was almost more significant than the deeds done. To perform the governmental roles of statecraft properly one had to be properly bred. . . . With theatrical gravity, noble gentlemen should stand before the people and win support by virtue of their eloquence, the compelling aesthetical force of their rhetoric. . . .

The Idea of a Patriot King is an exercise in obscurantism—certainly as it pertained to the world of real politics.

Bolingbroke is one of the best examples of disdain for political parties among eighteenth century political writers (granted he had been an advocate of party government during Anne's reign). He concluded that the decline of seventeenth century ideological differences between Tory and Whig left only conflict over persons and power. Parties caused "even reasonable men to act on the most absurd, and honest men on the most unjustifiable principles," he wrote in *A Dissertation upon Parties* (1735). Instead of party distinction in Parliament, Bolingbroke advocated a division between a government party and an opposition. In his estimate, opposition was a duty and must be undertaken seriously and steadily and systematically. In like manner, he argued, an alternative program to that of the government party must be offered. Opposition must be clarified as not opposing the king, but rather the king's ministers, an idea that became reality in the eighteenth century as "His Majesty's (Loyal) Opposition." Bolingbroke defined the Crown as an essential part of the constitution, whereas the king's ministers were merely changeable parts of the government. The constitution consisted of the institutions, customs, and laws that "compose the general system, according to which the community hath agreed to be governed," he wrote. A government is merely the "particular tenor of conduct" by which officers administer public affairs.

SIGNIFICANCE

If Edmund Burke is the epitome of conservatism at the end of the eighteenth century, First Viscount Bolingbroke was in many ways the same thing at the century's beginning. Bolingbroke believed that the position and authority of aristocratic-landed men as well as the Church of England was necessary for the well-being of England.

Burke asked whether anyone read Bolingbroke, or whether anyone ever read him through. John Adams had—five times, as he confessed in 1813. *A Dissertation upon Parties,* Adams wrote, "is a jewel, there is nothing so profound, correct, and perfect on the subject of government in the English or any other language." Bolingbroke's statement "to die the last of British freemen, [rather] than bear to live the first of British slaves" rang true to many Americans during the Revolutionary War. His opposition to political parties took root in American soil, as the revolutionary fathers believed that one of the worst fates to befall the young republic would be the rise of political factionalism. Certainly later British Tories and conservatives would find merit in Bolingbroke's

writings. His pamphleteering, with the help of friends, broadened the base of political awareness of the issues of public affairs in English society. The elegance of his style was widely recognized and highly recommended by Philip Stanhope, Lord Chesterfield. Moreover, the young William Pitt conceded that of all the literature of the past that was lost, he would be most happy to recover a speech of Bolingbroke.

Much of the stigma imposed on Bolingbroke for the Treaty of Utrecht is political bias. His behavior may have been unprincipled, but the treaty served England's national interest, both at the time and subsequently. In many ways Walpole's pursuit of trade was consistent with Bolingbroke's position. His opponents accused him of disingenuousness, but it was a charge of which they were guilty, too, by and large. There was much that both appeared and was contradictory in Bolingbroke, but Kramnick contends that fundamentally a large element of consistency runs through his career and particularly his thought. He was irreverent and a religious skeptic (or a Deist), but his defense of the church was a matter not of personal confession but rather of social necessity.

The judgment of history, especially Whig history, has been unkind to Bolingbroke. In his own time, however, he was regarded with the warmest admiration and affection by some of the most brilliant contemporaries of the Augustan Age.

—Jimmie F. Gross

FURTHER READING

Biddle, Sheila. *Bolingbroke and Harley*. New York: Alfred A. Knopf, 1974. An examination of the politics of Queen Anne's reign in general, and of the relationship and politics of Bolingbroke and Harley in particular. Biddle contrasts Bolingbroke's and Harley's personalities and policies.

Bolingbroke, Henry St. John, Viscount. *The Works of Lord Bolingbroke, with a Life, Prepared Expressly for This Edition, Containing Additional Information Relative to His Personal and Public Character, Selected from the Best Authorities*. 4 vols. Philadelphia: Carey and Hart, 1841. An excellent primary resource.

Cottret, Bernard, ed. *Bolingbroke's Political Writings: The Conservative Enlightenment*. New York: St. Martin's Press, 1997. Examines Bolingbroke's writings within the context of contemporary English and French thought. Includes an analysis and full reprinting of *A Dissertation upon Parties* and *The Idea of a Patriot King*.

Foord, Archibald S. *His Majesty's Opposition, 1714-1830*. New York: Oxford University Press, 1964. Informative concerning the historical development of political opposition beginning with Bolingbroke's time. Foord argues that there was no program of organized opposition, and the extent to which the opposition was united was largely determined by political prejudices. The opposition was composed of the "outs"; they were important for what they did and who they were, not for what they proposed.

Holmes, Geoffrey. *British Politics in the Age of Anne*. New York: St. Martin's Press, 1967. An analytical and interpretive work that explains the machinations of Whig and Tory politicians. The book is particularly mindful of the influence of Sir Lewis Namier and other revisionist historians of eighteenth century politics.

James, D. G. *The Life of Reason: Hobbes, Locke, Bolingbroke*. New York: Longmans, Green, 1949. A discussion of the literary and intellectual dimensions of three "Augustans" of the Age of Reason.

Kramnick, Isaac. *Bolingbroke and His Circle: The Politics of Nostalgia in the Age of Walpole*. Cambridge, Mass.: Harvard University Press, 1968. A critical assessment of Bolingbroke's political writings explained in the context of the social and economic milieu of the time. Bolingbroke should not be dismissed as inconsequential, for what he had to say was of significance, even if, as Kramnick concludes, he was inaccurate.

Pettit, Alexander. *Illusory Consensus: Bolingbroke and the Polemical Response to Walpole, 1730-1737*. Newark: University of Delaware Press, 1997. Pettit has studied pamphlets, plays, sermons, and newspapers published in the 1730's to examine the views of Bolingbroke and others who opposed Walpole. The author concludes that most people responded anxiously to Bolingbroke's concept of a unified opposition.

Stephen, Leslie. *History of English Thought in the Eighteenth Century*. 2 vols. New York: Harcourt, Brace & World, 1962. In volume 2, chapter 10, part 9, "The Walpole Era," Stephen offers a scathing denunciation of Bolingbroke.

See also: John Adams; Queen Anne; Edmund Burke; George I; George II; First Earl of Godolphin; First Duke of Marlborough; Montesquieu; Philip V; William Pitt the Younger; Alexander Pope; Jonathan Swift; Voltaire; Robert Walpole.

Related articles in *Great Events from History: The Eighteenth Century, 1701-1800:* May 26, 1701-September 7, 1714: War of the Spanish Succession; June 12, 1701: Act of Settlement; May 15, 1702-April 11, 1713: Queen Anne's War; March 23-26, 1708: Defeat of the "Old Pretender"; April 11, 1713: Treaty of Utrecht; 1721-1742: Development of Great Britain's Office of Prime Minister; 1726-1729: Voltaire Advances Enlightenment Thought in Europe.

CLAUDE ALEXANDRE DE BONNEVAL
French soldier, adventurer, and statesman

Bonneval was a brilliant soldier whose personal pride and drive for self-aggrandizement led him to betray all three of the nations that he served. His turbulent life and career as a professional mercenary reflected the convoluted geopolitics of early eighteenth century Europe.

Born: July 14, 1675; Coussac-Bonneval, France
Died: March 23, 1747; Pera, Constantinople, Ottoman Empire (now Istanbul, Turkey)
Also known as: Claude Alexandre de Bonneval de Blanchefort; Ahmed Pasha
Areas of achievement: Government and politics, warfare and conquest

EARLY LIFE
Claude Alexandre de Bonneval (klohd ah-lehk-zahn-duhr duh bawn-vahl) was the son of Jean-François de Bonneval de Blanchefort and Claude de Monceaux, members of old noble families from the central French region of Limousin. Sent to study at a Jesuit college when his father died, Bonneval developed a passion for history and Latin, demonstrating a remarkable memory that would later make him famous. His formal education, however, lasted only until he was eleven, when his uncle, Comte Anne-Hilarion de Costentin de Tourville, admiral of the French navy, made him enter the navy as a navy guard.

Life in the service appealed to the young man. In 1688, when the Wars of the League of Augsburg began, the minister of the navy, the marquis de Seignelai, noticed Bonneval in the ranks. Taking pity on so young a boy about to be sent into the horrors of naval battle, the minister told him that he was to be discharged because of his age. Bonneval, however, was too proud of his accomplishments and his family to accept dismissal, which he took as a personal affront. Haughtily, the boy responded, "One does not discard a man of my name!" Taken aback, but thoroughly pleased by the young man's enthusiasm, the minister replied, "Whatever, Sir, the king discharges you from the navy guard but makes you an ensign."

LIFE'S WORK

Fortunately for Bonneval, his sharp tongue and enormous self-importance were accompanied by a quick intellect, bravery, and martial skills that allowed him to distinguish himself in three of the many naval battles of the wars, the Battles of Dieppe (France), den Haag (Holland), and Cádiz (Spain). Unfortunately, his bad temper led him into self-destructive behavior. In 1697, feeling that he had been slighted and treated as a child by his lieutenant, the comte de Baumont, Bonneval provoked a duel in which Baumont was injured. Baumont was also a man whose family connections were impressive, and under pressure from Baumont's allies in the navy, Bonneval was forced to leave the service.

In 1698, at the age of twenty-three, Bonneval enlisted in the French Guards, where he served until the outbreak of the War of the Spanish Succession in 1701. Following the custom of the time, in which rich men outfitted regiments for national service, he purchased an infantry regiment for £33,000, though in an uncharacteristic fit of humility he did not take command, instead placing himself and his regiment under the orders of the maréchal de Catinat (who was soon replaced by the duc de Villeroi, and later by the duc de Vendôme).

Bonneval distinguished himself campaigning in Italy, where Prince Eugene of Savoy, commanding the army of the Holy Roman Emperor, could not help but admire the boldness and tactical genius of the young French officer whose daring had brought the French victory at Luzzara. Although Bonneval's superiors in his own army agreed on his bravery and admired his skills on the battlefield, however, they were hesitant to take tactical advice from one so young and inexperienced. When his regiment continued the war in Dauphiné, a region west of the Alps, Bonneval succeeded in forcing the capitulation of a region called Biélois. Finding himself cut off from his supplies, he used £3,000 of his own money to provide his

soldiers and the local military hospitals with necessary supplies.

Proud of both his success and his commitment to the well-being of his troops, Bonneval was outraged when the army superintendent refused to reimburse him for his costs. In a fit of temper, the young officer responded to the rejection of his request with a vindictive and passionate letter in which he threatened to offer his services to the Holy Roman Emperor if he was not reimbursed within three months. Only after the letter had been posted did he reflect on the implications of his threat to commit treason. To avoid being court-martialed, he requested and was granted a leave of absence, spending the winter of 1705-1706 in Italy. While in Venice, his attempts to use the offices of the French ambassador to resolve his problem failed; thus, when his funds were gone he followed the lead of another French officer, the marquis de Langallerie, who had deserted to the enemy, carrying out his impetuous threat to offer his services to the empire. Pleased to have the services of so capable an officer, the emperor gave Bonneval the same rank in his army that the young man had enjoyed in the French one.

By joining the enemy, Bonneval cut himself off from his estate in France, losing much more than the £3,000 that had precipitated his actions. With no place else to turn, he served the emperor ably. Soon rising to the rank of major general, Bonneval brought Emperor Joseph I victories at Turin and elsewhere in Italy, ultimately penetrating France and fighting at Dauphiné (1709) and Flanders (1710), where he interceded to save the lives of two wounded French officers who had been captured. Happily for him, his moments of chivalry and compassion helped build a counterbalance to his reputation as a turncoat.

When the war ended, Bonneval attended the meeting at which Charles VI, Eugene of Savoy, and the maréchal de Villars (representing Louis XIV) signed the Treaty of Utrecht (1713). In the following year, Austria engaged in a war against the Ottomans that sent Bonneval to Hungary, where his bravery and skills once again brought him fame. Back in Vienna, he discovered that the French ambassador to Austria was now a relative of his who could be persuaded to intercede on his behalf with the duc d'Orléans, regent of France for the young Louis XV. His petition was successful, and in February, 1717, Bonneval came back to France after an absence of sixteen years. His overjoyed mother immediately arranged a marriage with Judith de Biron, but it took Bonneval only ten days to realize that he was not cut out for a married existence. Abandoning his wife, he fled to Vienna and then to Hungary.

Resuming his position in the imperial army, Bonneval fought with distinction in Sardinia, Messina, and Genoa. Poorly adapted to life without battle, Bonneval, when peace came in 1719, made an insolent remark to Prince Eugene, which brought him into disgrace but not dismissal from the army. However, when he acted improperly toward the representatives of Prince Eugene while assigned to Brussels in 1724, he was jailed twice and court-martialed. His response was predictable; enraged by the slight to his honor, in 1729 he abandoned the empire to serve its enemies, the Ottomans. Converting to the Muslim faith and changing his name to Ahmed Pasha, Bonneval wrote a treatise suggesting changes in the tactics used by the Ottoman army that could increase their effectiveness against the troops of the Habsburgs. Never completely comfortable in his new country or truly committed to anyone other than himself, he made several unsuccessful attempts in the last years of his life to leave Turkey. He died on March 23, 1747, at the age of seventy-one in Pera, a neighborhood of Constantinople.

SIGNIFICANCE

Claude Alexandre de Bonneval was a colorful figure and an exemplar of the kind of professional mercenary that the convoluted military and political conditions of early eighteenth century Europe could produce. A man of great skills and even greater regard for his own importance, he reached positions of high rank and influence in three different armies because of his effectiveness on the battlefield. His military cleverness, bravery, and adventures, combined with his acts of personal gallantry on the battlefield, were widely admired during his lifetime.

However, his immense ego overshadowed all of his accomplishments; his actions demonstrated time and time again that his self-importance made it impossible for him to develop a primary commitment to any person, nation, or community. Failure of commitment—to nation, king, or wife—led to his lack of lasting impact on his world and to his essentially lonely and incomplete life, which ended unhappily in a land he was trying to escape.

—Denyse Lemaire and David Kasserman

FURTHER READING

Bell, David A. *The Cult of the Nation in France: Inventing Nationalism, 1680-1800*. Cambridge, Mass.: Harvard University Press, 2003. Examines the history of nationalism in France in the eighteenth century.

Frey, Linda, and Marsha Frey. *Societies in Upheaval: Insurrections in France, Hungary, and Spain in the Early Eighteenth Century*. Westport, Conn.: Greenwood Press, 1987. This book describes the tragic economic dislocations, oppression, and wars in Europe in the eighteenth century.

Jones, Colin. *The Great Nation: France from Louis XV to Napoleon*. New York: Penguin Books, 2003. Exhaustive account of the history of eighteenth century France.

Landes, Joan B. *Visualizing the Nation: Gender, Representation, and Revolution in Eighteenth-Century France*. Ithaca, N.Y.: Cornell University Press, 2003. Describes the role of woman in eighteenth century France.

See also: Charles VI; Eugene of Savoy; Louis XV; Mahmud I; Duc d'Orléans.

Related articles in *Great Events from History: The Eighteenth Century, 1701-1800:* May 26, 1701-September 7, 1714: War of the Spanish Succession; September 11, 1709: Battle of Malplaquet; November 20, 1710-July 21, 1718: Ottoman Wars with Russia, Venice, and Austria; 1736-1739: Russo-Austrian War Against the Ottoman Empire; December 16, 1740-November 7, 1748: War of the Austrian Succession.

DANIEL BOONE
American explorer and settler

In addition to opening Kentucky to settlement, Boone became a legendary symbol of the early American frontier and is considered a national hero.

Born: November 2, 1734; Berks County, Pennsylvania
Died: September 26, 1820; near St. Charles, Missouri
Areas of achievement: Exploration, geography, warfare and conquest, military

EARLY LIFE

Daniel Boone was the sixth of eleven children. His father, Squire Boone, was the son of an English Quaker who came to Philadelphia in 1717; his mother, Sarah Morgan, was of Welsh ancestry. Young Boone received little, if any, formal schooling, but he learned to read and to write, although his spelling was erratic. His real interest was in the forest, and as a boy he developed into an excellent shot and superb woodsman.

Squire Boone left Pennsylvania in 1750, and by 1751 or 1752, the family was settled on Dutchman's Creek in North Carolina's Yadkin Valley. Daniel hunted and farmed, and he was a wagoner in General Edward Braddock's ill-fated 1755 expedition against Fort Duquesne. He may have been a wagon master three years later, when General John Forbes took the fort. During the 1750's, Boone met John Finley, who captivated him with tales of the lovely land called Kentucky.

In young adulthood, Boone was about 5 feet, 9 inches in height and had broad shoulders and a broad chest. Strong and quick, he possessed marvelous endurance and calm nerves. He had blue eyes, a Roman nose, a wide mouth with thin lips, and dark hair that he wore plaited and clubbed. Boone detested coonskin caps and always wore a hat. Mischievous and fun-loving, he was a popular companion, but Boone was happiest when alone in the wilderness. Honest, courageous, quiet, and unpretentious, he inspired confidence, and he accepted the leadership roles thrust upon him.

On August 14, 1756, Daniel married Rebecca Bryan, four years his junior. Between 1757 and 1781, they had ten children, and Rebecca carried much of the burden of rearing them during Daniel's long absences. One child died in infancy, and sons James and Israel were killed in Kentucky by American Indians. Rebecca ended Daniel's interest in Florida by refusing to move there in 1766. Boone, sometimes accompanied by brother Squire and brother-in-law John Stuart, explored westward, always tantalized by stories of the fine lands and bountiful game to be found in Kentucky.

LIFE'S WORK

On May 1, 1769, Daniel Boone, John Finley, John Stuart, and three hired hands left Boone's cabin for his first extended visit into Kentucky. A successful hunt was spoiled by a band of Shawnee, who took their catch and most of their equipment. Stuart was later killed, and when the rest of the party went back for supplies in 1770, Boone remained behind to hunt and explore westward. In 1771, some hunters investigated a strange sound and found Boone, flat on his back, singing at full volume for sheer joy. The seizure of another catch by Native Americans was a small price to pay for such delights.

In September, 1773, Boone attempted to take his family and other settlers into Kentucky, but they turned back after an American Indian attack in which Boone's son James was among those killed. On the eve of Lord Dunmore's War in 1774, Boone and Michael Stoner were sent to warn hunters and surveyors in Kentucky of the impending danger. In sixty-one days, they covered more than 800 miles of wilderness, although Boone paused at the incipient settlement at Harrodsburg long enough to claim a lot and throw up a cabin. During the short Indian war, Boone's role as a militia officer was to defend some of Virginia's frontier forts.

During these years, Boone became associated with Judge Richard Henderson, who dreamed of establishing a new colony (to be called Transylvania) in the western lands claimed by the North Carolina and Virginia colonies. Boone helped persuade the Cherokees to sell their claim to Kentucky, and agreement was reached at Sycamore Shoals on March 17, 1775. Anticipating that result, Boone and thirty axmen had already started work on the famed Wilderness Road that brought thousands of settlers into Kentucky and helped destroy the wilderness solitude that Boone loved.

Boonesborough was soon established on the south bank of the Kentucky River, and crops were planted in hastily cleared fields. When Henderson arrived with a larger party, a government was set up with representatives from the tiny, scattered stations. Boone introduced measures for protecting game and improving the breed of horses. American Indian raids frightened many of the settlers into fleeing eastward, but during the summer of 1775, Boone brought his family to Boonesborough. Had

143

he joined the exodus, the settlements probably would have been abandoned. Even the capture of a daughter and two other girls by American Indians did not shake his determination to hang on. Henderson's grandiose scheme failed when Virginia extended its jurisdiction over the region by creating a vast Kentucky County in December, 1776.

The American Revolution was fought largely along the seaboard, but the British used American Indians to attack the Kentucky settlements; the war in the West was fought for survival. Boone accepted the new nation created in 1776, but he was later charged with Toryism and treasonable association with the enemy. A court-martial cleared him of all charges, and he received a militia promotion.

During a raid led by Shawnee chief Blackfish, Boone's life was saved by young Simon Kenton, one of his few peers as a woodsman. The indigenous peoples' incursions brought the settlers near starvation, given the danger of both hunting and farming. When Boone was captured near Blue Licks by a large Shawnee raiding party

on February 7, 1778, he persuaded his twenty-six salt makers to surrender to save their lives. Boone then convinced Blackfish to return home and that Boonesborough would capitulate in the spring. Boone was adopted by Chief Blackfish, who refused to sell him to the British in Detroit. Big Turtle, as Boone was called by the Shawnee, enjoyed American Indian life, but he escaped in June, 1778, to warn Kentuckians of an impending attack. First by horse, and then on foot, Boone covered 160 miles in four days with only one meal, and upon his arrival Boonesborough's defenses were hastily improved. In any event, the attacking party of four hundred American Indians and one dozen French Canadians did not arrive until September 7. The settlers prolonged negotiations, hoping help would arrive, and the nine-day siege was one of the longest in American Indian warfare. All hostile stratagems failed, and Boonesborough survived.

George Rogers Clark's 1778-1779 campaign in the Illinois country and later expeditions against American Indian towns eased some of the danger. Indeed, Boonesborough was becoming too crowded for Boone, and in October, 1779, he moved to Boone's Station, a few miles from the fort. Boone had acquired some wealth, but he and a companion were robbed of between $40,000 and $50,000 when they went east in 1780 to purchase land warrants. Boone felt honor-bound to repay the persons who had entrusted money to him.

His hunting exploits, escapes from American Indians, and other feats of skill and endurance made him a legend in his own time. Kentucky was divided into three counties in November, 1780, and Boone's importance was recognized by appointments as Fayette's sheriff, county-lieutenant, lieutenant-colonel of militia, and deputy surveyor, and by election to the Virginia legislature. Captured by the British in Charlottesville in 1781, Boone soon escaped or was paroled.

In August, 1782, after a failed American Indian attack on Bryan's Station, Boone's warnings went unheeded, and the rash pursuers were ambushed near Blue Licks; Boone's son Israel was among the sixty-four non-Indian casualties. Boone participated in expeditions across the Ohio River to curb the indig-

Daniel Boone. (The Granger Collection, New York)

enous, but he criticized Clark for not moving his head-quarters to the eastern settlements for better protection. This criticism failed to take into account Clark's responsibilities for the Illinois country as well as for Kentucky: Louisville was a central location from which Clark could move quickly in either direction.

About 1783, Boone moved to Livestone (Maysville) on the Ohio River, where he opened a store, surveyed, hunted, and worked on prisoner exchanges with the indigenous. His fame spread throughout the nation and to Europe after 1784, following John Filson's addition of a thirty-four-page Boone "autobiography" to *The Discovery, Settlement, and Present State of Kentucke* (1784). In 1789 or 1790, Boone moved to Point Pleasant, in what became West Virginia, but he was in the Blue Licks area by 1795. By then, defective land titles had cost him most of his good lands, and Boone ceased to contest any claims brought against him. Disappointed by his treatment and convinced that Kentucky, a state since 1792, was becoming too crowded, Boone decided to move to Missouri, where Spanish officials welcomed him. In 1799, just before he was sixty-five years old, Boone led a party across the Mississippi River and settled on land some 60 miles west of St. Louis.

The next few years were happy ones. Despite rheumatism, Boone could still hunt, and the wilderness lured him into long journeys westward, perhaps as far as the Yellowstone. He received large land grants, and as a magistrate he held court under a so-called Justice Tree. The old pioneer was incensed in 1812, when he was rejected as a volunteer for the War of 1812; he was seventy-eight years old but ready to fight. His wife Rebecca died in 1813, and Boone probably made his last long hunt in 1817. He had a handsome coffin made and stored for future use. After the Louisiana Purchase, through carelessness and a series of misunderstandings, he lost most of his Missouri land, just as he had earlier lost his holdings in Kentucky.

Boone probably made his last visit to Kentucky in 1817; he was reputed to have only fifty cents left in his pocket after he paid the last of his creditors. Two years later, Chester Harding painted Boone's only life portrait. Boone died at a son's home near St. Charles on September 26, 1820, after a brief illness. In 1845, his and Rebecca's remains were re-interred on a hill above Frankfort, Kentucky.

SIGNIFICANCE

Despite his preference for the wilderness, Daniel Boone contributed mightily to the end of the Kentucky frontier—by opening roads, building settlements, surveying land, and fighting American Indians. Without his leadership, Kentucky's settlement would have been delayed, for he inspired trust that kept settlers from fleeing to safety. This clash between the idea of wilderness as paradise and the restrictions of civilization has been a common theme in the history of the American frontier; it remains an issue still.

In addition to his notable accomplishments, Boone became the symbol of the American frontier during the first half-century of nationhood. James Fenimore Cooper and Lord Byron were only two of many authors whose work includes depictions of Boone. Both his character and his exploits made Boone a natural hero, and they marked a way of life, believed virtuous, that was rapidly vanishing.

—Lowell H. Harrison

FURTHER READING

Boone, Nathan. *My Father, Daniel Boone: The Draper Interviews with Nathan Boone*. Edited by Neal O. Hammon, with an introduction by Nelson L. Dawson. Lexington: University Press of Kentucky, 1999. Historian Lyman Draper interviewed Boone's only surviving child, Nathan, and Nathan's wife, Olive, in 1851, as part of Draper's research for a biography of Boone. This is an updated transcript of those interviews.

Chaffee, Allen. *The Wilderness Trail: The Story of Daniel Boone*. New York: T. Nelson and Sons, 1936. An account that tells much more about Boone than his connection with the Wilderness Trail, one of the major routes for pioneers who entered Kentucky.

Draper, Lyman C. *The Life of Daniel Boone*. Edited by Franklin Belue. Mechanicsburg, Pa.: Stackpole Books, 1998. Historian Draper died in 1891, leaving a massive but unfinished biography of Boone. Belue has transcribed and annotated Draper's manuscript. Although Draper presents a hagiographic account of Boone, his work was based on extensive research and interviews, and he vividly re-creates many details of Boone's life. Belue's chapter notes correct Draper's romanticism, and the seventy-six period drawings, engraving, photos, and maps enhance the text.

Eckert, Allan W. *The Court Martial of Daniel Boone*. Boston: Little, Brown, 1973. This well-researched and well-written historical novel reconstructs the charges brought against Boone and his successful defense. The trial record disappeared, but Eckert's version sounds plausible.

Filson, John. *The Discovery, Settlement and Present State of Kentucke: . . . To Which Is Added . . . the Adventures of Col. Daniel Boon*. Wilmington, Del.: James Adams, 1784. This rare book has been reprinted many times. Although the "autobiography" was written by Filson and contains many errors, he did interview Boone and a number of other Kentuckians.

Lofaro, Michael A. *Daniel Boone: An American Life*. Lexington: University Press of Kentucky, 2003. Lofaro published an excellent biography, *The Life and Adventures of Daniel Boone*, in 1979. This updated biography is more detailed and is based upon thirty years of research. Lofaro explains why Boone is considered the quintessential frontiersman and why the idea of the frontier remains a part of the American experience.

Thwaites, Reuben Gold. *Daniel Boone*. New York: D. Appleton, 1902. Despite its age, this book provides a generally accurate biography. The author was one of the first Boone biographers to make use of the Lyman Draper manuscripts.

See also: Ethan Allen; Joseph Brant; George Rogers Clark; Alexander McGillivray.

Related articles in *Great Events from History: The Eighteenth Century, 1701-1800:* April 27-October 10, 1774: Lord Dunmore's War; July 4, 1776: Declaration of Independence.

JAMES BOSWELL
Scottish writer

Boswell wrote what many consider to be the English-speaking world's greatest biography, The Life of Samuel Johnson, LL.D., *and also was a distinguished autobiographer who penned voluminous journals and letters.*

Born: October 29, 1740; Edinburgh, Scotland
Died: May 19, 1795; London, England
Area of achievement: Literature

EARLY LIFE

James Boswell was the eldest son of Alexander Boswell of Ayrshire, a judge who, when raised to the bench of Scotland's highest court, took the courtesy title of Lord Auchinleck. Both James's parents descended from upper-class families with connections not only with nobility but also with royalty. His mother was weak and timid, while his father was a somber, stern disciplinarian who wanted his firstborn to follow him in a legal career and looked with consistent disfavor on both James's writing and his preference of London's society to Scotland's. The contour of Boswell's literary career reflects his divided allegiance between his pride in his ancient Scottish heritage and love of Highland characteristics on one hand and his zestful fascination with London's intellectual and sensual enticements on the other. This tension was to nourish his creative imagination.

From 1753 to 1758, Boswell took undergraduate arts courses at the University of Edinburgh and was accepted to the University of Glasgow in 1759 to study law. There, he much preferred the lectures on philosophy and rhetoric by Adam Smith, who had not yet published *The Wealth of Nations* (1776) but impressed Boswell with his *Theory of Moral Sentiments* (1759). In the spring of 1760, Boswell interrupted his academic term to run away for what became a three-month stay in London, during which he briefly embraced not only actresses but also the Roman Catholic faith.

Little is known about this first London sojourn, but much information is available concerning his next London trip, in 1762, for by then Boswell had begun the detailed diaries that he was to maintain for the rest of his life. *Boswell's London Journal, 1762-1763* (1950) highlights his encounters with prominent politicians and writers as well as his womanizing. The book is carefully organized according to the rise-and-fall rhythms of dramatic action, with Boswell featuring himself as a talented but directionless young man, not knowing whether to become a lawyer, guards officer, or author.

As a diarist, Boswell was devoid of pomp or even dignity; he was willing to show himself a fool or a boor. The reader is beguiled by Boswell's candor, high spirits, and capacity for vivid self-portraiture. The personality he disclosed is a deeply divided one, full of contrarieties—both cocksure and insecure, romantic about love yet rakish about women, conservative in his politics and religion yet anarchic in his conduct.

Boswell's first year in London included the pivotal event of his life: his meeting with Samuel Johnson on May 16, 1763. The scene is memorable, as described by Boswell in the greatest of literary biographies, *The Life of*

Samuel Johnson, LL.D. (1791). Young Boswell, in his twenty-third year, having heard that Dr. Johnson frequented John Davies's bookshop, had already gone there several times in the hope of meeting Johnson. When Davies saw Johnson through the shop's glass door, his awestricken voice in announcing the doctor's arrival reminded Boswell of Horatio announcing the arrival of his father's ghost to Hamlet: "Look, my Lord, it comes." Davies introduced the men to each other, roguishly indicating that Boswell came from Scotland. Aware that Johnson despised Scots, Boswell stuttered apologetically, "I do indeed come from Scotland, but I cannot help it." Johnson slammed back, "That Sir, I find, is what a great many of your countrymen cannot help." In *London Journal, 1762-1763*, Boswell records no further dialogue for this encounter; in *The Life of Samuel Johnson, LL.D.*, however, he relates two more pages of conversation on a variety of topics. He concludes, "I was satisfied that though there was a roughness in his manner, there was no ill-nature in his disposition." Eight days later, Johnson received Boswell in his Inner Temple chambers. By June 13, he invited him to "come to me as often as you can. I shall be glad to see you." The world's most famous literary friendship was sealed, with each man ultimately to owe his reputation to the other.

LIFE'S WORK

By August, 1763, James Boswell had left England for what was to become a three-year sojourn on the Continent, ostensibly to study civil law at Utrecht. He did maintain a studious regimen in Holland but also found time for a long affair with Zelide (Belle de Zuylen), though her Deism shocked his Presbyterian soul. After a chill ten months, Boswell left Holland to undertake—against his father's wishes—a Grand Tour of Europe. *Boswell on the Grand Tour: Germany and Switzerland, 1764* (1953) is Boswell's most interesting travel narrative, spotlighting his interviews with Jean-Jacques Rousseau and Voltaire in, respectively, Lausanne and Ferney.

Boswell was as determined to meet these two foremost contemporaneous European writers as he had been to meet Johnson; throughout his life, he was to pursue great men, usually with great success. His motives were multiple: He sought great men partly out of adventurousness and a curiosity to know extraordinary individuals (Boswell also pursued the philosophers David Hume and Lord Kames, authors Laurence Sterne and Oliver Goldsmith, politician John Wilkes, actor David Garrick, and General Pascal Paoli). Largely, however, Boswell was seeking a surrogate father, someone with whom he could

exchange the respect and affection his own censorious father denied him. The basically benign yet authoritative Johnson, thirty years his senior, satisfied this hunger admirably.

Boswell approached Rousseau by writing him a letter in French, in which he asked him how to lead the good life. The two met six times and parted on excellent terms. With Voltaire also he had several long talks, mostly consisting of debates on religion that Boswell instigated to provoke Voltaire's defense of his skeptical views. The rest of Boswell's continental travels are recounted in two overlapping books, both culled from his diaries: *An Account of Corsica: The Journal of a Tour to That Island* (1768) and *Boswell on the Grand Tour: Italy, Corsica, and France, 1765-1766* (1955). The latter text concentrates on his obsessive sexual profligacy, particularly his simultaneous pursuit of two women in Siena. The former focuses on the dignified and colorful leader of Corsica's battle for independence from Genoa, General Paoli, whom Boswell considers a heroic figure. When Paoli was later exiled from vanquished Corsica, Boswell arranged a warm welcome for him in London, where Paoli became a member of Johnson's inner circle. Boswell's *An Account of Corsica* proved a spectacular success, was translated into four languages, and made him well known at the age of twenty-seven.

Boswell in Search of a Wife, 1766-1769 (1956) has a self-explanatory subject: Back in Scotland, Boswell dallied with a number of women but finally married a distant cousin, Margaret Montgomery, of whom his father disapproved because she was poor. Boswell and Margaret were married on the same day—November 19, 1769—as his father was remarried, his first wife having died in 1766. Relations between the two couples remained cold. While Boswell cared for Margaret and continually resolved to improve his behavior, he neglected her for prostitutes, gambling jousts, and annual jaunts to jolly London.

In the autumn of 1773, Boswell and Johnson undertook a long-planned journey to western Scotland and the Hebrides. Both published accounts of this adventure: Johnson's *Journey to the Western Islands of Scotland* (1775) is a conventional, sober travel text, impersonal in perspective. Boswell's *The Journal of a Tour to the Hebrides, with Samuel Johnson, LL.D.* (1785) is much livelier, essentially constituting a vivid portrait of a great personality, the famous Johnson, on a rare holiday away from his intellectual labors and associates in London. The drama Boswell narrates revolves around the crusty, sedentary sixty-four-year-old literary dictator astride

A QUIET MOMENT IN THE GARDEN

James Boswell's The Life of Samuel Johnson, LL.D. *is not only a biography of its subject but also a story of the relationship between subject and author. In the excerpt below, Boswell recalls a simple moment between the two men. The inclusion of such minor incidents in literature, especially incidents lacking allegorical significance, was still unusual in the eighteenth century, and Boswell therefore follows his account with a comment on his decision to include it.*

One morning after breakfast, when the sun shone bright, we walked out together, and "pored" for some time with placid indolence upon an artificial water-fall, which Dr. Taylor had made by building a strong dyke of stone across the river behind the garden. It was now somewhat obstructed by branches of trees and other rubbish, which had come down the river, and settled close to it. Johnson, partly from a desire to see it play more freely, and partly from that inclination to activity which will animate, at times, the most inert and sluggish mortal, took a long pole which was lying on a bank, and pushed down several parcels of this wreck with painful assiduity, while I stood quietly by, wondering to behold the sage thus curiously employed, and smiling with an humorous satisfaction each time when he carried his point. He worked till he was quite out of breath; and having found a large dead cat so heavy that he could not move it after several efforts, "Come," said he, (throwing down the pole,) "YOU shall take it now;" which I accordingly did, and being a fresh man, soon made the cat tumble over the cascade. This may be laughed at as too trifling to record; but it is a small characteristick trait in the Flemish picture which I give of my friend, and in which, therefore I mark the most minute particulars. And let it be remembered, that Aesop at play is one of the instructive apologues of antiquity.

Source: James Boswell, in *Boswell's Life of Johnson*, edited by George Birkbeck Hill, vol. 3 (Oxford, England: Clarendon Press, 1887), p. 57.

---

horses in wild country or meeting provincial—even primitive—people in the Highlands. Boswell's method of composition was to jot down sketchy notes every evening during the trip, then fill them out the following morning while their references remained fresh to his memory. He showed considerable skill in stage-managing confrontations, as when he asked a man whose views he knew Johnson detested, Lord Monboddo, to invite them to his residence. The two elderly gentlemen at first clashed but gradually came to agree on several topics and parted warm friends. *Boswell's London Journal, 1762-1763* is not only his best sustained narrative but also a helpful trial run for the innovative fusion of memoir, character sketches, and literary history that characterizes his master work, *The Life of Samuel Johnson, LL.D.*

This biography, six years in the writing, demonstrates superlative literary skills. It treats the main events of Johnson's life until his death in 1784, emphasizing John-son's often brilliant and always forceful conversational powers. Boswell was fortunate in his central subject: Johnson had vigor, courage, assertiveness to the point of dogmatism, odd mannerisms, a grotesque appearance, an eruptive temper, a profound mind, and striking wit—his was a great personality. Other strong characters have been weakly portrayed, however, and Johnson had already been inadequately depicted in Sir John Hawkins's *The Life of Samuel Johnson* (1787), which Boswell resented as often inaccurate as well as injurious to Johnson's reputation in falsely stressing his preference for inferior companions.

Four-fifths of Boswell's long book covers the last twenty years of Johnson's seventy-five years, when Boswell knew him; Hawkins's biography treats the earlier period far more fully. Boswell was in Johnson's company a total of 425 days, including the 101 days of their Scotland travels. Yet Boswell was assiduous and indefatigable in collecting letters and reminiscences that accounted for all of Johnson's years. Boswell's revolutionary approach to his protagonist was to describe him precisely as he was, warts and hairs on warts, at close range, under a strong light of observation, largely in his own words and on his own terms. He recounts individual episodes to reveal Johnson in conversation or correspondence with such eminent persons as Sir Joshua Reynolds, Edmund Burke, and Lord Chesterfield, or with the members of his own literary club (including Goldsmith, Edmund Malone, and Edward Gibbon). The deeply affectionate bond between biographer and subject helps to unify what is sometimes a static, dull, and surely overlong work.

Most impressive is Boswell's genius for dramatizing Johnson's characteristic words, gestures, and tonalities, his theatrical forte in organizing many-voiced and rounded scenes, with Boswell often acting as contriver of the episode and director of the plot as well as cast member and audience. Perhaps the most vivid production of this type was the dinner party orchestrated by Boswell to bring together Johnson and a radical, controversial politician whose views he hotly condemned, John Wilkes. Boswell traps Johnson into attending the gathering by suggesting that he reject the invitation, since the abominated Wilkes might also be present; always contradictory, Johnson insists on attending the dinner. Wilkes sat next to Johnson at the table and charmed him by suggesting the choicest cuts of the served veal. Johnson reluctantly softened, "'Sir, Sir, I am obliged to you, Sir,' cried Johnson, bowing, and turning his head to him with a look for some time of 'surly virtue,' but, in a short while, of complacency"; the two men proceeded to exchange anecdotes, to discuss Horace, and to tease Boswell, busy jotting down his notes.

By 1784, Johnson's consistently poor health had deteriorated markedly. The two friends bade each other farewell on July 1, and Johnson, after having left Boswell's carriage, "sprung away with a kind of pathetic briskness . . . which seemed to indicate a struggle to conceal uneasiness, and impressed me with a foreboding of our long, long separation." Five and a half months later, Johnson died.

The final ten years of Boswell's life were mostly dismal. In 1788, he moved from Scotland to London, was admitted to the English bar, but never practiced in the city. His wife's death in 1789 left him with five children, the oldest of whom was then sixteen. He divided his time between them, his diverse dissipations, and work on his life of Johnson. After its 1791 publication, he became increasingly morose and alcoholic, dying when not yet fifty-five years old.

SIGNIFICANCE

Until the 1920's, a number of critics maintained that James Boswell's *The Life of Samuel Johnson, LL.D.* was an accidentally great work, that Boswell was no more than a fortunate or inspired idiot who had the opportunity of listening to and the energy to record the many wise sayings of the world's greatest social talker. Yet the discovery of the past few generations of a mountain of Boswell's personal papers has caused a drastic elevation of critical evaluation.

While most of Boswell's papers remained in the archives of his estate at Auchinleck, about one-third became mixed up with the documents of one of his executors, Sir William Forbes. In 1905, Auchinleck was inherited by Lord Talbot de Malahide, who moved the archives to Malahide Castle, outside Dublin. A wealthy American collector, Lieutenant Colonel Ralph Isham, bought what was then thought to be all the Boswell papers from Lord Talbot in 1927. Further batches of Bos-

well's manuscripts, letters, and notes were found at Malahide, however, in 1930, 1939, and 1949; Isham also bought these. Meanwhile, the Forbes collection of Boswelliana had been accidentally discovered, and Isham acquired these papers in the 1930's and 1940's.

All these documents have provided overwhelming evidence that Boswell is a magnificent writer of major status. He was not only the English-speaking world's greatest biographer but also its most revealing autobiographer—a complex person capable of astounding self-understanding and singular honesty, a writer with a uniquely expert dramatic sense, comparable to Rousseau in his need to confess the truth combined with his talent to convey it.

In 1949-1950, Isham sold all of his Boswell accumulations to Yale University. From 1950 on, Yale has published, through McGraw-Hill, a series of volumes containing the more interesting papers, beginning with *Boswell's London Journal, 1762-1763.*

—Gerhard Brand

FURTHER READING

Bate, W. Jackson. *Samuel Johnson.* New York: Harcourt Brace Jovanovich, 1977. A brilliantly executed narrative of Johnson's life, character, and work, which interprets Boswell's connections with Johnson incisively and persuasively.

Boswell, James. *Boswell's Life of Johnson.* Edited by R. W. Chapman. New York: Oxford University Press, 1960. The most convenient single-volume edition of the biography, including an authoritative introduction by Chauncey B. Tinker, the first of Yale University's distinguished modern scholars of eighteenth century English literature.

_____. *The Heart of Boswell: Six Journals in One Volume.* Edited by Mark Harris. New York: McGraw-Hill, 1981. Novelist Harris has chosen fascinating highlights from the first six of Boswell's autobiographical volumes in the Yale series, covering events from November, 1762, to September, 1774.

Brady, Frank. *James Boswell: The Later Years, 1769-1795.* New York: McGraw-Hill, 1984. A sequel to Frederick Pottle's biography written by Brady, who sometimes collaborates with a protege of Pottle. An authoritative treatment of the second half of Boswell's life.

Clifford, James L., ed. *Twentieth Century Interpretations of Boswell's Life of Johnson.* Englewood Cliffs, N.J.: Prentice-Hall, 1970. Boswell, as well as Johnson, has been fortunate in attracting the attention of first-rate scholars and critics. Clifford, himself a distinguished Johnsonian, has collected a judiciously chosen collection of essays that students will find illuminating.

McAdam, E. L., Jr. *Johnson and Boswell: A Survey of Their Writings.* Boston: Houghton Mifflin, 1969. A scholarly critical text in the Riverside Studies in Literature series. McAdam devotes eighty pages to Boswell's writings, assessing them thoroughly and lucidly.

Martin, Peter. *A Life of James Boswell.* New Haven, Conn.: Yale University Press, 2000. A detailed account of Boswell's often complicated life.

Pottle, F. A. *James Boswell: The Earlier Years, 1740-1769.* New York: McGraw-Hill, 1966. For two generations, Pottle was the world's leading authority on Boswell. This is a standard work, to be read before Frank Brady's sequel.

Redford, Bruce. *Designing the "Life of Johnson."* New York: Oxford University Press, 2002. Redford reconstructs Boswell's methods and models for writing his biography, analyzing the various stages leading to the first edition and the impact of portrait and drama on the book's structure. Based on a series of lectures delivered in 2001-2002.

Sisman, Adam. *Boswell's Presumptuous Task: The Making of the Life of Dr. Johnson.* New York: Penguin Putnam 2000. Sisman describes how Boswell wrote his acclaimed biography, questions why Boswell wanted to write the book, and discusses why he persisted in finishing the book despite years of adversity after Johnson's death.

See also: Edmund Burke; Robert Burns; Adam Ferguson; David Garrick; Edward Gibbon; Oliver Goldsmith; David Hume; Samuel Johnson; Flora MacDonald; Jean-Jacques Rousseau; Anna Seward; Adam Smith; Voltaire; John Wilkes.

Related articles in *Great Events from History: The Eighteenth Century, 1701-1800:* 1726-1729: Voltaire Advances Enlightenment Thought in Europe; 1746-1755: Johnson Creates the First Modern English Dictionary; March 20, 1750-March 14, 1752: Johnson Issues *The Rambler*; Beginning April, 1763: The *North Briton* Controversy; August, 1763-April, 1765: David Garrick's European Tour.

LOUIS-ANTOINE DE BOUGAINVILLE
French explorer

Bougainville is best known as the leader of the first French expedition to sail around the world. He fought the British during the French and Indian War and later during the American Revolutionary War.

Born: November 12, 1729; Paris, France
Died: August 31, 1811; Paris, France
Areas of achievement: Exploration, warfare and conquest

EARLY LIFE

Louis-Antoine de Bougainville (lwee-ahn-twahn duh bew-gan-veel) was the youngest of four children. His father was a notary in the Paris Courts of Justice. Although his mother died while Louis-Antoine was an infant, he seems to have had a happy childhood.

His biographers have generally been kind to Bougainville. He was short, inclined to be plump or, by some accounts, even fat. His portrait shows him as a splendid French gentleman with a filled-out face, rosy cheeks, and a reddish, somewhat bulbous nose. He is described as tactful, compassionate, and good-humored. He seems to have been an adventurer, a gambler, and somewhat of a ladies' man. Loyal to his friends, king, and country, he was concerned for the welfare of his companions and those under his command. The translations of his writings indicate that he was a better-than-average journalist.

At his father's urging, he studied law and mathematics at the University of Paris. In 1755, he published a treatise on integral calculus that brought him academic honors, the most notable being his election to membership in the Royal Society of London. It is not known whether he ever practiced law, but he did have influential friends in law, politics, and government who helped him gain important positions. Bougainville spent several months as secretary to the French ambassador in London, where he enjoyed an active social life, perfected his English, and made the acquaintance of (and often befriended) many prominent Englishmen. He read the accounts of English naval explorers, particularly the account of Admiral George Anson's voyage around the world.

LIFE'S WORK

Bougainville lived at a trying time for his country. Yet if France had been on the rise, he might not have had his moment in the sun. In 1756, at the beginning of the Seven Years' War, General Louis-Joseph de Montcalm was appointed military commander of the French forces in what was then France's colony in North America, a large tract of land consisting of Canada, the Great Lakes region, and the Mississippi basin, including Louisiana. Bougainville was Montcalm's aide-de-camp and friend from 1756 until the end of 1759, when Montcalm was killed in the Battle of Quebec. As Montcalm's aide, he learned to deal with the American Indians. He did this so successfully that he was adopted by an Iroquois tribe. He visited most of the French forts of this territory and took part in many of the skirmishes and battles. He was wounded in the Battle of Ticonderoga.

Since he spoke English and had diplomatic experience, he frequently would be sent to negotiate the terms of surrender in these battles. As the years passed, he watched France's power fade and the friction between the French military and colonial government increase. At this juncture, General Montcalm sent Bougainville to France with two objectives: to defend Montcalm from the accusations of Governor Philippe de Rigaud de Vaudreuil and to encourage the French government to support the war effort in North America or risk losing Canada to the English. He accomplished the former aim but succeeded only in getting lip support for Montcalm. Returning empty-handed to Canada, he took part in the losing defense of Quebec against General James Wolfe. After the death of Montcalm, he rose to second in command of the remaining French forces and eventually played a part in negotiating France's surrender of Canada to the English, then commanded by Lord Amherst.

The Pacific was the next stage in the European rivalry between France and England. On his return to France, Bougainville convinced King Louis XV that despite France's defeat in the Seven Years' War, it still might be possible to block the English from the Pacific. Bougainville was given permission to try but was not given money to establish a French settlement in the Malouine (Falkland) Islands. He raised his own funds and, with a small group of French Canadians, in 1764 landed on and

Louis-Antoine de Bougainville. (Library of Congress)

took possession of the Malouine Islands for France. The English, who had claimed but not settled these islands, demanded that France withdraw its colony. The French, thoroughly drained by the Seven Years' War, were powerless to resist. Instead, they negotiated an agreement with Spain to turn the settlement over to Spain rather than give it to the English. As part of this political maneuvering, Bougainville was given the job of handing over another French colony to another foreign power. In return, he was given two ships and orders to sail around the world—and in the process explore the South Pacific for France. It was this voyage that brought renown to Bougainville as the first Frenchman to circumnavigate the globe.

Bougainville was not alone in the exploration of the South Pacific. The English in the same year sent an expedition under Samuel Wallis and Phillip Carteret. They became separated during bad weather while passing through the Straits of Magellan and each continued alone, unaware of the other's progress. Bougainville followed closely behind. Bougainville finally caught up with and passed Carteret off the west coast of Africa, returning to home port first. Several colorful and complimentary accounts, including his own, have been made of Bougainville's voyage. He unsuccessfully searched for the then legendary southern continent and discovered several new islands and channels. One of the islands today bears his name. He visited Tahiti and his description of it and its people captivated the French imagination. His supply ship carried Jeanne Baret, the first woman to sail around the world. She was apparently the mistress of the expedition's naturalist, Philibert Commerson, who had successfully disguised her as his valet. She was not discovered until they had reached Tahiti. Bougainville brought a Tahitian back with him to Paris, and the Tahitian became the talk of Paris. Commerson, a botanist, found a brightly flowered vine in Brazil that he named Bougainvillea. While Bougainville's voyage added little to what was known of the Pacific, it was of importance to the French. It gave them a small victory after a series of dismal failures in the international power struggles of the eighteenth century.

Shortly after Bougainville had completed his account of the journey, he was again pressed into military service for France. In 1778, the French, at the urging of Benjamin Franklin, signed a treaty with the fledgling United States of America to take their part against the English. Bougainville was given the command of a French battleship and again went to war against the British. This French adventure was, on the whole, less than successful. The one success was the naval battle in Chesapeake Bay, which led to the surrender of First Marquess Cornwallis to George Washington in 1781. Thus, the French were instrumental in depriving their enemy of a large colony in North America in revenge for their loss of Canada twenty years earlier.

Bougainville married at the age of fifty and had four sons by this marriage. One of them, Hyacinthe, followed in his father's footsteps, joining the navy, and making several voyages of exploration, including a trip to Tahiti. Bougainville, a supporter of the royalty during the French Revolution, barely escaped the guillotine. He spent the last eighteen years of his life in good health, honored by Napoleon I and the people of France. He was preceded in death by his second son and by his wife. Bougainville died on August 31, 1811, in his home in Paris.

SIGNIFICANCE

Louis-Antoine de Bougainville can be described as a model eighteenth century aristocrat. He was intelligent, well educated, adventurous, socially outgoing, and, in the latter part of his life, financially comfortable. He dedicated most of his life to public service, first as a junior army officer and later as naval commander. In his public life, he was a patriot, loyal to his country, king, and commanding officers, and in return he received their loyalty.

He is most renowned for being the first Frenchman to command a vessel that circumnavigated the globe. This voyage was noteworthy for a reason that was given little or no public acclaim but in retrospect was more important than any real or imagined victory over the English. Bougainville made accurate notations of the longitude of the places he visited. He used a method suggested by Galileo and Jean Cassini's tables of the eclipses of the moons of Jupiter to determine the time it was in Paris compared to the time it was where they were. Unfortunately, this method of establishing the longitude of a place did not become widely used, partly because of the difficulty of the astronomical observations needed. Once this practice, pioneered by Bougainville, became commonplace, navigators were able to determine their destination accurately, as well as where they were in relation to their destination. Thus, the guesswork was taken out of overseas transportation and trade became more practical.

—*Theodore P. Aufdemberge*

FURTHER READING

Allen, Oliver E., et al. *The Pacific Navigators*. Alexandria, Va.: Time-Life Books, 1980. The third chapter of this book relates biographical material on Bougainville, centering on his part in the exploration of the South Pacific. Contains his portrait and a map tracing his voyage across the Pacific. Also includes references to the solution to the longitude problem.

Bougainville, Louis-Antoine de. *Adventure in the Wilderness: The American Journals of Louis-Antoine de Bougainville, 1756-1760*. Edited and translated by Edward P. Hamilton. Norman: University of Oklahoma Press, 1964. A very readable translation of Bougainville's American journal. Also contains a short but valuable introduction that describes Bougainville and sets the historic and geographic stage for his journal. Contains several portraits, two of Bougainville, and several sketch maps, including a very useful place-name map of New France and the British Colonies.

_____. *The Pacific Journal of Louis-Antoine de Bougainville, 1767-1768*. Translated and edited by John Dunmore. London: Hakluyt Society, 2002. An English translation of Bouganville's journal of his voyage across the Pacific. Dunmore provides introductory material about the ships, participants, and other aspects of the voyage. Illustrations.

Brown, Lloyd A. *Map Making: The Art That Became a Science*. Boston: Little, Brown, 1960. The chapter "The Science of Longitude" describes the method used by Bougainville to establish the longitudes of the places he visited.

Dunmore, John. *French Explorers in the Pacific*. Vol. 1, *Eighteenth Century*. New York: Oxford University Press, 1965. Relates the stories of seven French navigators of the eighteenth century, including a chapter on Bougainville. The majority of the chapter deals with his voyage across the South Pacific.

_____. *Monsieur Baret: First Woman Around the World, 1776-1768*. Auckland, New Zealand: Heritage Press, 2002. Recounts the story of Jeanne Baret, who disguised herself as a valet and accompanied Bougainville on his voyage around the world.

Hammond, L. Davis, ed. *News from New Cythera: A Report of Bougainville's Voyage*. Minneapolis: University of Minnesota Press, 1970. This short but valuable book contains a long introduction to the translation of a newsletter written by Bougainville, in which he describes his encounter with the island of Tahiti. In the introduction Hammond cites the historic significance of this voyage and gives a short biography of Bougainville.

Kimbrough, Mary. *Louis-Antoine de Bougainville, 1729-1811: A Study in French Naval History and Politics*. Lewiston, N.Y.: E. Mellen Press, 1990. Kimbrough examined research conducted in France since 1964 to prepare this biography focusing on Bougainville's place in French naval history. Includes chapters on Bougainville's participation in the Seven Years' War and his voyage around the world, as well as illustrations.

See also: Lord Amherst; Lord Anson; First Marquess Cornwallis; Benjamin Franklin; Louis XV; Louis-Joseph de Montcalm; George Washington; James Wolfe.

Related articles in *Great Events from History: The Eighteenth Century, 1701-1800*: May 28, 1754-February 10, 1763: French and Indian War; June 8-July 27, 1758: Siege of Louisbourg; December 5, 1766-March, 16, 1769: Bougainville Circumnavigates the Globe; April 27-October 10, 1774: Lord Dunmore's War; April 19, 1775: Battle of Lexington and Concord; May, 1776-September 3, 1783: France Supports the American Revolution; July 4, 1776: Declaration of Independence; September 6-7, 1776: First Test of a Submarine in Warfare; August 6, 1777: Battle of Oriskany Creek; September 19-October 17, 1777: Battles of Saratoga; February 6, 1778: Franco-American Treaties; October 19, 1781: Cornwallis Surrenders at Yorktown.

JOSEPH BOULOGNE
Caribbean-born composer and revolutionary commander

A product of French and African parents, Boulogne overcame racial challenges to become a master swordsman and prominent musician in France, as well as one of the most celebrated personalities of the Enlightenment era.

Born: c. 1739; Basse-Terre, Guadeloupe
Died: June 9 or 10, 1799; Paris, France
Also known as: Chevalier de Saint-Georges
Areas of achievement: Music, military

EARLY LIFE
Joseph Boulogne (zhoh-zehf bew-lohn-yuh) was born in the Basse-Terre region of Guadeloupe to a beautiful Senegalese slave woman and an aristocratic plantation owner. His paternity within the extensive Boulogne fam-

ily is also disputed, but it seems most likely that his father was the planter Guillaume-Pierre Tavernier de Boulogne, who had properties in the French colonies of Guadeloupe and Saint-Domingue.

Joseph's earliest childhood was spent in both these colonies, but in 1748, with his mother, Nanon, in tow, Joseph accompanied his father to Bordeaux and then to Paris, where he began a life and career that vaulted him to the highest levels of French society. As occasionally happened even within the oppressive slave systems of the Caribbean, Joseph's father was fond of his son and undertook to secure for him privileges that were rare for people of color in eighteenth century France.

At age thirteen, Joseph became a boarding student with the Parisian fencing master Nicolas Texier de La

Böessière, and in a few years his form and athleticism had earned him plaudits as France's premier swordsman. For the next several decades, he maintained this reputation, giving exhibitions of his dazzling technique and often defending himself against those who doubted his prowess with the foil. He also regaled audiences with his displays of dancing, swimming, skating, riding, and pistol marksmanship. He became a knight of the king's Royal Guard, earning the title chevalier de Saint-Georges, and his mastery of arms earned him a teaching position at the Royal Academy.

Boulogne's musical potential had been recognized during his childhood in the Caribbean, when he had received fiddle lessons from the plantation steward. Later, in France, his father arranged for him to study with Jean-Marie Leclair, the doyen of French violinists. He also began a long association with the most influential French musician of the era, François-Joseph Gossec, who seems to have cultivated Boulogne's interest in composition.

LIFE'S WORK

The irrepressible Joseph Boulogne was soon a master musician, violin virtuoso, composer, and conductor of two of France's leading orchestras. In 1769, he was awarded the position of first violin and ensemble timekeeper with the Concert des Amateurs, a symphonic orchestra comprising more than seventy amateur and professional performers; after Boulogne was appointed its conductor (1773-1781), it became one of the premier ensembles in Europe. Following this, he conducted a new orchestra founded by the Freemasons, Le Concert de la Loge Olympique, and often performed at the Royal Palace.

Boulogne's own concerti, quartets, and operas were played and admired throughout Europe on programs that also included selections by Wolfgang Amadeus Mozart and Joseph Haydn. Though Mozart was in Paris during the peak of Boulogne's celebrity, there is no evidence that the two ever met. Mozart was certainly aware, however, of the musical innovations being advanced by Boulogne and other French musicians. In 1786, Boulogne visited Haydn in Vienna to commission six "Parisian" symphonies, which were premiered by Le Concert de la Loge Olympique. Boulogne and Gossec pioneered in the composition of string quartets and *symphonies concertantes*, which feature soloists with orchestras. Boulogne occasionally conducted another major orchestra, the Concert Spirituel, which presented his works, and in 1775 he became director of the theater and orchestra of Madame de Montesson, wife of the duc d'Orléans. He was also music adviser to Marie-Antoinette, wife of King Louis XVI.

With the charisma of a matinee idol, Boulogne skillfully navigated the nuanced waters of upper-class French society. Welcomed into the Lodge of the Nine Sisters of the Grand Orient of France, he became the first person of color within the ranks of French Freemasonry. Counting the king and Marie-Antoinette among his many patrons and friends, he was the toast of the Parisian salon world. A dashing favorite of the ladies, from whom he did not withhold his charms, he was also known to bestow much of his fortune on both his friends and the unfortunate. He was well received at the influential salons of Madame de Vauban, the marquise de Montalembert, and the celebrated painter Élisabeth Vigée-Lebrun. In a different arena, there is evidence that he served the duc d'Orléans as a secret agent in Belgium and England.

Though theoretically enjoying the rights and freedoms of other French subjects, people of color in eighteenth century France generally experienced declining mobility as France's role in the international slave trade increased. The prevalence of Enlightenment ideals did little to soften government rules limiting the presence of Africans and biracial people in France. Exceptional as he was, Boulogne was never beyond the snares of racial prejudice. Although he was often referred to as "the famous Saint-Georges," he was equally "the Black Don Juan" or simply "the Mulatto." When Louis XVI wanted to appoint Boulogne director of the Paris Opera, three women artists informed the queen that they would never submit to the orders of a mulatto. The position remained vacant.

Notwithstanding his aristocratic connections, in 1789 Boulogne espoused the republican ideals of the French Revolution. He joined the national guard in Lille and served as an officer under the marquis de Lafayette. In September, 1792, the national assembly authorized the formation of a contingent of one thousand free people of color, to be known as the National Legion of the South. Boulogne was appointed colonel in command of the unit, which soon came to be known as the Saint-Georges Legion. Second in command was Thomas Rétoré Davy de La Pailleterie, the mulatto father of Alexandre Dumas, *père*, who wrote *Les Trois Mousquetaires* (1844; *The Three Musketeers*, 1846).

In his military capacity, Boulogne helped the Army of the North defend against the Austrians, but later elements of the Saint-Georges Legion were dispatched to Nantes to punish aristocratic enemies of the revolution. By the spring of 1793, Boulogne found himself denounced for his aristocratic associations and forced to defend his loyalty to the revolution. In September, he forfeited his command, and several days later he was arrested. After eighteen months in prison, Boulogne recovered his liberty but not his military charge.

In 1796, Boulogne returned to the Caribbean to greet the Haitian Revolution, which had erupted in the late summer of 1791. Accompanying Julien Raimond, the leading champion of people of color in the French world, he found the former colony still in the delirium of emancipation but also beset with factious strife. Disappointed, he soon returned to France to recover some of the acclaim that had hitherto been his constant companion; he became musical director of the Circle of Harmony and once again received praise for his performances. Three years later, in 1799, his own death from abdominal ailments just preceded the end of the century of the Enlightenment that he had helped to glorify.

SIGNIFICANCE

Virtually without peer, Joseph Boulogne embodied superior athletic skill, musical creativity, and courtly charm. His was an extraordinary story in a society where several thousand people of color, whether enslaved or free, could expect only servile and domestic roles. Unfortunately, Boulogne departed the eighteenth century leaving little personal account of his life and age.

Boulogne's life enhanced his art. With his remarkable accomplishments in music and athletics and his engaging presence, Boulogne overcame the social disadvantage of his mixed ancestry to become one of the most visible and popular figures in eighteenth century French aristocratic society. His life is a testament to the challenges faced by people of color in a land prominent for Enlightenment ideals, but his story equally reveals the possibilities that talent and character can create even in an unwelcoming environment. In addition to his varied compositions, Boulogne helped to pioneer eighteenth century music techniques such as the *symphonie concertante* for soloists and orchestra, and his music heralded the advent of the Romantic era.

—*William H. Alexander*

FURTHER READING

Guédé, Alain. *Monsieur de Saint-George: Virtuoso, Swordsman, Revolutionary*. Translated by Gilda Roberts. New York: Picador, 2003. An appreciative, comprehensive study by a journalist at the forefront of the international movement to restore Boulogne's glory. It differs from other works in identification of his birth year and paternity.

Ribbe, Claude. *Le Chevalier de Saint-George*. Paris: Éditions Perrin, 2004. A major work by a Guadeloupean intellectual living in France, based considerably on unpublished documents. In French.

Smidak, Emil. *Joseph Boulogne, Called Chevalier de Saint-Georges*. Lucerne, Switzerland: Avenira Foundation, 1996. A sympathetic treatment by a recognized musicologist, focusing on Boulogne's musical accomplishments within the context of his life.

See also: Johann Sebastian Bach; George Frideric Handel; Joseph Haydn; Louis XVI; Marie-Antoinette; Wolfgang Amadeus Mozart; Duc d'Orléans; Toussaint Louverture; Élisabeth Vigée-Lebrun.

Related articles in *Great Events from History: The Eighteenth Century, 1701-1800*: January, 1762-November, 1766: Mozart Tours Europe as a Child Prodigy; July 14, 1789: Fall of the Bastille; August 22, 1791-January 1, 1804: Haitian Independence; April 20, 1792-October, 1797: Early Wars of the French Revolution; September 20, 1792: Battle of Valmy; January 21, 1793: Execution of Louis XVI; March 4-December 23, 1793: War in the Vendée.

MATTHEW BOULTON
English inventor and businessman

Boulton created one of the first factories in England, made varied housewares of high artistic quality available to the middle class, modernized the coining process, and helped James Watt manufacture and merchandise an improved steam engine.

Born: September 3, 1728; Birmingham, England
Died: August 18, 1809; Birmingham, England
Areas of achievement: Business, science and technology, art

EARLY LIFE

Matthew Boulton's father was a successful maker of buckles and buttons. After studying at a private academy, in 1742, at age fourteen, Boulton was apprenticed to his father's business. By age seventeen, Boulton had already invented the inlaid buckle, which significantly increased his father's trade. At that time, European fashions were individualized by small details of ornament, such as buckles and buttons, and much of Birmingham's economy depended on the buckle trade. The younger Boulton's invention of inlaid buckles foreshadowed traits that would later be the key to his historical significance: He was inventive, and he was sensitive to public tastes in a way that would be commercially successful.

As a young man, Boulton was of above average height and had a receding forehead, gray eyes, and a prominent nose. He won others over as much by his sociability, intelligence, and kindness as by good looks. He was clearly regarded as an eligible young bachelor. In 1749, when he was twenty-one years old, he married Mary Robinson, a distant cousin from a wealthy family. When she and Boulton's father died in the same year, Boulton inherited a business and stood to inherit a small fortune. Yet Boulton was never one to rest comfortably in financial security or to yield to a life of idleness he associated with the "gentlemen" of his time. Instead, he was planning methods to increase his business and provide the beautiful objects he produced to a much wider clientele.

Boulton sought a site near Birmingham suitable for a factory, to be called the Soho Manufactory. It would be an early product of, and contributor to, the Industrial Revolution. The factory brought together a group of skilled metalworkers, provided a unified power source in a nearby brook, coordinated its activities at a single location through a group of supervisorial personnel, and, eventually, through a later partnership, provided a means of merchandising its goods to the broadest possible national and international clientele.

LIFE'S WORK

By 1762, Matthew Boulton had constructed the Soho Manufactory and found a partner in John Fothergill, whose skill in languages and experience in foreign travel would help him influence buyers of the fine metal items Boulton was already producing. Boulton was the energetic innovator of the two, continually proposing new schemes and underbidding his competition, but often undertaking projects that left the partnership in debt. He was the perennial optimist, writing letters of encouragement to the perennial pessimist Fothergill.

One way of alleviating the financial straits in which the partnership often found itself was marriage. In 1767, Boulton married Anne Robinson, his first wife Mary's sister. When Mary and Anne's brother, Luke, died, Boulton inherited £16,000 and significant holdings in real estate. This second marriage also provided Boulton with his only children, Anne and Matthew.

Boulton's first significant commercial expansion was the manufacture of Sheffield plate—a process by which silver is bonded to copper, giving the elegant appearance and durability of silver while costing far less. Boulton's Soho plant now began turning out candlesticks, tureens, bread baskets, urns, communion cups—all silverplated items that could make daily life pleasant and impress others with the purchaser's taste for beautiful things. Because these objects contained and advertised themselves in terms of precious metals, they had to be assayed. Dissatisfied with the inefficiency of long, slow travel to assay offices in London or Chester, in 1773, Boulton successfully pressured the House of Commons to create an assay office in Birmingham.

The promotion of Birmingham was one of Boulton's chief desires and accomplishments, for he deplored the arrogance and dominance of London. Birmingham had acquired a reputation for cheap, shoddy trinkets; in fact, the city had given its name to the term "brummagem" (cheaply showy or spurious). Boulton was embarrassed by this association and strove to produce goods that were artistic and precision-made. After becoming the largest producer of silverplate in Birmingham, Boulton added a line of ormolu, a metal usually made of brass or bronze and simulating gold. Though gilded pieces were sold to King George III of England and Catherine the Great of

Russia, this line produced a net loss. Boulton then experimented with other items to manufacture, such as clocks, copying devices, and lamps. Despite this variety, Boulton's ventures failed to be consistently profitable until he became associated with James Watt and the steam engine. The steam engine solved a number of problems that the Industrial Revolution had created. New markets were forming among the middle class, vast numbers and varieties of goods were beginning to be produced, and the metals composing these goods required mines at greater depths. The improved steam engine provided an efficient source of power to mine the metals and manufacture the metal goods. Watt's steam engine, by adding a condenser, made the engines pioneered by Thomas Newcomen and Thomas Savery much more efficient. Watt's first partner, John Roebuck, however, did not propel the manufacture or merchandising of the engine sufficiently to produce profits or give Watt the time to perfect his prototype engines. Roebuck eventually went bankrupt, and Boulton purchased the patent and, along with Fothergill, became partners with Watt in 1774-1775.

Still, Boulton perceived that ownership of the patent for the steam engine and partnership with its inventor were useless financially without sufficient time to refine and market the product. Watt's original patent was set to expire in eight years (of the original fourteen years); thus, Boulton and Watt successfully pressured the British government for a special bill to extend the patent twenty-five years, to 1800. Boulton also encouraged Watt to develop the rotative steam engine; this had much wider use than the original Watt engine, used primarily to pump water from mines. The rotative engine was first produced in 1783 and soon became widely employed in foundries and mills.

The steam engine represented the movement from "natural" power to mechanical power, a development aptly illustrated by the last significant chapter in Boulton's life as an industrialist, the application of the steam engine to the problem of coinage. Previous to Boulton's effort, coining was labor-intensive, using a fly press and two men to strike a single coin; coins varied in quantity and were easily counterfeited. Simultaneously, the growth of a laboring class created a need for numerous small coins to pay weekly salaries. Boulton discovered that Jean-Pierre Droz had improved the coining press and developed a "split collar" to hold and shape the coin uniformly; Boulton encouraged this Frenchman, took out a patent for the coining press (1790), added a steam engine for power, and redesigned the coining process so that Boulton's Soho Foundry was virtually an assembly line

and could mint twelve hundred tons of coins per year. Ultimately, in 1799, Boulton fitted the Royal Mint with his devices and even manufactured coins for foreign nations, such as Russia.

Boulton had come a long way from a small maker of buckles in Birmingham to an internationally known craftsman and manufacturer. He had known many of the great scientists and industrialists of his time and helped to found an intellectual discussion group in Birmingham called the Lunar Society. Its membership was graced at times by such notaries as Benjamin Franklin, Josiah Wedgwood, and Joseph Priestley. In his later years, Boulton withdrew more from daily oversight of his business, eventually developed kidney disease, and died on August 18, 1809, at the age of eighty-one, leaving most of his fortune and his share in the business to his son.

SIGNIFICANCE

Matthew Boulton's career began at a time when beautiful objects were made one at a time by highly skilled craftsmen for a few wealthy individuals, usually royalty. In response to this, Boulton both created and embodied virtually every significant change that led to modern industrial organization and the factory system. He is best known for his contribution to the development of the steam engine, but this accomplishment is merely one example of his particular genius, a genius for improvement, facilitation, and organization.

Boulton began as a silversmith and shopkeeper and ended as a lord of industry. He realized that through centralization of power, political pressure, and reduction of costs, one could make luxurious and graceful objects widely available. His manufacture of silverplate and ormolu made elegant candlesticks for not only King George III or Catherine the Great but also for the middle class.

Furthermore, Boulton was sensitive to the situation of workers in the changing social structure. He paid his employees liberally for the times, with department heads receiving £9 a week, and he established, in 1792, one of the first insurance societies for workers. The favor was returned by his employees, many of whom stayed with him throughout their careers and working lives.

Boulton was a fond father to his children and a father figure to his employees, but he was not above exploiting his influence, wealth, and foresight. Thus, he was able to pressure the British government to extend Watt's patent for twenty-five years, when the normal running time was fourteen years. He was willing to supply jobs to orphans and "plain country lads" but also expected twelve-year-old boys to work ten hours at night on his coining press.

The development of silverplate, the steam engine, and the coining press reflect Boulton's skill as improver, manager, and industrialist. These inventions did not originate with Boulton, yet he was the key to their development. Thomas Boulsover had originated silverplate; Watt saw the advantage in efficiency that a condenser could add to the steam engine; Jean-Pierre Droz had invented a device to coin efficiently and uniformly. It was Boulton, however, who found the capital, obtained extended patents, and manufactured products in such numbers as to make profits and benefit a growing populace. The middle class wanted fine housewares to impress friends; other industrialists needed steam engines to unearth raw materials or refine them profitably; the entire economy needed a source of dependable coinage, which could not be counterfeited, to use as a medium for wages and purchases. Boulton foresaw and satisfied these needs.

—*Jonathan L. Price*

FURTHER READING

Boulton, Matthew. *The Engine Partnership, 1775-1825.* Vol. 1 in *The Selected Papers of Boulton and Watt.* Edited by Jennifer Tann. Cambridge, Mass.: MIT Press, 1981. An edited collection of papers pertaining to the Boulton and Watt firm.

Delieb, Eric, and Michael Roberts. *Matthew Boulton: Master Silversmith.* New York: Clarkson N. Potter, 1971. This work includes some biographical detail, particularly of Boulton's early years, but focuses on the work of Boulton's firm in silver and other metals. Excellent descriptions and full-color plates of candlesticks, tureens, cups, and vases.

Dickinson, H. W. *Matthew Boulton.* Cambridge, England: Cambridge University Press, 1937. Though dated, this book remains the best biography of Boulton. Explains in detail his projects in silverplate, the steam engine, and coinage. Makes good use of original documents but is often uncritically positive in its judgment of Boulton's character.

Goodison, Nicholas. *Ormolu: The Work of Matthew Boulton.* London: Phaidon Press, 1974. Similar to Eric Delieb and Michael Roberts's work in its emphasis on artistic production. Contains little biographical detail but many full-page color plates and a sophisticated description of individual works as well as of the state of the ormolu trade in the mid-eighteenth century.

Lord, John. *Capital and Steam Power, 1750-1800.* London: P. S. King and Son, 1923. Reprint. New York: Augustus M. Kelley, 1965. An intelligent, though dated, discussion of the social and economic milieu that fostered the Industrial Revolution and the invention of the steam engine. Credits the Boulton and Watt firm with the primary contribution to this development.

Marsden, Ben. *Watt's Perfect Engine: Steam and the Age of Invention.* New York: Columbia University Press, 2002. Includes information about Boulton and Watt's partnership, describing how the men held a twenty-five-year monopoly on steam power that stymied innovation and destroyed competition.

Schofield, Robert E. *The Lunar Society of Birmingham: A Social History of Provincial Science and Industry in Eighteenth Century England.* Oxford, England: Clarendon Press, 1963. Investigates the society of scientists and intellectuals Boulton helped to found. Though this text comments on Boulton's role, primary emphasis is on other luminaries, such as Josiah Wedgwood, Joseph Priestley, and Erasmus Darwin.

Uglow, Jenny. *The Lunar Men: Five Friends Whose Curiosity Changed the World.* New York: Farrar, Straus, and Giroux, 2002. Recounts how Boulton and his friends established the Lunar Society of Birmingham, where they and other scientists and inventors could share knowledge. Unlike Robert Schofield's book, Uglow's work emphasizes Boulton's contribution to the group and provides a great deal of information about his life and inventions.

See also: Robert and James Adam; John Baskerville; Hester Bateman; Catherine the Great; John Fitch; Benjamin Franklin; George III; Thomas Newcomen; Joseph Priestley; Paul Revere; John Roebuck; James Watt; Josiah Wedgwood.

Related articles in *Great Events from History: The Eighteenth Century, 1701-1800:* 1701: Plumier Publishes *L'Art de tourner*; 1705-1712: Newcomen Develops the Steam Engine; 1759: Wedgwood Founds a Ceramics Firm; 1765-1769: Watt Develops a More Effective Steam Engine; October 23, 1769: Cugnot Demonstrates His Steam-Powered Road Carriage; 1781-1784: Cavendish Discovers the Composition of Water; April, 1785: Cartwright Patents the Steam-Powered Loom; 1793: Whitney Invents the Cotton Gin; 1797: Wollaston Begins His Work on Metallurgy; 1800: Volta Invents the Battery.

JOSEPH BRANT
Mohawk chief and military leader

Brant demonstrated the impact an educated Native American leader could have on his people's destiny, as he led the way for a great Mohawk migration to Canada after the American Revolution, in which he fought for the British against American revolutionaries.

Born: 1742; Ohio Country
Died: November 24, 1807; near Brantford, Ontario, Canada
Also known as: Thayendanegea (birth name); Kayendanegea; Two Sticks of Wood Bound Together
Areas of achievement: Government and politics, warfare and conquest, military, diplomacy

EARLY LIFE

Known to his Mohawk kin as Thayendanegea, meaning "he who places two bets," Joseph Brant was the son of Argoghyiadecker (also known as Nickus Brant), a prominent leader on the New York Indian frontier during the mid-eighteenth century. He had an older sister known as Molly Brant who became an extremely influential tribeswoman. She combined her own political acumen with her role as consort to the American Indian superintendent for the British, William Johnson, to build a powerful network within the tribe. Some observers believed she was capable of influencing tribal decisions in a major way. Major Tench Tilghman, an American observer in the Iroquois Country in 1776, observing Molly Brant and the other Iroquois women, reflected that "women govern the Politics of Savages as well as the refined part of the world."

Brant grew up in the Mohawk village of Canojohare, where he enjoyed the traditional teachings of the tribal elders as well as the efforts of Anglican missionaries who came to convert the indigenous peoples to Christianity and to teach them basic educational skills. So bright was the young Brant, however, that this village education was insufficient. Accordingly, when David Fowler and Samson Occum visited the Mohawk country as representatives of the Reverend Eleazar Wheelock's school in Lebanon, Connecticut, Brant was one of three young Mohawks designated to return eastward for additional education.

Upon their arrival in Lebanon, Brant and his Mohawk companions were so frightened by their surroundings that they kept their horses ready at a moment's notice for flight back to their village. Of the three new students, the schoolmaster had the highest praise for Brant: "The other being of a family of distinction among them, was considerably cloathed, Indian-fashion, and could speak a few words of English."

Within three months, Brant's two companions returned to the safety of their home country, but Brant remained to study and to help teach the Mohawk language to a young missionary named Samuel Kirkland. When Kirkland went west in November on a recruiting mission, Brant went along to interpret and help persuade two more Mohawks to attend school. During his sessions in Lebanon, Brant improved his written Mohawk and his English skills, which would serve him well as both interpreter and then spokesperson for his people. As early as March of 1768, he assisted Ralph Wheelock in conferring with an Onondaga chief, to the visitor's obvious approval: "By Joseph Brant's help I was able to discourse with him, and delivered to him my discourse to this nation."

Brant's stay at school was curtailed by the outbreak of war in the West. When Pontiac and his followers attempted to drive the British out of the Ohio Country, Brant's sister Molly urged her brother to come home, lest some revenge-seeking colonist murder him.

Although he never returned to Wheelock's school, Brant retained not only his literary skills but also his belief that education was the key to success and survival for his people. In time he was regarded as the most able interpreter in the British northern American Indian department. He had the advantage of being a respected Mohawk who could attend such important meetings as the tribal council at Onondaga, where he could take notes on the proceedings and then report them accurately to the British officials.

In the years before the American Revolution, Brant married Margaret, daughter of the Oneida chief Skenandon. At her death, he married her sister Susanna, who cared for Brant and his young children until her death. His third wife was Catherine Croghan, the Mohawk daughter of George Croghan, a member of the British Indian department and a confidant of William Johnson.

LIFE'S WORK

The coming of the American Revolution turned the world of Joseph Brant and the Mohawks upside down. He would emerge from his position as an official in the

British Indian department to become the most feared Mohawk warrior of the time. Indeed, some historians have since described him as the most ferocious American Indian leader of the colonial period. Such accusations, however, were largely frontier hyperbole.

What Brant did during the American Revolution was accompany Guy Johnson, who had succeeded to the office of Indian superintendent at the death of his uncle in 1774, to London in 1775-1776. Feted by the royal court, Brant dined with the famous and had his portrait painted, both alone and as a figure in the background when Benjamin West painted Colonel Guy Johnson. In both cases, the depiction of a powerful and dignified young man suggests the sagacity Brant would use to lead the Mohawks through the difficult war years.

When Brant finally made his way back to America, he had to slip through the countryside in disguise to avoid capture. To his dismay he found the Mohawk country in an uproar over the war, with many Mohawks already planning to emigrate to the British post at Niagara. Brant first went to Niagara to secure the safety of his family and then recruited warriors to return with him to the Mohawk country, where they might attempt to drive out American invaders and aid British expeditions coming through American Indian country. Despite the accusations of frontiersmen in later years, there is no evidence to support the contention that Brant was a bloodthirsty killer. For most of 1777 and 1778, Brant was active in the Mohawk country with his band of warriors. In 1779, however, they had to withdraw toward Niagara in the face of the major expedition launched through the Iroquois country by the Americans under General John Sullivan.

After he had a disagreement with his old friend Guy Johnson in 1780, he withdrew to the Ohio Country in an attempt to rally the indigenous peoples of that territory. In 1781 he joined an attack on an American flotilla on the Ohio River, destroying supplies destined for George Rogers Clark in the Illinois country. This success, however, did not change the plight of the Ohio Indians, for as Brant heard at Detroit late in 1781, many of the western tribal leaders believed the British would walk away from them when the end of the war came. As Brant soon came to know, the fear was well-founded, for the rumors of peace first heard in late 1781 were confirmed in early 1782.

Immediately, Brant wrote to General Frederick Haldimand in Canada, seeking to hold the British officer to his promise of sanctuary in Canada for the Mohawks. A man of his word, Haldimand agreed that Brant and

his people had sacrificed too much. By March, 1783, Brant and Haldimand agreed on a Mohawk homeland along the Grand River in present-day Ontario. As a reward for his faithful service, Brant was commissioned by Haldimand as captain of the Northern Confederate Indians.

With this commission in hand and with the general's help in clearing title to the land, Brant began leading the Mohawks and others to Canada. By virtue of his newfound rank, Brant assumed the role of spokesperson for all the pro-British Iroquois, especially those migrating to Canada. In his role as tribal leader and frontier entrepreneur, Brant would have his critics. Some accused him of profiting from the establishment of the Mohawks in Canada, and his opponents were especially bitter when he opened unused Mohawk lands for settlement by whites, from whom he collected a kind of real estate commission. Others may have resented the baronial style he had copied from William Johnson, as the following attests:

> Captain Brant . . . received us with much politeness and hospitality. . . . Tea was on the table when we came in, served up in the hansomest China plate and every other furniture in proportion. After tea was over, we were entertained with the music of an elegant hand organ on which a young Indian gentleman and Mr. Clinch played alternately. Supper was served up in the same gentel stile. Our beverage, rum, brandy, Port and Maderia wines . . . our beds, sheets, and English blankets, equally fine and comfortable. . . . Dinner was just going on the table in the same elegant stile as the preceding night, when I returned to Captain Brant's house, the servants dressed in their best apparel. Two slaves attended the table, the one in scarlet, the other in coloured clothes, with silver buckles in their shoes, and ruffles, and every other part of their apparel in proportion.

In the face of criticism, Brant often countered by using his support system within the traditional Iroquois matriarchy, the mothers and aunts who dominated village politics, nominated the sachems, and influenced the councils. With their assistance, he silenced opposition. Since his sister was the brilliant and powerful Molly Brant and his wife, Catherine, was from a prominent Iroquois family, he well understood the most effective means of playing politics within the Iroquois council.

One of Brant's long-term goals was advancing the cause of Christianity and advancing education among the Iroquois. Within a few years after his relocation in Canada, he was joined by his longtime friend and supporter, Daniel Claus, in editing the Prayer Book of the Anglican Church in Mohawk. This new volume, published in 1786, contained not only the Mohawk version of the Book of Common Prayer but also the Gospel of Mark.

In the 1780's, funds were obtained to build a church in the Grand River settlement. Then, in 1788, the former Anglican missionary at Canojohare, the Reverend John Stuart, came to visit, bringing with him some of the silver communion plates that once had been in the Mohawk church at Fort Hunter in New York. According to Stuart, the church Brant had seen constructed "in the Mohawk village is pleasantly situated on a small but deep River—the Church [is] about 60 feet in length and 45 in breadth—built with squared logs and boarded on the outside and painted—with a handsome steeple & bell, a pulpit, reading-desk, & Communion-table, with convenient pews." Stuart had no great love for Brant; he was convinced that Brant would accept no clergyman for the Mohawk church whom he could not dominate. Indeed, believed Stuart, the Mohawks "were afraid of the restraint which the continued residence of a Clergyman would necessarily lay them under." Evidently there was some substance to this belief, since the number of white missionaries at Grand River remained quite low as long as Brant was in a position of influence there.

Brant remained the active frontier speculator until the last years of his life. Constantly involved in land transactions, travel, and farming, he never lacked for activity, yet his home was always the place of choice for visitors. As many callers pointed out, he lived in a grand style, and when he decided to build a new home early in the nineteenth century, it closely resembled Johnson Hall, the home of Sir William Johnson in New York where Brant had spent so much time as a child and as a young adult. From youth to death, Brant lived in two worlds.

SIGNIFICANCE

Joseph Brant's life was a success story, judged by most standards. He grew up among the elite of the Iroquois. His father was a prominent leader and his sister Molly Brant a respected woman among the Mohawks. Because of his intellectual ability, he was offered a chance for an education enjoyed by few of his contemporaries. Once he had acquired that education, he chose to walk the extremely narrow path between the two worlds of his own people and the neighboring new Americans and the European immigrants.

One of the most powerful role models in his life was Sir William Johnson, whose splendid home was the center of conviviality, diplomacy, and trade in the Mohawk Valley. Watching the success with which Johnson played patron to the Iroquois, military leader, land speculator, colonial politician, and wilderness baron had to have an impact on Brant. During the course of his travels, Brant was always careful to cultivate his patrons and the right politicians. Such adroitness served him well in maintaining his leadership position in the face of all opposition.

While Brant had his enemies and his detractors, he succeeded in surviving and in guaranteeing the survival of the Mohawks who followed him. While a strictly traditionalist tribal leader might not have approved of Brant's feet being in two worlds, others might agree that he found the only way for Native American peoples to survive in a world of rapid change.

—*James H. O'Donnell III*

FURTHER READING

Fenton, William N. *The Great Law and the Longhouse: A Political History of the Iroquois Confederacy*. Norman: University of Oklahoma Press, 1998. A comprehensive history that also examines Brant's role in Iroquois relations with the British and with American revolutionaries from 1760 to 1794.

Fischer, Joseph R. *A Well-Executed Failure: The Sullivan Campaign Against the Iroquois, July-September 1779*. Columbia: University of South Carolina Press, 1997. A military analysis of the Continental army's first expedition against the American Indians, focusing on field operations.

Graymont, Barbara. *The Iroquois in the American Revolution*. Syracuse, N.Y.: Syracuse University Press, 1972. An overview of the Iroquois in the American Revolution by the leading student of Six Nations affairs. While a bit naive about the motives of the missionaries, it is extremely useful for its accounts of the battles in which the Iroquois took part.

Johnson, Charles. *The Valley of the Six Nations*. Toronto, Ont.: Champlain Society, 1964. An indispensable source for understanding Brant and the Mohawks in Canada. Reprints a number of sources that reveal the tensions with which Brant had to contend.

Mintz, Max M. *Seeds of Empire: The American Revolutionary Conquest of the Iroquois*. New York: New York University Press, 1999. Focuses on the military campaigns against the Iroquois and their Tory allies from 1777 through 1779. Mintz contends the American Revolution was not only a struggle for freedom but also a battle for American Indian lands, "and the jewel was the upstate New York domain of the Iroquois' Six Nations."

O'Donnell, James H., III. "Joseph Brant." In *American Indian Leaders: Studies in Diversity,* edited by R. David Edmunds. Lincoln: University of Nebraska Press, 1980. An analysis of Brant, his role models, and his career.

Stone, William L. *The Life of Joseph Brant, Thayendanegea.* New York: G. Dearborn, 1838. The classic nineteenth century account, in which the author tries to unearth every story and scrap of evidence, both real and imagined, about Brant. It is still the place to start for anyone doing serious research on Brant.

See also: George Rogers Clark; Pontiac; Thanadelthur; Benjamin West.

Related articles in *Great Events from History: The Eighteenth Century, 1701-1800:* April 19, 1775: Battle of Lexington and Concord; May 24 and June 11, 1776: Indian Delegation Meets with Congress; August 6, 1777: Battle of Oriskany Creek; 1799: Code of Handsome Lake.

JAMES BRINDLEY
English engineer

The first modern English canal engineer, Brindley designed and engineered the canal network necessary for the industrialization of the Midlands and therefore essential to eighteenth century England's Industrial Revolution.

Born: 1716; Turnstead, Derbyshire, England
Died: September 27, 1772; Turnhurst, Staffordshire, England
Areas of achievement: Engineering, science and technology

EARLY LIFE

James Brindley was born in a remote section of Derby, England, an area populated by small tenant farmers, transient hawkers, and squatters. Brindley's father made an indifferent living on a small leasehold, and impoverishment seems to have been the family's general circumstance. As the eldest, James received some instruction from his mother. Nevertheless, he remained barely literate throughout life, although there is scant evidence that this was a handicap to him. Until he was seventeen years old, Brindley worked as a laborer but displayed a keen interest in the operations of waterwheels, cog wheels, drum wheels, and related machinery, frequently making models of them.

In 1733, Brindley entered a seven-year apprenticeship to a millwright near Macclesfield, the most prominent town in his native district. Doubtless, Brindley carefully chose his craft: In the England of his day, there were no provisions for the formal training of professional engineers, and millwrights, who were obliged to design, construct, and maintain the varieties of machinery and power sources on which their livelihoods depended, afforded the most proximate practical experience. While Brindley was probably unaware of it, the route he had chosen was identical to the route other renowned early engineers—William Meikle, William Fairbairn, and John Rennie, for example—also had chosen.

In any event, thanks to the indolence of his master, Abraham Bennett, within a few years, Brindley displayed skills and ingenuity that won for him high repute throughout Derby. Brindley contrived a flint mill, which proved of great value to Josiah Wedgwood and other potters. He also drained the Clifton coal mines, improved a silk mill, and experimented with enhancing the performance of early steam engines. After nine years in his trade as an apprentice and two as a journeyman, the twenty-six-year-old Brindley launched his own business in Leek as a master wheelwright and millwright, continuing his versatile dealings with mechanical problems. He constructed drain systems for mines, improved the smelting of industrial metals, and resolved mechanical problems in the industries of nearby Cheshire and Lancashire, earning a still wider and admirable reputation as "The Schemer."

LIFE'S WORK

The intersection of James Brindley's skills and the duke of Bridgewater's entrepreneurial needs signaled the concentration of his work upon canals and his movement to national prominence. Young, well-traveled, and eccentric, the duke of Bridgewater was eager to capitalize on the coal under his Worsley estate. His problem, like that of all the hopeful mine owners and small manufacturers of the Midlands, was the region's almost complete absence of transportation facilities. Waterways were largely unimproved; canals, such as there were, were short, inadequate for heavy traffic, and for the most part private monopolies with tolls regulated accordingly. The few roadways or highways were similarly unpromising, usable only in the fairest weather or seasons, ill-maintained, usually monopolized, and invariably prohibitively expensive. Thus, the survival, not to mention prosperity, of the Midlands' fledgling textile, pottery, and metallurgical industries hinged upon the development of reliable, inexpensive transportation: first, to Manchester and Liverpool to the west; second, southward to London and the Thames River.

Brindley's survey for the Duke's Canal began in 1759. Parliament passed enabling legislation in 1760, and work began immediately from Worsley southeast across the River Irwell to a point about 5 miles west of Manchester. From there, one spur led east to the city itself; the other led westward to gain access to the River Mersey, Liverpool, and port facilities. The canal was an engineering novelty in several respects. It was the first in England to consist of navigable trenches cut in dry land, freeing transport from dependence on natural waterways. Indeed, Brindley made it a principle to avoid mixing other waters with those of the canal, except to ensure adequacy of supply. Navigation, therefore, was not subject to periodic flooding.

Despite voiced doubts and opposition from other "experts," Brindley constructed the first canal aqueduct, a stone span of three arches across the Irwell, for the passage of canal barges. Water flowing through the aqueduct was contained by puddled clay and earthworks, another novelty. A third new feature of the canal was the construction of an embankment across treacherous land, 2,700 feet long, 112 feet broad at the base, and 17 feet high. As was true of the aqueduct, the waters were sealed in the earthen embankment by puddled layers of clay faced with sand and earth. The process of puddling, previously unknown, consisted of reducing well-tempered clay and sand to a viscous state, chopping and working it with spades, and covering the viscous material with earth, thereby completely sealing in the canal waters. Finally, instead of carting coal from the mines at Worsley to canal barges, Brindley drove the canal itself into the mines, eventually creating a network 40 miles long,

James Brindley. (Library of Congress)

allowing the coal to be loaded virtually at the coal faces where it was hewn.

Together, these innovations established the hallmarks of Brindley's engineering: careful observation, practical good sense combined with critical reflections on experience, and great ingenuity. These qualities were brought to bear by unremitting attention to work in progress. Like all engineers of his day, indeed well into the following century, Brindley, from start to finish, lived on the job site. In what time was available, he nevertheless shuttled to other work in the district, redesigning mills and improving or repairing waterwheels, steam engines, and heavy-duty cranes.

While the Duke's Canal was under way, the indefatigable Brindley had already surveyed a much greater work for Earl Gower and a number of other Midlands investors and entrepreneurs, a work that sought to link the Mersey with the Trent, then both with the Severn, thereby linking three of England's four major rivers, and in the process joining the ports of Liverpool, Hull, and Bristol by inland water communication. In 1766, Wedgwood turned the first sod for the project and Brindley named it the Grand Trunk Canal, the most monumental undertaking of its kind in England. Completed in 1771, the Grand Trunk extended nearly 140 miles north and south across the west of England. The lay of the land required five major canal tunnels, the most notable of which—Harecastle Tunnel—was 1.5 miles in length, along with major aqueducts over the rivers Trent, Dove, and Dane, 160 minor aqueducts, and 109 road bridges. The western approaches to England were effectively opened to the now interconnected Midlands enterprises, and they in turn were opened to the sea. Though Brindley would build more canals, the Grand Trunk was his last great work.

The extraordinary demands of his calling seriously curtailed Brindley's social and family life. At fifty years of age, he married the nineteen-year-old Anne Henshall, daughter of his assistant surveyor, and she bore two daughters. It is doubtful, however, if Brindley enjoyed much of his family or his small estate, Turnhurst, since he continued daily on-site direction of the Grand Trunk and subsequent canals. Moreover, the physical and mental stresses of his compulsive ways at times seriously debilitated him, however briefly. Anxiety attacks caused him simply to flee work on occasion and hide away. Yet there is abundant evidence that Brindley was enormously self-confident, at times arrogant—this, despite his inability to enter the conversational, mannered circles of his time or to enter the life of the mind fed by literature or science. His portrait, drawn late in life, reveals a full face, rising on an ample double chin, and a rather vacuous stare. It is a portrait whose merit is belied by Brindley's enormous achievements raised on the humblest of beginnings. His death was brought on by exhaustion and exposure but was attributed to diabetes.

SIGNIFICANCE

James Brindley's practical genius and ingenuity were responsible for laying the foundations of English industrialization. He devised and constructed the reticulation of canals that opened the way for fuller exploitation of the coal resources upon which industry came to rely for its energy. In the process, he liberated the latent commercial and industrial potential of the Midlands and bound them, as he did three of England's major rivers, into a coherent, reliable, relatively inexpensive network leading to both internal and external markets. There was a direct correlation between the startling increase in the number of enterprises and in the population of the Midlands and completion of Brindley's canals.

Much less well equipped than successors such as Thomas Telford, a greater canal builder and intellectually a worthier founder of the civil engineering profession, Brindley appears all the more impressive for the deficiencies he mastered. Had he not been available to launch his pioneering work when he did, by extending to the limits his practical genius and hard-earned experience, industrialization, which is so vitally dependent upon communications, might have been delayed twenty years or more.

—*Clifton K. Yearley*

FURTHER READING

Boucher, Cyril T. G. *James Brindley*. Norwich, England: Goose Publications, 1968. Readily available but brief, this work's strength lies in the attention given Brindley's technical expertise.

Boughey, Joseph. *Hadfield's British Canals*. 8th ed. Stroud, England: Alan Sutton, 1994. An updated version of a book originally written by Charles Hadfield, a noted historian of the British canal system. Provides an overview of how canal engineering emerged from the Industrial Revolution of the eighteenth century through current times, including information about Brindley and the duke of Bridgewater.

Clark, Ronald W. *Works of Man*. London: Viking Press, 1985. A handsome, sweeping, well-written and well-illustrated volume that is available in most major libraries. Clark spends only six pages on Brindley but manages to place his work in excellent perspective in the chapter "Engineering Artificial Waterways."

Karwatka, Dennis. "James Brindley and Early Canal Construction." *Tech Directions* 63, no. 6 (January, 2004): 10. A tribute to Brindley and his engineering achievements.

Maynell, Laurence. *James Brindley: The Pioneer of Canals*. London: Werner Laurie, 1956. This work is popularly written but undocumented, so it is not useful in assessing controversial decisions by Brindley or in resolving debates about his work. It is readily available, however, and often cited in engineering bibliographies.

Rolt, L. T. C. *Thomas Telford*. New York: Viking Penguin, 1959. Rolt was a distinguished professional engineer and a major engineering historian. While Brindley is not the subject of this work, Rolt does much to place him and the engineering problems and practices of Brindley's day in perspective. Readily available in engineering and general undergraduate libraries. Well written, well documented, and authoritative.

Smiles, Samuel. *Lives of the Engineers*. 4 vols. London: John Murray, 1862-1865. Though old, this set is available in most major libraries and nearly all engineering libraries. For generations it was the best-documented, best-written history of major engineers. Volume 1, containing a full "Life of James Brindley," is rewarding, if not technically detailed, critical, or ca-

pable of the fresher perspectives that later scholarship makes available.

See also: Thomas Newcomen; James Watt; Josiah Wedgwood.

Related articles in *Great Events from History: The Eighteenth Century, 1701-1800:* 1759-1766: Construction of the Bridgewater Canal; 1767-1771: Invention of the Water Frame; November, 1777-January 1, 1781: Construction of the First Iron Bridge.

LANCELOT BROWN
English architect

Building on the pioneering work of William Kent, Brown perfected the "natural" school of landscaping. Using only arranged trees, water, and lawns, the natural school sought to transform the estates of the English gentry into vast prospects that, while appearing to be the work of nature, were meant to be superior, aesthetically, to anything created by nature.

Born: August 30, 1716 (baptized); Kirkharle, Northumberland, England
Died: February 6, 1783; London, England
Also known as: Capability Brown
Areas of achievement: Landscape architecture, art

EARLY LIFE

Lancelot Brown's nickname, Capability, came from his habit of speaking, as he rode his horse over an estate, of an estate's "capabilities" for improvement under his hands as a landscaper. He was born in a remote area of northern England sometime in 1716. Little is known of his family. Presumably, his father was a yeoman farmer. One biographer, Thomas Hinde, conjectures, on the basis of various bits of circumstantial evidence and a local tradition, that Brown was the illegitimate son of the local squire, Sir William Loraine. Brown attended school until the age of sixteen, far beyond the age customary for lads of his social class. His education, together with his native intelligence, served him well all of his life, giving him the mathematics necessary for his profession and enabling him to consort easily with the great figures of the age.

After his schooling ended, Brown worked locally as a gardener. It was in this early period that he learned the essentials of his profession: the use of tools, the raising of

young plants and transplanting of mature ones, the draining of marshy areas, and in general, a sense about plants and what they can do for a landscape. Already in this early period of his life, he began to practice landscaping, in which his great talent, indeed genius, soon became apparent.

Brown's ambition and drive led him to leave Northumberland and move south when he was only twenty-three years old. He soon took employment in Stowe, the historic seat of the Grenville family, and in the twentieth century was one of the great English public schools. Stowe was already famous in England in the eighteenth century for the beauty of its garden and landscaping. According to legend, Brown began as a lowly kitchen gardener, but modern authorities believe that his skills as a landscaper were already known when he was taken on at Stowe. In a short time he was head gardener. At Stowe he implemented William Kent's designs and thereby mastered the principles of this great innovator in the art of landscaping. As Brown's reputation grew, aristocrats began to "borrow" him to work on their own estates. By 1751, Brown's reputation was such that he was able to move to London and set himself up in business as a landscaper for the wealthy English gentry.

Already in his youth he showed those features of personality and character that played so large a role in his career. He was scrupulously honest, there being in all of his many business dealings only two known occasions when he and his customers quarreled over a bill. Sometimes clients voluntarily paid Brown a bonus to show their appreciation for the good work he had done. Although of very humble origins, he moved easily in the highest levels of society, even becoming a valued companion of

King George III. Horace Walpole wrote with a kind of amused respect that "Mr. Brown's flippancy diverted one, the first peer that experiences it laughs to conceal his being angry at the freedom; the next flatters him for fear of being treated as familiarly; and ten more bear it because it is so like Brown."

He was an affectionate husband and devoted father, giving his sons an excellent education and extending to at least one daughter a freedom of choice unusual in the eighteenth century in choosing a mate. His employees esteemed him. Intelligent, humorous, calm, loving, self-confident—and a genius in his field—Brown was a paragon of a man.

LIFE'S WORK

When the eighteenth century began, the English were slavishly copying the French geometric garden, of which Versailles, designed by André Le Nôtre, is the prime example. This kind of garden, reflecting the Scientific Revolution's belief that humans could master nature, was laid out in rigid geometric shapes, all arranged in perfect symmetry. The straight line, least likely to be found in nature, predominated.

The natural landscape is, in a sense, also the progeny of the Scientific Revolution in that it shows humans in harmony with a nature that, with the advent of scientific understanding, need no longer be feared. Some authorities trace the taste for the natural landscape to Chinese influence, while others, pointing to passages in the work of Joseph Addison and other eighteenth century writers, insist that the idea is wholly native to England. Perhaps the most judicious conclusion is that the eighteenth century English gentry saw in Chinese gardens something for which it was already seeking. Probably the continental landscape painters played a role also by influencing English landscapers to create in reality what the painters had created on their canvases, an image of nature actually better than anything nature, unaided by humans, could do.

In general, the elements of the designed "natural" landscape, a scene that would come to be known as the picturesque, are as follows: First, the park is bounded at a great distance by an encircling belt of woodland, which excludes from sight any agricultural land, but which can be opened to allow a glimpse of a distant object, perhaps a ruin, of pictorial interest. The inner belt of trees is irregular, receding or projecting according to the contours of the land. Specimen, that is, individual trees, and clumps of trees, the clumps varying greatly in size, add diversity to the view. The middle distance is enlivened by water, its source added if necessary. Great sweeps of grass connect all the elements. All lines are curved. The beauty is enhanced by the generous English rainfall, which keeps the grass green.

The modern observer is struck first by the enormous labor involved. Created before modern power machinery, the parks were made by hundreds of laborers employing shovels, carts, and wheelbarrows. On occasion, as at Chatsworth, an entire hill was removed from the setting so that the view would correspond to Brown's vision. Flat areas were transformed into contours. To change the course of a river was an ordinary task in Brown's eyes. Lakes were formed by digging out the depression and then puddling clay, so that the water would not be lost by seepage. Formal gardens, no longer in fashion, had to be ruthlessly destroyed to make way for the new park. Hedgerows, too, were swept away. New trees were brought in by the thousands. Brown insisted that the trees be native species, with special use made of oaks, beeches, chestnuts, birches, and elms. He used evergreens intensively, for contrast with the paler greens of the deciduous trees and for winter color. All the colors had to be native to Great Britain, thus excluding the bluish tints of various North American conifers.

Lawns were created, not by employing turf, but by planting hayseed. The grass was cut by men wielding scythes and by grazing sheep, kept from the area of the house by the "haha," or fosse, a trench that would not interrupt the line of sight from the house, as would a fence or hedgerow. Modern Brown lawns, now more than two-hundred years old, contain an extremely wide diversity of plants. The lawns run smoothly into the rivers or lakes, which were not to have reeds or brambles along their edges, since these would interrupt the continuity of view.

The exact number of parks created by Brown cannot be determined because of faulty records, but they number more than one hundred. Many, fallen victim to neglect, have reverted to a more "natural" state. Others, fortunately, are intact. A prime example of a Brown park still in existence is Blenheim, the seat of the dukes of Marlborough. Brown expended probably his greatest efforts on this park, and it is generally regarded as the epitome of his achievement. Blenheim Park is a superb example of the design effect known as "surprise." Coming from the urban setting of Woodstock, one steps through an archway and at once encounters an astonishing picture, composed of the lake, the great vistas, the lawns, the thousands of trees (arranged in forest belts, clumps, and as individuals), and finally the great palace, framed by the "natural" landscape. Part of the transformation required the radical altering of the small Glyme River; Brown gave it the proportions and curved outline of a large river, and then pridefully commented, "Thames, Thames, you will never forgive me."

The whole park takes up 2,700 acres and is 12 miles in circumference. Nothing on this scale had ever been attempted before, for even the gardens at Stowe comprised a mere 200 acres. The transformation took ten years to complete and decades more for the trees to grow to maturity. The entire gigantic project cost more than £20,000, an enormous sum for the eighteenth century. It should be noted that Brown's work rested on the wealth created by the Agricultural Revolution and by the gentry's profits from investment or family connections in England's commerce.

As Brown's fame grew, English aristocrats outdid themselves to acquire his services. One tried to hire him to redesign his estate in Ireland, but Brown refused, noting in his humorous way that he "had not yet finished England." Growing wealth enabled Brown in 1767 to buy his own estate, Fenstanton, in East Anglia. The manor carried certain old seignorial rights, so that Brown in a sense joined the aristocracy. His greatest honor came from George III, who appointed him the royal master gardener, with the right to live in Hampton Court, in the Wilderness House, which still stands. The post carried various horticultural responsibilities, including the raising of pineapples. The monarch and the landscaper got along very well together, so well that Brown was able on occasion to intercede in political questions for his friends, including William Pitt the Elder.

Brown used his success to foster his family fortunes. Helped by contacts, and one hopes not lacking in ability themselves, one son became an admiral in the British navy and the other served as a member of Parliament.

Brown, who had long suffered from asthma, collapsed and died in a London street at the age of sixty-seven. Upon hearing the news, Walpole wrote to a friend, "Your Dryads must go into black gloves, Madam. Their father-in-law, Lady Nature's second husband, is dead! Mr. Brown dropped down at his own door yesterday." An obituary concluded with the words, "Such, however, was the effect of his genius that when he was the happiest man, he will be least remembered; so closely did he copy nature that his works will be mistaken."

SIGNIFICANCE

Unlike Humphry Repton, his great successor in landscaping in the nineteenth century, Lancelot Brown left no extended statement of his principles. He did speak once of the need for a landscape to be fit not only for the owner but also for "the poet and painter." There were to be no flowers to distract the eye, no collecting of large amounts of sculpture, but only lawns, woods, and water put together in a harmonious way in curved lines that seem so natural, but which are artificial. Brown was as much an artist as any eighteenth century composer or painter, except that he never got to see his creations in finished form.

His work was not universally esteemed. William Chambers, a contemporary critic, complained that his landscapes were so close to "vulgar nature" that they showed a poverty of imagination. Chambers, alluding to Brown's low social origins, lamented that "peasants emerge from the melon-ground to take the periwig and turn professor," and further that "this island is abandoned to kitchen gardeners well skilled in the culture of salads." Brown made no known reply. Because of changing tastes, Brown's reputation declined during Queen Victoria's reign, to the extent that he came to be remembered mainly as a destroyer of formal gardens, and for his distinctive nickname. One modern and unsympathetic critic, N. F. Clark, comments that Brown's "fault lay in endless repetition of a formula, the most obvious features of which were circular clumps of trees, the boundary ride or belt, serpentine rivers and his undulating lawns brought up to the very walls of the house." One can also complain about Brown's work worsening the social injustices so deeply embedded in England's class structure, in that his vast parks most effectively cut off the gentry from any contact, even visual, with ordinary people.

Since beauty is in the eye of the beholder, one must judge Brown's work for oneself. In the eighteenth century, Brown had, as noted, countless admirers in his homeland. Foreign supporters included such disparate people as Catherine the Great of Russia and Thomas Jefferson of the United States. Both invoked his principles in their respective countries. The huge number of visitors to those Brown parks that are still intact in the early twenty-first century show a revival of interest in Brown and his work. A vigorous movement to maintain those parks that still exist has come into being. Those who love Brown's parks will be thankful for such a movement when they realize that the trees, put out by the tens of thousands in the eighteenth century, have now passed their prime and will have to be replaced according to plans based on Brown's principles. One hopes that the English will do their duty by their great landscaper, for the kind of beauty created by Brown is sorely needed in this industrial, urban age.

—*Roland V. Layton, Jr.*

FURTHER READING

Chambers, Douglas. *The Planters of the English Landscape Garden: Botany, Trees, and the Georgics.* New Haven, Conn.: Yale University Press, 1993. Chambers examines how new developments in horticulture as well as scientific advances and renewed interest in ancient texts, created a distinctive philosophy of gardening in England between 1650 and 1750. Good background for understanding Brown's ideas and of other gardeners of the period.

Hinde, Thomas. *Capability Brown: The Story of a Master Gardener.* New York: W. W. Norton, 1986. A good summary and beautifully illustrated.

Hyams, Edward. *Capability Brown and Humphry Repton.* New York: Charles Scribner's Sons, 1971. An excellent book by an author who has written extensively on gardening.

Laird, Mark. *The Flowering of the Landscape Garden: English Pleasure Grounds, 1720-1800.* Philadelphia: University of Pennsylvania Press, 1999. Laird describes how the English mania for flowering shrubs and conifers from North America created a distinctively English type of garden. Includes information on Brown and his work. Illustrated.

Stroud, Dorothy. *Capability Brown.* London: County Life, 1950. Rev. ed. London: Faber and Faber, 1984. Stroud's book is the pioneering work on Brown and still the standard.

Turner, Roger. *Capability Brown and the Eighteenth Century English Landscape.* New York: Rizzoli, 1985. A lovely book, with many helpful old prints as well as modern photographs. Especially good for its descriptions of individual Brown parks.

See also: Robert and James Adam; Joseph Addison; Catherine the Great; Sarah Churchill; George III; Nicholas Hawksmoor; Thomas Jefferson; First Duke of Marlborough; William Pitt the Elder; William Stukeley; Sir John Vanbrugh.

Related articles in *Great Events from History: The Eighteenth Century, 1701-1800:* 1715-1737: Building of the Karlskirche; 1719-1724: Stukeley Studies Stonehenge and Avebury; 1748: Excavation of Pompeii; 1762: *The Antiquities of Athens* Prompts Architectural Neoclassicism.

JAMES BRUCE
Scottish explorer

Bruce explored extensively along the Blue Nile River and in Ethiopia, and his endeavors helped direct European attention to the interior of Africa in the late eighteenth century.

Born: December 14, 1730; Kinnaird, Stirlingshire, Scotland
Died: April 27, 1794; Kinnaird, Stirlingshire, Scotland
Areas of achievement: Exploration, geography

EARLY LIFE

James Bruce was the son of a Scottish laird whose unpretentious home at Kinnaird, in Stirlingshire, looked out over the Forth. His childhood—indeed his entire life—was marked by an extraordinary number of problems, yet early unhappiness was a primary motivating factor for his travels. His mother died when he was a baby, and his father, David Bruce, quickly remarried. The younger Bruce was never close to his father, but one suspects that he inherited some of his sense of adventure from a man who had been a participant in the Jacobite uprising of 1715 and was lucky to escape with his life.

A sickly youth, Bruce began his formal education in London and enrolled at the noted English public school, Harrow, a few years later. Subsequent study at the University of Edinburgh made him an intellectually well-rounded man. In some ways he was a fine example of the Scottish Enlightenment, but his lonely childhood, spent almost entirely away from home, tended toward the creation of a cold, aloof individual who later evinced a certain lack of humanity. This is understandable given the way trouble continued to plague him. He was ill during much of his time at the university, but a much crueler blow came when his pregnant wife died of tuberculosis after the couple had been married only nine months. Disconsolate, Bruce soon sought release from his grief in solitude. He vowed to immerse himself in what he considered the noblest of all occupations, that of explorer,

James Bruce. (Library of Congress)

and his vision fixed on the age-old mystery of the Blue Nile River's sources.

LIFE'S WORK

Once set on the course of locating the fountains from where the Nile sprang, nothing—not even the 1758 death of his father—could lure James Bruce back to Europe or distract him from his purpose. A period spent in Algiers as British consul served him as a sort of apprenticeship in preparing for African exploration, and by 1768, he was in Cairo ready to begin his grand venture. Dressed as a dervish, Bruce set about planning the tremendous undertaking that would carry him into the heart of Ethiopia, much of which remained terra incognita.

In 1769, Bruce commenced his incredible journey at the port of Mesewa on the Red Sea, and in just over three months he had penetrated the Ethiopian hinterland and reached the capital city of Gonder on Lake Tana. He soon ingratiated himself with local authorities, thereby establishing connections that enabled him to travel with relative impunity. During 1770, he explored Lake Tana and its immediate environs. He discovered the Blue Nile's outflow from the lake, observed the spectacular Tissisat Falls, and saw most of the other significant features of the river's headwaters. In addition, he encountered people and customs that were alien to him. He saw people who wore rings in their lips, who used cow blood as a body ornamentation, and he witnessed hordes of tiny flies driving men and animals before them. He also was told of men who hunted other men and of mothers who were not yet ten years old. Even though he was generally accurate in his descriptions of the scenes he witnessed, the time would come when Bruce wished that he had never shared his experiences with the public. Indeed, in England (though not at home in Scotland or on the European continent) he would be mocked and disparaged as an inveterate liar for the remainder of his days.

Bruce had no inkling of what lay before him, however, as he completed his travels by following the Blue Nile downriver to its juncture at Khartoum (now in Sudan) with its sister White Nile River. His initial reception in Europe was one of warm acclamation accompanied by keen scientific and public interest. He had been away from home for a full decade, and he envisioned himself returning as a conquering hero. In truth there was much of the egomaniac in Bruce, but certainly he deserved praise for his massive labors.

For a time he did receive praise. He met the renowned naturalist, comte de Buffon, on his return, and the two of them journeyed together to Paris for a reception with King Louis XVI. For weeks Bruce was the rage of the Parisian smart set, and his presence in fashionable salons assured hostesses of social success. Things changed, though, not long after he reached London in June of 1774. Astonishment at the tales of his feats soon turned to amusement, and within a few weeks he became the butt of malicious jokes. Perhaps the supreme insult came from the renowned wit, Dr. Samuel Johnson. He accused Bruce of never even visiting Ethiopia, suggesting that the land of Prester John was little more than a figment of Prestidigitator Bruce's imagination. Not surprisingly, Bruce decided that he had had enough of London society and fled to his native Scotland.

Bruce fared better in Scotland, where learned men in Edinburgh and elsewhere listened to him carefully and compared his accounts with the concept of the "noble savage" advanced by Frenchman Jean-Jacques Rousseau and other philosophers. He was similarly most welcome at his own inherited estates at Kinnaird. Although they had declined alarmingly, these included valuable coal mines, and Bruce found, to his pleasant surprise, that he was a wealthy man. In short order he settled down to being a benevolent laird; within two years he had married Mary Dundas, a beautiful young woman twenty-four years his junior, and in due time the union was blessed with several children.

Fate, which heretofore had been so unkind to him, seemed to have taken an abrupt turnabout, and Bruce spent his ample leisure time entertaining, playing with his offspring, and indulging himself in the finest traditions of Scottish eccentricity, working through his African collections and pursuing a passion for astronomy while wearing a turban and robed in Ethiopian dress.

Still, the old slights rankled, and the bitter sense of outrage that burned deep within him would not die. Time and again Bruce returned to his carefully maintained journals, but a combination of stubborn pride and fear of negative reaction in England stayed him from publication. When his still young wife died in 1788, however, even amid his sorrow a new spirit moved within Bruce. Fourteen years had passed since he had borne the brunt of the critics' wrath, and with his wife gone he had less concern regarding how family sensitivities might be affected by renewed controversy and hostility. He would publish—English skepticism notwithstanding—and the book would be his final justification.

The resultant magnum opus, published in five sumptuous volumes, was entitled *Travels to Discover the Source of the Nile, in the Years 1768, 1769, 1770, 1771, 1772, and 1773* (1790). Bruce dedicated the book to King George III and anticipated his critics in the preface by saying that he would not lower himself to respond to "any cavills, captious or idle objections . . . what I have written I have written." Critics there were, and in abundance, and a new edition of Baron Munchausen's fictitious travels was brought out dedicated to James Bruce. Yet in retrospect, the book must be viewed as a splendid achievement, as were the travels it describes.

Publication of the book was the final important act of Bruce's life, and in many ways the most important. Tragedy would stalk him to the very end. While entertaining a number of house guests at Kinnaird, he fell on the great staircase of his home as he bid one of his visitors adieu. He struck his head and lapsed into an unconsciousness from which he never awoke. Death came on April 27, 1794, when he was sixty-three years of age. Bruce was thus denied the opportunity to see the vindication that eventually would be accorded all his seemingly preposterous claims.

SIGNIFICANCE

In his book, James Bruce left a careful, meticulously detailed record of his African endeavors, and there is no de-

nying the significance of his travels. He may have been laughed at and in some cases even disbelieved, but Bruce was by no means ignored. Ironically, the controversy that surrounded his work may actually have served to give it a greater impact than if his claims had been accepted at full value. He created excitement and focused attention on Africa. The French always took him seriously, and as a new age of scientific exploration dawned, the scoffing English learned that this Scotsman whom they had so crudely maligned had been miraculously accurate.

Bruce's greatest impact, though, may well have been on his fellow Scots, who chose to follow his footsteps into Africa. He had initiated the solution of and focused attention anew on the ancient enigma of the Nile. Henceforth, as European imaginations encompassed ever wider horizons, the question of the Nile's ultimate source, as well as Africa's other geographical mysteries, would remain well to the forefront in both public curiosity and geographical circles. That such was the case, and that ultimately the Scottish would play a predominant role in solving these puzzles, owed much to Bruce's pioneering example. He can justly be considered the progenitor of the great age of African exploration of the nineteenth century.

—*James A. Casada*

FURTHER READING

Bredin, Miles. *The Pale Abyssinian: A Life of James Bruce, African Explorer and Adventurer.* London: HarperCollins, 2000. Bredin seeks to rehabilitate Bruce's reputation by painting a portrait of the explorer as a brave, tough pioneer.

Bruce, James. *Travels to Discover the Source of the Nile.* Edited by Charles F. Beckingham. New York: Horizon Press, 1964. An abridged version of Bruce's work, with an introduction by the editor. Includes maps, illustrations, and an index.

Head, Francis Bond. *The Life of Bruce, the African Traveller.* London: John Murray, 1838. This old, standard biography remains useful and has not been entirely supplanted.

Hibbert, Christopher. *Africa Explored: Europeans in the Dark Continent, 1769-1889.* London: Allen Lane, 1982. This work provides an introduction to African exploration in the late eighteenth to late nineteenth centuries for general readers.

Moorehead, Alan. *The Blue Nile.* London: Hamish Hamilton, 1962. A beautifully written book that gives a credible, entertaining account of Bruce's part in the exploration of the Blue Nile.

COMTE DE BUFFON
French naturalist

Buffon wrote one of the earliest multivolume natural histories that considered nature a coherent entity. He also worked toward a concept of evolution and geological change that contributed to later investigations in the field.

Born: September 7, 1707; Montbard, France
Died: April 16, 1788; Paris, France
Also known as: Georges-Louis Leclerc (birth name)
Areas of achievement: Biology, science and technology

EARLY LIFE

The comte de Buffon (kohnt duh bew-foh) was born Georges-Louis Leclerc in the region of Dijon, France, to an upper-middle-class family, where his father was the lord of Buffon and Montbard. He was the eldest of five children and he grew up in a house in Dijon, where his family held an important position in society. Between 1717 and 1723, he attended a nearby Jesuit college, where he showed some promise in mathematics. He then began legal training for three years, a future career suited to his position in society. His career path was interrupted in 1727, when he became close friends with a Swiss mathematics professor and went to Angers to pursue his interest in medicine and botany. His activities during the next four years remain obscure, although there are unsubstantiated reports that he fought a duel and traveled extensively.

Buffon returned to Paris in 1732 and began to make rapid advancement in both political and scientific circles. His mother had died a year earlier and left him a sizable inheritance. Even though his financial future was secured, he devoted a considerable amount of time building on his inheritance and soon became a wealthy man. For the next few years, he directed his attention to areas of mathematics and physics. He wrote a paper on timber strength for the navy and contributed a study on probability theory. In 1734, he was elected as an associate to the French Royal Academy of Sciences, and for the following six years Buffon would follow his interests wherever they led him through a number of different scientific areas. Buffon worked in botany, mathematics, and chemistry, as well as performing microscopic research on animal reproduction. In 1739, he was appointed curator of the Royal Gardens of the king of France. This was a major turning point in Buffon's life, because from this point on he would concentrate more of his attention on biological and botanical areas. Also by this time, he completed his study of the physics of Sir Isaac Newton (1642-1727), including a translation of Newton's *The Method of Fluxions and Infinite Series* (1736) in 1740. Throughout his career, Buffon would view nature from a mechanical point of view.

LIFE'S WORK

The comte de Buffon returned to Montbard in 1740 to administer and enlarge his family estates. For the next forty-eight years, he divided his time between his financial concerns and his scientific interests. He spent summers on his estate and returned to his botanical responsibilities in the fall in Paris. During his tenure, he expanded the Royal Gardens extensively and saw them become an important center of scientific research. During this period of his life, he gradually began to publish his forty-four volume *Histoire naturelle, générale et particulière* (1749-1789; *Natural History, General and Particular*, 1781-1812). He became a leading scientist of his time and was a member of the many influential scientific societies of Europe. Louis XV made him comte de Buffon and ordered a statue made in his likeness. Although scientific and financial matters seemed to fill his life, he was married to a pretty, twenty-year-old woman in 1752. Their marriage lasted until her death in 1769, when he was left with a five-year-old son.

Buffon's life's work is contained in his monumental forty-four-volume natural history. He began work in

171

1740 on this unprecedented attempt to write a comprehensive history of all the natural sciences. He developed a network of correspondents throughout the world, who sent him summaries of scientific research. In Paris, he organized a team of collaborators, who helped him sort and digest the vast amount of information at hand. The first three volumes of *Natural History, General and Particular* were published in 1749, and these include titles on the theory of Earth's history and the history of humankind. These volumes were published by the royal press and hence were not examined by the censors. As a result, their publication brought a storm of protest from the Catholic clergy, who were incensed over Buffon's rejection of the Genesis view of creation. Yet he could not be considered an atheist; like many other thinkers of the Enlightenment, he remained a Christian despite his rejection of tradition. Indeed, Buffon wrote a retraction, but he then continued to publish volumes in his natural history without swerving from his commitment to scientific investigation.

Periodically throughout his life, volumes of his work would be published. Buffon worked on a series of volumes on quadrupeds (1753 to 1767). These were followed by volumes on birds between 1770 and 1783. A final series on minerals appeared between 1783 and 1788. In addition, there were a number of volumes called supplements, which were published between 1774 and 1789. Among this last group is one of his most famous works on the geological periods of Earth, *Époques de la nature* (1778; epochs of nature). Taken as a whole, these forty-four volumes make three major contributions to biological sciences: the rejection of a rigid system of identification and classification of biological forms; the opening of a continuing debate on the nature, formation, and diversification of biological species; and the entrance of the concept of evolution into the vocabulary of science through research on anatomy, fossil records, and a vastly extended geologic time.

Buffon began the first volume of his natural history based on the belief in the continuity and unity of nature. He declared in that volume that nature knows only individuals and cannot be placed into logical categories such as classes and genera. This assertion flies in the face of biological classification, which had reached a degree of success and scientific acceptance with the work of Carolus Linnaeus. Linnaeus saw the biological world as discontinuous, each species of organism separately created and placed in the world. For Buffon, each organism was not made according to some ideal design but functioned in the world in a practical manner. Thus, in 1749 Buffon

would claim that the classification of organisms was impossible, because it did not take into account the entire organism, only some structural parts. Yet he did not believe that organisms could evolve over time and pass on these traits to future generations. In time, as his knowledge of organisms grew, he would accept classifications of birds and other mammals, but always with the mental reservation that the system was artificial and arbitrary. Having lived a long and active intellectual life, Buffon would often reconsider his earlier conclusions. As a consequence, later commentaries would often disagree as to his precise thoughts on a specific subject.

One major problem in any classification system is that of how to split organisms into various categories: in other words, to identify each separate species or genus as distinct from another one. Linnaeus believed that each species of organism was separately created by God and continued through direct descent to his time. Buffon's concept of species, when he came to accept this concept, is closer to modern notions than to those of his own time. He argued on the basis of reproduction that those similar individuals that could constantly reproduce over time were a species. He also differed from Linnaeus in another aspect: Buffon thought that physical characteristics were less important than those of habit, temperament, and instinct. Buffon's ideas on species are closer to later biological descriptions of subspecies and varieties.

Buffon was also probably the first person to open discussion on a large number of questions surrounding evolution. While his answers to these questions were to result in a rejection of the concept of evolution, they nevertheless became part of the scientific literature. In his work *Époques de la nature,* Buffon attempted to establish a chronology that was vastly different from the accepted one. Biblical interpretation placed the age of Earth at somewhere between 6000 and 4000 B.C.E.; Buffon's experiments on the cooling of the Earth gave him a figure of seventy-five thousand years. In fact, in his notes he had worked out a figure of three million years, but he thought that he would be misunderstood by his readers. He also proposed a theory of how minerals were transformed by physical and chemical agents and suggested that coal was the product of organic matter. He raised questions regarding sedimentary rocks and fossils within these strata, and this led to questions with regard to the extinction of species. Through his investigations in these areas, Buffon opened the doors for future research that would produce major discoveries in the natural sciences.

SIGNIFICANCE

The comte de Buffon was a man of the Enlightenment who believed that rational thought and observation would provide answers to the mysteries of the natural world. He largely rejected the myths of the past and wanted to provide his carefully considered evaluation of the problems of nature. Because he believed that an organism should be treated as a whole, he suggested the possibility of comparative anatomy; the study of behavior followed, since an organism also responded to its environment.

Through his efforts, the attempt to measure the chronology of the Earth became a scientific enterprise on the part of geologists. Buffon had studied the human species by the same methods he applied to other organisms. In one of his volumes, he described the first humans as living on the Earth while the Earth was still hot; thus, they were black and capable of living in tropical temperatures. It was through the use of human intelligence that humans invented fire and tools that enabled them to adapt to all climates. Buffon saw his work as organizing and analyzing facts and following them to a rational and ordered conclusion; this is an intellectual and scientific framework that future investigators would use to advance their own discoveries.

—Victor W. Chen

FURTHER READING

Bowler, Peter J. *Evolution: The History of an Idea.* 3d ed., rev. and expanded. Berkeley: University of California Press, 2003. Traces theories of human evolution through history. Chapter 3, "Evolution in the Enlightenment," includes information about Buffon's concept of evolution.

Buffon, George-Louis Leclerc, comte de. *Three Hundred and Sixty-Eight Animal Illustrations from Buffon's "Natural History."* New York: Dover, 1993. Reprints some of the engravings of animals in their natural environments. The illustrations were originally published in Buffon's compilation of natural history.

Eisley, Loren. *Darwin's Century.* Garden City, N.Y.: Doubleday, 1958. The section on Buffon is brief and scattered in several parts of the text. Buffon is included in this work to provide the background for Charles Darwin's theory of evolution. This work is recommended as a general text on eighteenth century natural science, since the author's writing is highly accessible to the general reader.

Lovejoy, A. O. "Buffon and the Problem of Species." In *Forerunners of Darwin, 1745-1859,* edited by Bentley Glass, O. Temkin, and W. L. Strauss, Jr. Baltimore: Johns Hopkins University Press, 1959. This article describes in some detail the major problems associated with classification of species and how Buffon's ideas on species fit with those of his predecessors and of Linnaeus.

Mayr, Ernst. *The Growth of Biological Thought: Diversity, Evolution, and Inheritance.* Cambridge, Mass.: Harvard University Press, 1982. Written by a leading authority on Darwin and on the history of biological evolution. Each major section contains information on Buffon and his contributions to biology. The material is sometimes difficult, but the treatment is definitive.

Nordenskiöld, Eric. *The History of Biology.* New York: Tudor, 1928. Chapter 8 of this volume summarizes Buffon's major contributions. Even though the work is dated, the presentation of the materials is competent and provides useful information.

Roger, Jacques. *Buffon: A Life in Natural History.* Translated by Sarah Lucille Bonnefoi, edited by L. Pearce Williams. Ithaca, N.Y.: Cornell University Press, 1997. Biography providing a balanced view of Buffon's life and placing his work within the context of Enlightenment science.

Wilkie, J. B. "The Idea of Evolution in the Writings of Buffon." *Annals of Science* 12, nos. 1-3 (1956). This three-part article examines in some detail the questions of how Buffon may have considered the idea of evolution. Even though Buffon would have rejected the modern concept of evolution, there are concepts of transformation of species in Buffon that link him to later developments in evolutionary theory.

See also: Sir Joseph Banks; Carolus Linnaeus; Louis XV.

Related articles in *Great Events from History: The Eighteenth Century, 1701-1800*: 1704: Newton Publishes *Optics*; Beginning 1735: Linnaeus Creates the Binomial System of Classification; 1749-1789: First Comprehensive Examination of the Natural World; 1751: Maupertuis Provides Evidence of "Hereditary Particles"; 1757: Monro Distinguishes Between Lymphatic and Blood Systems; 1757-1766: Haller Establishes Physiology as a Science; 1760's: Beginning of Selective Livestock Breeding; 1779: Ingenhousz Discovers Photosynthesis.

EDMUND BURKE
Irish politician and philosopher

Burke criticized not only the abuse of royal power but also theories of radical democracy, which he thought threatened the stability of the social order. He opposed the use of force in dealing with the American colonies and advocated responsibility and humanity in dealing with subject peoples. He also wrote a classic work in aesthetic criticism.

Born: January 12, 1729; Dublin, Ireland
Died: July 9, 1797; Beaconsfield, Buckinghamshire, England
Areas of achievement: Government and politics, philosophy

EARLY LIFE

Edmund Burke was the son of a Protestant father and a Catholic mother. He was reared a Protestant, but he worked to obtain equal treatment for Catholics. Burke studied at Trinity College, Dublin, and in 1750 he went to London to pursue a career as a writer. His work, *A Philosophical Inquiry into the Origin of Our Ideas of the Sublime and Beautiful*, published in 1757, was hailed as a major piece of aesthetic criticism, and he became a friend of Samuel Johnson, David Garrick, Oliver Goldsmith, and other leading literary figures. Also in 1757, Burke married Jane Nugent, a doctor's daughter.

In 1758, Burke became the first editor of *The Annual Register*, a volume that contained a survey of the events of the year, including international affairs, domestic politics, economic and social developments, important scholarly or literary contributions, and a wealth of statistical information. Bound and indexed, *The Annual Register* became an important reference work, and it continues to be a useful source for historians. As a politician, Burke was noted for his industry and wide knowledge, attributes fostered by his long association with *The Annual Register*. He was also employed as secretary to William Hamilton, a member of the House of Commons, where he obtained firsthand experience of parliamentary politics.

Burke's political career began in 1765, when he became "man of business" to Lord Rockingham and entered Parliament for a borough controlled by Rockingham. In that year, Rockingham formed a ministry determined to restore the importance of the Whig aristocracy, which was thought to be threatened by the assertiveness of the young king, George III. Burke was intensely loyal to Rockingham, who throughout their long

association treated Burke with kindness and respect. The main achievement of the Rockingham ministry was repeal of the Stamp Act, a conciliatory measure intended to restore obedience in the American colonies. Thereafter, Burke held the view that government of English citizens overseas must be based not on the legal powers of the Crown and Parliament but on statesmanlike recognition of the colonists' experience in managing their own affairs. The next year the Rockingham ministry was cut short by intrigues at court. The dismissal of the Rockingham ministry colored Burke's view of politics, for he viewed "the influence of the Crown" as an insidious force corrupting the political process.

LIFE'S WORK

The major part of Edmund Burke's political career was spent in opposition or in preparing plans of reform. Philosophically he was a conservative, whose principal concern was to preserve the "mixed and balanced constitution" established in the revolution of 1688-1689. As a practical politician his views placed him in opposition to King George III, for Burke believed that the principal danger to the British constitution came from the Crown and the influence it could exert in Parliament.

From 1766 to 1782, the Rockingham group was in opposition, held together by the firmness of Lord Rockingham and the energy of Burke. Burke had enormous respect for the aristocratic members of his party, whom he regarded as the natural leaders of England. He became a prominent spokesman for Rockingham's views in the House of Commons, and he conducted an extensive correspondence to keep the party together in spirit and in parliamentary votes. In *Thoughts on the Cause of the Present Discontents* (1770), he expressed the view that early in the reign of George III a plan had been formed to use "the influence of the Crown" to make Parliament subservient to the king and his ministers. In an age when political parties were criticized as selfish or unpatriotic, Burke defended partisanship when it was devoted to achieving the public good.

The major issue that faced Great Britain in the 1770's was the unity of the British Empire. King George III and the ministry of Lord North (1770-1782) were determined to enforce the authority of the Crown, which was challenged by the American colonists. In *The Speech on Moving His Resolutions for Conciliation with the Colonies* (1775), Burke urged the North ministry to abandon the use of force and preserve harmony within the empire by accepting the reality that the Americans were determined to realize self-government. The War of Independence that broke out at Lexington and Concord in 1775 became a general maritime war with the entry of France (1778), Spain (1779), and the Netherlands (1780) into the conflict. As the war expanded, Burke and the Rockingham party were criticized for their support of the American cause, especially when Rockingham accepted the idea of American independence. The American Revolution led to resistance to British rule in Ireland. Burke supported the Irish, urging Parliament not to make the mistakes it had made with the American colonists. He also supported efforts to extend religious toleration to Catholics.

In 1774, Burke had been elected member of Parliament for Bristol. In his *Speech to the Electors of Bristol* (1774), he stated that a representative should be attentive to the needs and views of his constituents but that in legislative matters he should rely on his own judgment. Burke paid a price for adherence to this principle. In the election of 1780 he was not reelected, for his Bristol constituents objected to his views on the American war, political concessions to Ireland, and toleration of Catholics. Thereafter, Burke's seat in Parliament was provided by Lord Rockingham and his heir.

The most dramatic years of Burke's political career began in February, 1780, when he delivered his famous *Speech on Presenting to the House of Commons the 11th of February a Plan for the Economical Reformation of the Civil and Other Establishments*, followed by five bills that would make extensive reforms in British public finance. Burke believed that the public money was used to increase the political power of the Crown by offering employment, contracts, pensions, and other tangible benefits to members of Parliament. He concentrated his attention on the Civil List, which was money provided to the king and his ministers for the royal household and civil government. Burke advocated abolition of posts that were used primarily as political rewards, a policy he

---

SENTIMENTS AND JUDGMENTS ON TASTE

Edmund Burke, in addition to his substantial and important work in government and politics, is also known for his scholarship on the question of aesthetics, namely, taste, the sublime, and the beautiful. His criticism has influenced generations of art historians, aestheticians, philosophers, art critics, essayists, and others. In this excerpt, Burke introduces his discussion of "taste."

On a superficial view, we may seem to differ very widely from each other in our reasonings, and no less in our pleasures: but notwithstanding this difference, which I think to be rather apparent than real, it is probable that the standard of both reason and Taste is the same in all human creatures. For if there were not some principles of judgment as well as of sentiment common to all mankind, no hold could possibly be taken either on their reason or their passions, sufficient to maintain the ordinary correspondence of life.... But there is not the same obvious concurrence in any uniform or settled principles [as relates to truth and falsehood, for example] which relate to Taste.

... And my point in this enquiry is to find whether there are any principles, on which the imagination is affected, so common to all, so grounded and certain, as to supply the means of reasoning satisfactorily about them. And such principles of Taste, I fancy there are.

Source: Edmund Burke, "Introduction on Taste," in *A Philosophical Enquiry into the Origin of Our Ideas of the Sublime and Beautiful*, edited by James T. Boulton (Notre Dame, Ind.: University of Notre Dame Press, 1968), pp. 11, 13.

---

justified by need to reduce corruption in Parliament and to reduce the financial burdens of the nation. He also suggested improvements in fiscal management. The North ministry fought Burke's plan of "economical reform" vigorously, although North conceded that improved management of the finances was highly desirable. Burke's proposals were rejected, only to be revived two years later.

At the same time, a powerful movement arose to reform the House of Commons by abolishing many small boroughs and giving the seats to London and the populous counties. Burke opposed parliamentary reform on the grounds that the existing distribution of seats gave Great Britain a body of well-qualified leaders while representing adequately the substantial interests of the nation. Since Burke sat for a small borough, his critics charged that his views were based on self-interest. On this issue Burke revealed another facet of his conservatism: his opposition to popular democracy.

In 1782, Lord North resigned when the House of Commons turned against the American war. Lord Rockingham became prime minister and Burke took office as Paymaster of the Forces. In this office he reformed the army pay system. Parliament also passed his bill to reform the Civil List. Burke's plans were cut short when Lord Rockingham died three months after taking office. A year later, Burke was back as paymaster in a ministry led by Charles James Fox, heir to the mantle of Rockingham, and his former foe, Lord North. By this time Burke's major concern was the abuse of power in India by officials of the British East India Company. He was active in preparing a bill that King George III used as a pretext to dismiss the Fox-North coalition ministry in December, 1783. Burke never held public office again.

Once more in opposition, Burke became a leader of a lengthy and acrimonious impeachment brought against Warren Hastings, former governor-general of the East India Company. Though an injustice was probably done to Hastings, who had performed well under difficult circumstances, Burke's role in the impeachment was a public service, for he argued that Great Britain should govern with a sense of responsibility and humanity those peoples who had come under its jurisdiction.

Burke's political career changed dramatically in 1789, when a revolution broke out in France that soon turned radical and violent. Fox was sympathetic to the revolutionaries, a point of view objectionable to Burke, who deplored the "tyranny of the people" as much as the tyranny of kings. In his *Reflections on the Revolution in France* (1790), Burke sounded a note of alarm, which became more strident in his later works. In 1791, he broke politically with Fox, a step he justified in *An Appeal from the New to the Old Whigs*. Burke became a staunch supporter of the king and the Tory ministry of William Pitt the Younger. He opposed reforms that might stimulate a similar outbreak in Great Britain, and he advocated an ideological crusade against France in support of the historic institutions and civilization of Europe. He was praised by George III and rewarded with a pension. He justified his change from reformer to conservative in *A Letter to a Noble Lord on the Attacks Made upon Him and His Pension in the House of Lords by the Duke of Bedford and the Earl of Lauderdale* (1796). Burke retired from the House of Commons in 1794 and died three years later, revered by those whom he had formerly opposed and alienated from those who had been his closest friends.

SIGNIFICANCE

Edmund Burke was a hardworking parliamentary politician, who rose above ordinary by his ability to discern general principles of government and morality implicit in the practical concerns of politics. He was a conservative in that he supported the historic institutions of Great Britain when they appeared to be threatened by an assertive king, popular demagogues, or the ideology of the French Revolution. As a conservative, he believed that institutions must be reformed when they become corrupt, and most of his political life was devoted to reform of government and removal of abuses in Great Britain and the empire. His definition of the role of the statesman in his *Speech to the Electors of Bristol* is a classic, as is his justification of the role of political parties in representative government.

His opposition to the use of force against the American colonists is a model of practical statesmanship as opposed to rigid, legalistic policies out of touch with reality. His long involvement with the affairs of India showed his sympathy for subject peoples and fostered a sense of responsibility and humanity in imperial government. His attacks on the French Revolution, although marred by rhetorical excesses, have become the foundation of modern conservative political thought, for he made clear the fallacy in proposals for sweeping change and the importance of gradual political development within established institutions.

—*Earl A. Reitan*

FURTHER READING

Burke, Edmund. *The Correspondence of Edmund Burke.* Edited by Thomas Copeland. 9 vols. Chicago: University of Chicago Press, 1958-1972. A magnificently edited collection of correspondence that gives a detailed record of Burke's role as a practicing politician.

_____. *The Writings and Speeches of Edmund Burke.* Edited by Paul Langford and William B. Todd. Oxford, England: Clarendon Press, 1981-2000. Burke's role as a political thinker is best followed through his published works, which are available in many editions. This multivolume edition, completed in 2000, is the best.

Chapman, Gerald. *Edmund Burke: The Practical Imagination.* Cambridge, Mass.: Harvard University Press, 1967. A good study of Burke's thought.

Cone, Carl B. *Burke and the Nature of Politics.* 2 vols. Lexington: University Press of Kentucky, 1957-1964. A competent, balanced account of Burke's life.

Crowe, Ian, ed. *Edmund Burke: His Life and Legacy.* Dublin: Four Courts Press, 1997. A collection of essays examining Burke's life and political ideas. Includes essays about his views of the American and French Revolutions, his legacy in the debate over Irish affairs, and his influence on British conservatism in the nineteenth and twentieth centuries.

Dreyer, Frederick A. *Burke's Politics: A Study in Whig Orthodoxy*. Waterloo, Ont.: Wilfrid Laurier University Press, 1979. Places Burke within the context of eighteenth century political thought.

Fennesey, R. R. *Burke, Paine, and the Rights of Man*. The Hague, the Netherlands: Martinus Nijhoff, 1963. A study of Burke's opposition to the French Revolution.

Lambert, Elizabeth R. *Edmund Burke of Beaconsfield*. Newark: University of Delaware Press, 2003. Examines Burke's domestic life and private friendships from 1750 until the death of his wife, Jane, in 1812.

Lock, F. P. *Edmund Burke, 1730-1784*. New York: Oxford University Press, 1998. Recounts Burke's Irish upbringing, education, early writing, and parliamentary career through the time of the American Revolution.

O'Gorman, Frank. *Edmund Burke: His Political Philosophy*. London: Allen & Unwin, 1973. A clear, brief survey of Burke's political thought in relation to his career as a politician.

Reitan, E. A. "Edmund Burke and Economical Reform, 1779-83." In *Studies in Eighteenth-Century Culture*, edited by O. M. Brack. Vol. 14. Madison: University of Wisconsin Press, 1985. A detailed study of Burke as a reformer in economics.

See also: First Viscount Bolingbroke; Charles James Fox; David Garrick; George III; Oliver Goldsmith; Warren Hastings; Samuel Johnson; Lord North; Thomas Paine; William Pitt the Younger; François Quesnay.

Related articles in *Great Events from History: The Eighteenth Century, 1701-1800:* March 22, 1765-March 18, 1766: Stamp Act Crisis; April 19, 1775: Battle of Lexington and Concord; July 4, 1776: Declaration of Independence; September 17, 1787: U.S. Constitution Is Adopted; 1790: Burke Lays the Foundations of Modern Conservatism; February 22, 1791-February 16, 1792: Thomas Paine Publishes *Rights of Man*; April 20, 1792-October, 1797: Early Wars of the French Revolution.

CHARLES BURNEY
English scholar and historian

Inspired by the prodigious commentary on music contained in the French Encyclopédie, *Burney compiled an informative history of music that gave rise to a distinguished tradition of English musical criticism.*

Born: April 7, 1726; Shrewsbury, England
Died: April 12, 1814; Chelsea, Middlesex, England
Areas of achievement: Music, scholarship

EARLY LIFE

Charles Burney was born to a family that was descended from landed gentry in Shropshire. His father, James, was a portrait painter who, upon losing his first wife, married Ann Cooper. Burney had a twin sister, who died young. His parents settled in Chester, but Burney remained in Shrewsbury under the care of a nurse, and it was there that he began musical study with his half brother, James, who served as organist at St. Margaret's Church from 1735 to 1789. After attending Chester Free School (1739-1742), where he studied under Edmond Baker (organist of Chester Cathedral), Burney returned to Shrewsbury to study French and the violin under Nicholas Matteis.

In 1744, Burney left for London in the company of Thomas Augustine Arne, a noted composer; it was here that Burney made the acquaintance of David Garrick, the actor and theater director, and other luminaries associated with the Covent Garden and Drury Lane Theatres. Besides being active as a music teacher, Burney wrote some of the incidental music for a revival of James Thomson's masque *Alfred* (1740). He also contributed to the score of a masque written by Moses Mendez, *Robin Hood* (1749), and another, titled *Queen Mab* (1749), by Henry Woodward. A set of sonatas for two violins and bass was published in 1747, and Burney arranged "God Save the Queen" for a performance at Covent Garden.

Burney was an accomplished organist; this led to his appointment at St. Dionis-Backchurch in 1749. He was also enlisted as harpsichordist and conductor at the subscription concerts at the King's Arms, Cornhill. At this time, Burney married Esther Sleepe; the couple moved to Lynn, Norfolk, to protect Burney's health when he became consumptive. Their daughter Frances (Fanny), an accomplished writer who contributed to the development of the novel of manners, was born at Lynn in 1752.

Burney's wife died soon after the family returned, in 1760, to London, where he had a solid reputation as a music teacher and composer of works for the harpsichord. It was at this time that he began his friendship with Samuel Johnson, with whom he had corresponded since 1755. This friendship lasted until Johnson's death in 1784; according to James Boswell's *Life of Samuel Johnson* (1791), Burney was the recipient of one of Johnson's last letters. This may have been, in part, because of the great affection Johnson held for Fanny Burney; nevertheless, it is clear from Boswell's biography that Johnson had enormous respect for Burney's opinion and enjoyed his company on many occasions, along with that of Sir Joshua Reynolds and Edmund Burke. Boswell referred to Burney as "that ingenious and amiable man"; he was blessed with a lively sense of humor and a fine critical acumen, evidence of which is preserved in *A General History of Music* (1776-1789), the work for which he is best known.

LIFE'S WORK

Inspired by the numerous commentaries on music found in the pages of the French *Encyclopédie* (1751-1772), Charles Burney began to contemplate a plan for an extensive history of music, the first of its kind in England. In 1764, Burney was in Paris, where he hoped to enroll his daughters in a school. He was impressed by French opera, and upon returning to London, he adapted, in collaboration with Garrick, Jean-Jacques Rousseau's opera *Le Devin du village* (1752), which was thus produced in 1766 for the Drury Lane Theatre as *The Cunning Man*. This production did not match the success attained by Burney's musical version of Bonnell Thornton's burlesque *Ode on St. Cecilia's Day* (1760), performed at Ranelagh in the same year as the original. The ensuing disappointment deterred Burney from writing for the theater, and so, his curiosity for learning more about trends in continental music criticism undimmed, he turned his attention to gathering material for a projected history of music. Within a few years, he had exhausted whatever primary sources were available in England; for this reason, he planned to embark on a series of "musical tours."

In 1767, Burney married Mrs. Stephen Allen, a widow with two children. Two years later, the University of Oxford conferred upon him the bachelor's degree and doctorate in music. The work composed for the doctorate was an anthem with several overtures. It was favorably received and had numerous renditions at the Oxford Music Meetings, and Karl Philipp Emanuel Bach directed a

performance of the piece at Hamburg. Burney had been elected to the Royal Society of Arts in 1764 for his musical scholarship related to parish church music and annotated programs for the Anglican service, which had attracted the notice of Charles Wesley. Nine years later, he became a fellow of the Royal Society, partly for disseminating new ideas regarding the history of comets, a lifelong interest about which he eventually wrote an essay (1769) that included translations from the latest French treatises.

In June, 1770, Burney visited France, Switzerland, and Italy to consult libraries, attend concerts, and establish contact with musicians and scholars. He met Voltaire in Geneva and was introduced to Rousseau's *Dictionnaire de musique* (1767; *Dictionary of Music*, 1779), a copy of which he brought with him when he returned to England. The book proved to be an invaluable resource.

Burney's first success as a writer came with the publication, in diary form, of *The Present State of Music in France and Italy* (1771). Johnson was so taken with this conceit that he imitated it in his *Journey to the Western Islands of Scotland* (1775). Burney had been able to assimilate in his journal an extraordinary number of observations regarding musical performances. English readers were fascinated by his descriptions of Venetian street musicians, cello playing (*capotasto*), and Italian opera, about which he was highly enthusiastic. He examined subjects as diverse as scale harmonizing, placing of the voice (*messa di voce*), use of the trill, and different ways of applauding.

Elated by this success, Burney studied German and returned to the Continent in July, 1772. In Vienna, he met Christoph Gluck, Metastasio, and Johann Adolf Hasse, among other prominent librettists and composers. K. P. E. Bach performed for him at Hamburg. In later writings, Burney extolled the shaping of orchestral style formulated by Bach and his adherents of the Mannheim school. An account of this tour, entitled *The Present State of Music in Germany, the Netherlands, and the United Provinces*, which includes numerous details germane to his interest in music history, was published in two volumes in 1773 to wide acclaim.

With this impetus, Burney issued a prospectus to his publisher regarding a subscription plan for the sale of *A General History of Music,* of which the first volume appeared in 1776, a few weeks after the publication of Sir John Hawkins's *General History of the Science and Practice of Music.* Hawkins was a Middlesex magistrate who had been knighted in 1772. He wrote legal articles and musical texts, and his 1787 biography of Samuel Johnson was superseded only by that by Boswell. He was also an executor of Johnson's will. With these credentials, he was obviously not flattered when Burney's *A General History of Music* eclipsed his own. He accused his rival of being an opportunist, but the popularity of Burney's work can be attributed partly to the fact that it was sold in installments, whereas the cost of Hawkins's five-volume set was prohibitive. The two works are best seen as complementary, not competitive. Both represent sound scholarship and range over the entire field of musicology, from antiquity to the late eighteenth century. On the surface, Hawkins's work seems more theoretical, but it is stultified by a style that is listless and dry. Burney's history is keenly analytical and gains on second reading; moreover, it is informed with a fluent, kaleidoscopic intelligence and enhanced by an engagingly anecdotal style.

The second volume of *A General History of Music* was published in 1782; the remaining two volumes appeared seven years later. Because of the unusually long interval between installments, Burney had the advantage of being able to digest and absorb critical opinion regarding the preceding volumes. *A General History of Music* represents a mine of detailed information, some of it unavailable elsewhere. In the preparation of the first volume, Burney received considerable assistance from the Reverend Thomas Twining, a Greek scholar. In subsequent volumes, Burney's comments on improvisation (change in cadenza patterns), extemporaneous pieces, pianoforte playing, chamber music, and descant (counterpoint) not only reflect his astute critical perception but also point directly to later developments. Burney's history revived the reputations of Giovanni Palestrina, Robert White, and Josquin des Prez, composers whose works became standardized in permanent repertoire. Burney called attention to the merits of Johann Sebastian Bach, and in this, he was ahead of his time. He wrote extensively about George Frideric Handel (his account of the Handel Festival of 1784 was published separately), whom he met on several occasions, and about Joseph Haydn, who was not well known in England at that time.

After the great success of the completed *A General History of Music,* Burney continued to remain a prolific author. In 1789, he began writing for the *Monthly Review*; his three-volume *Memoirs of the Life and Letters of the Abate Metastasio* appeared in 1796, and he compiled an unpublished dictionary of music. In 1801, Burney began to contribute music articles to the *New Cyclopaedia*

(1802-1819), compiled by Abraham Rees, for which he received a large honorarium. He was granted a king's pension in 1806 and became a correspondent of the Institut de France (French Institute) in 1810. He worked on his memoirs until his death on April 12, 1814, the night of the official rejoicing for Napoleon's first abdication. He was buried in the cemetery at Chelsea College, having served as organist there since 1783. A tablet in his memory was later erected in Westminster Abbey.

SIGNIFICANCE

Charles Burney's compositions are punctilious and pleasant but of no lasting importance. Like many of his contemporaries, however, he recognized the need for a purely English musical idiom, over and against the prevailing Italian style. He admired early music, then called Barocco, and did much to resuscitate an interest in plainsong, madrigals, and fioritura. One weakness of *A General History of Music* is that it overlooked the large number of English ballad operas based primarily on plots from folk songs.

Burney was the preeminent musicologist of his age. His wide range of interests reflects the humanitarian ideals of the Enlightenment. In the essay on music criticism that introduces volume 3 of *A General History of Music,* Burney advocated a new mode of critical thinking with regard to established forms and practices. In this way, he represents the eighteenth century cosmopolitan spirit, intricately bound to a system of aesthetic values about music that he codified and expressed.

—*Robert J. Frail*

FURTHER READING

Brofsky, H. "Dr. Burney and Padre Martini: Writing a General History of Music." *Music Quarterly* 65 (July, 1979): 313-345. An informative account of the influence of Martini, a celebrated theorist, teacher, and composer, whom Burney met in Bologna.

Burney, Charles. *A General History of Music.* Edited by Frank Mercer. 2 vols. New York: Harcourt, Brace, 1935. Reprint. New York: Dover, 1957. Mercer's "Critical and Historical Notes" includes excerpts from Burney's correspondence as well as a biographical portrait.

_____. *The Letters of Dr. Charles Burney.* Edited by Alvaro Ribeiro. New York: Oxford University Press, 1991. Collection of letters written between 1751 and 1784, providing information about Burney's life and ideas, including his impressions of contemporary music and his friendships with Samuel Johnson and Sir Joshua Reynolds. Ribeiro has carefully edited and exhaustively annotated these letters, many of which have never before been published.

Kassler, Jamie Croy. "Burney's 'Sketch of a Plan for a Public Music School.'" *Musical Quarterly* 58 (April, 1972): 210-234. A description of Burney's project to institute musical training for children at the London Foundling Hospital, based on observations made in Naples and Vienna. The plan was rejected.

Lonsdale, Roger H. *Dr. Charles Burney: A Literary Biography.* New York: Oxford University Press, 1965. Using previously unpublished material, Lonsdale offers a chronicle of Burney's uphill struggle for recognition. Burney's profile is that of an "arriviste," striving to enter the mainstream of the extraordinarily fluid London literary society.

Ribeiro, Alvaro, and James Basker, eds. *Tradition in Transition: Women Writers, Marginal Texts, and the Eighteenth Century Canon.* New York: Oxford University Press, 1996. Collection of essays written in honor of Roger Lonsdale, a Burney biographer. Includes an essay examining the letters of Burney and Hester Thrale, an English writer, diarist, and close friend of Samuel Johnson.

Scholes, Percy A. *The Great Doctor Burney: His Life, His Travels, His Works, His Family, and His Friends.* New York: Oxford University Press, 1948. Reprint. Westport, Conn.: Greenwood Press, 1971. The definitive biography by the author of *The Life and Activities of Sir John Hawkins: Musician, Magistrate, and Friend of Johnson* (1953). A well-balanced overview of the eighteenth century context.

Woolf, Virginia S. "Dr. Burney's Evening Party." In *Collected Essays.* Vol. 3. London: Hogarth Press, 1966-1967. A marvelous vignette depicting an uproarious concert at no. 1, St. Martin's Street, with the famous Italian castrato soprano, Pachiarotti, leading the performance.

See also: Edmund Burke; Fanny Burney; Queen Charlotte; Denis Diderot; Christoph Gluck; George Frideric Handel; Joseph Haydn; Samuel Johnson; Wolfgang Amadeus Mozart; Georg Philipp Telemann.

Related articles in *Great Events from History: The Eighteenth Century, 1701-1800:* c. 1701-1750: Bach Pioneers Modern Music; April 13, 1742: First Performance of Handel's *Messiah*; 1746-1755: Johnson Creates the First Modern English Dictionary; March 20, 1750-March 14, 1752: Johnson Issues *The Rambler*; January, 1762-November, 1766: Mozart Tours Europe as a Child Prodigy; August 3, 1778: Opening of Milan's La Scala; 1795-1797: Paganini's Early Violin Performances.

FANNY BURNEY
British writer

Burney, one of the most significant writers of her time, wrote Evelina: Or, The History of a Young Lady's Entrance into the World, *admired as a first comedy of manners. Her diaries and letters remain fascinating records of the lives of the monied classes and the British aristocracy in the late eighteenth century.*

Born: June 13, 1752; King's Lynn, Norfolk, England
Died: January 6, 1840; London, England
Also known as: Frances Burney (birth name); Madame d'Arblay; Frances d'Arblay; Fanny d'Arblay
Areas of achievement: Literature, theater

EARLY LIFE

Fanny Burney was born the third child of Esther Sleepe Burney and Charles Burney, a well-known musician and scholar. Frances, best known as Fanny, soon had two younger sisters and a younger brother. When she was eight, Fanny recalled being teased by her older brother James for not knowing her letters, but two years later she was spending her free time either reading or writing.

In 1760, the family moved from King's Lynn to London, where father Charles drew his students from the highest levels of society and became acquainted with men such as lexicographer Samuel Johnson and the actor-playwright David Garrick. However, on September 29, 1762, Esther Burney died of consumption, and Fanny and her siblings were devastated. However, the bereft family found some consolation in the kindness of friends, including Samuel Crisp, who would often invite them to his home at Chessington in Surrey. Crisp was partial to Fanny, though her own father had always considered her his least promising child. Perhaps that was the reason Charles left Fanny behind in 1764, when he took his daughters Esther and Susan to be educated in Paris.

Meanwhile, Charles had been courting Elizabeth Allen, a wealthy widow from King's Lynn. They were married in October, 1767. The Burney children got along well with the young Allens but found their stepmother to be moody and difficult. In 1770, Elizabeth and Charles finally united their households, eventually settling down in a house near Leicester Square and just a few steps from the home of painter Sir Joshua Reynolds. Charles now had a doctorate in music from Oxford and, as Dr. Burney, was introduced to the wealthy Henry Thrale and his wife Hester. This association led to Fanny's friendship with Hester Thrale and with the Thrales' frequent guest, Samuel Johnson.

LIFE'S WORK

On her fifteenth birthday, Fanny Burney was ordered either by her father or by her future stepmother to burn everything she had written. It was probably at that time that Fanny's first novel, which she titled "The History of Caroline Evelyn," was lost and therefore never published. However, this attempt to diminish Fanny's obsession with writing failed miserably. She immediately began recording her observations in a diary, and after the move to London, she had ample material. The success of the travel book her father had published in 1771 brought the most prominent members of London society to his home for evening musical entertainments. Fanny's shyness served her well, however, as she observed without being observed, then re-created the social scene and sent her narratives to be read and admired by Samuel Crisp, or "Daddy," as she called him.

Fanny now began spending long hours doing secretarial work for her father, who published a second travel book in 1773 and then embarked upon a multivolume history of music. However, Fanny was determined to write, even if she had to stay up all night to do so. Working at first from fragments of a projected sequel to the unpublished "History of Caroline Evelyn," Fanny secretly developed her novel *Evelina: Or, The History of a Young Lady's Entrance into the World*. Only Crisp, her siblings, and a male cousin knew that she was writing this novel, and she even altered her handwriting when making a fair copy of the work. She had her brother Charles

Fanny Burney. (The Granger Collection, New York)

disguise himself before taking the manuscript to the bookseller, Thomas Lowndes. *Evelina* was published anonymously in January, 1778, and was an immediate success. It was several months before Dr. Burney, his friends, and finally the rest of London society learned that Fanny Burney was the author. She immediately became a celebrity, sought after by people in the highest ranks of society and welcomed into such important intellectual circles as the Bluestockings and Dr. Johnson's Literary Club.

Fanny then turned to writing for the theater. In 1779, she completed a satirical comedy called "The Witlings," but Crisp and Fanny's father feared it might offend someone important, so they dissuaded her from having it performed. Fanny's second novel, *Cecilia: Or, Memoirs of An Heiress* (1782), was an even greater success than her first. Her writing career was soon interrupted by what was meant as an honor, an appointment as Second Keeper of the Robes to Queen Charlotte, but to Fanny, the role was drudgery. After five years, she was permitted to retire.

In January, 1793, while visiting friends in Surrey, Fanny met a group of French émigrés. Among them was Alexandre-Jean-Baptiste Piochard d'Arblay, a handsome but penniless aristocrat and a Roman Catholic. On July 28, 1793, at the age of forty-one and despite her father's objections, Fanny Burney became Madame d'Arblay. The next year, she gave birth to a son, Alexander. The marriage was a happy one, but the couple desperately needed money. In 1795, Fanny wrote another play, *Edwy and Elgiva*, but it was dropped after one performance that same year. None of Fanny's other plays ever reached the stage during her lifetime. Her third novel, *Camilla: Or, A Picture of Youth* (1796), proved to be her most profitable venture. With its proceeds, the d'Arblays built a house in Surrey, christening it Camilla Cottage.

In 1802, hostilities that continued the Napoleonic era in Europe trapped the three d'Arblays in France, where they remained for a decade. In 1811, Fanny was diagnosed with breast cancer and underwent a mastectomy without anaesthetic. After returning to England, she published one more novel, *The Wanderer: Or, Female Difficulties* (1814), but it did not sell well. She nursed her father until his death in April, 1814, then rejoined her husband in France.

In October, 1815, after the Battle of Waterloo, the d'Arblays returned permanently to England, settling in Bath. After her husband's death in 1818, Fanny moved to London and assembled her father's memoirs, called *Memoirs of Dr. Charles Burney* (1832). Despite Fanny's best efforts, her son Alex could not find a purpose for his life, and he died suddenly in 1837, three years before his mother. Fanny died at her home in London on January 6, 1840.

SIGNIFICANCE

During her lifetime, Fanny Burney was known primarily as a novelist. However, after her death, when her niece Charlotte Barrett began bringing out her journals in installments, Fanny became known for her insightful descriptions of life in England and France during the late eighteenth and early nineteenth centuries.

It was not until the early twentieth century, when the English feminist writer Virginia Woolf referred to Fanny as the mother of English fiction, that scholars began to reassess her achievements. They came to realize that Fanny was primarily responsible for creating the novel of manners—in which realistic women characters are shown as they function in social settings—and that her works

had influenced the novels of the Irish writer Maria Edgeworth and those of Jane Austen, the author of *Pride and Prejudice* (1813). Feminist scholars have also drawn attention to a major theme in Fanny's novels and plays, the struggles of women to survive in a male-dominated society. Finally, the journals have been re-edited and are now studied as illuminating works on women in eighteenth and early nineteenth century English society—and particularly of talented women such as Fanny Burney—within the patriarchal structure of the Georgian family.

—*Rosemary M. Canfield Reisman*

FURTHER READING

Davenport, Hester. *Faithful Handmaid: Fanny Burney at the Court of King George III*. Stroud, England: Sutton, 2000. Focuses on the years when Burney was with Queen Charlotte, as recorded in Burney's letters and journals.

Doody, Margaret Anne. *Frances Burney: The Life in the Works*. New Brunswick, N.J.: Rutgers University Press, 1988. Doody's work is considered the major Burney biography. Includes a bibliography and an index.

Harman, Claire. *Fanny Burney: A Biography*. London: HarperCollins, 2000. A scholarly and entertaining work. Includes bibliographical references, an index, and illustrations.

Justice, George L. "Suppression and Censorship in Late Manuscript Culture: Frances Burney's Unperformed 'The Witlings.'" In *Women's Writing and the Circulation of Ideas: Manuscript Publication in England, 1550-1880*, edited by George L. Justice and Nathan Tinker. New York: Cambridge University Press, 2002. Justice contends that Burney's experience with "The Witlings" taught Burney that because the submission of manuscripts to a coterie could result in censorship, it was better to entrust one's work to the public.

Lane, Maggie. *Literary Daughters*. New York: St. Martin's Press, 1989. In a lengthy chapter on Fanny Burney, the author shows how Charles Burney's well-meaning interference in his daughter's career and in her relationships almost always worked to Fanny's disadvantage. Primary and secondary bibliographies. Illustrated.

Manley, Seon, and Susan Belcher. *O, Those Extraordinary Women! Or, The Joys of Literary Lib*. Philadelphia: Chilton, 1972. A lively re-creation of Burney's life and times. Illustrated.

Spencer, Jane. *The Rise of the Woman Novelist: From Aphra Behn to Jane Austen*. Oxford, England: Basil

Blackwell, 1986. One section of this book explains how Burney's fear of being criticized for unbecoming behavior affected her career, and a later section applies that analysis to *Evelina*.

Thaddeus, Janice Farrar. *Frances Burney: A Literary Life*. New York: St. Martin's Press, 2000. Argues that most biographers focus on just one aspect of Burney's personality, while in fact she shows varying characteristics, including timidity, confidence, and even explosive emotionality. Includes a genealogical table, bibliographical notes, and an index.

See also: Mary Astell; Charles Burney; Hester Chapone; Queen Charlotte; David Garrick; Samuel Johnson; Sophie von La Roche; Mary Wortley Montagu; Sir Joshua Reynolds; Mary Robinson; Mary Wollstonecraft.

Related articles in *Great Events from History: The Eighteenth Century, 1701-1800:* 1746-1755: Johnson Creates the First Modern English Dictionary; March 20, 1750-March 14, 1752: Johnson Issues *The Rambler*; 1792: Wollstonecraft Publishes *A Vindication of the Rights of Woman*.

ROBERT BURNS
Scottish poet and songwriter

Burns, writing his poetry and songs at the culmination of Scottish cultural tradition, made a major contribution to preserving Scottish culture, especially the folk song. His universal human appeal made him an internationally recognized as well as an intensely national poet.

Born: January 25, 1759; Alloway, Ayrshire, Scotland
Died: July 21, 1796; Dumfries, Scotland
Areas of achievement: Literature, music

EARLY LIFE

Legend has it that there was a severe storm on the night of Robert Burns's birth. Certainly the poet himself encouraged the legend and took it as emblematic of his later vicissitudes in life. Although his father, William Burnes (as he spelled it), was a man of character and intelligence, even writing a pamphlet of theological instruction in the form of a dialogue between father and son, he was not a successful farmer. The family went through a series of moves and endured humiliating poverty and debt.

Even in such straitened circumstances, Burns's education was not completely neglected. Statutes for universal education had been initiated by John Knox and the Reformation, so that all could read the Scriptures, but the actual schooling provided usually fell woefully short of the ideal. Often families made their own arrangements, giving the teacher board and a small stipend. William Burnes, with several other neighbors, employed William Murdoch, who was to remain for two and a half years. Burns had three brothers and three sisters, of whom Gilbert Burns (1769-1827) was closest to the poet. Later, Burns spent three weeks with Murdoch, polishing his English and learning enough French to continue reading

and studying the language, and he was always an avid reader. Among his favorite poets were Alexander Pope and William Shenstone. Clearly, Burns was far from being the "Heaven-taught ploughman" that his first critics perceived, a legend that he himself encouraged.

The Scottish attitude toward literacy also meant that Burns's potential readers were not entirely limited to an educated elite. Broadsides, chapbooks, and collections of songs were among the popular entertainment, and there was a flourishing oral tradition. An "old maid" of his mother's acquaintance (actually a widowed aunt who occasionally lived with them) fired his imagination with songs and legends. Early in his life, Burns began to write verses. In 1774, when he was fifteen, he wrote "Handsome Nell" for Nelly Kirkpatrick, whom he courted at harvest time, and, as he said, "Thus with me began Love and Poesy." From that time, Burns thought of himself as a poet.

LIFE'S WORK

A poet, however, must usually find another means of earning a living. In the summer of 1775, Burns's attempt to learn surveying and mathematics was not successful. In 1777, the family moved again, to Lochlie farm in Tarbolton parish. There Burns enjoyed the society of the Tarbolton Bachelors' Club, which he had helped to organize; he probably wrote the group's constitution. In the winter of 1781-1782, he and a partner settled in Irvine to learn flax dressing, a venture that proved disastrous. Penniless, Burns returned to the farm; here he began his first commonplace book, containing poems and remarks regarding his poetic development. After his father's death, in February, 1784, Burns and his brother Gilbert rented

Mossgviel farm from Gavin Hamilton, a young lawyer who was sympathetic to Burns's work. Shortly thereafter, Burns acquired the poems of Robert Fergusson, a promising Edinburgh poet whose poems greatly influenced Burns.

Burns and Fergusson were both indebted to the Scottish literary tradition, which went back to William Dunbar, Robert Henryson, and James I of Scotland, author of "The Kingis Quair" (1423?). Before the departure of the court of James I of England and James VI of Scotland for London in 1603, Scots had flourished as a literary language. Scots and the dialect of Northern England (Anglian) were virtually identical; the London dialect of Geoffrey Chaucer had not yet developed into standard English. There was no Scottish equivalent of the King James Bible to provide a widespread and influential example of cultured Scots, and it is somewhat ironic that one of the major influences in unifying English bore the name of a Scottish monarch. After the departure of the court and the onset of the Reformation, Scotland itself was divided both in language and religion between the predominantly Roman Catholic Gaelic-speaking Highlands and the predominantly Scots-speaking Protestant Lowlands. Yet Scottish literature continued to flourish through the seventeenth century, in many traditional

Robert Burns. (Library of Congress)

forms, including what is now called the Burns stanza but earlier was known as Standard Habbie, six lines rhyming *aaabab,* the first, second, third, and fifth lines in tetrameter and the fourth and sixth lines in dimeter. Burns used it to great effect in poems widely different in mood and tone, such as "To a Mouse" and "Address to the Deil."

Burns was a careful craftsman, both in his verse forms and in his use of the Scots vernacular, choosing words carefully for poetic effect. Critics differ as to whether Burns was speaking a particular dialect of Scots or attempting to reproduce the spirit of the vernacular rather than a literal representation of a specific local speech. Scotsmen spoke both languages, using the more formal English for communication in business, law, theology, and philosophy, and Scots for casual conversation, song, and some poetry.

For Burns, the year 1785 was a landmark year for both love and poesy. In that year, Elizabeth, Burns's daughter by Elizabeth Paton, was born; Burns wrote "A Poet's Welcome to His Love-Begotten Daughter." He then began courting Jean Armour and writing, among other poems, the epistles to Davie and Lapraik; "Holy Willie's Prayer," not published until after his death, a devastating satire of Calvinist piety and hypocrisy; and "The Cotter's Saturday Night," the poem most admired by his contemporaries for its elevated use of the English language and its moral tone. Although Armour was now pregnant, the family refused to let her marry Burns, and he, discouraged with both his personal situation and his professional prospects, planned to emigrate to the West Indies. In need of passage money, Burns decided to publish his poetry. *Poems, Chiefly in the Scottish Dialect,* now usually referred to as the Kilmarnock edition, was printed in July, 1786, by John Wilson of Kilmarnock. The edition of six hundred copies sold out in a month. In September, Armour gave birth to twins, Robert and Jean, and in November, Burns left for Edinburgh to seek his fortune in the capital and to try to bring out another edition of the poems.

The impact of this small volume of thirty-six poems was remarkable, considering that it was written predominantly in Scots by an unknown provincial poet. Despite, or perhaps in part because of, the sudden departure of Parliament from the capital with the union of England and Scotland in 1707, the Scottish Enlightenment that flourished in the eighteenth century became an intellectual force recognized both in England and in Europe, its major figures writing in polished English. Most critics maintained that Scots was an unsuitable language for literature. By the time Burns reached Edinburgh, the Enlightenment was in a state of transition. David Hume (1711-1776) was dead and Adam Smith (1723-1790) aged and ill, and Sir Walter Scott (1771-1832) was a sixteen-year-old boy who was later to write of his meeting with his famous contemporary. Nevertheless, there were many less towering figures, including Henry Mackenzie, whose *The Man of Feeling* (1771) was immensely popular.

The Scottish political eclipse also generated an intense interest in Scotland's past. One of Burns's finest poems, "Tam o' Shanter," was written at the request of an antiquary friend to accompany an illustration of Alloway Kirk. In general, Jacobite sympathies for the ill-fated Stuarts went with an interest in the glories of the Scottish past, and emphasis on English and the wider world of culture went with Whig or even Jacobin leanings, which did not, however, necessarily involve active support of the French Revolution. There were those, such as Burns, who combined an intense Scottish patriotism with a sympathy for the underdog, and managed to be Jacobite and Jacobin simultaneously. Many of Burns's songs reflect the former influence. "The Jolly Beggars," a "cantata" of poems and songs originally called "Love and Liberty," and "A Man's a Man for a' That" stress freedom of action and the intrinsic worth of all human beings. In a subtler and more genial way, the first poem in the Kilmarnock edition, "The Twa Dogs," a dialogue between a poor man's dog and a rich man's dog, expresses these sentiments. Other poems, such as his welcome for his daughter Elizabeth and "Holy Willie's Prayer," with its attack on a prominent church member, he suppressed. Religion was a very sensitive topic in Burns's Scotland. The established Presbyterian Church, or kirk, was divided between the Old Lights and the New Lights. It was not so much the complex theological disputes that involved Burns, but the social and sexual conservatism of the Old Lights. Both Burns and Armour, for example, had to confess their liaison in church and be reprimanded.

In Edinburgh, a combination of well-placed introductions, critical acclaim from Mackenzie, among others, and his compelling personality promptly made Burns the talk of the town. Because most of Edinburgh's residents crowded into the Old Town, a medieval warren of multistory houses, in which rank determined how high one lived in the houses, Edinburgh society was more open than that of London. There were numerous clubs for men, ranging through all classes and interests, and Burns was quickly made welcome. In addition, the publisher William Creech held a daily open house for members of the literary milieu.

Burns was shrewd enough to realize that interest in him was in part a result of his novelty and would soon wane, but now he took advantage of his situation to arrange for another edition of his poetry. Creech published *Poems, Chiefly in the Scottish Dialect* in April, 1787, with the addition of much new material, including some of the suppressions from the first edition. The use of the same title left many potential readers unaware of the substantial additions, though the editions did well enough to warrant a second Edinburgh edition and were issued with an impressive list of subscribers.

Before he left Edinburgh, Burns also met James Johnson, editor of *The Scots Musical Museum*, an important collection of Scottish songs, both words and music. Burns was eventually to produce more than two hundred songs for Johnson, some of which appeared in the first volume, published in May of 1787. Burns refused payment or credit for his work. In some cases, he made few changes in the songs, but some he rewrote extensively, some from one line, and some he wrote to fit music to which the words had been lost. Mastering the music before he began to write, Burns was extraordinarily sensitive in matching words to music, a point upon which all critics concur, though there is varying opinion on how much of the technical aspects of music Burns knew. Certainly he had mastered all the published material and, in his travels in Scotland in the fall of 1787 as well as at other times, he collected songs, both words and music.

Burns returned to Edinburgh in December, 1787, where he met Agnes M'Lehose (or McLehose), with whom he had an intense relationship, exchanging impassioned letters under the names of Sylvander and Clarinda. In March, 1788, however, Jean Armour again gave birth to twins, daughters who died within a few weeks. Burns left Edinburgh, leased Ellisland farm, near Dumfries, and married Armour in April, 1788. With a wife and family to support, Burns needed a more dependable source of income than either farming or poetry offered, and petitioned for a position in the Excise. Numerous products, both imported and domestic, were taxed, and the excisemen rode circuit, collecting taxes for a given district. Combined with farming, the severe physical strain of riding miles in all sorts of weather aggravated the rheumatic fever Burns had had since his youth. Yet he continued to write, devoting himself to continuing the collection, restoration, and preservation of Scottish songs.

In 1791, Burns, more secure with a promotion in the Excise, was able to move to Dumfries, a pleasant small city. Without the arduous farm duties, he had more time to write and, in the city, more intellectual companionship. In 1792, he began to work on songs for George Thomson, editor of *A Select Collection of Original Scottish Airs,* the first set of which was published in June, 1793. By September, 1795, Burns's health began to decline seriously, and on July 21, 1796, he died. He wrote until the last: "O Wert Thou in the Cauld Blast" for Jessie Lewars, who cared for him during his final weeks, and songs for the volume *The Scots Musical Museum,* which appeared after his death.

SIGNIFICANCE

Robert Burns's fame mirrors the conflict already noted in Scottish culture. On the one hand, he is the most intensely national of poets, claimed by the Scottish as their own. Even in the poorest household, there were likely to be two books—the Bible and Burns's poems. On the other hand, the universality of feeling and the clarity of his songs and poems have made him a poet known and loved throughout the world. He has been translated into at least two dozen languages, including Japanese and Russian. This very popularity, combined with an overemphasis on his numerous affairs, illegitimate children, and drinking bouts, has tended to influence his critics unduly. Most discerning criticism has tended either to be sweepingly adulatory and sentimental, obscuring appreciation of his tremendous intelligence and wit, or to dismiss all but his Scottish poetry as inferior, or to find fault with his work on grounds of his personal irregularities. Burns's earliest biographer, a temperance advocate, perpetuated the notion that Burns died of alcoholism. He evidently died of a heart condition related to his rheumatic fever, and his drinking was not excessive by the standards of the time.

Of his relationships with women, contemporary critics have observed that there were conflicting forces at work. Passionate in all of his attachments, intellectual and physical, he was accepted by men who were his intellectual equals if social superiors, but he was not able to marry a woman who could have given him intellectual as well as physical companionship.

Now criticism is more likely to maintain a balance between attention to his life and to his work, always a difficulty because Burns is an intensely personal poet, and knowledge of his life and the times in which he wrote are essential to understanding him. In addition to being appreciated as a poet appealing to universal sentiments, Burns is recognized as a satirist and a humorist, as being well-read despite the limitations of his formal schooling,

and, in the field of song, as a master. His place in world literature was well described by his first major European critic, Hans Hecht, as a "titanic fragment."

—Katharine M. Morsberger

FURTHER READING

Brown, Mary Ellen. *Burns and Tradition.* Urbana: University of Illinois Press, 1984. Relates Burns's writings to the Scottish literary tradition. Assesses Burns as a collector of folk songs in relation to the eighteenth century antiquarian movement.

Burns, Robert. *The Poems and Songs of Robert Burns.* Edited by James Kinsley. 3 vols. Oxford, England: Clarendon Press, 1968. A definitive edition with the poems and songs extensively annotated, arranged in chronological order. Melody lines given for the songs.

Butt, John. *The Mid-Eighteenth Century.* Edited by Geoffrey Carnall. Oxford, England: Clarendon Press, 1979. A brief but very useful chapter on Scottish poetry provides detailed background on the development of Scots as a literary language and Burns's place in that tradition. Includes a well-selected bibliography for authors discussed in the text.

Crawford, Thomas. *Burns: A Study of the Poems and Songs.* Stanford, Calif.: Stanford University Press, 1960. A detailed analysis of Burns's poetry and songs, stressing the social and political milieu in which they were written. Emphasizes Burns's wit and ideas.

Daiches, David. *Robert Burns.* New York: Rinehart, 1950. Critical study of Burns by a major Burns scholar. Much biographical and background material included.

_____. *Robert Burns and His World.* New York: Viking Press, 1972. A brief but very thorough account of Burns's life and times. Sections placing him in the Scottish literary and social traditions are particularly useful. The atmosphere of Burns's Scotland is well conveyed by the many well-chosen illustrations.

Dent, Alan. *Burns in His Time.* London: Thomas Nelson and Sons, 1966. An attempt to counterbalance an adulatory approach to Burns, perhaps too far in the opposite direction. Excellent on historical context, with detailed accounts of historical events and literary figures, and quotes from contemporary newspapers and other sources.

Fitzhugh, Robert Tyson. *Robert Burns: The Man and the Poet.* Boston: Houghton Mifflin, 1970. Full-length biography including quotations from many of the poems, with Scots words translated in marginal glosses.

Low, Donald A., ed. *Critical Essays on Robert Burns*. London: Routledge and Kegan Paul, 1975. A collection of essays on Burns by modern scholars. The three essays on Burns as a songwriter and on his knowledge of music are of particular interest.

McGuirk, Carol. *Robert Burns and the Sentimental Era*. Athens: University of Georgia Press, 1985. A study of Burns's work in the context of his literary contemporaries. McGuirk persuasively maintains that Burns's flaws were not a result of his lesser skill in standard English but of the sentimentality of thought and diction shared in varying degrees by most eighteenth century poets. Good bibliography, arranged by topics.

McIntyre, Ian. *Dirt and Deity: A Life of Robert Burns*. London: HarperCollins, 1995. Written to coincide with the bicentennial of Burns's death, McIntyre's biography is an honest examination of the poet's life. Exhaustively documented and written in a clear, precise style.

Mackay, James. *R. B.: A Biography of Robert Burns*. Edinburgh: Mainstream, 1992. Mackay argues that Burns's reputation has been unfairly destroyed by earlier studies depicting him as a drunk and womanizer.

Sprott, Gavin. *Robert Burns, Pride and Passion: The Life, Times, and Legacy*. Edinburgh: Her Majesty's Stationery Office, 1996. Explores Burns's life and the world in which he lived, using letters, manuscripts, paintings, and other materials available in the National Library of Scotland and the National Museums of Scotland.

See also: William Blake; James Boswell; Edmund Burke; David Hume; Alexander Pope; Anna Seward.
Related articles in *Great Events from History: The Eighteenth Century, 1701-1800:* March 1, 1711: Addison and Steele Establish *The Spectator*; March 20, 1750-March 14, 1752: Johnson Issues *The Rambler*.

JOSEPH BUTLER
English religious leader and philosopher

Butler was a moral philosopher who sought to demonstrate, by painting a comprehensive picture of human nature acceptable to common sense, that uprightness and benevolence were more congenial than exclusive preoccupation with oneself and one's own interests. Also, as a Christian advocate, he defended natural and revealed theology against Deism and skepticism. His work asked, Why be moral? Why be religious? Which morality? and Which religion?

Born: May 18, 1692; Wantage, Berkshire, England
Died: June 16, 1752; Bath, Somerset, England
Areas of achievement: Religion and theology, philosophy

EARLY LIFE

Joseph Butler was born at the market town of Wantage, the birthplace also of King Alfred. He was the eighth and youngest child of a prosperous retired draper, whose family was rising in status. Butler began his education at the town's grammar school under the tutelage of its master, the Reverend Philip Barton. The school's name was later changed to King Alfred's School. Butler's family was Presbyterian, and with a view to his entering the ministry Butler was subsequently sent to a dissenting academy—one of a number of private institutions that offered dissenters from the established church the equivalent of a university education. This academy was run by Samuel Jones, first at Gloucester and later at Tewkesbury.

There are no exact dates for Butler's earlier education, but he seems to have remained at Jones's academy until early in 1715. While at this academy Butler became dissatisfied with the principles of Presbyterianism, which led him later to join the Anglican Church. Among his fellow pupils were a number who subsequently became distinguished men, including several who, like Butler himself, came to be reconciled to the Church of England. The most notable, and the closest friend of Butler, was Thomas Secker, who later was appointed archbishop of Canterbury.

Toward the end of his time at Tewkesbury, Butler entered into his celebrated correspondence with Samuel Clarke, best known for *A Demonstration of the Being and Attributes of God* (1705), who was the most eminent philosophical theologian of his time. The peaceable and respectful tone of Butler's philosophical critique of Clarke's proofs of the unity and omnipresence of God, combined with the intellectual rigor with which Butler pursued it, impressed Clarke. The correspondence, initially anonymous on Butler's part, extended over four years and was published by Clarke in later editions of *A Demonstration*.

LIFE'S WORK

On March 17, 1715, despite his abandonment of Presbyterianism, and with his father's financial support, Joseph Butler was entered as a commoner at Oriel College, Oxford, intending to prepare for holy orders in the Church of England. At Oxford, Butler formed a close friendship with another student, Edward Talbot, the second son of William Talbot, bishop of Salisbury, and later of Durham. Edward Talbot died as a young man in 1720, but the Talbot family continued to be Butler's firm friends, and it was their patronage that facilitated his early ecclesiastical career.

Butler became dissatisfied with what he deemed as the pedantic technicalities of his philosophical and theological studies at Oxford and thought of going to Cambridge. Nevertheless, he stayed in Oxford, took his first degree on October 11, 1718, and soon was ordained deacon, then priest, by the bishop of Salisbury. On the recommendation of Clarke and Talbot, he was appointed preacher at the Rolls Chapel. The stipend was small, but his family continued to assist him. In 1722, William Talbot, bishop of Durham, made him rector of Haughton le Skerne and transferred him, in 1725, to the wealthy rectory of Stanhope. In 1726, Butler published *Fifteen Sermons Preached at the Rolls Chapel*, in which he pleaded the cause of moral virtue. The second edition of *Fifteen Sermons*, with an important new preface, was published in 1729, and a revised and enlarged edition, *Fifteen Sermons to Which Are Added Six Sermons Preached on Public Occasions*, was published in 1765.

Butler lived at his Stanhope rectory in complete retirement from the worlds of learning and of fashion for the next seven years. His extreme isolation led a contemporary clergy to describe him as not dead but buried. Apart from the duties of a parish priest, his principal occupation during those years seems to have been the writing of *The Analogy of Religion, Natural and Revealed, to the Constitution and Course of Nature* (1736). The book counters objections to natural theology and Christian theology by Deists and skeptics. In this work, Butler uses a method of drawing probabilities from analogies. It was *The Analogy of Religion*, rather than *Fifteen Sermons*, that made Butler's reputation for the next hundred years or so following its publication.

In 1733, Lord Chancellor Talbot, the elder brother of Butler's friend Edward, drew Butler from his reclusion by making him his chaplain. Butler's earlier friend,

Secker, was now a chaplain to the king. Through him Butler was brought into contact with Queen Caroline, who in 1736 appointed Butler her Clerk of the Closet. In his royal service, Butler had to attend the regular gatherings of men of wit and learning, which the queen was fond of assembling. In his short service to the queen, Butler won her respect and liking to such a degree that she spoke of him on her deathbed on November 20, 1737, and desired that he should be given preferment. Preferment came in the following year, but in the somewhat disappointing shape of the bishopric of Bristol, the poorest see in England. Early in 1740, not long after his disdainful acceptance of the Bristol bishopric, Butler was presented to the deanery of St. Paul's Cathedral in London. As dean of St. Paul's he was able to combine his duties at the cathedral with the attendances at court and in Parliament.

There are very few details about Butler's life in his last twelve years, apart from the official record of his appointments. He published no substantial work after *The Analogy of Religion*. In 1746, he was made Clerk of the Closet to the king, but there is no evidence that this appointment brought him into the same intimacy with King George II as he had enjoyed with the late queen. The offer of the bishopric of Durham, with which Butler's name is most often associated, came in 1750; it came under such ungrateful conditions that Butler came very close to declining the offer.

Ties at Bristol and in Parliament prevented Butler from establishing himself at Durham until June of 1751. His new dioceses was the occasion of Butler's last published work, the *A Charge Delivered to the Clergy of the Diocese of Durham* (1751), which offers interesting insights into the conditions of the church in the eighteenth century. Butler's health soon broke down, and on medical advice he traveled, first to Clifton and then to Bath. On June 16, 1752, after weeks of severe fever, digestive disorder, and unconsciousness, he died at Bath. Butler was buried in Bristol Cathedral on June 16, 1752.

SIGNIFICANCE

Joseph Butler did not publish extensively, and in the published corpus he did not present a full-fledged philosophical system. Although there are historical disputes as to whether Butler was widely read during his own lifetime, undoubtedly by the late eighteenth century Butler's work was widely studied in Scottish universities, and from the early nineteenth century at Oxford, Cambridge, and many colleges in the United States. Butler's impact on the American intellectual arena may be attributed to a strong Scottish influence. Butler's work impressed luminaries such as David Hume and John Wesley, and prominent figures such as Thomas Reid and Adam Smith considered themselves Butlerians.

Butler was a great favorite of the Tractarians in the nineteenth century, but the association with them may have conspired against his ultimate influence in England, especially since Cardinal John Newman attributed his own conversion to the Roman Church in 1845 to his study of Butler. The English Romantic poet and critic Samuel Taylor Coleridge was among the first to urge the study of Butler's *Fifteen Sermons* and to disparage *The Analogy of Religion*, yet the decline of interest in the latter during the late nineteenth century has not been satisfactorily explained. At its zenith, Butler's influence cut across Protestant denominational lines and party differences in the Church of England, but serious interest in *The Analogy of Religion* is now concentrated among certain Anglican writers. Generally, Butler is considered one of the very finest English ethicists, and, despite the waning of his reputation, he was for a long time considered to be a great philosophical theologian. He is seen as an icon of a highly intellectualized, even rarefied, theology.

—Majid Amini

FURTHER READING

Brown, David. *The Divine Trinity*. London: Duckworth, 1984. Brown's work relates the relevance of Butler's religious views to modern controversies concerning Deism and incarnational Christology.

Cunliffe, Christopher, ed. *Joseph Butler's Moral and Religious Thought: Tercentenary Essays*. Oxford, England: Clarendon Press, 1992. This collection addresses the significance and contribution of Butler's ideas and arguments to contemporary philosophical concerns and theological issues.

Darwall, Stephen. *The British Moralists and the Internal "Ought," 1640-1740*. New York: Cambridge University Press, 1995. Darwall offers a detailed analytical perspective on Butler's moral theory in relation to other significant ethical theories of that era.

Duncan-Jones, Austin. *Butler's Moral Philosophy*. Harmondsworth, Middlesex, England: Penguin Books, 1952. A comprehensive examination of Butler's ethical doctrines.

Gladstone, William Ewart, ed. *The Works of Bishop Butler*. New York: Continuum, 1997. A collection of Butler's major writings and correspondence, including Gladstone's own *Studies Subsidiary to the Works of Bishop Butler*, first published in 1896.

Mossner, Ernest Campbell. *Bishop Butler and the Age of Reason*. New York: Macmillan, 1936. Mossner presents a dissenting view on the originality of Butler's argumentation in philosophical theology, and in particular against Deism, and generally on his influence on the subsequent generations of Christian theologians.

Penelhum, Terence. *Butler*. New York: Routledge, 1999. An in-depth analysis and discussion of some of Butler's philosophical and theological positions.

See also: Mary Astell; Caroline; George II; David Hume; Adam Smith; Charles Wesley; John Wesley; John Witherspoon.

Related article in *Great Events from History: The Eighteenth Century, 1701-1800:* 1739-1740: Hume Publishes *A Treatise of Human Nature*.

CANALETTO
Italian painter

Among the most popular of the Old Masters, Canaletto preserved in his canvases the world of eighteenth century Venice. His realistic portrayal of the commonplace and his brilliant clarity influenced numerous artists in Italy and England.

Born: October 18, 1697; Venice (now in Italy)
Died: April 20, 1768; Venice
Also known as: Giovanni Antonio Canal (birth name)
Area of achievement: Art

EARLY LIFE

The son of Bernardo Canal and Artemisia Barbieri Canal, Giovanni Antonio Canal was nicknamed Canaletto (kah-nah-LAYT-toh), or little Canal, to distinguish him from his father. After nearly a century of artistic decline, Venice during Canaletto's youth was experiencing a renaissance. Luca Carlevaris, the city's most successful topographical painter of the early 1700's, was creating a local market for the kind of work Canaletto would produce. He may also have been Canaletto's teacher. Whether he taught Canaletto directly or not, however, it is clear that Carlevaris was an important influence on the painter.

A theatrical scene painter came to Venice in 1712 and introduced the idea of moving the vanishing point from the center of a backdrop to the side or even offstage. Afterward, Canaletto, who helped his father and his brother Cristoforo design sets for theatrical and operatic productions, frequently employed this device. In 1716, another topographical artist, Marco Ricci, settled in Venice. Ricci would affect Canaletto's early handling of light, shadow, and background. Ricci was among those who combined actual scenes with imaginary, romanticized landscapes to create the *capriccio*, a form Canaletto would adopt in the 1740's.

In 1719, Canaletto accompanied his father and brother to Rome, where they prepared the scenes for two of Alessandro Scarlatti's operas, both of which were performed during the 1720 Carnival. These were probably the last theatrical pieces Canaletto produced. While in Rome, he almost certainly saw the work of the Dutch painter Gaspar van Wittel, who had moved to Italy in 1699 and had helped popularize urban views. Canaletto may even have studied briefly under van Wittel, and at this time he may have executed the twenty-one Roman scenes that have been attributed to him.

LIFE'S WORK

By 1722, Canaletto was back in Venice, though the first work that is indisputably his dates from three years later. In 1725 and 1726, he executed four paintings for Stefano Conti, three of them offering views of the Grand Canal. These canvases are large: 1 yard (1 meter) tall and more than 4 feet (1.2 meters) wide; Canaletto did his best work on a large scale. Although he is famous for his luminous shadows, light backgrounds, and clear blue skies, his early works, including those for Conti, are painted on a dark, reddish-brown ground like that used by Ricci. Dark clouds hang in the sky, and figures are small.

In other respects, however, these early paintings exhibit characteristics of Canaletto's later work. He painted slowly, in part because he insisted on using only the best ingredients for his colors. For example, he is the only artist of the period known to have used the then newly discovered Prussian blue; after more than two and one-half centuries, his paintings have therefore retained their brightness. Also typical are the high viewpoint and the realism employed in these works: One sees the peeling stucco and worn bricks of a Venice past its prime.

For these four works, Canaletto received ninety sequins, a fairly high price for the time. Some two years later, in July, 1730, the future British consul Joseph Smith, Canaletto's greatest patron, wrote in a letter, "[Canaletto is] so much follow'd and all are so ready to pay him his own price for his work (and which he vallues himself as much as anybody)." According to one account, Carlevaris died of apoplexy brought on by the great success of his rival Canaletto.

As the French scholar Charles de Brosses was to complain in the late 1730's, the English on the Grand Tour were especially fond of Canaletto, and in the late 1720's the painter began catering to this audience by painting festivals and ceremonies. In such pictures, he drew on his experiences in the theater to convey a sense of drama and action, and he demonstrated great skill with both figures and architectural detail. This ability is evident in six large paintings of the Piazza San Marco, the first of many commissions Canaletto received from Smith. In these pictures one also finds another of Canaletto's traits: a willingness to sacrifice topographical accuracy for artistic needs.

The Stonemason's Yard (c. 1728) is the masterpiece and culmination of Canaletto's early phase, with its realistic portrait of Venetian squalor, its dramatic depiction of people working, and its mixture of sunlight and shade (chiaroscuro). Heightening the sense of everyday life are elements such as a half-naked baby squalling on the ground in front of its mother on the far left and a woman getting water from a well on the right.

By 1729, Canaletto was turning away from chiaroscuro in favor of luminosity, even in shadows. His painting of the reception of Count Bolagno is bathed in light. The background is white rather than reddish-brown; the colors are clear and bright, especially the gold and silver of the barges. The contrast of light and dark derives from the costumes of the figures, and the threatening clouds of the earlier works have vanished from a blue sky.

Between approximately 1727 and 1732, Canaletto prepared a series of fourteen paintings for Smith; these appeared in a book of engravings that includes twelve views of the Grand Canal with *A Regatta on the Grand Canal* (c. 1732) and *The Bucentoro at the Molo on Ascension Day* (c. 1732). Smaller than most of his earlier works, the twelve views of the Grand Canal seem wooden, lacking the sweep and drama of the other two paintings in the volume, which are painted on a larger scale and were probably added as an afterthought. The frontispiece to this volume contains the only definite portrait of Canaletto. His keen eyes (at the age of sixty-six he boasted of painting without glasses) gaze from an oval frame. Beneath long wavy hair, a high forehead, and a full nose, a faint smile suggests his contentment with being the city's most popular painter.

Smith apparently had the Venetian tourists in mind when he issued the volume, intending to suggest the type of work they could secure from Canaletto. In this regard, the pictures succeeded. Indicative of the artist's popularity are purchases by the fourth earl of Carlisle and the duke of Bedford. When the Swedish count Carl Gustaf Tessin wrote on July 16, 1736, about the leading Venetian painters, he placed Canaletto first and commented on the high prices he commanded. Demand for Canaletto's work increased to such an extent that he began to portray character types rather than individuals, to rely on assistants such as his nephew, Bernardo Bellotto, for much of the painting, and to use dots and dashes to suggest light.

The War of the Austrian Succession, which erupted in 1740 and reached Italy the next year, sharply reduced the number of visitors from northern Europe to Venice; even an expanded second edition of engravings failed to re-

A painting of Venice, Italy, by Canaletto. (The Granger Collection, New York)

vive business for Canaletto. He now turned to other forms and subjects, devoting himself to drawings and engravings. He may have paid a second visit to Rome about 1740, for shortly afterward he executed a number of pictures on Roman themes. These may, however, have been based on illustrations rather than observation. He definitely toured the Brenta Canal as far as Padua, an excursion that led to many of his best drawings, with fine lines that resemble engraving. The careful attention to detail and drama that recalls his paintings of the 1720's characterizes these efforts, many of which he later translated into oils.

Never reluctant to alter a view for aesthetic ends, Canaletto began to execute *capriccios*; among these is *The Ponti della Pescaria and Buildings on the Quay* (1742-1744), one of thirteen "overdoors" Smith commissioned, in which the artist moved statues from the library to the bridge. Even more fanciful is a view of the Rialto with the bridge Andrea Palladio had designed for the site; that structure had never been built. Canaletto did not altogether abandon topographical scenes, though. *Entrance to the Grand Canal: Looking East* (1744) is in many ways the finest of his renditions of this view, bathed in the Venetian sunlight as only Canaletto could render it and rich in painstaking detail, showing none of the haste that mars some of the other works of this phase in his career.

Perhaps Canaletto lavished time on this piece because orders from patrons other than Smith were limited. When he was told about the possibility of commemorating the nearly completed Westminster Bridge in London, Canaletto resolved to visit England to secure the commission. Two of his most important customers, the dukes of Richmond and Bedford, were involved in the construction, and if the English could not come to Venice, Canaletto would go to the English.

In addition to painting Westminster Bridge, Canaletto secured a number of commissions from the British aristocracy. For his patron, the duke of Richmond, he executed two of his most famous views in 1747, *Whitehall and the Privy Gardens* and *The Thames and the City of London from Richmond House*. New admirers also appeared, among whom where Sir Hugh Smithson, first duke of Northumberland, Lord Brooke, and the earl of Warwick, for whom Canaletto painted five views of Warwick Castle. From the dean of Westminster came a request to commemorate the procession of the Knights of the Bath from Westminster Abbey to the House of Lords.

Still, Canaletto's popularity had declined from its zenith. Antiquarian George Vertue even reported the rumor

that the painter claiming to be Canaletto was an impostor. Actually, the English were witnessing the change in Canaletto's style, particularly in his treatment of figures, which had begun a decade earlier.

Later commentators have also criticized Canaletto's English works, but the best, such as his *Old Walton Bridge* (1754), rival his greatest paintings. They also provide a record of a mid-Georgian London that has largely vanished and create a panoramic cityscape freed from smoke and suffused with Italian sunlight. Even if more than half of *The Thames and the City of London from Richmond House* consists of sky, the figures are wooden and small, and the vessels on the river are Italian barges rather than English craft, the picture still ably re-creates the sense of eighteenth century England, the crowded spires of Sir Christopher Wren's churches punctuating the horizon, with the great dome of St. Paul's serving as the focal center. With his views of Whitehall and Charing Cross, Canaletto captured what Samuel Johnson called in another context "the full tide of human existence" that London exhibited, conveying the city's mood as well as its topography.

In 1755, Canaletto returned to Italy, where his last years were difficult. Occasionally he received commissions, but at his death on April 20, 1768, he had twenty-eight unsold paintings. In 1760, John Crewe came upon the painter sketching in St. Mark's Place, probably hoping to attract passersby. If that was his motive, he apparently succeeded in this instance, for in 1836 Lord Crewe sold a Canaletto painting of the piazza; most likely it was the one acquired in 1760.

The Venetian Academy, founded in 1750, finally admitted Canaletto in 1763. For his reception piece he presented the academy with *Portico of a Palace* (1765), a complex study in perspective, rather than a more typical cityscape, because such work still lacked prestige. Had Canaletto painted historical scenes or portraits, he would probably have gained admission to the academy much sooner. The last recorded work by Canaletto, executed in 1766, shows that he could still draw firmly and well. The scene is full of life, and architectural features and human figures receive equally detailed attention. Although he depicts an interior, a rare setting for him, he fills the church with the light that is his trademark.

SIGNIFICANCE
French novelist Théophile Gautier called Venice the city of Canaletto, not because Canaletto was born, lived, worked, and died there but because he, more than any other artist, commemorated and celebrated it in his art.

An excellent technician—even in his oils he developed the ability to record his impressions without revision—he lovingly rendered every brick and ornament. Although he frequently repeated scenes in his eight hundred paintings and four hundred drawings, each version exhibits subtle differences because he shifted a building's proportions, added or removed figures, or changed the lighting. Always present is a sense of drama, for he saw Venice—and London—as the backdrop for human action.

Despite the decline in his popularity after 1740, Canaletto influenced a number of artists. Among the Italians are his nephew, Bellotto, Migliara Borasto, and Giambattista Cimaroli of Brescia. In England, where his impact was greater, Thomas Girtin, John Constable, and J. M. W. Turner learned from his work. In *Ducal Palace and Bridge of Sighs, Canaletto Painting* (1833), Turner pays tribute to the master in his first oil of Venice.

Although English art critic John Ruskin expressed the dominant Romantic dissatisfaction with Canaletto's neoclassicism, Édouard Manet admired his drawings, and James McNeill Whistler liked his paintings. The late twentieth century shared this enthusiasm, recognizing that Canaletto did not only paint "things which fall immediately under his eye," as Owen McSwiney claimed. Instead, he mixed sun and shade, palaces and laundry hanging out to dry, columns, bridges, and canals, and beggars and patricians, to create a personal view of his world. If the result is rarely profound, it is almost always pleasing in its ability to convey a mood as well as a sense of place.

—Joseph Rosenblum

FURTHER READING

Bomford, David, and Gabriele Finaldi. *Venice Through Canaletto's Eyes*. New Haven, Conn.: Yale University Press, 1998. This book was produced to accompany an exhibition of Canaletto's paintings of Venice that were displayed at London's National Gallery. The catalog contains reproductions of the paintings and essays describing Canelleto's painting techniques.

Constable, W. G. *Canaletto: Giovanni Antonio Canal, 1697-1768*. Rev. ed. Oxford, England: Clarendon Press, 1976. The definitive study of Canaletto's life and work, it provides a catalogue raisonné of Canaletto's output and reproduces the majority of his paintings, drawings, and engravings. Includes Owen McSwiney's letters to Lord March about the artist, a detailed account of Canaletto's estate at his death, and a selective bibliography.

Levey, Michael. *Canaletto Paintings in the Royal Collection*. London: Phaidon Press, 1964. The British Royal Family owns the most extensive collection of Canaletto's works. This catalog reproduces the holdings in black-and-white full-page illustrations and offers a short biography of the artist.

_____. *Painting in Eighteenth-Century Venice*. London: Phaidon Press, 1959. Rev. ed. Ithaca, N.Y.: Cornell University Press, 1980. Provides a well-illustrated overview of eighteenth century Venetian art. Arrangement is by type of work: historical painting, landscapes, views, genre, and portraits. Good section on Canaletto.

Links, J. G. *Canaletto*. 2d ed. London: Phaidon Press, 1999. A comprehensive study of the artist with illustrations conveniently located in the text. Drawing on recent research, Links clarifies some puzzles about Canaletto, such as his relationship with Joseph Smith and his activities in England.

Moschini, Vittorio. *Canaletto*. Milan, Italy: Aldo Martello, 1954. A lavishly illustrated text that reproduces many important paintings in full color. The detailed chronology is especially useful. Contains a bibliography of works dealing with the artist from 1733 to 1753.

Pedrocco, Filippo. *Canaletto and the Venetian Vedutisti*. New York: Riverside, 1995. Describes Canaletto's paintings of Venice.

See also: Hester Bateman; Johann Bernhard Fischer von Erlach; Jean-Honoré Fragonard; Thomas Gainsborough; Francisco de Goya; William Hogarth; Angelica Kauffmann; Sir Joshua Reynolds; George Romney; Giovanni Battista Tiepolo; Élisabeth Vigée-Lebrun; Antoine Watteau.

Related article in *Great Events from History: The Eighteenth Century, 1701-1800*: December 16, 1740-November 7, 1748: War of the Austrian Succession.

CAO XUEQIN
Chinese novelist

Cao Xueqin, China's greatest novelist, wrote the popular and illustrious novel, Dream of the Red Chamber, *a massive, encyclopedic work exploring a wide range of experiences from everyday life. It is a vast compendium of late imperial Chinese culture as well, and it introduces autobiographical elements and a unique psychological realism that were uncommon in Chinese literature.*

Born: 1715?; Nanjing, China
Died: February 12, 1763; Beijing, China
Also known as: Cao Zhan (birth name); Ts'ao Chan (Wade-Giles); Ts'ao Hsüeh-ch'in (Wade-Giles)
Area of achievement: Literature

EARLY LIFE

Cao Xueqin (chow sway-chin) was born in southern China. His exact date of birth, like much of his life, remains unclear, but it is thought to have been sometime in the spring of 1715. He was born into a rich and distinguished Han banner family, which had served under the control of the imperial household and had an unusual history. Banners (brigades) were companies of military units, including members' families, which were garrisoned around the country.

Cao's ancestors were from Liaoyang city, in northeastern China, in the area later known as Manchuria. In the early seventeenth century, family members became bond servants, or slaves, of the Manchu aristocracy and members of the Plain White Banner, which was directly under the command of the Manchu ruler. When the Manchu conquered China in 1644, members of this group rose in social status and became important officials and agents of the emperor.

For three generations, a total of forty-eight years, members of the Cao family were employed as textile commissioners in Nanjing. This post involved overseeing the huge imperial silk factories and managing the transportation of goods to the Imperial City in Beijing. The position was one of the most lucrative in the country and also required acting as a confidential informer to the emperor, reporting on the activities of other high-ranking officials in the region and keeping him abreast of local matters and rumors. The most renowned of these commissioners was Cao Xueqin's grandfather, Cao Yin (1658-1712), who was textile commissioner from 1690 to 1712, as well as a poet, dedicated bibliophile, dramatist, and accomplished calligrapher. A favorite of Emperor Kangxi (1662-1722), Cao Yin hosted Kangxi on an impressive four occasions during the emperor's celebrated tours of the south.

Because of the affluence of his family, Cao Xueqin grew up in very luxurious circumstances. The Cao family compound in Nanjing consisted of large gardens, thirteen separate houses, with 483 rooms, and 114 servants. The family even had its own theatrical group, which on occasion performed several plays written by Cao Yin. Cao Xueqin's father is now generally believed to have been Cao Fu, Cao Yin's nephew and adopted son.

In spite of the great wealth and power of the Cao family, its status was in the end dependent upon the caprice of the emperor. In 1728, Emperor Yongzheng (1723-1735) suddenly ordered that all Cao property be confiscated. Yongzheng disapproved of bond servants, thinking them corrupt and inefficient, but the exact reason for his action is still unclear. Some historians believe that the Cao family owed money and others believe that Yongzheng had concerns over its loyalty. Cao Fu was textile commissioner at this time, having inherited the position from Cao Yin's son Cao Young. Cao Fu was removed from office and charged with financial mismanagement. After this incident, the Cao family moved to Beijing, where it had several houses and some distant relatives. Cao Xueqin was thirteen years old during this dramatic reversal of his family's fortunes, and he never recovered economically or psychologically from its effects. Though well educated and extremely artistic, he had a great deal of difficulty finding steady employment and worked sporadically as a secretary in the imperial household bureau and as a teacher in the imperial clan's school for the children of the nobility and banner men. Little else is known of his life during the next few years, but it is believed that he began writing his famous novel *Hongloumeng* (1792; *Dream of the Red Chamber*, 1958; also known as *The Story of the Stone*, 1973-1982) in 1744.

LIFE'S WORK

Details regarding the composition and content of Cao Xueqin's great work *Dream of the Red Chamber* are fraught with controversy and unanswered questions. The novel's original title, *Honglou-meng*, means "dream of the red chamber," where "chamber" (*lou*) refers to a traditional two-storied building in which young women, usually unmarried, stayed or lived. The color "red" (*hong*) is significant because in China it symbolizes beauty, happiness, fortune, and youth. The word "dream" (*meng*) relates to one of the main themes of the novel—the illusionary and dreamlike nature of life and of everyday notions of truth and falsity.

Containing 120 chapters and more than 700,000 words covering 1,500 pages, the *Dream of the Red Chamber* also features more than thirty main characters and at least four hundred minor characters (more than in all of William Shakespeare's work). There has been a long-standing and intense debate among scholars over how much of the novel Cao Xueqin actually wrote. There are eleven manuscript versions of the first eighty chapters (frequently with revealing commentary by two unknown individuals), which were circulated among Cao's friends and relatives starting in 1754. When the novel was finally published in 1792, an additional forty chapters had been added by the publisher Cheng Weyiuan. Cheng claimed he had acquired the chapters from booksellers, and that he had his friend edit what he found. It is generally believed that his claim is true and that his friend heavily edited these chapters and altered parts of the novel's ending, probably for political reasons.

The plot of *Dream of the Red Chamber* concerns the rise and fall of the wealthy, aristocratic Jia family in Beijing. The main character is the indulgent aesthete and scion of the family, Jia Bao-yu (precious jade). The heart of the story concerns his love affair with his cousin Daiyu (black jade) and his prolonged but successful quest for identity and philosophical understanding.

However, the story is much more than a simple tale of love and redemption, for the narrative operates on many levels. It is also a tragedy, a metaphysical allegory with much foreshadowing, and an extremely realistic novel surprisingly modern in tone and much concerned with describing the minutiae of everyday life. In addition, the novel is a brilliant, dense, and vast compendium of late imperial Chinese culture, encompassing topics from clothing, food, sexual habits, religious practices, marriage and funeral rites, medicine, customs, festivals, and law to the educational and banking systems, all the traditional Chinese literary forms, music, and painting, as well as garden and architectural design. The work is also populated with precisely described individuals from all classes of society. Its linguistic and visual richness clearly demonstrates Cao Xueqin's deep interest in painting and drama. The distinguished *Dream of the Red Chamber* scholar Zhou Ruchang has compared the novel to a long, elaborate scroll, woven from the silken threads of the lives of the novel's many characters and their individual stories.

What makes the book even more remarkable for its time are the autobiographical elements in the story, which were rare in traditional Chinese literature, and the unique and sophisticated psychological realism of the characters, where the inner feelings and motivations of each person are deftly shown. (It is worth noting that while Cao Xueqin was working on *Dream of the Red Chamber*, the rise of the novel was beginning in England.)

Cao Xueqin never knew of the popularity of his work. He spent the last eight years of his life living in poverty in a small village in the western hills of Beijing while he struggled to support himself as a painter (of rocks) and finish his novel. He died on February 12, 1763, perhaps of grief caused by the death of his son the year before. He was described as rather stout, short, and mustached. He was fond of drink and was known as an entertaining and witty conversationalist.

SIGNIFICANCE

Cao Xueqin's *Dream of the Red Chamber* represents the highest achievement of Qing Dynasty literature, forming an essential part of Chinese culture. The novel is still very much a part of China's national culture. Plays, operas, ballets, and a widely watched television drama in 1987 have retold the story. It is the most studied work of Chinese literature, even claiming a special field of Chinese literary studies called Hongxue (redology). The entire novel has been translated into English and more than a dozen other languages.

The publication of *Dream of the Red Chamber* in 1792 created a sensation, but it was not until the advent of China's New Culture Movement (1916-1925), with its appreciation of the vernacular style in literature, that the work began to receive critical acclaim and analysis. The encyclopedic nature of the novel, as the scholar Zhou Ruchang has observed, makes it the best general and most enjoyable introduction to traditional Chinese culture and life available. Because of its psychological and philosophical sophistication and its sheer realism, the novel is comparable in scope and detail to such classics of world literature as Dante's *La divina commedia* (c. 1320; *The Divine Comedy*, 1802), James Joyce's *Ulysses* (1922), Miguel de Cervantes' *El ingenioso hidalgo don Quixote de la Mancha* (1605, 1615; *The History of the Valorous and Wittie Knight-Errant, Don Quixote of the Mancha*, 1612-1620), and Murasaki Shikibu's *Genji monogatari* (c. 1004; *The Tale of Genji*, 1925-1933).

—Ronald Gray

FURTHER READING

Cao Xueqin. *The Story of the Stone*. 5 vols. Translated by David Hawkes and John Minford. London: Penguin Books, 1973-1986. Generally considered the best English translation of the novel, with its alternate title in translation.

Ho, An. *Dream of the Red Chamber: An Experience in Traditional Chinese Aesthetics*. Atlanta: Oglethorpe University Museum of Art, 2000. An exhibition catalog that features the work of artist An Ho, who brings to life the twelve central female characters of Cao Xueqin's novel, including commentary on each of the characters and their roles in the book. Also includes an introductory essay.

Levy, Dore. *Ideal and Actual in the Story of the Stone*. New York: Columbia University Press, 1999. A good introduction to Cao Xueqin's novel.

Spence, Jonathan. *Ts'ao Yin and the Kang-hsi Emperor*. New Haven, Conn.: Yale University Press, 1966. A famous biography of Cao Xueqin's grandfather and the Cao family.

Yu, Anthony. *Rereading the Stone*. Princeton, N.J.: Princeton University Press, 1997. A well-written literary analysis of the novel, with many intriguing insights.

See also: Dai Zhen; Qianlong; Wang Zhenyi; Yongzheng.

Related articles in *Great Events from History: The Eighteenth Century, 1701-1800:* June 20, 1703: Chikamatsu Produces *The Love Suicides at Sonezaki*; April 25, 1719: Defoe Publishes the First Novel; 1740-1741: Richardson's *Pamela* Establishes the Modern Novel.

SIR GUY CARLETON
British military leader and administrator

Carleton's competent military leadership and adroit political sensitivity helped ease the transition of Canada from its position as conquered French province to prosperous English colony.

Born: September 3, 1724; Strabane, County Tyrone, Ireland

Died: November 10, 1808; Stubbings, Berkshire, England

Also known as: Lord Dorchester; First Baron Dorchester

Areas of achievement: Military, warfare and conquest, government and politics

EARLY LIFE

Guy Carleton was the son of Christopher Carleton, a member of the Irish landowning class, and Katherine Ball, from County Donegal. The first years of Guy's life were spent securely in the prosperity of the Irish country gentry. When he was fourteen, however, his father died. His mother then married the Reverend Mr. Thomas Skelton. Although his stepfather's biographer later would claim that Guy owed his education to Skelton's interest, the interval between his father's death and Carleton's commission as an ensign in the British army suggests otherwise. Since most young men of the eighteenth century had completed their education by the age of fourteen (unless they were bound for the university), it

seems unlikely that an unhappy adolescent could have been educated in four years.

Carleton began his long career in the British army on May 21, 1742, at age seventeen, when he became an ensign in the Twenty-fifth Regiment of Foot. The time at which Carleton entered the king's service would have been an exciting one for a young officer. England was engaged in a war that had begun in the Caribbean in 1739 and broadened into the War of the Austrian Succession by 1742. Against this background of crisis he was promoted to lieutenant within three years.

He did not experience his first foreign campaign until the French and Indian War. Promoted in 1757 to captain lieutenant in the First Regiment of Foot Guards, he would serve with that unit at the first Siege of Louisbourg in 1758. So impressive was his service there that he was promoted to lieutenant colonel in America.

LIFE'S WORK

Guy Carleton's career as officer and administrator in the British colonial service had begun. His outstanding service and bravery under fire earned for him a promotion to colonel in 1762 and the appointment to the post of lieutenant governor of Quebec in 1766.

With his succession to the governorship of Quebec after James Murray's resignation in 1767, Carleton inherited all the problems peculiar to governing a colony of foreign nationals. On the one hand, he had to administer the laws to the inhabitants who had populated Canada at the time of its transfer—French-speaking Roman Catholics accustomed to a rather tightly controlled government. On the other hand, there were his recently arrived countrymen, each seeking fortune in Great Britain's new acquisition. These newcomers would request special treatment. Further compounding Carleton's difficulties was factionalism within the English community.

In Governor Carleton's observation, the absence of a constitutional basis for government in Quebec demanded that action be taken by Parliament. The citizens of Canada could not be treated forever as conquered subjects. Some legislative foundation had to be laid, therefore, for building a peace-time government satisfactory to all—the king, Parliament, Governor Carleton, the French inhabitants, and the English settlers.

In August of 1770, however, Carleton returned to England on leave. He hoped that while in London he might consult the imperial authorities for assistance not only in settling disputes between the vying factions but also in persuading royal officials that constitutional legislation for Quebec was imperative. Not all of his time was spent consulting with members of officialdom, however, for during his sojourn, the handsome and aristocratic Carleton married Lady Maria Howard and fathered two children.

During his relatively brief experience as governor, he had drawn two conclusions that fundamentally shaped his perceptions about the nature of Canadian society. First, and most fundamentally erroneous, he concluded that the French Canadian landowners, known as seigneurs, were politically adroit and powerful as well as possessed of the military skill and the knowledge and influence of an English country squire. Second, he believed that in the light of increasing unrest in the colonies to the south, the best choice for the British Empire would be to keep Canada as French as possible and thus out of the arms of the American "troublemakers."

Accordingly, Carleton was instrumental in shaping the Quebec Act, which Parliament passed in 1774. Over time, the act has been called many things. American revolutionary leaders denounced it as a Jesuitical decree, English legislators regarded it as a necessary expedient, and some historians have judged it a piece of enlightened

Sir Guy Carleton. (Library of Congress)

statesmanship. One scholar describes the act as "drafted in close consultation with Guy Carleton, in accordance with the plans formulated by him during his administration of Quebec—plans formulated quite frankly with a view to military action on the continent as well as to defence against a French invasion."

Essentially, Quebec needed constitutional legislation, in part because earlier attempts by governors had failed to solve existing problems, but more significantly because permanent foundation for government was long overdue. Three basic matters needed to be addressed: laws and government, religion, and revenue. The last could be treated separately, and was, in the Quebec Revenue Act, which taxed imported rum and molasses.

The other two issues, however, would be addressed within the Quebec Act, which provided for law and government within a newly enlarged geographic region. By the stipulations of this legislation, the boundaries of Quebec included land already claimed by the Thirteen Colonies. Yet from the administrative viewpoint this extension was necessary in order to extend government to the former French settlements in the Illinois country. Throughout Quebec the populations would be subject to

English criminal law, but for purposes of civil suits, they would be regulated by the laws and customs of French Canada. The Roman Catholic Church was recognized, the clergy was allowed to administer the Sacraments, and communicants were extended civil equality. No representative legislature was provided, but a council was established, composed of twenty-three members who could pass ordinance with the consent of the governor.

Thus armed with a foundation for civil government, not to mention a French-educated wife and two infant children, Carleton returned to Quebec in 1774. Almost immediately he was confronted with resistance to the Quebec Act. The English merchant faction complained and petitioned for its repeal. They opposed the unfamiliar French civil law, which they could not manipulate. Protest was also voiced by newly arrived English settlers from the Thirteen Colonies, who saw the act as a check on traditional English liberties.

Such political considerations quickly were eclipsed by new military demands. To the south, the protests against England prompted General Thomas Gage, the British commander in chief in North America, to request regulars from Canada as reinforcements. In effect, Carleton stripped his colony of forces that he later would need.

At the time Carleton dispatched these units to Gage, he had no reason to hesitate. By the spring of 1775, however, Canada was being threatened. Reports reached Carleton that an American expedition was headed northward. Without his regulars, Carleton faced the necessity of ordering the Canadian militia into service. His earlier misperception of the influence of the seigneurs rose to haunt him. Because these landowners had no real power, the habitants simply refused to muster into the militia. In effect, Carleton was powerless, dependent on the whim of a fickle populace. The failure of the American invaders to capture all of Canada had as much to do with inadequate supplies, troop shortages, and difficult weather as with General Carleton's genius. Carleton and his spirited forces, however, did hold on until a rescue fleet arrived in the spring of 1776. Although Carleton was hailed as a hero and awarded the Order of the Knight of Bath, his detractors would note his failure to follow and crush the retreating invaders.

After the withdrawal of the Americans, Carleton still faced the difficulties of governing a divided colony. The French habitants were no more supportive than ever; indeed, the governor had to send investigators to seek out those who had aided the enemy during the invasion. In dealing with the habitants on this matter, as in other matters, the governor depended on the assistance of the Roman Catholic clergy, which was, by and large, supportive of the government that supported them.

One of Carleton's most acute problems resulted from his clash with Lord George Germain, the secretary of state for the colonies. From the time Germain took office in 1775, friction between the two arose as both issued commissions for government appointments in Canada, each assuming such to be his right. This difficulty reached a crisis point in 1778 when the chief justice of Canada, a Germain appointee named Peter Livius, challenged Carleton's authority. Already bitterly disappointed because he had been passed over for the command of an expedition from Canada into the Thirteen Colonies in 1777, the sensitive officer took this incident with Livius as the last straw; he dismissed the chief justice and returned to England in 1778.

Carleton's North American service was by no means over, for he would be asked to serve there in two more important assignments. First, in 1782, he was requested to return to North America as commander in chief, charged with the oversight of withdrawing British troops and emigrating Loyalists. His firm but humane handling of that crucial phase of the American war brought him the thanks of Parliament in the form of a pension of £1,000 a year for life. Earlier he had been promoted to lieutenant general and made governor of Charlemont in Ireland.

SIGNIFICANCE

Despite more than forty years of service, the still energetic Sir Guy Carleton was not ready to enter retirement at age sixty-two. Again he sailed for America in 1786, answering the king's call to govern Canada. So grateful was the king that he gave Carleton a title of nobility in 1786, naming him First Baron (Lord) Dorchester.

Lord Dorchester's term as governor of Canada would last for ten years, from 1786 to 1796. Still convinced that his assessment of Canadian society was accurate, he governed largely as he had before, depending on his highly popular pro-French wife to win the hearts of the Canadians. Even so, the old tensions were still there, with his staunch allies, the seigneurs, whom he called the "Canadian gentlemen," continuing to oppose an elected assembly, fearing representative government would deprive them of their vested status. The English merchants and their allies still clamored for an assembly and English commercial law.

The governor and his supporters, however, were opposing the inevitable, for England did not wish to lose its second empire as it had a large part of its first. Before the end of Carleton's second term, changes were in the making. Canada was to be divided into Upper Canada (now Ontario) and Lower Canada (now Quebec). In Parliament, moreover, legislation had been introduced that would establish an elected assembly, an appointed upper house, and a governor's executive council.

Whatever changes were to occur in Canada's future governmental development, Carleton could retire to England, confident that he had served both Quebec and England long and well. Indeed, while in Canada he had been promoted to the highest rank in the service, general in the army. He had presided effectively, even if in an authoritarian manner, over one of England's most important parts of empire during two extremely critical periods. The stability the soldier-statesman provided had assisted Quebec in a peaceful transition from defeat to prosperity within the growing British Empire.

A final note of irony may be found in his last journey back to England: Carleton's ship was wrecked while it was still in North American waters. Fortunately, no one was hurt, all on board were rescued, and Carleton and his party soon found passage on another vessel bound for home. Thus he had survived the military battlefield, the minefields of political dispute, and a shipwreck, in a lifetime of service to his king. Ever the heroic figure of military bearing, he could spend the last dozen years of his life in retirement content in the company of his wife and their nine sons and daughters.

—James H. O'Donnell III

FURTHER READING

Burt, Alfred L. *The Old Province of Quebec*. Minneapolis: University of Minnesota Press, 1933. This is the standard of scholarship on Quebec against which all other works are measured.

Coupland, Reginald. *The Quebec Act: A Study in Statesmanship*. New York: Oxford University Press, 1968. Originally published in 1925, this proimperial study is highly laudatory toward Carleton, whose "influence on the shaping of the future destinies of Canada was stronger than that of any man of his time." Coupland describes Governor Carleton as the "chief and the most closely questioned witness before the House of Commons" on the Quebec Act.

Lawson, Philip. *The Imperial Challenge: Quebec and Britain in the Age of the American Revolution*. Montreal: McGill-Queen's University Press, 1989. Examines how the conquest of Quebec affected British policies and imperial beliefs, eventually leading to the passage of the Quebec Act.

Mackesy, Piers. *The War for America, 1775-1783*. Cambridge, Mass.: Harvard University Press, 1964. In this study of the struggle for independence by the Thirteen Colonies, the author presents a balanced view of the contribution of Carleton and his role as governor, officer, and, ultimately, commander in chief.

Neatby, Hilda. *The Quebec Act: Protest and Policy*. Englewood Cliffs, N.J.: Prentice-Hall, 1972. Although basically a book of documents in a series on Canadian historical controversies, there is a useful assessment both of the Quebec Act and historians' attitudes toward it. Neatby's book is helpful to anyone who wishes to understand the act and Carleton's role in its adoption.

_____. *Quebec: The Revolutionary Age, 1760-1790*. Toronto, Ont.: McClelland and Stewart, 1966. A volume in the Canadian Centenary series, this study incorporates Carleton into the larger scope of Canada's history during the first three decades of its English history. Overall, it presents a balanced view of the general and governor.

Nelson, Paul David. *General Sir Guy Carleton, Lord Dorchester: Solider-Statesman of Early British Canada*. Madison, N.J.: Fairleigh Dickinson University Press, 2000. A thorough and scholarly biography of Carleton.

Smith, Paul H. "Sir Guy Carleton: Soldier-Statesman." In *George Washington's Opponents: British Generals and Admirals in the American Revolution*, edited by George A. Billias. New York: William Morrow, 1969. Although Smith is interested primarily in Carleton as a military commander, he cannot ignore his dual role as commander and governor.

See also: Lord Amherst; John André; Benedict Arnold; Sir Henry Clinton; Thomas Gage; William Howe; Louis-Joseph de Montcalm; William Pitt the Elder; John Graves Simcoe; George Washington; James Wolfe.

Related articles in *Great Events from History: The Eighteenth Century, 1701-1800:* 1713: Founding of Louisbourg; December 16, 1740-November 7, 1748: War of the Austrian Succession; May 28, 1754-February 10, 1763: French and Indian War; January, 1756-February 15, 1763: Seven Years' War; June 8-July 27, 1758: Siege of Louisbourg; May 20, 1774: Quebec Act; April 19, 1775: Battle of Lexington and Concord; 1783: Loyalists Migrate to Nova Scotia; 1791: Canada's Constitutional Act.

LAZARE CARNOT
French revolutionary politician, military leader, and mathematician

Carnot is credited with reorganizing the French Republican army so that it could successfully fight the Austrian army. He acted as minister of war during the Napoleonic era and minister of the interior during the Hundred Days. Cofounder of the École Polytechnique, Carnot popularized mathematics education and extended the synthetic geometry developed by Blaise Pascal.

Born: May 13, 1753; Nolay, Burgundy, France
Died: August 2, 1823; Magdeburg, Prussian Saxony (now in Germany)
Also known as: Lazare-Nicolas-Marguerite Carnot (full name)
Areas of achievement: Government and politics, warfare and conquest, mathematics, education

EARLY LIFE

Lazare Carnot (lah-zahr kahr-noh), the son of a lawyer, graduated in 1773 from the school of engineering in Mézières, where Gaspard Monge had been one of his instructors. In 1783, Carnot became a captain in the French army corps of engineers. He also published an engineering work, *Essai sur les machines en général* (1783; essay on machines in general), followed closely by *Dissertation sur la théorie de l'infini mathématique* (1785; dissertation on the theory of mathematical infinity). Carnot advocated a new geometry, involved with applying the general principles of transformation within geometrical systems to facilitate the design and construction of machines.

LIFE'S WORK

Lazare Carnot's career may be roughly divided into five parts: his early contributions in the field of mathematics, his political and military career during the French Revolution, his service under Napoleon I, his "retirement"—tutoring his sons and working in the field of mathematics—and his exile in Magdeburg, Germany. After being elected to the national assembly in 1791, Carnot was involved in several military and diplomatic missions. He then became a member of the Committee of General Defense, was placed in charge of armies, and worked at improving their organization and strategies, including the food supply and the armaments of the troops.

Prior to 1793, the French revolutionary armies had been unable to fight effectively against the Austrians. In April, 1793, Carnot took command of the Army of the North and was able to occupy Belgium. He publicly declared that it be "stripped" and exploited on behalf of the French Republic.

Carnot's efforts in defending the frontiers resulted in the accolade "Organizer of Victory," as he rejected the "Prussian Military School" traditions, streamlined the delivery of supplies to the armies, and instituted new strategy and tactics. During the winter of 1793-1794, he concentrated on improving discipline among new recruits.

Carnot's military focus was on recruitment, weaponry, discipline, and tactics. He appointed young generals and advocated taking advantage of numerical superiority, revolutionary ardor, and superior-quality weapons. He also advocated abandoning the system of deployment in line, instead favoring attacks from column formations. He rejected subtlety and long sieges, favoring massive attacks at a single point. Carnot's approach was employed effectively in the Austrian campaign when the French attacked Vienna at the Main and Danube Rivers.

Carnot became a member of the Committee of Public Safety (1793-1794). He did not take part in the debates concerning King Louis XVI's execution, but once the debates were over, he voted against an appeal to the people and in favor of executing the king. Carnot bluntly disagreed with Robespierre on several issues, including the concept of the Supreme Being. Robespierre in turn threatened that Carnot would lose his head as soon as he lost his first battle.

Together with Gaspard Monge, Lazare Carnot was cofounder of the École Polytechnique, which was established in 1794 to educate students to serve the republic. The school admitted students via a competitive entrance exam, and it educated many of the political, scientific, and military leaders of France during the next two hundred years. A few of the most famous early graduates of the École Polytechnique include André-Marie Ampère, François Arago, Gustave Gaspard de Coriolis, and Augustin Cauchy.

Continuing to direct the French army, Carnot became one of five members of the Directory (1795-1797). It was Carnot who gave Napoleon I command of the French army at Genoa. In 1796, however, Carnot opposed Napoleon's appointment as first consul for life, stating, "I am an irreconcilable enemy of all kings." Carnot left France prior to the coup d'état of September 4, 1797 (Fructidor

18, 1797, in the revolutionary calendar). After his departure, his colleagues stripped him of his chair in geometry, awarding it to Napoleon instead. While in exile, Carnot wrote *Réflexions sur la métaphysique du calcul infinitesimal* (1797; *Reflexions on the Metaphysical Principles of the Infinitesimal Analysis*, 1801). This work, a blend of mathematics and philosophy, became very popular and was reprinted in French in numerous editions and translated into a number of foreign languages. Carnot returned to France in 1799.

Carnot was appointed minister of war by Napoleon in early 1800 and accompanied Jean Victor Moreau early in the Rhine campaign. As minister of war, Carnot worked to reduce military expenditures, but he soon tired of the position. In 1801, Napoleon accepted his resignation, and Carnot devoted himself to his mathematical studies and tutoring his sons.

Carnot publicly opposed the monarchist sentiments of Napoleon, but when Carnot's colonial investments suffered reversals in 1809, he accepted a commission from Napoleon to write a treatise on fortifications. His famous military book *De la défense des places fortes* (1810; on the defense of strong places) was published the next year. In this book, Carnot suggested a novel defense construct, the "Carnot Wall." Following Waterloo, some forts were built incorporating Carnot Walls, including the Boyen Fortress in eastern Prussia and the Shoreham and Littlehampton Forts in East Sussex, England.

Carnot maintained his dislike for the Napoleonic monarchy. In 1812, he declared he would fight "for France," not for the Napoleonic French Empire. He was appointed minister of the interior during the Hundred Days in 1815 and served as governor of Antwerp. In 1816, under Louis XVIII, Carnot's Republican views forced him into exile at Magdeburg, and he took his young son Lazare Hippolyte Carnot (1801-1888) with him. In 1821, Carnot's older son Sadi Nicholas Léonard Carnot (1792-1832) visited Magdeburg, where he became interested in steam engines. Carnot himself had become interested in steam engines three years previously, when one had been brought to Magdeburg. For this reason, it is widely believed that the elder Carnot influenced Sadi's research into thermodynamics, especially the mechanics and efficiency of steam engines.

SIGNIFICANCE

Although Lazare Carnot's leadership roles in the French Revolution and during the Napoleonic era were historically significant, the paradigm shift he and Monge created within mathematics was historic. This paradigm shift was accomplished largely through the education of students at the École Polytechnique, where research and education were intertwined. The graduates of the École Polytechnique shared the ideology of its founders, as well as a new common approach to attacking problems mathematically. The École Polytechnique led to the acceptance of mathematicians and engineers (*ingénieurs-savants*) as highly respected members of society. This was a radical departure from the classical education of European aristocratic leaders outside France. After more than two hundred years, the École Polytechnique remains among the most internationally esteemed French universities.

Carnot's ultimate goal was to replace the aristocratic gentleman-scholar with the professional citizen-scientist in a meritocratic environment. His mathematical works, *Reflextions on the Metaphysical Principles of the Infinitesimal Analysis*, *De la corrélation des figures de*

Lazare Carnot. (Library of Congress)

géométrie (1801; on the correlation of geometrical figures), and *Géométrie de position* (1803; geometry of position), have been republished periodically during the last two hundred years. *Géométrie de position* evoked substantial interest among mathematicians. In this work, Carnot initiated the search for "intrinsic coordinates" and introduced a quantity now referred to as "aberrancy" or "angle of deviation." This work included Carnot's polygram theorem, which has led to several significant proofs.

Work done by Carnot's progeny is sometimes attributed to him. They achieved their own places in history, however: His elder son Sadi determined the formula for the efficiency of engines. Hippolyte went into exile in Magdeburg with his father, but in 1823 he returned to France, where he worked with his elder brother Sadi on writing about engines. In 1839, Hippolyte was elected deputy for Paris in the Governing Chamber, sitting with the Radical Left. He was named as a national assembly senator for life in 1875. Hippolyte's two sons also made significant contributions: Marie François Sadi Carnot (1837-1894) was president of the Third Republic. Under his grandson's presidency, Hippolyte's remains were entombed in the Panthéon in 1889. Hippolyte's younger son Adolphe Marie Carnot (1839-1920) was a prominent analytical chemist and geologist and dean of the École Nationale des Mines (1901-1907) who discovered an ore of uranium subsequently named "carnotite" in his honor. A. M. Carnot authored *Traité d'analyse des substances minerals* (1898-1904).

—*Anita Baker-Blocker*

FURTHER READING

Boyer, Carl B. *A History of Mathematics.* 2d ed. New York: Wiley, 1991. An excellent reference book on great mathematicians that devotes a chapter to Carnot's contributions to the fields of calculus and geometry.

Carnot, Lazare. *Révolution et mathématique.* Paris: L'Herne, 1984. A twentieth century French-language publication regarding Lazare Carnot's contributions to the field of mathematics.

Dhombres, Jean, and Nicole Dhombres. *Lazare Carnot.* Paris: Fayard, 1997. A 770-page comprehensive work in French, with an excellent portrait of a middle-aged Carnot on the cover.

Glas, Éduard. "Socially Conditioned Mathematical Change: The Case of the French Revolution." *Studies in History and Philosophy of Science, Part A* 33 (December, 2002): 709-728. Examines the mathematical accomplishments of Lazare Carnot and Gaspard Monge before, during, and after the French Revolution. Carnot and Monge, as engineers, realized that industrial technology required interchangeable parts, and needed to move to mathematical formulations, rather than "rules of thumb." Radical changes in political power enabled mathematician-engineer-scientists Carnot and Monge to create a new engineering-oriented mathematics curriculum taught to future French leaders at the École Polytechnique. Carnot's political prominence led to the wide readership of his mathematical works.

Goubert, Pierre. *The Course of French History.* Translated by Maarten Ultee. New York: Routledge, 2003. A review of Lazare Carnot's importance in the French Revolution and his interactions with Napoleon.

McLynn, Frank. *Napoleon: A Biography.* New York: Arcade, 2002. A good introduction to Carnot's role under Napoleon.

See also: Louis XVI; Gaspard Monge; Napoleon I; Robespierre.

CAROLINE
Queen of Great Britain and Ireland (r. 1727-1737)

During her long and colorful life, the intelligent and politically savvy Queen Caroline participated actively in politics and government during the reign of King George II and helped rule Great Britain.

Born: March 1, 1683; Ansbach, Brandenburg-Ansbach (now in Germany)
Died: November 20, 1737; London, England
Also known as: Wilhelmine Charlotte Caroline (birth name); Princess Karoline von Brandenburg-Ansbach; Markgravine of Brandenburg-Ansbach; Caroline of Ansbach; Electress of Hanover
Area of achievement: Government and politics

EARLY LIFE

Caroline was born Wilhelmine Charlotte Caroline to Eleanor Erdmuthe Louise of Saxe-Eisenach (1662-1696) and Johann Friedrich, margrave of Brandenburg-Ansbach (1667-1686). Caroline was orphaned at a young age, and she spent her early years primarily at Dresden and Berlin, where she formed a close attachment to Sophia Charlotte, queen of Prussia (r. 1701-1705).

In 1704, the twenty-one-year-old Caroline met mathematician and philosopher Gottfried Wilhelm Leibniz (1646-1716), Sophia Charlotte's friend who often visited the queen at her home at Lützenburg. Leibniz was to become Caroline's tutor, and the two remained friends until Leibniz's death in 1716.

Like all royal princesses, Caroline understood that her role in life was to make an advantageous marriage. Political and economic connections were of primary concern in royal marriages; love and romance took a distant back seat. Caroline turned down the opportunity to become queen of Spain because to do so would have meant changing her Protestant faith to that of Roman Catholicism. However, George Augustus (1683-1760), the Protestant son of the elector of Hanover and in line to become heir to the throne of Great Britain, seemed a perfect match. In 1705, Caroline married George Augustus in Hanover, Germany, and shortly thereafter, in 1707, she gave birth to their first child, Prince Frederick Louis (1707-1751).

LIFE'S WORK

In 1714, Caroline's father-in-law became the first British king from Hanover, George I, upon the death of the last Stuart monarch, Queen Anne. Caroline's husband became the prince of Wales and she became the princess of Wales. The couple set off for England, leaving behind Frederick Louis, who was just seven years old. Since there was no English queen, Caroline became the first lady of Britain and took on all the responsibilities of a sitting queen. Intelligent, witty, and astute, the young princess immediately became politically entrenched in government and court politics.

As the princess of Wales, but mostly as the first lady, Caroline gained political influence through her developing friendship with British prime minister Robert Walpole (1672-1745), a relationship that was to last the rest of her life. Indeed, it was Caroline who helped Walpole retain power during his turbulent tenure as the first British prime minister (1730-1742). Under Walpole's peaceful and prosperous term, the foundations of the Industrial Revolution were realized. Britain saw increased coal production, an increase in shipbuilding and in agriculture, and a rise in British colonization in the Caribbean and in India. Caroline could see the long-term advantages of political maneuvering, and so she encouraged political and religious appointments based on intelligence and experience rather than on cronyism.

When Caroline's husband became estranged from his father, King George I, Walpole made sure that Caroline nevertheless maintained a prominent political position and enjoyed a luxurious lifestyle at London's Leicester House. During her time at Leicester House, Caroline began a prominent intellectual salon for London's literary lights. At the same venue, a dissident Whig group headed by Walpole sprang up as well, further suggesting Caroline's powerful political influence.

Caroline sided with her husband in his continuing disputes with his father. So severe was the family infighting that Caroline and George were forced to leave court and live in their London residence, Leicester House. They even lost custody of their children. In time, the royal couple reconciled with the king in 1720, and seven years later, George was crowned King George II and Caroline became queen.

As queen, Caroline effectively ruled as regent in the absence of her husband, but she could not contain the family squabbling that characterized the royal Hanoverian family. Although it would seem that the family would have learned from their battle with George I, the hostilities continued into the next generation with Caroline's eldest son, Frederick, prince of Wales.

Caroline. (Library of Congress)

By 1728, when he finally was able to join his parents in England, Frederick was an adult and beyond their political influence. At every turn, he opposed his parents, especially Caroline, and turned instead to Parliament for support. Despite having personally picked her new daughter-in-law, Augusta of Saxe-Gotha (1719-1772), Caroline plotted to undermine the marriage. Of particular note was a strange episode concerning the birth of Caroline's first grandchild. Frederick had to smuggle Augusta—who was in labor—out of Hampton Court Palace to ensure Caroline would not disrupt the birth. Family quarrels continued to escalate, and they caused complete estrangement between Caroline and her son's family.

Scholars maintain that Caroline's marriage to George II was an unusually happy one, although no one doubted her intellectual superiority over her husband. Caroline maintained great patience with the king, putting up with, and even acknowledging, her husband's string of royal mistresses.

Caroline was also highly influential in scholarly matters. Indeed, in 1715, she had recommended a debate, conducted through a series of letters between Leibniz and Samuel Clarke—the English physicist, theologian, and friend of Sir Isaac Newton—in an effort to work out an unresolved dispute between Leibniz and Newton. In the letters, Clarke defended Newton's conceptions of space and time, ideas that Leibniz, Newton, and many others have argued over for centuries. The letters, published soon after the exchange, received a wide readership and are still read today.

On the domestic front, Caroline gave birth to eight children—three sons and five daughters—and died from a ruptured womb on November 20, 1737, in London. George had been so attached to Caroline that he arranged for matching coffins with removable sides to be built so that they could rest together upon his own death, which came twenty-three years later. The two are indeed buried together at Westminster Abbey. Caroline's troublesome son Frederick died in 1751, never having inherited the throne, and it passed in 1760 to Caroline's grandson, George III.

SIGNIFICANCE

Caroline became one of the most popular queens in the history of the English monarchy. She brought to light—and lived—the idea that queen consorts could be far more than bearers and mothers of royal children. Indeed, no one doubted that Caroline was intellectually superior to her husband, King George II, and he often relied upon her wisdom and support. From her childhood as the student of mathematical genius Leibniz, many acknowledged that Caroline was to become the real, behind-the-scenes decision maker in England during George's reign; she greatly influenced Prime Minister Walpole, who acted, it has been said, on her behalf.

In effect, the government was in Walpole's hands, but so great was Caroline's influence on him that upon her death in 1737, his power came to an abrupt halt and the country plunged into years of war, first with Spain and then with both Spain and France during the War of the Austrian Succession (1740-1748).

—*M. Casey Diana*

FURTHER READING

Clarke John, et al. *The Houses of Hanover and Saxe-Coburg-Gotha.* Berkeley: University of California Press, 2000. Volume 1 of this impressive five-volume series covers the reigns of British monarchs George I and George II. Very approachable and also full of illustrations, this work sheds light on the Hanover Dynasty and the long-lasting, deep influence of Queen Caroline of Ansbach.

Sinclair-Stevenson, Christopher. *Blood Royal: The Illustrious House of Hanover*. New York: Doubleday, 1980. A well-written account of the colorful House of Hanover, of which Caroline of Ansbach was a highly influential member as wife, mother, grandmother, and diplomat.

Treasure, Geoffrey. *Who's Who in Early Hanoverian Britain: 1714 to 1789*. London: Treasure Stackpole Books, 2002. An indispensable guide to the royal eighteenth century Hanover Dynasty. Considers all the major members of Caroline's family and also those who made up her political and social milieu.

Van der Kiste, John. *King George II and Queen Caroline*. London: Alan Sutton, 1998. This work recounts the marriage between King George II and Queen Caroline, their political and social milieu, and family fractions.

Wilkins, W. H. *Caroline the Illustrious, Queen-Consort of George II and Sometime Queen-Regent: A Study of Her Life and Time*. New York: Longmans, Green, 1901. A dated but wonderfully succinct account of Caroline, her life at the British court, and her lasting political influence.

See also: Queen Anne; Joseph Butler; Georgiana Cavendish; George I; George II; George III; George Frideric Handel; Robert Walpole.

Related articles in *Great Events from History: The Eighteenth Century, 1701-1800:* September 11, 1709: Battle of Malplaquet; 1721-1742: Development of Great Britain's Office of Prime Minister; 1739-1741: War of Jenkins's Ear; December 16, 1740-November 7, 1748: War of the Austrian Succession.

CHARLES CARROLL
American politician

With a rebellious spirit, a penchant for the law, and an ability to forecast social upheaval, Carroll fought for government reform, helping to bring about independence and religious freedom for an entire nation.

Born: September 19, 1737; Annapolis, Maryland
Died: November 14, 1832; Baltimore, Maryland
Also known as: Charles Carroll of Carrollton
Areas of achievement: Government and politics, law, religion and theology

EARLY LIFE

Charles Carroll was the only child born to Charles Carroll and Elizabeth Brooke. His grandfather had emigrated to the American colonies from Ireland, bringing with him the Roman Catholic faith that became a source of religious discrimination for the Carroll family. The signature term "of Carrollton" was added to Carroll's name in 1765 to distinguish him from his father, grandfather, and several other relatives of the same name. His name was equally important in verifying his paternity, given that his parents were not legally married until he was twenty years old.

Unlike his revolutionary counterparts, Carroll was educated mostly abroad, in part on the insistence of his father, who desired a traditional and proper education for his young son, and because Catholic teachings were prohibited in the colonies. At age eleven, Carroll was sent to France to his father's alma mater, the Jesuit English College of St. Omers, which he attended for six years. He remained in France studying classical literature, philosophy, and French civil law until 1759, when he enrolled at the Middle Temple in London to earn a degree in English law.

Much is known about Carroll's early years, his experiences abroad, and his political viewpoints because of the abundance of letters he exchanged with his parents. Aside from Carroll's Jesuit education, his father was his chief influence. His father, who had amassed a vast fortune, was determined to raise a son morally and intellectually fit to preserve the family estate; young Carroll was considered a life investment. Charles Carroll of Annapolis demanded excellence from his son. He instructed him in study habits, courtship, fashion, popular culture, and even his personal appearance (at one time urging Carroll to maintain his natural hair rather than wear a wig). The small, fine-featured Carroll consulted his father on everything.

In February, 1765, fifteen years after being sent away to school, Carroll returned to Annapolis and plunged into a life of aristocracy. In June, 1768, he married a nineteen-year-old cousin, Mary Darnall. His family's wealth and literary interests led him to memberships in prestigious clubs, where he formed a network of friends interested in American independence from England and civil liberties for Marylanders. Carroll was interested by the growing dissatisfaction with parliamentary government; his knowledge of English law provided him insight into the changing climate.

LIFE'S WORK

In 1773, Maryland governor Robert Eden enacted a high fee scale allowing public officials to impose fees for services. The ruling sparked controversy in light of the ongoing outrage toward Britain's taxation laws. Maryland attorney general and longtime Carroll family rival, Daniel Dulany, published an article in the *Maryland Gazette* defending the governor's actions. In the article, Dulany made reference to the "first citizen," a metaphor for Maryland's people. Inflamed by the legislation and Dulany's support, Charles Carroll countered Dulany in a series of articles entitled "The First Citizen," denouncing arbitrary power and supporting citizens' rights. Instantly, the public rallied around Carroll, thrusting him into extreme popularity and encouraging his continued efforts to represent the citizens' growing upset with tyrannical leadership.

During this period, Carroll developed strong opinions regarding the demise of England's government and was convinced that American independence was the only way of achieving civil and religious liberties for a people he felt were not properly represented. His inherited revolutionary spirit resulting from the religious persecution his family had endured fueled his political interests and involvement in the independence movement.

The recognition Carroll received from the First Citizen debate during the mid-1770's led to a series of public appointments to state committees, including, among others, the Committees of Safety and of Correspondence. His role in these "watchdog" organizations was to defend the rights of Marylanders to ensure they would not be governed in ways beyond their consent. He also felt that by coordinating with other colonies, a strong unity could be formed against British power. Carroll claimed, "[Our Constitution's] true spirit cannot be preserved without the most watchful care and strictest vigilance of the representatives over the conduct of administration." From September to October, 1774, Carroll went to Philadelphia as an honorary delegate to the Continental Congress; he would have been an elected member had it not been for his Catholic faith.

In March, 1776, Carroll was commissioned by the Continental Congress, along with Benjamin Franklin,

Samuel Chase, and his cousin John Carroll, to travel north on a mission to secure French-Canadian support for America's cause against Britain. Canada viewed the colonies as highly anti-Catholic and with American armies present in their homeland, the northern neighbors were reluctant to help. Carroll's religious background and fluency in the French language made him a fitting ally to incite Canadian sympathy for American independence—but to no avail. The mission proved a complete failure.

Carroll returned to Maryland to find that the state convention had voted to oppose national independence and had issued anti-independence instructions to the congressional delegation, which was preparing an official vote of separation from England. Carroll feverishly prepared an argument in favor of colonial sovereignty, citing that "the sole and exclusive right of regulating the internal government and police of [Maryland] be reserved to the people thereof." Carroll also prepared for Maryland a smaller version of the Declaration of Independence, formulating his ideals into an organized structure. By the end of June, 1776, Carroll had persuaded the convention to rescind its decision and amend its instructions in time for the July 4 vote in Philadelphia.

Carroll's longtime predictions were coming true— England had ignored the will of its people, forcing them to form their own representation. Within days, Carroll was awarded an official delegation to Congress and would participate in determining the future of the new United States. On August 2, 1776, Carroll, along with fifty-four other delegates, cast his signature on the Declaration of Independence, forever changing the course of America.

National sovereignty granted new freedoms to Americans, including religious liberties; without legal banishment, Carroll was free to pursue a formal political career. Immediately following the signing, he returned to the Maryland assembly seeking to reform the state's constitution and electoral process. He believed in a central form of authority, but that government should have a system of checks and balances, ensuring that no one entity functioned without representation. Most important, thought Carroll, government should provide everyone with equal protection under the law.

Carroll played an integral role in drafting a new state constitution, which was accepted in November, 1776. One month later, Carroll was elected to the state senate in the very manner that he had helped to establish. As senator, he participated in designing the stringent and highly controversial Legal Tender Act in the hopes of increasing currency worth. Passing in 1777, the law required debtors to pay creditors in paper money, essentially devaluing credit held in land and other personal property, thus creating a major financial loss for wealthy landowners. Carroll argued the law was the price to pay for the liberty and protection the Constitution would bring, although the issue caused a significant strain between him and his father.

In 1787, Carroll was elected a delegate to the federal Constitutional Convention but refused the position. He did, however, accept his election as state representative to the first United States Congress and served from 1789 to 1792. Carroll lost his state senate office in 1800.

With his father no longer alive to encourage his political ambitions, Carroll resigned himself to creating a business empire and preserving the family fortune. In 1800, he founded the First Bank of the United States, followed by the Second Bank in 1816. He further invested in the American infrastructure through organizations such as the Potomac Canal Company, Georgetown Bridge Company, and the extremely successful Baltimore Water Company. In 1828, at age ninety, he served on the board of directors for the Baltimore and Ohio Railroad. He died at age ninety-five in his daughter's house in Baltimore.

SIGNIFICANCE

Charles Carroll was a self-disciplined man determined to uphold the family rebelliousness instilled in him. Carroll persevered despite religious discrimination and served the public through extralegal organizations, coming full circle when his own influence granted him the freedom to hold elected public office.

His commitment to government reform was genuine and his strategy effective, but Carroll's revolutionary motives have often been questioned: His cumulative political record shows him to be a staunch Federalist and conservative, willing to ensure the natural rights of all citizens, while maintaining the power and distinctive class of the elite. His writings at times condemned America's revolution, claiming that anarchy was imminent and the states would be devastated by civil war. He was certain each state would not create proper leadership. By his own admission, he was more comfortable in the private sector, where he felt he could have greater impact. This could explain why his most measurable successes were in his business endeavors, notably establishing himself as the wealthiest citizen in the United States.

Although he did not gain the same level of eminence achieved by some of the other revolutionaries such as

Thomas Jefferson, Samuel Adams, and Benjamin Franklin, Carroll ultimately gained fame as the last surviving signer of the Declaration of Independence. He died in 1832, survived by two of his seven children and twelve grandchildren.

—Caralee Hutchinson

FURTHER READING

Hanley, Thomas O'Brien. *Charles Carroll of Carrollton: The Making of a Revolutionary Gentleman*. Chicago: Loyola University Press, 1982. This book provides in-depth coverage of Carroll's formative years and influences during his schooling. Special emphasis is placed on Carroll's intellect, culture, and earliest accomplishments. Includes documentary notes and index.

_____. *Revolutionary Statesman: Charles Carroll and the War*. Chicago: Loyola University Press, 1983. This book looks at Carroll's patriotic contributions to independence. The author focuses on Carroll's personal character and cites an extensive list of primary sources. Includes documentary notes and index.

Hawke, David Freeman. *Honorable Treason: The Declaration of Independence and the Men Who Signed It*. New York: Viking Press, 1976. A collection of profiles of each of the signers, providing equal detail on all fifty-five men. Good source for delegate comparisons. Includes bibliographical notes.

Hoffman, Ronald. *Princes of Ireland, Planters of Maryland: A Carroll Saga, 1500-1782*. Chapel Hill: University of North Carolina Press, 2000. Large, well-researched study of the Carroll family, beginning with its struggles in Ireland until its eventual financial success in eighteenth century Maryland. Describes Charles Carroll's decision to align with the revolutionary cause and his family's determination to maintain its Catholicism in the face of prejudice.

Hoffman, Ronald, Sally D. Mason, and Eleanor S. Darcy, eds. *Dear Papa, Dear Charley: The Peregrinations of a Revolutionary Aristocrat, as Told by Charles Carroll of Carrollton and His Father, Charles Carroll of Annapolis, with Sundry Observations on Bastardy, Child Rearing, Romance, Matrimony, Commerce, Tobacco, Slavery, and the Politics of Revolutionary America*. 3 vols. Chapel Hill: University of North Carolina Press, 2001. This collection of letters begins in 1740, when young Carroll writes his father while receiving his education in Europe. The letters chronicle young Carroll's rise to power during the American Revolution, the political and economic compromises he made, and details of his private life.

Maier, Pauline. *American Scripture: Making the Declaration of Independence.* New York: Alfred A. Knopf, 1997. A comprehensive narrative that examines the era, colonies, and delegates involved in the Declaration of Independence's formation. Provides only brief mentions of Carroll but includes a significant section on Maryland and extensive reference notes.

_____. *The Old Revolutionaries: Political Lives in the Age of Samuel Adams.* New York: Vintage Books, 1982. This account of six revolutionaries, including Carroll, provides insight into his personal identity and what influenced his political endeavors. The author concludes with a general discussion of revolutionary politics. Includes an index and some illustrations.

Van Devanter, Ann C. *Anywhere So Long As There Be Freedom: Charles Carroll of Carrollton, His Family, and His Maryland.* Baltimore: Baltimore Museum of Art, 1975. A catalog of an exhibition created to commemorate the U.S. bicentennial. Offers a biographical account of the Carroll family and catalogs family portraits, property, furniture, household items, and other memorabilia. Includes an exhaustive index of artists and an abbreviated chronology of the Carroll family tree. An excellent source for researching the family estate.

See also: Samuel Chase; Benjamin Franklin.

Related articles in *Great Events from History: The Eighteenth Century, 1701-1800:* September 5-October 26, 1774: First Continental Congress; May 10-August 2, 1775: Second Continental Congress; July 4, 1776: Declaration of Independence; September 17, 1787: U.S. Constitution Is Adopted; December 15, 1791: U.S. Bill of Rights Is Ratified.

CASANOVA
Italian adventurer

Although discounted by some as too bawdy to be literature, Casanova's twelve volumes of memoirs serve as a treatise on the manners and mores of society in eighteenth century Europe.

Born: April 2, 1725; Venice (now in Italy)
Died: June 4, 1798; Dux, Bohemia (now Duchcov, Czech Republic)
Also known as: Jean-Jacques; Chevalier de Seingalt; Giovanni Giacomo (or Jacopo) Casanova de Seingalt (full name)
Area of achievement: Literature

EARLY LIFE

Jean-Jacques, chevalier de Seingalt, whose other name, Casanova (kah-sah-NAW-vah), would become synonymous with the bon vivant and sexually proficient man, was a sickly child who was considered mentally deficient by his parents. He suffered from debilitating nosebleeds and was so unresponsive that he did not speak until he was eight years old. His parents made no secret of their wish that he would die.

Casanova was the eldest son of a Venetian actor of Spanish descent and Zanetta, the leading lady in the Comici troupe of comic actors. His father died when Casanova was very young, and soon after, Zanetta abandoned the young Casanova, his three brothers, and two sisters, leaving them with strangers while she toured Verona, St. Petersburg, and Dresden. After she left, she seldom saw the children.

After the death of his father and in his mother's absence, Casanova began to flourish academically and was sent to boarding school in Padua, where he studied law, although he wished to become a doctor. In his memoirs, he proudly claims that while at school, he experienced his first sexual encounter at age eleven and found his second love, the gaming tables. He soon lost his money, began gambling on credit, and wrote his grandmother for additional funds. Instead of sending money, Casanova's grandmother whisked him home to Venice and placed him in an abbey school in the hope that the church would alter his less-than-reputable passions. At age fifteen, Casanova had received three minor orders from the church, been introduced into society by his patron, and acquired the social graces that would serve him well throughout the remainder of his life. He excelled in his studies and was allowed to preach two sermons, but during the second sermon it became obvious that he was not sober, and he was dismissed from the program. Thanks to the intercession of his patron, he was transferred to a seminary but soon was expelled for a sexual tryst.

Because he obviously was not cut from clerical cloth, Casanova's next foray into the professional world was the Venetian army, which he entered as an ensign. This, too, proved to be a less-than-ideal choice; he resigned the post in 1745. Seeking a less structured position, he began to play the violin in a theater orchestra. During an evening performance, one of the theater patrons became ill, and Casanova, claiming to be schooled in the medicinal arts, saved the man's life. The gentleman was Senator Bragadin, a wealthy and influential politician, who showed his gratitude by moving Casanova into his home and his social circle and becoming his patron. After many false starts, Casanova had found his niche in the world and realized his true calling, which was to be supported and valued merely by virtue of being himself.

LIFE'S WORK

During his years at Bragadin's home, Casanova's main source of revenue was gambling, naturally with the senator's money. He reveled in his new social position, charmed the high society of the region, and dazzled all he met with his rugged good looks and the energy that seemed to radiate from his person. He was tall, unusually strong, and dark complected. His face bore several smallpox scars, and he had a high forehead, a long nose, a soft chin, large eyes, and full lips. He was a born orator, a good listener, and generous to a fault—particularly when the source of the generosity was not his own funds.

Casanova. (Library of Congress)

Although he was educated, Casanova used his knowledge for nothing more than to sparkle in conversation in the attempt to impress the wealthy and well connected now drawn to his circle. His energy was without bounds but undirected; he was intelligent but lacked the power of concentration. Within this new social sphere, his hedonism and narcissism flourished, and although he entertained everyone he met with his wit and carpe diem philosophy, he also exploited them. In the fluid social milieu of eighteenth century Europe, knowledge was a ticket to fame and fortune, and Casanova had a demonstrable talent for always being in the right place at the right time with the proper witticism.

Casanova's actions caught the attention of the police, who noted that the young man's libertine excesses had nearly ruined Senator Bragadin. Under the noted rogue's tutelage, the senator had acquired an interest in magic and the occult. In addition, Casanova had penned satirical and, by some accounts, atheistic poetry and was well-

known for his gambling and sexual conquests. With little provocation, the police raided Casanova's quarters, discovered books on magic, and, accompanied by forty archers, arrested him. Uninformed of the charges against him, which included bewitching Bragadin and being a corrupter of youth, and without benefit of trial, Casanova was escorted to Piombi prison under the roof of the Doges' Palace in Venice. The inquisitors of state sentenced him to a prison stay of five years. Casanova found prison less suited to his appetites than the church or the military, and he immediately began plotting an escape. With the aid of a cellmate, a monk called Balbi, the enterprising young man dug his way out and left Venice for almost twenty years.

Employing the graces he had acquired during his time at the senator's and his expertise as a "lover of women," Casanova traveled extensively in Europe, floating from one patron or patroness to another and increasing his circle of influence. During this period, he conversed with Voltaire, King George III, and Empress Catherine the Great and became a favorite of the upper classes. He wrote novels, plays, and scholarly treatises and dabbled in finance, organizing a national lottery in Holland.

Although successful by his standards, Casanova longed to return to his beloved Venice. Through his connections, he gained a reprieve on the condition that he would return as a secret agent, which he did, serving from 1774 to 1782. Ironically, however, he found that after twenty years of traveling, the home of his youth failed to hold his interest: Soon he yearned to wander once again, this time to England. The eight years Casanova spent in England proved to be his downfall. He failed to amuse and delight British society as he had the society of the Continent, and he encountered people more adept than he at being scoundrels. Penurious, he returned to Venice to find himself barred from gaining entry to the great halls where he had once enjoyed social success.

Without other recourse, Casanova accepted an invitation to become chateau librarian for Count von Waldstein in Bohemia. Unable to speak the language and thus stripped of his witty repartee, society's once-shining star was relegated to the periphery of the social world at the château of Dux. Miserable and isolated, Casanova removed himself from the milieu and began to compose his memoirs, a task that encompassed the final fourteen years of his life. He died at the château, broken and alone, in 1798.

SIGNIFICANCE

It is virtually impossible to separate Casanova the man from Casanova the literary artist, not only because the major portion of his work is autobiography, which is theoretically factual, but also because so much of Casanova's character is fiction. Although he disliked novels, he is the prototype of the picaresque, the charming rogue who slips and slides through encounters while envisioning, at best, an improved state in life and, at the least, survival at any cost.

Whether Casanova created the legend or vice versa remains a matter of scholarly debate; however, Casanova's memoirs clearly enumerate the manners, the ills, and the mores of the upper classes of eighteenth century Europe. Although some critics dismiss Casanova's memoirs as erotic or obscene, others believe the twelve volumes are great literature worthy of study and discourse.

Casanova died in 1798, but the manuscript did not appear until 1820, when Carlo Angiolini, about whom little is known, brought the handwritten bundles to Brockhaus Publishers in Leipzig. Although Angiolini presented the publishers with twelve bundles, which corresponded roughly to the original twelve volumes of the autobiography, it became apparent that sections were missing and that the work was probably incomplete, because the chronology ended in 1774. Some sources contend that Casanova burned the balance of the manuscript when age forced the writing to become less than perfect.

The work was translated into German and published between 1822 and 1828 as *Aus den Memoiren de Venetianers Jacob Casanova de Seingalt*. Before the memoir's publication in French, Jean Laforgue, a language professor, was hired to clean up the language, both grammatically and morally, and many of the original passages were deleted. When the French version was released, many doubted its authenticity and attributed the writing to Stendhal. Based on independent research and the restoration of the purged passages, the first "complete and unabridged English translation" was published privately in London (*The Memoirs of Jacques Casanova de Seingalt*, 1894). This original English translation by Arthur Machen was a numbered, limited run of one thousand copies, of which five hundred were earmarked for American distribution. It was reprinted numerous times by various private clubs and societies (because of its erotic content) and published publicly by Elek Books, London, in the early 1900's and by G. P. Putnam in New York (1959-1961). Abridged and edited versions of Machen's translation were also published throughout the twentieth century. *Histoire de ma vie*, an edition purporting to be the first complete and authentic publication of the original French memoir, was published by Brockhaus in 1960-1962.

Although many people may find the blatant sexuality of the memoirs offensive, each of the hundreds of vignettes in the work sheds light on the customs of the era. Also, many readers will find something admirable in the candor of a person who veils nothing, is ashamed of nothing, and is no hypocrite. Although Casanova provided no great boon for humanity, he obviously was pleased with a life well lived. Casanova is an enigma: He had no respect for authority or reputation, yet he wished to be well liked; he laughed at religion and convention, yet he was pious and intellectually defensive; he personified the quest for pleasure, yet he was known for his respect for women; he was a sensualist who lived life to the fullest, yet he was generous to a fault. This scholar, adventurer, gamester, vagabond, romantic, and rogue can be considered one of the first heroes of popular culture—the popular culture of the Enlightenment.

—Joyce Duncan

FURTHER READING

Casanova, Giacomo. *The Memoirs of Jacques Casanova de Seingalt*. Translated by Arthur Machen. 12 vols. Reprint. New York: G. P. Putnam's Sons, 1959-1961. Claims to be the first complete and unabridged translation of the work; employs new scholarship.

Dobree, Bonamy. *Three Eighteenth Century Figures: Sarah Churchill, John Wesley, Giacomo Casanova*. London: Oxford University Press, 1962. A rather fond rendering of Casanova's life, including an overview of his encounters, travels, and lifestyle.

Flem, Lydia. *Casanova: The Man Who Really Loved Women*. Translated by Catherine Temerson. New York: Farrar, Straus & Giroux, 1997. Presents Casanova's life as a psychobiography in an attempt to rationalize his activities based on his impoverished childhood and his perpetual search for a mother figure.

Nettl, Paul. *The Other Casanova: A Contribution to Eighteenth Century Music and Manners*. New York: Philosophical Library, 1950. Places Casanova within the cultural milieu of his era by discussing the music and other arts that he encountered and critiqued.

Parker, Derek. *Casanova*. Stroud, Gloucestershire, England: Sutton, 2002. Sympathetic biography, describing Casanova's abilities not only as a lover of women but also as a writer, playwright, mathematician, librarian, diplomat, and spy. Places Casanova's romantic activities within the context of eighteenth century sexual attitudes and practices.

Symons, Arthur. "Casanova at Dux." In *The Memoirs of Jacques Casanova de Seingalt, Venetian Years*. Vol. 1. New York: G. P. Putnam's Sons, 1959. The preface to this edition of the memoirs is worthy of note as an independent source, because it examines in detail the omission of the bawdy sections in the French translation and the process by which the materials were rediscovered and reincorporated.

See also: Jean-Jacques Rousseau; Marquis de Sade; Voltaire.

Related articles in *Great Events from History: The Eighteenth Century, 1701-1800*: April 25, 1719: Defoe Publishes the First Novel; 1740-1741: Richardson's *Pamela* Establishes the Modern Novel; 1782-1798: Publication of Rousseau's *Confessions*.

CATHERINE THE GREAT
Empress of Russia (r. 1762-1796)

One of the early enlightened monarchs, Catherine attempted to create a uniform Russian government with a modern Westernized code of laws that represented all levels of Russian society with the exception of the serfs. In the forty-four years of her reign, she sculpted Russia into one of the great world powers of the time and laid the foundation for what would become modern Russia.

Born: May 2, 1729; Stettin, Pomerania, Prussia (now Szczecin, Poland)

Died: November 17, 1796; Tsarskoye Selo (now Pushkin), near St. Petersburg, Russia

Also known as: Yekaterina Alekseyevna; Yekaterina Velikaya; Catherine II; Sophie Friederike Auguste von Anhalt-Zerbst (birth name)

Area of achievement: Government and politics

EARLY LIFE

Catherine the Great was born Sophie Friederike Auguste von Anhalt-Zerbst, in Stettin, a seaport in Pomerania. Her parents, Prince Christian August and Princess Johanna Elizabeth of Holstein-Gottorp, were minor members of the German aristocracy. As a result of her strained relationship with her mother, Sophie developed into an independent young woman. Russian monarchs held the prerogative of choosing their successors, and her cousin, Duke Karl Peter Ulrich of Holstein-Gottorp, had been summoned to Russia by the childless Empress Elizabeth as the heir to the throne. It only remained to find him a wife, and, after several months of searching, Elizabeth decided on Sophie: Both the fourteen-year-old princess and her mother were invited to Russia in January, 1744.

Elizabeth was pleased with her choice, and Peter fell in love with the princess. On June 28, 1744, Sophie converted to Russian Orthodoxy and was given the name Catherine, and on the following day the couple were publicly engaged. However, from the time he arrived in Russia, Peter, whose health was never good, had a series of illnesses that left him permanently scarred and most probably sterile. Their marriage, which occurred on August 21, 1745, was not consummated immediately and probably was not consummated at all.

Married to a man who displayed a mania for Prussian militarism and who would rather play with toy soldiers and conduct military parades than be with her, Catherine was left to develop her own interests. She began to read, a pastime almost unheard of in the Russian court, and mastered the technique of riding astride horses, an activity in which she took great pleasure, often going for long rides. Neither interest could overcome the lack of an heir, which, as the empress pointed out to her on more than one occasion, was Catherine's only reason for being. Starved for affection and aware that her position depended on producing a child, she took a lover, Sergei Saltykov. Twice she became pregnant and miscarried, but on September 20, 1754, Catherine gave birth to a male child, Paul Petrovich, who was probably the son of Saltykov.

The empress took control of the child from the moment he was delivered, and Catherine was once again left alone. Totally barred from any involvement in the political life of the court, she consoled herself with reading the works of such writers as Voltaire, Tacitus, and Montesquieu. Saltykov was replaced in her affections first by Count Stanisław August Poniatowski and then, in 1761, by Grigori Grigoryevich Orlov, with whom she fell in love. During this time, her husband's behavior became more and more eccentric. Russia was at war with Prussia, yet Peter made no secret of his pro-Prussian sentiments, even going so far as to supply Frederick II with information concerning Russian troop movements.

Elizabeth died in December, 1761, leaving Catherine's husband, Peter III, as the new emperor. Catherine was six months pregnant with Orlov's child at the time, a son who was born in April, 1762, although no one really noticed. Peter III immediately ended the war with Prussia and then allied himself with the Prussians to make war on Denmark, declaring himself more than willing to serve Frederick II. Adding to this insult to Russian patriotism, Peter outraged the church by reviling Russian Orthodox ritual and by ordering the secularizing of church estates and the serfs bound to those estates. Most important to his final overthrow, he offended the elite guards, dressing them in uniforms that were completely Prussian in appearance and constantly taunting the men.

In June, 1762, Catherine, with the support of the powerful Orlov family and the guards, acted. In a bloodless coup, she seized the Crown in St. Petersburg and published a manifesto claiming the throne. Dressed in a guard's uniform and astride her stallion, Brilliant, she led her troops against her deposed husband in his stronghold at Peterhoff. He offered his abdication, and, with its acceptance, Catherine became empress of Russia.

LIFE'S WORK

Catherine began her reign by declaring that she had acted only because it was the will of the people. Aware that she had come to the throne by the might of the powerful Orlov family and with the backing of the guards, she realized that she must avoid antagonizing the nobility or the church. As a result, her manifesto justifying her seizure of the throne claimed that it had been necessary in order to establish the correct form of government, an autocracy acting in accord with Russian Orthodoxy, national custom, and the sentiment of the Russian people. Although her words offered welcome relief from the brief reign of Peter III, her actions were not unilaterally accepted— after all, she was German by birth and had no blood claim to the throne, even if she was ultimately claiming it for her son. To complicate matters, Peter III died, in all probability murdered at the behest of the Orlovs, and in 1764, Ivan VI, himself deposed by Elizabeth, was killed in his prison cell during an abortive rescue attempt. Catherine

Catherine the Great. (The Granger Collection, New York)

ON THE STATUS OF SERFS

In 1767, the same year that Catherine issued her Instructions *to the legislative commission for reforming Russia's legal codes according to Enlightenment principles, she also issued a decree reaffirming the status of the empire's serfs. In the following excerpt, she declares that a serf's landlord is the ultimate authority concerning that serf: Any attempt to petition a higher authority for a redress of grievances by a serf is a crime.*

The Governing Senate . . . has deemed it necessary to make known that the landlords' serfs and peasants . . . owe their landlords proper submission and absolute obedience in all matters, according to the laws that have been enacted from time immemorial by the autocratic forefathers of Her Imperial Majesty and which have not been repealed, and which provide that all persons who dare to incite serfs and peasants to disobey their landlords shall be arrested and taken to the nearest government office, there to be punished forthwith as disturbers of the public tranquillity, according to the laws and without leniency. And should it so happen that even after the publication of the present decree of Her Imperial Majesty any serfs and peasants should cease to give the proper obedience to their landlords . . . and should make bold to submit unlawful petitions complaining of their landlords, and especially to petition Her Imperial Majesty personally, then both those who make the complaints and those who write up the petitions shall be punished by the knout and forthwith deported to Nerchinsk to penal servitude for life and shall be counted as part of the quota of recruits which their landlords must furnish to the army. And in order that people everywhere may know of the present decree, it shall be read in all the churches on Sundays and holy days for one month after it is received and thereafter once every year during the great church festivals, lest anyone pretend ignorance.

Source: Catherine the Great, from *A Source Book for Russian History: From Early Times to 1917*, edited by George Vernadsky, vol. 2 (New Haven, Conn.: Yale University Press, 1972), pp. 453-454.

was forced to deal with the doubts of many who thought she had murdered the legitimate claimants to the throne to gain it for herself.

At the time she took the throne, Catherine still retained much of her early beauty. She had a clear, very white complexion, which was set off by her brown hair and dark eyebrows. Her eyes were hazel, and in a certain light they appeared bright blue. She had a long neck and a proud carriage, and in her youth she was noted for her shapely figure. As she aged, she grew increasingly heavy: When she collapsed immediately before her death, it took several men to carry her to her bed.

Despite her rather tenuous hold on the throne, the new empress rapidly took charge of her empire. She ended the hated war against Denmark and quickly went to work trying to reform Russia into the nation that Peter the Great had envisioned. An advocate of economic growth and expansion and an opponent of trade restrictions, she abolished most state monopolies and authorized grain exports. Under her reign, Russia had some of the most liberal tariff policies in Europe. Determined to improve agriculture, in 1765 she established the Free Economic Society for the Encouragement of Agriculture and Husbandry.

Faced with the chaos of the Russian legal system, Catherine was determined to create an effective centralized government. She set to work codifying the laws of Russia, and in 1766, she published a work in which she drew freely from writers such as Montesquieu, Cesare Beccaria, and Denis Diderot. In it, she confirmed that autocracy was the best form of government to fill the needs of Russia, yet she also developed the idea that the government was responsible for meeting the needs of the people. All subjects, except the serfs, were entitled to equal treatment under the law, and all had the right to petition the sovereign. The standard use of torture in conjunction with legal proceedings and the common use of capital punishment were shunned—the only exception being in the case of a threat to national security.

Not content with this venture alone, Catherine set to work on a series of legal codes to cover nearly all aspects of the Russian social order. In 1782, she published a work that gave minute instructions for the administration of the urban population. This was followed in the same year by two charters that delineated the rights and obligations of the various levels of society. Despite these laws, she did not deal with the one level of society that by the end of the century made up 90 percent of the population—the peasantry. Russian serfs were bound to the nobles, who had complete control over them. The wealth of a noble was based on how many serfs, or souls, he owned, not on how much land he controlled. Catherine maintained her position through the support of the nobility. To create any law that interfered with the nobles' rights over their serfs would alienate the nobility and without any question would lead to her being deposed in favor of her son. For this reason, while she remained acutely aware of the serfs' plight, she did nothing to change their status as property and refused them the basic right to petition the monarch, a right held by all her other subjects.

Two major problems that plagued her reign were wars and the frequent threat of impostors making claims on her throne. In 1768, the Ottoman Empire declared war on Russia over the question of Russian troops in Poland, and the war continued until the Ottomans surrendered in 1774. Russian territory was greatly increased in the settlement, but in 1787 the Ottoman Empire again declared war on Russia, a conflict that lasted until 1791. In 1782-1783, the Crimea was under siege but was subdued and incorporated into Russia in 1784. In 1788, while Russia was at war with the Turks, war with Sweden erupted and lasted until 1790. In 1793, Catherine annexed part of Poland, and in 1794 a full-scale rebellion erupted in that country but was finally crushed by Russian troops, leaving the area firmly in Russian control.

From the beginning of her reign, rumors abounded that Peter III was not dead, and at intervals impostors came forward to claim the Crown. Some of these amassed considerable followings, especially in the case of Pugachev's Revolt (1773-1774), but all were quickly eliminated. Most of the impostors spent the rest of their lives in banishment in Siberia. Catherine was always aware of the fragility of her hold on the throne, and she reacted with fear to the news of the French Revolution, taking stern measures to ensure that no such events could occur in Russia. In 1793, she broke all relations with France, including the importation of any French goods, and, despite her earlier support of publishers, in 1796 she imposed rigid book censorship and limited the number of presses to those completely under government control. Any hint of republican thinking was immediately investigated, and anyone even remotely suspect was quickly banished.

At the height of this fear of French republicanism, and having outlived nearly all of her friends and advisers, Catherine suffered a stroke in November, 1796, and died at the Winter Palace in St. Petersburg. Her relationship with her son had always been strained, and there were rumors that she intended to remove him as her heir in favor of his son Alexander. If she left a testament to this effect it was never found, although forgeries of such a document continued to appear. The new emperor, Paul I, had his murdered father's body exhumed, and, after crowning the remains with his own hands, he had the bodies of his parents buried together at the Peter and Paul Cathedral in St. Petersburg.

SIGNIFICANCE

Under Catherine the Great, Russia was changed from a chaotic, badly managed nation to one of the major forces in Europe. Laws were codified and a powerful centralized government was formed. As a result of numerous wars, the nation's territory was greatly increased. There was also a great increase in national wealth.

Despite her failure to deal with the question of the serfs, Catherine can be viewed as one of the first enlightened monarchs, attempting to create a moral society and eliminating corruption in government. She introduced smallpox inoculation to Russia in 1768, and in 1786 she published a statute setting up general education in the twenty-six provincial capitals. In a highly illiterate nation, this was a radical step. She encouraged advancement in agriculture and made every effort to improve the lives of the Russian people.

—*C. D. Akerley*

FURTHER READING

Alexander, John T. *Catherine the Great: Life and Legend.* New York: Oxford University Press, 1989. Gives a largely unbiased portrait of a complex and powerful woman. Alexander considers all aspects of Catherine's life and manages to deal honestly with the reality of her legendary love life. Excellent bibliography.

Bergamini, John D. *The Tragic Dynasty: A History of the Romanovs.* New York: G. P. Putnam's Sons, 1969. A generally detailed look at the life of Catherine, although greater emphasis is given to her sexual appetites and her relationship with her two famous lovers than to the political aspects of her reign.

Cowles, Virginia. *The Romanovs.* New York: Harper & Row, 1971. Cowles deals with Catherine's love of opulence and the scandals of her life, emphasizing her love of grandeur and her numerous lovers.

De Madariaga, Isabel. *Catherine the Great: A Short History.* 2d ed. New Haven, Conn.: Yale University Press, 2002. This is not a conventional biography but a summary of De Madariaga's scholarship on Catherine the Great. The book focuses on Catherine's work as empress, including her involvement in administrative reform, foreign policy, and bringing the intellectual ideas of the Enlightenment to Russia.

Erickson, Carolly. *Great Catherine: The Life of Catherine the Great, Empress of Russia.* New York: Crown, 1994. Comprehensive popular biography. Erickson describes Catherine's complex personality and her reign as empress.

Grey, Ian. *The Romanovs: The Rise and Fall of a Dynasty*. New York: Doubleday, 1970. Catherine is depicted as a ruthless sovereign who plotted her way to the throne even before the death of Empress Elizabeth.

MacKenzie, David, and Michael W. Curran. *A History of Russia and the Soviet Union*. Chicago: Dorsey Press, 1978. Includes several detailed chapters on Catherine that place her life in historical perspective. Excellent bibliography of historical texts on the period.

Troyat, Henri. *Catherine the Great*. Translated by Joan Pinkham. New York: Meridian, 1994. Originally published in 1980, this is a reprint of a popular biography of Catherine.

See also: Cesare Beccaria; Denis Diderot; Elizabeth Petrovna; Mikhail Illarionovich Kutuzov; Montesquieu; Aleksey Grigoryevich Orlov; Grigori Grigoryevich Orlov; Peter the Great; Peter III; Grigori Aleksandrovich Potemkin; Yemelyan Ivanovich Pugachev; Aleksandr Vasilyevich Suvorov.

Related articles in *Great Events from History: The Eighteenth Century, 1701-1800*: May 27, 1703: Founding of St. Petersburg; November 20, 1710-July 21, 1718: Ottoman Wars with Russia, Venice, and Austria; August 10, 1767: Catherine the Great's Instruction; October, 1768-January 9, 1792: Ottoman Wars with Russia; September, 1773-September, 1774: Pugachev's Revolt; 1788-September, 1809: Russo-Swedish Wars.

GEORGIANA CAVENDISH
English politician and writer

Cavendish overcame a restrictive private life to become a respected politician who was determined to support the Whig cause despite her obligations to support her husband. Her visible and active presence highlight women's significant contributions to eighteenth century politics. She also wrote two novels.

Born: June 7, 1757; Wimbeldon, Surrey, England
Died: March 30, 1806; London, England
Also known as: Georgiana Spencer (birth name); Duchess of Devonshire
Areas of achievement: Government and politics, literature

EARLY LIFE

Georgiana Cavendish was born an aristocrat, being the eldest child of John, created the First Earl Spencer when his daughter was only eight, and Margaret, daughter of the Right Honourable Stephen Poyntz. As a daughter, her education concentrated upon her duty to make a suitable dynastic match, offering only a smattering of basics such as history, geography, and languages, coupled with the specifically feminine aspects of etiquette, deportment, music, and drawing. Georgiana was expected to be a pleasing and refined addition to any family rather than an educated companion and helpmate in a partnership of equals.

Georgiana and her sister Harriette, inseparable throughout their lives, were noted for their striking good looks, acclaimed charm, style, and sophistication. Coupled with their status within a strict hierarchy of rank, there was no doubt that they were very desirable "commodities" in the marriage market. At sixteen years old and before she had properly been launched as a debutante upon exclusive society as a way of promoting her eligibility, Georgiana caught the eye of the fifth duke of Devonshire, William Cavendish.

The Devonshires were one of the wealthiest families in the country, owning vast tracts of profitable land and six of the most magnificent estates and houses in England and Ireland. Georgiana was an obvious and acceptable choice for the duke and his family: The social status of her family, the Spencers, almost matched that of the Devonshires, and Georgiana was beautiful, popular, and young and thus ideal for bearing the next generation. However, no matter how illustrious the match, it was not a happy one. Georgiana was impulsive and demonstrative and the duke, though well respected, was famous for his reserve and awkwardness in public. A difference in age of ten years did little to smooth over the troubles in what was essentially a union of opposites.

LIFE'S WORK

Married at age sixteen, Georgiana Cavendish was defined by her marriage in all aspects. There had not been a duchess of Devonshire for twenty years, and Cavendish's new position catapulted her into the limelight of the overlapping social and political spheres of the fashionable elite. Because of her rank, charismatic youth, and good looks, Cavendish swiftly became the undisputed leader of the fashionable world. Her clothes, accessories, and even movements were slavishly followed by public and press alike. Her social success went some way to compensate for what appeared to be the duke of Devonshire's complete indifference to his lively wife. She published *Emma: Or, The Unfortunate Attachment—A Sentimental Novel* in 1773, an insider's look at the institution of arranged dynastic marriages, and published *The Sylph* in 1779, an epistolary novel clearly based on her own experiences with fashionable society.

Within a few months, though, she was a heavy drinker and addicted to both drugs and gambling. Her debts, even by eighteenth century standards, were astronomical, and they nearly crippled the vast wealth of the Devonshires. It was not until after her son became the sixth duke that the financial mess was finally resolved. Cavendish's personal life was further complicated by a series of miscarriages when her foremost social duty was to produce a male heir and by sharing her friendship, her home, and her husband with her friend Lady Elizabeth Foster, an arrangement—a ménage à trois—that could have become volatile.

Cavendish's role as politician came through fulfilling her role as wife to her politically important husband and through replacing her downward spiral of self-destruction with a determined sense of purpose. The Devonshires were major leaders of the opposition Whig Party, but peers, by law, were barred from actively campaigning for their own interests. It was therefore the role and responsibility of the wives to represent their husbands politically.

Cavendish's numerous obligations were split between town and country. When in London during the season that spanned the time Parliament was in session, she would host dinners and balls as a method of ensuring support and loyalty to the Whig Party, and she became an active patron of the arts as well. When in the country, she was expected to be involved in charity work, the dispensation of patronage, and presiding over "public days," those times when the Chatsworth estate was open to all the tenants and respectable passersby. Vast quantities of food and drink were available at the expense of the duke.

Cavendish was a successful ambassador for the Whig Party because of her personal touch. Her ability to mix and talk, with apparent sincerity, with all social classes made her extremely popular and very successful as a rallying focus for the party as a whole, earning her the epithet "head of opposition public."

What began as obligation for Cavendish became for her a staunch advocacy of the Whig causes: supporting a limited monarchy, personal liberty, and religious freedom. She extended what was initially an ambassadorial role on behalf of her husband's interests into a role of political activist for the Whig Party. She caused a sensation and a scandal when she campaigned for the statesman Charles James Fox during the Westminster elections of 1784. Fox recognized Cavendish as an astute propagandist with a flair for engaging with the public and an eye for the political potency of the symbolic: For example, she used her riding habit to represent a military uniform when forces were gathering against a French invasion in 1778, and she adopted the three feathers of the prince of Wales as decoration, demonstrating alliance during the Regency Crisis of 1788-1789. By successfully campaigning for Fox, Cavendish set a precedent while canvassing for a male nonrelative and being associated with a party in her own right; she exceeded the political ambitions of her husband.

In London, Devonshire House became the formal and informal headquarters of the Whig Party, and Cavendish moved beyond being a symbolic patriot to becoming a premier political hostess, confidante, and negotiator, using her connections and advantageous social position to bring together all that would further the interests and secure the future of the Whigs. It is a measure of her success that Cavendish was singled out by the opposition press to be vilified as nothing more than a common prostitute for making such a public "display" of herself when campaigning on behalf of the Whigs, which was swiftly becoming identified as her party.

SIGNIFICANCE

Georgiana Cavendish Chapone a vast amount of publicity, especially critical publicity. She was criticized because of her association with Fox and the Regency Crisis; she overstepped the boundary of female propriety by being too forward and public; and she was disgraced—facing two years' banishment abroad—because she had an affair with Earl Grey. Cavendish's later political activities as negotiator and facilitator occur at a more discreet level, behind the scenes.

Her correspondence reveals the extent of her political participation, and it shows just how much of a role she carved out for herself. Her letters also demonstrate the precarious nature of the public realm for women. Her involvement in eighteenth century politics ran counter to the prescribed social roles for women of the time, as the public and private spheres were gendered and marked out for both women and men. Cavendish's life is an example of, rather than an exception to, the mutually dependent and all-encompassing worlds of the social and the political.

—Leigh Wetherall

FURTHER READING

Cavendish, Georgiana, Duchess of Devonshire. *Emma: Or, The Unfortunate Attachment—A Sentimental Novel*. Edited by Jonathan David Gross. Albany: State University of New York Press, 2004. Cavendish first published her novel anonymously in 1773, almost prophetically from an aristocratic female viewpoint about the internal and external dynamics of an arranged dynastic marriage.

_____. *The Sylph*. York, England: Henry Parker, 2001. First published in 1779, this is a fascinating epistolary novel that draws upon Cavendish's own unhappy experiences of the fashionable world that transforms a gauche young girl into a sophisticated woman of the world. Introduction by Amanda Foreman.

Chapman, Caroline. *The Duke of Devonshire and His Two Duchesses*. London: John Murray, 2002. Despite the title, this work is more a vindication of Lady Elizabeth Foster but is an insight into the dynamics of the ménage à trois.

Foreman, Amanda. *Georgiana, Duchess of Devonshire*. London: HarperCollins, 1998. An excellent, well-balanced biography that charts, chronologically, Cavendish's development from birth to young wife to the foremost female politician of her day.

_____. "Georgiana, Duchess of Devonshire and the Whig Party." In *Roles, Representations, and Responsibilities*, edited by Hannah Barker and Elaine Chalus. London: Longman, 1997. This chapter examines Cavendish's political career, which is broken into two parts: the high public profile of campaigning at the end of the eighteenth century and the more discreet profile at the beginning of the nineteenth century, illustrating that her presence in the political arena was both individual and illustrative.

See also: Abigail Adams; Joseph Addison; Edmund Burke; Caroline; Charles James Fox; Catherine Macaulay; Sir Joshua Reynolds; Richard Brinsley Sheridan; Richard Steele; Mercy Otis Warren.

Related articles in *Great Events from History: The Eighteenth Century, 1701-1800:* June 2-10, 1780: Gordon Riots; July 14, 1789: Fall of the Bastille; 1790: Burke Lays the Foundations of Modern Conservatism.

Henry Cavendish
French-born English scientist

Cavendish, a reclusive character, made significant advances in the chemistry of gases and contributed to the study of electrical phenomena.

Born: October 10, 1731; Nice, France
Died: February 24, 1810; London, England
Areas of achievement: Chemistry, physics

Early Life

Little is known in detail about the personal life of Henry Cavendish. He was born into a leading aristocratic British family. His father, Lord Charles Cavendish, was the third son of the duke of Devonshire, while his mother, Lady Anne Grey, was the daughter of the duke of Kent. His mother's death when he was two years old left him totally in his father's care. He entered Dr. Newcombe's Academy in Hackney in 1742 and matriculated at St. Peter's College, Cambridge, in 1749, leaving in 1753 without taking his degree. Most biographers have speculated

that he refused the religious tests required for a degree, but no evidence exists concerning his religious convictions at any time in his life.

After leaving Cambridge, he resided with his father in London. Lord Charles Cavendish was a longtime member of the Royal Society and an avid investigator of meteorological and electrical questions, having received the society's Copley Medal for perfecting a registering thermometer. His father sponsored his election to the Royal Society in 1760; living in an all-male environment permeated with scientific conversation may very well have shaped both Cavendish's lifelong fascination with science and his strange social behavior.

Throughout his life, Cavendish was reclusive, shunning human society. He was restricted by his father to an extremely small allowance, forcing him to become very close with money, often attending Royal Society dinners with only the 5 shillings necessary to gain admission.

Following his father's death in 1783, he came into a large family inheritance. While very wealthy, he remained parsimonious in his personal expenditures and oddly indifferent to other uses of money, giving generously to charity but always checking the list of donors and giving precisely the amount of the largest donation. Abhorring any meeting with women—he even left notes for housemaids to avoid personal contact—Cavendish remained an eccentric and elusive person. Only in the Royal Society, where he attended regularly and participated fully, did he have any public life. He was responsible for a detailed description and analysis of the society's meteorological instruments in 1776 and served on a committee investigating lightning protection for the Purfleet powder magazine, using his own electrical research to recommend pointed rather than blunt lightning rods. Even at the Royal Society, however, he would flee if approached by a stranger, and he was often seen outside the meeting room, waiting for the moment when he could slip in unnoticed. To the end of his life he was so totally devoted to science that everything else was secondary.

Only one portrait of Cavendish exists, a watercolor sketch by Sir John Barrow done surreptitiously at a dinner meeting of the Royal Society. It shows a somewhat tall, lanky middle-aged man of a rather sharp and thrusting appearance, dressed in a greatcoat and three-cornered hat stylish in the 1750's. Apparently the dress was his usual, as he was noted for never changing the style of his clothing and purchased only one set of clothing at a time, following a precise schedule as the old garments were worn out.

LIFE'S WORK

In his lifetime, Henry Cavendish was known primarily for his research in chemistry and electricity, work reflected in a remarkably small number of papers in the *Philosophical Transactions of the Royal Society*. His first public work was in 1776, a series of papers on the chemistry of "factitious airs," or gases. Chemistry at the time was dominated by the idea that air was a single element, one of the four Greek elements. British chemists, from Robert Boyle, who first elucidated the gas laws in 1662, through Stephen Hales and Joseph Black in the eighteenth century, had made "pneumatic chemistry," manipulating and measuring "air" in its various states of purity, practically a national specialty.

Chemical research was also carried on around the organizing concept of the phlogiston theory put forward by Georg Ernst Stahl in 1723. Phlogiston was the element of fire, or its principle, which caused inflammability when present in a body. It was believed to be central to most

Henry Cavendish. (Library of Congress)

chemical reactions. Combustion was explained as a body releasing its phlogiston. In this dual context of pneumatic chemistry and phlogiston theory Cavendish presented his study of "factitious airs," or gases contained in bodies. Most important, he isolated and identified "inflammable air," now called hydrogen. Recognizing the explosive nature of "inflammable air," Cavendish went on to identify it as phlogiston itself. He cannot be said to have discovered hydrogen, as others had separated it before him, and he did not specifically claim its discovery.

In 1783, Cavendish, having heard of experiments by Joseph Priestley that generated a "dew" upon exploding "inflammable air" and "common air," presented a study of an improved eudiometer, or a device for testing the "goodness" of air. He demonstrated that "common air" was composed of constant proportions of different constituents, rather than being a single elemental substance. This research was followed the next year with two more papers on air, the research for which was principally concerned to find the cause of the absorption of gases in the eudiometer. When he mixed "inflammable air" with "common air," he created an explosion and he noticed a dew on the containing vessel. Where Priestley had mentioned the fact in passing, Cavendish focused on it, noting that "by this experiment it appears that this dew is plain water, and consequently that almost all the inflammable air, and about one-fifth of the common air, are turned into pure water." He had discovered that water was a compound of "airs," not one of the four elements.

Cavendish's priority of the discovery of the composition of water was soon disputed. He had done his experiments in the summer of 1781 but postponed publication because the resulting water was contaminated with nitric acid. Solving this problem eventually led him to his last chemical discovery, the isolation of nitric acid in 1785. He had told Priestley of his water results, and a friend had passed the same information to Antoine-Laurent Lavoisier in Paris, who repeated and extended the experiments, while James Watt also made the discovery independently. When all three published their investigations in 1784, Watt, Lavoisier, and Cavendish all laid claim to priority. A brief controversy ensued but was quickly extinguished, with each of the three rather politely deferring to the others. The controversy was rekindled in the mid-nineteenth century and continues in some scholarly circles. Cavendish should probably be conceded the right to claim the discovery of the compound nature of water, although his explanation was given in the context of the phlogiston theory. Lavoisier followed Cavendish chronologically but explained the composition of water in the radically different terms of his new antiphlogiston chemistry, as the union of oxygen and hydrogen.

Lavoisier's antiphlogiston explanation was indicative of a revolution in chemistry that he was leading on the Continent. In 1772, when he had weighed the product of calcination (oxidation in the new terminology), there was a weight gain in the calx. He offered the explanation that something was taken up in the process, rather than phlogiston being given off. This "something" he identified as oxygen and thereby created a new chemistry. Cavendish recognized that Lavoisier's oxygen-based chemistry was essentially equivalent to a phlogiston-based chemistry, but he rejected the new ideas to the end of his life. "It seems," he wrote, "the phaenomena of nature might be explained very well on this principle, without the help of phlogiston; . . . but as the commonly received principle of phlogiston explains all phaenomena, at least as well as Mr. Lavoisier's, I have adhered to that." In 1787, Lavoisier introduced his new chemistry in his *Nomenclature chimique*, and fully elaborated it in 1789 in *Traité élémentaire de chimie*. Again Cavendish rejected the ideas, stressing that arbitrary names and ideas, as he saw them, could only lead to great mischief. By 1788, Cavendish had published the last of his chemical researches.

The second major area of Cavendish's published research was in electrical phenomena, a near-craze sweeping through scientific and popular circles throughout Europe. In 1771, Cavendish published his first paper on electricity, putting forward a single-fluid theory of electricity, in opposition to the then popular two-fluid theory. He presented electricity as a single "fluid" that could be measured according to its compressibility, using the analogy of Boyle's gas law. He provided a quantitative measure of tension as well as quantity, surmising that this "fluid" followed an inverse square law for repulsion, rather than the first power law displayed by gases. This work was expanded in 1776, with a paper describing his effort to construct a model of the electrical torpedo fish to analyze whether its electrical effects were similar to electrostatic phenomena, then the center of scientific attention. He demonstrated that they were the same.

In 1783, he also published a series of papers on heat, focusing on the question of the freezing point of mercury. He was able to expand upon the idea of latent heat presented earlier in the century by Joseph Black. These papers were based on a series of experiments carried out at the request of Cavendish by officers of the Hudson's Bay Company in 1781 and after in northern Canada.

Finally, in 1798 he presented his final paper to the Royal Society, outlining his effort to measure the density of the Earth. Using an experimental torsional balance apparatus devised by John Michel, he was able to provide an extremely accurate estimate of Earth's density, while also providing the first experimental demonstration of Sir Isaac Newton's gravitational laws.

SIGNIFICANCE

Henry Cavendish was widely recognized by his contemporaries as a precise experimenter and a thorough researcher, despite his small output of published works. His international reputation was certified in 1803 by election as a foreign member of the Institut de France (French Institute). This reputation was further honored in the founding of the Cavendish Society in 1846 and his family's endowment of the Cavendish Laboratories and the Cavendish Professorship at Cambridge in 1871, where much of the fundamental research in atomic theory was carried out in the early twentieth century.

Unpublished manuscripts, discovered after his death, have significantly altered the perception of his scientific pursuits as limited solely to precise and narrow experimentation. The publication of these papers has deepened the appreciation of Cavendish's interests and abilities. Russell McCormmach has shown that Cavendish's work was rooted in a coherent and consistent vision of the scientific approach and theories of Newton. Newton had postulated a world made up of interacting particles, attracting and repelling one another according to strict mathematical laws. Cavendish pursued an integrated research program attempting to apply the Newtonian insight to the physical world.

Whether because he was simply shy about publishing or because he refused to publish until he was fully satisfied with the results, the world saw only a seemingly unrelated series of papers. Yet each, whether on "airs," heat, electricity, or the density of Earth, was firmly rooted in his Newtonian vision of the world. Cavendish was the most original and creative physical theorist of his age in a nation of empirical experimenters, yet he kept his ideas hidden behind a facade of the misanthropic rejection of humanity.

—William E. Eagan

FURTHER READING

Akroyd, Wallace Ruddell. *Three Philosophers: Lavoisier, Priestley, and Cavendish.* Westport, Conn.: Greenwood Press, 1970. Very readable account of the chemical revolution in relatively nontechnical terms. Focuses mainly on Lavoisier and Priestley, with a short chapter on Cavendish.

Conant, James Bryant. *The Overthrow of the Phlogiston Theory: The Chemical Revolution of 1775-1789.* Cambridge, Mass.: Harvard University Press, 1950. Case 2 of the Harvard Case Histories in Experimental Science series and an excellent, easily grasped, almost hands-on introduction to the experimental background of the chemical revolution.

Davis, Kenneth Sydney. *The Cautionary Scientists: Priestley, Lavoisier, and the Founding of Modern Chemistry.* New York: G. P. Putnam's Sons, 1966. Relatively brief, joint biography that traces the interaction of the Scientific Revolution. Fairly popular.

Guerlac, Henry. *Antoine-Laurent Lavoisier, Chemist and Revolutionary.* New York: Charles Scribner's Sons, 1975. Synthesis of a lifetime of work by the leading Lavoisier scholar. Technical and precise, yet accessible. Well worth the effort for the best understanding of the chemical revolution.

Jungnickel, Christa, and Russell McCormmach. *Cavendish: The Experimental Life.* Lewisburg, Pa.: Bucknell University Press, 1999. Examines Cavendish's discoveries within the context of the elite society in which he and his father developed their scientific interests.

McCormmach, Russell. *Speculative Truth: Henry Cavendish, Natural Philosophy, and the Rise of Modern Theoretical Science.* New York: Oxford University Press, 2004. Explores the new theories of natural philosophy that emerged in the second half of the eighteenth century, including Cavendish's mechanical theory of heat. Includes an edition of Cavendish's manuscript about the mechanical theory of heat.

McKie, Douglas. *Antoine Lavoisier: Scientist, Economist, Social Reformer.* New York: Henry Schuman, 1952. Older, comprehensive, relatively nontechnical biography of Lavoisier that is fair in its discussion of Cavendish. Widely available in a number of paperback editions.

Miller, David Philip. *Discovering Water: James Watt, Henry Cavendish, and the Nineteenth Century "Water Controversy."* Burlington, Vt.: Ashgate, 2004. Describes how Cavendish's and Watt's and Lavoisier's independent discoveries that water is a compound of "airs" and not a combination of elements became an issue of controversy among nineteenth century scientists.

Wilson, George. *The Life of the Honourable Henry Cavendish.* London: Cavendish Society, 1851. Reprint. New York: Arno Press, 1975. A very traditional life-and-times treatment. Excessive focus on composition-of-water controversy; interesting contrast to modern treatments.

See also: Joseph Black; John Fitch; Benjamin Franklin; Antoine-Laurent Lavoisier; Thomas Newcomen; Joseph Priestley; Georg Ernst Stahl; James Watt.

Related articles in *Great Events from History: The Eighteenth Century, 1701-1800:* 1718: Geoffroy Issues the *Table of Reactivities;* 1723: Stahl Postulates the Phlogiston Theory; 1733: Du Fay Discovers Two Kinds of Electric Charge; 1738: Bernoulli Proposes the Kinetic Theory of Gases; 1745: Lomonosov Issues the First Catalog of Minerals; June, 1752: Franklin Demonstrates the Electrical Nature of Lightning; 1781-1784: Cavendish Discovers the Composition of Water; 1786-1787: Lavoisier Devises the Modern System of Chemical Nomenclature.

Hester Chapone
English writer

Chapone was an important voice for women's rights. Her best-known work, Letters on the Improvement of the Mind, *laid out a plan for the education of young women. Her exemplary life made it clear that learned women were at least as virtuous as those whom society deliberately kept ignorant. Furthermore, her letters to the novelist Samuel Richardson, arguing against slavish filial obedience, were so persuasive that he altered his novel* Clarissa *to make it better conform to her thinking.*

Born: October 27, 1727; Twywell, Northamptonshire, England

Died: December 25, 1801; Hadley, Middlesex, England

Also known as: Hester Mulso (birth name)

Areas of achievement: Women's rights, literature, education

Early Life

Hester Chapone (sheh-POHN), born Hester Mulso, was the daughter of Thomas Mulso, a gentleman farmer, and his wife, whose family name was Thomas. Hester's mother is said to have been a beautiful but vain woman who did not approve of educating girls or women. Her daughter was not good-looking, but she was a precocious child. When Hester was nine, she wrote a romance, "The Loves of Amoret and Melissa." Although her mother disapproved of the work, indeed, of Hester's writing anything at all, her father and her three brothers were sure that it showed great promise.

It was undoubtedly because of the efforts of the men in her family that Hester received an education far better than that of most girls. She learned French, Italian, and Latin, as well as drawing and music. Because her voice was so lovely, she was soon nicknamed the "linnet," after the finch of the same name. Despite her mother's disapproval, Hester was writing serious poetry by the time she was just eighteen years old.

While she was attending the races in Canterbury, Hester met Elizabeth Carter, a classical scholar, much-published author, and a longtime friend of Samuel Richardson and the famous writer Samuel Johnson. Through Carter, Hester met other members of the group of literary and other intellectual women—named the Bluestockings after the literary club of the same name—and was introduced to their illustrious friends. Thus, by the time she had reached her early twenties, Hester had gained accep-

tance by some of the most brilliant writers, critics, and conversationalists of her time.

Life's Work

In the fall of 1750, Hester Chapone's verbal dispute with Samuel Richardson about his insistence on filial obedience in his novel *Clarissa* led Chapone to voice her objections in the form of three well-reasoned letters to him, the final one dated January 3, 1751. Though these letters were not published until after her death, they were widely circulated at the time they were written. Chapone had been called a "little spitfire" by Richardson, and she was not pleased. However, she did not back down, and when the third edition of his novel came out, he had modified the plot.

Chapone also had circulated some of her poems and composed a Pindaric ode asserting the superiority of the Christian view of life over that of the Stoics. (A Pindaric ode is an ode—or lyric poem—written especially for choral song and dance.) Chapone's collection was published in 1758 in Elizabeth Carter's *Epictetus*. In 1750, Chapone wrote four fictional letters for Johnson's literary magazine, *The Rambler*, and, in 1753, the "Story of Fidelia," a cautionary tale about a woman brought by Deists to the brink of damnation, appeared in *The Adventurer*. In 1755, Johnson published a quatrain of Chapone's poem "To Stella" in *A Dictionary of the English Language*.

It was in 1754 that Hester Chapone became engaged to John Chapone, a law student, whom she probably met through Richardson. However, her father did not feel that John would be able to support a wife, and even after her father allowed the marriage to take place six years later, the young couple had financial difficulties. Nevertheless, Hester Chapone was evidently deeply in love with her husband, and when he died in September, 1761, less than ten months after the wedding, she became desperately ill. Even after she recovered, she told her new friend Elizabeth Montagu, the leader of the Bluestockings, that she still missed him desperately.

Chapone was left so little by her husband that she had to sell her possessions, and she remained relatively poor the rest of her life. When her father died in 1763, she received a small bequest from him, but she did not have enough money to maintain a household, and from that time on she spent much of her days with friends and family members, including her uncle, the bishop of Winchester, who was in residence at Farnham Castle.

STUDYING WITH A FRIEND

In her best-known work, Letters on the Improvement of the Mind, *Hester Chapone advises her niece to seek out a companion when studying subjects such as history, because studying with another person allows for practicing, rehearsing, and recalling verbally what one has read—"to fix it in your memory." Chapone even offers herself as her niece's study partner.*

It would be a useful exercise of your memory and judgment, to recount these interesting passages to a friend, either by letter or in conversation; not in the words of the author, but in your own natural style—by memory, and not by book; and to add whatever remarks may occur to you. I need not say that you will please me much, whenever you are disposed to make this use of *me*.

The want of memory is a great discouragement in historical pursuits, and is what every body complains of. Many artificial helps have been invented, of which, those who have tried them can best tell you the effects: but the most natural and pleasant expedient is that of conversation with a friend, who is acquainted with the history which you are reading. By such conversations, you will find out how much is usually retained of what is read, and you will learn to select those characters and facts which are best worth preserving: for, it is by trying to remember every thing without distinction, that young people are so apt to lose every trace of what they read. By repeating to your friend what you can recollect, you will fix it in your memory.

Source: Hester Chapone, "On the Manner and Course of Reading History," in *Letters On the Improvement of the Mind, Addressed to a Young Lady,* new ed. (London: J. Walter and E. and C. Dilly, 1777), pp. 211-212.

Although her friend Montagu brought her offers to serve as a governess, Chapone declined them, deciding instead to see how well she could do with her writing. In 1770, with Montagu's encouragement, Chapone decided to publish the letters of advice about the education of girls that she had been sending to her niece Jane during the previous five years. Montagu volunteered to be her editor, and Chapone spent the next three years rewriting and revising *Letters on the Improvement of the Mind,* which she dedicated to Montagu. It was a great success, but because she had turned over the copyright to the publisher for just £50, she made little profit from the work. Chapone did better financially with *Miscellanies in Prose and Verse* (1775), which was dedicated to Elizabeth Carter. It was followed with *Letter to a New-Married Lady* (1777), which was later included in a subsequent edition of *Miscellanies.* Chapone continued to write, but she no longer attempted to augment her income by publishing her work.

During the next two decades, however, Chapone continued to attend the Bluestocking assemblies, and sometimes she would entertain them more modestly. She also exerted her considerable influence in the literary world by supporting other women writers. As late as 1789, she was still able to write a well-crafted poem, in which she urged Charlotte Smith and William Bowles to write less depressing sonnets.

During her final years, Chapone lived with her youngest niece in a rented house in Hadley, Middlesex. In 1799, when she was seventy-two years old, she had to admit that her memory had become untrustworthy, making it impossible for her to continue even with her correspondence. She died in Hadley on December 25, 1801. In 1807, her family published *The Posthumous Works of Mrs. Chapone,* consisting mostly of letters, including the series on filial obedience that had been sent to Samuel Richardson. The first collection of her works appeared that same year.

SIGNIFICANCE

As one of the early Bluestockings, Hester Chapone demonstrated to men of letters and to aristocrats of an intellectual bent that an educated woman could hold her own in rational discourse. Her intellectual brilliance, combined with her sparkling personality, made her an ideal advocate for women's rights. She was able to convince some of the most conservative members of a patriarchal society that a young woman should have at least the right of refusal when a father had chosen her future husband. In addition, both by her words and by her example, Chapone persuaded that same society that proper self-education would make women better wives and more devout Christians.

Chapone's works are read by scholars mostly. Her poetic abilities and her deft touch with the essay form made it clear to her contemporaries, however, that women could be writers, and writers on a par with men. She prepared the way for the next generation of Bluestockings, who would not hesitate to devote their lives to literature.

—*Rosemary M. Canfield Reisman*

FURTHER READING

Binhammer, Katherine, and Jeanne Wood. *Women and Literary History: "For There She Was."* Newark: University of Delaware Press, 2003. Essays on the way literary history has dealt with women's writing. Important background material for any study of the Bluestockings.

Chapone, Hester. *Letters on the Improvement of the Mind.* 1773. Reprint. Brookfield, Vt.: William Pickering, 1996. Volume 2 of the Female Education in the Age of Enlightenment series, this is a reprint of Chapone's classic work.

Myers, Sylvia Harcstark. *The Bluestocking Circle: Women, Friendship, and the Life of the Mind in Eighteenth-Century England.* Oxford, England: Clarendon Press, 1990. Chapone is one of four early Bluestockings on whom this book focuses. By proceeding chronologically and interweaving their life stories, the author explains their interconnectedness as well as their differences. Illustrated.

Pohl, Nicole, and Betty A. Schellenberg, eds. *Reconsidering the Bluestockings.* San Marino, Calif.: Huntington Library, 2003. This useful volume contains an introductory historiography of the Bluestockings, biographical sketches, a number of essays, a bibliography, and an index.

Wilson, Mona. *These Were Muses.* Port Washington, N.Y.: Kennikat Press, 1970. Chapone is discussed in the chapter "An Unaffected Blue-Stocking" in this lively, illustrated book.

Zuk, Rhoda, ed. *Catherine Talbot and Hester Chapone.* Vol. 3 in *Bluestocking Feminism: Writings of the Bluestocking Circle, 1738-1785.* Edited by Gary Kelly. London: Pickering and Chatto, 1999. Includes Chapone's "Letters on Filial Obedience," "A Matrimonial Creed," "A Letter to a New-Married Lady," and five of her published poems. The section on Chapone's life contains a general introduction, bibliography, and chronology, as well as comments and notes on each of her included works.

See also: James Boswell; Fanny Burney; Samuel Johnson; Sophie von La Roche; Mary de la Rivière Manley; Mary Wortley Montagu; Hannah More; Samuel Richardson; Anna Seward; Mary Wollstonecraft.

Related articles in *Great Events from History: The Eighteenth Century, 1701-1800:* 1746-1755: Johnson Creates the First Modern English Dictionary; March 20, 1750-March 14, 1752: Johnson Issues *The Rambler*; 1792: Wollstonecraft Publishes *A Vindication of the Rights of Woman.*

JEAN-SIMÉON CHARDIN
French painter

Perhaps the greatest French painter of the eighteenth century, Chardin drew his inspiration from the Dutch masters and the simple world of the Paris bourgeoisie that he knew so well. Yet he was not celebrated only as a genre painter—a painter of daily life. Many of the techniques that he employed both in his oils and in his pastels would be adopted and developed by generations of painters.

Born: November 2, 1699; Paris, France
Died: December 6, 1779; Paris, France
Also known as: Jean-Baptiste-Siméon Chardin (full name)
Area of achievement: Art

EARLY LIFE

Jean-Siméon Chardin (zhahn see-may-ohn shawr-dan) was the eldest surviving son of Jean and Jeanne Françoise David Chardin. He was baptized at the church of Saint Sulpice the following day, and he lived his entire life in the neighborhood of Saint-Germain-des-Près. His father was a master cabinet maker whose specialty was billiard tables, and one of his patrons was the king of France. Anxious to provide each of his children with a proper livelihood, the elder Chardin tried to persuade his namesake to train to take his place, but Jean would have none of it. His first love was art.

With reluctance Jean's father agreed to his son's choice of a career, but he did not understand the importance of the course of study pursued by aspiring artists. Without being consulted, young Jean was sent in 1718 to study with Pierre-Jacques Cazes, who was a professor at the Royal Academy but in all respects an inferior teacher. Cazes was so poor that he could not afford to hire models; instead, his students were forced to copy his sketches. Luckily, two years later, Chardin was able to leave the studio of Cazes to become the assistant of Noël-Nicolas Coypel, from whom he learned to paint directly from nature. There was always a refreshing spontaneity in Chardin's art, a quality not often found in the work of many of his contemporaries, who usually painted from sketches.

In 1723, Chardin fell in love with Marguerite Saintard, a young woman whose family included prosperous lawyers and minor government officials; against all odds, she accepted his proposal of marriage. The contract was drawn up that same year, and the elder Chardin, conscious that his family would soon improve its social status, once again took charge of his son's life. Without his knowledge or permission, the aspiring young painter's name was submitted for membership in the Academy of St. Luke in 1724. More a guild than an assembly of artists, this once-proud organization was the refuge of men whose talents placed them in the second rank. While his father's action was the result of ignorance of the hierarchy of the arts, Chardin was faced with the difficult task of bringing his talents to the attention of those who could advance his career.

Each summer, during the morning hours of Corpus Christi Day, young artists who were not members of the Royal Academy were allowed to exhibit their works in the Place Dauphine. On June 20, 1728, Chardin showed a number of his paintings, all of them in the lowest category sanctioned by the academy. Since he had little formal education or training, he might not aspire to paint historical or religious subjects, but he could perfect his mastery of the still life. His bid for recognition was successful; on September 25, 1728, he was admitted to membership in the Royal Academy as a painter skilled in animals and fruits. The following year, he resigned from the Academy of St. Luke.

LIFE'S WORK

Despite his admission to the Royal Academy at the lowest level of membership, Jean-Siméon Chardin was a loyal member until his death. Although he failed in his attempt to gain an assistant professorship, he considered the academy to be extremely valuable as a teaching institution for the training of young artists. He regularly attended its meetings and exhibited at its salons. By the time of his marriage in February, 1731, to Marguerite Saintard, Chardin was already popular with critics and the public alike for his still lifes, which sold for modest prices but were always in demand. Some even called him the French Rembrandt. Yet it was his technique that set him apart from his contemporaries and earned for him his special niche in the history of art.

From the study of the works of the Dutch and Flemish masters, which were available in numerous engravings, Chardin developed the same fascination for the effects of light on objects in nature that made the work of the Dutch painter Jan Vermeer so exciting. Some even mistook

Chardin's works for those of a Flemish painter. As he began to paint genre canvases, he often borrowed themes and compositions familiar in the works of the northern painters, but he achieved a freshness and originality that gave his work a special character. Always true to nature, Chardin nevertheless painted objects and figures according to his special vision. He rearranged his subjects to suit his exploration of the mysteries of light. Chardin placed his paints on canvas in a manner unlike any other artist of his day. Often he applied them rather thickly and blended his colors into one another with a subtlety that made it difficult to discern the subject of a painting when viewed at close range. When regarded at a distance, however, the various elements of his composition were easily recognizable.

Chardin's father died in the summer of 1731, and on November 18 of that year, Chardin's son Pierre-Jean was born. Two years later, on August 3, daughter Marguerite-Agnes was baptized. As his family grew, so did Chardin's reputation. The French ambassador to Spain commissioned two paintings, and in June, 1734, sixteen of his works were exhibited at the Exposition of Young Artists. His personal life, like one of his canvases, was a mixture of light and shadow. In April, 1735, at the age of thirty-eight, Marguerite Saintard Chardin died after a long illness. It is interesting to note that no painting bears the date 1735, a year of grief for Chardin, who always sought to reassure his public of the basic goodness of human existence through his art. By 1737, when he exhibited eight paintings at the salon of the Royal Academy, he had lost his daughter also. Some of his personal loss must have been assuaged by his professional success; his works were now appearing in engravings, and the circle of his admirers was growing ever wider.

He had no rival in the area of still life, but in the realm of genre painting there were several artists whose works were widely respected. To compete with them for the public's attention, Chardin had to develop a new approach to this category of art. Working with a rather narrow palette of soft and muted tones, he created works in which the composition was the central theme and the actual subject matter often secondary. These were works that appealed to artists, to connoisseurs such as the king of Prussia, the queen of Sweden, and King Louis XV of France, who obtained two Chardin canvases in 1740 for his collection. Because he devoted so much effort to perfecting a composition, Chardin often copied his earlier paintings at the request of patrons, giving him a lucrative and steady source of income for a man who only worked on one painting at a time. Since he was dealing with a familiar composition, he could work faster than normal.

Within the structure of the Royal Academy, Chardin's activities increased as his reputation grew. He was appointed in 1739 to a committee responsible for keeping accounts and assessing taxes. His expertise in finance eventually led to his appointment as the first treasurer of the Royal Academy in 1755. He was promoted in 1743 to the post of adviser to the Royal Academy of Painting and Sculpture. Five years later, Chardin served on a committee to examine the pictures at the academy salon. His diligent service, broken only by a six-month illness in 1742, earned for him the recommendation of an annual grant, in 1752, and living quarters in the Louvre, in 1757. Just as his professional life reached this zenith, his private life was filled with trouble and tragedy.

A modest inheritance passed to Chardin at his mother's death in 1743, which enabled him to marry, on November 26, 1744, Françoise Marguerite Pouget, a wealthy widow. The following October, their daughter Angélique-Françoise was born, and the Chardins settled down to a comfortable life. Chardin also took pride in the progress of his son Pierre-Jean, who showed a remarkable talent for painting. Pierre-Jean received all the advantages and opportunities that had been denied his father. In April, 1754, while studying to be a painter of historical subjects, the highest level of achievement in the Royal Academy, he was allowed to compete for the academy's grand prize, which he won in August. Three more years of work with the best teachers earned for Pierre-Jean Chardin the chance to study at the French Academy in Rome. He left Paris in December, 1757, and died in Venice ten years later under mysterious circumstances. During that stormy decade, he wasted his opportunities, caused a scandal among the members of the French community in Rome with his outrageous behavior, was captured briefly by pirates in 1762, and publicly accused his father of cheating him out of his inheritance.

From scenes of domestic life, Chardin turned to portraits, but they were not well received by the critics; at the end of his career, he therefore returned to the still life. In 1755, he had taken charge of hanging the pictures at the annual academy salon for a friend who was ill; the task was awarded to Chardin permanently in 1761. It was a duty he enjoyed, and one that gave him great power over his fellow artists. A painter's reputation could be enhanced or damaged by the placement of his works at the salon. Chardin became well known for his fairness and tact. As the years passed, Chardin continued to paint and to attend faithfully to his duties at the academy, but in-

creasingly the critics relegated him to the past, a pleasant old anachronism. They were wrong. At the very end of his life, Chardin discovered another area of artistic endeavor, the pastel. When his first pastel portraits appeared in the salon of 1771, they caused a sensation. Suffering from gallstones and plagued with failing eyesight, he continued to work until his death from edema on December 6, 1779.

SIGNIFICANCE

The art of Jean-Siméon Chardin moved through a few phases: from his mastery of the still life as a young man, to the charming pictures of domestic harmony and the artistically correct portraits of his mature years, and finally to the sensitive pastels at the end of his life. Yet the subjects that consumed six decades of creativity are unimportant when compared to the techniques that Chardin developed. Often he regretted that he had not received the training provided by the Royal Academy; yet that omission allowed him to explore the full measure of his media and to maintain his creativity in the face of the potentially stifling rules and regulations of the academy.

Chardin was inspired by the art of the Netherlands, by the subject matter, by the palette, and by the techniques of the Dutch and Flemish masters. He was particularly fascinated by the effects of light on nature. The object, whether animate or inanimate, was of little importance to Chardin; it was the light and the shadow that motivated him. In nearly every canvas he painted, Chardin dealt with his fascination with light and the problems it might cause the artist. He painted objects as they appeared to him, not as they necessarily were. Chardin sought to portray the essence of his subjects, not their reality. In this respect, he was the precursor of Impressionism. Many of his contemporaries did not understand or appreciate his art; it remained for their children's children to rediscover Chardin's fresh and original approach to the painter's craft.

Genre painting, the celebration of the simple life, had long enjoyed a popularity among all classes, but especially the bourgeoisie. Too often, however, scenes of domestic life possessed a cloying charm. Chardin gave genre painting dignity. He seemed to prefer the most commonplace subjects, but he gave them a timelessness by carefully divorcing them from contemporary events or definite fashions. The men, women, and children who people his canvases are more symbols than personalities. They are suspended in time and space, captives of the same light that held Chardin spellbound. He was not a revolutionary; his celebration of bourgeois life was not political in its intent. He simply painted what was readily at hand. His muted colors and delicate contrasts were the palette of one who adored the subtle loveliness that lay all around him, but particularly in simple things. For more than fifty years, Chardin was a member of the Royal Academy, for nineteen its treasurer. In the last analysis, however, he was the servant of beauty.

—*Clifton W. Potter, Jr.*

FURTHER READING

Chikamatsu, Colin B., Philip Conisbee, and Thomas W. Gaehtgens. *The Age of Watteau, Chardin, and Fragonard: Masterpieces of French Genre Painting.* New Haven, Conn.: Yale University Press, 2003. Catalog of an exhibition of 113 paintings that were first displayed at the National Gallery of Canada in 2003. Includes essays that explore the development of genre painting and examine paintings by Chardin and other eighteenth century French artists.

Conisbee, Philip. *Chardin.* Lewisburg, Pa.: Bucknell University Press, 1986. Perhaps the most complete treatment of Chardin and his contribution to the art of painting in eighteenth century France. The quality of the plates is quite good, and in a number of cases the reader is able to examine specific details of some of Chardin's more important works.

De la Mare, Walter. *Chardin, 1699-1779.* New York: Pitman, 1950. While only ten of Chardin's most famous domestic scenes are featured in this slender volume, it is nevertheless of interest because of the excellent essay and notes by de la Mare. The whole work is not merely informative; it is beautifully written as well. One of the best introductions to Chardin and his work.

Furst, Herbert E. A. *Chardin.* London: Methuen, 1911. While the style of this work is dated, this volume is an excellent treatment of the life and work of Chardin. The author obviously has a great admiration for Chardin, not only as an artist but also as a man; it is this quality of sensitivity that makes this book worthwhile.

Kalnein, Wend Graf, and Michael Levey. *Art and Architecture of the Eighteenth Century in France.* Harmondsworth, England: Penguin Books, 1972. Very useful as an introduction to the main events in the painter's life as well as to the elements of his style. More important, Chardin is placed in the context of his time, and his contemporaries in all the arts are given the same thorough and scholarly treatment.

Roberts, Warren. *Morality and Social Class in Eighteenth-Century French Literature and Painting.* Toronto, Ont.: University of Toronto Press, 1974. Chardin's works are examined in the light of the society in which they were produced. Roberts views Chardin's representations of bourgeois domestic life as the antithesis of the bedroom art that was so popular among some members of the French aristocracy. Chardin is viewed not as a political revolutionary but as the perfect representative of his class.

Roland Michel, Marianne. *Chardin.* Translated by Eithne McCarthy. New York: Abrams, 1996. A thorough biography by a French art historian and gallery director, including updated information about Chardin's life and paintings. Contains almost 300 illustrations.

Rosenberg, Pierre. *Chardin, 1699-1779.* Translated by Emilie P. Kadish and Ursula Korneitchouk. Cleveland, Ohio: Cleveland Museum of Art, 1979. Although this work is essentially a catalog of a remarkable exhibit of Chardin's works, it contains a tremendous amount of biographical and historical data useful to the student of the period. Each of the artist's works is described. Contains notes and a bibliography for each work. The general bibliography is also extremely valuable.

Schwarz, Michael. *The Age of the Rococo.* Translated by Gerald Onn. New York: Praeger, 1971. This remarkably well-translated version of an earlier German work is extremely valuable because it examines the various types of painting that flourished in the eighteenth century, not only in France but also throughout Western Europe. The treatment of Chardin and his work is balanced.

Wildenstein, Georges. *Chardin.* Translated by Stuart Gilbert. Rev. ed. Greenwich, Conn.: New York Graphic Society, 1969. The essay that begins this revised edition of Wildenstein's 1933 work is an excellent introduction to the life and work of Chardin. Also useful are the chronology that precedes the superb collection of plates—both in color and in black and white—and the catalog of Chardin's work, which is divided according to subject.

See also: Canaletto; Jean-Honoré Fragonard; William Hogarth; Louis XV; Antoine Watteau.

Related article in *Great Events from History: The Eighteenth Century, 1701-1800:* December 10, 1768: Britain's Royal Academy of Arts Is Founded.

CHARLES III
King of the Two Sicilies (r. 1734-1759) and king of Spain (r. 1759-1788)

Charles III's Bourbon Reforms rejuvenated the economic and political administration of Spain and its colonies. While upholding the doctrine of political absolutism, these reforms promoted Enlightenment ideals of humanitarianism, rationalism, and secularism in Spanish government and culture. As a consequence, Charles became the most successful of Europe's "enlightened despots."

Born: January 20, 1716; Madrid, Spain
Died: December 14, 1788; Madrid, Spain
Also known as: Charles VII; Don Carlos de Bourbon
Area of achievement: Government and politics

EARLY LIFE

Charles III was born in Madrid, Spain, on January 20, 1716, the first son of Phillip V of Spain and Elizabeth Farnese of Parma. He was born into Spain's Bourbon Dynasty, which was founded in 1700 by his father, who was the grandson of Louis XIV (r. 1643-1715), the great French Bourbon king. Phillip's accession to the throne was secured and legitimated by the War of the Spanish Succession (1701-1714). Charles's mother was very ambitious for her son, but her hopes for his accession to the Spanish throne seemed blocked by the aspirations of her older stepchildren, Louis and Ferdinand VI. As it happened, however, Louis died at a relatively young age, and Phillip and Ferdinand were both afflicted by melancholia, providing an opening for Charles eventually to emerge as king of Spain.

Charles's preparation for the Spanish monarchy began early. In October, 1731, he became duke of Parma and Piacenza, and in 1734 he became Charles IV, king of the Two Sicilies. In 1736, he married Maria Amalia of Saxony, niece of the Holy Roman Emperor. As monarch of the kingdom of the Two Sicilies, Charles imposed political absolutism on a very violent and contentious society, and he relied heavily on astute advisers to train him in the art of statecraft. His reign was characterized by a remarkable public building program, Enlightenment values, and subordination of the church to the state.

LIFE'S WORK

In August, 1759, Ferdinand VI of Spain died; Charles resigned as king of the Two Sicilies in favor of his third son, Ferdinand, and left for Spain to become Charles III. He was well received by the Spanish people, but this festive mood was dimmed by the death of Maria Amalia.

Charles never remarried. At this moment in life, he appeared homely and small in stature, colorless in personality, yet a man of considerable intelligence and devotion to duty and family. He reflected a curious blend of devout Roman Catholic faith and Enlightenment rationalism. He read extensively in history and economics, and he exhibited a deep passion for hunting and other sports.

Charles was appalled by Spain's political, economic, and cultural backwardness, and he resolved to restore his country to its former glory. He quickly initiated a road construction program to promote better communication within the country and a stronger national economy. He also built irrigation canals to help increase the amount of land under cultivation, and he erected numerous public buildings in Spain's urban centers.

Even so, Charles's popularity never extended to the rest of his government, which was dominated by Italian ministers. This was an unfortunate mistake on Charles's part, because he himself had not been in Spain since 1731 and was largely uninformed about the country and its people. His inattention to the attitudes of his subjects resulted in a number of unwise decrees that led to the Madrid Riot of March 23, 1766. This upheaval compelled the king to replace his Italian foreign advisers with talented and reform-minded Spaniards such as the conde de Aranda, the conde de Floridablanca, the conde de Campomanes, and Gaspar Melchor de Jovellanos. As a group, they reinforced Charles's notions of political absolutism, colonial and economic reform, and subordination of church and nobility to the state.

Charles's early efforts to restore Spanish pride and power were not completely successful. In 1761, he joined the Family Compact with France to prevent England's victory over France and its hegemony in the New World and Europe. In 1762, Charles formally entered the Seven Years' War (1756-1763) and experienced disastrous reverses in the Caribbean and the Philippines. During the Paris peace negotiations of 1762-1763, France ceded the western half of Louisiana to Spain, but Charles had to relinquish the Floridas to England in order to regain Havana. He also managed to regain Manila.

In spite of this debacle, Charles reaffirmed his commitment to the Family Compact over the next two decades. By 1770, he was forced to concede British dominion over the Falkland Islands. During the American Revolution, he joined France in supporting the rebels in order to weaken and embarrass England. In 1779,

Charles offered to mediate the dispute, but England's refusal led him to declare war and intervene militarily on the rebel side. The French-Spanish intervention proved decisive. Although a massive Spanish assault on Gibraltar was repulsed, Spain won a series of victories in North America and kept constant pressure on British military forces. In 1782, Spain captured Minorca. In 1783, Charles allowed the Family Compact to lapse, and in the Treaty of Paris (1783) he received the Floridas and Minorca and secured a British pledge to leave Honduras.

One primary goal behind Charles's diplomatic and military policies was to protect New Spain's (Mexico's) silver district in the north-central plateau. In order to secure this objective, Charles's advisers proposed that a series of buffer zones be established between the silver district and Spain's enemies, namely the Americans, British, and Russians. Consequently, Texas, New Mexico, and Louisiana were envisioned as buffers that would contain the British and Americans east of the Mississippi River and behind the Great Lakes, and, in 1769, the Spanish occupied California so it could serve as a buffer against the Russians heading southward from Alaska.

Charles also instituted a series of political, economic, and military reforms that are collectively known as the Bourbon Reforms. In 1767, Spain retrenched the fortifications of the northern frontier of New Spain to more defensible locations. This realignment of presidios would save the king some eighty thousand pesos annually.

Charles revived the captain-generalcy as an administrative unit and applied it to Cuba (including the Floridas and Louisiana), Guatemala, Chile, and Venezuela; he also established the Viceroyalty of La Plata (Buenos Aires) in 1776. Most important of these administrative reforms was the introduction of the intendant system, which streamlined imperial administration, made it more efficient, and eliminated graft and corruption. The intendants assumed responsibility for finances, justice, war, and administration and proved to be very successful in meeting their objectives.

In economic reforms, Charles sought to open trade within the empire while denying it as much as possible to foreigners. He broke the Cádiz monopoly on colonial trade and allowed other Spanish ports to participate in it. Restrictions on internal trade were relaxed, as were trading relations between the colonies and the mother country. Charles abandoned the obsolete flota system of colonial trade in favor of individual registered ships sailing from colonial ports to Spain. By freeing the internal economic system of the empire, Charles succeeded in increasing intercolonial trade and promoted a rising middle class in the colonies and Spain. In general, however, these reforms did not take hold in Spain itself because of internal opposition, war, lack of an industrial base, and competition from other European economic powers.

The Bourbon Reforms were directed at internal Spanish problems, many of which related to the Church. Just as in the Two Sicilies, Charles had become concerned by the concentration of economic and political power in the Church, and he and his officials resolved to make it subordinate to the will of the monarchy. Charles systematically struck at the Church. For example, he decreed that no papal bull would be published without the prior consent of the government. He curbed the activities of the Holy Council of the Inquisition, and he expelled the Society of Jesus (Jesuits) from Spain and its colonies in March or April, 1767. Charles's motivations in the latter action have never been clearly presented. He apparently resented the society's popularity among the Spanish people, and he resented its refusal to subordinate itself to the king. Moreover, he suspected that the Jesuits had been behind the Madrid Riot of 1766.

SIGNIFICANCE

On December 14, 1788, following two days of high fever, Charles III died in Madrid, leaving Spain in a far better position than it had been before his reign. Spain seemed well on its way toward political and economic recovery. The monarchy was stronger than ever before, and the privileges and power of the clergy had been contained. Prosperity was general throughout the land, and education flourished. Madrid had become a cleaner and more livable city, and the nation's road system had tied the country closer together than ever before. Moreover, Spain's cultural life had been deeply influenced by the Enlightenment. Yet this reform program did not long survive Charles, because his successors were not equal to the standards he had set for the monarchy and nation. Consequently, despite Charles's reign, Spain continued its slide into the nineteenth century.

—*Stephen P. Sayles*

FURTHER READING

Durant, Will, and Ariel Durant. *Rousseau and Revolution*. New York: Simon & Schuster, 1967. Although occupying a small portion of the volume, there is a fine and illuminating account of Charles's life and career. It reveals his character, personality, and cultural contributions to the Spanish Enlightenment.

Gibson, Charles. *Spain in America*. New York: Harper & Row, 1966. A fine overview of Spanish imperial policy with a good but brief section on Charles and the Bourbon Reforms. Oriented toward the nonspecialist.

Herr, Richard. *The Eighteenth Century Revolution in Spain*. Princeton, N.J.: Princeton University Press, 1958. An excellent look at the intellectual revolution that occurred in Spain under the Bourbons, especially Charles's reign. Determines that the origins of Spanish liberalism date from Bourbon rule and emphasizes the role of France in Spain's intellectual upheaval.

Hull, Anthony H. *Charles III and the Revival of Spain*. Washington, D.C.: University Press of America, 1980. Examines Charles's life and reign.

Petrie, Sir Charles. *King Charles III of Spain: An Enlightened Despot*. New York: John Day, 1971. The best biography of Charles; a very positive view of his life and career with extensive information on his early years.

Stein, Stanley J., and Barbara H. Stein. *Apogee of Empire: Spain and New Spain in the Age of Charles III, 1759-1789*. Baltimore: Johns Hopkins University Press, 2003. Examines Charles's attempts to reform Spain's political, economic, and social institutions and to modernize Spain's relationship with its colonies. Concludes that Charles's efforts ultimately failed, and Spain was ill prepared for future upheaval in Europe and its colonies.

See also: José de Gálvez; Philip V.

Related articles in *Great Events from History: The Eighteenth Century, 1701-1800*: May 26, 1701-September 7, 1714: War of the Spanish Succession; January 24, 1744-August 31, 1829: Dagohoy Rebellion in the Philippines; 1759: Charles III Gains the Spanish Throne; January 19, 1759-August 16, 1773: Suppression of the Jesuits; 1775: Spanish-Algerine War; 1776: Foundation of the Viceroyalty of La Plata; June 21, 1779-February 7, 1783: Siege of Gibraltar; 1780-1781: Rebellion of Tupac Amaru II; 1786: Discovery of the Mayan Ruins at Palenque.

CHARLES VI
Holy Roman Emperor and archduke of Austria (r. 1711-1740)

Much of Charles's reign was devoted to ensuring the survival of the Austrian Habsburg empire. To that end, he issued the Pragmatic Sanction in 1713 and then focused his efforts on persuading other European rulers to accept that document. He also expanded his imperial territory in the Netherlands and Italy.

Born: October 1, 1685; Vienna, Austria
Died: October 20, 1740; Vienna, Austria
Also known as: Karl VI; Charles III, king of Spain; Charles II, king of Bohemia
Area of achievement: Government and politics

EARLY LIFE
Charles VI, German emperor and archduke of Austria from 1711 until his death in 1740, was named after Karl Borromäus, archbishop of Milan, an important leader in the Catholic Counter-Reformation. He was the second son of Leopold I, the Habsburg archduke and Holy Roman Emperor (r. 1658-1705). His mother was Eleonore Magadalena (1655-1720), the daughter of Count Philipp Wilhelm of Pfalz-Neuburg, a member of the Wittelsbach family. Charles's mother was a pious member of a lay order of noble women devoted to the memory of Mary. His godfather was King Charles II of Spain (r. 1665-1700).

Seven years younger than his brother Joseph (1678-1711), Charles was Leopold's favorite son. Like his father, he took Communion often, and he loved music. Charles was more reserved and less decisive than his brother, nor was he as devoted to wine and women. Charles was a slim boy with dark brown hair who inherited the typical Habsburg lower lip and elongated face. Later in life, the envoy to the Viennese court from Savoy described Charles as ugly with an unmajestic walk. As early as age fourteen, he exhibited a devotion to formal ceremony, when he insisted that the Bavarian envoy to Vienna could not cover his head in his presence.

Charles received a carefully planned education, influenced by his mother, who had a close relationship with her second son. In contrast to his brother, he was educated by Jesuits. His education was supervised by Anton Florian, count of Liechtenstein, who instilled in Charles a belief that he was selected by God to rule Christian people. Charles also studied Latin, Italian, French, and Spanish, and later in life he learned Catalonian and Hungarian. At court, he favored formal Latin and Italian, although in private he used a Viennese dialect. He was never very interested in the philosophical debates of his time.

LIFE'S WORK

When Charles was twelve years old, his father wanted to send him to his godfather Charles II in Spain who was ill and without a direct heir. However, Charles did not travel to Spain until September, 1703, three years after Charles II died and left his throne to Philip of Anjou, the grandson of the French king Louis XIV (r. 1643-1715). When Charles left the court in 1703 to seize the throne of Spain from King Philip V, his mother lamented his departure. Arriving in Portugal with twelve thousand allied troops in late 1704, Charles began his lifelong effort to secure the future of the House of Habsburg, first in Spain and then in the Austrian Empire.

With the support of the English fleet, Charles entered Barcelona in November, 1705, and in 1706 his allies captured Madrid and proclaimed Charles king Charles III of Spain. The next year, however, Charles had to retreat to Catalonia, where he found popular support. In Barcelona, Charles married Princess Elisabeth Christine of Brunswick-Wolfenbüttel (1691-1750) on August 1, 1708. Elisabeth, a Protestant princess who converted to Catholicism, bore a son, Leopold Johann, who died in infancy, and two daughters who reached adulthood.

Charles's efforts in Spain came to an end when Charles's brother, Holy Roman Emperor Joseph I (r. 1705-1711), died on April 17, 1711, without a male heir. Although Charles was not eager to leave Spain, he returned to Frankfurt to claim the imperial crown on December 22, 1711, as Emperor Charles VI. On May 22, 1712, he was crowned king of Hungary in Pressburg and on June 5, 1723, he was crowned king of Bohemia in Prague. In addition to relying heavily on Spanish advisers and his close friend Count Michael Johann Althann, Charles VI continued to use his brother's counselors, particularly Prince Eugene of Savoy (1663-1736), a superb military leader.

At his court in Vienna, Charles dressed in Spanish regalia, with black and red socks and shoes and a hat with a feather, and he demanded strict adherence to protocol and etiquette. He worked diligently and wrote imperial instructions in his own hand. In religious policies, he supported the resettlement of Protestants to border regions, and he put pressure on the Greek Orthodox Christians in the southeastern military districts. For entertainment he enjoyed hunting, cards, music, and the theater.

Charles refused to accept the Treaty of Utrecht in 1713, which marked the first phase of the end the War of the Spanish Succession. In the Treaties of Rastatt and Baden in 1714, Charles made peace with the Bourbons,

although he did not renounce his claim to the Spanish throne until 1725. Charles obtained the Spanish Netherlands and Italian land for the Austrian Habsburgs, but after the War of the Polish Succession (1733-1735), he lost Naples and Sicily in exchange for northern Italian lands. He was much more successful against the traditional Habsburg enemies in the southeast, the Ottoman Turks. His military commander, Eugene of Savoy, defeated the grand vizier at Peterwardein on August 5, 1716. The Habsburgs made enormous territorial gains in the southeast by the Treaty of Peterwardein on July 21, 1718. Much of that gain, however, was lost in another war with the Turks in 1736-1739.

To ensure the survival of the House of Habsburg, Charles devoted much of his reign between 1713 and 1740 to ensuring the acceptance of the Pragmatic Sanction by all the major European powers. He first announced the Pragmatic Sanction on April 19, 1713, to his officials in Vienna. This decree declared that in the event that Charles died while there was no male Habsburg heir, his daughters would succeed to the throne. In case his daughters died, the succession would go first to the daughters of Joseph I and then to the daughters of Leopold I. The second important provision of the Pragmatic Sanction was that the Habsburg possessions would no longer be divided but would all be inherited by one person.

Charles devoted the rest of his reign, particularly after his son Leopold died six months after his birth in 1716, to ensuring the viability of his decree. Charles never experienced the failure of the Pragmatic Sanction, which had technically been accepted by all major European powers but was immediately violated after Charles died on October 20, 1740, following a hunting trip and, perhaps, the consumption of poisonous mushrooms.

SIGNIFICANCE

Charles VI sacrificed territorial, economic, and strategic Habsburg interests to ensure the acceptance of the Pragmatic Sanction, while failing to prepare the military and administrative reforms necessary to make the Pragmatic Sanction an effective document. He gave up the Habsburg East Indian Trade Company in 1731 to obtain the support of England and the Netherlands. To obtain the approval of Spain, Charles exchanged Naples and Sicily for the far less desirable northern Italian territories of Parma and Piacenza. To arrange the marriage of his daughter Maria Theresa to the duke of Lorraine, he forced his son-in-law to renounce all claim to Lorraine. His alliance with Russia led to a disastrous war with the Ottoman Turks.

It would have been more prudent for Charles to have continued a policy of economic and administrative modernization. Instead, he failed to integrate his Spanish lands, and he compromised with the regional Habsburg elites. He never limited church lands, which would have provided the empire with more tax money, and he did not support the agrarian reforms advocated by his advisers. He did support commercial growth, however, and he built the ports of Trieste and Fiume and constructed roads over the Brenner and the Semmering Passes to northern Italy and the Adriatic.

Charles failed to heed the advice of Eugene of Savoy that his daughter Maria Theresa should marry the duke of Bavaria in order to reduce the danger posed by Prussia. On the positive ledger, Charles's Pragmatic Sanction ensured that the Habsburg lands would no longer be divided among various heirs but would form a unified whole, thus allowing the Habsburg empire to survive into the twentieth century.

—Johnpeter Horst Grill

FURTHER READING

Hochedlinger, Michael. *Austria's Wars of Emergence: War, State, and Society in the Habsburg Monarchy, 1683-1797*. New York: Longman, 2003. Excellent Habsburg military history from the Turkish siege of Vienna in 1683 to the Treaty of Campo Formio in 1797; includes a section on Charles VI's wars.

Hughes, Michael. *Law and Politics in Eighteenth Century Germany: The Imperial Aulic Council in the Reign of Charles VI*. Wolfeboro, N.H.: Boydell Press, 1988. Important scholarly treatment of Charles VI's policies in the Holy Roman Empire.

Ingrao, Charles W. *The Habsburg Monarchy, 1618-1815*. New York: Cambridge University Press, 1994. A chapter on the Second Habsburg empire offers the best scholarly survey of Charles VI's reign in English.

Lindsay, J. O., ed. *The Old Regime, 1713*. Vol. 7 in *The New Cambridge Modern History*. Cambridge, England: Cambridge University Press, 1966. Charles VI's reign is briefly but competently surveyed in a chapter, "The Habsburg Dominions," by C. A. Macartney.

Roberts, Penfield. *The Quest for Security*. New York: Harper & Row, 1963. Blames Charles VI's personal failures and court rivalries for his inability to compete more effectively with European rivals.

See also: Eugene of Savoy; Maria Theresa; Philip V.

Related articles in *Great Events from History: The Eighteenth Century, 1701-1800*: May 26, 1701-September 7, 1714: War of the Spanish Succession; November 20, 1710-July 21, 1718: Ottoman Wars with Russia, Venice, and Austria; April 11, 1713: Treaty of Utrecht; March 7, 1714, and September 7, 1714: Treaties of Rastatt and Baden; 1715-1737: Building of the Karlskirche; October 10, 1733-October 3, 1735: War of the Polish Succession; 1736-1739: Russo-Austrian War Against the Ottoman Empire; November 18, 1738: Treaty of Vienna; October 20, 1740: Maria Theresa Succeeds to the Austrian Throne; December 16, 1740-November 7, 1748: War of the Austrian Succession.

CHARLES XII
King of Sweden (r. 1697-1718)

As one of the greatest kings of the Vasa Dynasty, Charles XII defended Sweden and won many victories for his country during the Great Northern War against Russia, Poland, and Denmark. He brought Swedish power to a high point, but he also initiated its decline.

Born: June 17, 1682; Stockholm, Sweden
Died: November 30, 1718; Fredrikshald (now Halden), near Oslo, Norway
Also known as: Karl XII; Alexander of the North; Charles XII of Sweden; Madman of the North; Lion of the North
Area of achievement: Government and politics

EARLY LIFE

The future Charles XII was born to loving parents, the reigning Vasa king of Sweden, Charles XI, and his wife, Ulrika Eleonora, a former Danish princess. As a child, Charles was frail but physically active. He survived a case of smallpox and throughout his life loved riding and hunting. Charles also appreciated and enjoyed his formal education. While he was uncomfortable and awkward speaking Swedish, he was learned in Latin, German, and French. He liked reading biography and military history and studying religion and mathematics (which he often applied to problems of ballistics and fortifications). His heroes were Alexander the Great and Julius Caesar. As a young man, he was often wild, extravagant, irreverent, and drunken, but as king he became pious and abstemious, drinking no alcohol stronger than beer. He was always strong-willed and stubborn.

Charles was the first king of Sweden born to absolutism, and from the beginning of his reign he expanded upon the absolutist powers of the Swedish throne. Charles XI died in 1697, and a regency was established for his fifteen-year-old son and successor, but it lasted only a few months. In 1697, at age sixteen, Charles XII crowned himself king in Stockholm rather than in Uppsala, as dictated by tradition, and he omitted the traditional oath as well. His first official acts were to build and restore several palaces, setting the stage for a lavish court life, and to enlarge and modernize the Swedish military establishment (for example, by introducing flintlocks and bayonets).

LIFE'S WORK

Unquestionably, the most important event of Charles's reign was the Great Northern War (1701-1721), yet he

had little directly to do with its coming about and was one of its casualties before it was over. The war was largely caused by the dynamic and ambitious czar of Russia, Peter the Great, who was ten years Charles's senior. Mistaking the new Swedish king's youth and inexperience for ineptitude, Peter gathered to his emerging Russian Empire two of Sweden's other historic rivals, Poland and Denmark, in an initial alliance and seized an apparent moment of vulnerability to go to war with Sweden.

In the opening weeks of the war, Charles moved swiftly and decisively, catching the enemy alliance almost completely off guard and proving himself to be a military genius. He soon came to be called the Lion of the North. In 1700, with the aid of England and the Netherlands, he defeated Denmark and quickly turned to Poland. The price for Anglo-Dutch support had been a pledge of Swedish neutrality during the War of the Spanish Succession (1701-1714), in which England and the Netherlands engaged France, whose King Louis XIV was Sweden's tacit ally.

In Poland, Charles quickly defeated the Polish-Lithuanian-Saxon armies and established a position of dominance, and the defeat of the Russians at Narva at the end of 1700 caused Peter to initiate a reorganization of his forces. In 1703, however, Russian victories along the Baltic Sea led to the founding of Peter's new capital, St. Petersburg. In 1704, Charles deposed the Saxon king of Poland, Augustus II, and replaced him with Stanisław I Leszczyński, forcing Poland into a temporary alliance with Sweden and clearing the Russians from Polish territory. The mastery of Poland at this time marks an important high-water mark of Swedish power in the seventeenth and eighteenth centuries. Charles secured his rear flank in 1707 by signing a treaty with Prussia and a convention with the Holy Roman Empire to protect his earlier invasion of Saxony.

After concluding a secret alliance with the Cossack leader Ivan Stepanovich Mazepa in 1708, Charles launched an invasion of the Ukraine. Peter's military reforms bore their first fruits with the great Russian victory over the Swedes and Cossacks at Poltava in 1709. The Swedish army was destroyed, Charles and Mazepa were forced to flee to the Ottoman Empire, and Augustus was reinstated as king of Poland. The Russo-Danish-Polish-Saxon alliance was reconstructed, and, in 1710, Charles responded by forming an alliance with Turkey. The Russians were then decisively defeated in a battle at the Pruth

River in which Peter the Great was captured in 1711. Consequently, the peace that followed was dictated by the Turks, and Charles returned to the Ottoman Empire. Russia mainly lost territory in the Azov region on the Black Sea, which it had secured from Turkey in 1700.

Sultan Ahmed III and Charles had a falling-out in 1713, all Russo-Turkish hostilities ceased, and Charles was forced to return to Europe in 1714 to defend Swedish-occupied Stralsund. In 1715, the Netherlands, Britain, Prussia, Bremen, Verden, Holstein, and Hannover declared war on Sweden, and Stralsund fell to the Danes and Prussians. Charles invaded Norway in 1716, and in 1717 Peter finally failed in his attempts to secure an alliance with Louis XIV. Charles was killed in the trenches at the Siege of Fredriksten in 1718.

While as a warrior-king on campaign Charles lived a spartan, sober, and even pious existence, the Great Northern War nevertheless took a formidable toll on Sweden and its Baltic empire. With the king's continued absence from Stockholm, the absolutism of the monarchy began to erode. Because Charles remained unmarried and had no direct heir to the throne, while he was away at the war his weaker sister, Ulrika Eleonora, became the de facto head of state. The resurging power of the Swedish parliamentary forces, especially of its upper house, and the increasing demands of the prolonged war began to force change on the monarchy. In 1711-1714, while Charles was in Turkey, administrative and economic reforms were enacted in Sweden, allowing for new taxes to pay for the war in return for economic and political concessions on the part of the monarchy. Perhaps Charles believed that he could reestablish the absolute authority of the monarchy upon his return to Stockholm, but he never did return. Upon Charles's death in battle, he was succeeded to the throne by Ulrika Eleonora. She gradually lost more power to the nobility and clergy under a new constitution.

After 1715, Russian successes in Finland and the Baltic area, which eventually came to threaten Stockholm itself, and the general political and economic exhaustion resulting from a war of more than two decades finally forced Sweden to agree to an end to the hostilities. Under the Treaty of Nystadt in 1721, peace was formally declared, and Sweden lost some parts of its Baltic empire (for example, the province of Ingria, surrounding St. Petersburg, was lost to Peter the Great's newly declared Russian Empire). The Treaty of Nystadt was by no means a victor's peace. Instead, it led to better relations in the changing spectrum of Baltic and other powers in Northern Europe, culminating in Sweden's participation in the allied coalition against Napoleonic France less than a century later.

SIGNIFICANCE

Charles XII was a single-minded and ambitious absolutist ruler and a formidable soldier who neglected the real needs of his kingdom and its empire for foreign adven-

Charles XII and men fighting Moldavian soldiers. (Library of Congress)

ture and personal glory. Of the twenty-one years of his reign, he spent all but three away from Stockholm fighting in the Great Northern War. Through his military triumphs, he revitalized, for a time, the power and status of the Swedish Empire. This revitalization recalled the days of the greatest Vasa king of Sweden, Gustavus II Adolphus, and the Thirty Years' War and has caused many historians to consider Charles second in importance only to Gustavus among the ruling members of the Vasa Dynasty.

However, the Great Northern War and Peter the Great also were Charles's and the Swedish Empire's undoing. The Russian victory and the Treaty of Nystadt marked Sweden's fall and its replacement as a great power by Peter's new Russian Empire. With this treaty, the tacit French-Turkish-Swedish anti-Habsburg coalition came apart too, and Poland was reduced to little more than a Russian puppet-state on the road to partition. Last, the reign of Charles signaled the beginning of Sweden's transition from an absolute to a constitutional monarchy under the later Vasa and Bernadotte Dynasties.

—Dennis Reinhartz

FURTHER READING

Bain, R. Nisbet. *Charles XII and the Collapse of the Swedish Empire, 1682-1719*. New York: G. P. Putnam's Sons, 1895. A standard biography of Charles, presenting a detailed account of his life and times. Dwells on his military prowess and sees his ambition as his undoing and that of the Swedish Empire.

Bengtsson, Frans G. *The Life of Charles XII, King of Sweden, 1697-1718*. London: Macmillan, 1960. A more modern, but nevertheless standard, biography. Bengtsson portrays Charles in a more positive light than Bain does, but on the whole Bain's life of Charles reveals more to the reader.

Buzzi, Giancarlo. *The Life and Times of Peter the Great.* Translated by Ben Johnson. London: Hamlyn, 1968. This popular account of Charles's principal rival includes several sections on Charles and the Great Northern War. Profusely illustrated.

Englund, Peter. *The Battle That Shook Europe: Poltava and the Birth of the Russian Empire.* New York: I. B. Tauris, 2003. Military history by a Swedish historian describing the decisive battle in the Great Northern

War. Examines the impact of the war on Russia and Sweden.

Hallendorff, Carl, and Adolf Schück. *History of Sweden.* Stockholm: C. E. Fritze, 1938. This standard history of Sweden has a good chapter on Charles and puts him into perspective with the rise and fall of the Swedish Empire under the Vasa Dynasty.

Hatton, R. M. *Charles XII of Sweden.* New York: Weybright and Talley, 1968. The best biography of Charles in English. A well-researched, well-documented, well-written, and balanced study of the man, his country, and his times.

Lisk, Jill. *The Struggle for Supremacy in the Baltic, 1600-1725.* New York: Funk & Wagnalls, 1968. Follows the rise of Swedish and then Russian power in the Baltic arena in the seventeenth century through the Great Northern War and the death of Peter the Great. Includes two important chapters on Charles and the Great Northern War.

Massie, Robert K. *Peter the Great: His Life and World.* New York: Ballantine Books, 1980. A Pulitzer Prize-winning biography of Peter the Great. Thorough and well written, with information on Charles primarily in chapter 24. Charles is treated fairly and not overshadowed by Peter when they are both center stage.

Roberts, Michael. *From Oxenstierna to Charles XII: Four Studies.* New York: Cambridge University Press, 1991. Collection of four essays about Swedish history, including an essay examining the controversy surrounding the death of Charles XII.

Warner, Oliver. *The Sea and the Sword: The Baltic, 1630-1945.* New York: William Morrow, 1965. Essentially a general modern naval history of the Baltic basin. Includes a good and rather extensive chapter on Charles, Peter, and the war.

See also: Ahmed III; Peter the Great.

Related articles in *Great Events from History: The Eighteenth Century, 1701-1800*: c. 1701-1721: Great Northern War; May 26, 1701-September 7, 1714: War of the Spanish Succession; May 27, 1703: Founding of St. Petersburg; June 27, 1709: Battle of Poltava; November 20, 1710-July 21, 1718: Ottoman Wars with Russia, Venice, and Austria.

QUEEN CHARLOTTE
Queen of the United Kingdom of Great Britain and Ireland (r. 1761-1818)

Queen Charlotte essentially ruled Great Britain and Ireland when her husband, King George III, became disabled in 1810.

Born: May 19, 1744; Mirow, duchy of Mecklenburg-Strelitz (now in Germany)
Died: November 17, 1818; Surrey, England
Also known as: Charlotte Sophia (birth name); Princess Charlotte Sophia of Mecklenburg-Strelitz
Area of achievement: Government and politics

EARLY LIFE

The German-born Charlotte Sophia had an unremarkable childhood in the duchy of Mecklenburg-Strelitz, where her uncle Frederick was the duke. She was schooled essentially by her mother and a few attendants, and she had an early interest in art. Charlotte could trace direct lineage to Marguerita de Castro y Sousa, a black member of the royal family of Portugal.

Brought up in a religious household, Charlotte venerated the church. Her displays of religious respect were apparent. For example, she always removed her jewelry before taking Holy Communion. When she and King George III were installed as king and queen of England, she wore a bejeweled headpiece. The king removed his crown before taking communion, and Charlotte was about to remove her tiara when the officiating priest excused her because the tiara was intricately woven into her hair.

Charlotte was seventeen years old when she married George III, who had assumed the throne upon the death of his father, George II, on October 25, 1760. George III delayed his coronation as long as was seemly—some eleven months following his father's death—because he was madly in love with Lady Sarah Lennox and desperate to marry her. Both his mother, Augusta, and his most influential adviser, the earl of Bute, opposed this union so strongly that George finally had the earl draw up lists of eligible marriage prospects for him among the Protestant princesses of Europe.

Augusta and the earl of Bute attempted to persuade George to marry Princess Caroline of Brunswick, but George resisted. Caroline would marry someone else. The two matchmakers, beginning to despair of finding a suitable bride for the twenty-three-year-old king, set their sights on Princess Charlotte, reputed to be a shy, retiring young lady, not dazzlingly beautiful but slender, dark-eyed, and reasonably attractive.

On July 8, 1761, the Privy Council formally approved of George's wish to marry Charlotte, who had never met the king. She arrived in court on September 8, 1761, unable to speak English, and was graciously received by George. The two embarked upon a marriage that lasted for fifty-seven years.

LIFE'S WORK

Queen Charlotte delivered her first child, George IV, on August 12, 1762, attended by various courtiers and two lady attendants she had brought to England with her. Charlotte bore her first child easily, scarcely crying out during the birth according to those attending her. Between 1762 and 1783, Charlotte bore fifteen children—nine sons and six daughters—of whom all but two sons survived to maturity.

The first duty of royal wives was to produce children, preferably sons, so that the royal line could continue. In part because of her continual pregnancies, Charlotte had little direct involvement in affairs of state. George III, whose mother was intimately involved politically during her husband's reign, did not encourage Charlotte's involvement in matters of state because George resented his mother's political meddling.

Charlotte became something of a nonentity during her childbearing years. She had a jealous nature and often harbored deep suspicions that George was being unfaithful to her, although nothing has surfaced to support such suspicions. George appeared to be genuinely devoted to his wife and, although he undoubtedly had a roving eye, he is generally thought never to have been unfaithful.

Added to George's reluctance to have Charlotte involved in affairs of state was that Charlotte lived in fearful awe of the king's mother, who had an overpowering personality. Fanny Burney, the diarist who was for several years a member of the household staff at Windsor, portrayed Charlotte as being unreasonably demanding. She imposed impossible protocols on members of the court, forbidding them from coughing or sneezing in the presence of the monarchs.

A dark cloud descended over the royal palace in the spring of 1788 when the king, suffering from a progressive disease later diagnosed as porphyria, became insane for about a year, during which he experienced brief intervals of rationality. The government had never been forced to deal with such a situation and was quite at odds

Queen Charlotte. (Library of Congress)

about how to handle it. In the earliest stages of this hereditary disease, George had been hyperactive, as sufferers from porphyria often are. This hyperactivity had helped to ignite his open conflict with the American colonies.

As the king became increasingly psychotic, Charlotte had little choice but to take on some of the matters that normally fell to her husband. Following a two-year period of reasonable lucidity that lasted from 1799 until 1801, George resumed most of his formal activities, but he lapsed into insanity in 1801 and by 1804 was in a grave mental state. His inhibitions were fading rapidly as his language and actions became uncharacteristically crude and increasingly obscene.

Charlotte suffered considerable humiliation as the king lapsed into these trying periods. She had long since ceased to share her bed with George, who now seemed intent on taking a mistress, although no evidence substantiates his having done so. At the celebration of the royal couple's forty-third wedding anniversary, some of the royal ministers tried to persuade the queen to resume conjugal relations with her husband, but she was

resolute in her refusal, going so far as to post two women in her bedroom in the early evening lest George, who sometimes became obsessed with her, try to enter her room.

George, humiliated by Charlotte's behavior, moved to a separate building on the grounds of Windsor Palace, declaring that he would never have a separate bed in the residence he shared with the queen. Also, the king was going blind as a result of his porphyria. By 1810, George was sufficiently disabled by his illness that he could no longer perform even the most rudimentary responsibilities of his office. Charlotte, with the knowledge and consent of Parliament, was officially empowered to take on most of the king's official duties. She served actively as his consort until her death in 1818, which came two years before George's death.

SIGNIFICANCE

Because of King George's illness and his subsequent inability to fulfill the duties of his office, Queen Charlotte graduated from being essentially a cipher whose chief activity was childbearing to becoming an increasingly active and contributing member of the royal family. Despite the relative isolation of her first thirty-five years as queen, Charlotte, who was intelligent, emerged as a woman capable of dealing with complex problems. She faced her domestic problems squarely and was resolute in her dealings with the king. Had she been equally resolute earlier in her dealings with George's mother Augusta, the course of her life might have been different.

Charlotte has been commemorated with a group of islands named for her (the Queen Charlotte Islands off the coast of British Columbia, Canada) as well the city of Charlotte, North Carolina. Queen's College in New Jersey, now Rutgers University, was also named in her honor. Because of her exotic appearance, she was a favorite subject of artists. Sixty-four major portraits of her exist in museums throughout the world. She also inspired a special type of cream-colored earthenware that Josiah Wedgwood produced, calling it Queen's Ware. Queen's Ware pieces are simply decorated and clean in appearance.

—*R. Baird Shuman*

FURTHER READING

Carretta, Vincent. *George III and the Satirists from Hogarth to Byron.* Athens: University of Georgia Press, 1990. A study of how King George III and Queen Charlotte were portrayed in various art forms by artists seeking to satirize them.

Graham, Jenny. *The Nation, the Law, and the King: Reform Politics in England, 1789-1799*. Lanham, Md.: University Press of America, 2000. Demonstrates how a monarch's deteriorating mental state affected world politics.

Long, J. C. *George III: The Story of a Complex Man*. Boston: Little, Brown, 1960. Although dated, this volume is well written and interesting. Long reveals the complex interactions between a reigning monarch and his somewhat subdued wife, showing how these interactions necessarily changed as the monarch declined both mentally and physically.

Macalpine, Ida, and Richard Hunter. *The "Insanity" of King George III: A Classic Case of Porphyria*. St. Alban's, England: Gainsborough Press, 1966. An excellent background study for understanding the problems facing Charlotte as her husband deteriorated mentally.

Tytler, Sarah. *Six Royal Ladies of the House of Hanover*. 2d ed. London: Hutchinson, 1898. Although this resource is more than one hundred years old, the material on Queen Charlotte provides valuable reading.

See also: Fanny Burney; Caroline; Thomas Gainsborough; George II; George III; Sarah Siddons; Josiah Wedgwood.

Related articles in *Great Events from History: The Eighteenth Century, 1701-1800:* 1774: Hansard Begins Reporting Parliamentary Debates; December, 1774-February 24, 1783: First Marāthā War; April 19, 1775: Battle of Lexington and Concord; May, 1776-September 3, 1783: France Supports the American Revolution; July 4, 1776: Declaration of Independence; June 21, 1779-February 7, 1783: Siege of Gibraltar; June 2-10, 1780: Gordon Riots; 1783: Loyalists Migrate to Nova Scotia; 1790: Burke Lays the Foundations of Modern Conservatism; May-November, 1798: Irish Rebellion; July 2-August 1, 1800: Act of Union Forms the United Kingdom.

SAMUEL CHASE
American jurist

Chase is the only U.S. Supreme Court justice to have faced an impeachment trial. He was both a partisan firebrand and a Founding Father whose political and legal theory helped shape the republic.

Born: April 17, 1741; Somerset County, Maryland
Died: June 19, 1811; Baltimore, Maryland
Areas of achievement: Law, government and politics

EARLY LIFE
Samuel Chase's mother, British-born Matilda Walker Chase, died the day he was born. Three years later, the young boy moved to Baltimore with his father, Thomas Chase, a British-born Church of England clergyman. The elder Chase's profession conferred on him the status of a gentleman, but father and son seemed always beset by money worries. From his father, Chase received both a good education in the classics and an ambivalent attitude toward wealth and aristocracy.

At age eighteen, Chase left for Annapolis, Maryland, to pursue a legal career. As was the custom, he did not attend law school but rather "read" law in the offices of legal practitioners, those of Arthur Hill in Chase's case. Four years later, in 1763, he was admitted to the Maryland bar.

One year earlier, Chase had married Ann Baldwin, whose father was a bankrupt farmer. The marriage produced seven children, only four of whom survived infancy, and lasted until Ann died sometime between 1776 and 1779. This union did little to further Chase's prospects, and he had a difficult time attracting wealthy clients. For several years, his practice focused on defending debtors from their creditors. Eventually, however, he built a successful law firm in Annapolis.

Like many lawyers, Chase was attracted to politics. In 1764, he was elected to the lower house of the Maryland assembly, where he would spend two decades representing Annapolis and Ann Arundel County. By the early 1770's, he had established himself as one of the colony's most important and most controversial politicians. His leadership of demonstrations against the city of Annapolis caused the mayor to call him a "busy, restless incendiary, a ringleader of mobs, a foul-mouthed and inflaming son of discord."

LIFE'S WORK
Samuel Chase was an early and enthusiastic supporter of the revolutionary cause. In 1774, he helped organize the Sons of Liberty, a militant group that demonstrated

against British rule. The same year, Maryland sent him as a delegate to the First Continental Congress. At age thirty-three, he was one of the youngest participants at the congress, where he signed the Declaration of Independence. He again represented Maryland at the Second Continental Congress in 1775, where he served on more than thirty committees and urged colonial unity in an economic boycott of English goods.

At the same time, Chase continued to serve in the state legislature and develop his legal practice. He was one of the authors of the Maryland constitution, a document that ultimately reflected his belief that governing should be left in the hands of an elite group of property holders. Later, the ruling senate he helped design opposed him, and Chase reverted to the role of champion of the common person. In 1788, he opposed Maryland's ratification of the state constitution because at the time it lacked a bill of rights, and the opposition cost him his seat.

Chase found himself out of office and bankrupt. For many years, he had lived beyond his means, attempting to transform himself into a property holder. In 1778, in fact, he had been suspended from the Continental Con-

gress owing to accusations of war profiteering connected with an attempt to corner the flour market. Now in his forties and just married to his second wife, Hannah Kitty Giles, who would bear two daughters, Chase sought a position that would bring him both public respect and financial security: He became a judge.

Chase first served as a local judge in Baltimore County. Then, in 1791, he also became chief judge of the Maryland General Court. Objecting to this dual role and annoyed by the overbearing manner Chase displayed on the bench, certain members of the state assembly attempted to remove him from both posts. In a preview of Chase's later judicial impeachment, the vote went in his favor by the narrowest of margins.

By all accounts Chase was a larger-than-life figure. More than 6 feet tall and broadly built, he had a brownish-red complexion that caused his detractors to refer to him as Old Bacon Face. More kindly, U.S. Supreme Court justice Joseph Story compared Chase to the legendary eighteenth century English man of letters Samuel Johnson "in person, in manners, in unwieldy strength, and severity of reproof, in real tenderness of heart; and above all in intellect."

On the bench, the once ardent Republican reverted to his earlier elitist orientation, aligning himself with the Federalists, who favored a strong central government. His intense commitment to the Federalist cause was one of the reasons President George Washington nominated Chase to the Supreme Court in 1796; it also nearly proved to be his undoing. Like all Supreme Court justices in his day, Chase was obliged to perform two roles: one as an appellate judge on the highest court in the land and the other as a circuit judge who heard cases in an assigned geographical area. In two cases for which he served a judge, Chase's Federalist partisanship caused him to conduct criminal trials in a highly questionable manner.

In 1798, the Federalist Congress passed the Alien and Sedition Acts, which were meant to quell political dissent during the war then raging between Britain and France. The United States was officially neutral, but Republicans, who supported the French, feared that the administration of President John Adams favored the British. Several publishers and editors of Republican newspapers were prosecuted under the act, which made it a punishable offense to oppose the federal government in word or deed. One of these

Samuel Chase. (Library of Congress)

journalists was John Callender, who had published a book claiming that President Adams was an "alleged aristocrat" who served British interests. When Chase, along with a district judge, heard the case against Callender in the spring of 1800, he repeatedly interfered with defense counsel's attempts to present its case, seating an admittedly biased juror despite objections and refusing to allow the testimony of one of the defense witnesses.

Only months earlier, Chase had presided over the Philadelphia trial of John Fries, who was accused of treason. The question before the court was whether Fries's leadership of a tax revolt amounted to treason. Chase, however, forestalled any debate on the issue by delivering an opinion defining the crime even before the trial began. As a result, Fries's attorneys withdrew from the case, whereupon Chase declared that the court would act as Fries's advocate. Not surprisingly, Fries was found guilty and sentenced to hang.

Chase's partisanship became more pronounced as the presidential election of 1800 approached. In August of that year, the start of the Supreme Court's term had to be delayed because Chase was detained in Maryland working for Adams's reelection. Despite Chase's efforts, the Republican candidate, Thomas Jefferson, was elected. Undeterred, Chase pursued his Federalist campaign, in 1803 delivering a charge to a Baltimore grand jury in which he openly, and egregiously, criticized Republican policy. Jefferson responded by suggesting to one of the leaders of the House of Representatives that Chase be impeached.

Under Article I of the U.S. Constitution, only the House is endowed with the power to impeach for offenses that Article II outlines as "treason, bribery, or other high crimes and misdemeanors." In 1804, the House voted to impeach Chase on eight charges, the most serious of which grew out of the Fries and Callender trials and the 1803 grand jury charge. Chase's trial was held in 1805 before the Republican-controlled Senate, where the justice was so well represented and the case against him so badly managed that even some Republicans voted not to impeach. In the end, many senators—both Federalists and Republicans—came to believe that the charges against Chase were either politically motivated or not serious enough to warrant his removal from the bench. Although eighteen—all of them Republicans—of the thirty-four members of the Senate voted in favor of convicting Chase, their votes did not constitute the two-thirds extraordinary majority the Constitution requires for conviction.

By the time of Chase's acquittal, the Supreme Court was dominated by Chief Justice John Marshall, who wrote most of the Court's major opinions. It is difficult, therefore, to know just how the impeachment trial affected Chase's participation in the affairs of the national judiciary. He did, however, continue to serve on the high court until his death from heart failure in 1811.

SIGNIFICANCE

Samuel Chase's acquittal scotched any further impeachment plans the Republicans might have been entertaining in an attempt to wrest control of the judicial branch from the Federalists. It has also had long-term significance in that it established the principle that impeachment was not to be used as a political weapon. No Supreme Court justice has ever been impeached, and the two presidents faced with an impeachment trial, Andrew Johnson and William Clinton, were likewise acquitted. Those who voted against impeachment in these two cases undoubtedly saw the trials as political and perhaps also recollected the partisanship that occasioned Chase's trial.

However, Chase's legacy does not stem solely from his impeachment trial. During his early years on the Supreme Court, he clearly was the intellectual leader of the bench. Before Justice Marshall enshrined the principle of judicial review in law in the case of *Marbury v. Madison* (1803), Chase had spoken out in support of the principle, which made the Supreme Court the final authority on the constitutionality of state and federal laws. Chase also helped to establish the doctrine of substantive due process, which holds that rights not expressly laid out elsewhere in the Constitution can be justified by the due process clause found in either the Fifth or the Fourteenth Amendments.

By nature a conservative, Chase adhered to the principle of judicial restraint, which holds that the Court should customarily defer to Congress with regard to changes in legislation, and advocated a strict, literal interpretation of the words of the Constitution. It is a mark of his genius that he was able to reconcile these seeming contraries, all of which remain vital in American jurisprudence.

—*Lisa Paddock*

FURTHER READING

Burger, Warren E. *It Is So Ordered: A Constitution Unfolds*. New York: W. Morrow, 1995. A historical look at the U.S. Constitution and constitutional law, with chapters on Chase's impeachment trial and the subpoena of President Jefferson's papers by Justice Marshall. Includes an index.

Chase, Samuel. *Trial of Samuel Chase*. 1805. Reprint. New York: Da Capo Press, 1970. Chase's own legal responses to the articles of impeachment filed against him in the House of Representatives.

Elsmere, Jane Shaffer. *Justice Samuel Chase*. Muncie, Ind.: Janevar, 1980. Still the best full-length biography of the justice.

Haw, James A., et al. *Stormy Patriot: The Life of Samuel Chase*. Baltimore: Maryland Historical Society, 1980. Includes valuable information about Chase's judicial and political career in his home state.

Malone, Dumas. *Jefferson the President: First Term, 1801-1805*. Boston: Little, Brown, 1970. The fourth installment of this multivolume biography of Jefferson provides an excellent historical and political backdrop for the drama of Chase's impeachment. Includes illustrations, maps, and an extensive bibliography.

Presser, Stephen B. *The Original Misunderstanding: The English, the Americans, and the Dialectic of Federalist Jurisprudence*. Durham, N.C.: Carolina Academic Press, 1991. A history of the federal courts in the late eighteenth century, focusing on Chase's career. The author describes how law, politics, and morality in the United States drew from, and contrasted with, that of England.

Rehnquist, William H. *Grand Inquests: The Historic Impeachments of Justice Samuel Chase and President Andrew Johnson*. New York: W. Morrow, 1992. Rehnquist provides a clear and concise exploration of the historical background and legal complexities of two significant impeachment trials in U.S. history.

See also: John Adams; Charles Carroll; Thomas Jefferson; Samuel Johnson; George Washington.

Related articles in *Great Events from History: The Eighteenth Century, 1701-1800:* September 5-October 26, 1774: First Continental Congress; May 10-August 2, 1775: Second Continental Congress; July 4, 1776: Declaration of Independence; October 27, 1787-May, 1788: Publication of *The Federalist*; June 25-July 14, 1798: Alien and Sedition Acts.

MARQUISE DU CHÂTELET
French writer and scholar

Largely self-educated, du Châtelet produced the definitive French translation of Sir Isaac Newton's Principia *as well as several scientific and cultural treatises of her own.*

Born: December 17, 1706; Paris, France
Died: September 10, 1749; Lunéville, Meurthe-et-Moselle, France
Also known as: Gabrielle-Émilie du Châtelet (full name); Gabrielle-Émilie Le Tonnelier de Bretueil (birth name)
Areas of achievement: Science and technology, physics, philosophy, mathematics

EARLY LIFE

The marquise du Châtelet (mahr-keez dew shaht-leh), the daughter of Louis-Nicholas, baron de Breteuiland, and Alexandra-Elisabeth de Froulay, spent her early years learning the ways of aristocratic life in the court of Louis XIV, where her father held several lucrative positions. As a girl, she received lessons in fencing, riding, and gymnastics and discovered her intellectual gifts, as indicated by mastery of English, Italian, Spanish, Greek, and Latin and by her interests in mathematics and metaphysics.

Not particularly attractive as a child, she blossomed into a beauty by the age of sixteen, when her father introduced her at court. At this time, she also began to read the works of René Descartes and became engaged in discussions of his philosophy with professors at the Sorbonne. At the age of nineteen, she entered into a marriage of convenience to the marquis Florent-Claude du Châtelet-Lomont, a military man with whom she had nothing in common. She bore a daughter in 1726 and sons in 1727 and 1733.

As was tolerated at the time, she took on a succession of lovers, including for a time her lifelong friend, the duc de Richelieu, a noted French statesman. During the course of their yearlong affair, which began in 1730, Richelieu encouraged du Châtelet to pursue her intellectual interests. She began to work on mathematical theorems and studied advanced physics and mathematics in private tutorials with members of the Royal Academy of Sciences. She also engaged in serious efforts to translate Latin poetry into French. About 1733, she began a long affair with Voltaire, the famous philosophe. Converted to the theories of physics of Sir Isaac Newton during a trip to England, Voltaire introduced du Châtelet to two French Newtonians, Pierre Louis de Maupertuis in 1734 and Alexis-Claude Clairaut during the 1740's, both of whom became her tutors. Voltaire and du Châtelet retired to the du Châtelet estate in Cirey, with du Châtelet's husband accepting a ménage à trois. Together, Voltaire and Madame du Châtelet threw themselves into studies that made Cirey an intellectual center.

LIFE'S WORK

At Cirey, du Châtelet and Voltaire pursued a variety of subjects, on which du Châtelet wrote several unpublished manuscripts. One was a free translation of Bernard Mandeville's *The Fable of the Bees: Or, Private Vices, Public Benefits* (1714), a work on moral philosophy to which she added her own reflections and points of view. The next year, 1736, she and Voltaire worked on *Grammaire raisonée* (reasoned grammar), of which the three extant chapters written by du Châtelet contain arguments that language should be considered a branch of logic.

As biblical criticism was popular during the eighteenth century, du Châtelet and Voltaire developed an interest in critical Deism. A five-volume manuscript written by du Châtelet, *Examen de la Genèse* (examination of Genesis), provided a thorough critique of the entire Bible. Copies were circulated, though no one attributed its authorship to du Châtelet. Toward the end of her life, she wrote another manuscript, *Essai sur le bonheur* (1797; a discourse on happiness), addressed to the elite of society.

Du Châtelet published several scientific works. Through her tutors and self-study, she acquired the same knowledge of analytic geometry and differential and integral calculus as many members of the Academy of Sciences, from which women were excluded. As her knowledge of mathematics soon exceeded Voltaire's, she provided him with the mathematical information necessary for his *Eléments de la philosophie de Newton* (1736; *Elements of Sir Isaac Newton's Philosophy*, 1738).

In 1737, the Academy of Sciences announced a competition to investigate the nature of heat and fire. In order not to anger Voltaire, who had decided to enter the contest, du Châtelet secretly worked on the questions posed by the academy, though she never tested her hypothesis in the laboratory. Neither du Châtelet nor Voltaire won, but both garnered honorable mentions. Once the competition was over, du Châtelet informed Voltaire of her entry, and he arranged for the publication of her essay, *Dissertation sur la nature et la propagation du feu* (1739; essay on the nature and propagation of fire), as well as of his.

Marquise du Châtelet. (Library of Congress)

Du Châtelet's approach to physics began to diverge from Voltaire's, as she was interested in the metaphysical underpinnings of science. In 1737, she began to work on *Institutions de physique* (1740; lessons in physics), a book designed to instruct her son in Newtonian physics. At this time, she found a new tutor, Samuel König, who introduced her to the metaphysics of Gottfried Wilhelm Leibniz, largely unknown in France. Leibniz's notions of the principle of sufficient reason and the *vis viva* (living force) appealed to du Châtelet. At the same time, she approved of René Descartes's attempt to unite his metaphysics with the physics of his mechanical philosophy, though she did not accept the particulars of his philosophy, especially his reliance on God as the first cause. Critical of revealed religion, she replaced Descartes's God with Leibniz's principle of sufficient reason in the metaphysical aspect of the work and substituted Descartes's physics, including the vortices and theory of motion, with Newtonian mechanics and Leibnizian dynamics.

In 1745, du Châtelet began her translation of the third edition of Sir Isaac Newton's *Philosophiae naturalis principia mathematica* (1687; *The Mathematical Principles of Natural Philosophy*, 1729; best known as the

Principia), a project in which she was engaged until the end of her life. She consulted both the first and second editions of the work and Newton's own commentaries and abridgment, as well as a number of commentaries and specialized mathematical treatises written by French and Swiss mathematicians. In the notes to the translation, she defended her choice of words and revealed a familiarity with possible solutions.

Included in du Châtelet's translation was an "Exposition abrégée" (abridged exposition), which provided three ways to understand Newton's physics. In the first, she provided the reader with a clear understanding of the basic ideas and the logic behind Newton's physics, avoiding the technical language of science and mathematics. The second explication presented algebraic equivalents of Newton's demonstrations and included du Châtelet's solutions of some problems through calculus. Finally, she synthesized the progress made in physics since Newton's death. The result of four years of work, *Principes mathematiques de la philosophie naturelle* (1759; mathematical principles of natural philosophy) was published first in an incomplete form in 1756.

By 1748, the relationship between Voltaire and du Châtelet had become quite strained. They went to Lunéville, the court of King Stanisław I Leszczyński. There, du Châtelet met Jean François, marquis de Saint-Lambert, a man ten years younger than she. She became pregnant by him and died on September 10, 1749, a few days after giving birth to a daughter.

SIGNIFICANCE

The marquise du Châtelet's translation is still the only French translation of Newton's *Principia*. Publication of the complete version in 1759 was eagerly awaited and was instrumental in providing the French with an understanding of Newtonian physics. Du Châtelet's name was included in a list of important Newtonians in the 1779 edition of the *Encyclopédie: Ou, Dictionnaire raisonné des sciences, des arts, et des métiers* (1751-1772; *Encyclopedia*, 1965). However, the acceptance of Newtonianism was not complete in France until the end of the eighteenth century.

It is significant that du Châtelet's male contemporaries accepted her as their intellectual equal. However, modern scholars have examined her life in the context of the restrictions imposed on women by society. She herself decried the lack of educational opportunities for women. Most of her important friends were men, and it was only through her association with them that she was able to attain prominence. On the other hand, her mar-

ginalization from the professional mainstream allowed her to carve out an original philosophical position, as expressed in the *Institutions de physique*.

—*Kristen L. Zacharias*

FURTHER READING

Harth, Erica. *Cartesian Women: Versions and Subversions of Rational Discourse in the Old Regime*. Ithaca, N.Y.: Cornell University Press, 1992. Discusses the efforts of intellectual women who, excluded from participation in the new learning by the founding of the Academy of Sciences in 1666, circumvented and challenged the dominant discourse. Includes a discussion of du Châtelet's reactions to Descartes's thought and her own ideas on physics.

Hutton, Sarah. "Émilie du Châtelet's 'Institutions de physique' as a Document in the History of French Newtonianism." *Studies in the History and Philosophy of Science* 35, no. 3 (September, 2004): 515-531. Examines the development of du Châtelet's Newtonianism from 1738 to 1742 and her view that Leibniz's metaphysics was compatible with Newton's physics.

Wade, Ira O. *Voltaire and Madame du Châtelet: An Essay on the Intellectual Activity at Cirey*. Reprint. New York: Octagon Books, 1967. Exhaustive study focused on du Châtelet's critique of Genesis and its influence on Voltaire.

Zinsser, Judith P. "Émilie du Châtelet: Genius, Gender, and Intellectual Authority." In *Women Writers and the Early Modern British Political Tradition*, edited by Hilda L. Smith. New York: Cambridge University Press, 1998. A discussion of difficulties faced by du Châtelet as a result of the exclusion of women from the learned academies.

_____. "Entrepreneur of the 'Republic of Letters': Émilie de Bretenil, Marquise du Châtelet, and Bernard Mandeville's *Fable of the Bees*." *French Historical Studies* 25 (Fall, 2002): 595-624. Discussion of du Châtelet as a philosophe and as an intermediary between French and English culture.

_____. "Translating Newton's *Principia*: The Marquise du Châtelet's Revisions and Additions for a French Audience." *Notes and Records of the Royal Society of London* 55, no. 2 (May, 2001): 227-245. An evaluation of the scope of du Châtelet's efforts to translate and explain Newton's great work on physics.

See also: Maria Gaetana Agnesi; Jean le Rond d'Alembert; Étienne Bonnot de Condillac; Denis Diderot;

Joseph-Louis Lagrange; Gaspard Monge; Montesquieu; Voltaire.

Related articles in *Great Events from History: The Eighteenth Century, 1701-1800*: 1704: Newton Publishes *Optics*; 1718: Bernoulli Publishes His Calculus of Variations; 1733: De Moivre Describes the Bell-Shaped Curve; 1740: Maclaurin's Gravitational Theory; 1743-1744: D'Alembert Develops His Axioms of Motion; 1748: Agnesi Publishes *Analytical Institutions*; 1748: Euler Develops the Concept of Function; 1751-1772: Diderot Publishes the *Encyclopedia*; 1781: Kant Publishes *Critique of Pure Reason*.

CHIKAMATSU MONZAEMON
Japanese playwright

Chikamatsu wrote more than one hundred plays for the puppet and Kabuki theaters, most of them concerned with the drama and emotional life of common, ordinary people.

Born: 1653; Fukui, Echizen Province, Japan
Died: January 6, 1725; Sakai, Japan
Also known as: Sugimori Nobumori (birth name); Sōrinshi; Heiandō
Areas of achievement: Literature, theater

EARLY LIFE

Chikamatsu Monzaemon (chi-kah-mah-tzoo mohn-zah-ay-mohn) was born the second son of Sugimori Nobuyoshi, to a line of samurai who had been temporarily without government employ several generations earlier. His father served Matsudaira Tadamasa, lord of Echizen province, in Fukui until Matsudaira's death when he began to serve one of his lesser sons, which was his position when Chikamatsu was born. Chikamatsu's father was of minor samurai rank. Chikamatsu's mother was the daughter of a physician. Chikamatsu's father moved to the provincial town of Yoshie (now Sabae City) when Chikamatsu was two. Chikamatsu probably lived comfortably there for the larger part of his childhood.

When Chikamatsu was fifteen or sixteen years old (1668 or 1669), it seems his father lost employment and moved the family to Kyoto. Chikamatsu began serving Ichijō Ekan, probably soon after their arrival. After Ekan's death in 1672 he served other high-ranking officials. Given his status as the son of a lordless samurai, it is unlikely that Chikamatsu expected to advance as a samurai himself. It is more probable that he was learning the life of an intellectual, the educated class, under the tutelage of the men he served. For example, a *haikai* poem (short verse of three lines) by him was published when he was age nineteen (the earliest known record of his writing). The men he served also had interest in the puppet theater (*jōruri*), and Chikamatsu surely gained his exposure to this world through them. One of the gentleman whom he served wrote a puppet play for the master Uji Kaga-no-jō, and it is believed that by around 1677, Chikamatsu did so as well, perhaps not as an independent writer but as one who corrected plays based on what Kaga-no-jō determined needed correcting.

His father's move to Kyoto and Chikamatsu's subsequent social intercourse while he was not yet twenty with men of education who had special interests in literature, especially the puppet theater, should be seen as life-defining, providing the stimulus and opportunity for Chikamatsu to leave the samurai tradition of many generations within his family to become a playwright.

LIFE'S WORK

The first play known to have been independently penned by Chikamatsu Monzaemon was a puppet play titled *Yotsugi Soga* (the soga successors), first performed in 1683 (pb. 1896). Chikamatsu's reputation began with this well-received play of morally sanctioned revenge. The following year, Takemoto Gidayū, who would later be known as the founder of the Gidayū tradition, used this play for the opening of his first theater house, the Takemoto-za, in Osaka. Staging this play prefaced a collaboration that would prove successful for both men.

Though Chikamatsu continued to write plays for the puppet theater, for the next twenty years the greater part of his energy was devoted to composing scripts for the more showy and increasingly popular Kabuki theater, through an association with the famous Kabuki actor of the era, Sakata Tōjūrō.

The play that would truly establish Chikamatsu's reputation, however, came in 1703, when he wrote, once again for the Takemoto Theater, the wildly popular *Sonezaki shinjū* (*The Love Suicides at Sonezaki*, 1961), the oldest puppet play still performed. He would thereafter be officially employed by that theater. Moving from Kyoto to Osaka in 1706, he continued to write puppet plays for the remainder of his life. *The Love Suicides at*

Chikamatsu Monzaemon's plays were performed in Kabuki theaters such as the one depicted in this eighteenth century woodblock print. (The Granger Collection, New York)

Sonezaki, loosely based on a pair of what had been recent suicides, had such a social impact that it is said similar love suicides increased after this play. In this story, a simple, overly trusting shop clerk refuses the marriage that has been arranged for him by his family because he is in love with a courtesan. His mother, unfortunately, has already accepted the dowry for the marriage. It is money he must return, but even though he manages to find the sum, he foolishly loans it to a friend, who then claims never to have received such a loan. The extreme predicament leads the clerk and his lover to decide that suicide is their only option. The description of the two luckless lovers as they walk toward the place where they intend to kill themselves is the moving climax, and a scene still highly regarded for its emotional impact and fine language.

Chikamatsu would write other plays that focus on domestic situations, including *Meido no hikyaku* (pr. 1711; *The Courier for Hell*, 1961), his masterpiece *Shinjū ten no Amijima* (1720; *The Love Suicides at Amijima*, 1953), and *Onnagoroshi: Abura jigoku* (pr. 1721; *The Woman-*

Killer and the Hell of Oil, 1961). He wrote at least twenty-four such plays. Chikamatsu explores in all these plays the strong emotions of ordinary people, with special emphasis on betrayal, revenge, and ill-conceived love. Though not considered morality plays as Western traditions might define them, such domestic plays (*sewa-mono*) do explore the painful and contradictory imperatives that derive from desperate personal needs and the immovable, strict requirements placed upon individuals by social norms. This friction between obligation (*giri*) and human feeling (*ninjō*) was the source of suspense and impact of many Chikamatsu plays.

In addition to his domestic plays, Chikamatsu wrote more than eighty historical plays (*jidai-mono*). Though based on historic events, these plays often have current, if concealed, political relevance. His most famous is *Kokusenya kassen* (pr. 1715; *The Battles of Coxinga*, 1951). Set in the year 1644 at the dramatic fall of the Ming Dynasty, the story deeply involves the forbidden country of China. The play's exoticism, variety of dramatic events, settings, and sheer beauty of language make this his most popular play, one that ran for seventeen months after opening.

Chikamatsu's aesthetic has been described in the following manner: "the space between fiction and truth is like that between the surface of skin and flesh" (*kyojitsu himaku*). That is, truthful art should not strive for perfect realism but rather present an alteration of reality that achieves truth. Chikamatsu made special effort to achieve a high literary level for his scripts. They are replete with words that have resonance with other nearby word choices (*engo*), additional meanings derived from using homonyms (*kakekotoba*), rhyming, and careful choice in rhythm to help set off the prose passages from poems.

According to the inscription on his tombstone, Chikamatsu had a wife who died in 1734. It appears that he also had two sons. Not a great deal is known about them, though it seems one son, Tamon, painted and the other, Taemon, served as a steward for an important family. (In 1741, however, he was removed to Izumi province for causing trouble during a parade.) Chikamatsu died at the Nichiren sect Buddhist temple called Kōsai, in present-day Amagasaki City, near Osaka, at the age of seventy-two.

SIGNIFICANCE

Chikamatsu Monzaemon's reputation during his lifetime was great enough that in one commentary he was called "the guardian god of writers." His influence extended throughout the puppet and Kabuki theater worlds. His impact on puppet theater is so great that it is with his *Shusse Kagekiyo* (pr. 1686, pb. 1890; Kagekiyo the victorious) that historians demarcate between old and new puppet theater. His introduction of the lives and emotions of a merchant class man and his prostitute lover in *The Love Suicides at Sonezaki* has been recognized as the beginning of premodern drama. His approach to the relationship of fiction to fact remained a central framework for Japanese writers as they began to import and interpret European literature with the establishment of an open country in the nineteenth century.

In part because of the later ascendancy of the Kabuki theater, many of Chikamatsu's plays themselves, however, were rewritten or not performed in later years. In the twenty-first century, while Chikamatsu is firmly established as an icon in the history of Japanese literature and theater, only a few of his works remain well known.

—*John R. Wallace*

FURTHER READING

Gerstle, Andrew C., trans. *Chikamatsu: Five Late Plays.* New York: Columbia University Press, 2001. Translations of plays never before translated into English. Includes annotations by the translator.

_____. *Circles of Fantasy: Convention in the Plays of Chikamatsu.* Cambridge, Mass.: Council on East Asian Studies, Harvard University, 1986. An analysis of Chikamatsu's approach to the puppet theater.

Heine, Steven. "Tragedy and Salvation in the Floating World: Chikamatsu's Double Suicide Drama as Millenarian Discourse." *Journal of Asian Studies* 53, no. 2 (May, 1994): 367-393. Heine's article studies suicide in the context of Confucian and Buddhist teachings.

Keene, Donald, trans. *Major Plays of Chikamatsu.* New York: Columbia University Press, 1990. Keene presents translations of eleven plays, with an introduction to Chikamatsu, his plays, and his era. Originally published in 1961.

_____. *World Within Walls: Japanese Literature of the Pre-modern Era, 1600-1867.* New York: Columbia University Press, 1999. Originally published in 1978, This book presents a history of the remarkable Genroku period, during which Chikamatsu wrote his plays. Includes a new preface.

Mueller, Jacqueline. "A Chronicle of Great Peace Played Out on a Chessboard: Chikamatsu Monzaemon's *Goban Taiheiki.*" *Harvard Journal of Asiatic Studies* 46, no. 1 (June, 1986): 221-267. Mueller examines this historical play.

Shinoda, Masahiro, dir. *Double Suicide.* Videorecording. Criterion Collection, 2000. A film director's interpretation of Chikamatsu's *The Love Suicides at Amijima.* Originally released in 1969. 103 minutes, black-and-white, subtitles in English.

Shively, Donald H. *The Love Suicide at Amijima: A Study of a Japanese Domestic Tragedy by Chikamatsu Monzaemon.* Ann Arbor: University of Michigan Press, 1991. An introduction to the puppet theater and a study and translation of this play. Originally published in 1953.

See also: Cao Xueqin; Hakuin; Honda Toshiaki; Ogyū Sorai; Suzuki Harunobu; Tokugawa Yoshimune.

Related articles in *Great Events from History: The Eighteenth Century, 1701-1800:* June 20, 1703: Chikamatsu Produces *The Love Suicides at Sonezaki*; 1740-1741: Richardson's *Pamela* Establishes the Modern Novel.

ÉTIENNE FRANÇOIS DE CHOISEUL
French statesman

Choiseul was an excellent military strategist and negotiator. He was responsible for the Pacte de Famille, uniting the Bourbon rulers of Europe against England, and for the Treaty of Paris, which ended the Seven Years' War. He preserved the West Indies for France and added Lorraine and Corsica to its possessions.

Born: June 28, 1719; Nancy, France
Died: May 8, 1785; Paris, France
Also known as: Comte de Stainville; Duc de Choiseul
Areas of achievement: Government and politics, diplomacy, warfare and conquest

EARLY LIFE

Étienne François de Choiseul (ay-tyehn frahn-swah duh shwah-zuhl) was a born into an influential family of Lorraine and known early in life as the comte de Stainville. He spent his childhood in the care of nurses, tutors, and governesses, a typical existence for children of the aristocracy in the eighteenth century, as French aristocratic parents rarely spent time with their children. For such parents, it was the family name that mattered, not the individual: Children were viewed simply as heirs to the family name and fortune. It was only once they became adults and distinguished themselves by bringing honor to the family that their importance as individuals increased.

Stainville's initial choice of a career that would honor his family was in the military. Having received a traditional aristocratic education, he entered the French army as an officer. In his mid-thirties, however, he was called to diplomatic service. In 1754, Stainville was appointed ambassador to Rome and remained in the position until 1757. From 1757 to 1758, he served as ambassador to Vienna.

LIFE'S WORK

At the court of Louis XV, Stainville came to the attention of both the king and his mistress Madame de Pompadour, who had enormous influence on the king. Stainville quickly became a favorite of Pompadour and enjoyed her protection until she died in 1764. As a result of his relationship with Pompadour and Louis, Stainville received the title of duke and was henceforth known as the duke of Choiseul. He is sometimes referred to as the duke of Choiseul-Stainville. In 1758, the same year he was raised to duke, he became secretary of state for foreign affairs, and in 1761 he was made secretary of war.

At this time, France was embroiled in the Seven Years' War against England and Prussia. In 1761, Choiseul concluded the Pacte de Famille among the Bourbon rulers of France, Spain, Parma, and Naples. This treaty enabled them to resist the British navy. Great Britain's navy was far superior to any navy of the Continent. The war did not go well for France; the country suffered defeat after defeat. It finally ended in 1763 with the signing of the Treaty of Paris on February 10.

Choiseul represented France in the negotiations to end the war, and although he had to cede the French territories of Canada and the left bank of the Mississippi River to England, he managed to keep the West Indies. These islands were essential to the continuing growth of the French economy, because they provided the raw material for France's sugar trade. Nevertheless, Choiseul was bitterly angered by France's defeat and the concessions he was forced to make. Once back in France, he immediately implemented reforms in the army and navy to prevent such defeats from occurring in the future.

In 1766, Stanisław I Leszczyński, the exiled former king of Poland and Louis XV's father-in-law, died. Choiseul carried through the arrangements made by Prime Minister André-Hercule de Fleury before his death. Lorraine, which had been an independent duchy ruled by Stanisław, once again became part of France. In 1768, Choiseul further increased French territory by purchasing Corsica from Genoa.

Choiseul did not easily accept France's defeat in the Seven Years' War. He wanted revenge. Thus he formulated a plan to humiliate England. He also hoped to improve France's financial situation and to restore its glory. His plan was to cause unrest in the British colonies, to bring about a revolt against England, and eventually to annex the colonies to France. As early as 1764, he sent two agents to the colonies to determine the needs of the colonists for a revolt. The report that came back in 1767 displeased him. There was no interest in revolting with the help of a foreign power.

Choiseul later devised a plan to invade England. However, as a result of the bumbling of his agents, the plan's existence was used by Charles d'Éon de Beaumont, chevalier d'Éon, to blackmail Louis XV. A dreadful scandal resulted, just at the moment the comtesse du Barry and her faction were working to discredit Choiseul with the king.

Choiseul was unable to quell the political unrest within France. The *parlements*, largely dominated by allies of the Jansenists, were constantly opposing the king. The

Jansenists and the Gallicans were once again vocally at odds with the Jesuits. The philosophes were at odds with the Jesuits. It happened that a member of the Jesuit order was implicated in a bankruptcy. The Parlement of Paris used this incident to suppress the Jesuits in 1762. Choiseul made no effort to intervene. His allegiance to Madame de Pompadour was undoubtedly a factor. She had been denied the sacraments by the Jesuits; she detested them and wished to see them ruined. Thus, Choiseul sacrificed the Jesuits to placate a number of factions and to gratify Madame de Pompadour.

The *parlements* continued to challenge the absolute power of the king. In 1764, this opposition intensified in the Affaires de Bretagne. In 1765, the parliamentarians of Rennes resigned. Louis-René de Caradeuc de La Chalotais, the *procureur-général* (attorney general), was arrested for making injurious remarks against the king. The Paris Parlement supported Rennes. Finally, on March 3, 1766, Louis XV addressed the Parlement and reaffirmed the absolute power of the king.

Madame de Pompadour, who had been in failing health for some years, died in 1764. Choiseul continued to support the parliamentarians. After the death of Madame de Pompadour, Louis XV took the comtesse du Barry as his mistress. She and Choiseul despised each other. Factions at court realigned and influence with the king shifted. Du Barry allied herself with the *dévot* faction, which had always been enemies of Madame de Pompadour and Choiseul. In December, 1770, on the advice of René Nicolas de Maupeou, one of du Barry's allies, Louis XV dismissed Choiseul. The disgraced Choiseul retired to his estate of Chanteloup. There, in his later years, he raised Swiss cattle. He died in Paris in 1785.

SIGNIFICANCE

Étienne François de Choiseul exemplified the lifestyle and values of the French nobility during the reign of Louis XV. He began his career as an army officer, found his way into the court, and used the favor he garnered at court to obtain positions in the government. He availed himself of the financial benefits to be had at court as well, being appointed to the lucrative position of colonel general of the Swiss Guards. His skill at diplomacy allowed Choiseul to give something back to his nation, as he negotiated the best possible terms for France in the Treaty of Paris, preventing the Seven Years' War from damaging French power and prestige even further.

Choiseul spent lavishly and despised avarice as the greatest antisocial vice. He loved his wife but was unfaithful to her. Charming yet quick of wit and capable of bitter sarcasm, he was at ease in the salons where intellectuals and aristocrats met to discuss philosophy, science, and literature. Possessed of a cosmopolitan culture, his interests included Chinese architecture, Flemish painting, and English gardens. Not devoutly religious, he counted the philosophes among his friends.

—*Shawncey Webb*

FURTHER READING

Algrant, Christine Pevitt. *Madame de Pompadour: Mistress of France*. New York: Grove Press, 2002. Details life of Pompadour. Discusses her role in administration of French government and her relationship with Choiseul.

Butler, Rohan d'Olier. *Choiseul*. New York: Oxford University Press, 1980. Intended as the first volume of what was to be a longer study, this excellent biography in English details Choiseul's early life, from 1719 to 1754.

Doyle, William. *Old Regime France: 1648-1788*. New York: Oxford University Press, 2001. A wealth of information on France's overseas involvement, politics and public life, Choiseul, and the American colonies.

Jones, Colin. *The Great Nation: France from Louis XV to Napoleon*. New York: Columbia University Press, 2003. Looks at the reigns of Louis XV and Louis XVI as periods of effective royal power, military achievement, and cultural prestige. Chapter 6 focuses on Choiseul, his military achievements and his scapegoats (*dévots* and Jesuits).

_____. *Madame de Pompadour: Images of a Mistress*. New York: Metropolitan Museum of Art, 2002. Scholarly biography recounts her life and role at court using the paintings of her to show how she utilized her image to advance her career.

Roche, Daniel. *France in the Enlightenment*. Translated by Arthur Goldmann. Cambridge, Mass.: Harvard University Press, 2000. Highly detailed cultural history examines lives of all classes: the king, nobility, bourgeoisie, peasants. Looks at the period as important in its own right, not just as a prelude to the revolution.

See also: André-Hercule de Fleury; Jean-Baptiste Vaquette de Gribeauval; Louis XV; Madame de Pompadour.

Related articles in *Great Events from History: The Eighteenth Century, 1701-1800*: January, 1756-February 15, 1763: Seven Years' War; February 10, 1763: Peace of Paris; February 24, 1766: Lorraine Becomes Part of France; May, 1776-September 3, 1783: France Supports the American Revolution.

CHŎNG SŎN
Korean landscape painter

Chŏng Sŏn revolutionized Korean art by painting realistic Korean landscapes, using a popular Chinese style but choosing not to copy the customary Chinese scenes of this genre. He influenced generations of Korean painters and contributed to the success of authentic Korean national art in the eighteenth century.

Born: January 3, 1676; Seoul, Korea
Died: March 24, 1759; Seoul, Korea
Also known as: Wŏnbaek; Kyŏmjae; Kyŏmcho; Kŏymno; Kyŏmja; Nankok
Areas of achievement: Art, patronage of the arts

EARLY LIFE

Chŏng Sŏn (chuhng suhn) was born into a family of land-owning scholars. His father, Chŏng Si-ik, was a government official who rose to the lower fourth rank and was responsible for handling government documents, sitting on the Royal Education Council, and working as royal secretary. His mother, Choe, came from a family of prominent Confucian and Neo-Confucian philosophers. Chŏng Sŏn's family lived in the Samch'ongdong district of Seoul, which had become capital of Korea with the rise of the Yi (or Choson) Dynasty in 1392. His first name, Sŏn, means "healing" or "completing."

Chŏng's ancestors on his father's side had been provincial governors and a professor of a Confucian school. Learning, government service, and relative material security were part of his family background. He received a classical education, stressing calligraphy, literature, philosophy, and the arts. Upon reaching maturity he took the adult name of Wŏnbaek.

Some time between 1694 and 1703, Chŏng Sŏn joined the royal Korean painters' academy upon the recommendation of Kim Ch'ang-jip, a high official of ruling king Sukchong. Chŏng was one of the few painters appointed on merit alone under the Chongo rule, which stated that once every three years, in the first month of the year (generally February according to the Western calendar), high government officials, such as his sponsor Kim, could recommend three candidates to join the academy.

Chŏng Sŏn was one of the few young artists chosen to join the academy under this rule—an indication of his talent. He chose Kyŏmjae, meaning "modest studio," as his first artistic name with which he signed his paintings.

LIFE'S WORK

Chŏng Sŏn's art, particularly his landscape paintings, soon stood out because they combined elements of the two opposed artistic styles of the period as well as adding a definite Korean dimension. Court painters, like those trained at the academy, generally followed the Northern Song style from China. They were expected to paint Chinese landscapes and follow rigid rules regarding theme, style, composition, and technique. On the other hand, literary painters like Chŏng's teacher Yun Tu-sŏ, who painted for aesthetic pleasure and appreciation, followed the new techniques of the Chinese Southern Song style.

Chŏng Sŏn painted landscapes, as expected, but defied tradition by not faithfully copying Chinese masters. Instead, he turned to the techniques of the Southern Song School, incorporating Mi Fu drops, or dots, named after the Chinese painter who used this technique. Chŏng Sŏn also used "axe stroke" brushstrokes to depict the steep, barren granite mountainsides of his native Korea.

In 1705, a trip to the famous rugged Mount Kŭmgang (Mount Diamond) in northern Korea decisively influenced Chŏng Sŏn. Taking in the majestic scenery provided inspiration for his decision to depict real Korean landscapes rather than copied or imagined Chinese scenes in his paintings. Filled with impressions and concrete ideas of the natural beauty of his own country, Chŏng Sŏn returned to his studio to create realistic Korean landscapes. According to artistic tradition, painters worked in their studios rather than on location, adding a layer of reflection to their immediate impressions. The thirteen eaves of his album *P'ung-akdo* (c. 1705) represented Chŏng Sŏn's first creative reaction to his trip to Mount Kŭmgang.

By 1731, Chŏng Sŏn's painting of a Korean embassy making its way through the mountains on its way to Beijing symbolized the national importance of his art. Like the ambassador it depicted, his painting reflected Korean national self-assertiveness. Even though his decision to depict realistic Korean landscapes followed the groundbreaking tradition of an earlier Korean painter, Cho Sok (b. 1595), Chŏng's paintings captured the spirit of the times. The paintings also won the favor of the new king, Yŏngjo. The fifty-eight leaves of *Kyo-nam-myongs ngch' op* (1734; album of diamond mountain paintings) contained some of Chŏng Sŏn's masterpieces.

The decade from 1740 to 1750 is considered Chŏng Sŏn's great creative period. His landscape paintings showed full development of his vigorous, Southern School brushstrokes and his individual ink technique. His opposition to Chinese stereotypes and abstractions and his innovative depiction of real Korean natural scenes, including human figures in Korean instead of Chinese dress, solidified his fame.

As was Korean custom, court painters also worked as government officials, one of the attractions of the profession. By 1742, at age sixty-six, Chŏng Sŏn was administrator of the Yangchon district, north of Seoul. In November, 1742, he joined a fellow magistrate to welcome a visiting high royal official, and the three men took a boat trip that inspired two landscape drafts, which some critics consider Chŏng Sŏn's most important literary painting. While drinking on the boat, the three men were reminded of a similar scene in Chinese literature. Chŏng Sŏn's paintings depicted this famous literary incident within a Korean landscape. Following tradition, friends wrote the circumstances of its inspiration directly on Chŏng's painting.

Some time between 1742 and 1755, King Yongjo promoted Chŏng Sŏn to the rank of chomjong, or supervisor, for the royal grain supply in Sadosi. Yongjo's patronage supported the famous painter, who used the artist's name of Kyŏmno (modest old man) by this time. Chŏng Sŏn felt confirmed in his artistic choices. His painting of a pavilion in 1748, for example, was widely praised for its realism in depicting a Korean building. His album *Sakondo sip'um* (1749) featured paintings inspired by Korean literary poems based on Chinese models, yet the landscapes depicted in the album were clearly and identifiably Korean.

A contemporary Korean biographer asserts that Chŏng Sŏn made a fortune from his paintings. The date of Chŏng Sŏn's marriage is no longer known, but both his son, Chŏng Man-su, and his grandson, Chŏng Hwang, became well known in Korea. In March, 1759, Chŏng Sŏn died at age eighty-three in his native city of Seoul.

SIGNIFICANCE

Chŏng Sŏn's national Korean art boldly followed the path of Cho Sok and represented real Korean landscapes instead of Chinese landscapes that were copied or imagined, giving eighteenth century Korean art a major creative impulse. His ability to render the Korean landscape in an artistic style most suitable to its realistic depiction, including his "axe stroke" brushstrokes to paint granite mountains and his portrayal of wind-bent pine trees rather than the straight Chinese version, created a major

stylistic shift in Korean painting of the period. More than five hundred of his works have survived.

Chŏng Sŏn's individual style and the composition of his landscape paintings deeply influenced both his contemporaries and his successors. He taught literary painters such as Sim Sa-chŏng and the accomplished Kim Hong-do. Chŏng Sŏn's legacy survived through his art and the generations of future artists who were inspired by his choice of theme and artistic execution.

By the end of the nineteenth century, with Chinese traditionalists winning the favor of the artistic community, Chŏng Sŏn's reputation lost some of its brilliance. It was not until Korean independence from Japanese colonial rule in 1945 that appreciation for Chŏng Sŏn's Korean landscapes reemerged.

—*R. C. Lutz*

FURTHER READING

Ahn, Hwi-joon. "A Scholar's Art: The Chinese Southern School." In *Fine Arts*. Vol. 1 in *Korean Cultural Heritage*, edited by Chu-hwan Park. Seoul: Samsung Moonhwa, 1994. Explores the traditional Chinese influence on Korean landscape painters of the eighteenth century, with a good discussion of Chŏng Sŏn's artistic development and significance. Illustrated with reproductions of some of his major paintings.

Huh, Young-hwan. "Choson Landscape and Genre Painting." In *Fine Arts*. Vol. 1 in *Korean Cultural Heritage*, edited by Chu-hwan Park. Seoul: Samsung Moonhwa, 1994. Places Chŏng Sŏn in the context of Korean painting of the period and discusses his influence and legacy. Illustrated.

Portal, Jane. *Korea: Art and Archaeology*. London: Thames & Hudson, 2000. Written upon the occasion of the opening of a new gallery for Korean art at the British Museum in London, the text provides a good account of Chŏng Sŏn's achievements. Valuable for placing the artist in context and discussing the adaptation of Chinese artistic traditions in Korea in the eighteenth century. Illustrated, with an index and a bibliography.

Pratt, Keith. *Korean Painting*. New York: Oxford University Press, 1995. Discusses the work of Chŏng Sŏn in light of his significant contributions to realistic Korean landscape painting and places him in the context of Korean art. Provides a useful history of painting style in the period and after. Includes illustrations and a map.

See also: Dai Zhen; Haikun; Suzuki Harunobu.

SARAH CHURCHILL
Duchess of Marlborough

Churchill, duchess of Marlborough, was the wealthiest and most powerful woman in early eighteenth century England. The duchess's early friendship with Anne, princess and later queen, helped the Churchills rise to prominence, wealth, and power. Churchill's ambition and controlling personality caused breaches with her children, grandchildren and, most important, Queen Anne.

Born: June 5, 1660; St. Albans, Hertfordshire, England
Died: October 18, 1744; London, England
Also known as: Sarah Jennings or Jenyns (birth name); Duchess of Marlborough; Countess of Marlborough
Area of achievement: Government and politics

EARLY LIFE

Sarah Churchill was born to Richard Jennings and Frances Thornhill. Her father was a member of the House of Commons but had fallen on hard times. Thus, Sarah grew up in an unstable financial environment and lacked formal education. However, she was spirited, independent, strong willed, and beautiful, which attracted attention when she became maid of honor in October, 1673, to Mary Modena, the second wife of James, duke of York and Albany, heir to the throne as James II. This brought Sarah into contact with James's daughters from his first marriage—Mary, age ten, and Anne, age eight—and initiated a friendship with Anne that lasted until its irreparable breach in April of 1710.

Sarah attracted the attention of the extremely handsome page, John Churchill, ten years her senior, and after initially rejecting his proposal, she accepted, and the two secretly married, perhaps as early as November, 1677. Thus began one of the most remarkable personal and political partnerships in English history.

Married life was characterized by periods of separation caused by John's accompanying James and in later years conducting military and diplomatic operations on the Continent. This caused them great heartache, as Sarah was in England giving birth to their seven children. She attempted to procure good marriages for them, but her meddling in their lives caused familial friction.

LIFE'S WORK

During the Exclusion Crisis (1679-1681), when the Whigs attempted to exclude James from the succession to the throne because of his Catholic beliefs, Sarah exhibited sympathy for Whig political ideals, although she was closely attached to James's household. Because of her marriage, Sarah had to resign her position, but when Princess Anne married Prince George of Denmark in 1683, this necessitated an expansion of Anne's household, and Sarah became one of the ladies of the bedchamber, beginning an official connection that lasted until Sarah was forced to resign her positions in January, 1711. Anne sought a friend and confidante while Sarah benefited from Anne's position. Eventually, to create a more equal standing between them, Anne suggested that they use slang names in their correspondence—Anne became "Mrs. Morley" and Sarah became "Mrs. Freeman."

After James II (r. 1685-1688) ascended the throne, Anne elevated Sarah to a salary of £400 per year and gave Sarah greater financial independence. As James II's policies worried leading Protestants that he intended to restore Catholicism, William of Orange, leader of the Netherlands and husband of Anne's older sister Mary, led an invasion of England initiating the Glorious Revolution (1688-1689), which elevated William III (r. 1689-1702) and Mary II (r. 1689-1694) as joint sovereigns after James II fled into exile. John and Sarah performed notable services for William and Mary, as John had deserted James II and brought the army to William. Sarah had helped Anne escape from London ahead of attempts to place Anne and James under guard. However, Sarah and John did not benefit as much as they desired; John was elevated to earl of Marlborough. Suspicions that John was in contact with James and fear of John's ambitions caused William III to strip John of his positions and briefly imprison him in the Tower of London. William and Mary asked Anne to dismiss Sarah, but Anne's steadfast refusal to comply caused friction between the royal sisters.

When Anne became queen in 1702, the Marlboroughs benefited from Anne's friendship. Sarah became keeper of the privy purse and ranger of Windsor Park, with an annual income of £6,000. Since Sarah held these posts independently of John, it gave her financial independence. John was elevated to duke of Marlborough and named commander of English troops in the War of the Spanish Succession (1701-1714). The couple wielded tremendous influence. To commemorate John's victory at Blenheim (1704), Anne rewarded him with the royal manor at Woodstock. This became the site of their tremendous residence, Blenheim Palace, but it became a burden to them and occupied their attention the remainder of their lives, spawning acrimonious battles with the architect Sir John Vanbrugh and lawsuits over payment to the workers. After the Marlboroughs' fall from favor, Anne ordered a halt to construction in 1712.

While John was on the Continent for a good part of the year because of his military and diplomatic responsibilities, Sarah, highly political and a supporter of the Whigs, attempted to influence Anne, a moderate Tory. Sarah's constant badgering of Anne over appointments and policy caused Anne to seek a new confidante, Abigail Hill Masham, Sarah's cousin, and gradually Sarah's influence with the queen waned. Sarah was not above using Anne's funds, about £22,000 for construction of Blenheim Palace, and when it became apparent that Abigail was now Anne's favorite, Sarah "accused" Anne of having lesbian relations with Abigail.

In 1710, Anne began replacing Whigs in her administration with Tories and the breach with Sarah became permanent. Anne and the Tories sought to end the War of the Spanish Succession and secure commercial and territorial gains by reaching a secret agreement with France. John became a liability because of his support for continuing the war, and the Marlboroughs were brought to heel. Sarah was forced to resign her positions in January, 1711; John, accused of seeking to prolong the war for his personal financial benefit, was formally stripped of his posts and command in December, 1711, and January, 1712. In late 1712, John left England for the Continent and Sarah joined him in early 1713.

When Anne fell ill in July of 1714, the Marlboroughs made preparations to return to England; they arrived the day of Anne's death, August 1, 1714. The Marlboroughs were disappointed that they did not gain greater favor under George I (r. 1714-1727), but the king did order resumption of work on Blenheim Palace in 1716. However, in May and November of 1716, John suffered strokes and Sarah cared for him until his death on June 16, 1722. Sarah's shrewd investments in land and stock substantially increased her wealth, but lawsuits over Blenheim Palace and poor health troubled her in the 1720's.

She rejected marriage proposals because marriage would end her independence. Although she no longer possessed the political clout she once held, Sarah did have electoral influence because of her many estates, but her last attempt at intervention in politics in 1734 by supporting candidates opposed to Prime Minister Robert Walpole was not successful, although she did live to see him resign in 1742. She published *An Account of the Dowager Duchess of Marlborough* in 1742 to elucidate the ill treatment she felt she had received. On October 18, 1744, Sarah died and was buried at Blenheim Palace. The body of her beloved husband John, buried at Westminster Abbey, was moved and buried next to her.

SIGNIFICANCE

Sarah Churchill left a phenomenal fortune—estimated at £400,000 in estates, £250,000 in capital, and £12,000 in annuities—that sparked lawsuits over its disposition. Her friendship with Queen Anne was one of the

Sarah Churchill, Duchess of Marlborough. (Hulton Archive/Getty Images)

most significant between royalty and a commoner and provided the couple with tremendous advantages, but Sarah was unable to perceive that her hectoring and badgering of the queen had driven a wedge between them that contributed to loss of favor. In many ways, Sarah was her own worst enemy.

Her remarkable life and her marriage to John Churchill make her one of the most influential women in English history. She had mused what would have happened if she were a man and could run for Parliament. Sarah's combination of intelligence, ambition, loyalty to her husband, tempestuous personality, and passion for life made her a force to be reckoned with. Her influence continued beyond her own lifetime, as the most illustrious of her descendants, English prime minister and statesman Winston Churchill, honored John with a massive biography. Winston Churchill applied lessons learned from his study of John's dealings with King Louis XIV to his own dealings with Adolf Hitler and the English war effort in World War II.

—Mark C. Herman

FURTHER READING

Bucholz, R. O. *The Augustan Court: Queen Anne and the Decline of Court Culture*. Stanford, Calif.: Stanford University Press, 1993. Bucholz examines how and why court culture declined in importance by the early eighteenth century despite Anne's efforts to restore it to its former glory. Maintains that Anne was not dependent upon her female favorites but was able to exert independence over Sarah Churchill and Abigail Hill Masham.

Butler, Iris. *Rule of Three*. London: Hodder and Stoughton, 1967. This work provides valuable psychological insight into the characters of Anne, Sarah Churchill, and Abigail Masham. It is rich with many previously unpublished items.

Field, Ophelia. *The Favourite: Sarah, Duchess of Marlborough*. New York: St. Martin's Press, 2003. A popular biography that is strong on Sarah's relationships with her children.

Gregg, Edward. *Queen Anne*. 1980. Reprint. New Haven, Conn.: Yale University Press, 2001. The first work to offer a major reassessment of Queen Anne's political influence, containing an extensive treatment and analysis of the relationship between Sarah and Anne.

Harris, Frances. *A Passion for Government: The Life of Sarah, Duchess of Marlborough*. Oxford, England: Clarendon Press, 1991. This extremely analytical, scholarly biography, based on extensive archival research, provides a complete treatment of Sarah's life and influence.

Hibbert, Christopher. *The Marlboroughs: John and Sarah Churchill, 1650-1744*. New York: Viking Press, 2001. This dual biography from the well-known biographer Hibbert details the relationship and careers of this remarkable couple.

See also: Queen Anne; Lancelot Brown; George I; First Earl of Godolphin; Mary de la Rivière Manley; First Duke of Marlborough; Sir John Vanbrugh; Robert Walpole.

Related articles in *Great Events from History: The Eighteenth Century, 1701-1800:* May 26, 1701-September 7, 1714: War of the Spanish Succession; February, 1706-April 28, 1707: Act of Union Unites England and Scotland; March 23-26, 1708: Defeat of the "Old Pretender."

GEORGE ROGERS CLARK
American military leader

Clark's successful attack against British forts in 1778-1779 served as the basis for the American claim to the Northwest Territory during negotiation of the Treaty of Paris of 1783. His leadership of the Northwest campaign led in turn to the founding of Louisville, Kentucky, and Clarksville, Indiana.

Born: November 19, 1752; near Charlottesville, Virginia
Died: February 13, 1818; Louisville, Kentucky
Areas of achievement: Military, warfare and conquest, government and politics

EARLY LIFE

George Rogers Clark was the second of ten children born to John and Ann Rogers Clark. Both parents were of British stock whose roots went deep into Virginia's past. In 1757, the family moved to an inherited plantation in Caroline County. Young George attended a school there conducted by a Scottish schoolmaster named Donald Robertson. Clark studied mathematics and surveying and showed a strong interest in history and geography. The Clark family was moderately prosperous, but John Clark believed in instilling in his children a sense of discipline and responsibility. Thus, when George was fifteen years old, his father gave him his own tobacco crop and then charged the youth's clothing and other personal expenses against it.

The most important element of Clark's education was his early frontier experience. In 1772, after receiving training in surveying from his grandfather, John Rogers, Clark made his first trip west with a party that descended the Ohio River and explored and surveyed land in the vicinity of the Kanawha River. Over the next two years, Clark spent much time surveying wilderness land, acquiring in the process a substantial knowledge of natural history and an understanding of American Indian ways.

No early portraits of Clark exist, but contemporary descriptions suggest that he was a tall, powerfully built man with reddish or sandy-colored hair. His strong physical appearance complemented a winning personality that inspired confidence in others and quickly marked him as a leader.

LIFE'S WORK

George Rogers Clark's military career began in 1774 when he was commissioned a captain in the Virginia colony during Lord Dunmore's War, a conflict between the Shawnee and the settlers on the Kanawha River frontier. Clark missed the critical Battle of Point Pleasant and saw little or no fighting otherwise, but he displayed a gift for command and acquired a knowledge of American Indian fighting tactics and military organization.

With the end of Lord Dunmore's War, Clark joined the Ohio Company and spent several months surveying in central Kentucky and aiding in the organization of Kentucky County. Meanwhile, fighting had erupted between American colonists and British troops in Massachusetts. As the rebellion intensified, Clark joined the Kentucky County militia. By 1777, he was a major and temporary ranking officer in Kentucky. He spent several months trying to defend scattered settlements against American Indian raids instigated by the British north of the Ohio. As the attacks increased, however, Clark sought ways to take the war to the enemy.

In June, 1777, he sent spies to obtain the intelligence necessary to plan a long-distance strike. Using their information, Clark formulated his strategy and presented it to Virginia governor Patrick Henry in December. Impressed with the boldness of Clark's scheme, Henry persuaded the legislature to appropriate funds for the campaign, without revealing the purpose of the expenditure. The governor then promoted Clark to lieutenant colonel and gave him secret orders to raise the troops necessary to attack the British fort at Kaskaskia, located on the Kaskaskia River near the Mississippi.

On May 12, Clark and his regiment of 150 men, along with about one dozen civilian families, sailed for the Falls of the Ohio, located about 400 miles downriver from Pittsburgh. After picking up a few more recruits along the way, the flotilla landed at Corn Island near the falls on May 27. A month later, Clark and his regiment departed for the Illinois country, leaving behind the civilians.

By July 4, Clark was poised at the outskirts of Kaskaskia. During the night his troops broke into the fort and captured its garrison without firing a shot. The following day, one of Clark's companies captured Cahokia, about 40 miles away, in a similar manner. In August, the British-controlled French garrison at Vincennes, 240 miles east on the Wabash River, surrendered to Clark after learning of the French-American alliance of 1778. Now Clark turned his attention to Detroit, headquarters of Lieutenant Governor Henry Hamilton, the chief British official in the Northwest Territory. Before he could march, however, Clark had to deal with the expiring enlistments of many of his troops and to provide for the administration of the posts under his command. The funds appropriated by the Virginia legislature long since exhausted, he used his personal resources and borrowed heavily from friends to continue the campaign. Meanwhile, Hamilton counterattacked, recapturing the inadequately defended post at Vincennes in mid-December. With winter setting in, Hamilton decided to wait until spring to retake Kaskaskia and Cahokia. It was a fatal decision.

While Hamilton waited, Clark plotted a surprise attack against Vincennes. In early February, 1779, he crossed the Kaskaskia River with about 170 men. The troops marched for two weeks through rain-swollen swamps and rivers. On February 23, they arrived at Vincennes, and Clark delivered a surrender ultimatum. Hamilton proposed a truce, but Clark, having deployed his forces in a manner that made their number appear much larger, rejected the proposal and returned surrender conditions that he demanded Hamilton to accept. Realizing that Clark would not be moved, Hamilton capitulated.

Clark began planning immediately to attack Detroit. His plans collapsed, however, because of a lack of troops, and he returned to the Falls of the Ohio in August, 1779. His destination was not Corn Island but the tiny village of Louisville, which had been established a few months earlier when the settlers on the island heeded Clark's message to move to the Kentucky shore. Using Louisville as his base, Clark spent most of the remainder of the war conducting defensive operations along the Ohio. In 1779-1780, he supervised construction of Fort Jefferson on the Mississippi near the mouth of the Ohio. During mid-1780, he coordinated the defense of the Ohio Valley against a British counterattack from Detroit. Later that year Clark began anew planning a campaign against Detroit, but the effort was thwarted again when he became temporarily involved in defending the James River valley in Virginia and when Virginia and continental officials refused the necessary financial assistance. The objective of taking Detroit was achieved finally through the Treaty of Paris in 1783, during whose negotiations American diplomats used Clark's capture of the Northwest forts as the basis for claiming the entire territory.

Many of Clark's postwar activities were extensions of his wartime service. A skilled negotiator with American Indians, he worked out the Treaty of Fort McIntosh in 1785 and the Treaty of Fort Finney in early 1786. Later in

1786, he joined Benjamin Logan in an expedition against the Wabash Confederacy in southwestern Indiana. Victimized by inadequate supplies and poor discipline, the campaign was a fiasco. Nevertheless, the pressure prompted the tribes to ask for a council, and peace was arranged in the spring of 1787.

Meanwhile, Clark had become involved in a second venture in town development. In 1783, the Virginia legislature awarded Clark and his regiment a grant of 150,000 acres on the Indiana shore at the Falls of the Ohio. One thousand acres was designated as Clarksville, which ranks as the oldest Anglo-American municipality in the old Northwest. A board of trustees was appointed to govern the town, and a board of commissioners was created to survey the land. Clark chaired both bodies for more than two decades.

Despite his accomplishments, Clark's star sank quickly after 1787. Pressured by creditors for repayment of loans he had obtained for the Illinois campaign, Clark sought assistance from the Virginia legislature. Rebuffed again and again, he became increasingly addicted to alcohol. His intense bitterness and dire financial straits led to participation in schemes that caused many to question his loyalty. In 1789, Clark became involved in an abortive plot to establish American colonies on Spanish soil west of the Mississippi. In 1793, he accepted a commission to command a French revolutionary legion that would descend the Mississippi River and seize Spanish possessions. The U.S. government, however, thwarted the operation before it began.

Clark spent the remainder of the century on his parents' Louisville estate, supervising farmwork and attempting to untangle his finances. In 1803, he built a cabin on his Clarksville land overlooking the Falls of the Ohio. There he received numerous visitors and accomplished some competent studies in natural history, but his heavy drinking steadily eroded his health. In February, 1809, he suffered a stroke and fell into his fireplace, causing burns that necessitated the amputation of his right leg. Disabled, Clark moved to Locust Grove, the Louisville home of his sister and brother-in-law, Lucy and William Croghan. In 1812, the Virginia legislature awarded him a sword and an annual pension of $400 in recognition of his wartime service. He died at Locust Grove on February 13, 1818.

SIGNIFICANCE

George Rogers Clark's achievements were among the most remarkable and least understood of the American Revolution. Barely thirty years old when the war ended, he had captured a major portion of the Northwest region and commanded the successful defense of the Ohio Valley. These accomplishments resulted from a unique combination of strategic vision, personal courage, and persuasive ability. Yet he was not, as some have claimed, the "conqueror of the Northwest," nor did his victories alone guarantee American control of that area through the peace negotiations. Because Clark was unable to capture Detroit, the British maintained a foothold in the Northwest. Moreover, the American peace commissioners—John Jay, Benjamin Franklin, and John Adams—were under instructions from Congress to follow the lead of the French, who had no desire to see the American domain expand to the Mississippi. When Jay and Adams learned that their ally was negotiating secretly with the British, they convinced Franklin that the Americans should deal directly with the British, in violation of their congressional orders. The British, wanting to reestablish trade and avert future conflict with the Americans, agreed to provisions in the Treaty of Paris that extended the western boundary of the United States to the Mississippi.

The significance of Clark's accomplishments, however, cannot be diminished if placed in their proper perspective. Without his victories the American diplomats would have had difficulty mustering the bargaining power to secure the Northwest. By the middle of the nineteenth century, this territory had been carved into the states of Ohio, Indiana, Illinois, Michigan, Wisconsin, and Minnesota. Clark's exploits also contributed to the creation of a bistate urban region, which by 1980 numbered nearly one million people. Louisville is Kentucky's largest city. Clarksville, Indiana, grew slowly during the nineteenth century, overshadowed by neighboring Jeffersonville and New Albany, both of which are within Clark's Grant. Clarksville mushroomed after World War II, though, and became the second largest incorporated town in Indiana and a major commercial center. Certainly, the long-term consequences of Clark's achievements outweigh the tragic circumstances of his postwar years.

—*Carl E. Kramer*

FURTHER READING

Bakeless, John. *Background to Glory: The Life of George Rogers Clark.* Philadelphia: J. B. Lippincott, 1957. This detailed biography provides an accurate account of Clark's Northwest campaign.

Carstens, Kenneth C., and Nancy Son Carstens, eds. *The Life of George Rogers Clark, 1752-1818: Triumphs and Tragedies.* Westport, Conn.: Praeger, 2004. A collection of essays about various aspects of Clark's life and military career, including his relationship with his wife, his role in the settlement of Kentucky, and his control of the Northwest Territories. Includes a bibliography.

English, William Hayden. *Conquest of the Country Northwest of the River Ohio, 1778-1783.* Indianapolis, Ind.: Bowen-Merrill, 1896. This two-volume work is the classic heroic account depicting Clark as the "conqueror of the Northwest." Although dated in interpretation, it is useful for its abundant illustrations, biographical sketches, lengthy quotations from original documents, and detailed roster of Clark's regiment.

Harrison, Lowell H. *George Rogers Clark and the War in the West.* Lexington: University Press of Kentucky, 1976. This brief, synthetic essay pictures Clark as one of the few revolutionary figures who understood the strategic significance of the frontier and as the person most responsible for saving Kentucky from the British.

James, James Alton. *Life of George Rogers Clark.* Chicago: University of Chicago Press, 1928. Based upon extensive research in primary sources, this is still the most accurate and most complete biography of Clark. Very readable and sympathetic to Clark, it includes a detailed discussion of his financial problems and participation in the Spanish and French conspiracies.

Jones, Landon Y. *William Clark and the Shaping of the West.* New York: Hill & Wang, 2004. This biography of George Roger Clark's brother, William, includes a chapter about George's life between 1772 and 1789 and his Northwest campaign.

Quaife, Milo M., ed. *The Capture of Old Vincennes.* Indianapolis, Ind.: Bobbs-Merrill, 1927. Essentially a firsthand account of the capture of Vincennes, based upon Clark's and Hamilton's memoirs of the event. Clark's peculiar syntax and spelling have been recast for easy reading.

Sosin, Jack M. *The Revolutionary Frontier, 1763-1783.* New York: Holt, Rinehart, and Winston, 1967. Contextualizing Clark's exploits, this volume explores the roles of land speculation, settlement patterns, Anglo-American politics, development of local government, and American Indian affairs on the frontier during the revolutionary period.

Waller, George Macgregor. *The American Revolution in the West.* Chicago: Nelson-Hall, 1976. Based upon secondary sources, this brief narrative is especially useful in establishing the relationship between Clark's victories in the Northwest and the decision of the American peace commissioners to seek a separate peace with the British.

See also: John Adams; Daniel Boone; Joseph Brant; Benjamin Franklin; Patrick Henry; John Jay.

Related articles in *Great Events from History: The Eighteenth Century, 1701-1800:* April 27-October 10, 1774: Lord Dunmore's War; April 19, 1775: Battle of Lexington and Concord; February 6, 1778: Franco-American Treaties; September 3, 1783: Treaty of Paris; May 20, 1785: Ordinance of 1785; July 13, 1787: Northwest Ordinance.

SIR HENRY CLINTON
Canadian-born British general

Clinton, the most successful British general during the American Revolution, drafted strategic plans that if properly implemented could have saved Britain's North American colonies. Yet Clinton's failure to command his subordinates was one major reason for Britain's defeat.

Born: April 16, 1730; Newfoundland, Canada
Died: December 23, 1795; Gibraltar
Areas of achievement: Military, warfare and conquest

EARLY LIFE

Henry Clinton was born in the British province of Newfoundland, where his father, British naval officer George Clinton, was governor. This accident of geography made Henry Clinton the only senior British general in the American Revolution to have a natural connection with North America.

In 1743, after intense lobbying by his influential kinsman, the duke of Newcastle, George Clinton was named governor of New York. Young Henry Clinton attended the Reverend Samuel Seabury's School at Hempstead, Long Island, and entered military service as a lieutenant of fusiliers in the New York militia when he was fifteen. In 1746, he was promoted to captain and served with troops garrisoning Louisbourg, the important fortress at the mouth of the St. Lawrence River captured from the French. Clinton volunteered for an expedition to Prince Edward Island, where the British were ambushed by the French and their Indian allies; he escaped only by abandoning his weapons and swimming to a nearby British ship.

The exploit did not dampen Clinton's enthusiasm for a military career. In 1749, he left for England and in 1751 was commissioned captain-lieutenant in the elite Coldstream Guards. In 1756, he was appointed aide-de-camp to Sir John Ligonier, commander in chief of the British army. Although Clinton's duties were largely ceremo-

nial and he spent much of his time in London, his career continued to advance, and in 1758, he was promoted to lieutenant colonel in the First Regiment of Foot Guards.

As the Seven Years' War (known as the French and Indian War in North America) reached its climax, Clinton's regiment was sent in 1760 to fight in Germany. Clinton distinguished himself as aide-de-camp to Prince Charles of Brunswick, was promoted to colonel in June of 1762 and was wounded at the Battle of Johannisburg in August of the same year. It was in Germany that Clinton learned military strategy and tactics; during this same period, future generals such as John Burgoyne and William Howe were learning quite different lessons on colonial battlefields. This difference in professional background later caused problems for the British during the American Revolution.

Returning to England, Clinton continued his rise. In 1764, he was named groom of the bedchamber to William Henry, duke of Gloucester (the king's favorite brother), and so acquired another influential patron to go with his Newcastle relatives.

Clinton's appearance was far from imposing. Described by one historian as "smallish, paunchy, and colorless," his portraits show a man of average height for the period, with a round face, large and rather expressive eyes, and double chin. His contemporaries and biographers have noted that while Clinton had many acquaintances, he had few close friends.

On February 12, 1767, Clinton married Harriet Carter, a young woman of a good but hardly distinguished family. There is speculation that she may have been pregnant at the time. It is certain that the Clintons had four children following the marriage: two daughters, Augusta and Harriet, and two sons, William Henry and Henry. Both of the sons followed in their father's footsteps by pursuing careers in the military and, like him, rose to the rank of general and were inducted into the Order of the Bath.

The flexible attitudes of the time permitted Clinton, an army officer, to participate directly in politics, and in 1772, he was both promoted to major general and elected to Parliament. However, in August, he was plunged into despair when his wife died after giving birth to their second daughter. The event was a catastrophe from which Clinton never fully recovered. For a time, his friends feared for his sanity, and it was perhaps with a sense of relief that Clinton received orders in 1775 to embark for America, where the colonies were in open rebellion.

LIFE'S WORK

In May, 1775, one month after the Battles of Lexington and Concord, Henry Clinton joined British commander in chief Thomas Gage in Boston. The American Continental army had laid siege, and Clinton argued for a swift seizure of Dorchester Heights, which commanded Boston from its position south of the city. Gage rejected this advice and the next month, when American troops seized Breeds and Bunker Hills north of Boston, was forced to launch a frontal attack against them. Clinton personally led a column in the final attack that cleared the hills.

Clinton was promoted in September to the local rank of lieutenant general and made second in command to the new commander in chief, William Howe. The two generals were soon at odds, a situation that Clinton frequently found himself in throughout his career. In part to resolve this conflict and also to advance British strategy, Clinton was sent south to seize Charleston, South Carolina.

The expedition was a fiasco. The sea approach to Charleston was protected by a partially built fort of palmetto logs on Sullivans Island. The infantry under Clinton landed north of Sullivans Island to outflank the Americans while the British fleet bombarded them from the sea. However, an unfordable inlet prevented Clinton from attacking, and the cannonballs of the ships proved useless against the soft palmetto wood. After receiving severe punishment from the fort, the fleet retired, and the British returned to Boston.

Despite this setback, Clinton was again promoted, this time to the local rank of full general. He was outstanding in the New York campaign of 1776, providing exceptional leadership in the Battle of Long Island and subsequent actions in Manhattan and New Jersey. He continued to press his suggestions on Howe, who again sent him on an amphibious expedition, this time a successful movement against Newport, Rhode Island.

However, Clinton, still haunted by the Charleston debacle, returned to England and threatened to resign. The government responded by awarding him a knighthood, inducting him into the Order of the Bath, and promoting him to lieutenant general. Clearly, Clinton was valued for his military skills and abilities as well as for his powerful connections.

In July of 1777, Clinton returned to New York as Howe's second in command at a time when Britain's most ambitious plan to suppress the revolution was under way. General Burgoyne was advancing south from Canada, and Howe struck against the colonial capital of Philadelphia. Kept on the defensive by Howe's orders, Clinton finally won approval to mount an expedition in support of Burgoyne against American positions along the Hudson River. It was well conceived and conducted but too late; before it was over, Burgoyne had surrendered at Saratoga and the revolution had passed its turning point.

Clinton succeeded Howe as commander in chief in May, 1778. The government in London gave him secret orders to abandon Philadelphia, go on the defensive in

Sir Henry Clinton. (Library of Congress)

the northern colonies, and concentrate his efforts in the south where there were believed to be substantial numbers of Loyalists. On his return to New York, Clinton fought and won the Battle of Monmouth on June 28, 1778, the last major engagement of the revolution in the northern colonies.

For the next year, Clinton remained on the defensive, partly in deference to his orders from London and partly because the French, encouraged by Saratoga, had entered the war on the American side. Clinton successfully dispatched strong raiding parties to harass the countryside. A single expedition destroyed more than £300,000 (roughly $600,000) worth of property along the Chesapeake. Had such naval-land tactics been continued, they might have turned the tide in favor of Britain; however, that was not to be the case.

In the summer of 1779, Charles Cornwallis arrived as Clinton's second in command and was already designated as Clinton's successor. In this difficult situation, Clinton sailed south in December and attacked Charleston in early 1780. He was brilliantly successful, bottling up American general Benjamin Lincoln and his army of almost five thousand, which surrendered on May 12. The campaign was Clinton's masterpiece, for the British had destroyed a major American army, captured a vital port city, and opened the way into the presumably Loyalist south with a loss of less than three hundred troops.

Leaving Cornwallis in command in the south, Clinton returned to New York. Against Clinton's wishes (although, significantly, Clinton did not expressly forbid it), Cornwallis embarked upon an aggressive strategy that led to major British defeats at Kings Mountain (October 7, 1780) and Cowpens (January 17, 1781). Cornwallis then headed north into Virginia, where he was brought to bay at Yorktown and forced to surrender on October 20, 1781. Although Cornwallis must bear the major portion of blame for the disaster that lost the war for the British, Clinton's indecisiveness and contradictory orders certainly contributed to the result.

In May, 1782, Sir Guy Carleton succeeded Clinton as commander in chief, and Clinton returned to England where he was widely blamed for the disaster at Yorktown. He had a falling out with Newcastle and lost his seat in Parliament only to regain it on his own initiative in 1790. Although his reputation may have been marred, his career was not destroyed: He was promoted to full general in 1793 and the next year appointed governor of Gibraltar. He died there on December 23, 1795.

SIGNIFICANCE

According to military historian Mark Boatner, Henry Clinton held a crucial position longer than any general on either side except George Washington, and he has been hailed as "the most successful British general in the War of Independence" by no less an authority than John Keegan. Yet, in the end, Clinton proved unequal to the task of subduing the rebellious American colonies. There are several reasons for this failure.

The first is military. Except at the very beginning of his campaigns, Clinton lacked the strength to either defeat the American army in open battle or capture and hold key strong points, most of them ports, that would have cut off supplies and reinforcements from Europe. The second is political. Inconsistent policies by the British government, especially its favoritism of subordinates such as Cornwallis, deprived Clinton of the authority he needed to implement a consistent strategy that might have proven effective.

The most damaging reason, however, was psychological. Although Clinton was a talented and imaginative soldier, as second in command, he was unable to have his plans adopted; as a commander, he could not impose his plans upon his subordinates, most notably Cornwallis, who persisted in campaigns that ruined Britain's American empire. Known throughout his career for his quarrels with his fellow officers, Clinton's most fatal quarrel seems to have been with himself.

—*Michael Witkoski*

FURTHER READING

Boatner, Mark M. *Encyclopedia of the American Revolution.* New York: David McKay, 1975. The biographical entry on Clinton is supplemented with more detailed examinations of specific campaigns, such as his foray into the New York highlands and his great victory at Charleston in 1780. The numerous cross-references are extremely helpful.

Bobrick, Benson. *Angel in the Whirlwind: The Triumph of the American Revolution.* New York: Simon & Schuster, 1997. Although written from the American point of view, this volume contains a clear and fair account and assessment of Clinton's role, including his successes and failures, during the conflict.

Fortescue, John, Sir. *The War of Independence: The British Army in North America.* Vol. 3 in *History of the British Army.* London: Greenhill Books, 2001. Reprint of the nineteenth century history compiled by a British military historian. This comprehensive survey of Britain's role in the American Revolution includes information about Clinton's failures in New York and his Charleston campaign.

Keegan, John, and Andrew Wheatcroft. *Who's Who in Military History: From 1453 to the Present Day*. New York: William Morrow, 1976. In addition to a brief biography of Clinton, this volume also offers valuable cross-references to help the reader place the general within the context of the American Revolution.

Willcox, William B. *Portrait of a General: Sir Henry Clinton in the War of Independence*. New York: Alfred A. Knopf, 1964. The most extensive individual work on Clinton and his role during the revolution, especially as commander of the British forces during

most of the war. Willcox argues that Clinton was psychologically predisposed to failure through feelings of inadequacy.

See also: John André; Benedict Arnold; Sir Guy Carleton; First Marquess Cornwallis; Thomas Gage; Nathanael Greene; William Howe; George Washington.

Related articles in *Great Events from History: The Eighteenth Century, 1701-1800:* January, 1756-February 15, 1763: Seven Years' War; April 19, 1775: Battle of Lexington and Concord; September 19-October 17, 1777: Battles of Saratoga; October 19, 1781: Cornwallis Surrenders at Yorktown.

ROBERT CLIVE
English soldier and administrator

Clive's military success against the French at Arcot and the Bengalese at Plassey, along with his rule over Bengal, created the basis for the vast British Empire in India in the eighteenth century.

Born: September 29, 1725; Styche, Shropshire, England
Died: November 22, 1774; London, England
Also known as: First Baron Clive of Plassey
Areas of achievement: Diplomacy, warfare and conquest, military, government and politics

EARLY LIFE
Robert Clive was born on his family's estate in Shropshire. His father was a country squire by inheritance and a lawyer by profession. As the son of a gentleman, Clive received a public school education and entered boarding school at age twelve. His father, financially unsuccessful, either had little hope for his teenage son at home or considered him unsuited for the professions, and therefore sent young Clive abroad to make a fortune in the British East India Company. In 1744, at age eighteen, Clive became a clerk for the company, serving first in Madras, in southern India.

In the mid-eighteenth century, India was in turmoil. The Mughal Empire deteriorated after the death of Emperor Aurangzeb in 1707, and the internal anarchy, along with the presence of the French, made conditions difficult for the British East India Company. The French, trying to dominate southern India, were the immediate problem. During the War of Austrian Succession, in the 1740's, fighting broke out between the French and British. Clive took advantage of the hostilities, quit his clerk's position, and joined the military in 1745. Yet the French practiced Indian politics deftly and were formidable opponents. The French leader in India, Joseph-François Dupleix, learned that interference in the dynastic struggles of Indian states proved profitable. Siding with one candidate and supporting him with troops usually meant success for the French. The victorious Indian prince paid huge sums to Dupleix and the Compagnie Française des Indes (French East India Company). The British soon copied the French tactics and enhanced their military presence in India. The East India Company recruited Indian troops for a company army and a few years later used regular British army troops. By 1749, however, the troop total only reached three thousand. In the Carnatic, these British forces came into conflict with the French by supporting a rival candidate. The British suffered military reverses attributable to inexperience and weak officers. Clive seized this opportunity. Although taken prisoner in 1746, when the French took Madras, Clive escaped to Fort St. David. In 1747, he was promoted to the rank of ensign.

The War of Austrian Succession ended in 1748, but the Treaty of Aix-la-Chapelle did not stop the British-French rivalry in India. By then, precedents important to Clive's career in India had been established. European powers interfered in the internal affairs of Indian states and backed up that interference with well-trained troops. In the Carnatic, the seat of French strength, Clive excelled as a military leader, and by 1749, he was made a lieutenant. His first important military success came in

1751 at Arcot, the capital of the Carnatic. The British needed relief at Trichinopoly and hence the British company sent twenty-five-year-old Clive to lead a diversionary force of five hundred men against Arcot. Taking it by surprise, he did not have to fire a shot, and he held it during a fifty-day siege. The following year, the French surrendered, and Clive installed the British candidate as ruler of the Carnatic. Success in the Carnatic proved that the British company could handle rough Indian politics and that Clive was a resourceful and decisive military leader. Arcot established his reputation of invincibility, so important later for intimidating his opposition. His quality of leadership was important for British success in India. Indians respected him as ruler and friend. Along with his legendary courage and valor, Clive also exhibited a darker side. Recklessly ambitious, hot-tempered, proud, and egotistical, Clive's drive for power and wealth created enemies in the years ahead in India. His self-control and optimism were offset by moods of depression during which he became introverted, sullen, selfish, and unstable. Physically, he was not an imposing figure: He was of medium height, stout, and, as a result of heavy features, not a handsome man.

Fresh from the triumph in the Carnatic, Clive spent a three-year interval in England. In 1753, the same year he sailed for England, he married a woman whose family had East India Company connections. With his financial and military successes in India, he was elected in 1754 to Parliament after political intrigue and aristocratic infighting, only to be expelled by the Commons. Clive then set his eyes once again on India.

LIFE'S WORK

Robert Clive's return to India marked the beginning of the most successful phase of his life. He returned in 1755 to Madras as deputy governor of Fort St. David and as a lieutenant colonel in the Royal Army. The next year, Clive was called on to improve the British position in Bengal, the real source of wealth in India. Calcutta also was a vital center for export trade. The key figure, the nawab of Bengal, had granted trade concessions to both the French and the British. These various forces all vied for greater control of the commerce in Bengal. In 1756, the nawab of Bengal, Siraj-ud-daula, attacked Calcutta, site of a British trading station, and the British surrendered to his force of fifty thousand men. After plundering the city,

Robert Clive. (Library of Congress)

the nawab's forces locked more than one hundred British prisoners in a cell designed only for a few. Their deaths were remembered as the infamous atrocity—the Black Hole of Calcutta.

The British East India Company responded by sending Clive with a force of twenty-four hundred troops, five men-of-war, and five transports. By January, 1757, he recaptured the city with little difficulty. For good measure, a French trading station was captured. After the fighting, the nawab made large concessions to the British, but despite his restoring and extending the company's trading privileges in Bengal, Clive deviously schemed to undermine him. The nawab had been too inconsistent in his relations with the company and could not be trusted. To make the company's position stronger for the future, Clive supported a rival to the throne, the old general Mir Jafar. To conduct the negotiations with Mir Jafar, Clive used an intermediary whom he promised rewards, but in the end Clive double-crossed his middleman by forging a treaty. Clive feared the consequences if the nawab uncovered the treachery, and therefore, secrecy was essential. Furthermore, Clive avoided future obligations to his negotiator with the forged treaty. Clive demonstrated his mastery of political intrigue in eighteenth century British India. He had sensed a weakness in Siraj-ud-daula, whom merchants and military officers increasingly distrusted, and he took advantage of it.

Clive completed his scheme against Siraj-ud-daula at the Battle of Plassey. On June 23, 1757, Clive led an army of eight hundred Europeans and twenty-two hundred Indians against the nawab's Bengal army of more than sixty thousand. The nawab's army folded against the company's forces and his subjects deserted him. When Mir Jafar held back his forces, Siraj-ud-daula fled. Though Clive achieved victory virtually by default, and the outcome was never in doubt, the Battle of Plassey became the epic military triumph of his career.

The results were important for Clive and for the East India Company. On June 28, 1757, the company placed Mir Jafar on the throne as a mere puppet. The new nawab of Bengal reaffirmed privileges granted earlier by Siraj-ud-daula, made an alliance with the British, pledged to fight the French in Bengal, promised large compensations for the earlier loss of Calcutta, and paid huge sums to officials of the East India Company. Clive himself received £234,000 in cash and rights to lucrative land rents. The company, because of Clive's exploits, named him governor and commander in chief in Bengal.

In 1760, after one term as governor, Clive returned to England as a hero and a wealthy man. He purchased a controlling interest in the East India Company and in 1761 was elected to the House of Commons as a member from Shrewsbury. The following year, he was given an Irish peerage as Baron Clive of Plassey and in 1764 was made a Knight of the Bath.

In 1764, conditions so worsened in Bengal that the public demanded his return to India, and the next year his second governorship began. His method of ending the chaos was to strike at corruption. For internal trade, the company had tax exemptions, but company employees stretched it for private individual transactions. These individuals enriched themselves at company expense with tax-exempt trading, and politicians and shareholders became concerned. Clive had support within the company to end this wheeling and dealing. He restricted the size of gifts for political favors, regulated private trade, reduced company allowances, and ended the mutiny of officers. Although Clive initiated these reforms, the salaries for company employees remained low and private trading continued to be financially important for them.

Also during his second governorship, the company secured its position in Bengal. With the French threat practically gone, the company defeated an alliance of the nawab with the king of Oudh and the Mughal emperor at the Battle of Buxar, in 1764. Afterward, the company had the right to collect revenues for all of Bengal and had the power of administration over Bengal through its Indian agents. The company pensioned the nawab and paid off the Mughal emperor.

In January, 1767, Clive, then forty-one years old, his health broken, emotionally drained, left India for the last time for England. His retirement, however, ended in scandal. Parliament's attitude turned against servants of the East India Company who had accumulated vast fortunes in India, especially since some of the money was spent to buy seats in Parliament. In the eighteenth century, success on the battlefield often brought financial rewards, and in that tradition the East India Company had permitted their officials to enrich themselves. Yet Clive's fortune was enormous, despite the financial problems in Bengal. In 1772, the company faced bankruptcy, and committees of Parliament investigated his actions during his first governorship.

With news of his riches from Bengal in the press, the public and Parliament questioned whether Clive had swindled the company. Committees in Parliament questioned his actions in Bengal from 1757 to 1760, and their reports generally condemned Clive's actions. Prominent members of Parliament such as Lord Chatham and Colonel John Burgoyne joined in the assault, and Parliament also passed resolutions critical of private individuals acquiring during wartime vast fortunes that should have gone to the state. Although references to Clive's character were deleted from the resolutions, the huge sum he received as commander in chief in Bengal was included, a mild censure in itself. As to the charges of corruption, Clive defended himself by pointing to his moderation, given the temptation of vast riches at his disposal. Still a member of the Commons with a strong following in that body, Clive survived the attack from Parliament. There was no criminal prosecution, and in 1773, Parliament concluded the proceedings by passing a resolution praising his great service to his country.

Nevertheless, Clive's life ended on a tragic note. In London, on November 22, 1774, at the age of forty-nine, he committed suicide as a result of his poor health and the strain of defending himself before Parliament.

SIGNIFICANCE

Both hero and villain, Robert Clive was a man of contrasts; he deserves both recognition and condemnation. His leadership in Bengal provided the basis for the enormous British colonial empire. His service in India included victories over both French and Indian challenges. Clive's contribution to Arcot and Plassey was probably a combination of military genius and good fortune.

The tragic aspect of Clive's life reflected the moral deficiencies of his time. His recklessness and opportunism were acceptable for the mid-eighteenth century British Empire. Unfortunately for Clive, the British attitude toward empire changed in the late eighteenth century from an emphasis on acquisition and trade to reasonable administration of colonies. The British at home and in India were sensitive to morality in Indian affairs. Clive had been caught in the transition. New laws affecting India illustrated the new mood. In 1773, Parliament passed laws regulating the finances of the East India Company and creating a new constitution for it. To prevent future scandals, the company paid higher salaries to its servants. Clive's misfortune led to this first attempt by the Crown to control the East India Company's rule of India.

—*Douglas Carl Abrams*

FURTHER READING

Davies, A. Mervyn. *Clive of Plassey*. New York: Charles Scribner's Sons, 1939. A generally critical biography of Clive. The author attributes Clive's military successes not to genius but to luck. Comprehensive in its coverage of Clive's career in India.

Edwardes, Michael. *The Battle of Plassey and the Conquest of Bengal*. New York: Macmillan, 1963. Focuses on Clive's victory in 1757. Edwardes covers more of the political intrigue surrounding the battle than the actual battle itself. Plassey is seen as decisive for British and Indian history.

Harvey, Robert. *Clive: The Life and Death of a British Emperor*. New York: Thomas Dunne Books, 2000. Popular biography recounts the story of Clive's life, without offering new information or the Indian perspective of events. However, the book provides an introduction for readers who want a general overview of Clive's life.

Huttenback, Robert A. *The British Imperial Experience*. New York: Harper & Row, 1966. A solid analysis of various topics associated with the full span of the British Empire, geographically and chronologically. The first chapter includes an excellent assessment of Clive.

Lawson, Philip. *The East India Company: A History*. London: Longman, 1993. This study of the company includes information about Clive's role in the company and in India and his political legacy.

Lloyd, T. O. *The British Empire, 1558-1983*. New York: Oxford University Press, 1984. One of few excellent narrative histories of the British Empire from the sixteenth century to the twentieth century. Scholarly and thorough, the work provides proper background for an evaluation of Clive, although it is short on analysis.

Marshall, P. J. *East Indian Fortunes: The British in Bengal in the Eighteenth Century*. New York: Oxford University Press, 1976. A close look at the private side of British expansion in India. Focuses on the small British communities in eighteenth century Bengal and on East India Company employees.

Mason, Philip. *The Men Who Ruled India*. New York: St. Martin's Press, 1954. Begins with the founding of the East India Company in 1600 and continues through the Sepoy mutiny in 1858. Combines history with biography and is favorable to the English in India.

Sutherland, Lucy Stuart. *The East India Company in Eighteenth Century Politics*. New York: Oxford University Press, 1952. Based on company records and massive private correspondence, a comprehensive and scholarly examination of the company in the context of the times. Looks at Westminster politics and company actions in East India.

See also: First Marquess Cornwallis; Joseph-François Dupleix; Warren Hastings.

Related articles in *Great Events from History: The Eighteenth Century, 1701-1800:* 1746-1754: Carnatic Wars; June 23, 1757: Battle of Plassey; August, 1767-May, 1799: Anglo-Mysore Wars; December, 1774-February 24, 1783: First Marāthā War.

ÉTIENNE BONNOT DE CONDILLAC
French philosopher

Through writings famed for their precision, clarity, and persuasiveness, Condillac became the only major figure of the French Enlightenment to create a systematic theory of knowledge and to exhibit a professional command of the issues of philosophy.

Born: September 30, 1715; Grenoble, France
Died: August 2, 1780; Château Flux, Beaugency, France
Also known as: Abbé de Condillac
Area of achievement: Philosophy

EARLY LIFE

Étienne Bonnot de Condillac (ay-tyehn baw-noh duh kohn-dee-yok) was the third son of Gabriel de Bonnot, vicomte de Mably, a magistrate and member of the *noblesse de la robe* in the Dauphiné provincial *parlement*. The name Condillac, by which he would be known for the rest of his life, was added in 1720, when his father bought the nearby estate and domain of that name. As a child, his health was poor, his eyesight was bad, and he was painfully shy. His education did not begin until after he was twelve, when a local priest taught him the basics. His mother, about whom virtually nothing is known, died when he was quite young, and his father died in 1727, when he was thirteen.

After his father's death, he went to live with his eldest brother, Jean Bonnot de Mably, a royal official in Lyons, but his personal situation does not seem to have improved. His shy nature was apparently mistaken by his brother and family for simplemindedness. Jean-Jacques Rousseau, who was hired by Jean to tutor his children for a short time, was able to see what the family had missed, and so began a long friendship.

Condillac's other brother, Gabriel Bonnot, had taken holy orders and styled himself the Abbé de Mably. He, too, saw something in Condillac, and, a few years later, Condillac went to Paris to live with Gabriel. Gabriel entered Condillac first at Saint-Sulpice and then at the Sorbonne to study theology. By 1740, Condillac had completed the course of studies and was ordained a priest.

While he wore a cassock and called himself the Abbé de Condillac for the rest of his life, it was reported that he said mass only once and otherwise chose not to exercise the office. This was not unusual in France at that time. Condillac was a man of pleasant but unremarkable appearance. His portrait shows large, wide-set eyes, a high forehead, and a modest smile. Other evidence indicates that he was of average height but slightly built. He wore neither a beard nor a mustache and kept his hair long and curled in the fashion of the day.

LIFE'S WORK

Condillac was twenty-six years old when he left the Sorbonne, and, under the sponsorship of his brother, was introduced to the social and literary life of Paris. He soon decided that his education was inadequate to move in that circle and began educating himself, reading the works of René Descartes, Gottfried Wilhelm Leibniz, Baruch Spinoza, and Nicolas Malebranche. Sometime during this course of study, he developed a profound disapproval of their speculative systems of thought.

The English philosophers, whom he read next, were much more to his liking. Because he read no English, however, he had to rely on translations or someone's summary and commentary. John Locke's *An Essay Concerning Human Understanding*, published in 1690, had been translated into French in 1700 by Pierre Coste. It was this work that made the deepest impression on Condillac. He also read Voltaire's summary and commentary *Éléments de la philosophie de Newton* (1738; *The Elements of Sir Isaac Newton's Philosophy,* 1738), which also introduced him to the Idealism of Bishop George Berkeley's *A Treatise Concerning the Principles of Human Knowledge* (1710). He was also quite impressed with several works by Francis Bacon.

During these years, Condillac sometimes joined in the social life of the Paris salons, where he renewed his friendship with Rousseau, who introduced him to Denis Diderot. The three became good friends and met often. Later writings by both Rousseau and Diderot reflect Condillac's influence. Condillac does not seem to have made much of an impression on the other intellectuals at the salons, probably because of his acute shyness and timidity. Condillac, however, would make his reputation with the printed word.

In 1746, Condillac published his first book, *Essai sur l'origine des connaissances humaines* (*An Essay on the Origin of Human Understanding*, 1756), and his second, *Traité des systèmes* (treatise on systems), in 1749. These two books were very well received and brought Condillac recognition as a major philosopher. Shortly after publishing the second book, he was honored by election to membership in the Academy of Sciences and Literature of Berlin.

What Condillac sought was a philosophy that was an exact science. He thought philosophy should be clear, precise, universal, and, above all, verifiable. *An Essay on the Origin of Human Understanding* was a systematic elaboration of Locke's theory that all human knowledge was derived from two sources: the information received by the mind through the senses and the mind's ability to reflect upon that information and understand its meaning. It was a brilliant study, using only empirical evidence and a strictly logical methodology. Condillac's essay established empirical sensationism as the prevailing analysis of the working of the human mind for the Enlightenment.

His *Traité des systèmes* was a vigorous criticism of the metaphysical systems of Descartes, Leibniz, and others that were rationalistic and not empirical. He attempted to show that there was no empirical evidence for such ideas as Descartes' innate ideas or for Leibniz's monads, that these ideas were mere speculations without basis in fact. Condillac accused these philosophers of having used vague words that had no clear and precise meaning, thereby producing only confusion and misunderstanding.

In 1754, after some delay because of trouble with his eyes, Condillac published his most advanced work on the theory of empirical sensationism, *Traité des sensations* (*Condillac's Treatise on the Sensations*, 1930). To help illustrate the role of sensation in the acquisition of knowledge, he described what it would be like if a person were encased in marble and his mind had never received any sensory information and, therefore, was completely blank. Condillac then imagined what would happen when the nose was uncovered and how the person's mind would react to a flood of olfactory information. That person's perceptions, comparisons, memories, recognitions, and abstractions would consist only of odors. He then uncovered the other sense organs, one at a time, describing how the mind would react to the new data and correlate it with the data from the other sense organs. Condillac described how—when all senses were functioning together—these sense impressions produced pleasure and pain, and desires and aversions; he also described how all aspects of a person's mental life were derived from sensations.

After his first book on Locke's theory, he had discovered a problem that he attempted to correct in this work. Diderot had pointed it out to him. Locke had written about two sources of knowledge, sensory impressions and the reflection of the mind on these impressions. If sensation did not imprint knowledge directly on the mind but required the reflection of the mind, this meant that the mind was conscious of itself and its operations of thinking, doubting, reasoning, and willing. Condillac thought that this implied the existence of innate ideas, which he denied. In this book, he sought to avoid that issue by making language the means by which sensation passed into reflection to become knowledge. Language was the cause of the most complex operations of the mind, including attention, memory, imagination, and intuition. Since all language was learned, there could be no innate ideas.

In his *Treatise on the Sensations,* Condillac moved from being merely a student of Locke, having produced the most rigorous demonstration of sensationalist theory of his century. When it was pointed out that his work could be interpreted as advocating materialism and atheism, Condillac published two works in 1755 to refute the claim. In the brief *Dissertation sur la liberté,*

Étienne Bonnot de Condillac. (Library of Congress)

and then in *Traité des animaux,* Condillac denied that animals were mere machines and possessed no spiritual soul. Condillac never agreed that his theories eliminated free will or the spiritual side of the human experience.

After 1754, Condillac's work was being discussed by intellectuals in other countries and by high officials of France. In 1758, he was invited to Parma to tutor the duke of Parma's son, Ferdinand, who was a grandchild of the king and queen of France. He remained there until January of 1767, during which time he wrote the impressive sixteen-volume *Cours d'études pour l'instruction du prince de Parme* (1775) for the young Ferdinand. The set included a grammar, a handbook of writing style, a book on the scientific method, an analysis of the psychology of thought, a philosophy of history, and history texts. In appreciation of his services, the duke obtained the revenue of the Premonstratensian Abbey of Mureau for Condillac. This liberal income removed all personal financial worries for the rest of Condillac's life.

In 1768, Condillac, back in Paris, was elected to the French Academy. He was asked to become tutor to the three sons of the dauphine, who included the future kings Louis XVI, Louis XVIII, and Charles X, but he refused. Instead, he devoted himself to the publication of the *Cours d'études pour l'instruction du prince de Parme* and rarely attended the academy or the salons. Condillac's criticisms of church politics had apparently earned for him the hostility of the bishop of Parma, who delayed publication of the works. With the intervention of several of his philosophe friends, Condillac received permission to publish his books in Paris. In 1773, he left Paris for the peace and quiet of the château, where he remained for the rest of his life.

In 1776, Condillac published a book on political economy, *Le Commerce et le gouvernement considérés relativement l'un à l'autre,* in which he presented the novel idea that value was a matter of utility and not labor. That same year, he joined the Société Royale d'Agriculture d'Orléans. Condillac returned to Paris for a short visit each year; his last trip was in the summer of 1780. While there he fell ill and returned to Château Flux. When his condition worsened, he sent for a priest to reaffirm his Catholic faith. He died of a fever on the night of August 2, 1780, at the age of sixty-five.

SIGNIFICANCE

Building on the work of Locke, Étienne Bonnot de Condillac contributed more to a synthesis of epistemology and psychology than did any other writer of philos-ophy of the Enlightenment. His method was empirical observation. His ideas and methodology inspired the philosophes, and reflections of his work are found throughout their works. The goal of the philosophes was to bring about a revolution in the way people thought and to end superstition, prejudice, and ignorance. They hoped to teach people to think clearly, rationally, and scientifically. The major theoretician behind this new way of thinking was Condillac. He established its epistemological foundations, which he had derived with a methodology that he hoped would not only withstand criticism but also be applicable to all the fields of knowledge available to humankind.

Condillac's influence extended beyond his own time. Jeremy Bentham incorporated Condillac's concept of pleasure and pain as motivating forces into his philosophy of Utilitarianism. James Mill and John Stuart Mill also borrowed ideas from Condillac. His philosophy and methodology of history inspired a number of nineteenth and twentieth century historians in their attempts to make the writing of history scientific. The Enlightenment made important and productive contributions to philosophy and to a better understanding of how the human mind works. Condillac's work, which was central to the Enlightenment, is an important part, therefore, of the Western intellectual tradition.

The contrast between Condillac's work as a philosopher and his personal life makes his achievements remarkable. As a philosopher he was a stringent empiricist, but privately he was a devout Catholic. He believed that humans had souls without any empirical evidence to support such a belief. His ideas were among the most radical and progressive of his age, yet politically he was a conservative monarchist. As a philosopher his work concerned all the myriad sensations and experiences a person could have and how knowledge grew from them, but Condillac himself was virtually a one-dimensional person. He never married and was virtually a recluse who shunned contact with all but a very few people. He preferred the quiet and solitude of the countryside to the excitement of the city. With the few close friends he did have, he seems to have discussed only philosophical issues. For Condillac, philosophy was his life.

—*Richard L. Hillard*

FURTHER READING

Brewer, Daniel. *The Discourse of Enlightenment in Eighteenth-Century France: Diderot and the Art of Philosophizing.* New York: Cambridge University

Press, 1993. Describes how French Enlightenment writers attempted to rationally critique and demystify all knowledge. While it focuses on Diderot, the book also contains information about Condillac.

Cassirer, Ernst. *Philosophy of the Enlightenment*. Translated by Fritz A. C. Koelln and James P. Pettegrove. Princeton, N.J.: Princeton University Press, 1951. A brilliant and perceptive work of intellectual history. Cassirer does not present a lengthy discussion of Condillac in any one place. Instead, he integrates his discussion of Condillac into topically arranged analyses, in which he reveals a fine appreciation for what is important and what is peripheral in Condillac's thought.

Condillac, Étienne Bonnot de. *Commerce and Government Considered in Mutual Relationship*. Translated by Shelagh Eltis. Cheltenham, England: Edward Elgar, 1997. English translation of Condillac's economic treatise, in which he argued that commerce and industry, in addition to agriculture, contributed to France's wealth. Includes an introductory essay by Shelagh Eltis and Walter Eltis about Condillac's life and contributions to economics.

Gay, Peter. *The Enlightenment: An Interpretation*. 2 vols. New York: Alfred A. Knopf, 1966-1969. A lively and brilliant interpretation of the Enlightenment organized by topic. Less critical of the philosophes than some historians, but a gold mine of information.

_____. *The Party of Humanity: Essays in the French Enlightenment*. New York: W. W. Norton, 1971. A series of essays on various aspects of the Enlightenment by one of the period's most renowned historians. See especially the essay on "The Unity of the French Enlightenment."

Hazard, Paul. *The European Mind, 1680-1715*. Translated by J. Lewis May. Cleveland, Ohio: World, 1963. An interesting and well-respected treatment of the origins and early days of the Enlightenment. Often treats the philosophes with cynical amusement, which interferes with an appreciation of the book's positive qualities.

Knight, Isabel F. *The Geometric Spirit: The Abbé de Condillac and the French Enlightenment*. New Haven, Conn.: Yale University Press, 1968. This is the closest there is to a biography of Condillac in English. Focuses primarily on Condillac's ideas concerning the origins of knowledge and gives little attention to his personal life. Perceptive in spots, but pedestrian in others.

Krieger, Leonard. *Kings and Philosophers, 1689-1789*. New York: W. W. Norton, 1970. An excellent, well-written history of the Enlightenment age. Explains how the Enlightenment was made possible, in part, by the political stability that resulted from the end of the Reformation wars and the rise of the centralized state, and how the ideas of the Enlightenment came into conflict with divine right monarchies and produced the French Revolution.

Woloch, Isser. *Eighteenth-Century Europe: Tradition and Progress, 1715-1789*. New York: W. W. Norton, 1982. One of the best general histories of the age with a good annotated bibliography. Recommended for the reader who needs an understanding of the entire age before concentrating on the intellectual history of Condillac and the Enlightenment.

See also: Jeremy Bentham; George Berkeley; Denis Diderot; Louis XVI; Jean-Jacques Rousseau; Voltaire.

Related articles in *Great Events from History: The Eighteenth Century, 1701-1800*: October, 1725: Vico Publishes *The New Science*; 1739-1740: Hume Publishes *A Treatise of Human Nature*; 1754: Condillac Defends Sensationalist Theory; April, 1762: Rousseau Publishes *The Social Contract*; July, 1764: Voltaire Publishes *A Philosophical Dictionary for the Pocket*; 1770: Publication of Holbach's *The System of Nature*; 1781: Kant Publishes *Critique of Pure Reason*; 1784-1791: Herder Publishes His Philosophy of History; 1792-1793: Fichte Advocates Free Speech.

MARQUIS DE CONDORCET
French mathematician, philosopher, and revolutionary

Condorcet's works synthesized the thinking of the philosophes of the Enlightenment. He spent his life promoting educational, political, social, and religious change in France.

Born: September 17, 1743; Ribemont, France
Died: March 29, 1794; Bourg-la-Reine, France
Also known as: Marie-Jean-Antoine-Nicolas de Caritat (birth name); Marie-Jean-Antoine-Nicolas Caritat
Areas of achievement: Social reform, education, mathematics, government and politics, philosophy

EARLY LIFE

The marquis de Condorcet (mahr-kee duh kohn-dawr-seh) was born into the very old aristocratic family of Caritat, which took its title, Condorcet, from a town in Dauphiné. The marquis spent his early years in pursuits typical of his class. He received his early education at the Jesuit school in Reims and then entered the Collège de Navarre in Paris. There he developed a lifelong commitment to science. In 1769, he was elected to the Academy of Sciences, followed by membership in the French Academy for his work in the science of statistics and the doctrine of probability. As a result of his reputation in mathematics, he was appointed inspector general of the mint in Paris.

While serving as inspector general, Condorcet met and married Sophie de Grouchy in 1786. Twenty years his junior and considered one of the great beauties of the day, Madame Grouchy presided over a salon of notable reputation, which attracted many of the leading personalities in Paris. There Condorcet conversed with people such as David Hume, the great British philosopher. At this time, Condorcet wrote the biographies, *Vie de M. Turgot* (1786; *The Life of M. Turgot*, 1787) and *Vie de Voltaire* (1789; *The Life of Voltaire*, 1790). These works reflected his appreciation for Anne-Robert-Jacques Turgot's Physiocratic economics and Voltaire's revolutionary religious and social theories. Condorcet had become a philosophe.

He also frequented the Paul-Henri-Dietrich d'Holbach's salon, the Café de l'Europe, where wide-ranging discussion included political and social reform, religion, education, science, and the arts. He wrote for Denis Diderot's *Encyclopédie: Ou, Dictionnaire raisonné des sciences, des arts, et des métiers* (1751-1772; *Encyclopedia*, 1965). While he respected Jean-Jacques Rousseau's

work, it was Jean le Rond d'Alembert's ideas that influenced him most strongly. When the marquis de Lafayette returned from his American success, it was with Condorcet that he conferred about the American Revolution and the future of France. Condorcet also knew Thomas Jefferson and Benjamin Franklin and thought that the United States was the place most likely to implement the ideals of the Enlightenment. Not surprisingly, when the French Revolution began, Condorcet repudiated all the religious and aristocratic ideals of his background and became one of the few philosophes actively involved in the revolution.

LIFE'S WORK

Although he would not survive the revolution, Condorcet is best remembered for the work that he produced during its first five years. On the eve of revolution, Condorcet and Emmanuel-Joseph Sieyès founded the '89 Club, a salon that became the meeting place for the politically moderate Girondists. Condorcet was elected as a representative from Paris to the legislative assembly. As secretary of this body, he wrote the address in 1791 which explained the revolution to the European powers. The following year, he drafted the declaration that suspended the monarchy, disbanded the assembly, and called for a new government, the national convention, to formulate a constitution for France. Though ultimately defeated in favor of the more radical proposal from the Jacobins, Condorcet's was the first of the constitutions presented to the convention. In this government, Condorcet represented the Department of Aisne.

Although the first person to declare for republican government, Condorcet voted against the execution of the king and queen. By 1793, his independent and moderate attitude and his enormous prestige made him dangerous to Robespierre, who was by then in control of the revolution. When Condorcet objected to the arrest of his Girondist friends, Robespierre had him outlawed.

During these hectic but creative early years, Condorcet wrote his two most influential works. The first of these was his educational plan, submitted to the legislative assembly in 1792, which detailed a system for state education. It divided the proposed educational system into four parts: primary, secondary, higher, and adult education, all of which would be coeducational. All instruction would be based in free inquiry under the control of a corporation of scholars, independent of supervision by either the church or the state. The curriculum would be secular in emphasis. Primary education was to be free and compulsory for all children of the state. Characteristic of Jean-Jacques Rousseau's educational theory, students were to be allowed considerable freedom of choice in their curriculum, and administration would be minimal. The higher education component included a system of technical, medical, and teacher-training schools, which when finally implemented became the best in Europe. Condorcet assumed that all people would want and appreciate the opportunity to attend school and that they, like him, would recognize that only through education could the ideal of progress be attained. Although revolution and war prevented its immediate implementation, the plan became the basis of the education system ultimately adopted, not only by the French but also by other nations.

Equally influential was Condorcet's *Esquisse d'un tableau historique des progrès de l'espirit humain* (1795; *Sketch for a Historical Picture of the Progress of the Human Mind*, 1955), written just before his death in 1794. In this work, Condorcet analyzed all human history, past, present, and future; he used history to find evidence to justify his confidence that human progress was inevitable. The work is particularly significant, as it synthesized the major strains of Enlightenment thought and the goals of the French Revolution. It reflects the extent of Condorcet's optimism.

Condorcet divided the history of humankind into ten epochs, eight in the past, the ninth in his own age, and the tenth in the future. Up to the Middle Ages, Condorcet thought that humankind had made great progress. For example, the Greeks had opened the way for humankind's search for truth through the greatest of inventions, philosophy. Then the Dark Ages fell, thought to be shrouded in superstition, ignorance, and clericism. Condorcet saw only the unintended development of precision in argumentation made by the Scholastics and the contributions to poetry, nobility of spirit, and individual freedom made by Dante in *La divina commedia* (c. 1320; *The Divine Comedy*, 1802) as worthy contributions of this epoch.

The fourteenth and fifteenth centuries brought renewed light to human understanding. Witness the development of the printing press, the tool that reawakened the mind of humans, creating, according to Condorcet, "cultural revolution." The ninth epoch was his own, in which the revolution would destroy old ideas and institutions, thus paving the way for the tenth epoch, in which the perfect human would live in a perfect civilization.

All this progress was possible because science had revealed the secrets of nature and technology, which would relieve humans of labor so that they might use their free time for self-improvement. Although Condorcet conceded that the intellectuals would dominate paternalistically until all people had the benefit of education, he believed that once educated, each individual would use his or her time constructively. The improvement of the individual would lead to social and political progress, stop exploitation, and produce true equality. Condorcet recognized that this process was not an easy one and that often there were periods when things seemed bleak, but he firmly believed that the spirit and reason of humans would prevail, that the perfectibility of humans and society was inevitable. He believed in the unity of all knowledge and in the continuity of progress. He thought that this was the consummate lesson of human history.

SIGNIFICANCE

As the youngest of the philosophes, marquis de Condorcet embodied the principles of the Enlightenment. He represented the moderate Girondist position in the French Revolution. Thus, he voted against the execution of the king, while still being one of the first revolutionaries to promote republicanism. He worked hard in several capacities to achieve the goals of the revolution. He was the leading educational theorist of the revolution and the creator of a secular education system that became the model for many state systems established during the nineteenth and twentieth centuries. Condorcet insisted that education and science were crucial to social progress and human perfectibility. His theory of history particularly influenced Auguste Comte and the development of sociology.

Outlawed with other Girondists during the Reign of Terror, Condorcet went into hiding. He spent the last weeks of his life writing the *Sketch for a Historical Picture of the Progress of the Human Mind*, which he is said to have been holding in his hands when he died. On March 24, believing that his hiding place had been discovered, Condorcet fled Paris and hid in the countryside for three days. On March 27, he wandered into the village of Clamart, where he was captured and taken to the prison in Bourg-la-Reine to await execution. Whether by poison or from exhaustion, Condorcet was found dead in his cell two days later. Despite this dismal death, Condorcet never lost his faith in the revolution or his optimism about the progress of the human spirit.

—*Shirley F. Fredricks*

FURTHER READING

Becker, Carl. *The Heavenly City of the Eighteenth Century Philosophers*. New Haven, Conn.: Yale University Press, 1932. Reprinted many times and readily available, this provocative and brilliantly insightful essay has stimulated much research about the nature and influence of Enlightenment thinkers, including Condorcet. Any study of Enlightenment thinkers should begin with this book.

Bury, J. B. *The Idea of Progress: An Inquiry into Its Origins and Growth*. 2d ed. New York: Macmillan, 1932. This now-classic work on the idea of progress as the basic characteristic of Enlightenment thought contains an excellent analysis of Condorcet's role in the development of this idea.

Condorcet, marquis de. *Sketch for a Historical Picture of the Progress of the Human Mind*. Translated by June Barraclough with an introduction by Stuart Hampshire. New York: Noonday Press, 1955. This is an excellent translation of Condorcet's best-known work, which strongly influenced the work of Auguste Comte and the development of sociology.

Durant, Will, and Ariel Durant. *The Age of Voltaire*. New York: Simon & Schuster, 1965. This intelligent, urbane, highly readable, and readily available account of the Enlightenment contains excellent insights into the role and contributions of Condorcet.

Gay, Peter. *The Party of Humanity: Essays in the French Enlightenment*. New York: Alfred A. Knopf, 1964. This stylistically excellent, soundly researched book is a brilliant synthesis of the various threads of Enlightenment thought. It clearly illustrates the environment that produced Condorcet as well as his contributions to the revolutionary quality of his age.

Goodell, Edward. *The Noble Philosopher: Condorcet and the Enlightenment*. Buffalo, N.Y.: Prometheus Books, 1994. Examines Condorcet's life and work. Goodell places special emphasis on *Sketch for a Historical Picture of the Progress of the Human Mind* as an example of Condorcet's thought and contributions to Enlightenment philosophy.

Lovejoy, Arthur O. *The Great Chain of Being: A Study of the History of an Idea*. Cambridge, Mass.: Harvard University Press, 1936. This standard work details the history of the ideas of natural law and progress.

Martin, Kingsley. *French Liberal Thought in the Eighteenth Century: A Study of Political Ideas from Bayle to Condorcet*. New York: Harper & Row, 1963. Based almost exclusively upon primary sources, this book remains the best analysis of the development of liberal thought in the eighteenth century. As such, it describes Condorcet's contributions, particularly his theories of history, social progress, and human perfectibility.

Shapiro, J. Salwyn. *Condorcet and the Rise of Liberalism*. New York: Harcourt, Brace, 1934. This biography is a thorough study of Condorcet and his contributions to the tradition of liberal thought in Western society.

Williams, David. *Condorcet and Modernity*. New York: Cambridge University Press, 2004. Analysis of Condorcet's political theory, examining the connection between Condorcet as a visionary idealist and a pragmatic legislator.

See also: Jean le Rond d'Alembert; Denis Diderot; Benjamin Franklin; Paul-Henri-Dietrich d'Holbach; David Hume; Thomas Jefferson; Robespierre; Jean-Jacques Rousseau; Emmanuel-Joseph Sieyès; Anne-Robert-Jacques Turgot; Voltaire.

Related articles in *Great Events from History: The Eighteenth Century, 1701-1800*: 1739-1740: Hume Publishes *A Treatise of Human Nature*; 1743-1744: D'Alembert Develops His Axioms of Motion; 1751-1772: Diderot Publishes the *Encyclopedia*; June, 1752: Franklin Demonstrates the Electrical Nature of Lightning; April, 1762: Rousseau Publishes *The Social Contract*; July, 1764: Voltaire Publishes *A Philosophical Dictionary for the Pocket*; 1770: Publication of Holbach's *The System of Nature*; July 4, 1776: Declaration of Independence; 1782-1798: Publication of Rousseau's *Confessions*; June 20, 1789: Oath of the Tennis Court; July 14, 1789: Fall of the Bastille; 1790: Burke Lays the Foundations of Modern Conservatism; April 20, 1792-October, 1797: Early Wars of the French Revolution; July 27-28, 1794: Fall of Robespierre.

JAMES COOK
English mariner and explorer

With his inspired seamanship and his practical grasp of scientific method, Cook added greatly to world knowledge of geography and oceanography. His voyages led to British colonialism in the Pacific.

Born: October 27, 1728; Marton, Yorkshire, England
Died: February 14, 1779; Kealakekua Bay, Hawaii
Also known as: Captian Cook
Areas of achievement: Exploration, geography, cartography, astronomy, mathematics

EARLY LIFE

James Cook was born in the small village of Marton in the northern county of Yorkshire, England, but he spent most of his boyhood in the nearby village of Great Ayton. His father was a Scottish farm laborer who had married a Yorkshire woman. His father's employer, spotting young Cook's potential, paid for the boy to attend the Great Ayton village school.

At sixteen years old, Cook was apprenticed to a grocer and haberdasher in the tiny Yorkshire fishing village of Staithes, but after eighteen months he persuaded his employer to release him, and with his parents' backing he was reapprenticed to John Walker, a master mariner and coal shipper, at the nearby seaport of Whitby.

During the following nine years, Cook gained a wide experience in the harsh conditions of the North Sea and was promoted to serve as mate. In 1755, Walker invited him to command one of his ships—a major career opportunity that would have saved him, since talk of war was in the air, from the press gangs. He chose instead to volunteer for the navy as an able seaman, sharing the rough conditions and low pay of the mainly impressed crews. He soon rose to the rank of master—the most responsible noncommissioned rank in the navy of that time.

England and France in the mid-eighteenth century were the keenest rivals in an intense struggle among European nations for trade and territorial rights. In 1758, when war broke out between them over French conquests in North America, Cook set sail for Nova Scotia as master of HMS *Pembroke*. His meticulous survey of the St. Lawrence River contributed to the British victory at Quebec. After the peace treaty, he was sent back to Newfoundland as ship's surveyor. Before Cook set sail, he married Elizabeth Batts, and a family house was eventually established in London's Mile End. The couple had six children, but three died in infancy and the two oldest sons were killed at sea.

The authorities were impressed by Cook's work in Newfoundland—his accurate charting and his observations of an eclipse of the sun—which showed him to combine a flair for seamanship and navigation with an understanding of scientific principles. In 1765, he was chosen to lead the first of the three voyages of discovery that were to make him a legend in his lifetime.

Portraits painted during Cook's peak years depict him as a man with a commanding presence, a strong, bony face and prominent nose, piercing eyes, and the firm mouth of a strict disciplinarian. He was much admired and respected by the officers and men who sailed under his command, not only for his seamanship and leadership but also for his fair-mindedness and individual acts of kindness. They criticized him, however, for his tendency to favor secrecy over consultation and for his harsh excesses of discipline, especially on the final voyage.

LIFE'S WORK

James Cook's first voyage was sponsored by the Royal Society, a body of distinguished figures devoted to the furtherance of scientific inquiry, in conjunction with the Admiralty. Its official purpose was to sail to Tahiti (previously located by Captain Samuel Wallis) to observe the transit of Venus, an infrequent phenomenon in which the planet transverses the sun's disc. It was thought that accurate observations of the transit, which were to be undertaken by observers from many different countries and vantage points, would contribute to the art of plotting longitude. This was of major importance to the seagoing nations, for despite the celebrated voyages of discovery over the centuries, land has been "discovered" and then "lost" again, because of the problems of longitude charting without adequate instruments for seafarers lacking Cook's understanding of astronomy. Cook also had sealed orders to sail south from Tahiti in search of Terra Australis Incognito—a vast, paradisiacal, southern continent that philosophers had dreamed of and explorers had sought through the ages.

Cook, now commissioned as a lieutenant, set sail from Plymouth on August 25, 1768, in HMS *Endeavour*, with a company of ninety-four, including an eleven-man party from the Royal Society headed by the wealthy botanist Sir Joseph Banks, with an astronomer, an artist, and various servants. In the course of the voyage to follow, the observation of the transit of Venus was not wholly successful, and there were no sightings of the mysterious unknown continent. The main triumph of the voyage was Cook's circumnavigation of New Zealand and his charting, despite being nearly shipwrecked on the then unknown Great Barrier Reef, of the east coast of New Amsterdam (Australia), thereby adding to the work on the other three coasts previously pioneered by the Dutch. When the *Endeavour* returned to Great Britain on July 13, 1771, Cook and Banks were welcomed back as heroes.

Despite an unsuccessful first try, neither Cook nor the Admiralty had given up hope of discovering the unknown continent. Admiralty orders for the second voyage again included a search for the unknown continent, this time in the Antarctic regions. A specially designed chronometer was supplied by the Admiralty to be tested as an aid to plotting longitude.

Cook, promoted to captain, was given command of HMS *Resolution*, which left Plymouth on July 13, 1772, accompanied by HMS *Adventure*, under Captain Tobias Furneaux. For three summers, the ships pummeled away at the Antarctic, reaching a latitude of seventy-one degrees, ten seconds—farther south than anyone had previously sailed—with the crews suffering excruciatingly harsh conditions. "I am now fully satisfied," Cook wrote to John Walker, "that there is no Southern continent."

In the winter months, Cook and company sailed the Pacific, putting in at various anchorages for repairs and supplies, making contact with the local populations, bartering beads, red feathers, and much sought after iron nails and axes, and distributing livestock and seeds. New islands identified included the Friendly Islands, the Hervey Islands, and New Caledonia, and Cook was able to explore New Zealand in further detail. During a long stay in Tahiti, Furneaux took on board a young Tahitian man, Omai, who would become the toast of London society.

Cook returned to England on July 29, 1775, and was again feted as a hero. The Royal Society elected him a member, and the Admiralty awarded him a retirement position as fourth post captain at Greenwich Naval Hospital, with a generous salary that was to ensure his family's future. He accepted the position on condition that he be allowed to command an expedition again if the occasion arose.

Cook's next opportunity came in 1776, while he was getting his journals ready for publication. The Admiralty was preparing an expedition to the North Pacific to try to establish a northwest passage from the Pacific to the Atlantic. The expedition was also to return Omai to Tahiti. Cook was given command of the *Resolution;* the sister ship, HMS *Discovery*, was commissioned under Captain Charles Clerke. By the time of departure, the American War of Independence had set England and America at war with each other, but it was too late to cancel the voyage.

The *Resolution* sailed from Plymouth on July 12, 1776, with so much livestock aboard that Cook compared it to Noah's ark. A series of untoward circumstances, including damage to the *Resolution*'s masts and stormy seas, led to a six-month delay in reaching Tahiti, where Omai was returned to his people, and the loss of the first summer for Arctic exploration. Cook spent part of the voyage in further exploration; his major discovery was the Hawaiian group

Captain James Cook. (Hawaii State Archives)

INSTRUCTIONS FOR COOK'S AUSTRALIAN VOYAGE

James Cook received secret instructions from the British Admiralty, the Royal Navy board, ordering him to seek a continent between 40° latitude and the already discovered island of New Zealand. He was instructed to then explore and claim the new continent in the name of the British Empire.

If you discover the Continent above-mentioned either in your Run to the Southward or to the Westward as above directed, You are to employ yourself diligently in exploring as great an Extent of the Coast as you can; carefully observing the true situation thereof both in Latitude and Longitude, the Variation of the Needle, bearings of Head Lands, Height, direction and Course of the Tides and Currents, Depths and Soundings of the Sea, Shoals, Rocks, &ca and also surveying and making Charts, and taking Views of such Bays, Harbours and Parts of the Coast as may be useful to Navigation.

You are also carefully to observe the Nature of the Soil, and the Products thereof; the Beasts and Fowls that inhabit or frequent it, the fishes that are to be found in the Rivers or upon the Coast and in what Plenty; and in case you find any Mines, Minerals or valuable stones you are to bring home Specimens of each, as also such Specimens of the Seeds of the Trees, Fruits and Grains as you may be able to collect, and Transmit them to our Secretary that We may cause proper examination and Experiments to be made of them.

You are likewise to observe the Genius, Temper, Disposition and Number of the Natives, if there be any, and endeavour by all proper means to cultivate a Friendship and Alliance with them, making them presents of such Trifles as they may Value, inviting them to Traffick, and Shewing them every kind of Civility and Regard; taking Care however not to suffer yourself to be surprized by them, but to be always on your guard against any Accident.

You are also with the Consent of the Natives to take possession of Convenient Situations in the Country in the name of the King of Great Britain; or, if you find the Country uninhabited take Possession for his Majesty by setting up Proper Marks and inscriptions, as first discoverers and possessors.

Source: "Additional Instructions for Lt. James Cook, Appointed to Command His Majesty's Bark The Endeavour." Secret Orders from the Admiralty. http://www.geocities.com/TheTropics/7557/secret.html. Accessed September, 2005.

of islands, which he called the Sandwich Islands, after Lord Sandwich, at the Admiralty.

In the second summer, the two ships probed the whole of "New Albion"—the northwest coast of America—to see if there was any navigable eastward passage, and then sailed in appalling weather to the Bering Strait. Prevented from further Arctic exploration by solid ice, the ships returned to Hawaii intending to try again the following summer.

Cook's reception by the Hawaiians was extraordinary. As soon as he stepped ashore, indigenous peoples prostrated themselves before him. He was treated with great pomp and ceremony, the significance of

which he had little understanding. Historians have since suggested that Cook may have been mistaken for one of the Hawaiian gods, Orono, who, it was predicted, would return to the island by ship. The generosity of the Hawaiians was so great that they depleted their own stores, and after a month they hinted that it was time for the ships to leave. Not long after the departure, however, the *Resolution* developed rigging trouble and had no option but to return to the island.

During the third voyage, Cook seems to have been under considerable nervous strain. He suffered from bouts of ill health, and the explosive fits of temper for which he was renowned among the seamen became more frequent and intense. He grew impatient of theft by the islanders and even, on one occasion, burned down houses in an effort to get stolen property returned. The strain was intensified when Cook returned to Hawaii. The Hawaiians, perhaps having, in the interim, become doubtful of Cook's status as a god, received the two ships with unexpected hostility. On February 14, 1779, during an onshore confrontation with them in Kealakekua Bay over some stolen property, Cook was stoned and stabbed to death. The Hawaiians were said to have shown deep regret for what had happened in the heat of the moment, and to have held Cook's memory in high esteem.

After a funeral ceremony at sea, the expedition continued toward the Arctic with Captain Clerke in charge of the *Resolution* and John Gore, Cook's second-in-command, heading the *Discovery*. The ships were again defeated by ice, and on the return voyage, Clerke died of tuberculosis. The two ships finally reached home in October, 1780.

SIGNIFICANCE

Captain James Cook has captured the popular imagination over the centuries as a person of humble origins who rose through his own efforts to become one of the world's great navigators. The second half of the eighteenth century was a period not only of intense rivalry between European nations for trade and conquest but also of dramatic expansion of scientific and geographical knowledge, aided by rapid advances in the development of instruments and navigational techniques. Cook's genius for seamanship, combined with his capacity for meticulous surveying and charting and his understanding of astronomy and mathematics, exactly matched the needs of the moment.

Cook's three great voyages of discovery brought prestige to Great Britain and helped to consolidate its position as a leading maritime and trading nation. By annexing territories for the Crown—usually by such simple ceremonies as carving an inscription on a tree or leaving a written declaration in a bottle on a mound of stones, according to the custom of the times—he laid the foundation for British colonial development in the Pacific. At the same time, it must be said, he sowed the seeds of destruction of the indigenous Pacific cultures.

Practical and down-to-earth, Cook dispelled two long-standing romantic illusions about world geography. His proof that there was no unknown continent and no navigable passage through the North American mainland was as valuable as his more positive findings. The imagination with which Cook conjured names for every new bay, river, or headland he charted was one of the few indications of romanticism in his own makeup. His log books and journals, giving vivid descriptions of the terrains he explored and of the lives and customs of the peoples he met, added greatly to the store of human knowledge, as did the botanical specimens and exotic artifacts brought back by Joseph Banks from the first voyage.

By strict control of his ships and ships' companies, with rigid rules about hygiene and diet, Cook was able to eliminate scurvy from his vessels, thereby making an important contribution to the future health of the British navy. He was less successful, however, in his attempts to prevent his sailors from infecting the island communities with sexually transmitted diseases, and he was humane enough to express deep worry and regret about this in his journals.

Of all Cook's achievements, perhaps the most important one for his century was his demonstration—especially on the second voyage, during which he sailed the equivalent of three times around the world and reached farther south into the Antarctic than had any previous explorer—that with proper management of men and resources, a ship could stay at sea almost indefinitely.

—*Nina Hibbin*

FURTHER READING

Barrow, John. *A Chronological History of the Voyages into the Arctic Regions*. London: J. Murray, 1818. Reprint. London: Newton Abbott, David and Charles, 1971. The reprint edition includes an introduction by Christopher Lloyd. The original title page explains that the voyage was "undertaken chiefly for the purpose of discovering a north-east, north-west or polar passage." Provides historical and geographical context for Cook's last voyage.

Beaglehole, John Cawte. *The Life of Captain James Cook*. London: Adam and Charles Black, 1974. This is the definitive account of Cook's life and exploits, with an abundance of detail providing the historical, scientific, and geographical context. Includes reprints of charts, maps, paintings, and sketches, some by Cook himself. The text is so comprehensive and detailed that it is difficult to identify key points; chapter summaries would have been a useful addition.

Carrington, Hugh. *Life of Captain Cook*. London: Sidgwick and Jackson, 1939. A good, standard account of Cook's life and voyages, but it glosses over negative aspects. There are useful appendices on the personnel of the *Endeavour*, Cook's family, and his ships, and comments on his controversial reputation in Hawaii. Contains a reproduction of a chart of the Pacific Ocean, drawn in 1756 and used by Cook on the first voyage, showing the limitation of geographical knowledge before Cook.

Collingridge, Vanessa. *Captain Cook: A Legacy Under Fire*. Guilford, Conn.: Lyons Press, 2002. Collingridge disputes the claim that Cook was the first person to discover Australia by recounting the story of her distant cousin, British aristocrat George Collingridge. In 1883, Collingridge visited Australia and found maps dating from 1542 through 1546. After some research, he discovered the maps were made by Dutch cartographers, based upon previous Portuguese maps. Collingwood intersperses the story of Cook's explorations with the story of her cousin's attempts to prove that the Dutch had discovered Australia long before Cook.

Cook, James. *The Journals of Captain James Cook on His Voyages of Discovery*. Edited by John Cawte Beaglehole. 4 vols. Cambridge, England: Hakluyt Society and Cambridge University Press, 1955-1967.

Includes the full texts of Cook's holograph journals as well as journals of Captain Clerke and others, and reprints of correspondence, documents, drawings, and paintings. A long introduction by Beaglehole assesses Cook's strengths and weaknesses. The best primary source for the study of Cook.

Hough, Richard. *Captain James Cook*. New York: W. W. Norton, 1995. A popular biography, written in a readable narrative style. Hough argues that Cook provided a link between eighteenth century science and the coming Industrial Revolution.

_____. *The Murder of Captain James Cook*. London: Macmillan, 1979. A very full account of the third voyage with a detailed analysis of Cook's death, putting forward the theory that the tragedy was a result of a change in Cook's character.

Jopplen, Rodigar, and Bernard Smith. *The Art of Captain Cook's Voyages*. 2 vols. New Haven, Conn.: Yale University Press, 1985. A beautifully bound and produced book, with superb reproductions of prints and paintings associated with the voyages. Also contains a descriptive catalog of all the known original drawings of peoples, places, artifacts, and events connected with Cook and his voyages.

McCormick, Eric Hall. *Omai: Pacific Envoy*. Auckland, New Zealand: Auckland University Press and Oxford University Press, 1977. A comprehensive study of how Omai was brought to London and why his presence created so much interest. The analysis of the clash of cultures is of particular interest. Illustrations include reprints of all known likenesses of Omai.

MacLean, Alistair. *Captain Cook*. New York: Doubleday, 1972. A popular and very readable biography.

See also: Sir Joseph Banks; Vitus Jonassen Bering; William Bligh; James Bruce; Edward Jenner; Sir Alexander Mackenzie; Arthur Phillip; George Vancouver.

Related articles in *Great Events from History: The Eighteenth Century, 1701-1800:* 1714-1762: Quest for Longitude; April 5, 1722: European Discovery of Easter Island; 1752-March, 1756: Mayer's Lunar Tables Enable Mariners to Determine Longitude at Sea; December 5, 1766-March, 16, 1769: Bougainville Circumnavigates the Globe; August 25, 1768-February 14, 1779: Voyages of Captain Cook; January 26, 1788: Britain Establishes Penal Colony in Australia.

JOHN SINGLETON COPLEY
American painter

Copley achieved a striking realism in his portraits and a vibrant excitement in his historical paintings. In gaining international acclaim, he showed that America could have a distinguished cultural life.

Born: July 3, 1738; Boston, Massachusetts
Died: September 9, 1815; London, England
Area of achievement: Art

EARLY LIFE
John Singleton Copley's English ancestors migrated to Ireland in the 1660's. His parents, Mary Singleton and Richard Copley, were married there in 1735 and then came to Boston about a year later, where they ran a tobacco shop. Richard Copley died a few years later. John Singleton Copley, who had been born in 1738, was still a small boy, and his mother was left to run the tobacco shop alone. They lived in very modest circumstances until the boy was ten.

When his mother remarried in 1748, John's life took a crucial turn. His new stepfather was Peter Pelham

(c. 1695-1751), who already had something of an artistic career under way. He had been a moderately successful mezzotint engraver in London for some years when he decided to emigrate to Boston in 1727. There he found little public interest in his engravings, but he was a versatile man who undertook various other activities to make a living, including teaching.

Pelham had a number of artistic friends, including the distinguished portraitist John Smibert (1688-1751), whom he had known in London. Smibert was the foremost of a number of painters who were in Boston at the time, doing portraits and family groups from which engravings were often made. All of them, including Robert Feke (c. 1705-c. 1750), John Greenwood (1727-1792), and Joseph Badger (1708-1765), were household acquaintances of the Pelham family. Their influence on the talented and impressionable boy can be seen in the early work he did in his own artistic career.

The young Copley was a studious, industrious, somewhat introverted person, who read his stepfather's books on art and learned to use the engraver's tools. He was rather a good-looking boy who could manage the pleasant expression and good manners expected of him, while, like many teenagers, in his private thoughts he resented the great limitations of the provincial community in which he lived. Some time later, he expressed this resentment by declaring that in Boston painting was regarded mainly as a way of preserving likenesses of favored persons. The people seemed to think of painting, he complained, as simply another trade, like that of a carpenter, tailor, or shoemaker, rather than as one of the noble arts of the world.

Into this household a son, Henry Pelham, was born, in 1749. Then, in December, 1751, Peter Pelham died. Copley, at thirteen, again had no father. While there were older stepbrothers, Copley felt strongly that he should do all he could to support his mother and the new half brother. Within a year or two, he used Pelham's tools and studio to produce a few portraits and other pictures. Thus, his artistic career was launched at an astonishingly early age, as he was driven by a combination of natural zest and ability for the work, and by adverse personal circumstances.

LIFE'S WORK

It was natural that the young Copley's first efforts at engraving and painting should be a virtual continuation, both in subject and in style, of the work of Peter Pelham. After doing only one engraving, however, he devoted himself exclusively to painting. For some time, his work was much like that of other artists; yet, already, there were subtle but distinct differences. His idea of the painter's art, prompted by his reading about the Renaissance and the various old masters of European fame, went well beyond the portraiture that dominated colonial American fashion. He experimented with paintings from prints of scenes depicting classical mythology, but no one was much interested in them. Bostonians wanted portraits, and so he worked energetically to paint them. His portraits, beginning with one of his stepbrother, Charles Pelham (1754), were well received, and he was given frequent commissions within a short time. Among those early portraits were those of Joshua Winslow (1755), William Brattle (1756), and Mr. and Mrs. Jonathan Belcher (1756), all prominent members of society whose names are familiar to historians. Copley was not yet twenty years old.

It was in the 1760's that his talent burst forth into genuine distinction. His portraits of the Reverend Edward Holyoke (1759-1761) and of Epes Sargent (1759-1761)

show a striking realism and great insight into human nature, qualities that eventually became distinguished features of Copley's work. The young John Hancock had just inherited a fortune from his wealthy merchant uncle, Thomas Hancock, when he sat for a portrait by Copley (1765). He was very pleased, and this led to his request that Copley paint a portrait of his Uncle Thomas, to be presented to Harvard College, which had been a particular interest of the late merchant. That huge canvas, more than 8 feet high, was praised by many people. Copley's fame was rising.

It was in 1765 that Copley painted the picture that changed his life, a portrait of his younger half brother, Henry Pelham; it later became known as *Boy with a Squirrel*. He sent this work to a friend in London, apparently hoping that a favorable reception of it would make him known beyond the colonies, and it did. Exhibited in 1766, it was strongly praised by the great Sir Joshua Reynolds, and also by the brilliant young Benjamin West (also born in 1738), an American whose precocious achievements as a painter had brought him to Europe a few years earlier. Both offered constructive criticisms, relatively minor ones. West, for his part, also began a correspondence with Copley, in which he repeatedly urged the Bostonian to come to London. Yet Copley was making a large amount of money by this time, for he had become much in demand as the premier portraitist of America. On Thanksgiving Day, 1769, Copley married Susanna Farnham Clarke, daughter of the well-to-do Richard Clarke, a merchant and agent for the British East India Company. It was a loving, solid marriage, which sustained both of them during the troublesome years that were to come. Three of their six children lived, as did their mother, beyond the age of ninety.

The times had become turbulent in Boston, especially since the Stamp Act riots (1765), boycotts, demonstrations by the radical Sons of Liberty (including the Boston Tea Party in 1773), and, finally, the arrival of British troops to keep order. Earlier, in 1770, there had been a confrontation with the troops in which five civilians were killed (the Boston Massacre). Copley probably, in a general way, shared the hostility to British policies, but he did his best to stay out of politics. His wife's family and friends were nearly all Loyalists, some of them prominent and outspoken ones.

Copley's artistic talents at this time were still growing. He was doing more and more pastels, wherein his gift as a colorist became especially impressive. He went to New York at the behest of Myles Cooper, president of King's College (whose portrait he had painted when

Cooper visited Boston). There, in seven months, he painted thirty-seven portraits, which included, he believed, some of his best work. Yet, as people in all social and political ranks became ever more preoccupied with the escalating troubles over British authority in America, the commissions became fewer. Copley had long had friends on both sides of the Anglo-American quarrels, but increasingly it was difficult to maintain neutrality.

At last, he made a difficult decision: He left Boston in June, 1774, for a study trip to Europe, the move that Benjamin West had urged so long as necessary for Copley's professional growth. Copley always insisted that he left Boston only to improve his art. Along with many people of the time, he probably believed that the political troubles would pass, and he could return in a year or two to resume remunerative work. Instead, Parliament's policy became much more severe, and Americans reacted strongly, leading to actual war by April, 1775. Late in May, Copley's wife and children sailed for England; her Loyalist father and brothers came afterward. In October, Copley returned to London from his European tour, which had indeed been enriching, and there was a joyous family reunion. His American career was finished; he never returned to his native land.

Copley's English career began in most promising circumstances. His reputation in England was high, he had friends among the most prominent men in artistic circles, his work habits were excellent and well established, and he was eager to paint. At first, for the sake of income, he painted mostly portraits. Later, he was able to do the historical paintings for which Americans had shown little interest. The first of these, *Watson and the Shark* (1778), received high critical acclaim, and it was a quick popular success. This painting was soon followed by *The Death of the Earl of Chatham* (1779-1781), a bold effort to portray on a heroic scale a recent (1778) event. It was fraught with political danger (Chatham had his enemies), the setting of the picture (the House of Lords) was known to many, and there were fifty-five portraits of public figures in it. Nevertheless, it was a great success, and it assured Copley's reputation as one of the two great historical painters of the time. The other was his friend and fellow American, West. Other historical paintings that followed were also praised, including *The Death of Major Peirson* (1782-1784) and *The Siege of Gibraltar* (1783-1791).

In 1783, Copley was admitted to full membership in the Royal Academy. He moved his family to a fine new house. He received permission (though not a commission) to paint members of the royal family. That painting, known as *The Three Youngest Daughters of King George III* (1785) would, he assumed, bring him actual royal commissions; at the least, it would surely bring much business from the highest nobility, who would be pleased to have portraits done by one who painted for the royal family. His painting received poor reviews, however, and, while he continued to paint portraits, rarely were his sitters from the upper nobility.

At this time, Copley began to be plagued with other disappointments, as well. Both of the two children who had been born in England died within two weeks, late in 1785. Another picture was severely criticized in 1786. Copley had offended the Royal Academy when he exhibited his *Death of the Earl of Chatham* privately, before it could be shown in an Academy exhibition. Then, he repeated the offense with his huge *The Siege of Gibraltar* (it was truly a spectacle, nearly 18 feet high and 24 feet wide), for which he had a huge tent erected for public exhibition. Finally, a rift began to develop between him and West, whose political sagacity at least equaled his artistic talent, for he was on his way to becoming the president of the Royal Academy.

Copley continued his assiduous labors for the remainder of his life. Many of his last paintings were excellent, although none surpassed and few equaled his earlier best work. The prolonged wars with France (1793-1815) became more and more disruptive for Copley and his circle. His living costs remained high and even increased to the point at which they exceeded his income. Some artistic decline accompanied his physical decline. He died on September 9, 1815.

SIGNIFICANCE

Copley rose from modest circumstances to become, in a twenty-year period, the foremost painter in America. He achieved distinction in his portraits, with his close attention to exact detail, lifelike realism, and insight into personality and character. Furthermore, many of the portraits have inestimable historical value: Paul Revere, sitting in shirt sleeves, holding his teapot, tools before him; Samuel Adams, in a good but plain suit, papers in hand, pointing to more papers before him, about to speak (one supposes) against British tyranny; these and other images make the men and women, and the times, come alive. His portrait of John Adams, painted later in England, also has this lifelike quality. In his English career, Copley became regarded as among the foremost painters of the time, virtually the peer of Reynolds, Thomas Gainsborough, and George Romney. His historical paintings contain multiple masterpieces of portraiture, and they excite interest in significant events.

At a time when pride in America was crucially needed, Copley contributed to that pride. He always denied that he was a Loyalist, and there are passages in his letters and traditional anecdotes that support him. After the war, he had cordial relationships with visiting Americans, and he painted some of their portraits. His daughter married a Boston merchant, and Copley's contacts with Boston continued. Yet his impact on a rising American culture was found in his demonstration that an American could achieve renown in the arts. This example provided inspiration to many aspiring American artists, who wanted their new country to share in full measure the richness of civilization and culture.

—*Richard D. Miles*

FURTHER READING

Amory, Martha Babcock. *The Domestic and Artistic Life of John Singleton Copley, R. A.* Boston: Houghton Mifflin, 1882. Family traditions and personal information by Copley's granddaughter. Although some information is erroneous, this book enhances one's understanding of Copley through its many anecdotes and the letters reprinted here.

Flexner, James Thomas. *American Painting: First Flowers of Our Wilderness.* Boston: Houghton Mifflin, 1947. Illustrated survey of colonial American painting, especially good on problems faced by aspiring artists. Chapters 9 and 10 are on Copley, and they provide a lively story of the artist to 1774.

_____. *John Singleton Copley.* Boston: Houghton Mifflin, 1948. A brief biography that is especially good reading. The author revised and enlarged his treatment of Copley from an earlier book, *America's Old Masters: First Artists of the New World* (1939). Includes thirty-two black-and-white plates plus a frontispiece in color.

Frankenstein, Alfred. *The World of Copley, 1738-1815.* Alexandria, Va.: Time-Life Books, 1970. A well-written, relatively brief account of Copley's life that emphasizes the art as much as the man. Effectively portrays the context of Copley's work, both the world into which he arrived and the quite different world at the time of his death. Includes beautiful illustrations, some in color.

Jones, Guernsey, ed. *Letters and Papers of John Singleton Copley and Henry Pelham.* Vol. 71. Boston: Massachusetts Historical Society, 1914. Indispensable material for a serious study of Copley.

Neff, Emily Ballew. *John Singleton Copley in England.* Houston, Tex.: Museum of Fine Arts, 1995. The catalog that accompanied an exhibition of the work Copley created during his years in England. Includes an essay.

Prown, Jules David. *John Singleton Copley.* 2 vols. Cambridge, Mass.: Harvard University Press, 1966. The most valuable single source of reliable, detailed information about the artist and his work. Brings together biographical information and informed aesthetic commentary. Impressive scholarship, and delightful to read. Appendices are invaluable, including checklists of pictures and 678 illustrations.

Rebora, Carrie, et al. *John Singleton Copley in America.* New York: H. N. Abrams, 1995. The catalog that accompanied an exhibition of the works Copley created while living in the colonial United States. Includes essays describing his life, art training, and techniques, and reproductions of the paintings, pastels, and miniatures displayed in the exhibition.

Weekley, Carolyn J. *John Singleton Copley: An American Painter Entirely Devoted to His Art.* Williamsburg, Va.: Colonial Williamsburg Foundation, 1994. A 31-page illustrated pamphlet examining Copley and his work.

See also: John Adams; Samuel Adams; Thomas Gainsborough; George III; John Hancock; Charles Willson Peale; Paul Revere; Sir Joshua Reynolds; George Romney; Benjamin West.

Related articles in *Great Events from History: The Eighteenth Century, 1701-1800:* March 22, 1765-March 18, 1766: Stamp Act Crisis; March 5, 1770: Boston Massacre; December 16, 1773: Boston Tea Party; April 20, 1792-October, 1797: Early Wars of the French Revolution.

FIRST MARQUESS CORNWALLIS
British military commander and colonial governor

Cornwallis served his country on three continents, combining military skill with private and public probity as the chief civil administrator in India and Ireland.

Born: December 31, 1738; London, England
Died: October 5, 1805; Ghazipur (now in Uttar Pradesh), India
Also known as: Charles Cornwallis (full name); Viscount Brome; Lord Cornwallis; Earl Cornwallis
Areas of achievement: Government and politics, military

EARLY LIFE

Charles Cornwallis was the eldest son of the Fifth Baron Cornwallis and Elizabeth, daughter of the Second Viscount Townshend. When his father rose in 1753 to become Earl Cornwallis and Viscount Brome, Charles received the courtesy title of Viscount Brome. The family estates lay in Suffolk, where an ancestor had built Brome Hall in the sixteenth century and where the larger and more recent inheritance of Culford Hall stood.

Cornwallis attended Eton, where, while playing hockey, he received an eye injury that gave him a heavy-lidded appearance. Before his eighteenth birthday, he determined upon a military career, and on December 8, 1756, he became an ensign in the Grenadier Guards. Cornwallis sought to broaden his professional knowledge through formal instruction. Since England had no military academies, he crossed the channel to Europe in the summer of 1757 to attend one. He journeyed on the Continent and then entered the military academy at Turin, where he studied for several months. Cornwallis left to travel to Europe again when the Seven Years' War erupted. After he learned that his regiment had departed to join an Anglo-German army commanded by Prince Ferdinand of Brunswick, he joined the prince's force directly. Cornwallis then secured an appointment, on August 6, 1758, as aide-de-camp to the Marquess of Granby, who would next year command the British forces in Germany.

LIFE'S WORK

First Marquess Cornwallis served almost continuously throughout the war in Germany. He became a captain in the Eighty-fifth Foot in 1759 and lieutenant colonel commanding the Twelfth Foot in 1761. In the latter capacity, he distinguished himself at the battles of Kirch Donkern

and Grebenstein. When in the summer of 1762, however, he learned that his father had died, he returned to England and, as Second Earl Cornwallis (he had thus far been known as Brome), entered the House of Lords.

In 1768, Cornwallis married Jemima Tullekin Jones, the daughter of Colonel James Jones of the Third Regiment of Foot Guards. Their happy marriage produced two children, Mary and Charles. Cornwallis's service in the colonies during the American Revolution would interrupt their felicitous family life. During his absence, Lady Cornwallis would grow so ill that he would come home in 1778 to attend her. She would die in February of 1779, to his unbounded grief.

During the 1760's, Cornwallis consistently championed American liberty, voting against the Stamp Act in 1765 and in 1766 voting for the repeal of the Stamp Act and for outlawing general warrants. He was one of only five peers who opposed the Declaratory Act. Yet Cornwallis still received governmental favors. He became aide-de-camp to the king in 1765, the next year colonel of the Thirty-third Regiment of Foot, and in 1770 privy councillor and constable of the Tower of London. When the American Revolution began, he was promoted to major general and then to lieutenant general in America. Despite his opposition to the government's American policy, his sense of duty caused him to volunteer to go to America to crush the rebellion that broke out in 1775.

Cornwallis arrived off the North American coast on May 3, 1776, to come under the command of General Henry Clinton during the bungled British campaign against Charleston, South Carolina. Thereafter, he sailed with Clinton's force to New York, where General William Howe was commander in chief. Under Howe, Cornwallis fought at the Battle of Long Island, and he led Howe's forces when they chased George Washington across New Jersey. After Washington defeated the Hessians at Trenton, Howe sent Cornwallis to catch him, but Washington eluded him yet again. Cornwallis's next major campaign did not come until autumn, 1777, when he ably seconded Howe's crushing victory over the Americans at the Battle of Brandywine. After a trip to England in December, 1777, Cornwallis returned to America, on June 3, 1778. By then, command in America had devolved upon Clinton (who had by this time been knighted). Ordered to evacuate Philadelphia, Clinton led his army overland toward New York. During that march, he fought the hotly contested Battle of Monmouth Courthouse, in which American artillery severely pounded a charge that Cornwallis led.

Monmouth Courthouse was Cornwallis's last major battle under another officer's direct command. After returning to England in December of 1778 because of his wife's fatal illness, he came back to the United States in July of the next year to bury himself in activity and forget his grief. Anxious for an independent command, he got one after Clinton besieged and then captured Charleston, South Carolina, in May of 1780. When Sir Henry returned north in June, he left Cornwallis in charge in the South. Clinton expected him to pacify the two Carolinas and then subdue Virginia. For these tasks, he had a woefully inadequate number of troops. Yet he began well, smashing the Americans at the Battle of Camden. Cornwallis then entered North Carolina, believing that regular American armies to his north kept rebellion alive in the South. Unfortunately for him, the defeat of his subordinates, Major Patrick Ferguson at King's Mountain in October, 1780, and Lieutenant Colonel Banastre Tarleton at Cowpens in January, 1781, combined with his costly victory over General Nathanael Greene at Guilford Courthouse in March of 1781, severely crippled his army. Believing that he could do little in the Carolinas, Cornwallis pushed northward into Virginia. There, he took over forces Clinton had previously dispatched. The earl now commanded about five thousand men and again undertook an offensive war. In late June, however, he received Clinton's orders to fortify a defensive station. Cornwallis chose Yorktown, and in August he began building fortifications there.

By the middle of September, a large French fleet lay in the Chesapeake Bay and a French army larger than his own camped at Williamsburg, while the forces of Washington approached. Cornwallis planned to break out from his position, when he received a dispatch from Clinton promising reinforcements. That dispatch caused the earl to abandon his plans and to await the relief that never came. Once Washington's army arrived, the odds against him were overwhelming. The Siege of Yorktown followed, lasting only a few weeks. On October 19, 1781, Cornwallis surrendered, virtually ending the struggle for American independence.

The earl returned to England seeking new employment. Negotiations with the Pitt government, continuing spasmodically for five years, eventually resulted in Cornwallis's appointment as governor general and commander in chief in India, where he arrived in 1786. A man of the utmost integrity, he now worked to rid the British East India Company of the profiteers who had defrauded

it. Through reform and retrenchment in administration and through commercial expansion and improvements in communications, he sought to gain the company a profit and give the Indians an honest government. He established the controversial "permanent settlement" of the revenues in Bengal. Cornwallis also enacted reforms in criminal and civil justice. Since he thought—typically for his class and time—that the British would not respect Indians in positions of authority, he decreed that no native person or half-caste could hold civil or military office. Although he lacked the authority to stop slavery, a practice he loathed, Cornwallis ended the slave trade in children. He tried but failed to effect major changes in the military system because many entrenched interests opposed him. Finally, he waged successful war against Tippu, the Muslim ruler of Mysore, after the latter in 1789 attacked a native ruler allied to the British. Although he defeated Tippu in battle initially, he had to suspend operations because of shortages of supplies and the imminence of the monsoon season. When he resumed the campaign, however, he showed himself a master of logistics, using elephants to better advantage than any previous British commander, establishing supply depots, and employing more than fifty thousand human bearers. He then besieged Tippu's capital and forced his surrender in February, 1792.

First Marquess Cornwallis. (Library of Congress)

The earl now seemed to mark time until he left India in August, 1793, arriving in Great Britain on February 3, 1794. In the meantime, the king had advanced him to marquess in 1792 (he had previously bestowed on him the Order of the Garter). The East India Company in 1793 voted him their thanks and an annuity of £5,000 per year for twenty years. Also in 1793, Cornwallis gained the rank of general.

The marquess soon found new work at home. In February of 1795, he became master general of the ordnance. His responsibilities included providing ordnance for the army and the navy, control of Woolwich Academy (which trained engineer and artillery officers), and command of the engineers and artillery. During his tenure, he strengthened England's coastal defenses and raised the standards of admission to Woolwich. He also served as the only professional soldier in the cabinet and its chief military adviser. Although he held the master general-ship officially until 1801, he left most of the work to subordinates in 1798, when the government called upon him for a new venture.

In Ireland in 1798, a rebellion exploded. In June, Cornwallis took the joint appointment of lord lieutenant and commander in chief there. By the time he arrived, the major uprising had failed, but a small French army had landed, hoping to encourage further rebellion. Cornwallis, however, captured it before it could reach Dublin. After that, he worked mainly to effect a legislative union between Great Britain and Ireland, necessarily using methods he found highly repugnant. Under the proposed union, Ireland would give up its own Parliament but have one hundred seats in the British House of Commons. Some large landholders who "owned" boroughs in the Irish legislature thereby stood to lose those seats. To these disenfranchised "owners" went an outright monetary payment of £15,000 each; Cornwallis also promised them posts and pensions. The resulting Act of Union went into effect on January 1, 1801; unfortunately, it excluded Catholics, the majority of the Irish, from voting for or sitting in the new parliament. Cornwallis had sought, and even had led some people to believe, that Catholic "emancipation" would come about with union. King George III stubbornly refused to permit it. As a result, Cornwallis resigned.

By the time the marquess returned to England, negotiations had already begun for a peace with Napoleon's France. In the autumn, the government asked Cornwallis to conclude the arrangements. He accepted without enthusiasm, beginning official talks with the French at Amiens in December of 1801. The treaty eventually signed in March, 1802, scarcely favored Great Britain, but the British government approved it. Cornwallis returned to England shortly after its ratification.

Although by that time he was more than sixty years old, the marquess still desired employment. In January of 1805, he again accepted appointment as governor general and commander in chief in India. He reached Madras in July, but almost at once his health began to decline. By late September, his condition deteriorated rapidly, and at Ghazipur he died, on October 5, 1805.

SIGNIFICANCE

First Marquess Cornwallis, truly an imperial figure, was a man of integrity and humanity. In America, he displayed great tactical ability as a general but suffered the frustration of never holding the supreme command. There and only there, and only partly through his own fault, he suffered defeat. In India, he showed his character through his many reforms and his considerable military skill in defeating Tippu. In Ireland, he faced less of a military threat, but his character showed again in his clemency toward rebels and in his attempt to gain emancipation for Catholics. He did not display outstanding skills as a diplomat, yet the peace he concluded at Amiens was one the British government desperately needed and the only one Great Britain had with France between 1793 and 1815.

—Mary B. Wickwire

FURTHER READING

Aspinall, Arthur. *Cornwallis in Bengal.* Manchester, England: Manchester University Press, 1931. Deals with Cornwallis's administrative and judicial reforms in India.

Cornwallis, Charles. *The Correspondence of Charles, First Marquis Cornwallis.* Edited by Charles Ross. 3 vols. London: John Murray, 1859. The most important published edition of Cornwallis's letters.

List and Index Society. *Gifts and Deposits, Part 1.* Vol. 10. London: Swift, 1966. An important research tool that describes the Cornwallis Papers available in the Public Record Office.

Patterson, Benton Rain. *Washington and Cornwallis: The Battle for America, 1775-1783.* Lanham, Md.: Taylor Trade, 2004. A military history of the major campaigns and battles in the American Revolution. Contrasts the characters of Cornwallis and Washington and analyzes their performance as military commanders.

Seton-Karr, W. S. *The Marquis Cornwallis and the Consolidation of British Rule.* Oxford, England: Clarendon Press, 1914. Studies the regulations for the settlement of land revenue in Bengal.

Stevens, Benjamin Franklin, comp. *The Campaign in Virginia 1781: An Exact Reprint of Six Rare Pamphlets on the Clinton-Cornwallis Controversy.* 2 vols. London, 1888. A specialized study of the dispute between Clinton and Cornwallis.

Ward, Christopher. *The War of the Revolution.* Edited by John R. Alden. 2 vols. New York: Macmillan, 1952. A good overall study of the American Revolution.

Wickwire, Franklin, and Mary Wickwire. *Cornwallis: The American Adventure.* Boston: Houghton Mifflin, 1970. The first part of a two-volume biography, this study goes through the surrender at Yorktown.

_____. *Cornwallis: The Imperial Years.* Chapel Hill: University of North Carolina Press, 1980. Completes the biographical study of Cornwallis, dealing with India, the ordnance, Ireland, and Amiens.

See also: Sir Henry Clinton; Robert Clive; George III; Nathanael Greene; Jean-Baptiste Vaquette de Gribeauval; William Howe; George Washington; Anthony Wayne.

Related articles in *Great Events from History: The Eighteenth Century, 1701-1800:* 1746-1754: Carnatic Wars; June 23, 1757: Battle of Plassey; August, 1767-May, 1799: Anglo-Mysore Wars; December, 1774-February 24, 1783: First Marāthā War.

FRANÇOIS COUPERIN
French composer

Couperin was the chief representative of French musical classicism in the waning years of the reign of Louis XIV and during the regency that followed.

Born: November 10, 1668; Paris, France
Died: September 11, 1733; Paris, France
Also known as: Le Grand
Area of achievement: Music

EARLY LIFE

François Couperin (frahn-swah kew-pra) was the most famous member of a family of musicians sufficiently long-lived and well known that they constituted a musical dynasty much like the Bach family in Germany, to whom they have frequently been compared. The prominence of François within this group was acknowledged by the unofficial title "Le Grand," a sobriquet well established by the late eighteenth century and probably in use as early as 1710.

Couperin's early musical training and first professional experience centered on the organ at the Church of St. Gervaise, where his uncle, Louis Couperin, had served as organist, as had his father, Charles Couperin, since 1661. Charles died in 1679, and his son's musical training was continued by Jacques Thomelin, himself a famous organist, who became a second father to François. The young Couperin's talents were such that the council of St. Gervaise determined that he should inherit his father's position when he became eighteen, although they engaged Michel-Richard de Lalande as principal organist for the interim period. In 1685, the council extended to François an annual stipend of three hundred livres until a formal contract could be issued, an act which, considering Lalande's many other activities, suggests that the seventeen-year-old Couperin may have been assuming the role of organist in all but name for several years. He continued to occupy the organist's house of St. Gervaise and in 1689 married Marie-Anne Ansault. His spouse was to bear him four children, two of whom became prominent musicians in their own right, and also brought to Couperin contacts in the business world that would later become advantageous for some of his publishing ventures.

LIFE'S WORK

In 1690, François Couperin obtained a royal privilege to print and sell his music, which led to the publication of the *Pièces d'orgues consistantes en deux messes: Messe pour les paroisses et messe pour les couvents,* two organ masses that represent his first published work and his only known compositions for this instrument. He was active as an organist for most of his life, and in 1693 he gained entry to the court of Louis XIV through a royal appointment as one of four court organists, each responsible for organ music in the royal court and chapel for one quarter of the year.

At about the same time, he was at work on several trio sonatas (two violins and continuo), some of which were later incorporated into the set entitled *Les Nations* (1726). These sonatas, conceived around 1693, reflect Couperin's awareness of the difference between French and Italian styles, his enduring admiration for Arcangelo Corelli, the quintessential composer of the Italian Baroque, and presumably the introduction into France of the genre that, for many, typifies Baroque instrumental chamber music.

Couperin's appointment as a court organist brought him into contact with the aristocracy; he subsequently became harpsichord instructor to many noble families and in 1694 was appointed Maître de Clavecin des Enfants de France. He took advantage of an edict by Louis XIV offering ennoblement to any person in respectable employment who could pay for it. About 1702, he was further honored as Chevalier de l'Ordre du Lateran. Such titular recognition must have been important to him, for upon his ennoblement he fashioned a family coat of arms, and the Lateran Cross is prominently displayed in the famous portrait by Andre Boüys by which Couperin generally is known.

Between 1693 and the king's death in 1715, Couperin established himself as the leading French composer. The esteem in which he was held is documented by the number of musical works dedicated to him at that time. He

continued as organist at court and at St. Gervaise and was firmly established as the foremost teacher of harpsichord and organ.

His first book of harpsichord pieces, an accumulation of works written over a period of several years—and the literature by which he is best known in the modern era—was published in 1713. Couperin had for some time been assisting Jean-Henri d'Anglebert, the king's harpsichordist, in his duties at court, and when d'Anglebert withdrew because of ill health, Couperin officially replaced him in 1717. His second book of harpsichord pieces appeared at this time; it was no doubt his increasing responsibilities as harpsichord teacher that led to his famous treatise *L'Art de toucher le clavecin* (1716, 1717). This work, essentially pedagogical, endures as one of the most influential treatises on performance practice of the eighteenth century. Most keyboard tutors of the period concentrate on the realization of a figured bass and in that context offer instruction in the rudiments of harmony for the keyboard player. Couperin addresses performance itself, treating fingering, ornamentation, and style of performance to a degree uncommon until after mid-century.

Book 3 of Couperin's harpsichord pieces (1722) contained as a supplement the *Concerts royaux,* a series of trio-sonata movements written for two upper-range instruments (violin, flute, oboe) and continuo (keyboard plus viola da gamba or bassoon). *Les Goûts-réunis* (1724) continued in much the same vein; the varied movements represent a juxtaposition of French and Italian styles more than any inherent blending or unification.

The two trio-sonata sets *Le Parnasse: Ou, L'Apothéose de Corelli* (1724) and *Concert instrumental sous le titre d'apothéose composé à la mémoire immortelle de l'incomparable Monsieur de Lully* (1725) are tributes to the composers Couperin regarded as defining his musical world. Titles to individual movements are quasi-programmatic in their reference to these composers and to their place among the gods and scenes of classic mythology, presumably their rightful place in Couperin's view. *Les Nations,* written almost thirty years prior to its publication, was Couperin's first effort in this type of instrumental chamber music. It is probable that many of the other collections published in the 1720's also had been written and performed at an earlier time, as references to such works appeared in some concerts during 1714 and 1715.

The *Pièces de violes avec la basse chifrée* (1728) are among Couperin's last works. They consist of two suites for solo bass viola da gamba and continuo (harpsichord and a second bass gamba).

François Couperin. (Library of Congress)

The fourth book of harpsichord pieces (1730) was Couperin's last publication. In the preface to this volume, he referred to the illness that had been sapping his strength for some time, and the variety of pieces included here suggests less concern for consistency than in most of his earlier collections of instrumental music for any medium.

Very little substantive information exists concerning the composer's last years. He was buried in the Church of St. Joseph, a dependency of the parish of St. Eustache. Shortly before his death, he had obtained a new privilege for ten years to cover further publication of his works. Obviously there remained works awaiting publication, or he had further plans for new compositions, or both. Couperin's family did not pursue the project and, as no manuscripts of Couperin are known to remain, it is probable that a substantial body of music was irretrievably lost.

SIGNIFICANCE

François Couperin's music was very much a reflection of the social milieu from which it emerged. There was much that was frivolous in the reign of Louis XIV; there was also an element of order that was imitated throughout the Western world. It is possible to hear Couperin's music and note only the care and attention given to ornamentation for the purpose of achieving a given effect; underlying the thin texture and careful decoration, however, one finds a technical control and artistic balance equal to that achieved in any age. Couperin expressed musically the conflict in the *grand siècle* between personal passion and self-control.

He claimed priority in introducing the sonata to France. He recognized and defined for his contemporaries the differences between French and Italian style and, in some of his instrumental chamber music, he achieved a balance, if not a synthesis, between those styles. In his four books of harpsichord pieces, the individual dance movements were organized into *ordres*, a grouping by key rather than by a stereotypical plan of dance movements. Here Couperin broke away from the literalness of choreography, both in the musical patterns of these works and in their sequence. They represent musical conceptions far more than stylized dance pieces.

Couperin devoted much of his effort to teaching, an involvement reflected in his published treatise on playing the harpsichord. Couperin's advice and established procedure in teaching children to play the instrument before they were taught to read printed music anticipated by more than two centuries developments in instrumen-

tal teaching in Japan that have gained so much favor in the musical community of the last half of the twentieth century.

—Douglas A. Lee

FURTHER READING

Abraham, Gerald, ed. *Concert Music, 1630-1750*. Vol. 6 in *The New Oxford History of Music*. New York: Oxford University Press, 1986. Focuses on Couperin's solo harpsichord music. Provides a substantive exploration of the four books of harpsichord pieces, marked by some historical background and a sensitive description of many individual works.

Anthony, James R. *French Baroque Music: From Beaujoyeulx to Rameau*. New York: W. W. Norton, 1974. One of the most important studies of French music available. The author treats Couperin within his collective study of the various genres, forms, and idioms to which he contributed. The stylistic analysis of many of Couperin's important works is among the best, both in the treatment of individual works and in the exploration of their social context.

Beaussant, Philippe. *François Couperin*. Translated by Alexandra Land. Portland, Oreg.: Amadeus Press, 1990. Translation of French biography, placing Couperin's life within the context of French baroque society and culture.

Bukofzer, Manfred F. *Music in the Baroque Era from Monteverdi to Bach*. New York: W. W. Norton, 1947. This popular study of Baroque music examines Couperin and his musical works in the context of his time and musical milieu. Offers a broad description of Couperin's works, encompassing those for organ and chamber music as well as the better known harpsichord pieces.

Mellers, Wilfred. *François Couperin and the French Classical Tradition*. London: Denis Dobson, 1950. The principal English-language study of Couperin since its first appearance in the mid-twentieth century. Contains three chapters addressing the artistic environment of Couperin's years in Paris, taste during the *grand siècle*, and an overview of music, the court, and the theater during Couperin's life. Includes a sweeping study of Couperin's oeuvre, seven valuable appendices, a list of works, and a useful bibliography.

Newman, William S. *The Sonata in the Baroque Era*. Rev. ed. Chapel Hill: University of North Carolina Press, 1966. As the title suggests, this work treats only Couperin's works known as sonatas, but that in effect encompasses the majority of his chamber music. The text offers a concise description of these works with thorough documentation.

Tunley, David. *Couperin*. London: British Broadcasting Corporation, 1982. There is no significant attempt here at biography. The author examines the prevailing musical scene in which Couperin worked and then discusses the works by genre. A good overview, liberally illustrated with musical examples.

_____. *François Couperin and "the Perfection of Music."* Burlington, Vt.: Ashgate, 2004. Updates and expands Tunley's previous work, providing an analysis of Couperin's entire musical output. Include a discussion of seventeenth- and eighteenth century musical

theory, demonstrating how Couperin combined the French classical tradition with the Italian Baroque.

See also: Johann Sebastian Bach; Jean-Philippe Rameau.

Related articles in *Great Events from History: The Eighteenth Century, 1701-1800*: c. 1701-1750: Bach Pioneers Modern Music; c. 1709: Invention of the Piano; April 13, 1742: First Performance of Handel's *Messiah*; January, 1762-November, 1766: Mozart Tours Europe as a Child Prodigy; 1795-1797: Paganini's Early Violin Performances.

HANNAH COWLEY
English playwright and poet

Cowley excelled in writing farce, comedy of manners, and tragedy. In addition to being a poet, she was a key figure in the transition of the London stage from the neoclassic to the Romantic period.

Born: March 4, 1743; Tiverton, Devonshire, England
Died: March 11, 1809; Tiverton, Devonshire, England
Also known as: Hannah Parkhouse (birth name); Aunt Matilda (pseudonym)
Areas of achievement: Theater, literature, women's rights

EARLY LIFE

Little is known about Hannah Cowley's early life. Her father, Philip Parkhouse, was a bookseller and student of the classics, whose literary interests and extensive family library provided Hannah with an independent education rare for girls and women of the time.

In 1772 she married Thomas Cowley, several years her junior and a newspaper writer and clerk in the Stamp Office. Soon after marriage, the couple moved to London, where Cowley lived until her retirement from the London stage. It seems the couple lived happily, and they had three, and possibly four, children. However, they evidently suffered financially, as Thomas's annual salary of £50 from the Stamp Office and another £50 from hack writing hardly sufficed.

Three years into the marriage, Cowley determined to supplement the family income. In the preface to her posthumous *The Works of Hannah Cowley* (1813), Cowley audaciously boasted to her husband, during one tedious evening at the theater, that she could write a better play

than the one they had just watched. Encouraged by Thomas, a theater critic, she did just that, producing three weeks later *The Runaway* (1776) and thereby increasing the family's income.

LIFE'S WORK

Hannah Cowley's theatrical career was a long one, 1776 to 1801, and included fifteen plays, but her reputation has been based primarily on five plays: *The Runaway* (1776), *Albina* (1776), *Who's the Dupe?* (1779), *The Belle's Stratagem* (1780), and *A Bold Stroke for a Husband* (1783). These plays represent a broad range of Cowley's art and include first-rate farce, comedy of manners, and tragedy.

Probably no one was more surprised than Cowley when the great theater manager and actor David Garrick responded to a draft of *The Runaway* with encouragement. The play premiered on February 15, 1776, and had a very respectable run of seventeen performances and three benefits. Cowley earned a surprising £500 from the play, which was the only new play produced by Garrick in his final season. It featured Sarah Siddons in her first role.

The runaway of the play is a young woman of position fleeing a tyrannical father and the man, George, he chose for her to marry. By wonderful comic chance, she is the same young beauty with whom young George was smitten upon seeing her once before at a masquerade. George, too, is the victim of a tyrannical father planning to wed him to a much older woman, Lady Diana. Three parallel plots follow, involving pairs of lovers who overcome objections from their parents and prove they are socially and economically worthy of each other. The star of the play for a twenty-first century audience would be, no doubt, Bella, the delightful, worldly cousin who facilitates the various romantic relationships. Cowley's first play shows her skill, developed early in her career, in working comic contrivances and delightful coincidences to significant artistic effect.

Despite her success in 1776, a new theater manager, Richard Brinsley Sheridan, had less enthusiasm for playwrights who were women and refused to restage *The Runaway* in 1777. He further delayed staging Cowley's second play, *Albina*, a tragedy.

The eighteenth century was a great age for tragedy despite its lack of appreciation by twentieth century modernist critics. Cowley's tragedy *Albina* was one of the best of her time. It naturally follows the basic neoclassic norm for regularity and unity, ensuring the rewarding of goodness and the thwarting of evil. What the original audience perceived from the tragedy and what postmodern audiences perceive, however, are quite different.

Albina, a young widow devoted to the memory of her husband killed in battle, is persuaded by her father to accept a profitable proposal from the rich, handsome young hero of the wars, Westmoreland. She does not need much convincing. What makes the play appealing especially to twenty-first century audiences, however, is the secondary plot. Editha, a young woman of equal rank to Albina, has lost her fortune in the war. Albina has undertaken to be Editha's protector, but her unmotivated goodness and her unmerited fortune understandably smother Editha. Desperate, Editha, along with Egbert, another victim of Albina's virtue, plots her means for justice. Cowley's contemporary audience would have called Editha's plot revenge. The play ends with a plot twist worthy of Hollywood. Editha and Egbert perish whereas Westmoreland and Albina live happily ever after, but a later audience would consider with horror that Albina's innocent oppression of Editha was an oppression forced by the flawed social norms of the day. The blank verse is competent and majestic, and, while not necessarily intentional, it ennobles the plight of those oppressed by social propriety. *Albina* surely ranks as one of the great tragedies of the century alongside such earlier plays as James Thomson's *Tancred and Sigismunda* (pr. 1745) and Edward Young's *The Brothers* (wr. 1724, pr. 1753).

Cowley's next play was delayed by Sheridan so that she could not profit from it, but ultimately it became one of her most popular, being performed 126 times between 1779 and 1800. With *Who's the Dupe?* Cowley showed that she had learned much from the master of English farce, Garrick, for the play surely rivals such Garrick farces as *The Lying Valet* (pr. 1741) and *Miss in Her Teens* (pr. 1747). Farce works by denying its intellectual significance through dehumanizing all characters into mere mechanical props for producing laughter, and *Who's the Dupe?* meets these expectations perfectly. Once again, Cowley develops a strong female character, Elizabeth, who is being forced to marry the pedantic Gradus by a father desperate for a son-in-law who is highly learned, unlike him. Of course, Elizabeth manipulates matters so that her true love, Granger, earns the father's approval. The best scene in the play occurs as Granger fools the father by displaying his impressive but utterly bogus learning while outwitting Gradus.

The Belle's Stratagem proved to be Cowley's most popular comedy, and it is often rated as her best play. Indeed, along with *A Bold Stroke for a Husband*, *The Belle's Stratagem* should have secured Cowley's reputation along with the other great playwrights of the age—George Colman Senior, Oliver Goldsmith, and Sheridan. The fortunes of gender, though, precluded scholars in the past from seriously considering the works of eighteenth century women playwrights.

The belle in this comedy is Letitia Hardy, betrothed to the honorable Doricourt since childhood, though she has not seen him in years. When he returns from abroad ready to perform his honorable duties with his betrothed, he finds that Letitia is, however, dull and unexciting. She is in fact a lively young girl who is testing him by developing a stratagem for capturing his love. The stratagem carries the plot and the laughter as Doricourt is smitten deeply by an exciting beauty who turns out to be the erstwhile insipid Letitia herself. A delightful subplot keeps the comedy lively throughout.

After the success of *The Belle's Stratagem*, Cowley experienced a series of failures, one play actually being hissed off the stage during a performance. By 1783, however, she was regaining her reputation as one of the top comic playwrights of the day with the production of *A Bold Stroke for a Husband*. The bold stroke consists of bold strokes by two of Cowley's best scheming comic heroines. The traps each sets for her respective lover are not original, but Cowley's sense for comic timing and ingenuity makes them effective. Victoria's philandering husband has pursued an affair with Laura in which he condemned his family to financial ruin by deeding to Laura his property, and thus his fortune. Victoria determines to make him fall in love with her again and reclaim the property from Laura. Earlier critics often condemned such plot schemes as sentimental. At the same time, Olivia is being forced by her father to choose among various suitors, none of whom is the one she truly loves. Her stratagem consists of imitating the character of Kate in William Shakespeare's *The Taming of the Shrew* (1594) and driving her suitors away while gaining her father's approval for her own true love. Thus the play provides two strong women, comic characters who dominate the men for their own purposes.

SIGNIFICANCE

While Hannah Cowley often professed disinterest toward the theater, she was closely connected with theater business and theater affairs throughout her long career. Among other things, she carried on a lengthy rivalry with fellow playwright Hannah More, accusing More of plagiarism on at least two occasions.

While her work at one time was dismissed along with much of the rest of eighteenth century drama as being sentimental, a postmodern sensibility provides for a reevaluation of one of the most significant and popular playwrights of the eighteenth century. Later centuries have responded to Cowley's plays not in ways she or her audience intended but by looking for what she could not intend. While she would never be considered a revolutionary feminist, she created strong women characters forced to work within the unjust status quo to survive. Cowley's dramatic art, then, lives on, and it is not merely a series of artifacts from a bygone era.

—Paul Varner

FURTHER READING

Anderson, Misty G. *Female Playwrights and Eighteenth-Century Comedy: Negotiating Marriage on the London Stage.* New York: Palgrave, 2002. Anderson examines the marriage conventions depicted in the comedies of female playwrights.

Bolton, Betsy. *Women, Nationalism, and the Romantic Stage: Theatre and Politics in Britain, 1780-1800.* New York: Cambridge University Press, 2001. Bolton explores the political themes in Romantic theater of the last twenty years of the eighteenth century.

De la Mahotière, Mary. *Hannah Cowley: Tiverton's Playwright and Pioneer Feminist, 1743-1809.* Tiverton, England: Devon Books, 1997. A brief account of Cowley's life and work in the light of her early, implicit, feminism.

Donkin, Ellen. *Getting into the Act: Women Playwrights in London, 1776-1829.* New York: Routledge, 1995. Donkin examines the proliferation of women playwrights in London between 1776 and 1829.

Feldman, Paula R., ed. *British Women Poets of the Romantic Era: An Anthology.* Baltimore: Johns Hopkins University Press, 1997. In addition to her plays, Cowley wrote poetry. This anthology includes some of her poems.

Folger Collective on Early Women Critics, ed. *Women Critics, 1660-1820: An Anthology.* Bloomington: Indiana University Press, 1995. A comprehensive collection that includes discussion of Cowley's writings and the work of her contemporaries.

Link, Frederick M., ed. *The Plays of Hannah Cowley.* 2 vols. New York: Garland, 1979. A collection of reprints of Cowley's complete plays.

See also: Fanny Abington; Fanny Burney; David Garrick; Oliver Goldsmith; Charlotte Lennox; Mary de la Rivière Manley; Hannah More; Anne Oldfield; Richard Brinsley Sheridan; Sarah Siddons; Peg Woffington.

Related articles in *Great Events from History: The Eighteenth Century, 1701-1800:* December 7, 1732: Covent Garden Theatre Opens in London; 1742: Fielding's *Joseph Andrews* Satirizes English Society.

DAI ZHEN
Chinese philosopher

Dai Zhen offered unprecedented and highly critical evaluations of Song-Ming neo-Confucianism by reinterpreting the classical, idealist Confucian philosophy, especially that of Mencius. In so doing, he elucidated his own philosophical ideas, which, above all, valued and validated human feelings, passions, and desires.

Born: January 19, 1724; Huining, Anhui Province, China

Died: July 1, 1777; Beijing, China

Also known as: Tai Chen (Wade-Giles); Dai Dongyuan (Pinyin) or Tai Tung-Yüan (Wade-Giles)

Areas of achievement: Philosophy, scholarship

EARLY LIFE

Dai Zhen (day-zehn) came from a small merchant family with no scholarly tradition. It is said that he was unable to talk until the age of ten and only then did he begin to read and study Confucian classics (the Four Books, or the Four Classics, edited by Zhu Xi) under the guidance of a private tutor. Endowed with an unusually good memory and an inquisitive mind, he made rapid progress in learning. Doubtful and critical of what he was told by his teacher were the meanings of the words in the classics, he attempted to verify them himself. He often asked questions that puzzled the teacher. At the age of sixteen or so, Dai Zhen had already read most of the basic Confucian texts.

Roughly between 1742 and 1745, Dai Zhen was away from home, helping his father do business and also working as a tutor. During this time period, he traveled widely in southern China and came to know more about society, especially the lives of common people. In 1745, Dai Zhen returned to his hometown for full-time study under Jiang Yong (1681-1762), a scholar famous for his textual criticisms based on phonology. He extended his academic inquiry to astronomy, arithmetic, trigonometry, hydrography, and phonology. In 1751, Dai Zhen passed the civil service examination for the budding-talent degree (*xiucai*, equivalent of the bachelor's degree). In 1754, he left for Beijing to escape being persecuted by a clansmen with whom he had become involved in a lawsuit.

LIFE'S WORK

Between 1754 and 1757, Dai Zhen stayed in Beijing and acquainted himself with many distinguished scholars and scholar-officials, including Qian Daxin, Ji Yun, Wang Mingsheng, and Wang Anguo. He discussed scholarship, conducted academic research, and worked as a tutor for some of the sons of these scholars.

After 1757, Dai Zhen spent most of his life in Beijing and in Yangzhou, a prosperous commercial city in Jiangsu Province. In 1762, Dai Zhen passed the prefectural-level civil service examination and obtained the lifted-person degree (*juren*, equivalent of the master's degree). In the next twelve years, Dai Zhen took but failed, six times, the metropolitan-level (national-level) examination for the presented-scholar degree (*jinshi*, equivalent of the doctorate), largely because of his nonconformist philosophical ideas. Given his erudition, however, a special imperial decree granted him a presented-scholar degree and appointed him an editor of the prestigious encyclopedic work, the *Siku Quanshu* (eighteenth century; complete collection of the four treasures). In addition to working on this project, Dai Zhen continued his scholarly research.

Dai Zhen had extensive knowledge of the humanities and the social and natural sciences, excelling in philology, phonology, and classic poetry. Not only did he annotate ancient works on astronomy, mathematics, biology, engineering, geography, and hydrography, he also wrote on some of these subjects and published extensively on ancient political institutions. Methodologically, he was a master of textual criticism, a method to help determine the authenticity of ancient texts as well as the texts' authors.

Dai Zhen's most important and inspiring scholarly achievements were in the field of philosophy. His major philosophical works include *Yuan shan* (1765; *Tai Chen's Yuan shan*, 1969) and "*Mengzi zi yi shu zheng* (1777; *Tai Chen on Mencius: Explorations in Words and Meaning*, 1990). Dai Zhen continued the philosophical tradition (as represented by Wang Fuzhi) that stressed the material or empirical nature of the universe and human society. What is most striking about Dai Zhen's philosophy is its categorical rejection of some fundamental ideas of the neo-Confucianism of the Song Dynasty. Dai Zhen revealed and denounced the distorted readings and interpretations of neo-Confucianists of early or classical Confucian writings.

Neo-Confucianism centered on the concept of *li* (principle or heavenly principle). *Li*, held to be something metaphysical and universal, originated from heaven and produced and dominated all material things (*qi*). Thus, material things (*qi*) were believed to be inferior to *li*. Also, *li* was believed to be present in humans and to constitute the rational part of human nature, which was good and should be preserved. Feelings and desires—the irrational—were considered evil and in need of suppression or elimination. This view was best embodied in the notorious neo-Confucian statement, "preserve the heavenly principle and eliminate human desires."

Dai Zhen completely rejected this neo-Confucian perception of *li*. He believed that things in the universe were produced not by *li* but from the interaction between the two substantial forces called yin and yang. In fact, Dai Zhen did not believe in the existence of a universal and transcendental *li*. He did adopt the term *li*, but he used it to refer to patterns (or principles) of concrete things (and affairs). His conceptualization of *li* was highly individualistic and empirical. *Li* did not come from outside (for example, from heaven) but existed in concrete things, and each different thing had a different *li*, which explained the variety of things in the universe. Also, Dai Zhen's *li* was open to human understanding.

For Dai Zhen, humans, like all other things, are products of the natural interaction between yin and yang. Humans are unique (in comparison with animals) because they are moral beings. Human morality, which could be understood as *li*, was predicated on or existed in human desires (for food, clothes, music, sex, and so forth). Humans would need no concept of morality had they no desires. These desires were part of human nature, stemming from the natural need of humans to sustain life. It is necessary and natural for humans to satisfy their desires. However, in attempting to satisfy one's own desires, an individual must follow certain moral principles, such as benevolence and righteousness, to avoid doing harm to others. These moral principles (*li*) should be used to regulate rather than replace or eliminate desires.

Dai Zhen pointed out that the "heavenly principle" in neo-Confucianism was not a universal truth, but instead was developed through the personal opinions of those who endorsed it. Neo-Confucian philosophers invented the notion of heavenly principle and then imposed it upon others, especially the common people, depriving them of their right to seek their personal interests; the principle also protected the vested interests and power of the elite.

SIGNIFICANCE

Dai Zhen was the first philosopher who systematically and straightforwardly criticized and rejected neo-Confucianism. Since neo-Confucianism had long been adopted as the state ideology and used by the rulers to justify their rule, its rejection represented a challenge to and negation of the existing political order.

Dai Zhen can be considered a modern Chinese Humanist, comparable to the Humanists of Renaissance Europe, given that he placed humans at the center of his philosophy and that he acknowledged and affirmed the rights and efforts of individuals to seek personal happiness and, particularly, to fulfill their personal feelings and desires.

Dai Zhen's philosophy has had a significant influence on Chinese scholars and political activists in later generations. For example, Zhang Taiyan (1868-1936), a scholar, reformer, and revolutionary, had high regard for Dai Zhen and borrowed his ideas in denouncing the monarchical system and in preparing public opinions for the anti-Qing revolution. Liang Qichao (1873-1929), a reformer and an accomplished scholar, believed that Dai Zhen's thoughts represented a new direction in the development of Chinese culture. Many of Liang's philosophical ideas echoed those of Dai Zhen. Hu Shi and Lu Xun, two principal leaders of the May Fourth movement (1919), were all admirers of Dai Zhen, drawing inspiration from him to reevaluate traditional Chinese culture.

—Yunqiu Zhang

FURTHER READING

Chan, Alan K. L., ed. *Mencius: Contexts and Interpretations.* Honolulu: University of Hawaii Press, 2002. Includes the chapter "Mencius, Xunzi, and Dai Zhen: A Study of the *Mengzi zi yi shu zheng*," which examines Dai Zhen's commentary on Mencius and his philosophy of human nature.

Cheng, Chung-ying. *Tai Chen's Inquiry into Goodness.* Honolulu: East-West Center Press, 1971. A study of Dai Zhen's philosophical treatise *On Original Goodness*.

Dai Zhen. *A Complete Collection of Dai Zhen's Works.* Beijing: Qinghua University Press, 1991. Contains Dai Zhen's extant writings.

_____. *Tai Chen on Mencius: Explorations in Words and Meaning.* New Haven, Conn.: Yale University Press, 1990. An updated translation of Dai Zhen's work on Mencius, with a critical introduction by Annping Chin and Mansfield Freeman.

Ewell, John Woodruff, Jr. *Re-inventing the Way: Dai Zhen's "Evidential Commentary on the Meanings of Terms in Mencius (1777)."* Unpublished Ph.D. dissertation, University of California, Berkeley, 1990.

An analysis of Dai Zhen's interpretations of Mencius's philosophy. Includes bibliographical references.

Ivanhoe, Philip J., ed. *Chinese Language, Thought, and Culture: Nivison and His Critics*. Chicago: Open Court Press, 1996. A collection on Chinese philosophy, with a chapter on Dai Zhen and contemporary intellectual debate.

Meng, Peiyuan. *The Evolution of Neo-Confucianism: From Zhu Xi to Wang Fuzhi and Dai Zhen*. Taibei: Wenjin Press, 1990. Contains a chapter on Dai Zhen's philosophy.

Xu Sumin. *Dai Zhen and Chinese Culture*. Guiyang: Guizhou People's Press, 2000. An examination of Dai Zhen's philosophy and its influence on Chinese culture.

See also: Cao Xueqin; Chŏng Sŏn; Étienne Bonnot de Condillac; Hakuin; Claude-Adrien Helvétius; Qianlong; Wang Zhenyi.

Related articles in *Great Events from History: The Eighteenth Century, 1701-1800:* 1754: Condillac Defends Sensationalist Theory; July 27, 1758: Helvétius Publishes *De l'esprit*.

GEORGES DANTON
French revolutionary leader

Danton was one of the principal leaders and shapers of the French Revolution. He became influential in molding modern conceptions of democracy, revolutionary politics, and the nation-state.

Born: October 26, 1759; Arcis-sur-Aube, France
Died: April 5, 1794; Paris, France
Also known as: Georges-Jacques Danton (full name)
Areas of achievement: Government and politics, social reform

EARLY LIFE
Georges Danton (zhawrzh dahn-tohn), like most of his future revolutionary associates, was born into a comfortably middle-class, provincial family. His father, Jacques Danton, who died when Georges was two years old, worked as a clerk for a local court. His mother, née Jeanne-Madelaine Camut, was remarried to an Arcis merchant, Jean Recordain, when Danton was ten. As the oldest male child, Danton received the best education his family could afford. After attending a local school for the primary grades, he was sent in 1773 to the Oratorian seminary at Troyes to complete his education. There, he studied a curriculum emphasizing science, history, and modern languages. Later, his critics would brand him "uneducated," probably because of his inability to read Latin and Greek and his unfamilarity with classical texts. Nevertheless, by modern standards Danton's schooling was first rate. He mastered English and achieved a reading knowledge of Italian. As an adult, he showed an extraordinary command of the contemporary works of the Enlightenment, especially those of Voltaire, the comte de Buffon, and Jean-Jacques Rousseau.

Danton chose civil law as his career. After being graduated from Troyes, he attended the University of Reims and received his law degree in 1784. He then resided in Paris, where he competed with hundreds of other provincials for scarce legal business that barely provided a living. In 1787, however, Danton recouped his fortunes in an enterprising manner which would come to characterize him. On June 9, he was married to Antoinette-Gabrielle Charpentier, the daughter of a prosperous Parisian café proprietor. Using her dowry and loans from his father-in-law and a former mistress, Danton earlier had purchased an office as attorney to the King's Councils, a position that entitled him to present cases before the royal councils and commissions. When the French Revolution erupted in 1789, Danton owned a lucrative law practice and enjoyed the prestige proceeding from a close association with the Versailles court.

LIFE'S WORK
As befitted a beneficiary of the established regime, Danton was slow to involve himself in the revolutionary fervor rising around him. Once immersed in the enthusiasm that followed the storming of the Bastille (July 14, 1789), however, Danton rivaled all others in his fanaticism and devotion to political reform. Soon he became renowned for his unique oratory. Utilizing natural attributes—commanding height, intimidating size, and a stentorian voice—he demonstrated a capacity for incisive speech that motivated Parisian artisans, shopkeepers, and laborers to participate actively in the revolution.

During this early period of revolutionary involvement, Danton's attentions were principally focused on

Parisian politics. Although a supporter of the newly established constitutional monarchy, he rapidly developed a reputation for rabble-rousing and corruption. It was at this time that he pioneered the techniques of mob incitement and control that have since come to characterize successful revolutions. As an advocate of freedom of speech and of association—and to sustain his personal ambitions—he harangued the crowds and directed the resulting anger against more conservative constitutional monarchists, such as the marquess de Lafayette and Jean-Sylvain Bailly.

The flight of the royal family to Varennes in June, 1791—King Louis XVI considered himself a prisoner of the revolutionaries—was a major turning point in Danton's career. Like many Frenchmen, he regarded the flight and other questionable royal deeds as evidence of Louis's treason. The king's actions radicalized Danton. He soon directed his demagogic activities toward deposing Louis and establishing a republic. The national as-

French revolutionary leader, Georges Danton. (Hulton Archive/ Getty Images)

sembly's charade that the royal family had been kidnapped further aroused Danton and many like-minded radicals. Against the constitutional monarchists' determination to preserve Louis's powers, Danton helped organize a massive demonstration on July 17, at the Field of Mars, where thousands signed a petition demanding a new executive power. When the national guard arrived to break up the crowd, shots were fired that killed fifty demonstrators. Hunted as one of those responsible for the incident, Danton fled to England, where he remained for only a short time.

By September, he had returned to Paris. During the next eleven months, the king and the constitutional monarchists played into the hands of the radicals, the former by vetoing the assembly's attempts to enforce clerical conformity to the nationalization of church property and activities, and the latter by declaring (April, 1792) and waging an unsuccessful war against Austria and Prussia. In July, the allied armies, assembled on the frontier preparing to invade France, issued the infamous Brunswick Manifesto, which threatened Paris with destruction if the people did not obey the will of the king. Danton and other republicans had little trouble transforming Parisian fear at the prospect of an allied invasion into a violent hysteria and hatred for Louis, whose communications with the Austrians and the French émigrés were well known. Danton was one of the principal organizers of the assault upon the Tuileries, the king's residence, on August 10. With the mob in control of Paris, direction of the revolution fell largely into the hands of the radicals. The legislative assembly voted for the suspension of the king and for the calling of a national convention to draw up a new constitution. Danton was named minister of justice in the provisional executive council. A period of great personal achievement was to follow for him.

Danton served as minister of justice for only two months. During that time, he wielded greater power than Louis XVI had ever possessed. Relying on his abundant energy and determination, he dominated the provisional executive, requisitioning vast supplies of arms and recruiting thousands of volunteers for the French armies. On September 20, the allied invasion was turned back at the Battle of Valmy, a victory reflective of Danton's efforts. Shortly thereafter, he abandoned the ministry for a seat in the national convention, where he and his followers aligned themselves with Robespierre and the Jacobins—the most famous of the revolution's radicals.

As a deputy, Danton continued to strive tirelessly for the revolutionary cause. Denying charges of corruption—which were probably true—he involved himself deeply in foreign affairs. Between December, 1792, and March, 1793, he traveled to conquered Belgium four times to direct the installation of a revolutionary government there. In March and April—responding to French defeats in both Holland and Belgium—he mobilized 300,000 men for the armies and was instrumental in the creation of the Revolutionary Tribunal and the Committee of Public Safety, judicial and executive bodies designed to use authoritarian means to expedite and maximize the mobilization of people and resources for the war effort. During this period as a member of the Committee of Public Safety he supervised two departments, national defense and foreign affairs, making him for the second time the most powerful man in France.

These hours of triumph were marred by tragedy. In February, while in Belgium, Danton learned that his wife, Gabrielle, had died in childbirth. He was overcome with grief upon receiving the news but soon buried himself in politics and state business. A few months later, he married Louise Gely, who was fifteen years old and a friend of his family. His interest in his new wife probably lay mainly in the need to provide a mother for his two young sons.

On June 2, the Montagnards (radicals who included the Jacobins and Dantonists) purged the convention of the more moderate Girondins, leaving the direction of France completely under the control of Parisian extremists whose views were anathema to the majority of Frenchmen. Danton was a principal instigator of this coup. This was the high point of his power, however, as the Jacobins in subsequent months came increasingly to distrust his growing moderation.

By the summer of 1793, France had become once again a nation under siege. Great Britain and Spain had joined the powers already aligned against it, while counterrevolutionary movements controlled much of western and southern France. In response to the crisis, the Montagnards ruled the nation dictatorially through the Committee of Public Safety and the use of the Reign of Terror—the rounding up and executing of those suspected of opposing the revolution or obstructing the war effort. Danton's solution to France's troubles was to negotiate with the enemies, whose armies were pressing upon the frontier. The Jacobins considered his views to be a sign of weakness. They preferred to impose economic controls and mobilize the nation for an all-out struggle with internal and external foes. In July, Danton failed to win reelection to the committee, signaling his deteriorating political position. In October, Danton committed a fatal, inexplicable error by retiring to Arcis with his family for

two months. In his absence, Robespierre and Louis de Saint-Just consolidated Jacobin control over the revolution. When Danton returned in mid-November, they were powerful enough to move against him whenever they pleased.

By the early spring of 1794, the allied armies had been pushed back in several areas, while within France counterrevolutionary regions were undergoing slow pacification. As the crisis thus eased, Danton, seemingly unaware of the precariousness of his position, publicly called for relaxation of the Reign of Terror. His opponents moved swiftly against him. On March 30, he was arrested as an "enemy of the Republic." His trial before the Revolutionary Tribunal was farcical, and several times Danton jeered at absurd attempts to portray him as a "counterrevolutionary." Nevertheless, he was convicted and died, on April 5, 1794, on the guillotine.

SIGNIFICANCE

Georges Danton's ambition found expression in pure demagoguery. A skillful orator and an adroit politician, he consistently demonstrated an uncanny ability to ascertain the desires of the Parisian lower classes and to identify himself quickly with them. Although Danton gained and retained power through unscrupulous manipulation of the electorate—and occasionally utilized the *sans culottes* as the bludgeon for his policies—his political career was distinguished by remarkable achievements in a very short time. Destruction of the monarchy, establishment of the republic, universal manhood suffrage, and abolition of imprisonment for debt—all of these landmarks of French history were given impetus through Danton's energy, both in his role as a popular mob leader and during his two brief tenures as unofficial chief minister of France. He was truly an architect of modern democracy and of the nation-state.

—*Michael S. Fitzgerald*

FURTHER READING

Christophe, Robert. *Danton: A Biography*. Translated by Peter Green. Garden City, N.Y.: Doubleday, 1967. A highly readable, dramatic account of Danton's life that captures the essence of his personality. Somewhat unreliable as to dates and facts.

Doyle, William. *The Oxford History of the French Revolution*. 2d ed. New York: Oxford University Press, 2002. Comprehensive history, from Louis XIV's accession to the throne in 1774 to Napoleon's assumption of power in 1802. Includes a chronology of events and an essay examining the historiography of the French Revolution.

Hampson, Norman. *Danton*. New York: Holmes & Meier, 1978. Scholarly and reliable, an excellent companion to the biography by Christophe. The bibliography cites nearly all the printed contemporary sources on Danton's life and the most important works by later historians.

Lefebvre, Georges. *The Coming of the French Revolution, 1789*. Translated by R. R. Palmer. New York: Random House, 1947. Introductory material for novices of the French Revolution. Although many historians disagree with Lefebvre's Marxist views, his interpretation continues to be popular in France. Covers only the early stages of the revolution, 1787-1789.

Palmer, R. R. *Twelve Who Ruled: The Year of the Terror in the French Revolution*. Bicentennial ed. Princeton, N.J.: Princeton University Press, 1989. Revised edition of the book originally published in 1941, containing a new preface by the author. Focuses on the twelve members of the Committee of Public Safety.

Sydenham, M. J. *The French Revolution*. New York: G. P. Putnam's Sons, 1965. An introduction to its topic that emphasizes the role of personalities and factions in shaping the revolution. Includes a large bibliography and other valuable references for the beginner such as a detailed chronology, a map of Paris at the time of the revolution, and an explanation of the revolutionary calendar.

Thompson, J. M. *The French Revolution*. 1943. Rev. ed. Oxford, England: Basil Blackwell, 1985. An older narrative introduction with an updated (1985) bibliography. The latter cites the major printed primary sources on the revolution while stressing more recent secondary works. Contains a host of valuable references.

See also: Jean-Sylvain Bailly; Comte de Buffon; Louis XV; Louis XVI; Robespierre; Jean-Jacques Rousseau; Louis de Saint-Just; Voltaire.

Related articles in *Great Events from History: The Eighteenth Century, 1701-1800*: 1749-1789: First Comprehensive Examination of the Natural World; January, 1759: Voltaire Satirizes Optimism in *Candide*; April, 1762: Rousseau Publishes *The Social Contract*; July, 1764: Voltaire Publishes *A Philosophical Dictionary for the Pocket*; May 5, 1789: Louis XVI Calls the Estates-General; June 20, 1789: Oath of the Tennis Court; July 14, 1789: Fall of the Bastille; October, 1789-April 25, 1792: France Adopts the Guillotine; April 20, 1792-October, 1797: Early Wars of the French Revolution; September 20, 1792: Battle of Valmy; January 21, 1793: Execution of Louis XVI; March 4-December 23, 1793: War in the Vendée; July 27-28, 1794: Fall of Robespierre; November 9-10, 1799: Napoleon Rises to Power in France.

ABRAHAM DARBY
English industrialist and inventor

Darby solved the problem of substituting coal for wood in the making of iron. His use of coke, after further improvements made by his son, Abraham Darby II, and others, changed English iron making from a declining industry into the second leading sector, along with cotton production, of the first Industrial Revolution.

Born: c. 1678; Wren's Nest, near Dudley, Worcestershire, England

Died: March 8, 1717; Coalbrookdale, Shrophire, England

Areas of achievement: Science and technology, business

EARLY LIFE

Abraham Darby was born in the Midlands of England in a village southwest of Birmingham. This area, dotted with small furnaces and forges, would in later years contain such a concentration of metalworking establishments as to be called the Black Country, for its constant noise and clouds of smoke. Abraham was the only son of John Darby, a farmer who also worked as a nail maker and locksmith. The family were Quakers. The network of faith, mutual aid, and business dealings supported by this religious sect was central to Darby's subsequent career. As a young boy, Darby worked in the family forge and gained a good knowledge of various kinds of iron working. When he was old enough, the boy was apprenticed to Jonathan Freeth, a Quaker malt mill maker in Birmingham. At the end of his term in 1698, Abraham married Mary Sergeant of Dudley. They moved to Bristol, at that time the second seaport in the country, and there Abraham set up as a malt mill maker in partnership with a number of Quaker merchants, many of whom were also connected with the iron trade.

It seems probable that in 1704, Darby spent some time in Holland, then well known for the skill of its metal casting. There he studied the Dutch method of casting brass pots and even brought back with him some Dutch workers to Bristol.

LIFE'S WORK

In 1706, and back in England, Abraham Darby formed a new partnership, again with Quaker businessmen. They set up a brass works at Baptist Mills. The following year, 1707, Darby and his longtime worker and friend John Thomas were granted a patent for the casting of iron pots in sand, rather than using loam or clay. The importance of this breakthrough was that a cheaper, quicker method had been developed at a time when casting iron was rare, the demand for pots was increasing, and the import of expensive brass pots from Holland was becoming more difficult. Unfortunately, Darby's partners were not sufficiently impressed, so he sold his shares in Baptist Mills and looked for a place to work on his own.

The place Darby chose for his new business, Coalbrookdale, had many advantages. It lay along the greatest commercial waterway in England, the River Severn. Large deposits of iron and coal lay near the surface within a mile of his works, and there was an abundant supply of wood nearby. In addition, a swift stream descended through the site, a source of power for Darby's machinery. Iron making had been established there for some time, so premises were already constructed. Important markets were close by at Bridgenorth, Shrewsbury, Bewdley, and Welshpool along the Severn, and at various inland towns. Finally, there were many Quakers active in the area.

Despite all this, Darby chose to enter an industry that had been in decline for almost a century. The principal reason for this decline was that iron making depended on the use of wood. Great quantities of wood were needed to make charcoal. The use of wood for charcoal and the expansion of English agriculture were responsible for clearing many forested areas. By 1600, iron makers in the traditional iron centers of the Forest of Dean and the Sussex Weald had to find wood from farther and farther afield. New, more remote iron districts grew up in the Midlands and Yorkshire, but these, too, suffered shortages in raw materials. The decline of iron production was enhanced by the import of cheap, high-quality iron from Sweden, Russia, and, to a lesser extent, the American colonies. The advantageous position of Coalbrookdale was thus doubly important for the survival of Darby's

business and for the support of his experiments to replace charcoal with coke.

Darby was, above all, a religious man. His entire life was immersed in the Quaker faith. His social contacts were mainly with other Friends; his business partnerships were all with Quakers; his largest customer, Nehemiah Champion of Bristol, was also a coreligionist. At Coalbrookdale, Darby attracted families of Quakers to settle and work for him. Generations of workmen continued to work for the Coalbrookdale Company. All managers until 1897 were Quakers. Weekday meetings were held in the company offices at the works, and on Sundays Darby would take his place with the workers at the meeting. Later visitors confirmed that the friendliness and fellowship of the Quaker meeting carried over into the work situation. Darby's other great quality was his concern for his family. He and Mary, his wife, had five sons and six daughters.

Darby leased Coalbrookdale in 1708. Almost from the beginning, he used coke in iron making on a commercial scale. Throughout his career at Coalbrookdale, Darby financed his capital requirements and purchased equipment through forming partnerships and taking out mortgages. Operating expenses such as wages were paid out of cash received from sales. From the beginning, Coalbrookdale proved to be modestly successful.

The England of Darby's day was divided into regional markets limited by problems of communication in the days before the canal, road, and railway booms. Darby and his manager, Richard Ford, traveled the countryside selling their wares. They concentrated particularly on the regional fairs that served as the principal markets for the exchange of goods. Close to Coalbrookdale was the great annual fair at Stourbridge, where goods from all over the country and even from Europe were bought and sold, and then distributed to smaller merchants in the locality. There, Darby and Ford would meet personally with their customers to take orders and collect accounts. The partners found that dealing personally with customers enhanced their business. Furthermore, the method of casting any small iron ware to the customers' individual specifications, direct from the furnace, and the substitution of coke for coal in many instances meant that Darby was able to satisfy his customers and sell more cheaply than his competitors. Through his modest business success, Darby was able to expand Coalbrookdale considerably. By the time of his death, it was a thriving business.

For the last eighteen months of his life, Darby was seriously ill. His son-in-law and manager, Richard Ford, and the workers ran the business for him. At the end,

Darby died intestate. His widow took out papers of administration but half the works were mortgaged to the Bristol banker and longtime Darby partner, Thomas Goldney, who demanded payment and was given more shares in the business. When Mary died, shortly after Abraham, her brother Joshua Sergeant bought three shares (out of sixteen) so that the children might be left something from their father's efforts. At the time of his father's death, the oldest son, Abraham Darby II, was six years old.

SIGNIFICANCE

Abraham Darby was not a great industrialist, and he profited but little from his invention. For many years, his claim to have been the first to solve the technical problems of using coke in iron making was also in dispute. For this reason, many accounts of the iron industry in Great Britain spend much less space than one would expect on the inventor of a process that served to revolutionize not only the whole industry but also society itself.

There are several reasons for this. To begin with, starting in the early seventeenth century, many individuals took out patents for processes that they claimed successfully used coal or coke to make iron. Beginning with Simon Sturtevant in 1612, through the tragicomic Dud Dudley, who died in 1684 but who may have found a solution, to William Wood in 1728, patents were taken out using coal in the iron-making process. No process, however, proved as successful as that of Abraham Darby. Furthermore, during his own lifetime, Darby did not publicize his invention. In fact, the first public account of Darby's method did not appear until 1747, thirty years after his death, in a letter to the Royal Society from a visitor to Coalbrookdale.

Darby's reticence, in part a product of his Quaker background, also resulted from the nature of his business. The many false starts to iron making with coal or coke made potential customers suspicious of an end product that was often characterized by defects and brittleness. From Darby's own, incomplete business records, it appears that there was a high wastage rate; he was constantly experimenting to improve the quality of his product. In his own day, Darby was unable to produce good bar iron capable of being pounded in a forge; all products were cast directly from the furnace. Darby was also more fortunate than he probably realized in that the local coal he used was particularly pure, with a low sulfur content, and the resulting coke allowed for an acceptable form of iron. When he offered his invention to other ironmasters in Cumberland in northwest England and in Dolgelly, South Wales, they preferred to continue the use of charcoal, largely because the results from their own coke were so poor. Finally, Darby restricted his business to one branch of the English iron industry. It was by far the smallest branch and was confined to domestic users. Most iron makers worked with malleable, not cast, iron and used forges as well as furnaces. For them, during Darby's lifetime, the use of coal was not an option except to produce a fire in the forge to shape iron made with charcoal.

Improvements in the use of coke were carried out by Abraham Darby II, who, until the discovery of his own wife's diaries, was thought to deserve the credit for the successful use of coke in iron making. He was able to produce iron of much higher quality than his father, even bar iron for forge work. Further improvements by the great ironmasters later in the eighteenth century and the invention of the puddling process by Henry Cort meant that it was after 1780 before the use of coke in iron making became general.

Coalbrookdale continues to be a functioning ironworks, a living museum operated by the Ironbridge Gorge Trust. It is honored as one of the best in Europe, visited by thousands of tourists, schoolchildren, and scholars, and exhibiting the iron-making activities of the Darby family in the eighteenth century. Through the museum, Abraham Darby and his achievements live on.

—*Stephen Burwood*

FURTHER READING

Ashton, T. S. *Iron and Steel in the Industrial Revolution.* 2d ed. Manchester, England: Manchester University Press, 1954. An excellent work on the iron industry in Great Britain. Ashton's work is strong in providing the context of Darby's inventions. A good discussion of Darby's importance in the preface, with a first-rate treatment of Darby in chapters 1 and 2.

Boyns, T., ed. *The Steel Industry.* 4 vols. New York: I. B. Tauris, 1997. Volume 1 of this history of the steel industry examines Darby and the coal iron industry in eighteenth century England.

Deane, Phyllis. *The First Industrial Revolution.* 2d ed. New York: Cambridge University Press, 1979. The best short account of the Industrial Revolution by one of England's most distinguished economic historians. Chapter 7 is about the iron industry.

Flinn, M. W. "Abraham Darby and the Coke Smelting Process." *Economica,* n.s. 26 (1959): 54-59. Surveys the evidence concerning the date of Darby's successful use of coke in iron making.

Hyde, C. K. *Technological Change in the British Iron Industry, 1700-1870*. Princeton, N.J.: Princeton University Press, 1977. A comprehensive analysis that explains the slow adoption of coke for iron making and the significance of the myriad technological advances that led to the rapid growth of the industry by 1800.

Mantoux, Paul. *The Industrial Revolution in the Eighteenth Century: An Outline of the Beginnings of the Modern Factory System in England*. Translated by Marjorie Vernon. New York: Harcourt, Brace, 1927. Rev. ed. Chicago: Chicago University Press, 1961. A brilliant, clearly written, comprehensive account by a famous French historian and first published in French in 1905. Still unsurpassed on most aspects of the Industrial Revolution. Mantoux sheds light on the regional nature of England's economic life and its iron industry.

"Out of the Cauldron." *New Scientist* 160, no. 2164 (December 12, 1998): 58. Focuses on Darby's patent for casting iron bellied pots and his use of coal to produce iron.

Raistrick, Arthur. *Dynasty of Ironfounders: The Darbys and Coalbrookdale*. London: Longmans, Green, 1953. A standard account that is excellent on the Darby family and informative about the workings of the company despite patchy evidence for some periods.

_____. *Quakers in Science and Industry*. Newton Abbot, England: David and Charles, 1950. Reprint. New York: Augustus M. Kelley, 1968. Very good for explaining the importance of Darby's Quaker beliefs and the network of which he was a part.

Trinder, Barrie. *The Darbys of Coalbrookdale*. London: Phillimore, 1974. A short, popular account of the ironmaster family that draws on some information not available to Arthur Raistrick.

_____, ed. *"The Most Extraordinary District in the World": Ironbridge and Coalbrookdale*. London: Phillimore, 1977. An anthology of visitors' impressions dealing mainly with the century following 1750. Good for a flavor of the physical surroundings. Augmented by prints and photographs.

See also: Thomas Newcomen; Paul Revere; John Roebuck; Eli Whitney; John Wilkinson.

Related articles in *Great Events from History: The Eighteenth Century, 1701-1800:* 1709: Darby Invents Coke-Smelting; November, 1777-January 1, 1781: Construction of the First Iron Bridge; 1783-1784: Cort Improves Iron Processing.

JEAN DAUBERVAL
French dancer, ballet master, and choreographer

Dauberval choreographed and performed highly acclaimed ballets in France and England. His La Fille mal gardée, *a masterpiece of* ballet d'action *and one of the oldest ballets in the modern repertoire, premiered at the Grand-Théâtre in Bordeaux on July 1, 1789.*

Born: August 19, 1742; Montpellier, France
Died: February 14, 1806; Tours, France
Also known as: Jean Bercher (birth name); Jean d'Auberval; Jean d'Aubervel; Jean Doberval
Area of achievement: Dance

EARLY LIFE

Jean Bercher, later known by his stage name Jean Dauberval (zhahn doh-bur-vahl), was born out of wedlock in Montpellier, France, on August 19, 1742. His parents were both quite young at the time and did not marry until about eleven years later. His father, Étienne-Dominique Bercher, an aspiring actor, probably introduced him to the world of theater at an early age. Jean received professional training as a dancer and choreographer under renowned ballet master Jean-Georges Noverre and performed in Lyons as a leading male dancer in Noverre's choreography of *La Toilette de Vénus* (1757; Venus at her toilet) in November of 1757.

While still in his teens, Jean found temporary employment at the Royal Theater of Turin as director of ballets and principal male dancer in 1759, then returned to train under the guidance of Jean-Barthélemy Lany and Gaetano Vestris at the Royal Academy of Music in Paris. He made his debut at the Paris Opera as a dancer in the heroic ballet *Zaïs* (1761) and subsequently appeared in a variety of productions, including *Armide* (1761), *Les Indes galantes* (1762; the courtly Indies), *Acis et Galatée* (1762), and *Iphigénie en Tauride* (1762; Iphigenia among the Taurians).

After dancing under Noverre in Stuttgart in 1762 and 1763, Dauberval migrated to England and served as a leading dancer and choreographer for the King's Theatre at the Haymarket in London from 1763 to 1764. By the following season, he was back in Paris performing in opera-ballets and lyric tragedies set to the fashionable music of André Campra, Jean-Philippe Rameau, and Jean-Baptiste Lully. Over a period of ten years, he advanced from the rank of first dancer in character roles (1763) to that of *premier danseur noble* and assistant ballet master (1773).

LIFE'S WORK

From 1765 to 1782, Jean Dauberval performed in numerous pieces at the Paris Opera, ranging from comic interludes and pastoral scenes to heroic ballet and lyric tragedies. A master of pantomime, he was particularly admired for his skill in the portrayal of character, emotion, and dramatic action. One measure of his importance, both as a choreographer and as a dancer, can be found in the theatrical success of a *pas de deux* he performed together with Marie Allard in the popular opera-ballet *Sylvie*, first at the court of King Louis XV in 1765 then at the Paris Opera in 1766. A contemporary gouache painting by Louis Carrogis de Carmontelle captured the couple's memorable performance, transforming it into an iconographic legend that was soon reproduced in popular engravings.

Influential critics of theater and dance, such as the Englishman John Weaver, the Italian Carlo Goldoni, and the Frenchman Jean-Georges Noverre, had condemned the use of painted masks, cumbersome wigs, unwieldy hoopskirts, and extravagant costumes common in eighteenth century theater, calling for more attention to plot, greater realism, the artistic expression of emotions, and a general ban on gratuitous technical virtuosity and pageantry. If one judges by Carmontelle's vision of Dauberval and Allard on stage, *demi-caractère* dancers (character dancers) had succeeded in discarding their masks and adopting somewhat more natural attire by the mid-1760's. This newfound freedom of facial expression combined with a greater attention to plot contributed to the triumph of *ballet d'action* (narrative ballet) later in the century.

In his *Lettres sur les arts imitatives* (1807; letters on the imitative arts), Noverre looked back on Dauberval's performance in *Sylvie* as a milestone in the transition to *ballet d'action* in Parisian theater, adding appreciatively:

> It was thus Dauberval who first had the courage to oppose preconceived notions, to vanquish long-standing prejudice, to triumph over opera's outdated rules, destroy masks, adopt a more authentic costume, and so reveal his inner self in accordance with Nature.

Noverre considered himself the leading theorist of *ballet d'action* and considered Dauberval its first practitioner. In response to these claims, however, historians point out that the transition from theatrical *divertissement* to *ballet d'action* was a gradual one and that many of Dauberval's contemporaries also played important roles as catalysts of innovation. Thus Marie Sallé, Marie Carmago, Maximilien Gardel, and Gasparo Angiolini, among others, deserve credit alongside Dauberval for the transformation in ballet that took place in the eighteenth century.

Serving under Vestris and Noverre, Dauberval found only limited opportunities for work as a choreographer at the Paris Opera. He created minor interludes in 1771 and 1772, mythological and pastoral ballets for the Royal Theater of Turin in 1771 and 1775, and a ballet-pantomime, *Alcimadure*, in 1778. Sensing that he could achieve nothing more by remaining, he took leave of the Paris Opera in the summer of 1783, married his former pupil, Madeleine-Louise Crespé (known to the public as Mademoiselle Théodore), and accepted a new appointment as ballet master at the King's Theatre in London. Between December, 1783, and July, 1784, he produced eight ballets for the English public, including *Le Déserteur* (the deserter) and *Le Coq du village* (the village beau).

Upon the expiration of his contract in London, Dauberval and his wife returned to France, where Dauberval was hired as ballet master of the newly erected Grand-Théâtre in Bordeaux. During his tenure there, from 1785 to 1790, he staged some of his greatest artistic achievements: *Le Bonheur est d'aimer* (1786; happiness is being in love), *Le Page inconstant* (1786; the unfaithful servant), *Le Ballet de la paille* (1789; ballet of straw), and revivals of *Le Déserteur*. A major success, his *Ballet de la paille* was renamed *La Fille mal gardée* (the ill-guarded girl) two years later and has retained that name ever since. When his contract expired in 1790, Dauberval signed on as ballet master at London's Pantheon Opera House and staged more new ballets, including *Telemachus in the Island of Calypso* (1791) and *Le Siège de Cythère* (1791; the siege at Cythera).

In 1796, Dauberval returned from semiretirement to serve one last term as ballet master at the Grand-Théâtre in Bordeaux, but he created no new ballets during that time. After his wife's death two years later, he maintained an active interest in promoting ballet, traveling on occasion between Bordeaux and Paris to keep abreast of new developments. He succumbed to sudden illness during a return trip from Paris and died at the Boule d'Or inn in Tours, France, on February 14, 1806.

SIGNIFICANCE

Jean Dauberval was a leading practitioner of the ground-breaking aesthetics of performance developed by Jean-Georges Noverre. He thus played an important role in the gradual triumph of *ballet d'action* in France and England during the second half of the eighteenth century, which marked a new era in the history of professional dance: As choreographers and dancers discovered new ways to express ideas and emotions without recourse to the spoken word, ballet began to assert its independence from opera.

As a ballet master and teacher, Dauberval contributed to the formation of outstanding dancers—Charles-Louis Didelot, Salvatore Viganò, Jean Aumer, Eugène Hus, and James Harvey d'Egville—who in turn helped disseminate *ballet d'action* throughout Europe. At the height of his creative activity in Bordeaux and London, he demonstrated a singular talent for transforming dance and pantomime into instruments of coherent narration. Several of his ballets remained popular well into the next century, and *La Fille mal gardée* has maintained its place as one of the oldest *ballets d'action* in twenty-first century repertoires. Because Dauberval and his contemporaries possessed no adequate system of notation, however, all of the original choreography for his ballets is now lost. Modern versions of *La Fille mal gardée* rely mainly on the printed scenario.

—Jan Pendergrass

FURTHER READING

Bremser, Martha, Larraine Nicholas, and Leanda Shrimpton, eds. *International Dictionary of Ballet.* 2 vols. Detroit, Mich.: St. James Press, 1993. Contains detailed biographies and iconographic resources on major figures in eighteenth century ballet, including Dauberval.

Chazin-Bennahum, Judith. "Wine, Women, and Song: Anacreon's Triple Threat to French Eighteenth-Century Ballet." *Dance Research* 5 (1987): 55-64. Compares Dauberval's anacreontic ballet *Le Bonheur est d'aimer* with works by Eugène Hus and Charles Didelot.

Costonis, Maureen Needham. "Dauberval's *Le Siège de Cythère*, 1791: A Commentary and Translation." *Dance Chronicle* 14 (1991): 175-202. Discusses a rare scenario of *Le Siège de Cythère* bearing annotations in Théodore Dauberval's handwriting.

Guest, Ivor. *The Ballet of the Enlightenment: The Establishment of the Ballet d'Action in France, 1770-1793.* London: Dance Books, 1996. Essential reading, with chapters focusing on Dauberval's career and his contributions to classical ballet.

_____, ed. *La Fille mal gardée.* London: Dancing Times, 1960. Chapters by nine dance historians on Dauberval's most successful piece, preceded by an English translation of the 1803 scenario.

Milhous, Judith. "Dancers' Contracts at the Pantheon Opera House, 1790-1792." *Dance Research* 9 (1991): 51-75. Examines Dauberval's contracts for two seasons with the Pantheon Opera House, based on papers preserved at the Bedford Estates Office in London.

Milhous, Judith, Gabriella Dideriksen, and Robert D. Hume. *The Pantheon Opera and Its Aftermath, 1789-1795.* Vol. 2 in *Italian Opera in Late Eighteenth-Century London.* Oxford, England: Clarendon Press, 2000. Includes substantial discussion of Dauberval's activities as ballet master at the Pantheon.

Price, Curtis, Judith Milhous, and Robert D. Hume. *The King's Theatre, Haymarket, 1778-1791.* Vol. 1 in *Italian Opera in Late Eighteenth-Century London.* Oxford, England: Clarendon Press, 1995. Focuses on the operation and management of the King's Theatre, but includes discussion of Dauberval's engagement there.

See also: Joseph Boulogne; François Couperin; Louis XV; Jean-Philippe Rameau.

Related articles in *Great Events from History: The Eighteenth Century, 1701-1800*: January 29, 1728: Gay Produces the First Ballad Opera; December 7, 1732: Covent Garden Theatre Opens in London; May 15, 1738: Foundation of St. Petersburg's Imperial Ballet School; October 5, 1762: First Performance of Gluck's *Orfeo and Euridice*; August 3, 1778: Opening of Milan's La Scala; April 27, 1784: First Performance of *The Marriage of Figaro*.

DANIEL DEFOE
English novelist

Because of his inventiveness, his eye for detail, and his stylistic adeptness, Defoe was a great journalist and creator of fiction, including the popular Robinson Crusoe, *which set the standard for the English novel.*

Born: 1660; London, England
Died: April 26, 1731; London, England
Also known as: Daniel Foe (birth name)
Area of achievement: Literature

EARLY LIFE

Daniel Defoe was the son of James Foe, a tallow chandler who later acted as an auditor for the Butchers' Company (Daniel changed his name to Defoe in 1695). Little is known about Daniel's mother, Alice, except that she came from Dissenting stock and, like her husband, was a Presbyterian. She died when Daniel was eight.

Daniel's formal education began at the Reverend James Fisher's school at Dorking, Surrey. Since Dissenters were refused admission to the universities at Oxford and Cambridge, Defoe then went to the Reverend Charles Morton's small college at Newington Green, which, Defoe later commented, lacked the intellectual stimulus of the great universities.

Unlike his classmates, most of whom entered the ministry, when he left school in 1680 Daniel went into trade as a hose-factor, seeking out and distributing various sorts of goods. The business necessitated extensive travel in Europe. Since he was a keen observer, he thus gained knowledge of people and places that would be useful in his writing. In 1684, he married Mary Tuffley, the daughter of a prosperous wine-cooper, who provided her with a considerable dowry. Mary was to bear her husband eight children.

The young merchant then became increasingly active on the political scene. In 1683, he published his first journalistic effort, a political tract. Two years later, he joined the army of Charles II's illegitimate son, the Protestant duke of Monmouth, who was attempting to seize the throne from Catholic James II. When the rebellion failed, Daniel may have fled the country; in any case, two years later a Daniel Foe was pardoned for taking part in the uprising. In 1688, when William of Orange and Mary, both staunch Protestants, became England's monarchs, Daniel Foe was a highly visible supporter of the new regime.

His political contacts served him well, for his business affairs were in dire straits, in part because of imprudent ventures, in part because of heavy shipping losses incurred during a war with France. In 1692, Foe declared bankruptcy, and for a time only his income from appointments in the Whig government enabled him to support his family. He added the prefix to his name in 1695, perhaps to suggest to his new associates that he had an aristocratic background. During this period, Defoe also became a secret agent for William III; at the same time, he was again involved in a business venture, a brick and roof-tile factory near London. When it prospered, Defoe was able to pay off most of his debts, to buy a new house, and even to keep a coach. However, like the characters in his novels, he was soon to discover how abruptly Providence could change the direction of one's life. At thirty-seven, Defoe became a writer.

LIFE'S WORK

Daniel Defoe's new life began in 1697 with the publication of his first signed work, *An Essay upon Projects*. In this work, he suggested that the nation would benefit by educating women, providing care for those with mental disabilities, setting up insurance, and instituting an income tax. The book is still of interest, demonstrating as it does Defoe's original mind, his attention to detail, and the clarity of his prose. There is also much of lasting value to be found among the propaganda pieces that Defoe began turning out, for example, the long doggerel poem *The True-Born Englishman* (1701), a brilliant work that countered attacks on William as a foreigner by pointing out that the English themselves were of mixed ancestry. The poem was extremely popular; according to the author, the first edition alone sold more than eighty thousand copies.

After William died in 1702 and the Tories rose to power, the Dissenters found themselves threatened by Tory extremists, and Defoe responded by writing *The Shortest Way with Dissenters*. Though the pamphlet appeared to urge the Tories to further action against nonconformists, it was actually a parody of the Tories at their most intolerant. When his intent became clear, Defoe was arrested, convicted of seditious libel, and sentenced to stand three times in the pillory, pay a large fine, and remain in jail for an indeterminate period. Defoe's response was to write a poem in praise of liberty called "A Hymn to the Pillory." Although Defoe was roundly cheered by the populace while he was in the pillory, he was deserted by the Whig leadership. It was the Tory leader Robert Harley who obtained a pardon for Defoe and also found him financial aid, for during his six months in prison the factory had failed, and Defoe was once again bankrupt.

Defoe now became a full-time professional journalist in the service of the Tories. It is difficult to believe that a single person could write so much, and so well, as Defoe did during this period. From 1704 to 1713, he composed and edited *The Review*, a landmark in the history of journalism. He was also turning out hundreds of highly effective political pamphlets and writing accounts such as *A True Relation of the Apparition of One Mrs. Veal, the Next Day After Her Death, to One Mrs. Bargrave . . .* (1706), which many consider his finest work as a reporter. Among Defoe's many book-length publications were the political allegory *The Consolidator* (1705); *Jure Divino* (1706), a poem about the principles of government; and *The History of the Union* (1709), which drew upon the author's knowledge of Scotland, where Harley had sent him while the two countries were negotiating over unification.

As long as the Tories were in power, Defoe felt secure; whenever he was arrested, his friends could secure his release. When George I succeeded Queen Anne and

Daniel Defoe. (Library of Congress)

the Whigs took over the country, however, Defoe found it necessary to make peace with his old Whig enemies. He became a double agent, taking orders from the Whig leader Robert Walpole while still pretending to be a Tory. Not only did Defoe gather information from his Tory associates, but he also placed articles in Tory journals that would subvert their policies. It is ironic that at this time Defoe also produced a morally edifying book entitled *The Family Instructor* (1715), which became his most popular didactic work. In fact, it sold so well that he soon followed it with a sequel.

Since he had now become a master of subterfuge, perhaps it was appropriate that Defoe should try his hand at fiction. In 1719, he published *Robinson Crusoe*, which many scholars consider the first true English novel. Though purely fictional, *Robinson Crusoe* was presented as a true story of travel and adventure, so detailed that its veracity could hardly be doubted and so well provided with moral and religious content that not even a Dissenter could find it less than edifying. Some months later came a sequel, *Further Adventures*.

In these and in the novels that followed, Defoe, like many earlier storytellers, used a first-person narrator. What sets Defoe's fiction apart from its predecessors, however, is a new complexity in characterization, especially where the narrator is concerned. Defoe's narrators change and develop as the story progresses, thus providing a kind of unity and interest that simpler narratives did not have. Like Crusoe, the narrator-protagonists of *Captain Singleton* (1720), *Colonel Jacque* (1722), and *Memoirs of a Cavalier* (1724) describe the exterior landscape in painstaking detail, but they also take their readers into the interior landscape, confiding their fears, self-doubts, and moral confusion. These revelations make each protagonist distinct from the others. The narrator of *A Journal of the Plague Year* (1722), for example, is shown as a practical man who totals up horror like an accountant, almost certainly preserving his sanity in the process. Defoe's female characters are just as interesting and just as distinct. The title character of *Roxana* (1724) describes her glittering past with regret and dies poor and penitent. However, the narrator in *Moll Flanders* (1722), who, along with Crusoe, is probably Defoe's finest creation, is so adept at justifying her actions that one wonders if she has tricked even Providence, for the book ends with her rich and happy enough to indulge in a little repentance.

Defoe produced these great novels over the course of just five years and then turned back to nonfiction, rapidly producing books on subjects ranging from *Conjugal*

SHIPWRECKED ON AN ISLAND

In Daniel Defoe's most famous work, Robinson Crusoe, *the title character is the sole survivor of a shipwreck. In the passage excerpted below, Crusoe sets out for the first time to explore the area in which he is stranded.*

My next work was to view the country, and seek a proper place for my habitation, and where to stow my goods to secure them from whatever might happen. Where I was, I yet knew not; whether on the continent or on an island; whether inhabited or not inhabited; whether in danger of wild beasts or not. There was a hill not above a mile from me, which rose up very steep and high, and which seemed to overtop some other hills, which lay as in a ridge from it northward. I took out one of the fowling-pieces, and one of the pistols, and a horn of powder; and thus armed, I travelled for discovery up to the top of that hill, where, after I had with great labour and difficulty got to the top, I saw my fate, to my great affliction-viz. that I was in an island environed every way with the sea: no land to be seen except some rocks, which lay a great way off; and two small islands, less than this, which lay about three leagues to the west.

I found also that the island I was in was barren, and, as I saw good reason to believe, uninhabited except by wild beasts, of whom, however, I saw none. Yet I saw abundance of fowls, but knew not their kinds; neither when I killed them could I tell what was fit for food, and what not. At my coming back, I shot at a great bird which I saw sitting upon a tree on the side of a great wood. I believe it was the first gun that had been fired there since the creation of the world. I had no sooner fired, than from all parts of the wood there arose an innumerable number of fowls, of many sorts, making a confused screaming and crying, and every one according to his usual note, but not one of them of any kind that I knew. As for the creature I killed, I took it to be a kind of hawk, its colour and beak resembling it, but it had no talons or claws more than common. Its flesh was carrion, and fit for nothing.

Source: Daniel Defoe, *Robinson Crusoe.* University of Virginia Library Electronic Text Center, 2000. Chapter 4. http://etext.lib.virginia.edu/toc/modeng/public/DefCru1.html. Accessed September, 2005.

tery of the language, though he had that gift, too. Defoe was responsible for supporting both himself and his family, and when his businesses failed, not once but twice, he could not quit. In desperation, he looked for other ways to make money, and he found two: political intrigue and writing.

It would be easy to brand Defoe as an opportunist who wrote whatever would sell and who in his own life ignored the principles he professed. That would be profoundly unfair. Defoe often wrote that his own difficult life had demonstrated how Providence operated. Like Robinson Crusoe and Moll Flanders, Defoe felt himself guided by God. He did not live to realize that his financial failures paved the way for him to become one of England's greatest writers, breaking ground and producing works of lasting value in not one but two areas. However, as he said in a letter written from his hiding place just a few months before his death, his faith never failed. At the last, he trusted the God who had been with him in adversity and danger, on the pillory and in prison, to guide him safely to his eternal rest.

—*Rosemary M. Canfield Reisman*

Lewdness (1727) to *A Plan of the English Commerce* (1728). However, despite his industry, in the summer of 1730 Defoe was again in financial difficulty. Though his health was failing, he had to leave his family and go into hiding to escape an old creditor. The following April, he died alone in a rented room. Defoe was buried in a cemetery favored by Dissenters, not far from another literary genius well acquainted with prison life, the author of *The Pilgrim's Progress* (1678, 1684), John Bunyan.

SIGNIFICANCE

Although scholars are still uncertain about attribution in a few cases, they have identified a total of 566 separate works by Daniel Defoe. So huge an output cannot be explained either by the author's intellectual curiosity, though certainly he possessed that quality, or by his mas-

FURTHER READING

Backscheider, Paula R. *Daniel Defoe: His Life.* Baltimore: Johns Hopkins University Press, 1989. A lengthy biographical study of the author and his place in the eighteenth century literary tradition. A work of major importance.

Bastian, F. *Defoe's Early Life.* Totowa, N.J.: Barnes & Noble Books, 1981. A detailed discussion of Defoe's family background, youth, and involvement in politics. Ends in 1703, with Defoe imprisoned in Newgate.

Bloom, Harold, ed. *Daniel Defoe.* New York: Chelsea House, 1987. A volume in the Modern Critical Views series. Thirteen essays represent three decades of criticism. Subjects include point of view, theme, style, and characterization. Harold Bloom's introduction, Leo Braudy's "Daniel Defoe and the Anxieties of Autobiography," and John J. Burke, Jr.'s "Observing the Observer in Historical Fictions by Defoe" are of particular interest.

Curtis, Laura A. *The Elusive Daniel Defoe*. London: Vision, 1984. Prompted by Defoe's habit of writing in the first person, Curtis hopes to discover the true identity of the author by looking for repeated patterns in his novels. Voluminous notes point out similarities between Defoe and other writers and possible influences. A highly original study.

Earle, Peter. *The World of Defoe*. London: Weidenfeld & Nicolson, 1976. Though not new, this work is still valuable for its comments about the author's society and his relationship to it. Helpful notes and good index.

Novak, Maximillian E. *Daniel Defoe, Master of Fictions: His Life and Ideas*. New York: Oxford University Press, 2001. Definitive, scholarly biography written by a noted Defoe scholar. Focuses on Defoe's writing career, integrating details of his life with information about his fiction, travel literature, and other written works. On a par with, and a supplement to, Paula Backscheider's biography.

Richetti, John J. *Daniel Defoe*. Boston: Twayne, 1987. Argues that examination of Defoe's fiction should be balanced by careful study of his nonfiction. This book looks at both, noting both similarities and inconsistencies.

Rogers, Pat, ed. *Defoe: The Critical Heritage*. 1972. Reprint. London: Routledge and Kegan Paul, 1995. This comprehensive collection of comments about Defoe is essential for the understanding of such a complex figure. The editor's introduction provides an excellent overview.

West, Richard. *The Life and Strange Surprising Adventures of Daniel Defoe*. London: Flamingo, 1998. A nonscholarly biography providing a detailed and sympathetic portrait of Defoe. Focuses on his travel books and journalism, with less emphasis on his novels and other literature.

See also: Joseph Addison; Queen Anne; Henry Fielding; George I; Charlotte Lennox; Ann Radcliffe; Samuel Richardson; Robert Walpole.

Related articles in *Great Events from History: The Eighteenth Century, 1701-1800:* April 25, 1719: Defoe Publishes the First Novel; 1726-1729: Voltaire Advances Enlightenment Thought in Europe.

AAGJE DEKEN
Dutch writer

Deken, along with Betje Wolff, wrote the realistic epistolary novel De historie van Mejuffrouw Sara Burgerhart, *often considered the first modern novel produced in the Netherlands. The work satirized Dutch society and delved into the inner workings of the middle class.*

Born: December 10, 1741; Amstelveen, the Netherlands
Died: November 14, 1804; The Hague, the Netherlands
Also known as: Agatha Deken (birth name)
Area of achievement: Literature

EARLY LIFE
Aagje Deken (AHG-yuh DAY-kihn), born to parents who died when Aagje was four years old, was cared for and educated by De Orange Appel, a pietistic orphanage in Amsterdam. Some sources suggest that she remained in the orphanage until 1767, when she would have been twenty-six years old.

Upon leaving the orphanage, Deken had little hope of being anything more than a domestic worker. She served several families in domestic capacities but yearned for a life of greater independence. While still working as a domestic, Deken became an entrepreneur, establishing a business marketing coffee and tea.

In 1769 she joined the Baptist Church and became active in Amsterdam's Baptist community. Feeling isolated and alienated, Deken was searching for companionship. She had experienced some lesbian contact in the orphanage, and once she was out on her own she sought women for intimacy.

Deken never gave up her quest for companionship. Her early introspection led her to writing, mostly poetry, which led to self-understanding and realizing her place in society. She was not satisfied with her life, but the course it followed had been predestined by the premature deaths of her parents. She was alone in the world but was determined to take control of her own life.

The orphanage in which she was raised demanded from her obedience and acquiescence. As she embarked upon a more independent existence, her behavior was colored by tactics she developed to survive in the constricted institutional life of the orphanage.

LIFE'S WORK

At age twenty-nine, Aagje Deken found compatible and rewarding work. In 1770 she was employed by the upper-middle-class Bosch family to nurse their sickly daughter, Maria. Deken established an immediate rapport with Maria, who was the same age as she. The two shared an enthusiasm for poetry, and both had dabbled in writing poems before they met. Deken spent two good years with the Bosch family, and she remained close to them even after Maria died in 1773.

Deken and Maria worked together on their poems for the two years preceding Maria's death. Deken published their poetry in a book called *Stichtelijke gedichten* (1775; edifying poems), a volume of predominantly didactic verse. Meanwhile, Deken had read some of the radical writings of Betje Wolff, a highly controversial writer in her day.

Wolff came from a prosperous merchant family, whom she had disgraced by spending a single unchaperoned night with a naval ensign named Matthijs Gargon. This act brought upon her the scorn of her conservative community, Vlissingen, and of members of her family, who were strict Calvinists. In 1759, to distance herself from the disdain of her community and family, Betje married a widowed clergyman, Adrian Wolff, some thirty years her senior. This marriage, presumably a loveless union, lasted until Adrian's death twenty-five years later. During the last fifteen years of that marriage, Betje Wolff published extensively and became a well-known writer. The early trials she endured would provide considerable material for her later collaborations with Deken.

Deken's initial contact with Wolff was in 1776, the year before Wolff's husband's death. Deken was shocked by many of the radical ideas she found in Wolff's writing. Having yet to escape the bonds of her pietistic upbringing in the orphanage, she wrote to Wolff, chiding her for her controversial views on education, religion, the status of women, and society in general. Much of Wolff's most stinging satirical writing was aimed at established religion, to which Deken still adhered.

Rather then being offended by Deken's criticism, Wolff detected in it an incisive intelligence and a clear understanding of her sometimes elusive satire. The two women corresponded regularly and met for the first time in October, 1776. Early in 1777, Wolff's husband died. Wolff then invited Deken to live with her. The two lived together until their deaths (which were nine days apart) in 1804.

During their early relationship, Wolff, already an established author, and Deken, who had published but had not garnered the critical acclaim enjoyed by Wolff, continued to write independently. Soon, however, the two collaborated on novels based on their joint experiences: Deken's in the orphanage and as a household servant and Wolff's as a scorned and controversial woman. Their first collaborative effort was *Brieven* (1778; letters).

Another collaboration, *De historie van Mejuffrouw Sara Burgerhart* (1782; the history of Miss Sara Burgerhart), placed the two among the most significant writers in the Netherlands. The eighteenth century was a period in which most Dutch writing was stylized and mediocre, largely because of the complacency brought about by the commercial ascendancy of the Netherlands. *De historie van Mejuffrouw Sara Burgerhart* would see three editions by 1786. The novel was reportedly influenced by British author Samuel Richardson's novel *Pamela* (1740-1741), but it was clearly not derivative.

The Deken-Wolff collaboration would continue and result in three more epistolary novels, the most successful being *De historie van den Heer Willem Leevend* (1784-1785; the history of Mr. William Leevend), an eight-volume work that began well but became increasingly long-winded and philosophical as it progressed. Never again did the pair achieve the success they experienced with *De historie van Mejuffrouw Sara Burgerhart*.

A successful pastoral book grew out of their ten-year residence in France, to which they fled during the Prussian invasion of the Low Countries in 1788. They lived in Trévoux and recorded some of that experience in *Wanderlingen door Bourgogne* (1789; strolling through Burgundy).

Although Deken received an inheritance of thirteen thousand guilders in 1781, that money was gone by the time she and Wolff fled to France. They produced another multivolume epistolary novel, *De historie van Mejuffrouw Cornelia Wildschut* (1793-1796; the history of Miss Cornelia Wildschut) while in France, but tastes had changed. This novel failed to attract the large following of enthusiastic readers garnered by their first novel.

Financially strained, Deken and Wolff finally returned to the Netherlands in 1798, settling in The Hague until their final year. Barely surviving by doing translations, they were helped by the charity of various friends and admirers. Wolff died on November 5 and was followed in death nine days later by Deken. The two women were buried next to each other in Scheveningen, a Dutch seaside resort in The Hague along the North Sea.

SIGNIFICANCE

Aagje Deken and Betje Wolff's writing of the first modern novel in the Netherlands, *De historie van Mejuffrouw Sara Burgerhart*, assured their niche in Dutch literary history. Filled with keen insights into human behavior, the work nevertheless avoids being oversentimental. It is a realistic novel that draws heavily on Wolff's experience as a satirist, producing the subtle and often humorous characterizations for which it gained quick acceptance by a reading public eager for a compelling tale.

Deken is recognized for her farsighted views on women's rights and her honesty in dealing with her own sexuality. She was a woman of character who refused to live a life of deceit and apology. Her relationship with Wolff was the most important aspect of her existence, and she struggled to preserve it against daunting odds.

—*R. Baird Shuman*

FURTHER READING

Kors, Alan Charles, ed. *Encyclopedia of the Enlightenment*. 4 vols. New York: Oxford University Press, 2003. This four-volume encyclopedia includes an entry about Deken.

Meijer, Reinder P. *Literature of the Low Countries: A Short History of Literature in the Netherlands and Belgium*. The Hague, the Netherlands: Nijhoff, 1978. This is one of the few books in English on Dutch literary history. A useful presentation of Deken's contributions to literature.

Nisbet, H. B., and Claude Rawson, eds. *The Eighteenth Century*. Vol. 4 in *The Cambridge History of Literary Criticism*. New York: Cambridge University Press, 2001. Chapter 9, a survey of prose fiction in the Netherlands and Germany, includes discussion of Deken and Wolff.

Wilson, Katharina M., ed. *An Encyclopedia of Continental Women Writers*. New York: Garland, 1991. Wilson is to be commended for her comprehensive coverage of her topic. Her examination of Deken and Wolff is accurate, clear, and easily accessible.

See also: Daniel Defoe; Sophie von La Roche; Mary Wortley Montagu; Samuel Richardson; Mary Wollstonecraft.

Related articles in *Great Events from History: The Eighteenth Century, 1701-1800:* 1740-1741: Richardson's *Pamela* Establishes the Modern Novel; 1792: Wollstonecraft Publishes *A Vindication of the Rights of Woman*.

JOHN DICKINSON
American legal scholar and politician

At a crucial point in the development of the American Revolution, Dickinson stated the colonists' arguments against England in a new and compelling way and became, for a while, a spokesman for all the colonies. Later, he helped draft and win ratification of the U.S. Constitution.

Born: November 8, 1732; Crosiadore Plantation, Maryland
Died: February 14, 1808; Wilmington, Delaware
Areas of achievement: Government and politics, law

EARLY LIFE

John Dickinson was born on a plantation in Maryland that had been in his family for three quarters of a century. Eight years later, John's father, Samuel, moved his family to Delaware, where he hired an Irish tutor named William Killen to teach his children classics and history. Samuel Dickinson was a lawyer as well as a gentleman farmer, and Killen, too, was attracted to the law (he later became chief justice of Delaware), so it is not surprising that the young John Dickinson chose law as a career.

When he was eighteen years old, John Moland, one of Philadelphia's leading attorneys, accepted Dickinson as a student. The three years that he spent in Moland's office introduced him to a much wider world than he had known before, and he began to meet other young men who would become important in revolutionary Pennsylvania and Delaware. His fellow students in Moland's office, for example, included Samuel Wharton and George Read.

To complete his legal training, Dickinson left America in 1753 to study at the Inns of Court in London. Five years later, he returned to Philadelphia and opened his own law office. A bookish and intelligent man, he was apparently as interested in studying and writing history, especially English constitutional history, as he was in trying cases. Nevertheless, he quickly became one of the most successful lawyers in the city. A portrait of him done years later reveals a man with the somewhat portly build typical of successful men in the eighteenth century. His mental abilities, his training, and his understanding of history and constitutional law, however, were anything but typical.

The popular, talented, and wealthy young attorney soon ran for office and won election to the Delaware legislature in 1760. Two years later, he became a delegate to the Pennsylvania Assembly, representing Philadelphia, where he opposed Joseph Galloway and Benjamin Franklin in their attempts to have King George III convert Pennsylvania from a proprietary colony ruled by the Penn family to a royal colony run by a royal governor. Dickinson had little love for the Penns, whom he (and most Pennsylvanians) regarded as a particularly rapacious clan, much too prone to place their own welfare above the public good. Yet Dickinson thought the remedy Franklin proposed would make things worse, for it would strip Pennsylvanians of the protection that their proprietary charter afforded them from direct royal (and parliamentary) interference in their affairs.

Dickinson's stand was not popular, and he lost his seat at the next election. On the sidelines and out of public favor, he began to write about the emerging struggle between the colonies and England. That struggle would change Dickinson's life and career and led him away from the practice of law toward a life of revolutionary politics and public service.

LIFE'S WORK

In 1765, John Dickinson published the pamphlet *The Late Regulations Respecting the British Colonies on the Continent of America Considered*. In it, he denounced both the Sugar Act (1764) and the Stamp Act (1765) as ill-advised and economically senseless attempts by Parliament to raise revenues in the American colonies. The popular pamphlet made Dickinson one of Pennsylvania's leading opponents of the stamp tax, and so when the legislature chose delegates to attend the Stamp Act Congress in New York, Dickinson was among them. That congress so closely reflected the cautious Dickinson's views, and so respected his talents as a constitutional scholar and essayist, that it permitted him to draft its formal resolutions. In them, Dickinson stated the colonies' objections to the Stamp Act but avoided any suggestion that colonists ought to resist the law until it was (as the congress hoped it would be) repealed.

Parliament did repeal the Stamp Act in 1766, but soon a new threat to colonial liberties arose when England again tried to raise a revenue in the colonies. The Townshend Revenue Act of 1767 imposed taxes on English goods imported into the colonies. In December, 1767, Dickinson began publishing in the *Pennsylvania Chronicle* a series of letters signed "A Farmer in Pennsylvania" that opposed the Townshend taxes. Dickinson was not a farmer in Pennsylvania, but was a lawyer in Philadelphia. Yet the overwhelming majority of colonists (90 percent or more) lived in rural areas, not cities, and were not likely to be much impressed by "Letters from a Philadelphia Lawyer." Dickinson wisely chose a more appealing pen name. In any case, that he was the "Pennsylvania farmer" quickly became public knowledge.

In the "farmer's letters," as they came to be called, Dickinson accomplished two things. First, he summarized and stated the colonists' claim that English attempts to tax them were not merely inexpedient and ill-advised, but were flatly unconstitutional—and he summarized that claim more clearly and succinctly than any colonist before. "It is *inseparably essential to the freedom of a people*," he wrote at the Stamp Act Congress and repeated in Letter IV, "that NO TAX be imposed on them, *except with their own consent*, given personally, or by their representatives." Second, he pointed out that the form of any tax England attempted to lay upon American colonists to raise revenues was irrelevant. What mattered in deciding if a tax was or was not constitutional was the purpose for which it had been passed. If England taxed, for example, colonial imports to restrict American trade with foreign nations, then the purpose of that tax was primarily to regulate trade—and few colonists, and certainly not Dickinson, as yet challenged England's right to regulate the colonies' trade. If England laid a tax on colonial imports to raise money, however (as it did in the Townshend Act), then the tax was unconstitutional. Dickinson added that it was the colonists' right to determine for themselves what Parliament's intent had been in passing any colonial tax.

The "farmer's letters" were immensely popular. Nearly every colonial newspaper published them. A pamphlet version appeared in Philadelphia in 1768 and was republished at least six times in other American cities, while editions also came out in London, Paris, and Dublin. When most colonial assemblies endorsed Dickinson's ideas, he became the first American who could, with some justice, claim to speak for the American colonies, rather than for only a few of them. In the letters, Dickinson laid the foundation for an emerging sense of American "nationality" among the colonists. He brought much closer the day when colonists would think of them-

John Dickinson. (Library of Congress)

selves not as New Yorkers or Virginians or Rhode Islanders first, but as one people, sharing common ideas, interests, and goals. This was the most important contribution of the letters to the developing American Revolution and to the nation it created.

For a while, Dickinson was the most popular individual in the colonies. Praised by town meetings, toasted by county committees, honored by legislatures, Dickinson found himself hailed from Massachusetts to Georgia. In the letters, he had staked out the most advanced constitutional ground and had placed himself at the cutting edge of the incipient revolution against England. Dickinson's exceptional popularity, however, did not last. He opposed, publicly and often, any open resistance to English law and especially any violent resistance. Perhaps influenced by his family's Quaker heritage, he held to that opinion, insisting that conciliation, patience, and petitions, along with trade boycotts, were the proper means of changing England's mind even after the Tea Act and the Boston Tea Party. Not even the passage of the Coercive (Intolerable) Acts, the imposition by England of martial law in Massachusetts and the military occupation of Boston, changed his mind. By the spring of 1775, Dickinson was being denounced for his caution as a Loyalist sympathizer and a coward throughout much of New England, while many ardent rebels in Pennsylvania became suspicious, if not of his loyalty, then at least of the depth of his commitment to the rebel cause.

By late 1774 even Dickinson knew that war might be unavoidable and that the colonists had best prepare for the worst even as they tried to avoid it. He served that year as a Pennsylvania delegate to the First Continental Congress, as chairman of his colony's Committee of Safety and Defense and as colonel of the first battalion of revolutionary militia raised in Philadelphia. Yet even after the war began at Lexington in April, 1775, Dickinson still sought a peaceful resolution of the troubles between England and the colonies, and he still refused to support a declaration of American independence. In December, 1775, for example, after eight months of war, Dickinson arranged to have Pennsylvania's delegation to the 1776 Continental Congress (which included himself) forbidden by the Assembly to consider independence at Congress.

By the end of 1775, Dickinson had come to fear what England's armies might do to America in a revolutionary war declared too soon, without sufficient preparation, planning, and unity and without a single guarantee of foreign assistance. He also worried about what colonists might do to themselves during and after such a war. Dickinson was well aware of the jealousies and antagonisms among colonists that had characterized most of colonial history, problems that had not dissolved when the war began. He worried that thirteen petty, independent states might eventually make war on one another, and that anarchy or tyranny might follow. He worried, in short, that the liberties that colonists were fighting to preserve might be destroyed by the revolution intended to secure them. Thus, when Congress took a preliminary vote on independence on July 1, 1776, Dickinson spoke eloquently in opposition and voted no. When the final vote came the next morning, however, it was clear that independence would pass overwhelmingly, so Dickinson abstained; he took no part in the vote that finally, after fifteen months of war, declared the American colonies free and independent states.

Dickinson still had misgivings about the revolution following independence, especially when Congress rejected his draft of a proposed constitution for the new nation, which would have created a relatively strong central government. Instead, Congress adopted articles of confederation that left most significant powers in the hands of the separate states. Widely suspected of being a lukewarm rebel at best, his advice ignored by Congress, and his seat there taken from him by the end of 1776, Dickinson withdrew from public life for a time, resigning his commission and his place in the legislature.

In 1779, however, Dickinson returned to Congress as a delegate from Delaware. Two years later, he became president of that state's Supreme Executive Council, and he soon won the same post in Pennsylvania, although he despised the state's radical revolutionary constitution. His troubled experience as president of the council merely reinforced his conviction that the states and the nation could neither survive nor prosper without stronger, more stable governments.

When Delaware chose him as a delegate to the federal Constitutional Convention at Philadelphia in the summer of 1787, Dickinson accepted. He took an active part in the convention's deliberations and played an important role in arranging the compromises among the various factions represented there (and particularly between the large and small states) that made any agreement on a new national constitution possible. Never as ardent an advocate of national government power (as opposed to state power) as James Madison or Alexander Hamilton, Dickinson nevertheless worked at the convention to create a more vigorous central government than existed under the Articles of Confederation.

After the convention presented the new national Constitution to the states for their approval, Dickinson wrote a series of letters signed "Fabius," which began appearing in newspapers in the fall of 1787. They urged ratification of the Constitution on the grounds that it would provide the stability of government that the ineffective Articles of Confederation manifestly had not, and so protect liberty, ensure the due power of each state within the Union, and guarantee stability. That done, he all but retired from public life, though he continued to follow public affairs closely and to express his opinions in letters and essays. When he died in February, 1808, he was seventy-six years old.

SIGNIFICANCE

John Dickinson was, all of his life, cautious and conservative. In 1776, he did not so much embrace revolution as accept it when events left him no choice. Never much attracted by the possibilities that revolution offered to create new liberties, Dickinson instead feared the threat revolution posed to liberties he already enjoyed, liberties solidly grounded in English history, law, and tradition.

The "farmer's letters" united the colonists behind a single constitutional doctrine in opposition to England, a necessary condition for independence and an American nation. At the same time, Dickinson upheld the power of law, peaceful persuasion, and public discourse as the proper means by which colonists might see their grievances redressed.

As late as July, 1776, Dickinson opposed the Declaration of Independence, which his own writings had helped make inevitable. Yet once his fellow colonists chose to establish a new nation, he stood with them. Once he understood, as John Adams, Benjamin Franklin, and others did before him, that the fact of imminent tyranny outweighed the dangers of resistance and even independence, commitment to the revolution did not waver. He spent the remainder of his public life helping to secure independence and working to prevent the liberties he valued from being consumed by the revolution or undermined in its aftermath. At the federal Constitutional Convention of 1787, he worked to enhance the power of the central government without unduly limiting the autonomy of the states. Once a stable national frame of government had been agreed upon at Philadelphia, Dickinson campaigned to have it accepted by the states. After ratification, with the republic safe, at least for a while, Dickinson retired to his home in Delaware as one of the founders of a new republic in a world of monarchies.

—Robert A. Becker

FURTHER READING

Berkin, Carol. *A Brilliant Solution: Inventing the American Constitution.* New York: Harcourt, 2002. Recounts the events of the Constitutional Convention, featuring information on Dickinson's role in the proceedings. Includes an appendix with short biographies of convention delegates.

Bradford, M. E. *Founding Fathers: Brief Lives of the Framers of the United States Constitution.* 2d rev. ed. Lawrence: University Press of Kansas, 1994. A five-page biography of Dickinson is included among the biographies of the fifty-five delegates to the Constitutional Convention. Examines the delegates' constitutional theories and visions for a new nation.

Dickinson, John, and Richard Henry Lee. *Empire and Nation: Letters from a Farmer in Pennsylvania; Letters from the Federal Farmer.* Englewood Cliffs, N.J.: Prentice-Hall, 1962. Contains the text of all the "farmer's letters." Forrest McDonald's introduction is useful for putting the letters in context.

Flower, Milton E. *John Dickinson, Conservative Revolutionary*. Charlottesville: University Press of Virginia, 1983. The first full biography of Dickinson since 1891 and the only one readily available. Scholarly and not particularly easy reading. Flower portrays Dickinson in the usual manner, as a conservative, and offers few new insights. Yet Flower provides far more, and more accurate, information about Dickinson than any other single source.

Jacobson, David L. *John Dickinson and the Revolution in Pennsylvania, 1764-1776*. Berkeley: University of California Press, 1965. Not a full biography. Scholarly yet surprisingly readable. Treats Dickinson as less conservative than do most historians.

Jensen, Merrill. *The Articles of Confederation: An Interpretation of the Social-Constitutional History of the American Revolution, 1774-1781*. Madison: University of Wisconsin Press, 1959. Includes a detailed account of Dickinson's draft of articles of confederation submitted to Congress shortly after independence. Chapter 4 deals exclusively with Dickinson's draft. Places the Articles of Confederation and the debate over them within the larger context of the revolution. Though somewhat dated, the book is still useful for understanding Dickinson and the political climate in which he lived.

Van Doren, Carl C. *The Great Rehearsal: The Story of the Making and Ratifying of the Constitution of the United States*. Westport, Conn.: Greenwood Press, 1982. Originally published in 1948, this nicely written, largely narrative account provides a good background for understanding Dickinson's role at the federal Constitutional Convention and in the ensuing ratification debates.

See also: John Adams; Sir William Blackstone; Benjamin Franklin; George III; Alexander Hamilton; James Madison; James Wilson.

Related articles in *Great Events from History: The Eighteenth Century, 1701-1800:* 1712: Stamp Act; March 22, 1765-March 18, 1766: Stamp Act Crisis; June 29, 1767-April 12, 1770: Townshend Crisis; December 16, 1773: Boston Tea Party; September 5-October 26, 1774: First Continental Congress; April 19, 1775: Battle of Lexington and Concord; July 4, 1776: Declaration of Independence; March 1, 1781: Ratification of the Articles of Confederation; September 17, 1787: U.S. Constitution Is Adopted.

DENIS DIDEROT
French philosopher and writer

As editor of and contributor to the Encyclopedia, *Diderot codified and promulgated the views of the French Enlightenment. His posthumously published fiction, moreover, has earned for him a prominent place in the pantheon of eighteenth century writers, and his philosophical works remain challenging and influential.*

Born: October 5, 1713; Langres, France
Died: July 31, 1784; Paris, France
Also known as: Pantophile
Areas of achievement: Scholarship, philosophy, literature

EARLY LIFE

The son of Didier Diderot, a master cutler, and Angélique Vigneron Diderot, a tanner's daughter, Denis Diderot (duh-nee dee-droh) was born into a family of tradesmen. In addition to this trade connection, quite a few of his relatives had entered the Church, among them the canon of the cathedral at Langres. Diderot's brother, Didier-Pierre, and his sister, Angélique, would follow this ecclesiastical path, the former becoming a priest and the latter a nun. Diderot, despite his later atheism, also showed early religious inclinations. Tonsured at the age of twelve, he made the 150-mile (240-kilometer) journey north to Paris three years later to study at the Jesuit Collège de Louis-le-Grand or the Jansenist Collège d'Harcourt; he may have taken courses at both. When he received his degree in 1732, though, it was from the University of Paris, and his interest had shifted to philosophy and rhetoric.

Since Diderot had abandoned a career in the Church, his father apprenticed him to the Parisian lawyer Clément de Ris. This field suited him no better than religion, however, and after enduring two years of legal studies, Diderot turned to a life of letters. His father refused to approve of so uncertain a course, so for the next decade, Diderot survived on the meager earnings he garnered as a tutor and hack writer, supplemented by occasional small sums from his mother. On November 6,

1743, he married Anne-Toinette Champion, the daughter of a poor linen-shop owner; the marriage further alienated his father, who so opposed it that he had Diderot locked up in a monastery to prevent the wedding. Diderot escaped; he realized, however, that he could not rely on his parents to support his family and recognized that he needed a secure source of income.

LIFE'S WORK

Denis Diderot turned to the booksellers, offering his fluency in English and his literary talent. In 1743, he translated Temple Stanyan's *Grecian History* (1707) for a publisher named Briasson, who was sufficiently pleased with the result to ask Diderot for a French version of Robert James's *Medical Dictionary* (1743-1745). At the same time that he was translating James's treatise, he adapted the third earl of Shaftesbury's *An Inquiry Concerning Virtue or Merit* (1699). Much in Shaftesbury's work appealed to Diderot and deeply influenced his views. He admired the Englishman's tolerance and emphasis on reason, and he adopted the notion that religion and morality should be judged according to their social effects. Diderot also agreed with Shaftesbury that emotions play an important role in fostering socially proper conduct. He was less prepared to accept Shaftesbury's optimism, his notion of innate aesthetic appreciation, and his criticism of organized religion.

Diderot's first original philosophical work, *Pensées philosophiques* (1746; English translation, 1819), which was written over Easter weekend, 1746, to earn fifty gold pieces for his mistress Madame de Puissieux, was built on his encounter with Shaftesbury's text. Diderot was still not prepared to reject the Church—the fifty-first *pensée* reaffirms his belief in Catholicism—but he does urge that faith be tested by reason and that the passions, deemed by the orthodox to be dangerous, be seen as necessary to morality and creativity. Published anonymously, it was sufficiently impressive to be attributed to such well-known intellectuals as Voltaire or Étienne Bonnot de Condillac. It was also regarded as sufficiently radical to be condemned by the Parlement of Paris in July, 1746.

La Promenade du sceptique (wr. 1747, pb. 1830; the skeptic's walk) revealed Diderot's increasing doubts about religion; the manuscript was seized before publication, and the police began to watch Diderot closely. His bawdy satire on Louis XV and Madame de Pompadour, *Les Bijoux indiscrets* (1748; *The Indiscreet Toys*, 1749), further antagonized the authorities, and his *Lettre sur les aveugles* (1749; *An Essay on Blindness*, 1750;

also as *Letter on the Blind*, 1916), which questioned the Deistic argument that cosmic order proves God's existence, led to his arrest and solitary confinement for three months in the fortress of Vincennes.

Diderot's imprisonment shook him deeply. Previously, he had published his controversial works anonymously; henceforth, he would rarely publish them at all. His reputation in the eighteenth century, therefore, was lower than it would become after his death. Much of his contemporary acclaim derived from the project that would occupy him for the next fifteen years: His translations and other writings not only had exposed Diderot to new knowledge but also had made him a logical choice to be coeditor with Jean le Rond d'Alembert of the ambitious project to translate and supplement Ephraim Chambers's five-volume *Cyclopaedia: Or, Universal Dictionary of the Arts and Sciences* (1728). The finished work, comprising seventeen volumes of text and eleven volumes of plates, was published as *Encyclopédie: Ou, Dictionnaire raisonné des sciences, des arts, et des métiers* (1751-1772; partial translation *Selected Essays from the Encyclopedy*, 1772; complete translation *Encyclopedia*, 1965).

As conservative opponents, who twice succeeded in having the *Encyclopedia* condemned, realized, the work

Denis Diderot. (Library of Congress)

was not an innocent compilation of existing knowledge. In its pages, nature replaced Providence and determinism superseded God's will as the guiding forces of the world. Instead of relying on authority and tradition, Diderot and his fellow philosophers urged readers to judge by experience and experimentation. In a world of monarchies, the article "Political Authority" proclaimed that "no man has received from nature the right to command other men. Freedom is a present from heaven, and every individual of the same species has the right to enjoy it as soon as he enjoys reason." By 1758, d'Alembert was sufficiently frightened by official reaction to the *Encyclopedia* to resign as coeditor, leaving Diderot with the sole responsibility for writing and soliciting contributions to complete the massive project.

In the midst of these labors, Diderot found time to produce a number of other works. The theater had long interested him. Late in life, he would state that he had debated between studying at the Sorbonne and becoming an actor, and in his *Lettre sur les sourds et muets* (1751; *Letter on the Deaf and Dumb*, 1916) he claimed to know much of French drama by heart. In the latter half of the 1750's, he indulged his interest by writing two plays, *Le Fils naturel: Ou, Les Épreuves de la vertu* (pr., pb. 1757; *Dorval: Or, The Test of Virtue*, 1767) and *Le Père de famille* (pb. 1758, pr. 1761; *The Father of the Family*, 1770; also known as *The Family Picture*, 1871). As the subtitle of *Dorval* reveals, Diderot regarded these works, as he did all of his writings, as having a moral purpose. In an article in the *Encyclopedia*, he had spoken of actors' ability to engender in audiences the love of virtue, and an essay on Geneva by d'Alembert, also in the *Encyclopedia*, urged the city to permit dramatic productions because they promote morality.

In addition to reforming society, Diderot hoped that his plays would alter theatrical techniques and practices, which he regarded as unrealistic. To the published version of each play he added comments on stagecraft, urging actors to pretend that no audience faced them. He wanted the people onstage to interact naturally with one another, not perform for observers. Diderot also argues, in *Paradoxe sur le comédien* (wr. 1773, pb. 1830; *The Paradox of Acting*, 1883), that the actor must be ruled by the intellect rather than by his emotions if he wishes to convey passion consistently. This view incidentally might suggest that Diderot was beginning to question his earlier agreement with Shaftesbury on the primacy of sentiment in guiding action.

Questioning does not, however, mean rejecting. As he matured, Diderot would become increasingly skeptical—

of his own views as well as the views of others, stating that "skepticism is the first step toward the truth." In *Le Neveu de Rameau* (1821, 1891; *Rameau's Nephew*, 1897), he seems to prefer Apollonian reason to Dionysian passion, but he also acknowledges the necessity of emotion for creativity. This same ambivalence shows itself in the aesthetic criticism that he wrote for Friedrich Melchior Grimm's *Correspondance littéraire*, a newsletter that circulated in manuscript, from 1759 to 1781. In an essay from 1766 on painting, Diderot instructed artists, "Move me, astonish me, rend me; make me shudder, weep, tremble; fill me with indignation." At the same time, he recognized that reason must balance enthusiasm.

Though uncertain about the means by which art should achieve its effects, Diderot had no doubt that its end must be the promotion of virtue. Hence, for example, he preferred the sentimental paintings of Jean-Baptiste Greuze to the more sensuous works of François Boucher. Greuze appealed to the heart, Boucher only to the eye. Similarly, though he was an atheist, he admired religious art, because it inspired virtuous feelings.

By the time his role in the *Encyclopedia* ended in 1765, Diderot had gained the reputation of being an important French intellectual. A flattering sign of Diderot's growing reputation came from Jean-Honoré Fragonard and Russia's Catherine the Great. In his series of paintings honoring the various arts, Fragonard chose Diderot to represent literature. His hair short, his forehead high, his mouth turned up in an enigmatic smile of reason, the philosopher holds a volume of the *Encyclopedia* and appears to be a Roman citizen wearing an eighteenth century dressing gown. Catherine the Great relieved Diderot of financial concerns in 1765 by buying his library for fifteen thousand livres and appointing him as its curator for life at a salary of another one thousand livres a year. She agreed not to take formal possession until after Diderot's death.

In 1773, Diderot went to Russia to thank the empress for her patronage. The trip inspired a number of works reflecting on politics and education, and during this time Diderot probably completed his best-known novel, *Jacques le fataliste et son maître* (wr. c. 1771, pb. 1796; *Jacques the Fatalist and His Master*, 1797). A clever, picaresque work, it once more reveals Diderot's skepticism. Although he had, like Jacques, believed in determinism earlier in his life, he now questioned this view. Despite Jacques's claim that no one has free will, he behaves in the novel as if he can choose whatever course of action he wishes to pursue, and authorial intrusions indicate that chance rules the world. Readers may draw their own conclusions—or conclude nothing.

Similar doubts characterize other writings of this period. "Beware of those who impose order," Diderot warned in *Supplément au voyage de Bougainville* (1796; *Supplement to Bougainville's Voyage,* 1926). The dialogue form, which Diderot used repeatedly, allows for the presentation of various positions without requiring the author to endorse any. This method, drawn from Plato, appealed to Diderot because it was safe should authorities secure a copy of the manuscript, and it also permitted Diderot to explore various viewpoints. *Est-il bon? Est-il méchant?* (pr. 1781, pb. 1834; is he good? is he mean?), his last and best play, questions, without deciding, whether one can be virtuous if one performs good deeds in a manner that embarrasses their beneficiaries. Skeptical to the end, Diderot's last words to his daughter were, "the first step toward philosophy is disbelief."

SIGNIFICANCE

Since his death on July 31, 1784, Denis Diderot's reputation has grown. With the benefit of the perspective brought by time, one can recognize the truth of Carl Becker's observation that Diderot epitomized his age, both in the profundity of his thought and in the occasional shallowness of his observations. One can appreciate more fully his courage in speaking out, guiding the *Encyclopedia* to completion despite an official ban, telling Catherine the Great that she should abandon autocracy for democracy, and the like. One of his essays was sufficiently bold in its criticism of the ancien régime to earn for him a severe reprimand from the police commissioner of Paris. With the publication of many of his best works, one can at last see his greatness as a writer as well as a thinker.

Even more important to the increasing appreciation of Diderot is the fact that his empiricism and skepticism matched the modern mood. In his own day, Voltaire referred to him as Socrates, a name that fits well. Like Socrates, Diderot questioned the accepted wisdom of his day, risked much for his beliefs, and contributed to the intellectual progress of his age. Writing of eccentrics, Diderot remarked, "If one of them appears in company, he is like a piece of yeast which ferments and restores to everyone a portion of his natural liberty. He shakes and stirs things up; he calls forth praise and blame; he brings out the truth." In these lines from *Rameau's Nephew,* Diderot wrote his own epitaph.

— *Joseph Rosenblum*

FURTHER READING

Becker, Carl. *The Heavenly City of Eighteenth Century Philosophers.* New Haven, Conn.: Yale University Press, 1932. Classic source on eighteenth century philosophes, placing Diderot in the context of the general Enlightenment project of building a new ideal on the wreckage of medieval philosophy.

Blom, Philipp. *Enlightening the World: "Encyclopédie," the Book That Changed the Course of History.* New York: Palgrave Macmillan, 2005. Relates the history of the *Encyclopedia,* describing the book's conception, efforts to suppress its publication, and the authors who faced exile, jail, and censorship to complete the work.

Blum, Carol. *Diderot: The Virtue of a Philosopher.* New York: Viking Press, 1974. Focuses on Diderot's concern for a moral life and his intellectual quest to define what such an existence involves. A well-written study that draws on biography, letters, and published writings. Makes some useful comparisons between Diderot and Jean-Jacques Rousseau on the nature of virtue.

Brewer, Daniel. *The Discourse of Enlightenment in Eighteenth-Century France: Diderot and the Art of Philosophizing.* New York: Cambridge University Press, 1993. Describes how French Enlightenment writers attempted rationally to critique and to demystify all knowledge. Focuses on Diderot, discussing his experiments in applying Enlightenment critique to his studies of philosophy, science, and fine arts.

Darnton, Robert. *The Business of Enlightenment: A Publishing History of the "Encyclopédie," 1775-1800.* Cambridge, Mass.: Harvard University Press, 1979. This massive, prizewinning history of Diderot's great project is an important contribution to the growing number of studies devoted to publishing, bookselling, the reading public, and similar topics, placing ideas in the context in which they are disseminated. Illustrated, with a narrative bibliography and an index.

Fellows, Otis. *Diderot.* Boston: Twayne, 1977. A chronological overview touching briefly on almost all Diderot's works. Stresses Diderot's modernity and traces the evolution of his thought. A helpful, annotated bibliography concludes the work.

France, Peter. *Diderot.* New York: Oxford University Press, 1983. A good, short introduction concentrating on Diderot's ideas. Arranged topically rather than chronologically, covering Diderot's political, social, and aesthetic views. Includes a useful bibliography with brief annotations.

Furbank, P. N. *Diderot: A Critical Biography.* New York: Alfred A. Knopf, 1992. Survey of Diderot's life, focusing on an examination of his major works. Furbank argues that Diderot's ideas anticipate the philosophies of later French thinkers.

Undank, Jack, and Herbert Josephs, eds. *Diderot: Digression and Dispersion, a Bicentennial Tribute*. Lexington, Ky.: French Forum, 1984. Presents nineteen essays that cover Diderot's many activities and interests. In their diversity, the contributions mirror the editors' view that Diderot did not seek unity but rather regarded diversity as the rule of nature.

Wilson, Arthur M. *Diderot*. New York: Oxford University Press, 1972. The definitive biography. Places Diderot within the context of the Enlightenment and emphasizes his courage in remaining the editor of the *Encyclopedia*. Considers the development of Diderot's ideas on such matters as religion, emotion and reason, order and diversity, determinism, and chance.

See also: Jean le Rond d'Alembert; Catherine the Great; Étienne Bonnot de Condillac; Jean-Honoré Fragonard; David Hume; Louis XV; Montesquieu; Madame de Pompadour; Jean-Jacques Rousseau; Voltaire.

Related articles in *Great Events from History: The Eighteenth Century, 1701-1800*: 1743-1744: D'Alembert Develops His Axioms of Motion; 1749-1789: First Comprehensive Examination of the Natural World; 1751: Maupertuis Provides Evidence of "Hereditary Particles"; 1751-1772: Diderot Publishes the *Encyclopedia*; 1754: Condillac Defends Sensationalist Theory; January, 1759: Voltaire Satirizes Optimism in *Candide*; July, 1764: Voltaire Publishes *A Philosophical Dictionary for the Pocket*; December 5, 1766-March, 16, 1769: Bougainville Circumnavigates the Globe.

JOSEPH-FRANÇOIS DUPLEIX
French colonial administrator

As the governor-general of French India, Dupleix dreamed of achieving French hegemony in southern India. To that end, he fought for more than a decade against the British East India Company for control of the region but ultimately failed.

Born: January 1, 1697; Landrecies, France
Died: November 10, 1763; Paris, France
Also known as: Marquis de Dupleix
Areas of achievement: Government and politics, warfare and conquest

EARLY LIFE

Joseph-François Dupleix (zhoh-zehf frahn-swah dyew-plehks), was the son of François Dupleix, a director of the French East India Company. Through his father's connections, he was appointed senior councillor of the Superior Council at Pondicherry, the company's headquarters in India, and arrived there on August 22, 1722. After almost a decade in Pondicherry, Dupleix was appointed in 1731 superintendent at Chandernagore in Bengal, where he remained for eleven years. His helpmate during that time was a biracial woman, Jeanne Albert, called "the Begam Jeanne," known for her strong will and intelligence. Throughout Dupleix's years in India, she was his most trusted adviser.

Appointed governor-general of Pondicherry in 1740, Dupleix assumed his duties in January, 1742. In 1743,

marauding Marāthās invaded the Carnatic, killing the nawab, Dost Ali, overlord of both the French at Pondicherry and the English at Madras. Then, news arrived that the War of the Austrian Succession (1740-1748) was in full flow in Europe: The French and English in India found that they were officially at war.

LIFE'S WORK

When Dupleix returned to Pondicherry from Chandernagore, he was forty-five years old with twenty years' experience of India. He may have been one of the first Europeans to diagnose the collapse of the Mughal state-system, due principally to the fact that, while military technology in contemporary Europe was rapidly changing, the armies of Indian rulers remained little better than undisciplined rabbles, armed with medieval weaponry and led by commanders who were often inept and cowardly. Dupleix divined that quite small, well-armed European forces or European-led Indian forces must always be superior to indigenous armies, and he dreamed of French political hegemony in South India. Such hegemony would require weakening the British in the region.

Both nations were at war in Europe, presenting Dupleix—as he thought—with the opportunity to crush English pretensions in India once and for all. Dupleix resolved to take Madras with the help of the French governor of Île de France (Mauritius), Bertrand-François La

Bourdonnais, who blockaded Madras by sea, enabling land forces from Pondicherry to enter the city on September 21, 1746. The French occupied it for the next two years, although failure to capture Fort St. David, near Cuddalore, left the English with a base on the coast.

Meanwhile, events of great significance for Dupleix's future were occurring inland. Dost Ali, nawab of the Carnatic, had perished in battle in 1743. The overlord of the nawab of the Carnatic was the Mughal viceroy of the Deccan, Asaf Jah, known by his honorific title of Nizam al-Mulk (r. 1719-1748). Following the death of Dost Ali, Asaf Jah had appointed a new nawab, Anwar al-Din. The new nawab, enraged to learn of Dupleix's aggression against Madras (both French and English were under his protection), marched a large force to the relief of Madras, only to discover that the French were already in possession. Confrontation at the River Adyar proved disastrous for the nawab, but in the history of European imperialism it was of immense significance, for it demonstrated conclusively Dupleix's contention: A troop of 450 Frenchmen was able to disperse an indigenous force of thousands. Not long afterwards, news of the Treaty of Aix-la-Chapelle reached India, and Madras was restored to the English. Overt conflict with the English was forbidden.

Since the engagement at the River Adyar, Dupleix regarded the nawab as an enemy. Fortuitously, Chanda Sahib, Dost Ali's son-in-law, returned from Marāthān captivity in 1748, and Dupleix enlisted him as an ally. Combining their forces, they defeated and killed Anwar al-Din at Ambur (August, 1749). Dupleix then installed Chanda Sahib in Arcot (the capital of the Carnatic) as the new nawab. Dupleix was now master of the Carnatic, but part of his plans miscarried: Anwar al-Din's son, Muhammad Ali, escaped the carnage at Ambur and fled south to the fort of Trichinopoly, where he allied himself with the local rajas, reckoning that the nizam would confirm his succession.

Asaf Jah died in 1748, and his second son, Nasir Jang, assumed the sovereignty of the Deccan. His claim, however, was disputed by a nephew, Muzaffar Jang, who enjoyed the support of Dupleix and who entered into an alliance with Chanda Sahib, Dupleix's other client. Nasir Jang marched on the Carnatic (March, 1750), attempting to force Muzaffar Jang into submission, but Nasir Jang was assassinated in December, 1750, and Dupleix provided French troops to accompany Muzaffar Jang to Hyderabad. Muzaffar Jang was installed as nizam at Hyderabad by the French commander, Charles-Joseph Patissier, marquis de Bussy, but he was in fact a puppet

of the latter Frenchman. From 1751 until he was recalled in 1758, Bussy was the virtual ruler of Hyderabad.

In 1751, Muzaffar Jang was killed in a skirmish with hostile nobles, and Bussy swiftly substituted Muzaffar Jang's uncle, Salabat Jang (r. 1751-1761), as the fourth nizam. Salabat Jang was as much a French client as Chanda Sahib, but from Dupleix's point of view he was easier to handle—paradoxically, as a result of the fact that Hyderabad was farther away than Arcot, and the English had not yet reached the Deccan. However, Bussy's contingent was a heavy drain on the company's resources. He therefore prevailed upon the nizam to lease the Northern Circars to cover its expenses.

Dupleix could rely upon Bussy to take care of Hyderabad. The Carnatic, however, proved more intractable. With Muhammad Ali on the loose in Trichinopoly, Chanda Sahib's position remained precarious. He therefore marched on Trichinopoly to overcome his rival, aided by a succession of indifferent French commanders.

Although it was not apparent at the time, Trichinopoly was to prove Dupleix's Achilles' heel. At first, all of Dupleix's schemes went well, but there then appeared an English military genius in Robert Clive (1725-1774). In 1751, Clive was a British East India Company writer (a junior clerk) at Madras, who, bored, had been permitted to enlist in the company's military service, attaining the rank of captain. Clive now proposed a diversion, the seizure of Chanda Sahib's capital of Arcot while Chanda Sahib was busy besieging Trichinopoly. Learning from the action on the River Adyar, Clive marched a force of some two hundred European troops and three hundred *sepoys* (European-trained Indian troops) to Arcot in midsummer, capturing the city with ease. Predictably, Chanda Sahib drew off a force from the siege of Trichinopoly to recover his capital, which Clive held during a fifty-three-day siege (September-October, 1751).

In Trichinopoly, matters now went badly for Dupleix. The initial French commander, Dupleix's nephew d'Auteuil, fell ill and was replaced by Jacques Law, who belied his later impressive military reputation by timidity and prevarication in the face of a determined resistance by Muhammad Ali and his allies, who now included an English contingent. Unwisely, Law withdrew across the Kaveri River to the island of Srirangam to await reinforcements but was himself besieged. A relieving force under d'Auteil was ambushed (June 9, 1752), and Law was forced to capitulate. Taken with him was Chanda Sahib, who was promptly beheaded.

The execution of Chanda Sahib left Dupleix without a protégé, but he remained as resolute as ever, and by December, 1752, the siege of Trichinopoly was renewed. French and English forces countermarched across the Carnatic, each with some success, but Dupleix was ill-served by his commanders. The French had the edge in numbers of European troops, but the English had supremacy at sea.

For Dupleix, time was running out. His vision of French hegemony in South India with Indian puppet rulers providing the revenue base with which to fuel the company's operations was at variance with the priorities of his masters in Paris. Moreover, he had foolishly failed to explain his audacious schemes to those masters. It appears that the first time he communicated his plans to the homeland was in a dispatch of October 16, 1753, when his recall had already been determined, and Charles-Robert Godeheu had been named his successor.

Godeheu landed at Pondicherry on August 1, 1754, and by December had negotiated a provisional treaty with the English, which, although subsequently derided by Dupleix's partisans, retained for the French everything that Dupleix had striven to secure, including territories providing a total revenue of 68 lakhs (one lakh was equal to 100,000 rupees) and Bussy retaining power in Hyderabad; thus ended the Second Carnatic War.

Dupleix left India with his family on August 15, 1754. He was given an honourable reception in Paris, but he died an embittered man in straitened circumstances on November 13, 1763.

SIGNIFICANCE

Had Joseph-François Dupleix succeeded in his schemes and had he been succeeded by men of equal ability and foresight, it is not too far-fetched to imagine that India might have been a French dependency rather than a British one for the next two centuries. The French East India Company, however, unlike its English rival, was an unenterprising state-managed bureaucracy, and the French were never able to retain the initiative at sea. The victory on the River Adyar was certainly a turning point

in European expansion, but it was Clive, learning from Dupleix and Bussy, who reaped the advantages of that victory. For all that, Dupleix's ambitions and his initiative in attempting to realize them place him among the great empire builders of the eighteenth and nineteenth centuries.

—Gavin R. G. Hambly

FURTHER READING

Dodwell, Henry. *Dupleix and Clive: The Beginning of Empire*. London: Methuen, 1920. Reprint. Hamden, Conn.: Archon Books, 1968. Still the best narrative in English of the struggle between Dupleix and Clive for control of India.

Martineau, Alfred. "Dupleix and Bussy." In *The Cambridge History of India*, vol. 5. Cambridge, England: Cambridge University Press, 1929. Detailed brief narrative summary by the author of a definitive, four-volume study in French.

Price, J. Frederick, and K. Rangachari. *The Private Diary of Ananda Ranga Pillai*. 12 vols. 1904-1928. Reprint. New Delhi: Asian Educational Service, 1985. Pillai was Dupleix's *dubash* (interpreter). A unique record of his thoughts and actions.

Sen, S. P. *The French in India*. Calcutta: University of Calcutta Press, 1947. A useful narrative.

Thompson, Virginia M. *Dupleix and His Letters, 1742-1754*. New York: R. O. Ballou, 1933. Useful biographical material.

Vigié, Marc. *Dupleix*. Paris: Fayard, 1993. A later study, in French, incorporating late twentieth century scholarship.

See also: Robert Clive; Hyder Ali; Shāh Walī Allāh.
Related articles in *Great Events from History: The Eighteenth Century, 1701-1800*: December 16, 1740-November 7, 1748: War of the Austrian Succession; 1746-1754: Carnatic Wars; June 23, 1757: Battle of Plassey.

JONATHAN EDWARDS
American theologian

The greatest Puritan theologian in America, Edwards tried to establish an intellectual foundation for Puritanism, to find a rational interpretation of predestination, and to justify the ways of God to humankind.

Born: October 5, 1703; East Windsor, Connecticut
Died: March 22, 1758; Princeton, New Jersey
Area of achievement: Religion and theology

EARLY LIFE

Jonathan Edwards was born in East Windsor, along the Connecticut River, an area that was still a frontier. Worshipers carried muskets to church. Edwards was the only boy among ten sisters, but there were seven boy cousins living next door and a number of boys attending school under Edwards's father, the Reverend Timothy Edwards. Educated by his father, Edwards was a precocious boy who was ready for college at the age of thirteen. When he was eleven, he wrote a paper on flying spiders that is remarkable for both its scientific observation and its literary skill. As a teenager, Edwards was already dedicated to religion as his unquestioned calling. Sober and meditative by temperament, he had a private place of prayer deep in the woods.

In 1716, he entered Yale College, founded only fifteen years earlier, with a freshman class of ten. At this time Edwards experienced an intense religious struggle, which he later described in his "Personal Narrative"; in particular, he had been "full of objections against the doctrine of God's sovereignty, in choosing whom he would to eternal life, and rejecting whom he pleased; leaving them eternally to perish, and be everlastingly tormented in hell." This doctrine appeared horrible to him, but somehow he managed to accept it and to delight in God's absolute sovereignty. After graduating from Yale at age seventeen, in 1720, Edwards studied theology for two years in New Haven, after which he served for a year and a half as pastor to a Presbyterian church in New York City. For the next two years, Edwards was a tutor at Yale. On February 22, 1726, he was ordained at Northampton, Massachusetts, as assistant minister to his eighty-four-year-old grandfather, Solomon Stoddard. About 25 miles north of East Windsor, on the Connecticut River, Northampton was then an isolated frontier village, cut off by forests from the wider world.

In July of 1727, Edwards married Sarah Pierrepont, the daughter of a founder of Yale. Edwards was then twenty-three years old, his bride age seventeen. She was apparently the ideal wife for him, a capable manager, a devoted mother to their surviving three sons and seven daughters, a deeply religious person able to share her husband's spiritual life. When the famous Evangelist George Whitefield visited the Edwards family in 1740, he was so impressed with Sarah Edwards that he wished he could marry someone like her. When Solomon Stoddard died in 1729, Edwards, at twenty-six, became the minister of the chief parish of western Massachusetts.

LIFE'S WORK

Coming of age when the Puritan oligarchy had crumbled and when Puritan theology was being challenged by Deism and by more liberal Christian denominations, Jonathan Edwards tried to create a philosophical justification for Calvinist dogma. Calvinism can be summed up in the acronym TULIP: total depravity, unconditional election, limited atonement, irresistible grace, and perseverance of the saints. First proclaimed in John Calvin's *Institutes of the Christian Religion* (1536), these doctrines had been the backbone of Puritanism. The most thorny of them were the ideas that humanity is not merely in a state of Original Sin (which is not total and is balanced by human goodness) but is totally depraved; everyone deserves damnation, and most will receive it; only a limited few will be saved by God's inscrutable mercy. Along with this doctrine is the idea of predestination; there is no free will, and every detail of each individual's life is predetermined by God, including salvation and damnation, which are ordained before birth, so that no amount of good works can merit salvation for one who is not among the elect.

Calvin offered no proof of these grim doctrines; he merely maintained that God's majesty is so great that humanity is nothing beside it. By Edwards's time, the Puritans had lost their monopoly on the northern colonies; other denominations preached a more merciful creed, according to which salvation was available (though not guaranteed) for everyone, while Deism threw out Christianity altogether, denying miracles, original sin, the incarnation and resurrection, and proclaiming that "whatever is is right."

Edwards has been maligned as the quintessential "hell-fire and brimstone" preacher, chiefly because of a sermon entitled "Sinners in the Hands of an Angry God," which he gave at Enfield, Connecticut, on July 8, 1741.

In it he dramatized the concept of total depravity, arguing that everyone deserves to be cast into Hell, so that divine justice never stands in the way, for sinners are already under a sentence of condemnation and only God's restraints keep them out of Hell. Yet people cannot count on those restraints, for "the God that holds you over the pit of hell, much as one holds a spider, or some loathsome insect over the fire, abhors you, and is dreadfully provoked." The flaming mouth of Hell gapes wide, "the bow of God's wrath is bent," the wrath of God is like great waters damned but ready to be released. Edwards piles up more metaphors for God's wrath but then urges his congregation to repent so that they may receive divine mercy.

Indeed, it is that mercy that Edwards stressed in most of his work. In his entire career, he gave only two sermons on hellfire, the other being "The Justice of God in the Damnation of Sinners" (1734). Edwards was no ranter; he was slender and shy, with a thin, weak voice; he spoke his sermons with quiet intensity. What made them eloquent was his immense preparation, his ability to paint pictures that made the abstract visible in terms of familiar experience, and the sense of authority that made him seem merely the mouthpiece for God. He was not a fiery preacher, nor was he an ecclesiastical scold giving lurid exposés of community sins and laying down blue laws.

The problem that Edwards tried to cope with was that of reconciling a loving and merciful God with a God who predestined most of humankind to Hell before they were even born. If salvation or election is already determined, why should individuals strive for salvation, when they have no free will? Why should ministers call sinners to repentance?

Nevertheless, Edwards tried to answer, stressing "the excellency of Christ," and, in 1734, he preached so eloquently that a revival broke out in Northampton (though he had not calculated to start one) and quickly spread to other towns. Seemingly wholesome at first, it turned to frenzied hysteria, with numerous suicides and attempted suicides. Edwards tried to tone down such bizarre behavior and "bodily manifestations," writing in *A Faithful Narrative of the Surprising Work of God* (1737) that "multitudes" felt suicide "urged upon them as if somebody had spoke to them, 'Cut your own throat. Now is a good opportunity.'"

The Northampton revival foreshadowed a much broader one, ushered in in 1740 by the visiting Evangelist George Whitefield, who, unlike Edwards, was an itinerant preacher using the devices of theatrical show-manship; Lord Chesterfield said Whitefield could make people weep simply by the way he said "Mesopotamia." Following Whitefield, a revival frenzy broke out all over New England, called the Great Awakening. After its initial inspiration passed, novelty took over, with ecclesiastical juvenile delinquents trying to take over services and with zeal considered more important than knowledge, so that there was danger that fanaticism would triumph.

In response, Edwards wrote one of his major works, *A Treatise Concerning Religious Affections*, preached in 1742-1743 and published in 1746, in which he tried to distinguish between genuine and false religious experiences. Edwards said that the church should be concerned with souls, not bodily symptoms. He did not study the bizarre details but tried to examine the laws of human nature behind such behavior. Turning to John Locke's *An Essay Concerning Human Understanding* (1690), Edwards denied innate ideas and said that all knowledge comes through sensation, whereby one apprehends those ideas that God has willed to communicate. Accordingly,

Jonathan Edwards. (Library of Congress)

the imagination conjures up things that are not present objects of sense, and here is "the devil's grand lurking place." Edwards divided the mind into the understanding and the will; reason belongs to the former, and though it is important, it is not, as the Deists maintained, sufficient, for Edwards believed that true religion comes from "holy love," which is not in the understanding but in the will. Thus, echoing Saint Paul, Edwards wrote that "he that has doctrinal knowledge and speculation only, without affection, never is engaged in the business of religion." The person who has received a divine light does not merely notionally believe that God is glorious, but instead has a sense of the gloriousness of God in his or her heart. Rational understanding alone is insufficient. There is, then, an essential emotional element in religion.

Edwards attempted to distinguish between the false emotionalism of revivalism, generated by mass hysteria, and a true religion whereby regenerate individuals receive a supernatural light from divine grace and are touched by the Holy Ghost, which acts within them as an indwelling vital principle. Therefore, enthusiastic delusions and bodily manifestations are merely from the imagination, not of love from and for God.

For modern readers, *Religious Affections*, which has been greatly condensed here, is likely to be the most meaningful of Edwards's works. In his day, *Freedom of Will* (1754) was thought to be his masterpiece. In it he tries to reconcile human choice with the doctrine of predestination. Briefly, his reasoning is that each act of the will depends upon a preceding act of the will, back to the original act of creation in the mind of God. Accordingly, he concluded that one is free to do what one will but not to will what one will.

In 1747, when David Brainerd, missionary to the American Indians, died, Edwards edited his life and diary, producing a popular book that spurred missionary activities. Then, in June of 1750, Edwards's congregation dismissed him after twenty-three years as minister. He had been too aristocratic for Northampton tastes, but the actual break came over the question of whether the unconverted should be admitted to Communion. When Edwards refused to admit those who would not acknowledge faith, he was defeated by a rigged election. Afterward, he moved to Stockbridge, Massachusetts, as missionary to the American Indians. He did not consider the indigenous peoples depraved; he respected their customs, was an able administrator, and earned the friendship and trust of the Stockbridge Indians, who protected him when the French and Indian War broke out in 1754. At Stockbridge, Edwards wrote *Freedom of Will* and

"The Nature of True Virtue" (1765), in which he argues that true virtue must be disinterested benevolence. Unlike his contemporary, Benjamin Franklin, a Deist who tried to make himself morally perfect by a thirteen-point program of good works, Edwards argued that true virtue comes not from repeated good choices but only from the grace of God.

In 1757, Edwards was offered the presidency of the College of New Jersey (which later became Princeton). A week after his induction on February 16, 1758, he allowed himself to be inoculated against smallpox; a month later, he died of smallpox at age fifty-four. A week later, his daughter Esther Burr also died of smallpox, and the following autumn, Mrs. Edwards died in Philadelphia. One of Edwards's grandsons, Timothy Dwight, became a poet and president of Yale; another, Aaron Burr, became vice president of the United States.

SIGNIFICANCE
Though Perry Miller has traced a line of influence from the Puritan Edwards to the Transcendentalist Ralph Waldo Emerson, most leading nineteenth century thinkers reacted against Edwards; Herman Melville, Oliver Wendell Holmes, Leslie Stephens, and Harriet Beecher Stowe were all hostile to his Puritan doctrines, chiefly predestination, total depravity, and limited atonement. Among other things, Moby Dick (of Melville's novel of the same title, 1851) symbolizes the Puritan God of wrath and vengeance; to the novel's Captain Ahab, this God is a tyrant whose "right worship is defiance." Nathaniel Hawthorne never wrote directly about Edwards, but his somber theology and psychology may have influenced such Hawthorne tales as "The Minister's Black Veil."

The twentieth and twenty-first centuries, with their horrors, have in some measure rediscovered original sin ("from whose visitations," wrote Melville, "in some shape or other, no deeply thinking mind is always and wholly free. For, in certain moods, no individual can weigh his or her world without throwing in something, somehow like Original Sin, to strike the uneven balance"), and Edwards has had a reappraisal, though few scholars any longer accept Calvinism uncritically. In the age of the early twenty-first century, with its militant Fundamentalism and biblical literalism as well as its cults and gurus, Edwards's *Religious Affections* takes on a new relevance, and though his reasoning in *Freedom of Will* may seem logic-chopping, many modern doctrines—behaviorism, Freudianism, communist dialectical materialism, to name a few—deny free will on secular but similar grounds. Edwards is now recognized not only as a writer of poetic prose but as the major philosophical and psychological thinker and writer of the colonial era in America.

—Robert E. Morsberger

FURTHER READING

Davidson, Edward Hutchins. *Jonathan Edwards: The Narrative of a Puritan Mind*. Cambridge, Mass.: Harvard University Press, 1968. A slim volume in the Riverside Studies in Literature series, this work presents Edwards as struggling against and rejecting the rationalism of the Enlightenment.

Edwards, Jonathan. *A Jonathan Edwards Reader*. Edited by John H. Smith, Harry S. Stout, and Kenneth P. Minkema. New Haven, Conn.: Yale Nota Bene, 2003. An anthology of Edwards's treatises, sermons, letters, and autobiographical writing.

Elwood, Douglas J. *The Philosophical Theology of Jonathan Edwards*. New York: Columbia University Press, 1960. Explores Edwards's response to the problem of evil and his consuming awareness of God's majesty and the ecstasy of divine grace.

Fiering, Norman. *Jonathan Edwards's Moral Thought and Its British Context*. Chapel Hill: University of North Carolina Press, 1981. A study of seventeenth century moral philosophy and its influence on Edwards.

Levin, David. *Jonathan Edwards: A Profile*. New York: Hill & Wang, 1969. Contains Samuel Hopkins's book *The Life and Character of the Late Rev. Mr. Jonathan Edwards* (1765), articles by Edwards's biographers Perry Miller and Ola Elizabeth Winslow and other modern writers, and two poems by Robert Lowell.

McClymond, Michael J. *Encounters with God: An Approach to the Theology of Jonathan Edwards*. New York: Oxford University Press, 1999. Analyzes various issues in Edwards's theology within the intellectual context of Enlightenment culture. The book's six chapters examine Edwards's concepts of spiritual perception, metaphysics, spirituality, ethics, redemption, and other ideas.

McGiffert, Arthur Cushman. *Jonathan Edwards*. New York: Harper and Brothers, 1932. A portrait of Edwards as a religious psychologist.

Marsden, George M. *Jonathan Edwards: A Life*. New Haven, Conn.: Yale University Press, 2003. A comprehensive biography, using newly available sources from Yale University to examine Edwards's life within the context of the religious and cultural battles in colonial New England. Edwards is depicted as a complex thinker who struggled to reconcile his Puritan background with the secular world of the Enlightenment.

Miller, Perry. *Jonathan Edwards*. New York: William Sloane Associates, 1949. The chief interpretive biography, by the leading scholar on American Puritanism.

Tracy, Patricia J. *Jonathan Edwards, Pastor*. New York: Hill & Wang, 1980. A brief biography that focuses on Edwards's pastoral role in Northampton.

Winslow, Ola Elizabeth. *Jonathan Edwards, 1703-1758*. New York: Macmillan, 1940. A Pulitzer Prize-winning biography and one of the most detailed studies of Edwards's life and times.

See also: Francis Asbury; Cotton Mather; Increase Mather; Charles Wesley; John Wesley; George Whitefield.

Related articles in *Great Events from History: The Eighteenth Century, 1701-1800:* 1739-1742: First Great Awakening; May 28, 1754-February 10, 1763: French and Indian War; 1790's-1830's: Second Great Awakening.

ELIJAH BEN SOLOMON
Lithuanian rabbi and theologian

Elijah ben Solomon contributed to Talmudic and rabbinic literature by solving the most complicated questions of Jewish law and by writing commentaries and annotations to biblical, Talmudic, and Kabbalistic texts.

Born: April 23, 1720; Sielec, Lithuania
Died: October 9, 1797; Vilna (now Vilnius), Lithuania
Also known as: Ha-gaon Rabbi Eliya-hu; Gaon of Vilna; Ha-gra; Elijah ben Solomon Zalman (birth name)
Areas of achievement: Religion and theology, scholarship, law

EARLY LIFE

Elijah ben Solomon was born on the first day of Passover, 1720, to Treina Zalman and Rabbi Solomon Zalman. Rabbi Solomon named his son Elijah in memory of his grandfather. Early in his childhood, Elijah manifested an intellect of great potential. At the age of six, Elijah was able to study the Bible and the Talmud by himself. At six and a half, he delivered a lengthy discourse on Jewish law in the great synagogue in Vilna. When the boy was seven, Rabbi Abraham Katzenellenbogen of Brest Litovsk took him to study under Rabbi Moses Margalioth. Sometimes Elijah's comprehension was so swift that it was impossible for others to follow his thought. While most Jewish boys of his age were still laboring through the Torah, Elijah could navigate through the vast sea of the Talmud and the Kabbala.

Elijah also studied secular subjects—algebra, astronomy, geometry, geography, history, anatomy, and philosophy—to understand certain Talmudic laws and discussions. His main reason for studying astronomy, for example, was to comprehend the regulations of the Jewish calendar.

At age eighteen, Elijah married Hannah, the daughter of a rabbi. There is no doubt that much of Elijah's success was attributable to his happy marriage with Hannah. She was often the only person who had access to the secret retreats Elijah selected for his meditations. She brought him food and informed him about the happenings in the community. Elijah had full confidence in his wife, and she, an exceptionally pious and valorous woman, gave him her full empathy.

At the age of twenty, Elijah decided to leave his wife and home in Vilna and wander throughout Europe. He had concluded that his store of knowledge was inadequate because of his seclusion. He wanted to gain a fuller understanding of Judaism by witnessing Jewish life in its various aspects, seeing the customs and traditions of diverse peoples. For eight years, he traveled, impoverished, through the kingdoms of Europe. For a while, he served as a tutor to Jewish children in an isolated village. There are interesting but unverified stories about Elijah helping perplexed scholars to solve complicated problems. In one tale, a professor accosted him in Berlin and requested his help in solving an abstruse astronomical problem. Elijah solved the professor's problem with a sketch on a scrap of paper.

Elijah returned to Vilna as a recognized authority in Jewish law. Rabbis from all over Europe turned to him with their rabbinic legal difficulties. Again and again Jews in Vilna urged him to become the rabbi of Vilna, but Elijah refused. He would not even accept membership in the rabbinical board, but his opinion was sought on all important questions. Only on rare occasions would he publicly assert his great, though unofficial, authority. He preferred his status as a layperson.

LIFE'S WORK

Elijah ben Solomon settled in Vilna, where he would live for the remainder of his life. He received a weekly stipend from the community so that he could devote his entire time to study and writing. The money came from a legacy of his great-great-grandfather, Rabbi Moses Rivkes, to the community and was intended to help any descendant who devoted himself to the study of Judaism. Scholars soon acclaimed Elijah as the Gaon (Talmudic scholar par excellence), while the people called him Hasid (saint). These titles gradually took the place of his personal name.

Elijah lived in Vilna as a recluse; he slept two hours a day and took little nourishment. Despite his asceticism, Elijah was acclaimed throughout the Jewish world as the Talmudic scholar whose opinions on Jewish law were considered final. His views on contemporary communal problems were sought far and wide. In 1755, when Elijah was thirty-five years old, he was asked by the sixty-five-year-old Rabbi Jonathan Eybeschuetz to render an opinion concerning a controversy between Eybeschuetz and Rabbi Jacob Emden.

Elijah was confronted with the problems of two eighteenth century movements, the Haskalah (enlightenment) and Hasidism. The Hasidic movement was founded by Baʿal Shem Tov. Baʿal Shem Tov taught that God should be served with joy and that asceticism might be the root of evil. Rabbis and scholars of the time were perplexed by the Hasidic movement, which gave a preeminent place in Judaism not to learning but to emotion and sentiment. It valued religious exultation over holy knowledge. As Hasidism extended its foothold in Eastern Europe, there emerged an antagonist movement, the Haskalah. Haskalah called for rationalism and realism and opposed the antirationalistic tendency of Hasidism. In their nascent forms, Hasidism and Haskalah endangered the integrity of established Judaism; there was too much exultation in Hasidism and too much rationalism in Haskalah—either extreme undermined the Jewish tradition. Elijah, confronted with these extremes, tried to harmonize between the heart and the mind to prevent Judaism from being crushed between Haskalah and Hasidism. He vehemently opposed Hasidism, which rejected the scholarly approach to the Torah that Elijah thought so important, and he supported the effort to excommunicate followers of Hasidism.

Elijah wrote more than seventy works and commentaries. More than fifty have been published, though others are no longer extant. He considered Joseph ben

Elijah ben Solomon. (Library of Congress)

Ephraim Karo's *Shulḥan arukh* (1565; *Code of Jewish Law*, 1927) to contain the authentic gist of Talmudic law. Elijah wrote a commentary on the *Shulḥan arukh* known as the *Beʿur ha-Gra* (1803; the commentary of Ha-gaon Rabbi Eliya-hu). In his commentary, he traced every statement, decision, custom, and tradition expressed or validated in the former work to its source in the Talmud and Talmudic thought.

Elijah wrote commentaries on nearly all the books of the Old Testament and on several books of the Mishnah. Elijah's writings cover the Kabbala, algebra, trigonometry, astronomy, and grammar. He urged the translation of Euclid into Hebrew and examined the historical works of Flavius Josephus rendered into Hebrew. His favoring of secular study, however, does not place him in the camp of the Haskalah, which aimed at the substitution of reason for faith. He was, however, a critic of those scholars who relied too much on spiritualist speculation. He was even critical of Moses Maimonides (1135-1204) for having interpreted certain passages of the Bible or Talmud in a philosophical manner, ignoring their literal meanings.

After Elijah reached the age of forty, he devoted most of his time to educating his disciples. He surrounded himself with a number of students who were gifted with brilliant minds and exhibited genuine piety. They became messengers in spreading the teachings of their beloved master. Elijah warned his students against wasting their precious time in *pilpul* (dialectic excess). He taught them to use clear thinking and to search for truth painstakingly. He provided his students with his corrected texts of the great books of halakic literature, the result of years of studying the Talmud. Elijah showed clearly that corrections made in a passage of the Talmud could change one's interpretation of the text. He opened to his students a new frontier: critical examination of the text. Elijah advocated not only proper intellectual training but also the cultivation of morality. He held that, in order for Judaism to have its divine effect, the heart must be pure. He compared the Torah to rain. Just as rain nourishes the earth so the Torah nourishes the soul.

Elijah also inspired Jews to emigrate to Israel. It was his lifelong dream to settle in the Holy Land. He once undertook the dangerous and arduous trip but for unknown reasons decided to return to Vilna. The Vilna emigration that he had encouraged began in 1808, eleven years after his death; hundreds of Lithuanian Jews settled in Palestine. Six of his disciples headed the movement.

In a well-known legend, Elijah was passing through a crowd of playing children and noticed that they were shouting, "*Der Vilner Gaon, Der Vilner Gaon.*" He stopped and said to the children, "If you only will it, you too, will become *Geonim*" (preeminent scholars). Elijah's humbleness belied his great intelligence and piety; few scholars have been as influential.

SIGNIFICANCE

It is rare in Jewish history for one man to leave behind a legacy of great works in rabbinic literature, significant individual contributions, noble deeds, and outstanding personal attributes. Elijah ben Solomon, revered by all, was such a man. His creations and involvement are those of a complicated individual and not simply reflections of the time and place in which he lived. An outstanding rabbi, legal codifier, scholar, thinker, author, and humanitarian, Elijah shared in the political, social, communal, and cultural trials and tribulations of his time, but he transcended these in continuing humanity's age-old examination of its purpose in life and its relationship to God and to one another. His spirit and writings made important contributions to his generation, and they continue to have meaning and will remain inspiring to future generations as well. His impact on Torah scholarship and on the establishment and maintenance of rabbinical seminaries is immeasurable. His contributions to rabbinic literature show him to be one of the most prolific and influential Talmudic scholars in history.

—*Lester Eckman*

FURTHER READING

Dubnow, S. M. *History of the Jews in Russia and Poland.* Translated by I. Friedlander. Vol. 1. Philadelphia: Jewish Publication Society of America, 1916. An excellent history of the period based on primary documents on the life and work of Elijah.

Etkes, Immanuel. *The Gaon of Vilna: The Man and His Image.* Translated by Jeffrey M. Green. Berkeley: University of California Press, 2002. Seeks to demystify Elijah by tracing the various myths surrounding him and revealing the "real" life and character of the man. One of the few books devoted to Elijah that has been translated into English.

Graetz, Heinrich. *History of the Jews.* Vol. 5. Philadelphia: Jewish Publication Society of America, 1895. A scholarly source on the life of Elijah. Contains important information on the controversy between Elijah and the proponents of Hasidism.

Malamet, A., et al. *A History of the Jewish People.* Edited by H. H. Ben-Sasson. Cambridge, Mass.: Harvard University Press, 1976. Provides some background on Elijah's life and is an excellent source on the controversy over Hasidism.

Schochet, Elijah Judah. *The Hasidic Movement and the Gaon of Vilna.* Northvale, N.J.: J. Aronson, 1994. Discusses the conflict over Hasidism in the eighteenth century and examines why Elijah opposed the Hasidic movement.

Waxman, Meyer. *From the Middle of the Eighteenth Century to 1880.* Vol. 3 in *A History of Jewish Literature.* New York: Thomas Yoseloff, 1960. An excellent work. Contains information on the life and writings of Elijah.

Zinberg, Israel. *Hasidism and Englightenment, 1780-1820.* Vol. 9 in *A History of Jewish Literature.* Translated by Bernard Martin. Cleveland, Ohio: Press of Case Western Reserve University, 1972-1978. A discussion of Elijah's thoughts on the controversy over Hasidism.

See also: Baʿal Shem Tov; Moses Mendelssohn.

Related articles in *Great Events from History: The Eighteenth Century, 1701-1800*: October 30, 1768: Methodist Church Is Established in Colonial America; 1773-1788: African American Baptist Church Is Founded; July 28-October 16, 1789: Episcopal Church Is Established.

ELIZABETH PETROVNA
Empress of Russia (r. 1741-1762)

After taking control of Russia in a palace coup, Elizabeth ruled as empress with the assistance of capable advisers and department officials. Her reign heralded a new era in which Russia enjoyed greater domestic stability, as well as successful military and foreign policies.

Born: December 29, 1709; Kolomenskoye, Russia
Died: January 5, 1762; St. Petersburg, Russia
Also known as: Elizaveta Petrovna; Yelizaveta Petrovna
Areas of achievement: Government and politics, warfare and conquest

EARLY LIFE

Elizabeth Petrovna (pyih-TRAWV-nuh), a daughter of Peter the Great, was born prior to the official, public marriage of her parents, rendering her technically illegitimate in the eyes of the Russian Orthodox Church and royal circles. Her gender and status as the youngest of several children also reduced Elizabeth's rights as a possible successor to the Russian throne. She was an attractive young woman who showed comparatively little interest in politics in her youth and early adult years, apparently willing to leave political matters to others. She shied away from politics deliberately, however, to avoid possible problems with those in power, who might otherwise have seen Elizabeth as a threat to their position and might have taken steps to isolate or even arrest her.

Elizabeth's interests during those early years emphasized comfort, ease, luxury, and indolence, and these priorities continued throughout her reign as Russia's monarch. Her court arranged frequent balls and other entertainments in which Elizabeth took an active part as an accomplished dancer. She also liked to ride and hunt. She knew German and French as well as her native Russian but believed that excessive reading was harmful to one's health. Fancy clothing became a lifelong obsession for Elizabeth, who possessed a vast number of expensive dresses: A fire at her Moscow residence in the 1740's destroyed four thousand of her dresses, yet another fifteen thousand outfits were found at her death in 1762.

LIFE'S WORK

Elizabeth never married, leaving room and opportunity for those who enjoyed her intimate favors. Her amorous interests before and after she became empress were known among the inner court circle, although the public remained ignorant of this aspect of her private life. She gave titles, money, and vast estates (including serfs as property) to her favorites.

She also found solace in religion and periodically went to religious sites in Russia on pilgrimages in which fasting played an important part. When such pilgrimages were over, however, she would overeat and drink excessively, which caused her many health problems.

Elizabeth Petrovna's position as empress of Russia, rather than her personal life, makes her a historical figure worthy of attention. The death in 1725 of Czar Peter the Great plunged Russia into a period of weak and ineffective leadership and divisive palace politics. Prominent families and influential political advisers vied for power. Four monarchs came to the Russian throne between Peter's passing and early 1741, a recipe for uncertainty and confusion. These conditions, compounded by the mediocre quality of the several rulers, destabilized the government and consequently weakened the nation.

By 1740, a new phase in Elizabeth's life emerged with the naming of a new czar, Ivan VI. Since he was only an infant, real power resided in the hands of his mother, Anna Leopoldovna, and her influential but unpopular advisers. Several prominent aristocrats approached Elizabeth with a scheme to seize power and place her on the throne. Being the daughter of Peter the Great would be an asset in convincing the nation of the legitimacy of her claim to the throne. Moreover, the secret support of France, conveyed via the French ambassador and Elizabeth's French physician, strengthened her chances of success.

The virtually bloodless coup occurred on December 6, 1741. Loyal regiments in the capital played a vital role in this event. The infant czar, his mother, and leading officials were quickly detained or arrested. Elizabeth placed her supporters in key positions to manage the affairs of state. Since they were all Russians, this decision immediately imparted a strong national character to Elizabeth's administration when compared with those of prior rulers who relied on many Germans in central governmental roles. Elizabeth's supporters included Nikita Trubetskoy, procurator general and leader of the senate, and Peter Shuvalov, who shaped domestic policy. Shuvalov's brother, Ivan, became the empress's lover by the late 1740's, but he is important in his own right for his ac-

Empress Elizabeth Petrovna. (Hulton Archive/Getty Images)

The Elizabethan years were especially important to Russian foreign policy. Russia's relations with neighboring Turkey always were difficult, as their competition for territory led to periodic wars between the two nations. A war with Sweden in the 1740's affected the northwest boundary between the two states. Historically suspicious of France and Austria, Russia during Elizabeth's reign eventually reached workable and significant accommodations with both states. Russia played a minor role in the War of the Austrian Succession (1740-1748). By the 1750's, however, Russia became a significant player in European power politics, participating in the major confrontation of the mid-eighteenth century, the Seven Years' War (1756-1763).

In the Seven Years' War, Russia and its French and Austrian allies opposed the enemy coalition of the rising state of Prussia under Frederick the Great and its ally Britain. Despite occasional military defeats, Russian forces won significant victories in 1759 and briefly occupied the Prussian capital of Berlin in 1760. By the time of Elizabeth's death in 1762, Russia occupied substantial portions of Prussian territory, but her nephew and successor as monarch, Czar Peter III, quickly made peace with the Prussian king and returned these conquered lands. Within six months, the czar's wife had deposed and killed him, ascending the throne herself as Empress Catherine the Great.

Russia's economy expanded during Elizabeth's rule, especially in the iron and textile industries. However, the extravagance of the royal court and a bloated and inefficient bureaucratic system, as well as large military expenses, created serious financial problems for the government. The government periodically raised taxes to cope with its huge deficits but consistently failed to balance the budget. Also, repressive laws and harsh treatment of the serfs and lower classes created antagonism and occasional riots against the authorities, but these were suppressed forcefully. Elizabeth had no sympathy for those who questioned her autocratic rule, and the quality of life for millions of Russians remained bleak in contrast to the favored economic and social position that the nobility enjoyed.

Nonetheless, scholars generally interpret Russia's Elizabethan era positively. The empress ruled for two decades, a tribute to both her staying power and her abilities compared with those of her immediate predecessors. She also utilized the talents of capable advisers to make her lengthy reign one of the more noteworthy in modern Russian history. However, her vanity and self-centered personality meant that she increasingly neglected impor-

tive support of Russian cultural life. Other key figures in the new administration included Prince Ushakov, the director of the Secret Chancellery, or secret police, and Alexei Bestuzhev-Ryumin, vice-chancellor and later chancellor of Russia.

Empress Elizabeth reconstituted the senate in St. Petersburg as a leading agency of the government, possessing both legislative and executive functions under her supervision. The nation, however, too often depended on the decisions of powerful individuals rather than government agencies and a system of laws. The system of autocracy, designed to keep authority in the hands of the monarch, remained fundamentally unchanged.

Under Elizabeth, there was a marked growth in Russian education, culture, and intellectual life. The first Russian scientific and literary journal appeared in 1755, the same year as the establishment, with Elizabeth's support, of the University of Moscow as Russia's first university. Her regime also promoted Russian theater and art. Famous works of public architecture constructed during her reign includes the impressive new Winter Palace in St. Petersburg, designed by the architect Francesco Rastrelli, as well as his improvements to the royal residence at Czarskoe Selo, outside the capital.

tant domestic and foreign issues. Fortunately, Elizabeth left many decisions to government officials who acted in her name.

In her older years, Elizabeth gained excessive weight, suffered from edema, fainting, and occasional convulsions, and had several strokes. She died on January 5, 1762 (or, by the "Old Style" Russian calendar, December 25, 1761, Christmas Day). Her body lay in state at the Winter Palace before its burial at the royal chapel in St. Petersburg, where her crypt can be seen today near the remains of her father and mother.

SIGNIFICANCE

Russia grew during the eighteenth century in size, power, and influence. From the rule of Peter the Great earlier in the era to the latter decades of the century under Catherine the Great, the nation grew from a comparatively unsophisticated and sometimes crude nation into a robust and impressive state whose achievements were felt beyond its borders. As Russia's empress for two decades, Elizabeth Petrovna, like her father, played a prominent role in this development.

Elizabeth's administration succeeded to a high degree in stabilizing Russian politics, promoting intellectual and cultural life, expanding Russia's borders, and playing a significant role in the diplomatic and military affairs of Europe as a whole. She thus helped to place Russia as an equal (or at least a contender) among the powerful and influential states of eighteenth century Europe, including Austria, Britain, France, and Prussia. Elizabeth believed strongly in the concept of autocracy, the widely practiced political theory of the period, which justified her domination of her country. All authority came from the top, and limitations or checks rarely existed. The most negative aspect of Elizabeth's legacy, however, is that her successors inherited economic and social problems that were obvious but not adequately understood and therefore difficult to resolve.

—*Taylor Stults*

FURTHER READING

Anisimov, E. V. *Five Empresses: The Women Who Made Modern Russia*. Westport, Conn.: Praeger, 2004. Translation of a Russian biography of five women who ruled Russia.

Brennan, James F. *Enlightened Despotism in Russia: The Reign of Elizabeth, 1741-1762*. New York: Peter Lang, 1987. Interprets Elizabeth as a progressive and able ruler.

Coughlan, Robert. *Elizabeth and Catherine: Empresses of All the Russias*. New York: Putnam, 1974. Traces the personalities and private lives of the two great eighteenth century empresses.

Longworth, Philip. *The Three Empresses: Catherine I, Anne, and Elizabeth of Russia*. New York: Holt, Rinehart and Winston, 1973. Compares the lives of three eighteenth century monarchs.

The Memoirs of Catherine the Great. Translated by Mark Chase and Hilde Hoogenboom. New York: Modern Library, 2005. Covers the years when young Catherine lived in the Elizabethan court and conveys Catherine's impressions of her forebear.

Rice, Tamara Talbot. *Elizabeth, Empress of Russia*. New York: Praeger, 1970. Excellent biography of Elizabeth's life and reign.

Troyat, Henri. *Terrible Tsarinas: Five Russian Women in Power*. New York: Algora, 2001. Colorful comparison of five eighteenth century rulers, with several chapters on Elizabeth.

See also: Catherine the Great; Frederick the Great; Peter the Great; Peter III.

Related articles in *Great Events from History: The Eighteenth Century, 1701-1800*: November 20, 1710-July 21, 1718: Ottoman Wars with Russia, Venice, and Austria; 1736-1739: Russo-Austrian War Against the Ottoman Empire; December 16, 1740-November 7, 1748: War of the Austrian Succession; January, 1756-February 15, 1763: Seven Years' War.

OLAUDAH EQUIANO
Ibo slave, writer, and abolitionist

Equiano was kidnapped in 1756, enslaved in Virginia, purchased by an English naval lieutenant, and subsequently sold to a Quaker. He purchased his freedom in 1766 and later published an autobiography. He exposed the Zong disaster, in which a captain drowned 132 slaves to recover insurance money. In 1788, he presented an antislavery petition to England's Queen Caroline.

Born: c. 1745; Essaka, Kingdom of Benin (now in Nigeria)
Died: March 31, 1797; London, England
Also known as: Gustavus Vassa
Areas of achievement: Literature, social reform

EARLY LIFE

The father of Olaudah Equiano (oh-LOW-duh ehk-wee-AHN-oh) was an elder (an *embrenché*) of their African tribe who served as a judge. His father held many slaves and had numerous children, seven of whom remained alive by Equiano's eleventh year. Equiano claimed himself to be from a nation that celebrated music, dance, and poetry. He equated his people, the Ibo, with the ancient Jews. In warfare, his people carried shields that could cover a man from head to foot. He had been trained to fight with javelins. The land was fruitful, but workers had to walk several hours to reach the fields, where they tilled the land by hand, without oxen or machines.

When he was eleven years of age, while the adults were away, kidnappers captured children of the village and carried off Equiano and his sister; they were soon separated as they were transferred or sold from one slaveholder to another. Equiano soon found himself on a slave ship bound for Barbados. Once there, he was auctioned off to the highest bidder. His autobiography, *The Interesting Narrative of the Life of Olaudah Equiano: Or, Gustavus Vassa, the African* (1789), describes the chaotic nature of the slave auction. Sold to a Virginia slaveholder, he saw a kitchen worker unable to eat or drink the food she was preparing because her face was encased in an iron muzzle. Equiano was next purchased by a lieutenant in the Royal Navy, Michael Henry Pascal. Throughout his adventures, Equiano developed a knowledge of languages and was able to adjust himself to each new situation. On his trip to England, Richard Baker, a boy sixteen or seventeen years old, taught him to read and write English.

LIFE'S WORK

Olaudah Equiano was subjected to the oppression of the slave trade and the whims of slaveholders until he gained his freedom. However, his experience sailing with Michael Henry Pascal gave him knowledge of trade and sufficient education in sailing, in military warfare, in transcontinental business—including the slave trade—and in mercantilism. His experience would later enable him to become a successful businessman in his own right.

Near the age of twelve, in Falmouth, England, Equiano made the discovery that white people did not sell each other into slavery. He was also moved by attendance at a Methodist church service, where he learned of the concept of God. These experiences, as recounted in *The Interesting Narrative of the Life of Olaudah Equiano*, provide readers with an appreciation of Equiano's view of life, but they also introduce engaging anecdotes. To entertain visitors on the ship, Equiano and a white sailor were forced to fight with each other, and they were paid from five to nine shillings for their effort. It was the first time he had a bloody nose.

Equiano learned the art of modern warfare on the *Roebuck*, a man-of-war that sailed the French coast and captured seventeen ships. He was permitted to fire the guns. On the warship *Namur*, Equiano witnessed the defeat of the French fleet at Louisbourg, off Nova Scotia, in 1758. He recognized the mayhem of war, with men falling thick about him and ships' masts and main sails torn apart. So skillfully did he serve that he was ultimately appointed steward of the *Namur*.

Baptized in St. Margaret's Church, Westminster, in February, 1749, Equiano was given Thomas Wilson's book *A Guide to the Indians* (1740) by his friends the Guerin sisters, for religious study. His wartime experiences had increased his faith in Providence, for he had seen a woman with a baby at her breast fall from the upper deck of the *Jason* into the hold near the keel and suffer no injury; he himself had fallen headlong from the upper deck of the *Etna* into the after-hold; those who saw him fall assumed that he had been killed. Equiano attributed the woman's and his survival to God's will. Success as a seaman and as a crew member gave him confidence to perform other work. In Georgia, he conducted a funeral for the dead child of a black woman who could get no white minister to perform the ceremony. He also gained skill as a barber.

After the war, Equiano was sold to a slaveholder in the West Indies, where he saw the horrors of slavery. One slave who had earned enough money to purchase a boat for himself in turn had the boat confiscated by an angry slaveholder who refused to allow him his property. Another slave was staked to the ground and flogged for not giving up a paycheck to his owner soon enough. Shocked at the oppression, extortion, and cruelty of the slaves' owners, Equiano gained relief when he was sold to the Quaker Robert King. Equiano was to handle many of King's affairs in the slave trade. Equiano had difficulty reconciling the Christian beliefs of these slaveholders with their conduct toward their slaves. Having gained wealth working for the Quaker, Equiano purchased his freedom from King in 1766, at the age of twenty-one.

Equiano sought to end the slave trade and soon found himself involved in numerous abolitionist ventures, supported by the Methodist Church. He acted essentially as a world ambassador, advancing the cause of abolition in places such as Turkey, Italy, Genoa, Portugal, London, and Nicaragua. His travels, however, were not without the constant worry of being kidnapped again and sold back into slavery. In Savannah, Georgia, for example, two white men accosted him, maliciously identifying him as a missing slave.

Equiano exposed to the world the affair of the slave ship *Zong*. The *Zong* had sailed from Saõ Tomé, near West Africa, in September, 1781, with 440 slaves. Deadly disease spread through the ship, killing seven crew members and sixty slaves. When the ship reached the Caribbean, disease had spread so widely through its "cargo" that the captain of the ship knew the ship's owners would suffer at the slave market because sick slaves would not sell profitably. Instead of bringing them to market, therefore, he chained 132 of them (in groups of 54, 42, and 36) and had them thrown overboard, thus collecting insurance money from their supposedly accidental drowning. The story told by Equiano rallied the abolitionists.

Equiano saw numerous organizations formed to seek the abolishment of slavery, including the Society for the Abolition of Slavery in England and the French Société des Amis de Noirs. In Massachusetts, New York, and Pennsylvania, legislators banned slavery. Slave revolts took place in the French colony of Saint Domingue (1791-1803) and in Richmond, Virginia (1800). By 1807, Great Britain had officially abolished the slave trade.

SIGNIFICANCE

Olaudah Equiano helped to drive the international abolition movement in the eighteenth century, a time when the attitude of the world toward the slave trade was indeed changing. Slavery came to be seen by some as the antithesis of their religious beliefs and of democratic idealism. The

---

EMBRACING ENGLISHNESS

In The Interesting Narrative of the Life of Olaudah Equiano, *Olaudah Equiano describes his changing attitudes toward English people and the circumstances under which he was baptized into the Church of England.*

I could now speak English tolerably well, and I perfectly understood everything that was said. I now not only felt myself quite easy with these new countrymen, but relished their society and manners. I no longer looked upon them as spirits, but as men superior to us; and therefore I had the stronger desire to resemble them; to imbibe their spirit, and imitate their manners; I therefore embraced every occasion of improvement; and every new thing that I observed I treasured up in my memory. I had long wished to be able to read and write; and for this purpose I took every opportunity to gain instruction, but had made as yet very little progress. However, when I went to London with my master, I had soon an opportunity of improving myself, which I gladly embraced. Shortly after my arrival, he sent me to wait upon the Miss Guerins, who had treated me with much kindness when I was there before; and they sent me to school.

While I was attending these ladies their servants told me I could not go to Heaven unless I was baptized. This made me very uneasy; for I had now some faint idea of a future state: accordingly I communicated my anxiety to the eldest Miss Guerin, with whom I was become a favourite, and pressed her to have me baptized; when to my great joy she told me I should. She had formerly asked my master to let me be baptized, but he had refused; however she now insisted on it; and he being under some obligation to her brother complied with her request; so I was baptized in St. Margaret's church, Westminster, in February 1759, by my present name. The clergyman, at the same time, gave me a book, called a Guide to the Indians, written by the Bishop of Sodor and Man. On this occasion Miss Guerin did me the honour to stand as godmother, and afterwards gave me a treat.

Source: Olaudah Equiano, *The Interesting Narrative of the Life of Olaudah Equiano: Or, Gustavus Vassa, the African* (London: Author, 1789), pp. 132-134.

English mainland law and the establishment of a nation that professed all individuals equal provided an opportunity for some to see an inherent hypocrisy in espousing religious morality while maintaining that the slave trade was an economic necessity.

Equiano's greatest frustration lay in the difficulty of gaining freedom for those enslaved. He could not prevent William Fitzpatrick's men in 1774 from carrying away his friend John Annis and returning him to slavery at St. Kitts, where he was subjected to torture and death, despite having gained his freedom in England. Feeling guilty for not saving Annis, Equiano seemed about to give up the struggle. In a stirring and prolonged passage at the end of chapter 10 of *The Interesting Narrative of the Life of Olaudah Equiano*, relating events of October 6, 1774, Equiano explains why he continued to fight. He compares himself to Jacob wrestling with the angel and relates a vision of Christ that reaffirmed his faith and sustained his fight for the freedom of the slave.

—*Irving N. Rothman*

FURTHER READING

Allison, Robert J., ed. *The Interesting Narrative of the Life of Olaudah Equiano: Written by Himself*. Boston: Bedford/St. Martin's, 1995. Reading Equiano's narrative is the most important first task in studying his life and work. This text is annotated with a comprehensive introduction in five parts.

Carretta, Vincent. *Equiano, the African: Biography of a Self-Made Man*. Athens: University of Georgia Press, 2005. An informative and engrossing study of Equiano's life and times that also provides an in-depth examination of Equiano's slave narrative.

Costanzo, Angelo. *Surprizing Narrative: Olaudah Equiano and the Beginnings of Black Autobiography*. Westport, Conn.: Greenwood Press, 1987. Equiano's work is in the Spanish picaresque tradition of a traveller engaged in private and public affairs, a useful vehicle for objectifying slave narratives.

Potkay, Adam. "Olaudah Equiano and the Art of Spiritual Autobiography." *Eighteenth-Century Studies* 27 (1994): 677-690. Equiano's "talking book" topos has African books talking to each other across time. The added integer is the spiritual lesson these books teach the African and Equiano's religious commitment.

Sollors, Werner, ed. *The Interesting Narrative of the Life of Olaudah Equiano: Or, Gustavus Vassa, the African, Written by Himself*. New York: W. W. Norton. Equiano's authorship of *The Narrative* is confirmed with contemporary accounts (1789) extracted from the *Monthly Review*, the *General Magazine and Impartial Review*, and the *Gentleman's Magazine*.

See also: Benjamin Banneker; Joseph Boulogne.

Related articles in *Great Events from History: The Eighteenth Century, 1701-1800*: 18th century: Expansion of the Atlantic Slave Trade; January, 1756-February 15, 1763: Seven Years' War; June 8-July 27, 1758: Siege of Louisbourg.

FIRST BARON ERSKINE
Scottish lawyer and social reformer

Combining eloquence with strong liberal leanings, Erskine became the most famous and accomplished trial lawyer and defender of individual rights in English history.

Born: January, 10, 1750; Edinburgh, Scotland
Died: November 17, 1823; Almondell, Linlithgow (now West Lothian), Scotland
Also known as: Thomas Erskine (full name)
Areas of achievement: Law, social reform, government and politics

EARLY LIFE

Thomas Erskine's mother, née Agnes Stuart, was of distinguished English parentage: One of her grandfathers was Sir Thomas Browne, the author of *Religio Medici* (1642, 1643). Henry David Erskine, his father, was the tenth earl of Buchan and the descendant of a historically significant Scottish clan. By the time Erskine was born, however, his father's income had diminished considerably, and Erskine did not receive the same education as did his two older brothers, one of whom, Henry, was destined to become an outstanding barrister in Scotland. Unable to purchase a commission in the army, which he would have preferred, his family did secure a position for him in the navy. At fourteen Erskine went to sea on the *Tartar*, commanded by a nephew of Lord Mansfield, who later was to encourage Erskine's legal ambitions.

After four years at sea, which he spent primarily in the West Indies, Erskine left naval service and bought a commission as ensign in the First Royal Regiment of Foot. At the age of twenty he married, despite her father's objections (Erskine's prospects were hardly promising at the time), Frances Moore, who was from a good though relatively poor family. After the marriage the Erskines went to Minorca, where his regiment was stationed. During this two-year stint there, Erskine unwittingly prepared himself for his future success in law. Continuing a practice he had established before his marriage, he served as preacher to his men; the art of organizing material and adjusting content to an audience was to stand him in good stead when he later "preached" before judges and juries. In addition, he did much reading especially in "classic" English literature, and many Miltonic and Shakespearian quotations, sentiments, and rhetorical devices subsequently appeared in his summations before juries.

In 1772, he left Minorca and obtained a six-month leave, which he spent in London. Because of Lord Mansfield's encouragement, his brother Henry's success, his awareness that military advancement would be unlikely, his need to support his family, and the nature of his talents, Erskine determined to become a lawyer. Being the son of a nobleman, he was entitled to a degree at one of the universities, and his work at Trinity College, Cambridge, shortened the length of time it took to be admitted to the bar. In 1775, he became a student at Lincoln's Inn (one of the Inns of Court, where the study of law was conducted), sold his commission in the army, and matriculated at Trinity in 1776. While at Cambridge he continued his study of English literature and concurrently read law, and in 1778 he received his honorary master of arts degree and was admitted to the bar. During those three years he lived in relative poverty, but his fortunes were to change radically when he took his first case, one which was to prove typical in that he defended a victim of the privileged classes and that the case involved freedom of the press and freedom of speech.

LIFE'S WORK

Thomas Baillie, who was the lieutenant governor of the Greenwick Hospital for sailors, charged fraud and corruption in the earl of Sandwich's administration of the hospital and was subsequently charged with libel. Because Baillie overheard Erskine attack the earl of Sandwich in a dinner conversation, he inquired about Erskine's identity and upon learning of Erskine's legal training and naval experience engaged him as one of

First Baron Erskine. (Library of Congress)

his barristers. Although his other counsel advised a compromise, Baillie agreed with Erskine's advice to seek an acquittal, and when Baillie's case appeared lost, Erskine made an impassioned defense that tied Baillie's fate to national security and naval morale, thereby winning his client's case and ensuring his own future success.

Within a few months, Erskine, again serving in a secondary capacity, wrote the speech that cleared Admiral Keppel of "incapacity" charges, and when he successfully defended Lord George Gordon, who was tried for high treason for his alleged participation in the anti-Catholic riots of 1781, he established himself as the foremost English barrister of his time. His was a lucrative practice, involving both civil domestic cases and maritime and commercial cases related to the animosity between England and France. His success and his response to it—he was fastidious in dress, convivial and self-assured in behavior, and a bit of an actor before an audience—did produce some critics, whose jealousy led them to term him "Counselor Ego."

Among Erskine's detractors was William Pitt the Younger, who had served under him and whose personality formed a distinct contrast to the joking, carefree, open Scot. The personality conflict had political implications as well: Pitt, a Tory, became King George III's prime minister; Erskine, a Whig, allied himself with Richard Brinsley Sheridan (the playwright-politician) and Charles James Fox, and was a favorite of the prince of Wales (later King George IV). The conflict between the two surfaced when Erskine made his first speech in the House of Commons. Pitt's contemptuous response to his speech—he made a point of failing to take notes during the speech—crushed Erskine's ego, but he more than compensated for his subsequent political defeat by his courtroom victories over Pitt's repressive measures against freedom of the press and freedom of speech. In a libel case involving Pitt, Erskine was successful in reducing the judgment against the *Morning Herald* to £250, and he won an acquittal for John Stockdale, who had been charged with libel relating to the prosecutors of Warren Hastings, who was being tried for high crimes in India.

Erskine's belief in freedom of the press was such that he defended, despite the advice of his friends, Thomas Paine, the American patriot who had in 1791 published the first part of *The Rights of Man*, a response to Edmund Burke's negative *Reflections on the Revolution in France* (1790), and followed it with part 2, an attack on hereditary government. Without even waiting for his summation, the jury, which feared that the excesses of the French Revolution could be repeated in England, found the absent Paine (wisely in France) guilty. Erskine was subsequently asked to resign as attorney general to the prince of Wales, who had expressly requested him not to defend Paine. In his espousal of the liberal cause—at a time when Francophobia was at its height—Erskine effectively cut his ties with the people in power. When he lost the John Frost "no king" case, Erskine's fortunes were at their lowest.

The Fox Libel Act of 1792, which left to the jury rather than judges the question of libel, played a large part in reversing the tide against English liberties, for the principle of trial by jury democratized justice and also allowed Erskine, who had come to be the defender of governmental victims, greater latitude in establishing their innocence. In the *Morning Chronicle* trial of 1792, for example, he even overcame the judge's direction to convict by moving the jury to return a verdict of not guilty. When Pitt persisted in his suppression of "domestic enemies" and charges of high treason were brought against Thomas Hardy, John Horne Tooke, and John Thelwall for their participation in the London Corresponding Society, Erskine defended all three successfully, though his methods varied with his clients (he allowed the brilliant

Horne Tooke to conduct his own defense, thereby absolving himself of charges of egotism).

In 1797, Erskine reversed himself with Paine and acted, for once, as prosecutor in the case of Paine's *The Age of Reason* (1794-1795), which was itself an indictment of the Christian faith. Apparently, the freedom of the press had some limits for Erskine, whose Christian zeal outweighed Paine's right to free speech and Williams's right to sell the book. Although Erskine won the case, he was not cut out for the role of prosecutor and unsuccessfully attempted to intervene on behalf of Williams. The case is noteworthy because it is the only blot on Erskine's record as a champion of individual rights, and also because it brought about reconciliation with the prince of Wales.

Three years later, Erskine defended James Hadfield, who had shot at and missed George III in an apparent assassination attempt. In this trial, which was his last state case, Erskine provided a landmark insanity defense in which he distinguished between "total" insanity and "partial" or temporary insanity and explained Hadfield's violent act as temporary insanity attributed to severe head wounds suffered serving his country in battle. Because of the array of witnesses and the impeccable logic of Erskine's argument, Hadfield, whose conviction had been a foregone conclusion, was found innocent, although he was institutionalized for the remainder of his life.

In 1805, Pitt, who had resigned as prime minister in 1801, died, and a new ministry was formed under the leadership of Fox and Grenville. The new ministry contained some Whigs, and, in 1806, Erskine was named lord chancellor, a post he held for a scant fourteen months. His appointment was not greeted with much enthusiasm, for while he had been an outstanding barrister, his success resulted more from his eloquence, wit, and logic than from his knowledge of law. He seemed to his critics to be particularly unsuited for his new post, which concerned equity and property law. While he did not distinguish himself as lord chancellor, he knew his limitations, exercised caution, sought advice, and exercised his honesty and good sense. As a result, none of his decisions was subsequently overturned. His most noteworthy performance was his handling of the trial of Lord Melville, which was conducted more professionally than a similar trial involving Warren Hastings, which lasted seven years.

After resigning as lord chancellor, Erskine turned increasingly away from his public life—he was often absent from the House of Lords and rarely took part in debates—to his private life. In 1817, however, he became active once again to oppose repressive governmental measures, including the Seditious Meetings Bills, and on one occasion urged his colleagues in the House of Lords to "confide yourselves in the people." Despite his general decline in influence and popularity he returned to center stage during the trial of Queen Caroline, in which his defense of the queen briefly restored the popularity he once enjoyed. Soon after the trial, however, he retreated from the limelight and was in financial straits and understandably out of favor with the king. On a voyage to visit his brother, he became ill and died at his brother's residence on November 17, 1823.

SIGNIFICANCE

While his "apprenticeship" for his legal career may hardly have seemed appropriate, First Baron Erskine found that his gifts as an orator, his lively wit, and his ability to adjust a message to an audience made him the ideal advocate to represent his clients before a jury. As is often the case with influential figures, he seemed created for his time, a time in which English laws began to allow lawyers greater opportunity to affect the course of justice but also a time in which hard-won English liberties were threatened not only from without but also from within. As well-intentioned government officials sought to avoid an English counterpart to the French Revolution, they unfortunately and ironically created their own "reign of terror." In the face of Pitt's assaults on English liberty, Erskine defended the victims of governmental oppression and championed the liberal cause, whether the issue was cruelty to animals, freedom of the press, or slavery.

While he had no peer as a barrister, Erskine did not enjoy equal success as a judge, a position for which he lacked not only the training but also the temperament. Ever the actor, he was more at home before the bar, and his appointment as lord chancellor, which should have served as the culmination of his career, actually signaled the beginning of his decline. Nor did he experience success in politics, a field seemingly well suited to a person of his oratorical skills. Temperamentally, however, he was not a politician, for his principles were too fixed, and he seemed unable to temper his enthusiasm to the prevailing national moods. By remaining active, perhaps because of his vanity, long after he had reached his peak as a barrister, he experienced the inevitable decline that accompanies old age and that made him easy prey for the enemies he had made in the defense of English liberties.

—*Thomas L. Erskine*

FURTHER READING

Brown, Philip Anthony. *The French Revolution in English History*. New York: Barnes and Noble Books, 1965. A sympathetic account of Erskine's defense of Paine and his role in defending the English victims of Pitt's repressive measure. Describes the profound effect of the French Revolution on England.

Browne, Irving. *Short Studies of Great Lawyers*. Littleton, Colo.: Fred B. Rothman, 1982. A reprint of a book originally published in 1878, this book includes a chatty, anecdotal treatment of some of Erskine's greatest court cases and a favorable portrait of Erskine's character. Browne tends to be effusive in his praise: "Erskine's place among lawyers is as peculiar and unrivaled as Shakespeare's in literature."

Eyck, Erich. *Pitt Versus Fox: Father and Son, 1735-1806*. Translated by Eric Northcott. London: G. Bell and Sons, 1950. Eyck places Erskine in the political fray between the Whigs and Tories and praises his contribution to liberalizing the libel laws.

Hostettler, John. *Thomas Erskine and Trial by Jury*. Chichester, England: Barry Rose, 1996. An updated biography of Erskine, written by an English lawyer and focusing on Erskine's legal career. A readable, well-researched book, containing reprints of some of Erskine's speeches.

Roscoe, Henry. *Lives of Eminent British Lawyers*. Littleton, Colo.: Fred B. Rothman, 1982. A reprint of a book originally published in 1830, Roscoe's "life" is a favorable account of Erskine's many court cases and includes many lengthy speeches, which makes it an especially valuable source. Roscoe's life is essentially the source for most subsequent biographical study of Erskine, who is treated as the model English barrister: "The genius of Erskine seems to have been created at the very period which enabled it to shine forth in its brightest lustre."

Speer, Emory. *Lincoln, Lee, Grant, and Other Biographical Addresses*. New York: Neale, 1909. A baccalaureate address delivered at the Mercer University Law School Commencement in 1908, Speer's address is an "appreciation" of Erskine's abilities as a "forensic orator." The address concentrates on Erskine's cases and law career.

Stryker, Lloyd Paul. *For the Defense: Thomas Erskine*. Garden City, N.Y.: Doubleday, 1947. An extremely favorable life of Erskine, the book criticizes his foes, notably Pitt, and dismisses criticism as the product of jealous minds. Stryker provides a wealth of historical background which is essential to assessing Erskine's achievements in terms of the turbulent times in which he lived.

See also: Jeremy Bentham; Sir William Blackstone; Adam Ferguson; Maria Anne Fitzherbert; George III; Warren Hastings; David Hume; First Earl of Mansfield; Montesquieu; Thomas Paine; Jean-Jacques Rousseau; Granville Sharp; Richard Brinsley Sheridan; Adam Smith; John Wilkes.

Related articles in *Great Events from History: The Eighteenth Century, 1701-1800:* 1726-1729: Voltaire Advances Enlightenment Thought in Europe; 1739-1740: Hume Publishes *A Treatise of Human Nature*; 1748: Montesquieu Publishes *The Spirit of the Laws*; April, 1762: Rousseau Publishes *The Social Contract*; Beginning April, 1763: The *North Briton* Controversy; September 10, 1763: Publication of the *Freeman's Journal*; January 10, 1776: Paine Publishes *Common Sense*; January 4, 1792-1797: The *Northern Star* Calls for Irish Independence; May-November, 1798: Irish Rebellion; July 2-August 1, 1800: Act of Union Forms the United Kingdom.

EUGENE OF SAVOY
French-born Italian noble and general

A great general and statesman, Eugene was successful in numerous engagements against the Turks in Central and Eastern Europe. Although born in France, he was an opponent of Louis XIV's expansionist foreign policy and saw extensive action during the War of the Spanish Succession. Later, he was governor of the Austrian Netherlands and president of the Imperial War Council.

Born: October 18, 1663; Paris, France
Died: April 20 or 21, 1736; Vienna, Austria
Also known as: François-Eugène de Savoie-Carignan (full name)
Areas of achievement: Warfare and conquest, government and politics, patronage of the arts

EARLY LIFE

The lack of any surviving personal papers or memoirs has made it difficult for biographers and historians to gain an understanding of Eugene of Savoy (ew-GEEN uhv sah-VOY), and little is known of his early years. He was small and slight in stature but very dignified and quiet in his bearing. Born in France to parents of Italian heritage who produced five sons and two daughters, Eugene was the youngest son of Cardinal Mazarin's niece, Olympia Mancini, and her husband Eugene Maurice, prince of Savoy-Carignan, count of Soissons, a soldier in the French army.

Before Olympia's marriage to Eugene Maurice, King Louis XIV (r. 1643-1715) had fallen in love with her. Because the young Eugene was not the oldest son, he was, as often was the case with younger sons of nobility, prepared at first for a career in the church, which may account for his love of learning and books. However, in 1683, he applied to serve in Louis XIV's military. He was rejected, which caused Eugene and his close friend, the prince of Conti, to attempt to leave France without Louis's permission in July, 1683. When the two young nobles were detained near the border, Conti returned to France, but Eugene continued on and entered the service of Leopold I, Holy Roman Emperor and emperor of Austria (r. 1658-1705). Eugene's cousin prince Louis of Baden was an important imperial general, and Eugene's older brother Louis had served in Austria's army until his death in July, 1683, while fighting the Turks.

Eugene's first military experience came in the fighting to relieve the Siege of Vienna (1683), as the Ottoman Turks attempted to push deep into Central Europe. Because of his personal bravery, he was awarded a pair of golden spurs and given command of one of the regiments that pushed eastward into Hungary in the wake of the Turkish retreat. For the next five years, Eugene would be heavily involved in this theater, and he rose steadily in the ranks, becoming a major general in 1685. After a successful counterattack at Berg Harsan that drove the Turks from the field in 1687, he was elevated to field marshal lieutenant at age twenty-four. He was seriously wounded at the Siege of Belgrade (1688) and was forced to recover from his wound in Vienna. His attentions would soon shift westward, as his service was needed in Italy during the Wars of the League of Augsburg (1689-1697).

LIFE'S WORK

Eugene convinced his cousin Victor Amadeus II of Savoy (r. 1675-1730) to enter the Grand Alliance against France in 1689. Savoy's entry in the alliance put pressure on France's southeastern border and opened Italy as a major theater in the wars. Although Eugene advised Leopold I to conclude peace with the Turks, Leopold pursued military actions in the west against France and in the east against the Turks. Consequently, Eugene saw action in Italy and in Eastern Europe. In 1693, Eugene was promoted to field marshal because of his successes against the French in Italy, but Savoy's shift of allegiance from the Grand Alliance to France in 1696 caused the emperor to negotiate an armistice in Italy in order to concentrate on the Turks.

The imperial armistice opened the opportunity for Eugene's greatest military victory, at Zenta, Hungary, on September 11, 1697, on his first independent command. By devastating the Turkish army, Eugene opened the way for the Treaty of Karlowitz (1699) between Austria and the Turks, which brought large areas of Hungary and Transylvania to Austria and helped accelerate its development as a major European power. Eugene built a sumptuous palace in Vienna and settled into society for several years, until the War of the Spanish Succession broke out and necessitated the services of the imperial supreme commander, which Eugene had become in 1700.

Eugene of Savoy. (Library of Congress)

Eugene operated in northern Italy, defeating the French at Carpi (1701) and later relieving Turin (1706). During the early stages of the war, Leopold named him president of the Imperial War Council in 1703, and he held that post until his death in 1736. During the war, Eugene and John Churchill, first duke of Marlborough, the great English commander, formed a remarkable partnership that produced substantial victories at Blenheim (1704) and Oudenarde (1708). However, when Eugene negotiated with the French in 1709, he demanded such stiff terms that the French continued the war.

Eugene and Marlborough presided over the allied victory at Malplaquet (1709), the bloodiest battle of the eighteenth century. Because the French had taken such heavy losses, Eugene advised attacking Paris, but his advice was not heeded. When England surprised the allies with the news that it had negotiated the terms of a potential peace agreement with France in October, 1711, Eugene urged Emperor Charles VI to oppose the agreement. Plans were made for Eugene to travel to England to present the emperor's case in person. Before he arrived in January, 1712, Marlborough—who also opposed ceasing hostilities—had been stripped of command by Queen Anne.

Eugene's two-month stay in England did not produce the desired result, and when he returned to the Continent to continue the war against France, he suffered a serious defeat at Denain, in the Spanish Netherlands, on July 24, 1712. England made good its plan to withdraw from the war when it signed the Treaty of Utrecht (April 13, 1713). The emperor did not follow suit. Marlborough traveled to Europe in January, 1713, to enlist support for an invasion of England to overthrow the government to prevent the restoration of James, the Pretender. Eugene informed Marlborough that Charles VI would not support his invasion plan but would support the Hanoverian Protestant succession. Meanwhile, Eugene continued the war against France until he negotiated the Treaties of Rastatt and Baden on March 7, 1714.

When the Turks renewed an offensive against Austria, Eugene returned to Eastern Europe, where his victories at Peterwardein (1716) and Belgrade (1717) added to his reputation and brought additional territory to Austria, which the Turks ceded in the Treaty of Passarowitz (1718). From 1716 to 1724, Eugene was governor of the Austrian Netherlands, which Austria gained via the War of the Spanish Succession. His days on campaign were largely over, but during the War of the Polish Succession (1733-1735), he helped prepare the defense of the southern German states of the Holy Roman Empire. Living in Vienna, he enjoyed the company of friends because he never married and had no children, and he patronized the arts until his death in 1736.

SIGNIFICANCE

As a statesman and military commander, Eugene of Savoy was highly regarded by most of his contemporaries and was esteemed by such towering figures as Frederick the Great of Prussia and France's Napoleon I (r. 1804-1815), who considered him one of history's seven greatest generals. Eugene produced tremendous victories against the declining Ottoman Empire that brought Austria substantial territorial gains in the Treaties of Karlowitz and Passarowitz, thereby enabling Austria to take its place among the great powers of Europe. Eugene's partnership with the first duke of Marlborough during the War of the Spanish Succession and their notable victories over France helped England procure tremendous advantages in the Treaty of Utrecht. However, neither man could accept the terms of the treaty, and they urged the continuation of the war.

Once the threat from the Turks had subsided, Vienna was rebuilt and developed as one of Europe's great capitals. Eugene's palaces, the winter palace on the Himmelpfortgasse in central Vienna, the Belvedere in southeastern Vienna, and the one on the island of Czepel in the Danube River, were magnificent structures, with the Belvedere becoming the talk of Europe. These residences were adorned with beautiful paintings, sculpture, decorations, and furniture, which made Eugene one of Europe's most influential patrons. He acquired great libraries of the finest books available in Europe.

Despite his accomplishments, which made Eugene one of the great men of his time, and despite his bravery, personal charm, and skill on the battlefield, some military historians fault him for failing to improve and modernize the Austrian army during the last two decades of his life. The result of this failure came in the 1740's and

beyond, when Austria suffered military setbacks at the lands of Prussia and the Turks.

—Mark C. Herman

FURTHER READING

Chandler, David. *The Art of Warfare in the Age of Marlborough*. New York: Hippocrene Books, 1976. An essential starting point for understanding the military context of Eugene's time.

Henderson, Nicholas. *Prince Eugen of Savoy*. Reprint. London: Phoenix Press, 2002. A full-length study that is especially strong on military matters and his patronage of the arts.

Lynn, John. *The Wars of Louis XIV*. London: Longman, 1999. An excellent survey of two wars, the War of the Grand Alliance (1689-1697) and the War of the Spanish Succession (1701-1714), in which Eugene fought against France.

McKay, Derek. *Prince Eugene of Savoy*. London: Thames and Hudson, 1977. The most complete biography in English, providing balanced coverage of Eugene as soldier, statesman, and patron.

Roider, Karl A. *Austria's Eastern Question, 1700-1790*. Princeton, N.J.: Princeton University Press, 1982. This study examines Austria's wars and diplomacy with Turkey, in which Eugene played a significant role.

See also: Queen Anne; Charles VI; Frederick the Great; First Duke of Marlborough.

Related articles in *Great Events from History: The Eighteenth Century, 1701-1800*: May 26, 1701-September 7, 1714: War of the Spanish Succession; August 13, 1704: Battle of Blenheim; March 23-26, 1708: Defeat of the "Old Pretender"; September 11, 1709: Battle of Malplaquet; November 20, 1710-July 21, 1718: Ottoman Wars with Russia, Venice, and Austria; April 11, 1713: Treaty of Utrecht; March 7, 1714, and September 7, 1714: Treaties of Rastatt and Baden; October 10, 1733-October 3, 1735: War of the Polish Succession.

LEONHARD EULER
Swiss mathematician and physicist

Euler had a tremendous impact on almost all fields of mathematics, opening new and more fruitful courses of inquiry. One of the most prolific mathematical writers ever, his founding of the field of analysis was particularly important, and his notations remain in common use in mathematics.

Born: April 15, 1707; Basel, Switzerland
Died: September 18, 1783; St. Petersburg, Russia
Areas of achievement: Mathematics, physics, science and technology

EARLY LIFE

Leonhard Euler (LAY-awn-hahrt OY-luhr) was born to a Calvinist minister, Paul Euler, and his wife, Marguerite Brucker, the daughter of a minister, in Basel, Switzerland, on April 15, 1707. The family soon moved to the suburb of Riehen. Little is known of Euler's childhood, but the information that is available indicates that his interest in mathematics was quite logical, because his father was an excellent mathematician in his own right.

Paul Euler had studied under Jakob I Bernoulli, a member of the famous Bernoulli family of mathematicians, while he was studying for his degree in theology. The elder Euler gave Leonhard his first instruction at home. During this period, the younger Euler studied some of the most difficult texts in mathematics available at the time. He later went to live with his grandmother in Basel, where he went to the local school (*Gymnasium*). Euler was not satisfied with the mathematics instruction offered there and received private tutoring from Johann Burckhardt.

When Euler was almost fourteen, at his father's wish he entered the University of Basel to study theology. Although Leonhard was quite devout and worked dutifully, he had no desire to become a minister, and he filled his free time with mathematics. In fact, in time he received limited tutoring from Johann I Bernoulli. Bernoulli suggested texts for Euler and agreed to explain any difficulties during his free time on Saturdays. Since Euler did not want to disappoint Bernoulli, he worked very hard to ensure that he did not waste the professor's time.

LIFE'S WORK

In 1724, at age seventeen, Euler received a master's degree. His father was concerned about the progress Leonhard was making in theology, but the Bernoullis convinced Paul Euler that the young man was extremely gifted in mathematics and that the gift should not be wasted. Thus, Euler was free at a very young age to pursue a career in mathematics. Euler began working independently and submitted a solution to a problem in navigation proposed by the Academy of Sciences in Paris in 1727. Although he received only an honorable mention from the academy, his name was placed before many of the people who could influence his career.

Unfortunately, there were many mathematicians who were not ready to accept one so young. When Euler applied for a post as professor of mathematics at the University of Basel, his name was not forwarded, probably because of his age. As such positions were rare in his home country, Euler was very discouraged, but the Bernoullis encouraged him with news of the newly formed Academy at St. Petersburg in Russia. This institution had a twofold purpose: Its members received a stipend to continue their own work, and, from time to time, the czar might pose practical problems to be solved by the members. Both Nikolaus and Daniel Bernoulli held positions there, and they wrote to Euler that there would soon be an opening in medicine. Therefore, Euler began to study anatomy so that he would be qualified for the position when it became available. He received the appointment in 1727, and he traveled to Russia, intending to accept this medical position. The reigning monarch, Catherine I, died before he could take up his appointment, however, and he instead joined the mathematical group, unnoticed in the change of regimes.

Although the political situation in Russia was not entirely satisfactory, the Russian academy offered Euler security and a comfortable lifestyle, and he was able to marry Catharina Gsell and begin a family. Except for a two-decade stint in Berlin, he made St. Petersburg his permanent home. His work for the first six years was fairly routine as a member of the physics staff, but in 1733 he became the leading member in mathematics when Daniel Bernoulli left to return home.

Euler threw himself into his work with fervor. (Indeed, when the Swiss prepared to publish Euler's writings in the twentieth century, the project's editors were stunned by the amount of material found in St. Petersburg.) His work at the Russian academy was diverse, spanning navigation, cartography, ballistics, mechanics, measurement, and especially mathematics. During this first, fourteen-year period in Russia, Euler wrote nearly one hundred articles and memoirs for publication. He

Leonhard Euler. (Library of Congress)

also maintained correspondence with the most widely known European mathematicians, both for himself and in the name of the Academy of Sciences. Indeed, as the result of his strenuous pursuit of a Parisian prize in the field of astronomy, Euler developed an illness that resulted in the loss of sight in one eye.

In 1741, Euler was invited to Berlin by Frederick the Great of Prussia as part of the reorganization and refurbishing of the Berlin Academy. Euler accepted this position, which he filled from 1741 until 1766. He also maintained his membership in the St. Petersburg Academy, as well as in the Royal Society of London, to which he was elected in 1749. He continued to write for the Russian academy during this time, as he was still in their employ. While living abroad, Euler received a stipend from Russia in addition to his recompense for his post in Berlin. While in Russia, he was supported well enough to have several servants. Euler and Frederick got along so poorly that at least once Frederick tried to remove him as the director of the academy but was convinced by others that this would be a mistake. Nevertheless, Euler more than earned his pay. He worked on many applications for

Frederick, including coinage, insurance, and pensions, and he held several administrative posts. In addition, he produced almost three hundred mathematical papers and tutored some of Frederick's relatives.

By 1766, however, the situation with Frederick had become so bad that Euler, then fifty-nine, decided to accept the invitation of Catherine the Great to return to Russia. Because he had regularly sent memoirs back to that country and had enjoyed its financial support while in Berlin, the move seemed logical. He was to live there for the remainder of his life.

Soon after his return, Euler began to develop a cataract in his remaining eye. For a man of lesser gifts, blindness would have been a career-ending disability. Euler, however, began to train himself to solve problems mentally and dictate the results to others, principally his sons Johann Albrecht and Christoph, who were also mathematicians. He succeeded so completely that he was able to work in this fashion for another fifteen years, holding his post at the academy and actually producing more papers than ever before. During this time, Euler produced some of his best work, including his analysis of the effects of the gravitational pull of the Earth and the Sun upon the motion of the Moon. Although he did benefit from discussions with his peers, all the work had to be done without the aid of writing partial results or ideas. He also produced a monograph on integral calculus, work on fluid mechanics, and won a prize for work in astronomy.

Despite a lifetime of work, Euler was most comfortable with his family. A devoted family man, he even held his children while working on mathematics when they were still small. Working with his sons in his later life was also quite fulfilling for him. Although he had chosen not to pursue theology as a youth, Euler never left his church, and he held daily services with his family. Euler's wife died in 1776, and he soon was married to his first wife's sister, with whom he lived until his death in St. Petersburg on September 18, 1783.

SIGNIFICANCE

The extent of Leonhard Euler's work was vast. In mathematics, he developed much of the notation in current use, in addition to a considerable amount of theory. Euler was the first to treat trigonometry as a field in itself rather than a branch of geometry, and he developed spherical trigonometry. Thus, he led the way in its development as a discipline. He made great progress in calculus, writing two texts, *Institutiones calculi differentialis* (1755) and *Institutiones calculi integralis* (1768-1770), that are still used by mathematicians as reference works. Included in these books are several discoveries Euler made concerning differential equations and partial differential equations. Euler made significant refinements to the fundamental theorem of algebra. He was also extremely interested in summation of infinite series and developed much of the basis upon which convergence theories would later be founded.

Although he produced a great quantity of work in physics, in part in response to requests by monarchs, Euler's major contribution in this field was his imposing analysis of mechanics. He was far more interested in the mathematical aspects of physical problems and thus was able to systematize his study. Euler published his results in *Mechanica sive motus scientia analytice exposita* (1736) and *Theoria motus corporum solidorum seu rigidorum* (1765). The former work was the first attempt to establish clear solutions to mechanical problems. Other sciences in which Euler worked include astronomy, navigation, and optics, yet Euler's foremost field was mathematical analysis, a field that owes its foundation to Euler's book *Introductio in analysin infinitorum* (1748; *Introduction to Analysis of the Infinite*, 1988-1990). Of particular interest to mathematicians is his development of function theory and notation.

The republication of Euler's work began in 1911 in Leipzig, Germany, and moved to Lausanne, Switzerland, in 1942. Three series have been produced, *Opera mathematica, Opera mechanica et astronomica*, and *Opera physica*, in which each work is reproduced in the original language of publication. Although only those papers that Euler personally prepared for publication are included, it is estimated that to include them all would take more than fifty volumes. Euler ranks as one of the most prolific mathematicians in history.

—*Celeste Williams Brockington*

FURTHER READING

Bell, Eric T. "Analysis Incarnate." In *Men of Mathematics*. New York: Simon & Schuster, 1937. Each chapter in this book deals with a major mathematician, dating from ancient Greece to the early twentieth century. This chapter on Euler includes biographical information and a limited discussion of his work.

Boyer, Carl B. *A History of Mathematics*. 2d ed., rev. New York: Wiley, 1989. Boyer's book is a standard though extensive history, and his discussion of Euler and his work is both interesting and clear.

Dunham, William. *Euler: The Master of Us All*. Washington, D.C.: Mathematical Association of America, 1999. In this book aimed at readers with a knowledge of mathematics, Dunham describes Euler's many contributions to the field. Topics include number theory, logarithms, infinite series, complex variables, algebra, and geometry.

Eves, Howard. *An Introduction to the History of Mathematics*. 5th ed. Philadelphia: Saunders College, 1983. Although the treatment of Euler is extremely brief, Eves is excellent in placing Euler within the evolution of mathematics.

Havil, Julian. *Gamma: Exploring Euler's Constant*. Princeton, N.J.: Princeton University Press, 2003. Euler first described how gamma was a constant in many areas of mathematics. Almost three hundred years later, however, the nature of this constant remains a mystery. Havil examines Euler's discovery and subsequent developments in the understanding of gamma.

Struik, Dirk J. *A Concise History of Mathematics*. 4th rev. ed. New York: Dover, 1987. A standard history of mathematics; the treatment of Euler and his work is concise yet informative.

Youschkevitch, A. P. "Leonhard Euler." In *Dictionary of Scientific Biography*. Vol. 4. New York: Charles Scribner's Sons, 1971. This article is of particular note for at least two reasons. First, Youschkevitch was a fellow of the Soviet Academy of Sciences, an outgrowth of the St. Petersburg Academy. As such, he had easy access to Euler's work. Second, the article contains an extensive bibliography (seventy entries).

See also: Maria Gaetana Agnesi; Benjamin Banneker; Catherine the Great; Frederick the Great; Joseph-Louis Lagrange; Colin Maclaurin.

Related article in *Great Events from History: The Eighteenth Century, 1701-1800*: 1724: Foundation of the St. Petersburg Academy of Sciences.

DANIEL GABRIEL FAHRENHEIT
German scientist

In addition to developing the temperature scale that bears his name, Fahrenheit made considerable advances in thermometer technology, greatly increasing the accuracy of measurements of temperature.

Born: May 24, 1686; Gdańsk (now in Poland)
Died: September 16, 1736; The Hague, Dutch
    Republic (now in the Netherlands)
Also known as: Gabriel Daniel Fahrenheit
Area of achievement: Science and technology

EARLY LIFE

Daniel Gabriel Fahrenheit (DAHN-yehl GAHB-ree-ehl FAHR-ehn-hit) was born in Gdańsk (Danzig), a free city under Polish protection located within East Prussia. He was the eldest son of a merchant with connections to the nobility. The early death of his parents forced him to go into business at a young age in order to earn a living. However, his strong interest in the natural sciences led him into scientific studies and experimentation, and he eventually found his place as a maker of fine instruments for scientific measurements. Because his background was that of a tradesman rather than a "natural philosopher," or scientist, Fahrenheit felt little compulsion to make extensive or detailed records of his researches. As a result, very little is known of his methods or procedures, and they have become the subject of much conjecture and folklore.

LIFE'S WORK

During the first decade of the eighteenth century, Fahrenheit spent considerable time in Denmark, where he visited the famous Danish astronomer Ole Rømer, whose most notable achievement was the discovery that light did not propagate instantaneously, as many had supposed, but in fact had a finite speed, albeit an extraordinarily rapid one.

Unlike Fahrenheit, Rømer was a keeper of meticulous notes, jotting down his experiments and calculations in a small notebook that ultimately would make its way to the University of Copenhagen after his death. This notebook, and particularly the annotations made in it by his successor, Peter Horrebow, are the best source of information on this critical period in the development of the modern thermometer. Rømer was particularly interested in creating a reproducible thermometer, so that experiments and observations from

widely differing locales could be reliably compared to one other.

Because the hollow glass tubes that were used in making thermometers were hand-blown, it was impossible to make them physically identical. As a result, it was necessary to find some means other than simple physical comparison to determine when multiple thermometers were in perfect calibration with one another. Rømer's solution was to calibrate each thermometer against known reference points, such as the melting point of ice and the boiling point of water. If the rate of expansion of the measuring fluid (whether mercury, alcohol, or some other substance) were precisely known, and each thermometer was calibrated from the same reference point, it would be possible to ensure that different thermometers would produce identical measurements, even if they were not structurally identical.

The next step was to assign specific numerical values to the various points on the temperature scale being used. Rømer experimented with a number of different scales, setting various numbers for the reference points. Rømer still had not settled upon a workable scale when Fahrenheit arrived to discuss questions of measurement with him. Historians of science would subsequently argue intensely about the extent of Rømer's role in inspiring Fahrenheit's work in thermometers and temperature scales, until the discovery of a letter in an archive in Leningrad (St. Petersburg) in which Fahrenheit himself recounted experiments that he and Rømer had performed together. These experiments led him to an interest in improving the mechanism of both thermometers and barometers. Although there were some discrepancies between the descriptions of these experiments in Fahrenheit's letter and those in Rømer's notebook, which have led some scholars to try to diminish the role of Rømer in Fahrenheit's work, the letter was written some time after the fact, and time may have blurred some of the details of Fahrenheit's memory of the events.

After Rømer's death in 1710, Fahrenheit continued his work in developing a rational scale that would provide convenient numbers for the most commonly observed temperatures. Since he was working primarily with thermometers to be used in meteorological observations, it was desirable to reserve the numbers 0-100 for temperatures that would commonly be observed in the environment. It therefore seemed most prudent for the boiling point of water to be a much higher number than

100, since it represented a temperature significantly beyond those relevant to meteorological observations. By the same token, setting the zero point of the scale at the freezing point of water was undesirable, since it would force meteorologists to use negative numbers to denote the temperatures of northern European winters.

While it is thus apparent why the Fahrenheit scale developed along the general lines that it did, it remains a subject of great conjecture how exactly Fahrenheit determined that 32 and 212 were the best numbers to represent the freezing and boiling points of water. The only definitive account of the process is found in a paper written years after the fact to be delivered at the Royal Society. There, Fahrenheit described his discovery of the supercooling phenomenon, in which water may remain liquid after it has become cooler than its normal freezing temperature, only crystalizing upon the introduction of a trigger, such as air bubbles.

According to his description, Fahrenheit assigned the zero point of his scale to the coldest temperature he could attain with a mixture of ice, water, and either of two kinds of salts. He noted, however, that the experiment worked better in winter than in summer, suggesting that he was providing less than completely accurate information. During his lifetime, much of the work of the instrument maker was still essentially a trade secret, and the habit of secrecy may well have overcome the scientist's drive to share his discoveries with his colleagues, leading him deliberately to obscure his methods. Many historians have suggested that the melting point of water and the normal body temperature of the human being, also referred in his paper, were Fahrenheit's real fixed points for determining his scale.

Among Fahrenheit's customers for thermometers was noted chemist Herman Boerhaave, who bought both a mercury thermometer and an alcohol thermometer from him. After subjecting them to careful experimental observation, Boerhaave noted that they did not always quite agree in their readings. When he informed Fahrenheit of this discrepancy, Fahrenheit became curious as to the reason behind it but could not determine the cause. At length, he concluded that the discrepancy must result from the thermometers being made from two different kinds of glass. He missed entirely the real cause, namely that mercury and alcohol do not expand proportionately to one another.

Two thermometers credited to Fahrenheit have survived to modern times, but their authenticity is doubtful. One, signed by Fahrenheit, has a scale running from 0 to 600, the latter point of which is indicated as being the boiling point of mercury. However, the tube is filled with a darkish liquid that is probably not mercury, and it is often surmised that while the backing board with its engraved temperature marks is probably authentic, the glass parts have been replaced by some unknown hand at a later point.

SIGNIFICANCE

Daniel Gabriel Fahrenheit greatly improved temperature-measuring techniques by inventing a scale that could be used to denote temperatures in different times and places and compare them accurately. His immediate goal was to improve the science of meteorology, but the development of a method of objective measurement of temperature and a rational scale by which to measure it was of utmost importance to a great many areas of science and technology, far beyond the meteorological. With a practical thermometer, physicians could determine a patient's actual temperature, rather than being limited to feeling the forehead and trying to decide if it felt hotter than normal. Chemists could determine the temperature at which reactions took place or control the temperature of a reagent.

—Leigh Husband Kimmel

FURTHER READING

Balestrino, Philip. *Hot as an Ice Cube*. New York: Crowell, 1971. Basic concepts of temperature measurements, including experiments that effectively replicate Fahrenheit's development of thermometer calibration.

Fahrenheit, Daniel Gabriel. *Fahrenheit's Letters to Leibniz and Boerhaave*. Edited, translated, and annotated by Pieter van der Star. Amsterdam: Rodopi, 1983. A collection of Fahrenheit's correspondence with the Dutch chemist and the German philosopher, reproduced in the original language and translated into English with commentary by the editor.

Frisch, Joy. *Temperature*. Mankato, Minn.: Smart Apple Media, 2003. Introduction to scientific concepts of temperature, including a laboratory exercise in building a thermometer very similar to Fahrenheit's original work.

Knowles-Middleton, W. E. *A History of the Thermometer and Its Uses in Meteorology*. Baltimore: Johns Hopkins University Press, 1966. An older book, but with a wealth of references to primary sources in the original languages, showing the depth of research performed by its author.

Royston, Angela. *Hot and Cold*. Chicago: Heinemann Library, 2002. Includes a bibliography of other books accessible to young readers.

Walpole, Brenda. *Temperature*. Milwaukee, Wis.: Gareth Stevens, 1995. Introduction to concepts of temperature and its measurement, including the history of temperature measurement and thermometers.

See also: Sir Richard Arkwright; John Baskerville; Henry Cavendish; Abraham Darby; James Hargreaves; John Kay; Antoine-Laurent Lavoisier; Nicolas Leblanc; Mikhail Vasilyevich Lomonosov; Gaspard Monge; Jacques-Étienne and Joseph-Michel Montgolfier; Thomas Newcomen; John Roebuck; Georg Ernst Stahl.

Related articles in *Great Events from History: The Eighteenth Century, 1701-1800*: 1705: Halley Predicts the Return of a Comet; 1714: Fahrenheit Develops the Mercury Thermometer; 1714-1762: Quest for Longitude; 1723: Stahl Postulates the Phlogiston Theory; 1735: Hadley Describes Atmospheric Circulation; 1742: Celsius Proposes an International Fixed Temperature Scale; 1786-1787: Lavoisier Devises the Modern System of Chemical Nomenclature.

ADAM FERGUSON
Scottish philosopher

Ferguson was a leading figure of the eighteenth century Scottish Enlightenment. He was not simply the contemporary of David Hume and Adam Smith but also esteemed as their peer. Widely regarded as a founder of modern sociology, he was the forerunner of, and a significant influence upon, such later thinkers as Auguste Comte, Herbert Spencer, and Karl Marx.

Born: June 20, 1723; Logierait, Perthshire, Scotland
Died: February 22, 1816; St. Andrews, Fife, Scotland
Areas of achievement: Sociology, philosophy, scholarship

EARLY LIFE

Adam Ferguson was born in a village in the foothills of the Scottish Highlands. His father, also named Adam, was the local Presbyterian (Church of Scotland) minister; his mother, the former Mary Gordon, was a farmer's daughter. After attending the local parish school and a grammar school in Perth, Ferguson won in 1738 a competitive examination for a bursary at Saint Andrews University. He received the master of arts degree in 1842, and at his father's behest went on to study divinity first at Saint Andrews and then at the University of Edinburgh.

His father owed his post to the patronage of the duke of Athole, and that link was responsible for Ferguson's appointment in 1745 to a chaplaincy with the newly formed "Black Watch" regiment and for his obtaining a special dispensation from the General Assembly of the Church of Scotland allowing his ordination as a minister, despite his having completed only the first two years of the regular four-year divinity course. In 1754, when the regiment was transferred to America, Ferguson resigned his commission, left the ministry, and moved to Edinburgh to try his fortunes there as a man of letters.

For the next five years, Ferguson eked out a living through a series of makeshift jobs. In 1759, thanks to the support of influential friends led by the philosopher David Hume, he was elected professor of natural philosophy at the University of Edinburgh. Although he had no prior qualifications for teaching the natural sciences, he proved a successful and popular lecturer. In 1764, he won election to the chair of moral philosophy—his primary interest. His lectures attracted not simply a large student audience but also leading figures from Edinburgh and even London society.

Yet his status as "court philosopher" to the establishment resulted primarily from his growing list of publications. His first book, *An Essay on the History of Civil Society* (1767), was a pioneering exercise in comparative history that traced the process of social evolution through the three stages of savagery, barbarism, and civilization. During the next fifty years, the volume would go through nine English editions and reprintings and be translated into French and German. Two years later, he published an expanded version of his lectures under the title *Institutes of Moral Philosophy* (1769), a work that added to his reputation. In 1783, he brought out the massive *History of the Progress and Termination of the Roman Republic*, covering the period from the beginning of the First Punic War through the end of the reign of Augustus. His best-known though least popularly successful work, *Principles of Moral and Political Science*, appeared in 1792.

LIFE'S WORK

Adam Ferguson was not a systematically consistent thinker. His views changed over time, and there were tensions and contradictions in individual works. There was, however, a reasonably well-defined general tendency in his opinions. In accord with the dominant spirit of his time, he was optimistic about the potential for human improvement. He was sufficiently influenced by the Calvinist tradition in which he had been reared to acknowledge the baneful influence of humankind's "evil passions." He averred that "perfection is no where to be found short of the infinite mind" of God, nor did he look ahead to any time in which humans would live in blissful harmony. Conflict among individuals and among nations was natural, even beneficent. Competition between individuals stimulated ambition and enterprise; war between nations fostered social cohesion. Yet Ferguson affirmed that "progression is the gift of God to all his intelligent creatures and is within the competence of the lowest of mankind." Such progress was not inevitable. Adverse geographical and climatic conditions could result in stagnation.

Similarly, nations could and did decay when unwise policies were followed "that crush [the individual's] spirit; that debase his sentiments, and disqualify his mind for affairs." The thrust of human nature, however, was progressive, with persons "perpetually busied in reformations." "Not only the individual advances from infancy to manhood," Ferguson summed up, "but the species itself from rudeness to civilization."

Linked with this optimism about human potentialities was the Newtonian vision of a law-governed universe. Although reaffirming that "every circumstance or event in the order of nature" served "to manifest, and to extol the supreme wisdom and goodness of God," Ferguson emphasized that this "wise providence" operated by the "fixed and determinate laws" of nature. Just as Sir Isaac Newton had revealed the laws governing the physical world, Ferguson aspired to discover the laws governing the social world. His aim, in short, was to rest moral philosophy upon a similarly empirical basis. As he wrote, "Before we can ascertain the rules of morality for mankind, the history of man's nature, his dispositions, his specific enjoyments and sufferings, his conditions and future prospects, should be known." The most important fact that Ferguson discovered about humans is that they are social animals. "It appears from the history of mankind that men have always acted in troops and companies. . . . [W]hile they practice arts, each for his own preservation, they institute political forms and unite their forces for common safety." Thus, he denied the existence of a state of nature in which humans lived without social bonds.

> From society are derived not only the force, but the very existence of man's happiest emotions; not only the better part, but almost the whole of his rational character. Send him to the desert alone, he is a plant torn from its roots; the form indeed may remain, but every faculty droops and withers; the human personage and the human character cease to exist.

The corollary was that "most of the opinions, habits, and pursuits of men, result from the state of their society." The proper study of humankind, therefore, was the study of groups rather than individuals. More important, Ferguson concluded that the structure of any given society was an "adventitious" historical product rather than a planned creation. "The crowd of mankind are directed in their establishments and measures, by the circumstances in which they are placed . . . and nations stumble upon establishments which are indeed the result of human action, but not the execution of any human design." He accordingly had no patience with those who would reconstruct the social order upon a priori ideals. While paying lip service to the principle that government must rest upon the consent of the governed, he came close to holding that the successful exercise of authority was self-legitimating.

> The consent, upon which the right to command is founded may not be prior to the establishment of government; but may be obtained under the reasonable exercise of an actual power, to which every person within the community, by accepting of a customary protection, becomes bound to pay the customary allegiance and submission. Here is a compact ratified by the least ambiguous of all signs, the whole practice, and continued observance of an ordinary life.

There is no question that Ferguson's defense of the status quo was influenced by the milieu in which he lived. The wealth produced by the growth of commerce and industry in Scotland during the second half of the eighteenth century supplied the material basis for the remarkable outburst of intellectual activity of which Ferguson was part. Yet the accompanying strains and tensions roused grave anxieties about the stability of the social fabric. Indeed, Ferguson—like his fellow intellectuals of the Scottish Enlightenment—was dependent upon the patronage of the well born and powerful. The practical import of his

Adam Ferguson. (Library of Congress)

companying pursuit of individual gain, and the resulting inequalities of wealth threatened social cohesion, but he thought that the benefits outweighed the disadvantages. Freeing the poor from the exigencies of labor "would be to frustrate the purpose of nature in rendering toil and the exercises of ingenuity necessary to man; it would be to cut off the sources of wealth, and, under pretence of relieving the distressed, it would be to reject the condition upon which nature has provided that the wants of the species in general shall be relieved." Ferguson, however, rested the sanctity of private property upon a higher justification than simply this prudential calculus. Inequality in the distribution of property reflected "the unequal dispositions of men to frugality and industry." The individual was born with an inherent right "to use of his faculties and powers."

> Whilst we admit, therefore, that all men have an equal right to defend themselves, we must not mistake this for an assumption that all men have equal things to defend, or that liberty should consist in stripping the industrious and skillful, who have acquired much, to enrich the lazy and profligate. . . . It is impossible to restrain the influence of superior ability, of property, of education, or the habits of station. It is impossible to prevent these from becoming to some degree hereditary; and of consequence, it is impossible, without violating the principles of human nature, to prevent some permanent distinction of ranks.

Ferguson's reputation as a founding father of sociology rests primarily upon his analysis of the process of social evolution. Since human nature was everywhere the same and had always been the same, progress everywhere followed the same path. He postulated three major stages through which society passed: the savage, the barbarian, and the "polished." The most important determinative force responsible for the transformation from one stage to the next was change in the "means of subsistence." Savage societies depend for their livelihood upon hunting, gathering, and fishing; thus such possessions as exist are communally owned. The shift from a food-gathering to a pastoral economy results in the institution of private property. Barbarian societies "having possessed themselves of herds and depending for their provision on pas-

teachings was thus the necessity of upholding the existing sociopolitical order. "It has pleased Providence for wise purposes," he preached, "to place men in different stations, and to bestow upon them different degrees of wealth. Without this circumstance there could be no subordination, no government, no industry. Every person does good, and promotes the happiness of society, by living agreeable to the rank in which providence has placed him." Any reform should come gradually through orderly legal processes; the alternative was a descent into chaos followed by despotism. "The present government may have its defects, as the walls or roof of the building in which we lodge may be insufficient or threaten to fall on our heads. Then set about the necessary repair." "But," he continues, "it is a wise maxim: Beware you take not away so much of your support at once as that the roof may fall in."

A major theme recurring through Ferguson's writings was his warning against any attempt at equalizing wealth. He recognized that the commercial spirit, the acture, know what it is to be poor or rich. They know the re-lations of patron and client, of servant or master, and suffer themselves to be classed according to the measure of wealth." Once individual possession of herds is ac-cepted, its extension over land follows. People abandon their migrations and societies and become settled and ag-ricultural. The growth of commerce and manufacturing leads to the next stage. Its hallmark was a vast expansion in the division of labor whereby there is "committed to different persons, the several tasks, which require a pecu-liar skill and attention." As a result, "the sources of wealth are laid open; every species of material is wrought up to the greatest perfection, and every commodity is produced in the greatest abundance."

Along with this identification of the division of labor as the crucial distinguishing feature of the modern commer-cial and manufacturing economy, Ferguson's other major contribution lay in his analysis of the causal link between a society's economic base and its governmental forms. In savage societies, the absence of property meant loosely defined patterns of subordination with leaders chosen ad hoc to meet temporary exigencies. The accumulation of property in private hands accustomed men to the "dis-tinction of rank" and thus paved the way for the more for-malized relationship between ruler and ruled represented by the rise of hereditary monarchy. Ferguson pictured as the appropriate government for the commercial and man-ufacturing society the "mixed" British constitution of his own day; he believed that the exercise of unrestrained power trampling upon established rights stifled enterprise. There was, however, no threat to a commercial economy when the power of the monarch was checked by the no-bility, represented in the House of Lords, and the proper-tied classes, represented in the House of Commons.

Ferguson married Katherine Burnet in 1766. That same year he was awarded an honorary LL.D. by the University of Edinburgh; in 1793 he was elected an hon-orary member of the Berlin Academy. A pamphlet that he wrote upholding the British side against the rebellious American colonies was published at government ex-pense in 1776. Two years later, he was appointed secre-tary to the Carlisle Commission sent to America in an abortive bid at negotiations. Although suffering a near-fatal paralytic stroke in 1780, he recovered sufficiently to return to his work. In 1785, he was appointed to the chair of mathematics at the University of Edinburgh—in real-ity a sinecure that allowed him to give up teaching. The death of his wife in 1795 was followed by his own depar-ture from Edinburgh for retirement in the countryside. On February 22, 1816, four months before his ninety-

third birthday, he died in St. Andrews, where he had moved eight years before to live under the care of friends because of his failing eyesight. His last words were, re-portedly, "There *is* another world."

SIGNIFICANCE

Adam Ferguson's most important short-run contribu-tion—like that of his fellow luminaries of the Scottish Enlightenment such as Adam Smith—lay in formulating the ideological underpinnings for the emerging capitalist order. He would also, however, have a longer-range in-tellectual impact transcending the immediate circum-stances shaping his thinking. Ferguson's ideas greatly in-fluenced many writers' efforts to discover the laws of social development. Claude Henri de Saint-Simon ap-pears to have derived from Ferguson his thesis regarding the evolution from military to industrial societies. Auguste Comte paid homage to him as a pioneer in the search for a positivist science of society. Herbert Spencer was another nineteenth century giant who drew heavily upon Ferguson. Karl Marx rightly acknowledged his debt to Ferguson on the crucial importance of the divi-sion of labor in the rise of capitalism. Ludwig Gump-lowicz hailed him as the founder of the "group struggle" theory of social development. In addition, most histori-ans of sociology agree that he was a—if not *the*—father of the discipline in its modern shape.

—John Braeman

FURTHER READING

Bryson, Gladys. *Man and Society: The Scottish Inquiry of the Eighteenth Century*. Princeton, N.J.: Princeton University Press, 1945. A landmark study of the role played by the writers of the Scottish Enlightenment in establishing an empirical basis for the study of hu-mans and society. Includes an extended treatment of Ferguson as "representative" of the group.

Buchan, James. *Crowded with Genius: The Scottish En-lightenment, Edinburgh's Moment of the Mind*. New York: HarperCollins, 2003. Ferguson is one of the Scottish Enlightenment figures discussed in this ex-amination of intellectual life in eighteenth century Edinburgh.

Camic, Charles. *Experience and Enlightenment: Social-ization for Cultural Change in Eighteenth-Century Scotland*. Chicago: University of Chicago Press, 1983. A penetrating analysis of the broader social forces and individual life experiences responsible for shaping the leaders of the Scottish Enlightenment.

Kettler, David. *The Social and Political Thought of Adam Ferguson*. Columbus: Ohio State University

Press, 1965. The most detailed analysis of Ferguson's thought, but the author's long-windedness and abstruse style make for difficult reading.

Lehmann, W. C. *Adam Ferguson and the Beginnings of Modern Sociology: An Analysis of the Sociological Elements in His Writings with Some Suggestions as to His Place in the History of Social Theory.* New York: Columbia University Press, 1930. An exploration of Ferguson's role in the foundation of sociology and social theory as modern academic disciplines.

Ox-Salzberger, Fania. *Translating the Enlightenment: Scottish Civic Discourse in Eighteenth-Century Germany.* New York: Oxford University Press, 1995. Examines how Ferguson's theories were received in Germany. Although German thinkers misread Ferguson's work, they were able to reveal new philosophical insights.

Snell, John. *The Political Thought of Adam Ferguson.* Wichita, Kans.: Municipal University of Wichita, 1950. A handy, brief introduction with a survey of Ferguson's later influences.

See also: George Berkeley; Joseph Black; James Boswell; Marquis de Condorcet; First Baron Erskine; David Hume; Adam Smith; Giambattista Vico.
Related articles in *Great Events from History: The Eighteenth Century, 1701-1800:* 1726-1729: Voltaire Advances Enlightenment Thought in Europe; 1739-1740: Hume Publishes *A Treatise of Human Nature*; September 10, 1763: Publication of the *Freeman's Journal*; March 9, 1776: Adam Smith Publishes *The Wealth of Nations*; February 22, 1791-February 16, 1792: Thomas Paine Publishes *Rights of Man*.

JOHANN GOTTLIEB FICHTE
German philosopher

Fichte's philosophy of ethical idealism served as the pivotal theory in the development of idealism within the German philosophical community. His emendations of Immanuel Kant's conception of the human mind paved the way for the development of Absolute Idealism by Georg Wilhelm Friedrich Hegel.

Born: May 19, 1762; Rammenau, Saxony (now in Germany)
Died: January 29, 1814; Berlin, Prussia (now in Germany)
Area of achievement: Philosophy

EARLY LIFE

Johann Gottlieb Fichte (yoh-HAHN GAWT-leep FIHKH-tuh) was born into poverty. His father, Christian Fichte, managed only a meager living by making and selling ribbons. At an early age, Johann displayed severe conscientiousness, stubbornness, and tremendous intellectual talents. As legend has it, a local nobleman, Baron von Miltitz, missed the Sunday sermon and was informed that Johann could recite it verbatim. The baron was so impressed with this feat that he undertook to have the poor boy formally educated. Fichte was sent to the school at Pforta (1774-1780).

After Pforta, Fichte studied theology at the Universities of Jena, Wittenberg, and Leipzig. No longer supported by Miltitz, Fichte was forced to terminate his edu-

cation in 1784 and support himself by tutoring. Yet his proud temperament and radical ideas forced him to change locations frequently. In 1788, he traveled to Zurich as a tutor for a wealthy hotel owner. There he befriended Johann Kasper Lavater, the most important pastor of Zurich, with whom he came to share theological interests. Lavater in turn introduced him to Inspector Hartman Rahn (a brother-in-law of the poet Friedrich Gottlieb Klopstock). Fichte fell in love with the inspector's daughter Johanna. Because of his financial situation, however, they remained unmarried for several years.

LIFE'S WORK

During his engagement, Fichte studied the work of Immanuel Kant, the dominant philosopher in Germany during this period and the figure responsible for Fichte's intellectual development. Initially, Fichte endorsed the doctrine of determinism. He became convinced, however, that a philosophical reconciliation between determinism and human freedom was possible within a Kantian framework. In fact, Fichte was so enthusiastic about Kant's philosophy that he traveled to Königsberg to meet the aging savant but received a rather cold reception.

In spite of this rebuff, Fichte immediately went to work on his first major philosophical treatise, *Versuch einer Kritik aller Offenbarung* (1792; *Attempt at a Critique of All Revelation*, 1978), in which he interpreted revealed religion in terms of Kant's moral theory. He argued that the experience of duty (the analysis of which he deduced from Kant) is the real supernatural element in human life; in short, one's experience of the moral law is one's experience of the divine. Thus, revealed religion amounts to an acknowledgment of being bound by a principle (of morality) that cannot be deduced from the world of sensation.

When the work was published, the author's name was omitted and the reading public assumed that Kant was the author. Eventually, Kant denied authorship, praised the work, and cited the rightful author. This error on the part of the publisher made Fichte's career.

The year after publication he married Johanna. After their marriage, Fichte and Johanna continued to live in Switzerland. During this time, Fichte published two pamphlets anonymously, *Zurückforderung der Denkfreiheit von der Fürsten Europens* (1793; reclamation of the freedom of thought from the princes of Europe) and *Beitrag zur Berichtigung der Urteile des Publikums über die französische Revolution* (1793; contributions designed to correct the judgment of the public on the French Revolution). In these works, he was influenced by Gotthold Ephraim Lessing's concerns with freedom of thought and toleration and defended the ideal of free speech as an inalienable right. Unfortunately, these political views earned for him the label of a radical.

In 1794, at the age of thirty-two, he was appointed to a professorship at the University of Jena on the recommendation of Johann Wolfgang von Goethe. Fichte had been working on foundational problems in epistemology and metaphysics for some time and now combined these domains of philosophical investigation into a science of knowledge, the *Wissenschaftslehre*. His first major texts on the subject, *Über den Begriff der Wissenschaftslehre and Grundlage der gesamten Wissenschaftslehre*

(combined translation as *The Science of Knowledge*, 1868), were published the same year of his appointment.

Kant lies at the basis of all Fichte's writings, but even though Fichte embraced Kant's moral philosophy, he completely rejected Kant's metaphysical notion of the thing-in-itself (*Ding-an-sich*). This concept refers to that which lies "behind" and causes experience. Yet there can be no answer to the question of whether the world is identical to the way it is experienced (because an answer would entail taking a viewpoint that stands above experience and measuring its correspondence). Since one can-

---

OUTLINE OF THE DOCTRINE OF KNOWLEDGE

Near the end of his life, Johann Gottlieb Fichte published a summary of the epistemological ideas he had worked out in earlier texts. The following excerpt makes clear Fichte's place within the history of German philosophy. By conceiving of God as absolute knowing, Fichte anticipates Georg Wilhelm Friedrich Hegel's later formulation, but by conceiving of this knowledge as unchanging, he remains rooted within the eighteenth century. Hegel's nineteenth century epistemology would emphasize that absolute knowing comes only at the end of history, as a result of the evolution of reality over time.

The Doctrine of Knowledge, apart from all special and definite *knowing*, proceeds immediately upon Knowledge itself, in the essential unity in which it recognises Knowledge as existing; and it raises this question in the first place—How this Knowledge can come into being, and what it is in its inward and essential Nature?

The following must be apparent:—There is but One who is absolutely by and through himself,—namely, God; and God is not the mere dead conception to which we have thus given utterance, but he is in himself pure Life. He can neither change nor determine himself in aught within himself, nor become any other Being; for his Being contains within it all his Being and all possible Being, and neither within him nor out of him can any new Being arise.

If, therefore, Knowledge must be, and yet be not God himself, then, since there is nothing but God, it can only be God *out of* himself,—God's Being out of his Being,—his Manifestation, in which he dwells wholly as he is in himself, while within himself he also still remains wholly such as he is. But such a Manifestation is a picture or *Schema*.

If there be such a Schema—and this can only become evident through its immediate being, seeing that it is immediate—it can only be because God is; and, so surely as God is, it cannot but be. It is, however, by no means to be conceived of as a work of God, effected by some particular act, whereby a change is wrought in himself; but it is to be conceived of as an immediate consequence of his Being. It is absolutely, according to the Form of his Being, just as he himself is absolutely; although it is not he himself, but his Schema.

Source: Johann Gottlieb Fichte, *Outline of the Doctrine of Knowledge.* In *The Popular Works of Johann Gottlieb Fichte* (London: Trübner, 1889). http://www.marxists.org/reference/subject/philosophy/works/ge/fichte.htm. Accessed September, 2005.

not know in principle if there is perfect correspondence between one's experience and the thing that causes that experience, one is forced to conclude that the thing-in-itself is absolutely unknowable. Because Fichte rejected the notion of such a cause of experience, only the phenomenal realm was left. This is the starting point of all idealistic philosophies, the world as it appears in one's experience.

The great problem for Fichte was to account for the fact that experiences are of two sorts, namely subjective and objective, or what appears as coming from one's own mind and what does not. The philosopher conceptually isolates the two fundamental facts of experience, the subject and the object, and attempts to explain all experience in terms of one or the other. The attempt that begins with the object (of experience) must ultimately make recourse to the thing-in-itself and is labeled dogmatism by Fichte. The other approach, idealism, begins with the subject (of experience) and explains experience ultimately through recourse to the thought that lies behind the conscious subject. Only this approach allows for freedom of action. Most important, Fichte argued that the choice between these two is ultimately based on the character of the philosopher. Since freedom belongs to the realm of the subject, a philosopher aware of and concerned with the fact of freedom will choose idealism.

Within this general idealistic approach, Fichte argued that there are three fundamental principles that characterize the metaphysical structure of the universe. All the particular sciences are derived from these principles, which do not admit of further justification or grounding. The first and, logically, ultimate principle is "the ego posits itself," or, in effect, reality is conceived of as activity.

Fichte already had ruled out the thing-in-itself, so reality is not ultimately material, it is ideal, or thought or spirit. Yet even as ideal, the fundamental nature of reality is not substance, it is thought activity. This activity is the absolute ego, by which Fichte does not mean the individual self, soul, "I," or whatever might be meant by the term "ego" in contemporary psychology. He means the primordial, total, infinite activity of existence.

The second principle is that this prime activity creates for itself a "field." The transcendental ego posits the non-ego and in so doing limits and defines itself by creating the domain within which it realizes itself. The third principle is that the absolute spirit posits a limited ego in opposition to a limited non-ego. One now has the particular subjects and objects of empirical knowledge, that is, knowers and what is known.

In Kant's philosophy, the concept of the transcendental ego had served the function of making the experience and moral action of the individual possible. Fichte argued that a trans-experiential, unindividuated ego was the ground or source of all being, including finite, experiencing selves.

In the following years, Fichte developed the ethical aspect of his philosophy. In 1796, he published *Grundlage des Naturrechts nach Principien der Wissenschaftslehre* (*The Science of Rights*, 1886, 1889) and in 1798 he published *Das System der Sittenlehre nach den Principien der Wissenschaftslehre* (*The Science of Ethics as Based on the Science of Knowledge*, 1897).

In Fichte's moral philosophy, the choices of the individual are expressions of the striving of the absolute ego, if the individual acts in accord with the moral law. The free activity of the absolute spirit has as its end increased self-determination or definition (as free, self-defining activity). Since the absolute ego expresses its free, determining activity through individual selves, each individual self strives to determine itself to strive after complete freedom. Thus, freedom itself becomes the end of moral activity. With these developments of his moral philosophy, Fichte had become the preeminent philosopher in Germany.

While at Jena, Fichte coedited a monthly philosophical journal, the *Philosophisches Journal einer Gesellschaft teutscher Gelehrten*. In 1798, he published an article in this journal entitled "Concerning the Foundation of Our Belief in Divine Government of the World," in which he argued that if the world is considered from a standpoint outside itself, then it is seen to be only a "reflection of our own activity." Accordingly, God is not needed to explain the existence of the sensed world.

Fichte iterated an identification of God with the moral order of the universe (equating God with the absolute ego). On the basis of these claims, he was charged, in a series of anonymous pamphlets, with atheism and unfitness for teaching. The Saxon government ordered the Universities of Leipzig and Wittenberg to impound all copies of the journal in which the articles appeared and requested the governments of the neighboring German states to follow suit. Fichte responded by publishing two essays insisting that his views were not atheistic though they differed from the Judeo-Christian conception of a personal God.

The grand duke of Weimar was finally approached concerning the issue and, because he was dedicated to free research, would have been content with a censure of Fichte. Anticipating this, Fichte declared in writing to the authorities that he would not submit to censure that, when acknowledged by the government, was tantamount to dismissal. Fichte left the university in 1799 and settled in Berlin. Surprisingly, though Goethe had supported Fichte's acceptance at Jena, he now became an ardent supporter of his dismissal. In addition, Kant published a statement in which he emphatically separated his own philosophy from that of Fichte.

In the year after his dismissal, Fichte published a popularization of his moral views, *Die Bestimmung des Menschen* (1800; *The Vocation of Man*, 1848). In 1805, Fichte accepted a professorship at Erlangen. Yet within two years he returned to Berlin and shortly thereafter published *Reden an die deutsche Nation* (1808; *Addresses to the German Nation*, 1922). In this work, he advocated national educational policies that emphasized the development of the individual's conscience and capacity for moral action. When these traits were fully realized in adulthood, according to Fichte, the German people would be worthy of being spiritual leaders of the world. Fichte believed that the German people were best fitted for such leadership because Napoleon I had betrayed the ideals as expressed in the French Revolution.

Fichte's metaphysics took on deeply religious overtones toward the end of his life. He came to equate the absolute ego with the God of traditional religion. In 1806, he published *Die Anweisung zum seligen Leben: Oder, Auch die Religionslehre* (*The Way Towards the Blessed Life*, 1844). In this work, Fichte claimed that the whole purpose of life is to attain knowledge of and love of God.

The final university appointment came for Fichte in 1811, when he was made rector of the newly formed University of Berlin. Because his temperament made it difficult to work with him, he did not remain at this post for long. He did continue to lecture throughout 1812-1813. During these years, Johanna worked at a hospital nursing the sick and those wounded in the Napoleonic Wars. In the course of her work, she contracted a fever, and while Fichte was nursing her back to health he also became ill. The malady proved fatal in his case, and he died on January 27, 1814.

SIGNIFICANCE

Johann Gottlieb Fichte exercised a tremendous influence on philosophy in Germany. He personally knew the leading figures of the Romantic movement. Friedrich von Schlegel, Fichte's student in 1796, closely followed the intellectual footsteps of his master. Schlegel later turned to Baruch Spinoza and Gottfried Wilhelm Leibniz and eventually became the most prominent leader of the German Romantic movement. Friedrich Wilhelm Joseph von Schelling, a professor at Jena, argued that the absolute ego could be apprehended in a direct intuition (and not merely posited by pure practical reason as in Fichte's system). One of Schelling's early journal articles was a comparison of the philosophies of Fichte and Spinoza. Fichte met Friedrich Schleiermacher during his Berlin years. He was, however, very critical of the free morals and glorification of sentimentality of the Romanticists and quickly dissociated himself from the movement.

Most important, Fichte influenced Georg Wilhelm Friedrich Hegel, who had succeeded Fichte in 1800 as professor of philosophy at Jena. Hegel's first book was a comparison of the philosophies of Fichte and Schelling. Fichte's change of the Kantian transcendental ego into an unindividuated absolute activity paved the way for Hegel's development of Absolute Idealism. Fichte's philosophy also influenced Thomas Carlyle.

In his own day, Fichte was respected as much for his moral character as for his philosophy. He was regarded as extremely conscientious, self-demanding and disciplined. The epigraph on his tomb reads, "Thy teachers shall shine as the brightness of the firmament, and they that turn many to righteousness as the stars that shine for ever and ever."

—*Mark Pestana*

FURTHER READING

Adamson, Robert. *Fichte*. Edinburgh, Scotland: William Blackwood and Sons, 1881. Contains a long biography. Traces the evolution of *The Science of Knowledge* from its early to later phase. Argues that the work's philosophy never rids itself of subjective idealism and that it was influential only in its earlier formulations.

Breazeale, Daniel, and Tom Rockmore. *New Essays on Ficthe's Later Jena Wissenschaftslehre*. Evanston, Ill.: Northwestern University Press, 2002. Collection of essays analyzing Fichte's *Wissenschaftslehre Nova Methoda*, published in 1796-1799.

Everett, Charles Carroll. *Fichte's "Science of Knowledge": A Critical Exposition*. Chicago: S. C. Griggs, 1884. Compares Hegel's and Arthur Schopenhauer's philosophies to Fichte's. Argues that Fichte fails to reconcile the concept of finitude with the doctrine of the absolute. More than half of the work is devoted to exposition of Fichte's three fundamental principles.

Fichte, Johann Gottlieb. *Fichte: Early Philosophical Writings*. Translated and edited by Daniel Breazeale. Ithaca, N.Y.: Cornell University Press, 1988. Contains a long biographical introductory essay by the translator and a substantive preface to each of the ten selections.

Hohler, T. P. *Imagination and Reflection, Intersubjectivity: Fichte's "Grundlage" of 1794*. The Hague, the Netherlands: Martinus Nijhoff, 1982. Devoted to the problem of finitude and the philosophy of the "I" in Fichte's early writings. Argues that the transcendental "I" is essentially and inherently intersubjective; that is, intersubjectivity is argued to be a transcendental constituent of "I-ness."

La Vopa, Anthony J. *Fichte: The Self and the Calling of Philosophy, 1762-1799*. New York: Cambridge University Press, 2001. Biography recounting Fichte's life from birth until his resignation from the university at Jena in 1799. Examines Fichte's philosophy, tracing his ideas in German Lutheranism, eighteenth century culture and philosophy, revolutionary politics, and the emergence of German universities.

Talbot, E. B. *The Fundamental Principle of Fichte's Philosophy*. New York: Macmillan, 1906. Concentrates on the changes Fichte made in his fundamental principle between the early and later periods of his development. Argues that differences noted by critics are overstated and the fundamental characterization as activity remains constant throughout.

Zöller, Günter. *Ficthe's Transcendental Philosophy: The Original Duplicity of Intelligence and Will*. New York: Cambridge University Press, 1998. Examines Fichte's philosophy of the self and its place in the world, using information found in his recently discovered lectures. Describes how Fichte integrated the acts of thinking and willing into a unified system of freedom.

See also: Johann Wolfgang von Goethe; Immanuel Kant; Friedrich Gottlieb Klopstock; Gotthold Ephraim Lessing.

Related articles in *Great Events from History: The Eighteenth Century, 1701-1800*: October, 1725: Vico Publishes *The New Science*; 1739-1740: Hume Publishes *A Treatise of Human Nature*; April, 1762: Rousseau Publishes *The Social Contract*; July, 1764: Voltaire Publishes *A Philosophical Dictionary for the Pocket*; 1770: Publication of Holbach's *The System of Nature*; 1781: Kant Publishes *Critique of Pure Reason*; 1784-1791: Herder Publishes His Philosophy of History; 1792-1793: Fichte Advocates Free Speech.

HENRY FIELDING
English novelist

Fielding developed the novel as a carefully plotted form with fully developed characters, dramatic scenes, and serious intent. He also was an effective journalist, a successful dramatist, and, with his brother John, was responsible for establishing the London police force that developed into Scotland Yard.

Born: April 22, 1707; Sharpham Park, Somersetshire, England
Died: October 8, 1754; Lisbon, Portugal
Areas of achievement: Literature, theater, law

EARLY LIFE

Henry Fielding was born at the home of his mother's father near Glastonbury. His ancestry was distinguished. His father was related to the earl of Denbigh and to Lady Mary Pierrepont (Mary Wortley Montagu), who later encouraged his literary efforts. His paternal grandfather was archdeacon of Dorset and a chaplain of King William. Following a family tradition, Henry Fielding's father, Edmund, became a military officer, serving under the first duke of Marlborough at Blenheim and rising eventually to the rank of lieutenant general. Henry's maternal grandfather was a judge of the Queen's Bench, Sir Henry Gould. Although the match between Sarah Gould and Edmund Fielding was an elopement, evidently the judge was reconciled to the match; nevertheless, he took steps to guard his daughter's inheritance from her rather imprudent husband.

Henry was born the year after Sarah and Edmund were married; six other children followed in rapid succession, five daughters and a son. (It was the third daughter, Sarah, who was so close to Henry in later years.) The children were reared on a country estate in Dorsetshire, living a happy life, despite the frequent absence of their restless father, until their mother's death in 1718. After the colonel's remarriage to a woman of dubious social rank, a Roman Catholic as well, the children were placed in various schools to remove them from the unhappy home environment and finally became wards of their grandmother. Henry remained on good terms with his father, as well as with his grandmother. At Eton, he developed a love of the classics, which was later consistently reflected in his works. There, too, he grew into a tall, well-built, graceful man, with brown hair and sparkling eyes that suggested his habitual optimism. Fielding's intelligence, his fascination with human nature, and his perception of the comic side of life were already evident; these qualities would pervade the later poems, pamphlets, plays, and novels that he wrote.

Choosing not to proceed immediately to a university, Fielding lived the life of a gentleman of leisure for several years after leaving Eton. Alternating between country life with his grandmother and exciting visits to London, he postponed the decision as to his life's work. Probably he studied some law; certainly he continued to read and to write. He was unsuccessful in the planned abduction of an heiress in Lyme Regis; he was more successful in charming his cousin, Mary Wortley Montagu, who enjoyed his enthusiasm and encouraged his writing. Because she was one of the most interesting women in London, the friend of wits and nobles alike, she could help her young relative both with advice and with influence. Early in 1728, Fielding's poem "The Masquerade" appeared, supposedly written by Jonathan Swift's character, Lemuel Gulliver. Not surprisingly, it was a burlesque. Less than three weeks later, Fielding's comedy *Love in Several Masques* was produced. It was dedicated to Lady Mary.

Despite his success in London, Fielding decided to complete his education and enrolled in the University of Leiden. At the end of a year and a half, his father was evidently unable to continue remittances, and Henry returned to London, faced with the necessity of earning his own living. As he later remarked, he had to choose between being a hackney writer and a hackney coachman. He chose to write. For him, and for the English novel, it was a momentous decision.

LIFE'S WORK

During the period from 1730 to 1737, Henry Fielding produced more than two dozen plays, including translations of Molière, satirical comedies, burlesques, and farces. The most notable of these was the hilarious literary burlesque, *Tom Thumb: A Tragedy* (1730), which was revised and enlarged the next year under the title *The Tragedy of Tragedies: Or, The Life and Death of Tom Thumb the Great*. The plays delighted his audience, particularly the Tory opposition to Robert Walpole, the powerful prime minister whose spokesman Fielding became.

Henry Fielding. (Library of Congress)

Meanwhile, Fielding had fallen in love with Charlotte Cradock, one of the beauties of Salisbury, where his grandmother, Lady Gould, lived. For four years he courted "Celia," in poetry and in person. Impulsively, in 1734, they eloped and married. It was Charlotte who became the model for Fielding's finest women characters, such as the lovely Sophia Western in *The History of Tom Jones, a Foundling*, which was published in 1749, five years after Charlotte's death. In 1736, Henry and Charlotte had a daughter and, in 1737, another. It was at this point, however, that Fielding lost his livelihood. Infuriated by his ridicule, the Whig government passed the Theatrical Licensing Act, which permitted England's lord chamberlain to censor the theater, thus driving Fielding from the stage.

Desperate, Fielding began to read law, meanwhile beginning his journalistic career by editing the opposition journal *The Champion: Or, British Mercury* as well as turning out any kind of translation or essay that might help to support his family. Although he was called to the bar in 1740, Fielding found that his legal fees were insufficient for his needs and so continued his writing career as well. By 1741, his situation had worsened. His health was failing, probably from overwork; his debts were troubling; and his older child was ill. Disgusted by the popular success of Samuel Richardson's novel *Pamela:*

FIELDING ON MODERN PHILOSOPHY

In an interlude in Tom Jones, *Henry Fielding comments upon the modern, dispassionate skepticism with which the subject of love and the passions has been treated by contemporary philosophers. His commentary is, characteristically, as ironic as it is insightful.*

In our last book we have been obliged to deal pretty much with the passion of love; and in our succeeding book shall be forced to handle this subject still more largely. It may not therefore in this place be improper to apply ourselves to the examination of that modern doctrine, by which certain philosophers, among many other wonderful discoveries, pretend to have found out, that there is no such passion in the human breast.

Whether these philosophers be the same with that surprising sect, who are honourably mentioned by the late Dr. Swift, as having, by the mere force of genius alone, without the least assistance of any kind of learning, or even reading, discovered that profound and invaluable secret that there is no God; or whether they are not rather the same with those who some years since very much alarmed the world, by showing that there were no such things as virtue or goodness really existing in human nature, and who deduced our best actions from pride, I will not here presume to determine. In reality, I am inclined to suspect, that all these several finders of truth, are the very identical men who are by others called the finders of gold. The method used in both these searches after truth and after gold, being indeed one and the same, viz., the searching, rummaging, and examining into a nasty place; indeed, in the former instances, into the nastiest of all places, A BAD MIND.

But though in this particular, and perhaps in their success, the truth-finder and the gold-finder may very properly be compared together; yet in modesty, surely, there can be no comparison between the two; for who ever heard of a goldfinder that had the impudence or folly to assert, from the ill success of his search, that there was no such thing as gold in the world? whereas the truth-finder, having raked out that jakes, his own mind, and being there capable of tracing no ray of divinity, nor anything virtuous or good, or lovely, or loving, very fairly, honestly, and logically concludes that no such things exist in the whole creation.

Source: Henry Fielding, *The History of Tom Jones: A Foundling*. Vol. 1 (New York: P. F. Collier & Son, 1917), book 4, section 1, paragraphs 1-3. http://www.bartleby.com/301/. Accessed September, 2005.

virtuous Joseph, the novel soon transcended mere mockery of Richardson, to create a panorama of English society, high and low, virtuous and vicious, ranging from scoundrelly lawyers and hypocritical ladies to the saintly but human Parson Adams, who is generally considered to be Fielding's finest character, illustrating Fielding's faith that virtue will at last triumph, however it may be tested.

Fielding's own trials were not over. His older child, Charlotte, died just after *Joseph Andrews* was published, and his wife died in 1744. For a time he continued his journalistic efforts, which were now devoted to support the Hanoverians against the Jacobites. In 1747, Fielding married Mary Daniel, his housekeeper, who had formerly been his wife's maid. Although she bore him five children, she could never take the place of Charlotte, either in his heart or in his works.

In 1748, however, Fielding's Hanoverian loyalties were repaid when he was appointed a Bow Street magistrate and later magistrate of Middlesex. With his blind half brother John, who soon joined him, Fielding could now attempt in actuality to protect the innocent and to punish the guilty, just as Providence did in his novels. It is interesting that in a short novel published in 1743 (but perhaps written much earlier), *The History of the Life of the Late Mr. Jonathan Wild the Great*, Fielding had dealt with a real criminal who had been hanged at Tyburn in 1725 and who was compared to Robert Walpole, much like Peachum in John Gay's *The Beggar's Opera* (1728). As magistrate, Fielding attempted to break up the street gangs who terrorized London. His effective Bow Street Runners eventually developed into the London police force known as Scotland Yard.

In 1749, Fielding published the second of his three major novels, the rollicking *Tom Jones*, whose innocent young hero is initiated into the ways of lust, love, and fi-

Or, Virtue Rewarded (1740-1741), Fielding published a parody, *An Apology for the Life of Mrs. Shamela Andrews* (1741). Although it did not solve his financial problems, the short work was significant, for with it Fielding had embarked upon fiction. Prompted by his desire to continue the satire of *Pamela*, he now began a novel about her brother, titled *The History of the Adventures of Joseph Andrews, and of His Friend Mr. Abraham Adams*. It was published in February, 1742. With it Fielding won his rank among the world's greatest writers. Beginning with Lady Booby's attempts to seduce the

nally restraint for the sake of love. In contrast to his essentially decent Tom, Fielding exposes dozens of hypocrites, all of whom, however, are convincing as people as well as targets of satire. Magnificently plotted, *Tom Jones* takes its characters on the road, as *Joseph Andrews* had done, thus enabling Fielding to bring together people from every level of life.

Fielding's final novel, *Amelia*, was published in 1751. Although it was his most popular novel, it lacks the comic grandeur of *Joseph Andrews* and *Tom Jones*. The story of a married couple who innocently fall afoul of the law, it takes the noble Amelia Booth, again a portrait of Charlotte, and her frailer husband through temptations to safety and prosperity.

In 1754, because of illness, Fielding was forced to resign his judicial position. In search of health, he traveled to Portugal, writing the travel book *The Journal of a Voyage to Lisbon* (1755) as he proceeded. He did not live to see it published, however, dying in Lisbon on October 8, 1754.

SIGNIFICANCE

Before Henry Fielding, the novel generally related a series of adventures in the life of a single character who was also the narrator; this pretense of autobiography guaranteed the work's respectability. The scene was sketchy; atmosphere was almost nonexistent; characters were not fully developed. It is true that Daniel Defoe's *Moll Flanders* (1722) and *Robinson Crusoe* (1719) do seem to spring into a fuller life than earlier characters and that Richardson's *Pamela* and *Clarissa* (1747-1748) reveal psychological complexities not previously found in fiction. When Fielding invented his "comic prose epic," however, he was appropriating for the novel the careful plotting and the satirical purpose of classical comedy along with the stylistic devices and the high purpose of the traditional epic. No longer would the novel pretend to be real and thus worthwhile. Without apology, Fielding asserted that his works were fiction, but like Sir Philip Sidney before him, he insisted that they were therefore even more true, even more instructive, because they were an imitation of nature.

Admitting that his novels were fictional, Fielding could exploit all the possibilities of authorial omniscience. When he liked, he could stop the story to make an observation about life or literature. If he wished, he would address the reader as a friend, so skillfully that even William Makepeace Thackeray could not successfully imitate him. Although his plots were flawless, Fielding could choose to interpolate a seemingly unre-

lated story, concealing from the reader that the characters, the events, and the themes of the story were essential to the central situation of his novel.

Because of Fielding, novelists had a new respect for their art and a new license to experiment with technique. Above all, they began to discover that all of society and all of human life were their province. Perhaps more than any other writer of the eighteenth century, Fielding gave the world the modern novel.

—*Rosemary M. Canfield Reisman*

FURTHER READING

Allen, Walter. *The English Novel: A Short Critical History*. New York: E. P. Dutton, 1954. A clear, well-written history of the novel that underlines Fielding's place in its development. The introductory chapters, as well as those on Richardson and Fielding, provide a background for the study of any individual novel.

Bertelsen, Lance. *Henry Fielding at Work: Magistrate, Businessman, Writer*. New York: Palgrave, 2000. Describes how Fielding's experiences as a magistrate, businessman, and writer affected his literature.

Butt, John. *Fielding*. London: Longmans, Green, 1954. A brief but penetrating evaluation of Fielding's place in literary history. Integrates the pattern of Fielding's life with the pattern of his novels.

Cross, Wilbur L. *The History of Henry Fielding*. 3 vols. New Haven, Conn.: Yale University Press, 1918. Reprint. New York: Russell and Russell, 1963. Still the standard biography of Fielding, this work is scholarly and readable. Fascinating as well as essential because Cross summarizes and quotes Fielding's plays and less easily available works, and because he includes contemporary comments (and gossip) about Fielding and his works.

Dudden, F. Homes. *Henry Fielding: His Life, Works, and Times*. 2 vols. Oxford, England: Clarendon Press, 1952. This work is particularly valuable for its description of Fielding's England, especially the plight of the poor, the problem of crime in eighteenth century London, and the deficiencies of the judicial system. Dudden details Fielding's effective responses to these problems.

Pagliaro, Harold E. *Henry Fielding: A Literary Life*. New York: St. Martin's Press, 1998. Pagliaro demonstrates how Fielding's complex personality and attitudes contributed to the style and content of his novels and plays.

Paulson, Ronald. *The Life of Henry Fielding: A Critical Biography*. Malden, Mass.: Blackwell, 2000. Paulson explains how Fielding used his storytelling to alter his personal experiences, including his experiments with different professions.

Paulson, Ronald, and Thomas Lockwood, eds. *Henry Fielding: The Critical Heritage*. London: Routledge and Kegan Paul, 1969. Like the other books in the Critical Heritage series, this one collects comments about a writer and his works from contemporary sources, ranging from published reviews to personal letters. The statements by other writers, such as Alexander Pope, Samuel Richardson, Samuel Johnson, Tobias Smollett, Thomas Gray, and Horace Walpole, are illuminating.

Stevenson, Lionel. *The English Novel: A Panorama*. Boston: Houghton Mifflin, 1960. Stevenson's book is organized chronologically rather than in separate chapters for each writer, so it can more easily show relationships and influences. Includes an interesting

discussion of the relationship between Sarah Fielding, also a writer, and her brother Henry.

Van Ghent, Dorothy. *The English Novel: Form and Function*. New York: Harper & Row, 1953. Contains essays on eighteen novels, including *Tom Jones*, and Miguel de Cervantes's *Don Quixote de la Mancha* (1605, 1615), which was an important influence on Fielding's work. Van Ghent's analysis of structure is outstanding.

See also: Joseph Addison; Daniel Defoe; Samuel Johnson; Charlotte Lennox; Mary Wortley Montagu; Alexander Pope; Samuel Richardson; Jonathan Swift; Robert Walpole.

Related articles in *Great Events from History: The Eighteenth Century, 1701-1800:* January 29, 1728: Gay Produces the First Ballad Opera; 1740-1741: Richardson's *Pamela* Establishes the Modern Novel; 1742: Fielding's *Joseph Andrews* Satirizes English Society.

JOHANN BERNHARD FISCHER VON ERLACH
Austrian architect

The founder of the Austrian Baroque movement, Fischer von Erlach was the pivotal figure in the artistic life of late seventeenth century and early eighteenth century Austria, creating an architectural style that embodied the imperial pride of the revived Habsburg Dynasty.

Born: July 20, 1656 (baptized); Graz, Austria
Died: April 5, 1723; Vienna, Austria
Area of achievement: Architecture

EARLY LIFE
Johann Baptist Fischer, the father of Johann Bernhard Fischer von Erlach (yoh-HAHN BURN-hahrt FIHSH-ur fohn UR-lahkh), was a sculptor in Graz, Austria. He had sufficient means to send his son, whom he had trained as a sculptor and stucco worker, to Italy to complete his artistic education. It was natural that the younger Fischer should go south for his apprenticeship. The lands of the Austrian crown had long been little more than an artistic extension of the Italian Baroque, with itinerant architects, painters, and stucco workers from northern Italy, especially from the Como region, disseminating there the aesthetic canons of the Jesuit-dominated Counter-Reformation. Fischer would be the first native Austrian to challenge this virtual monopoly of the Italians, and in so doing he would become the father of the Austrian and German Baroque.

Nevertheless, Fischer's sojourn in Italy proved immensely rewarding. Although the exact length of his stay is unknown, he seems to have spent at least twelve years there between the early 1670's and around 1686, working and studying first in Rome and then in Naples. In Rome, Gian Lorenzo Bernini was still alive, and Francesco Borromini was not long dead. The work of both men greatly influenced the young Fischer, but he seems to have been especially fascinated by Borromini. Italy had much to teach him, but he was no mere architect's apprentice or a hanger-on in artists' ateliers. Already, he possessed a voracious appetite for reading and learning and a boundless intellectual curiosity that, in time, would make him something of a Renaissance man.

By 1687, Fischer had returned to Graz and, by 1690, he was established in Vienna. Between 1688 and 1689, he worked (with the Italian Lorenzo Burnacini) on the Dreifaltigkeitssaule, or Pestsaule, the sculptured column erected by Leopold I in the Graben to remember a recent plague epidemic. In 1688, he also began his first major architectural commission for Count Michael Althan at Schloss Frain (Vranov, Czechoslovakia), on a magnificent cliff-top site, where he designed a freestanding domed Ahsensaal, a hall in which the count's ancestors were commemorated, with ten niches in which stood life-size statues of ancestors and with a frescoed ceiling representing the familial virtues of the Althans. The painter was Johann Michael Rottmayr, a native Austrian from the Salzkammergut, who later worked with Fischer in Salzburg and in the Karlskirche.

By now, Fischer had attracted the attention of the Habsburg court, and on the occasion of the crowning of Leopold's heir (the future emperor Joseph I) as king of the Romans in 1690, he was commissioned to construct an elaborate triumphal arch, for which the exuberant design still exists. Thereafter, he was appointed architectural tutor to Joseph, presumably on the strength of his growing reputation as the first Austrian architect to rival the ubiquitous Italians (Leopold was committed to reducing French and Italian influences at his court). He was also ennobled, aquiring the title "von Erlach." On his accession in 1705, Joseph I appointed Fischer von Erlach chief imperial inspector of buildings and festivities. The emperor stood as godfather to the architect's eldest son, Joseph Emanuel, who was to pursue a distinguished career as an architect in his own right. It was Joseph I who requested Fischer von Erlach to design for him a palace at Schönbrunn to outshine Versailles. Although the palace was never built, the design survives and has been described as "one of the great visions of architectural history."

LIFE'S WORK

During the first fifteen years of the eighteenth century, Fischer von Erlach achieved his full stature as an architect. It was during these years that he set his distinctive mark upon Vienna, executing many commissions for town palaces for the nobles of the empire, who were eager to employ the emperor's favorite to build residences that would advertise both their wealth and their taste. The first of these commissions was the palace he built for Prince Eugene of Savoy between 1695 and 1700 on the narrow Himmelpfortgasse, later to be enlarged by his rival, and the prince's favorite architect, Johann Lucas von Hildebrandt. He gave it a Roman facade of the kind that would become his hallmark and designed a *Treppenhaus* (an entrance hall with a double staircase) that ranks as one of the finest examples of a form for which the Austrian and German Baroque is rightly famous. The upper level of the staircase is supported by magnificent muscular *atlantes*, which Fischer von Erlach would employ again to great effect in the Batthyány and Trautson palaces and in the Bohemian Chancellery.

Eugene's town palace was followed by the construction of the Batthyány palace (1699-1706), the Klesheim palace at Salzburg (1700-1709), the Bohemian Chancel-

lery (1708-1714), the Trautson palace (1710-1716), the Schwarzenberg palace (1713), and the Clam-Gallas palace in Prague (begun in 1713). Notwithstanding these secular commissions, mainly in Vienna, Fischer von Erlach had also established a reputation as an ecclesiastical architect, primarily through his work at Salzburg. Largely because of an idiosyncratic dislike of Italian craftspeople on the part of the reigning prince-archbishop of the city, Johann Ernst von Thun-Hohenstein, Fischer von Erlach replaced Johann Caspar Zuccalli as court architect and was commissioned to build there the Dreifaltigkeitskirche (the Church of the Holy Trinity, 1694-1707), the Kollegienkirche (the Collegiate Church of the Benedictine University, 1696-1707), and the Ursulinkirche (the Church of the Ursuline Convent, 1699-1705). In 1709, the archbishop died, and since his successor preferred to employ Hildebrandt, Fischer von Erlach's connection with the archiepiscopal city came to an end. There was also a hiatus in his church-building until 1715, when he began work upon his ecclesiastical masterpiece, the Karlskirche.

By then, he had become by far the most celebrated architect in the emperor's dominions. With his acute intelligence and his wide-ranging interests, there was much of the scholar about him, as well as the artist, and it should come as no surprise to find him a correspondent of the philosopher Gottfried Wilhelm Leibniz. Indeed, it has been suggested that Fischer von Erlach aspired to create in stone a transcendent vision of the harmony and order inherent in the mind of the Leibnizian "Divine Mover."

In 1712, Fischer von Erlach dedicated to Charles VI the preliminary manuscript version of his lavishly illustrated history of architecture, *Entwurff einer historischen Architektur* (pub. 1721; *A Plan of Civil and Historical Architecture in the Representation of the Most Noted Buildings of Foreign Nations Both Ancient and Modern*, 1730). The treatise was to be one of the most influential architectural works of the eighteenth century. It was characteristic of Fischer von Erlach's intellectual curiosity that his researches led him far beyond the world of classical antiquity to Egypt, the Middle East, and Asia. He seems, for example, to have had an appreciation for Islamic architecture that was rare among Europeans at that time and indeed for the following two centuries.

In 1713, the plague again struck Vienna, and in fulfillment of a vow made at that time to Saint Carlo Borromeo for the city's deliverance, the emperor determined to construct a great basilica for the saint facing across what was then open ground toward the Hofburg, the imperial palace. Leading architects of the day such as Hildebrandt were invited to submit designs, but it was Fischer von Erlach's plan for the basilica that was accepted, and in 1715 he began work upon his masterpiece. The foundation stone was laid in 1716, but it was not until 1738 that the Karlskirche was finally dedicated. At the time of Fischer von Erlach's death in 1723, however, the frame of the church was already standing (the dome and the dome drum being completed during 1723-1724), and under the direction of Joseph Emanuel Fischer von Erlach, the dead architect's son whom Charles VI held in great esteem, the project went forward in accordance with the original design.

The internal arrangements of the Karlskirche center on a longitudinal oval at right angles to the facade, crowned by a mighty dome, but it is the facade of the Karlskirche that gives it a unique place among Baroque churches. As was his custom, Fischer von Erlach designed the front exterior with great care. The central section was to consist of a Roman portico, behind which would be seen the great high-drummed dome above the nave. The portico was then linked to two rather squat campanili by concave walls, in front of which were to stand two immense columns derived from Trajan's column in Rome and similar to a pair that had originally been incorporated into his grandiose design for Schönbrunn. Both columns were to be encircled, like their Roman original, by commemorative bas reliefs, in this case illustrating the life of Saint Carlo Borromeo.

Just as Fischer von Erlach did not live to see the completion of the Karlskirche, so he did not see the completion of his other masterpiece, the Hofbibliothek or imperial library. The Hofburg, for generations the Vienna residence of the Habsburgs, had deteriorated greatly, and Charles VI turned to Fischer von Erlach for a master plan for its renovation. Between 1716 and 1720, therefore, the latter drew up designs for an imperial library as the first stage of the rebuilding. It was to represent, symbolically, a temple of knowledge and science, perhaps reflecting the ideas of Leibniz, who certainly took a great interest in its design. Delays resulting from lack of funds and the declining health of the architect meant that the finished building, erected between 1722 and 1738, was as much the work of Joseph Emanuel Fischer von Erlach as it was of his father. Nevertheless, the son was meticulous in following his father's original plan, although he himself deserves full credit for the quality of the finished interior, with its ceiling frescoes by Daniel Gran, who had worked with both father and son on the Schwarzenberg palace.

SIGNIFICANCE

One of the most original architects of the late Baroque period, Johann Bernhard Fischer von Erlach was the founder of the *Kaiserstil*, or imperial style, which spread from Austria, in one form or another, throughout the Holy Roman Empire. Possessing an equal aptitude for ecclesiastical and secular building, he left an indelible mark upon the landscape of Vienna. Yet unlike many of his contemporaries, Fischer von Erlach was no mere technician: Rather, he was the embodiment of the notion (perhaps derived from Leibniz) that the architect could be both the formulator and the interpreter of the ideals of the age, an assumption as implicit in his great treatise on world architecture as it was in the elaborate symbolism of the Karlskirche and the Hofbibliothek.

—Gavin R. G. Hambly

FURTHER READING

Aurenhammer, Hans. *J. B. Fischer von Erlach.* Cambridge, Mass.: Harvard University Press, 1973. This is the only book available in English devoted solely to Fischer von Erlach. As such, it must be regarded as an invaluable study.

Fergusson, Frances D. "St. Charles' Church, Vienna: The Iconography of Its Architecture." *Journal of the Society of Architectural Historians* 29 (1970): 318-326. A detailed account of the imperial symbolism attached to the building and decoration of the Karlskirche. Essential reading.

Fischer von Erlach, Johann Bernhard. *Entwurff einer historischen Architektur, in Abbildung unterschiedener berühmten Gebäude, des Alterthums und fremder Völcker.* Ridgewood, N.J.: Gregg Press, 1964. Fischer von Erlach's treatise on the history of architecture, reprinted in the second edition of 1725, together with the English translation of 1730, entitled *A Plan of Civil and Historical Architecture, in the Representation of the Most Noted Buildings of Foreign Nations, Both Ancient and Modern.*

Hift, Fred. "Salzburg." *Europe* no. 358 (July/August, 1996): 36. Describes Schloss Klessheim, the ducal palace designed by Fischer von Erlach.

Norberg-Schulz, Christian. *Late Baroque and Rococo Architecture.* New York: Harry N. Abrams, 1974. An outstanding survey of its subject, excellently illustrated with photographs and ground plans.

Sedlmayr, Hans. *Johann Bernhard Fischer von Erlach.* Vienna: Herold, 1956. The definitive monograph on the architect. In German.

Tapié, V. L. *The Age of Grandeur: Baroque and Classicism in Europe*. Translated by A. Ross Williamson. London: Weidenfeld & Nicolson, 1960. Virtually an instant classic upon publication, this book provides the best general background to the art and aesthetics of Baroque Europe.

Wangermann, Ernst. *The Austrian Achievement, 1700-1800*. London: Thames & Hudson, 1973. An excellent introduction to Austria's golden age, setting Fischer von Erlach's activities in historical perspective.

Weber, N. F. "Baroque Splendors of Vienna's Schwarzenberg Palace." *Architectural Digest* 47, no. 10 (September, 1990): 116. Photo essay about the palace, designed by Fischer von Erlach and Johann Lucas von Hildebrandt.

See also: Charles VI; Johann Lucas von Hildebrandt.
Related articles in *Great Events from History: The Eighteenth Century, 1701-1800*: 1715-1737: Building of the Karlskirche; May, 1720-December, 1721: Last Major Outbreak of Plague; 1748-1755: Construction of Istanbul's Nur-u Osmaniye Complex; 1762: *The Antiquities of Athens* Prompts Architectural Neoclassicism.

JOHN FITCH
American inventor

Fitch was one of the earliest inventors to produce serviceable steamboats. Although an adept inventor, he was unable to demonstrate the steamboat's economic value and thus cultivate support for his work. Instead, Robert Fulton is remembered as the inventor in 1807 of the American steamboat, many years after Fitch's pioneering work, which went unacknowledged by Fulton and others.

Born: January 21, 1743; Windsor (now South Windsor), Connecticut
Died: July 2, 1798; Bardstown, Kentucky
Area of achievement: Architecture

EARLY LIFE

The younger son of a Connecticut Yankee farmer, John Fitch was taken out of school at age eight and pressed into field chores. Despite a lack of encouragement by his poor and penny-pinching father and stepmother—his mother having died when the boy was less than five years old—Fitch was sufficiently self-motivated to acquire and master a book on elementary arithmetic and another on geography. At age seventeen he ran off to Rocky Hill, Connecticut, and was hired as a sailor, but the unbearable conditions and a storm prompted his early return home.

In Rocky Hill he became apprenticed to two watchmakers, the Cheany brothers, who overworked, bullied, and starved him. Fitch was assigned primarily work in the fields and household chores rather than being taught the clock trade—except for some handicrafts in metals. Buying his way out of his apprenticeship, Fitch started to

journey and wander beginning in 1769. From New England, he went to Trenton, New Jersey, where he stayed until 1775, spending part of the time in Bucks County, Pennsylvania. He made brass buttons for a tinsman, was apprenticed to a silversmith, cleaned and helped repair clocks, was an itinerant peddler, and engaged in other occupations.

During the Revolutionary War years of 1775-1780, Fitch served intermittently in the militia and as a gunsmith repairing weapons. The years 1780-1781, 1782, and 1783-1784 found him undertaking three Western trips as frontiersman, land surveyor, and land jobber. On his second expedition, he became a captive of American Indians in Kentucky but managed to escape. However, his occasional savings and land acquisitions were depleted through currency devaluation and amendments to land allotment laws.

The year 1785 was to change Fitch's life. Observing a stagecoach try to negotiate a bumpy road, Fitch got the idea of applying steam power to drive it. However, given the deplorable highway conditions at the time, he soon shifted to steamboats and expressed surprise on being informed that inventors such as Thomas Savery, Thomas Newcomen, and James Watt in England had already conceived the idea of harnessing steam power for performing useful work. That is when Fitch, with practically no formal schooling or training of any kind in engineering, became a steamboat inventor. The series of difficulties, misfortunes, and injustices that Fitch was to experience in the remaining thirteen years of his life were compounded by his personal circumstances.

This towering man with a twitching face had the appearance and manners of a crank, a lack of social graces and political savvy, and poor judgment of his fellow human beings. Among other things, his marriage to Lucy Roberts, by many accounts a woman with a temper who ridiculed and scorned him, was a failure. He deserted her as she was expecting the birth of their second child. Later, Fitch was befriended by a widow and the mistress of his friend and business partner, a German immigrant watchmaker named Henry Voigt who was to assist Fitch closely—and later be his rival—in much of his steamboat work. When Fitch offered to marry Mary Kraft to legitimize her status and that of the child she had borne to Voigt, she refused, even though she occasionally signed as "Mary Fitch." Eventually, Voigt and his mistress made Fitch the scapegoat of the scandal and turned on him.

With all this going on, Fitch still found the energy to promote his Deist "universal society" for the free discussion of religious, philosophical, social, and political ideas "for the benefit of mankind and the support of civil government." However, in this universal society, he proposed to stimulate freedom of thought by throwing out any fellow member for "improper conduct," just like the churches he wished to supplant.

John Fitch. (Library of Congress)

LIFE'S WORK

In 1785, Fitch built a 23-inch model steamboat that he presented to the American Philosophical Society in Philadelphia as well as to public figures and scholars. He received only indifferent moral support from the Founding Fathers of the American republic, including George Washington and Benjamin Franklin, to whom Fitch had appealed in person. In fact, Washington and Franklin were backing a suave and polished Virginian and competing steamboat inventor, James Rumsey, who never produced a practical working model. Rumsey and Fitch would have a heated published argument over which of them had first invented the steamboat.

Fitch was equally unsuccessful in getting any funding for his navigation project from the American legislatures. However, between March, 1786, and November, 1787, he obtained fourteen-year exclusive rights for the

building and use of all kinds of watercraft driven by "fire or steam" from New Jersey, Delaware, New York, Pennsylvania, Virginia, and, finally, from the U.S. Congress in 1791. Congress simultaneously granted rights to James Rumsey without recognizing Fitch's seniority.

Fitch's first working model in September, 1785, was a small skiff. The craft had a double-acting cylinder 3 inches in diameter made of brass. Steam was injected at both ends of a piston enabling the engine to make a power stroke. The skiff was driven by means of an endless chain and floats and paddle boards, this method being adopted after abortive experiments with spiral paddle wheels.

The second model, the *Perseverance*, built in 1786, was 45 feet long with a 12-foot beam. The engine now had a single horizontal double-acting 12-inch cylinder. It had six vertical oars on each side attached to an endless chain. The front bank of oars, three on each side, was cranked to dip into and rise from the water to provide propulsion and was followed by the six rear oars in canoe style. The boiler held 500 gallons of water set in 3.5 tons of brickwork.

The third model, called *Steamboat* and built in 1788, was 60 feet long with an 8-foot beam. It had a new boiler of coiled iron pipes to replace the old pot-shaped one. The brickwork now became unnecessary, lightening the load considerably. This boat could run from Philadelphia to Burlington, New Jersey, a distance of some 20 miles, in about three hours, a record at the time. A later version of the boat, the *Experiment*, built in 1790 with an improved engine and boiler, had four broad paddles at the stern operated by a series of gears and chain belts. It reached a record 8 miles per hour upstream. Even though the advertised, regularly scheduled service was extended to Trenton, New Jersey, and the boat was used for excursions on Sundays, the thirty paid passengers whom it carried were insufficient to make it a viable enterprise. The opposition of the competing stagecoach and sailboat operators and, especially, the refusal of stockholders to invest more funds in the company contributed to the financial—not technical—failure of the undertaking.

For other reasons, too, the years 1790-1791 turned out to be critical for Fitch. His petition for the position of master-at-arms was turned down by the Senate, and Congress had decided to grant a patent similar to his to rival inventor Rumsey. Accordingly, an angry and frustrated Fitch wished to "end the fight." He therefore moved back to Kentucky and earned his living as a good silversmith. Yet even as the inventor was filling six notebooks in what was to become his autobiography and which he willed to be unsealed thirty years after his death, he still could not give up his dream of steamboating. He decided to try his luck in Europe.

In 1793, Fitch sailed for France, where he met with his customary misfortunes. His major sponsor—a French public figure named Jacques-Pierre Brissot de Warville—was guillotined in the French Revolution. Shipwrights to build him a boat were impossible to find. His side trip to England, where he had hoped to purchase a more efficient Boulton and Watt engine, was equally unsuccessful because the British government prohibited the engine's export. Moreover, Fitch had been denied permission to return to France.

He thus sailed to Boston, where he worked on the waterfront. Eventually, he was to return to Kentucky, revisiting his hometown in Connecticut along the way. After his quarter century absence, however, his wife and son were barely on speaking terms with him.

In New York in 1796, Fitch made an attempt to experiment with a screw-driven boat on Collect Pond. The craft was 18 feet long with a 6-foot beam. He was now using a two-cylinder engine and an iron boiler. The connecting rod drove a crank on the forward end of the propeller shaft. Fitch failed to get backing for this effort; he built another boat in Bardstown, Kentucky, a side-paddle-wheeler, in 1797-1798. Even though a tavern-keeper had agreed to feed him and provide him a pint of whisky daily, as he was in abject poverty and suffered from rheumatism and despair, he committed suicide. Using his death as an excuse, Chancellor Livingston, Robert Fulton's chief backer, managed to have New York State's patent monopoly to Fitch transferred to Fulton, ostensibly for the public good.

SIGNIFICANCE

Although John Fitch's steamboats proved to be reliable, he had been careless about building and operating costs and about cultivating influential contacts. Thus, he failed to demonstrate the economic value of steam navigation. For all that, the words of this disheartened inventor harboring an overwhelming sense of injustice turned out to be prophetic. He had predicted that someday a more powerful individual would reap fame and fortune from the very invention whose rewards were denied to him. Indeed, in 1807, some twenty years after Fitch had demonstrated to the delegates of the Constitutional Convention in Philadelphia his first working model of a steamboat, the world hailed Robert Fulton's *Clermont* as the first American steamboat, giving Fitch, on whose patent and ideas Fulton may have infringed, no credit whatever.

—Peter B. Heller

FURTHER READING

Boyd, Thomas. *Poor John Fitch, Inventor of the Steamboat*. New York: G. P. Putnam's Sons, 1935. A sympathetic profile of the early inventor. Illustrated.

Deeson, A. F. L. *An Illustrated History of Steamships*. Bourne End, England: Spurnbooks, 1976. Deeson briefly examines contributions to steam navigation made by Fitch and other early inventors. Illustrated.

Fitch, John. *The Autobiography of John Fitch*. Philadelphia: American Philosophical Society, 1976. The inventor's semiliterate account of his life and unrecognized contribution to steam navigation through 1791. Illustrated.

Shagen, Jack L. *Who Really Invented the Steamboat? Fulton's Clermont Coup, a History of the Steamboat Contributions of William Henry, James Rumsey, John Fitch, Oliver Evans, Nathan Read, Samuel Morey, Robert Fulton, John Stevens, and Others*. Amherst, N.Y.: Humanity Books, 2004. Shagen, an engineer, provides a comprehensive history of the steamboat and its many worthy inventors.

Sutcliffe, Andrea. *Steam: The Untold Story of America's First Great Invention.* New York: Palgrave Macmillan, 2004. Sutcliffe focuses on Fitch's invention of the steamboat almost twenty years before the time of Robert Fulton. Examines the significance of Fitch's invention and the brutal competition he faced from rival inventors.

Ward, Ralph T. *Steamboats: A History of the Early Adventure.* Indianapolis, Ind.: Bobbs-Merrill, 1973. Written with attractive line drawings for young readers, with quotations from Fitch and other contemporaries showing how recognition and thus fame and fortune bypassed the steamboat inventor. Illustrated.

Westcott, Thompson. *The Life of John Fitch: The Inventor of the Steamboat.* Philadelphia: J. B. Lippincott, 1878. This work focuses on the injustice done by elevating Fulton, described in the book as a mere "imita-

tor and copyist," to the status of inventor of the steamboat instead of Fitch. Illustrated.

See also: Sir Richard Arkwright; Matthew Boulton; Henry Cavendish; Thomas Newcomen; James Watt; Eli Whitney.

Related articles in *Great Events from History: The Eighteenth Century, 1701-1800:* 1705-1712: Newcomen Develops the Steam Engine; 1738: Bernoulli Proposes the Kinetic Theory of Gases; 1764: Invention of the Spinning Jenny; 1765-1769: Watt Develops a More Effective Steam Engine; 1767-1771: Invention of the Water Frame; October 23, 1769: Cugnot Demonstrates His Steam-Powered Road Carriage; April, 1785: Cartwright Patents the Steam-Powered Loom; 1790: First Steam Rolling Mill; 1795: Invention of the Flax Spinner.

LORD EDWARD FITZGERALD
Irish rebel leader

Fitzgerald, born into an aristocratic family, became a leader of the movement for Irish independence from England and repudiated his title of nobility in an act of defiance. He was part of the attempt to pursuade France to invade England and thus incite rebellion in Ireland.

Born: October 15, 1763; Carton House, near Maynooth, County Kildare, Ireland
Died: June 4, 1798; Newgate Prison, Dublin, Ireland
Areas of achievement: Government and politics, warfare and conquest, military

EARLY LIFE
Lord Edward Fitzgerald was the scion of the upper echelons of the Anglo-Irish aristocracy. His father, James Fitzgerald, was earl of Kildare and later, as first duke of Leinster (1766), became the highest-ranking Irish peer. His mother was Emilia Mary, daughter of the second duke of Richmond. As the fifth son, Edward led a life of opulence and ease without the undue pressures of responsibility, moving back and forth between the many Fitzgerald estates at places including Carton House in Kildare, Leinster House in Dublin City, and Frascati House near Blackrock, County Dublin.

Fitzgerald apparently developed egalitarian ideas at an early age and, perhaps encouraged by his mother, became deeply absorbed in the philosophy of Jean-Jacques Rousseau. He never abandoned his attachment to the

idea of the pure, unsullied "noble savage" struggling for freedom against an artificial class system. In 1779 he embarked on a military career, journeying to America with the Sussex Volunteer Militia. In one of the last battles of the American Revolutionary War, a brutally contested fight at Eutaw Springs, South Carolina, on September 8, 1781, Fitzgerald was seriously injured and left for dead on the field. He was providentially rescued and nursed back to recovery by an escaped slave named Tony Small, who later accompanied the young man back to Ireland and became a lifelong friend.

LIFE'S WORK
Returning to Ireland after the ending of the American Revolution by the Treaty of Paris in 1783, Edward Fitzgerald took up a seat in the Irish parliament, representing Athy. Soon bored, however, he went on a Grand Tour of Europe, falling in love with a cousin, Georgina Lennox. After a brief affair, their relationship fizzled. Out of disappointment, Fitzgerald returned to military service, and he was stationed in Canada as a major in the infantry. While on this tour of duty, he persuaded the colonial authorities to allow him to undertake an expedition of discovery into unmapped territory. He journeyed from Quebec, down the Mississippi River to Louisiana, and became an "adopted" member of the Huron nation in the process.

His ardor for military glory and adventure seemed to leave him for a while, and he refused a commission from the prime minister to command a British expedition against Cádiz in Spain. Instead, he returned to parliamentary politics and also took a romantic interest in Elizabeth Linley, the wife of a noted author and fellow Irishman. A daughter was born out of this affair but, strangely, no violent rift seems to have been created between Sheridan and Fitzgerald.

Neglecting his parliamentary and military duties, the young noble again traveled abroad, this time taking a deep interest in the unfolding drama of revolutionary France and frequenting radical circles and debating clubs in Paris. He then began advocating a break of Ireland from England, by violent revolution if necessary, and marked himself as a subversive in 1792 by denouncing the British administration and renouncing his title of nobility. That same year saw the overthrow of King Louis XVI, the replacement of the monarchy by the First Republic, and a general war in Europe, which pitted England against France. Edward Fitzgerald was deprived of military rank and henceforth kept under surveillance. In France he had become enamored to Pamela Seymour, who is said to have been the daughter of Philippe Égalité, duke of Orleans, through a liaison with the courtesan, Madame de Genlis. Fitzgerald and Seymour were married in 1792, and upon his return to his native land shortly thereafter, he was suspected of engaging in subversion.

Certainly he made no secret about his political sympathies. However, he made no definitive move until 1796, when he joined the the Society of United Irishmen, a predominantly Protestant revolutionary nationalist organization founded by Wolfe Tone, James Napper Tandy, and others. He is known to have been present at a secret meeting in Hamburg, Germany, between United Irish leaders and French agents to set down plans for French assistance in fomenting an Irish rebellion. (However, how significant his role in the meeting was remains subject to debate.) It is believed that the abortive landing of General Louis Lazare Hoche and Tone in Bantry Bay, County Cork, in December of 1796 might have been one of the main items on the agenda.

Though a latecomer to politics, Fitzgerald's exalted station in society assured him of a place within the movement's leadership. From that time on he concentrated on pulling together an underground military apparatus that could be set to rise in revolt throughout Ireland and would coordinate with landings of French troops. Plans for such a rising, set for late spring of 1798, were far from complete when an informer, Thomas Reynolds, revealed that the main governing revolutionary unit, the Leinster Directory, was to meet in Dublin on March 12, 1798. As-

sembled at the home of Oliver Bond, the unit's directors were arrested. However, Fitzgerald, the unit president, was warned by Reynolds himself and evaded the net; Fitzgerald was given the opportunity to leave the country before martial law was declared. Reynolds may have been acting at the behest of government officials, who undoubtedly hoped to avoid the embarrassment of prosecuting a member of such a prominent family. Fitzgerald chose to not compromise and thus remained in hiding for more than two months, despite the imposition of martial law on March 30. He made plans as best he could on the run and spirited himself from house to house within the city, under the very noses of his adversaries.

Finding Fitzgerald to be less than obliging and being forced to hunt him down, officials allowed a bounty to be put upon his head; a lawyer named Francis Magan revealed his whereabouts at Thomas Street. On May 19, a group of men led by the constable, Major Henry Charles Sirr, went to his hideaway and burst into his bedroom to apprehend him. Fitzgerald put up a determined struggle to escape, slashed at his opponents with his knife, and mortally wounded one of them. Major Sirr drew a pistol, shot Fitzgerald in the shoulder, and incapacitated him. Fitzgerald was taken to Newgate Gaol, where it was initially assumed that his injury was not life-threatening. However, the wound became infected, and the rebel leader died in his cell on June 4, 1798, even as the revolt he was planning had broken out and was raging through counties Kildare and Wexford.

SIGNIFICANCE

Lord Edward Fitzgerald was considered neither a dynamic nor an effective a leader nor an imaginative thinker in comparison to contemporary revolutionaries Wolfe Tone, Arthur O'Connor, or Thomas Addis Emmett, among others. He acted as a blue blood turned amateur revolutionary, who in the end proved too reckless to coordinate an effective underground movement.

His untimely capture and death, however, constitute one of history's major "what ifs." Like his equally ill-fated colleague-in-arms, Tone, Fitzgerald is the most revered and the best known of the 1798 rebels, and he has served as a role model for Irish Republican nationalists of all stripes for the last two centuries.

—*Raymond Pierre Hylton*

FURTHER READING

Curtain, Nancy J. *The United Irishmen: Popular Politics in Ulster and Dublin, 1791-1798*. Oxford, England: Clarendon Press, 1994. The most definitive study of the United Irish as a grassroots movement.

Knox, Oliver. *Rebels and Informers: Stirrings of Irish Independence.* New York: St. Martin's Press, 1997. An excellent time line and useful information on the diversity of opinions, the degree of commitment, and the quality within the leadership of the Irish nationalist movement of the late eighteenth century.

Newsinger, John, ed. *United Irishman: The Autobiography of James Hope.* London: Merlin Press, 2001. A contemporary account by one of the participants in the rebel organization that also sheds light on the leadership and personalities involved in the nationalist struggle.

Smyth, Jim, ed. *Revolution, Counterrevolution, and Union: Ireland in the 1790's.* New York: Cambridge University Press, 2000. A collection that brings together different slants on aspects of what was, even for early modern Ireland, a tumultuous decade.

Tillyard, Stella. *Citizen Lord: The Life of Edward Fitzgerald, Irish Revolutionary.* New York: Farrar, Straus and Giroux, 1998. A biography that seeks to resolve or at least explain some of the contradictions in the psychological makeup of an aristocrat turned radical revolutionary.

See also: Henry Grattan; Louis XVI; Duc d'Orléans; Jean-Jacques Rousseau; Wolfe Tone.

Related articles in *Great Events from History: The Eighteenth Century, 1701-1800:* April 19, 1775: Battle of Lexington and Concord; January 4, 1792-1797: The *Northern Star* Calls for Irish Independence; April 20, 1792-October, 1797: Early Wars of the French Revolution; January 21, 1793: Execution of Louis XVI; July 2-August 1, 1800: Act of Union Forms the United Kingdom.

MARIA ANNE FITZHERBERT
English aristocrat

Based upon her wealth, social skills, and "secret" marriage to the prince of Wales (later King George IV), Fitzherbert maintained a respected and influential position in late Georgian society. Their marriage, technically illegal and punishable under English law, was both tacitly recognized and used as a threat in the politics of the era. Despite Fitzherbert's ambiguous public status, she managed to maintain her moral and religious integrity in a profligate era.

Born: July 26, 1756; place unknown
Died: March 27, 1837; Brighton, England
Also known as: Maria Anne Smythe (birth name); Maria Anne Weld
Area of achievement: Government and politics

EARLY LIFE

Maria Anne Fitzherbert was born into the country gentry of Shropshire. Her father, Walter Smythe, the second son of Sir John Smythe, inherited both money and land. His 1755 marriage to Mary Ann Errington increased the family's holdings. Maria Anne was born the next year. She apparently had a happy childhood, growing up in a spacious country house, Bambridge, with younger siblings.

Still under legal disabilities and popular suspicion, English Catholics like the Smythes moved within a social world largely of their coreligionists. Twelve-year-old Maria Anne attended a French convent school in Dunkirk. At age eighteen she married Edward Weld, a thirty-two-year-old widower with large landholdings. A brief three months after the wedding, Edward died, leaving Maria Anne with an annual income of £1,800.

In 1778 she married Thomas Fitzherbert, heir to a great Catholic family. The marriage seemed harmonious, with rounds of visiting and party-giving interspersed with country life. Thomas, however, was tubercular, and in 1781 he died in Nice. At age twenty-six, Maria Anne was a widow twice over. Financially, her second husband left her an even better income than she already received from Edward Weld's estate. Thomas also left her the house they had shared on fashionable Park Street in London, making it relatively easy for her to ease slowly into the social scene during her obligatory two years of mourning.

LIFE'S WORK

Eighteenth century women of Maria Anne Fitzherbert's class did not follow a profession, but their interests were not limited to domestic matters. Her marriages had already provided for her financial security and an assured place in English society. By moving back to London and joining the lively, highly placed subculture soon to be called "the ton," Fitzherbert entered a setting where the social world intertwined with political power and politi-

The Prince of Wales restrains Maria Fitzherbert (the two figures on the left) in this British cartoon lampooning her rivalry with a German queen. (Library of Congress)

cal developments. A major player in "the ton's" round of parties, racetrack visits, and other entertainments was the prince of Wales, the future King George IV (r. 1820-1830), who was quite unlike his dour father, King George III.

The prince claimed he immediately fell in love with Fitzherbert upon seeing her at the opera. He soon courted her relentlessly. For her part, Fitzherbert had mixed feelings toward him. Six years older than George and with more life experience, she recognized the potential pitfalls for herself and the political pitfalls for the monarchy should they marry. Unwilling to become a royal mistress, Fitzherbert was deeply aware that the 1701 Act of Settlement and subsequent laws forbade a royal heir to marry a Roman Catholic. Still, she could not help but be flattered by the attentions of "the most accomplished prince of his age" and be swayed by his charm. George even staged a suicide attempt, and Fitzherbert had been called. Under duress, she accepted a ring borrowed from the duchess of Devonshire as a pledge to marry him.

Afterward, sobered by the implications of her engagement, Fitzherbert fled to the Continent with her friend Lady Anne Lindsay. For a year the two traveled in France, the Netherlands, and Switzerland, while Fitzherbert tried to ignore George's passionate letters, which reached her by courier. Eventually, worn down by his pleas, she agreed to return to England and marry him.

The wedding had to be held in secret because there would be severe penalties for participating in such a ceremony. George had trouble finding a clergyman to perform the wedding, but he eventually persuaded John Burt, an Anglican cleric imprisoned for debt, to do so in exchange for paying off his debts. Fitzherbert's uncle and brother were witnesses; an armed guard stood at the door during the furtive ceremony, and the only official record kept was a statement written by George, and then signed by him, Fitzherbert, and the witnesses.

The ceremony, valid in the eyes of both Anglicans and Catholics, satisfied Fitzherbert's worries about morality.

For obvious reasons the couple could not live together, although between 1785 and 1794 they managed to live in nearby houses, give parties together, and be accepted as a couple by most of society's arbiters. They spent much time in Brighton, where the prince's presence spurred the town's transformation from a decrepit fishing village into a fashionable resort.

Fitzherbert was welcomed by most nobles, and even the royal family was kind to her, especially George's brothers Clarence (later King William IV) and Frederick. Her personality—gracious, witty, and soft-spoken—no doubt made her more acceptable. With so much at stake, some in the political realm were eager to flog a scandal. The marriage mystery nearly faced examination in the House of Commons in 1787, when debts from the prince's extravagance had been discussed. George acted far from honorably on this occasion. First, to his supporter Charles James Fox, George had denied that he was married to Fitzherbert. Then, when Fox repeated George's denial, he let Fox take the blame for impugning Fitzherbert. Finally, George gave a younger member, Charles Grey, the impossible task of refuting Fox without actually saying a marriage existed. This triple betrayal had political consequences, causing the first rift between George and his erstwhile champions, the Whigs.

Pressured to make a state marriage and mollify the king, George left Fitzherbert in 1794. His marriage to Caroline of Brunswick was disastrous, but not until 1800 did he and Fitzherbert resume their relationship. In the meantime, Fitzherbert led a largely private life. In later years she recalled the eight years after the reconciliation as the happiest of her life. Again, the couple created a fair imitation of domestic bliss, while overseeing projects such as George's Royal Pavilion at Brighton.

George refused to resist the charms of other women, however. Eventually the strain wore on Fitzherbert. When, in 1811, the king's incapacity appeared permanent, a regency for the prince appeared imminent. His domestic situation now took on a different light, aggravated by Fitzherbert's lack of rank. At a state reception for exiled Louis XVIII, Fitzherbert was to be seated "below the salt." Defending her dignity against this slight, she wrote a letter of protest to the prince, but to no avail. Although they exchanged some letters later, the end of their personal relationship had arrived.

Fitzherbert had always led a partially independent life, and this stood her in good stead in these later years. She was not a naturally vindictive person but she found some balm for her injured pride by remaining in Brighton and entertaining lavishly while the embarrassed prince hovered in his pavilion. She mothered her two adopted children, Minney and Marianne, traveled, did charitable works, and became notably more devout.

Fitzherbert outlived George, who finally inherited the throne at age sixty. She died of a fever in March, 1837, still officially Maria Anne Fitzherbert, a woman who sustained her unique position graciously through wit and will.

SIGNIFICANCE

Maria Anne Fitzherbert had no pretensions to feminism, but her insistence on living by her own standards set a strong example of female integrity. For most of her adult life she had her own household, managed her own financial interests, and treasured her own web of friendships. In an era when women were believed to need a man's "protection," she pioneered an independent manner.

George IV lived in the midst of a slow shift in Britain from a directly ruling monarchy to parliamentary government. He was an admirable patron of the arts and a brilliant man-about-town, but his political instincts were not particularly good. Neither of his marriages served him well politically. Although Fitzherbert took no direct part in politics, the very existence of her bond with the prince had major impact upon the nation. In youth, George IV was viewed as a Whig sympathizer. He supported the American colonists' cause, and progressives saw in him a future king who would enact peaceful reforms. That did not happen. The reasons were numerous, but some date back to the alienation between George IV and the Whig Party stemming from his relationship with Fitzherbert. His behavior made liberals realize they had to work directly for democratic reforms instead.

Whether Fitzherbert's role helped loosen the strictures against Catholics is uncertain. In fact, when George IV came to power, he decided that abolishing the strictures would be too "upsetting." Nonetheless, anti-Catholic laws soon were modified. If Fitzherbert played any part, it was surely just by force of example. She was an amiable and tolerant woman, a far cry from the scary "Papist" stereotype of popular fears.

Fitzherbert's life has fascinated the public and historians alike in subsequent years. She was the only woman George ever loved. Until the early twentieth century no evidence was known of their actual marriage, so the lure of mystery burnished the romanticism. Fitzherbert remains a unique kind of romantic heroine, brave and self-assured in her own way, her story falling midway between fortunate and tragic.

—*Emily Alward*

FURTHER READING

Leslie, Shane. *Mrs. Fitzherbert: A Life Chiefly from Unpublished Letters*. London: Burns, Oates, 1939. A favorable biography that draws on previously unavailable letters.

Munson, James. *Maria Fitzherbert: The Secret Wife of George IV*. New York: Carroll & Graf, 2001. A detailed biography that also explores the social setting and influences in Fitzherbert's life.

Smith, E. C. *George IV*. New Haven, Conn.: Yale University Press, 1999. A personal and political account of the prince's life that explores Fitzherbert's impact in some depth.

See also: First Baron Erskine; Charles James Fox; George III.

Related article in *Great Events from History: The Eighteenth Century, 1701-1800:* June 12, 1701: Act of Settlement.

ANDRÉ-HERCULE DE FLEURY
French cardinal and statesman

As prime minister of France from 1726 to 1743, Fleury restored economic prosperity and stability to the country, and he maintained peace both domestically and internationally. Using his power and experience as both statesman and clergyman, he quieted the outbreak of Jansenist unrest and brought accord between the Crown and the French judiciary.

Born: June 22, 1653; Lodève, France
Died: January 29, 1743; Paris, France
Also known as: Cardinal de Fleury
Areas of achievement: Government and politics, religion and theology, education

EARLY LIFE

André-Hercule de Fleury (ahn-dray ehr-kewl duh flew-ree) was born into a well-connected family that had ties to the Church, the Crown, the legal profession, and the provincial landed gentry. He received an excellent education, attending the Collège de Navarre, the Collège Louis le Grand, and the Collège d'Harcourt. From birth, Fleury was destined to the priesthood. In 1668, he became canon of Montpellier. In 1675, he became the queen's chaplain. The next year, 1676, he received his degree of theology. In 1678, he was appointed as one of the eight chaplains of King Louis XIV, and in 1680 he became a deputy to the assembly of the clergy.

In 1699, Louis XIV appointed Fleury to the diocese of Fréjus, and he spent the next fifteen years as bishop of Fréjus. During this time, he was very involved in his religious duties. He looked after the needs of the poor and paid special attention to the education of the children of his diocese. However, Fleury missed Paris and life at court. Early in 1715, he resigned his position as bishop, and in July he left Fréjus and returned to Paris.

LIFE'S WORK

Fleury's career had seemed to come to a standstill at Fréjus. When he returned to Paris, he was sixty-two years old and probably believed that he was approaching the end of his career, but it was at this somewhat late time in his life that his most important work began. During Fleury's earlier sojourn at the court, Louis XIV had found him too worldly. In spite of this earlier opinion, shortly before the king died, he chose Fleury as the future tutor of his heir apparent, who would become Louis XV. Madame de Maintenon, the former Françoise d'Aubigné and wife of Louis XIV at the time, is credited with strongly influencing her husband in this decision.

It was not until 1717 that Fleury actually began his work as tutor to the young Louis XV. Fleury concentrated on instilling in his pupil religious piety and respect for the Church, concern for the happiness of his subjects, and a distaste for wars of expansion. Louis developed an extraordinary amount of confidence in Fleury and consistently followed his advice about most affairs of state. It was at Fleury's suggestion that, upon the death of the duc d'Orléans in 1723, the duc de Bourbon became prime minister. It was also Fleury who saw to it that Bourbon was disgraced in 1726. In June of 1726, Louis XV appointed Fleury prime minister of France. Fleury now officially exercised the duties and power that had already been his for years. In the same year, he was also made a cardinal of the Church.

During Fleury's ministry, France enjoyed domestic economic prosperity and freedom from war abroad. As a result of the extravagant spending of Louis XIV and the disastrous financial scheme of John Law during the Regency, France was in serious economic difficulty when Fleury came to power. To remedy the situation, Fleury returned to the practices employed by Jean-Baptiste Colbert. During the middle years of the previous reign, Colbert, in a process that came to be called Colbertisme, had succeeded in stabilizing the budget and in expanding commerce in spite of the extravagances of the king. Fleury wisely availed himself of experienced ministers such as Philibert Orry and Jean Frédéric Phélypeaux, comte de Maurepas, to implement his programs.

The problem of Jansenism had never been settled in France. Although it had been declared heretical in the papal bull *Unigenitus*, that bull had never been officially registered in France. The French clergy's aversion to bowing to the dictates of Rome was responsible for this situation. Consequently, there were still many Jansenists among the clergy, as well as in the secular world, especially in the judicial class. Throughout his clerical career, Fleury had been opposed to the sect. In 1726, he had taken control of the *feuille de bénéfice*, which made appointments within the Church. He routinely excluded Jansenists from promotion. Though not fanatical in his opposition to Jansenism, he wished to purge the church in France of Jansenists.

In 1730, Fleury brought about the declaration of the bull *Unigenitus* as law in France. The Parisian parliamentarians immediately took issue with this stratagem and protested vehemently. Fleury exiled them from Paris. In August, 1731, the Parisian lawyers went on strike. In 1732, Louis XV promulgated a law denying the reiteration of remonstrance to Parlement and forbade strikes by lawyers. Toward the end of 1732, an agreement was reached between the Crown and the Parlement. Fleury permitted its members to return to Paris; they submitted to the will of the state, and the decree of 1732 was suspended. Thus, using a policy that was firm but moderate in the severity of action taken, Fleury silenced the Jansenist quarrel.

In international affairs, Fleury believed in the benefits of the peaceful coexistence of nations. However, he was still able to expand French territory. Through negotiation, he acquired the duchy of Lorraine by first obtaining it for Louis XV's father-in-law, Stanisław I Leszczyński, the dethroned king of Poland. Stanisław was to enjoy sovereignty in Lorraine until his death, at which time the duchy would lose its independence and become a part of France.

During the last years of his life, Fleury saw France drawn into the War of the Austrian Succession (1740-1748). Against Fleury's advice, Louis XV decided to align himself with Prussia in opposition to Maria Theresa, who had the support of England. The war brought France many more problems than benefits, but Fleury did not live to lament over this situation. He died January 29, 1743.

SIGNIFICANCE

André-Hercule de Fleury was an exceptional statesman. He succeeded in quelling the Jansenist unrest and subduing the Parlement. He accomplished these aims with a minimum of force when the legal community rose up in opposition to the bull *Unigenitus* as law and thus in opposition to the king.

Fleury understood the importance of centralization and unity to the existence of an absolute monarchy. Such a monarchy had to function on the principle of "one king, one will, one religion." Any schism in the scheme would erode the absolute power of the king.

War was, in Fleury's opinion, detrimental to a country. It strained finances and placed an enormous tax burden on the people. Fleury came from a family whose members had been engaged in the collection of both ecclesiastical and secular taxes. His father was a *receveur de tailles royales* (royal tax collector). War also shifted attention outward, away from the domestic needs of the country.

Fleury wisely delegated authority to experts who were able to achieve the ends that he sought. He also availed himself of policies that had been successful in the past. By implementing Colbert's methods, he stabilized the French economy during his ministry.

Fleury inspired confidence. Louis XV relied upon him to set policy and essentially govern France for seventeen years. Even the years before he appointed Fleury prime minister, he relied upon his former tutor's advice in matters of state.

—*Shawncey Webb*

FURTHER READING

Campbell, Peter R. *Power and Politics in Old Regime France, 1720-1745*. Rutgers, N.J.: Rutgers University Press, 1996. Based on thorough archival research. Comprehensive treatment of the ministry of Fleury, with discussion of the Jansenism crisis.

Jones, Colin. *The Great Nation: France from Louis XV to Napoleon*. New York: Columbia University Press, 2003. Looks at the reigns of Louis XV and Louis XVI as periods of effective royal power, military achievement, and cultural prestige. Chapters 2 and 3 cover Fleury's role in the reign of Louis XV.

McManners, John. *The Clerical Establishment and Its Ramifications*. Vol. 1 in *Church and Society in Eighteenth Century France*. New York: Oxford University Press, 1999. Along with volume 2, presents every aspect of religious life in eighteenth century France.

_____. *The Religion of the People and the Politics of Religion*. Vol. 2 in *Church and Society in Eighteenth Century France*. New York: Oxford University Press, 1999. Discussion of Jesuit-Jansenist struggle.

Roche, Daniel. *France in the Enlightenment*. Translated by Arthur Goldmann. Cambridge, Mass.: Harvard University Press, 2000. Detailed cultural history, examining the lives of all classes: the king, nobility, bourgeoisie, and peasants. Looks at the period as important in its own right and not just a prelude to the French Revolution.

Wilson, Arthur McCandless. *French Foreign Policy During the Administration of Cardinal Fleury, 1726-1743*. Reprint. Westport, Conn.: Greenwood Press, 1972. A study in Fleury's expertise in diplomacy and commercial development.

See also: Étienne François de Choiseul; Louis XV; Louis XVI; Maria Theresa; Duc d'Orléans.

Related articles in *Great Events from History: The Eighteenth Century, 1701-1800*: September 8, 1713: Papal Bull *Unigenitus*; September, 1720: Collapse of the South Sea Bubble; May, 1727-1733: Jansenist "Convulsionnaires" Gather at Saint-Médard; November 9, 1729, and February, 1732: Treaty of Seville; October 10, 1733-October 3, 1735: War of the Polish Succession; 1736-1739: Russo-Austrian War Against the Ottoman Empire; November 18, 1738: Treaty of Vienna; September 18, 1739: Treaty of Belgrade; October 20, 1740: Maria Theresa Succeeds to the Austrian Throne; February 24, 1766: Lorraine Becomes Part of France.

CHARLES JAMES FOX
English politician

Spending decades of his political career in opposition, Fox associated aristocratic Whiggery and the Whig Party, which he came to lead, with the defense of liberty against the exercise of arbitrary power by the king and the king's ministers.

Born: January 24, 1749; London, England
Died: September 13, 1806; Chiswick, Devon, England
Area of achievement: Government and politics

EARLY LIFE

Charles James Fox was the third and favorite son of Henry Fox, later first Lord Holland, who had earned a well-deserved reputation for venality as paymaster of the Forces and manager of the House of Commons. With his father's abundant wealth placed at his disposal, Fox was reared in an atmosphere of luxury and privilege exceptional even by the standards of the eighteenth century aristocracy. He attended Eton in 1758 and four years later accompanied his father on an extended journey to the Continent. He enrolled in Hertford College, Oxford, in 1764, and in the spring of 1766 left for several years of touring in France and Italy, living a life of unfettered luxury and often of dissipation. He was a dandy, and his large frame, not yet resembling the corpulent figure so familiar from the portraits and caricatures of his mature years, was often noticed at the gaming clubs of the day. Gambling was to remain his most enduring vice, and despite his considerable wealth, it often left him in straitened financial circumstances. His dissolute life as a gambler was complemented by his sexual escapades.

Even in his early manhood, however, debauchery was tempered by more refined pleasures. He had worked hard at Oxford in mathematics and in the classics, which he mastered beyond the mere collection of felicitous Latin phrases that embellish the oratory of eighteenth and nineteenth century politicians. He had a facility for languages, read poetry, and developed a love for the theater that may well have contributed to the powerful impact he was to have as an orator, if not to his acknowledged dexterity in debate. He was, in short, an eighteenth century "man of parts." In addition, he acquired the comforts of domesticity as a result of his prolonged liaison with his mistress, Elizabeth Armistead. Theirs was a relationship that began in the early 1780's and lasted until Fox's death, their secret marriage of 1795 not disclosed publicly until 1802.

LIFE'S WORK

In March, 1768, while still underage, Charles James Fox was elected a member of Parliament for the family's pocket borough of Midhurst in Sussex. While his career was later to be identified with relentless opposition to governmental infringement on liberty, in his early years Fox was a loyal supporter of the government and a reliable member of what was then called the court interest. Despite the repeated election to Parliament in 1769 of the outlaw John Wilkes by the defiant freeholders of the county of Middlesex, Fox supported seating Wilkes's opponent. He argued for the independence of the House of Commons as a branch of the constitution (along with the Crown and the House of Lords) and reasserted the traditional right of the House to choose its own members. The House of Commons, in this case, was to be independent of the electorate, a member of Parliament presumably being an independent representative rather than a mere delegate executing the instructions of a constituency. Fox's interpretation of representative government was to be expanded subsequently, but the independence of the House of Commons—albeit from the alleged influence of the Crown if no longer from the people—was to remain one of his constant concerns.

Already a junior lord of the treasury, Fox was promoted to a lordship of the Admiralty in February, 1770, in the new government led by Lord North. He seemed to be following the pattern expected of a son of a famous officeholder, well on his way to an even greater place in government. Yet even in these early years, Fox displayed considerable political independence. He opposed the Royal Marriages Act of 1772, whereby the marriage of a royal prince or princess required the approval of the sovereign. (Perhaps he was influenced by the example of his parents' romance and elopement.) He supported the claims of Dissenters for relief of ministers and university students from the requirement of subscription to the Thirty-nine Articles. Fox resigned his office in February, 1772, possibly because of his intended opposition to the Royal Marriages Bill, but was recruited once again as a lord of the treasury in December of that year. His final departure from the North government resulted from his insistence upon punitive measures being pressed against a printer, whose paper imputed improprieties to the speaker of the House. Forcing North to fulfill a pledge and pursue the matter, Fox embarrassed the prime minister, and George III directed that he be dismissed.

After his dismissal, Fox became associated with the grievances of the American colonists. He did not question the right of Parliament to legislate for the colonies or the propriety of the doctrine of virtual representa-

tion, but he thought it inexpedient for Parliament to exercise such power. Fox seems to have been particularly influenced by the argument of Edmund Burke, then one of the marquess of Rockingham's lieutenants, that the bonds of empire rested upon ties of custom and affection between the colonists and the mother country. He also welcomed the growing respectability of the idea of party as publicized by Burke—a body of principled and honorable men in opposition to the government. During the years of the American Revolution, Fox gravitated toward the Rockingham faction, an opposition group that supported the Americans. It also attempted, with some success, to arrogate to itself exclusively the historic name of the Whig Party, which was associated with the Revolution Settlement and the limitation of royal power.

Just as Fox had defended the independence of the Commons from the people during the Wilkite affair, he came to associate the government's disastrous American policy with the excessive and adverse influence of the Crown upon the House of Commons. The Associations movement of 1779-1780 facilitated that argument. Various county associations, primarily composed of respectable country gentlemen, objected to excessive taxation and sought to remedy the problem by reducing the allegedly wasteful expenditure of the Crown. Fox argued that the best way to do so was to reduce the number of placemen, those who held office under the Crown and also had seats in the House of Commons. This advocacy of "economical reform," as it was called, was taken up by the Rockingham Whigs. Fox went beyond most of his new colleagues, however, in advocating parliamentary reform, which then signified reducing the duration of parliaments and redistributing parliamentary constituencies, particularly adding members to the counties. During this time of countrywide meetings by country associations, Fox helped to organize the householders of Westminister, one of the most open parliamentary constituencies, which also contained some radical elements. Returned as a member of Parliament for the city of Westminister in October, 1780, Fox continued to represent it until his death. Thus, the man who had opposed their excessive influence a decade earlier was now hailed as a man of the people.

The North government collapsed in early 1782, humiliated by defeat at the hands of the Americans. It was succeeded by a coalition of Rockingham Whigs and followers of Lord Shelburne. The death of Lord Rockingham after only a few months in office and the personal animosity between Fox and Shelburne, however, led Fox

Charles James Fox. (Hulton Archive/Getty Images)

to resign when Shelburne was chosen by George III as his prime minister. Fox justified his resignation by contending that the cabinet should be collectively responsible for recommending a minister to the king, and by inflating his differences with Shelburne about the terms of the prospective peace with America to a matter of great principle.

At the head of the Rockingham Whigs in opposition early in 1783, Fox joined forces with his old opponent, Lord North, to defeat the Shelburne government after it had negotiated the Treaty of Paris (1783). Fox and North then forced themselves on the king, who could find no other ministers to command the Commons. The alliance was looked upon as a cynical grab for power by men who had for so long opposed each other, presumably on matters of principle. Fox once again became foreign secretary, now in the coalition government nominally led by the duke of Portland. The unpopularity of the Fox-North alliance was intensified by the government's proposed India Act in late 1783, originally drawn up by Burke. It would have replaced the existing administration of India with a board of seven commissioners, named in the bill, who, for a stipulated period, would control the vast patronage associated with Indian affairs. Each of the prospective commissioners was associated with either Fox

or North. Fox, then, was open to the charge of venality. Moreover, by naming the commissioners in the bill, the ministers were perceived as having gone too far in redressing the balance of the constitution and infringed on the king's rightful powers. George III, intent upon ridding himself of a ministry forced upon him and reclaiming the king's prerogative to name his own ministers, persuaded the House of Lords to defeat the India Act, dismissed his ministers, and appointed William Pitt the Younger as his prime minister.

In 1783, then, Fox commenced a period in opposition that would last more than two decades. During almost all of that time, William Pitt was prime minister, and politics assumed the dimension of a personal feud between the two. Fox was unable to take advantage of Pitt's initially weak support in the Commons, and the election of 1784 produced a majority for the king's ministers. The opposition, composed of the former Rockingham Whigs led by Fox and many of North's supporters who joined them, cultivated the idea that Pitt had acquired control unconstitutionally and that the king and his ministers were engaged in the flagrant abuse of power.

The Regency Crisis of 1788-1789 provided Fox with a seemingly splendid opportunity. George III had apparently gone mad. Fox, the champion of limiting royal power, now argued that the prince of Wales become regent immediately, with the full powers of the monarch. In the tradition of eighteenth century filial opposition, the prince of Wales had attracted a coterie of followers opposed to the court. Fox, foremost among them, expected to be carried into office by the prince. The king recovered and resumed power, however, and Fox, whom he detested and blamed for his son's dissolute life, was once again consigned to the political wilderness.

Fox welcomed the outbreak of the French Revolution, which he, like most Englishmen, associated with England's Glorious Revolution a century earlier. As it became more violent and democratic, and as radical activities by extraparliamentary groups became more widespread in England, popular enthusiasm for the revolution was transformed into opposition. When the war between Great Britain and France came to be perceived as a war for national survival, Fox persisted in defending the revolution and continued to emphasize its similarity to the Glorious Revolution and to the American Revolution. He painfully witnessed the reduction of the Whig opposition, as former colleagues began to join or support Pitt's government. Burke had denounced the revolution as early as 1790, and the substantial group of Whigs led by the duke of Portland joined the Pitt government in 1794.

Throughout the years of revolution, Fox vigorously defended freedom of speech and association from the infringement of government. He was outspoken in opposition to such repressive legislation as the Treason and Sedition bills and opposed the prosecution of treason trials. At the same time, while he recognized that the revolution was not an unqualified benefit, he supported negotiations with France and an end to hostilities. He was increasingly beleaguered, however, and, in 1797, Fox and the rump of Whigs who had remained loyal to him seceded from Parliament. Fox remained barred from office by the animosity of George III, even when Pitt resigned in 1801 and when Pitt himself wished to recruit Fox as a cabinet minister in 1804. A realignment of political factions and Pitt's death in 1806 finally resulted in a coalition government of the Foxite Whigs and the supporters of Lord Grenville. It was called the Ministry of All the Talents, and Fox became foreign secretary once again. He died a few months thereafter, in September, 1806, and was buried in Westminster Abbey.

SIGNIFICANCE

Having spent most of his political career in opposition, Charles James Fox had become associated with a variety of causes: limiting the power of the Crown, maintaining the independence of the House of Commons, supporting a formed party in opposition, and advocating collective responsibility of the cabinet rather than a government of departments. He had also supported parliamentary as well as economical reform.

While his association with most of these causes was rooted in the practical political necessity of finding issues that could rally support in opposition to the king's ministers, Fox and the Whig Party eventually came to regard some of them as important principles. Above all, Fox and his attenuated Whig Party thought of themselves as the party of liberty, which they were to defend against the arbitrary assaults of the king and his ministers—hence, Fox's passionate defense of individual liberty, which he believed was endangered in the 1790's by policies of Pitt's government. Nor is it surprising that the one achievement of the Talents' Ministry was the abolition of the slave trade, passed only a few months after Fox's death. It was a measure that Fox had ardently supported since it had first been raised in Parliament in 1789. The slave trade and slavery, he contended, violated the individual's fundamental right to personal liberty, much less the civil and religious liberties that he

and his colleagues so eloquently defended. Fox's passion for liberty, however, did not signify a predilection for democracy. Above all, Fox was an aristocrat. Indeed, he thought of the Whig Party as an aristocratic group that could mediate between the Crown on the one hand and the populace on the other.

Fox became at least as important in death as he had been in life. His memory was kept alive by Fox clubs that commemorated his association of the Whig Party with liberty. His nephew, Lord Holland, became a custodian of his uncle's memory. He and others sought, successfully, to associate the Whig Party in the early nineteenth century with the name of Fox and with the defense of civil and religious liberties.

—Abraham D. Kriegel

FURTHER READING

Carswell, John. *The Old Cause: Three Biographical Studies in Whiggism.* London: Cresset Press, 1954. An attempt to place Fox in the tradition of the seventeenth century Whigs who defended the "old cause" of English liberty against the arbitrary exercise of royal power.

Christie, Ian R. *Wars and Revolutions: Britain, 1760-1815.* Cambridge, Mass.: Harvard University Press, 1982. An outstanding treatment of the political history of the period, which diminishes the role of political parties and of Fox, who emerges as an ineffective politician, deficient in character.

Derry, John W. *Charles James Fox.* London: Batsford, 1972. A detailed, highly unsympathetic treatment of Fox, who is portrayed as a rogue, an opportunist, and an inept politician.

_____. *Politics in the Age of Fox, Pitt, and Liverpool: Continuity and Transformation.* Houndsmills, Basingstoke, England: Macmillan, 1990. Describes how the British political system was able to withstand the challenges of war, the French Revolution, and the social and economic transformations of the late eighteenth century.

Mitchell, L. G. *Charles James Fox.* New York: Oxford University Press, 1992. Mitchell assesses Fox's political achievements and contributions to the Whig Party, describing how Fox became a politician through circumstance rather than inclination.

_____. *Charles James Fox and the Disintegration of the Whig Party, 1782-1794.* London: Oxford University Press, 1971. Considers Fox as a man of great principle, who often sacrificed opportunities for office. The author argues that the Whigs developed their creed in these dozen years of opposition, and makes the case for Fox as an astute political leader.

O'Gorman, Frank. *The Whig Party and the French Revolution.* New York: St. Martin's Press, 1967. A highly detailed study of parliamentary politics in which Fox emerges favorably.

Reid, Loren. *Charles James Fox: A Man for the People.* Columbia: University of Missouri Press, 1969. A favorable treatment of Fox based upon an analysis of his parliamentary speeches.

See also: Edmund Burke; Georgiana Cavendish; Maria Anne Fitzherbert; George III; Lord North; William Pitt the Younger; Richard Brinsley Sheridan; John Wilkes.

Related articles in *Great Events from History: The Eighteenth Century, 1701-1800:* Beginning April, 1763: The *North Briton* Controversy; June 2-10, 1780: Gordon Riots; September 3, 1783: Treaty of Paris; July 14, 1789: Fall of the Bastille; 1790: Burke Lays the Foundations of Modern Conservatism.

Jean-Honoré Fragonard
French painter

Fragonard was one of the foremost painters of the eighteenth century and has been particularly praised for the gaiety of his style and composition. He is renowned for his depictions of French high society in the years immediately preceding the revolution.

Born: April 5, 1732; Grasse, France
Died: August 22, 1806; Paris, France
Area of achievement: Art

Early Life

The son of a Grasse merchant, Jean-Honoré Fragonard (zhahn-aw-naw-ray frah-gaw-nahr) was brought to Paris at the age of fifteen. His father had been ruined by bad investments, and Fragonard was apprenticed to a notary. Showing no talent for the law but already exhibiting signs of his artistic gift, he was taught by several important French masters, including the great landscape painter François Boucher. Boucher's influence proved the strongest, and Fragonard's work has often been compared to his teacher's, especially in its delightful depiction of frivolous French court life and the pleasures of the flesh.

A precocious talent, Fragonard won the Prix de Rome (one of the most coveted prizes in France) when he was only twenty. Beginning in 1756, he spent six years in Italy drawing monuments, ruins, Italian gardens, and copying works by Giovanni Battista Tiepolo and learning to emulate his sunny palette and sense of drama. For the most part, Fragonard was not drawn to Renaissance art but rather to landscapes and bacchanalian scenes.

Shortly after his return from Italy in the early 1760's, Fragonard painted a series of landscapes in rather dark, realistic tones to presage a shift in public taste away from the elaborate and fanciful decorativeness of rococo art. It may have been in response to this new seriousness in the

public mood that the artist searched for a safe subject that would guarantee his full membership in the French Academy.

Life's Work

To become a member in the French Academy, Fragonard painted *Corésus Sacrificing Himself to Save Callirhoé* (c. 1761-1765), which was soundly praised by the critics and satisfied the Royal Academicians, who were looking for first-rate history painters to serve the needs of the state. Marion L. Grayson has called the painting "a scene of strange and violent pagan passions," and R. H. Wilenski has referred to it as "rather simple and severe with few of the impetuous curves that characterise his later drawing." Yet it is recognizably in Fragonard's manner, rendered with his characteristic flair for presenting voluptuous women. The painting pleased Fragonard's conservative contemporaries, but this stylish artist never returned to this kind of conventional work. Instead, he changed almost immediately to portraying risqué scenes from private life that made him something less than a respectable figure.

The Swing (c. 1766), perhaps Fragonard's most famous painting, epitomizes the artist's willingness to delineate titillating scenes that his contemporaries avoided. Gabriel-François Doyen had been approached by Baron de Saint-Julien to paint his mistress on a swing being pushed by a bishop, and the baron wanted himself put somewhere in the composition, where he could have a good view of the charming lady's legs. Doyen was taken aback by the proposition and did not accept the commission, although he suggested the witty innovation of having the lady's slipper fly into the air to be caught by cupids. Fragonard not only accepted the baron's salacious conceit but also exaggerated it by showing the lady at the height of her swing kicking one leg high up against a cloudy background, sending her slipper upward toward a statue of a cupid while the baron (reclining on the ground) obtains a tantalizing glimpse of his lover. On the lady's other side, her husband (who seems to be amused) thrusts his arms forward, having pushed her high into the air. The picture forms a neat triangle, with the lady at its apex, her companions below taking different sorts of pleasure from her own happy recreation.

This has been called a naughty picture. It is also a brilliant evocation of sophisticated French court society before the French Revolution, in which ladies and gentlemen indulged their fantasies, took lovers with considerable panache, and in general adopted a worldly attitude toward sin. If this painting was shocking, it was so only in the sense that an artist of Fragonard's stature would indulge his patron's whims so directly and flamboyantly. Technically, the artist's contemporaries recognized that his painting was a tour de force. The setting is beautifully realized: The lady swings into the light out of the cozy shadiness of the bushes and trelliswork. In the flowing folds of her dress, she appears as an airy creature, suspended between the yearning arms of two men. Indeed,

the entire effect of the painting is of lightness and of fancy—the playfulness of desire.

With *The Swing,* Fragonard gained a reputation for pandering "to the tastes of a morally and esthetically decadent few," as Grayson puts it. His work provided elegant decoration for the residence of the rich and the highborn. Between 1770 and 1775, he painted the *Progress of Love* series of Madame du Barry, the mistress of Louis XV. His portraits rival those of Peter Paul Rubens in their supple rendering of human flesh, yet Fragonard's expressionistic brushwork gives his female figures an ethereal, almost spiritual quality—especially in portraits where a young woman is posed, quill in hand, about to write a letter, or is pictured with a letter in one hand while she places her other hand to her cheek as she reads with a serene, contented expression. In such works, the paint looks as though it has been swirled onto the canvas in one extremely graceful movement. Fragonard is said to have accomplished some of these portraits in an hour's time, a stunning feat of artistic inspiration and control.

Fragonard married in 1769, an important step for a painter who could have continued to frequent the salons of his patrons and remain outside the realm of respectable domesticity. Instead, he chose to pursue a more conventional existence, which had remarkable consequences for his work. Beginning in the 1770's, the painter turned to scenes of home life and family life. In *The Good Mother* (c. 1770-1772), for example, he took up Jean-Jacques Rousseau's conceit that the best education was to be got at home and that society should return to its origins in nature. Rousseau was reacting against the elaborate artifice of a society that had paid Fragonard handsomely for celebrating its sexual games and intrigues. Now Fragonard, with a home life of his own, and in a society moving toward the utter seriousness of a revolution that would overthrow the decadent court, was showing that he, too, had values that transcended what was merely fashionable. In a country that was gearing up for massive social change, *The Good Mother* emphasized continuity, security, and protectiveness. The subject is pictured in a luxuriant garden—more a fantasy or wish fulfillment than a real place—with a babe on her lap, another asleep beside her, and a third wide-awake, somewhat older child behind her pouring water into a bowl while the mother dips a cloth, evidently about to wash her infant's face. The harmony and peacefulness of this scene is echoed in many other paintings—in settings where a motherly figure is portrayed with children gathered about her teaching them the alphabet, where daily

Jean-Honoré Fragonard. (Library of Congress)

life and domestic pursuits are given a uniquely sincere value.

Horace Shipp has pointed out that these two phases of Fragonard's work—his erotic portrayals of courtly society and his charmingly serious evocations of family life—constitute different veins of influence stemming from his apprenticeship to Chardin (the man of the people who found in their homely lives and scenes his inspiration) and Boucher (the fantastic colorist and decorator who gave a rococo flourish to the sexually titillating lives of the richly privileged). For a time, in other words, Fragonard was able to mirror and to capitalize upon the contradictions of his society that was, at turns, attracted to domestic stability, dignified and historical themes, moralizing stories based on pagan subject matter, romantic landscapes, and classical subjects (Roman ruins and sculpture). It was only in his last years, in the period of the revolution, that the artist's complex attitude toward his paradoxical culture was incapable of coping with enormous, abrupt change.

SIGNIFICANCE

In his last years, Jean-Honoré Fragonard came under the protection of Jacques-Louis David, who became, in Wilenski's words, the "art-dictator" of the revolution. David believed that Fragonard had painted many masterpieces, and he was able to secure for his older contemporary a position as a museum curator. Yet the temper of the times had clearly turned against an artist who could easily, if unfairly, be accused of frivolousness and of idealizing the lives of the idle rich. The very gorgeousness of Fragonard's technique, his extraordinary facility with paint, was condemned for its seductiveness. By 1806, when Napoleon decreed that all artists and their studios must be removed from the Louvre, Fragonard, then seventy-four, was forced to find a new home and place to work. On August 22, 1806, Fragonard, hot from a long walk, sat down at a café for some relief and died of a stroke.

In the years since his death, Fragonard has come to be valued for his style, for the way he is able to endow the slightest subject matter with elegance and wit. In discussing one of his great landscapes, *The Fête at Saint-Cloud* (c. 1778-1780), Raymond Mortimer marvels at the witty, seductive, and kind look at nymphs, at a "Nature in gauze and feathers, a millinery of trees, under which to be private" and imagines a modern rake exclaiming, "Oh, to have lived when frivolity could be thus poetical." Mortimer notes that Fragonard's scenes never really existed, that they are highly idealized—

expressions of fantasy, not reality. Fragonard's work still has the power to disturb viewers who demand a politically engaged and socially responsible art and to indulge viewers who find satisfaction in admiring the artist's technique and his ability to suggest a world where the art of living and where the artist's talent predominate.

—*Carl Rollyson*

FURTHER READING

Bailey, Colin B., ed. *The Age of Watteau, Chardin, and Fragonard: Masterpieces of French Genre Painting*. New Haven, Conn.: Yale University Press and the National Gallery of Canada, Ottawa, 2003. Comprehensive survey of eighteenth century French genre painting, with detailed descriptions of paintings, and 230 color and 60 black-and-white reproductions. Also features essays placing Fragonard and other artists within the context of their time.

Fragonard, Jean-Honoré. *Fragonard Drawings for Ariosto*. Essays by Elizabeth Mangan, Philip Hofer, and Jean Seznec. New York: Pantheon Books, 1945. The essays discuss Fragonard as draftsman, examines illustrated editions of Ariosto's *Orlando Furioso,* and discuss Fragonard as an interpreter of Ariosto's long narrative poem that features the adventures of Roland and Charlemagne's other knights in wars against the Saracens. Notes, a bibliography, and 137 black-and-white plates make this a comprehensive study of the artist as illustrator.

Grappe, Georges. *Fragonard: La Vie et l'œuvre*. Monaco: Les Documents d'Art, 1946. Contains thirty-two large black-and-white plates of the artist's most important works. In French.

Grayson, Marion L. *Fragonard and His Friends*. St. Petersburg, Fla.: Museum of Fine Arts, 1982. A catalog of an exhibition, held November, 1982-February, 1983. Sixty black-and-white plates document the place of Fragonard's art in his time, with examples of his painting and of engravings made by others of his work. Included in the exhibition is work by Boucher, Chardin, and many of Fragonard's other contemporaries and teachers. Notes on individual plates explain the background of the work. Grayson's biographical and critical introductions to Fragonard and his contemporaries are succinct and insightful and make this catalog an extremely valuable study.

Massengale, Jean Montague. *Jean-Honoré Fragonard*. New York: H. N. Abrams, 1993. Art historian Massengale provides a study of Fragonard's life and work, comparing the artist's gift and temperament to those of Wolfgang Amadeus Mozart, his near contemporary.

Muehsam, Gerd, ed. *French Painters and Paintings from the Fourteenth Century to Post-Impressionism.* New York: Frederick Ungar, 1970. Contains two illustrations of Fragonard's work and excellent excerpts from studies of his painting. A detailed bibliography and indexes help organize and structure this anthology of criticism.

Shipp, Horace. *The French Masters: A Survey and Guide.* London: S. Low, Marston, 1931. One of the older histories of French art, but still a competent and succinct treatment of Fragonard's place in the context of his teachers and successors. Several black-and-white plates, a chronology of important dates in French history, and an index make this a convenient, accessible source of study.

Wilenski, R. H. *French Painting.* Rev. ed. Boston: Charles T. Branford, 1949. Contains an excellent section on Fragonard's life, his oeuvre, and his accomplishments as an artist. Several black-and-white plates give a representative survey of his work. A judicious and well-indexed study.

See also: Jean-Siméon Chardin; Louis XV; Jean-Jacques Rousseau; Giovanni Battista Tiepolo; Antoine Watteau.

Related articles in *Great Events from History: The Eighteenth Century, 1701-1800*: April, 1762: Rousseau Publishes *The Social Contract*; December 10, 1768: Britain's Royal Academy of Arts Is Founded; 1782-1798: Publication of Rousseau's *Confessions*; 1785: Construction of El Prado Museum Begins; 1787: David Paints *The Death of Socrates*.

BENJAMIN FRANKLIN
American statesman, scientist, and philosopher

Franklin helped shape most of the important political, social, and intellectual developments in eighteenth century America. He became a veritable symbol of the United States by the end of his life, both at home and abroad, and he remains an influential folk hero.

Born: January 17, 1706; Boston, Massachusetts
Died: April 17, 1790; Philadelphia, Pennsylvania
Areas of achievement: Government and politics, diplomacy, business, science and technology, philosophy

EARLY LIFE
Among Benjamin Franklin's English ancestors, one had owned a bit of land only 12 miles from the English ancestral seat of the Washingtons. Franklin's father, Josiah, had repudiated the Church of England and left England for Boston in the 1680's; Franklin's mother's forebears had arrived somewhat earlier. When Franklin was born in 1706, the modest household was already teeming with children, for he was a tenth son—and, incidentally, the youngest son of the youngest son for five generations back. The salient facts of Franklin's life were extraordinary from the start.

Although his father was a struggling tradesman (a candle maker and soap boiler), there was much in the way of reading, thinking, and discussing as well as hard

work in his home. Franklin learned to read when very young, and by the age of twelve he had progressed through the Bible, the works of John Bunyan, Plutarch's *Parallel Lives* (105-115), and certain essays of Daniel Defoe and of Boston's Cotton Mather. He had very little formal schooling, and his family could not afford to send him to Harvard College.

Instead, an effort was made to bring him into the family business. He disliked the work, and he hated the smell. At that point, an older brother, James, returned from London, where he had been trained as a printer. Thus, the restless, bright, bookish twelve-year-old Benjamin Franklin was apprenticed to his high-spirited brother, who in 1721 started a newspaper, *The New England Courant.* It was the fourth newspaper in the colonies. These years were supremely important in shaping the man who later became so famous. He learned a trade that would bring him profits and prominence. He had access to many books, especially those loaned by patrons and friends. He discussed and debated matters with men who loitered in the shop and also with friends after hours. The principal subjects were the two that would be commonly avoided centuries later: religion and politics. He worked hard at learning to write and he experienced the thrill of seeing his first piece, an anonymous letter to the editor, in print. When the pugnacious James got into trouble with the authorities and was jailed, his brother, then sixteen, functioned as the paper's editor.

The brothers often quarreled, and the younger Franklin, a mere apprentice, was often treated severely. He resented this and decided to run away, arriving in Philadelphia in October, 1723, munching on a large roll, with one Dutch dollar and a copper shilling in his pocket. The scene became a memorable passage in the memoir he later wrote, which included the fact that his future wife happened to see him and laughed at the ridiculous sight he made. He soon found work, for he was an excellent printer, and he soon found adventure as well. An eccentric governor of the province, William Keith, proposed that Franklin go to England to purchase equipment for a new printing business Keith hoped would outdo all competition. He would send letters of credit and letters of introduction.

Franklin was in London by Christmas, 1724, but no letters came from the governor. The eighteen-year-old did find work, however, in a printing house, and as always he read intensively and grappled with ideas. After setting type for a religious book, he became convinced that the author was all wrong. In response, Franklin composed and printed a pamphlet that set forth a radical refutation. He later regarded this as a mistake, but it did gain him some attention and some new acquaintances, a few of them prominent writers of the day.

Franklin returned to Philadelphia in 1726 and was soon employed again in his old shop. Before long, he left the shop to form a new business with a partner, on credit. By dint of very long hours of work, ingenious planning, and excellent workmanship, they survived—barely. Then the partner wanted to leave, and Franklin, borrowing money, bought him out. By July, 1730, he was the sole proprietor of a promising business, which included the printing of a newspaper begun the year before, *The Pennsylvania Gazette*. Six weeks later, he married Deborah Read, the daughter of his first landlady. Though she was uneducated (thus never an intellectual companion), she was frugal, industrious, and loving. Franklin, at twenty-four, had become a solid Philadelphia burgher.

LIFE'S WORK
The foundation of Benjamin Franklin's renown was his success as a businessman. Both he and Deborah worked very hard, and they lived frugally for some time. It was, however, more than routine drudgery, for new projects were always appearing: Franklin established a stationery shop; Deborah collected and prepared rags for the paper makers; he imported books in both English and foreign

Benjamin Franklin. (Library of Congress)

languages; he printed almanacs for those who compiled them, and then decided to compile his own. *Poor Richard's Almanack*, begun in 1732 and published between 1733 and 1758, was ultimately to become the best known of the many that were printed in eighteenth century America. Franklin enjoyed borrowing and reworking phrases from his reading and sometimes wrote new adages, which delighted his readers. For many, he and his fictional wise man, Richard Saunders, became one. The central themes of Richard's concern were thrift, industry, and frugality, and Franklin at the time appeared to be practicing what "Poor Richard" preached.

Political connections quickly became an important feature of Franklin's business success. He printed much of the provincial government's work: laws, records of legislative voting, and even the new paper currency in favor of which Franklin had argued in his first political pamphlet, *A Modest Enquiry into the Nature and Necessity of a Paper Currency* (1729). He became clerk of the Pennsylvania Assembly in 1736. The following year, he secured an appointment as postmaster for Philadelphia, a position that gave him immediate access to the latest news—very helpful in his newspaper business. Later, he was deputy postmaster general for all the colonies (1753-1774), and under his administration the governmental department showed a profit. He was always heavily involved with public affairs and often managed to influence their course.

It was during his years as a businessman that Franklin's remarkable flair for civic improvement by private initiative appeared. In 1727, he founded a discussion group, or club, of tradesmen, clerks, and mechanics, which he called the Junto. Often Franklin would first propose to his friends at the Junto for discussion an idea for a public project, and then follow his proposal with an article in his newspaper. Soon the project would be under way. He was prominent in the founding of a circulating library, a fire company, a hospital, and an academy that evolved into the University of Pennsylvania, among many other projects. Ever the keen observer of daily life in his beloved city, he was always alert to possibilities for improvement.

Franklin was also a particularly astute observer of nature, and this ultimately led him to the forefront of certain branches of the sciences of his day. On an early transatlantic voyage, he kept careful records of temperatures, of the flora and fauna of the sea, of the positions of the Moon and the stars; later he made a map of the Gulf Stream. He believed that knowledge must be useful, and actual inventions came out of many of his studies, including the improved Franklin stove, bifocal spectacles, a glass harmonica (a musical instrument for which even Wolfgang Amadeus Mozart wrote music), and other gadgets.

His main interest, though, was electricity. His famous kite experiment in 1752 demonstrated the identity of lightning and electricity and gave him an international reputation. He was, as always, interested in practical application, which in this case became the lightning rod. Nevertheless, he was also responsible for naming the concept of polarity, negative and positive, to describe the behavior of electricity.

In 1748, Franklin was able to retire from business, expecting to devote himself to his favorite scientific pursuits. Public affairs, however, became the dominant force throughout the remainder of his life. When the threat of war with France led to a gathering of delegates at Albany in 1754, Franklin was there representing Pennsylvania. He proposed a plan for an intercolonial union that the Albany Congress approved, only to see it rejected by both the various colonial governments and the imperial authorities in London. Franklin always believed that if these governments had not been so shortsighted,

the American Revolution might have been avoided. In 1757, as a result of a quarrel between the Pennsylvania Assembly and the proprietors of the colony, he was sent to London as spokesman for the assembly, the members of which wanted the authorities there to intervene. In this he achieved a partial success. While in England, he received honorary degrees from St. Andrews and Oxford. He was very happy in England and seriously considered a permanent move, but he came home to Philadelphia in 1762.

Another political quarrel in Pennsylvania led to Franklin's return to England in 1764, where he soon became involved in efforts to forestall the new imperial policies toward the colonies, which Americans regarded as outrageous. For ten years, Franklin was torn between his profound pride in America and things American, and his enthusiasm for English culture. As the foremost American of his day, he was looked to for the preservation of American rights: He became an agent for Georgia, New Jersey, and Massachusetts, as well as the Pennsylvania Assembly. As Anglo-American relations deteriorated, Franklin revealed in private his growing conviction that the American colonists' claims were sound and that their resistance was justified, while he continued to make every diplomatic effort possible for accommodation.

Early in 1774, however, news arrived of the destruction of tea at Boston Harbor, in an act known as the Boston Tea Party. This was quickly followed by a mighty personal attack on Franklin, occasioned by his part in obtaining and circulating certain letters written by Governor Thomas Hutchinson of Massachusetts, the contents of which inflamed opinion against Hutchinson and led to a petition for his recall. Franklin was dismissed by the royal government from his postal appointment and subjected to a searing public humiliation before a committee of the Privy Council (January, 1774). For another year he tried in many ingenious ways to achieve a reconciliation, but to no avail. He sailed for America in March, 1775.

When Franklin arrived home, the Continental Congress, which had first convened during the preceding fall, was now into its second session at Philadelphia. The deliberations were becoming extremely anxious because the unthinkable had happened: Actual fighting had broken out with British soldiers at Lexington and Concord. Franklin was made a member of the congress the day after he arrived, and he immediately undertook important work. He drew up a plan of colonial union, something similar to an early version of a national constitution. He organized a post office and became postmaster general.

A MODERATE, MEATLESS DIET CLEARS THE HEAD FOR STUDY

Benjamin Franklin, in his Autobiography, *wrote about coming across a book as a teen that recommended a vegetable, or vegetarian, diet, which he took to heart. His refusal "to eat flesh" led to his being ridiculed because it was odd for one to not eat meat. He adds in this excerpt that eating and drinking in moderation helped him make "greater progress" in his studies.*

When about sixteen years of age I happened to meet with a book, written by one [Thomas] Tryon, recommending a vegetable diet. I determined to go into it. My brother, being yet unmarried, did not keep house, but boarded himself and his apprentices in another family. My refusing to eat flesh occasioned an inconveniency, and I was frequently chid for my singularity. I made myself acquainted with Tryon's manner of preparing some of his dishes, such as boiling potatoes or rice, making hasty-pudding, and a few others, and then proposed to my brother that if he would give me, weekly, half the money he paid for my board, I would board myself. He instantly agreed to it, and I presently found that I could save half what he paid me. This was an additional fund for buying books. But I had another advantage in it. My brother and the rest going from the printing-house to their meals, I remained there alone, and, despatching presently my light repast, which often was no more than a bisket [biscuit] or a slice of bread, a handful of raisins or a tart from the pastry-cook's, and a glass of water, had the rest of the time till their return for study, in which I made the greater progress from that greater clearness of head and quicker apprehension which usually attend temperance in eating and drinking.

Source: Benjamin Franklin, *The Autobiography of Benjamin Franklin*, electronic edition, p. 6. Independence Hall Association, Philadelphia. http://www.ushistory.org/franklin/autobiography/index.htm. Accessed June, 2005.

He served on a number of important committees, including one that in 1776 was to draft the Declaration of Independence. He was, at the age of seventy, the oldest signer. Toward the end of that year, he was sent by the congress, along with Arthur Lee and Silas Deane, to solicit French support for the American cause.

Franklin was well known in France. He had visited that country before, but more important was his reputation as a scientist, writer (Poor Richard's witticisms had been translated), and apostle of the latest ideas of the Age of Reason. He played the part well, with fur hat and simple clothes, a genial manner, and appropriate bons mots (witticism), and he exuded the spirit of liberty—a veritable backwoods Socrates spreading the truths of nature. Following the American victory at Saratoga (October, 1777), the French became receptive to American suggestions, and by February of 1778, France had become a formal ally. This meant that France was now at war with Great Britain.

Franklin became the sole American ambassador in September of 1778 and, as always, found many interests beyond his principal work. He managed, nevertheless, to keep French-American relations good; France provided America with material aid, an army, and, in the crucial autumn of 1781, a navy. After the British defeat at Yorktown (October, 1781), peace negotiations with Britain began. Franklin was joined by John Adams and John Jay in the final talks, but on several occasions the wily old Philadelphian's role was decisive. It was an excellent treaty for Americans, gaining them a formal acknowledgment of independence and generous boundaries.

When Franklin returned to Philadelphia in September, 1785, he was nearly eighty years old. Yet he was chosen president of the executive council of Pennsylvania, and he became the president of an antislavery society. He was chosen as a Pennsylvania delegate to the Philadelphia Convention, which drew up the U.S. Constitution in 1787, and he gave his prestigious support to its ratification. His last public act was signing a petition to Congress for the abolition of slavery. He died on April 17, 1790.

SIGNIFICANCE

Benjamin Franklin's life was so varied and his achievements so diverse that it seems as though there were several Franklins, though one tends to overlap the other. The most familiar is the successful businessman who rose from humble circumstances to dine with kings, substantially by his own efforts. His life symbolized the rags-to-riches success of a self-made man, a theme of great importance in American thought. His version of his life, as presented in the didactic *The Autobiography of Benjamin Franklin* (1791) and in the sayings of Poor Richard, stressed thrift, industry, and frugality, which were important elements of his own Puritan heritage, rendered in secular, easily understood forms. His zest for useful knowledge became the main style of American science and technology, yet he had great respect for learning and for intellectual curiosity, and he believed that educational opportunity was indispensable for a great future nation.

He was civic-minded from the start. He demonstrated what could be done by private, voluntary community effort to care for human needs, but he also stressed the importance of alert participation in the prevailing political system. His style was egalitarian, tolerant, and democratic before such a style was expected and common; yet he understood well the importance of dignity and deference in human affairs. Americans, during his later years, repudiated kings and hereditary aristocrats, but they also yearned for heroes. Franklin provided them with a hero unlike any other known before.

—Richard D. Miles

FURTHER READING

Aldridge, Alfred Owen. *Benjamin Franklin: Philosopher and Man*. Philadelphia: J. B. Lippincott, 1965. An effort to explain Franklin's human qualities as much as his achievements, this is a judicious, authoritative biography by an author who has done much to expand knowledge of Franklin and who has written extensively about him.

Cohen, I. Bernard. *Franklin and Newton*. Cambridge, Mass.: Harvard University Press, 1966. In this reprint of the excellent 1956 study of eighteenth century scientific thought, Cohen, a historian of science, places Franklin in the context of prevailing notions about scientific method. He appreciates Franklin as a scientist without overstating the case. Especially good depiction of human qualities that affect scientific work.

_____. *Science and the Founding Fathers: Science in the Political Thought of Jefferson, Franklin, Adams, and Madison*. New York: W. W. Norton, 1995. Cohen explains how Franklin and other Founding Fathers were affected by the Age of Reason, seeking to discover the links between scientific principles and constitutional government.

Conner, Paul W. *Poor Richard's Politics: Benjamin Franklin and His New American Order*. New York: Oxford University Press, 1965. A systematic discussion of Franklin's political ideas. This is a thoughtful, well-informed book, filled with materials regarding Franklin's intellectual world. Strong effort to arrive at balanced judgments about Franklin as a thinker.

Crane, Verner W. *Benjamin Franklin and a Rising People*. Boston: Little, Brown, 1954. A succinct, extremely informative, and reliable work, which is especially strong on philosophical, social, and political ideas.

Franklin, Benjamin. *The Autobiography of Benjamin Franklin*. Edited by Leonard W. Labaree et al. New Haven, Conn.: Yale University Press, 1964. Franklin's memoirs (the word "autobiography" was not used in the eighteenth century) have been printed a bewildering number of times, and most readers may well believe that they are familiar with them. It is one of those classics, however, that deserve repeated readings, even though it presents only one of several sides of Franklin's life.

Granger, Bruce I. *Benjamin Franklin: An American Man of Letters*. Ithaca, N.Y.: Cornell University Press, 1964. A skilled presentation of Franklin's literary achievements. Each chapter is devoted to a kind of writing, such as essays, letters, and almanacs. Strong claims are made for Franklin, many of them persuasive.

Isaacson, Walter. *Benjamin Franklin: An American Life*. New York: Simon & Schuster, 2003. In this bestselling popular biography, Isaacson depicts Franklin as "the founding father who winks at us." Clearly written, well researched, and an enjoyable read.

Lopez, Claude-Anne. *Mon Cher Papa*. New Haven, Conn.: Yale University Press, 1966. An unusually charming account of Franklin's life in France during the American Revolution by one of the editors of the Franklin papers. The author does a good job of dispelling some of the myths about Franklin and makes a strong case for his greatness as a diplomat.

Middlekauff, Robert. *Benjamin Franklin and His Enemies*. Berkeley: University of California Press, 1996. Middlekauff presents Franklin as a man of passionate anger who drew the enmity of William Penn, the "founder" of Pennsylvania, and John Adams, among others.

Morgan, Edmund S. *Benjamin Franklin*. New Haven, Conn.: Yale University Press, 2002. Morgan focuses on Franklin's public life, detailing his activities as a politician and diplomat.

Srodes, James. *Franklin: The Essential Founding Father*. Washington, D.C.: Regnery, 2002. Srodes describes Franklin's evolution from "striving craftsman to daring diplomat, spy, and national master builder" in generally favorable terms.

Stourzh, Gerald. *Benjamin Franklin and American Foreign Policy*. Chicago: University of Chicago Press, 1954. A searching, learned analysis of some major features of Franklin's thought. Begins with a review of prevailing currents of thought in the eighteenth century, such as the Great Chain of Being and the belief in progress and reason, then describes how Franklin developed such materials in the course of his diplomatic career.

Van Doren, Carl C. *Benjamin Franklin*. New York: Viking Press, 1938. A magisterial biography, massive and still impressive. This is the kind of book to which one might turn for reliable information about nearly anything regarding Franklin's life. An excellent literary achievement containing profound, extensive scholarship.

See also: John Adams; Samuel Adams; John André; Benjamin Banneker; Charles Carroll; Henry Cavendish; Samuel Chase; George Rogers Clark; John Dickinson; Jonathan Edwards; Richard Howe; Thomas Hutchinson; John Jay; Thomas Jefferson; John Paul Jones; Wolfgang Amadeus Mozart; Thomas Paine; William Pitt the Elder; Benjamin Rush; Alessandro Volta; George Washington; John Peter Zenger.

Related articles in *Great Events from History: The Eighteenth Century, 1701-1800:* 1729: Gray Discovers Principles of Electric Conductivity; 1733: Du Fay Discovers Two Kinds of Electric Charge; October, 1745, and January, 1746: Invention of the Leyden Jar; June, 1752: Franklin Demonstrates the Electrical Nature of Lightning; June 19-July 10, 1754: Albany Congress; December 16, 1773: Boston Tea Party; September 5-October 26, 1774: First Continental Congress; April 14, 1775: Pennsylvania Society for the Abolition of Slavery Is Founded; April 19, 1775: Battle of Lexington and Concord; April 19, 1775-October 19, 1781: American Revolutionary War; May 10-August 2, 1775: Second Continental Congress; May, 1776-September 3, 1783: France Supports the American Revolution; July 4, 1776: Declaration of Independence; July 2, 1777-1804: Northeast States Abolish Slavery; September 19-October 17, 1777: Battles of Saratoga; February 6, 1778: Franco-American Treaties; October 19, 1781: Cornwallis Surrenders at Yorktown; September 3, 1783: Treaty of Paris; September 17, 1787: U.S. Constitution Is Adopted.

FREDERICK I
Elector of Brandenburg (r. 1688-1713) and king of Prussia (r. 1701-1713)

Building on the achievements of his father, Frederick I continued to strengthen the army, to centralize the administration of his possessions, and to support Prussian cultural achievements. He enhanced Prussia's position, obtaining additional jurisdictional powers at the expense of the Holy Roman Empire.

Born: July 11, 1657; Königsberg, East Prussia (now Kaliningrad, Russia)
Died: February 25, 1713; Berlin, Prussia (now in Germany)
Also known as: Frederick III, elector of Brandenburg
Areas of achievement: Government and politics, patronage of the arts

EARLY LIFE
Frederick I was the third son of Frederick William, the Great Elector, and of Louisa Henrietta of Orange-Nassau. As the result of an accident during infancy, Frederick had a deformed spine. His mother did her best to comfort the frail and asthmatic child, supervising his education and introducing him to the arts. She arranged for

excellent tutors, notably Otto von Schwerin and Eberhard von Danckelmann. Danckelmann would serve as Frederick's principal adviser until he fell out of favor in 1697. When Frederick's mother died in 1667 and his father married Dorothea of Holstein-Glücksburg, Frederick's position at court took a turn for the worse, as his new stepmother sought to promote the interests of her own children.

When Frederick's older brother, apparently his father's favorite, died in the course of a military campaign in 1674, the physically unimpressive Frederick became the crown prince. Still, relations between father and son remained cold and distant. To escape the hostile environment at court—his scheming stepmother allegedly had tried to poison him—Frederick spent a considerable amount of time away from home and returned only when his father's health was deteriorating.

After his first wife died in 1683, Frederick married the sixteen-year-old Sophia Charlotte of Hanover. Although intelligent and witty, she was also openly contemptuous of her new environment and of the culture of the Hohenzollern court. In 1688, the Great Elector died after a lengthy illness, and Frederick now assumed the duties of the elector of Brandenburg as Frederick III.

LIFE'S WORK

Frederick's principal goal was to enhance the importance of his far-flung, disjointed possessions and forge them into a kingdom. Building on the financial and military legacy of his father, he strove to strengthen his army and to centralize his administration. He had a strong sense of loyalty to the Holy Roman Emperor, the Habsburg Leopold I, and participated in several military ventures directed against the ambitions of Louis XIV of France.

Although Frederick's well-trained troops performed with distinction in the Wars of the League of Augsburg, he was to be disappointed when the members of the Grand Alliance offered him only minor territorial awards at the Treaty of Ryswick in 1697. Moreover, although he engaged in lengthy negotiations with the emperor over a royal title, he made little progress in actually acquiring such a title, a fact that contributed to the fall of his trusted adviser Danckelmann. Obtaining a royal title became all the more urgent when the elector of Saxony converted to Roman Catholicism and thereby became king of Poland.

An opportunity arose when, following the death of Charles II of Spain in 1700, Leopold I claimed the throne of Spain for Austria. The emperor needed Prussia's troops in the coming conflict, which became known as the War of the Spanish Succession. Appreciative of the eight thousand well-trained Prussian soldiers with which he was provided, Leopold consented to Frederick's assumption of a royal title. Prince Eugene of Savoy, for one, recognized the potential ramifications of a new kingdom in the north and suggested that those who had advised Leopold to agree to Frederick's request should all be hanged.

In 1701, Frederick staged an elaborate coronation ceremony in Königsberg with all the pomp and splendor befitting a baroque prince. However, the new King Frederick I was only allowed to call himself "king in Prussia," because West Prussia was still part of Poland: His royal title was based on the Duchy of Prussia, which lay outside the Holy Roman Empire and was a sovereign territory ruled by the Hohenzollerns. Frederick also emphasized his independence from the Church by placing the crown on his head with his own hands before he similarly crowned the electress.

Compared to the meager territorial gains he made— rewards for his substantial military contributions—Fred-

erick's efforts to raise the cultural level of Brandenburg Prussia met with far greater success. The University of Halle, now a center of Pietism, would train future administrators committed to serving the public good in the spirit of a tolerant Christianity. Here, August Hermann Francke introduced numerous reforms that had a significant impact on the future development of education in Prussia. The university attracted scholars such as the international jurist Christian Thomasius, who argued that an enlightened absolutist ruler's only duty was to rule for the well-being of his subjects.

In 1696, Frederick founded the Prussian Academy of Arts, which attracted the Gdańsk sculptor Andreas Schlueter, the architect of the Charlottenburg Palace. A few years later, Frederick created a society of sciences under the leadership of the philosopher Gottfried Wilhelm Leibniz, who had been called to Berlin on the urging of Sophia Charlotte. Another of the many distinguished personages at his court was the international jurist Samuel von Pufendorf, who made major contributions in the field of historiography.

Unfortunately, all these efforts, as well as the increasingly costly trappings of royal power, required substantial funds, which had to be obtained as subsidies from other powers. Following the dismissal of the fiscally conservative Danckelmann, Frederick's administration was marked by gross mismanagement, wasteful projects, and a series of corrupt officials. These officials took advantage of a king who seemed to be more interested in maintaining a splendid representational court than in the day-to-day operations of his government, resulting in an ever-worsening financial situation.

After the death of Sophia Charlotte in 1705, Frederick, apparently prompted by fears that Crown Prince Frederick William might not be able to produce any more offspring, decided to marry the twenty-three-year-old Sophia Louisa of Mecklenburg-Schwerin. As it turned out, the birth of a grandson, the later Frederick the Great, soon laid his fears to rest. However, the worsening financial situation in the country, exacerbated by bad harvests and the outbreak of the plague in East Prussia in 1709, resulted in a major crisis, which the government was powerless to meet. During the last year of his life, Frederick's health rapidly deteriorated and he died at age fifty-five with his son and successor at his bedside.

SIGNIFICANCE

Compared to the achievements of his father, as well as those of his son and of his grandson, Frederick I's record appears to be modest. Obsessed with maintaining the image of a proper Baroque prince in the style of Louis XIV of France, "crooked Fritz," as the Berliners called the small hunchbacked man, relied on foreign subsidies, greatly limiting his freedom of action. Still, although often poorly served by corrupt officials and pursuing ruinous financial policies, he managed to achieve all of his major objectives.

Acquiring a royal crown clearly enhanced the prestige of Prussia, while establishing primogeniture protected the indispensable foundations for the future growth of Prussia under his son, the so-called Soldier King. Assisted by Sophia Charlotte, he helped to elevate the cultural level of Prussia by attracting intellectuals, artists, and architects to his court. By extending his royal patronage to universities and academies and by supporting the creation of a variety of educational institutions, Frederick had a decisive impact on the future growth and development of Prussia.

—*Helmut J. Schmeller*

FURTHER READING

Dwyer, Philip G., ed. *The Rise of Prussia, 1700-1830*. Harlow, Essex, England: Pearson Education, 2000. Of particular interest in this collection is the essay by Christopher Clark, which analyzes Frederick's role in the establishment of Pietism in Prussia and its influence on society and its institutions.

Fischer-Fabian, S. *Prussia's Glory: The Rise of a Military State*. Translated by Lore Segal and Paul Stern. New York: Macmillan, 1981. The first three chapters of this lively account offer a good description of Frederick's efforts to obtain a royal crown and of the general nature of his rule. Useful genealogical and chronological tables.

Frey, Linda, and Marsha Frey. *Frederick I: The Man and His Times*. Boulder, Colo.: Eastern European Monographs, 1984. Based on extensive archival research, this comprehensive biography of Frederick differs from earlier highly critical assessment by offering a more balanced treatment of Frederick. Excellent discussion of Frederick's foreign policy. Extensive notes but no bibliography.

Gawthrop, Richard L. *Pietism and the Making of Eighteenth Century Prussia*. New York: Cambridge University Press, 1993. Offers an excellent analysis of the evolution of the Hohenzollern state under Frederick I and of the reform efforts of August Hermann Francke. Comprehensive bibliography.

Koch, H. W. *A History of Prussia*. New York: Longman, 1978. This general history of Prussia offers a concise and thoughtful treatment of Frederick as elector and king. Contains excellent maps and genealogical tables.

Neumann, Hans-Joachim. *Friedrich I*. Berlin: Quintessenz Verlag, 2001. This volume focuses on Frederick's contributions towards raising the cultural and intellectual level of his kingdom, including his impact on the architecture of Berlin. The author, a professor of medicine at Humboldt University in Berlin who has written extensively on the Hohenzollern dynasty, also analyzes Frederick's various afflictions.

See also: Eugene of Savoy; Frederick the Great; Frederick William I; Maria Theresa.

Related articles in *Great Events from History: The Eighteenth Century, 1701-1800*: May 26, 1701-September 7, 1714: War of the Spanish Succession; May 31, 1740: Accession of Frederick the Great; October 20, 1740: Maria Theresa Succeeds to the Austrian Throne; December 16, 1740-November 7, 1748: War of the Austrian Succession.

FREDERICK THE GREAT
King of Prussia (r. 1740-1786)

As king of Prussia, Frederick raised the power and prestige of his relatively obscure state, transforming it—through despotic but progressive policies at home and spectacular military victories—into one of Europe's most powerful nations.

Born: January 24, 1712; Berlin, Prussia (now in Germany)

Died: August 17, 1786; Sanssouci, near Potsdam, Prussia (now in Germany)

Also known as: Frederick II

Areas of achievement: Government and politics, warfare and conquest

EARLY LIFE

One of Prussia's greatest kings, Frederick the Great was the son of Frederick William I and Princess Sophia Dorothea of Hannover. As prince and heir to the throne, Frederick had to study government and military matters, as his father prescribed, but the prince found them boring. Frederick William was anti-intellectual and cared only for his army, but Prince Frederick, under the influence of his tutor Duhan de Jandun, developed a passionate love for French language and culture. Relations between father and son became extremely hostile, and the king often beat his son and berated him in public. The queen, on the contrary, encouraged her son's cultural inclinations.

As tensions with his father became unbearable, the prince tried to flee to England with two companions, but all were caught and arrested. Frederick William threatened to remove Prince Frederick from the royal succession if he ever rebelled again, and he imposed upon his son a regimen of training in state and military affairs, which his instructors pursued mercilessly.

At his father's insistence, Frederick married Princess Elizabeth Christina of Brunswick-Bevern in 1733, a loveless union without progeny. By that time, Frederick had capitulated to paternal demands, and, through services he performed in the province of Neumark, he gained a measure of respect from his father.

From 1735 to 1740, Frederick lived at Rheinsberg, an estate north of Berlin. There he enjoyed fellowship with learned friends, played his flute, read, and wrote under the influence of the French philosophes. He corresponded with the brilliant French scholar Voltaire, and he composed *Anti-Machiavel* (1740), a critique of amoral politics. While at Rheinsberg, Frederick im-

proved his relationship with the king by completing all assigned duties competently.

LIFE'S WORK

On May 31, 1740, the quasi-reformed prince became King Frederick II, monarch of Europe's thirteenth largest state. He brought to the throne the conviction that the ruler was the first servant of the state. An atheist, he rejected the theory of divine right monarchy and began to cement his rule. He worked relentlessly for the kingdom, and he expected his subjects to do the same. Frederick made heavy demands upon the nobles, especially for military service. He managed to increase the army from 80,000 eventually to 200,000 men.

Although while at Rheinsberg Frederick had written against amoral politics, as king he made pragmatism the basis of his policy. A striking evidence of this may be seen in his seizure of Silesia from Empress Maria Theresa, which initiated the War of the Austrian Succession. His late father had allowed Austria to decide his foreign policy and had signed a pragmatic sanction, by which he recognized Maria Theresa's right to succeed to the Habsburg throne. Frederick, however, revived a dubious Prussian claim to parts of Austrian Silesia, which he invaded in December, 1740. In this struggle, Prussia allied with France and Bavaria, both of which Frederick deserted once he had realized his objective. Victory enabled him to increase his kingdom by about one third and thereby acquire territory rich in agricultural lands and mineral resources. His skillful military leadership and the performance of his army impressed all the great powers. In his memoirs, the king admitted that he had taken Silesia simply to strengthen Prussia, and he did not think it necessary to justify that move morally.

Frederick's impressive triumph over Austria produced a general alarm about his intentions toward Europe as a whole. The Habsburgs remained unreconciled to their losses, and Maria Theresa branded Frederick "the robber of Silesia." She concluded alliances with Russia, Saxony, and France. Frederick had unwittingly effected a diplomatic revolution, which confronted Prussia with a coalition of Europe's three largest states. Although Frederick was able to gain the support of Great Britain, the future looked bleak for Prussia. Rather than wait to be attacked, Frederick launched a preemptive strike against Saxony, thereby beginning the Seven Years' War (1756-1763).

Frederick had no illusions about the dangers that confronted Prussia. He instructed his mistress to pay no ransom should he be captured and his army to wage war as though he were there. He carried poison, apparently to end his life rather than fall into enemy hands. He led combat operations personally and often exposed himself to danger. The king's heroism had an inspiring effect upon his troops and contributed to some amazing victories over much larger enemy forces.

At first, the Prussian armies won resounding victories and inflicted heavy casualties upon their foes. Finally, however, the sheer weight of numbers took its toll, and Prussia could not replace its losses. Defeat appeared certain, but Empress Elizabeth Petrovna of Russia died in 1762 and left the throne to Peter III, a peculiar personality with an obsessive admiration for Frederick the Great. Russia withdrew from the war. This reenergized the Prussian effort, and by 1763 all combatants were nearing exhaustion. The Treaty of Hubertsburg ratified Prussian possession of Silesia and left Frederick's kingdom the chief power in central Europe.

By 1763, the prestige of Prussia and its heroic king were at their height. No other power could afford to ignore Prussia, whose interests would have to be considered in all significant international matters. Frederick knew this and took full advantage of this hard-won status.

After his great victory of 1763, Frederick made the security of his domain his chief concern. His kingdom was powerful and prosperous as a result of success in postwar reconstruction, and he intended to keep it that way. National security required rapprochement with recent enemies; Frederick therefore turned to Russia, where Catherine the Great had replaced Peter III, her murdered husband, in 1762. Catherine required, as the price of an agreement, Frederick's cooperation in the partition of Poland, over much of which Russia exercised control, and where a succession crisis had erupted. In 1772, Russia, Austria, and Prussia collaborated in dividing about a third of Poland among them.

In domestic affairs, Frederick's achievements are almost as impressive as his triumphs in war and diplomacy. Frederick aspired to be an enlightened ruler. He sought the good of his subjects, but he never relinquished despotic authority over them. He maintained the traditional class structure by relying upon the nobles to fill the army officer corps and the most important posts in the state. He nevertheless enacted many reforms that improved life for all classes of society.

To combat waste and corruption, Frederick eliminated the sale of government offices and conducted regular audits of state funds. He protected peasants against abusive landlords, made the dispensation of justice more equitable, and banned the use of torture for crimes other than treason.

Frederick had no faith, but he believed that religion had social utility by teaching public morality. He respected the rights of Catholics in occupied Silesia, but he pressured priests to support his policies. He employed Jesuits to teach in some schools even after the pope had dissolved that order. The king granted both toleration

Frederick the Great. (Library of Congress)

and citizenship to Jews in his dominions, although Protestantism remained the dominant faith in Prussia. Frederick actually ridiculed Christianity as a superstition. Some of his French critics complained that the only real liberty in autocratic Prussia was the freedom to scorn religion. Frederick could afford to tolerate diverse religions because he was indifferent toward all of them.

Frederick's economic policies reflect his subscription to mercantilism, a government-regulated economy. Salt, coffee, and tobacco were state monopolies, and families were required to buy a stipulated amount of salt annually. When he opened Crown lands to settlement, the king required colonists to pay him dues. They could not leave the land without finding replacements, and they were subject to forced labor. Many features of feudalism remained in Prussia long after they had disappeared in France.

The king owned a third of Prussia's agricultural lands, and he regulated timber, iron, and lead production. Frederick required farmworkers to learn the art of wool spinning, and he gave free looms to immigrant weavers. He was a paternalist who sought to direct the profits from state enterprises toward the public welfare. He assumed that no one knew better than he what was good for his subjects. Yet his economic policies protected the old class structure and thereby retarded the growth of a vigorous middle class. The king placed taxation in the hands of French revenue agents, who were more efficient than any officers who might have been recruited in Prussia. Although government income increased considerably, the presence of foreign officials caused much resentment, which the monarch chose to ignore.

The Seven Years' War exhausted Frederick, and he retired to the seclusion of Potsdam and thereafter seldom appeared in public. In old age, he became irritable and sometimes irrational. When, for example, some Berlin magistrates rendered a verdict that angered him, the king sentenced them to forced labor for a year, despite his subscription to the rule of law.

SIGNIFICANCE

Voltaire, who had been a sort of philosopher-in-residence at the palace from 1750 to 1753, bestowed upon Frederick the title "the Great." The king's remarkable achievements surely justify that appellation, but Frederick was, nevertheless, an authoritarian ruler, a militarist at times, and an advocate of enlightenment only insofar as it would strengthen the state and his control over its affairs. In military matters, he was one of the greatest commanders in history.

Subsequent events seem to indicate that Frederick's Prussia depended too much upon him personally, and when he was gone, his far less able successors were unable to maintain the strength it needed. The Napoleonic Wars brought humiliating defeats, but on the foundation that Frederick the Great laid, Otto von Bismarck built the mighty German Empire, Europe's most powerful state, by the opening of the twentieth century.

—James Edward McGoldrick

FURTHER READING

Asprey, Robert B. *Frederick the Great*. New York: Ticknor & Fields, 1986. A work of fine scholarship and extensive research, placing Frederick in the context of his times and skillfully evaluating his role in history. The lucid style makes it accessible reading for anyone interested in the subject.

Daniels, Emil. "Frederick the Great and His Successors." In *The Cambridge Modern History*. Vol. 6, edited by A. W. Ward et al. Cambridge, England: Cambridge University Press, 1909. Although this treatment appeared years ago, it remains a highly useful analysis containing extensive coverage of Frederick's economic policies and their far-reaching effects. Frederick is portrayed as a progressive ruler with a keen understanding of his nation's needs who improved the quality of life for his subjects and greatly enhanced Prussia's international standing.

Fraser, David. *Frederick the Great: King of Prussia*. New York: A. Lane, 2000. Fraser, a general and biographer, focuses on Frederick's military career. The book contains detailed descriptions of battles and military strategy, placing these conflicts within the context of eighteenth century European diplomacy and political history.

Horn, D. B. *Frederick the Great and the Rise of Prussia*. New York: Harper & Row, 1964. A delightfully written work combining a biography with a political history of eighteenth century Prussia. Intended for general readers, it nevertheless displays erudite research and scholarship.

Johnson, Hubert C. *Frederick the Great and His Officials*. New Haven, Conn.: Yale University Press, 1975. Scholarly examination of Prussia's development under Frederick's scrupulous and relentless direction, aimed at readers who have some previous knowledge of Frederick and this period in history. Johnson explains how Frederick demonstrated unusual managerial abilities in supervising the political and economic administration of his state.

MacDonogh, Giles. *Frederick the Great: A Life in Deed and Letters*. New York: St. Martin's Press, 2000. Comprehensive biography, based on meticulous research into primary documents, including Frederick's correspondence. Readers already familiar with Frederick will not find new revelations, but the book is a useful introduction for students and others who want to know more about the man and his times.

Paret, Peter, ed. *Frederick the Great: A Profile*. New York: Hill & Wang, 1972. Despite his overwhelming importance in European history, Frederick has always been a controversial figure. Paret unites diverse interpretations of Frederick's policies and his role in history, allowing readers to ascertain how Frederick's career has impressed a variety of scholars.

Ritter, Gerhard. *Frederick the Great: A Historical Profile*. Translated by Peter Paret. Berkeley: University of California Press, 1968. Widely acclaimed critical biography by a renowned scholar of German history, best understood by readers with some previous acquaintance with Prussian history and Frederick's role in it.

Schieder, Theodor. *Frederick the Great*. Edited and translated by Sabina Berkeley and H. M. Scott. New York: Addison Wesley Longman, 1999. Abridged English translation of a biography published in 1983. Although the original notes, bibliography, and a chapter on Frederick and the concept of "historical greatness" have been deleted, the remaining book provides a useful introduction to Frederick's life and career.

See also: Catherine the Great; Elizabeth Petrovna; Frederick I; Frederick William I; Maria Theresa; Peter III; Voltaire.

Related articles in *Great Events from History: The Eighteenth Century, 1701-1800*: May 31, 1740: Accession of Frederick the Great; October 20, 1740: Maria Theresa Succeeds to the Austrian Throne; December 16, 1740-November 7, 1748: War of the Austrian Succession; January, 1756-February 15, 1763: Seven Years' War; January, 1759: Voltaire Satirizes Optimism in *Candide*; July, 1764: Voltaire Publishes *A Philosophical Dictionary for the Pocket*; August 10, 1767: Catherine the Great's Instruction.

FREDERICK WILLIAM I
King of Prussia (r. 1713-1740)

Frederick William I was responsible for developing Prussia into a legendary military power. He created the militaristic civil institutions and nationalistic discipline that eventually led to the unification of Germany under Prince Otto von Bismarck and the aggressiveness of Germany under Kaiser Wilhelm II and Adolf Hitler.

Born: August 15, 1688; Berlin, Prussia (now in Germany)

Died: May 31, 1740; Potsdam, Prussia (now in Germany)

Also known as: Friedrich Wilhelm von Hohenzollern (full name); the Soldier King

Areas of achievement: Government and politics, military

EARLY LIFE

Frederick William I, the son and heir of the first king in Prussia, Frederick I, was raised in the strict military environment that was the legacy of his grandfather, Frederick William, the Great Elector, whose policies and successes, from the end of the Thirty Years' War in 1648 until his death in 1688, ultimately enabled his son Frederick to found Prussia in 1701 as Europe's first secular military kingdom. Frederick I did not possess the great elector's military and political genius, but Frederick William's talents and inclinations resembled his grandfather's more than his father's.

As crown prince, Frederick William married his cousin, Sophia Dorothea, daughter of King George I of Great Britain, on November 28, 1706. He fought under John Churchill, first duke of Marlborough, in the War of the Spanish Succession (1701-1714), relishing his role in Marlborough's Pyrrhic victory at Malplaquet on September 11, 1709, and seeming to delight in the butchery. Eventually, he would be known as the Soldier King. In 1710, disgusted at the fiscal mismanagement wrought by several of his father's advisers, notably Augustus Wittgenstein and Johann Kasimir Graf von Wartenberg, and even more disgusted that his father remained blind to their corruption and incompetence, Frederick William preempted the king's authority to engineer their dismissal. Such unilateral decisiveness characterized his life.

LIFE'S WORK

When Frederick William I ascended the Prussian throne on February 25, 1713, he set as the goal of his monarchy the restoration of Prussia to the power and prestige that Brandenburg had enjoyed under his grandfather. When he became king, the army numbered between twenty-five thousand and forty thousand men, or about 1 percent of the population, and the country was nearly bankrupt. Frederick William was convinced that a renewal of the militaristic policies of the great elector would refill the national coffers and restore national morale.

Where his father had been extravagant and impulsive, Frederick William was frugal and restrained. To bring Prussia out of the financial crisis that his father's mistakes and inattention had created, he immediately imposed economic austerity on the kingdom and personally shared in the privations that his subjects suffered. He governed as an absolute monarch, imposing his strict Pietist-Calvinist ideals of severity and diligence on the entire citizenry, but he did not "live like a king." Instead, he shared their burden. Frugal almost to the point of miserliness, Frederick William never wore fine clothes, ate fancy meals, or indulged in frivolous pastimes. He fired so many palace servants that the queen and princesses themselves had to wash the dishes. According to Thomas Carlyle, Frederick William ruled like a drill sergeant.

Frederick William worked assiduously on administration, reform, and especially military matters. He instituted important reforms in agriculture, industry, and commerce, but his main aim was to transform the entire country into an armed camp with the largest and best-trained standing army in Europe. He invented or improved several methods of drill for the Prussian army, and his aide, Prince Leopold of Anhalt-Dessau, invented the "goose step" that would become notorious under the Nazis. The king replaced the feudal hierarchy with a military one and changed the system of royal favors from a hereditary or plutocratic basis to a strict meritocracy. This had the advantage of ensuring that the officers of the Prussian army were all supremely qualified by education, character, and discipline, since commissions could no longer be inherited or bought. He made military education readily available to all, even peasants. As he was especially fond of tall soldiers, he paid bonuses and sometimes resorted to subterfuge to enlist tall men.

Among Frederick William's earliest acts as king was to conspire with Russia against Sweden. The small but strong Prussian army, commanded by Anhalt-Dessau, entered the Great Northern War in 1715 and helped the Danish-Russian-Saxon alliance defeat Sweden at the Battle of Stresow. Frederick William intimidated Charles XII of Sweden enough to gain the city of Stettin in 1715 and most of the province of Pomerania by 1720. This was the only time that Prussian troops took to the battlefield during his reign. He kept out of the other two major European conflicts of his time, the War of the Quadruple Alliance (1718-1720) and the War of the Polish Succession (1733-1735), but was friendly with the winning side in both cases.

Frederick William was a bully as a boy, and throughout his life he remained mean, bad-tempered, boorish, physically violent, and usually angry. He had no love of art, literature, music, science, intellectual activity, or culture, especially French culture. He expected all of this to be sacrificed for the sake of military greatness. Yet curiously, he was himself a fairly accomplished painter. He suffered from gout, migraine, indigestion, insomnia, heart trouble, depression, and several other chronic ailments. Toward the end of his life, he became overweight and had to use a wheelchair. He seemed to be in constant mental, emotional, and physical pain. He inscribed his famous self-portrait "in tormentis pinxit," which means "painted in pain" in Latin.

Frederick William's love of anything military and hatred of almost everything nonmilitary even extended to physical abuse of eminent practitioners of nonmilitary interests, including his own heir, the future Frederick the Great. His cruelty toward his elder son was notorious. He tortured the prince with chokings, kickings, public beatings, humiliations, threats of disinheritance and even execution, and overt preference for his other son, August William. Young Frederick tried to run away three times, but he survived his brutal upbringing to rule Prussia for forty-six years as Frederick the Great.

Even though Frederick William despised nearly everyone, he always dutifully provided for the well-being of all Prussians. The profound mutual hatred between him and his cousin and brother-in-law, George II of Great Britain, influenced the foreign policies of both nations, but the Prussian monarch was able to make an objective decision when necessary.

SIGNIFICANCE

Frederick William I did not fight any battles himself as king, but when he died, Prussia was the strongest military power in central Europe. He bequeathed to his son a huge treasury and a mighty army of between eighty-one thousand and eighty-five thousand superbly trained soldiers. The average population of Prussia during his reign was about 2.5 million, and the average size of his standing army was about eighty thousand, just over 3 percent of the population, or about 11 percent of the able-bodied men. His culture of discipline and obedience developed the regimented society that eventually unified Germany and started the Franco-Prussian War (1870-1871), World War I (1914-1918), and World War II (1939-1945).

Despite his inclinations to the contrary, Frederick the Great maintained the military establishment as his father wished and even developed it further, fighting many battles along the way. The irony is that his father's army provided Prussia with the security that allowed Frederick to become a major patron of European art and literature.

—Eric v.d. Luft

FURTHER READING

Büsch, Otto. *Military System and Social Life in Old Regime Prussia, 1713-1807: The Beginning of the Social Militarization of Prusso-German Society*. Translated by John G. Gagliardo. Atlantic Highlands, N.J.: Humanities Press, 1997. A political analysis centered on the pervasive military atmosphere in all aspects of Prussian culture.

Carsten, Francis Ludwig. *The Origins of Prussia*. Westport, Conn.: Greenwood Press, 1981. Explains the origins of the nationalistic and imperialistic attitudes and the political, social, and economic instititions that provided the conditions for the emergence of modern Germany.

Dorwart, Reinhold August. *The Administrative Reforms of Frederick William I of Prussia*. Westport, Conn.: Greenwood Press, 1971. A political history rather than a biography.

Dwyer, Philip G., ed. *The Rise of Prussia, 1700-1830*. Harlow, England: Longman, 2000. A seamless collection of commissioned chapters by leading historians, explaining and sometimes justifying Frederick William's reasons for his policies.

Ergang, Robert Reinhold. *The Potsdam Führer: Frederick William I, Father of Prussian Militarism*. New York: Octagon, 1972. The standard biography.

Feuchtwanger, E. J. *Prussia: Myth and Reality: The Role of Prussia in German History*. Chicago: Henry Regnery, 1970. An evaluation of Prussia's and early Germany's role in the geopolitics of Central Europe.

Frey, Linda, and Marsha Frey. *Frederick I: The Man and His Times*. New York: Columbia University Press, 1984. Includes a clear account of Frederick William's life as crown prince.

MacDonogh, Giles. *Frederick the Great: A Life in Deed and Letters*. New York: St. Martin's Press, 1999. Contains stunning stories of Frederick William's relentless cruelty to his son and heir.

Nelson, Walter Henry. *The Soldier Kings: The House of Hohenzollern*. New York: Putnam, 1970. The standard history of this royal family.

Oppenheim, Walter. *Habsburgs and Hohenzollerns, 1713-1786*. London: Hodder & Stoughton, 1993. Introduction to the diplomatic and military intrigues among the Holy Roman Empire, Austria, Prussia, and the various Protestant German states.

Thadden, Rudolf von. *Prussia: The History of a Lost State*. Translated by Angi Rutter. New York: Cambridge University Press, 1987. A general but authoritative survey.

See also: Charles XII; Frederick I; Frederick the Great; George I; George II; First Duke of Marlborough.

Related articles in *Great Events from History: The Eighteenth Century, 1701-1800*: c. 1701-1721: Great Northern War; May 26, 1701-September 7, 1714: War of the Spanish Succession; September 11, 1709: Battle of Malplaquet; October 10, 1733-October 3, 1735: War of the Polish Succession; May 31, 1740: Accession of Frederick the Great; October 20, 1740: Maria Theresa Succeeds to the Austrian Throne; December 16, 1740-November 7, 1748: War of the Austrian Succession.

THOMAS GAGE
English military leader and administrator

A skillful organizer and an efficient administrator, Gage helped to establish Great Britain's first empire on a solid footing through service as governor at Montreal and military commander in America.

Born: 1721; Firle, Sussex, England
Died: April 2, 1787; London, England
Areas of achievement: Military, warfare and conquest, government and politics

EARLY LIFE

Thomas Gage, whose precise date of birth is unknown, was the son of Thomas Gage, first Viscount Gage (in the Irish peerage), and Benedicta Maria Theresa Hall. In January, 1728, young Thomas and his brother William, who was two years older, were enrolled in the school at Westminster. For the next eight years, Thomas Gage labored through the curriculum, achieving competence but not brilliance. Far more important to him than studies were the influential friends he made while at school. Many of them would rise to high rank in the army or in politics, where they could be of service to him in later life. Furthermore, Westminster made a lasting impression, for Gage would later send his four sons there.

Even before leaving school in 1736, he had decided upon a career in the army. Through the influence of the duke of Newcastle, who was a family friend, Gage obtained his first appointment. By January 30, 1741, he purchased a lieutenant's commission in the regiment known as the First Northampton. Within eighteen months he transferred to Battereau's Regiment, becoming a captain lieutenant in May, 1742. Eight months later, he obtained a captaincy in that same unit. Gage's first exposure to battle occurred in 1744, when his regiment served in France under the duke of Albemarle. The duke was the father of Gage's school friends, George and Augustus Keppel. After the bloody Battle of Fontenoy in 1745, Gage accompanied Albemarle on an expedition against the Scottish. At the Battle of Culloden, he witnessed the second rout by British troops within a year. When Albemarle returned his army to the Continent in 1747, Gage accompanied him.

LIFE'S WORK

In 1748, Thomas Gage transferred to the Forty-fourth Regiment, where he was able to purchase a commission as major. After three years of service, he was promoted to the rank of lieutenant colonel on March 2, 1751. Like many officers in the permanent army establishment, he was stationed in Ireland during the late 1740's and 1750's. Stationing troops in Ireland served the purposes of avoiding the objections of the English to peacetime standing armies, maintaining troops ready for the possibility of renewed warfare, and providing forces sufficient to intimidate the Irish.

The slender, aristocratic young officer, of medium height, did not mind his Irish sojourn, but he was pleased with his unit's relocation to North America in 1754. The century-old Anglo-French conflict was about to erupt anew. An officer seeking promotion was eager for service wherever there was the promise of battlefield action.

On the western border of Virginia, Colonel George Washington's troops had been turned back in their attempt to stop construction of a French fort located near what is now Pittsburgh, Pennsylvania. Consequently, General Edward Braddock was ordered to lead an expedition against the new Fort Duquesne. Gage's Forty-fourth Regiment was instructed to join Braddock. Although the unit sailed in mid-January, 1755, it did not reach the American frontier until August. Trapped in a crossfire by the French and their allies, the English were slaughtered and turned back. Although Gage bravely commanded the advance guard, as well as the contingent trying to cover the retreat, he could save neither the expedition nor the mortally wounded Braddock. After withdrawing into Pennsylvania, Gage's regiment was ordered into winter quarters at Albany, New York.

Largely because of ineffective army leadership in 1755 and 1756, Gage and his troops spent two winters in Albany, broken only by an expedition designed to relieve the British post at Oswego, a venture that failed because the post fell to the French first. During his long periods of inactivity, Gage reflected on improvements in the army. Like other young officers, Gage believed that the army needed more light-infantry units that would respond quickly to tactical changes on the battlefield, a need demonstrated by his experience on the Braddock expedition. Partly to create such a unit and partly to obtain promotion to colonel, Gage offered to raise a regiment of light troops that he called "chasseurs." With the approval and assistance of his commander, he began recruiting for this new Eightieth Regiment. Late in 1757, he established his recruiting headquarters at New Brunswick, New Jersey, which was, not coincidentally, the home of the Kemble family, whose daughter, Margaret, would become his bride.

In 1758, Gage's courtship was temporarily interrupted by the summer's campaign. Gage and his troops joined the unsuccessful British expedition against Fort Ticonderoga. By the fall of that year, however, he returned south to New Jersey. En route, he stopped in New York, where he learned that he had been promoted to brigadier general on the American establishment. After being married on December 8, he and his bride journeyed to Albany, New York, where he was commander during winter quarters.

During most of the 1759 campaign, Gage served on the staff of General Jeffrey Amherst, but when the commanding officer of a British expedition against Niagara was killed, Gage replaced him. In his new command Gage was ordered to advance eastward toward La Gallete. Underestimating his own strength and fearing the onset of winter, he failed to advance as instructed. When bad weather closed operations for the year, he returned to Albany, again the commander of winter quarters.

Although he was fortunate in being able to spend the season with his wife, he was ordered back into the field in the spring of 1760. He commanded the rear guard in the army of General Amherst that reached Montreal on Sep-

General Thomas Gage. (Library of Congress)

tember 6, 1760, two days before the French surrender. Before Amherst returned to his headquarters in New York, he appointed Gage military governor for Montreal.

For three years, from October, 1760, to October, 1763, Gage governed Montreal. As the official responsible for twenty-five thousand French civilians, Gage faced the endless trivialities of civilian administration. Life was not altogether mundane, however, for his bride joined him late in 1760. In March, 1762, their first child, Henry, was born: He would later become the third Viscount Gage. In the course of their marriage, the Gages would have four boys and four girls.

As a career officer in the army, Gage was concerned about promotions. With his brother's support, he managed advancement to major general in 1761; the next year, he secured the colonelcy of the Twenty-second Regiment. Despite these preferments, Gage worried about peacetime placement. He raised this matter with Amherst, who advised patience. Amherst knew that he was taking a leave from which he had no intention of returning. Once in England, Amherst resigned and had Gage appointed commander in America. The general and his family then moved to New York, taking up residence in a large house on Broad Street, where they resided happily from 1763 to 1772.

The first major crisis facing Gage as commanding general was an American Indian war that had erupted even before Amherst's departure. On the Western frontiers the charismatic Ottawa leader named Pontiac had achieved dramatic victories. Numerous British outposts had been overwhelmed, leaving only Pittsburgh and Detroit intact.

Under the strategy envisioned by Amherst and adopted by Gage, troops were to move westward from Niagara under General Bradstreet to crush the upper Ohio tribes in one-half of a pincer movement. From the south, the pincers would be closed by General Henry Bouquet and his force advancing into the Ohio Country from Fort Pitt. Unfortunately, both of Gage's commanders accepted peace overtures before any American Indian leaders or tribes had been punished. Many colonials questioned the presence of British regulars who could not even punish Indians. Through negotiation and diplomacy, however, Gage did manage to bring a conclusion to the hostilities.

Colonial protests against parliamentary policies, however, were pushing the Americans toward rebellion. There were riots from Massachusetts to Virginia. In New York, Gage improved the defenses of a long-unused fort in the harbor and exchanged letters with several governors about the situations in their respective colonies. He understood that he could not simply exercise his power as commander; in the best English tradition, he had to cooperate with the civilian authorities. Thus, when the colonials assembled in New York to protest against the Stamp Act, Gage could only observe. Indeed, he and his troops remained quietly in defensive positions during the riots of November, 1765.

During the next three years, however, relations between Great Britain and the Thirteen Colonies worsened. Protests in Boston became so violent by 1768 that the British government stationed more troops there. For the next five years, Gage labored to assist the civilian authorities throughout the colonies, to the loud denunciations of the colonial protesters.

In the summer of 1773, after more than seventeen years in America without leave, Gage and his wife sailed to England. Gage consulted at length with officials about the dangerous American situation. By the spring of 1774, Parliament had passed legislation designed to bring Boston back to order. Gage's role would be crucial, since he was to return as both military commander and as governor of Massachusetts. Soon after his return he concluded that the colonials would not yield to parliamentary demands, that the Bostonians were ready to fight, and that the colonists to the south would support them. In the face of this determination, Gage insisted that he would not be responsible for war; he would act only on instructions from London.

Accordingly, not until orders from London arrived in April, 1775, did Gage send troops out from Boston, resulting in the shots heard around the world. When this news reached London, Gage's enemies, such as Lord George Germain, actively sought his replacement. The king delayed his decision until he learned the cost of the British victory on Bunker Hill; he then agreed that Gage should come home. In the fall of 1775, therefore, Gage returned to England technically to aid in planning the campaign for 1776 that he would lead, but actually never to return. He lived quietly in London for the next eleven years at his home in Portland Place, where he died on April 2, 1787, ever the faithful servant of the Crown.

SIGNIFICANCE

The career of Thomas Gage was inexorably interwoven with the growth of the British Empire. He entered public service as Great Britain was concluding more than a century of war with France, a struggle that continued for the first twenty-five years of his service. During his early

years, he witnessed many British soldier-civil servants who succeeded largely through sheer determination. Like his fellow junior officers, he benefited from the achievements of the brilliant General James Wolfe. Gage, however, was no Wolfe, but a patient organizer and administrator. In these capacities he shone, first as governor at Montreal, then as peacetime military commander at New York. Both citizenries applauded Gage as a humane, efficient public servant. Although such pedestrian activities seldom yield laurels, empires must have such leaders or the empires will not last beyond the lifetimes of those tireless bureaucrats who make the system work. The colonies seized by the mailed fists of commanders such as Wolfe had to be integrated into the empire by the gloved hands of administrators such as Thomas Gage.

—*James H. O'Donnell III*

FURTHER READING

Alden, John Richard. *General Gage in America: Being Principally a History of His Role in the American Revolution*. Baton Rouge: Louisiana State University Press, 1948. An early attempt at a biography of Gage, which remains the standard account of the general's leadership at the beginning of the American Revolution. It is basically a sympathetic treatment, suggesting that, given the circumstances, Gage did the best he could.

_____. *A History of the American Revolution*. New York: Alfred A. Knopf, 1969. In this account of the revolution, Alden provides a balanced analysis of the role played by Gage at the outset of the war. Although basically sympathetic to Gage, Alden nevertheless informs the reader of London's critical attitude toward the general and of the commander's intentions regarding the American war and his role in it.

Gage, Thomas. *The Correspondence of General Thomas Gage with the Secretaries of State, 1763-1770*. Edited by Clarence Carter. 2 vols. New Haven, Conn.: Yale University Press, 1931-1933. A valuable selection of correspondence, well edited by Carter. Indispensable because it makes Gage accessible. Simply browsing through the volumes makes the reader aware of the scope of the general's responsibilities.

Gipson, Lawrence H. *The British Empire Before the American Revolution*. Vols. 1-3. Caldwell, Idaho: Caxton, 1935. Vols. 4-15. New York: Alfred A. Knopf, 1939-1970. While this monumental work deals with the larger questions of empire, it takes note of the army and its leaders in the prelude to the American Revolution. It will be helpful to the student who wishes to understand the imperial context of decision making.

Gruber, Ira D. *The Howe Brothers and the American Revolution.* New York: W. W. Norton, 1972. Although this is a book about Gage's successor, William Howe, and his brother, Admiral Richard Howe, the study provides insight into the army's decision-making process and offers a comparison of the two generals. It is useful to reflect that the Howes fared little better in solving American problems than did Gage.

McCue, Michael Westaway. "The Spy Who Wasn't There." *American History* 36, no. 4 (October, 2001): 56. Examines the mystery surrounding John Howe, an alleged spy for the British army before the start of the American Revolution. In his journal, Howe claimed that Gage asked him to perform surveillance activities in Massachusetts in April, 1775. The article contains information about Gage's actions and attitudes before and during the revolution.

Shy, John. "Thomas Gage: Weak Link of Empire." In *George Washington's Opponents: British Generals and Admirals in the American Revolution.* Edited by George Billias. New York: William Morrow, 1969. Shy's study is as critical of Gage's failures in leadership as Alden's is sympathetic. Shy's research on the nature of the British army in the eighteenth century makes his work a particularly useful supplement to Alden's more supportive assessment.

_____. *Toward Lexington: The Role of the British Army in the Coming of the Revolution.* Princeton, N.J.: Princeton University Press, 1965. Shy explains how the British army was an imperial institution whose leaders and soldiers were instrumental in shaping the course of empire. This volume conveys the sense in which officers such as Gage were controlled by a system from which they could not escape.

See also: Samuel Adams; Lord Amherst; Benedict Arnold; Sir Guy Carleton; Sir Henry Clinton; First Marquess Cornwallis; George III; Nathanael Greene; John Hancock; Richard Howe; William Howe; Pontiac; Paul Revere; George Washington; James Wolfe.

Related articles in *Great Events from History: The Eighteenth Century, 1701-1800:* March 22, 1765-March 18, 1766: Stamp Act Crisis; June 29, 1767-April 12, 1770: Townshend Crisis; March 5, 1770: Boston Massacre; December 16, 1773: Boston Tea Party; May 20, 1774: Quebec Act; April 19, 1775: Battle of Lexington and Concord; October 19, 1781: Cornwallis Surrenders at Yorktown; September 17, 1787: U.S. Constitution Is Adopted.

THOMAS GAINSBOROUGH
English painter

Through his landscapes and portraits, Gainsborough became one of the most creative English painters of his age and an inspiration to many significant artists of the nineteenth century.

Born: May 14, 1727 (baptized); Sudbury, Suffolk, England
Died: August 2, 1788; London, England
Area of achievement: Art

EARLY LIFE

Thomas Gainsborough (GAYNZ-buhr-oh) was born in a small Suffolk village, some 50 miles northeast of London. The exact date of his birth is unknown, but records show that he was baptized on May 14, 1727, at the local Independent Meeting House. Born into a large Dissenter family of nine children, Thomas was the fifth and youngest son.

Thomas's father, John Gainsborough, was engaged in the wool trade. His mother, born Mary Burroughs, was a cultivated woman who enjoyed painting flowers and who encouraged her son's artistic inclinations. The young Gainsborough attended the local grammar school run by his uncle, the Reverend Humphry Burroughs, but he displayed no significant academic ambitions and preferred to wander through the countryside with his sketchbook.

Convinced that Thomas's artistic abilities showed sufficient promise, the Gainsboroughs sent their thirteen-year-old son to London in 1740, where he initially lived in the household of a respectable silver engraver. For a while he worked with the engraver and draftsman Hubert Gravelot, a Frenchman trained in the rococo style. He was also influenced by Francis Hayman, an English painter and engraver who dabbled in theatrical scenery. It was Hayman, with his rather dissolute reputation, who introduced Gainsborough to the more risqué aspects of London life, initiating his lifelong affinity for women and drink.

The young Gainsborough briefly attended an art school sponsored by William Hogarth, then England's most famous living artist, but it remains uncertain whether the two ever met. Evidently, Gainsborough's natural abilities enabled him to become self-supporting soon after his arrival in London. As his proficiency increased, art dealers hired him to repair old paintings, which afforded him the opportunity to study works by the old masters in detail. He was particularly attracted to the works of Dutch landscape painters such as Jacob van Ruisdael.

By 1745, the eighteen-year-old artist had his own fledgling business. He preoccupied himself with portraits and landscapes, a few of which sold for modest sums. Convivial, lively, and impulsive, Gainsborough showed no inclination to mingle with the elite of English society. Throughout his life, he preferred the companionship of musicians and theater people. He seldom read a book and generally avoided London's active literary circles (although he became good friends with the playwright Richard Brinsley Sheridan), nor did he develop any significant political inclinations. Self-portraits from this period reveal a handsome young man, dignified without being pretentious.

On July 15, 1746, Gainsborough married Margaret Burr, an eighteen-year-old of great charm and beauty who was evidently the illegitimate daughter of the duke of Beaufort. The duke provided Margaret with an annual annuity of £200, a handsome sum that provided the young couple with some financial security while Gainsborough struggled to become financially successful as an artist. His initial efforts to obtain lucrative commissions proved unsuccessful, and when his father died in the autumn of 1748, the young artist decided to return to his native Sudbury to help settle the family estate.

LIFE'S WORK

Thomas Gainsborough's productive career encompassed three basic phases. From 1748 through 1759, he remained a relatively obscure painter in Suffolk. After a few years in Sudbury, he moved his family, which by now included two daughters, to the nearby village of Ipswich. A thriving community of some eleven thousand, Ipswich boasted many citizens who had become wealthy in the wool trade. Gainsborough undoubtedly hoped that they and the local gentry would provide him with sufficient commissions to make a credible income.

Gainsborough had become convinced that portraiture was the only type of painting likely to lead to financial security, although his lifelong preference was for landscapes. He initially experimented with a format that depicted his clients amid a lush setting of English countryside. Although some eighty portraits of this Suffolk period have been identified, they did not bring him sufficient income to prevent his experiencing financial difficulties throughout much of the 1750's.

Gainsborough led a fairly quiet and inconspicuous existence in Ipswich. His chief recreation consisted of long walks in the countryside to indulge his penchant for sketching and participation in a local society of musicians. Although it remains uncertain whether he learned to read music, he became an accomplished fiddler and evidently learned to play several other instruments.

One of the most influential friends Gainsborough made during this period was Philip Thicknesse, the governor of nearby Landguard Fort, who was one of the first to recognize the young painter's gifts. At the urging of Thicknesse, Gainsborough sold his house and goods at Ipswich in 1759 and moved his family to Bath, thus beginning the second phase of his career. Bath was England's most fashionable winter resort. Almost immediately, Gainsborough's portraits attracted the attention of the fashionable and wealthy Englishmen who wintered in the town, and he quickly rose to become the most prominent artist in the area. Within seven years, he was living in luxurious quarters at the Circus, the city's most prestigious address.

The growing success of Gainsborough's portraiture increased his reputation in the capital. In 1761, he submitted a portrait for exhibition at the newly formed Society of Artists in London, and one of the works he sent the following year brought him his first significantly favorable attention in the London press. By 1768, his reputation was sufficiently established for him to be invited to become one of the thirty-six original members of the Royal Academy, the only non-London resident so honored. For the next several years, he regularly sent works to the academy's annual exhibition, and by the time he finally decided to move to London in 1774, he was one of England's most famous artists. The move to London inaugurated the third and most successful phase of Gainsborough's career. He secured prestigious lodgings at Schomberg House, part of a ducal mansion on Pall Mall, one of the city's most fashionable streets. By 1777, he had his own carriage and footman, signs of a highly advanced social status.

Soon after his arrival in London, Gainsborough was invited to the palace and became the favorite painter of the royal family. He produced eight portraits of George

III and many others of the rest of the numerous members of the royal family. No courtier by nature, Gainsborough basically found his work at the palace tedious and seemed artistically inspired only by Queen Charlotte.

During these London years, Gainsborough's only significant rival was Sir Joshua Reynolds, the first president of the Royal Academy. Contemporary newspapers and many subsequent works exaggerated the degree of their rivalry. Unlike Reynolds, Gainsborough never studied in Italy and was not enamored of the classical tradition that so dominated Reynolds's style. Although competitors in the same market, the two recognized each other's talent. In 1782, Reynolds even purchased Gainsborough's *Girl with Pigs* (1782) for 100 guineas, 40 more than the original asking price.

Although his relationship with Reynolds remained gentlemanly, Gainsborough did quarrel repeatedly with the Royal Academy. Even after his election to the governing council in 1775, he never bothered to attend an academy meeting. The chief difficulty concerned the manner in which the academy chose to hang Gainsborough's pictures at its annual exhibitions.

Gainsborough objected to some of the rigid rules regarding the placement of portraits and other works because he judged they did not always display his paintings in the best manner. He boycotted the exhibitions of 1773 through 1776, and in 1784 a final quarrel over the hanging of a portrait of three of King George's daughters led Gainsborough to withdraw all of his works. He refused to exhibit with the academy for the rest of his life and instead opened his own public exhibition room at Schomberg House.

Although he enjoyed considerable financial success and public recognition during these years, Gainsborough's home life was far from idyllic. His wife became increasingly demanding, and both of his daughters grew into unstable young women. Margaret, the elder, an eccentric, died unmarried in 1820; her younger sister, Mary, had a brief, unsuccessful marriage to a musician of whom her father disapproved and eventually became totally insane before her death in 1826.

During his final years, Gainsborough was able to command princely sums for his portraits: 40 guineas for a head, 80 for a half-length, and 160 for a full-length rendition. In contrast, his portraits from his Suffolk period had brought him only 8 to 15 guineas.

Gainsborough's final illness began in the spring of 1788, when he noticed a lump on the back of his neck. Initially diagnosed as merely a swollen gland, it proved to be cancer. He continued painting almost to the end and had a final emotional farewell with Reynolds before dying at Schomberg House on August 2. Six of his fellow artists, including Reynolds, served as pallbearers. Four months afterward, Reynolds made Gainsborough the chief subject of his fourteenth discourse to the students at the academy, the only English artist he ever so honored.

SIGNIFICANCE

Along with William Hogarth and Sir Joshua Reynolds, Thomas Gainsborough ranks as one of the giants of eighteenth century English painting. His lifetime output was prodigious, including more than seven hundred known portraits, between two hundred and three hundred landscape paintings, and numerous landscape drawings. His portraits, many of them clearly inspired by the style of Sir Anthony Van Dyck, provide posterity with an incredible panorama of personalities from the great age of English oligarchy. Figures as diverse as Samuel Johnson, Benjamin Franklin, Edmund Burke, and actor Sarah Siddons all posed for the great master. When inspired by his subject, Gainsborough frequently achieved a remarkable degree of inventiveness and spontaneity in his portraits, especially in those of elegant women. Above all, he liked to incorporate his subjects within scenes

Thomas Gainsborough. (Library of Congress)

from nature in a far less formalized manner than was the norm.

Although portraiture was the bulk of his work and was his chief source of income, Gainsborough's persistent passion was landscape painting. His earlier works resembled the great Dutch masters in their precision. After his move to Bath, he developed a more fluid style similar to that of Peter Paul Rubens, whose work he greatly admired. Gainsborough's landscapes did not copy nature directly but rather as it existed in his imagination. He frequently painted from little models of moss, pebbles, and even broccoli stalks that he meticulously constructed in his studio.

In his last years, Gainsborough experimented with a new genre of so-called fancy pictures. Whereas peasants had previously occupied only a small place in his landscapes, they now dominated the picture. These sentimental paintings, peopled with bucolic and often sad visages, reflected Gainsborough's sincere concern with the plight of the poor. His glorification of the lower classes anticipated the work of Gustave Courbet some seventy years later.

Refusing to abide by any rigid rules, Gainsborough ranks as one of the most innovative artists of his age. In his later works, his brushwork became increasingly rough and indeterminate, clearly foreshadowing the Impressionists. He left no specific school of followers, his only known pupil being his nephew Gainsborough Dupont. In his love of the English countryside, however, he was clearly an inspiration for such nineteenth century painters as John Constable and Joseph Mallord William Turner. Above all, the hundreds of portraits that Gainsborough produced constitute a priceless historical record, opening a window into the aristocratic world of eighteenth century England.

—*Tom L. Auffenberg*

FURTHER READING

Besley, Hugh. *Thomas Gainsborough: A Country Life*. New York: Prestel, 2002. Focuses on Gainsborough's early life in Suffolk, where he indulged his passion for painting landscapes and developed a more natural approach to portraiture. Includes 80 reproductions of his paintings.

Gainsborough, Thomas. *The Letters of Thomas Gainsborough*. Edited by Mary Woodall. Greenwich, Conn.: New York Graphic Society, 1963. Definitive edition of Gainsborough's correspondence, containing numerous examples of letters he wrote to his friends, family, and clients. These letters are carefully annotated. See also Woodall's *Gainsborough's Landscape Drawings*, published in London by Faber and Faber in 1939.

Hays, John. *Gainsborough: Paintings and Drawings*. London: Phaidon Press, 1975. Contains a brief biography and essay on Gainsborough's style, coupled with helpful bibliographic information. Includes reproductions of 140 of his works, with comments on each, presented in chronological sequence to demonstrate his development as an artist.

Leonard, Jonathan Norton. *The World of Gainsborough*. Alexandria, Va.: Time-Life Books, 1969. This highly readable volume provides useful information on the life and style of Gainsborough and some of his leading contemporaries, such as Hogarth and Reynolds. It clearly describes the artistic environment in which these men flourished, including a section on eighteenth century Bath.

Lindsay, Jack. *Thomas Gainsborough: His Life and Art*. New York: Universe Books, 1980. A popular work that follows a standard chronological format in an easily understandable style. Lindsay, who has also written biographies of Hogarth and Turner, asserts that Gainsborough was the most creative English artist of his day.

Postle, Martin. *Thomas Gainsborough*. Princeton, N.J.: Princeton University Press, 2002. An eighty-page illustrated introduction to the artist's life and work.

Thicknesse, Philip. *A Sketch of the Life and Paintings of Thomas Gainsborough, Esq*. London, 1788. Written in only one day, this biography by Gainsborough's longtime eccentric friend and benefactor is heavily anecdotal and self-serving. Yet it remains a highly useful source from a man who knew Gainsborough intimately for thirty-five years.

Vaughan, William. *Gainsborough*. New York: Thames & Hudson, 2002. Vaughan recounts Gainsborough's life in relation to political and social movements in eighteenth century Britain. Includes 176 illustrations of Gainsborough's art.

Waterhouse, Ellis. *Gainsborough*. London: Spring Books, 1958. The most important general study of the artist, written by a leading authority on the period. The book is lavishly illustrated and is especially useful for its thorough topical catalog of more than one thousand of Gainsborough's works.

Whitley, William T. *Thomas Gainsborough*. London: John Murray, 1915. Long the standard biography, this work is based on years of research and incorporates much material from the newspapers of the era. The major focus of the volume is on Gainsborough's life rather than his style.

See also: Edmund Burke; Queen Charlotte; Benjamin Franklin; George III; William Hogarth; Samuel John- son; Sir Joshua Reynolds; Richard Brinsley Sheridan; Sarah Siddons.

Related article in *Great Events from History: The Eigh- teenth Century, 1701-1800:* December 10, 1768: Britain's Royal Academy of Arts Is Founded.

LUIGI GALVANI
Italian physician and physicist

Galvani contributed to physiological studies on the electrical stimulation of nerves and muscles. His most important discovery was the production of electric current from the contact of two different metals attached to a frog, which led to the invention by Alessandro Volta of the electric battery.

Born: September 9, 1737; Bologna, Papal States (now in Italy)

Died: December 4, 1798; Bologna, Cisalpine Republic (now in Italy)

Also known as: Alyosio Domenico Galvani (birth name)

Areas of achievement: Biology, physics, science and technology

EARLY LIFE

Luigi Galvani (lew-EE-jee gahl-VAH-nee) was born on the via de' Maggi in Bologna. He was the third of four children born to Domenico and Barbara Foschi Galvani and was baptized Alyosio Domenico. His family was well known in Bologna, going back in local records to 1267. Deciding early to pursue a medical career, he en- tered the University of Bologna, where he studied philos- ophy and medicine under some of the leading teachers of his time.

Under Domenico Galeazzi, Galvani developed a spe- cial interest in anatomy. After receiving his degree in medicine and philosophy in July, 1759, he wrote his doc- toral thesis on the structure, function, and pathology of the human skeleton. He described human bones, their an- atomical and chemical composition, their growth pat- terns, and their diseases.

In 1762, Galvani married Lucia Galeazzi, the only daughter of his teacher. Professor Galeazzi had served four terms as president of the Bologna Academy of Sci- ence. For several years, Galvani served as an honorary lecturer in anatomy at the University of Bologna and as an instructor at the affiliated Institute of Science while maintaining a medical and surgical practice and conduct- ing anatomical research. He was installed by the Senate of Bologna in 1766 as curator of the anatomical museum at the university. In 1768, he became a paid lecturer, and in 1773 he was promoted to the rank of professor of anatomy and surgery. His demonstrations made his lectures popu- lar, though he was not regarded as an eloquent lecturer.

Galvani's early research efforts were devoted mostly to bird anatomy. He published an article on the kidneys of birds in 1767 that described the three-layered ureteral wall and its peristaltic and antiperistaltic movements (contractions) when irritated. He also devoted several papers to the anatomy of the ear in birds. When Galeazzi died in 1775, Galvani succeeded him as lecturer in anat- omy, having already succeeded him as president of the academy in 1772. Finally, in 1782, the Senate of Bolo- gna elected him professor of obstetric arts at the Institute of Science.

LIFE'S WORK

Galvani's most important work began in the 1770's with a shift in emphasis from anatomical concerns to physio- logical studies on nerves and muscles in frogs, leading to a particular interest in animal electricity. In 1772, he pre- sented a paper to the Institute of Science concerning the Swiss physician Albrecht von Haller's theory of irritabil- ity. Haller had demonstrated muscle contractions by stimulating muscle and nerve tissues. Galvani presented two more papers to the institute in 1773 and 1774 on muscle movements in frogs and on the effect of opiates on frog nerves. These studies led him to conduct a series of experiments in the late 1770's on electrophysiology; he stimulated frog muscles by electrical means.

Earlier work on animal electricity had been done by several other Italian researchers. Electricity had been used to stimulate muscles in 1756 at Bologna, and it had been suggested that nerves conduct a so-called electric fluid and perhaps even excite it. Giambattista Beccaria, professor of physics at the University of Turin, used elec- tricity to stimulate the muscles of a living rooster and published correspondence on his electrical research that

Luigi Galvani. (Library of Congress)

supported and extended the ideas of Benjamin Franklin on atmospheric electricity.

By 1780, Galvani had acquired an electrostatic machine and a Leyden jar for producing and storing electric fluid, and after 1783 his major field of research became animal electricity. He prepared frogs for electrical stimulation by dissecting the lower limbs as a unit with the spinal column attached by the crural nerves (the nerves that act on the leg muscles). By touching the conductor of his electrostatic machine to the spinal cord resting on a pane of glass, he could observe the contractions of the muscles in the legs when the machine was discharged. Galvani also experimented with the effects of atmospheric electricity on warm-blooded animals, assisted by his nephew Camillo Galvani. In September, 1786, he recorded a frog-muscle contraction when the nerve was touched by scissors during an electrical storm.

In autumn of 1786, Galvani began to observe some surprising phenomena that led to his discovery of current electricity in contrast to the static electricity used in his experiments. These observations started when an assistant touched a scalpel to the medial crural nerve of a frog preparation and observed violent contractions even

though the electrostatic machine was disconnected and at some distance away on the table. Another assistant—his wife, Lucia, according to some accounts—noticed that this happened at the same moment that a spark was discharged from the electrical machine. Galvani confirmed this effect with several experiments in which contractions were induced whenever the nerve was touched by a grounded conductor at the same time that a spark was drawn from a disconnected electrical machine.

To see if this induction effect would result from natural electricity, Galvani fastened some prepared frogs by brass hooks in their spinal cord to an iron railing surrounding a balcony of his house and observed contractions when lightning flashed. The most surprising result was that contractions continued to occur even after the sky cleared, and these were intensified when the brass hook in the spinal cord was pressed against the iron railing. At first, Galvani viewed the frog preparation as a sensitive electroscope, but then he suggested that perhaps electric fluid was produced within the assembly of frog and metals, independent of any external electrical source.

Galvani confirmed this result indoors by placing the frog preparation on an iron plate and pressing the brass hook against it. He found that the strength of the contractions depended on the kinds of metals used and that nonmetals such as glass and resin produced no effect. He also performed a series of experiments in which metallic arcs were connected between the leg muscles and the hook in the spinal cord and again showed that the kinds of metals in the arc and hook determined the strength of the contractions. Thus, Galvani clearly demonstrated the main features of what came to be known as "galvanism" by producing an electric current from the contact of two dissimilar metals in a moist environment. He thought, however, that this environment must include animal tissues and that they were the source of the electricity. Thus, he believed that he had confirmed the existence of "animal electricity," which some thinkers in the eighteenth century believed to be a vital force, separate and distinct from other, inorganic forms of electricity such as lightning or static electricity.

After five years of careful research, Galvani published the results of his work, *De viribus electricitatis in motu musculari commentarius* (1791; *Commentary on the Effect of Electricity on Muscular Motion*, 1953). This four-part essay reviewed the effects of artificial electricity on muscular motion, similar effects produced by atmospheric electricity, his observations and ideas in support of animal electricity, and his final conclusions and conjectures. In the last section, he asserted that the muscle was like a Leyden jar in which the nerve becomes positively charged while the muscle becomes negatively charged: A metal simultaneously contacting both nerve and muscle would cause a discharge of electric fluid, which in turn would account for the contractions he had observed in his experiments.

Galvani's *Commentary on the Effect of Electricity on Muscular Motion* aroused considerable interest among scientists, and his experiments were repeated by many. Alessandro Volta, professor of physics at the University of Pavia and already famous for his work in electricity, pursued the theory of animal electricity but became skeptical after it occurred to him that the metals might be the source of the electric fluid, with the frog legs serving only as a kind of electroscope. By the end of 1793, Volta had rejected animal electricity in favor of his "contact" theory, in which electric fluids were produced by the mere contact of two dissimilar metals.

A long debate followed from these two interpretations, leading to many ingenious experiments being conducted by both Galvani and Volta. Galvani showed that contractions resulted from two pieces of the same metal, which Volta explained by differences in metal composition. Much of Galvani's defense was continued by his nephew Giovanni Aldini, son of his sister Caterina and later professor of physics at Bologna. The controversy spread: Other scholars at Bologna disagreed with those at Pavia; physiologists argued against physicists, and animalists argued against metalists. Despite their differences, Galvani and Volta remained on friendly terms.

In the last years of his life, Galvani suffered many difficulties, but he managed to continue his work. His wife died childless in 1790 at the age of forty-seven. In 1794 and 1797, he announced two experiments in which contractions were produced merely by touching frog nerves to muscles without any metals. During this time, he made a sea voyage along the Italian coast to collect marine torpedoes and showed that their strong electrical discharge was generated by structures similar to nerves and muscles. Although these results supported Galvani's theory of animal electricity, they also led Volta to invent the bimetallic pile (electric battery) in 1799. Galvani died in the house of his birth the year before Volta's invention. Earlier that year, he was dismissed from the university and lost his salary when he refused to take an atheistic oath of allegiance to the Cisalpine Republic created by Napoleon I. He left his microscope to Aldini, his electrical machine to his nephew Ludovico Galvani, and his manuscripts to another nephew, Camillo Galvani.

SIGNIFICANCE

Luigi Galvani was a modest and deeply religious man whose achievements were the result of hard work and careful experimentation. His many contributions are often obscured by Volta's discovery of a source of constant electric current, which ushered in the electrical revolution of the nineteenth century; Galvani, however, provided the generative spark that made Volta's discovery possible. Moreover, his early contributions to the pathology of bones and the comparative anatomy of birds alone would have been sufficient to secure his reputation. His investigations of birds' ears included many original and valuable observations.

All of Galvani's writings demonstrate the thoroughness of his scientific method, but this is especially true of those concerning his electrical experiments. His observations of electrostatic induction, including the inductive effects of lightning discharges on his frog preparations, anticipated the discovery of the propagation of radio waves. His most important contribution, however, was his observation and description of the production of electric fluid from the contact of two metals with frog muscles. These experiments led directly to the investigations by Volta of what he called "galvanism" and the invention of the electric battery. Thus, Galvani's name has been immortalized in words such as "galvanometer" and "galvanize."

The publication of Galvani's *Commentary on the Effect of Electricity on Muscular Motion* and the subsequent Galvani-Volta debate stimulated much further research in both physics and physiology. Although Galvani failed to see the full significance of his discovery of galvanism, he demonstrated the electrical nature of the nervous fluid. His defense of animal electricity led to experiments that in effect marked the beginning of electrophysiology as a science. His demonstrations that frog leg contractions resulted from contact between nerve and muscle even without metals led to the discovery in the 1840's of the electrical nature of nerve impulses by Emil Du Bois-Reymond and others. The life and work of Luigi Galvani are too important to be dismissed as merely a confused preface to the discovery of methods to produce electric current and the electrical revolution that followed.

—*Joseph L. Spradley*

FURTHER READING

Dibner, Bern. *Galvani-Volta: A Controversy That Led to the Discovery of Useful Electricity.* Norwalk, Conn.: Burndy Library, 1952. Contains a brief description of the historical background and scientific work of Galvani, the defense of his ideas by Aldini, and the controversy with Volta, as well as an original translation of the first experiment establishing the existence of electricity in living tissues, published anonymously in 1794.

Fara, Patricia. *An Enlightenment for Angels: Electricity in the Enlightenment*. Lanham, Md.: Totem Books, 2002. Provides brief explanations of experiments conducted by Galvani, Volta, Benjamin Franklin, and other seventeenth and eighteenth century scientists who studied electricity.

Galvani, Luigi. *Commentary on the Effect of Electricity on Muscular Motion*. Translated by Robert Montraville Green. Baltimore: Waverly Press, 1953. The twelve-page introduction discusses and evaluates Galvani's life and work. Includes an original work by Aldini. Also translated by Margaret Foley for Burndy Library in 1953.

Keithley, Joseph F. *The Story of Electrical and Magnetic Measurements: From 500 B.C. to the 1940's*. New York: IEEE Press, 1999. Historical survey of significant discoveries regarding electricity and magnetism. Chapter 10 outlines Galvani's experiments with frog legs.

Lenard, Philipp. "Luigi Galvani and Alessandro Volta." In *Great Men of Science: A History of Scientific Progress*. New York: Macmillan, 1933. This twelve-page chapter gives a brief account of the life and work of Galvani and the development of his work by Volta.

Pera, Marcello. *The Ambiguous Frog: The Galvani-Volta Controversy on Animal Electricity*. Translated by Jonathan Mandelbaum. Princeton, N.J.: Princeton University Press, 1992. Recounts how the two scientists offered different theories to explain why a dead frog's muscles contracted when stimulated by electricity. Pera describes theories of electricity in the 1790's, and compares the careers and laboratory procedures of Galvani and Volta.

Potamian, Michael, and James Walsh. "Galvani, Discoverer of Animal Electricity." In *Makers of Electricity*. New York: Fordham University Press, 1909. This twenty-nine-page chapter gives an interesting and readable account of Galvani's life and work, though it contains some historical inaccuracies.

See also: Benjamin Franklin; Alessandro Volta.

Related articles in *Great Events from History: The Eighteenth Century, 1701-1800*: 1704: Newton Publishes *Optics*; 1723: Stahl Postulates the Phlogiston Theory; 1729: Gray Discovers Principles of Electric Conductivity; 1733: Du Fay Discovers Two Kinds of Electric Charge; October, 1745, and January, 1746: Invention of the Leyden Jar; June, 1752: Franklin Demonstrates the Electrical Nature of Lightning; 1757-1766: Haller Establishes Physiology as a Science; 1800: Volta Invents the Battery.

JOSÉ DE GÁLVEZ
Spanish colonial administrator

Gálvez reorganized New Spain's tax system, strengthened New Spain's defenses of its northern border, created a government tobacco monopoly that poured money into the Spanish treasury, and formed expeditions that developed the first nonindigenous settlements in Alta California.

Born: January 2, 1720; Vélez-Málaga, Spain
Died: June 17, 1787; Aranjuez, Spain
Also known as: José Bernardo de Gálvez Gallardo (full name); José Gálvez; Marqués de la Sonora
Areas of achievement: Government and politics, economics

EARLY LIFE
Born into a humble family, José de Gálvez (hoh-SAY thay GAL-vehs or GAL-veth) showed considerable promise as a young child and soon came to the attention of two of Málaga's bishops, who made it possible for him to receive a solid education. Gálvez received his primary and some of his secondary education in Málaga, after which he went to Salamanca to continue his studies.

Gálvez entered the law school of the University of Madrid and eventually received a degree in law. His ecclesiastical protectors in Málaga, proud of the accomplishments of this son of impoverished parents, used their influence to have him appointed secretary to the Spanish minister of state, a post roughly equivalent to that of the secretary of state in the United States. This post was extremely important for Gálvez's political and administrative development, for it would expose him to Spain's international relations, most significantly to the country's relations with the New World.

New Spain, as Mexico was called by the Spanish, was a territory rich in resources. Spain's rulers realized that revenues from New Spain could greatly enhance their position as an international force, but great changes in the administrative structure of the area had to be accomplished before Spain could benefit directly and substantially from the riches of the new world.

Gálvez, a bright young man with considerable administrative potential, was also an acquiescent supporter of the Spanish monarchy, which made him, after considerable administrative exposure at home, a logical choice to serve the monarchy's interests effectively in the Americas. That the need for such service was great was driven home emphatically in 1762 when Spain lost the critically important seaport of Havana to the British. This defeat solidified Spanish king Charles III's determination to become stronger militarily in the New World and to shore up the relatively ineffective military system then in place in New Spain.

LIFE'S WORK

José de Gálvez would soon be a seasoned statesman, appointed inspector general of all the judiciary councils and royal coffers of New Spain in 1765, taking over from Inspector General Juan de Villalba, who had been charged with establishing a professional army and a militia in the region. Villalba accomplished what was expected of him, but he created great resentment among many of the indigenous people by treading roughshod over local customs and by ignoring the political interactions required for unity. His troops were abusive to the indigenous, and were arrogant.

The new inspector general, Gálvez, also served as quartermaster general of Spain's military forces in New Spain. He would hold these two posts until 1771. During his tenure, Gálvez increasingly realized the need for drastic reorganization and reform and set out to achieve this end. Among his early reforms was the reorganization of the customs houses that had been running inefficiently for decades, weakened by both nepotism and graft, or illegal or unfair gain. Gálvez replaced most of the administrators of these facilities with salaried employees who were held to very strict standards of professional conduct. He put the monopoly that made playing cards and the monopoly that manufactured and distributed *pulque*, a popular alcoholic beverage, under royal supervision. He replaced corrupt officials in the gunpowder industry with hand-picked, salaried employees.

The tobacco monopoly had been among the most important in New Spain and was said to employ fifty-six hundred workers in Mexico City alone and more than twelve thousand workers throughout New Spain. The monarchy had already taken steps toward reforming this monopoly before Gálvez arrived, but he intensified these reforms, arousing large numbers of the local populace. Nevertheless, the reforms achieved the economic ends the monarchy envisioned. Between 1768 and 1789, income from the tobacco monopoly credited to the royal treasury quadrupled.

Gálvez granted generous tax exemptions to the mining industry after the discovery of large mercury deposits in Spain, which enabled him to cut in half the price of mercury that was used in the production of silver in New Spain. His favoritism toward the mining industry caused considerable unrest, but it resulted in increases in the territory's silver production, thereby enhancing the coffers of the Spanish monarchy substantially.

The reforms Gálvez imposed created smoldering resentment throughout New Spain, but it was his expulsion of the Jesuits from the country that sparked eruptions of violence in 1767. Indigenous insurgency gripped San Luis Potosí and Michoacán. The Jesuits had contributed a great deal to local society, particularly in their establishment of schools and medical facilities for local peoples. The Society of Jesus, as the Jesuits were designated, was a self-governing group of highly intelligent clergymen who defied the Papacy with considerable regularity.

The indigenous people had a strong sense of their own rights, and the Jesuits were often their supporters in opposition to the ruling government. The indigenous regarded the Jesuits as their advocates. When uprisings occurred in 1767, Gálvez ignored the traditional ways the indigenous had solved such problems, and he authorized Spanish troops to put down the uprisings with maximum force. The results were devastating. Some 85 local people were hanged, 73 were publicly flogged, 117 were exiled, and 674 were imprisoned. Putting down simple rioting by such draconian means sowed the seeds for considerable future resentment and unrest.

Gálvez reinstated Spain's sovereignty in the high courts. He sought to control the municipal governments by appointing honorary aldermen and magistrates. He also reinforced the systematic collection of taxes, enhancing Spain's wealth. He revoked many tax exemptions that had been in effect for years, causing considerable resentment. Gálvez's methods for enforcing tax collection were so successful that by the end of the eighteenth century, New Spain was yielding 70 percent more in taxes than was the Iberian Peninsula.

When Gálvez returned to Spain at the end of his service in New Spain, he became active in the council of the Indies, rising to be its president in 1774. He was appointed minister in general and councillor of state to the Indies in 1775. He continued to serve until shortly before his death in 1787. Two years before he died, he received the title marquess of Sonora.

SIGNIFICANCE

José de Gálvez will be remembered for his radical changes to New Spain's tax system, a reorganization that was to become the basis for the Bourbon Dynasty's economic reforms in Spain and in other European venues. Also, he created and maintained a monopoly on the government's trade in tobacco, which added great sums to Spain's treasury.

Under Gálvez's leadership, Spanish forces occupied parts of Alta (Upper) California (now the U.S. state of California). His most memorable reforms, however, included establishing intendancies, official governments modeled on the French system and set up to control colonial provinces to ensure European supremacy in governmental administration.

Largely through Gálvez's influence, his brother, Matias de Gálvez, and his nephew, Bernardo de Gálvez, were appointed viceroys of New Spain during the 1780's. The city of Galveston, Texas, is named after the Gálvez family.

—*R. Baird Shuman*

FURTHER READING

Beerman, Eric. *José de Gálvez: The First Marques of Sonora.* Sonora, Calif.: Tuolumne County Historical Society, 1980. Interesting for the local color relating to Gálvez being named marques of Sonora.

Cheetham, Nicolas. *Mexico: A Short History.* New York: Crowell, 1971. Although somewhat dated, this resource offers an overview that should help readers who are unfamiliar with Mexican history.

Kirkwood, Burton. *The History of Mexico.* Westport, Conn.: Greenwood Press, 2000. Kirkwood's treatment of the colonial period is concise and well controlled. A useful source for building a background.

Meyer, Michael C., and William H. Beezley, eds. *The Oxford History of Mexico.* New York: Oxford University Press, 2000. Three contributions contain valuable information about Gálvez. The fullest account is in Virginia Guedea's "The Old Colonialism Ends, the New Colonialism Begins." Also useful are accounts by Mark A. Burkholder in "An Empire Beyond Compare" and Robert Patch in "Indian Resistance to Colonialism."

Mills, Kenneth, and William B. Taylor, eds. *Colonial Spanish America: A Documentary History.* Wilmington, Del.: Scholarly Resources, 1998. A comprehensive resource of primary documents relating to the colonial history of New Spain. Chapter 39 provides "José de Gálvez's Decrees for the King's Subjects in Mexico (1769, 1778)." Includes illustrations, a bibliography, and an index.

Priestley, Herbert I. *José de Gálvez, Visitor-General of New Spain, 1765-1771.* Berkeley: University of California Publications, 1916. Despite its age, this extraordinary biography by one of the leading scholars in Mexican history remains the best book on Gálvez. An outstanding achievement in biographical writing.

_____. *Mexican Nation: A History.* New York: Macmillan, 1923. Priestley delves into Gálvez's role in the history of Mexico with keen insight and clarity. A valuable resource.

See also: Charles III; Philip V; Guillaume-Thomas Raynal; Junípero Serra.

Related articles in *Great Events from History: The Eighteenth Century, 1701-1800:* 1759: Charles III Gains the Spanish Throne; January 19, 1759-August 16, 1773: Suppression of the Jesuits; July 17, 1769-1824: Rise of the California Missions; 1776: Foundation of the Viceroyalty of La Plata; 1780-1781: Rebellion of Tupac Amaru II; 1786: Discovery of the Mayan Ruins at Palenque.

DAVID GARRICK
English actor

Garrick raised acting to a new level of expression and respectability, further popularized the plays of William Shakespeare, and brought creative management to the Drury Lane Theatre in London.

Born: February 19, 1717; Hereford, Herefordshire, England
Died: January 20, 1779; London, England
Area of achievement: Theater

EARLY LIFE

David Garrick came from a French Huguenot family who had migrated from the arid lands of southern France when their religion was banned in 1685. The family name was changed from Garric to Garrick when David's grandfather was naturalized in 1695. David's father, Peter, was commissioned in the British army and met Arabella Clough while stationed in Lichfield. They were married in 1706 and had seven children. Although David was born in Hereford, his true family home was Lichfield—also the home of his famous contemporary Dr. Samuel Johnson.

Peter Garrick was assigned to military duty in Gibraltar for much of David's youth. In his father's absence, Johnson and Gilbert Walmesley (a court official in Lichfield) had great influence on the young Garrick. Garrick was enrolled for a brief time in Johnson's school at Edial. Early in 1737, Johnson and Garrick departed for London, where Walmesley had made arrangements for Garrick to enter Rochester School in preparation to study law at Lincoln's Inn. Within weeks, Garrick's father died, and his brother Peter went to London, where the two began a wine business—David working London and Peter, the Lichfield area.

Garrick's wine shop was located in the theater district, later to be the site of the Adelphi, his town house. Because of his shop's location, Garrick made contact with several people involved in dramatic arts. Meanwhile, Johnson's editor was encouraging Garrick to write and act. In addition, Charles Macklin, a well-known actor, became Garrick's friend and acting coach. In 1741, Garrick played a Harlequin (his mask concealing his identity) and authored a short play, *Lethe: Or, Aesop in the Shades* (1740), a farce, for Henry Gillard, an actor-manager who had helped him obtain wine business at the Bedford Coffee House. In the summer of 1741 he played a number of parts at Ipswich under the name Lyddall. His decision to act anonymously or under a false name can be attributed both to the low reputation of actors and to concern about his family's opposition.

Garrick was about five feet, four inches tall, reasonably well proportioned until he put on weight in his later years. As an actor, he did not appear short. His eyes were dark yet piercingly bright. For acting purposes, he kept his head shaved except for a ponytail to which wigs could be attached. He dressed stylishly but not extravagantly so. He was a witty, lively conversationalist and liked to play practical jokes and mimic friends. He wished to please others and disliked criticism and disputes. Although he did not come from wealth and noble status, Garrick was a gentleman, and he cultivated well-bred companions.

LIFE'S WORK

On October 19, 1741, Shakespeare's *Richard III* (1592-1593) was performed at Goodman's Fields Theatre with "a gentleman (who never appear'd on any stage)"—David Garrick—playing the leading role. Garrick was instantly acclaimed as an actor, and the fashionable theater crowd abandoned the licensed establishments of Drury Lane and Covent Garden to witness his Shakespearean performance. By December, he was playing the lead in the premiere of his own farce, *The Lying Valet*. Early in 1742, his success led to offers from both of the licensed theaters. After contracting with Charles Fleetwood, the owner of the Drury Lane Theatre, to act during the 1742-1743 season, he spent the summer season acting at the Smock Alley Theatre in Dublin, Ireland, where his costar was Peg Woffington, an actor with a questionable personal reputation.

Upon their return to London, Garrick, Woffington, and Macklin took a house together. When Fleetwood failed to pay his actors, Garrick led his fellow actors on a strike against him. The eventual settlement returned all the performers to the stage except Macklin, who was viewed as the ringleader. In December, 1744, Garrick was interrupted onstage by a riot instigated by supporters of Macklin. Two days later, Fleetwood used thirty prizefighters to prevent a similar outbreak. Garrick and Macklin were less friendly thereafter, even though the former had offered financial assistance and later would direct Macklin in plays that he had written. Garrick continued to live with Woffington until 1745; he probably wished to marry her but was concerned about her reputation and his respectability. They remained friends until her death in 1760, never discussing their affair.

In March, 1746, a dancer from Vienna, Austria, became the lead performer at the Haymarket Opera House and was immediately acclaimed by aristocratic English audiences. As the two most popular stage performers of the day, "Violette" (Eva Maria Veigel) and Garrick were invited to a party, where they first met. Garrick was instantly enamored of Violette. Before he could marry her, however, he needed to convince Dorothy, countess of Burlington, who had given Violette a home, that he was a proper mate. They were married June 22, 1749, and in the course of their life together, they were never known to have spent a single night apart. She was quiet, gentle, and supportive, a perfect counterpoint to his ebullience and flamboyance. The one obstacle to their happiness was the absence of children, particularly painful because they both adored them.

While Garrick was acting at Drury Lane during the 1744-1745 season, Fleetwood sold the theater to James Lacy. In April, 1745, illness forced Garrick to stop acting; poor health increasingly interfered with his work as he got older. Soon after, he rejected a proposal to join other actors in buying Lacy's interest in the Drury Lane operation. Instead, he went back to Ireland to act, and receive part of the profits from his roles. In May, 1746, Garrick was back in London acting at Covent Garden, where he also performed during the 1746-1747 season. On April 9, 1747, he signed a contract to become half owner of the Drury Lane (with Lacy), paying £8,000 for his share.

From 1747 to December, 1776, Garrick was joint owner-manager of the Drury Lane patent. (The patent was the government-ordained right to sell entertainment in the theater.) Lacy served as the financial administrator and saw after the physical properties—costumes, scenery, lighting; Garrick performed, directed, and produced. He had a good grasp of the audience's tastes and while catering to them still was able to revive a number of plays from the sixteenth and seventeenth centuries. He was good at organization and effectively managed temperamental actors and actresses by demanding their participation in rehearsals and imposing fines for tardiness. He recruited the best musicians and scene painters and hired such experts as Philippe Jacques de Loutherbourg, a Frenchman, to perfect lighting. Loutherbourg introduced footlights and silk screens for colored light effects. In 1762, Garrick redid the interior of the theater, enlarging its capacity to an estimated two thousand; in 1775, he commissioned Robert Adam, an architectural innovator, to redecorate the inside once again and to add a streetside facade entryway. Garrick attempted to halt the traditional practice of permitting half-price entrance after the third act but gave up when riots caused damage at Drury Lane and Covent Garden. One other failure occurred in 1755, when he imported a troop of French dancers to perform Jean-Georges Noverre's *The Chinese Festival* and was forced to abandon the project when anti-French riots caused £4,000 worth of damage. Finally, Garrick established a theatrical fund comprising money earned from benefit shows to be used for disabled, retired performers. The fund was given legal status by an act of Parliament in 1776 through the efforts of his friend Edmund Burke, whose maiden speech, supporting the American colonists, he had witnessed.

In the period of his co-ownership of Drury Lane, Garrick limited his acting to about thirty performances per year. From August, 1763, to April, 1765, he and his wife were on tour of France, Italy, Austria, and other European states. Much of the time, however, was spent recovering from illness. Late in 1775, Garrick decided that he would retire at the end of the season. Beginning in April, 1776, he performed a series of his most famous roles before packed, emotionally enthralled audiences. His final performance was on June 19, when he played Don Felix in Susannah Centlivre's *The Wonder: A Woman Keeps a Secret*. In 1777, he helped prepare the premiere performance of Richard Brinsley Sheridan's *The School for Scandal*. (Sheridan was one of the purchasers of his share in Drury Lane.) In January,

---

GARRICK'S EPITAPH FOR JAMES QUINN

In addition to being a foremost actor and playwright, David Garrick was known for his wit and sardonic humor. These characteristics are embodied in his famous epitaph for James Quinn, reproduced below.

> Here lies James Quinn. Deign, reader, to be taught,
> Whate'er thy strength of body, force of thought,
> In Nature's happiest mould however cast,
> To this complexion thou must come at last.

Source: Arthur Murphy, *The Life of David Garrick, Esq.* (London: J. Wright, 1801), vol. 2, p. 38.

1779, Garrick became fatally ill. He returned to his London apartment, where he died on January 20. His funeral, on February 1, 1779, attracted a throng of onlookers, stretching from the Adelphi to Westminster Abbey, where he was buried. In 1797, a monument was placed in Poets' Corner near his grave.

SIGNIFICANCE

David Garrick raised acting to a new height. He made a fortune at his profession, leaving an estate of £100,000 at his death. He became the ultimate Shakespearean: reviving and staging original versions of plays such as *Macbeth* (1606); erecting his Temple of Shakespeare on the lawn of Hampton House (his country home); collecting editions of plays for his, and other, libraries; directing a Stratford-upon-Avon Jubilee in 1769 (which was rained out but which created an opportunity to stage *Ode*, a poem that Garrick had written to be performed and that packed Drury Lane for 153 performances over a three-year period—more than any Shakespeare play during his twenty-nine years as manager); and seeking to popularize the Bard in France, despite the criticism of Voltaire (the most influential French writer of the day).

Since actors were not by profession considered important personages, the striking feature of Garrick's life is the breadth of his acquaintanceships and influence. The Garricks were friends with some of the most powerful political aristocrats, with whom they stayed in the summers. He met and corresponded with a number of leading literary lights of the age, among them Edward Gibbon, James Boswell, Hannah More, and Henry Fielding. Garrick continuously supported the arts, not only employing artists at Drury Lane and his residences—the Adam brothers as designers, Lancelot Brown in landscape architecture—but also finding patrons for their creative work. Johann Zoffany, for example, was discovered by Garrick and obtained the patronage of King George III. Thomas Gainsborough, the founder of the English school of painting and the Royal Academy, painted a number of portraits and landscapes for Garrick. Garrick was also elected to the select club, founded by Johnson in 1764, that would later be the Literary Club.

As a man of wealth, Garrick was generous in support of others, starting with his family. His brother George made a comfortable living as his assistant at Drury Lane. He watched over the financial well-being of his nieces and nephews. He found employment for down-and-out actors, playwrights, and friends. He gave his troupe the chance to earn extra money through benefit perfor-

mances at Drury Lane and elsewhere. Thus, in his generosity, Garrick not only supported his immediate family and friends but also, more important, bequeathed a valuable cultural legacy to future generations.

—Lance Williams

FURTHER READING

Benedetti, Jean. *David Garrick and the Birth of Modern Theatre*. London: Methuen, 2001. Benedetti maintains that Garrick was the father of modern theater, reforming theater practice to become its first international superstar.

Boas, Frederick S. *An Introduction to Eighteenth-Century Drama, 1700-1780*. London: Oxford University Press, 1965. An account of dramatists of the period, with chapters devoted to Joseph Addison, John Gay, Henry Fielding, Richard Brinsley Sheridan, and other playwrights. Boas analyzes the characters of some of Garrick's plays and his performances in them.

Garrick, David, and George Colman. *Plays by David Garrick and George Colman the Elder*. Edited by E. R. Wood. New York: Cambridge University Press, 1982. Includes a short sketch of Garrick and Colman, a biographical chart, and a full listing of writings. Plays by Garrick reprinted are *The Lying Valet*, *The Irish Widow* (1772), *Bon Ton: Or, High Life Above Stairs* (1775), and *The Clandestine Marriage* (1766; with Colman).

Kendall, Alan. *David Garrick: A Biography*. London: Harrap, 1985. A heavily illustrated account with particular emphasis on the use of letters to tell the story. The bulk of the middle part is treated topically, rather than chronologically.

McIntyre, Ian. *Garrick*. New York: Penguin Putnam, 1999. An exhaustively detailed, well-researched recounting of Garrick's life, career, and circle of friends.

Nicoll, Allardyce. *A History of Late Eighteenth Century Drama, 1750-1800*. Cambridge, England: Cambridge University Press, 1927. Places Garrick in the context of the general developments of theater during the era. A standard reference source for the subject containing details on the variety of forms, individual drama houses, and extensive lists of plays written and performed.

Parsons, Florence M. *Garrick and His Circle*. 2d ed. New York: Benjamin Blom, 1969. Parsons first published this account in 1906, utilizing *The Private Correspondence of David Garrick* (1831), unpublished letters from the Victoria and Albert Museum—where much Garrick memorabilia is held—four packs of Garrick material sold at Christie's auctioneers in 1905, and the four prior biographies. It is a sympathetic account with considerable insight into eighteenth century drama.

Price, Cecil. *Theatre in the Age of Garrick*. Totowa, N.J.: Rowman and Littlefield, 1973. A survey of the nature of the theater, including acting styles, costuming, its role as entertainment, ways of the audiences, non-London forms, and opera and ballet's place. Price describes in detail the mannerisms, voice inflections, and facial expressions that made Garrick the dominant performer.

Smith, Helen R. *David Garrick, 1717-1779*. London: British Library Board, 1979. A brief sketch on the occasion of the bicentennial of Garrick's death. Essentially, a book that deals with him topically as actor, author, book collector, manager, and supporter of the visual arts. Includes a number of illustrations.

Woods, Leigh. *Garrick Claims the Stage, Acting as Social Emblem in Eighteenth-Century England*. Westport, Conn.: Greenwood Press, 1984. An analytical look at Garrick and his profession using the tools of modern disciplines such as sociology, anthropology, and psychology. Woods's perspective is suggested by the title of the last chapter, "The Actor as Trickster: Illusionism on the Eighteenth-Century English Stage."

See also: Robert and James Adam; Joseph Addison; James Boswell; Lancelot Brown; Fanny Burney; Edmund Burke; Hannah Cowley; Henry Fielding; Thomas Gainsborough; George III; Samuel Johnson; Hannah More; Anne Oldfield; Richard Brinsley Sheridan; Sarah Siddons; Peg Woffington.

Related articles in *Great Events from History: The Eighteenth Century, 1701-1800:* January 29, 1728: Gay Produces the First Ballad Opera; August, 1763-April, 1765: David Garrick's European Tour.

GEORGE I
Elector of Hanover (1698-1727) and king of Great Britain and Ireland (r. 1714-1727)

George I became king at a time when the constitutional settlement brought about by the Glorious Revolution of 1688-1689 made it necessary for the Crown and Parliament to learn to work together. His firmness and moderation at a time of bitter partisanship stabilized the Hanover Dynasty on the British throne. While maintaining the authority of the king in foreign policy and the appointment of ministers, George I was willing to give his ministers wide discretion in domestic policy and public finance, where the major consideration was the support of Parliament. In so doing he contributed to the development of cabinet government.

Born: May 28, 1660; Osnabrück, Hanover (now in Germany)
Died: June 11, 1727; Osnabrück, Hanover
Also known as: George Louis (birth name)
Area of achievement: Government and politics

EARLY LIFE

George Louis, elector of Hanover, was already an experienced ruler in 1714 when he became King George I of Great Britain and Ireland. Through his father he inherited the electorate of Hanover, a medium-sized north German state. His mother was the granddaughter of King James I of England, and as the closest Protestant descendant of the Stuart family, she and her heirs were named in the Act of Settlement (1701) as successors to the British throne should Queen Anne (r. 1702-1714) die childless. In 1682, George Louis married Sophia Dorothea, of the neighboring duchy of Celle, a marriage intended to extend the Hanoverian territories. The marriage produced an heir, George Augustus, who later became King George II. In other respects the marriage was unhappy, and when Sophia Dorothea was found guilty of adultery, she was shut up in a castle for the rest of her life.

George Louis succeeded his father as elector of Hanover in 1698. As a young man George Louis gained military experience fighting against the Turks and in war against King Louis XIV of France, whose power and ambitions made him the dominant force in European affairs. When he succeeded to the electorate of Hanover in 1698, George Louis continued to be active in opposition to Louis XIV, joining with Great Britain and other states in the alliance that eventually stopped Louis XIV in the War of the Spanish Succession (1701-1714).

When his mother died in 1714, George Louis became the lawful successor to Queen Anne. Despite the Act of Settlement, the intense partisan politics of the period gave reason to think that the death of Queen Anne might be followed by an effort to restore the Stuart claimant, James Edward, son of King James II. James Edward was Catholic, and as such he was objectionable to the British people. He was also dependent on the national enemy, Louis XIV of France. For these reasons most British leaders, Whig or Tory, regarded the Hanoverian succession as inevitable. Queen Anne resented the Hanover family, and the Tories, who held office during her last four years, kept George Louis at arm's length. The Whigs seized the opportunity to gain favor with the successor. The Whig case was strengthened when the Tory ministry of Queen Anne negotiated a peace treaty with Louis XIV that George Louis and the Whigs regarded as a betrayal of the allies. When Queen Anne died in 1714, George Louis was firmly attached to the Whigs, and he relied upon the Whigs for the duration of his reign.

LIFE'S WORK

Accession to the British throne enhanced the influence of George Louis and Hanover in the affairs of the German states, but his role as king of Great Britain and Ireland is the basis for his historical importance. As she lay dying in August, 1714, Queen Anne conferred power upon a group of moderate political leaders, and the accession of George I to the throne passed without serious challenge in England. In 1714 the Stuart claimant, James Edward, landed in Scotland and rallied considerable support before the uprising was subdued. James Edward returned to France and eventually died in Rome.

The new king spoke English, although haltingly, and he preferred to conduct business in French, which at that time was the universal language of the European ruling class. He was short and stocky, with the bluff manner of a soldier. He enjoyed himself in Hanover, but in England he was shy and withdrawn, preferring the company of his Hanoverian advisers. He was always accompanied by two Turks—Mohammed and Mustapha—who were his personal servants and bodyguards. He enjoyed music and was a patron of George Frideric Handel, but he was uncomfortable with political chatter and the elegance of court life and preferred to associate quietly with a few close friends. George I continued to govern Hanover personally and made five visits there during his reign.

George I brought with him from Hanover his son, George Augustus, who became prince of Wales; a group of Hanoverian advisers; and two German women who played an important part in his life and reign. Madame Melusine Schulenburg (later duchess of Kendal) was the king's mistress and bore him three illegitimate daughters. Madame Sophia Charlotte Kielmansegge (later countess of Darlington) was an illegitimate half sister of the king. In reference to their figures the British public called them "the Maypole" and "the Elephant." British politicians soon recognized the importance of remaining on good terms with them, and they in turn accumulated substantial wealth by providing access to the king.

The major importance of the reign of George I was the establishment of the Hanover Dynasty on the British throne. At his accession George I placed the Whigs in office, and his occasional efforts to bring moderate Tories into the ministry were frustrated by the intensity of party feeling. The Whigs gratified the king by persuading the House of Commons to vote a generous civil list, which was the financial support for the royal family, royal household, and civil government. Supported by the electoral influence of the Crown, the Whigs won a decisive victory in the election of 1715. The Whigs consolidated their power by the Septennial Act (1716), which extended the term of the House of Commons to a maximum of seven years, and the Riot Act (1715), which gave local authorities increased power to suppress disorders by calling in the army. Excluded from power and accused of loyalty to James Edward, the Tory Party declined as a political force although Toryism remained strong among the people.

The unity of the Whigs, and the security of the Hanover monarchy, were shaken by disputes between the Whig leaders. The active foreign policy of Lord Stanhope led to a split within the Whig Party in 1717, with lords Stanhope and Sunderland continuing in power while Lord Townshend and Robert Walpole curried favor with the prince of Wales and went into opposition. Walpole made so much trouble for the ministers in the House of Commons that in 1720 a reconciliation took place and Townshend and Walpole returned to office. Later that year a financial boom and crash occurred, which was called the South Sea Bubble. The king, his mistress, and many prominent politicians were implicated, and the outrage of those who lost money in the Bubble threatened the Hanover Dynasty. Walpole became first lord of the treasury in 1721 and masterfully restored financial stability and public confidence. When Stanhope died in 1721 and Sunderland died in 1722, the ascendancy of Townshend and Walpole was assured. Under the watchful leadership of Walpole, the Hanover monarchy was secure.

The reign of George I was important for the development of cabinet government. The word "cabinet" referred to a meeting of the king with the principal ministers to discuss policy. Queen Anne presided at her weekly cabinet meetings, but George I was not fluent in English and for that reason his ministers usually met without him, communicating their advice later. The king was expected to exercise the powers of the Crown personally, but the need to work with Parliament made it essential to govern through ministers with parliamentary support. The king had the deciding voice in the appointment of ministers, although George I's freedom of choice was limited by his commitment to the Whigs. George I dominated foreign policy, but he was willing to leave to his ministers most of the details of politics, elections, administration, and public finance. The ministers were also members of the House of Lords or the House of Commons, and as such they exercised a dual role as officers of the Crown and members of the legislative body. The cabinet became the informal group that worked to keep the Crown and Parliament in harmony. Although more than a century was required before the modern conventions of cabinet government were firmly established, the origins of these conventions are to be found in the political necessities of the Hanoverian period.

The accession of George I brought a new direction to British foreign policy. The death of Louis XIV in 1715 led to weak government in France, and Stanhope was able to restore good relations with that country. The main concern of George I was the Great Northern War, then raging between Sweden and Russia. He used the opportunity to gain the territories of Bremen and Verden for Hanover. Attempts of Peter the Great of Russia (r. 1682-1725) to extend his influence into northern Germany were resisted. Steps were taken to secure British trade in the Baltic area, which produced maritime supplies that were essential for the British navy and merchant marine. With the accession of George I, Great Britain became actively involved in the affairs of northern and central Europe, much to the dismay of those who favored a "blue water" policy that avoided continental entanglements.

In the reign of George I, the religious dissension that had marked the reign of Queen Anne began to subside. As a Protestant, George I had no difficulty in conforming to the Church of England, as required by law. The king favored broad religious toleration, but in Great Britain religion was intensely political, and the king's efforts to remove religious disabilities were frustrated by party politics. Protestant Dissenters, primarily Presbyterians, Congregationalists, and Baptists, were entitled to religious toleration but were excluded from political office under the Crown or in local government. Although the Dissenters were strong supporters of the Whigs, the Whig ministers found it politically expedient to support the privileged position of the Church of England, and the Dissenters settled into the niche provided for them. Catholics enjoyed neither political rights nor religious toleration, and the claim of James Edward to the Crown tarred Catholics with charges of disloyalty. George I's efforts to reduce Catholic disabilities were frustrated by the intense anti-Catholicism of the British public and Walpole's fear that Catholics would support another attempt at a Stuart restoration.

The final step in the establishment of the Hanover monarchy was the peaceful succession of the heir. In 1717, George I quarreled with his son, the prince of Wales, for the prince felt politically ignored and inadequately supported financially. George I banished the prince and his family from the royal court and took custody of their children. The prince and his charming wife, Princess Caroline, set up a separate court at Leicester House where dissatisfied politicians gathered. When they left the Whig ministry in 1717, Townshend and Walpole conspicuously courted the favor of the prince, but when they returned to office in 1720, they brought about a reconciliation of the king and his heir. George I was in Hanover in June, 1727, when he became ill and died. The prince of Wales was in England, where he was immediately proclaimed King George II. James Edward, residing in Rome, made no attempt to return to England, and the accession of the new king passed without incident. George I was buried in Hanover, where he had spent most of his life and which was always closest to his heart.

SIGNIFICANCE

King George I was important for the institutional developments of his reign. His claim to the British throne was clearly established in law; his achievement was to avoid the mistakes that might have revived the succession to the throne as a controversial issue. George I was a workaday king, who lacked the divine-right majesty of his Stuart predecessors or the romantic aura that gathered around Queen Victoria. The "mixed and balanced constitution" of eighteenth century Great Britain required a king who would be personally involved in government while keeping the support of Parliament and the people.

George I maintained those powers essential to personal monarchy: leadership in foreign policy and control of the appointment of ministers. His firm rule and steady reliance on the Whigs gave him capable ministers and a solid political base. By expecting his ministers to maintain support in Parliament, he contributed to the origins of cabinet government. His concern for Hanover brought

Great Britain more fully into the balance-of-power relationships of the European states. When the Crown passed peacefully to his son, his major goal was accomplished: establishment of the Hanover family on the British throne.

—Earl A. Reitan

FURTHER READING

Hatton, Ragnhild. *George I: Elector and King*. London: Thames and Hudson, 1978. The definitive biography.

Holmes, Geoffrey. *The Making of a Great Power: Late Stuart and Early Georgian Britain, 1660-1722*. London: Longman, 1993. Examines the economic advances, scientific and intellectual developments, and political changes that enabled Great Britain to become a major European power during George I's reign. Holmes explains how a more socially cohesive and constitutionally stable country was able to withstand the Jacobite Rebellion of 1715-1716 and the South Sea Bubble.

Mangan, J. J. *The King's Favour: Three Eighteenth Century Monarchs and the Favourites Who Ruled Them*. New York: St. Martin's Press, 1991. Describes how George I, Catherine the Great of Russia, and Louis XV of France relied on favored politicians to rule their countries.

Plumb, J. H. *The First Four Georges*. Boston: Little, Brown, 1975. Interesting, well-written chapters on the Hanover monarchs by the outstanding authority on the period. The 1975 edition is profusely illustrated.

_____. *Sir Robert Walpole: The Making of a Statesman*. London: Cresset Press, 1956. A masterful biography of the great Whig politician who rose to power in the reign of George I.

Williams, Basil. *The Whig Supremacy, 1714-1760*. 2d ed. Revised by C. H. Stuart. Oxford, England: Clarendon Press, 1962. A good overview of the period.

See also: Queen Anne; Second Duke of Argyll; First Viscount Bolingbroke; Caroline; Catherine the Great; Charles XII; Sarah Churchill; Eugene of Savoy; George II; George III; First Earl of Godolphin; George Frideric Handel; Louis XV; Peter the Great; Philip V; First Earl Stanhope; Robert Walpole.

Related articles in *Great Events from History: The Eighteenth Century, 1701-1800:* May 26, 1701-September 7, 1714: War of the Spanish Succession; June 12, 1701: Act of Settlement; May 15, 1702-April 11, 1713: Queen Anne's War; February, 1706-April 28, 1707: Act of Union Unites England and Scotland; March 23-26, 1708: Defeat of the "Old Pretender"; September 6, 1715-February 4, 1716: Jacobite Rising in Scotland; September, 1720: Collapse of the South Sea Bubble; 1721-1742: Development of Great Britain's Office of Prime Minister; 1736: *Gentleman's Magazine* Initiates Parliamentary Reporting.

GEORGE II
Elector of Hanover (1727-1760) and king of Great Britain and Ireland (r. 1727-1760)

George II continued the relationship of Crown and Parliament developed under his father George I, which gave the king extensive powers in foreign affairs and the appointment of ministers but required him to appoint ministers and follow policies that the Parliament would support. Under George II this system of government was adapted to the needs of a dynamic, expanding nation that, by the end of his reign, had established itself as a major European power and the dominant force in overseas trade and colonies.

Born: November 10, 1683; Herrenhausen Palace, Hanover (now in Germany)
Died: October 25, 1760; London, England
Also known as: George Augustus (birth name)
Area of achievement: Government and politics

EARLY LIFE

Unlike his father, George I, George II (born George Augustus) was given an opportunity to know his kingdom before he ascended the throne. He was born in Hanover, a medium-sized north German state. His father, George Louis, was elector of Hanover and lawful successor to Queen Anne. His mother was accused of adultery and was shut up in a castle, where she spent the rest of her life. George Augustus was never permitted to see his mother, which was one of many grievances he held against his father. He performed bravely in the War of the Spanish Succession (1701-1714), in which Hanover was allied with Great Britain and other states against the ambitions of King Louis XIV of France. When Queen Anne died in 1714, George Louis of Hanover became King George I. George Augustus came with his father to England, where he was created prince of Wales and recognized as heir to the throne.

In 1705, George Augustus married Caroline of Ansbach, a German princess, who became his close partner in politics and one of the most remarkable women of the time. Caroline grew up at the courts of the elector of Saxony and the king of Prussia, where she was well educated and developed a warm, cheerful personality and broad intellectual and cultural interests. She was a handsome woman, with fair skin, blue eyes, rich blonde hair, and a buxom figure. George was quite dependent upon her—politically, personally, and sexually—although he kept mistresses whom he flaunted openly. Their eldest son, Frederick Louis, was born in 1707, and seven other children followed. Although her life with George was often personally unhappy, Caroline knew that her husband relied on her for political advice and encouragement.

Antagonism between father and eldest son was characteristic of the Hanover monarchs, and it was soon revealed to the British public. When George I made his first return visit to Hanover, in 1716, he refused to designate the prince of Wales as regent, appointing him Guardian of the Realm with closely restricted powers. Father and son broke openly in 1717, when George I banished the prince and princess from the palace and seized custody of their children. About the same time, a split took place in the Whig ministry, as Lord Townshend and Robert Walpole went into opposition. It was also characteristic of Hanoverian politics that opposition groups would rally behind the prince of Wales, who disposed of significant patronage and parliamentary influence and who represented the future. The prince and his charming wife established a lively court at Leicester House in London, which became the center of political opposition and polite society. Three years later, Townshend and Walpole rejoined the Whig ministry and the king and the prince were reconciled. The prince believed that Walpole had abandoned him for the sweets of office, but Walpole had established himself in the confidence of Princess Caroline, a relationship that bore political fruit as long as she lived.

George II. (Library of Congress)

LIFE'S WORK

George I died in June, 1727, and the prince succeeded to the throne as King George II. George I had realized that the power of the Crown in the British system of government was limited, not only by law but also by the need to obtain parliamentary support for the ministry and its policies. George I relied upon the Whigs to provide leadership in Parliament, for their loyalty to the Hanover Dynasty was unquestioned. The Whig leader, Robert Walpole, was a master at using patronage and partisanship to maintain a strong following in the House of Commons. Under George I, the ministers normally met without the king, which was an important step toward the modern system of cabinet government.

George II struggled against the dependence that George I had accepted, but usually without success. Unlike his father, he was active and talkative, with an astonishing memory for genealogies, dates, treaties, regimental symbols, and European courts. He was physically brave but a political coward, and Walpole, with the support of Queen Caroline, learned that he could usually get his way. George II's first attempt at an independent exercise of royal power was a humiliating failure. The new king asked Sir Spencer Compton, a Leicester House intimate, to prepare his opening speech to Parliament. Robert Walpole had resigned, and it was expected that Compton would be designated to lead the ministry. Compton confessed that he did not know how to proceed, and Walpole obligingly stepped in and wrote the speech. When Parliament reassembled, Walpole proposed a large addition to the Civil List, which was the financial provision for the king, the royal family, the royal household, and the civil government. George II was so pleased that he reappointed Walpole first lord of the treasury, a post from which Walpole established a strong personal grip on the cabinet and the House of Commons. Although some politicians tried to influence the king through his mistresses, Walpole possessed the confidence of Queen Caroline, which was decisive. Walpole once remarked that he "took the right sow by the ear."

In the reign of George I, the principal concern of British government had been to establish the Hanover Dynasty and restore political stability after a period of bitter partisanship. When George II took the throne, these objectives had been achieved. The reign of George II was dominated by the problems that arose in a dynamic, expanding nation that was no longer satisfied with the cautious, defensive policies of the previous reign. As the years passed, the rigid domination of Walpole was resented, and he was accused of being a "prime minister," a charge he vigorously denied. An energetic political opposition arose, led by the former Tory leader, Lord Bolingbroke, and dissident Whigs. They made effective use of the press and public agitation to attack the power and policies of Walpole. The opposition found an eloquent voice in William Pitt the Elder, a brilliant orator, who attacked Walpole's policy of peace and the king's partiality for Hanover. When Frederick Louis, prince of Wales, came of age in 1737, he followed the trail blazed by his father, making Leicester House again the center of opposition politics. The death of Queen Caroline, the same year, weakened Walpole at court while the emergence of the prince gave legitimacy to the opposition.

In this period of partisanship, George II generally supported Walpole, although his temperament inclined him to greater agressiveness than Walpole usually displayed. The major issues arose in foreign policy, where the king normally exercised the most influence. As elector of Hanover, George II wished to intervene in the War of the Polish Succession (1733-1735), but he was dissuaded by Walpole, who wished to avoid costly continental entanglements. In 1739, a crisis arose with Spain as a result of the efforts of British merchants and sea captains to expand the illegal trade with the Spanish colonies. George II was eager for war with Spain, in which he was supported by the duke of Newcastle, secretary of state. Walpole was overruled, and Great Britain entered jauntily into a war for which it was ill-prepared. The next year, war broke out between Austria and Prussia; this conflict, known to historians as the War of the Austrian Succession, was to last from 1740 to 1748. George II rushed to the aid of the Austrians to protect Hanover against threats from France and Prussia. Walpole was swept along by the tide, and when the war went badly and the House of Commons turned against him, he found it best to resign.

The resignation of Walpole, in 1742, was a landmark in British constitutional development. Despite the acknowledged right of the king to appoint his own ministers, it demonstrated that the king could not keep in office a minister who had lost the confidence of the House of Commons. In the political crisis that followed, George II was forced to come to terms with the hated prince of Wales and bestow office upon politicians who had opposed him. In 1746, George II quarreled with a ministry led by the duke of Newcastle and Henry Pelham, successors to Walpole as leaders of the Whigs. The king asked two personal favorites, Lord Carteret and Lord Bath, to form a ministry, but he was compelled to back down when they could not obtain parliamentary support. Newcastle and Pelham returned to office, stronger than before. George II had learned an important lesson. Although he grumbled that "the people are king in this country," thereafter he kept in mind the limits within which the king could control the composition of ministries.

In the meantime, George II was actively involved in the War of the Austrian Succession. His main concern was to protect Hanover from French threats. In 1743, he personally commanded an army of British and Hanoverian troops in the Rhineland, where he led his soldiers into a French trap. George II fought bravely in the face of French gunfire and turned certain defeat into victory when the French cavalry charged prematurely. The Battle of Dettingen was the last time that any British king led his troops on the battlefield.

In 1745, George II was confronted with the last important challenge to the Hanover Dynasty when Prince Charles (Bonnie Prince Charlie), the Stuart claimant to the throne, landed in Scotland. The Highlanders rose in support of the man they regarded as their rightful king, and Prince Charles was crowned in Edinburgh. Leading his motley army southward, Prince Charles entered England, advancing into the Midlands before being compelled to withdraw. George II, with his usual resolution and courage, participated actively in organizing military resistance. In April, 1746, the Highlanders were crushed at the Battle of Culloden by a force of redcoats led by the king's favorite son, the duke of Cumberland. Prince Charles was compelled to flee to France and eventually to Rome, where he died a lonely exile in 1788. The result of the Forty-five, as it was called, was to rally the English behind their German-born king.

Prior to 1744, British efforts in the War of the Austrian Succession had been as allies of Austria and Hanover against France. In 1744, Great Britain and France declared war upon each other and the conflict was extended to the colonies. By the end of the war, British seapower had gained control of the seas, but the ground warfare on the Continent favored the French. All parties were ready for peace, which was signed in 1748. The War of the Austrian Succession was indecisive. Another more intensive struggle was likely between Austria and Prussia for supremacy in Europe and Great Britain and France for supremacy in the colonial arena. Hanover continued as a hostage to the fortunes of European conflict.

The last two decades of the reign of George II were marked by population increase, economic growth, and colonial expansion. For a time political controversy declined. Frederick, prince of Wales, died in 1751, leaving the opposition without a rallying point. The duke of Newcastle and his brother, Henry Pelham, provided capable parliamentary leadership and adopted "broad-bottom" policies that won widespread support. In 1754, the period of peace and progress ended: War broke out with France in North America and Henry Pelham died. "Now I shall have no more peace," George II commented. He was right.

In 1756, the war with France in America, known to Americans as the French and Indian War (1754-1763), was absorbed into a general European conflict called the Seven Years' War (1756-1763). France, Austria, and Russia joined against Frederick the Great of Prussia, who fought valiantly to stave off defeat. George II, concerned as always for the security of Hanover, came to the aid of Prussia. As usual, Great Britain got off to a bad start, which precipitated a political crisis at home. William Pitt, now at the peak of his power, attacked the mismanagement of the war and made it impossible for Newcastle to govern. When Newcastle resigned in 1756, George II was compelled to accept Pitt as leader of the ministry, even though Pitt had been a constant critic of the king's preoccupation with Hanover. Newcastle, as leader of the Whigs, was able to block Pitt. Eventually reason prevailed and, in 1757, a coalition government was formed in which Pitt managed the war and Newcastle managed Parliament and the finances. George II had lost his control of ministries, for the Pitt-Newcastle ministry rested upon the support of Parliament and public opinion.

George II had the good fortune to live long enough to preside over the most successful war in British history. Pitt was a superb war leader, and news of victories flowed into Great Britain in a steady stream. The French were driven out of North America, the French West Indian islands were captured, and the British East India Company defeated the French in India, gaining the great province of Bengal in the process. Despite his previous strictures against continental involvements, Pitt supported Frederick the Great of Prussia with money and sent an army to defend Hanover. The British navy swept the seas, and when Spain came to the aid of France in 1761, the British captured Florida, Cuba, and Manila.

By that time, King George II was no more. On October 25, 1760, shortly before his seventy-seventh birthday, the king finished his morning chocolate and fell over dead. The prince of Wales was proclaimed King George III, and a new era in British history began.

SIGNIFICANCE

The long reign of King George II established firmly the process by which Crown and Parliament worked together in the "mixed and balanced constitution" of eighteenth century Great Britain. Despite his attempts to assert himself, George II accepted the reality that government must be exercised by ministers who had the support of Parliament. Normally the king could guarantee such support, for the influence that the Crown exercised through patronage, honors, and other benefits gave ministers a core of loyal supporters, and the independent members were inclined to give the king and his ministers the benefit of the doubt. At times of political crisis, as in 1742, 1746, and 1757, the king would have to yield. George II did not accept defeat gracefully, but he did so nevertheless. The ministers continued the practice of meeting apart from the king, and the cabinet became the place where the main issues were discussed and decided. When George II died, cabinet government was well established, and the long career of Walpole demonstrated the advantages of one recognized leader—a prime minister.

The main importance of the reign lay outside the realm of government: in the growth of the economy, imperial expansion, and remarkable achievements in philosophy, science, literature, theater, and the arts. Apart from his love of music and support of George Frideric Handel, George II had little direct effect in these areas, but the provision of a government which provided both stability and freedom was undoubtedly an important factor in the other developments of the Georgian age.

—Earl A. Reitan

FURTHER READING

Black, Jeremy, ed. *British Politics and Society from Walpole to Pitt, 1742-1789*. New York: St. Martin's Press, 1990. Eight essays explore the history of the period, including the position of parliament, the British empire, the church, popular political movements, Scotland, and Ireland.

Hervey, John. *Some Materials Towards the Memoirs of the Reign of King George II*. 3 vols. Edited by Romney Sedgwick. Reprint. New York: AMS Press, 1970. Fascinating court memoirs also available in an abridged edition by Peter Quennell.

Marples, Morris. *Poor Fred and the Butcher: The Sons of George II*. London: Michael Joseph, 1970. Dual biography of Frederick, prince of Wales, and the duke of Cumberland.

Plumb, J. H. *The First Four Georges*. Boston: Little, Brown, 1975. Interesting, well-written chapters on the Hanover monarchs by the outstanding authority on the period. Profusely illustrated.

_____. *Sir Robert Walpole: The King's Minister*. London: Cresset Press, 1960. The second volume of Plumb's masterful biography takes the story to 1734.

Quennell, Peter. *Caroline of England: An Augustan Portrait*. New York: Viking Press, 1940. A delightful and fascinating biography with much about George II.

Trench, Charles Chenevix. *George II*. London: Allen Lane, 1973. A good scholarly biography of George II is lacking, but this work provides acceptable coverage and is written in an interesting style.

Van der Kiste, John. *King George II and Queen Caroline*. Stroud, England: Sutton, 1997. Biography of the royal couple explores their relationship with their sons and the governance of their country. Van der Kiste describes how George II delegated political business to Walpole and Pitt, and how Caroline worked with Walpole to rule Great Britain.

Williams, Basil. *The Whig Supremacy, 1714-1760*. 2d ed. Revised by C. H. Stuart. Oxford, England: Clarendon Press, 1962. A good general overview of the period.

See also: Queen Anne; Second Duke of Argyll; First Viscount Bolingbroke; Caroline; Frederick the Great; George I; George III; First Earl of Godolphin; George Frideric Handel; Henry Pelham; Philip V; Robert Walpole.

Related articles in *Great Events from History: The Eighteenth Century:* 1721-1742: Development of Great Britain's Office of Prime Minister; October 20, 1740: Maria Theresa Succeeds to the Austrian Throne; December 16, 1740-November 7, 1748: War of the Austrian Succession; August 19, 1745-September 20, 1746: Jacobite Rebellion; January, 1756-February 15, 1763: Seven Years' War.

GEORGE III

Elector of Hanover (1760-1814), king of Great Britain and Ireland (r. 1760-1820), and king of Hanover (r. 1814-1820)

George III's forty-year reign covered a period of remarkable political, economic, social, and cultural change. He was conservative in his views, but his efforts to prevent changes in the role of the monarchy were frustrated by forces beyond his control. By standing for traditional values, he helped make the changes of his time more acceptable to his people.

Born: June 4, 1738; London, England
Died: January 29, 1820; Windsor Castle, Berkshire, England
Also known as: George William Frederick (full name)
Area of achievement: Government and politics

EARLY LIFE

George III was the eldest son of Frederick, prince of Wales, and Princess Augusta. In typical Hanoverian fashion, bitter antagonism arose between Frederick and his father, King George II. Frederick became a leader of the opposition to George II and his ministers, and he contributed to the fall of the king's domineering minister, Robert Walpole. When Frederick died in 1751, George became prince of Wales and heir to the throne. At Leicester House, where he lived with his mother, he imbibed the ideas of Frederick. He grew up with the firm conviction that it was his duty to restore the constitutional power of the monarchy and set an example of propriety and morality in public and personal life.

When George II died on October 25, 1760, George III was proclaimed king. He immediately called upon Lord Bute, his tutor for many years, for advice. At that time, Great Britain was involved in the Seven Years' War (1756-1763), which is known in American history as the French and Indian War (1754-1763). Great Britain was led by the imperious William Pitt the Elder, who directed the war to a series of magnificent victories, and the duke of Newcastle, who was a master of the politics of parliamentary and electoral management. Pitt had nothing but contempt for Newcastle's kind of politics, and Newcastle feared the domineering manner of Pitt. George III and Lord Bute regarded both these ministers as obstacles to the restoration of the royal power, but in the tide of victory they could not be removed from office.

The young king and Lord Bute were convinced that the war should be ended as soon as possible. In September, 1761, Pitt wanted to attack Spain, for he had reason to believe that Spain was preparing for war. The cabinet, including Newcastle, rejected his proposal and Pitt resigned. A few months later Spain entered the war, which led to additional British victories and conquests. In April, 1762, the cabinet again showed its determination to end the war by refusing to agree to additional financial support for Great Britain's hard-fighting ally, King Frederick the Great of Prussia. At this point, Newcastle resigned, for he insisted that the nation needed a continental ally. Bute became leader of the ministry. In this way, Pitt and Newcastle left office, but in both cases the king and Bute had the support of the cabinet.

As principal minister of George III, Bute's major concern was to make peace with France and Spain. The peace treaty brought vast colonial acquisitions for Great Britain, including Canada, the area between the Appalachians and the Mississippi River, Florida, several West Indies islands, and a dominant position in India. Pitt and Newcastle criticized the treaty, but ineffectively. The treaty was approved overwhelmingly by Parliament, but by using the kind of political corruption that George III and Bute had criticized earlier. At this point Lord Bute resigned. He complained of ill health, but also he had no stomach for the difficult decisions and bitter disputes that occur in politics. For several years thereafter, George III occasionally turned to Bute for advice, but essentially he had "dropped the pilot" and was on his own.

In the meantime, the young king had married Charlotte of Mecklenburg-Strelitz, a minor German principality. Charlotte was selected for George by his mother and Lord Bute, but he accepted her as a suitable consort and the marriage was a happy one. Her appearance was plain and her conduct modest and proper. They had fifteen children and were devoted parents.

LIFE'S WORK

The major objective of King George III was to maintain the power of the monarchy as an independent and active factor in the British political process. The key was the right of the king to appoint his own ministers, for the powers of the Crown were exercised through ministers who were also members of the House of Lords or House of Commons. Under the rule of George I and George II, politicians had used their political support in Parliament to impose ministers and policies upon the king against his wishes. George III was determined to preserve his freedom of action in this respect. To accomplish his purpose he eventually found it necessary to build his own body of supporters in Parliament.

The king's second concern was to establish his role as the leader and symbol of the nation. He was proud that he was the first of his family who was born in England and who spoke English as a native language. His responsibility in this respect, as he conceived it, was to be accessible to the public and to set a good example in his political and personal conduct. As such, he was a forerunner of Queen Victoria.

The first decade of the reign of George III was one of political instability, as one short-lived ministry followed another. Some of the responsibility lay with the king, for he lacked political experience, and he was inclined to judge ministries on personal grounds rather than political competence. In part, the responsibility lay with a group of contentious political leaders, who magnified their differences and reacted to the king in a testy manner. A major factor was the rise of divisive issues: popular radicalism at home, economic distress aggravated by poor crops and high food prices, resistance in the North American colonies, growing discontent in Ireland, and abuses of power by the British East India Company in India. France and Spain were awaiting their opportunity to

King George III. (Library of Congress)

avenge the defeats of the Seven Years' War, and Great Britain lacked a reliable continental ally. Any government would have faced serious problems, but the situation was aggravated by a young, insecure, inexperienced, but determined king.

In this fluctuating political climate George III learned that he would have to play politics too, and gradually he collected about him a group of parliamentary politicians and hardworking administrators whose primary allegiance was to the Crown. One of the most able of this group was Frederick, Lord North, who became leader of the ministry in 1770. North was willing to accept the leadership of the king, and the king was willing to delegate extensive responsibility to North, whose loyalty and competence he trusted. As George III gained maturity and confidence, he became a strong and effective ruler, and under Lord North the Crown built a following in Parliament that guaranteed safe majorities on almost all issues.

The American Revolution presented George III with a crisis that seemed to destroy all he had worked to achieve. George III was determined that the unity of the British Empire should be preserved, for he and most of his people were convinced that the power and prosperity of Great Britain depended on the empire. The king and his ministers espoused a domino theory, which held that the loss of the thirteen American colonies meant that Canada and the British West Indies would soon follow. Ireland would then demand independence, British trade and seapower would decline accordingly, and Great Britain would be left a minor state comparable to Sweden. Since the Crown and Parliament had the legal right to govern the empire, it seemed essential to enforce that power against colonial resistance and mob violence.

After a decade of controversy, the Boston Tea Party (1773), in which Bostonians boarded a ship of the British East India Company and threw its cargo of tea into the harbor, was seen in London as the last straw. Coercive measures were taken against Massachusetts, the colonies joined together in the Continental Congress, and in April, 1775, shots were fired at Lexington and Concord. At first the American colonists insisted that their quarrel was with Parliament and the king's ministers. The Declaration of Independence (1776), however, was directed against King George III, making it clear that the Americans were determined to break all ties with the mother country. In these disputes George III consistently advocated firm enforcement of royal authority. The king was determined to use military force to subdue the rebellion if necessary, although he was prepared to be generous to the colonists if they would admit the supremacy of the British crown.

The war that began in the American colonies became a general maritime war with the involvement of France (1778), Spain (1779), and the Netherlands (1780). In Ireland, the Volunteers, who were organized to defend the country against invasion, became a political pressure group seeking more self-government. In India, the British East India Company was fighting for survival against a coalition of Indian princes organized and supported by France. At home, the opposition, led by Lord Rockingham, criticized the North ministry for political corruption and bad management. In 1780, Edmund Burke's plan of "economical reform" almost brought about the resignation of the North ministry.

Through all of these discouragements and defeats, George III was the constant advocate of courage and resolution, but as one crisis followed another, the country lost heart. In October, 1781, Lord Cornwallis surrendered his army at Yorktown, and in March, 1782, the House of Commons turned against the war. Lord North resigned, advising the king that his predecessors had often given way to the wishes of the House of Commons, and that it was necessary to do so again. This was not the message the king wanted to hear. George III had no choice but to accept a ministry led by Lord Rockingham and pledged to American independence. It was the most bitter defeat of his life, for he had lost his control of the appointment of ministries and the shaping of policy. He never forgave Lord North for abandoning him at that crucial moment.

The fall of North's ministry brought a new period of political instability. The Rockingham ministry was determined to reduce the resources of patronage by which the Crown had developed a body of loyal followers in the House of Commons. The king accepted some of these measures, but he opposed Edmund Burke's bill for control of the Civil List, which was the money provided for support of the king, the royal family, the royal household, and the civil government. The Civil List was voted to the king for life at the beginning of his reign, and it was regarded as uniquely personal to the king. As such, George III regarded Burke's Civil List Act (1782) as a personal rebuke, although he had no choice but to sign it.

In June, 1782, Lord Rockingham died and George III had an opportunity to reassert his right to control the appointment of ministers. He offered leadership of the ministry to Lord Shelburne, who was formerly linked with Rockingham. Most of the followers of Rockingham, however, refused to support Shelburne and followed Charles James Fox, a strong critic of the king and of royal power. Shelburne advocated a generous peace treaty with the American colonists, and when the treaty was presented to Parliament, he was severely criticized for his concessions. Shelburne was forced to resign by a coalition of Fox and North. Shelburne's first lord of the Admiralty, William Pitt the Younger, earned the respect and goodwill of George III by holding out a few weeks longer, but when Pitt resigned in March, 1783, the king again was forced to accept a ministry not of his own choosing.

The new ministry was based on a coalition of Fox, supported by most of the former followers of Rockingham, and Lord North, who still had the confidence of many who had supported his former ministry. George III detested Fox, and North's alliance with Fox he regarded as a second betrayal.

Shortly, however, George III found the opportunity to rid himself of the hated Fox-North ministry. Fox introduced a bill for reform of the East India Company that was unpopular in both houses of Parliament. The king also learned that Pitt would lead a new ministry if he were guaranteed the open support of the king and an election to strengthen his position in the House of Commons. George III agreed, and in December, 1783, the Fox-North ministry was dismissed. Pitt took office as leader of a ministry, despite the opposition of a majority of the House of Commons.

The king had succeeded only partially in restoring his own power. Pitt never forgot that he was the king's man, but his ability and integrity gave him an independent position in Parliament that the king had to respect. The alternative to Pitt was Fox, however, so George III had little choice but to stand behind his young but able prime minister. Despite their differences on many issues, the king relied increasingly on Pitt. In 1788, George III suffered his first attack of mental illness. When he recovered, he learned that Pitt and the queen had loyally protected his interests, while the prince of Wales had behaved abominably, preparing to take power as regent and promising offices to Fox and his friends. Thereafter, George III reduced his activities to preserve his health, and his dependence on Pitt was even greater.

In 1789, a revolution broke out in France that soon became violent at home and aggressive toward neighboring states. Great Britain declared war in 1793, joining with most of the states of Europe to contain French militarism and revolutionary zeal. The war further diminished the political power of the king, for the Pitt ministry had to take responsibility for conducting the war. On the other hand, the role of the king as symbol of the nation was enhanced. Unlike the war of the American Revolution, the war against revolutionary France was popular, and for the first time, the king became an admired figure.

In 1801, a political crisis arose concerning the Act of Union, which joined Great Britain and Ireland. Pitt insisted that the measure could work only if Catholics received political rights. When George III refused to agree, Pitt resigned and the king suffered another attack of mental illness. Thereafter, mental breakdowns came more frequently, and by 1811, the king was permanently insane. His son, the prince of Wales, now overweight, cross, and petulant, exercised the royal powers as regent.

By this time, a different Great Britain was emerging. The long wars with revolutionary and Napoleonic France, the Industrial Revolution, and the Romantic movement were transforming British life and thought. A new empire was arising in India and Australia to replace the thirteen rebellious colonies, lost long before. Old, blind, mad, and lonely, George III wandered the drafty halls of Windsor Castle, wearing a skull cap and dressing gown, sometimes playing the organ, sometimes living with memories of the past. His faithful queen, who died the year before he did, was fearful of him and lived apart. When he died in 1820, King George III was little more than a memory.

SIGNIFICANCE

George III's long struggle to maintain the independent role of the monarch was frustrated by the growth of cabinet government and the increasing power of Parliament. Pitt's long tenure of power helped establish the role of the prime minister as the effective national leader. George III could not stop the evolution of the British constitution, and the practices that began in the reigns of George I and George II became generally accepted in the long reign of George III.

When the king did intervene in the political process, he was often stubborn and wrongheaded. His inexperience contributed to the political instability of his first decade. He undoubtedly prolonged the American war and paid a political price for it. He resisted movements for parliamentary reform, religious toleration, and abolition of the slave trade. He made the union of Great Britain and Ireland unworkable by refusing to concede political rights to Catholics. On the positive side, his determination to fight the power and ideology of revolutionary France served the national purpose by strengthening resistance to a dangerous foe.

As a symbol of the nation, the personal conduct of George III gave dignity to the Hanover Dynasty that previously, despite its merits, had not been popular with the British public. George III's John Bull nationalism was shared by his people, and he won respect by his probity of conduct and concern for his family. Even his personal quirks, such as his jerky mode of speech and his homespun hobbies, struck a sympathetic chord. His profligate sons, who succeeded him as George IV and William IV, aroused disdain. His true successor was Queen Victoria, who continued to give the British monarchy dignity and respect.

—Earl A. Reitan

FURTHER READING

Ayling, Stanley. *George the Third*. New York: Alfred A. Knopf, 1972. A well-written and informative biography.

Brooke, John. *King George III*. London: Constable, 1972. A well-written personal biography by a leading scholar of the period.

Hibbert, Christopher. *George III: A Personal History*. New York: Addison-Wesley, 1997. Hibbert refutes the popular conception that George III was a tyrant, madman, or unsophisticated rube. Instead, Hibbert maintains the king was a hardworking constitutional monarch, a patron of the arts and sciences, and a loving husband and father.

Macalpine, Ida, and Richard Hunter. *George III and the Mad Business*. London: Pimlico, 1991. George III has often been depicted as a raging lunatic, with serious mental problems. The authors, two psychiatrists, examined the king's medical records and concluded he suffered from porphyria, a rare blood disease that was not properly treated and was responsible for his odd behavior.

Namier, Sir Lewis. *The Structure of Politics at the Accession of George III*. 2d ed. London: Macmillan, 1957. Seminal study of parliamentary politics in 1760.

Pares, Richard. *King George III and the Politicians*. Oxford, England: Clarendon Press, 1953. The best study of the political role of the king.

Plumb, J. H. *The First Four Georges*. Rev. ed. Boston: Little, Brown, 1975. Interesting, well-written chapters on the Hanover monarchs by the outstanding authority on the period. Profusely illustrated.

Reitan, E. A. *George III: Tyrant or Constitutional Monarch?* Lexington, Mass.: D. C. Heath, 1964. Introduction and selections illustrating historical interpretations of the character and purposes of King George III.

Watson, J. Steven. *The Reign of George III, 1760-1815.* Oxford, England: Clarendon Press, 1960. A good general overview of the period.

See also: Queen Anne; Queen Charlotte; First Marquess Cornwallis; Charles James Fox; Benjamin Franklin; George I; George II; Thomas Jefferson; Lord North; William Pitt the Younger; Robert Walpole; George Washington.

Related articles in *Great Events from History: The Eighteenth Century, 1701-1800:* May 28, 1754-February 10, 1763: French and Indian War; January, 1756-February 15, 1763: Seven Years' War; June 29, 1767-April 12, 1770: Townshend Crisis; March 5, 1770: Boston Massacre; December 16, 1773: Boston Tea Party; 1774: Hansard Begins Reporting Parliamentary Debates; December, 1774-February 24, 1783: First Marāthā War; April 19, 1775: Battle of Lexington and Concord; July 4, 1776: Declaration of Independence; June 21, 1779-February 7, 1783: Siege of Gibraltar; June 2-10, 1780: Gordon Riots; March 1, 1781: Ratification of the Articles of Confederation; October 19, 1781: Cornwallis Surrenders at Yorktown; 1783: Loyalists Migrate to Nova Scotia; September 17, 1787: U.S. Constitution Is Adopted; 1790: Burke Lays the Foundations of Modern Conservatism; December 15, 1791: U.S. Bill of Rights Is Ratified; May-November, 1798: Irish Rebellion; July 2-August 1, 1800: Act of Union Forms the United Kingdom.

ELBRIDGE GERRY
American statesman and politician

Gerry was an ardent and early supporter of American independence, first in Massachusetts and then in the Continental Congress. He signed the Declaration of Independence and, at the Constitutional Convention, he helped forge compromises that would lead to the establishment of a stronger federal government. His life was devoted to public service as a vice president, a representative, and a governor of Massachusetts.

Born: July 17, 1744; Marblehead, Massachusetts
Died: November 23, 1814; Washington, D.C.
Area of achievement: Government and politics

EARLY LIFE
Elbridge Gerry was the son of Elizabeth Greenleaf and Thomas Gerry, a British immigrant and Marblehead merchant respectively. He entered Harvard College at the age of fourteen, graduated in 1762, and received a master's degree from there in 1765. In his thesis, Gerry argued for opposition to British restrictions on commerce in the colonies. He joined his father and brothers in the family business, shipping dried fish to Spanish and Portuguese ports and trading for other goods. He accumulated a modest fortune but spent much of it as his interests shifted to politics and public service.

Elected to the General Court in 1772, Gerry met Samuel Adams and through his influence became an early leader in the Committee of Correspondence system, first in Marblehead and then in the Massachusetts state committee. His faith in democratic governance, however,

was shattered during months of mob violence in Marblehead. In response to a local smallpox epidemic, Gerry and other businessmen built a private hospital. Townspeople feared the spread of disease and attributed it to the hospital. Mobs threatened the lives of Gerry and his partners and burned down the hospital. Gerry's reaction to the smallpox war and to the fatal illness of his father was to withdraw temporarily from politics.

Patriot sympathies were renewed after the British parliament's Coercive Acts closed the port of Boston. Gerry led relief efforts and organized local merchants to assist their colleagues in Boston. In October, 1774, he was elected to the Massachusetts Provincial Congress, an extralegal body set up after Governor Thomas Gage dissolved the Massachusetts legislature. Appointed to several committees regarding governance and military preparedness, Gerry worked to acquire and store military supplies. On April 18, 1775, Gerry met with Adams, John Hancock, and other members of the Committee of Safety in Menotomy (now Arlington). Gerry slept at the tavern that night but awoke with the arrival of a raiding party on its way to Lexington and Concord. Half-clothed, Gerry escaped out the back and hid in a cornfield as British soldiers searched the buildings.

LIFE'S WORK
Elected to the Continental Congress (1776-1781, 1783-1785), Elbridge Gerry aligned with Samuel Adams and John Adams. He was critical of the Massachusetts delegation's shift away from lagging support for indepen-

dence. Gerry signed the Declaration of Independence, and he later viewed this as the most important act of his life. In addition, Gerry signed the first American constitution, the Articles of Confederation, which formed a weak national government. In Congress, he asserted a leadership role and guided the new nation with his experience as a merchant, particularly in the areas of finance and military supply.

Gerry married Ann Thompson, a New York merchant's daughter, on January 12, 1786. They moved to Cambridge and had six daughters and three sons. Gerry left Congress and retired from business, but he was elected to the Massachusetts house of representatives. In 1786-1787, Revolutionary War veteran Daniel Shays led a rebellion of farmers in western Massachusetts to stop mortgage foreclosures. Like most members of the economic and social elite, Gerry was disturbed by the violence and the inability of the nation to respond under the Confederation, but he also feared the unchecked power of a strong central government.

Initially opposed to reforms for a stronger national government, Gerry accepted an appointment as a delegate to the Philadelphia Convention of 1787. During the constitutional debates, he favored more balanced power between national and state governments. He distrusted reform efforts proposing greater democracy (such as popular election of the Senate or the president), yet argued for a bill of rights to protect citizens from governmental encroachment. Gerry preached the virtue of compromise and chaired the committee that resolved the issue of representation of large and small states. He also cast the deciding vote in the Massachusetts delegation in favor of the Connecticut Compromise, which in turn was decided by a 5-4 vote among the states.

In the end, however, Gerry was one of only three delegates who refused to sign the new federal Constitution. His primary complaint was that the document lacked a bill of rights, a demand that anti-Federalists pressed during ratification. Gerry, however, was elected to the new government's House of Representatives (1789-1793) and helped frame the provisions of what would be the Bill of Rights.

In 1797, President John Adams nominated Gerry, John Marshall, and Charles Cotesworth Pinckney as ministers to Paris to negotiate growing disputes between France and the United States. During this controversial mission, known as the XYZ affair, Gerry was conciliatory with the French, who were angered by Jay's Treaty with Britain in 1795. Gerry conducted secret negotiations with French minister Charles Maurice de Talleyrand-

Périgord, even as Marshall and Pinckney abandoned their posts and returned home. Gerry believed that his negotiations prevented war with France, but his political opponents argued that he was duped by Talleyrand and the French agents.

After Adams recalled Gerry and his dispatches were published, Gerry become more suspicious of an aristocratic and a pro-British bias of the Federalists. His political ideology moved closer to the Jeffersonian Republicans, but as a candidate he still appealed to moderate Federalists. Gerry was elected as governor of Massachusetts for two terms (1810-1812). His first term was characterized by moderation and conciliatory politics, but his second term became synonymous with partisan politics. Gerry signed into law a bill that redrew electoral districts. It effectively concentrated Federalist voters within a few constituencies and thus gave Gerry's Democratic-Republicans an electoral advantage. After observers likened the district that included Marblehead and the northeastern coast to a salamander, redistricting for partisan advantage became known as a "gerrymander."

Although he lost the gubernatorial election of 1812, the Republican Congressional Caucus nominated Gerry as vice president on the ticket with incumbent President James Madison. He was elected with Madison just as the War of 1812 with Britain raged. Gerry was in poor health

Elbridge Gerry. (Library of Congress)

during his term as vice president, but he continued to fulfill his duties as president of the Senate. After entering the Senate chamber on the morning of November 23, 1814, Gerry suffered chest pains. He had a hemorrhage of the lungs and died shortly thereafter. During his last few months, he had been a strong supporter of Madison, the Republicans, and the war with Great Britain.

SIGNIFICANCE

Elbridge Gerry was a central figure before and during the American Revolution and the founding of the republic. His political philosophy, however, epitomized the inherent contradictions of the new government. Gerry opposed the monarchy and strong central authority, but he also feared popular democracy and its tendency toward mob rule. Gerry argued against establishing a federal standing army and a naval power, yet he advocated military conflict with Britain during the revolution and the War of 1812.

His leadership in the Philadelphia Convention forged key compromises and the ultimate approval of the federal Constitution, but, insisting on the inclusion of a bill of rights and other provisions, he refused to sign the document. Remembered primarily as an early practitioner of partisan redistricting, Gerry disliked political parties and factional divisions. His life in public service stemmed from his belief in a superior moral character produced by the American experience, yet his career could also be viewed as an exercise in political expediency.

—*James W. Endersby*

FURTHER READING

Austin, James T. *Life of Elbridge Gerry*. Boston: Wells and Lilly, 1828-1829. An extended treatment of Gerry's early life, through the end of the American Revolution, written by his son-in-law. This two-volume set also includes copies of some of Gerry's correspondence to friends and associates.

Billias, George Athan. *Elbridge Gerry: Founding Father and Republican Statesman*. New York: McGraw-Hill, 1976. This standard biography is based on Gerry's correspondence and other manuscripts from numerous archives and collections. It argues that his republicanism was an organizing principle in his life and sheds lights on how republicanism influenced nonintellectuals.

McCullough, David. *John Adams*. New York: Simon & Schuster, 2001. This biography of one of Gerry's closet contemporaries sheds light on events of the times as well as Gerry's own life.

Madison, James. *Notes of Debates in the Federal Convention of 1787*. Athens: Ohio University Press, 1993. There are many editions of Madison's description of what occurred behind the closed doors of the Constitutional Convention in Philadelphia. The understanding of Gerry's political thought and the thoughts of other framers comes chiefly through Madison's description of them.

Morison, Samuel Eliot. "Elbridge Gerry, Gentleman-Democrat." *New England Quarterly* 2 (1929): 3-33. A discussion of Gerry's place in the early Republic and the development of political parties. The article characterizes Gerry as inconsistent and irresolute.

Rush, Mark E. *Does Redistricting Make a Difference?* Baltimore: Johns Hopkins University Press, 1993. Reprint. Lanham, Md.: Lexington Books, 2000. Gerry entered the lexicon as a symbol of partisan and unfair redistricting. The argument in this work is that the presumed consequences of a gerrymander are unsubstantiated.

Stinchcombe, William. *The XYZ Affair*. Westport, Conn.: Greenwood Press, 1980. The undeclared naval war with France threatened the future of the American Republic after independence. This book discusses the negotiations of Gerry and others with Talleyrand and his agents.

See also: John Adams; Samuel Adams; Thomas Gage; John Hancock; John Jay; James Madison; Daniel Shays; Mercy Otis Warren.

Related articles in *Great Events from History: The Eighteenth Century, 1701-1800:* September 5-October 26, 1774: First Continental Congress; April 19, 1775: Battle of Lexington and Concord; May 10-August 2, 1775: Second Continental Congress; May, 1776-September 3, 1783: France Supports the American Revolution; July 4, 1776: Declaration of Independence; February 6, 1778: Franco-American Treaties; March 1, 1781: Ratification of the Articles of Confederation; September 3, 1783: Treaty of Paris; September 17, 1787: U.S. Constitution Is Adopted; 1790's: First U.S. Political Parties; December 15, 1791: U.S. Bill of Rights Is Ratified; November 19, 1794: Jay's Treaty; October 27, 1795: Pinckney's Treaty; September 17, 1787: U.S. Constitution Is Adopted; October 4, 1797-September 30, 1800: XYZ Affair.

EDWARD GIBBON
English historian

Combining immense learning with a polished style and a gently ironic wit, Gibbon wrote The History of the Decline and Fall of the Roman Empire, *which proved a durable landmark in historiography.*

Born: May 8, 1737; Putney, Surrey, England
Died: January 16, 1794; London, England
Areas of achievement: Historiography, scholarship, literature

EARLY LIFE

Edward Gibbon's mother, née Judith Porten, was the daughter of a London merchant who lived in Putney. His father, also named Edward Gibbon, was a country gentleman. The future historian grew up at Buriton, the Hampshire manor that his grandfather Gibbon had saved from the wreck of his first fortune and to which his father retired on the death of his first wife, whose eldest and only surviving son was the young Edward. The little boy was sickly and bookish. If he did not regret his frequent confinements, and even secretly rejoiced in the illnesses that kept him off the playing fields, still he always carried the scars of the bleeding and caustics of those early days, as well as the scar left by a dog strongly suspected of madness.

His education began at home and continued there during the long vacations from Westminster School and later Magdalen College, Oxford. He dreaded being torn away from his reading, and he therefore dreaded the full moon, which meant the practicality of navigating dirt roads to visit neighboring county families. On such visits he occupied himself in his host's library. He wrote of one such occasion, "I was immersed in the passage of the Goths over the Danube, when the summons of the dinner-bell reluctantly dragged me from my intellectual feast."

Not quite fifteen years old, Gibbon was packed off to Magdalen College "with a stock of Erudition that might have puzzled a doctor, and a degree of ignorance of which a schoolboy would have been ashamed." This early reader of *The Arabian Nights' Entertainments* had thought of doing Oriental (Asian) studies, but he was dissuaded, and instead did nothing. At the end of a second academic year, during which he applied himself steadily to questions about transubstantiation, he was received into the Roman Catholic Church. He had changed his mind about religion. He was barely sixteen. He was the proud convert of his own scholarship. Yet that was not an argument to offer his father.

Sent off to the Continent without ceremony, Gibbon recommenced his formal education, improving his Latin, beginning Greek, and learning conversational French. At Lausanne, guided by his Protestant Swiss tutor, Gibbon's reconversion was accomplished. Redeemed from popery, he pledged a temporary allegiance to the Church of England, in which he had been brought up, before moving on to skepticism. During this exile of nearly five years, there was time for more than study, and the short young man with the sensitive face fell in love with Suzanne Curchod. His summons home broke up the romance of which he later wrote that he sighed as a lover but obeyed as a son. There was a happy ending. Suzanne became Madame Necker, mother of Madame de Staël. Gibbon had an affair with Marie Jeanne de Chatillon, wife to Pierre Bontemps, and, later, a flirtation with Lady Elizabeth Foster.

On returning home, and without any vocation he was yet ready to declare, Gibbon followed his father into the militia, obtaining the rank of captain for himself and bestowing a Latin motto on the South Hampshire Grenadiers. With the peace of 1763, Gibbon left the militia, keeping his commission and taking with him the first symptoms of the hydrocele that, neglected for thirty years, killed him before he was fifty-seven. He went abroad again, and, as he later depicted it,

> It was at Rome on the 15th of October, 1764, as I sat musing amidst the ruins of the Capitol, while the barefooted friars were singing vespers in the Temple of Jupiter, that the idea of writing the decline and fall of the city first started to my mind.

That is the way he told it years later. He was wrong about the Temple of Jupiter, and a letter of June, 1764, shows that he had thought of a history of ancient Italy as early as that. His father's death in 1770 left him means and freedom to pursue and even to expand his historical blueprint. Back in England, he became a member of the House of Commons, but this was irrelevant to his main purpose, like his romance with Suzanne and his captaincy in the militia: He never married, never fought, and, in Parliament, never spoke.

LIFE'S WORK

In February, 1776, Edward Gibbon wrote to his friend and executor John Holroyd (later First Baron Sheffield), announcing the forthcoming publication of his first volume. It appeared in March to stand company with three other works of 1776: Adam Smith's *The Wealth of Nations*, Jeremy Bentham's *Fragment on Government*, the Declaration of Independence, and Thomas Paine's *Common Sense*—as remarkable a set of publications as ever came off the presses of the English-speaking world in a given year.

The genesis of *The History of the Decline and Fall of the Roman Empire* (1776-1788) is not in doubt. Gibbon had been thinking of some such project since 1764. Yet his first reaction to the Roman ruins is worth recalling: It had been one of profound distaste. He qualified that judgment, as he changed his mind about the very nature of history as he worked his way through the grand design for what proved to be a six-volume work.

He was convinced that there was an underlying intelligibility in history, the perceptible interaction of cause and effect. He was not a philosopher, but he aspired to be a philosophical historian. His general ideas were clearly derivative from the philosophes. One rule to which he clung with perfect consistency was that a narrative should include only facts that were either interesting or important. What could be applied to the instruction of his own age was important. Such instruction assisted the march of progress, and Gibbon believed in progress though he was writing about a decline. He believed in perfectibility and in an irreducible core of civilization. Indeed, after dealing with Rome's collapse, he offered the view that every period increases human knowledge and possibly human virtue. This view has to be set beside his definition of history at the beginning of his first volume as scarcely more than a record of human crime, folly, and misfortune. He was not consistent. Some of the inconsistency, however, reflects Gibbon's continuing development as a historian.

For example, Gibbon's contempt for the religiosity of the Middle Ages and his thesis that the fall of Rome came with the triumph of barbarism and religion are well known. Yet some years after he had completed his history, he pleaded for a scholarly edition of the medieval English chronicles. He wrote, "For the losses of history are indeed irretrievable: when the productions of fancy or science have been swept away, new poets may invent, and new philosophers may reason; but if the inscription of a single fact be once obliterated, it can never be restored by the united efforts of genius and industry." His subject required him to deal with continental migrations, the wars of an empire, and the religion of the masses. Incalculable numbers of anonymous people were creating the framework within which day-to-day decisions had to be made. Working out his synthesis in such terms, Gibbon outgrew this earlier attitude toward the Middle Ages and his first impression of the Roman Empire itself.

How Gibbon handled his sources would require a separate essay. Happily, J. B. Bury's critically annotated edition of Gibbon's history goes a long way toward answering the question. Gibbon never supplied his own critical bibliography. He concentrated on telling a story. His moral reflections are neatly worked into the narrative, as ballast for the flights of rhetoric. There are also two different histories in *The History of the Decline and Fall of the Roman Empire*. There is the original conception, a history of Rome, expanded to cover the later empire in the West, throughout which the historian is always in Rome, looking outward; then there is the history of Constantinople (modern Istanbul) and the Byzantine Empire, which he had never visited and with which he had only a kind of literary sympathy.

Gibbon was biased in favor of success. If he considered the Antonine age a golden age, he also applauded the level of civilization at which the nations of Western Europe, and their settlement colonies, the true heirs of Rome, had arrived in 1776. Constantinople, to him, had

Edward Gibbon. (Library of Congress)

been a failure without respectable issue. Yet its history was reminiscent of *The Arabian Nights' Entertainments*, and Gibbon's style was adapted to do it literary, if not historical, justice. Gibbon explained how hard he worked on style, revising the first chapter of volume 1 three times and the second and third chapters twice, to achieve his desired effect. His discussion of three centuries of Roman history is constantly animated by his understanding and frequently his admiration for the Romans, both lacking when he shifted the scene to Constantinople. Then, composition was an exercise of style alone, shorn of sympathy, and his interest perceptibly flagged before he had covered the 980 years of eastern history, to which he allotted no more pages than he had to the three centuries dealing with Rome.

By the time he had completed his master work, in June, 1787, Gibbon had left London for Lausanne, where his modest income enabled him to live in greater style than was possible in England. His life and work were disrupted, however, by the death of his friend and companion, Georges Deyverdun, and by the French Revolution. It was not only the refugees, swarming into Lausanne by 1790 but also the actual threat of French invasion that made Gibbon look back to England, to which he returned in 1793. Much of his last summer he spent in the company of John Holroyd, Lord Sheffield, and his children. By autumn, his hydrocele had become such a painful deformity as to make surgery unavoidable. The third operation was fatal, and Gibbon died in London, January 16, 1794. He was buried among Holroyds at Fletching in Sussex.

SIGNIFICANCE

In his own lifetime, Edward Gibbon was often compared to David Hume and William Robertson. Certainly, Gibbon read and learned from those of their works that antedated his own, and in significant ways he imitated them. Hume, as a philosopher as well as a historian, brought a deeper intellect to bear on questions concerning historical causation. Robertson had already popularized the style that Gibbon made his own. Nevertheless, granting the sources available to him and his linguistic limitations, he accomplished as much as any single writer could have done in writing his epic. Contemporaries, not only in England, saluted him. The reception of his work is separable from the history of its genesis and content. Apart from the clergymen who instantly attacked the first volume, only to be crushed by the weighty learning of Gibbon's retort, the reception was favorable. Gibbon obviously glowed with pleasure at Richard Brinsley

Sheridan's complimentary remarks made on the floor of the House of Commons.

After Gibbon's death, anonymous editors chopped and changed his masterpiece. Thomas Bowdler bowdlerized it. By the end of the nineteenth century, German historical scholarship had sapped the foundations of many parts of *The History of the Decline and Fall of the Roman Empire*. Simultaneously, critical emphasis changed, and Gibbon was rebuked not for scoffing at Christianity but for taking sides at all. Early in the nineteenth century, the young William Ewart Gladstone confessed to preferring the intellectual vigor of Hume to Gibbon's ornate style. Yet late in the same century, the young Sir Winston Churchill begged his mother to include Gibbon among the books to be sent out to him in India, where he was striving to compensate for the brevity of his own formal education.

In the end, what brings historians, whether Roman specialists or not, back to Gibbon is their perennial fascination with the splendor of his solution to his problem: how to handle immense themes, spread over a vast chronological canvas, in a way likely to interest the general public.

—*Barry McGill*

FURTHER READING

Bond, Harold L. *The Literary Art of Edward Gibbon.* Oxford, England: Clarendon Press, 1960. A doctoral dissertation submitted at Harvard University and revised for publication.

Bowersock, Glen W., et al., eds. *Edward Gibbon and "The Decline and Fall of the Roman Empire."* Cambridge, Mass.: Harvard University Press, 1977. Though there is no bibliography for the volume as a whole, the footnotes to the various chapters provide a guide to writing on Gibbon. The chapters by Steven Runciman, "Gibbon and Byzantium," and Bernard Lewis, "Gibbon on Muhammad," are particularly notable.

Gibbon, Edward. *The Autobiographies of Edward Gibbon.* Edited by John Murray. London: John Murray, 1896. Includes the six full versions and a fragment of a seventh that show how Gibbon kept polishing up the image he wished to present to posterity.

_____. *Gibbon's Journal to January 28th, 1763.* Edited by David Morrice Low. New York: W. W. Norton, 1929. An improvement over the extracts printed earlier by John Sheffield.

_____. *The History of the Decline and Fall of the Roman Empire.* Edited by J. B. Bury. 7 vols. New York:

Macmillan, 1896-1902. Bury examines the scholarship on Gibbon since Gibbon's time and evaluates his use of sources.

_____. *Letters*. Edited by J. E. Norton. 3 vols. London: Cassell, 1956. Supersedes previous, less complete collections.

_____. *The Miscellaneous Works of Edward Gibbon*. Edited by John Sheffield. London: B. Blake, 1837. Includes juvenile writings, some letters, extracts from journals, and one version of the autobiography.

McKitterick, Rosamond, and Roland Quinault, eds. *Edward Gibbon and Empire*. New York: Cambridge University Press, 1997. Essays by historians interpreting *The History of the Decline and Fall of the Roman Empire*. Gibbon's ideas of empire, working methods, appreciation of the past, and other aspects of the book are considered in light of current research into eighteenth century intellectual history and the history of the Roman Empire, Byzantium, and the Middle Ages.

Wormersley, David. *Gibbon and the "Watchmen of the Holy City": The Historian and His Reputation, 1776-* *1815*. New York: Oxford University Press, 2002. Describes the conflict between Gibbon and critics who disliked his view of Christianity in *The History of the Decline and Fall of the Roman Empire*. Gibbon derisively labeled these critics the "watchmen of the holy city."

Young, George M. *Gibbon*. London: Rupert Hart-Davis, 1948. This was first published in 1932 and reissued with a new introduction in this edition.

See also: Jeremy Bentham; Denis Diderot; Oliver Goldsmith; David Hume; Catherine Macaulay; Thomas Paine; Richard Brinsley Sheridan; Adam Smith; Madame de Staël; William Stukeley; Giambattista Vico; Johann Joachim Winckelmann.

Related articles in *Great Events from History: The Eighteenth Century, 1701-1800:* 1719-1724: Stukeley Studies Stonehenge and Avebury; 1726-1729: Voltaire Advances Enlightenment Thought in Europe; 1751-1772: Diderot Publishes the *Encyclopedia*; 1762: *The Antiquities of Athens* Prompts Architectural Neoclassicism.

CHRISTOPH GLUCK
German composer

Gluck established a new style of opera that marked the end of the Baroque and the beginning of the classical era in music. Many of his stage works represent a turning point in the balance between counterpoint and homophony, between vocal display and musical drama.

Born: July 2, 1714; Erasbach, Upper Palatinate, Bavaria (now in Germany)
Died: November 15, 1787; Vienna, Austria
Also known as: Christoph Willibald Gluck (full name)
Area of achievement: Music

EARLY LIFE

Christoph Gluck (KRIHS-tahf GLOOK) was the son of a forester and huntsman, a profession followed by several of his ancestors. The young Gluck's early training remains a matter of conjecture, but he traveled to Prague in late adolescence and probably enrolled at the University of Prague, though he did not complete his studies there. In Prague, he studied music privately and obtained a position as church organist. He was also exposed to Prague's vigorous musical life, which was dominated by Italian composers, operas, and oratorios.

Gluck then traveled to Milan, where he was engaged in the private orchestra of Prince Antonio Melzi and where he came under the influence of the Italian symphonist Giovanni Battista Sammartini—through association, if not through direct study. It was in Milan that Gluck composed his first opera, *Artaserse* (1741). This successful production was followed by seven more Italian operas in the next four years. In 1745, he visited London and produced two more operas there, works derived largely from his Milan scores. The composer's later views on melody may have been born at this time: Gluck is said to have noticed that simplicity in composition exerted the greatest effect on English audiences, and he subsequently tried to write for the voice in a simpler, more natural manner.

Many of Gluck's works during the following years were constructed with borrowings from his own earlier compositions, but *Semiramide riconosciuta* (1748) was performed with great success in Vienna and was recognized as a totally new work both in its musical materials and in the sense of musical drama that it projected. Gluck traveled to Hamburg and Copenhagen later that same year, establishing a widening reputation as an opera composer and conductor. In Copenhagen, he met the critic Johann Adolph Scheibe, who probably influenced Gluck to some degree in the question of the connection between an opera's overture and the music of the opera proper, an idea later promoted by Gluck himself.

In 1750, Gluck married the daughter of a wealthy Viennese merchant. This marriage brought him both a dowry and connections at the Viennese court that ensured his financial independence, a consideration important for any composer contemplating new ventures.

LIFE'S WORK

In 1752, Gluck was appointed Konzertmeister in the household of the imperial field marshal in Vienna, a position giving him a secure base of operations in the very heart of the Austrian Empire. In the ensuing years, he produced a number of operas that won the favor of the royal family, and his growing reputation led to a commission for an opera to be presented during the 1756 carnival season in Rome. Through the influence of one of his Roman patrons, Gluck was awarded the papal title cavalier of the golden spur. Upon his return to Vienna, an appointment to adapt several French *opéras comiques* for the stage brought him into contact with a good troupe of French actors. His first original *opéra comique, La Fausse Esclave* (1758), was a success noted for its coordination of music and drama. Around 1760, Gluck was introduced to the Italian author and dramatist Raniero Calzabigi; their first collaboration, the ballet-pantomime *Don Juan: Ou, Le Festin de Pierre* (1761), was unusually well received.

Don Juan was followed by *Orfeo ed Euridice* (1762), a major success that marked a turning point in the history of opera and formed the cornerstone of Gluck's lasting fame as an opera composer. It is probable that some of the traditions of vocal display to which singers and audiences were accustomed endured in early performances of this work, yet the score avoided the then-entrenched pattern of alternating recitative and aria. The work's comparatively uncluttered vocal lines allowed the audience to develop a sense of dramatic projection of the text. The orchestra, moreover, supported the dramatic events onstage, and chorus and ballet were incorporated into the score in a masterful way.

Gluck continued to work at adapting French *opéras comiques* for the Viennese stage, traveling frequently between Paris and Vienna. He collaborated once again with Calzabigi for *Alceste* (1767), a second reform opera in the spirit of *Orfeo ed Euridice*. In the preface to the pub-

Christoph Gluck. (Library of Congress)

lished score of *Alceste,* Gluck set forth his musical goals in matters of opera: Music, he said, should follow the poem, not be overburdened with ornaments. The tripartite aria should not interfere with the sense of the plot, the overture should be in keeping with the action that follows, and all should be executed with the goal of achieving a beautiful simplicity. Gluck later acknowledged that Calzabigi was responsible for many of these ideas. It is also clear that similar thoughts were widespread among the literati of the time. Yet, to the composer's lasting credit, it was the unusually expressive quality of the music in both *Orfeo ed Euridice* and *Alceste* that established them as milestones in the history of opera.

Gluck continued his operatic activity in Vienna; his third reform opera, *Paride ed Elena* (1770), was less successful than its predecessors, and possibly as a result, it represented Gluck's last joint venture with Calzabigi. In spite of the personal fortune achieved with the aid of his wife's dowry, Gluck, always noted for a degree of parsimony, felt driven to exert extra effort to recover his losses on some theatrical investments in Vienna. The operatic scene in Paris seemed to offer the most ready profits, and he spent most of the next decade in travels between Vienna and the French capital. *Iphigénie en Aulide* and a French version of *Orfeo ed Euridice,* both produced in Paris in 1774, show a continued development of his sense for music and drama.

In 1777, Gluck was once again in Paris, where he was drawn into a controversy between his own supporters and those favoring the older Italian opera as it was represented in the works of Niccolò Piccinni. It was proposed that both composers should set the story of *Roland,* by Philippe Quinault, but Gluck, upon learning that Piccinni was already at work on that libretto, withdrew and put forth instead his setting of Quinault's *Armide* (1777). This work was performed four months before Piccinni's *Roland*; while it did little to affirm the superiority of one style over another in the opinion of the factious Parisian public, *Armide* did establish a distinction between the style of Gluck's operas and the traditional *opéra seria.* On his next sojourn in Paris, Gluck had his single greatest success with another setting of a classic tragedy, *Iphigénie en Tauride* (1779). His musical depiction of characters and the suggestion, by the orchestra, of character traits and ideas not directly present on stage were qualities later expanded by nineteenth century opera composers, particularly Richard Wagner.

Gluck's last years in Vienna were marked by continuing composition and several efforts to revive some of his earlier works for the Paris stage, despite a series of debilitating strokes. He was in contact with the young Wolfgang Amadeus Mozart, an aspiring composer for the stage whose natural gifts far surpassed Gluck's, but who still must have assimilated much from the many rehearsals of the German version of *Iphigénie en Tauride* he attended. A few days before his death, Gluck gave to Antonio Salieri, his supposed successor, a *De profundis,* which Salieri conducted at the composer's funeral on November 17, 1787. Gluck's tombstone reflected something of the esteem he enjoyed in the eyes of his contemporaries; he was described as "An upright German man, a devout Christian, a faithful husband . . . great master of the noble art of music."

SIGNIFICANCE

Christoph Gluck, with the possible exception of Claudio Monteverdi, may be described as the earliest composer of opera to maintain a place in the functioning repertory. He effectively wrought significant and lasting changes in what was a widespread yet decadent art form. For all his influence, though, his work represents a synthesis at least as much as an innovation: Many of his ideas had been expressed by others before he gave them musical shape and substance. However, Gluck's reform operas of the

1760's realized the ideals of the eighteenth century Enlightenment in matters of naturalness, balance, and clarity, and he continued this development in varying degrees in the works that followed.

In specifically musical matters, Gluck achieved in the opera a new balance between music and drama; he avoided the vocal display and stereotyped librettos that had made opera into a notorious spectacle. His orchestral arrangements contributed to the dramatic presentation of his works through careful use of instrumental timbre and thematic interplay with the vocal parts, and his overtures became integral parts of his scores rather than mere dispensable introductions. These changes in style mark Gluck as one of the major creative figures who established the principles that underlay musical classicism in the late eighteenth century.

—*Douglas A. Lee*

FURTHER READING

Brown, Bruce Alan. *Gluck and the French Theater in Vienna.* New York: Oxford University Press, 1991. Recounts Gluck's involvement with Vienna's first French theater, founded in 1752. Describes theatrical life in Vienna and the influence of the French musical theater on *Orfeo ed Euridice* and other Gluck operas.

Cooper, Martin. *Gluck.* New York: Oxford University Press, 1935. An extended monograph by a recognized authority on Gluck and his music. Contemporary events are chronologically presented to illustrate the composer's activities as a response to the milieu of the musical theater in which he worked. Most valuable is the closing chapter examining Gluck's position in the history of music.

Einstein, Alfred. *Gluck.* Translated by Eric Blom. London: J. M. Dent, 1936. Reprint. New York: McGraw-Hill, 1972. Although somewhat dated in its style, this remains a standard and comprehensive English-language monograph on Gluck. Supplemented by useful appendices, including a catalog of works, a list of persons with whom Gluck worked, a bibliography, and an excerpt from Gluck's correspondence.

Grout, Donald Jay, and Hermine Weigel Williams. *A Short History of Opera.* 4th ed. New York: Columbia University Press, 2003. A concise, direct approach to the complete scope of opera, with a significant portion devoted to Gluck, his works, and his influence. One of the most accessible and current sources available.

Howard, Patricia. *Gluck: An Eighteenth Century Portrait in Letters and Documents.* New York: Oxford

University Press, 1995. Gluck's life and work is explored through the letters he wrote and received and through other documents, translated into English from German, French, and Italian.

_____. *Gluck and the Birth of Modern Opera.* London: Barrie & Rockliff, 1963. A stylistic study cast in a historical perspective that treats Gluck and his works, particularly his reform operas, as part of the second (modern) stage of opera following its beginning in the early seventeenth century.

_____, ed. *C. W. von Gluck: "Orfeo."* New York: Cambridge University Press, 1981. Essays by various authors addressing the first and most famous of Gluck's reform operas. The essays can be grouped into the historical, the analytical, and those examining the impact of critical writing about this particular work. Select bibliography and discography, the latter all too often omitted in critical studies of major musical works.

Ratner, Leonard G. *Classic Music: Expression, Form, and Style.* New York: Schirmer Books, 1980. Within a comprehensive examination of musical style in the eighteenth century, Gluck and his operatic achievements are presented as the principal manifestation of a "high style" in musical theater specifically and in the later years of the classical era in general. Comparisons between settings by Gluck and others of the same plot, *Iphigénie en Tauride,* serve to illustrate the specific stylistic differences between Gluck and his contemporaries.

Wellesz, Egon, and Frederick Sternfeld, eds. *The Age of Enlightenment.* Vol. 7 in *The New Oxford History of Music.* London: Oxford University Press, 1973. Gluck's Italian and French operas are addressed separately; the discussion of Gluck's work in Paris is particularly valuable, because he is presented clearly as a musical iconoclast facing an aristocratic, autocratic society rather than a prophet of later operatic venues for a middle-class public. Perhaps the best discussion available of his French operas.

See also: Luigi Boccherini; George Frideric Handel; Wolfgang Amadeus Mozart; Alessandro Scarlatti.

Related articles in *Great Events from History: The Eighteenth Century, 1701-1800*: January 29, 1728: Gay Produces the First Ballad Opera; April 13, 1742: First Performance of Handel's *Messiah*; October 5, 1762: First Performance of Gluck's *Orfeo and Euridice*; August 3, 1778: Opening of Milan's La Scala.

FIRST EARL OF GODOLPHIN
English politician

Without seeking fame or personal compensation, Godolphin created the structural power base that would later become, officially, the office of prime minister, and served as the prototype for this evolution in English government.

Born: June 15, 1645 (baptized); Breage, Cornwall, England

Died: September 15, 1712; St. Albans, Hertfordshire, England

Also known as: Sidney Godolphin (full name)

Areas of achievement: Government and politics, diplomacy

EARLY LIFE

The first earl of Godolphin, named Sidney Godolphin at birth, was born to Dorothy Berkeley of Yarlington, Somersetshire, and William Godolphin. The family name, Godolphin, originally spelled "Godalgahn" (Cornish for "white eagle"), signifies high standards and originates from the first Godolphin manor possessed at the time of the Norman Conquest by John de Godolphin. Sidney Godolphin could count among his ancestors a high sheriff, a steward of the mines in Cornwall and Devon, and a comptroller of coinage who was decorated for bravery under Henry VIII. Godolphin's grandfather, Sir Francis Godolphin, the founder of the family fortune, presented plans to Elizabeth I for increasing the strength of England's shoreline defense. Although he was instrumental in aiding the future king Charles II in escaping from the perils of Cromwellian England, William Godolphin's primary distinction lay in rearing the future lord high treasurer and consolidator of the office of prime minister, Sidney, the first earl of Godolphin.

Although not much is known about his early and adolescent years, at seventeen, the short, awkward, and somewhat melancholy Godolphin was appointed page of honor to the restored king on September 29, 1662, for a salary of £120. This appointment marked the beginning of a lifelong career at court. Almost immediately, he seemed eager to find ways in which he could be useful. Roused by the threat of a Dutch invasion in 1667, Godolphin felt the call of patriotism and applied for a commission in the army. Because of a serious fall from his horse, his military career was brief. In October of 1668, Godolphin represented Helston in the so-called Long Parliament of the Restoration, which continued until 1679; in the Short Parliament, from 1679 to 1681, Godolphin represented St. Marves. As a courtier, Godolphin advanced steadily. In 1672, he was groom of the bedchamber and in 1678, Master of the Robes. Neither of these positions was of great political significance, but they offered Godolphin direct personal influence with the king. During this apprenticeship period of Godolphin's life, he courted Margaret Blagge, the maid of honor to the duchess of York. After a nine-year engagement, on May 16, 1675, the couple consummated their relationship in marriage. Because Godolphin did not feel financially ready to establish a household, the marriage was kept a secret until June of 1676.

Godolphin demonstrated an eagerness to serve and a willingness to bear greater responsibility. After being refused the office of auditor of Wales, Godolphin, in January of 1678, was appointed envoy extraordinary to the duke of Villa-Hermosa, governor of the Spanish Netherlands. Also during this year, Godolphin corresponded with William of Orange and took part in some of the negotiations leading to the Treaty of Nijmegen.

On September 3, 1678, his son and only child, Francis, was born. On September 9, Margaret Godolphin died from a childbirth-related illness. Overcome by grief, Godolphin neither arranged nor attended his wife's funeral. Later, he traveled to Cornwall, where she was buried, remaining until early in 1679. Rumors circulated that Godolphin remarried. There is no substantial evidence for this. This early period of Godolphin's life establishes his reputation as a silently virtuous man, more eager for service than notoriety.

LIFE'S WORK

The first earl of Godolphin served four different monarchs. Charles II appointed him a lord of the treasury on March 26, 1679. In November, Laurence Hyde, the earl of Rochester, became the first lord. At this point, Hyde, Robert Spencer, the second earl of Sunderland, and

First Earl of Godolphin. (Library of Congress)

Godolphin were in the king's deepest confidence. They were called "the chits" and conducted the business of the government. On April 24, 1684, Godolphin was made secretary of state. After Rochester became lord president, Godolphin was advanced to the head of the treasury. On September 28, 1684, Charles made him Baron Godolphin of Rialton and praised him as being "never in the way and never out of the way."

After Charles II died, Rochester was made lord high treasurer. James II appointed Godolphin chamberlain to the queen, Mary of Modena. As an example of his selflessness, Godolphin attended mass with the queen without a qualm. Godolphin was loyal to his sense of duty even when his own reputation was in jeopardy. He was one of James's most trusted ministers, supporting and corresponding with James even after his abdication during the Glorious Revolution, which brought William III and Mary II and to the throne. Godolphin continued his involvement in various diplomatic missions. He took part in negotiations in which French king Louis XIV conceded the legitimacy of William III as king of England.

Godolphin's political neutrality served him well under William III's ministry. He was named a commissioner of the Treasury in 1689. In March, Godolphin retired for reasons that are unknown but was brought back in November and placed at the head of the commission. By 1695, even though the only Tory in the Treasury, he was actually the most important commissioner, because of his experience. In 1696, Godolphin was implicated by Sir John Fenwick in a plot to assassinate William, and Sunderland coerced him to resign. Godolphin's feeling of betrayal was not alleviated until the Tories returned to power and he resumed his position as head of the Treasury on December 9, 1700.

Godolphin's career reached its zenith under the reign of Queen Anne. His close association with John Churchill, the first duke of Marlborough, and the marriage between his son, Francis, and Marlborough's daughter, Henrietta, strengthened the bond between the two men. This friendship benefited Godolphin with increased support from Anne, as the duke and duchess of Marlborough dominated the sway of the queen's opinions at this time. On May 6, 1702, Queen Anne appointed Godolphin as lord high treasurer; he became the de facto head of the home government. The Marlborough-Godolphin ministry, as it may be called, met with great success in the War of the Spanish Succession (1701-1714). Godolphin managed Parliament and patronage in such a way that financial and political support for the war was always available. In 1707, Godolphin was the key figure in instrumenting the most outstanding legislative and diplomatic achievement of Anne's reign, the Act of Union with Scotland. Also in 1707, Godolphin reorganized the British East India Company.

Because he broke with the High Tories, who wanted limited warfare rather than a continuation of Marlborough's expensive campaigns of attrition, and because he was dependent upon the Whig majority, the Godolphin ministry became unpopular. Also by this time, Godolphin had lost the support of the queen. Because he was not as notorious a figure as Marlborough, Godolphin could be more easily dismissed. In August of 1710, by letter, Anne commanded him to break his staff of office. He died unnoticed two years later.

SIGNIFICANCE

The first earl of Godolphin inhabited one of England's most significant political epochs. Ironically, this virtuous, prudent man came to prominence during the Stuart Restoration, a period known for its bawdy excess and frivolity. His achievements were those of a man well acquainted with the inner corridors of power, yet, unlike such notable successors as Robert Walpole, he remained person-

ally uncorrupted. Though obscured by Marlborough's overbearing personality and military stature, Godolphin's management provided the base for the duke's brilliant initial victories in the War of the Spanish Succession. The same quiet diplomatic skill is imprinted on the agreement to unify England and Scotland, an achievement that not only brought increased trade revenues but also, by eliminating England's only land frontier, raised the country's sights toward international imperialism.

Though his personality and that of Queen Anne, along with his close association with the stellar Marlborough, make Godolphin one of English history's least-known major figures, his accomplishments and responsibilities established him as the prototype of the prime minister. It is at least doubtful that the office itself could have evolved when it did had Godolphin not consolidated so much authority in his own hands. It was not until England was ruled by a truly apathetic monarch (George I) that the actual office of prime minister could flourish; its longevity is Godolphin's legacy.

—*Phyllis Ann Thompson*

FURTHER READING

Coxe, William. *Memoirs of the Duke of Marlborough*. 3 vols. London: George Ball and Sons, 1908. Includes many of the earl of Godolphin's letters to the duke of Marlborough.

Dickinson, William Calvin. *Sidney Godolphin, Lord Treasurer, 1702-1710*. Lewiston, N.Y.: E. Mellen Press, 1990. Focuses on Godolphin's service to Queen Anne, demonstrating how he essentially functioned as Great Britain's first prime minister.

Evelyn, John. *The Life of Mrs. Godolphin*. Edited by Harriet Sampson. London: Oxford University Press, 1939. Offers insight into Mrs. Godolphin's view of her husband and their courtship and marriage. The biographical supplement in the appendix offers helpful material on various relatives and friends of the Godolphins.

Holmes, Geoffrey. *British Politics in the Age of Anne*. New York: Macmillan, 1967. A comprehensive view of the rise of the parties, with a helpful index and appendices.

Levin, Sir Tresham. *Godolphin: His Life and Times*. London: John Murray, 1952. Concentrates on Godolphin's life from 1662, when he arrived at court, until his death. Needs to be read with supplementary sources (such as Geoffrey Holmes and Robert Walcott) for an accurate picture of the political background.

Sundstrom, Roy A. *Sidney Godolphin: Servant of the State*. Newark: University of Delaware Press, 1992.

Examines the unprecedented power Godolphin wielded as minister to Queen Anne. Recounts his political successes, including his overhaul of the treasury and his ability to generate the revenue needed to finance Britain's participation in the War of the Spanish Succession.

Walcott, Robert. *English Politics in the Early Eighteenth Century*. New York: Russell and Russell, 1972. Detailed and valuable as a supplement. Differs in approach and conclusions from Holmes; the two works should be read together for a broad view.

See also: Queen Anne; George I; First Duke of Marlborough; Robert Walpole.
Related articles in *Great Events from History: The Eighteenth Century, 1701-1800:* May 26, 1701-September 7, 1714: War of the Spanish Succession; May 15, 1702-April 11, 1713: Queen Anne's War; February, 1706-April 28, 1707: Act of Union Unites England and Scotland; March 23-26, 1708: Defeat of the "Old Pretender."

WILLIAM GODWIN
English writer and scholar

Having changed his thinking from radical Protestantism to revolutionary atheism, Godwin developed libertarian socialism. His work would influence profoundly the individualism of English Romanticism and later ideas of anarchism, communism, socialist economics, and Marxism. His friendship with and marriage to Mary Wollstonecraft contributed to early feminist thought, and his ideas stimulated nearly all the Romantic poets.

Born: March 3, 1756; Wisbech, Isle of Ely, Cambridgeshire, England
Died: April 7, 1836; London, England
Areas of achievement: Philosophy, government and politics, literature, women's rights, social reform

EARLY LIFE

William Godwin was the seventh of thirteen children of John Godwin, a Dissenting minister in the Calvinist tradition. Like his father before him, the young Godwin moved with his family to Debenham in 1758 and to Guestwick in Norfolk in 1760. At the age of eight, Godwin began three years of school at Hindolveston near Guestwick; in 1767, he began three years of private tutoring in classical education with the Calvinist preacher Samuel Newton at Norwich.

When Godwin was fifteen, he returned to Hindolveston, serving for nearly a year as an usher in a small school administered by his former teacher, Robert Akers. After the death of his father on November 12, 1772, Godwin moved with his mother to London in April, 1773. He had intended to enter Homerton Academy, but he was rejected for his Sandemanian views, which opposed the authority of church and state, espoused a belief in communal property, and endorsed the progressive reform of individual morality and action.

Accepted for training in the ministry at Hoxton Academy, a Dissenting college founded because of the refusal of the established universities to admit Nonconformists, Godwin spent the next five years completing his formal education. Continuously under the influence of the Sandemanians (a sect that had been expelled by the Presbyterians) and resisting the liberal views of noted scholar Andrew Kippis, Godwin was graduated from Hoxton in 1777 and became a Sandemanian minister in East Anglia and Home Counties from 1778 to 1783. At Hoxton, he had gained a reputation for his immodest passion in intellectual argument, often asserting an unusual view that combined Tory conservatism, radical Calvinist theology, and materialistic philosophy. Diligent and disciplined, Godwin rose at five in the morning and often engaged in heated metaphysical discussions until after midnight. While he was generally regarded as sensitive and respectful, his fellow students noted his hunger for recognition and his obsession with winning arguments, usually with a seemingly cold detachment. Godwin was neither a particularly gifted debater nor a spontaneous conversationalist; his intellectual genius was more the product of deliberate study and dedicated willpower than intuitive insights.

In an era when religious dissent was also political dissent, Godwin attempted to carry on the profession of his father. In 1777 he preached at Yarmouth each Sunday morning and at Lowestoft each afternoon. In 1778 he secured his first regular appointment as Dissenting minister in Ware, Hertfordshire; Godwin, however, was not a popular minister and, in 1779, he left Ware for London, where he attended speeches by leading politicians, among them Charles James Fox (the emerging leader of the Whig Party) and Edmund Burke (the leading Tory spokesman). Moving freely and engaging in discussions within various radical circles, Godwin soon exhausted his meager savings and had to leave London later in 1779 to support himself as a minister at Stowmarket in Suffolk.

Godwin's reading over the next three years was to change profoundly his religious and political views, although he was to carry many of his Sandemanian views into his secular philosophy. After reading the political discourses of Jonathan Swift and the Latin historians, Godwin became convinced that monarchy was a corrupt system, and his Tory beliefs eroded rapidly. As a result of reading Jean-Jacques Rousseau, Claude-Adrien Helvétius, and Paul-Henri-Dietrich d'Holbach, Godwin's faith not only in Calvinism but also in the existence of God was so severely shaken that, by 1782, he could no longer sustain the ministry at Stowmarket, resigning after a minor dispute regarding church discipline.

Godwin left Stowmarket for London, hoping to pursue a literary career, but he was unsuccessful and was forced to accept a post as clergyman at Beaconsfield in 1783. Despite retaining his theological role there until 1788, he was determined to develop his writing career. From 1783 to 1789, he wrote (often anonymously) three novels (none of which has survived), a number of pamphlets, a biography of William Pitt, a prospectus for a private-school curriculum, political commentaries for a Whig review, and historical entries for the liberal *New Annual Register*, edited by his former tutor Kippis and published by George Robinson. Relieved from poverty—despite his writing, preaching, and tutoring in the early 1780's—by being employed by Robinson, his role seemed to be that of a modestly successful hack writer.

By the age of thirty-one and as a result of conversations from 1787 to 1789 with Thomas Holcroft, a republican reformer, Godwin had become essentially an atheist. Dropping his title "Reverend" and breaking with his orthodox family, the short, stocky Godwin presented the figure of a self-absorbed, contemplative, even aloof, soberly dressed man of dignity and detachment. His large brow, long nose, and pointed chin seemed indicative of an overbearing intellectual, but Godwin was, for the most part, unknown and unrecognized among most of his intellectual contemporaries in 1789.

LIFE'S WORK

Like many of the liberals in England, William Godwin responded to the onset of the French Revolution, the fall of the Bastille on July 14, 1789, with an enthusiastic par-

ticipation in meetings and sympathetic approval of the Jacobins (violent French extremists in the revolution). As the revolution proceeded, Godwin welcomed the declaration of France as a republic by the national convention in 1792. He had, however, characteristically already turned his industriousness to going beyond even the consensual views of the radicals with whom he associated. In July, 1791, he had persuaded George Robinson to take the unusual step of supporting him while he pursued a philosophical treatise on political justice. With an unflagging faith in reason, a belief in the gradual, inevitable perfection of humanity, and an egalitarian view of economics and politics that denounced the identification of private property with happiness, Godwin spent the next eighteen months defining and developing his ideas.

In January, Godwin published his most important work, the eight-volume *Enquiry Concerning Political Justice, and Its Influence on General Virtue and Happiness* (1793). Almost overnight, Godwin became a celebrity among the radical intellectuals, who saw his treatise as the definitive response (among some thirty others) to Edmund Burke's reactionary *Reflections on the Revolution in France* (1790), far exceeding (at the time) the impact of Thomas Paine's earlier reply to Burke, *The Rights of Man* (1791, 1792). Godwin's attacks on marriage, property, God, and the state were tempered by complex, anarchistic affirmations of individual freedom, cultural determinism, economic egalitarianism, and the liberating role of education—all of which, he claimed, nurtured a universal, moralistic benevolence among human beings. That he rejected God in favor of materialism and the authority of government in favor of individual moral judgment did not hinder his popularity among the liberals. Political societies purchased the book communally, and passages read aloud were frequently the centerpiece of meetings. In five years, the treatise went through three revised editions (1793, 1796, and 1798). So strongly stated were Godwin's opinions that only Prime Minister William Pitt the Younger's refusal to believe that a cheaply produced book could incite public political opinion prevented Godwin's prosecution for treason.

Godwin was to continue in the center of intellectual debate for much of the 1790's. His work appealed to young radicals and poets, among them Samuel Taylor Coleridge and William Wordsworth. His own literary reputation came with the publication of *Things as They Are: Or, The Adventures of Caleb Williams* (1794), one of the first mystery novels. In it, Godwin fashioned one of the most memorable characters in English fiction of the period: Falkland, a man whose sense of honor leads him to betray his own moral standards when he chooses to murder rather than to lose his good name. In the didactic passages of the novel, Godwin achieved in fiction what his work in philosophy had accomplished: He further cemented his reputation as a tough-minded, controversial thinker.

In 1794, Godwin also intervened in a famous trial of parliamentary reformers, among them his old friend Thomas Holcroft and John Horne Tooke, one of the leading liberal scholars, who were charged with treason. His anonymously published *Cursory Strictures on the Charge Delivered by Lord Chief Justice Eyre to the Grand Jury* (1794) was widely attributed as leading to the acquittal of all twelve defendants. While he was studious and contemplative, Godwin never hesitated to involve himself actively in the public affairs of his day.

Continuing to enjoy his notoriety and to write pamphlets and essays as well as substantially revise his major work for its second edition, Godwin met Mary Wollstonecraft in 1796. Wollstonecraft, author of *A Vindication of the Rights of Woman* (1792) and *An Historical and Moral View of the Origin and Progress of the French Revolution* (1794), had earned a reputation nearly as widespread as Godwin's own when she left the American captain Gilbert Imlay with her daughter Fanny Imlay to live with Godwin. With compatible and complementary democratic philosophies, Godwin and Wollstonecraft became the epitome of London's radical society. When she became pregnant, however, Godwin and Wollstonecraft shocked the radical intellectuals by announcing their marriage of March 29, 1797. Startled by the seeming contradiction to their ideals, previous followers—dismayed at their conventional response to the pregnancy—began to indulge in the critical rejection of Godwin and his ideas. With the birth, however, of their daughter Mary on August 30, Wollstonecraft developed complications from the delivery, and she died on September 10, 1797. Daughter Mary Wollstonecraft Shelley, who later married poet Percy Bysshe Shelley, wrote and published the novel *Frankenstein* in 1818.

The tragedy of Wollstonecraft's death and the increasingly conservative reaction in England to the violent excesses of the French Revolution and the rise of Napoleon marked the onset of Godwin's decline in reputation. Left with two small children and denounced by former supporters, Godwin—after having been rejected by several other women—married Mary Jane Clairmont, a widow with two children of her own, in 1801. He had continued, however, to write, publishing *Memoirs of the Author of a Vindication of the Rights of Woman* (1798), a

loving portrait edited anonymously, and *St. Leon: A Tale of the Sixteenth Century* (1799), his second-best novel, which recast the character of Caleb Williams in medieval France. Burdened with literary quarrels, financial disasters, and an unhappy second marriage, Godwin produced a steady stream of books, including histories of Greece, Rome, and England, and a biography of Geoffrey Chaucer as well as novels and plays; none of them, however well written, was a commercial success, and he was twice bankrupt.

His previous stature with Wordsworth and Coleridge had disappeared, although Godwin had, by 1800, accepted a vague belief in theism as a result of his reflections on Coleridge's philosophy. Shelley, who had provided generous financial support and who had assimilated much of Godwin's radicalism into his poetry, outraged Godwin by eloping with his daughter, Mary, in 1814. When Fanny, his stepdaughter from the Wollstonecraft marriage, committed suicide in 1816 and Shelley married Mary at the end of the same year shortly after his wife's death, Godwin had already been nearly forgotten by his contemporaries. Suffering a slight stroke in 1818, he did keep writing, but he was never again to have any but modest success.

Godwin outlived a son, William Godwin, by his second marriage, and it was not until 1822 that Mary Wollstonecraft Shelley (after her husband's death in Italy) returned to care for him. While Godwin continued to write until two years before his death, his poverty went largely unrelieved until a minor government appointment in 1833. After three decades of personal disappointment and relative obscurity, Godwin died in London on April 7, 1836, and was buried beside Mary Wollstonecraft.

SIGNIFICANCE

Of the nearly forty books William Godwin published in his lifetime, only *An Enquiry Concerning Political Justice, and Its Influence on General Virtue and Happiness* and *Things as They Are* have survived to attest his genius. More often than not, Godwin is known primarily as the inspiration for Shelley's ideas, the husband of Mary Wollstonecraft, and the father of Mary Wollstonecraft Shelley. Yet Godwin's accomplishment was far greater than merely his association with more famous luminaries: His meteoric rise and fall in the 1790's is a barometer for one of the most tumultuous decades in English history.

Godwin's synthesis of eighteenth century idealism and his systematic analysis of revolutionary democratic principles far exceeded the controversy and notoriety of his lifetime. Later democratic, communist, anarchist, and feminist theoreticians owe Godwin a considerable debt, for many of the most important developments in English liberal thought have their seeds in Godwin's philosophical speculations.

While Godwin's prose is likely to strike modern readers as pedantic and verbose, students of the Romantic period cannot omit him from their consideration. His work is informed by the dispute between reason and feeling, the optimism of the imagination, the imperative of the will, and the egalitarian idealism that were to characterize his age. Any reading of the Romantics ignores Godwin at its own peril, because Godwin—more than any thinker of the day—defined the major issues of his time, responded to them systematically, and speculated beyond mere paraphrase. Those ideas that so shocked conservatives and rallied liberals in the 1790's—a just economic distribution of goods as prerequisite to a healthy democracy, marriage as an insidious form of property, the sanctity of individual morality, and the eventual waning of all formal government—seem almost commonplace in latter-day political thought. Perhaps Godwin's optimistic faith in individual reason as more important than social and political institutions is his enduring legacy, both unique in its thorough consideration and speculative presentation and entirely representative of the revolutionary turmoil in his era.

—Michael Loudon

FURTHER READING

Brailsford, H. N. *Shelley, Godwin, and Their Circle.* 2d ed. London: Oxford University Press, 1951. A rigorous analysis of the intellectual and political climate in the 1780's and 1790's. Locates and defines the major currents and conflicts in relation to Godwin and Shelley. Includes balanced discussions of Thomas Paine and Mary Wollstonecraft. Excellent on the English reaction to the French Revolution.

Brown, Ford K. *The Life of William Godwin.* London: J. M. Dent and Sons, 1926. A sympathetic but detached scholarly biography and a basic introduction to Godwin's ideas, but limited in its reliance on anecdote and its intellectual and literary analysis. More thorough on the formative years than other biographies. Good bibliography of primary materials.

Clemit, Patricia, Harriet Devine Jump, and Betty T. Bennett, eds. *Lives of the Great Romantics III: Godwin, Wollstonecraft, and Mary Shelley by Their Contemporaries.* 3 vols. Brookfield, Vt.: Pickering & Chatto, 1999. A compilation of reviews, articles, correspondence, and portions of biographies and autobiographies by eighteenth and nineteenth century writers. Most of the information about Godwin is contained in volume 1, which features observations by Charles Lamb, Aaron Burr, William Hazlitt, and others.

Fleisher, David. *William Godwin: A Study in Liberalism.* New York: A. M. Kelley, 1951. Still the best analysis of Godwin's ideas and system. Commentary well supported by generous quotation from critically important passages. More thorough in discussing and clarifying political thought and philosophical ideas than in evaluating how Godwin used those ideas in his literary works.

Grylls, Rosalie G. *William Godwin and His World.* London: Odhams, 1953. Average in biographical data and limited information on later life, but excellent discussion of social and political milieu in which Godwin rose to fame. Scholarly analysis links Godwin with the thought of the late Enlightenment era rather than with the Romantics of the early nineteenth century.

Hazlitt, William. *The Spirit of the Age: Or, Contemporary Portraits.* In *The Complete Works of William Hazlitt,* edited by P. P. Howe. 21 vols. London: J. M. Dent and Sons, 1930-1934. The most complete account of Godwin and his friends from his own time, originally published in 1825. Often rhetorical and satirical, the anecdotes relate Godwin to Wordsworth, Coleridge, Shelley, and George Gordon, Lord Byron. Hazlitt's own style reveals the controversial attitudes that surrounded Godwin.

Paul, Charles Kegan. *William Godwin: His Friends and Contemporaries.* 2 vols. London: Henry S. King, 1876. Still the best source for Godwin's journals, letters, and autobiographical writings. Commentary at times is overly sympathetic and eulogistic but gathers basic biographical data. Attests to Godwin's later stature. The only available source for much of Godwin's personal writing, yielding anecdotes on the Romantic poets.

Preu, James Arthur. *The Dean and the Anarchist.* Tallahassee: Florida State University Press, 1959. An excellent study of Jonathan Swift's influence on Godwin. Provides a lucid summary of the philosophical and political debates in the social climate that pushed Godwin to write his major work. Scholarly and balanced; focuses on the primary ideas, summarizing them clearly and succinctly.

Smith, Elton E., and Esther G. Smith. *William Godwin.* New York: Twayne, 1965. Scanty in biographical data, but offers a thorough overview and accessible discussion of the political theory. Includes discussions of novels, plays, and children's books usually omitted from other studies. Good on elucidating the political ideas as they are applied in later literary works. Good bibliography of secondary studies.

St. Clair, William. *The Godwins and the Shelleys: The Biography of a Family.* New York: Norton, 1989. In his preface, St. Clair describes the book as "an account of two generations whose influence on each other was intense." He devotes considerable space to Godwin's life and career, and includes a bibliography of his works.

Woodcock, George. *William Godwin: A Biographical Study with a Foreword by Herbert Read.* London: Porcupine, 1946. A scholarly, balanced, and accessible presentation of both the life and ideas. More sympathetic to liberal traditions than Brown's earlier biography. Excellent in establishing Godwin as a seminal thinker who is important to later develop-

ments in liberalism and in relating Godwin to and distinguishing him from other liberals in his own time.

See also: Edmund Burke; Charles James Fox; Claude-Adrien Helvétius; Paul-Henri-Dietrich d'Holbach; Thomas Paine; William Pitt the Younger; Jean-Jacques Rousseau; Jonathan Swift; Mary Wollstonecraft.

Related articles in *Great Events from History: The Eighteenth Century, 1701-1800:* April, 1762: Rousseau Publishes *The Social Contract*; January 10, 1776: Paine Publishes *Common Sense*; July 14, 1789: Fall of the Bastille; 1790: Burke Lays the Foundations of Modern Conservatism; February 22, 1791-February 16, 1792: Thomas Paine Publishes *Rights of Man*; 1792: Wollstonecraft Publishes *A Vindication of the Rights of Woman*; April 20, 1792-October, 1797: Early Wars of the French Revolution; November 9-10, 1799: Napoleon Rises to Power in France.

JOHANN WOLFGANG VON GOETHE
German writer, poet, and scholar

Goethe, whose lyric, dramatic, and narrative talents produced literary works of lasting influence on the Western tradition, is considered one of the greatest of all German writers. An amateur scientist and able administrator, Goethe was a truly gifted man of his time.

Born: August 28, 1749; Frankfurt am Main (now in Germany)
Died: March 22, 1832; Weimar, Saxe-Weimar-Eisenbach (now in Germany)
Areas of achievement: Literature, theater, science and technology

EARLY LIFE
Johann Wolfgang von Goethe (yo-HAHN VAWLF-gahng fawn GUHR-tuh) was born into a financially well-established family in the cosmopolitan city of Frankfurt am Main. His father, Johann, was a serious man, who retired from his law practice early and devoted himself to the education of his children. His mother, Katharine Elisabeth, was of a more lighthearted nature and stimulated the imaginative and artistic faculties of her children. From 1765 to 1768, Goethe studied law (at his father's request) at the University of Leipzig. In August, 1768, he became gravely ill with a lung ailment and returned to

Frankfurt to recuperate. He remained there with his family until March, 1770, and then moved to Strassburg to complete his studies.

LIFE'S WORK
From April, 1770, to August, 1771, Goethe studied law in Strassburg; the period was a pivotal one for his development. He was of a literary nature and had never been interested in pursuing a law career. In Strassburg, he met Johann Gottfried Herder, an intense and brilliant man of letters, who encouraged Goethe's writing efforts. In Sesenheim, a small village outside the city, Goethe wooed a young woman, Frederike Brion, who inspired some of his best early poetry. His poems brought a vitality and freshness of image and theme to the discourse of the lyric. During the first half of the eighteenth century, German letters had reached a stasis in that the various genres had become rather mannered and stylized, often under the influence of prior Latin and French models. Goethe's older contemporaries, such as the poet Friedrich Gottlieb Klopstock and the dramatist Gotthold Ephraim Lessing, had begun to create a new vision of the literary arts, and Goethe brought this impetus to fruition. He is considered the major representative of the dynamic Sturm und Drang (storm and stress) period of German literature.

Filled with youthful bravado and creative energy, the young Goethe was a genial spirit—discussion of the creative genius was current at the time—and his early poems and plays are populated with titanic individuals involved in great deeds. His play *Götz von Berlichingen mit der eisernen Hand* (1773; *Götz von Berlichingen with the Iron Hand,* 1799) is fueled by the dramatic energy of the Shakespearean stage and portrays the monumental life of a renegade knight in the late Middle Ages as he struggles to maintain his independence against the imperial intrigues of the Bamberg court. After receiving his law degree, Goethe began a practice in the city of Wetzlar and became involved with another woman, Charlotte Buff, who was engaged at the time. In great emotional distress, he left the city in 1772. His epistolary novel *Die Leiden des jungen Werthers* (1774; *The Sorrows of Young Werther*, 1779) is partly autobiographical and relates the tragic fate of a young man who is caught in a love triangle and whose intense emotions drive him to suicide. The book was a European best-seller and the favorite reading matter of Napoleon I.

In 1775, Goethe was appointed adviser to Karl August, the young duke of Weimar, and moved to that city. He became involved with various administrative projects (such as road construction and mining) in the small duchy. In Weimar he also made the acquaintance of an older woman, Charlotte von Stein, who sought to cultivate the rather impetuous young writer. At the Weimar court, Goethe matured under her guidance, and his literary production exchanged its Sturm und Drang intensity for the more measured tone and form of the neoclassical movement of the late eighteenth century. His play *Iphigenie auf Tauris* (1779; *Iphigenia in Taurus*, 1793) was written in iambic meter and presents an adaptation of the play by Euripides that deals with a part of the legendary Trojan War. Iphigenia was the daughter of King Agamemnon, who sacrificed her to the gods so that the Greek fleet might find favorable winds for their journey to besiege Troy. Goethe's version stresses in the title figure a vision of the ethically exemplary individual whose behavior exerts a morally didactic influence of moderation and mutual respect upon those around her.

From 1786 to 1788, Goethe traveled extensively in Italy and then returned to the Weimar court. In July, 1788, he met a young woman, Christiane Vulpius, with whom he lived in a common-law marriage for many years and with whom he had several children. Goethe continued to serve in various official capacities (including theater director) in Weimar, while working on his literary projects.

After Goethe returned from his trip to Italy, he composed the *Römische Elegien* (1793; *Roman Elegies*, 1876), love poems that were modeled after the classical elegy form.

Goethe's *Bildungsroman*, or novel of education, *Wilhelm Meisters Lehrjahre* (1795-1796; *Wilhelm Meister's Apprenticeship*, 1824), established the model for this narrative subgenre. It deals with the developmental years of a businessman's son as he seeks his place in life and becomes involved with a group of actors on their travels through Germany. Through a series of trials and errors, he encounters a number of different individuals and attains in the end what Goethe held to be a well-rounded personality, that is, one whose contemplative-artistic and practical-committed sides have achieved a degree of harmony. A life dedicated to the service of humanity is presented as the ultimate goal of Wilhelm's development.

Goethe befriended the contemporary German poet and dramatist Friedrich Schiller, and the two maintained an active correspondence and collaborated on a well-known literary journal. During these years, Goethe was also actively engaged in various kinds of scientific research, especially comparative morphology and the theory of light refraction. He is credited with the discovery of a particular small bone in the human jaw. In *Zur Farbenlehre* (1810; *Theory of Colors*, 1840), he sought, in a fanciful way, to counter the prevailing light refraction theory of Sir Isaac Newton.

Johann Wolfgang von Goethe. (Library of Congress)

In 1809, Goethe started writing his autobiography, *Aus meinem Leben: Dichtung und Wahrheit* (1811-1814, 1833; *The Autobiography of Goethe*, 1824). During this same year, he also wrote another novel, *Die Wahlver-wandtschaften* (1809; *Elective Affinities*, 1849), a complex text that uses the symbolic image of chemical attraction and repulsion to examine the conflicting interactions of fated passion and moral self-restraint in four individuals. In the following years, Goethe published another volume of poetry, *West-östlicher Divan* (1819; *West-Eastern Divan,* 1877), a collection of love lyrics influenced by the fourteenth century Persian poet Hafiz.

In 1808, Goethe published the first part of his dramatic poem *Faust: Eine Tragödie* (1808; *The Tragedy of Faust*, 1823), his best-known and most widely read work. The final editions are written in a variety of metrical patterns and rhyme schemes. He had begun working on an early version of the story—a late medieval legend that had become a popular chapbook in 1587—during his student stays in Strassburg. It is the story of a learned man, a scholar and professor named Heinrich Faust, who makes a pact with a devil, Mephistopheles, in order to gain a godlike understanding of the universe.

In the first part of the poem, the devil rejuvenates the aging Faust, and the latter falls in love with an innocent young girl named Gretchen. Through the diabolical aid of Mephistopheles that leads to the deaths of Gretchen's mother and brother, Faust manages to seduce Gretchen, and she becomes pregnant. Faust abandons her; she murders her baby and goes insane with guilt. The first part concludes with Gretchen's execution and Faust's despair over what he has done. The second part of the Faust tragedy was published in 1833 and is a highly symbolic text in which Faust falls in love with the beautiful Helen of Troy. As an old man, he devotes himself to working on behalf of humanity. When Mephistopheles comes to claim his soul at the moment of death, God intervenes and Faust receives the pardon of divine grace.

Earlier versions of the Faust story, such as the chapbook or Christopher Marlowe's *Doctor Faustus* (c. 1588), are didactic tales that illustrate the essentially corrupt nature of humans. These Faust figures seek wealth and secular power. In these versions, Faust's soul is condemned to Hell. The character of Goethe's Faust, however, remains unique and is intended to represent the true spiritual nature of all human beings, that is, a striving for godlike perfection. His Faust seeks divine knowledge and not merely wealth and worldly prestige.

The beginning of the poem contains a prologue in Heaven, in which Mephistopheles wagers with God that he can corrupt Faust, and the latter becomes thereby a kind of Everyman figure. The terms of the pact Mephistopheles makes with the scholar is that the former can satisfy Faust and cause him to say yes to the moment and cease striving for ever-greater knowledge. Although Faust makes serious mistakes in his quest for absolute knowledge, he never stops his efforts and is thus true to his divine nature. He is therefore saved from eternal damnation.

During Goethe's later years, he was honored as an internationally respected man of letters. Goethe died in Weimar on March 22, 1832. His last words were reputedly "More light!"

MEPHISTOPHELES' LAMENT

In The Tragedy of Faust, *Johann Wolfgang von Goethe created a memorable portrayal of Mephistopheles, the devil who tempts Faust with damnation. In the excerpt below, Mephistopheles complains that evil is, so far, fighting a losing battle in the world.*

> And, to say truth, as yet with small success.
> Oppos'd to naught, this clumsy world,
> The something—it subsisteth still;
> Not yet is it to ruin hurl'd,
> Despite the efforts of my will.
> Tempests and earthquakes, fire and flood, I've tried;
> Yet land and ocean still unchang'd abide!
> And then of humankind and beasts, the accursed brood,—
> Neither o'er them can I extend my sway.
> What countless myriads have I swept away!
> Yet ever circulates the fresh young blood.
> It is enough to drive me to despair!
> As in the earth, in water, and in air,
> A thousand germs burst forth spontaneously;
> In moisture, drought, heat, cold, they still appear!
> Had I not flame selected as my sphere
> Nothing apart had been reserved for me.

Source: Johann Wolfgang von Goethe, in *The Tragedy of Faust, Part 1*. Translated by Anna Swanwick (New York: P. F. Collier, 1909-1914), lines 1032-1048.

SIGNIFICANCE

Johann Wolfgang von Goethe is a good example of the eighteenth century ideal of the Renaissance man. Like his American contemporary Thomas Jefferson, Goethe sought to encompass many fields of endeavor, from science and political affairs to the various genres of literature. It is in this latter area that he is most famous, and his role in the history of German literature is unparalleled. His literary production in poetry, drama, and fiction set standards that following generations of authors found hard to surpass.

Goethe revitalized the German lyric tradition. His *Erlebnislyrik*, or poetry of the individual's emotional or subjective experience, established a tradition that influenced nineteenth century German poets such as Annette von Droste-Hülshoff, Nikolaus Lenau, and Eduard Mörike. His dramatic works, along with those of Schiller, form the core of today's repertoire of classical German theater. His version of the Faust story has been seen as an exemplary tale of the true nature of modern humanity. His narrative texts, especially the novel of education *Wilhelm Meister's Apprenticeship*, influenced nineteenth century examples of this genre such as the works of the Austrian Adalbert Stifter and the Swiss Gottfried Keller. His highly symbolic yet realistic narrative *Elective Affinities* also helped to further the tradition of the modern novel.

Goethe's personal philosophy—as expressed in his literary works—went through a development that echoes the general trends of European culture. His early works, with their emphasis on feeling over intellect as a mode of knowing, are essentially Romantic and follow the rebellious and emotional spirit of other writers and thinkers such as Jean-Jacques Rousseau. As he grew older, and in the bloody aftermath of the French Revolution, Goethe tended toward a more conservative point of view and believed that a stoic attitude of self-control, as well as hard work in the service of humankind, was the best that an individual could contribute to the progress of history. Goethe seemed to prefigure the spirit of resignation that informed much of German and European culture and philosophy during the latter half of the nineteenth century. As a leading figure in the literary arts of his age and beyond, Goethe helped to direct the course of German literature and thought.

—*Thomas F. Barry*

FURTHER READING

Bloom, Harold, ed. *Johann Wolfgang von Goethe*. Philadelphia: Chelsea House, 2003. One in a series of books aimed at high school and college literature students. Includes an introductory essay by Bloom, essays by critics analyzing Goethe's major works, a short biography, and a chronology.

Boyle, Nicholas. *Goethe: The Poet and the Age*. New York: Oxford University Press, 1991-2000. This highly praised biography, a lengthy and exhaustively detailed study, combines biographical details, literary criticism, and analysis of political and social developments during Goethe's lifetime. The first volume, subtitled *The Poetry of Desire*, covers the period from 1749 until 1790; volume 2, *Revolution and Renunciation*, recounts events from 1970 until 1803.

Fairley, Barker. *A Study of Goethe*. New York: Oxford University Press, 1947. An older but classic introduction to Goethe and his writings that is organized by both topics and periods of the author's life. Contains an index.

Gray, Ronald. *Goethe: A Critical Introduction*. Cambridge, England: Cambridge University Press, 1967. An excellent, thorough study of Goethe's life and major writings by a respected scholar. Contains a selected bibliography and notes.

Hatfield, Henry. *Goethe: A Critical Introduction*. New York: New Directions, 1963. A well-respected introductory survey of the author's life and works that is organized chronologically and gives some background information on the period. Contains a brief bibliography and illustrations.

Reed, T. J. *Goethe*. New York: Oxford University Press, 1984. A brief but informative and well-written introduction to Goethe's life and works that covers all the major texts and is organized by topics. Contains annotated suggestions for further reading and an index.

Sharpe, Lesley, ed. *The Cambridge Companion to Goethe*. New York: Cambridge University Press, 2002. Collection of essays about Goethe's life and work. Some of the essays examine the world in which he lived; his poetic, dramatic, autobiographical, and other works; his ideas about religion and philosophy; and his reception in Germany and abroad.

Van Abbé, Derek. *Goethe: New Perspectives on a Writer and His Time*. London: Allen & Unwin, 1972. A brief yet interesting overview of Goethe's life and works organized in terms of thematic topics. Contains background information on the period.

Williams, John R. *The Life of Goethe: A Critical Biography*. Malden, Mass.: Blackwell, 1998. A comprehensive overview of Goethe's life and work, describing his scientific and public activities as well as his literature. Williams places Goethe's creative work within the context of his life and the literary and political movements of the time. The text cites portions of Goethe's work, translated into English; contains a bibliography of English-language books about Goethe.

See also: Johann Gottfried Herder; Thomas Jefferson; Friedrich Gottlieb Klopstock; Gotthold Ephraim Lessing; Jean-Jacques Rousseau; Friedrich Schiller.

Related articles in *Great Events from History: The Eighteenth Century, 1701-1800*: April 25, 1719: Defoe Publishes the First Novel; 1726: Swift Satirizes English Rule of Ireland in *Gulliver's Travels*; 1740-1741: Richardson's *Pamela* Establishes the Modern Novel; 1742: Fielding's *Joseph Andrews* Satirizes English Society; January, 1759: Voltaire Satirizes Optimism in *Candide*; 1782-1798: Publication of Rousseau's *Confessions*; 1784-1791: Herder Publishes His Philosophy of History.

OLIVER GOLDSMITH
English writer and historian

As a novelist, poet, dramatist, and essayist, Goldsmith stands in the first rank. His Life of Richard Nash, Esq. *pioneered a new type of biography, and his historical writings helped educate generations of schoolchildren and adults.*

Born: November 10, 1728 or 1730; Pallas, County Longford(?), Ireland
Died: April 4, 1774; London, England
Areas of achievement: Literature, historiography, education

EARLY LIFE

Many uncertainties linger about Oliver Goldsmith. Among them are the date and place of his birth. He was the fifth child and second son of the Reverend Charles Goldsmith and Ann Jones Goldsmith, and he grew up in the Irish village of Lissoy, the model for the imaginary Auburn of the poem *The Deserted Village* (1770). Goldsmith was fond of his father, who became the model for the benevolent Dr. Primrose in *The Vicar of Wakefield* (1766) and the kindly father of The Man in Black of *The Citizen of the World* (1762). The village curate in *The Deserted Village* is also based partly on the Reverend Charles Goldsmith, in addition to Goldsmith's brother Henry, to whom he dedicated his poem *The Traveller: Or, A Prospect of Society* (1764). The less flattering portrait of Mrs. Primrose in *The Vicar of Wakefield* reflects Goldsmith's estrangement from his mother, who grew disillusioned with her son's improvidence—a trait inherited from his father. When Ann Goldsmith died, Oliver supposedly wore only half-mourning (again the facts are unclear) because he regarded her as a distant relative.

A large part of his mother's disappointment stemmed from Goldsmith's reluctance to apply his obviously great talents. By age seven, he was already composing witty poetry and showing unusual ability at the village school run by Thomas Byrne, the wise schoolmaster of *The Deserted Village*. Goldsmith also was revealing his lifelong love of nature, which culminated in the eight-volume *An History of the Earth, and Animated Nature* (1774), an ambitious project that remained unfinished at his death. In that posthumously published work, Goldsmith recalled chasing dragonflies, distinguishing the songs of the various waterfowl, and observing the bees gathering pollen. Always in his London days he would seek some rural retreat, and his writings herald the Romantic turning away from the city in favor of the countryside.

From 1741 to 1745, Goldsmith studied under the Reverend Patrick Hughes at Edgeworthstown, Ireland. Returning to school after a summer vacation, he supposedly stopped one evening at the village of Ardagh and asked directions to the best house in town. His interlocutor happened to be the local wit, Cornelius Kelly, who willfully misunderstood Goldsmith's inquiry for an inn; Kelly sent him to the best house indeed, that of Squire Featherstone. Thinking that this private residence was an inn, Goldsmith behaved accordingly, ordering the owner about. This episode served as the basis of Goldsmith's brilliant comedy, *She Stoops to Conquer: Or, The Mistakes of a Night* (1773)—unless the story was manufactured because of the comedy. Yet the account is plausible, for throughout his life Goldsmith was extremely gullible. When he was working on his *The Grecian History, from the Earliest State to the Death of Alexander the Great* (1774), he asked Edward Gibbon the name of the Indian prince who fought against Alexander. When Gibbon flippantly replied, "Montezuma," Goldsmith credulously wrote down the name.

After leaving Hughes's school, Goldsmith matriculated at Trinity College, Dublin, in 1745; he was graduated without distinction four years later. From 1749 to 1752, he failed in halfhearted attempts to become a minister, a teacher, and a lawyer; from this period dates his alienation from his mother. In 1752, he went to Edinburgh to study medicine, but he neither enrolled as a regular student nor took a degree. In 1754, he traveled to Leiden, supposedly to complete his medical education, but again he neither officially enrolled at the university nor received a diploma.

How much medicine Goldsmith learned in these years remains questionable. In 1758, he failed an examination for the post of hospital mate. In the 1760's, when he was trying to establish a practice, he was angered by a lady's preferring the advice of her pharmacist to his and vowed never again to prescribe for his friends. To this assertion Topham Beauclerk replied, "Do so, my dear Doctor. Whenever you undertake to kill, let it be only your enemies." Certainly Goldsmith hastened his own death by prescribing for himself a heavy dose of James's Fever Powders.

What Goldsmith did learn at Edinburgh, at Leiden, and in his subsequent tour of Europe (1755-1756) was much about human nature and geography. *The Traveller* reveals a careful observer of landscape and national character, *An Enquiry into the Present State of Polite Learning in Europe* (1759) shows an acquaintanceship with the literatures of the Continent, and his essays draw upon his European experiences.

Settling in London in 1756, Goldsmith attempted to establish a medical practice, but his poverty limited his patients to the poor. Not only were his shabby clothes against him; so, too, was his appearance. Short and stocky, he had a protruding forehead. His homely face was further disfigured by a childhood attack of smallpox. Frances Reynolds, sister of the famous artist Sir Joshua Reynolds, said that Goldsmith looked like a tailor, and Mary Cholmondely claimed that he was the ugliest person she knew.

Unable to make a living as a doctor, he supplemented his meager income by working as a proofreader for the novelist and printer Samuel Richardson. As Goldsmith wrote to his brother-in-law Daniel Hodson, "Nothing [is] more apt to introduce us to the gates of the muses than Poverty."

Still struggling, Goldsmith eagerly snatched at the offer of a teaching position in Peckham, Surrey. There he met Ralph Griffiths, publisher of the *Monthly Review*. Griffiths offered Goldsmith £100 a year to serve as the magazine's reviewer. By April, 1757, he was living above Griffiths's shop in Paternoster Row, London, and writing.

LIFE'S WORK

Six months of working for Griffiths was enough for Oliver Goldsmith: Griffiths was demanding, and he took liberties with Goldsmith's essays. In 1758, Goldsmith returned briefly to his teaching post and also secured a commission to serve as a physician in India. To earn money for his passage, he completed *An Enquiry into the Present State of Polite Learning in Europe*. This work surveys education and literature, particularly in France and England. Goldsmith saw a decline in both countries but believed that the great power of booksellers in England was especially pernicious. No doubt he was thinking of his earlier experience with Griffiths.

Other booksellers were proving more generous, though. John Wilkie was starting a new thirty-two-page weekly magazine, *The Bee*, and asked Goldsmith to serve as its editor, by which he meant sole contributor. For the periodical's eight numbers (October 6, 1759, to November 24, 1759), Goldsmith churned out a variety of essays. As if this work were not enough, he was also writing for *The Critical Review* and *The Lady's Magazine*.

Although *The Bee* was short-lived, Goldsmith's work had attracted the notice of John Newbery, the publisher

Oliver Goldsmith. (Library of Congress)

433

of children's books. What unsigned work Goldsmith may have done for him is unclear; *Goody Two-Shoes* (1765), a children's classic, has been attributed to Goldsmith. Newbery definitely wanted Goldsmith to write for his new daily newspaper, *The Public Ledger*, offering £100 for two essays a week. Since the Seven Years' War had put an end to Goldsmith's hopes for India—heavy fighting between the French and the English there precluded his assuming a post on the subcontinent—this commission was welcome. Goldsmith seized the opportunity to create a philosophical tale capitalizing on the vogue for things Chinese. In a series of letters supposedly by Lien Chi Altangi, Goldsmith surveyed English society as an outsider. While Goldsmith knew nothing about China, he did know what it was like to be a stranger in England, since he himself was one. Though he criticizes the dirt of London or English imperialism, he also praises English generosity to French prisoners of war (letter 23) and urges his readers to accept life as it is (letter 44). These pieces were collected in 1762 under the title *The Citizen of the World.*

In that year, too, appeared Goldsmith's *The Life of Richard Nash, Esq.* Goldsmith had met Nash in Bath, and shortly after Nash's death, in 1761, he returned to that resort and talked with George Scott, the executor of Nash's estate. In part, Goldsmith found Nash interesting because Nash had refined the manners of the town and so played an important role in the social history of the country. Even more important for Goldsmith, though, was that Nash "was just such a man as probably you or I may be." In choosing a common man and then offering "a recital neither written with a spirit of satire nor panegyric" (as he put it in his preface), Goldsmith was forging a new style of biography. *The Life of Richard Nash, Esq.* looks ahead to the early nineteenth century view of the importance of the average person.

A third work dating from 1762 is *The Vicar of Wakefield*, though it was not published until four years later. This work, which went through two hundred editions in the nineteenth century and elicited the highest praise from Johann Wolfgang von Goethe and Sir Walter Scott, was sold to John Newbery's nephew Francis Newbery for £60 to rescue Goldsmith from debtors' prison. In this sentimental yet comic tale, Goldsmith drew on the scenes and people of his childhood, and he included himself in the guise of George Primrose. The praise of true benevolence corresponds to the age's growing concern for the unfortunate, whether orphans, the insane, the poor, or animals.

The Traveller, the first publication to carry Goldsmith's name, appeared in 1764 and earned for him in-

stant fame as one of the greatest poets of the century. After hearing Samuel Johnson read the poem, Mrs. Cholmondely declared, "I never more shall think Dr. Goldsmith ugly." T. S. Eliot pointed out that in *The Traveller*, Goldsmith fuses the traditional and the new. The poem is a verse epistle in the manner of Horace and Alexander Pope; it also relies upon conventions of eighteenth century topographical poetry in its descriptions and moral purpose. Yet it looks ahead to the Romantics in stressing the poet's own feelings and in attempting to free the couplet from Augustan rigidity.

In *The Traveller*, Goldsmith spoke of the enclosure of small fields to create large estates. This consolidation of land led to rural depopulation, urban overcrowding, and increased crime. The criticism of enclosure in *The Traveller* served as the basis of Goldsmith's other major poem, *The Deserted Village*. Here again the old and the new meet as Goldsmith uses an Augustan prospect poem to portray the poet's own feelings for the loss of rural simplicity and, beyond that, the destruction of innocence. The pastoral lament looks back to Vergil's *Georgics* (c. 39-27 B.C.E.), but it also anticipates William Wordsworth's *Michael* (1800).

Successful as an essayist, novelist, and poet, Goldsmith turned his pen to history and the stage. In history, his work was popular but hardly original. *A History of England in a Series of Letters from a Nobleman to His Son* (1764), *The Roman History, from the Foundation of the City of Rome to the Destruction of the Western Empire* (1769), *The History of England, from the Earliest Times to the Death of George II* (1771), and *The Grecian History* were all compilations drawn from secondary sources. Like *An History of the Earth, and Animated Nature*, they aimed "to drag up the obscure and gloomy learning of the cell to open inspection; to strip it from its garb of austerity, and to shew the beauties of that form, which only the industrious and the inquisitive have been hitherto permitted to approach." This desire to expand the realm of knowledge to the great middle class is characteristic of the age. One may compare Joseph Addison's statement in *The Spectator* (no. 10, March 12, 1711), that "I shall be ambitious to have it said of me, that I have brought Philosophy out of Closets and Libraries, Schools and Colleges, to dwell in Clubs and Assemblies, at Tea-Tables and in Coffee-Houses." So accessible were Goldsmith's books that they remained in use as school texts a century after his death.

While Goldsmith's histories were conventional, his plays were not. In *The Westminster Magazine* for January, 1773, he published "An Essay on the Theatre," in which he attacked the vogue for sentimental, moralistic comedies. His first play, *The Good-Natured Man* (1768), had parodied this genre: The hero, Honeywood, repents of his generosity and promises to be more selfish in the future. The plot thus inverts the typical prodigal's reformation in sentimental comedy. *The Good-Natured Man* enjoyed a respectable run but could not overshadow Hugh Kelly's *False Delicacy* (1768), which David Garrick was running opposite Goldsmith's play. *She Stoops to Conquer*, however, swept all before it. Its farcical elements violated the proprieties of sentimental comedy—and the audiences loved it. Sentimental comedy did not vanish immediately, but laughing comedy could now reassert itself on the stage and did so, most notably in the plays of Richard Brinsley Sheridan that shortly followed Goldsmith's.

She Stoops to Conquer earned for Goldsmith some £500; characteristically, he promptly spent the money. By early 1774, he was deeply in debt, by some £2,000, and his health was fragile. At a party he challenged Garrick to a battle of extemporaneous epitaphs, and Garrick replied, "Here lies Nolly Goldsmith, for shortness called Noll, Who wrote like an angel, but talked like poor Poll." Goldsmith, who was indeed a poor conversationalist, could not immediately respond. Instead, he turned to his pen and began *Retaliation: A Poem* (1774), a series of witty observations about his friends and acquaintances. Of Garrick he wrote, "On the stage he was natural, simple, affecting; / 'Twas only that, when he was off, he was acting." Before he could complete the poem, Goldsmith required a real epitaph; he died on April 4, 1774, and was buried quietly to prevent his creditors from seizing his body.

SIGNIFICANCE

The Latin inscription on Oliver Goldsmith's memorial in Westminster Abbey says that he "left scarcely any kind of writing untouched and touched nothing that he did not adorn." Though its author, Samuel Johnson, maintained that in lapidary inscriptions one is not upon oath, here he wrote no more than the truth.

Goldsmith was certainly a hack writer; in a three-month period in 1760 he turned out forty essays. Yet he left a novel that endures as a classic, two poems that rival any of the century, a comedy that still enjoys frequent revivals, and essays that continue to delight and instruct. The man who lamented the decline of literature gave ample testimony to its vitality.

He was a keen observer. In *An History of the Earth, and Animated Nature* he predicted the French Revolu-

tion, and elsewhere he foresaw the antagonism between Russia and Western Europe. Despite his gentleness, he could be a sharp social critic, as when he wrote in *The Deserted Village*, "Ill fares the land, to hastening ills a prey, / Where wealth accumulates, and men decay." His sympathy with the common individual and his experiments with traditional verse forms are as forward-looking as his political and social observations. He was not without his faults: He was feckless toward his mother, improvident, credulous, and vain. Yet, as Samuel Johnson wrote of him in a letter to Bennet Langton, "Let not his frailties be remembered; he was a very great man."

—*Joseph Rosenblum*

FURTHER READING

Ginger, John. *The Notable Man: The Life and Times of Oliver Goldsmith.* London: Hamilton, 1977. An interesting account that examines both the life and the works and adds new information about and insights into both.

Mikhail, E. H., ed. *Goldsmith: Interviews and Recollections.* New York: St. Martin's Press, 1993. The recollections of Goldsmith's friends and associates are reprinted in chronological order to create a composite biography. Many of these recollections have never before been published.

Quintana, Ricardo. *Oliver Goldsmith: A Georgian Study.* New York: Macmillan, 1967. Because Quintana concentrates on Goldsmith the writer and his works, he devotes only about ten pages to the first twenty-five years of Goldsmith's life. Emphasis is on Goldsmith's social and literary criticism.

Reynolds, Sir Joshua. "Reynolds on Goldsmith." In *Portraits*, edited by Frederick W. Hilles. New York: McGraw-Hill, 1952. Reynolds was Goldsmith's closest friend, the one to whom Goldsmith dedicated *The Deserted Village*. In this memoir, written two years after Goldsmith's death, Reynolds does not hide his friend's flaws, but he argues that Goldsmith was "a man of genius" and that even rarer thing as well, a charming companion.

Scott, Temple. *Oliver Goldsmith Bibliographically and Biographically Considered.* New York: Bowling Green Press, 1928. Using the extensive Goldsmith collection assembled by William M. Elkins, Scott presents an entertaining biography around the writings. Still a standard bibliography, even though some of the biographical material has been superseded.

Taylor, Richard C. *Goldsmith as Journalist.* Rutherford, N.J.: Fairleigh Dickinson University Press, 1993. Examines Goldsmith's journalistic career and the essays and other works he wrote for newspapers and magazines.

Wardle, Ralph M. *Oliver Goldsmith.* Lawrence: University Press of Kansas, 1957. First scholarly biography of Goldsmith and still a standard source. A sympathetic interpretation and a readable one as well.

Wibberly, Leonard. *The Good-Natured Man: A Portrait of Oliver Goldsmith.* New York: William Morrow, 1979. Intended for the general reader rather than the scholar. Wibberly uses his considerable novelistic abilities to weave a fascinating narrative that presents Goldsmith within his time. Although Wibberly is not beyond creating dialogues, and his facts are not al-

ways reliable, he wrote the book to show his admiration for Goldsmith, and that feeling comes through clearly.

See also: Anna Barbauld; James Boswell; Edmund Burke; David Garrick; Edward Gibbon; Johann Wolfgang von Goethe; Samuel Johnson; John Newbery; Sir Joshua Reynolds.

Related articles in *Great Events from History: The Eighteenth Century, 1701-1800:* 1726-1729: Voltaire Advances Enlightenment Thought in Europe; December 7, 1732: Covent Garden Theatre Opens in London; March 20, 1750-March 14, 1752: Johnson Issues *The Rambler.*

FRANCISCO DE GOYA
Spanish painter

A painter and engraver, Goya was not only one of Spain's greatest artists but also one of Western art's most original practitioners. His aesthetic range was so comprehensive that he anticipated major artistic schools from the French Romantics to the German Expressionists.

Born: March 30, 1746; Fuendetodos, Spain
Died: April 16, 1828; Bordeaux, France
Also known as: Francisco de Paula José de Goya y Lucientes (full name)
Area of achievement: Art

EARLY LIFE
Francisco de Goya (frahn-THEES-koh thay GOH-yah) was born in the desolate hills of northeastern Spain, in the province of Aragon, a parched and barren land. His father was a gilder of Basque origin and was frequently unemployed. The family possessed little property, and poverty forced them to work in the fields to feed themselves. It was Goya's lifelong terror of returning to the indigence of his early youth that later stimulated him to negotiate complex political maneuvers during several of Spain's stormiest changes of government in order to retain his comfortable household. When Goya was five years old, his father moved the family to the nearby town of Saragossa, where the boy spent the rest of his youth.

Because of his family's financial needs, the fourteen-year-old Goya was apprenticed to the highly successful church artist José Luzán. After four years of grinding colors, he began composing his own pictures, most of which

were imitations of his master, Luzán; he also created skilled reproductions of paintings by old masters. It was also in Saragossa that Goya met and became close friends with Martin Zapater, a classmate. Their mutual correspondence over many years, though far from complete, provides the basis of historians' knowledge of Goya's complex personality. The years of hard and monotonous work that he spent in Luzán's studio contributed to the characteristic rapidity and proficient technical craftsmanship that Goya was able to maintain throughout his creative life. He would become famous for his ability to complete a portrait during one long morning session. He corrected virtually nothing substantial because his hand and his eye were so practiced.

Despite his long years of grueling apprenticeship, Goya was unable to advance his career as quickly as he wished. In 1763 and 1766, he entered contests for scholarship admittance to the Royal Academy of San Fernando in Madrid and failed both times. Frustrated and angry, he left Spain for Rome, where he assiduously studied, copied, and absorbed the influences of the Italian masters, particularly Correggio and the Venetian Giovanni Battista Tiepolo. Indeed, many critics attribute the warmer and richer colors in Goya's paintings of this period to Tiepolo's influence.

Another, possibly more compelling reason for Goya's quick departure from Spain was the increasing pressure he and other free-spirited liberals were under from the reactionary proponents of the Inquisition. The Italians were considerably more appreciative of the young artist's talents and awarded him second prize in a contest sponsored by the Academy of Art of Parma in 1770. It seems that Goya then left Rome suddenly, because he had become involved in several exciting but dangerous romantic escapades, a habit he never relinquished.

After ten years of neglect and failure, Goya's dogged tenacity prevailed, and he managed to gain recognition outside his own country. He returned to Saragossa and was promptly commissioned to paint frescoes in the Cathedral of Our Lady of the Pillar. He had returned home with honor and now had a promising project that would last for the next ten years. Goya painted the commissioned frescoes in the prevailing Baroque-rococo style of the day but was still able to lend his personal touch to them; they were, even at this early stage in his career, unmistakably Goya's work.

From 1770 to 1773, the young artist pursued further studies with the well-known and highly influential painter Francisco Bayeu, a fellow Aragonese. He married Bayeu's sister, Josefa, in 1773, a move that did nothing to hurt his steadily growing reputation. Indeed, it was through his brother-in-law that Goya received an important commission to create the enormous mural paintings of the Carthusian Charterhouse of Auli Dei in Saragossa, work that dramatically caught the attention and respect of both the artistic and the royal community in Madrid. Again, because of the influence of Bayeu, Goya was summoned to Madrid in 1774 by the reigning artistic dictator of the court of Charles III, the powerful German-Czech exponent of neoclassicism, Anton Raphael Mengs. Mengs commissioned him to participate in preparing fifty cartoons to be submitted to the royal tapestry factory of Santa Barbara, a project that brought him into direct contact with King Charles III and the royal household. By 1774, the twenty-eight-year-old Goya found himself at the threshold of a career that would eventually lead him to the post of first painter to the king.

LIFE'S WORK

The year 1775 marked two significant events in Goya's life. One was the birth of his son, Xavier, the only one of his children to live beyond infancy. The other was the painting of his first self-portrait, a strikingly optimistic one that would turn out to be the first of many. He also drew cartoons for the tapestry factory of Santa Barbara that demonstrated the emergence, in a relatively short time, of his own, unique style. To achieve this style, Goya had to overcome an initial aesthetic timidity and to stop trying to imitate the flaccid neoclassicism of his brother-in-law. With his success in these endeavors,

Goya not only forged a new phase of Spanish art that started with El Greco but also managed to imprint his own character on everything he touched. Several of the Santa Barbara cartoons have come to be thought of as exemplary of Goya's early phase, notably *The Parasol* and *The Washerwoman*.

During this early phase, from 1776 to 1780, Goya was received into the court of the intelligent and kindly Charles III and given the opportunity to examine in depth the royal collection of paintings. The first and perhaps most revolutionary influence he was to encounter in the collection was the work of Diego Velázquez. The influence of the latter upon Goya was immediate and permanent. Goya's subsequent paintings displayed a deft handling of reflected light and atmospheric effects that had been absent from his earlier pictures. Goya stated on several occasions that he acknowledged only three masters: "Rembrandt, Velázquez, and Nature!" His adaptations of effects and techniques from earlier masters eventually enabled him to synthesize the neoclassical and Baroque-rococo elements in his work into his own, quasi-Romantic treatment of even the most banal subjects.

Late in the next decade, after winning several competitions and gaining important positions in the Royal Academy of San Fernando, Goya became painter of the royal household under Charles IV (r. 1788-1808), Charles III's considerably less sensitive and more frivolous son. The work that was to win for him these lucrative positions was a series of portraits he had begun in 1783. The first, *Portrait of the Count of Floridablanca*, secured nationwide fame for Goya. It was also the first major portrait in which he portrayed himself, an act simultaneously imitating and paying tribute to his spiritual master Velázquez. It was also an unmistakable sign that Goya saw himself, quite consciously, as the next successor in a line of great Spanish painters beginning with El Greco and Velázquez.

Other portraits followed quickly, and Goya's work was in great demand by every level of the aristocracy. It was in these portraits, particularly the justly famous *Portrait of Don Manuel Orsorio* (1788) and *The Duke and Duchess of Osuna* (1789), that Goya successfully developed a quality of luminescent impressionism that ultimately became his hallmark. With this quality, he managed to avoid any suggestion of mere prettiness or sentimentality but at the same time beautified, without decorating, his sense of the world about him.

Just as Goya was concluding his work on the tapestries of Santa Barbara, he contracted a mysterious malady that manifested itself in the form of enormous noises in his head. The illness, along with the monstrous

Francisco de Goya. (Library of Congress)

sounds, eventually disappeared but left him permanently deaf. Critics have theorized that, like Ludwig van Beethoven's deafness, Goya's terrible misfortune isolated him from much of society, whose darling he had been up to that point. At the same time, however, the deafness deepened the content of Goya's works, and his isolation forced him into areas beyond the realm of mere, albeit brilliant, portraiture.

It was shortly after his recovery from the illness that robbed him of his hearing that Goya began a series of etchings, the first of three extended studies that have come to be considered his major intellectual contributions not only to eighteenth century art but also to the general history of ideas and images of Western Europe. He called the series *The Caprices* (1793-1796), and it consisted of eighty aquatint etchings detailing with satiric savagery humankind's inhumanity to humankind and "existence as catastrophe." The etchings employed techniques and procedures that would later be called surrealistic and expressionistic, modes that recalled the hallucinatory terror of Hieronymus Bosch. They expressed a sense of existential emptiness, but one in which the void is actively corrosive. The etchings presented humans as victims of not only all ideologies and beliefs but also the pincers of their own minds. In retrospect, the

etchings became prophetic warnings of what civilization was sliding into during the eighteenth century.

Although *The Caprices* became the map of his own and Europe's fall into spiritual torpor, Goya's career as a portrait painter flourished as he produced what would later be regarded as prototypical Goyaesque works. His relationship with the royal house of Alba and specifically his love for the duchess of Alba, who may or may not have been his actual lover, inspired two masterpieces portraying the duchess and spilled over into two even more famous portraits that unquestionably established his reputation, the stunningly sensuous *The Clothed Maja* and *The Naked Maja*.

The climax of Goya's career occurred with his appointment as first court painter in 1799, the same year in which he produced the two Maja paintings. The artist had been waiting and maneuvering at court for this appointment for years. The year after he finally received it, he produced what most critics see as his greatest single painting: *Portrait of the Family of King Charles IV*. In this huge work, he accomplished the task of rendering the members of this venal, not very bright, and distinctly ugly family with pitiless accuracy. A more sensitive and intelligent patron and his family would have been highly insulted, but Goya's genius was so sure-handed that he was able to blind the royal family to their own ineffectual self-indulgence while demonstrating it to the rest of the world. Moreover, he vividly portrayed the disastrous effects that genetic inbreeding, both physical and spiritual, had had on the great house of Bourbon and, by implication, the equally destructive forces that were bringing all the great houses of Europe to ruin within the next fifty years. In this single magnificent portrait, Goya verified the beginning of the end of what had started as the Holy Roman Empire in 800 C.E.

With the death of the duchess of Alba and the chaos created by the Franco-Spanish War, Goya began his second series of etchings, known as *The Disasters of War* (1810). These further deepened and certified the despair of *The Caprices* but depicted the horrors of the atrocities, agonies, and starvation of actual war. By 1814, Goya had painted perhaps the greatest and most compelling images of war in all of Western art, *The Executions of May Second* and *The Executions of May Third*. Both series of etchings and the execution paintings demonstrated a darkening of Goya's vision, a darkening that produced its most despairing depictions in his final series of etchings, known as *The Proverbs* (1815-1816).

In *The Proverbs*, Goya expressed his profound grief and dismay in eighteen viciously satiric allegories that seem to be utterly disengaged from any rational foundations. His penultimate statement on the human condition he saved for the walls of his own house, which he named Quinta del Sordo (House of the Deaf Man). He called these works *The Black Paintings*, and they depict apocalyptically hallucinatory visions that seem to foretell the fall of Western civilization. The delirium of these paintings is so great that it almost seems as though they could have been rendered by Salvador Dali or Pablo Picasso in either artist's most surreal period.

During the Peninsular War (1808-1814), Goya had remained at court and painted under the occupying French government that had been installed in power by Napoleon I. Once Spain regained its independence and Ferdinand VII took back his throne, Goya feared reprisals and exiled himself to France temporarily. Once he saw that it was safe, though, he returned and was received kindly by Ferdinand VII, who gave Goya a hefty pension for life. Goya found life under the new regime too repressive, however, and moved back to Bordeaux, where he produced his final masterpiece. He returned to the subject of his youth, the common folk, and created *The Milkmaid of Bordeaux* (1827), a work that brought together all the styles within which he had worked and created, centering them within an autumnal but hopeful serenity. He died peacefully at age eighty-two on April 16, 1828.

SIGNIFICANCE

Francisco de Goya shared with the English poet and engraver William Blake and the great German composer Ludwig van Beethoven the unenviable position of connecting two of the stormiest centuries of the Christian era: the eighteenth and the nineteenth, the Age of Enlightenment and the Romantic Age. He, like the other two geniuses, was more than a mere transitional figure. His work, because of the vividly regenerative power of his imagination, created an intellectual and spiritual world in which the work of later great French artists such as Eugène Delacroix, Théodore Géricault, and Honoré Daumier could draw sustenance and find validation. Goya's major achievement was, in short, the enlargement of the possibilities of the Western imagination to an almost limitless degree. Like Beethoven in his early formalistic work, Goya moved from safe traditional forms into later projects where form and content became extensions of each other. In one dramatic lifetime, Goya advanced art from the highly traditional Baroque-rococo to the openness and complexity of the Romantic mode, which, in turn, made possible the modern sensibility.

Goya's direct influences on later artists are varied and sometimes remarkably surprising. His work prefigures that of Delacroix by embodying the principle that the personal is always the political, certainly a controlling idea in Delacroix's and other Romantics' work. Goya's sardonic satires paved the way for the work of another French social satirist, Daumier, while his impeccable handling of light and shade and his uniquely luminescent textures undoubtedly influenced the major French Impressionists, such as Édouard Manet, Claude Monet, and Pierre-Auguste Renoir. Indeed, Manet derived from Goya's *The Executions of May Third* his own *Execution of Maximilian*, and he offered no apologies. Finally, Goya's nightmarish and hallucinatory etchings, *The Proverbs*, *The Caprices*, and *The Disasters of War*, unquestionably anticipate the work of such major nineteenth and twentieth century European Expressionists as Käthe Kollwitz, Edvard Munch, Emil Nolde, and Paul Klee. Without Goya's aesthetic permission, his fellow Spanish surrealists, Picasso and Dali, could not have flourished. Goya was unquestionably one of the major revolutionary figures in the history of European art, and his rich legacy continues to resonate.

—*Patrick Meanor*

FURTHER READING

Chabrun, Jean-François. *Goya*. Translated by J. Maxwell Brown John. New York: Tudor, 1965. A highly readable novelistic narrative with much biographical information. Amply illustrated with both color and black-and-white prints. Excellent for beginners.

Connell, Evan S. *Francisco Goya*. New York: Counterpoint Press, 2004. Connell uses Goya's career to illustrate the decline of Spain by the end of the eighteenth century. Offers little analysis of Goya's art, but provides a lively, well-researched account of his life.

Glendinning, Nigel. *Goya and His Critics*. New Haven, Conn.: Yale University Press, 1977. The most intelligent treatment of the artist from the point of view of his place and influence within the history of art and European intellectual traditions. The author has spent much effort in tracking down every reference to Goya in the works of many other artists.

Goya, Francisco de. *Goya*. Text by José Gudiol. New York: Harry N. Abrams, 1965. A handsome volume with vivid and exceptionally well-produced reproductions of many of Goya's major masterpieces. The introduction traces Goya's life chronologically and offers intelligent, if sometimes stuffy, analyses of the works.

Hughes, Robert. *Goya*. New York: Alfred A. Knopf, 2003. An interpretive biography by a prominent art historian. Hughes traces Goya's development as a person and artist and analyzes his work.

Klingender, Francis D. *Goya in the Democratic Tradition*. New York: Schocken Books, 1968. An unashamedly partisan treatment of Goya in relation to his intellectual and social background. Thoroughly grounded in historical fact and stimulating.

Lewis, D. B. Wyndham. *The World of Goya*. London: Michael Joseph, 1968. Tends to be told in a quasi-novelistic narrative but done with much closer adherence to historical facts than Chabrun's work. Excellent cross-reference system. Densely illustrated.

Licht, Fred. *Goya: The Origins of Modern Temper in Art*. New York: Universe Books, 1979. A comprehensive and scholarly book that is unfortunately marred by illustrations in black and white only. Each chapter is concerned with only one group of works—cartoons, religious paintings, and so on—thus helping the reader focus on the similarities and differences found within the groups. Extremely helpful and thoroughly grounded in historical facts.

_____, ed. *Goya in Perspective*. Englewood Cliffs, N.J.: Prentice-Hall, 1973. An intelligent and comprehensive collection of essays written by art critics and historians. The essays offer a variety of views on Goya, from the poetic to the sociological.

Tomlinson, Janis A. *Francisco Goya y Lucientes, 1746-1828*. London: Phaidon, 1999. Tomlinson, who has written several books about Goya and Spanish art, discounts the popular theory that Goya's art darkened after he became deaf. She emphasizes the continuity of his work before and after his illness, and she shows how his deafness strengthened his resolve to explore and use his creativity.

See also: William Blake; Charles III; Giovanni Battista Tiepolo.

Related article in *Great Events from History: The Eighteenth Century, 1701-1800*: November 9-10, 1799: Napoleon Rises to Power in France.

HENRY GRATTAN
Irish politician and reformer

A key figure in Irish political life in the last quarter of the eighteenth century, Grattan helped establish Irish legislative independence and championed free trade and civil rights for Roman Catholics. A voice of moderation among Irish nationalists, he was renowned for the elegance of his oratory.

Born: July 3, 1746 (baptized); Dublin, Ireland
Died: June 6, 1820; London, England
Areas of achievement: Government and politics, church reform, religion and theology, social reform

EARLY LIFE

Henry Grattan was the only son of James Grattan, recorder of Dublin and member of Parliament for the city, and Mary Marley, daughter of the lord chief justice. The family was prosperous but lacked extensive landed property or influential connections. Grattan attended private day school in Dublin, showing early promise as a scholar, and entered Trinity College in 1763, intending, against the wishes of his father, to study classical literature. When his father died in 1766, he left most of his estate to his four daughters, and Henry, faced with the necessity of pursuing a profession, chose law. Upon graduation from Trinity College in 1767 he was admitted to read law at the Middle Temple in London.

Although he qualified for the Irish bar in 1772, he lacked success in the courtroom. Of more importance to his future career was the education he received by frequent attendance in the visitor's gallery of the English House of Commons, where he witnessed debates on the worsening crisis in the American colonies, imbibing both the style and the sympathies of the pro-American Whig opposition party.

Returning to Dublin during recesses, he gravitated toward the nascent Irish opposition party, headed by George Lucas, Henry Flood, James Caulfield, and others, who were embroiled in a dispute with the viceroy, Lord Townsend. For half a century, Ireland had been controlled by the Undertaker System, in which a viceroy appointed by the British crown ruled through a small number of Anglo-Irish landowning families, who in turn controlled the Irish house of commons through patronage. Townsend's determination to govern without intermediaries forced an uneasy alliance between aristocrats and radicals. Grattan joined the fray with his literary talents, but lacking wealth or crucial family connections, his entry into Parliament seemed problematical. His opportunity came when the man representing one of Caulfield's boroughs died suddenly in 1775, and Grattan was invited to fill the vacancy. Thereafter he was an active member of the Irish parliament, first for Caulfield and later for Dublin. He so made his mark that the era of Irish legislative independence, 1782-1800, is often referred to as "Grattan's parliament."

LIFE'S WORK

In 1775, the Irish parliament's overriding aim was its own legislative independence, without which no progress toward social or economic reform was possible. A Tudor statute known as Poyning's Law required all legislation initiated in Ireland to be approved in England, while the Irish parliament had no power to undo the dictates of the English parliament. Henry Grattan was foremost among the legislators advocating repeal of this law. He quickly distinguished himself by the elegance of his oratory, which owed much to his classical education. His lengthy speeches, written in advance, memorized, and delivered in theatrical style, were as much admired for their literary quality as for their arguments.

The outbreak of war in North America provided the Irish with leverage. England was forced to remove most of its troops from Ireland, leaving it vulnerable to domestic unrest and foreign invasion. To fill the vacuum, Irish Protestants formed the Volunteer Corps, an efficient paramilitary force, 100,000 strong at its height, with its own independent governing system. In 1782, advocates of legislative independence, led by Grattan, presented their demands for repeal of Poyning's Law to the Dungannon Convention of Ulster Volunteers amid threats of a martial nature uncomfortably reminiscent of America a decade earlier. The newly constituted Whig government in London capitulated, and "Grattan's parliament" was born.

Irish nationalists almost immediately split into two camps: those who felt that the revolution of 1782 went far enough and those who felt that the revolution should be followed by sweeping social and electoral reforms. Grattan's position, which fell somewhere between these extremes, was further compromised by his acceptance of the £50,000 voted him by the Irish parliament. This was a large sum of money, especially for someone so vocal in his opposition to pensions and sinecures.

From 1782 onward, Grattan's main causes were free trade and Catholic emancipation. On the subject of parliamentary reform he followed the moderate line adopted by William Pitt the Younger, the English Tory prime

Henry Grattan. (Library of Congress)

minister. He decried a system in which only a third of the seats in the Irish lower house were elected, and the remainder were frequently bought and sold, but he was no friend of universal franchise.

Grattan's parliament had a solid record as a reforming body. Beginning with revoking the remaining penal laws against Catholics, the Irish parliament went on to grant them the franchise and entry into professions in 1793. Revisions in the poor laws, criminal law, laws governing debtors, and the founding of a Catholic seminary at Maynooth made Ireland, on paper at least, more socially advanced than the parent country in the late 1790's.

Unfortunately, radical extremism and the resultant reaction swamped the voices of moderation. In 1795, the Whig opposition, now coalesced into a genuine political party under the leadership of Grattan, saw its opportunity in the appointment of a radical Whig as viceroy. Earl Fitzwilliam dismissed his predecessor's advisers, ensuring the enmity of key powerful families, and embarked on a sweeping program of complete Catholic emancipation. Pitt recalled him abruptly, unleashing a storm of recrimination and returning the conservatives to power. Finding themselves in a dwindling minority, their calls for reform eclipsed by an attempted French invasion in December of 1796 and the increasing militancy of Irish separatists, Grattan and his fellow Whig nationalists withdrew from the Irish parliament on May 1, 1797.

Grattan took no part on either side in the 1798 rebellion. He thus escaped the stigma attached to quelling the uprising, but he also removed himself from the stage at a critical juncture. By the time he returned to Ireland in 1799, the process of abolishing the Irish parliament was well under way. Purchasing himself a seat, Grattan made a dramatic entry into Parliament on May 26, 1800, delivering his impassioned speech against the proposed Act of Union from a sitting position because of poor health. It was a futile gesture. Possibly a majority of the respectable electorate of Ireland, still reeling from the horrors of the 1798 rebellion and fearing a French invasion, really supported union; in any case, corruption proved its own undoing when venial members were bought out.

Nationalist biographies of Grattan end here, with the lone Irish patriot on the bridge of the sinking ship. Grattan's subsequent political career was hardly a postscript. In retirement for five years, he entered United Parliament in 1805. Joining the opposition, he dedicated himself single-mindedly to the cause of Catholic emancipation, already partially in effect in Ireland but stalled in Britain as a whole because of opposition by British king George III. In 1813, at the height of the Napoleonic Wars, an unlikely alliance between Grattan, his nemesis Lord Castlereagh, author of the Act of Union, and George Canning, of Parliament for Liverpool, nearly succeeded in getting Catholic emancipation passed by the House of Commons, and did succeed in passing a key free trade measure breaking the monopoly of the British East India Company. No subsequent attempt at Catholic relief fared as well during Grattan's lifetime, partly because more and more Catholics turned to the banner of the extremist Daniel O'Connell, and many questioned whether Grattan's cautious program still had support.

Subsequently, declining health forced curtailment of political life. Dublin voters reelected Grattan in 1818. In 1820, the prospect of a revival of the Catholic question induced him to travel to London, against the advice of his physicians. His health deteriorated on the journey, and he died in London on June 6, 1820. He is buried in Westminster Abbey. In 1782 he had married Henrietta Fitzgerald, by whom he had two sons and two daughters.

SIGNIFICANCE

Henry Grattan's influence is measured more by the impact of his reputation than by his actual achievements.

His son published a carefully edited version of his speeches as well as a five-volume laudatory biography. The image of the electrifying orator, the courageous advocate for Catholic rights, and the determined if ineffective opponent of the Act of Union struck a respondent chord among nineteenth century Irish nationalists. Consequently, Grattan became something of a cultural icon.

In retrospect, his actual accomplishments are limited to the 1782 repeal of Poyning's Law and his support of social legislation. It is tempting to base the reputation of an opposition political figure upon the unsuccessful causes for which he advocated, but this practice pertains more to the way in which history is constructed for purposes of persuasion, than it pertains to history itself.

—*Martha A. Sherwood*

FURTHER READING

Herman, Neil. "Henry Grattan, the Regency Crisis, and the Emergence of a Whig Party in Ireland, 1788-89." *Irish Historical Studies* 32, no. 128 (1999): 478-497. Focuses on a brief but crucial episode in Grattan's career, and explores the complex relationship between Irish and English governments in the late eighteenth century.

McDowell, R. B. *Grattan: A Life.* Dublin: Lilliput Press, 2001. A thorough and very readable biography, good for Grattan's antecedents and early life. Corrects the nationalist and mythologizing trend of standard early biographies.

Madden, Daniel Owen. *The Speeches of the Right Hon. Henry Grattan, to Which Is Added His Letter on the Union, with a Commentary on His Career and Character.* Dublin: J. Duffy, 1874. The introduction to this work exemplifies the mythologizing of a historical figure.

Powell, John Stocks. "Henry Grattan: Enlightenment in Ireland." *History Today* 27, no. 3 (1977): 159-166. An overview of Grattan's career, aimed at a general audience. Examines the "Grattan mystique."

See also: Georgiana Cavendish; Lord Edward Fitzgerald; Charles James Fox; George III; William Pitt the Younger; Richard Brinsley Sheridan; Wolfe Tone.

Related articles in *Great Events from History: The Eighteenth Century, 1701-1800:* April 19, 1775: Battle of Lexington and Concord; January 4, 1792-1797: The *Northern Star* Calls for Irish Independence; May-November, 1798: Irish Rebellion; July 2-August 1, 1800: Act of Union Forms the United Kingdom.

NATHANAEL GREENE
American military leader

Greene was one of George Washington's most trusted military leaders throughout the Revolutionary War, playing significant roles as a field commander and as the Continental army's quartermaster general.

Born: August 7, 1742; Potowomut (now Warwick), Rhode Island

Died: June 19, 1786; Mulberry Grove plantation, Georgia

Areas of achievement: Warfare and conquest, military

EARLY LIFE

Nathanael Greene was one of the numerous descendants of the Quaker John Greene, who followed Roger Williams to Rhode Island in 1636 in search of religious freedom. He was born in Potowomut (modern Warwick), Rhode Island. Because of his father's suspicion of learning, Greene was largely self-educated, his early reading being directed by a chance meeting with Ezra Stiles, later president of Yale College. The young Greene was five feet, ten inches tall and well built, with an oval face, blue eyes, a straight nose, a full and determined mouth, a large forehead, and a firm double chin. A stiff right knee gave him a slight limp, but neither this nor periodic bouts of asthma prevented him from engaging in normal physical activity.

Like his brothers, Greene spent most of his youth working in the prosperous family forge and mills. In 1770, his father gave him control of the family forge in Coventry, Rhode Island, where he built his own house, including a library of 250 volumes. From early youth he had shown a fondness for dancing and an interest in things military; some time after his father's death, the Quaker meeting in Coventry dismissed him for attending a military parade.

Greene lived as a typical young man of his class, being elected to the Rhode Island General Assembly in 1770, 1771, 1772, and 1775. On July 20, 1774, he married Catharine Littlefield, and the two had two sons and three daughters. Greene was aware of the growing tensions between the American colonies and the mother country, becoming convinced as early as October, 1775, that a break with Great Britain was necessary to preserve American liberties. He was instrumental in the formation of the Kentish Guards, a militia company organized in response to the Boston Port Act of 1774; he served as a private when some members indicated that a captain who limped would be a blemish on the company.

LIFE'S WORK

Nathanael Greene's military career, which occupied the rest of his life, began when he was commissioned brigadier general of Rhode Island's three regiments on May 8, 1775. He took his troops to Boston, where he first met George Washington, and, on June 22, was appointed one of the eight brigadier generals of the Continental army. He commanded in Boston after the British evacuation in March of 1776; by May, he was supervising the building of fortifications on Long Island, though a three-week bout with fever kept him out of the battles there. He was made major general on August 9 and by mid-September was commanding his division during the retreat from New York. At this point, as commander of Forts Lee and Washington, Greene was confident that both could be held, and Washington took his advice. However, on November 16, Fort Washington surrendered, Fort Lee had to be evacuated, and Washington's army retreated through New Jersey.

Greene's division crossed the Delaware River with Washington, and Greene led the left column against Trenton, capturing the Hessian artillery. In early January, he delayed Lieutenant General Cornwallis while Washington made his night march to Princeton. At the Battle of Brandywine on September 10, Greene's division covered four miles in forty-five minutes to aid the right wing, covered the retreat, and saved the artillery. Arriving late at the October 4 dawn attack on Germantown, Greene's left column fought in the two-hour battle and then protected the rear for five miles of the retreat, without losing a gun. On December 19, 1777, the army went into winter quarters at Valley Forge.

On February 25, 1778, Greene reluctantly agreed to become quartermaster general (officially appointed on March 2). A difficult job at best, it was much involved with the politicking and intrigue swirling around Washington and in the Continental Congress; the eddies alone could destroy a reputation, and Greene preferred military activity. Yet his realization of the importance of the work and his strong sense of obligation to Washington and the revolutionary cause kept Greene in the position for eighteen months. During this time, he set up a system of supply depots and required monthly reports from his deputies. He was as effective as congressional politics, intercolonial squabbling, and inadequate financing allowed. On the march to Monmouth, for example, he picked good campsites and had them prepared with wood, straw, barrels of vinegar, latrines, and stone-walled springs, while seeing to the repair of equipment and the collection of fodder.

For the Battle of Monmouth on June 28, Greene resumed his line command and led the right wing, pushing back Sir Henry Clinton's line. Sent to Rhode Island to further a projected French-American push, Greene commanded the right wing on August 11, when American troops were defeated while count d'Estaing refused to disembark his four thousand French soldiers. Greene acted as peacemaker in the subsequent arguments and again as right wing commander in an unsuccessful engagement on August 29. The ensuing military lull did not extend to the quartermaster department, Greene administering approximately $50 million in 1779; his effectiveness at supply helped to support the army during winter quarters in Morristown and to keep it mobile during the summer's maneuvering. When Congress adopted a plan to reorganize the department, Greene's resignation (the last of several) was accepted, on August 3. During September, while performing quartermaster duty until his successor took over, Greene also presided over the board of general officers that condemned Major John André to be hanged as a spy.

The war in the North wound down after 1778 as the British shifted their major operations to the South, taking Augusta and Charleston and setting up a chain of interior posts. After General Horatio Gates's defeat at Camden, Washington appointed Greene to the Southern command on October 14, 1780, and Congress ratified this to include control of all troops between Delaware and Georgia. In Philadelphia, Greene arranged for a medical department, engineers, artillery, clothing, horses, and equipment; in Richmond, he established cooperation with Governor Thomas Jefferson; in North Carolina, he ordered the building of boats and established cooperation with the patriot organizations.

On December 2, in Charlotte, he took formal command, which was marked almost immediately by cooperation with the partisan leaders General Andrew Pickens, General Thomas Sumter, and Colonel Francis (Swamp Fox) Marion, and by his use of able subordinates such as General Daniel Morgan, Colonel Otho H. Williams, and Colonel William Washington, with General Henry (Light-Horse Harry) Lee's Legion as his intelligence arm. Throughout his tenure as the commander of the Southern Department, Greene made effective use of these brilliant and independent-minded leaders while maintaining good relations with political leaders in several states and paying his usual careful attention to the lo-

Nathanael Greene. (Library of Congress)

gistical details that made his strategy possible. A nationalist, the Rhode Islander felt no constraint in the South; more diplomatic as commander than he was as quartermaster general, he was able to get maximum cooperation from detached and independent forces.

American losses at Charleston and Camden had seriously reduced both numbers and morale, so Greene appointed good quartermaster officers and added to the strength of his forces, having about two thousand Continentals and between five hundred and one thousand partisans. Moving his camp to the Cheraw Hills, South Carolina, on the Pedee River, he once again faced Lieutenant General Cornwallis. Like Greene, Cornwallis did not have enough men to control the South, and his serious supply problems were never solved; although popular with his troops (with whom he shared privation and hardship) and fearless in battle, he did not plan in detail for long campaigns and often blundered.

Greene took the initiative and divided his army, sending off half under Morgan to the victory at Cowpens on January 17, 1781. Cornwallis burned his baggage and set off in pursuit. Both armies raced for the Dan River, but Greene had provided boats and Cornwallis had not. Greene, maneuvering while waiting for reinforcements, took a strong position near Guilford Courthouse on

March 15; he used his 4,200 men well, but few were veterans. Cornwallis attacked with two thousand veterans, but although Greene retreated after three hours of hard fighting, Cornwallis lost a quarter of his force and had to withdraw toward the coast, unable to resume the offensive in the Carolinas.

Greene was physically exhausted after six weeks with little sleep and no change of clothing, but after some rest he planned the best use of his limited resources: He was left with about 1,450 troops and the partisans. Cornwallis's subordinate Lord Francis Rawdon attacked Greene's new position (near Camden) on April 25; because of Colonel John Gunby's injudicious order to fall back, Greene was forced to make a general retreat from Hobkirk's Hill. Rawdon, however, his communications and supply lines threatened, was forced to move off. Greene's detachments took the British posts and Lee's Legion took Augusta; Greene besieged Ninety-six but Rawdon relieved the garrison on June 19. This was Rawdon's second Pyrrhic victory, for he had to abandon the post. Thus, by July, Greene held nearly the entire lower South, having forced Cornwallis to leave the theater of operations. After the campaign's long marches and short rations, Greene took his army to camp at the High Hills of Santee for six weeks of recuperation, drill, and discipline.

The army moved out on August 23 and on September 8 surprised Lieutenant Colonel Alexander Stuart at Eutaw Springs, fighting a bloody battle against an army of equal size. The militia fought well, British regulars were pushed back in open fighting, and an American bayonet charge was successful. When, however, Lee's Legion and the artillery advanced beyond troops who stayed to enjoy the food and rum in the abandoned British camp, Greene was forced to leave the field. This indecisive battle, at best a draw, marked the end of the fighting in the lower South, as Stuart withdrew to Charleston. Congress later voted Greene thanks for the victory, along with a gold medal and a British standard, and Washington congratulated him in a letter.

With the onset of the cool season, Greene brought his army down from the Santee camp to besiege Charleston on January 2, 1782, holding a superior British force in the city until the end of the war. Supplying his army, aiding the restoration of civil government, and attempting to prevent mistreatment of Loyalists occupied Greene until all troops began to leave in July of 1783. The legislatures of Georgia and of North Carolina and South Carolina had voted to grant him land in gratitude. Greene rode home to Rhode Island in November, but in 1784 had to return and sell the South Carolina plantation to settle claims made on him stemming from his arrangements for supplying the army before Charleston. (Congress granted, to his widow, the financial relief for which he had asked, in June, 1796.)

In the autumn of 1785, Greene moved his family to the Mulberry Grove plantation granted him in Georgia. He settled in to the life of a gentleman farmer, but on June 14, 1786, after walking in the afternoon sun, he developed head pains and inflammation, and he died five days later. He was buried in the cemetery of Christ Episcopal Church in Savannah, and in 1902 was re-interred under the Greene monument in Johnson Square in that city. The Marquis de Lafayette, a longtime friend of Greene, educated his son George Washington Greene in France until 1794; shortly after his return, at the age of nineteen, the boy drowned in the Savannah River. On June 28, 1796, Greene's widow married Phineas Miller; she died in 1814.

SIGNIFICANCE

In many respects, Nathanael Greene exemplified the American experience. Descended from early English settlers fleeing religious persecution, he was continuing the economic and educationally upward mobility that characterized colonial society when the Battle of Lexington and Concord in 1775 interrupted an essentially undistinguished life. Appointed a brigadier general despite an almost complete lack of experience, Greene quickly demonstrated his military value to Washington. Throughout the revolution he held important commands, in all of them giving his country unstinting service despite personal and financial hardships.

On many points he was somewhat ahead of general public opinion. Early in the conflict, he urged independence as a goal. He saw the need of a strong central government, and, equally in vain, advocated a large regular army, enlisted for the duration, with central command and adequate supply and financial support. In this he differed from both contemporary and historical opinion, which was that the traditional militia was an effective military force expressing the popular nature of American society without endangering American liberties. Military historians have come to see the revolutionary patriot militias as a cross section of the colonial yeomanry, the "nation-in-arms" proficient with weapons and familiar with its home terrain, fighting well with its own officers and in its own way. For example, its usual casual "desertions," to deal with farm and business needs, produced not only a constantly fluctuating troop strength but also far less pressure on slender resources than a consistently large regular army would have.

Yet a commander and quartermaster general was bound to concentrate on the militia's weaknesses, even when planning them into his tactics, as Greene placed mostly raw militia in his first two lines at Guilford Courthouse: He wanted then to retreat after a few volleys, knowing that militia usually broke and ran in the face of an enemy advance, particularly of a bayonet charge, "grim lines of scarlet-coated men emerging from the mist and heading straight toward . . . them with naked steel," wrote historians Mary Wickwire and Franklin Wickwire. As quartermaster general, Greene was too preoccupied with shortages and inefficiencies to feel grateful that he had to provide for forces that were smaller than they would have been, had militiamen been metamorphosed into duration-of-the-war Continentals.

Quartermasters general, however efficient, are rarely remembered except by the troops whom they contrive somehow to supply. Even secondary commanders, however much relied upon by their chiefs, do not decide strategy: While Washington accepted Greene's assurance that Fort Washington could be held, it was Washington's own decision to attempt to block British operations in New Jersey. As commander of the Southern Department after the Camden debacle, Greene came fully into his own, demonstrating great abilities in tactics and strategy, as well as what in a military leader is called "character": courage, determination, dominating one's opponent, and taking the psychological initiative. Greene chose his subordinates well, dealt diplomatically with both political and partisan leaders, and achieved results truly remarkable in the light of his command, which consisted of a small and inadequately supplied army supplemented by independent partisan groups and undisciplined militia.

In the South, Greene lost every major engagement he personally commanded, usually through the failure of troops at crucial points in the battle, when victory seemed imminent. Frustrating as these situations must have been to him—he had an impulsive temperament and was easily angered—he remained a cautious tactician, never risking a desperate continuation that might have won a battle but might as easily have destroyed his force. Like Washington, he realized the necessity of retaining an army able to fight again; he was willing to retreat, even run, but always to return to the conflict.

Despite his defeats, his Southern strategy achieved all the objectives of his campaigns; Cornwallis and Rawdon won battles but lost control of the lower South. By rapid movement, constant pressure on the enemy, and the use of a variety of methods (raids, harassing supply lines, siege, battles), Greene kept Cornwallis off balance, prevented his controlling the lower South and protecting its Loyalists, and possibly contributed to Cornwallis's decision to attempt a Virginia offensive rather than one in the Carolinas. That decision brought Cornwallis finally to Yorktown, where he surrendered in 1781.

—*Marsha Kass Marks*

FURTHER READING

Alden, John R. *A History of the American Revolution.* New York: Alfred A. Knopf, 1969. A basic general history, providing the necessary perspective. Includes a very clear section describing Greene's campaigns in the South.

Golway, Terry. *Washington's General: Nathanael Greene and the Triumph of the American Revolution.* New York: Henry Holt, 2005. Golway maintains that Greene's appointment as the commander of the revolutionary forces in the South was the decisive moment of the Revolutionary War.

Greene, Francis Vinton. *General Greene.* New York: D. Appleton, 1893. Reprint. Port Washington, N.Y.: Kennikat Press, 1970. A biography as slanted as one would expect from a late nineteenth century descendant of Greene. Nevertheless, well written and reasonably objective, with a nice balance of information on Greene's personal life and military career, the political background, and the prominent individuals whose lives intersected with his.

Greene, George Washington. *The Life of Nathanael Greene, Major-General in the Army of the Revolution.* 3 vols. New York: Hurd and Houghton, 1871. The late nineteenth century flavor of this work by Greene's grandson is amply compensated for by the author's intuitive grasp of his subject's character and development. Includes numerous quotations from primary sources. At age seventeen, the author knew Lafayette, was a friend of Henry Wadsworth Longfellow, and spoke at length with Greene's brothers and contemporaries in their old age.

Hairr, John. *Guilford Courthouse: Nathanael Greene's Victory in Defeat, March 15, 1781.* Cambridge, Mass.: Da Capo Press, 2002. One in a series of books about famous American battlefields, this work recounts the military exploits of Greene and Cornwallis at Guilford Courthouse. Chapter 1, "The Man from Rhode Island: Nathanael Greene," provides a brief overview of Greene's life and military career.

Higginbotham, Don. *The War of American Independence*. New York: Macmillan, 1971. A basic work on the Revolutionary War, but with a certain tendency to draw parallels between the revolution and twentieth century warfare, stretching the comparisons slightly. However, the book has an effective presentation of the overall military situation, specific battles, and the general political background of the time.

Ketchum, Richard M. "Men of the Revolution: III." *American Heritage* 23 (December, 1971): 48-49. A brief but comprehensive biographical sketch accompanied by Charles Willson Peale's portrait of Greene.

McCullough, David. *1776*. New York: Simon & Schuster, 2005. McCullough focuses on one year in the American Revolution, 1776, describing the battles between America's ragtag troops and British forces. Using letters, journals, diaries, and other primary sources, he describes the leadership of Nathanael Greene, George Washington, and General William Howe, as well as the heroic struggles of American soldiers.

Miller, John C. *Triumph of Freedom 1775-1783*. Boston: Little, Brown, 1948. A standard overview of the period, including an effective analysis of both Greene and Cornwallis.

Snow, Richard F. "Battles of the Revolution: Guilford Court House." *American Heritage* 24 (June, 1973): 17. A good summary of the military action at Guilford Courthouse, with color paintings of soldiers of the Delaware Regiment and the Seventy-first Regiment of Foot.

Wickwire, Franklin, and Mary Wickwire. *Cornwallis: The American Adventure*. Boston: Houghton Mifflin, 1970. A major study of Cornwallis, this work presents the war from the British perspective, with attention to the problems of the British political and military system. Although in style somewhat reminiscent of nineteenth century literature, thus giving a quaint flavor to the eighteenth century narrative coupled with twentieth century psychological insights, it is quite clear, explaining without explaining away Cornwallis's failures.

See also: John André; Sir Henry Clinton; First Marquess Cornwallis; William Howe; Thomas Jefferson; George Washington.

Related articles in *Great Events from History: The Eighteenth Century, 1701-1800:* April 19, 1775: Battle of Lexington and Concord; October 19, 1781: Cornwallis Surrenders at Yorktown.

JEAN-BAPTISTE VAQUETTE DE GRIBEAUVAL
French military leader and reformer

After rising through the ranks in the artillery branch of the French army and witnessing the poor performance of French arms in the Seven Years' War, Gribeauval was placed in charge of the branch and initiated many important reforms in the design, production, and use of artillery.

Born: September 15, 1715; Amiens, France
Died: May 9, 1789; Paris, France
Areas of achievement: Military, science and technology

EARLY LIFE
Jean-Baptiste Vaquette de Gribeauval (zhah bahp-teest vah-keht duh gree-boh-val) was the second child of Adrien Vaquette de Freschencourt and Catherine Romanet, both members of the lower French nobility. The family's patent of nobility was only a dozen years old when Jean-Baptiste was born. Adrien, like generations of Vaquettes, was active in local politics, having served as mayor of Amiens in 1711 and as a magistrate on the city's council. When his uncle, a military captain, died, Adrien assumed his title, de Gribeauval.

The younger sons of the family were destined for military careers. At age ten, Jean-Baptiste was placed with an excellent tutor, the Abbé Valart, and later with a fine teacher of mathematics and science. From this point the boy was being primed for a career with the French royal artillery, the branch most likely to advance a young man with few social connections. Adrien placed his son in the artillery school at La Fère when Gribeauval was seventeen.

There Gribeauval underwent mathematical and practical training to prepare him for a career as an engineer and artillery officer. Gribeauval completed his studies after three years and left La Fère with the rank of captain. Appointed a leader of others of his rank, Gribeauval spent the next five years in quiet garrison duty. This changed in 1740 with the onset of the War of the Austrian Succession.

LIFE'S WORK

On April 15, 1743, Gribeauval was named *commissaire extraordinaire*, essentially a wartime promotion. He participated as an artillery officer in several battles of the War of the Austrian Succession, including the French loss at Dettingen in Bavaria, and later in a string of sieges in the Netherlands, including Courtrai, Ypres, Ghent, Bruges, Ostende, Berg op Zoom, and Maastricht. His outstanding military service earned him a permanent promotion (*commissaire ordinaire*) on February 20, 1747. Throughout this period he was in close contact with Joseph de Vallière, who succeeded his father, Jean-Florent de Vallière, to the highest position in the royal artillery corps in 1747.

Over the next few years Gribeauval was garrisoned at Cherbourg, Valognes, and Arras, where he began working on the development of light or field artillery. For nearly a century the French army had depended almost exclusively on huge, heavy, and very cumbersome cannon and mortar that were quite effective during sieges but largely useless on the battlefield. King Frederick the Great of Prussia had been a pioneer in the use of lighter, mobile guns with shorter barrels, which were employed to great effect at Fontenoy in 1745.

Approached in 1752 by two English cannon founders who had developed prototypes, Gribeauval arranged a demonstration for the king at Choisy. However, these light guns failed to match the standard larger guns for range, accuracy, or endurance. In April, 1755, Vallière sent Gribeauval to Prussia to observe Frederick's artillery corps at work. The French officer and Prussian king got along well, and Gribeauval left firmly convinced of the possibilities of mobile field artillery.

When the Seven Years' War broke out in May, 1757, Gribeauval was posted to semiautonomous Danzig to help strengthen its fortifications against the Prussians. Along the way he was hijacked to Vienna, however, where he was promoted to lieutenant colonel and became a close client of the French ambassador Étienne François de Choiseul. He continued to Danzig in July, but his mission failed, and he returned to Vienna.

Maria Theresa (1717-1780), archduchess of Austria and queen of Bohemia and Hungary, convinced the French king to release Gribeauval into her service, and he became an adviser to her imperial artillery service at the rank of colonel major. He participated in the Siege of Neiss and the defense of Dresden, where he proved himself a master of defensive fortification. While still in Austrian service, he was promoted to *commissaire* of the French Royal Artillery and Miners, with the rank of

marchal-de-camp. He remained in Austria, however, where he unsuccessfully defended Schweidnitz in the late summer of 1762. His preparations and actions impressed even Frederick, who arrived to complete the operation. Frederick happily dined with Gribeauval, and Maria Theresa promoted him to lieutenant general. After a short imprisonment at Königsberg, Gribeauval returned to Vienna, and Maria Theresa offered him a position overseeing the construction of new fortresses and establishing new artillery schools. He decided to return to France, however, having been away for seven years. The king awarded him an annuity of twenty-four thousand livres and the new position of inspector general of the Royal Corps of Artillery and commander in chief of the Miners.

With Choiseul in power at Versailles, Gribeauval had a true friend at court. Choiseul had already begun reforming the French artillery system. In 1758 the artillery corps had been divided into thirty companies of one hundred cannoneers each, and this group, in turn, was divided into six brigades of five companies each. In 1761, Choiseul expanded the corps to nine brigades, with the additional firepower added to coastal defense. Vallière, who held the position of director general of the artillery, refused to separate the artillery from the engineers and otherwise stood in the way of changing his father's system.

Given French losses in men and materiel in the war, Choiseul and Gribeauval understood that this was the perfect time to overhaul the entire corps. The result would become known as the Gribeauval system. The first phase in the system was the introduction of guns made of a new metal that was 90 percent copper and 10 percent tin. The gun barrels were cast solid, without decorative casting; the solid barrels were bored with a precision that casting could not accomplish, and the lack of decoration allowed for a smooth turning for the process. The process and the machinery were made uniform across France, so that barrels and ammunition would be completely interchangeable. Gribeauval limited the number of calibers of the guns, giving them the shortest, lightest, and therefore most manageable barrels possible. He also standardized the gun carriages, maintaining the elevation screw and the prepackaged ammunition box that was fitted to the carriage itself.

Vallière and his allies opposed these changes, sparking a pamphlet war over artillery reform. Upon gaining authority in 1772, Vallière held up or rolled back many of the changes. Back in power in 1774, Gribeauval and his allies, including many forward-thinking philosophes, continued on their path. In the end, Gribeauval held the title first inspector general of the Royal Artillery Corps and served as vice president of the King's Council of War.

Gribeauval never married, and in 1769 he bought the estate of Bovelles near Amiens. Among other distinctions, he was awarded the Austrian Grand Croix of the Order of Maria Theresa and the French Grand Croix of the Royal and Military Order of St. Louis. He died in his Paris townhouse after a four-month illness.

SIGNIFICANCE

The Gribeauval system brought French artillery to a state of efficiency that surpassed any in Europe. It remained in place until 1827 and played a key role in the victories of the Revolutionary and Napoleonic armies. Gribeauval's insistence on developing field artillery alongside siege and coastal batteries gave the French a balance that was badly needed in battle. The independence and specialization of the artillery companies—rank and file as well as officers—made them extremely effective and provided an esprit de corps. His insistence on interchangeable gun parts was extended to small arms and allowed for both mass production and the provision of standard ammunition on a scale never seen before. Through treatises written by Heinrich Otto de Scheel, a Danish author who supported Gribeauval's reforms, and other writers, the reforms found their way across Europe and to the Americas, where they played an important role in military developments in the United States.

—Joseph P. Byrne

FURTHER READING

Alder, Ken. *Engineering the Revolution: Arms and Enlightenment in France, 1763-1815*. Princeton, N.J.: Princeton University Press, 1997. Presents a close study of the Gribeauvalist-Vallièrist controversy and the resulting Gribeauvalist reforms. Especially good in outlining the ways the conflict affected the French military during the French Revolution and the Napoleonic period.

Jones, Colin. "The Military Revolution and the Professionalization of the French Army Under the Ancien Régime." In *The Military Revolution and the State, 1500-1800*, edited by Michael Duffy. Exeter, England: Exeter Studies in History, 1980. Broad overview placing Gribeauval and his reforms in the context of the changing patterns in eighteenth century military science and training.

Kennett, Lee. *The French Armies in the Seven Years' War: A Study in Military Organization and Administration*. Durham, N.C.: Duke University Press, 1967. Valuable for understanding the environment from which Gribeauval came just prior to his rise to authority and the blatant weaknesses in the French system.

Nardin, Pierre. *Gribeauval, lieutenant général des armées du roi, 1715-1789*. Paris: Fondation pour les Études de Défense National, 1982. This book is the only modern monograph dedicated to Gribeauval and the evolution of French artillery in the eighteenth century.

Scheel, Heinrich Otto de. *De Scheel's Treatise on Artillery*. Translated by Jonathan Williams, edited by Donald E. Graves. Alexandria Bay, N.Y.: Museum Restoration Service, 1984. De Scheel was a Danish Gribeauvalist whose very influential treatise of 1777 encapsulated the Gribeauval system. It is thus a key primary source. Gribeauval is discussed in both the introduction and the text.

See also: Étienne François de Choiseul; First Marquess Cornwallis; Maria Theresa; Gaspard Monge; Marquis de Montalembert.

Related articles in *Great Events from History: The Eighteenth Century, 1701-1800:* December 16, 1740-November 7, 1748: War of the Austrian Succession; January, 1756-February 15, 1763: Seven Years' War.

HAKUIN
Japanese religious leader, writer, and artist

Revered as the father of modern Rinzai Zen Buddhism, Hakuin revived the Rinzai sect through his teaching and writings and his emphasis on the need to practice meditation, or the art of zazen, *with the aid of koans, or Zen riddles. His system of koan arrangement transformed Zen teaching, and his lectures drew huge crowds. Hakuin was also a brilliant painter, poet, and calligrapher.*

Born: 1685/1686; Hara, Suruga Province (now Shizuoka Prefecture), Japan
Died: 1768/1769; Hara, Suruga Province (now Shizuoka Prefecture), Japan
Also known as: Nagasawa Iwajiro (birth name); Hakuin Ekaku; Hakuin Zenji
Areas of achievement: Philosophy, religion and theology, art, scholarship

EARLY LIFE

Hakuin (hah-koo-een) was born Nagasawa Iwajiro in a small village at the foot of Mt. Fuji in Japan. This village, Hara, was a post station on the Tokaido road linking Kyoto and Edo (now Tokyo), and Hakuin's parents owned an inn used as a stopover for travelers. Hakuin was the youngest of five children in the Nagasawa family. His father was from the Sugiyama samurai family, but he had adopted the Nagasawa surname of his wife's family.

As a young child, Hakuin regularly accompanied his devout mother to the local Zen Buddhist temple. Hakuin was highly intelligent, and at the age of four he had already memorized hundreds of songs and could recall temple sermons. At the age of seven, a temple priest recited a sutra (scripture attributed to Buddha), which graphically described the punishment of sinners in the horrifying Eight Hot Hells. Hakuin was so frightened that he began daily religious exercises, such as reciting sutras, praying, and performing prostrations. He hoped that such a strict regimen would help him escape hell. However, after a few years, he realized that the only way to avoid hell was to become a monk and devote all of his time to religion.

On March 16, 1699, Hakuin received his preliminary ordination at Shoin-ji, the local temple. Soon he went to another temple, where he studied classical Chinese—the language of the Buddhist texts—for the next few years.

LIFE'S WORK

By Hakuin's time, Zen Buddhism had already existed in Japan for centuries. Originally developed in China, where it took its name (*Ch'an* or *Qan*) from the Sanskrit word *dhyana* (seated meditation), Zen emphasized the value of meditation, rather than adherence to doctrine and verbal concepts, as a means to enlightenment (satori). These teachings, which blended South Asian and East Asian meditative traditions, had been influential in Japan, but by the early eighteenth century, Zen Buddhism in Japan was in a serious decline. All three major Zen traditions—Soto, Obaku, and Rinzai—saw fewer and fewer students and temples.

During his early pilgrimages, Hakuin studied Buddhist scriptures and traveled from temple to temple to hear discourses by priests. He was disappointed with the state of Zen Buddhism, particularly his Rinzai sect, whose priests seemed too worldly, passive, and quietist. They appeared unwilling to help students strive for satori, and their practice of *zazen* and koan lacked energy.

At the age eighteen Hakuin read about the great Chinese Zen master Yantou, who could not escape being brutally murdered by bandits. This story convinced Hakuin that Buddhist enlightenment could not save him from hell's torments. Disillusioned, Hakuin rejected religion and decided to study literature, painting, and calligraphy.

That year, Hakuin studied poetry and calligraphy with the celebrated scholar-priest Bao. While at Bao's temple, the news came that Hakuin's beloved mother had died suddenly. Deeply grieving, Hakuin thought about hell and thus was led to prayer. When he saw a group of books piled up in the temple courtyard, he picked up *Changuan cejin* (c. 1600; *Meditating with Koans*, 1992), a work by Zhuhong (1535-1615), and then found and read the story of the famous Chinese monk Ciming, who prevented the extinction of the Linji school of Zen Buddhism during the Sung Dynasty.

Hakuin's Rinzai sect was the Japanese branch of the Chinese Linji tradition, established by the Zen patriarch Linji in ninth century China. During the twelfth century, the Linji line had spread to Japan, where it became the Rinzai sect (or Rinzai school) of Buddhism. Hakuin was inspired and encouraged by the Ciming story to resume his own search for religious awakening, leading him to reform and revive the Rinzai tradition, just as Ciming had saved the Linji line.

He continued his travels from temple to temple. In 1708, at the age of twenty-three, Hakuin visited the Eigan-ji temple in Takada, a coastal city. While meditating, he heard the sound of a distant bell and finally experienced his first satori, the deep and sudden awareness of one's true nature that is the spiritual goal of Zen Buddhism.

Soon after leaving Eigan-ji, Hakuin studied eight months with the elderly monk Shoju Rojin (1642-1721), who lived in a remote hermitage. Shoju was a demanding, uncompromising teacher who emphasized that religious attainment was not as easy as Hakuin thought. Shoju assigned difficult koans, insulted Hakuin, and always pushed him to practice to attain satori. In the winter of 1708, Hakuin left Shoju's hermitage to continue his journey. He never again saw Shoju, and only years later did he realize the value of Shoju's teaching. At the age of forty-one, Hakuin acknowledged Shoju as his most significant spiritual influence, and in his late fifties, Hakuin called Shoju the only genuine Zen teacher of the time.

From 1709 to 1716, between the ages of twenty-four and thirty-one, Hakuin engaged in practice subsequent to satori, attempting to integrate the tranquil part of his life with the active or everyday life. Hakuin returned to Shoin-ji temple, the temple where he had been ordained. Shoin-ji was destitute, with no priest and hardly any temple furnishings; Hakuin became its head priest. For the next decade, he lived in poverty at the temple. Ten years later, in 1726, he experienced the final, great enlightenment while reading the *Lotus Sutra*, Buddha's supreme preaching. Having achieved total enlightenment, he now dedicated himself to teaching others.

For the next forty-two years, from 1726 to 1768, Hakuin lectured at Shoin-ji, taught throughout Japan, and published his writings. Shoin-ji eventually became a religious center, attracting hundreds of students. Hakuin certified more than eighty disciples. Sometime in 1768 or 1769, he died.

SIGNIFICANCE

Hakuin revitalized and reformed Japanese Zen Buddhism after several centuries of decline and deterioration. Two years after he died, an imperial order granted him the title of Zenshi, or Zen master. Patriarch of modern Rinzai Zen Buddhism, Hakuin also was a dynamic teacher, writer, and artist who worked to bring Zen learning to all people.

A commoner himself, Hakuin produced writings and calligraphy to teach his lay followers, and he often wrote in vernacular, popular styles to reach the common people. As one of the most influential and celebrated Zen artists as well, Hakuin produced thousands of beautiful paintings, including humorous self-caricatures. In addition, he was radical in his belief that meditation and religious awakening in the midst of daily living within society was superior to the experience of monks or hermits in solitude or living outside society.

Instead of the intellectual and worldly preoccupation of contemporary monks, Hakuin's teaching and practice emphasized the rich, spiritual essence of Zen and the tradition of rigorous meditation in conjunction with rigorous koan practice. Hakuin revolutionized koan training by organizing traditional koans by level of difficulty. In this new system, the student had to resolve koans in a specific order. Hakuin also invented new koans, including the most famous: the paradox of hearing the sound of one hand clapping. His systematized koan study became the standard, and it continues into the twenty-first century.

—*Alice Myers*

FURTHER READING

Cleary, Thomas. *Secrets of the "Blue Cliff Record": Zen Comments by Hakuin and Tenkei*. Boston: Shambhala, 2000. First published in China in the twelfth century, the *Blue Cliff Record* is a Zen classic consisting of koans that deeply challenge the mind. Bibliography.

Hakuin. *Essential Teachings of Zen Master Hakuin: A Translation of the Sokko-roku Kaien-fusetsu (Lectures on the Records of Old Sokko)*. Translated by Norman Waddell. Boston: Shambhala, 1994. A significant text that provides insight into Hakuin's vision and fundamental teachings. Illustrated, with a bibliography and an index.

_____. *Hakuin's Commentary on "The Heart Sutra."* Translated by Norman Waddell. Boston: Shambhala, 1996. The text of *The Heart Sutra* is included after Hakuin's commentary. Although very brief, *The Heart Sutra* is believed to contain the essence of Buddhist teaching on wisdom and is one of the most popular religious texts in East Asia. Includes illustrations, with a self portrait by Hakuin.

_____. *Wild Ivy: The Spiritual Autobiography of Zen Master Hakuin*. Translated by Norman Waddell. Boston: Shambhala, 1999. The translator's long introduction provides useful background information to supplement the spiritual autobiography, which Hakuin wrote at the age of eighty-one. Illustrations include

Hakuin's calligraphy and ink drawings. Extensive chapter notes, index, and a bibliography of sources in Japanese and English.

Miura, Isshu, and Ruth Fuller Sasaki. *The Zen Koan: Its History and Use in Rinzai Zen.* New York: Harcourt, Brace & World, 1993. Originally published in 1965, this is the first scholarly study of the origin and development of traditional koan practice. The second of three chapters is devoted to Hakuin and the Rinzai koan system. Ten ink drawings by Hakuin.

Stevens, John. *Zen Masters: A Maverick, a Master of Masters, and a Wandering Poet.* New York: Kodan-

sha International, 1999. Very readable biographies of three celebrated—and very different from each other—Zen masters: Hakuin, Ikkyu Sojun (1394-1481), and Ryokan Taigu (1758-1831). Illustrated.

See also: Chikamatsu Monzaemon; Chŏng Sŏn; Dai Zhen; Honda Toshiaki; Ogyū Sorai; Suzuki Harunobu; Tokugawa Yoshimune.

Related articles in *Great Events from History: The Eighteenth Century, 1701-1800:* June 20, 1703: Chikamatsu Produces *The Love Suicides at Sonezaki*; December, 1720: Japan Lifts Ban on Foreign Books.

ALEXANDER HAMILTON
American politician

Hamilton served as aide-de-camp to Washington during the American Revolution and was a delegate to the Philadelphia Convention of 1787 and signer of the Constitution. An early advocate of a strong national government, he coauthored The Federalist *and was the first secretary of the U.S. treasury.*

Born: January 11, 1755; Nevis, British West Indies
Died: July 12, 1804; New York, New York
Areas of achievement: Government and politics, military

EARLY LIFE
Alexander Hamilton was the illegitimate son of a Scottish ne'er-do-well and a woman previously arrested for adultery. He was born in 1755, although at times he claimed that his birth year was 1757. Hamilton spent his early years in abject poverty on the Caribbean island of his birth, Nevis. After his mother's death, he worked for a merchant family on St. Croix, where he flourished, as his unusual abilities brought him to the attention of his employers. Hamilton quickly rose to be something more than a clerk but less than a partner. By age sixteen, he was giving orders to ship captains, making decisions on when cargoes should be sold, and firing and hiring company lawyers. When not working, he studied on his own.

In 1773, Hamilton's employers, recognizing his precocious genius, sent him to the mainland for his first formal education. From 1773 to 1774, he lived with Elias Boudinot, a future president of the Continental Congress, and studied at a Presbyterian academy in Elizabethtown, New Jersey. In this period, Hamilton socialized with

such future patriots and political leaders as William Livingston, Richard Stockton, Philip Schuyler, and Henry Brockholst Livingston. In 1774, Hamilton entered Kings College (now Columbia University) as a sophomore. In 1775, he anonymously published a pamphlet supporting the patriot cause; this was Hamilton's first political activity.

LIFE'S WORK
In March, 1776, Alexander Hamilton dropped out of college to become an artillery captain in the New York militia. He quickly came to the attention of senior officers, and in 1777 he joined George Washington's staff. Hamilton's relationship with the general was complex. The childless Washington often treated Hamilton as the son he never had. Hamilton, whose father was never present in his life, revered Washington, but at the same time he felt stifled working for "The Great Man," as his staff officers called him. As Washington's aide-de-camp, Hamilton had a unique view of the war and the politics of the revolution. It was during this period that he became a committed nationalist, as he saw the states squabbling over issues while the national army went without adequate food and other provisions.

The young Hamilton was short, slim, and not particularly athletic. He was brilliant as an administrator but hardly suited to frontline command. Yet he longed for the opportunity to achieve battlefield glory. This desire strained his relationship with Washington, and in February, 1781, he resigned his position. In July, Hamilton returned with his rank of lieutenant colonel to command a battalion, and at Yorktown he was finally given his opportunity for combat glory. Hamilton led his battalion in a brief and heroic assault on a British position. He was thrilled with his exploit but bitter that Congress never saw fit to award him a medal for his heroism. Shortly after the victory at Yorktown, Hamilton returned to civilian life.

In 1780, Hamilton was married to Elizabeth Schuyler. His father-in-law, General Schuyler, was one of the richest men in America and a powerful politician in New York. This family connection eliminated the taint of his illegitimate birth. In April, 1782, he began preparing for a career as a lawyer, and in July he was admitted to the bar. At first, Hamilton was ambivalent about his new profession, writing to the Marquis de Lafayette that he was "studying the art of fleecing my neighbours." Hamilton quickly threw himself into his law practice and was soon representing many of the wealthiest men in his state. Many of his clients were former Loyalists who sought to regain property taken during the revolution, yet Hamilton had few scruples about representing his former enemies. Between 1783 and 1789, he was involved in massive litigation over huge land claims in upstate New York. He also represented banks, shippers, and merchants. Hamilton's fundamentally conservative nature was reflected by his clients and his law practice.

During this period, Hamilton ventured into politics. The New York legislature chose him as a delegate to the Continental Congress (1782, 1783, 1787, 1788) and to the Annapolis Convention of 1786. Through his political connections, he served a short time as a collector of taxes for the Congress. In 1787, Hamilton was also elected to the New York legislature. With the exception of his election to the convention called to ratify the Constitution, this was the only popular election Hamilton ever won. Although a brilliant political theorist, his personal style prevented him from being a popular candidate.

The Annapolis Convention of 1786 was called to negotiate a trade agreement among the American states under the Articles of Confederation. The convention failed: Most of the states did not bother to send delegates. The meeting at Annapolis led to a call for another convention, however, to be held in Philadelphia the following year. That convention would write the Constitution.

Hamilton was one of three delegates from New York to the Philadelphia Convention of 1787. He received the unanimous support of the state legislature. Even his political enemies (and he had many by this time) believed that Hamilton was one of the ablest men in the state. At the beginning of the convention, a fellow delegate wrote that "Colo. Hamilton is deservedly celebrated for his tal-

Alexander Hamilton. (Library of Congress)

ents. He is a practitioner of the Law, and reputed to be a finished Scholar. . . . His manners are tinctured with stiffness, and sometimes with a degree of vanity that is highly disagreeable." While haughty and arrogant, Hamilton was also exceedingly handsome, with auburn hair, deep blue eyes, and a charming smile.

At Philadelphia, Hamilton was limited in his effectiveness. The other two New York delegates, John Lansing and Robert Yates, were opposed to a strong national government, which Hamilton supported. Thus, Hamilton was able to participate in debates, but his votes on the developing document were canceled by the rest of New York's delegation. In his first major speech, Hamilton argued for an extremely strong central government and a narrow and limited role for the states. Hamilton asserted his belief "that the British Govt. was the best in the world: and that he doubted much whether any thing short of it would do in America." He argued that the "hereditary interest of the King" prevented the dangers of corruption in England and that, for the American chief executive, "the English model was the only good one on this subject." His plan of government, which never received the support of any other delegates, called for a chief executive to serve for life and the appointment of state governors by the national government. This speech has led Hamilton's detractors to conclude that he was a monarchist. While that is perhaps an exaggeration, it is clear that Hamilton did favor a lifetime chief executive and that he leaned toward ruling over the people, rather than the people ruling themselves.

On June 29, Hamilton left the convention, in part because it was not headed in the direction he favored and in part because Yates and Lansing had outvoted him on most issues. Hamilton also wanted to return to his political base in New York and to the Continental Congress. Early in July, however, Yates and Lansing left the convention, and three days later, Hamilton returned. For the rest of the summer, Hamilton moved in and out of the convention. The rules of the convention required that each state have at least two delegates present to vote on the emerging document. Thus, Hamilton could debate but not vote. His most important contributions came in the debates that took place in September and in his work on the committee of style. At the end of the convention, he persuaded his fellow delegates to sign the document, even though New York as a state was not represented under the convention rules.

After the convention, Hamilton actively supported the new Constitution. In collaboration with fellow New Yorker John Jay and with Virginian James Madison, Hamilton planned and wrote a series of essays collectively known as *The Federalist* (1787-1788). All three authors wrote under the pen name Publius. Of the eighty-five separate essays, Hamilton wrote fifty-one and collaborated on another three. Madison's contributions, which included the famous numbers 10, 14, and 51, ended when he left New York in March, 1788, while Jay's writings were limited by illness. Hamilton continued the project without Madison and Jay, producing the last twenty-one essays on his own, including the powerful number 78, which explained the role of the judiciary in the constitutional system. *The Federalist* was written to convince New York voters to support the Constitution, but this goal was not really achieved. The majority of those elected to the New York ratifying convention opposed the Constitution. Neither the essays of Publius nor Hamilton's own speeches at the ratifying convention convinced the delegates to support the Constitution. Ultimately, New York ratified it by a slim three-vote margin, because a number of opponents of the Constitution concluded that with the ratification in Virginia and Massachusetts they had no choice but to ratify. While it was not persuasive in New York, *The Federalist* is generally con-

sidered to contain the single most important contemporary analysis of the Constitution and has been cited repeatedly by scholars and courts in the twentieth century.

With the organization of the new government, Hamilton became the nation's first secretary of the treasury. In his first two years in that office, Hamilton organized the nation's finances, established a mint and a system of creating money, and convinced the Congress and the president to support a national bank. He attempted to create a national program to support manufacturing and economic development, but this was defeated.

Hamilton's *Report Relative to a Provision for the Support of Public Credit* (1795), presented to the Congress in January, 1795, laid out a program for putting the nation on a sound financial footing. Hamilton urged that the national government pay off all foreign and domestic debt incurred by the Congress and the states during the revolution and confederation period. Two aspects of this report were particularly controversial. Hamilton recommended that all bondholders receive the face value of their bonds. This meant that speculators who had purchased war bonds at far below their original value would reap great profits, while those who had actually risked their money to support the American Revolution would not even get their original investment back. Hamilton also recommended that the national government pay off all unpaid state war debts. This proposal offended Virginia, which had paid off most of its debts and did not want to have to pay the debts of other states as well. Congressmen from states with small debts, such as Georgia, North Carolina, and Maryland, also opposed this plan. Representatives from states with large debts, including South Carolina, New York, and Massachusetts, naturally supported the plan.

Hamilton's goals in his debt-funding plan were not to aid one section of the nation and harm another. Nor did he seek to enrich speculators at the expense of patriotic investors who were forced, because of a postwar depression, to sell their bonds at low prices. Hamilton simply sought to put the nation on a sound economic footing. Nevertheless, high motives and sound economic policy were not enough to push through his proposal, and Congress adopted it only after much political maneuvering, which included an agreement to move the nation's capital from New York City closer to Virginia. Besides offering some political advantages, the Virginians hoped that the move would stimulate economic development in the Chesapeake region.

The creation of the Bank of the United States was Hamilton's second major accomplishment as secretary of the treasury. In the cabinet, Secretary of State Thomas Jefferson and Attorney General Edmund Randolph both opposed the bank. Congressional opposition was led by Madison, Hamilton's former collaborator on *The Federalist*. Hamilton's arguments in favor of the bank were more than economic: They were also constitutional. He asserted that the Constitution needed to be read broadly, and he argued that Congress must have the power to go beyond the specific "enumerated powers" in the Constitution through the "necessary and proper clause" of the document. In the cabinet debate, Hamilton prevailed, and Washington signed the bank bill into law.

Hamilton's "Report on Manufactures," delivered to the Congress in December, 1791, argued in favor of stimulating manufacturing in the nation through tariff and tax policies. Hamilton's report detailed the types of manufacturing needed, including iron, leather, textiles, sugar, gunpowder, paper, and books. The report anticipated an America in which manufacturing, not agriculture, would be the dominant economic activity. This report was unacceptable, however, to the agrarian America of the 1790's.

In the cabinet, Hamilton proved a tireless and ruthless advocate of expanding national power. He came close to accusing Jefferson of treason when the secretary of state publicly indicated his disagreement with Hamilton. As a cabinet official, Hamilton helped organize the Federalist Party to support his economic and political policies. In 1794, he advocated the use of massive military force against hard-pressed western farmers who opposed his policy of taxing the producers of whiskey. Hamilton's role in the Whiskey Rebellion, was, in the end, almost comical. He led a large army into western Pennsylvania, where a handful of farmers were arrested and then released. Hamilton once again sought military glory, but this time he appeared to be an oppressor of the people; instead of glory, he won contempt.

In 1795, Hamilton left Washington's cabinet for the private practice of law. He quickly became one of the most successful attorneys in New York. In 1798, he became inspector general of the army when it appeared that a war with France was likely. This was his last public position. Once again, however, military glory eluded Hamilton, and he returned to law after the crisis with France ended.

In his law practice, he was enormously successful, with clients begging for his services. In 1802, Hamilton earned nearly $13,000, an incredibly large sum for the period. Most of his law practice centered on marine insurance, banking law, and other litigation tied to commerce. Hamilton remained involved in politics, but his aggressive personal style and his penchant for intrigue served only to undermine the Federalist Party that he had helped to build in the early 1790's. Hamilton's public and private attacks on John Adams did little except to aid the fortunes of the Democratic-Republicans led by Jefferson and Aaron Burr. In 1804, he vigorously opposed Burr's attempt to gain the governorship of New York, so Burr challenged him to a duel, which took place on July 11. Hamilton once again had an opportunity for glory on the field of "combat." Once again, however, he was unsuccessful. He died, on July 12, of his wounds.

SIGNIFICANCE

Alexander Hamilton was one of the great figures of the revolutionary era. He was brilliant, charming, and a first-rate administrator. Yet he was also vain, overly ambitious, arrogant, and insecure over his status and place in the world. Hamilton's influence was undermined by his inability to get along with other leaders of the age. He was also something of a misfit.

Reared in the West Indies, Hamilton was a monarchist when he first came to America. Although he quickly joined the patriot cause, his political views, as expressed in the Constitutional Convention and in Washington's cabinet, were almost always anti-Republican; he had less faith in representative government than any of the other Founding Fathers. More than most public figures of the period, Hamilton favored a strong chief executive, if not a king. He was similarly out of step with America in his grandiose plans for the nation's economy. Nevertheless, his contributions to American politics, economics, and constitutional theory make him a towering figure of his age.

—*Paul Finkelman*

FURTHER READING

Bowen, Catherine Dinker. *Miracle at Philadelphia: The Story of the Constitutional Convention, May to September, 1787*. Boston: Little, Brown, 1966. Probably the best narrative history of the convention, and especially appropriate for high school and undergraduate students. Includes good details on convention delegates.

Brookhiser, Richard. *Alexander Hamilton, American*. New York: Free Press, 1999. Brookhiser provides an appreciation and assessment of Hamilton, demonstrating why he was one America's most important Founding Fathers.

Chernow, Ron. *Alexander Hamilton*. New York: Penguin Books, 2004. A comprehensive and meticulously detailed biography, offering new information about Hamilton's ancestry, personality, and relationships with George Washington, Thomas Jefferson, John Adams, and Aaron Burr. Chernow calls Hamilton "the father of the American government," the Founding Father who set the United States on a course of liberal democracy and capitalist economy.

Cooke, Jacob E. *Alexander Hamilton: A Biography.* New York: Charles Scribner's Sons, 1982. A short, readable biography by one of the nation's leading Hamilton scholars. An excellent place to begin research on Hamilton.

_____, ed. *Alexander Hamilton: A Profile.* New York: Hill & Wang, 1967. Contains essays on Hamilton by a wide range of scholars, with articles both favorable and unfavorable to Hamilton.

Emery, Noemie. *Alexander Hamilton: An Intimate Portrait.* New York: G. P. Putnam's Sons, 1982. Much like the James Thomas Flexner biography, although this volume gives more attention to Hamilton's later life.

Flexner, James Thomas. *The Young Hamilton: A Biography.* Boston: Little, Brown, 1978. A superbly written study by the author of a leading biography of George Washington. Focuses on Hamilton's early years and on his psychological development. A fascinating, accessible study.

Hamilton, Alexander. *The Reports of Alexander Hamilton.* Edited by Jacob E. Cooke. New York: Harper & Row, 1964. Contains Hamilton's reports on public credit, the Bank of the United States, and manufacturers. Also contains Hamilton's constitutional arguments in favor of the bank. The reports are models of lucidity and can be read by students, nonspecialists, and scholars.

Hamilton, Alexander, James Madison, and John Jay. *The Federalist.* Edited by Henry B. Dawson. New York: J. and A. McLeon, 1788. Reprint. Cambridge, Mass.: Belknap Press, 1961. Various editions are available in both paperback and clothbound formats, generally including introductions by major scholars. *The Federalist* papers reveal much of Hamilton's political philosophy, although they should be read with care because they were originally written to gain support for the Constitution and not as political theory.

Harper, John Lamberton. *American Machiavelli: Alexander Hamilton and the Origins of U.S. Foreign Policy.* New York: Cambridge University Press, 2004. Focuses on Hamilton's influence on American foreign policy, placing Hamilton's character, personality, and vision in relation to the Renaissance diplomat and thinker Machiavelli.

Mitchell, Broadus. *Alexander Hamilton: A Concise Biography.* New York: Oxford University Press, 1976. An excellent one-volume study by one of Hamilton's major biographers. Mitchell is also the author of a more elaborate two-volume study of Hamilton. This book covers the same ground, but with less detail.

See also: John Adams; John André; John Jay; Thomas Jefferson; James Madison; Robert Morris; George Washington.

Related articles in *Great Events from History: The Eighteenth Century, 1701-1800:* September 17, 1787: U.S. Constitution Is Adopted; October 27, 1787-May, 1788: Publication of *The Federalist*; 1790's: First U.S. Political Parties; July-November, 1794: Whiskey Rebellion.

JOHN HANCOCK
American politician and businessman

The first signer of the Declaration of Independence, Hancock was a wealthy Boston merchant and a notable example of those aristocratic patriots who invested much money as well as much time in the cause of liberty. Hancock was a leader in Massachusetts colonial politics, president of the Second Continental Congress, and governor of Massachusetts.

Born: January 12, 1737; North Braintree (now Quincy), Massachusetts
Died: October 8, 1793; Quincy, Massachusetts
Areas of achievement: Government and politics, business

EARLY LIFE

John Hancock was born in what is now Quincy, Massachusetts, just south of Boston. The gentle hills, streams, and tidal marshes led to coves and beaches of the coastal plain. It was a pleasant place for a young boy to grow up. He started his education in a "dame school," where he learned the rudiments of reading, writing, and arithmetic. At the age of seven, his life was suddenly altered with the death of his father, the minister of the local congregation.

John, along with his mother and his two siblings—Mary and Ebenezer, ages nine and three—had to vacate the local parsonage, and so went to live with the paternal grandparents in the Lexington parsonage. Both father and grandfather were Congregational (Puritan) ministers, and both were named John Hancock.

Thomas Hancock, the one remaining son and John's uncle, was a wealthy merchant and the proprietor of the Bible and Three Crowns, a book bindery and retailer for English publications in America. He had no children of his own and, well aware of his responsibilities to his family, adopted his young nephew John and brought him to live in the palatial Hancock mansion on Beacon Hill in Boston. There he was tutored for a year before entering the public Latin School, where he translated from Julius Caesar's *Commentaries* and Cicero's *Orations* and read history, philosophy, and theology from seven o'clock in the morning until five o'clock in the afternoon. In his spare time he learned the fine art of handwriting, the result of which can be seen in his signature on the Declaration of Independence.

At the age of thirteen, Hancock entered Harvard College. He was described as "graceful and aristocratic" in bearing, of medium height for the time (5 feet, 4 inches), of medium build, and with carefully groomed brown hair, a handsome face, and well-tailored, expensive clothing.

In 1760, Hancock was twenty-three years of age. He had finished college and had worked hard in his uncle's importing business for six years. It was time, Thomas thought, for his nephew to take an extended business trip to London to learn how the business operated overseas. He needed to become acquainted with British merchants and traders who could help him prosper. He also needed the direct exposure to British culture. The trip took from June 3 to July 10 just to get to London. There followed an entire year of business meetings and social gatherings, and in July, 1761, Hancock returned to the colonies satisfied that he had represented the company well and had expanded its contracts. Hancock maintained the reputation established by his uncle, and his associates in London believed that his uncle would have an able successor.

The succession was to take place sooner than anyone had anticipated. On January 1, 1763, Thomas announced that his nephew was being taken into full partnership in the business. Thomas had just enough time to work a smooth transition of leadership to his nephew before he died in 1764, at the age of sixty-one. The result was that John Hancock was the proprietor of a lucrative business and a very wealthy man. He inherited two-thirds of an estate valued at £100,000.

LIFE'S WORK

John Hancock's uncle's death not only pushed him into management of a large business but also quite naturally prompted him to take a more active role in politics. From 1739 to 1752, his uncle had been a selectman (the equivalent of a city councilman). Involving himself as he did in the various social and political clubs in his uncle's stead, it was no surprise that Hancock was elected selectman in March, 1765. At the age of twenty-eight, he was the youngest of the five selectmen on the town council.

These events coincided with the beginning of the revolutionary era, which historians usually peg at 1763, with the conclusion of the French and Indian War (1754-1763) and problems of the enlarged British Empire. The Sugar Act was enacted in 1764, the year of Thomas Hancock's death. The first real crisis of the revolutionary period followed Parliament's passage of the Stamp Act in 1765, which Boston sharply opposed. The issue was political sovereignty, and the principle was that the colonists could be taxed only by their own assemblies. The

Massachusetts General Court called for an intercolonial assembly to meet in New York in October, 1765, as the Stamp Act Congress. The Boston Sons of Liberty intimidated Andrew Oliver, the brother-in-law of Lieutenant Governor Thomas Hutchinson, into resigning his post as stamp master, and a mob demolished the furnishings in Hutchinson's home.

Meanwhile, Hancock wrote letters to his London correspondents criticizing the Stamp Act. He refused to send his ships to sea "under a stamp," demanding his rights under the English constitution. He sent his usual orders for goods but with the stipulation that the orders would automatically be canceled if the Stamp Act were not repealed. He and some 250 other Boston merchants joined a nonimportation agreement refusing to buy a long list of British items. Since some of the British merchants were also members of Parliament, the boycott was one of several significant influences in persuading the British government to repeal the hated law. Hancock provided food and wine on the Common, fireworks displays, and the like to encourage a patriotic spirit. He was also generous in extending credit to members of the non-importation agreement.

In 1766, Hancock was chosen as one of Boston's representatives to the Massachusetts General Court, the colonial legislature. There he served on some thirty committees besides continuing as a member of the Boston town council and managing one of the largest businesses in the area. In 1767, he was reelected to both political positions.

In the same year, he bought Clark's Wharf and renamed it Hancock's Wharf. His was the second largest docking facility in Boston and brought in usage fees and rents of £150 a year. It was also in the year 1767 that Parliament passed the Townshend Acts, levying revenue tariffs on tea, lead, paper, glass, and paint. Hancock joined with most of the other members of the General Court in declaring these acts to be an infringement on the "natural and constitutional rights" of Americans, since they were not represented in the legislature (Parliament) that created the laws; only local assemblies had the right to tax their constituents. One of the most objectionable portions of the law, however, was that the revenue was to pay the salaries of royal governors, judges, and other Crown appointees in the colonies, thereby making them less dependent on the colonial assemblies.

Hancock's political involvement made him a special target for British crown officials enforcing the customs laws. He probably did his share of smuggling to avoid what he considered unconstitutional customs duties, but

as a good businessman, he kept good records and traded in mostly nontaxable goods. On April 8, 1768, customs officials boarded and seized Hancock's ship *Lydia* (named after his aunt and mother by adoption). The colonies, though, were ruled by correct legal procedure, and Attorney General Jonathan Sewell ordered the ship released and the charges dropped because the officials lacked the legal authority to go below deck.

The *Liberty* incident, however, was not so easily resolved. On May 9, 1768, the *Liberty*, a small single-masted vessel owned by Hancock, reached the port of Boston inbound from Madeira at sunset. Customs officials had to wait until the next day to board the ship. Under cover of darkness, the crew worked unloading much of the cargo. Oddly enough, the captain collapsed and died on deck, and thus could not testify in the case. When the customs officers boarded the *Liberty,* they found only twenty-five pipes (very large casks) of wine. Hancock was accused of landing one hundred pipes (12,600 gallons valued at £3,000). He was further charged in June with loading whale oil and tar without first giving bond that the cargo's destination was within the limits of the trade laws. Although that was a technical violation of the law, the custom had always been to load first and give bond later before clearing port. Thus, Hancock stood by helplessly while Crown officials sailed the sloop away from his dock and anchored it under the covering guns of a British man-of-war.

Most Americans at the time were so preoccupied with arguing about who was going to levy taxes and under what circumstances that they overlooked the most ominous aspect of the case, namely, that Hancock was tried in an Admiralty court without jury rather than in a common-law court by a jury of his peers. It was almost as if a civilian were being court-martialed. This violated one of the most cherished and important rights of Englishmen who lived in America. Hancock's defense attorney, John Adams, hammered away at both points: the limitations of legislative authority of Parliament in America and of Admiralty Court jurisdiction in America. Adams was particularly eloquent, charging the British government with attempting to deprive Englishmen living in America of their cherished rights. The presiding judge found against Hancock and ordered the *Liberty* sold and the proceeds divided one-third to the colony, one-third to Governor Francis Bernard, and one-third to the informers (in this case, the customs officials). Hancock thus lost his vessel and cargo, but not his fortune, his prestige as a patriot, or his influence in Massachusetts.

When the *Liberty* was put up for sale, not a single person in the colonies bid for it. Not to be outdone, the customs commissioners finally bought it themselves and armed the *Liberty* as a patrol vessel. The anger, however, had spread far beyond Massachusetts. The *Liberty*, turned into a coast guard cutter, came into port at Newport, Rhode Island, in July, 1769, and was confronted by a mob that stormed the vessel and burned it to the waterline.

Nervous about the unrest and mob actions in Massachusetts, Governor Bernard sent to General Thomas Gage in New York requesting two regiments of British troops to keep order in Boston. The governor also refused to convene the colonial assembly, so the Boston town meeting called a special convention of all the towns in Massachusetts. Nearly one hundred towns sent delegates to the meeting at Faneuil Hall in Boston on September 22, 1768. The next month tensions were high when twelve hundred British troops occupied the town of Boston, which had only fifteen thousand citizens. Events finally exploded at the Boston Massacre on March 5, 1770,

when British troops, menaced by a mob, fired into the crowd, killing five and wounding several others. John Adams demonstrated his integrity and fairness in defending the British soldiers. So did the colonial jury, which acquitted them except for minor punishments. That same month, the British parliament repealed the Townshend Acts except for the tax on tea.

In April of 1770, Hancock was reelected to the General Court by an incredible 511-2 vote. In August, he was elected moderator to preside over Boston town meetings. Numerous letters were sent from the assembly stating public positions of the elected representatives. In the fall of 1773, a subcommittee was formed, including Hancock, and submitted to the assembly for unanimous approval the following statement: "We are far from desiring that the connection between Britain and America should be broken. *Esto perpetual*, is our ardent wish, but upon terms only of Equal Liberty. . . ."

As if he were not already busy enough, Hancock was elected treasurer of Harvard College that same fall. About the same time, four merchant ships, the *Dartmouth*, the *Eleanor*, the *Beaver*, and the *William*, all heavily loaded with East India tea, were making their way across the Atlantic toward Boston. The Tea Act of 1773 gave the British East India Company (partially owned by the British government) a monopoly on tea sales in America but sharply cut the price of tea. The controversial tea tax (set by the Townshend Acts) would continue to be levied but the actual price, including the tax, paid in America for tea would only be about one-half that paid by a Londoner for his or her tea. For Hancock, the issue was broader than the constitutional one of control over taxation, for it now included the issue of free trade versus monopolies established by government fiat.

In the turmoil over the attempt to land the tea, four hundred Bostonians crowded into Faneuil Hall for a town meeting. Hancock was again elected moderator. So high were emotions running that even he had difficulty maintaining order. Hancock and five other delegates were directed by the town to demand the resignations of the five merchants given the tea monopoly in Boston, including Governor Hutchinson. Unsuccessful in forcing the tea to be returned to England, an unidentified group of colonists thinly disguised as "Indians" dumped thousand of pounds of tea overboard. Hancock's contribution

John Hancock. (Library of Congress)

was to shout, "Let every man do what is right in his own eyes."

The response of the British parliament in passing the Coercive (or Intolerable) Acts of 1774 inflamed the colonists all along the Atlantic coast in a way that nothing else could have. Four laws were passed: The Boston Port Act closed the port of Boston until the tea was paid for, moving the Custom House to Plymouth and the capital to Salem; the Massachusetts Bay Government Act dealt serious blows to self-government; the Quartering Act gave local authorities the responsibility for housing British troops; and the Administration of Justice Act permitted the governor to send to England for trial Crown officials accused of crime, placing them beyond the reach of local courts. As a final means of control, King George III appointed General Gage as the civil (and military) governor of Massachusetts. Gage promptly dismissed Hancock as commanding colonel of the local militia. Hancock's company responded by returning the standard to the general and by disbanding.

The Massachusetts assembly met and "resolved themselves" into a Provincial Congress, electing Hancock as president. This was a dramatic step toward self-government in Massachusetts. From October, 1774, to December, 1774, the Provincial Congress met first in Concord and then in Cambridge. The Congress ordered taxes withheld from royal collectors. They organized the Committee of Public Safety, with Hancock as a key member, and formed a militia, the Minutemen. Rumor had it that General Gage was preparing to arrest Hancock.

Meanwhile, in Philadelphia, the First Continental Congress met. The fifty-six delegates represented all the colonies except Georgia and adopted several resolutions, declaring the new British-controlled government of Massachusetts "tyrannical and unconstitutional." Similarly, since the Intolerable Acts were a usurpation of power, Americans need not obey them. They urged the boycott of all trade with England and advised the people to "learn the art of war." In December, 1774, merchants formed the Continental Association, agreeing to import no goods from Great Britain and to halt all exports to Great Britain.

Hancock was with his wife and aunt at his grandfather's parsonage in Lexington when the shots that set off the American War of Independence were fired on Lexington green. He wanted to fight with the foot soldiers but was persuaded that he had more useful work to do. Several times in the next hectic days he barely escaped capture by the British.

When the Second Continental Congress met in Philadelphia on May 10, 1775, Hancock was one of the new delegates there. When Peyton Randolph of Virginia returned home suddenly, Hancock was unanimously elected president of the Second Continental Congress. In that capacity he was able to mediate between differing factions and helped secure passage of the "Olive Branch" petition to the king, demonstrating the colonists' willingness to accept self-governing status within the British Empire. In the midst of all these momentous events, Hancock was married to Dorothy Quincy at Fairfield, Connecticut, on August 28, 1775. Their honeymoon was like their courtship, sandwiched between political and business activities.

On July 4, 1776, "The Unanimous Declaration of the Thirteen United States of America," the Declaration of Independence, was approved by the Second Continental Congress, and John Hancock's signature was the very first. (In fact, he was the only one who signed on July 4; the other fifty-five signatures came at intervals until November 4.)

In 1777, Hancock retired from Congress to return to Boston. In 1778, he commanded five thousand Massachusetts militiamen in an unsuccessful joint effort with the French fleet to capture Newport, Rhode Island. The fleet withdrew, and so did the militia. In 1779, Boston sent Hancock as a delegate to help write a new state constitution. In the fall of 1780, Hancock was elected the first governor of the Commonwealth of Massachusetts, receiving more than ninety percent of the vote. From 1780 to 1793 (with the exception of two years, 1785-1787), Hancock served as governor. He was not a distinguished leader, but he managed to keep the government running smoothly, reconciling differences and avoiding excessive controversy.

During the war, in 1777, Hancock's daughter Lydia, not yet one year old, became ill and died. The next year, a son was born, John George Washington Hancock. One Sunday afternoon in January, 1787, when the young John was eight years old, he took his skates to go skating on a nearby pond. He slipped on the ice, struck his head, and died within hours. The trauma for the parents is easy to imagine.

When the debate over ratification of the U.S. Constitution came to Massachusetts, Hancock at first was noncommittal, listening to the debates. As the weeks went by, he finally, with Samuel Adams, proposed the addition of a Bill of Rights and spoke in favor of a national government powerful enough to act for the good of the nation. Even with the support of two of the most influential politicians in Massachusetts, ratification won by only a narrow margin, 187 to 168. Considering how close the vote was in New York and Virginia (after the Massachusetts vote), Hancock's support for federalism may have been one of his most historically significant decisions.

Hancock's poor health continued to deteriorate, and five years later he died, at the age of fifty-six, on October 8, 1793. He was survived by his wife, mother, brother, and sister, but no children.

SIGNIFICANCE

John Hancock was the right person in the right place at the right time to play one of the key roles in establishing the United States of America as a free and independent republic. He was one of those who pledged their "lives, their fortunes, and their sacred honour" for that one great cause. Although he did not lay down his life, he invested it in the cause of liberty and self-government. He was wealthy and invested much of his fortune to come to the aid of his country. When he died, he had scarcely half the fortune that had been bequeathed to him by his Uncle Thomas.

More than any other state (except possibly Virginia), Massachusetts led the way in opposing British control of the colonies. The leading city in Massachusetts was Boston, and certainly Hancock was one of the leading citizens of Boston. He was much involved in resisting the Stamp Act, in boycotting, in opposing the Townshend Acts, and in forming united intercolonial opposition. His stand in the *Liberty* incident brought him fame beyond Massachusetts. The king knew who he was, and so did the leading members of Parliament. He was a thorn in the side of the king's ministers, but a respectable and prestigious rallying point for the common people of Boston as they sought high-placed support in resisting what they considered encroachments on their liberties as free Englishmen.

—William H. Burnside

FURTHER READING

Allan, Herbert S. *John Hancock: Patriot in Purple.* New York: Macmillan, 1948. One of several standard works on Hancock. Useful for its full account and picturesque descriptions.

Bailyn, Bernard. *The Ideological Origins of the American Revolution.* Cambridge, Mass.: Harvard University Press, 1967. One of the most useful works for explaining why the war was fought and what motivated the colonists to risk their lives and property for such a cause. Hancock was steeped in the ideological and constitutional questions of the day.

Baxter, W. T. *The House of Hancock.* Cambridge, Mass.: Harvard University Press, 1945. A business history of the Hancock mercantile interest. The book ends with the beginning of the American Revolution.

Brandes, Paul D. *John Hancock's Life and Speeches: A Personalized Vision of the American Revolution, 1763-1793.* Lanham, Md.: Scarecrow Press, 1996. Brandes reexamines Hancock's career by analyzing his papers. Includes reprints of thirty-one of Hancock's speeches.

Carlton, Mabel M. *John Hancock: Great American Patriot.* Boston: John Hancock Mutual Life Insurance, 1922. A standard, corporate biography of Hancock.

Fowler, William M., Jr. *The Baron of Beacon Hill: A Biography of John Hancock.* Boston: Houghton Mifflin, 1980. Although borrowing heavily from earlier works, this biography includes updated interpretive scholarship.

Galvin, John R. *Three Men of Boston.* New York: Thomas Y. Crowell, 1976. A retelling of the events leading up to the revolution in Boston through the significant roles played by Thomas Hutchinson, James Otis, and Samuel Adams. John Hancock's involvement also is clearly seen.

Morgan, Edmund S., and Helen Morgan. *The Stamp Act Crisis.* Chapel Hill: University of North Carolina Press, 1953. The definitive work explaining the events surrounding the Stamp Act and opposition to it.

Rakove, Jack N. *The Beginnings of National Politics: An Interpretive History of the Continental Congress.* New York: Alfred A. Knopf, 1979. Examines the important role of the Congress in the conduct of the American Revolution. Since Hancock was president of the Second Continental Congress, understanding the position of Congress is essential to evaluating Hancock's place in history.

Sears, Lorenzo. *John Hancock: The Picturesque Patriot.* Boston: Little, Brown, 1912. Another biography of Hancock written during the Progressive Era.

Unger, Harlow Giles. *John Hancock: Merchant King and American Patriot.* New York: John Wiley & Sons, 2000. Unger explains how Hancock, an aristocratic, foppish Anglophile and "the least likely man in Boston to start a rebellion," became an ardent supporter of the American Revolution.

Woodbury, Ellen C. D. *Dorothy Quincy: Wife of John Hancock.* Washington, D.C.: Neale, 1901. Looks at Hancock's life from a perspective quite different from that provided by biographies of the patriot himself.

See also: John Adams; Samuel Adams; Thomas Gage; George III; Thomas Hutchinson.

Related articles in *Great Events from History: The Eighteenth Century, 1701-1800:* 1712: Stamp Act; March 22, 1765-March 18, 1766: Stamp Act Crisis; June 29, 1767-April 12, 1770: Townshend Crisis; March 5, 1770: Boston Massacre; December 16, 1773: Boston Tea Party; September 5-October 26, 1774: First Continental Congress; April 19, 1775: Battle of Lexington and Concord; May 10-August 2, 1775: Second Continental Congress; July 4, 1776: Declaration of Independence; March 1, 1781: Ratification of the Articles of Confederation; September 17, 1787: U.S. Constitution Is Adopted; December 15, 1791: U.S. Bill of Rights Is Ratified.

GEORGE FRIDERIC HANDEL
German composer and musician

One of the most gifted composers in music history, Handel gave to the world some of the most beautiful music ever written, including the Messiah, Water Music, *and* Fireworks Music.

Born: February 23, 1685; Halle, Brandenburg (now in Germany)
Died: April 14, 1759; London, England
Also known as: George Frederick Handel; George Frideric Hendel; Georg Frideric Handel; George Frideric Händel
Area of achievement: Music

EARLY LIFE

George Frideric Handel, the eighteenth century composer to whom the world owes thanks for some of its best-known and most beloved music, both sacred and secular, was born in Halle, Brandenburg. His father at times must have seemed more like a grandfather to his young son, since he was sixty-three years old when the future composer was born. His first wife had died after many years of marriage and several children, and he had then married a daughter of the Lutheran pastor in Halle, Dorothea Taust.

George's aunt, Anna Taust, introduced the young George to good music. She took him regularly to the Liebfrauenkirche (the Lutheran church), where he loved to listen to the wonderful organ played by a competent musician, Friedrich Zachow. Anna apparently also helped George smuggle a small clavichord into his attic, where, against his father's wishes, he played quietly, often late at night.

The father was the barber-surgeon at the court of Saxe-Weissenfels, and George's half brother, thirty-six years older than George, was also an employee of the duke. George often visited the court chapel, and the organist, realizing that the child was intelligent and had un-

usual musical talent, allowed him to play the organ. One Sunday service, George played a voluntary at the end of the service and so amazed the duke that he pressured the father into giving George a musical education. "To ignore gifts like these in a child is to fly in the face of God," the duke argued.

While attending school in Halle, George was tutored by Zachow, the organist at the Liebfrauenkirche. Zachow was a conscientious musician, capable of playing all the instruments then in general use, especially the organ, harpsichord, violin, and oboe. In three years he taught Handel everything he knew, including part of his style, counterpoint, and harmony.

At eleven years of age, George and his father journeyed to Berlin to the Prussian court. The future King Frederick I of Prussia offered Handel a lifetime musical position, but his father did not want him to live so far from home, and they returned to Halle. Still, George Frideric Handel's reputation as a composer and musician was already being established. The next year his father died at the age of seventy-five.

Handel enrolled at the University of Halle and just after his seventeenth birthday was appointed organist at the Schlosskirche, the Calvinist cathedral there. His duties gave him valuable experience. He played the organ at all services and kept it in good working order. He also composed and directed tunes for psalms and cantatas for all Sundays and festivals at the church.

An accomplished musician, Handel left Halle for Hamburg, an important commercial and cultural center, with the only regular opera company in Germany outside the royal courts. Handel played second violin and later harpsichord. Supplementing that income by giving private music lessons, he managed to support himself and even occasionally sent home a little money to his widowed mother. He lived a frugal life and busied himself in his work, ignoring the frivolities of such a bustling university town. He was sociable, however, and attracted the notice of many. Once he fought a duel with a friend over who was to play the harpsichord at an opera. Handel's life and career could suddenly have ended with a sword thrust, but as his friend later explained, "By God's mercy my sword [broke] . . . on a hard metal button." Handel himself escaped unscathed.

It was at Hamburg that Handel wrote his earliest important work, the *St. John Passion*, in 1704. His first two operas, *Almira* and *Nero*, he wrote in 1705—the first a success, *Nero* a failure. He also wrote many sonatas, arias, and cantatas. In Halle and Hamburg, the foundation was laid for one of the greatest musical lives in all history. The development of Handel's style, however, was yet to come—in Italy, in the greatest musical centers of the world.

LIFE'S WORK

While he was still in Hamburg, George Frideric Handel met the son of the grand duke of Tuscany, Prince Ferdinand de' Medici, who invited him to visit Italy. In his beautiful villa at Pratolino, the prince had built a magnificent theater for operatic performances. The love of Italian nobility for opera was well known, and with such high-ranking support Handel could expect an audience immediately. Thus Handel, at the age of twenty-one, went to Florence in the autumn of 1706. There he wrote and produced *Rodrigo*, his first Italian opera. From Florence he went to Rome and played the organ before enthusiastic listeners in the Church of St. John Lateran.

By that time Handel was becoming well known in Italy. The Marquess Francesco Ruspoli employed the young man as household musician at his palace in Rome and his country estates, from 1707 to 1709. Handel had flexibility to compose and move about as he pleased, but he was expected to write cantatas for weekly performance on Sundays. In this period Handel wrote some fifty cantatas, mostly with Spanish and French words. His most famous production for Ruspoli was the oratorio *La Resurrezione*, celebrating the resurrection of Christ, produced at Ruspoli's palace in Rome in April, 1708. A theater with scenery and a curtain were constructed in the palace, and a very large orchestra (for the time) was assembled, performing with at least forty-five players. The conductor was Arcangelo Corelli,

one of the most famous violinists and composers of the period. Fifteen hundred copies of the libretto were printed; the audiences must have been substantial.

The Italian years were particularly significant in Handel's career. He learned much of opera, oratorio, and cantata as well as concerto and sonata forms. In Florence, Rome, Naples, and Venice he became closely acquainted with the great Italian composers and musicians, including not only Corelli but also Alessandro and Domenico Scarlatti, and Antonio Vivaldi. Handel arrived in Italy a gifted but inexperienced composer. He left as a mature artist in command of his own rich, melodic style, having mastered the techniques for writing for voice. His writing was relaxed and flexible. He was ready for his distinguished English career.

Handel left Italy in February, 1710, to return briefly to Germany. The elector of Hanover (heir to the English throne) appointed him as Kapellmeister at a substantial salary, with the understanding that Handel would spend the next several months in England. Handel was favorably received at Queen Anne's court and in the new opera house, the Queen's Theatre in London. *Rinaldo*, his

George Frideric Handel. (Library of Congress)

first Italian opera composed for London, was first performed in 1711 and was a sensational success, performed fifteen times. Handel returned to his duties in Germany for a year, writing chamber and orchestral music and giving lessons to Princess Caroline of Ansbach (later Queen Caroline of England).

Back in London in 1712, Handel took up residence at Burlington House in Piccadilly, composing during the day and performing in the evenings. He continued his opera career and began writing English church and ceremonial music on the direct commission of the queen, who gave him an annual salary. On August 1, 1714, Queen Anne died, to be succeeded by Handel's other royal employer, the elector of Hanover, now King George I of England.

In 1719, Handel became the musical director of the Royal Academy of Music, a new enterprise designed to establish Italian operas in England. Squabbling among singers and disagreements within the directorship finally caused the venture to collapse after nine years, but Handel saw many spectacular successes in opera performances. In working for excellence, Handel tended to be forceful and somewhat dictatorial; rehearsals were often stormy, but performances were excellent. Typical of Handel's management style was a most unusual incident when his two prima donnas engaged in a shouting match before a crowded house, including many of the nobility and the princess of Wales. Some of the audience joined in the battle, tearing down part of the scenery as the two women tore at each other's hair.

As composer to the Chapel Royal, it fell to Handel to write four anthems for George II's coronation, considered some of the most spectacular such pieces ever written. He used forty-seven singers and an exceptionally large orchestra of 160 members. The archbishops of Canterbury and York sought to supply the words for the anthems, but Handel told them, "I have read my Bible very well and shall choose for myself."

Handel's magnum opus was the *Messiah*, written in the summer of 1741. The libretto, compiled by Charles Jennens, is entirely from Scripture. It includes several prophesies of the Old Testament concerning the coming of the Messiah, such as "Unto Us a Child Is Born," followed by the announcement by the angels of the birth of Christ, "Glory to God in the Highest." Arias, recitatives, and choruses depict the life and crucifixion of Christ followed by his resurrection and ultimate triumph, especially "I Know That My Redeemer Liveth," "Worthy Is the Lamb," and the chorus known popularly as the "Hallelujah Chorus." Handel wrote the stirring music that is

so perfectly tuned to the words of Scripture in only twenty-four days, working day and night, hardly stopping to eat. Handel wrote of his experience in composing the *Messiah*, "I did think I did see all Heaven before me, and the great God Himself!" First performed in Dublin in April, 1742, for the benefit of three charitable institutions, the *Messiah* was an instant success in Ireland (though less so initially in England) and has been performed every Christmas season throughout the English-speaking world. Indeed, the "Hallelujah Chorus" is probably the most widely performed Easter piece.

After nine months in Ireland, Handel returned to his work in London, work that included the preparation of ceremonial music for the English court. The most spectacular example was probably the writing of *Fireworks Music* for the Green Park celebration of April 27, 1749, commemorating the Treaty of Aix-la-Chapelle. A huge building more than 100 feet high was specially constructed for the event, and 101 brass cannon sat nearby for the royal salute. Handel put together a band such as is seldom seen: forty trumpets, twenty French horns, twenty-four oboes, sixteen bassoons, eight pairs of kettledrums, and one bass cornet eight feet long. The crowd of many thousands was enchanted with the music, and the celebration went well until the fireworks were lit and burned the pavilion. Given the huge crowd, there were surprisingly few injuries.

By 1751, it was clear that Handel was going blind; by 1753, he had completely lost his sight. He continued to work steadily, though, dictating his work to his secretary, Christopher Smith. He played his harpsichord by the hour and continued his habit of attending St. George's Church in Hanover Square. His last season began in March, 1759, and ended with a last performance of the *Messiah*. Friends came to see him, including the staunchly Methodist countess of Huntington, who wrote, "I have had a most pleasing interview with Handel. . . . He is now old, and at the close of his long career; yet he is not dismayed at the prospect before him [because of] the comforts and consolations which the Gospel affords. . . ."

"I want to die on Good Friday," he told his friends, "in the hope of rejoining the good God, my . . . Lord and Saviour, on the day of His resurrection." One day he bade farewell to his friends and told his servant not to admit anyone else to his chambers, saying, "I have now done with the world." He died on April 14, 1759, and was buried in Poets' Corner in Westminster Abbey. The marble statue above his monument shows Handel writing part of the *Messiah*, depicting the music and words of "I Know That My Redeemer Liveth." Handel left £20,000 and, as always, was generous to his servants, relatives, friends, and charities.

A large, portly man, Handel was rather ungraceful in his walk but dignified and kindly in his appearance. Somewhat quick and impetuous, he was also of good humor and sharp wit. He had great vitality and was an energetic worker. He had a reputation for absolute integrity and paid his singers and orchestra well. He was exceptionally generous, especially to charities, widows, and orphans, and although he never married, no aspersions were therefore cast on his morals. Handel was a devout Christian, a pious Lutheran who attended church regularly and was very familiar with his Bible. He was quick-tempered, but he quickly recovered as well. He never carried a grudge and was quick to admit that he was wrong when the occasion warranted. He was somewhat awkward in English at first, but later in life he wrote well. His fame as a composer has obscured the fact that he was as accomplished a musician as any of his contemporaries, particularly on the organ and harpsichord.

Handel lived for thirty-four years on Brook Street, Hanover Square, with two servants. His rugged simplicity was reflected in his plain furniture (in contrast to the ornateness of much of his music). His collection of paintings by Rembrandt was worth £8,000. His workroom was furnished with a few tables, half a dozen old chairs, his harpsichord, and a wall desk. He dressed modestly but well, typically in a gold-laced coat, ruffles, and a three-cornered hat.

SIGNIFICANCE

Melody, harmony, and beautiful sound (euphony) were always George Frideric Handel's goals in his music. He consciously sought to express the meaning and tone of his librettos musically. He complained occasionally of an inappropriate libretto, saying, "How is a musician to create anything beautiful if he has no beautiful words? . . . There is no spirit in the *verse*, and one feels vexation in setting such to *music*." One of the reasons the *Messiah* was and is so successful is the majesty of the words so appropriately chosen from the King James Bible. Handel's music seems to capture perfectly the meaning and grandeur of the lyrics. The medium captures the message.

Characterized by the ornate style of the Baroque and given to the splendor of Italian opera, Handel's music nevertheless reveals the sublimity of the simple things of life. That simplicity captured the hearts of his world. Handel delighted in wandering through art museums, and it is not surprising that Rembrandt was his favorite artist. Both he and Handel celebrate the goodness and joy

of the simple things of life. Another secret of his art is the use of contrast, at which Handel excelled: Majestic choruses, dramatic silences, and sublime, simple melodies all contribute to the rich diversity within the unity of a Handel composition. Handel's music is international in scope, both in its sources—German, Italian, French, and English influences are all clear to the discerning listener—and in its appeal.

—William H. Burnside

FURTHER READING

Burrows, Donald. *Handel*. New York: Oxford University Press, 1994. An examination of Handel's life and music. Burrows describes Handel's transition from a church-trained musician in Germany to an opera composer in London, and the evolution of his theater career from opera to oratorio composition.

_____, ed. *The Cambridge Companion to Handel*. New York: Cambridge University Press, 1997. A collection of essays that explore the musician's life and music, including discussions of the political, social, and cultural life of Handel's London, and the composer's arias, oratorios, and concertos.

Cudworth, Charles. *Handel: A Biography, with a Survey of Books, Editions, and Recordings*. Hamden, Conn.: Linnet Books, 1972. Part of the series The Concertgoer's Companions, designed to provide background information for greater appreciation of a concert. Consists of a brief survey of Handel's life, an annotated bibliography, an exhaustive list of Handel's music, and a dozen pages of recordings of his music.

Dean, Winton. *The New Grove Handel*. New York: W. W. Norton, 1982. The best brief technical analysis of Handel's compositions. Strives to be more analytical than historical, but contains six excellent pages describing Handel's character and personality.

Deutsch, Otto Erich, ed. *Handel: A Documentary Biography*. New York: W. W. Norton, 1955. A collection of documents by and about Handel. Includes excerpts from John Mainwaring's biography of 1760.

Flower, Newman. *George Frideric Handel: His Personality and His Times*. London: Cassell, 1923. Reprint. New York: Charles Scribner's Sons, 1948. The most readable, entertaining biography of Handel. Well written. Includes much anecdotal material.

Hogwood, Christopher. *Handel*. 1984. Reprint. New York: Thames and Hudson, 1996. A comprehensive biography by a musician and conductor. Includes about one hundred illustrations, reprints of contemporary documents, and a chronological table of Handel's life.

Myers, Robert Manson. *Handel's "Messiah": A Touchstone of Taste*. New York: Macmillan, 1948. Reprint. New York: Octagon Books, 1971. An analysis of Handel's most famous composition and its place in history.

Smith, Jane Stuart, and Betty Carlson. *A Gift of Music: Great Composers and Their Influence*. Westchester, Ill.: Cornerstone Books, 1978. An entertaining and thought-provoking book on twenty of the great composers in Western civilization, including Handel. Includes recommended reading and listening for each chapter.

Streatfeild, Richard A. *Handel*. New York: New Library of Music, 1907. Reprint. New York: Da Capo Press, 1960. A standard scholarly work that is arranged chronologically.

Weinstock, Herbert. *Handel*. New York: Alfred A. Knopf, 1946. Another carefully researched, carefully written biography.

See also: Queen Anne; Johann Sebastian Bach; Luigi Boccherini; Charles Burney; Caroline; Jean-Honoré Fragonard; Frederick I; George I; George II; Christoph Gluck; Joseph Haydn; Wolfgang Amadeus Mozart; Jean-Philippe Rameau; Alessandro Scarlatti; Antonio Stradivari; Georg Philipp Telemann; Antonio Vivaldi.

Related articles in *Great Events from History: The Eighteenth Century, 1701-1800:* c. 1701-1750: Bach Pioneers Modern Music; January 29, 1728: Gay Produces the First Ballad Opera; April 13, 1742: First Performance of Handel's *Messiah*; October 18, 1748: Treaty of Aix-la-Chapelle; January, 1762-November, 1766: Mozart Tours Europe as a Child Prodigy; October 5, 1762: First Performance of Gluck's *Orfeo and Euridice*; August 3, 1778: Opening of Milan's La Scala; April 27, 1784: First Performance of *The Marriage of Figaro*; 1795-1797: Paganini's Early Violin Performances.

JAMES HARGREAVES
English inventor

Hargreaves invented the spinning jenny, which greatly multiplied the output of spinners and initiated a period of rapid growth in the textile industry that marked the onset of the Industrial Revolution in Great Britain.

Born: January 8, 1720 (baptized); possibly Stanhill, near Oswaldtwistle, Lancashire, England
Died: April 22, 1778; Nottinghamshire, England
Also known as: James Hargraves
Areas of achievement: Science and technology, business

EARLY LIFE

Very little of the early life of James Hargreaves is known, except for his date of baptism and the possible place of birth. It also appears that he was employed from 1740 to 1750 as a carpenter and handloom weaver at Standhill, a town near Blackburn. The first certain record of Hargreaves's life—besides baptismal records—is his employment in 1760 by Robert Peel, an experienced spinner and calico printer in Blackburn and the grandfather of statesman Sir Robert Peel. Peel wished to have an improved machine for carding, the process of disentangling fibers prior to spinning.

In about 1760, the English weaving industry, centered in Lancashire, faced a crisis because spinners could not produce enough thread to satisfy weavers' needs and permit their businesses to operate profitably. This imbalance had been caused by the introduction in the 1730's of John Kay's flying shuttle, which greatly facilitated weaving. Adding to the crisis was that fabrics could not be made from cotton alone because of the lack of sufficiently strong cotton fibers. One indication of the industry's determination to overcome these problems is that the Society for the Encouragement of Arts, Manufactures and Commerce offered handsome premiums to inventors of improved spinning machinery, but it only received several unsuccessful designs. The invention that would prove revolutionary was not among them, for it belonged to an illiterate and humble cottage weaver, James Hargreaves, who invented his machine, the spinning jenny, in 1764.

LIFE'S WORK

The spinning jenny was James Hargreaves's one significant contribution, but it proved a major one. Historian Sir Edward Baines has written that it showed "high mechanical genius": For the first time, it permitted weavers to spin, simultaneously and in one operation, several threads of such materials as wool, cotton, and flax.

The spinning jenny was a sophisticated engineering feat, and it required great physical skill of the operator. It consisted of two creels, or racks, of bobbins set in a wooden frame. One rack held roving, the drawn-out and slightly twisted pieces of the raw material to be spun. The bobbins in the other rack received the yarn that had been drawn out by a carriage with one hand and spun with the other. The spinning was controlled by a wheel attached to a gear-and-pulley system. Returning the carriage to its original position after drawing out and spinning the roving caused the second set of bobbins to rotate and draw in the yarn.

It is popularly held that the spinning jenny was conceived as a result of happenstance. Coming into the kitchen, the story goes, Hargreaves startled his wife and caused her to knock over her single-thread spinning wheel. The wheel and the spindle continued to spin as the machine lay horizontal on the floor, and this is supposed to have suggested to Hargreaves the idea of building a horizontal spinning wheel that would be able to spin eight threads at a time. In effect, the machine provided the spinner with the equivalent of extra hands.

The new invention gave a great advantage to Hargreaves and his family over other cottage weavers. They used the spinning jenny to make weft—a coarse, weak yarn that they worked on their own loom in combination with stronger warp yarn. The Hargreaves's machine originally handled eleven threads of yarn at once. Evidently they used it in secrecy, fearing that other spinners in the region, which was the center of the English fabric and weaving industries, would become envious. When Hargreaves became financially pinched, however, he decided to make extra jennies and sell them to other spinners. This led to the sacking of his home in 1768 by a mob fearful that the machine would put many spinners out of work. The mob reportedly scoured the Blackburn area to locate and destroy other jennies as well as other recent inventions, such as carding engines and water-frames, that they believed would decrease the industry's dependence on human labor. The mob spared, however, jennies of twenty spindles or less, considering only those of greater capacity to be "mischievous."

His family factory destroyed, Hargreaves moved south to Nottingham, which was not a center of textile manufacture, and opened a small cotton mill in association with Thomas James, a joiner who appears to have helped Hargreaves to apply for a patent, which was taken out in July, 1770. The patent was for a jenny capable of spinning sixteen threads at once.

The origin of the name of the spinning jenny is disputed. Some historians claim that the name commemorates Hargreaves's wife, but her name is nowhere recorded. An almost contemporary commentator, Richard Guest, claimed that the machine was named for the daughter, named Jane, of a spinner from Leigh, Lancashire, Thomas Highs. Also disputed is whether Hargreaves actually invented the spinning jenny or merely improved an existing machine. Guest argued that Highs invented the spinning jenny in 1764 and that Hargreaves had merely improved the design. The most compelling arguments, however, are made by Baines. He states that Hargreaves's machine differed greatly from the machines of others who laid claim to the invention, and he argues that it must have predated the machines of other claimants. Baines also argues that the spinning jenny was so brilliantly conceived and executed that it undoubtedly took several years to conceive; since it was perfected by 1768, he says, Hargreaves must have been inventing prototypes several years earlier, and before other competitors' machines were developed.

After Hargreaves took out a patent on his invention, he discovered, nevertheless, that it was being used by many manufacturers in Lancashire. A legal dispute ensued, and those breaching Hargreaves's copyright offered him £3,000. Hargreaves at first demanded £7,000, though he later reduced his claim to £4,000. In any case, he refused to settle the case. His claims foundered, however, when the court learned that the inventor, forced to find funds to feed his six or seven children, had sold several jennies to manufacturers before taking out the patent.

Opinion varies as to Hargreaves's subsequent fate. The most dependable source, Baines, basing his account on an inquiry by the son of Hargreaves's partner, James, says that the partnership continued after the unsuccessful lawsuit "with moderate success," and that Hargreaves lived modestly on its profits. When he died in April, 1778, he left his wife £400.

Hargreaves's only other contribution to the rapidly evolving technology of fabric manufacture was the cylinder carder, a device soon superseded by better machines.

SIGNIFICANCE

After James Hargreaves's death, spinning jennies such as he had invented were soon being used throughout England. That machine, together with the water-frame developed by Sir Richard Arkwright, permitted pure cotton cloth to be made for the first time and promoted a rapid advance in cotton manufacture. Spinning jennies soon permitted spinners to work as many as 120 threads onto spindles at once, and the product was of a highly improved quality. As a result, spinners were able to increase their wages greatly. The invention also sparked a period of intense interest in aiding the manufacture of fabrics through machinery. Many weavers opposed these developments, but the new machinery actually increased the number of people employed in the fabrics industries.

Hargreaves's invention was one of a few which sparked the beginning of the factory system in England. Before its development, the manufacture of thread had been a cottage industry. A small spinning jenny could be used in the weaver's home, and a larger one could be placed in an adjoining workshop, but some of the other inventions that were sparked by its appearance could only be placed in larger, sturdier mills. The invention also encouraged greater division of labor, which again hastened the advent of the factory system. The factory system quickly became essential, as no cottage industry could compete with the efficiency and bulk output of the factories.

—*Peter Monaghan*

FURTHER READING

Baines, Sir Edward. *History of the Cotton Manufacture in Great Britain*. London: Frank Cass, 1966. A reprint of a work that originally appeared in 1835. A standard history of the cotton industry and the best source for Hargreaves's history. Compares his contribution to the advent of the Industrial Revolution to that of Sir Richard Arkwright and others.

Berg, Maxine. *The Age of Manufactures: Industry, Innovation, and Work in Britain, 1700-1820*. 2d ed. New York: Routledge, 1994. An excellent survey of eighteenth century British industry, featuring two chapters on the textile industry, with information on Hargreaves.

Guest, Richard. *A Compendious History of the Cotton-Manufacture*. Manchester, England: Joseph Pratt, 1823. Argues that Thomas Highs was the inventor of the spinning jenny as well as Arkwright's water-frame. Presents a history of the Lancashire cotton industry consonant with that argument, including testimony from Highs's unsuccessful lawsuit against Arkwright. In some respects more a curiosity than a dependable source. Contains illustrations of machinery.

Lipson, E. *The History of the Woollen and Worsted Industries*. London: A. and C. Black, 1921. Contains only a brief description of Hargreaves's contribution to the history of the industry but provides a useful description of the context of his invention.

Smelser, Neil J. *Social Change in the Industrial Revolution*. Chicago: University of Chicago Press, 1959. An application of a model of social change, the general theory of action, to the British cotton industry in Hargreaves's time.

Wadsworth, Alfred P., and Julia De Lacy Mann. *The Cotton Trade and Industrial Lancashire, 1600-1780*. Manchester, England: Manchester University Press, 1931. A standard text on the history of the industry in the years leading up to the Industrial Revolution. Describes the advent of the inventions of Hargreaves and others and the effect they had on the society and economy of the region.

See also: Sir Richard Arkwright; John Kay; James Watt; Eli Whitney.

Related articles in *Great Events from History: The Eighteenth Century, 1701-1800:* 1733: Kay Invents the Flying Shuttle; 1764: Invention of the Spinning Jenny; 1779: Crompton Invents the Spinning Mule; April, 1785: Cartwright Patents the Steam-Powered Loom; February 14, 1788: Meikle Demonstrates His Drum Thresher; December 20, 1790: Slater's Spinning Mill; 1793: Whitney Invents the Cotton Gin; 1795: Invention of the Flax Spinner.

WARREN HASTINGS
English colonial administrator

As the first governor-general, Hastings consolidated British rule in India by intervening in the internal politics of Indian states and by meeting threats elsewhere in the Indian subcontinent.

Born: December 6, 1732; Churchill, Oxfordshire, England
Died: August 22, 1818; Daylesford, Worcestershire, England
Area of achievement: Government and politics

EARLY LIFE

Warren Hastings had a difficult childhood: His mother died in childbirth, and his father deserted him. In turn, a foster mother, his grandfather, and his aunt all cared for him until he went to live with his uncle at Westminster at age eight. His uncle provided for his boarding school education. In 1749, Hastings' uncle died, and a guardian helped him become a clerk in the British East India Company. In 1750, at age eighteen, Hastings sailed for India.

Young Hastings worked in Bengal, an area important to Great Britain for its wealth. He rose quickly in the company's service. In 1755, he was promoted to the factory council as secretary and storekeeper. By 1757, the year of Robert Clive's triumph at Plassey, Hastings was appointed to the position of company representative at the court of the nawab of Bengel. Increasingly successful financially, Hastings served on the company's directing council in Calcutta after 1760 as the East India Company became a ruling as well as a trading body. In 1764, with his fortune in doubt and after losing a political battle, he resigned and sailed for England, where he spent the next four years. In 1769, he returned to India as deputy governor of Madras. His reserved and controlled temperament helped him overcome adversity, and his love for India brought him back to that land. Physically, Hastings did not appear able to withstand the rigors of India's climate.

LIFE'S WORK

The major break in Warren Hastings's East India Company service came in 1771 with his appointment to the governorship of Bengal. During the early 1770's, British policy toward India was undergoing great change. In the first half of the eighteenth century, East India Company employees were unscrupulous in their financial, diplomatic, and military actions in India. After Parliament investigated Clive in 1772-1773 for misconduct earlier in his service in India, a more honest administration in India

and better government in the empire were important. Perhaps the Wesleyan revival in England made the public more conscious of morality and the aristocrats resented the company officials, the nouveaux riches, garnering great wealth through unsavory means. The company continually faced financial problems with wars, famine, and problems with the employees. Parliament passed two laws in 1773 to address those problems. With one act, the government not only loaned the East India Company funds for its debts but also limited its dividends and promised to scrutinize its treasury. Another act provided a new constitution for the East India Company, which meant more Crown control over the company and higher salaries to discourage the temptation for corruption. Also in 1773, Hastings was chosen as the first governor-general to rule over all of British India—Bengal, Madras, and Bombay.

As he began his tenure as governor-general, Hastings faced tough problems. Through the work of men such as Clive, the East India Company had become the dominant force in India, and Hastings had the task of resolving the problems of company rule. The Regulating Act of 1773 that made Hastings governor-general also created a council to control him, and the three council members from London, appointed by the government, were suspicious of the company and antagonistic toward Hastings. Hastings also had power over the other two presidencies in Madras and Bombay concerning questions of war and peace, but envy and distance made relations with them difficult. Hastings, more interested in Indian culture and language than most British officials, sought to rule India for the Indians, and he declared that he loved India a little more than England. Through reforms of taxes, trade, administration, education, and postal service, he sought better relations between the company and native Indians. In the Indian subcontinent, the governor-general dealt successfully with the continued French threat, helped Bombay survive a challenge from a new ruler in the Marāthās, and defended Madras from attacks by the forces of Mysore. Military affairs occupied most of his attention, and through diplomatic skills, Hastings succeeded despite financial distractions and the drain of the American Revolution on the rest of the empire.

During his eleven years as governor-general, Hastings was confronted with several crises. These difficulties kept him from striving toward any long-term goals, and they frustrated his vision for imperial India. The

Rohilla War was his first major controversy. In 1772, and again in 1773, the Mārāthas attacked the Rohillas, a tribe that had taken land north of the state of Oudh. A combination of Rohilla, Oudh, and company forces pressured the Mārāthas to withdraw to their homes in central India. Until the Mārāthas invaded, the state of Oudh had not bothered with the Rohillas, but during that war the nawab of Oudh increasingly distrusted his neighbors to the north and wanted them defeated. For this task, the nawab enlisted the support of Hastings and the East India Company. The nawab of Oudh paid the company £500,000 for the return of lands that Clive had given the Mughal emperor, pledged £400,000 in exchange for its support against the Rohillas, and pledged more funds for use of a company brigade. Hastings considered his actions proper. The nawab was justified in attacking the Rohillas, he argued, and a threat was eliminated; meanwhile, the company made a profit. The successful war also enhanced the position of the company's ally—the state of Oudh.

Three new council members, however, did not share Hastings's opinion. They bitterly opposed the Rohilla War and stubbornly fought Hastings in the council. They

Warren Hastings. (Library of Congress)

overruled him and, more seriously, charged him with corruption. In 1775, an old Brahmin nemesis of Hastings, Nandakumar, accused the governor-general of bribery, and his enemies on the council seized on this charge in their persecution of Hastings. His political enemies were behind the council's actions, and the government and the company did little to defend him. Yet Hastings fought back vigorously, with the chief justice of Bengal on his side. For his false charges, Hastings ordered Nandakumar arrested and, on rather slim evidence, convicted for conspiracy. Next, Hastings charged him with forgery, found him guilty, and sentenced him to death. Though guilty of forgery, Nandakumar had only committed a crime common in India, and even though British law prescribed the death penalty, it had never been used in Bengal. Hastings's response was excessive, but his friends on the council did not come to Nandakumar's defense and he was executed. Hastings's firm action increased his public stature, however, and afterward ended his persecution from the council.

Expensive wars against the Mārāthas and Mysore brought financial pressures for Hastings, and the company did not support him financially. For funds, Hastings looked elsewhere and put pressure on tributaries. His unfortunate victim was Chait Singh, the raja of Benares, who since 1775 had been obligated to the company for the acquisition of lands. The raja's annual tribute was £225,000. In 1778, Hastings, desperate for more money for war, extorted additional funds from Chait Singh, and despite the raja's resistance, he demanded even more money the following year. Such demands were traditional among Asian princes, but this action by Hastings violated the 1775 agreement between Chait Singh and the company.

In 1779, Hastings received his funds when he threatened to invade Benares with British troops. The following year, Hastings demanded more money and troops. When the raja did not comply, Hastings arrested him. Chait Singh's soldiers in Benares resisted and massacred British troops, and the raja fled. Hastings placed the raja's nephew on the throne and made similar demands on him. The governor-general's appetite for money reached extremes when he used British troops to force the mother and grandmother of the nawab of Oudh to yield a treasure of more than £1 million to satisfy debts owed to the company.

For such actions, Hastings was severely criticized. Just as Clive's conduct led to new legislation, Hastings's record revealed weaknesses in the British rule of India. The remedy was the proposed India Act of 1784, which would have placed the East India Company under a board of control based in England.

Hastings returned to England in 1785 and encountered opposition from his enemies, who charged him with corruption and oppression in India. Edmund Burke and William Pitt the Younger led the attack in Parliament. Accused of improper conduct in the Rohilla and Mārāthā Wars, Hastings was acquitted, but in 1786, Parliament charged him with extortion of Chait Singh by a comfortable margin. Other charges of corruption followed, and by 1787, the Commons impeached Hastings and tried him before the House of Lords. The trial began in 1788 and lasted eight years because of elections, wars, and quarrels among his enemies. The House of Lords accused Hastings of high crimes and misdemeanors on the basis of British moral standards. Hastings's defense was that he acted like an Indian ruler, and he produced witnesses who so testified. The trial personally bankrupted him, but vindication came in 1795 when the lords acquitted him of all charges.

After the trial, Hastings avoided publicity and lived for twenty-three years in retirement at his estate, a broken man, worried about his health and finances. There were moments of public rehabilitation, such as when the Royal Society made him a member and when the royal family befriended him. In 1813, he was honored with an appearance before the Commons with testimony concerning India, and he received an honorary degree from Oxford. Having outlived most of his enemies, Hastings died in 1818 at the age of eighty-five.

SIGNIFICANCE

Clearly the accusations against Warren Hastings had substance, but in his favor, historians argue as his contemporary defenders did, that his conduct compared well with that of others involved in imperial Indian affairs. Perhaps the problem was not Hastings himself but the shifting public attitude in Great Britain toward the empire. The Wesleyan revival sweeping the country heightened its sense of morality in public affairs, especially concerning India. Just administration became more important than territorial acquisition and financial aggrandizement, actions previously acceptable for imperial officials. Hastings nevertheless consolidated British rule in India after the conquests of earlier leaders such as Clive. As a result of his policies, the British became increasingly involved in the politics of their Indian states and also in the affairs of the entire subcontinent. Though he spent most of his time responding to a series of crises, Hastings left as his legacy a greater role for the British in India. The India Act of 1784 corrected a basic problem that plagued Hastings. As governor-general, his commercial role with the East India Company conflicted with his political duties. A board of control in England would hereafter set policy for the East India Company in India, and in that way future governors-general reflected the moral and humanitarian concerns of the British public. In the end, Hastings's misfortunes brought positive changes.

—*Douglas Carl Abrams*

FURTHER READING

Bernstein, Jeremy. *Dawning of the Raj: The Life and Trials of Warren Hastings*. Chicago: Ivan R. Dee, 2000. A popular, well-written biography that includes some updated material about Hastings's private life.

Davies, Alfred Mervyn. *Strange Destiny: A Biography of Warren Hastings*. New York: G. P. Putnam's Sons, 1935. Lengthy, well-documented biography of Hastings, focusing on and defending his twenty-five years in India.

Freiling, Keith. *Warren Hastings*. Hamden, Conn.: Archon Books, 1954. Based primarily on Hastings's papers. A favorable, straightforward overview of his life. However, weak on analysis and interpretation.

Huttenback, Robert A. *The British Imperial Experience*. New York: Harper & Row, 1966. A solid analysis of various topics associated with the full span of the British Empire, geographically and chronologically. The first chapter includes an excellent assessment of Hastings.

Keay, John. *The Honourable Company: A History of the East India Company*. London: HarperCollins, 1991. A history of the company, containing information on Hastings, whom the author describes as a "misunderstood" figure.

Lloyd, T. O. *The British Empire, 1558-1983*. New York: Oxford University Press, 1984. One of few excellent narrative histories of the British Empire from the sixteenth century to the twentieth century. Scholarly and thorough, the work provides proper background for an evaluation of Hastings.

Marshall, P. J. *The Impeachment of Warren Hastings*. New York: Oxford University Press, 1965. The first part deals with the impeachment process, and the second part evaluates the charges against Hastings. Marshall's work is the result of extensive research and examines Hastings in the context of his times.

Moon, Perderel. *Warren Hastings and British India*. New York: Macmillan, 1949. Rather than a biography, this work is an interpretation of the major episodes in Hastings's career in India. No notes.

Sutherland, Lucy Stuart. *East India Company in Eighteenth Century Politics.* New York: Oxford University Press, 1952. Based on East India Company records and massive private correspondence, Sutherland's work is a comprehensive and scholarly examination of the company in the context of the times. Looks at Westminster politics and company activities in East India.

See also: Edmund Burke; Robert Clive; First Marquess Cornwallis; Joseph-François Dupleix; William Pitt the Younger.

Related articles in *Great Events from History: The Eighteenth Century, 1701-1800:* 1746-1754: Carnatic Wars; June 23, 1757: Battle of Plassey; August, 1767-May, 1799: Anglo-Mysore Wars; December, 1774-February 24, 1783: First Marāthā War.

NICHOLAS HAWKSMOOR
English architect

Overshadowed by Sir Christopher Wren and Sir John Vanbrugh for two centuries, Hawksmoor became recognized in the twentieth century as one of the three greatest English Baroque architects. His daring originality and eccentric brilliance mark him as the innovator of his time.

Born: c. 1661; probably East Drayton, Nottinghamshire, England
Died: March 25, 1736; London, England
Area of achievement: Architecture

EARLY LIFE

Nothing is known particularly of the early life of Nicholas Hawksmoor. The family name was, in fact, Hawksmore, and his father, also called Nicholas, was probably a farmer. The family has a history in the northeast corner of Nottinghamshire, but Hawksmoor's exact age and date of birth are unknown, since the parish records for the years 1659 to 1663 for East Drayton are missing.

He seems to have had some education, and, at the time of his death, it was stated that he was bred as a "scholar" and knew the "modern tongues." There was a grammar school in the nearby town of Dunham, and he may have been educated there. While still a young boy, he was employed as a clerk by Justice Samuel Mellish at Doncaster, which suggests that he had some education.

At the age of eighteen, he joined the most important architect in London, Sir Christopher Wren. How he got the position is not known, but a professional acquaintance of Wren, Edward Gouge, had done some plaster work for Justice Mellish and may have brought Hawksmoor to Wren's attention. At any rate, it was the chance of a lifetime, and he was to work with Wren for the next forty years. When Hawksmoor joined him, Wren was at the height of his creative powers; he was serving as surveyor-general in charge of Crown buildings, including the construction of St. Paul's Cathedral, and he had the ancillary task of supplying parish churches for the city as a result of the loss caused by the Great Fire of London of 1666. Hawksmoor was brought along slowly, starting off with simple office duties, but the late 1680's found him working as a draftsman, and by the early 1690's he was preparing designs for Chelsea Hospital and working as Wren's clerk and draftsman for St. Paul's and the city churches.

As early as 1685, he was preparing designs for his first important private commission, Easton Nexton House in Northamptonshire, owned by Sir William Fermor. The chance probably came to him through Wren, who was a distant relation of Fermor and was himself uninterested in domestic jobs. In 1689, he was made clerk of works at Wren's Kensington Palace project and was in charge of the drawing office at St. Paul's from 1691 onward. These major works went on for years, and he was, for example, clerk of works at Greenwich Hospital (Wren's last great commission). Just how much he contributed artistically to these works, particularly during Wren's life, is uncertain, but at Greenwich the King William Block and the Queen Anne Block look stylistically to be his, and the Orangery at Kensington Palace is probably his.

He was married in the 1690's, to a woman called Hester, and they had one daughter, Elizabeth. In 1699, established as Wren's closest associate and as an architect of some reputation in his own right, Hawksmoor entered into his second association as a subordinate, this time with the popular playwright Sir John Vanbrugh. It may seem surprising that a man without any technical training should consider himself, as Vanbrugh did, an architect, but it was not uncommon; Wren originally had a career as a scientist before deciding to design buildings. Hawksmoor, trained step-by-step in the intricacies of the profession by Wren, was in a sense better educated as an architect than either of the men whom he seconded. As in his association with Wren, Hawksmoor was to follow, and Vanbrugh was to be the gentleman-designer. Born to a humble farm family, it seemed to be temperamentally sufficient for Hawksmoor to follow the lead set by the gentlemen.

LIFE'S WORK

The two great buildings of the Vanbrugh-Hawksmoor collaboration were Castle Howard in Yorkshire and Blenheim Palace, the gift of the British nation to the duke of Marlborough for his military service during the war against Louis XIV. Castle Howard, which is familiar to many because of its use in the television version of Evelyn Waugh's *Brideshead Revisited*, is mainly Vanbrugh's, although Hawksmoor's Mausoleum, one of the splendid garden buildings, is an example of his later work. Blenheim, on the other hand, seems to have strong Hawksmoor elements in its wall decoration (where Hawksmoor always was more imaginative than either Wren or Vanbrugh) and in its numerous, extravagant towers, not only on the roofline but also on various ornamental structures throughout the park.

Both Vanbrugh and Hawksmoor were ordered off the Blenheim site by the imperious duchess of Marlborough (Sarah Churchill) in 1716, and Vanbrugh, its principal architect, was never to get back. Hawksmoor was brought back in 1722, designing ceilings, finishing rooms, and contributing what is considered the finest interior, the Long Library, as well as Woodstock Gate, the main entrance to the park.

Through these years of collaboration with Wren and Vanbrugh, Hawksmoor was involved in several independent projects, including the building of six churches in the London area that were to be the eventual touchstones of his public reputation.

He tried to work at Oxford but was rarely chosen, although the Old Clarendon Press (1712-1713) is his, and ironically, Radcliffe Camera, designed by a smoother rival, James Gibbs, looks unnervingly like Hawksmoor's proposal for the same job. Losing commissions to others, who were often less deserving, was an old story for Hawksmoor. In 1702, he lost to Vanbrugh for the job of comptroller of the King's Works, and as the young architects of Palladian persuasion came in the second decade, he lost his Whitehall positions as clerk and secretary to the Board of Works. He got his secretaryship back in 1725 but failed to succeed to Vanbrugh's office at the time of his collaborator's death. There is considerable

evidence in Hawksmoor's correspondence of his unhappiness about the way in which he was treated in the public domain, which was quite as much a matter of politics and influence as it was a matter of capability and prevailing aesthetic taste.

Through the succeeding centuries the reputation of Wren and, to a slightly lesser extent, that of Vanbrugh were to flourish; that of Nicholas Hawksmoor was to slip badly, and he was seen as not much more than an eccentric assistant to the grander talents of the other two men. Eccentric was, in fact, not an inappropriate way to see him. In fact, the Baroque itself is eccentric, an improvisatory manipulation of Renaissance classical ideas that can be viewed as inconsistent with the idea of propriety, which has always been strong in architecture. Baroque, on the Continent, was often saucily excessive, taking classical motifs to their most extravagant length, allowing the curves to swing wildly and the lines of the buildings to affect distended, swelling proportion, as a kind of reaction, in part, to the severity of classical rules, particularly those laid down by the great Italian Palladio.

The Baroque came late to England. There were modest signs of it in the mid-seventeenth century, but Wren was its first great British practitioner, and there is always a sense of rational control in his work. What distinguishes Hawksmoor is not so much his tendency to follow more emotionally the examples of continental Baroque practitioners, but his own, really quite peculiar, imaginative leaps, which make his buildings, both inside and out, so eccentrically original. On occasion, it is not inaccurate to see his work as verging on the weird and fantastic. Eclectic, as all Baroque artists were, he not only would exaggerate certain elements in a design but also would mix modes, so that it is not unusual to see classical, Renaissance, and Gothic bits and pieces brought together with surprising success in his buildings.

The London churches, all begun in the second decade of the eighteenth century and all extant in one form or another (near the end of the twentieth century, four of them were in various forms of interior and exterior scaffolding, indicating the determination to retrieve them) despite long-term neglect, the damage occasioned by World War II bombing, and the unfortunate location of three of them in Stepney, east of the city and subject to urban decay and poverty, are perhaps the best examples of what Sir John Summerson in his book *Georgian London* (1962) calls the imaginative unreason of Baroque. Many of Wren's churches are close at hand for comparison, and such comparison clearly indicates that though Hawksmoor was a true and faithful servant when working with Wren, he was, on his own, clearly and excitingly his own man.

Particularly adept at dealing with odd and awkward sites, such as those with which he was faced at St. Mary Woolnoth, and to a slightly lesser extent at St. George, Bloomsbury, and St. Alfege, Greenwich, he was always able to make an aesthetic advantage out of the liabilities. This is particularly true of St. Mary Woolnoth, which is literally crammed onto a pie-shaped site in the narrow streets across from the Bank of England. It possesses a strange, rusticated, fortresslike facade, topped by two low, embryonic towers that give it both a dramatic thuggishness and a sophisticated wittiness in the interplay of the ascending elements of the design. The same wittiness is applied to the problem of the sides, particularly to the north, where the street is so narrow, so angled that windows would be irrelevant and which Hawksmoor decorated with three deep niches in which finely carved concave aediculae are placed.

Nothing about the powerful, squat exterior of Woolnoth is sufficient preparation for the surprise of the squared richness of its archetypally Baroque interior. Indeed, surprise is a constant in his churches, particularly in design of the steeples, which range from a copy of the stepped, pyramidal Tomb of Mausolus at Halicarnassus at St. George, Bloomsbury, through the daring, sharp-angled, almost parodic steeples at St. Anne, Limehouse, and St. George-in-the-East.

Dismissed as vulgarly out of style by the new Palladians he may have been, but Hawksmoor often used Palladian motifs, particularly variations on the rounded Venetian windows, with arrogant virtuosity. Christ Church, Spitalfields, uses the arched window at both ends of the building: to the east, most conservatively as window, but at the west end on a much larger scale, as portico, which he repeats in the belfry story. At St. Alfege, Greenwich, it reaches even larger proportion as a portico, which is unusually placed, not at the west end, but abutting on the eastern chancel, since the main road passes along the eastern end of the site.

Hawksmoor was always particularly sensitive to the decorative, sculptural potential of exterior walls. Windows and window surrounds are fair game for all sorts of play, particularly in the use of oversized, almost Brobdingnagian keystones, for which he had a peculiar penchant. If he hated the Palladians, pushing into power and proclaiming their determination to purify architecture, it was not because he did not know what the rules were or

could not use them. His misuse of motifs, of any and every kind, was always deliberate, always calculated to remind, to resonate with echoes of their proper use. On the other hand, Woodstock Gate is as fine an example of the true triumphal arch as anything ever produced in the original glory of the Roman Empire.

The Woodstock Gate is helpful in coming to an understanding of Hawksmoor's aesthetic imagination. If Hawksmoor is often the most extravagantly moving of the English Baroque architects, he is not to be taken, therefore, as most inclined to follow European influences. He is, in fact, much the solidest, dourest, most monumentally inclined of the English group. The very weight of the Woodstock Gate, its obvious celebration of classical sources, is always present in his work. Whatever mix he may make of classical, Gothic, and Renaissance sources always has an unmistakable English stolidity about it. Fantastic he may be, but never frivolous. Wren is more graceful, Vanbrugh is more playful, and both are more grandiose than Hawksmoor.

Perhaps his working-class background held Hawksmoor to the ground; for all of his flights of wild surprise, there is always a sense in his buildings of sturdy craftsmanship. The weight, however, is never of such a nature as to diminish the unexpectedness of his buildings inside or out. Despite their Baroque sonority, there is often a graceful élan about the buildings that is at its best at St. George-in-the-East, which seems to ride, as Alastair Service puts it, like a great ship alongside the slightly sunken road on its south side. If one mark of the great artist is an immediately recognizable style that never palls, Hawksmoor had such a gift. What he also possessed was the capacity to be enchantingly different from work to work, and the London churches best exemplify this gift for "making it new" over and over again. With an eye fixed on the belfry stage of the monumentally towering portico and spire at the west end of Christ Church, Spitalfields, one can step slightly to the side and watch solidity turn into the flat of a stage set, architecture being quicker than the eye.

In the 1730's matters did not much improve for him, but he did gain the commission for the important design of the West Towers of Westminster Abbey, which were completed after his death. He died in March, 1736, and was buried, as he requested, at the village of Shenley in the county of Hertford.

SIGNIFICANCE

The drama of the Hawksmoor churches has not stopped working. It has, rather surprisingly, flowed into literature: It is St. Mary Woolnoth of which T. S. Eliot speaks in "The Burial of the Dead" section in *The Waste Land* (1922). Even more intriguing is the use that Peter Ackroyd makes of the London churches in his novel *Hawksmoor* (1985), in which all the London sites and buildings are used in a bizarre mystery of eighteenth and twentieth century murders, connected directly to the churches.

Some architectural historians have protested these literary depictions, primarily because what is known of Nicholas Hawksmoor suggests that he was a gentle, modest, uncomplicated man. On the other hand, his buildings are not, and there is something appropriate about them appearing in a modern gothic novel, a form of literature that developed in the later eighteenth century and that Hawksmoor's churches anticipated as not improper settings for the grotesqueries of that literary form.

—Charles H. Pullen

FURTHER READING

Downes, Kerry. *Hawksmoor*. New York: Praeger, 1970. The best popular critical biography by the scholar most responsible for putting what little is known of Hawksmoor in order. Generously illustrated.

_____. *Hawksmoor*. Cambridge, Mass.: MIT Press, 1980. A fuller, more scholarly study. Contains many illustrations. Despite its scholarship, it is gracefully written and highly readable.

DuPrey, Pierre de la Ruffinière. *Hawksmoor's London Churches: Architecture and Theology*. Chicago: University of Chicago Press, 2000. Examines Hawksmoor's six extant London churches, describing how their design reflects Hawksmoor's desire to connect with a pure Christianity.

Fletcher, Sir Banister. *A History of Architecture on the Comparative Method*. London: B. T. Batsford, 1954. This book, which is widely available in reference libraries, takes the mystery out of the movements, bringing the entire history of the scientific art to one book with many helpful illustrations.

Goodhart-Rendel, Harry Stuart. *Nicholas Hawksmoor*. London: E. Benn, 1924. The first breakthrough text that began the movement toward retrieving a reputation that had for centuries been ignored. Quite short, impassioned, and determined to put Hawksmoor in his proper place.

Hart, Vaughan. *Nicholas Hawksmoor: Rebuilding Ancient Wonders*. New Haven, Conn.: Yale University Press, 2002. Hart, an architectural historian, explains Hawksmoor's architectural theory and his role in the development of English architecture. Published for the Paul Mellen Centre for Studies in British Art.

Little, Bryan. *English Historic Architecture*. New York: Hastings House, 1964. A survey in some detail of the history of British architecture from the Saxon period to 1914, putting the English Baroque movement into the context needed to understand why it was not quite the same thing as the continental Baroque movement. Well-chosen illustrations.

Service, Alastair. *The Architects of London*. London: Architectural Press, 1979. This volume can be lugged about on a tour of London. It begins its survey in 1066 and ends with late-twentieth century architects. Includes sections on Hawksmoor, Wren, and Vanbrugh, setting out the important buildings and their locations. The comments are concise and sensible, and are often apt and incisive.

Summerson, John. *Georgian London*. London: Penguin Books, 1962. London in the eighteenth century flourished under the tasteful determination of a society, flush with money, that wanted to make the perfect town. Summerson's work is the best study of that adventure in social aesthetics, and he puts the English Baroque movement in its city context.

White, Roger. *Nicholas Hawksmoor and the Replanning of Oxford*. Oxford, England: Oxford University, Ashmolean Museum, 1997. Describes Hawksmoor's vision for rebuilding Oxford, with drawings and schematics of the architect's plan to remodel six colleges.

See also: Robert and James Adam; Lancelot Brown; Sarah Churchill; Johann Bernhard Fischer von Erlach; Johann Lucas von Hildebrandt; Antônio Francisco Lisboa; First Duke of Marlborough; Sir John Vanbrugh.

Related articles in *Great Events from History: The Eighteenth Century, 1701-1800:* 1715-1737: Building of the Karlskirche; 1762: *The Antiquities of Athens* Prompts Architectural Neoclassicism.

JOSEPH HAYDN
Austrian composer

For nearly fifty years, Haydn expressed his joy of life and love of beauty through music. Considered the father of instrumental music, he developed the form of the string quartet. Haydn's collected works include 17 operas, 68 string quartets, 62 sonatas, and 107 symphonies.

Born: March 31, 1732; Rohrau, Austria
Died: May 31, 1809; Vienna, Austrian Empire (now in Austria)
Also known as: Franz Joseph Haydn (full name)
Area of achievement: Music

EARLY LIFE
Joseph Haydn (YOH-zehf HID-n) was born in 1732 to Mathias Haydn and Maria Koller Haydn. Mathias, a wagon maker, though not poor by the standards of the day, was nevertheless unable to provide the education or training that his son so obviously needed. The young Haydn's musical talents were noted at an early age and, when he was six years old, he was given the opportunity to study at the Church of St. Philip and St. James in Hainburg. At the age of eight, fortune smiled on him again, and he was chosen to become a member of the boys' choir at St. Stephen's Cathedral in Vienna. There, his musical talents were nurtured, and his love of beauty was stimulated. There also, his love of mischief flourished, and a combination of boyish pranks and a changing voice led to his dismissal in 1749.

On his own at the age of seventeen, Haydn found that the world of Vienna offered a variety of opportunities for an industrious and talented musician. Haydn earned his keep by giving music lessons and by playing with the strolling musicians who populated Vienna. Haydn's talent and teaching (and a certain amount of luck) brought him into contact with an ever larger and more important circle of musical patrons in Vienna, and, in 1859, he was hired as musical director for Count Ferdinand Maximilian von Morzin. Through this position, he met and married Anna Aloysia Apollonia Keller. Haydn had loved Anna's younger sister, but she chose to become a nun rather than wed. He then married Anna and was thus bound into a loveless marriage.

When financial reverses led Count Morzin to give up his orchestra, Haydn moved into the service of the family with which he was to be associated for the fifty years of his greatest musical development. In 1761, Prince Pál Antal Esterházy hired Haydn as vice-chapel master, and

Haydn, with his wife, moved to the great estate of Eisenstadt, where he had his own church, opera house, choir, and orchestra. When Prince Miklós József Esterházy succeeded his brother, Haydn found in him the perfect patron, a man whose passion for music equaled his own. Most of his early works were composed for Prince Miklós, for whom Haydn developed the form of the string quartet. It was also for Prince Miklós that Haydn wrote his *Surprise Symphony* (1791), as a subtle hint that he and his musicians needed a vacation from the isolation imposed by Miklós's sojourn at the remote, fairy-tale palace at Esterháza. Each of the performers, as he completed his part, quietly blew out his candle and left the orchestra.

LIFE'S WORK
Joseph Haydn's fortune and fame grew under the Esterházys's patronage. Becoming chapel master in 1766, Haydn happily lived a rather isolated existence, but one in which his musical style grew and developed, while meeting a rigorous schedule of two concerts per week. In 1781, Haydn met the young Wolfgang Amadeus Mozart. Though vastly different in age, temperament, and musical development, these two men shared an enormous respect for each other, and each influenced the other's work. Haydn, by the 1780's, had a reputation that had spread beyond the Esterházy estates and even beyond Vienna and Austria.

In 1790, Prince Miklós died. His successor, Prince Antal, had great love neither for music nor for the enormous and remote palace of Esterháza. He paid Haydn a pension that kept him nominally in service to the family but that, in fact, left Haydn free to move to Vienna, which he did almost at once. Scarcely had Haydn settled himself and his wife when he was invited to visit and perform both in Italy and in England. Faced with the choice, Haydn accepted the offer to journey to London. When Mozart protested, saying that Haydn had no experience with travel and could not speak the language, Haydn replied, "But my language is understood all over the world."

At the age of fifty-eight, Haydn set forth for London, where some of his greatest music was composed and where he expanded his genius into the new musical form of oratorios. Haydn was young in spirit and in good health, and his two years in London were happy and spectacularly successful. He composed dozens of new works and gave a variety of public concerts, all of which were well received by the English. For the first time, Haydn, who had always been a servant of princes, moved in royal circles as a free and equal man. He was a house guest of the prince of Wales and was awarded an honorary doctor of music degree from Oxford. As always, he was admired by women, and his diary contains many love letters from a wealthy London widow.

Haydn was short but solidly built—his legs seemingly almost too short to support his body. His face was characterized by a strong nose, a broad forehead, and remarkably bright eyes. In spite of the smallpox scars that marred his face, his portraits show a not unattractive man of pleasant visage wearing the curled wig of his day. Far more appealing than his features were Haydn's naïve pleasure in his surroundings, his love of beauty, his zest for life, and his frank admiration of women. Especially strong were his ties to Maria Anna von Genzinger, to whom he wrote long letters that reveal both his daily activities and his observations on music and the world. His letters to her from London provide an especially valuable insight into Haydn's state of mind, as well as a record of his many activities in England.

Joseph Haydn. (Library of Congress)

Haydn was enormously successful in London. The warm adulation of the crowd nourished his creative talents. Among the triumphs of his sojourn in England were the symphonies inspired by the visit, which mark the peak of Haydn's instrumental compositions and the height of his maturity as a composer. In London, also, Haydn attended a performance of George Frideric Handel's *Messiah* (1742) in Westminster Abbey, with a choir of more than one thousand voices. He was greatly moved by this performance and musical style and was stimulated and challenged to emulate it. Haydn soon began work on his own masterpiece, *Die Schöpfung* (1798; *The Creation*).

As he returned to Austria in 1792, Haydn met the young Ludwig van Beethoven, who made plans to join Haydn and study under his direction in Vienna. In 1794, Haydn again returned to London, where he remained extremely popular. Though encouraged to make his home in London, Haydn returned to Vienna in 1795 at the behest of his nominal employer, Prince Miklós II, who had succeeded to the title and who, like his more illustrious ancestor, was eager to use his world-famous chapel master.

Haydn's duties upon his return were not arduous, consisting largely of the requirement that he compose masses for the prince and works for special occasions. Meanwhile, Haydn began work on his great oratorio, *The Creation*, basing the libretto on John Milton's *Paradise Lost* (1667, 1674). For three years, Haydn labored over this work. When the premier performance was given in 1798 to selected guests in Vienna, twelve policemen and eighteen mounted guards were necessary to contain the excited crowds of music lovers who thronged outside. *The Creation* was a triumph, and it was performed for many years, with the considerable proceeds going largely to charity.

The work on *The Creation* drained Haydn both physically and emotionally, but still the master continued to work. Another oratorio, *Die Jahreszeiten* (1801; *The Seasons*), followed, as did various orchestral works. Haydn's health, however, continued to decline, and on May 31, 1809, he died. Napoleon I (whose troops occupied much of Austria) sent members of the French army to form an honor guard around the catafalque, a tribute to a truly international man.

There was a curious epilogue to Haydn's death. When his body was removed to Eisenstadt for reburial in 1814, it was discovered that his head was missing. It had been removed by two of Haydn's admirers and was eventually bequeathed to the museum of the Society of Friends of Music in Vienna. In 1954, it was finally united with the body in the mausoleum built for Haydn by Prince Esterházy.

SIGNIFICANCE

Joseph Haydn was a man who enjoyed life, and this attitude was reflected in his music. His talent matured slowly; by the time he reached the age at which Mozart died, Haydn had barely begun to compose. His long life and robust health enabled him to compose many works, an accurate accounting of which is made all the more difficult by the unfortunate habit minor composers had of publishing their own works under Haydn's name in the hope of encouraging sales. Haydn was primarily an instrumental composer, and his major works include at least 37 concerti, 62 sonatas, 107 symphonies, 68 string quartets, and 45 piano trios, as well as other works. In addition to these instrumental pieces, he composed 17 operas, 2 oratorios, 60 songs, and 14 masses.

The whimsical Haydn also composed lovely small works, including a symphony for toy instruments and strings to delight children. He composed small pieces for musical clocks as well, and these were often gifts to his patron prince. A staunch patriot, Haydn was especially impressed during his sojourn in London by the stirring strains of "God Save the King," and he felt strongly the lack of a similar anthem for his own land. As the advances of Napoleon I threatened his beloved Austria, Haydn authorized the writing of a patriotic text that he set to music as the Austrian national anthem. It was first played for the emperor's birthday in 1797 and enjoyed great popularity. A variation of the familiar tune (made notorious through its use by the Nazi movement) formed the basis for one of Haydn's string quartets (op. 76), but it is most often enjoyed in the English-speaking world as the church hymn "Glorious Things of Thee Are Spoken."

Haydn was a truly remarkable individual whose musical style influenced two generations of composers. He developed and perfected the intimate form of the string quartet, arguably more difficult to write even than symphonies. Haydn worked with the different voices of the four instruments and the ways in which they could be blended together. It was a musical form uniquely his own.

Haydn's own style grew and changed as he studied and experimented with music. The tranquil years at Esterháza were especially valuable for the isolation and the time they provided him for this study. He was fundamentally interested in structure for its own sake, and this interest expressed itself in his music. His works are joyous and forthright in mood, seldom delving into the complex emotional conflicts of the Romantic composers, who so often despised Haydn's singleness of style and purpose. His rare ability to use the different sounds and range of each instrument in the orchestra makes Haydn's instrumental music especially fine. Haydn has often been rebuffed by musicians and critics for his style and for the supposed lack of seriousness in his adaptation of folk music to his symphonies, but the twentieth century saw a rebirth of Haydn's reputation and a new appreciation of his greatness. Haydn's life, reflected so perfectly in his music, was joyous and optimistic and was inspirational both to his era and to the future.

—Carlanna Hendrick

FURTHER READING

Barrett-Ayers, Reginald. *Joseph Haydn and the String Quartet*. London: Barrie & Jenkins, 1974. A specialized book for serious students of music. Nevertheless, because of its size, simplification of approach, and manageability of subject, this is an excellent book devoted to special areas of Haydn's music.

Geiringer, Karl, with Irene Geiringer. *Haydn: A Creative Life in Music*. 1946. Rev. ed. Berkeley: University of California Press, 1968. This book is by far the best single-volume treatment of Haydn's life. Includes updated scholarship and evaluation of available manuscripts as well as a sympathetic portrayal of the composer. Almost half of the book is devoted to a brief analysis of Haydn's work and the stylistic development throughout his life.

Griesinger, G. A., and A. C. Dies. *Joseph Haydn: Eighteenth-Century Gentleman and Genius*. Translated by Gernon Gotwals. Madison: University of Wisconsin Press, 1963. A delightful firsthand report on Haydn, often in his own words, by two men who knew him and worked with him. Griesinger, a business associate of Haydn, emerged as the official biographer to whom Haydn recounted the major events of his life. Dies was an art gallery director employed by Prince Esterházy who counted at least thirty visits with Haydn.

Hughes, Rosemary. *Haydn*. Rev. ed. New York: Farrar, Straus & Giroux, 1970. This short biography includes an analysis of Haydn's music in its various forms. The author credits the Geiringers as the inspiration for the biography, and this book follows much the same pattern as that earlier work. A worthwhile study of both

Haydn and his music. Possibly the most readily available source for the life of Haydn.

Landon, H. C. Robbins. *Haydn*. New York: Praeger, 1972. A slim volume, easily read, and a good introduction to Haydn. Includes brief musical bars and references to incorporate his music into a brief sketch of his life.

_____. *Haydn: Chronicle and Works*. 5 vols. Bloomington: Indiana University Press, 1980. Absolutely invaluable to serious students of Haydn. The definitive work on Haydn, this book takes advantage of the best available publications of Haydn's music. Provides a strong framework of Austrian history and culture, as well as that of England during Haydn's visits. Very detailed research on Haydn's music makes these volumes difficult for general readers but invaluable for the trained musician.

Sisman, Elaine R., ed. *Haydn and His World*. Princeton, N.J.: Princeton University Press, 1997. Collection of essays by musicologists, including an examination of Haydn's chamber music, oratorios, and symphonies. Also includes a list of the contents of Haydn's library.

Webster, James, and Georg Feder, eds. *The New Grove Haydn*. New York: Grove Press, 2002. The section about Haydn that originally was published in the *New Grove Dictionary of Music and Musicians* has been updated to appeal to general readers and reprinted in this individual volume. Also includes a list of Haydn's works, a bibliography, and illustrations.

See also: Johann Sebastian Bach; George Frideric Handel; Wolfgang Amadeus Mozart.

Related articles in *Great Events from History: The Eighteenth Century, 1701-1800*: c. 1701-1750: Bach Pioneers Modern Music; April 13, 1742: First Performance of Handel's *Messiah*; January, 1762-November, 1766: Mozart Tours Europe as a Child Prodigy; November 9-10, 1799: Napoleon Rises to Power in France.

CLAUDE-ADRIEN HELVÉTIUS
French philosopher

Helvétius was a materialist and sensualist philosophe who patronized many of the French Enlightenment's major figures and was part of the Encyclopedia *project. His major work,* De l'esprit, *angered French authorities and intellectuals alike for its uncompromisingly Epicurean view of human knowledge and understanding.*

Born: January 26, 1715; Paris, France
Died: December 26, 1771; Voré Estate, Collines des Perches, France
Areas of achievement: Philosophy, religion and theology

EARLY LIFE

Claude-Adrien Helvétius (ehl-vays-yewhs) was born to the chief physician of the queen of France, Jean-Claude-Adrien, in Paris. After initial education by tutors, he enrolled in the famed Jesuit Collége Louis-le-Grand. Since his parents destined him for a career in public finance, they sent him to live with an uncle, who was the director of the tax farms in the region around Caen in Normandy.

At the age of twenty-three, Helvétius received a gift from the queen in the form of a tax farm, worth annual revenues of 100,000 livres. Over the next thirteen years he worked a number of regions and amassed a considerable fortune. Some of his time he spent at court, but he was on the road for most of each year. While in Paris, Hélvétius befriended many of the great intellectuals of the age, such as Friedrich Melchior von Grimm, Jean-Jacques Rousseau, and Charles-Pinot Duclos, and in the course of his business travels he visited them in their rural retreats. To some of these he provided pensions of several thousand pounds per year as a way of subsidizing their philosophical efforts. He also became an early subscriber and contributor to the *Encyclopédie* project, which was under the direction of Denis Diderot and Jean le Rond d'Alembert. As a result of his conversations and correspondence with these figures, and spurred by the success of Montesquieu's *De l'esprit des loix* (1748; *The Spirit of the Laws*, 1750), he developed a set of radical ideas and decided to leave public life to cultivate the life of the philosopher. He purchased a position as maître d'hôtel to the queen, which should have provided a kind of legal protection and assured him of her patronage.

In 1749, Helvétius bought an estate of seventy-five-hundred wooded and arable acres at Voré. He resigned his tax farm in 1751, married (on August 17), and established himself as a landed gentleman at Voré. His wife was Anne-Cathérine de Ligniville, a well-educated and liberal aristocrat with whom he had two children.

LIFE'S WORK

Eight months of each year the couple attended to rural matters at Voré, and Claude-Adrien Helvétius spent much of his time reading and writing. The other four months they spent in Paris, where they held a salon each Tuesday evening at their townhouse at 18 rue Ste-Anne. They met with the likes of Montesqueiu, Voltaire, Rousseau, and the other lights of Paris intellectual life, and the gathering gained the reputation for being the most radical of the Paris scene. Helvétius himself was an outspoken opponent of the Catholic Church and the state, and he employed little of the tact that allowed others to launch their critiques without fear.

He gathered his thoughts in a book called *De l'esprit* (1758), which he considered a companion piece to Montesquieu's *De l'esprit des loix*. The work rapidly gained infamy as philosophes feared the official reaction it would provoke. The French authorities condemned its explicitly atheistic, materialistic, and hedonistic content. Though he shared most of his ideas with his fellow intellectuals, Helvétius stated these ideas in the baldest fashion, without regard for anyone's sensibilities. Prince Louis expressed his outrage; both the Sorbonne and the Parlement of Paris condemned the work, as did the pope in a letter of January 31, 1759. On February 10, Parlement had the book publicly burned, along with similar works by Voltaire and other authors. The queen revoked Helvétius's position at court, and even Voltaire publicly decried the work for its commonness and, where it provided new ideas, its obscurity.

On three separate occasions Helvétius was forced to recant the work, and he did so, though without conviction. The publication was also responsible for the closing down of the *Encylcopédie* project. Although he weathered the firestorm, Helvétius would not publish another work during his lifetime. In 1764 he paid a brief visit to England, where King George III pointedly welcomed the author but not the book. After this he spent about a year at the court of Frederick the Great in Berlin, dining often with the ruler, who also managed to distinguish his esteemed guest from his radical book. While there, Helvétius was inducted into the Berlin Academy and worked on a less "obscure" version of his work called *De l'homme* (*A Treatise on Man: His Intellectual Faculties and His Education*, 1777), published posthumously in 1773. His correspondence, numerous short works, and *Les progrès de la raison dans la recherche du vrai* (1775; the progress of reason in the search for truth) also were published shortly after his death. After his return to Paris he founded the Masonic lodge called The Sciences (1766). Even after his death in late 1771, his salon continued to attract the intellectual elite. Unlike so many intellectuals, he died a very wealthy man, leaving an estate worth 4,000,000 livres.

Helvétius's thought as expressed in *De l'esprit* was in many ways right in the mainstream of French Enlightenment thinking. In many ways it was an updated form of Epicureanism, a Hellenistic philosophy that had been revived during the Renais-

---

REDISTRIBUTING WEALTH

In a tract on economic inequality, Claude-Adrien Helvétius proposes ways not only to equalize income between the classes but also to make people happier. He argues for reduced work hours and increased wages, and for "diminishing" the economic resources of the rich to "augment" the income of the working poor.

The almost universal unhappiness of man, and of nations, arises from the imperfections of their laws, and the too unequal partition of their riches. There are in most kingdoms only two classes of citizens, one of which want necessaries, and the other riot in superfluities.

The former cannot gratify their wants but by excessive labour: such labour is a natural evil for all; and to some it is a punishment.

The second class live in abundance, but at the same time in the anguish of discontent. Now discontent is an evil almost as much to be dreaded as indigence.

Most countries, therefore, must be peopled by the unfortunate. What would be done to make them happy? Diminish the riches of some; augment that of others; put the poor in such a state of ease, that they may by seven or eight hours' labour abundantly provide for the wants of themselves and their families. It is then, that a people will become happy as can be.

Source: Claude-Adrien Helvétius, in *The Enlightenment: The Culture of the Eighteenth Century*, edited by Isidor Schneider (New York: George Braziller, 1965), p. 231.

sance. Helvétius's version was directly influenced by the empiricism of John Locke and its application and development by the French thinker Étienne Bonnot de Condillac, especially in his *Traité des sensations* (1754; *Condillac's Treatise on Sensations*, 1930). In brief, Epicureans believe that what a person knows, or can know, is attained through the senses alone: Individuals have no preexisting, inborn, or innate ideas, nor can a person learn from other faculties. This, of course, undermined Catholic teaching on both spiritual enlightenment and reliance on Church authority. As a materialist, Helvétius went further, adopting the modern form of the ancient Greek idea that all that exists must be made of matter, which is a clear denial of any "spiritual" world or entities, including a nonmaterial soul or spirit.

A person learns about the world by experiencing the world through the senses, and "human nature" is not an absolute but a construct composed of accumulated discrete experiences. The social (and political) environment and education—both formal and informal—create the person, and if these forces are reformed and directed properly, humankind can be transformed or even perfected. Some philosophes, however, were bothered by the radicality of Helvétius's materialism, for if all human nature is constructed, from what source do human rights stem?

On a moral level, Helvétius reduced the concepts of good and bad to the sensations of pleasure and pain. Thus, the moral life consisted of pursuing physical pleasure and avoiding physical pain. This supported his unconventional hedonism, which virtually required sexual license. Social organization—itself a purely human construct—at its most fundamental is founded on this principle as well, though without the sex. The problem, of course, was reconciling self-interest and personal pleasure with the public interest. Here is where the public control of education became necessary. Properly focused education could shape experiences in such a way as to manipulate the young person to accept the public interest as his or her own. Laws, which inflicted pain for the commission of unapproved acts, would act similarly to shape behavior. Rousseau reacted to this assault on his "natural man" model by branding Helvétius, quite rightly, an atheist.

Helvétius branded as vile all forms of education and governance that shaped behavior to turn away from the true public interest and the pursuit of greatest liberty and pleasure. He linked the intellectual and even aesthetic worlds with the political, and he posited that any true "republic of letters" required a republican form of govern-ment. This kind of thinking would lead to political revolution as the radical response to social ills. It was no mere whim that led the revolutionary government in France to rename rue Ste-Anne, as rue Helvétius.

SIGNIFICANCE

Claude-Adrien Helvétius's ideas were in themselves far from novel or revolutionary, but what was revolutionary was his blunt expression of these ideas. In tearing away the veil he exposed the atheistic and materialistic foundations of much enlightened thinking, and he exposed the philosophes to the dangers of a repressive regime. Though heavily criticized in his own day, one may see his emphasis on individual happiness as the goal of a society reflected in Thomas Jefferson's alteration of John Locke's "life, liberty and property" to "life, liberty and the pursuit of happiness" in the U.S. Declaration of Independence. Helvétius's works also had a major influence on the ideas of Jeremy Bentham and the ethical components of English utilitarian thought in the nineteenth century.

—*Joseph P. Byrne*

FURTHER READING

Cumming, I. *Helvétius: His Life and Place in the History of Educational Thought.* London: Routledge, 1955. Provides a biography and intellectual history of Helvétius and his philosophical materialism.

Grossman, Mordecai. *The Philosophy of Helvétius: With Special Emphasis on the Educational Implications of Sensationalism.* New York: AMS Press, 1972. Based on the author's doctoral dissertation, originally published in 1926, though still a cogent discussion of Helvétius's thought and its impact on behavioralism.

Helvétius, Claude-Adrien. *De l'esprit: Or, Essays on the Mind.* Sterling, Va.: Thoemmes, 2000. A reprint of the 1810 edition of Helvétius's controversial work.

Smith, David Warner. *Helvétius: A Study in Persecution.* Westport, Conn.: Greenwood Press, 1982. A study of French society's reaction to *De l'esprit* and other expressions of Helvétius's thought.

See also: Jeremy Bentham; Comte de Buffon; Étienne Bonnot de Condillac; Marquis de Condorcet; Dai Zhen; Denis Diderot; George III; David Hume; Louis XVI; Montesquieu; Jean-Jacques Rousseau; Anne-Robert-Jacques Turgot; Voltaire.

Related articles in *Great Events from History: The Eighteenth Century, 1701-1800:* 1726-1729: Voltaire Advances Enlightenment Thought in Europe; 1748: Montesquieu Publishes *The Spirit of the Laws*; 1749-

1789: First Comprehensive Examination of the Natural World; 1751-1772: Diderot Publishes the *Encyclopedia*; 1754: Condillac Defends Sensationalist Theory; July 27, 1758: Helvétius Publishes *De l'esprit*; January, 1759: Voltaire Satirizes Optimism in *Candide*; April, 1762: Rousseau Publishes *The Social Contract*; July, 1764: Voltaire Publishes *A Philosophical Dictionary for the Pocket*; 1782-1798: Publication of Rousseau's *Confessions*.

PATRICK HENRY
American attorney and politician

Expressing his libertarian ideas through a uniquely powerful oratory, Henry was a principal architect of the American Revolution. He is especially remembered for his poignant words before the revolutionary convention in Virginia in 1775: "Give me liberty, or give me death!"

Born: May 29, 1736; Studley Plantation, Hanover County, Virginia
Died: June 6, 1799; Red Hill Plantation, Charlotte County, Virginia
Areas of achievement: Government and politics, law

EARLY LIFE
Patrick Henry was born in Hanover County, Virginia, the second son of John Henry, a well-educated Scotsman from Aberdeen, and Sarah Winston Syme, the young and charming widow of Colonel John Syme. Henry's early years were characteristic of a farm boy in colonial Virginia. Hunting and fishing were consuming enthusiasms for him, although he also received a sound education (focused on mathematics and the Latin classics) from local schoolmasters, his uncle Patrick Henry (a minister), and his father.

At the age of fifteen, he was apprenticed as a clerk in a country store. A year later, he joined his older brother as a partner in a similar venture, which, however, failed. Meanwhile, Henry had fallen in love with Sarah Shelton, the daughter of nearby landowner John Shelton, and the two were married in the fall of 1754. The young couple took up residence on a small farm that had been given to them by Sarah's father. For three years they eked out a marginal existence, but worse was to come. In 1757, their house was destroyed by fire. Destitute, they moved into the large tavern owned by Sarah's father at Hanover Courthouse, where Henry for a time supported himself and his family, now including four children, by helping manage the tavern for his father-in-law.

By all accounts, Henry was a charming and convivial taverner, but there is otherwise little in his life to this point to foretell the kind of impact he would have on American history. Proximity to a busy provincial courthouse and frequent association with those who came and went there must have inspired his latent abilities, for by the age of twenty-four he had resolved upon becoming a lawyer. The normal course for a young man of such ambitions would have been to apprentice himself to an established lawyer who had attended one of the Inns of Court of London (there were no law schools in the American colonies; the first would be established in 1779 in Virginia at William and Mary College).

Henry, however, attempted his project through a program of self-study and, miraculously, succeeded within a year. His board of examiners was headed by the illustrious brothers Peyton and John Randolph. Impressed more by the force of natural genius he displayed in his examination than by his spotty knowledge of law, they admitted him to the bar. Their somewhat reluctant confidence was more than justified, for within three years, Henry had become a successful lawyer. Having handled some 1,125 cases, most of which he won, he was, at the age of twenty-seven, poised to enter the arena of history-making events.

LIFE'S WORK
The case that catapulted Patrick Henry to widespread recognition as a bold political spirit with a singular gift for oratory was the Parson's Cause of 1763. In colonial America, as in England, the Anglican Church was supported by general taxation, and in Virginia, salaries for the clergy were tied to the price of tobacco. A 1758 act of the Virginia legislature had fixed the nominal price of tobacco for this purpose at two pence per pound. Since this was far less than the actual commodity value of tobacco, the clergy petitioned King George III and his Privy Council to overrule the act. George did indeed overrule the act, thereby allowing the Virginia clergy to sue for back pay.

Patrick Henry delivering his famous speech on the rights of the American colonies. (Library of Congress)

Henry was engaged to handle the defense in the pivotal case brought by the Reverend Mr. James Maury. The youthful attorney's argument asserted that the 1758 law was just and that in overturning it, the king was acting as a tyrant. The jury of sturdy farmers was so impressed that it awarded the plaintiff Maury only a penny in damages. Henry's fame soon spread throughout Virginia, thereby laying the ground for his entry into the forefront of colonial politics.

In May, 1765, Henry entered the House of Burgesses, only a few weeks after Britain had passed the notorious Stamp Act. On his twenty-ninth birthday, only ten days after taking his seat as a representative, he proposed a number of resolutions against the Stamp Act, based on the assumption that only colonial legislatures had the right to levy colonial taxes. A lean six-footer, with plain angular features and dark, deep-set eyes, the somewhat ungainly and roughly dressed young legislator climaxed his defense of the resolutions with the threatening words (as reported by Thomas Jefferson), "Caesar had his Brutus, Charles the First his Cromwell, and George the Third—"

whereupon, interrupted by cries of "Treason!" Henry concluded, "may profit by their example. If this be treason, make the most of it." His daring speech galvanized the House of Burgesses into adopting his resolutions, and Virginia became an example to the other colonies in the rising resistance to taxation without representation.

Over the next few years, Patrick Henry's fame and authority as a revolutionary leader increased, as from his seat in the House of Burgesses he continued to oppose British encroachment upon the autonomy of the colonies. In September, 1774, he served as a member of the First Continental Congress that met in Philadelphia to deal with new British coercive measures imposed in the aftermath of the Boston Tea Party. Some six months later, he was an organizer of the revolutionary convention convened in Richmond to decide how Virginia should respond to the worsening situation, and it was in this setting, on March 23, 1775, that he made the speech that served as a call to arms for the colonies in the coming struggle. Arguing for the need to raise armed forces immediately, he concluded,

---

CALLING FOR WAR AGAINST THE BRITISH

Before the 1775 revolutionary convention in Virginia, and with British troops massing in Boston, convention organizer Patrick Henry gave a rousing, passionate speech that has become legendary in American history. In this excerpt, Henry calls for an end to British tyranny and colonial American subservience. To win freedom, he says, Americans need to take up arms and fight. He ends his speech with the infamous words, "Give me liberty, or give me death!"

Let us not, I beseech you, sir, deceive ourselves longer. Sir, we have done everything that could be done to avert the storm which is now coming on. We have petitioned; we have remonstrated; we have supplicated; we have prostrated ourselves before the tyrannical hands of the ministry and parliament. Our petitions have been slighted; our remonstrances have produced additional violence and insult; our supplications have been disregarded, and we have been spurned, with contempt, from the foot of the throne. In vain, after these things, may we indulge the fond hope of peace and reconciliation. There is no longer any room for hope. If we wish to be free—if we mean to preserve inviolate those inestimable privileges for which we have been so long contending—if we mean not basely to abandon the noble struggle in which we have been so long engaged, and which we have pledged ourselves never to abandon until the glorious object of our contest shall be obtained, we must fight! I repeat it, sir, we must fight! An appeal to arms and to the God of Hosts is all that is left us.

Source: Patrick Henry, 1775 speech, in *Living History America*, edited by Erik Bruun and Jay Crosby (New York: Tess Press, 1999), p. 135.

Is life so dear or peace so sweet as to be purchased at the price of chains and slavery? Forbid it, Almighty God! I know not what course others may take, but as for me, give me liberty, or give me death!

Swayed by the dramatic impact of this speech, the members of the convention authorized the formation of companies of militia, one of which was led by Henry himself in May to demand restoration of the gunpowder seized from the Williamsburg magazine by the Loyalist governor, Lord Dunmore. Although he succeeded, he was not cut out for military leadership. After a short appointment as a regimental commander, and burdened by grief for the death of his wife, he resigned his commission and returned home on February 28, 1776.

His absence from public life was only brief; in May, he took part in drafting the new constitution of Virginia, and on June 29 he was elected the first governor of the newly constituted commonwealth, a position in which he served for three years (retiring in 1779) and to which he was reelected for two years in 1784. Meanwhile, he had

married again, to Dorothea Dandridge, and had taken up residence on a huge tract of land in the mountainous western area of the state. A representative of the Virginia legislature from 1786 to 1790, he declined a nomination to the Constitutional Convention, while from his legislative seat he bitterly opposed Virginia's adoption of the Constitution in 1788, fearing its restrictive effect upon the sovereignty of the states, particularly those of the South. His vehement and sustained opposition was insufficient to prevent adoption, but it did prompt a general recognition of the need for constitutional amendments, leading to the framing of the first ten amendments; the Bill of Rights passed in 1791.

From 1790 to 1795, Henry returned to private law practice. The last years of his life were spent in semiretirement at his Red Hill plantation in Charlotte County. He refused the positions of both secretary of state and chief justice offered to him in 1795 by George Washington, but, increasingly reconciled to the principles of Federalism in his last years, he agreed in 1799 to run for the Virginia legislature once again. Elected, he did not live to serve his term, dying on June 6, 1799.

SIGNIFICANCE

The American Revolution was produced by heroic talents and energies that together achieved critical mass; within this process, the oratory of Patrick Henry was catalytic in effect. In an era of great public speakers, it was his voice in particular that provided a rallying cry for the colonial patriots at critical moments, especially in 1765, during the Stamp Act controversy, and, ten years later, on the eve of the battles of Lexington and Concord. His oratory was legendary in its own time. Characterized, according to contemporary accounts, by extraordinary dramatic nuance and force, it stands as an enduring example of the power of an individual speaker to influence large-scale events.

Henry's resistance to the principles of Federalism in later years is also indicative of a deep strain both in his character and in American society. Born in a picturesque but still largely "wild" region of Virginia, his first love was the land—its topography and vegetation, its creatures, and its seasons. The concept of liberty for him was rooted in a deep respect for nature and the individual autonomy nurtured by the frontier environment. His opposition to British rule and to federal authority should be seen as the two sides of a single coin. His anti-Federalist speeches in the Virginia assembly were a main influence behind the passage of the Bill of Rights. Yet the same kinds of sentiments divided the nation half a century later on the issue of states' rights—a controversy that even the Civil War did not eradicate.

In many ways, Henry's achievements are the stuff of which American legends have been forged. Son of colonial Virginia, self-made forensic genius, patriot, and lifelong spokesman for individual rights, even at the expense of national unity, his life is part of the national mythology of America, and his famous words "Give me liberty, or give me death" have etched themselves on the national psyche.

—*Charles Duncan*

FURTHER READING

Axelrad, Jacob. *Patrick Henry, the Voice of Freedom.* New York: Random House, 1947. A book for the general reader, somewhat dated in approach but useful for its economical account of Henry's career and its informative commentary on contemporary historical events.

Beeman, Richard R. *Patrick Henry: A Biography.* New York: McGraw-Hill, 1974. A solid, thoroughly researched, academic history. Beeman's vision of Henry is somewhat deconstructionist; he is not the legendary hero but a man more characteristic of his times. Beeman deals especially well with the less celebrated aspects of Henry's career, such as his role as governor and administrator.

Campbell, Norine Dickson. *Patrick Henry, Patriot and Statesman.* New York: Devin-Adair, 1969. The value of this work lies in its sense of the living presence of history as well as in the occasional emphatic detail produced by devoted research.

McCants, David A. *Patrick Henry, the Orator.* New York: Greenwood Press, 1990. An analysis of Henry's oratory within its historical and political contexts.

Mayer, Henry. *A Son of Thunder: Patrick Henry and the American Republic.* New York: Franklin Watts, 1986. A substantial, well-researched, and absorbing biography that places Henry in the context of his time.

Emphasizes his roots in the "evangelical revolt" against Virginia's aristocratic establishment.

Mayo, Bernard. *Myths and Men: Patrick Henry, George Washington, Thomas Jefferson.* Athens: University of Georgia Press, 1959. A collection of perceptive commentaries on the major leadership of the American Revolution. The essay on Henry is valuable as an economical, balanced overview of the issues of scholarship and historiography surrounding his biography.

Meade, Robert Douthat. *Patrick Henry.* 2 vols. Philadelphia: J. B. Lippincott, 1957-1969. The most comprehensive biography of Henry to appear in the twentieth century, likely to become the standard authoritative reference work. Meade's coverage of his subject is meticulous, based on definitive research into all aspects of Henry's private and public life.

Tyler, Moses Coit. *Patrick Henry.* Boston: Houghton Mifflin, 1887. A masterpiece of nineteenth century historiography, the first modern biography of Henry, and best for the general reader. The worshipful view of Henry, though old-fashioned, is deeply sincere.

Vaughan, David J. *Give Me Liberty: The Uncompromising Statesmanship of Patrick Henry.* Nashville, Tenn.: Cumberland House, 1997. Vaughan's book is divided into three sections. Part 1 provides an overview of Henry's life, part 2 describes his character traits, and part 3 assesses his legacy.

Willison, George F. *Patrick Henry and His World.* Garden City, N.Y.: Doubleday, 1969. Probably the best all-around general study. Willison's title is appropriate; the coverage of background historical material is thorough and illuminating. The book is well-paced, admirably written, and spiced with colorful, often amusing anecdotes.

See also: George Rogers Clark; George III; Alexander Hamilton; Thomas Jefferson; James Madison; George Mason; George Washington.

Related articles in *Great Events from History: The Eighteenth Century, 1701-1800:* 1712: Stamp Act; March 22, 1765-March 18, 1766: Stamp Act Crisis; March 5, 1770: Boston Massacre; December 16, 1773: Boston Tea Party; September 5-October 26, 1774: First Continental Congress; April 19, 1775: Battle of Lexington and Concord; May 10-August 2, 1775: Second Continental Congress; July 4, 1776: Declaration of Independence; September 17, 1787: U.S. Constitution Is Adopted; December 15, 1791: U.S. Bill of Rights Is Ratified.

JOHANN GOTTFRIED HERDER
German philosopher and theologian

Herder was a major figure in the transitional period in German letters that encompassed the second half of the eighteenth century. He was a universalist whose writings dealt with many areas of human thought.

Born: August 25, 1744; Mohrungen, East Prussia (now Morag, Poland)
Died: December 18, 1803; Weimar, Saxe-Weimar (now in Germany)
Also known as: Johann Gottfried von Herder
Areas of achievement: Philosophy, literature

EARLY LIFE

Johann Gottfried Herder (yoh-HAHN GAWT-freet HUR-duhr) was born on August 25, 1744, in the small East Prussian town of Mohrungen. He came from a family of modest financial resources; his father worked as a teacher, organist, and church warden. Both parents were pious people, and Herder grew up influenced by the moderate Pietist ideas common in the clergy at this time, which were opposed to orthodoxy and dogma in favor of a more personal, inner-directed religious life.

Herder had two sisters, who married and remained in Mohrungen. He showed his great desire to study rather early in life. While in Latin school, he became the favorite student of the stern schoolmaster, and at the age of sixteen he obtained free lodging with a vicar named Sebastian Trescho in exchange for work as a copyist. This arrangement was particularly advantageous for Herder because the vicar had an excellent library, where Herder could satisfy his avid desire to read.

Although Herder wished to attend the university, family finances might have made that impossible. Fortunately, when the Russian troops moved into the region in 1762, the regimental surgeon met Herder and generously offered to pay for his medical studies at Königsberg. In the spring of that year, Herder enrolled in medicine at the university, but he was clearly not suited to that field. Changing his field to theology, he lost his benefactor's support but was able to finance his own studies with a stipend and money earned by tutoring at the Collegium Fridericianum.

In Königsberg, Herder met Johann Georg Hamann, whose ideas greatly influenced him even though his own philosophical views differed from Hamann's, for example, on the origin of language. Hamann's thoughts on the Bible inspired some of Herder's early attempts at a better understanding of the book through its poetic medium and

an understanding of its social and historical context. During those same years, Herder attended lectures by Immanuel Kant on a wide range of subjects, which offered stimulus to his thought, as did contact with humanistic and humanitarian ideas, such as those of the Deutsche Gesellschaft (German Society).

LIFE'S WORK

In 1764, Herder began his professional life in the Domschule of Riga. He stayed for five years, during which time he became a successful teacher and preacher and published his first two books, *Über die neuere deutsche Literatur: Fragmente* (1767; on recent German literature: fragments) and *Kritische Wälder* (1769; critical forests), which brought him recognition and also criticism. His ideas about language became central to many other parts of his thinking as well. In his literary criticism, Herder rejects absolute standards and argues instead that the critic must enter into the spirit of the literary work, judging it from the point of view of its intentions.

In 1769, Herder departed from Riga for France. He spent several months in Nantes, where he wrote a type of diary of his voyage, revealing important parts of his inner life (not for publication). His intended destination was Paris, which he found that he disliked, and he soon left to accompany the prince-bishop of Oldenburg-Eutin's son on a three-year tour. He first went to the Netherlands and then continued on to Hamburg, where he met Gotthold Ephraim Lessing and Matthias Claudius. The companion role did not suit Herder, so he soon separated from the prince; however, the tour did bring him in contact with his future wife, Karoline Flachsland, in Darmstadt. After an unsuccessful eye operation in Strasbourg, he met Johann Wolfgang von Goethe in 1770. Herder's ideas on language, the historical development of humanity, and Hebrew poetry in the Old Testament had a great influence on the young Goethe. Herder was working on *Abhandlung über den Ursprung der Sprache* (1772; *Treatise upon the Origin of Language*, 1827), which was awarded a prize from the Prussian Academy of Sciences and which was something of a nucleus for future works. Through his organic philosophy of history and his recourse to the senses, Herder became recognized as a leading figure of the Sturm und Drang (storm and stress) literary movement.

Also in 1771, Herder decided to accept a church position as a *Hofprediger,* or court preacher, in Bückeburg so that he could be married, and he began a period of intensive writing. Herder's views put him in conflict with Count Wilhelm of Schaumburg-Lippe, since Herder defended the rights of the Church. At the same time, the clergy found him too liberal. When he was unable to move to Göttingen as a theology professor because of opposition from the other clergy, he took a position in Weimar, which Goethe helped him obtain.

Herder moved to Weimar in 1776, where he remained, although he complained that his efforts—in church and school reform, for example—were not appreciated. Herder's relationship with Goethe was difficult now that they were peers, but a period of friendship and collaboration followed, which lasted from 1783 to 1789. A serious rift occurred in 1794, when Goethe's friendship with Friedrich Schiller deepened. Jealousy created part of the conflict; however, another part was clearly a difference of philosophical opinion.

Herder was extremely productive in Weimar, writing some of his most important works, including *Ideen zur Philosophie der Geschichte der Menschheit* (1784-1791; *Outlines of a Philosophy of the History of Man*, 1800), often considered his most important work. His plan to write a fifth part was abandoned with the outbreak of the

Johann Gottfried Herder. (Library of Congress)

French Revolution. Instead, he began his *Briefe zu Beförderung der Humanität* (1793-1797; *Letters for the Advancement of Humanity*, 1800), in which he included some indirect commentary on events of the time. Herder saw human history as a natural development according to universal laws. His point of view was a religious humanism based on his conviction that creation was an indivisible whole. Furthermore, although he wished to take into account advances in science, he did not accept a mechanistic view of nature. Herder believed that both history and nature reflected the working of a divine spirit and that gradual progress was taking place. The French Revolution, however, caused him to doubt his views. His most mature religious ideas, making explicit his conception of God by combining a dynamic concept of nature with the idea of a divine immanence, appeared in his work *Gott: Einige Gespräche* (1787; *God: Some Conversations*, 1940).

Herder joined Goethe and Schiller in their project of a nonpolitical journal, *Die Horen* (1795-1797), but withdrew after an argument with Schiller about the role of literature in society. Also during this time, Herder became more and more hostile to Immanuel Kant's ideas. In 1785, Kant harshly reviewed the first two parts of Herder's major work, *Outlines of a Philosophy of the History of Man*, and in 1799, Herder retaliated by criticizing several of Kant's major works.

Herder's later work includes many shorter pieces. His last collection, *Adrastea* (1801-1804), which remained unfinished, comprised a discussion of eighteenth century history, culture, and religious ideas, including New Testament studies. His criticism of his times is also evident.

Herder felt isolated in Weimar after his break with Goethe and his criticism of the classical movement, although his friendship with Jean Paul Richter lessened this feeling somewhat. Toward the end of his life, Herder was interrupted in his work by illness. He died on December 18, 1803, leaving behind an extensive body of work.

SIGNIFICANCE

Johann Gottfried Herder was a major figure of the eighteenth century whose ideas had an impact on his age and on the nineteenth century in many areas of thought. Most commonly, he is acknowledged as a stimulus for the Sturm und Drang writers, including Goethe, and is counted among the critics of Kant's philosophical ideas as well as of German classicism.

In his writing, Herder attempted to achieve a type of synthesis that is associated with the universality of a Renaissance man. He wrote on religion, society, history, literary criticism, psychology, science, education, aesthetics, and the arts. He attempted to capture the totality of human experience, seeing creation as an organic whole, and rejected rationalism and any type of philosophical system, such as that proposed by Kant. Although maintaining his religious ties, he saw religion as something that should serve humanity, and he was equally opposed to orthodoxy (dogmatism) and antireligious secularization. Herder viewed the human soul as an entity where a person's powers are in harmony. The body is the mediator for the soul in its relationship with the material world, but the soul is the center of creative powers and has within it the drive toward perfection (*Humanität*).

As a thinker, Herder constantly sought to reconcile opposing currents in the intellectual community and within his own views. For example, he attempted to reconcile the early influence of Hamann's transcendental ideas with empiricism, gained in part by Kant's early influence; he synthesized religious and scientific elements; and he tried to balance some of the irrationalism of Sturm und Drang with more rationalist ideas. The result is an important body of writing with a rather consistent view developed from his first major works through his final essays. Herder influenced many of his important contemporaries, especially Goethe, but, unfortunately, by the 1790's his ideas were in conflict with the dominant values of classicism and the beginnings of Romanticism. Still, he was a keen observer of historical and cultural movements. His greatest importance may well be in sowing ideas which others later brought to fruition.

—*Susan L. Piepke*

FURTHER READING

Barnard, F. M. *Herder's Social and Political Thought: From Enlightenment to Nationalism.* Oxford, England: Clarendon Press, 1965. A study of the development of Herder's concept of organism and organic politics, ending with an assessment of his impact on German political Romanticism and of his immediate influence outside Germany. The discussion also includes a separate chapter on the central concept of *Humanität* in relation to religion, ethics, and politics.

Clark, Robert T. *Herder: His Life and Thought.* Berkeley: University of California Press, 1955. The most detailed Herder biography available in English, including a characterization of his important works set against the intellectual background of his time. Contains many quotations from Herder's work in English

translation as well as an extensive bibliography, with a listing of available translations.

Fugate, Joe K. *The Psychological Basis of Herder's Aesthetics.* The Hague, the Netherlands: Mouton, 1966. A discussion of the aesthetic questions considered by Herder from the perspective of his psychological ideas and principles. Fugate argues that in Herder's work, human endeavors in the arts cannot be understood without taking into account the powers inherent in the human soul. A bibliography includes general works and individual studies pertaining to Herder, some in English.

Herder, Johann Gottfried. *God: Some Conversations.* Translated with an introduction and notes by Frederick H. Burkhardt. New York: Hafner Press, 1949. The book's introduction discusses Herder's development and places this work in the context of his times, relating it specifically to Immanuel Kant and Baruch Spinoza. Serving as a table of contents, there is a brief summary of each of the five conversations and the epilogue.

_____. *Philosophical Writings.* Translated and edited by Michael N. Forster. New York: Cambridge University Press, 2002. Features some of Herder's essays on the philosophy of language, the mind, history, and politics. Includes an introductory essay.

Koepke, Wulf. *Johann Gottfried Herder.* Boston: Twayne, 1987. A general introduction for the nonspecialist. Koepke follows the unity in Herder's ideas and concerns through his life in historical sequence and emphasizes the importance of Herder's own achievements rather than viewing him mainly as Goethe's mentor or as a figure whose ideas were incorporated and improved by his successors. Useful annotated bibliography.

_____, ed. *Johann Gottfried Herder: Innovator Through the Ages.* Bonn, Germany: Bouvier, 1982. Eleven articles by different authors, reflecting some of the concerns of North American scholarship on Herder. Among the topics are the concept of *Humanität,* Herder's language model, and his theological writings. Includes a bibliography of mostly German-language sources and a useful index of names and works.

Nisbet, H. B. *Herder and the Philosophy and History of Science.* Cambridge, England: Modern Humanities Research Association, 1970. A detailed consideration of Herder's place in the history of the social, biological, and physical sciences. Nisbet argues that far from subscribing to Johann Hamann's antiscientific irrationalism, Herder affirmed the value of science in human history. Extensive bibliography on the subject, including works in German and English.

Schick, Edgar B. *Metaphorical Organicism in Herder's Early Works: A Study of the Relation of Herder's Literary Idiom to His World-View*. The Hague, the Netherlands: Mouton, 1971. A focused study of Herder's essays up to 1778, showing metaphors of organicism as central to an understanding of the work. Schick applies his thesis to Herder's writings on language, aesthetics, literary criticism, and historical development, concluding with an assessment of the conservative and innovative elements in Herder's organicist thought.

Zammito, John H. *Kant, Herder, and the Birth of Anthropology*. Chicago: University of Chicago Press, 2002. Examination of Herder's friendship with his teacher Kant, which eventually ended in bitter rivalry. Compares and contrasts their differing philosophies, describing how Herder's reinterpretation of Kant's ideas created the new science of anthropology.

See also: Johann Wolfgang von Goethe; Immanuel Kant; Gotthold Ephraim Lessing; Friedrich Schiller.

Related articles in *Great Events from History: The Eighteenth Century, 1701-1800*: October, 1725: Vico Publishes *The New Science*; 1739-1740: Hume Publishes *A Treatise of Human Nature*; April, 1762: Rousseau Publishes *The Social Contract*; July, 1764: Voltaire Publishes *A Philosophical Dictionary for the Pocket*; 1770: Publication of Holbach's *The System of Nature*; 1781: Kant Publishes *Critique of Pure Reason*; 1784-1791: Herder Publishes His Philosophy of History; 1792-1793: Fichte Advocates Free Speech.

CAROLINE LUCRETIA HERSCHEL
German-born English astronomer

Herschel was an astronomer and mathematician who spent years assisting her better-known brother William Herschel in his astronomical observations. However, she also independently scanned the sky for new objects, discovering two galaxies, several open star clusters, and eight comets. After her brother's death, she completed the Herschel catalog of twenty-five hundred nebulae, which was included in her nephew John Herschel's General Catalogue.

Born: March 16, 1750; Hanover (now in Germany)
Died: January 9, 1848; Hanover
Areas of achievement: Astronomy, music, mathematics

EARLY LIFE
Caroline Lucretia Herschel (KEHR-eh-lihn lew-KREE-shee-ah HUR-shehl) was the younger of two girls born to Isaac and Anna Ilse Herschel. She also had four brothers as well as three other siblings who died. Isaac, a musician and professor of music, encouraged his children to become educated. As the youngest daughter, Caroline was expected by her mother to do most of the housework, who generally treated Caroline as she would a servant.

When Caroline was seven, her brothers William and Alexander went to England when their regimental band was ordered there and her father fought in the war against France. At age ten, Caroline contracted typhoid fever, which stunted her growth and caused her to stoop slightly. She was only four feet, three inches tall as an adult, and her father predicted that she would likely never marry. In spite of her mother's attempts to enslave Caroline to domestic duties, her father educated her in music and mathematics and introduced her to astronomy. By 1760 her father had returned from the war, but he remained in poor health until his death in 1767.

In spite of her mother's attempts to keep her in servitude and after her father's death, Caroline decided to take more control of her own life and so learned dressmaking, planning to become a governess. Her brother William had been hired as organist in Bath in 1766, and by 1772 he decided to invite Caroline, now twenty-two years old, to live with him. Against her mother's protests she moved to England, where her brother gave her voice lessons and tutored her in English and mathematics.

She soon began a singing career under her brother's direction. She was a first soprano singing George Frideric Handel's *Messiah* and *Judas Macabaeus*, among other works, and was often engaged several nights a week. She turned down offers from other directors, reserving her singing for performances directed by her brother. During this time she also began helping William with his telescope projects. She learned to grind and polish lenses and construct the finished telescopes.

LIFE'S WORK

As she learned the skills needed to help William in the shop, Caroline also continued her studies in mathematics, focusing almost exclusively on topics applicable to astronomy, her brother's growing passion. William's obsession with his telescopes became so consuming that Caroline sometimes had to feed him while he continued his work, and other times she would read to him to pass the time productively as he laboriously turned yet another lens for a new telescope.

By 1781, William was spending more and more time gazing through his telescopes at the night sky, and Caroline was often by his side taking notes on his observations. In this same year, William made his breakthrough discovery, the planet Uranus. The astronomical community praised his discovery and King George III awarded William an annual salary of £200. William resigned his position as organist, and soon thereafter Caroline gave up her music career to devote her time to astronomy as well.

As William built ever-larger telescopes and needed increased workspace, he and Caroline moved to larger quarters, first to Clay Hall and then to Slough. Although

Caroline Herschel, at age ninety-two. (Library of Congress)

Caroline spent most of her time assisting her brother by taking records during their nightly observations and doing calculations during the day so the night's objects could be cataloged, she was still able to find time for her own observations. William encouraged her in this direction. She discovered her first new object on February 26, 1783, an open star cluster in the constellation Canis Major. Over the next several years she discovered more than ten other objects, including a large spiral galaxy and another smaller galaxy.

Caroline also spent a considerable amount of effort sweeping the sky methodically for comets, a common pursuit of amateur and professional astronomers alike. On August 1, 1786, she discovered her first comet, the first comet discovered by a woman. Between 1786 and 1797 she discovered seven more comets. Six of the eight she found in total bear her name. In recognition of her continuing work with her brother, King George III granted her an annual salary of £50, £150 less than William. When William married in 1788, Caroline lamented the change in her relationship with her brother. She moved to private lodgings nearby but continued to work with William and in time got along well with his wife, at which point she moved back into William's home.

After 1797, Caroline devoted most of her effort to other pursuits. In 1798 she published a work that cross-referenced and corrected John Flamsteed's *Historia coelestis Britannica* (1725). In addition to revising Flamsteed's well-known catalog, she added an additional 560 stars to the list. Over the next twenty-five years, until her brother's death in 1822, Caroline devoted most of her time to helping educate her brother's son, John, who was born in 1792.

When her brother died she returned to Hanover, resumed her work, and produced the Herschel catalog, listing twenty-five hundred nebulae, many of them discovered by William. The catalog was completed and then published as *General Catalogue of Nebulae and Clusters of Stars* in 1864 by nephew John.

For her foundational work she received the gold medal in science 1828 from the Royal Astronomical Society. Additional honors followed in 1835, when she was elected an honorary member of the Royal Society, and in 1838, when she was elected to the Royal Irish Academy. In 1846 she received a gold medal in science from the king of Prussia.

During the remaining two years of her life her health gradually worsened. She died on January 9, 1848. Her epitaph, which she composed herself, reads, "The eyes of her who is glorified here below turned to the starry heavens."

SIGNIFICANCE

Caroline Lucretia Herschel's fame and significance certainly were muted after living and working in William's more famous shadow. Although she made important astronomical discoveries of her own, those discoveries are not considered comparable in significance to those of William. Separating William's discoveries from her own, though, may be unfair. The two worked side by side for years, sharing in their work. Without her devotion to William's work, it is possible that his accomplishments would have been minimized. Certainly he could have worked with a different assistant, but Caroline's skills were so extraordinary that she could be considered more a colleague than an assistant. She certainly would have had greater opportunities for education if she were born male. Nevertheless, her perseverance enabled her to surmount many of the usual barriers to women's intellectual advancement. Her brother also helped remove her from the domestic life in which her mother attempted to trap her. Her illness as a child left her disfigured and ruined her chances at marriage, but it also allowed her the time to pursue a career.

Discovering several new objects in the sky and eight comets would have assured any astronomer some degree of fame. What makes Caroline's work more impressive is that she received recognition as a woman. Caroline Lucretia Herschel represents the first well-known woman astronomer, breaking ground for other women to follow. Her life was commemorated in 1889 with an asteroid bearing her middle name, Lucretia. In 1935 a lunar crater was also named for her.

—*Bryan D. Ness*

FURTHER READING

Herschel, Caroline Lucretia. *Caroline Herschel's Autobiographies*. Cambridge, England: Science History, 2003. Contains annotated editions of the two autobiographies penned by Herschel.

Higgins, Frances Lowry. *Sweeper of the Skies: A Story of the Life of Caroline Herschel, Astronomer*. Chicago: Follett, 1967. A biography of Herschel focusing primarily on her astronomical work.

Hoskin, Michael A. *The Herschel Partnership: As Viewed by Caroline*. Cambridge, England: Science History, 2003. A biographical work that focuses on the partnership between Caroline and William.

Lubbock, Constance A. *The Herschel Chronicle: The Life-Story of William Herschel and His Sister, Caroline Herschel*. Cambridge, England: Cambridge University Press, 1933. A biography of William and Caroline with material drawn from their own records.

Wearner, Robert G. *Caroline Herschel: First Woman Astronomer*. Austin: University of Texas Press, 1989. A biography focusing primarily on Herschel's astronomical work.

See also: Jean-Sylvain Bailly; Benjamin Banneker; George III; George Frideric Handel; William Herschel; Joseph-Louis Lagrange; Colin Maclaurin; Wang Zhenyi.

Related articles in *Great Events from History: The Eighteenth Century, 1701-1800:* 1704: Newton Publishes *Optics*; 1704-1712: Astronomy Wars in England; 1705: Halley Predicts the Return of a Comet; 1725: Flamsteed's Star Catalog Marks the Transition to Modern Astronomy; 1787: Herschel Begins Building His Reflecting Telescope; 1796: Laplace Articulates His Nebular Hypothesis.

WILLIAM HERSCHEL
German-born English astronomer

Herschel discovered Uranus and six of its moons. Using several large telescopes that he designed and manufactured, he made numerous planetary observations and also discovered that the Milky Way has a cloud-like appearance because of its numerous distant stars. He also identified double and triple stars, nebulae, star clusters, and other celestial objects, and made detailed studies of the structure of comets and the surface of the Sun.

Born: November 15, 1738; Hanover (now in
  Germany)
Died: August 25, 1822; Slough, Buckinghamshire,
  England
Also known as: Friedrich Wilhelm Herschel (birth
  name)
Areas of achievement: Astronomy, science and
  technology, mathematics, music

EARLY LIFE

William Herschel was one of six surviving children of Isaac and Anna Ilse Herschel. Isaac was a skilled musician and professor of music, and his talents seemed to have passed to several of his children, including William, who studied oboe, violin, and organ. William also loved mathematics and gained an interest in astronomy from his father.

In 1755, William and his brother Jacob, members of the Hanoverian regimental band, traveled to England when their regiment was ordered there. Initially, William's pay was barely enough to avoid poverty, but as his musical abilities gained recognition he was invited to be bandmaster in a militia regiment in northern England. He forged relationships with wealthy families in the area, which led to even more musical involvement, including teaching instrument lessons, and to better fortunes.

In 1764, Herschel paid a brief visit to his family in Germany. Upon his return to England in 1765 he was appointed organist at Halifax, further securing his economic fortunes. Within a year he moved up to the more lucrative position of organist at the Octagon Chapel in Bath. His sister Caroline Lucretia Herschel joined him in 1772. By this time William Herschel's life was extremely busy. What most would have considered a heavy, full-time job as a talented and popular musician was supplemented in Herschel's case with his pursuit of mathematics.

LIFE'S WORK

Soon after receiving a small telescope, William Herschel began the work that would gradually consume him for the rest of his life. His new thirst for exploring the night sky led him to build a larger telescope, since ready-made models were too expensive. After studying optics and experimenting with lens and mirror production, he settled on making an 18- to 20-foot telescope.

Soon Herschel's obsession consumed not only much of his free time but also several rooms of the house that were converted into workshops. Caroline, along with brother Alex, were also drafted to work on his projects. All of this activity was taking place amid Herschel's numerous musical responsibilities. His fixation on completing the 20-foot telescope was so intense that he would not stop turning a lens to eat, and Caroline often fed him or read to him while he worked. However, she was not simply a secretary and helpmate; she was also was an astronomer in her own right, and she possessed many of the observational and mathematical skills of her brother.

On the night of March 13, 1781, Herschel discovered the planet Uranus, initially named Georgium Sidus in honor of King George III. Consequently, he was awarded the Copley Medal and was elected a fellow in the Royal Society. The following year George III appointed him King's Astronomer and awarded him an annual pension of 300 guineas and a home nearer the king. With a steady, dependable income, Herschel finally made a permanent switch to astronomy, resigning his post as organist at Bath.

Herschel's next major project was to construct a more powerful 40-foot telescope. He eventually received funding of £2,000, and, by 1786, he and his sister had moved to Slough, where he built a better observatory and began constructing a larger telescope. Because of the size and great weight of this larger telescope, everything about it had to be specially designed. The end product was so cumbersome that Herschel needed assistance to adjust it for viewing specific portions of the sky. Caroline continued to assist him, devoting her life to his work. She was his primary record keeper, spending most nights by his side at the telescope. Because of Herschel's growing popularity, King George also provided funds to hire work assistants, who also gave tours to the growing numbers of visitors who came to see the large telescope and observatory.

Herschel's primary interest was in the planets, but he also made observations of the Sun and developed theories about its surface appearance. He performed experiments using a prism to separate sunlight into its component colors, measuring the temperature of each. As a result, he discovered infrared radiation—invisible rays beyond the red end of the spectrum—and showed they possessed heat.

He observed the surface of the Moon in great detail and attempted to measure the height of some of its surface features. He believed that some of the Moon's bright spots were volcanoes, a theory now known to be incorrect. He determined the shapes and approximate sizes of several of the "minor" planets, and believed that they were too small to be planets. He coined the term "asteroids" for these bodies, a name still used. He made detailed observations of comets, noting especially their nuclei and the apparent production of their own light.

In 1788 he married a woman with a large inheritance, which enabled him to devote his time completely to astronomy. His new marriage briefly strained his relationship with his sister. She moved out for a time but later rejoined the household and continued her work with Herschel.

Herschel was awarded an honorary degree from Oxford, and in 1816 he was knighted, becoming Sir William Herschel. In 1820 he was elected the first president of the Astronomical Society. By this point Herschel's health was beginning to fail; he died on August 25, 1822. Both Caroline and Herschel's son John carried on his work after his death, preparing a number of his documents for posthumous publication.

SIGNIFICANCE

William Herschel has taken his place among the great astronomers primarily because of his discovery of Uranus and six of its moons. His meticulous nature, both as an observer and as a telescope-builder, helped him in his discoveries. His lesser-known, though no less important, discoveries stem from these same, almost obsessive, tendencies. It is fair to say that his successes also lay in large part with his sister, Caroline. Her devotion to his work, along with her own abilities in astronomy and mathematics, enabled him to accomplish much more than he might have on his own.

Herschel's superior telescopes also helped him see objects never before observed by other astronomers. Most notable was his discovery that many hazy objects in the sky are actually groups of stars, often with clouds of gas accompanying them (nebulae). He discovered many nebulae and showed that the Milky Way is composed of millions of stars. Some of his speculations, however, about the Moon, the Sun, and the planets have not withstood the test of time. One of his wildest speculations was that all planets, and even the Sun, were inhabited.

Herschel's work has been commemorated by several objects bearing his name, including a crater on the Moon and one on Mimas, a moon of Saturn; a large impact basin on Mars; and an asteroid. The William Herschel telescope, located in La Palma on the Canary Islands, also bears his name. In 2007 the European Space Agency plans to launch the Herschel Space Observatory, which will be the largest space telescope of its kind.

—*Bryan D. Ness*

FURTHER READING

Armitage, Angus. *William Herschel*. Garden City, N.Y.: Doubleday, 1963. A biography of William Herschel focusing on his musical as well as his astronomical work.

Dreyer, John Luis Emil, ed. *The Scientific Papers of Sir William Herschel*. Bristol, England: Thoemmes Continuum, 2003. A collection of previously unpublished papers edited under the direction of a joint committee of the Royal Society and the Royal Astronomical Society. Includes a brief introductory biography.

Hoskin, Michael A. *William Herschel and the Construction of the Heavens*. London: Oldbourne, 1963. A biography of William Herschel focusing primarily on his astronomical work.

Lubbock, Constance A. *The Herschel Chronicle: The Life-Story of William Herschel and His Sister, Caroline Herschel*. Cambridge, England: Cambridge University Press, 1933. A more personal biography of Herschel and his sister, with material drawn from their respective records.

See also: Jean-Sylvain Bailly; Benjamin Banneker; George III; Caroline Lucretia Herschel; Joseph-Louis Lagrange; Colin Maclaurin.

Related articles in *Great Events from History: The Eighteenth Century, 1701-1800:* 1704: Newton Publishes *Optics*; 1704-1712: Astronomy Wars in England; 1705: Halley Predicts the Return of a Comet; 1725: Flamsteed's Star Catalog Marks the Transition to Modern Astronomy; 1787: Herschel Begins Building His Reflecting Telescope; 1796: Laplace Articulates His Nebular Hypothesis.

JOHANN LUCAS VON HILDEBRANDT
Austrian architect

One of the supreme architects of the Austrian Baroque movement, Hildebrandt specialized in the design and construction of palaces and pleasure gardens for the Austrian and German nobility. His finest achievement was the Belvedere Palace, built for Eugene of Savoy in Vienna.

Born: November 14, 1668; Genoa (now in Italy)
Died: November 16, 1745; Vienna, Austria
Area of achievement: Architecture

EARLY LIFE

A Genoa-born Austrian of mixed parentage, Johann Lucas von Hildebrandt (yoh-HAHN LEW-kahs fahn HIHL-duh-brahnt) was born in 1668. When his family returned to Austria, Hildebrandt found that, with few exceptions, both the secular and the ecclesiastical patrons of the arts within the Habsburg Dynasty employed only Italian architects, decorators, and painters. As a result of this situation, he became one of several Austrian artists who developed a distinctly Austrian version of the Baroque style to compete with the dominant Italian style. This Austrian Baroque has come to be known as the *Kaiserstil*, or imperial style, because it was associated with the Habsburg Dynasty and with the rebuilding of Vienna as an imperial capital in the late seventeenth and early eighteenth centuries.

Hildebrandt's father was a German captain who served first in the Genoese and then in the imperial army. His mother is presumed to have been Italian. In Italy, the young Hildebrandt studied architecture, city planning, and engineering, and for a time was a student of Carlo Fontana. Besides being much influenced by Fontana, Hildebrandt was also greatly impressed by Guarino Guarini, who was associated with Turin, a city where Hildebrandt may have spent some of his early years. By the 1690's, Hildebrandt was earning his living as a military engineer with the imperial army, and it was in this capacity that he attracted the attention of Prince Eugene of Savoy, with whom he campaigned in northern Italy in 1695-1696.

It was probably with Eugene's encouragement that Hildebrandt left the army to pursue the career of a professional architect. He reached Vienna in 1697, and within a year, presumably on Eugene's recommendation, he was appointed an imperial councillor and, in 1700, a court architect. By that date, however, the imperial family had already bestowed their architectural favors upon Johann

Bernhard Fischer von Erlach, and following the latter's death in 1723 they transferred their loyalty as patrons to his son, Joseph Emanuel Fischer von Erlach. In part because of the intense rivalry between Hildebrandt and the Fischer von Erlachs, the former received few commissions from the Habsburgs. He did, however, receive a lifelong salary from the court, and he was ennobled in 1720.

Soon after his arrival in Vienna in 1697, Hildebrandt received his first commission, to build a garden palace outside the city for Count Heinrich Franz Mansfeld-Fondi. Drawing upon his extensive knowledge of both Italian and French architecture and landscaping, he developed a striking design for a residence at the lower end of a slope, a triangular piece of property off the Rennweg that would rise from the residence in a series of terraces.

Hildebrandt continued to work on this first project while other commissions were raining upon him thick and fast, but he failed to complete it before the count died in 1715. The next owner of the still unfinished residence turned it over to Fischer von Erlach for completion. Thus, it is from the original plans rather than from the present structure that Hildebrandt's intentions can best be gauged. No doubt, he must have resented having to hand this project over to his rival, but by this time he was fully occupied elsewhere, particularly on behalf of Prince Eugene, who had become the emperor's greatest subject in his various roles as commander in chief, governor in absentia of the Spanish Netherlands, and a prince of the ruling house of Savoy.

It seems that Eugene's first commission for his young protégé was to enlarge his town house and official residence, built for him by Fischer von Erlach on the Himmelpfortgasse. There is no evidence of a quarrel between Eugene and Fischer von Erlach, but from 1701 onward it was to Hildebrandt that the prince turned with all his major architectural commissions. Meanwhile, the prince had purchased the island of Czepel, on the Danube River below Budapest, and had instructed Hildebrandt to design a summer retreat there at the village of Ráckeve. The architect drew up plans for a single-story, three-sided structure with a cupola and proceeded with its construction, but despite the idyllic rustic setting, Eugene lost interest in the project, perhaps as a result of the Hungarian uprising under Ferenc Rákóczi II between 1703 and 1711: He is recorded as having visited it only once, in 1717. By then, however, Hildebrandt had already embarked upon the building of what would eventually be his masterpiece.

LIFE'S WORK

The Habsburg nobles of the early eighteenth century each had several homes. They had town palaces, cramped within the confines of the old city of Vienna, and country palaces, located on the nobles' estates throughout the empire. In addition to these, it had become fashionable to build garden palaces in the suburbs of Vienna. Such had been the Mansfeld-Fondi Palace, Hildebrandt's first commission.

Since 1693, Prince Eugene had been buying plots of land off the Rennweg, plots that were now consolidated into an extended triangle of land on which he planned to build a sumptuous residence. The prince commissioned Hildebrandt to help him build this residence, but, to perhaps an even greater extent than with most patrons of this period, Eugene himself had definite ideas about what he wanted. The first part of the complex to be completed (between 1714 and 1716) was the elegant Lower Belvedere, intended to house the prince's paintings (Eugene was one of the greatest art collectors and connoisseurs of the age). Its rooms opened directly onto the garden, which swept upward to where, between 1721 and 1725, the much more elaborate Upper Belvedere was erected. Both prince and architect conceived of the landscaping in the grandest terms, and a French pupil of the great André Le Nôtre, Dominique Girard, was brought from Munich to assist in the work.

The Upper Belvedere provided the setting for Prince Eugene's almost regal entertainments. "The Belvedere," the art critic Anthony Blunt has written, "is Hildebrandt's supreme achievement and shows him at the height of his powers, finally in possession of an idiom wholly his own." Not that Hildebrandt's work for the prince ended there. In 1725, just when the Upper Belvedere was nearing completion, Eugene purchased a dilapidated property known as Schlosshof on the March River to serve as a country palace where he could entertain guests with hunting and *fêtes champêtres*. Between 1725 and 1732, Hildebrandt added two new wings to the old seventeenth century palace and laid out gardens of exquisite beauty and originality. Unfortunately, little remains of the palace, apart from the plans, to indicate what Schlosshof was originally like.

Throughout the years when Hildebrandt was occupied with these major undertakings for Eugene, there was no lack of commissions from other members of the Viennese nobility, although frequently he handed over projects for completion to his deputy, the master mason Franz Jänggle. Eugene never attempted to monopolize Hildebrandt's time or talent, and in addition to his friendship with the prince, the architect established a close connection with the powerful ecclesiastical dynasty of the Schönborns. In 1705, Friedrich Carl von Schönborn was appointed vice-chancellor of the empire, a post he held until 1734, by which time he was also prince-bishop of Bamberg and Würzburg.

The vice-chancellor had a passion for building that amounted to an obsession. He greatly admired Hildebrandt, enjoyed his company, and consulted him on matters of architecture, decoration, and furnishings for the best part of four decades, an extraordinary example of an enduring friendship between patron and artist. In 1705, Hildebrandt began building a magnificent garden palace for the vice-chancellor in the suburbs, and although neither palace nor garden survives in its original form, the plans suggest that this may have been one of the most original exercises in landscaping of the period. Then, in 1710, Schönborn purchased an estate at Göllersdorf in the country to the north of Vienna, and from 1712, Hildebrandt worked intermittently on restoring the former palace, enlarging it, and laying out the gardens.

Meanwhile, during the period when Schönborn was acquiring Göllersdorf, his uncle, Lothar Franz von Schönborn, imperial chancellor, elector-archbishop of Mainz, and prince-bishop of Bamberg, decided to build for himself a palace at Pommersfelden, in the country a few miles outside Bamberg. For the overall design, Lothar sought the services of Johann Dientzenhofer, whose work included the cathedral at Fulda, the Benedictine Abbey at Banz, and the design for the Neumünster at Würzburg. In addition, perhaps at the urging of his nephew, he engaged Hildebrandt, as well as the court architect from Mainz, Maximilian von Welsch, who had been involved with Hildebrandt at Göllersdorf and who would work with him again at the Würzburg Residenz. Johann Michael Rottmayr was summoned to paint the ceiling of the spectacular *Marmorsaal*. In the end, Hildebrandt's contribution to Pommersfelden was relatively small, but it was of outstanding quality: He was responsible for the central staircase, built between 1713 and 1715. In an age when the *Treppenhaus* (an entrance hall with a double staircase) often provided the focus for an entire palace, Hildebrandt's creation at Pommersfelden was without equal, including his own later staircases at Schloss Mirabell and Göttweig.

In 1719, Johann Philipp Franz von Schönborn, brother of Friedrich Carl, became prince-bishop of Würzburg and immediately began to plan a city residence for himself as an alternative to the former episcopal castle across the river. Characteristic of the Schönborns as patrons, he involved more than one architect in the project. Baltasar Neumann, who, like Hildebrandt, had been trained originally as a military engineer, was to have overall responsibility, but Hildebrandt, von Welsch, and Dientzenhofer were all involved at one time or another, along with several others. There seems to have been considerable friction between Hildebrandt and Neumann; in the end, Neumann's ideas prevailed, and it is uncertain how much of the Residenz is Hildebrandt's work, although certainly the Hofkapelle contains features by both men. When, in 1743, engravings of the Residenz were published, attributing the achievement to Neumann, Hildebrandt wrote bitterly to Friedrich Carl von Schönborn, "It grieves me very much, that another should parade himself in my clothes."

Although primarily associated with secular commissions, Hildebrandt also designed several ecclesiastical buildings, of which the most important were the Dominican Church of St. Laurence in Gabel (modern Czechoslovakia), built between 1699 and 1711; St. Peter's Church off the Graben in Vienna; and the Piarist Church of Maria-Treu in Vienna. He competed unsuccessfully against Fischer von Erlach, both to design the Karlskirche and to oversee the rebuilding of the Hofburg, but in 1718 a fire damaged much of the Benedictine Abbey of Göttweig, and its abbot, Gottfried Bessel, a former protégé of Lothar Franz von Schönborn, called upon Hildebrandt for its rebuilding.

Encouraged and assisted by Friedrich Carl von Schönborn, the architect immediately began drawing up plans for the abbey, and although today they exist only on paper, potentially they constituted Hildebrandt's most ambitious undertaking. The immense project proved to be beyond the abbot's means, however, and between 1724 and 1739 only the north and east wings and a *Treppenhaus* were completed. This stairway, however, ascending to a frescoed vault by Paul Troger, is one of Hildebrandt's finest conceptions and a token of one of the great "might-have-beens" of architectural history.

SIGNIFICANCE

It was Johann Lucas von Hildebrandt's achievement to be able to draw together Italian, French, and native Austrian elements into an architectural synthesis that was both dynamic and fluid. As a designer, he demonstrated a tireless virtuosity; as a decorator, he evinced inventiveness on the grandest scale combined with close attention

to detail. These qualities are perhaps most conspicuously displayed in his celebrated stairways at the Upper Belvedere, Schloss Mirabell, Pommersfelden, and Göttweig. The Belvedere is almost the only surviving monument to Hildbrandt's extraordinary gifts for combining architecture and landscaping as a single art form. Many of his projects were left unfinished, were modified by others, or have been allowed to fall into decay. His magnificent plans and drawings, preserved in the Hofbibliothek, most of them never undertaken or abandoned before completion, are reminders of the constraints imposed upon even the most successful artists by changing circumstances or the whims of a patron.

Hildebrandt, though, was exceptionally fortunate in his patrons. Prince Eugene and the Schönborns were enlightened and discriminating men, well able to appreciate the ideas and suggestions of an employee whom they respected as an artist and, in some sense, treated as a friend. It must have helped that Hildebrandt seems to have possessed an equitable temperament and obliging, courtly manners, notwithstanding the odd flash of temper and an enthusiasm for the grandiose that led extravagant spenders into even greater extravagance. His relations with his patrons were surely very different from the dealings of the scholarly, withdrawn Fischer von Erlach with his dour Habsburg masters.

Inevitably, the two rivals invite comparison: Fischer von Erlach, Roman and academic; Hildebrandt, the creator of an architecture of fantasy and enchantment. Yet, as Victor L. Tapié has expressed it, "Fischer von Erlach and Hildebrandt are complementary, and one is inevitably reminded of Bernini and Borromini, for here again are two artists with incompatible genius both working at the same time to beautify and transform a capital city."

—*Gavin R. G. Hambly*

FURTHER READING

Blunt, Anthony, et al. *Baroque and Rococo Architecture and Decoration.* New York: Harper & Row, 1978. This is a sumptuously produced volume, with beautiful illustrations, which while doing full justice to the Austrian Baroque, places it clearly in a broader European perspective. Strongly recommended.

Grimschitz, Bruno. *Johann Lucas von Hildebrandt.* Vienna: Herold, 1959. This remains the definitive monograph on the architect, though it is available only in German.

Hempel, Eberhard. *Baroque Art and Architecture in Central Europe.* Translated by Elisabeth Hempel and Marguerite Kay. Baltimore: Penguin Books, 1965. A volume in the Pelican History of Art series, this is the standard work in English on Austrian and German Baroque.

Henderson, Nicholas. *Prince Eugene of Savoy*. London: Weidenfeld & Nicolson, 1964. An excellent general biography of the prince, emphasizing his role as a patron as well as a military commander. Hildebrandt's commissions are discussed.

McKay, Derek. *Prince Eugene of Savoy*. London: Thames & Hudson, 1977. This biography places emphasis upon the prince as a statesman. Chapter 20, however, deals with him as a patron and discusses Hildebrandt.

Norberg-Schulz, Christian. *Late Baroque and Rococo Architecture*. New York: Harry N. Abrams, 1974. An outstanding survey of the subject, this book gives due weight to Hildebrandt's originality and his contribution. Excellent illustrations with photographs and ground plans.

Powell, Nicolas. *From Baroque to Rococo: An Introduction to Austrian and German Architecture from 1580 to 1790*. London: Faber & Faber, 1959. A literate and perceptive general introduction to the subject. Good for beginners.

Sitwell, Sacheverell, ed. *Great Houses of Europe*. New York: G. P. Putnam's Sons, 1961. This anthology on European palaces includes essays by Monk Gibbon on Pommersfelden and the Würzburg Residenz, both superbly illustrated.

Tapié, Victor L. *The Age of Grandeur: Baroque and Classicism in Europe*. Translated by A. Ross Williamson. London: Weidenfeld & Nicolson, 1960. Virtually an instant classic upon publication, this book provides the best general background to the art and aesthetics of Baroque Europe.

See also: Eugene of Savoy; Johann Bernhard Fischer von Erlach.

Related articles in *Great Events from History: The Eighteenth Century, 1701-1800*: 1703-1711: Hungarian Revolt Against Habsburg Rule; 1715-1737: Building of the Karlskirche; 1762: *The Antiquities of Athens* Prompts Architectural Neoclassicism.

WILLIAM HOGARTH
English painter and scholar

Hogarth's vivid sense of detail and dramatic construction enabled him to create paintings and engravings that were entertainingly comic as well as devastatingly satiric. He also wrote a treatise analyzing the concept of beauty.

Born: November 10, 1697; London, England
Died: October 26, 1764; London, England
Areas of achievement: Art, scholarship

EARLY LIFE

William Hogarth was born in the Smithfield Market section of London, the city that was his lifelong home and also the recurrent setting for the folly and wickedness satirized in much of his work. His father, Richard Hogarth, was a struggling schoolmaster and hack writer whose marriage with his landlord's daughter, Anne Gibbons, only marginally improved his financial circumstances. Richard's imprisonment for debt and the inescapable poverty of the family even when the father was not in Fleet Prison left a deep impression on the younger Hogarth, evident not only in his pictures capturing the squalor and horror of Grub Street life but also in his me-

ticulous concern for protecting his financial interests when he began to have some success.

Unable to afford a university education or to attend an art academy, Hogarth entered into an apprenticeship with a silversmith in 1714, engraving heraldic ornaments on silver plate and occasionally designing and executing illustrations for cheap novels and shop cards. He took steps, though, to ensure that his career, unlike that of his father, would not be limited to hack work. In 1720, he began to further his education in painting, a much more socially respectable skill than engraving, by affiliating himself with the artists at St. Martin's Academy, especially Sir James Thornhill, whose daughter Jane he married in 1729. He did not leave engraving behind but rather turned it to his own purposes, designing and selling satiric engravings that comically ridiculed some contemporary fashions and fiascos. His single plate (in 1721) on the South Sea Bubble, a disastrous investment scandal, and his series of plates (of 1725-1726) illustrating Samuel Butler's poem *Hudibras* (1663, 1664, 1678), continuing that poem's mockery of Puritanism, were very popular and perhaps helped convince him that there was indeed a profitable and aesthetically respectable future in such engravings.

It is no slur on Hogarth's personal inventiveness and industriousness to say that he was fortunate to live in circumstances that favored the development and appreciation of his particular type of genius. Such important writers as Alexander Pope, Jonathan Swift, and Henry Fielding helped to create an audience interested in, and a market capable of, supporting the kind of satire in which Hogarth excelled: concrete, detailed satire that could be savage or genial but was preeminently comic, always as entertaining as it was railing. It is no surprise that Hogarth's achievement is often linked with those authors, in part because he accomplished in visual form what they accomplished in literary form. Nor is it any surprise that Hogarth's first major success is associated with a literary work, whose tone and subject he captured perfectly: His painting of a scene from John Gay's *The Beggar's Opera* (1728) coincided with the enormous popularity of that comically satiric play, brought him into contact with patrons who would support him by commissioning or buying paintings, and, perhaps more important, also gave him the confidence to develop his work in such a way that he might become independent of such patronage.

LIFE'S WORK

The crucial turning point of William Hogarth's career came when, after some success painting so-called conversation pictures of people and scenes of interest to wealthy art collectors, he dedicated himself to (in his own words) "painting and engraving modern moral Subjects." These works typically involve a series of highly detailed pictures that tell a dramatic story about a person's sudden rise and fall, and it is a sure sign of Hogarth's skill that in a few carefully realized scenes he could reveal an astonishing amount about a character's temperament, vices, social milieu, and fate.

A Harlot's Progress (1731-1732), for example, requires only six plates to follow a young country woman's decline: from her arrival in town, which places her immediately in the hands of a bawdy woman; through several stages as an increasingly dependent, pathetic, and sickly prostitute; then finally to her funeral in a room filled with other prostitutes oblivious to the dismal lesson of her life. The moral intention may well have attracted many people to this work, although Hogarth is rarely "preachy," and much of his satire presupposes a world that refuses to turn from its folly and wickedness. *A Harlot's Progress*, though, instantly caught on for many reasons, not the least of which is that in it Hogarth

expertly pictured a seedy but instantly recognizable part of London life and populated it with likenesses of real people who were currently infamous for their vices or crimes.

Because of its tremendous popularity, *A Harlot's Progress* was not only imitated but also pirated, reproduced in editions that brought no profit to Hogarth or to his publisher. As a result, Hogarth delayed the publication of his next major work until the adoption of a parliamentary act in 1735 safeguarding at least minimal copyright protection for engravers. His active involvement in lobbying for this act illustrates his shrewd business sense and independence. Though he perhaps could have lived reasonably well supported by his wealthy patrons, he used these contacts to help devise and enact a law that would make such dependence unnecessary. His work in hand, *The Rake's Progress* (1735), was not only an imaginative work of art but also a valuable property, and Hogarth was very careful about its marketing as well as its creation.

Analogous to *A Harlot's Progress*, *The Rake's Progress* follows a young man through a predictable, though dramatic, decline. Material success, Hogarth seems to suggest, is no substitute for humility and common decency: The Rake has all the advantages of wealth as he inherits an estate from his miserly father, but he wastes himself in a series of debaucheries, powerfully anatomized in eight engravings, that end not in death but in madness. Hogarth returned to the pattern of these two "progresses" later in his career: *Marriage à la Mode* (1745) shows the disintegration of an arranged marriage between two prideful and irresponsible people, and *Industry and Idleness* (1747) contrasts the fates of two men, one of whom prospers through hard work while the other wastes his time and ends up hanged as a criminal. As interesting and dramatic as these later works are, though, it is the earlier "progresses" that seem to embody fully Hogarth's genius.

Hogarth's first self-portrait, *The Painter and His Pug* (1745), pictures the artist at the height of his powers. His features are rounded and softened, his eyes stare straight at the viewer in a confident, even bold manner, and his mouth has a trace of a smile, suggesting both benevolence and self-assurance. The top half of his body, all that is pictured, rests on three books, labeled Swift, Shakespeare, and Milton, indicating not only the crucial literary influences in his life but also his particular aspiration to achieve their kind of success. The subjects in the foreground also define two of his main concerns: His dog at one side adds a comic, affectionate touch (animals, espe-

BEAUTY IN VARIETY

A painter of both the comedic and the satirical, William Hogarth also wrote a treatise on the beautiful. This work of aesthetic criticism includes chapters on artistic concerns with "variety" and with "uniformity, regularity, and symmetry" in nature. He settles—in these two excerpts—on the beauty of variety, that is, on how individuals are pleased with the "composed," "designed" contrasts and ambiguities of works of art.

How great a share variety has in producing beauty may be seen in the ornamental part of nature.

The shapes and colours of plants, flowers, leaves, the paintings in butterflies wings, shells, &c. [etc.] seem of little other intended use, than that of entertaining the eye with the pleasure of variety.

All the senses delight in it, and equally are averse to sameness. The ear is as much offended with one even continued note, as the eye is with being fix'd to a point, or to the view of a dead wall.

Yet when the eye is glutted with a succession of variety, it finds relief in a certain degree of sameness; and even plain space becomes agreeable, and properly introduced, and contrasted with variety, adds to it more variety.

I mean here, and every where indeed, a composed variety; for variety uncomposed, and without design, is confusion and deformity.

We have, indeed, in our nature a love of imitation from our infancy, and the eye is often entertained, as well as surprised, with mimicry and delighted with exactness of counterparts: but then this always gives way to its superior love of variety, and soon grows tiresom[e].

If the uniformity of figures, parts, or lines were truly the chief cause of beauty, the more exactly uniform their appearances were kept, the more pleasure the eye would receive: but this is so far from being the case, that when the mind has been once satisfied, that the parts answer one another, with so exact an uniformity, as to preserve to the whole the character of fitness to stand, to move, to sink, to swim, to fly, &c. without losing the balance: the eye is rejoiced to see the object turn'd, and shifted, so as to vary these uniform appearances.

Source: William Hogarth, *The Analysis of Beauty* (London: J. Reeves, 1753), pp. 16-17, 18-19.

Beauty: Written with a View of Fixing the Fluctuating Ideas of Taste (begun in 1745 and published in 1753), to explain his theoretical principles. His compassion as well as his creativity flourished, and even as he was extremely busy with painting and designing engravings, he continued to serve as governor of a foundling hospital.

The latter part of his life, though, was not so encouraging. Despite the tremendous popularity of his engravings, which went through numerous editions, he found himself increasingly isolated and, he believed, neglected. He was not offered commissions he eagerly sought, and he repeatedly found that his call for a strong English style of painting resistant to stale classical techniques and subjects was not being heeded by a generation of artists who were moving toward the establishment of a Royal Academy of Art that would enfranchise much of what Hogarth despised: regulated artistic training based on what he believed would be unimaginative imitation of outmoded old masters.

Hogarth's appointment as Serjeant-Painter to the King (George II) in 1757 was not enough to bolster his spirits and in fact caused more trouble than anything else by leading him into a disagreeable confrontation with two satirists, John Wilkes and Charles Churchill, who attacked Hogarth's defense of court interests. He spent the last years of his life, it seems, fighting losing battles, defending his politics and his theories of art, but perhaps more generally trying to keep at an arm's length the assorted follies and evils he had satirized in his life's work. A late self-portrait, *The Artist Painting the Comic Muse* (1758), shows him in the process of trying to capture his noble subject, but his body is angular, almost contorted, radiating intensity but no confidence. His last engraving is a vision of failure: Like the ending of Pope's *The Dunciad* (1728-1743), where "Universal Darkness Buries All," and the end of Swift's *Gulliver's Travels* (1726), where

cially dogs, appear frequently in his works); at the other side is a palette, inscribed with a graceful S-curve, which he called the "Line of Beauty."

At this time in his life, from the 1740's through the 1750's, Hogarth had much about which to feel confident. His deep friendships with Fielding (who praised him in his novels) and the actor David Garrick were the source of much stimulation and support. He began to attract a group of followers, especially after he took over leadership of the art academy at St. Martin's Lane when Thornhill died. Always a teacher, he not only directed this group but also worked on a treatise, *The Analysis of*

Gulliver is mad, Hogarth's *The Bathos* (1764) pictures the inefficacy of all human effort and the end of the world. At the time of his death on October 26, 1764, Hogarth may well have felt overwhelmed by the combined forces of decay he had so energetically contested.

SIGNIFICANCE

William Hogarth is rightly regarded as one of the greatest comic artists, even though his works are filled with violent images and prideful, desperate, or otherwise ridiculous characters who are capable of great cruelty or stupidity and who end their lives unhappily. Hogarth's satire is, to say the least, barbed and serious, and his recurrent themes sound like an unrelenting indictment of a fallen world and an inveterately foolish species, humans. Again and again, he presents stunning pictures of humankind's dishonesty, preference for illusion over reality, pride, concern for material and sensual rather than moral comfort, and general unwillingness to be anything more than a beast to others. No one can feel confident in escaping Hogarth's penetrating, satiric gaze.

Where, then, is the comedy? Hogarth is often compared to William Shakespeare, but the essential correctness of this comparison appears only after a few important differences are noted. Hogarth does not often show a light comic touch. His characters are not often capable of redemption or change. Most important, he envisions no broad movement of comic reconciliation, as in the marriages that end Shakespeare's *Twelfth Night: Or, What You Will* (c. 1600-1602) and *As You Like It* (c. 1599-1600). Hogarth failed to complement the dismal view presented in *Marriage à la Mode*: He planned but was never able to complete a sequence called "The Happy Marriage."

There is more to comedy, though, than lightness and happy endings. Hogarth shares with Shakespeare a deep immersion in the physical world and the life of the body, displayed in abundant details. His pictures are filled with liveliness and energy, often misdirected, it is true, but perpetually intriguing. The actions portrayed are not always enviable—the suffering of a criminal or the posturing of fops at the pretentious soirée, for example—but they are always captivating. William Hazlitt, one of Hogarth's great admirers, called this liveliness of subject and style "gusto," and that term suits Hogarth perfectly.

Like the greatest comic and satiric artists, Hogarth had a basic willingness to acknowledge the ridiculous, and he did so without resorting to caricature. He broke through all proprieties to reveal basic, unclothed human traits, few of which are attractive. Through most of his

career, he was not cynical but honest, concerned less with sympathy than with accuracy. At its best and most characteristic, Hogarth's work is provocative and problematic, allied more closely with the comic interludes of Shakespeare's tragedies and history plays than with his benevolent and hopeful comedies.

—Sidney Gottlieb

FURTHER READING

Antal, Frederick. *Hogarth and His Place in European Art*. New York: Basic Books, 1962. An extensive discussion of the contemporary contexts of Hogarth's art, in England and abroad. Counters approaches that study Hogarth in limited and exclusively British settings.

Bindman, David. *Hogarth*. New York: Oxford University Press, 1981. A brief, reliable, well-illustrated introduction to Hogarth's life and works. In contrast to most works, Bindman's study emphasizes Hogarth's achievement as a painter rather than an engraver.

Cowley, Robert L. S. *Hogarth's "Marriage à la Mode."* Ithaca, N.Y.: Cornell University Press, 1983. A lavishly illustrated study of one of Hogarth's most important works. Includes a full background on the sources of this particular work, as well as detailed analysis, but also contains much commentary on other works by Hogarth.

Craske, Matthew. *William Hogarth*. Princeton, N.J.: Princeton University Press, 2000. A thematic analysis of Hogarth's satiric works. Craske describes how Hogarth's art comments on liberty, the ideals and realities of self-improvement, an affinity for "nobodys," and other ideas.

Hallett, Mark. *Hogarth*. London: Phaidon Press, 2000. Part of the Arts & Ideas series. Hallett examines in this work the dual nature of Hogarth's art, describing his portraits and history paintings as well as his satiric prints.

Hogarth, William. *The Analysis of Beauty*. Edited by Ronald Paulson. New Haven, Conn.: Yale University Press, 1997. A modern edition published for the Paul Mellon Centre for Studies in British Art. Includes an introductory essay by the editor of Hogarth's 1753 book on aesthetics. Includes bibliographical references and an index.

Paulson, Ronald. *Hogarth: His Life, Art, and Times*. 2 vols. New Haven, Conn.: Yale University Press, 1974. Paulson's two-volume work is the definitive critical biography, fully documented and illustrated. It is the starting place for serious work on Hogarth.

General readers and students may prefer to consult the one-volume abridged version, less fully documented but still comprehensive.

_____. *Hogarth's Graphic Works*. 2 vols. Rev. ed. New Haven, Conn.: Yale University Press, 1970. An authoritative edition of Hogarth's prints. Each plate is fully annotated with information about its subject and printing history.

_____. *Popular and Polite Art in the Age of Hogarth and Fielding*. Notre Dame, Ind.: University of Notre Dame Press, 1979. A valuable study of the interaction of popular and high culture in eighteenth century art and literature. Hogarth provides one of Paulson's best examples of how so-called low, or popular, art forms became modified by but also invigorated so-called higher art forms.

Quennell, Peter. *Hogarth's Progress*. New York: Viking Press, 1955. An accessible introduction to Hogarth's life and works, aimed especially at the general reader. Useful and interesting, but not as detailed, reliable, or well illustrated as Paulson's biography.

Shesgreen, Sean, ed. *Engravings by Hogarth: 101 Prints*. New York: Dover, 1973. Presents full-size re-productions of many of Hogarth's important plates, and includes a lengthy critical introduction, an annotated bibliography, and detailed commentary.

Uglow, Jenny. *Hogarth: A Life and a World*. New York: Farrar, Straus, and Giroux, 1997. Examines Hogarth's life and art within the context of eighteenth century London, describing how Hogarth was shaped by, and how his art reflected, the society in which he lived.

See also: Jean-Siméon Chardin; Henry Fielding; Thomas Gainsborough; David Garrick; George II; Alexander Pope; Sir Joshua Reynolds; Jonathan Swift; John Wilkes.

Related articles in *Great Events from History: The Eighteenth Century, 1701-1800:* September, 1720: Collapse of the South Sea Bubble; 1726: Swift Satirizes English Rule of Ireland in *Gulliver's Travels*; January 29, 1728: Gay Produces the First Ballad Opera; 1742: Fielding's *Joseph Andrews* Satirizes English Society; January, 1759: Voltaire Satirizes Optimism in *Candide*; December 10, 1768: Britain's Royal Academy of Arts Is Founded.

PAUL-HENRI-DIETRICH D'HOLBACH
German-born French philosopher

Holbach hosted the most renowned philosophical salon in Paris for four decades, was a major contributor to the Encyclopedia, *launched a relentless attack against Christianity, and developed a secular moral and political philosophy. He influenced the French Revolution and later anticlerical writers.*

Born: December, 1723; Edesheim, Rhineland-Palatinate (now in Germany)
Died: January 21, 1789; Paris, France
Also known as: Paul-Henri Thiry d'Holbach; Baron d'Holbach
Areas of achievement: Philosophy, religion and theology

EARLY LIFE

Paul-Henri-Dietrich d'Holbach (pawl-ah-ree-dee-treek dawl-bahk) was the son of Johannes Jacobus Thiry and Jacobea Holbach. Losing his mother at the age of six, he was brought to Paris at twelve by a wealthy, childless uncle, Franciscus-Adam d'Holbach, who had taken French citizenship and purchased noble status. Paul later studied not at the Sorbonne (still mired in Scholasticism), but the cosmopolitan University of Leiden, in the Netherlands, a great center of scientific research. The university was both tolerant and a safe haven for free-thinkers.

Holbach, blessed with an extraordinary memory, acquired broad expertise in the physical sciences, exceptional command of English—partly through enduring friendships formed with English students—and religious disbelief. Returning to Paris in 1749, he became a French citizen and, on February 3, 1750, married his second cousin, Basile-Geneviève-Suzanne d'Aine. Disconsolate when she died at twenty-five, he married her younger sister, Charlotte Suzanne d'Aine, two years later (1756). Holbach was coheir with his cousin (also his mother-in-law), inheriting his uncle's name and large fortune in 1753. Through his wife, he acquired Grandval, an estate in Sucy, southeast of Paris, where he typically lived from spring to autumn each year. Financially independent, happy in marriage, and passionately committed to the intellectual tasks he took up, Holbach would never seek recognition for his writings or his innumerable discreet acts of charity.

LIFE'S WORK

Cherishing the intellectual comradeship he had found in Leiden, Holbach re-created it soon after marrying. He formed an intellectual coterie by hosting a salon that would endure for four decades and generate the freest, most probing philosophical discussions of the French Enlightenment. It was dubbed the Café d'Europe, because it attracted not only the greatest philosophes of France but also brilliant individuals from Britain and across the Continent. It was also known as "the synagogue" for its unfettered discussion of religion.

At the heart of the group were the encyclopedists, including editor Denis Diderot (1713-1784), who became Holbach's close friend and lifelong intellectual comrade-in-arms. They shared broad interests in science, as well as a faith in science's ability to better humankind by destroying superstition and discovering solutions to persistent problems. They believed that religion is not simply untrue but a great impediment to human progress.

From the early 1750's, Holbach became a major contributor to the *Encyclopédie: Ou, Dictionnaire raisonné des sciences, des arts, et des métiers* (1751-1772; *Encyclopedia*, 1965). He wrote 376 articles in fifteen years. He also translated and published numerous German scientific books during these years, and most of his encyclopedia articles were based on German research, particularly in the fields of chemistry, mineralogy, and metallurgy, but he ranged over many other subjects as well. When clerical opposition to the *Encyclopedia* brought suppression of the great enterprise in 1759 and some, such as Voltaire, withdrew, Holbach worked with Diderot through the clandestine effort needed to complete this proud achievement of the French Enlightenment.

By then, Holbach's career was taking a new course. Appalled by the Catholic Church's power of censorship, control of education, and resistance to scientific progress, he threw himself into the most intense, relentless attack on Christianity—and religion in general—that Europe had ever witnessed. With coworker Jacques-André Naigeon (1738-1810), who had already been helping him prepare material for the *Encyclopedia*, he unleashed such a torrent of antireligious books that Diderot quipped that it was raining bombs on the house of the Lord.

Holbach published thirty-five such "bombs" in a decade; most were printed in Amsterdam and smuggled into France. Many of these volumes were translations of works by seventeenth and eighteenth century English

Deists or were French manuscripts that had already circulated surreptitiously. Eleven, all pseudonymous, were written by Holbach himself, beginning with *Le Christianisme dévoilé: Ou, Examen des principes et des effets de la religion chrétienne* (1761; *Christianity Unveiled*, 1795). His most important work was *Système de la nature: Ou, Des Lois du monde physique et du monde moral* (1770; *The System of Nature*, 1797). This multivolume edition was condensed as *Le Bon-sens: Ou, Idées naturelles opposée aux idées surnaturelle* (1772; *Common Sense*, 1795).

Collectively, Holbach's onslaught was a compendium of rationalistic attacks on Christianity and religion in general. Inconsistencies in the Bible were cataloged, the "cruel, vindictive, tribal" divinity of the Old Testament was challenged, and the failure of an "omnipotent, omniscient" God to prevent undeserved suffering was repeatedly questioned. In the face of the emerging scientific picture of nature ruled by unvarying physical laws, accounts of miracles that seemed to violate such laws, including those at the core of Christianity, were ridiculed and dismissed.

Holbach went further, affirming an unflinching materialism and atheism that rejected free will and any hope of a hereafter. Promises of a happier life to come were a cruel fraud, he declared; in admonishing individuals patiently to endure injustice and oppression, priests, typically in league with tyrannical rulers, were cheating them of their only chance for happiness. Like most ancient Greek philosophers, Holbach believed the universe had always existed. While granting that this concept is perplexing, he declared that it was more irrational to assert that the vast physical universe was created out of nothing by a spiritual Being whose own origin was more problematic than an uncreated universe.

To those who contended that religion was an indispensable ground for morality, Holbach put forward a secular ethical and political philosophy, a task that occupied the final portion of his career. Like his ancient counterpart, the antireligious materialist Epicurus (341-270 B.C.E.), Holbach's ethics rested on the self-interested pursuit of happiness. He believed such happiness could best be achieved by meeting human needs, individual and social, which science was best equipped to understand. He judged acceptable all pleasures that do not harm oneself or others but stressed the importance of contributing to society, because each individual depends on others and needs their approbation.

Holbach believed that, as part of nature's uninterrupted web of cause and effect, the human mind and human actions are determined by natural law, and one's moral sense, no less than any other aspect of the mind, is shaped by one's experiences in life. This denial of free will and any sort of innate conscience did not lead him to hopeless fatalism, however. He asserted that people are not simply buffeted by external causes: A just society will help mold good consciences within each individual, as will enlightened education, which frees people from superstition and teaches them to trust in reason and scientific knowledge, the surest guides to the greatest happiness nature permits.

The kind of political order Holbach judged most likely to sustain an enlightened, happy society was constitutional monarchy, in which a parliament prevents tyranny by either the monarch or a reckless populace. Since sovereignty derives from the people's consent, he believed, a government that fails to preserve the common welfare may be overthrown. He thought, however, that enduring progress can only come though slow, careful reform, rather than political upheaval. Nevertheless, Holbach favored numerous then-radical changes in government, including the abolition of hereditary aristocracies, progressive taxation to reduce great disparities in wealth, laissez-faire commercial policy, ending torture and excessive punishments, legalized divorce, complete separation of church and state, absolute religious tolerance, inviolable freedom of thought and the press, and state-provided universal secular education.

These reforms were advocated in Holbach's last books, including *La Politique naturelle: Ou, Discourse sur les vrais principes du gouvernment* (1773; natural politics: or, discourse on the true principles of government) and *La Morale universelle: Ou, Les Devoirs de l'homme fondé sur la nature* (1776; universal morality: or, the duties of man grounded in nature). Like all his other works, these did not bear his name. Thus, the man who produced perhaps the most systematic exposition of materialism and atheism ever penned, and who produced a generous-minded, humanistic social philosophy, lived unknown to most of his countrymen.

SIGNIFICANCE

The philosophes believed that reason and scientific knowledge would lead to human progress and counted themselves "friends of humanity." Their vision of a more just, more enlightened society gave important impetus to the French Revolution and is an enduring legacy in the modern world. Paul-Henri-Dietrich d'Holbach's passionate participation in their enterprise epitomizes the unusual confluence of wealth and philosophy that made the philosophes so influential. His crusade against religion helped shape the revolution's harsh treatment of the Church and helped account for the fact that unbelief was more common in France over the next two centuries than elsewhere in Europe. Because he published so many antireligious books by others, many of them Deists; because long after his death his books were republished without his name; and because his style was often prolix and repetitious; many have failed to recognize the unity and scope of his philosophy. While his belief in determinism and the social implications he drew from this belief are still not widely accepted, they seem less shocking in an age of neuroscience, and they find echoes in our criminal justice system.

—*R. Craig Philips*

FURTHER READING

Crocker, Lester. *The Embattled Philosopher: A Biography of Denis Diderot*. East Lansing: Michigan State College Press, 1954. A fine biography that illuminates the relationship between Holbach and the engaging Diderot.

Joshi, S. T. *Atheism: A Reader*. Amherst, N.Y.: Prometheus Books, 2000. Provides a wider perspective on the skeptical tradition in which Holbach figures so prominently.

Kors, Alan Charles. *D'Holbach's Coterie: An Enlightenment in Paris*. Princeton, N.J.: Princeton University Press, 1976. Useful corrective to conspiratorial characterizations of "the synagogue."

Outram, Dorinda. *The Enlightenment*. New York: Cambridge University Press, 1995. Good brief introduction to Holbach's era informed by recent interpretations.

Topaz, Virgil W. *D'Holbach's Moral Philosophy: Its Background and Development*. Geneva, Switzerland: Institut et Musée Voltaire, 1956. Informative about impact of English writers and French materialism on Holbach.

Wickwar, W. H. *Baron d'Holbach: A Prelude to the French Revolution*. London: George Allen & Unwin, 1935. Still the basic English monograph on Holbach; lists his publications.

See also: Jean le Rond d'Alembert; Jeremy Bentham; Étienne Bonnot de Condillac; Denis Diderot; Johann Gottlieb Fichte; Johann Gottfried Herder; David Hume; Immanuel Kant; Jean-Jacques Rousseau; Voltaire.

Related articles in *Great Events from History: The Eighteenth Century, 1701-1800*: 1739-1740: Hume

Publishes *A Treatise of Human Nature*; 1748: Montesquieu Publishes *The Spirit of the Laws*; 1754: Condillac Defends Sensationalist Theory; July 27, 1758: Helvétius Publishes *De l'esprit*; April, 1762: Rousseau Publishes *The Social Contract*; July, 1764: Voltaire Publishes *A Philosophical Dictionary for the Pocket*; 1770: Publication of Holbach's *The System of* Nature; 1781: Kant Publishes *Critique of Pure Reason*; 1784-1791: Herder Publishes His Philosophy of History; 1790: Burke Lays the Foundations of Modern Conservatism; February 22, 1791-February 16, 1792: Thomas Paine Publishes *Rights of Man*; 1792-1793: Fichte Advocates Free Speech.

HONDA TOSHIAKI
Japanese political economist and scholar

Honda advocated policies to modernize and strengthen Japan at a time when foreign encroachment was a national concern. He taught practical skills such as mathematics, mapmaking, and navigation to cadres of elite students who became leaders in the nation's development. His writings helped set the course for modernization, and he helped establish the idea that Japan was a nation of the world rather than an isolated feudal land.

Born: 1744; Echigo Province (now Murakami, Nigata Prefecture), Japan
Died: 1821/1822; Edo (now Tokyo), Japan
Also known as: Honda; Saburouemon
Areas of achievement: Government and politics, economics, scholarship, geography, education

EARLY LIFE

Eighteenth century Japanese intellectuals became increasingly concerned over foreign incursions, as well as over internal corruption and disorder because of the gradually deteriorating capabilities of the Tokugawa shogunate. Neo-Confucian scholars had advocated national reforms under the slogan *keisei-saimin* (political economy coming to the aid of the people), but their plans were never implemented. A new generation of *keiseika* (political economists), led by Honda Toshiaki (hohn-dah toh-shee-ah-kee), set out to implement national reforms and strengthen national defense.

At the age of eighteen, Honda had come to Edo to study mathematics and astronomy, but he had learned also about recent developments in Western science and technology as well as European history and geography from reading classical Chinese translations of European books. This knowledge of the West led him to enter the field of Rangaku (Dutch studies), through which Japanese students became specialists in various areas of European science, technology, and general education.

Honda lived at a time when Western ships had attempted to land in Japan during the eighteenth century. Sometimes they were repelled, and sometimes they were allowed to land briefly if they were in distress, but their reception was largely determined by the strength of the local authorities. In areas where there was little or no coastal defense, some landings of foreign crewmen ended in brawls or skirmishes.

Russian explorers and traders were moving southward by land and sea from Sakhalin, and in 1792-1793 a Russian naval vessel visited several northern Japanese ports in an abortive attempt to conclude agreements with the shogunate. Armed Russian landing parties were met by local feudal forces and regional shogunate officials. The negotiations ended in standoffs, however, because the Russians had insufficient strength to enforce their requests, while the local Japanese forces were not strong enough to force the Russians to leave.

LIFE'S WORK

In 1766, not long after he had completed his own basic studies, Honda opened his own school in Edo, where he taught mathematics and astronomy. Using his background in these two disciplines, he also learned and then taught the principles of Western navigation. He then developed his own program for the modernization of Japan. Honda was unlike the political economists in the tradition of Ogyū Sorai, who thought more in terms of coordinating the activities of the various feudal domains so the shogunate could more effectively run the country and who favored increased internal trade among different regions of Japan. Honda, instead, advocated an outward-looking policy and the development of foreign trade.

Though he was opposed to and alarmed by possible foreign encroachments into Japanese territory, Honda did not favor continuing the old policies of trying to lock out all foreigners. He began traveling through the areas in the far north of Japan, where Japanese and Russian interests faced one another, to find out for himself exactly what the situation was. He lobbied for the shogunate to hire specialists on these northern areas, and in 1786 his student Mogami Tokunai (1755-1836) was given a position to explore and map the northern territories using the technical training in navigation and mapmaking that he had received at Honda's school. In 1798, the shogunate annexed northern territory inhabited by the Ainu, and Mogami went on to become a shogunate expert, advising the shogun and holding administrative positions supervising the northern territories.

Honda was greatly concerned about the Tenmei Famine, which peaked in 1786, and he traveled around northern Honshu to observe the situation. He used the famine problems in the north, combined with the threats of Russian encroachment, to argue for a policy of Japanese expansion from northern Honshu into Hokkaido and the development of trade and commerce in the northern territories. He believed that improvements in the standard of living in that area, as well as in the rest of Japan, combined with advances in navigation and foreign trade, would strengthen Japan enough internally so that it would be in a better position to withstand external pressure from foreign powers as well. In addition to favoring stronger coastal defense, Honda advocated the widespread, nonmilitary use of explosives to open roads and facilitate national public works efforts.

In 1798, Honda wrote the two-volume *Keisei hisaku* (confidential strategies for use in political economy), a detailed program for national reform and progress. In this work and others like it that followed, Honda reflected on the practical experience he gained from his travels and studies and came up with a series of recommendations to improve conditions in Japan. In addition to calling for more public works, facilitated by modern explosives, Honda wanted the shogunate to develop a national mining effort—using Western methods—to extract metals, coal, and other resources essential for the development of modern national industry. He felt that the country should develop a modern shipbuilding industry and a merchant marine establishment that could carry on foreign trade on its own, rather than relying on European traders. He also promoted the development of national coastal defense, combined with the exploring of so-far-undeveloped territories that were part of or closely adjacent to Japan, with a view to national expansion and colonization.

Honda also advocated the establishment of a centralized national educational system, with an institution of higher learning to supervise the system and to train capable teachers and technical specialists. He felt that talented people should be educated and given key posts, regardless of class origins. Honda also proposed that Chinese-based cultural institutions should be replaced by modern Japanese ones, ones based on European models. He even suggested that the writing system based on the mastery of thousands of Chinese characters should be scrapped, to be replaced by a simple phonetic writing system that would allow greater numbers of people to master new knowledge and technology more rapidly and efficiently.

SIGNIFICANCE

Honda Toshiaki helped develop the concept of the private intellectual as one who promotes national progress and the bettering of society. Until Honda's time, most Japanese thinkers had relied on the backing and patronage of the shogunate or of individual feudal lords. Honda's leading predecessor in the realm of political economy, Ogyū Sorai, had become a private scholar late in life only because his former official patrons had lost power and died. Honda worked in the employ of the lord of the Kaga domain only briefly before he resigned.

The idea of a private intellectual who proposed change for the good of the nation as a whole, without attempting to cater to those in power, and yet could win the respect of national leaders, became a model for later modernizers to follow. Virtually all of Honda's ideas and proposals, apart from language reform, became realities two generations after his death.

Honda's greatest merit may have been that he foresaw the sorts of difficulties Japan would have after the country was forcibly opened to Western trade by Commodore Perry in 1853. Honda already had developed most of the plans for modernization that would be used to successfully cope with the West, and he did so a generation before Perry. Though many of his recommendations were not followed by the shogunate during his own lifetime, he is respected in Japanese history as the first to have the discernment and courage to warn of future problems for Japan, and he came up with the solutions that actually were used and the solutions that worked in the late Tokugawa and the Meiji eras.

—*Michael McCaskey*

FURTHER READING

Jansen, Marius. *The Making of Modern Japan*. Cambridge, Mass.: Harvard University Press, 2002. A standard text on the subject by a recognized authority on Japanese history.

_____, ed. *Japan in Transition: From Tokugawa to Meiji*. Princeton, N.J.: Princeton University Press, 1990. A definitive scholarly work on Japanese modernization.

Keene, Donald. *The Japanese Discovery of Europe, 1720-1830*. Stanford, Calif.: Stanford University Press, 1969. This special study was the first to acquaint Western readers with Honda's career and the importance of his role in the modernization of Japan. Includes helpful notes and a bibliography for those who wish to further explore Honda's life and work.

Kracht, Klaus, ed. *Japanese Thought in the Tokugawa Era: A Bibliography of Western-Language Materials*. Wiesbaden, Germany: Harrassowitz, 2000. An important reference for further independent research on Tokugawa thought, using sources in English and other Western languages.

Najita, Tetsuo, trans. and ed. *Readings in Tokugawa Thought*. Chicago: Center for East Asian Studies, University of Chicago, 1993. A standard collection of key texts reflecting Tokugawa intellectual life, compiled by a Japanese expert, using original sources.

Nakamura, Takafusa, and Oda Konosuke. *The Economic History of Modern Japan, 1600-1900*. New York: Oxford University Press, 2003. An updated, authoritative work on Japanese economic history, from the perspective of scholars in twenty-first century Japan.

Yoda, Yoshi'ie. *Foundations of Japan's Modernization: A Comparison with China's Path Towards Modernization*. Leiden, the Netherlands: Brill Academic, 1995. This study provides useful complementary analyses of Chinese and Japanese modernization.

See also: Hakuin; Ogyū Sorai; Tokugawa Yoshimune.

Related articles in *Great Events from History: The Eighteenth Century, 1701-1800:* December, 1720: Japan Lifts Ban on Foreign Books; 1786-1787: Tenmei Famine.

RICHARD HOWE
English admiral

One of England's foremost seamen of the Age of Sail, Howe won several noted victories over the French and Spanish but was unsuccessful in negotiating an end to the American Revolution.

Born: March 8, 1726; London, England
Died: August 5, 1799; London, England
Areas of achievement: Military, warfare and conquest, government and politics

EARLY LIFE

Richard Howe was born into a landed family. His grandfather, father, and brothers all distinguished—and enriched—themselves in service to the Whig regime of the eighteenth century. Richard's grandfather, Sir Scrope Howe, was rewarded for his role in the Glorious Revolution by being created an Irish viscount. The Irish title was purely an honorary one and did not indicate any particular interest in Ireland. Apparently, none of his descendants ever took a seat in the House of Lords in Dublin. Richard Howe's father, Emanuel Scrope, Second Viscount Howe, loyally was married to Mary Sophia von Kielmansegge, daughter of one of the two mistresses whom King George I brought with him from Germany at the Hanoverian succession. They had five sons and four daughters before the Second Lord Howe died at his post as governor of Barbados in 1735. Richard Howe was their second son.

Like his brothers, Howe was educated at home and, briefly, at Eton before beginning his career of service to the Crown. The navy was a popular choice for second sons of aristocratic families. Though its dangers were too great for the eldest son and heir to the family property, it offered a younger brother the chance to make his own fortune in prize money from the sale of captured ships. Even for a young aristocrat, though, it was a hard and dangerous apprenticeship. Howe joined his first ship, the *Severn*, at the age of fourteen, at the beginning of the War of the Austrian Succession. In 1740, the *Severn* sailed as part of Admiral Anson's famous round-the-world expedition but turned back after being damaged in a violent storm off Cape Horn. Howe spent the rest of his teenage years sailing and fighting in the Caribbean. His skill and connections gained for him early promotion to lieutenant just after his nineteenth birthday.

LIFE'S WORK

In the Royal Navy of the eighteenth century, promotion to admiral came by strict seniority among the post-captains. To command a fleet at sea, an officer had to attain that rank as young as possible. The surest way to accomplish that goal was to fight a desperate ship-to-ship action. Ordered back to England in 1745, Howe was given the command of the small sloop *Baltimore*. Along with another sloop, the *Baltimore* attacked two larger French frigates the following year. The two English ships were beaten off, but the badly wounded Howe won his promotion to postcaptain just after his twenty-first birthday.

During the years of the peace that soon followed, Howe's connections kept him constantly employed at sea, where he further developed his skills as commander of several frigates cruising the Caribbean and Mediterranean. By 1775, he was sufficiently senior to command a sixty-gun line-of-battle ship. In a fog off the mouth of the St. Lawrence, Howe's ship fell in with a larger French battleship sent to reinforce French Canada. Howe was there to thwart the French, and he fired on and captured the ship. Howe's was officially the "first shot" of the Seven Years' War, which was to have a profound effect upon Howe's career. During the rest of the war, Howe began to command groups of ships as commodore of several small squadrons covering expeditions against the French coast. His own ship led the van of Admiral Hawke's daring and triumphant attack on the French fleet in Quiberon Bay in 1759. Meanwhile, Howe's eldest brother, a brigadier general in the army, was killed leading British and American troops against the French near Fort Ticonderoga. This made Richard the Fourth Viscount Howe and head of his family. He married the daughter of another military family and ran successfully for a seat in the House of Commons, which he held for the next twenty-five years.

The twelve years of peace between 1763 and 1775 was the longest period of Lord Howe's life that he spent ashore. He fathered three daughters, held the lucrative political office of treasurer of the navy, and spoke regularly in Parliament. Howe became increasingly concerned with England's dispute with its North American colonists, with whom he felt a special link. His elder brother, George, had been killed in defense of the colonies against the French and American Indians; the province of Massachusetts had gratefully erected a monument to him in Westminster Abbey. His younger brother William had also distinguished himself serving in the army in America. One of his sisters was an eccentric spinster and occasional chess partner of Benjamin Franklin in London. Meeting secretly at her house in 1774,

Admiral Richard Howe. (Library of Congress)

Howe befriended Franklin and tried secretly to negotiate terms of reconciliation. Offered the naval command in North America, Howe was unenthusiastic about fighting the colonists. Instead, he believed that he and his brother, given joint command of the navy and army and also a commission to negotiate peace and individual pardons, could end the growing rebellion with a minimum of bloodshed. The cabinet agreed, and the Howe brothers arrived in America in the summer of 1776 as both military commanders and peace commissioners. They were too late. Howe had another secret negotiation with Franklin, John Adams, and Edward Rutledge at a house on Staten Island, but Congress had voted the Declaration of Independence two months earlier. Howe was neither inclined nor empowered to grant independence, and the talks failed. Still seeking to avoid much bloodshed, Howe imposed a loose blockade of the American coast and transported his brother's army in successful landings on the Long Island and New York shores and, in 1777, at Elkton, Maryland, for a march on Philadelphia.

When the French joined the war and sent a strong naval squadron to America in 1778, Howe was badly outnumbered. He moored his small fleet in a line across Sandy Hook at the mouth of New York Harbor and resolutely held off the French for eleven days, thus saving the main British base in North America. After reinforcements arrived, Howe went out hunting the French and successfully broke their siege of the British base on Rhode Island. In both cases, the French were outmaneuvered and declined battle. In 1778, the Howes were outraged to be superseded by another peace commission from England and resigned their commands to return home. King George III offered Howe Lord Sandwich's job as first lord of the Admiralty, but Howe demanded that Lord George Germain also be removed as head of the War Department. Failing that, he and his brother General William Howe went into opposition in Parliament, attacking the ministry's conduct of the war and defending their record in America.

Like many Whig admirals, Howe refused to serve again at sea until Sandwich was replaced. When Lord North's ministry finally fell after Yorktown, Howe was given command of the Channel fleet (the navy's senior command) and a seat in the House of Lords. In September, 1783, he sailed with thirty-three ships of the line to relieve Gibraltar from its four-year siege by the French and Spanish. Outmaneuvering the Franco-Spanish covering fleet of forty-six battleships, Howe escorted 183 transport ships in and out of Gibraltar without a battle.

At the end of the war, Howe was appointed first lord of the Admiralty and member of the cabinet of William Pitt the Younger. He was not happy as a peacetime administrator and drew political attacks on his economy measures. He also opposed the internal reforms of the navy proposed by Sir Charles Middleton, a troublesome subordinate. When the prime minister favored Middleton's ideas over his own, Howe resigned in 1788. George III made him an earl.

As the foremost admiral of the day, Howe was not allowed to retire. In 1790, at age sixty-four, he resumed command of the Channel fleet during a diplomatic crisis with Spain, and again in 1793 after the outbreak of the war against revolutionary France. In late May, 1794, Howe encountered an equal French fleet in the western approaches to the English Channel. After two days of skillful maneuvering in fog, Howe commanded a formal fleet attack that resulted in what is called the Battle of the Glorious First of June. Howe ordered his captains to break through the French line of battle in an attempt to annihilate the French. He nearly succeeded: Half of the twenty-six French ships surrendered or were dismasted; six were eventually towed into English ports as prizes.

England's first victory of the war caused a stir: George III himself came to Portsmouth to present Howe with a diamond-studded sword worth £3,000 and later made him a Knight of the Garter. Howe's captains received the first service medals ever given in the Royal Navy.

Later in 1794, Howe retired to Bath for his health, though remaining in nominal command of the fleet. This arrangement proved to be a mistake, as Howe was too distant to notice the growing discontent of the underpaid sailors. In 1797, the Channel fleet mutinied. Summoned to Portsmouth, Howe courageously went aboard the mutinous ships and negotiated a pay raise for the sailors, who then returned to their duties. This was his final victory. Troubled by gout, Howe turned to mesmerism for relief; he died on August 5, 1799, at the age of seventy-three.

SIGNIFICANCE

With his peerages and rewards from a grateful king and nation, Admiral Richard Howe certainly was a younger son who made good. He was popular with his sailors, who nicknamed him "Black Dick" because of his dark complexion. Although generally regarded as a conservative commander, he was associated with several innovations in the navy. As a young officer, he was one of the first to organize his ship's crew by divisions for better management. As admiral, he drilled his fleets rigorously and perfected the code of flag signals to convey his orders. At New York, Rhode Island, and Gibraltar, he showed himself to be a brilliant tactician who could gain his point by maneuver rather than by bloody battle. In battle, he was calm and determined, even at the First of June, when he was nearly seventy years old.

Howe was not a success as a politician. Long voyages tended to make naval officers taciturn, and Howe was no exception. Warm to his friends, he was neither personable to strangers nor a good public speaker. He never had a following in Parliament. Though genuinely based upon a sentimental attachment to America, his diplomatic efforts in the 1770's were ill-conceived. To Franklin, they appeared to be little more than an attempt at bribery. Later, Howe was a quarrelsome member of Pitt's cabinet and was not missed after his resignation.

Several of his strategic decisions have also been faulted as overcautious. He shares the blame of his father for the army's long cruise to attack Philadelphia in 1777. Had the Howes coordinated their strategy with John Burgoyne's invasion from Canada, the disaster of Saratoga might have been avoided. On the Glorious First of June, Howe concentrated on attacking the French warships, while failing to capture the vital grain convoy that they were escorting. This mistake may have saved the revolutionary regime. Finally, Howe was an opponent of the strategy of year-round close blockades of enemy fleets in port, which he thought was too dangerous for British ships and crews. Having experienced the first close blockade of Brest under Edward Hawke during 1759, Howe preferred to keep his main fleet in port, a strategy later criticized by John Jervis, earl of St. Vincent, Sir William Cornwallis, and the other great seamen of the Napoleonic Wars. Against Howe's caution, however, should be set the fact that while fighting in every war of the Hanover Dynasty in the eighteenth century, he never lost a battle at sea.

—John R. Breihan

FURTHER READING

Buchanan, John. *The Road to Valley Forge: How Washington Built the Army That Won the Revolution*. Hoboken, N.J.: John Wiley & Sons, 2004. Traces the development of the American revolutionary army from 1776 to 1778, describing troop movements and battlefield operations. Includes information on British military operations, including the Howe brothers' role as military commanders and peace commissioners.

Duffy, Michael, and Roger Morriss, eds. *The Glorious First of June, 1794: A Naval Battle and Its Aftermath*. Exeter, England: University of Exeter Press, 2001. Describes the naval battle from both British and French perspectives, including eyewitness accounts of the fighting.

Gruber, Ira D. "Howe Brothers: Richard Earl Howe/Sir William Howe." In *The Reader's Companion to Military History*, edited by Robert Cowley and Geoffrey Parker. Boston: Houghton Mifflin, 1996. Gruber, who has written a book on the Howe brothers' role in the Revolutionary War, describes how the Howes' hopes for a peaceful settlement of the conflict hampered their ability to wage a successful military campaign.

_____. *The Howe Brothers and the American Revolution*. Williamsburg, Va.: Institute of Early American History and Culture, 1972. Explores the links between the politics and strategy of the Howes' mission.

Mahan, Alfred T. *The Influence of Sea Power upon the French Revolution and Empire, 1793-1812*. 2 vols. Boston: Little, Brown, 1892. Reprint. *The Influence of Sea Power upon History*. New York: Hill & Wang, 1957. This classic work on naval strategy contains detailed narratives and charts for Howe's actions, as well as shrewd comments on his tactics and strategy.

Rodger, N. A. M. *The Wooden World: An Anatomy of the Georgian Navy*. Annapolis, Md.: Naval Institute Press, 1986. Although it mentions Howe only in passing, this is a groundbreaking book of the "new military history" that covers the whole world of life afloat during Howe's lifetime.

Warner, Oliver. *The Glorious First of June*. London: B. T. Batsford, 1961. A thorough review of the battle, based on extensive use of primary sources, as well as a thoughtful overview of Howe's whole career.

See also: John Adams; Lord Anson; William Bligh; Benjamin Franklin; Thomas Gage; George III; William Howe; Sir Alexander Mackenzie; Lord North; Arthur Phillip; George Rodney; George Vancouver.

Related articles in *Great Events from History: The Eighteenth Century, 1701-1800:* April 19, 1775: Battle of Lexington and Concord; July 4, 1776: Declaration of Independence; September 19-October 17, 1777: Battles of Saratoga; June 21, 1779-February 7, 1783: Siege of Gibraltar.

WILLIAM HOWE
British military leader

A model English officer of the eighteenth century, Howe gave his entire adult life to the service of the Crown. Upon such dedication the British Empire would be built.

Born: August 10, 1729; London, England
Died: July 12, 1814; Plymouth, England
Areas of achievement: Military, warfare and conquest

EARLY LIFE

William Howe was the son of Emanuel Scrope Howe, the Second Viscount Howe in the Irish peerage, and Mary Sophia, the eldest daughter of Baron Kielman-segge. Because his family was well connected at the Hanover court, where his maternal grandmother reportedly was a favorite of King George I, Howe enjoyed the favor of the court throughout his lifetime. During the long reign of King George III, the king was his most important ally. Howe's education was received from tutors and at Eton. Because his chosen profession was the army, there was no need for him to remain in school past his seventeenth year.

Shortly after his birthday in 1746, he purchased his first commission, a cornetcy in the duke of Cumberland's Light Dragoons. A year later the six-foot-tall, dark-complexioned young officer had made an impression sufficient to permit him to buy a lieutenancy in the same unit. After service with the Dragoons in Flanders during 1747-1748, Lieutenant Howe transferred to the Twentieth Regiment of Foot, where he obtained a commission as captain-lieutenant on January 2, 1750; within six months he was promoted to captain in that regiment. Fortunately for Captain Howe, his superior officer was the brilliant James Wolfe, lieutenant colonel commanding the unit and later the hero of the British victory at Quebec. In Howe's case, as in the case of other young officers, Wolfe's approval was a guarantee of promotion.

LIFE'S WORK

By January 4, 1756, the ambitious Howe had reached the rank of major, serving in the unit known as the Fifty-eighth Foot. Four years later, he achieved a promotion to lieutenant colonel while his regiment was stationed in Ireland. In 1758 he led his unit to North America, where he and his men served with distinction during the siege of the French fortress at Louisbourg on Cape Breton. Indeed, his old friend and commanding officer, General James Wolfe, judged that Howe led the best-trained bat-

talion in America. So convinced was Wolfe of Howe's abilities that he selected him to lead the assault up the path to the Plains of Abraham before sunrise on September 13, 1759. While the brave Wolfe's career would end that day, Howe's star continued to rise.

Soon after Quebec's capture, the specially selected light infantry led by Lieutenant Colonel Howe returned to their regular units. Resuming command of the Fifty-eighth Foot, Howe served in the defense of Quebec during the winter of 1759-1760. During 1760 he joined General James Murray's expedition against Montreal, after which he returned to England. There he enlisted in a force organized for assaulting Belle Isle on the French coast. Successful in that campaign, Howe declined the governorship of the island, to return to North America; as a young commander eager for combat and its rewards, he hoped for more military activity. His wish was fulfilled when he was ordered to Havana, where he served as adjutant general during the successful siege and capture of that port in 1762. Throughout this long service in France and America, Howe gained a reputation as a courageous officer whose troops were among the best disciplined in the army.

After the Treaty of Paris (1763), Howe used his skills to experiment with forming light companies out of each regiment. The economic cutbacks of peacetime made it impossible to carry out his proposed reforms to any great extent. Yet because of the esteem in which he was held by the young King George III, he was allowed to put the light companies through a review for the approving monarch at Richmond Park. During this interlude of peace he also married Frances Conolly of Castletown, County Kildare, Ireland.

One activity he might pursue in peacetime, however, was politics. His elder brother, George Augustus Howe, the Third Viscount Howe, had held the parliamentary seat from Nottingham. When Lord Howe was killed in battle near Ticonderoga in 1758, his seat became vacant. Lady Howe, mother of the fallen general as well as of the future general (William Howe) and admiral (Richard Howe), urged the electors of Nottingham to replace their late representative with his younger brother, even though he was absent in America. The appeal was successful: William Howe was returned from Nottingham from that time until 1780. Since he held this seat largely for purposes of personal glory he was seldom present in the Commons; he did not speak in Parliament until 1778, when he attempted to defend his actions as commander in America.

By the time of the American Revolution, William Howe, who had been promoted to major general in 1772, was one of Great Britain's brightest military minds. When political differences with the colonies exploded into rebellion, General Howe's initial reaction was sympathy for the Americans. His response was based in part on an emotional attachment to the colonies, and especially to Massachusetts, whose citizens had raised a monument to George Augustus Howe in Westminster Abbey.

No matter what his personal inclinations, however, General Howe was a soldier of the Crown, always loyal to the monarch. Because of his military reputation, more-

over, Howe was regarded by many as the leader who would act vigorously to crush the rebellion. Behind the scenes in London, Lord Germain, who thought General Thomas Gage needed a strong spur at the least, lobbied for the appointment of Howe to replace Gage.

Even if George III wished to accept Germain's recommendation, such a hasty action would have been politically unwise. The king could, however, send Howe to aid Gage; furthermore, a blank commission as commander in chief could be given General Howe so that he could assume command immediately upon Gage's departure. To make the move less obvious, two other major generals, John Burgoyne and Henry Clinton, were sent along with Howe, ostensibly to help General Gage plan his operations against the rebellion.

When they arrived in Boston, Howe and his two companions learned that the British army lay isolated in a city ringed by armed colonials. Especially alarming was the presence of entrenched troops on Charlestown Neck, a peninsula lying across a narrow channel from the city; artillery positioned there could damage civilian and military populations. Consequently, Howe joined in formulating a plan for a frontal attack against the colonials.

This assault on Charlestown Neck, known to the Americans as the Battle of Bunker Hill, was planned on the basis of erroneous assumptions held by British officers about colonial attitudes. Many British leaders shared the opinion that the colonial soldier was a weakling who would run at the sight of cold steel. Equally false, and probably far more damaging in the long run, was the ardently supported notion that most colonials still were loyal to the Crown, but that they had been intimidated and led astray by a fanatical minority who had seized power. According to the logic of this belief, the appearance of British troops would rally the loyal majority.

The misperception about American cowardice should have been dispelled by the battle on Charlestown Neck, for the colonials stood their ground and exacted a heavy toll on the king's forces. Despite courageous leadership under

General William Howe. (Library of Congress)

fire by the gallant Howe, his force was decimated, with a 40 percent casualty rate among the enlisted men and a staggering 60 percent loss of officers. The British had taken the American position, but only at a terrible cost.

Howe's bravery under fire brought him promotion to lieutenant general, a colonelcy in the Twenty-third Royal Welsh Fusiliers, and the badge of a Knight of the Order of the Bath. Nevertheless, when he succeeded Thomas Gage in October of 1775, the punishment his troops had met on Charlestown Neck had not been forgotten. That memory may have prompted his decision that his position at Boston was untenable. The better part of wisdom thus dictated that he withdraw to Halifax, Nova Scotia. At the beginning of the next year's campaign he could invade the American colonies at a more advantageous spot.

In the winter of 1775-1776, moreover, General Howe was victimized by his unquestioning acceptance of Loyalist assertions in planning the campaign for 1776. He accepted the idea that the rebellion was centered in New England. There it could be isolated and crushed by seizing New York and using that city as a base to control the Hudson River and the country north to Canada. Thus cut off, the New England rebellion would wither.

Numerous Loyalists had sought out Gage, especially visitors from the South, who emphatically insisted that there was a hidden Loyalist majority there. Send us a token force of regulars, they pleaded, and all the people will rally beneath the king's standard. Thus would Howe's campaign for 1776 rest on fallacious premises. Although he did manage to lead his army to victory in New York in the fall of 1776, the expedition dispatched southward under General Clinton failed miserably. Neither in New York nor in the Southern colonies did the Loyalists demonstrate their reported majority. Despite mounting evidence to the contrary, General Howe still believed prominent Loyalists such as Joseph Galloway, who promised that Philadelphia was definitely Loyalist. Besides rallying the Loyalists, argued Galloway, capture of that city would strike a blow at colonial morale by seizing their capital. Unfortunately, neither condition was true. In the final analysis, Philadelphia took Howe in 1777. By October, 1777, frustrated by what he perceived as lack of support from home, General William Howe sought to resign; allowed to do so early in 1778, he sailed for England on May 24.

SIGNIFICANCE

In many ways the experiences of General William Howe during his last American campaign reflected the quan-

dary of many officers of his generation. Most had entered the service during the French wars, in which they had demonstrated vigorous and daring leadership. Because the country and army needed such dynamic young officers in wartime, their careers had been notably successful. By the time conflict erupted with the colonials, however, they had attained the rank and age at which they were less willing to take risks, especially against fellow Englishmen. As General Howe stood amid the carnage at Charlestown Neck, he may have concluded that such death and destruction were unnecessary.

Whatever the reasons for his lack of success, his critics judged him to have had a failure of nerve, for during his campaigns against New York and Philadelphia he did not pursue his advantages. Especially harsh were those who condemned his failure to crush the Americans during the winter of 1777-1778 at Valley Forge. Yet given the procedures of eighteenth century warfare, where one campaigned in the summer and recuperated and refitted in the winter, Howe's inaction against Valley Forge seems less questionable. Indeed, all who commanded during the American Revolution—Gage, Howe, Clinton, and Guy Carleton—seemed stifled into inaction by the time and circumstances in which they found themselves.

Howe's American campaign was by no means, however, the end of his military service to his country. An official inquiry into his command ended inconclusively with his friends at court still supportive. Consequently, when war loomed with Spain over the Nootka Sound crisis in 1790, Howe was nominated for the command of the army. Even though there was no war, he was promoted to general on October 23, 1793. In that capacity he was actively engaged in preparations for the defense of England against possible French attack in the 1790's. During that same period he was governor of Berwick-upon-Tweed, from 1795 to 1805, and then governor of Plymouth from 1805 to 1814. He also bore the title Viscount Howe, to which he had succeeded at his brother's death in 1799. He died at Plymouth on July 12, 1814, less than a month before his eighty-fifth birthday, having served his country as an officer and a gentleman.

—*James H. O'Donnell III*

FURTHER READING

Alden, John R. *The American Revolution, 1775-1783.* New York: Harper & Row, 1954. A standard account of the military side of the American struggle for independence. The author's chapter on the campaign of 1777, "Philadelphia Takes Howe," shows the fatal consequences of the British policy of accepting Loyalist assessments. By doing things as the army had always done them, explains Alden, General Howe failed in his most important command.

Anderson, Troyer S. *The Command of the Howe Brothers During the American Revolution.* New York: Oxford University Press, 1936. Anderson's book emphasizes the difficulties in command presented to Howe by his twin responsibilities as both commanding general and, in tandem with his brother and admiral, commissioner for peace. Much more defensive of Howe than the study by Ira Gruber.

Brown, Gerald S. *The American Secretary: The Colonial Policy of Lord George Germain, 1775-1778.* Ann Arbor: University of Michigan Press, 1963. Paving the way for later research by Ira Gruber, Brown examines the secretaryship of Germain, a prominent politician and former military officer who was outspoken on his ideas about the conduct of the American war even before he became colonial secretary. Because this study is limited to the years coinciding with Howe's command, there is helpful material on the relationship between the two men.

Buchanan, John. *The Road to Valley Forge: How Washington Built the Army That Won the Revolution.* Hoboken, N.J.: John Wiley & Sons, 2004. Traces the development of the American revolutionary army from 1776 to 1778, describing troop movements and battlefield operations. Includes information on British military operations and the Howe brothers' role as military commanders and peace commissioners.

Fortescue, John W. *A History of the British Army.* 13 vols. London: Macmillan, 1899-1930. A classic work of military history, treating the British army from 1660 to 1918. Because it is an official publication, it has a predictable bias, wherein General Howe's difficulties in America are blamed on the ineptitude of parliamentary leadership.

Gruber, Ira D. "Howe Brothers: Richard Earl Howe/Sir William Howe." In *The Reader's Companion to Military History*, edited by Robert Cowley and Geoffrey Parker. Boston: Houghton Mifflin, 1996. Gruber, who has written a book on the Howe brothers' role in the Revolutionary War, describes how their hopes for a peaceful settlement of the conflict hampered their ability to wage a successful military campaign.

_____. *The Howe Brothers and the American Revolution.* New York: W. W. Norton, 1972. This work is the product of more than a dozen years of research. Gruber traces in detail the inner workings of imperial politics and decision making in London. He relates the American command of the Howe brothers to the machinations of imperial politics in London.

Jones, Maldwyn. "Sir William Howe: Conventional Strategist." In *George Washington's Opponents: British Generals and Admirals in the American Revolution*, edited by George A. Billias. New York: William Morrow, 1969. A brief account assessing General Howe's known military ability compared to his inability to defeat the colonial rebellion. Provides a suitable introduction to the larger question of British failure to crush the American rebellion.

McCullough, David. *1776.* New York: Simon & Schuster, 2005. McCullough focuses on one year in the American Revolution, 1776, describing the battles between America's ragtag troops and British forces. Using letters, journals, diaries, and other primary sources, he describes the leadership of Howe, George Washington, and Nathanael Greene, as well as the heroic struggles of American soldiers.

Willcox, William B. *Portrait of a General: Sir Henry Clinton in the War of Independence.* New York: Alfred A. Knopf, 1964. Because the author is defending General Clinton's failures in America, it is not surprising that Howe is criticized for ignoring Clinton's advice from 1775 to 1778. The book is useful not only for its insight into the decisions that led to Yorktown but also because it is a biography of a military figure in which the author has asked the necessary psychological questions.

See also: Sir Guy Carleton; Sir Henry Clinton; First Marquess Cornwallis; Thomas Gage; George I; George II; Nathanael Greene; Richard Howe; John Graves Simcoe; George Washington; James Wolfe.

Related articles in *Great Events from History: The Eighteenth Century, 1701-1800:* April 19, 1775: Battle of Lexington and Concord; July 4, 1776: Declaration of Independence; September 19-October 17, 1777: Battles of Saratoga; June 21, 1779-February 7, 1783: Siege of Gibraltar; 1783: Loyalists Migrate to Nova Scotia.

DAVID HUME
Scottish philosopher

Hume, whose philosophical writings on sentiment and the passions undermined the earlier reliance on reason as the sole guide for action, made major advances in the theory of perception and in ethics.

Born: May 7, 1711; Edinburgh, Scotland
Died: August 25, 1776; Edinburgh, Scotland
Area of achievement: Philosophy

EARLY LIFE

David Hume was born into a middle-class family, but his father died when he was quite young; this left him, as the second son, with a patrimony of £50 per year and a precarious living. He went to Edinburgh University with his older brother at the early age of twelve, and after three years of study he left without taking a degree, as was the custom at the time. Hume spent the next three years reading the Greek and Roman classics rather than the legal tomes he was supposed to master for a career in the law. Hume's reading of the classics inclined him to a career in letters (philosophy, history, criticism), and he set about reading at various libraries to prepare himself for the essays in philosophy and morals he planned to write. By 1729, he had already set out the plan for his first work, but such intensive study had an effect upon his health, so he began to exercise and transformed, in his own words, "a tall, lean and rawbon'd" young man into the "most sturdy, robust, healthful-like Fellow you have seen."

Hume had some difficulties in his first job as a clerk in Bristol. The work was not congenial, and he was named in a paternity suit as well. He therefore went to France in 1734, where his £50 would enable him to live more comfortably and where he could read and study more widely. He spent a year at Reims and two years at Anjou, where he took advantage of the Jesuit library where René Descartes had studied. After three years of studying and writing, Hume had almost completed his first major work, *A Treatise of Human Nature* (1739-1746), and he returned to England in expectation of "literary fame."

LIFE'S WORK

David Hume's *A Treatise of Human Nature* was published in 1739 but was, for the most part, ignored by the public. Hume said "it fell dead-born from the press." There is still some debate among scholars about Hume's intentions in the treatise. The most common view until the mid-twentieth century was that Hume was attempting to undermine or subvert the philosophies of John Locke and George Berkeley. Modern scholarship, however, has suggested that Hume was attempting to apply the Newtonian model developed in natural philosophy (now known as physics) to moral philosophy.

The most important aspect of Hume's program was an assault upon the primacy of reason in human affairs. As Hume said in his famous dictum, "Reason is and ought to be the slave of the passions, and can never pretend to any other office than to serve and obey them." What Hume attempted to do was banish that inaccurate reliance on reason and all formulations of "ought" in moral issues by showing how individuals really lived and acted. His philosophy is based on common sense, and not on deductive premises. Hume's solution is to propose that "custom" and the "passions" lead humans to act, not reason.

Other aspects of *A Treatise of Human Nature* that deserve special mention are Hume's attempt to construct a theory of perception based on sense impressions rather than innate ideas. For Hume, ideas are "derived from simple impressions." Nevertheless, while Hume believed in the existence of the objects of perception, he realized that he could not prove that they existed. Nicholas Capaldi has defended Hume's theory of perception, but even he acknowledges its problems and inconsistencies. More important for later philosophy is Hume's theory of causation, which attempts to destroy the Aristotelian theory of "essences" (what makes an object what it is when it is interacting with something else) and replace it with a Newtonian concept that defines an object by the qualities it appears to possess.

After the initial failure of *A Treatise of Human Nature*, Hume wrote political essays that were more successful and more lucrative, but he still needed a permanent position. He was encouraged to apply for the vacant professor of ethics position at Edinburgh University. He was obviously highly qualified but was rejected by the "zealots" for his supposed atheism. Hume defended his position in a pamphlet and accepted a position as tutor to the mentally ill marquess of Annandale. During these years he rewrote *A Treatise of Human Nature* to clarify certain positions and to tone down others that had offended some readers. The result of these revisions was published as *Enquiries Concerning Human Understanding* in 1748.

Enquiries Concerning Human Understanding clarifies some sections of *A Treatise of Human Nature*, adding two chapters as well. The chapters that were added, however, "Of Miracles" and "Of Particular Providence and Of a Future State," led to controversy. Hume tests all reports of miracles by the rules of evidence and logic and finds them so deficient that a person's belief in miracles is nothing less than miraculous. Hume is not as direct in his rejection of the arguments for God's providence; he simply sets it aside, saying that "No new fact can ever be inferred by the religious hypothesis." There is no evidence that Hume ever denied the existence of God, but he opposed basing religion on such dubious grounds.

Hume extended his common-sense approach to morality with the publication of *An Enquiry Concerning the Principles of Morals* in 1751. In his search for a viable source for morality, Hume changed the concept of "sympathy" in *A Treatise of Human Nature* to one of "benevolence—a common idea in the eighteenth century." He makes this change clear in *An Enquiry Concerning the Principles of Morals*: "Everything which contributes to the happiness of society, recommends itself directly to our approbation and good will. Here is a principle which accounts, in great part for the origin of morality: And what need we seek for abstruse and remote systems, when there occurs one so obvious and natural." Hume also contrasts the principle of "benevolence" to that of "self-love," and, he asserts, "I hate or despise him, who has no regard to any thing beyond his own gratifications and enjoyments."

During this period, Hume supported himself by taking a position first as judge advocate and later as aide-de-camp to General James St. Clair. The general's projected military expedition to Canada never became operational, but Hume did later take part in a military embassy with St. Clair to Vienna and Turin. Hume's *An Enquiry Concerning the Principles of Morals* was not immediately successful, so on his return to Scotland he began to write *Dialogues Concerning Natural Religion* (which was not published until three years after his death, in 1779) and *History of England*. *History of England* was published in six volumes from 1754 to 1762, and they did provide Hume with the literary fame for which he longed.

David Hume. (Library of Congress)

Hume's *History of England*, ironically, was far better known and respected in the eighteenth century than were his enduring philosophical works, which were ignored or denounced as atheistic.

The *Dialogues Concerning Natural Religion* is in the form of a Socratic dialogue with four speakers: Pamphillus (the narrator), Cleanthes (a Deist), Demea (an orthodox believer), and Philo (a skeptic). The subject of the dialogue is the "science of natural religion," which is based on scientific evidence and reasoning rather than revealed or institutional religion. Cleanthes advances the argument from design as proof of God's existence and nature. This argument is rejected by both the orthodox Demea and the skeptical Philo. At the end of the dialogue, Pamphillus acts as a sort of referee and states, "I cannot but think that *Philo's* principles are more probable than *Demea's*, but those of *Cleanthes* approach still nearer to the truth." This sudden shift at the end has puzzled many commentators, and as a result some have said

BEAUTY AND TASTE IN THE EYE OF THE BEHOLDER

David Hume proposed that disagreements about what is or is not beautiful, or what is or is not valuable, are relative. That is, it is a person's mind, however constituted—through education, disposition, or experience—that determines sensibility. He is certain of the relativity of beauty and such because, as his argument goes, no thing is inherently beautiful or ugly, desirable or lamentable, a truism confirmed by differences of opinion. Human sentiment—together with how one thinks about things—determines value and taste.

If we can depend upon any principle, which we learn from philosophy, this, I think, may be considered as certain and undoubted, that there is nothing, in itself, valuable or despicable, desirable or hateful, beautiful or deformed; but that these attributes arise from the particular constitution and fabric of human sentiment and affection. What seems the most delicious food to one animal, appears loathsome to another: What affects the feeling of one with delight, produces uneasiness in another. This is confessedly the case with regard to all the bodily senses: But if we examine the matter more accurately, we shall find, that the same observation holds even where the mind concurs with the body, and mingles its sentiment with the exterior appetite.

. . . You will never convince a man, who is not accustomed to Italian music, and has not an ear to follow its intricacies, that a Scotch tune is not preferable. You have not even any single argument, beyond your own taste, which you can employ in your behalf: And to your antagonist, his particular taste will always appear a more convincing argument to the contrary. If you be wise, each of you will allow, that the other may be in the right; and having many other instances of this diversity of taste, you will both confess, that beauty and worth are merely of a relative nature, and consist in an agreeable sentiment, produced by an object in a particular mind, according to the peculiar structure and constitution of that mind.

Source: David Hume, "The Sceptic" (1742), in *Essays, Moral, Political, and Literary*, edited by Eugene F. Miller, rev. ed. (Indianapolis, Ind.: LibertyClassics, 1987), pp. 162, 163.

that Philo speaks for Hume and others that Cleanthes does. Richard H. Popkin supports his view that Cleanthes speaks for Hume by comparing those views to Hume's other writings. If this is so, then the widespread notion that Hume rejected religion altogether is inaccurate, although he did oppose institutional religion throughout his life.

From 1763 until 1767, Hume served as private secretary to the earl of Hertford, who was appointed British ambassador to France. In France, Hume received the fame and even adulation he never found in England. The French recognized Hume as an important philosopher, and he had a receptive audience in the philosophes of Paris. He also had perhaps his closest relationship with a woman while in Paris. His friendship with the comtesse de Boufflers soon became a more intimate relationship;

they maintained a correspondence for many years, but marriage was impossible.

Hume returned to Scotland in 1767 and began revising the *Dialogues Concerning Natural Religion*. For once, he had no financial worries; his writing and appointments gave him an income of £1,000 per year. He became ill in 1775 and died on August 25, 1776, in a tranquil mood despite the impertinent questions about his beliefs posed by James Boswell and others.

SIGNIFICANCE

David Hume was a man of the eighteenth century—the Enlightenment, or the Age of Reason. It is often forgotten, however, that a major part of his work was intended to show the limits of reason. He extolled common sense and distrusted any theory that was not soundly based on experience. He never lapsed, however, into empiricism but instead retained a skeptical mind about the certainty of the objects of perception. Many critics have complained that Hume's philosophy is merely negative and skeptical, but Hume specifically rejected the extreme form of skepticism called Pyrrhonism, and many of his deconstructions prepared the way for other philosophers. For example, Immanuel Kant made his debt to Hume quite clear when he wrote, "I honestly confess that my recollection of David Hume's teaching was the very thing which many years ago first interrupted my dogmatic slumber." Hume also had a direct influence on eighteenth century Utilitarians such as Jeremy Bentham and nineteenth century Utilitarians such as John Stuart Mill. Mill's *Essay on Liberty* is clearly indebted to Hume.

There are lapses and inconsistencies in Hume's philosophy, and his psychological solutions to philosophical problems are of little value today. Nevertheless, Hume's achievement remains significant. He may not have solved the problem of the existence of the objects of perception, but he showed that Berkeley's idealism and Locke's empiricism were inadequate. In addition,

Hume's rejection of metaphysics is a favorite theme for the twentieth and twenty-first century poststructuralists. John Passmore summed up Hume's achievement when he wrote that "He [Hume] is pre-eminently a breaker of new ground: a philosopher who opens up new lines of thought, who suggests to us an endless variety of philosophical explorations."

—*James Sullivan*

FURTHER READING

Ayer, A. J. *Hume*. New York: Hill & Wang, 1980. Reprint. *Hume: A Very Short Introduction*. New York: Oxford University Press, 2000. This introduction to Hume's life and thought is both well-written and useful. The chapter on aims and methods is especially good.

Capaldi, Nicholas. *David Hume: The Newtonian Philosopher*. Boston: Twayne, 1975. The subtitle illustrates Capaldi's approach. He is very good in describing Hume's moral views. The book is thorough, with comparisons and contrasts to other thinkers.

Chappel, V. C., ed. *Hume: A Collection of Critical Essays*. Garden City, N.Y.: Doubleday, 1966. This collection of twenty-one essays by such acknowledged authorities as Ernest Mossner and Anthony Flew is a valuable source for students of Hume. There are many essays on Hume's theories of causality and morality.

Mossner, Ernest Campbell. *The Life of David Hume*. 2d ed. New York: Oxford University Press, 2001. Even though some of Mossner's speculations seem dubious, his life of Hume is a standard biography. It does not discuss in detail Hume's ideas but is superb on his life and background.

Norton, David Fate, ed. *The Cambridge Companion to Hume*. New York: Cambridge University Press, 1993. A collection of essays analyzing all aspects of Hume's philosophy, including the science of the mind, skepticism, moral psychology, and religion.

Noxon, James. *Hume's Philosophical Development*. New York: Oxford University Press, 1973. Noxon traces the changes in Hume's methodology and epistemology with clarity and cogency.

Passmore, John. *Hume's Intentions*. 3d ed. London: Duckworth, 1980. This is a well-written and invaluable discussion of what Hume said and intended. Passmore corrects earlier imprecise and biased views of Hume.

Popkin, Richard H. Introduction to *Dialogues Concerning Natural Religion*. Indianapolis, Ind.: Hackett, 1980. An excellent introduction and edition of one of Hume's most important works.

Price, John Valdimir. *The Ironic Hume*. Austin: University of Texas Press, 1965. Price investigates an oft-ignored aspect of Hume's practice, and suggests some important changes in interpretation that result from Hume's use of irony.

Schmidt, Claudia M. *David Hume: Reason in History*. University Park: Pennsylvania State University Press, 2003. Schmidt analyzes Hume's work in philosophy, political science, history, economics, and other disciplines to refute the belief that his writings lack coherence. She maintains that his work is unified by a belief in human reason and its historical dimension.

See also: Mary Astell; Jeremy Bentham; George Berkeley; James Boswell; Marquise du Châtelet; Étienne Bonnot de Condillac; Denis Diderot; First Baron Erskine; Adam Ferguson; Claude-Adrien Helvétius; Johann Gottfried Herder; Immanuel Kant; William Paley; Jean-Jacques Rousseau; Giambattista Vico.

Related articles in *Great Events from History: The Eighteenth Century, 1701-1800:* October, 1725: Vico Publishes *The New Science*; 1726-1729: Voltaire Advances Enlightenment Thought in Europe; 1739-1740: Hume Publishes *A Treatise of Human Nature*; 1748: Montesquieu Publishes *The Spirit of the Laws*; 1751-1772: Diderot Publishes the *Encyclopedia*; 1754: Condillac Defends Sensationalist Theory; July 27, 1758: Helvétius Publishes *De l'esprit*; April, 1762: Rousseau Publishes *The Social Contract*; July, 1764: Voltaire Publishes *A Philosophical Dictionary for the Pocket*; 1770: Publication of Holbach's *The System of Nature*; 1781: Kant Publishes *Critique of Pure Reason*; 1784-1791: Herder Publishes His Philosophy of History.

THOMAS HUTCHINSON
American politician and historian

As the last civilian to serve as royal governor of Massachusetts, Hutchinson had the tragic experience of watching the union between his province and Great Britain dissolve, in spite of his strenuous efforts. He wrote a remarkably objective and thoroughly documented three-volume history of Massachusetts, from its beginning to 1774.

Born: September 9, 1711; Boston, Massachusetts
Died: June 3, 1780; London, England
Areas of achievement: Government and politics, historiography

EARLY LIFE

Though a great-great-grandson of the brilliant Anne Hutchinson, who had been banished from the Massachusetts Bay Colony for her unorthodox religious views, Thomas Hutchinson was a man devoid of fanaticism, religious or otherwise. Born to the large family of a prosperous Boston merchant, and connected through marriage to similarly wealthy and prudent Rhode Islanders, Hutchinson presented the perfect picture of the Puritan turned Yankee. Studious and even scholarly from childhood, he entered Harvard College at the age of twelve, completed his degree at age seventeen, and earned a master of arts degree by completing a thesis at age twenty. By that time, he had already earned several hundred pounds by trading on his own account and was part owner of a ship. His main efforts, however, were on behalf of his father's firm, which he inherited while still in his twenties.

In 1734, Hutchinson married Margaret Sanford of Newport. Of their many children, five lived to maturity: Thomas, Elisha, William (Billy), Sarah (Sally), and Margaret (Peggy). His wife died shortly after the birth of Peggy in 1753, and Thomas Hutchinson never remarried. He remained, however, a most devoted family man, wearing himself out attending to the concerns of his children, with whom his commercial and political affairs were endlessly intertwined.

The prosperous young merchant began his political career in 1737 with election to two important posts: selectman for Boston and representative of Boston in the provincial legislature. There he quickly distinguished himself for his wide-ranging knowledge of political and commercial matters and for his patient and self-effacing industry. Though always eager to please, Hutchinson was also a man of principle, boldly defending the interests of Massachusetts in its boundary dispute with New Hampshire, and standing against any paper-money schemes that tended to defraud creditors or otherwise destabilize the currency. In 1741, Parliament dissolved a Massachusetts land bank whose creation Hutchinson had opposed. This dissolution brought about the financial ruin of the father of Samuel Adams and may partly explain the relentless and even obsessive zeal that Adams later showed for the autonomy of Massachusetts, and against the character of Hutchinson.

In 1749, Hutchinson's years of service in the legislature were rewarded by election to the council; Massachusetts was the only royal colony in which the right of nominating councillors rested with the elected representatives rather than with the royal governor. Hutchinson's term as councillor was followed by a series of other important offices, many held simultaneously: justice of common pleas for Suffolk County, probate judge, representative to the Albany Congress of 1754, and lieutenant governor of the province, from 1758. In all of these posts, Hutchinson acquitted himself with distinction; unfortunately, the career for which he is remarkable in American history was coincident with the rise of the American Revolution, whose progress Hutchinson, for reasons usually honorable and never contemptible, felt compelled to oppose at every step.

LIFE'S WORK

In 1760, Thomas Hutchinson accepted a still more distinguished position, the chief justiceship for Massachusetts. In accepting the offer from the new governor, Francis Bernard, Hutchinson knew that there had been some sort of prior understanding that the position, with its fixed salary and high prestige, was to have been offered first to the elder James Otis. Hutchinson was, however, remarkably well qualified, and he had no assurance that the elder Otis would receive the appointment if he himself declined it.

What Hutchinson could not realize was that his new post would immediately cast him as the villain in a political melodrama. The French and Indian War (1754-1763) had brought forth great exertions on behalf of the colonies of British North America, but the inspiration for those exertions, William Pitt the Elder, insisted on the enforcement of the acts of trade and navigation. To assist his customs collectors in their duties, he called for the use of open-ended search warrants, called writs of assistance; far from being foreign to the English constitution, these had been used in England for many years. The younger James Otis quit his own profitable position as attorney for the Boston Court of Vice-Admiralty in protest against these writs and argued in Chief Justice Hutchinson's court that the writs were in principle unconstitutional because they contradicted the English principle that one's home (and by extension a merchant's warehouse) was one's castle, and no officer of the law could invade it without a special warrant duly sworn, showing evidence presumptive of breaking the law.

Otis's appeal was too technical and too much restricted to the upper classes to produce a crisis at that time, but it set forth the arguments that the American colonies would use to deny to the Crown and Parliament of Great Britain sovereignty over their colonies. Otis invoked an authority higher than judges, courts, royal governors, prime ministers, or even parliaments and kings: He invoked the very spirit of the British constitution and the now-familiar doctrine of natural law, and he maintained with great vehemence that any laws or actions that violated such sacred principles must simply be nullified.

Hutchinson had absorbed the same general views of politics as Otis. He understood the principles of John Locke and the Glorious Revolution of 1688-1689. He was also a practical man who understood something of the workings of law and justice, and it occurred to him at the very outset of the revolution that, should each colony review for itself the acts of Parliament in the light of natural law, there would be an end to the empire, for with the best will in the world, no two people could exactly agree on how natural principles should be applied to particular cases. The chief justice therefore upheld the writs of assistance and thereby ensured the enmity of the Otises. They began to point out that, besides holding several lucrative and powerful offices himself, Hutchinson had close relatives in several others, notably his brother-in-law, Andrew Oliver, member of the council since 1746 and secretary of Massachusetts since 1756, and Andrew's brother Peter, a justice of the superior court since 1756. A young, ambitious, and agitated attorney named John Adams also pointed out that Hutchinson had never formally studied or practiced law.

With the Sugar Act of 1764 and the Stamp Act of 1765, Chief Justice Hutchinson became the object of continual public attack. He knew all too well how little he deserved such attacks, for he was nothing if not energetic in writing letters, and he had continually warned his correspondents in England that efforts to raise Crown revenues by direct taxation in Massachusetts would bring

The Boston home of Thomas Hutchinson. (Library of Congress)

trouble rather than money. Such was Hutchinson's conception of his duty, however, that he never made these opinions public and was, instead, obliged to enforce in his court the very revenue acts he had tried to forestall. Worse, Andrew Oliver, somewhat less sensitive to the issue than his brother-in-law, accepted the potentially lucrative stamp agency for Massachusetts. At least it would have been lucrative had the citizenry been prepared to pay the stamp tax, but they were not. On August 15, 1765, a crowd inspired by radical speeches (and perhaps some rum) hanged Oliver, along with one of England's prime ministers, Lord Bute, in effigy. Participants in the protest then demolished one of Oliver's commercial properties, believing it to be the future stamp office. Finally, they barraged the secretary's residence with stones until every window was broken and much was destroyed within. Hutchinson, never a coward, tried to disperse the mob, only to be driven back in a shower of stones himself.

Oliver prudently resigned the stamp agency, and no revenue stamps were sold between the passage of the Stamp Act and its repeal the next year. The mob sprang into renewed life, however, on August 26, attacking the homes of two customs collectors, taking special pains to destroy their records. That evening, the mob besieged the home of the chief justice himself, driving him and his family out, and either stealing or wrecking everything within. A friend rescued the manuscript of the second volume of Hutchinson's *The History of the Colony and Province of Massachusetts Bay* (1764-1828), which one of the marauders had dropped in the street. No one was ever indicted, let alone convicted, for the calculated destruction of private property in 1765, though Hutchinson much later received some compensation from the Massachusetts assembly. He received a vote of no confidence, and for the first time since the 1740's, neither Hutchinson nor Oliver was returned to the provincial council. Nine years before the Revolutionary War began, and ten years before the Declaration of Independence, to be both a paid servant of the Crown and a friend of the people of Massachusetts was impossible.

Furthermore, while Samuel Adams's majorities in the Boston town meeting and the Massachusetts assembly still stopped well short of denouncing the king, George III, or advocating independence, the royal law, as distinct from that of Massachusetts, was a nullity in Massachusetts. Attempts to revive it were met with swift, concerted action both in dignified resolutions drawn up in assemblies and by violence directed at any who presumed to defend the Crown's prerogatives.

Thus, in the wake of the Boston Massacre of March 5, 1770, it was not the townspeople who had provoked the riot who had to stand trial but the British soldiers who had fired their weapons in self-defense. Though the particular soldiers were acquitted, Samuel Adams made so much of the event that he was able to force Hutchinson to withdraw all six hundred troops from the city of Boston and keep them in barracks at Castle William. By this time, Hutchinson was acting governor, for Francis Bernard had fled to England, never to return. In 1771, Hutchinson accepted the governorship in his own right, though with reluctance and misgivings. Already under attack for calling the assembly to meet in Cambridge, to remove it somewhat from the turbulence and influence of the Sons of Liberty, he was now attacked for receiving his salary from the Crown. Virtually all the political wisdom of the eighteenth century argued for the independence of the branches of government, but Hutchinson was represented as a traitor to his native province for accepting and even defending the independence of the Massachusetts legislature.

Hutchinson's last effort to preserve British rule in Massachusetts was the cause of its final and irreversible collapse. He refused to allow three ships laden with tea to return to England until the new imperial Tea Act had been observed. By the time the Sons of Liberty had deposited the tea in Boston Harbor, Hutchinson's last shreds of reputation had been destroyed in Massachusetts by the publication of several of his private letters to England, stolen by Benjamin Franklin (whose reputation in England was subsequently ruined, making him a confirmed radical) and printed, against Franklin's express instructions, in Massachusetts. The letters were improved, for patriotic purposes, by selective editing, but they did not grossly misrepresent Hutchinson. He had frequently called for more British power, to overawe what always seemed to him a radical and wrongheaded minority.

In June, 1774, Hutchinson turned over the government of Massachusetts to General Thomas Gage and set sail for England. After war broke out in earnest in 1775, the provincial assembly of Massachusetts declared Hutchinson and his family outlaws and confiscated all of his property. He would never return. At first welcomed as a patriot and hero by the Crown, Hutchinson received an honorary degree from Oxford on, of all days, July 4, 1776. Soon enough he found himself an unimportant exile; to be sure, he had a comfortable pension, but all that he had spent a lifetime building was gone. Cruelest of all, his son Billy and his youngest daughter Peggy died in

England before he himself died in 1780. He did, however, have time to complete his history. Even though it told the story of the revolution that had driven him into exile, the third volume retained the objectivity and the love of Massachusetts that had characterized the work from its beginning.

SIGNIFICANCE

Thomas Hutchinson was a hardworking man of learning and high principle, but he was at least in part responsible for the tragedy that overtook him. However reluctantly he accepted high offices, he left himself open to the charge of using royal influence to support his personal power and wealth. Ultimately desiring the best of both worlds—power from the Crown and popularity with the people—he sacrificed the latter. The American Revolution was carried in public meetings; cut off from the people by his Crown appointments, Hutchinson lost his political standing in a community he had worked hard to build and actually celebrated in its first full-scale history.

—*Robert McColley*

FURTHER READING

Bailyn, Bernard. *The Ideological Origins of the American Revolution*. Cambridge, Mass.: Harvard University Press, 1967. The influential book that first explored revolutionary thought and accounted for its intensity.

_____. *The Ordeal of Thomas Hutchinson*. Cambridge, Mass.: Belknap Press, 1974. A modern biography, concerned especially with the character and thought of Hutchinson.

Calhoon, Robert McCluer. *The Loyalists in Revolutionary America, 1760-1781*. New York: Harcourt Brace Jovanovich, 1973. A comprehensive treatment of the Loyalists, and a book in which Hutchinson figures prominently. Calhoon shows that "all sorts and conditions of men" were Loyalists, not just wealthy Crown appointees, and they came from all parts of the colonies.

Freiberg, Malcolm. *Prelude to Purgatory: Thomas Hutchinson in Provincial Massachusetts Politics, 1760-1770*. New York: Garland, 1990. Freiberg examines Hutchinson's political activities before the Revolutionary War.

Galvin, John R. *Three Men of Boston*. New York: Thomas Y. Crowell, 1976. The story of the revolution in Massachusetts, focusing on Hutchinson, James Otis, and Samuel Adams. The writing is admirably clear, and the events are rendered in an exciting way.

Hutchinson, Thomas. *The Diary and Letters of His Excellency, Thomas Hutchinson*. 2 vols. London: Searle and Rivington, 1883-1886. Difficult to find, but an important collection of Hutchinson's writings. Hutchinson sometimes was more candid in his diary than in his historical writings or in official letters.

_____. *The History of the Colony and Province of Massachusetts-Bay*. Boston: Thomas and John Fleet, 1764-1828. Reprint. Edited by Lawrence S. Mayo. 3 vols. Cambridge, Mass.: Harvard University Press, 1936. Hutchinson's masterpiece in a fine modern edition.

McFarland, Philip. *The Brave Bostonians: Hutchinson, Quincy, Franklin, and the Coming of the American Revolution*. Boulder, Colo.: Westview Press, 1998. Examines the lives of Hutchinson, Benjamin Franklin, and archpatriot Josiah Quincy in 1774, the year following the Revolutionary War. McFarland uses excerpts from the men's papers to describe how and why they chose to be either Loyalists or patriots.

Norton, Mary Beth. *The British-Americans: The Loyalist Exiles in England, 1774-1789*. Boston: Little, Brown, 1972. A sad but interesting tale, encompassing both the trials of uprooted Americans and those British officials overwhelmed by claims for compensation, rewards, or mere subsistence.

Walmsley, Andrew Stephen. *Thomas Hutchinson and the Origins of the American Revolution*. New York: New York University Press, 1999. A biography that traces Hutchinson's decline from a respected Boston politician to one of the most vilified men in the colonies. Walmsley maintains Hutchinson's defeat was a classic political power struggle.

See also: John Adams; Samuel Adams; Benjamin Franklin; Thomas Gage; George III; John Hancock; William Pitt the Elder; William Pitt the Younger.

Related articles in *Great Events from History: The Eighteenth Century, 1701-1800:* May 28, 1754-February 10, 1763: French and Indian War; March 22, 1765-March 18, 1766: Stamp Act Crisis; March 5, 1770: Boston Massacre; April 19, 1775: Battle of Lexington and Concord; July 4, 1776: Declaration of Independence.

HYDER ALI
Ruler of Mysore (r. 1761-1782)

Hyder Ali was an uneducated Muslim soldier who became the de facto ruler of Mysore, in southern India. He established an efficient administration, a powerful modern army, and a small navy. He successfully fought against the Marāthās, the nizam of Hyderabad, and the powerful British East India Company, and he made himself the dominating power in southern India.

Born: 1722; Budikote, Mysore, India
Died: December 7, 1782; Chitor, India
Also known as: Haider Ali; Haidar Ali; Haider Ali Khan; Haider Naik
Areas of achievement: Government and politics, warfare and conquest

EARLY LIFE

Little is known about Hyder Ali's family, who were Muslims, or his early life, except that Hyder Ali's father, Fateh Muḥammad, was employed by Durgah Quli Khan, the Mughal commander of Sira, Karnatakata. He died when Hyder Ali was about seven years old. A member of his family, Hyder Sahib, was in the Mysore army in the service of the raja of Mysore, and so was Hyder Ali's elder brother, Shahbaz. About 1749, Hyder Ali joined them, also as a cavalry officer. Mysore had pledged allegiance to the Mughal emperor Aurangzeb (r. 1658-1707), so many Mughal officers, especially cavalry officers, became part of the Mysore forces. Indian muskets were inferior at this time, and the elite of Indian armies was the cavalry, that is, highly skilled archers mounted on fine breeds of horses. Hyder Ali proved himself a charismatic leader, full of energy, common sense, and sound judgment. He clearly recognized that the greatest danger to Mysore and other Indian states was the growing power of the British.

LIFE'S WORK

In 1749, Hyder Ali was involved in the Siege of Devanhalli and Arcot, where he observed and came to appreciate European military equipment, tactics, and organization. European armies were superior to Indian armies in the matter of discipline and *esprit de corps*. Soldiers trained as a group and were given uniforms and regular pay, which instilled loyalty. By contrast, Indian solders were often mercenaries, hiring out to one army after another. A soldier's greatest loyalty was to his horse, the means of his livelihood. European troops moved together by order, giving them greater confidence in num-

bers. They were drilled to fire in volleys and to load quickly, so they could fire two volleys before an Indian cavalry charge reached their lines. Hyder learned and adopted all these tactics.

In 1753, Hyder was appointed *faujdar* (military commander) of a Mysore stronghold, Dingidul. By 1755, he was hiring French military officers to organize his arsenal, his workshop, and his artillery. The combination of trained infantry drilled in the European manner equipped with flintlock muskets, unusual in India at that time, along with traditional Mughal cavalry, made his army a very powerful one. He attacked the surrounding poligars (petty chieftains), defeated them, and acquired a vast fortune. He became renowned for his audacity and courage.

In 1757, Hyder was appointed the commander in chief of the Mysore army when the state was attacked by the Marāthās. He repulsed them, thereby acquiring great renown and favors. The raja of Mysore was the nominal ruler of Mysore, but by 1761, Hyder Ali had supplanted him, and the raja was retired and placed under house arrest in his palace; he was shown to the people only once a year. Hyder Ali had become the de facto leader of Mysore.

Hyder Ali invaded his neighbors' lands and extended his territory, but in 1766 he was defeated by a coalition of the Marāthā Madhav Rao (d. 1773), the peshwa (head of the Marāthā polity); the nizam; and the British. In response, he paid tribute to the Marāthās, captured Mangalore, and defeated the British army of Bombay. He realized that the British—who had a growing army, an equally powerful navy, and control of Bengal after the Battle of Plassey (1757)—represented the greatest threat to his power. Accordingly, he allied with the nizam of Hyderabad and attacked the British in 1767, commencing the First Anglo-Mysore War *(August, 1767-April, 1769)*.

The British were intent on controlling Mysore and southern India after they had captured the northern Sarkars from the French in 1758. Although the nizam deserted Hyder at the beginning of the campaign, Hyder pushed the British back to the gates of Madras and forced them to sign a treaty very favorable to Mysore. It included a defensive alliance between the British and Mysore. In 1771, the Marāthās attacked again, and, much to Hyder's disgust, neither the nizam of Hyderabad nor the British came to his aid, in spite of the treaties they had signed with him. Hyder was forced to retreat to his fort at

Seringapatam to negotiate terms, which included paying a large indemnity and returning territory to the Marāthās. It was a humiliating defeat, and Hyder vowed revenge on the British.

Hyder attacked the British, sending some ninety thousand troops into the Carnatic and commencing the Second Anglo-Mysore War (1780-1784). A precipitating factor of the war was the British capture in 1779 of the French settlement at Mahe, which lay within Hyder's territory. This capture compounded the 1771 betrayal and the tendency of the British to march troops across his territory without permission. Hyder was beseiging Arcot when he learned through his military spies (*harkaras*) that Colonel William Baillie and his force were camped at Pullalur. On September 10, 1780, Hyder and Tipu with the cavalry and his French general Lally with the artillery attacked and annihilated the four-thousand-man army; only sixteen out of eighty-six European officers survived.

Baillie died in captivity on November 13, 1782. The British then sent another army under General Hector Munro (1726-1805), the hero of the Battle of Buxar (1764). Hyder defeated Munro too, even though the French, who had promised Hyder their support, deserted him. He inflicted the worst defeat on a British army in India. Munro fled back to Madras, leaving his artillery and baggage for Hyder to capture. Hyder celebrated his great victory by commissioning a wall-to-wall painting in his palace in Seringapatam, the "Baillie-Lally Yudh." He was now the supreme force in southern India.

When he heard of this disaster, the British governor-general, Warren Hastings, finally organized a formidable force under Sir Eyre Coote (1726-1783), who traveled to Madras by sea while another force marched by land. Coote met Hyder and defeated him in three battles in 1781 at Porto Novo, where Hyder lost more than ten thousand men, and at Pollilur and Sholinghur. A few months later, however, Hyder's son, Tipu Sultan, routed the British at the Coleroon River. Hyder retired to Arcot, and his son assumed power. Hyder died in December, 1782, after the British fleet had captured Nagappattinam, warning his son that the British were the greatest danger to Mysore.

SIGNIFICANCE

Along with the nizam of Hyderabad and the British, Hyder Ali at the height of his reign was one of the most powerful forces in southern India. Over the next half century, these three powers would fight to control the south of India. Although the British would defeat and kill his son Tipu Sultan in 1799 at the Battle of Seringapatam and incorporate much of Mysore into their empire, Hyder Ali is considered by some Indians to be their first nationalist freedom fighter. For thirty years, he was able to withstand the advance of the British. It has been believed by some historians that had he received better support from the French, Hyder Ali would have been able to drive the British from southern India completely, thereby preserving Indian independence in the south.

—Roger D. Long

FURTHER READING

Fernandes, Praxy. *The Tigers of Mysore: A Biography of Hyder Ali and Tipu Sultan.* New Delhi: Viking Press, 1991. Intended as a study of Tipu Sultan, the book was expanded to provide a background study of Hyder Ali as well.

Gordon, Stewart. *The Marāthās*, 1600-1818. New York: Cambridge University Press, 1993. This book is one of the volumes of *The New Cambridge History of India*. Provides an account of Hyder Ali's military techniques in the face of superior Marāthā military power.

Habib, Irfan, ed. *Confronting Colonialism: Resistance and Modernization Under Haidar Ali and Tipu Sultan.* New Delhi: Tulika, 1999. This volume of twenty-five essays came out of a conference to commemorate the bicentenary of Tipu Sultan's defeat by the British at Seringapatam in 1799. Seventeen years after his death, Mysore finally fell to the British.

See also: Robert Clive; Joseph-François Dupleix; Warren Hastings; Shāh Walī Allāh.

Related articles in *Great Events from History: The Eighteenth Century, 1701-1800*: 1746-1754: Carnatic Wars; June 23, 1757: Battle of Plassey; August, 1767-May, 1799: Anglo-Mysore Wars; December, 1774-February 24, 1783: First Marāthā War.

JOHN JAY
American jurist, diplomat, and politician

As president of the Second Continental Congress, ambassador to Spain, foreign secretary under the Articles of Confederation, first chief justice of the United States, and governor of New York, Jay contributed greatly to the political and judicial development of New York State and the American nation.

Born: December 12, 1745; New York, New York
Died: May 17, 1829; Bedford, New York
Areas of achievement: Law, diplomacy, government and politics

EARLY LIFE

John Jay was born in New York City, the sixth son in a family of eight children. His father, Peter Jay, was from one of the most influential families in the colony and had amassed a fortune as a merchant. His mother, née Mary Van Cortlandt, came from one of the oldest European families in the Hudson River Valley. Young Jay grew up as a member of the privileged class in New York, benefiting from private tutors and the most comfortable of surroundings. His father took a special interest in his education and decided that John should read the best of the classics, literature, and history. The youth attended King's College (now Columbia University), from which he was graduated in 1764. He decided upon the practice of law as his vocation and apprenticed himself to one of the most respected lawyers of the city, Benjamin Kissam.

Jay gained admission to the bar in 1768 and embarked upon a lucrative private practice. His family and social connections enabled him to associate with the elite of the colony. A tall, slender, and dark-complected young man of sensitive features, he soon captured the attentions of young ladies active in New York's social whirl. Although by nature a quiet, studious, and serious person, Jay had a quick wit and lively spirit that made him a person of popularity and an attractive bachelor. Sarah Van Brugh Livingston, daughter of William Livingston, the first governor of New Jersey, captured the young man's heart. She and Jay were married on April 28, 1774. They would eventually have two sons and five daughters.

By the time of his marriage, Jay had already become active in public affairs. His inherited wealth freed him from financial dependence on his law practice, and Jay was therefore able to devote himself to public service, a calling that would occupy most of his adult life. In 1773, he received appointment as member of a commission created to survey the boundary between New York and New Jersey. He served with distinction on this committee, which settled a long-standing border dispute between the two colonies. Jay impressed everyone with his diplomatic skills and negotiating abilities, talents upon which he would draw as a political leader. During the revolutionary crisis of the mid-1770's, Jay became an active member of the New York Committee of Correspondence. This resulted in his being elected as a delegate to the First and Second Continental Congresses.

LIFE'S WORK

John Jay's service in the First Continental Congress in 1774 marked the start of his major contributions to the creation of the United States of America as a free and independent nation. Initially, he represented the conservative commercial interests of his colony in the Continental Congress, and after the Declaration of Independence in 1776, Jay became one of the most vocal proponents of the new nation. In that year, he returned to New York, where he helped to draft the constitution of that state and served as chief justice of New York until he was reelected to Congress in 1778. His fellow delegates chose him as the president of the Continental Congress, a position he held from December, 1778, until September, 1779. During that time, he acted as the highest-ranking civil officer in the young government and, in concert with George Washington, directed the course of the Revolutionary War.

By 1779, the support of European nations, especially France and Spain, had become crucial to the success of the American cause. France had already entered the war as an American ally against Great Britain. Spain, however, vacillated and had only recently entered the conflict, refusing to ally itself formally with the United States. Jay was appointed ambassador to Spain in the fall of 1779 and was given the difficult task of winning Spanish support for the United States. As the largest colonial power in the Western Hemisphere, Spain was not eager to side openly with the American rebels. Jay therefore went to Spain prepared for difficult negotiations with the Spanish court. As ambassador, he spent two years in Spain, where he conducted talks with Count Floridablanca, the Spanish foreign minister, who did not want to assist the Americans. Nevertheless, Jay was able to convince Spain to make sizable "loans" to the United States and to continue sending large amounts of military supplies for General Washington's army. Although Jay's work in Spain never resulted in a formal treaty, he gained valuable diplomatic experience and secured significant assistance for the United States.

This work resulted in Jay being selected as a member of the U.S. delegation sent to Paris for the purpose of negotiating the peace treaty in 1782. Jay played an active role in these deliberations, along with John Adams and Benjamin Franklin. Jay was instrumental in convincing his fellow delegation members to conclude a separate treaty with Great Britain and not to include France in joint negotiations. This resulted in the United States signing a preliminary bilateral peace treaty with the British on January 20, 1783. (The Revolutionary War formally ended with the signing of the Treaty of Paris on September 3, 1783.) With the conclusion of this treaty, Jay rejected a congressional offer to become the ambassador to Great Britain. Instead, he returned home with the hope that he would resume the practice of law.

Upon his arrival in New York during the summer of 1784, he found that he had been appointed secretary for foreign affairs in the new U.S. government, which had recently been organized under the Articles of Confederation. He decided to accept this post and actively began the direction of American foreign policy. He served in this position during the remainder of the decade. Jay was chiefly concerned during these years with disputes along the U.S. borders with Canada and with Florida. England and Spain, as the colonial masters of these colonies, did not fully respond to his efforts to resolve these difficulties and draw firm boundaries. The government of the United States was perceived by European leaders as being so weak that Jay found it difficult to bring European diplomats to the bargaining table, much less obtain a favorable resolution. Jay did, however, negotiate successful commercial treaties with Denmark, Portugal, Austria, and Tuscany during his tenure as foreign secretary.

Between 1784 and 1789, Jay also conducted lengthy and extensive discussions with Diego Gardoquí, Spain's ambassador to the United States. Jay wished to resolve questions about the navigation of the Mississippi River and settlements in the western areas contiguous to Spanish Louisiana. Jay and Gardoquí drafted a preliminary treaty in 1789, which Congress refused to ratify because Jay had not insisted upon the free and unlimited navigation of the Mississippi by citizens of the United States.

Along with James Madison and Alexander Hamilton, Jay was an active supporter of the new Constitution, which was drafted in 1787. With these two colleagues, he wrote a series of essays arguing for adoption of the Constitution, essays that have become know as *The Federalist* papers (1787-1788). Jay was willing to continue as the nation's chief diplomat when the new document was implemented in 1789. Instead, President Washington appointed him to be the first chief justice of the United States. Most of the technical procedures and precedents under which the U.S. Supreme Court operates were established during Jay's term. In addition, he heard several influential cases, the most important being *Chisholm v. Georgia*, which affirmed the right of citizens of one state to sue citizens of other states in the federal court system.

Jay's greatest triumph while serving as chief justice came in the area of foreign affairs. In 1794, President Washington sent Jay to England on a special diplomatic mission for the purpose of discussing problems pending between the two nations. These included occupation by the Brit-

John Jay. (Library of Congress)

ish army of posts in U.S. territory northwest of the Ohio River, debts owed by Americans to English creditors, and seizures of neutral ships by the Royal Navy as a result of the Anglo-French War. In discussions with Lord Grenville, the British foreign minister, the American envoy drafted an agreement known as Jay's Treaty. This document provided for a mixed commission to hear maritime claims brought by citizens of the two nations, a British agreement to evacuate their northwestern posts inside the United States, the free navigation of the Mississippi by ships of English and American registry, and the use of special commissions to resolve future boundary claims between the two nations. This treaty became the object of a vigorous ratification debate in Congress during which Jay was vilified by political opponents of the Washington administration. The followers of Thomas Jefferson and Madison were incensed by this treaty, but, nevertheless, Congress ratified it.

Jay returned from England to find himself nominated as the Federalist Party candidate for the governorship of New York. While chief justice, Jay had played a role in supporting the Washington administration and the policies of Hamilton. This resulted in his becoming a leader of the Federalist Party, a party comprising those who agreed with Hamilton's program. Jay decided to run, resigning as chief justice. He served two terms as governor of New York, representing all the while the conservative concerns of the Federalist Party and the commercial interests of that state. As governor, he signed the law that abolished slavery in New York. In 1800, he decided to retire from public life and chose not to run for reelection. Jay retired to his farm at Bedford, Westchester County, only a few miles from New York City. There he spent the remainder of his life active in various organizations, including the American Bible Society and the Episcopal Church. He died in his rural home on May 17, 1829.

SIGNIFICANCE

As the highly educated son of a wealthy New York merchant, John Jay led a patrician life, the values of which were reflected in his diplomatic and legal accomplishments. He always had at heart the furtherance of American mercantile and commercial interests because he believed that the prosperity of the nation rested upon these activities. A quiet, deliberate, and studious man, he had natural skills as a diplomat and negotiator.

Jay was certain that the United States would have to stand alone as a free and independent nation, in control of its own international destiny. His dignified approach to American foreign relations brought a high moral tone which served the nation well. His discussions with Gardoquí and Grenville were conducted at a level that forced these European diplomats to accept Jay as an equal at a time when the recent, somewhat tentative independence of the United States did not always merit such treatment. He will always be remembered for his measured conduct of American foreign relations during the Confederation period, along with his successful negotiations of Jay's Treaty.

—*Light Townsend Cummins*

FOR A FEDERAL GOVERNMENT

John Jay argued in a 1787 essay, part of the well-known Federalist papers, for the adoption of the proposed U.S. Constitution. In this excerpt, he focuses on what he believes to be the inherent unity of the people of America and calls for a governmental union.

This country and this people seem to have been made for each other, and it appears as if it was the design of Providence, that an inheritance so proper and convenient for a band of brethren, united to each other by the strongest ties, should never be split into a number of unsocial, jealous, and alien sovereignties.

Similar sentiments have hitherto prevailed among all order and denominations of men among us. To all general purposes we have uniformly been one people; each individual citizen everywhere enjoying the same national rights, privileges, and protection. As a nation we have made peace and war: as a nation we have vanquished our common enemies: as a nation we have formed alliances and made treaties, and entered into various compacts and conventions with foreign States.

A strong sense of the value and blessings of Union induced the people, at a very early period, to institute a Federal Government to preserve and perpetuate it. They formed it almost as soon as they had a political existence; nay, at a time, when their habitations were in flames, when many of their Citizens were bleeding, and when the progress of hostility and desolation left little room for those calm and mature inquiries and reflections, which must ever precede the formation of a wise and well-balanced government for a free people.

Source: John Jay, *The Federalist*, no. 2, 1787, excerpted in *American Historical Documents, 1000-1904*, edited by Charles W. Eliot (New York: P. F. Collier & Son, 1938), p. 205.

FURTHER READING

Bemis, Samuel Flagg. *Jay's Treaty: A Study in Commerce and Diplomacy*. New York: Macmillan, 1923. Reprint. New Haven, Conn.: Yale University Press, 1962. This study, by a specialist in American colonial history, treats in detail Jay's role as a diplomat during the Confederation period and the Washington administration. It offers an almost day-by-day recounting of the negotiation of Jay's Treaty.

Brecher, Frank W. *Securing American Independence: John Jay and the French Alliance*. Westport, Conn.: Praeger, 2003. Brecher examines the American diplomatic efforts to end the Revolutionary War, focusing on the activities of John Jay and Charles Gravier de Vergennes.

Castro, William R. *The Supreme Court in the Early Republic: The Chief Justiceships of John Jay and Oliver Ellsworth*. Columbia: University of South Carolina Press, 1995. A history of the U.S. Supreme Court, from its creation through the appointment of its third chief justice. Includes an examination of the cases heard when Jay was chief justice, describing how the Court helped Washington's administration handle national security and foreign policy issues.

Jay, William. *The Life of John Jay: With Selections from His Correspondence and Miscellaneous Papers*. 2 vols. New York: J. and J. Harper, 1833. This biography, written by John Jay's son shortly after Jay's death, offers a unique view of Jay as a person and provides invaluable insights into his opinions, beliefs, and motivations.

Monagahan, Frank. *John Jay: Defender of Liberty*. New York: Bobbs-Merrill, 1935. Concentrates on Jay's public career and provides a factual, straightforward narrative of the events associated with his life. This work is the first scholarly biography of Jay and is based on primary sources and extensive research.

Morris, Richard B. *John Jay, the Nation, and the Court*. Boston: Boston University Press, 1967. The published version of the Bacon lectures, which the author presented at Boston University. Morris views Jay as a jurist who reflected the conservative commercial opinions of early American history. Highly interpretive, the lectures present few facts about Jay's life but instead comment upon his significance to American history.

_____. *The Peacemakers: The Great Powers and American Independence*. New York: Harper & Row, 1965. A general study of the diplomacy of the American Revolution that examines Jay's role as ambassador to Spain and peace commissioner within the context of the era. It provides an excellent assessment of his activities at the Paris Peace Conference of 1783.

_____, ed. *John Jay: The Making of a Revolutionary, Unpublished Papers, 1745-1780*. New York: Harper & Row, 1980. Volume 1 of a two-volume set.

_____. *John Jay: The Winning of Peace, 1780-1784*. New York: Harper & Row, 1980. Volume 2 of a two-volume collection of Jay's letters and papers, annotated by the editor. Each section contains a lengthy and extremely useful biographical and historical introduction.

Pellew, George. *John Jay*. Broomall, Pa.: Chelsea House, 1997. A reprint of a biography originally published in 1898, with an introduction by Jay scholar Richard B. Morris. Pellew was the nephew of Jay's grandson, and therefore able to read previously unexamined family papers and interview family members. His book provides a view of Jay's family life and his public career.

Smith, Donald Lewis. *John Jay: Founder of a State and Nation*. New York: Teachers College Press of Columbia University, 1968. A general study of Jay written especially for high school students. Based on secondary sources, it is a good starting place for those unfamiliar with Jay's career.

Stahr, Walter. *John Jay: Founding Father*. London: Hambledon and London, 2005. A comprehensive biography based, in part, on previously unavailable information. Stahr describes Jay's influence and importance in the early years of the American republic, examining his public career as well as his personal life.

See also: John Adams; George Rogers Clark; Benjamin Franklin; Alexander Hamilton; Thomas Jefferson; Alexander McGillivray; James Madison; Granville Sharp; Gilbert Stuart; Charles Gravier de Vergennes; George Washington.

Related articles in *Great Events from History: The Eighteenth Century, 1701-1800:* September 5-October 26, 1774: First Continental Congress; May 10-August 2, 1775: Second Continental Congress; May, 1776-September 3, 1783: France Supports the American Revolution; July 4, 1776: Declaration of Independence; February 6, 1778: Franco-American Treaties; March 1, 1781: Ratification of the Articles of Confederation; September 3, 1783: Treaty of Paris; November 19, 1794: Jay's Treaty.

THOMAS JEFFERSON
President of the United States (1801-1809)

A genuine revolutionary, Thomas Jefferson was one of the early and effective leaders of the movement to overthrow British rule in North America. After laboring to create a free, prosperous, enlightened, and agrarian republic, Jefferson served as the third president of the United States.

Born: April 13, 1743; Shadwell, Goochland (now Albemarle) County, Virginia

Died: July 4, 1826; Monticello, Albemarle County, Virginia

Areas of achievement: Government and politics, diplomacy

EARLY LIFE

The man generally considered the first thoroughgoing democrat in U.S. history began life as a Virginia aristocrat. His father, Peter Jefferson, had indeed come from yeoman stock but commended himself to the upper class as an expert surveyor, reliable county officer, and energetic planter. The elder Jefferson then joined that upper class by marrying Jane Randolph. From his parents, Thomas Jefferson inherited wealth, status, and a tradition of public service.

Educated at first in private schools kept by Anglican clergymen William Douglas and James Maury, Jefferson descended to Williamsburg in 1760, to study at the College of William and Mary. A proficient student, he completed the requirements for his degree within two years but stayed on to read law with George Wythe, an uncommonly learned and humane jurist. In his student years, Jefferson, along with his favorite professor, William Small, and Wythe, was frequently a guest in the governor's palace. Admitted to the bar in 1767, the young bachelor attorney became acquainted with all of Virginia by the strenuous but interesting practice of attending the quarter sessions of county courts. Jefferson soon stood among the leaders of his profession.

Entering the House of Burgesses in 1769, Jefferson already owned more than 2,500 acres inherited from his father, who had died in 1757. His marriage to the young widow Martha Wayles Skelton doubled his property in 1772, and the death of Martha's father in 1774 doubled it again, while increasing his slaves to more than two hundred. The Wayles inheritance also brought a large indebtedness, but in 1774, Jefferson might count himself the most fortunate of men, with a lovely wife and a robust baby daughter, a personal fortune, and a position near the top of Virginia's society and politics. He was imposing in appearance, standing more than six feet tall, with plentiful red hair, strong features, and an attitude of vitality and interest. Yet he was also shy and avoided public appearances whenever he could; he was at his very best in the cordial intimacy of the drawing room or the dining table.

LIFE'S WORK

In 1774, Virginia chose to support Massachusetts against the assaults of the Coercive (or Intolerable) Acts. To that support, Jefferson contributed the first of his major political writings, *A Summary View of the Rights of British America* (1774). In 1775, he was a delegate of Virginia in the Continental Congress in Philadelphia, supporting George Washington's newly formed Continental army in the defense of Massachusetts. Here, for a few months, Jefferson's sentiments were too radical for the majority, but when independence seemed all but inevitable in June, 1776, Congress placed him (with Benjamin Franklin and John Adams) on the special committee to draft a Declaration of Independence. Though slightly amended in committee and again on the floor of Congress, the Declaration of Independence is largely Jefferson's work.

For the next several years, Jefferson avoided continental service, preferring the considerable scene of action near his growing family and estate. With Wythe and Edmund Pendleton he drew up a new legal code for the state. He also prepared a plan for the gradual ending of slavery but declined to bring it before the House of Delegates. He also postponed his plans for a general scheme of education and for the separation of church and state. Elected governor in 1779, he found that office an ordeal. To the minor confusion of moving government from Williamsburg to Richmond was added the major trauma of a full-scale British military invasion of his state. Just before Jefferson's second term ended in June, 1781, he had to flee into the Blue Ridge Mountains to escape a raiding party sent to Monticello expressly to capture him.

Already discouraged by his last months as governor, Jefferson was cast into the deepest depression of his life by his wife's death in 1782. He never remarried, but he did accept reappointment to Congress, where, in 1783 and 1784, he worked on the monetary system of the United States, basing it on the plentiful Spanish dollar and applying the rational decimal system to fractional coins. He also drafted a comprehensive scheme for organizing the western territories of the United States. He introduced the idea of rectangular surveys and proposed local self-government from the start. His division of the terrain into eighteen jurisdictions, while convenient for the participatory democracy he had in view, would have long delayed statehood for any of them. A provision barring the introduction of slavery after 1800 failed to win the support of the nine states required under the Articles of Confederation, but Congress did adopt Jefferson's plan, replacing it instead with the Land Ordinance of 1785 and the Northwest Ordinance of 1787. Meanwhile, Jefferson had accepted a diplomatic mission to France; in 1785, he replaced the aged Benjamin Franklin as minister.

The five years in Europe were busy and happy. A tour of France and northern Italy confirmed Jefferson's architectural taste and enlarged his knowledge of agriculture. He flirted with an artistic Englishwoman, Maria Cosway, and enjoyed visiting John Adams in England, though he did not care for English society in general. By mail he kept up with the movement to disestablish religion in Virginia, where his own bill was finally passed under the expert guidance of James Madison. He also encouraged Madison and other correspondents in their drive toward a new federal constitution. In France, he sought help against the Barbary pirates and urged France to remove prohibitions or costly restrictions on such American commodities as tobacco and whale oil. His closest friends were liberal aristocrats such as the Marquis de Lafayette, whose leading role in the early stages of the French Revolution Jefferson followed with interest and encouragement.

Intending a brief visit only, Jefferson returned to the United States at the end of 1789, but he promptly accepted the post of secretary of state from President Washington. After settling his two daughters in Virginia, he took up his duties in the temporary capital, New York City. There he helped bring about the trade of votes that made possible Alexander Hamilton's federal assumption of state Revolutionary War debts and the permanent location of the Federal District on the Potomac River. The government then moved, temporarily, to Philadelphia.

JEFFERSON'S INAUGURAL ADDRESS

The third president of the United States, Thomas Jefferson, humbled himself before his audience during his inaugural address in 1801, excerpted here.

A rising nation, traversing all the seas with the rich productions of their industry, engaged in commerce with nations who feel power and forget rights, advancing rapidly to destinies beyond the reach of mortal eye—when I contemplate these transcendent objects, and see the honor, the happiness, and the hopes of this beloved country committed to the issue and the auspices of this day, I shrink from the contemplation, and humble myself before the magnitude of the undertaking. Utterly, indeed, should I despair did not the presence of many whom I here see remind me that in the other high authorities provided by our Constitution I shall find resources of wisdom, of virtue, and of zeal on which to rely under all difficulties. To you, then, gentleman, who are charged with the sovereign functions of legislation, and to those who associate with you, I look with encouragement for that guidance and support which may enable us to steer with safety the vessel in which we are all embarked amidst the conflicting elements of a troubled world.

Source: Thomas Jefferson, "Inaugural Address," March 4, 1801, in *Readings in Western Civilization*, vol. 2, edited by George H. Knoles and Rixford K. Snyder (New York: J. B. Lippincott, 1968), p. 594.

In 1791, Jefferson and Madison began to organize the first opposition party under the new Constitution. Their avowed object was to overturn not Washington but his secretary of the treasury, Hamilton. Washington almost always sided with Hamilton against his rivals, however, so it was really a case of going against a popular president by forcing him to fire a considerably less popular minister and change his policies. Vigorously protesting Hamilton's Bank of the United States and his avowed intention to reach a friendly understanding with Great Britain, Jefferson and his growing party accused Hamilton of secret designs to reestablish aristocracy and monarchy, and even return the United States to the British Empire.

In the spring of 1793, Jefferson opposed Washington's Neutrality Proclamation and initially supported the representative of the new French republic, Edmond Charles Genet. Genet, however, far overreached Jefferson's idea of propriety by licensing privateers to prey on British shipping, setting up prize courts in American seaports and raising an army based in Kentucky to attack Spanish Louisiana. Jefferson had the unpleasant task of opposing all this, while trying to contain the zeal of the many new Democratic societies that were supporting Genet. This crisis passed when Genet's group fell from power in France, and, after a harrowing yellow fever epidemic paralyzed the American government in the late summer, Jefferson returned to present Congress with his report on the foreign commerce of the United States. He then resigned and spent three years improving his estate and carrying on a lively exchange of letters with his political friends.

The odd workings of the original electoral system made Jefferson vice president in 1797, after he had finished a close second behind his now-estranged rival, John Adams, in the contest for president. Discreet in public, he acted behind the scenes to stiffen resistance to Adams and his Federalist majorities in Congress during the undeclared naval war with France. Jefferson wrote the Kentucky Resolutions against the partisan Alien and Sedition Acts of 1798; his friend John Breckinridge steered them through the Kentucky legislature. The resolutions contained the extreme doctrine that a state might nullify an act of Congress; the effect, however, was to let off steam until the Federalists and their acts passed from the scene.

Fearful that Adams might sneak in for a second term, every Jeffersonian elector cast one ballot for Jefferson and another for Aaron Burr of New York in the election of 1800. This produced a tie, unintended by the mass of voters, and threw the election into the lame-duck Congress that had been elected in 1798. Enough Federalist congressmen preferred Burr to Jefferson to produce a stalemate for several weeks, but Jefferson finally prevailed; Burr, as vice president, found Jefferson depriving him of federal patronage, and Governor George Clinton depriving him of influence in New York. Burr thus began on the course that led to his seeking Federalist support for his political comeback, which in turn produced the famous duel, fatal to Alexander Hamilton, and finally the adventures in the West that led Jefferson to arrest Burr and try him for treason.

Jefferson's first term in office was one of the most popular and successful in the history of the presidency. After many a bad turn, Washington and Adams had secured peace with all the major foreign powers and all the American Indian tribes capable of threatening America's frontiers. By cordially maintaining these arrangements—even with Britain—Jefferson presided over four years of peaceful and prosperous expansion. Yet he proved to be different from his predecessors. With the expert help of Albert Gallatin, secretary of the treasury, and James Madison, secretary of state, he greatly reduced the army, the navy, and the foreign diplomatic corps. His congressional majorities reduced the federal judiciary and repealed the unpopular excises, including the tax on distillations that had set off the Whiskey Rebellion in 1794. The Twelfth Amendment to the Constitution ended forever the confusion of presidential and vice presidential votes.

Jefferson did incur the expense of sending several ships to the Mediterranean, where various North African states were holding American sailors for ransom and demanding tribute that Federalist presidents, and various European governments, had customarily paid. Even in this, Jefferson hoped to save money in the long run, by putting a stop to criminal behavior that, he believed, civilized nations should never have tolerated in the first place.

In private life several years later, but hardly in retirement, Jefferson maintained an extensive political and philosophical correspondence, especially with John Adams, the two now fully reconciled. He also labored long and finally successfully to establish the University of Virginia in nearby Charlottesville. Jefferson and Adams both died on July 4, 1826, while their fellow citizens were celebrating the fiftieth anniversary of the Declaration of Independence.

SIGNIFICANCE

Thomas Jefferson was brilliant, versatile, energetic, and creative, but he was neither original nor systematic. He contributed no great books to the American tradition, but rather a number of ringing phrases about natural rights, the impositions of tyrants, the virtue of the people, and the beneficence of free inquiry. With Abraham Lincoln, he is the most quotable American public figure, and every conceivable political view has been bolstered by his maxims. Jefferson further helped this trend by being inconsistent in such important areas as the power of the national government, the proper treatment of dissenters, and the crucial question of slavery.

Yet he was perfectly consistent on many points. A true son of the Enlightenment, he believed that scientific study and education would cure the ills of humankind, and he rejected as superstitious all those parts of religion that dwelt on mysterious or miraculous interventions in human affairs. He detested the very idea of inherited power or status and believed that differences among races and national groups were the result of environment. He always believed that government should be kept to a minimum, that standing armies were not republican, and that the true strength of a people resided in the widest possible distribution of virtue, learning, and property; not in armies, national treasuries, or government agencies.

Early in life, he had supposed that the United States might not extend beyond the Appalachians, for he still shared the classical view that republics must be small. By the time he had retired from the presidency, however, he had conceived that all North America might be "an Empire for Liberty."

—*Robert McColley*

FURTHER READING

Boorstin, Daniel J. *The Lost World of Thomas Jefferson*. New York: Henry Holt, 1948. This is still the best introduction to the place of Thomas Jefferson in the American Enlightenment, written by a well-known American historian.

Ellis, Joseph J. *American Sphinx: The Character of Thomas Jefferson*. New York: Alfred A. Knopf, 1996. Ellis focuses on Jefferson's character to find the "real man" beneath the American icon. He portrays Jefferson as complex and sometimes devious.

Ferling, John E. *Adams vs. Jefferson: The Tumultuous Election of 1800*. New York: Oxford University Press, 2004. Ferling describes how the "contest of titans" between Jefferson and Adams marked a turning point in American history, with Adams's Federalists and Jefferson's Republicans battling over two different ideas of how the new nation should be governed.

Jefferson, Thomas. *The Papers of Thomas Jefferson*. Edited by Julian P. Boyd. 31 vols. Princeton, N.J.: Princeton University Press, 1950-2004. A splendid edition of Jefferson's writings.

Levy, Leonard. *Jefferson and Civil Liberties: The Darker Side*. Cambridge, Mass.: Belknap Press, 1963. Levy maintains that despite his advanced preaching about civil liberties, Jefferson acted very much the same as his contemporaries.

McCoy, Drew R. *The Elusive Republic*. Chapel Hill: University of North Carolina Press, 1980. An introduction to Jefferson's republican ideology and his special concern with economic policy as an expression of republicanism.

Malone, Dumas. *Jefferson and His Time*. 6 vols. Boston: Little, Brown, 1948-1981. Malone's work, by a considerable margin, is the longest and richest of the biographies.

Miller, John Chester. *The Wolf by the Ears*. New York: Oxford University Press, 1977. A balanced and thorough review of Jefferson's thoughts and actions regarding African American slavery.

Sheldon, Garrett Ward. *The Political Philosophy of Thomas Jefferson*. Baltimore: Johns Hopkins University Press, 1991. Sheldon describes Jefferson's views on democracy, federalism, freedom, slavery, and other political issues, placing these ideas within the context of his Virginia gentry class.

Wills, Garry. *Inventing America: Jefferson's Declaration of Independence*. Boston: Houghton Mifflin, 2002. Wills contrasts Jefferson's original draft of the declaration with the final accepted version. Wills argues that contrary to conventional assumptions, Jefferson was not a champion of individual rights but a believer in the interdependence of individuals within society.

See also: John Adams; Alexander Hamilton; James Madison; George Washington.

Related articles in *Great Events from History: The Eighteenth Century, 1701-1800:* September 5-October 26, 1774: First Continental Congress; April 19, 1775: Battle of Lexington and Concord; May 10-August 2, 1775: Second Continental Congress; July 4, 1776: Declaration of Independence; March 1, 1781: Ratification of the Articles of Confederation; May 20, 1785: Ordinance of 1785; January 16, 1786: Virginia Statute of Religious Liberty; July 13, 1787: Northwest Ordinance; September 17, 1787: U.S. Constitution Is Adopted; October 27, 1787-May, 1788: Publication of *The Federalist*; 1790's: First U.S. Political Parties; December 15, 1791: U.S. Bill of Rights Is Ratified; April 20, 1792-October, 1797: Early Wars of the French Revolution; July-November, 1794: Whiskey Rebellion; June 25-July 14, 1798: Alien and Sedition Acts.

EDWARD JENNER
English physician and scientist

Often called the father of immunology for his discovery that vaccination is a preventive measure against smallpox, Jenner pioneered the concept of using a modified form of a disease to produce immunity.

Born: May 17, 1749; Berkeley, Gloucestershire, England
Died: January 26, 1823; Berkeley, Gloucestershire, England
Areas of achievement: Medicine, science and technology

EARLY LIFE

Edward Jenner was born into an upper-middle-class family in Berkeley, England. His mother was the daughter of a clergyman, Henry Head; his father was the Reverend Stephen Jenner, a graduate of Oxford and the Anglican rector of Berkeley. Edward was the third and youngest son. His two older brothers, Stephen and Henry, became clergymen. He had three younger sisters, Mary, Sarah, and Ann; the youngest, Ann, was married to a clergyman.

In 1754, Edward's father died. Stephen took over as rector at Berkeley and became head of the family, supervising the education of his younger brothers and sisters. When he was about eight years old, Edward was sent to school at Wotton-under-Edge, a village near Berkeley, under the tutorship of the Reverend Mr. Clissold. Later, he was sent to Cirencester to study with another scholarly but rigidly strict clergyman, Dr. Charles Washbourn. The young Jenner was instructed in religion, history, Greek, and Latin but was most interested in reading books on scientific topics and collecting bird nests, dormouse nests, insects, and fossils in the hills and meadows surrounding the school.

In 1762, at age thirteen, Jenner was sent to Sodbury, about 15 miles from Berkeley, as an apprentice to Daniel Ludlow, a surgeon trained in London and competent in his profession. During the first several years he spent with Ludlow, the youth studied books on anatomy, helped the surgeon with simple operations, and dissected animals to improve his knowledge of anatomy. By the time he was eighteen, Jenner had acquired the skills that enabled him to assist Ludlow in more complicated surgical procedures and even to treat patients himself.

LIFE'S WORK

By 1770, Edward Jenner had learned all that Ludlow could teach him. His mentor suggested that this young

man of stocky build, medium height, blond hair, and heavy-lidded blue eyes, with a wide mouth and blunt nose, go to London and study with one of the most eminent surgeons of the day, John Hunter. Hunter was known throughout Europe for his treatment of aneurysms and gunshot wounds and for his descriptions of collateral circulation and the distribution of the olfactory nerve. Jenner studied anatomy and surgery with Hunter at St. George's Hospital for two years and also worked in Hunter's dissecting room preparing specimens for display.

In 1771, Jenner was asked to accompany Captain James Cook as a naturalist on Cook's second voyage, but the young physician decided instead to return to Gloucestershire in 1772 to assume the duties of a country doctor. Jenner soon established a successful practice in his home shire. He declined Hunter's offer of a partnership in 1775, preferring a rural lifestyle to the bustle of London.

While engaged in the pursuits of his medical calling, Jenner continued to contribute to the literature of natural science in his observations of the physiology of hibernating animals, the nesting habits of the cuckoo, and the migration of birds. In 1778, after dissecting the heart of a person who had died of angina pectoris, he described blockage and ossification of the coronary arteries of the heart as a contributory factor in the progression of the disease. After 1785, Jenner observed that his old friend and teacher, John Hunter, exhibited all the symptoms of progressive angina. Unwilling to inform Hunter of his findings because of the possible negative emotional impact upon Hunter (angina was considered incurable at that time), Jenner refused to publish his views on the symptomatology of the disease. His observations were vindicated after Hunter's death in 1793, when the autopsy report indicated that Hunter's coronary arteries were considerably ossified. It was in 1799 that Dr. Caleb Parry, in his publication *Inquiry into the Symptoms and Causes of the Syncope Anginosa*, gave Jenner credit for the earlier suggestion that angina was caused by a structural change in the heart.

Soon after he returned to Gloucestershire to begin his medical practice, Jenner began the observations and experiments that would lead to the discovery some twenty-five years later of the principle of vaccination. In much of rural eighteenth century England, an eruption of blisters on the udders of cows, cowpox, was quite widespread. The contagious disease, harmless to the dairy animals, was transmitted onto the hands of milkmaids, who themselves developed minor lesions and a mild fever, followed by complete recovery. It was believed locally that a person infected with cowpox could not contract the much more dangerous disease smallpox. This infectious, disfiguring, and potentially lethal malady had periodically swept Europe, resulting in some 400,000 deaths annually. The practice of inoculation, introducing matter from the pustules of a person with an active case of smallpox into the skin of a person to be immunized from the disease, had been known from ancient times in India and China. The person inoculated usually contracted a milder case of smallpox with its associated discomforts, but occasionally the inoculation, often performed on children, resulted in death. (As a young boy, Jenner had been inoculated when an epidemic swept Gloucestershire. As part of the treatment, six weeks before the actual inoculation Jenner was bled, purged, and starved. As a result of this debilitating experience, young Edward's health was shattered for many years.)

By 1780, Jenner was convinced that cowpox, which he differentiated from other lesions on the udders of cows and the hands of milkmaids, if introduced under the skin, would produce an immunity to smallpox, with few of the side effects associated with the inoculation process. Jenner had become convinced that a person who had contracted cowpox was indeed immune to smallpox, since he was unable to induce smallpox by inoculating persons who previously had contracted cowpox. When he discussed his theory in the scientific community, he was discouraged by the poor reception it received, and consequently he did not actively promote vaccination until the late 1790's.

In 1783, Jenner published an eleven-page pamphlet entitled *Cursory Observations on Emetic Tartar*. This paper was the result of his discovery of a new process of purifying the drug used for inducing vomiting in an age when purges were the fashion. Five years later, he published *Observations on the Natural History of the Cuckoo*, wherein Jenner described the manner in which the parasitic cuckoo hatchling ejected young birds from the nest of the host sparrows. This scholarly work in ornithology earned for Jenner a fellowship in the prestigious Royal Society in 1789.

At the age of thirty-eight, on March 6, 1788, Jenner married Catherine Kingscote, a niece of the countess of Suffolk and a daughter of a wealthy landowner in Cheltenham. On January 24, 1789, their first child, Edward, was born. On July 8, 1792, the country physician and surgeon was made a doctor in medicine by the University of St. Andrews, Scotland, upon the recommendation of his old friends, Caleb Parry of Bath and Dr. John Hickes of Gloucester. In 1794, Jenner's daughter, Catherine, was born. This same year he suffered a serious illness diagnosed as typhus fever, the third such episode in eight years. Jenner's second son, Robert Fitzhardinge, was born in 1797.

Jenner's growing reputation as a consulting physician enabled him to acquire a home in the aristocratic health spa of Cheltenham in 1795. He served as a member of the Cheltenham town council from 1806 to 1821 and practiced medicine there until 1820. As a result of the influential contacts that he made with the nobility and established physicians in Cheltenham, Jenner was able more easily to disseminate information about his controversial vaccination process.

On May 14, 1796, Jenner performed the first vaccination with cowpox serum on eight-year-old James Phipps, using material obtained from a pustule on the hand of Sarah Nelmes, a milkmaid who had contracted cowpox. Subsequently, Phipps was inoculated with smallpox material, but the disease did not develop in the boy. In 1798, Jenner continued his experiments with cowpox vaccine, convinced that immunity from smallpox for those inoculated with cowpox was the result. That same year, Jenner

Edward Jenner. (The Granger Collection, New York)

wrote a paper that listed the people vaccinated and the symptoms associated with induced cowpox. The work was submitted to the Royal Society, but that august body refused to publish it since the theory was considered too revolutionary. Jenner then published the treatise himself and titled it *An Inquiry into Cause and Effects of the Variolæ Vaccinæ, a Disease Discovered in Some of the Western Counties of England, Particularly Gloucestershire, and Known by the Name of Cow Pox* (1798).

The impact upon the world was immediate, although some opposition to the vaccination procedure resulted when a supply of vaccine contaminated with smallpox virus caused that disease to spread. By 1810, vaccination against smallpox was introduced in Austria, Germany, Switzerland, Hungary, Poland, Russia, Italy, France, Spain, India, the United States, and most of the rest of the world.

Jenner's fame and modest fortune increased proportionately, but these successes were tempered by the death of his wife in 1815. Edward survived his beloved Catherine by eight years, dying quietly at his home, the Chantry, in Berkeley, on January 26, 1823.

SIGNIFICANCE

On May 8, 1980, the World Health Assembly declared that the world was free from smallpox, the last case having been reported in Somalia in 1979. For the first time in the history of humankind, a dreaded disease had been conquered. This victory came as the result of Edward Jenner's discovery of an antigenically related, nontransmissible virus that provided protection against smallpox.

Jenner's historical impact should not be reckoned with only cold statistics regarding the tremendous numbers of lives saved as a result of his discovery of the principle of vaccination. Rather, he should also be remembered as the medical doctor who eschewed a monopoly of the cowpox vaccine and the great wealth that this exclusive knowledge would bring. He chose instead to disseminate the technique freely and selflessly to the whole world. He should be remembered not as the scholarly genius that some of his early biographers made him out to be but rather as a quiet, unassuming country physician whose observations of a disease over a twenty-five-year period resulted in one of the most beneficial medical discoveries ever.

Jenner was criticized in some quarters by those colleagues who, out of envy or ignorance, determined that his innovative discovery would result in a debacle. Those critics were silenced by the logic of Jenner's scientific method and the ultimate success that vaccination pro-

grams in the nineteenth century had in reducing the number of smallpox victims worldwide.

—*Charles A. Dranguet, Jr.*

FURTHER READING

Baron, John. *The Life of Edward Jenner, M.D.* 2 vols. London: Henry Colburn, 1827. The first major biography of Jenner, by a friend and associate of many years, and still the main source of information on the medical scientist. Written in the rather stilted style of early nineteenth century England, this two-volume work contains many of the letters by and to Jenner that were to form the basis of later studies of Jenner and his discoveries.

Baxby, Derrick. *Jenner's Smallpox Vaccine.* London: Heinemann Educational Books, 1981. Baxby examines the historical origins of smallpox vaccines used by Jenner and his associates. The material is presented in a readable style, without the jargon one might ordinarily expect in a work dealing with such specific medical topics.

Bazin, Hervé. *The Eradication of Smallpox: Edward Jenner and the First and Only Eradication of a Human Infectious Disease.* Translated by Andrew Morgan and Glenise Morgan. San Diego, Calif.: Academic Press, 2000. A history of smallpox, focusing on how Jenner created a vaccine that would ultimately—if temporarily—eradicate the disease.

Dolan, Edward F., Jr. *Jenner and the Miracle of Vaccine.* New York: Dodd, Mead, 1960. A readable, well-written work done in the style of a novel. Accurate details of Jenner's life have been garnered from primary and secondary sources.

Fisk, Dorothy. *Dr. Jenner of Berkeley.* London: Heinemann, 1959. This work by a British author is well-written and informative but is hampered by a somewhat ponderous style. There is, however, much information on Jenner's life that would be useful to general readers.

Jenner, Edward, and John Hunter. *Letters of Edward Jenner and Other Documents Concerning the Early History of Vaccination.* Edited by Genevieve Miller. Baltimore: Johns Hopkins University Press, 1983. An annotated collection of more than one hundred previously unpublished letters from Jenner to forty-five different correspondents, including medical colleagues, friends, and others dealing with his interests in vaccination, natural history, and a wide range of other topics. The collection also includes five letters written by John Hunter, Jenner's teacher and friend.

Kerns, Thomas A. *Jenner on Trial: An Ethical Examination of Vaccine Research in the Age of Smallpox and the Age of AIDS*. Lanham, Md.: University Press of America, 1997. Examines how a modern review panel using today's standards might judge the scientific and ethical design of Jenner's first smallpox vaccine. Questions how the panel might weigh the risks and benefits to James Phipps and the adequacy of Jenner's preliminary evidence. Compares eighteenth century standards of medical ethics review with review standards for AIDS research in the late twentieth century.

LeFanu, William R. *A Bio-Bibliography of Edward Jenner, 1749-1823*. London: Harvey and Blythe, 1951. A leading authority on Jenner discusses all publications by Jenner and, in addition, lists all letters known at the time by or to him in manuscript or printed form.

Roddis, Louis H. *Edward Jenner and the Discovery of Smallpox Vaccination*. Menasha, Wis.: George Banta, 1930. A small but informative offering with an introductory chapter on the history of smallpox. Written in a precise style, this work outlines Jenner's early life, his medical career, his discovery of vaccination, the honors he received, and the final years of his life. A fine introduction to Jenner, the individual and the physician.

Saunders, Paul. *Edward Jenner: The Cheltenham Years, 1795-1823*. Hanover, N.H.: University Press of New England, 1982. This well-documented chronicle of Jenner's vaccination campaign provides insights into the opposition and mistrust that Jenner met regarding vaccination. Fills the chronological gap that exists in John Baron's *The Life of Edward Jenner, M.D.*, during the height of his fame in Cheltenham and gives a new insight into Jenner's circle of friends and social life.

See also: Daniel Gabriel Fahrenheit; Mary Wortley Montagu; Benjamin Rush.

Related articles in *Great Events from History: The Eighteenth Century, 1701-1800:* 1714: Fahrenheit Develops the Mercury Thermometer; 1753: Lind Discovers a Cure for Scurvy; 1757: Monro Distinguishes Between Lymphatic and Blood Systems; 1765-1769: Watt Develops a More Effective Steam Engine; 1796-1798: Jenner Develops Smallpox Vaccination; 1799: Discovery of the Earliest Anesthetics.

SAMUEL JOHNSON
English writer and scholar

Johnson not only wrote some of the finest poetry, fiction, and essays of his time but also edited the works of William Shakespeare and compiled the first dictionary of the English language.

Born: September 18, 1709; Lichfield, Staffordshire, England
Died: December 13, 1784; London, England
Also known as: Dr. Johnson
Areas of achievement: Literature, scholarship

EARLY LIFE
Samuel Johnson's father, Michael Johnson, was an unsuccessful bookseller. As an infant, Johnson contracted tuberculosis from a wet nurse and lost sight in one eye and hearing in one ear. His physical appearance was not appealing; one of Johnson's aunts declared that she "would not have picked such a poor creature up in the street." Johnson's ill health and frightening appearance did not, however, prevent him from educating himself in the back room of his father's bookshop. He did very well in his studies at Lichfield Grammar School, and after a year at Stourbridge Grammar School as both student and teacher, he entered Pembroke College, Oxford. He was described by one of the dons there as "the best prepared pupil to have come up to Oxford." The small legacy from his mother was not enough to keep Johnson at Oxford, however, and he had to leave without a degree in 1731.

His prospects were very uncertain, but he did manage to get a job as an undermaster at Market Bosworth School. Johnson described this experience as a "complicated misery," and he soon left. It was during this period that Johnson fell into a psychological depression, a malady that was to plague him throughout his life. He did manage to break his depression long enough to translate into English the French version of Father Jerome Lobo's *A Voyage to Abyssinia*, in 1735. Also in 1735, he married a widow, Elizabeth Porter, who was older than he and not very attractive; in addition, her family opposed her marrying a younger man. With her money, he established Edial School; the school was not a success, however, and in 1737 he went to London with one of his pupils, the future great actor David Garrick.

Dr. Samuel Johnson. (Library of Congress)

LIFE'S WORK

In London, Samuel Johnson attempted to support himself with his pen. He wrote some essays for the *Gentleman's Magazine* and worked on his tragedy, *Irene* (1749). Johnson was living apart from his wife during this period, and the marriage, which was a very odd one to begin with, was never the same. Johnson wrote one of his better poems in 1738, *London: A Poem in Imitation of the Third Satire of Juvenal*. The poem is filled with horrifying descriptions of daily life in London, and it provides a picture of the type of life Johnson was then living. One couplet shows something about his attitude at this time: "This mournful truth is ev'ry where confess'd, / SLOW RISES WORTH, BY POVERTY DEPRESS'D." Johnson met Richard Savage in 1738, and the two of them wandered the streets living a hand-to-mouth existence. Savage was a poet, and he claimed to be the illegitimate son of the countess of Macclesfield. The moral Johnson and the amoral Savage made a strange pair, but Johnson had a close attachment to Savage, as is evident in *An Account of the Life of Mr. Richard Savage*, which Johnson published anonymously in 1744. W. J. Bate calls this work the first example of "critical biography" in English, and its combination of criminal biography with high-minded moral lessons has fascinated readers for two centuries.

Johnson was able to bring his wife to London in 1737, but he was still making a precarious living doing the journalism that Grub Street demanded. One of the most interesting examples of that type of writing was Johnson's reporting—or, more accurately, creating—the Parliamentary Debates. He did not attend the debates in Parliament, but learned the order of the speakers and the positions they took and then wrote them up in his very noticeable style. For more than two centuries some of those speeches were set forth as models of oratory, but they were really the product of a poor man who dashed them off when he could in a disheveled room in Grub Street.

In 1747, Johnson published *The Plan of a Dictionary of the English Language*. He intended to complete this monumental project in three years, and although it took eight years it remains one of the most impressive scholarly accomplishments of modern times. In contrast to Johnson's eight years, it took the forty members of the French Academy forty years to complete their dictionary. When Johnson's *Dictionary of the English Language* was published in 1755, it was greeted with critical praise and national pride. Johnson's reputation was established, and he could find some relief from the demands of Grub Street journalism. His financial circumstances began to improve once the dictionary project was supported by a group of booksellers. Johnson received £1,575 for the project, which enabled him to rent a house and place his wife in more pleasant surroundings; she was to die, however, in 1752, before her husband's great work was published. Johnson's feeling for her is evident in the following sentence he wrote in the preface to the dictionary:

> The English Dictionary was written with little assistance of the learned, and without any patronage of the great; not in the soft obscurities of retirement, or under the shelter of academick bowers, but amidst inconvenience and distraction, in sickness and sorrow.

Johnson's heroism and humanity were never more manifest.

In 1749, Johnson published his finest poem, *The Vanity of Human Wishes: The Tenth Satire of Juvenal Imitated*, which, like *London*, was based on one of Juvenal's Satires. Unlike *London*, however, which attacks the vices of the city, *The Vanity of Human Wishes* indicts all vain human desires. The poem is an inventory of those "wishes" and singles out such aspects of human life as power, military glory, and the life of the scholar and the poet. It concludes with a terrifying question: "Must helpless man, in ignorance sedate, / Roll darkling down the torrent of his fate?" The answer is that happiness can be obtained only by submitting to "heav'n" and abandoning vain desires. *The Vanity of Human Wishes* is not only a great poem but also a reflection of Johnson's own troubled mind; he fell into periodic depressions because he believed that he could not live up to the strong religious demands he made of himself. His only relief was to submit to "heav'n."

From 1750 to 1752, Johnson wrote hundreds of essays for his journal *The Rambler*. These essays were not in the manner of the light and personal essays that had been written earlier by Joseph Addison and Richard Steele for *The Spectator*; instead, Johnson wrote on moral issues with a more distant and impersonal style. For example, he wrote on such topics as old age, self-indulgence, and forgiveness. Some of the essays were on literary subjects such as modern fiction and biography, but they retained the high moral tone and the magisterial style. Johnson later said, "My other works are wine and water; but my *Rambler* is pure wine." A later venture into periodical writing in *The Idler*, in the vein of Addison and Steele, was not as successful, since it went against the Johnsonian grain.

In 1759, Johnson published his small masterpiece *Rasselas, Prince of Abyssinia*. *Rasselas* is very similar to a fairy tale. The title character leaves the "Happy Valley" to find "happiness." On this quest, Rasselas and his companions find not happiness but those vain human desires Johnson exposed in *The Vanity of Human Wishes*. Political power, learning, poetry, and the social world of pleasure are all found to be lacking in the capacity to bring happiness. It is only when Rasselas and the others can escape their own desires that they find something like happiness. The moral of the tale can also be applied to Johnson's own condition at the time. He wrote the tale in a few days to earn enough money to defray the expenses of his mother's funeral.

In October, 1765, Johnson's last great work, the long-delayed *The Plays of William Shakespeare*, was published. The textual editing of the plays has been superseded, but Johnson's own comments on specific plays and his preface are still discussed by Shakespearean scholars. The preface is especially important in its rejection of the neoclassical unities of time, place, and action. Johnson rejected the unities of time and space with typical common sense: "The objection arising from the impossibility of passing the first hour at Alexandria, and the next at Rome, supposes, that when the play opens, the spectator really imagines himself at Alexandria. . . ." His insistence on describing Shakespeare as a playwright whose works were taken from life rather than art and on the pleasure the audience receives from a Shakespearean play remains refreshing and illuminating. Moreover, he did not blindly worship Shakespeare; in fact, he criticized Shakespeare's excessive use of puns and his sometimes declamatory language.

The last period of Johnson's life is marked by the friends he made and talked with, especially the Thrales and James Boswell. Henry Thrale

---

A TRIBUTE TO SHAKESPEARE AND JONSON

In 1747, Samuel Johnson wrote a poem written to commemorate the opening of the Drury Lane Theatre. The poem was spoken on stage by David Garrick, the most famous actor of the eighteenth century, and was then published in Gentleman's Magazine. *It opens with these stanzas, paying tribute to Renaissance playwrights William Shakespeare and Ben Jonson.*

> When Learning's triumph o'er her barb'rous foes
> First rear'd the stage, immortal Shakespear rose;
> Each change of many-colour'd life he drew,
> Exhausted worlds, and then imagin'd new:
> Existence saw him spurn her bounded reign,
> And panting Time toil'd after him in vain:
> His pow'rful strokes presiding Truth impress'd,
> And unresisted Passion storm'd the breast.
> Then Jonson came, instructed from the school,
> To please in method, and invent by rule;
> His studious patience, and laborious art,
> By regular approach essay'd the heart;
> Cold Approbation gave the ling'ring bays,
> For those who durst not censure, scarce could praise.
> A mortal born he met the general doom,
> But left, like Egypt's kings, a lasting tomb.

Source: Samuel Johnson, "Drury-lane Prologue Spoken by Mr. Garrick at the Opening of the Theatre in Drury-Lane, 1747." *Representative Poetry Online*. http://eir.library.utoronto.ca/rpo/display/poem1097.html. Accessed September, 2005.

was a prosperous brewer, and his wife, Hester, had an interest in literature. They invited Johnson to stay at their country home and saved him from one of his periodic depressions. They became, in effect, his family, and their country home became his home. His own house in London provided him with little peace during this period, since it was inhabited by a group of quarrelsome dependents whom Johnson had charitably invited to live there.

In 1763, the famous meeting between Johnson and Boswell occurred. Boswell, the son of a Scottish laird, was a law student with an interest in literature. His relationship with Johnson was curious; Johnson was always teasing Boswell about being a Scot and about being naïve. Johnson also became a moral guide and confessor to Boswell; he patiently listened to tales of Boswell's romantic liaisons or doubts about religion and reassured him. Indeed, Boswell might be described as the son that Johnson never had. Boswell, for his part, spent a limited amount of time with Johnson, but he recorded the most telling and amusing stories and utterances by and about Johnson. Boswell's *The Life of Samuel Johnson, LL.D.* (1791) is a remarkable rendering of individual personality and thought, having earned for Boswell his own place in the history of letters. The reader of Boswell's biography comes away with a sense of a legendary man as a living being.

SIGNIFICANCE

Samuel Johnson was the last of the great neoclassical writers, and, as the last of his kind, he most fully embodied the values, style, and critical concepts of the period. He stressed the "grandeur of generality" in literature rather than the particular, and he insisted again and again that the purpose of literature is to "teach and delight." During the nineteenth century, this representative of his age came under attack as Romanticism displaced neoclassicism. For more than one hundred years, Johnson was seen as an oddity from an earlier and less important period. Fortunately, Johnson's fiction, poetry, and essays, as well as his criticism, are now read with a less prejudiced eye as readers continue to discover the Johnsonian values of common sense, humor, and morality.

Johnson the writer may not be to everyone's taste, but few can resist the appeal of Johnson the individual. The manner in which he practiced the moral precepts he taught, such as charity, is very rare. So, too, is the way in which Johnson fought off the depression that victimized him. He believed that "cheerfulness" was everyone's duty, and he maintained his good spirits in very trying

circumstances. Johnson was described by Hester Thrale as the most fun-loving person she had met. Surely, the impression any reader of Johnson or about Johnson receives is that of humor, good sense, and humanity.

—*James Sullivan*

FURTHER READING

Bate, W. J. *Samuel Johnson*. New York: Harcourt Brace Jovanovich, 1977. This full biography of Johnson is an essential supplement to James Boswell's biography. It is thorough and gracefully written, and discusses Johnson's psychology fully.

Bloom, Edward A. *Samuel Johnson in Grub Street*. Providence, R.I.: Brown University Press, 1957. The most informative book about Johnson's journalism and the practices of magazines and booksellers of the period.

Boswell, James. *The Life of Samuel Johnson, LL.D.* Edited by G. B. Hill. 6 vols. Oxford, England: Oxford University Press, 1934-1950. The standard edition of Boswell's great biography.

Clifford, James. *Young Sam Johnson*. New York: Oxford University Press, 1955. Clifford focuses on Johnson's early years, which were slighted by Boswell. Informative and readable.

Clingham, Greg, ed. *The Cambridge Companion to Samuel Johnson*. New York: Cambridge University Press, 1997. Collection of essays analyzing Johnson's major works; examining his views of women, politics, Christianity, and imperialism; and describing the critical reception for his writing.

Greene, Donald J. *The Politics of Samuel Johnson*. New Haven, Conn.: Yale University Press, 1960. A scholarly discussion of an important aspect of Johnson's career and life. It is the best book on the subject and corrects some false views of Johnson's Toryism.

Hudson, Nicholas. *Samuel Johnson and the Making of Modern England*. New York: Cambridge University Press, 2003. Johnson became a symbol of English national identity in the century following his death. Hudson explores Johnson's contributions to the creation of the modern English identity, including his opinions on class, feminism, party politics, nationalism, and imperialism.

Lipking, Lawrence. *Samuel Johnson: The Life of an Author*. Cambridge, Mass.: Harvard University Press, 1998. Biography describing how Johnson became a writer, rising from anonymity to fame and transforming the nature of authorship. Discusses the various works he wrote, including his dictionary, essays for

The Rambler, *Rasselas*, and *The Plays of William Shakespeare*.

Sledd, James H., and Gwin J. Kolb. *Dr. Johnson's Dictionary*. Chicago: University of Chicago Press, 1955. Still the best work available on the *Dictionary of the English Language*.

Voitle, Robert. *Samuel Johnson the Moralist*. Cambridge, Mass.: Harvard University Press, 1961. A full and revealing discussion of one of the most important aspects of Johnson's works and life.

Wimsatt, W. K. *The Prose Style of Samuel Johnson*. New Haven, Conn.: Yale University Press, 1942. Still the best discussion of Johnson's style, by an important literary critic.

See also: Joseph Addison; Mary Astell; George Berkeley; James Boswell; Charles Burney; Hester Chapone; Denis Diderot; David Garrick; Oliver Goldsmith; Charlotte Lennox; Flora MacDonald; Hannah More; Alexander Pope; Sir Joshua Reynolds; Samuel Richardson; Anna Seward; Jonathan Swift; Voltaire.

Related articles in *Great Events from History: The Eighteenth Century, 1701-1800:* 1746-1755: Johnson Creates the First Modern English Dictionary; March 20, 1750-March 14, 1752: Johnson Issues *The Rambler*; 1751-1772: Diderot Publishes the *Encyclopedia*; July, 1764: Voltaire Publishes *A Philosophical Dictionary for the Pocket*.

JOHN PAUL JONES
Scottish-born American military leader

Known in his own time for his daring raids on British territory and spectacular engagements with British vessels during the American Revolutionary War, Jones is now widely regarded as the founder of the U.S. Navy.

Born: July 6, 1747; Arbigland Estate, Kirkbean, Kircudbrightshire, Scotland
Died: July 18, 1792; Paris, France
Also known as: John Paul (birth name)
Areas of achievement: Warfare and conquest, military

EARLY LIFE

John Paul Jones, born John Paul, took the surname "Jones" as an adult. He was the fifth child of an estate gardener and a housekeeper. Growing up in Galloway, near Solway Firth, he evinced an early interest in the sea. At a very early age, he was apprenticed as ship's boy for merchant trading in the West Indies and the American colonies. Over the next several years, he learned navigation, improved his speech and writing, and learned gentleman's manners. On stopovers in Virginia, he stayed with his elder brother William, a tailor in Fredericksburg, and developed an abiding attachment to America. At age seventeen, he shipped for a time on slavers, but, by 1768, he was master of a merchant brig. Two years later, he became a Freemason in Kirkcudbright, and, in 1772, he was commander and part owner of a large merchant vessel sailing from London (where he then lived) to the West Indies. By the time he was twenty-five, he had made

£2,500 and wrote often of his desire to become a gentleman farmer in Virginia.

Jones was somewhat below average height (five feet, five inches) and had hazel eyes, sandy brown hair, high cheekbones, a sharp nose, and a cleft chin. He dressed well, read good literature, and developed a fairly elaborate writing style, also composing poetry; from an early age, he showed a determination to rise both economically and socially. Without money or family connections in an age when both were usually necessary for advancement, he achieved much, despite obstacles and opposition, by dint of hard work and ability. Yet his own character was also sometimes a handicap: He had a violent temper; he took offense easily; he incessantly bombarded others with complaints and unsolicited advice; and he was a perfectionist and an egotist.

In Tobago in October, 1773, during an altercation with his crew, John Paul (apparently accidently) killed the ringleader; fearing a trial by a jury of the crew's friends, he fled with only £50. About the following twenty months, there is little real information available about him; by late 1775, he was in America, had used the name John Jones, and had met some influential North Carolina and Virginia politicians. He was unemployed, and the battles at Lexington and Concord made it impossible for him to access his funds in Tobago. So, on December 7, 1775, John Paul Jones was commissioned a first lieutenant in the Continental navy and assigned to the ship *Alfred*.

LIFE'S WORK

The *Alfred* was part of the Continental navy's five-ship fleet. On its first cruise, it captured some cannon and powder at Nassau in the Bahamas, and damaged HMS *Glasgow*. On August 8, 1776, John Paul Jones was commissioned a captain and given command of the sloop of war *Providence,* taking sixteen prizes and destroying fisheries on the Nova Scotia coast. A second cruise in October, in command of the *Alfred,* also yielded several prizes.

From its beginnings, the Continental navy was plagued with serious difficulties. Not only did it suffer, as did the Continental army, from inadequate financing, but it also usually came off second best in competition with privateers, which offered crews less danger, looser discipline, and larger shares of prize money. Furthermore, advancement went to those with powerful friends and local connections, as Jones discovered when Congress, on October 10, 1776, placed him number eighteen on the seniority list and gave him command of the *Providence* rather than one of the thirteen new frigates then being built. As most of these frigates never got to sea, that was fortunate for Jones. He had no success, however, in getting Congress to listen to his ideas on naval strategy: to draw off the superior British fleet from American coasts by attacking undefended British areas, rather than by using American warships as commerce destroyers.

Amid the confusion, political intrigue, and charges and countercharges that usually enveloped Congress's naval arrangements, Jones was given command of the 110-foot, square-rigged sloop of war *Ranger,* on June 14, 1777 (the same day that Congress adopted the stars and stripes as the United States flag). It was November 1 before the *Ranger* could be fitted out to sail, during which time Jones had a coat of arms made and met, in Boston, the poet Phillis Wheatley. Having taken some prizes with the *Ranger,* Jones was in Paris in early December, where he met the American commissioners and became involved in the convoluted Euro-American diplomacy of the revolutionary period.

Having rerigged the *Ranger* completely (as he always did with his ships) to obtain greater speed and maneuverability, Jones left Brest on April 10, 1778. At dawn on April 23, Jones raided his old home port of Whitehaven, doing little material damage but considerably boosting morale. Later that morning, he landed near his old home in an attempt to capture the earl of Selkirk as a hostage, to force Britain to exchange naval prisoners (whom, unlike army captives, the British considered pirates and refused to exchange). As the earl was not home, some of the men prevailed on Jones to let them go to the mansion and take the family silver from the countess. The next day, as Jones remained in the same waters, there occurred a spectacular battle with the sloop of war HMS *Drake.* Using a tactic frequent with him, Jones moved close to the enemy vessels while his ship was disguised by covered gun ports and because the uniforms of officers and crew were similar to those of the British navy. The raid and the victory over HMS *Drake* provoked a general popular panic in British coastal areas, drove up shipping insurance rates, infuriated Britain, and made Jones well known from then on.

France, however, was not as enthusiastic about Jones's cruise as he had hoped, and for the next nine months he could get no new command, while experiencing major problems concerning the disposition of the prizes and the disinclination of the crew and some of the officers to accept naval discipline and naval, rather than financial, goals for future operations. Jones's own personality made things no smoother, and his irritation was increased by the lack of any official recognition of his exploits and by the fact that the French navy kept most of the British fleet in home waters while the remainder operated freely in American waters while Jones remained idle. Finally, in February, 1779, the French government

John Paul Jones. (Library of Congress)

gave Jones command of a refitted forty-gun East India-man, which, after six months of diplomacy and hard work, was finished and named the *Bonhomme Richard* (after Jones's friend Benjamin Franklin's "Poor Richard"). Jones had a squadron as well: the American frigate *Alliance* (commanded by Captain Pierre Landais) and three French ships (the frigate *Pallas*, the brig *Vengeance*, and the cutter *Le Cerf*). He was to make a diversion in northern England while a combined Franco-Spanish invasion fleet descended on southern England. As the projected invasion petered out without even a battle, Jones's exploits were to receive great attention.

Jones's cruise around the British Isles began in August with the taking of several prizes, an abortive attempt (because of a contrary wind in the Firth of Forth) to demand ransom from Leith (the defenseless port of Edinburgh), and a general alarm of the coastal population. The other captains refused to attack Newcastle; such general insubordination and lack of cooperation were common in fleets of the time, especially if the commander, like Jones, was unconventional. The *Richard*'s officers and crew, however, were enthusiastic and loyal. On September 23, off Flamborough Head on the Yorkshire coast, a forty-four-ship British merchant fleet from the Baltic was sighted, convoyed by the sloop of war *Countess of Scarborough* and the fifty-gun copper-bottomed frigate *Serapis*. By the time that a nearly full harvest moon rose, the *Richard* and the *Serapis* had engaged with broadsides; when the *Richard*'s bowsprit plowed into the *Serapis*'s stern, its captain, Sir Richard Pearson, asked, "Has your ship struck?" to which Jones replied, "I have not yet begun to fight." The *Richard* finally grappled the *Serapis*, which could not break loose to bring its superior firepower to bear; the two-hour battle was watched from Flamborough Head by many who had come from nearby towns. The *Serapis* continued firing its below-deck eighteen-pounders into the topsides of the *Richard*, which (in the words of historian Samuel Eliot Morison) became "little more than a battered raft."

In the meantime, the *Pallas* successfully engaged the *Countess of Scarborough*, but Landais, in the *Alliance*, sailed around the battle and deliberately fired into the *Richard* several times, doing major damage. By 10:30 that night, the *Richard* was in desperate shape, but Jones was determined to fight on, serving one of the three nine-pounders himself; with the *Serapis* mainmast about to go, Captain Pearson struck. Jones, the better captain in a worse ship, won; he transferred to the *Serapis* the next day, and, on the following day, the *Bonhomme Richard* sank. It had been a bloody battle: Half of the *Richard*'s

crew and a third of the crew of the *Serapis* had been killed.

When the American task force came into port in Holland, Jones became a hero in France. The British press was angry, calling him a pirate and printing much misinformation about him, but simultaneously he became a hero in British popular opinion, with several ballads produced about him. His position in neutral Holland, however, complete with his squadron, prisoners, and prizes, presented diplomatic difficulties and complicated the matter of prize money even more than usual. (The *Richard*'s share later came to $26,583, of which Jones got $2,658.) A brief cruise on the *Alliance* (from January 16 to February 10, 1780) was both unprofitable and unhappy. In mid-April, Jones spent six weeks in Paris, trying unsuccessfully to settle the problems of the prizes. During that brief period, he was generally lionized, presented to Louis XVI (who gave him the Order of Military Merit and a sword), had a new coat of arms made, mixed happily in sophisticated Paris society, was the subject of a mezzotint by Jean Michel Moreau and a bust by Jean-Antoine Houdon, and conducted at least one major love affair.

Jones's return to the port of Lorient opened a confused time in which Landais took command of the *Alliance* by a coup and took it to America and a court-martial conviction. Jones took over the sloop of war *Ariel* on June 20, rerigged it completely, and, by December 18, sailed, with two merchant brigs, carrying military supplies for the Continental army. (Jones was later repaid $4,249.23 by Congress for his expenses since 1777.) Off the West Indies, he surprised and took a faster and stronger British privateer, the *Triumph*, but it managed to escape; this was to be Jones's last battle under the American flag. He arrived in Philadelphia on February 18, 1781, in time for his cargo to be used at Yorktown. Congress passed several complimentary resolutions, and Charles Willson Peale painted his portrait.

The *Ariel*, on loan from the French navy, was sent back. Jones was given command of the ship-of-the-line *America*, being built at Portsmouth, but when a French ship ran aground nearby, Congress voted to replace it with the *America*. Congress also reimbursed Jones for his pay and expenses since 1775 (in the sum of $20,705.27), but the envy of the other captains blocked his promotion to rear admiral. A brief cruise as guest and pilot with a French fleet in the West Indies at the end of 1782 enabled him to study fleet evolutions and naval tactics, but the Revolutionary War ended in April of 1783.

Back in Philadelphia, Jones became one of the original members of the Society of the Cincinnati, and, in November, Congress sent him back to Paris to recover the prize money still due (of which Jones got his $22,435 share in July, 1786). During his three years in Paris, Jones invested in unsuccessful merchant ventures, had a love affair with a widow (by whom he probably had a son), and, in 1786, presented to King Louis XVI his *John Paul Jones' Memoir of the American Revolution Presented to King Louis XVI of France* (published in manuscript form in 1979), a brief autobiography, which did not, however, get him a post in the French navy. On his brief visit to the United States in 1787 (still trying to clear up the prize money account), Congress voted to award him a gold medal; the next year, he spent some time in Copenhagen on the same business.

In April of 1788, Jones accepted the post of kontradmiral (rear admiral) in the imperial Russian navy from Empress Catherine the Great (r. 1762-1796), then involved in the Russo-Turkish War. He commanded a squadron, comprising a flagship, eight frigates, and four armed vessels, in two battles of the Liman, in the Black Sea, in June. His successes there, however, went largely unrecognized. His short-lived Russian naval career, marked throughout by confusion, dissension, and intrigues, ended with him writing an angry letter to Grigori Aleksandrovich Potemkin in October. In August, 1789, in the wake of a St. Petersburg scandal probably arranged by his rivals, he left Russia, stopping at various cities until he reached Paris in May of 1790.

In revolutionary France, Jones, short of funds and with nothing to do, irritated busy people such as the Marquis de Lafayette and the American minister Gouverneur Morris, and wrote letters, especially to Catherine and to his two married sisters in Scotland. Documents appointing Jones consul to Algeria, to negotiate for the ransom of United States captives, did not reach Paris until the end of July. On July 18, 1792, Jones died, of nephritis and bronchial pneumonia. City officials organized a funeral procession and burial in the Protestant cemetery outside the walls. In 1905, President Theodore Roosevelt became interested in the exhumation of Jones's body (which had been preserved in alcohol in a lead coffin) and had it brought back to the United States. On January 26, 1913, it was placed in an elaborate tomb in the chapel at Annapolis.

SIGNIFICANCE

John Paul Jones had a complex and often contradictory character. From unimpressive beginnings, he educated himself, to a great degree, and developed sophistication and elegant manners, although he was rough and loud on shipboard. He never found a bride who could aid his social ambitions but engaged in numerous affairs, rarely having difficulty attracting women at any level of society. He frequently disavowed any interest in rank, wealth, or fame, yet insisted on every penny of prize money and expenses due him and his crews; was sensitive to public opinion about himself; and had ambitions of entering high society, signing himself "le Chevalier Paul Jones" after receiving the Order of Military Merit.

A complete egotist, he saw the world in terms of the scope it afforded for his talents and ideas. He had few friends and only a few patrons (such as Robert Morris, Benjamin Franklin, and Thomas Jefferson). Assertive, vain, and insecure, he was also courageous and considerate of inferiors and captives; his constant concern for his men, overbalanced by his temper and demands for perfection, did not gain for him their loyalty.

He had an eighteenth century attachment to concepts of liberty and asserted that he was a citizen of the world; he also claimed the title of an American patriot and found no inconsistency in serving under the despot Catherine the Great and spending the last years of his life in Europe. He began to be a legend even in his lifetime yet was always blocked and frustrated by lack of recognition for his achievements. Never a democrat, he found the insistence of American ex-merchant crews on majority voting for naval decisions infuriating. Little attention was paid to his long-range concepts, whether that of the destiny of the United States as the world's major sea power, the organization of naval command and administration, or the overall strategy that would benefit the revolutionary war effort.

A fighting sailor, he was never given full fleet command, and so could function only as a naval tactician; in this area he excelled. Although all revolutionary naval captains had problems similar to those of Jones, not surprising in a new and difficult service plagued by localism, politics, and competition for prize money, there was none who could match Jones's record in actual ship-to-ship combat. His abilities and ideas were often discounted during his lifetime; only later, as the importance of the Navy began to increase for the United States, did Jones begin to receive the recognition denied him in life, as the real founder of the U.S. Navy.

—*Marsha Kass Marks*

FURTHER READING

Bowen-Hassell, E. Gordon, Dennis M. Conrad, and Mark L. Hayes. *Sea Raiders of the American Revolution: The Continental Navy in European Waters.*

Washington, D.C.: Naval Historical Center, Department of the Navy, 2003. A brief (73-page) account of the naval campaigns waged by Jones and other sailors and admirals.

Chapelle, Howard I. *The History of the American Sailing Navy.* New York: W. W. Norton, 1949. Chapter 2, "The Continental Navy," is especially good. Much illuminating detail about the general naval situation and the ships themselves, with several detailed sketches of the ships.

Halliday, Mark. "An Agreeable Voyage." *American Heritage* 21 (June, 1970): 8-11, 70-76. A good account of the Whitehaven raid and the Selkirk affair. Includes contemporary drawings.

Jones, John Paul. *Memoir of the American Revolution.* Translated and edited by Gerard W. Gawalt. Washington, D.C.: Library of Congress, 1979. Jones's autobiography, presented to Louis XVI of France, is a valuable text, as it shows Jones's style, ideas, and perspective on the events of his life.

Lorenz, Lincoln. *John Paul Jones.* Annapolis, Md.: United States Naval Institute, 1944. Despite the style and nebulous speculations and commentary, this 700-page work is apparently the first reliable biography of Jones written in the twentieth century.

MacKay, James. *"I Have Not Yet Begun to Fight:" A Life of John Paul Jones.* New York: Atlantic Monthly Press, 1999. MacKay portrays Jones as a "bit of a bore," a self-absorbed man who was obsessed by rank.

Morison, Samuel Eliot. *John Paul Jones: A Sailor's Biography.* Boston: Little, Brown, 1960. Almost every aspect of Jones's life—because of malice or misunderstanding—is accompanied by numerous false stories and outright fictions. Morison, in this work, provides a text based on meticulous research and in-depth knowledge of maritime matters. As an expert sailor himself, the author includes detailed passages on ship handling and other naval esoterica. The best biography of Jones, completely reliable, clear, and well written.

Morris, Richard B. "The Revolution's 'Caine Mutiny.'" *American Heritage* 11 (April, 1960): 10-13, 88-91. An effective account of Pierre Landais, the paranoid martinet who fired on the *Bonhomme Richard* during the battle off Flamborough Head, took over the *Alliance,* and became so irrational on the voyage to the United States that the officers took over the ship. A 1780 court-martial convicted Landais and dismissed him from the navy.

Snow, Richard P. "Battles of the Revolution: Flamborough Head." *American Heritage* 25 (October, 1974): 53-56. Points out that the grappling of the *Serapis* was a result of Jones's deliberate intention and superb seamanship. Includes excerpts from Nathaniel Fanning's account; Midshipman Fanning was hostile to Jones, and much of what he wrote was biased and inaccurate, but this part of his story is reliable.

Thomas, Evan. *John Paul Jones: A Sailor, Hero, Father of the American Navy.* New York: Simon & Schuster, 2003. Thomas portrays Jones as a tortured warrior and self-made man, and argues for a renewed appreciation of Jones's role in the American Revolution.

Warner, Oliver. "The Action off Flamborough Head." *American Heritage* 14 (August, 1963): 43-47, 105. A chapter from Warner's *Great Sea Battles* (1963), this is a very good, succinct summary of Jones's life and an account of the battle. Includes excerpts from some eyewitness accounts and an illustration of a 1780 painting by a French artist.

See also: Catherine the Great; Benjamin Franklin; Thomas Jefferson; Louis XVI; Gouverneur Morris; Robert Morris; Charles Willson Peale; Grigori Aleksandrovich Potemkin; Phillis Wheatley.

Related articles in *Great Events from History: The Eighteenth Century, 1701-1800:* October, 1768-January 9, 1792: Ottoman Wars with Russia; April 19, 1775: Battle of Lexington and Concord; April 20, 1792-October, 1797: Early Wars of the French Revolution.

JOSEPH II
King of Germany (r. 1764-1790) and Holy Roman Emperor (r. 1765-1790)

Joseph II contributed to the enlightened reform of the Habsburg monarchy at the end of the eighteenth century, enabling it to survive as a great power until the end of World War I.

Born: March 13, 1741; Vienna, Austria
Died: February 20, 1790; Vienna, Austria
Area of achievement: Government and politics

EARLY LIFE

Joseph (YOH-zehf) II was born while the far-flung and relatively backward Habsburg monarchy was in deep crisis, its northern province, Silesia, invaded by Frederick the Great of Prussia, and its other borders threatened by hostile neighboring states. His father was Francis Stephen, duke of Lorraine until 1736, when he became grand duke of Tuscany. Joseph's mother was Maria Theresa, daughter of Charles VI, the Holy Roman Emperor, from whom she inherited, in 1740, the Habsburg dynastic lands if not the imperial title. Joseph grew to maturity while his mother was trying to unify the monarchy in order to repel its invaders and to recover Silesia.

As Francis Stephen and Maria Theresa's oldest male child, Archduke Joseph was expected to succeed his mother as ruler and was accordingly prepared for the task. Much of his early instruction was too pedantic to arouse a love of learning. He became fluent, however, in Italian, Czech, and French. The study that most significantly touched him was natural law, as expounded by the noted Austrian jurist Karl Anton von Martini, whose disciple, Christian Beck, tutored the young archduke. Joseph adopted their enlightened idea that a ruler, the first servant of the state, should be governed by considerations of social utility. Martini and Beck also inclined Joseph toward religious toleration as well as toward the reform of the monarchy's ecclesiastical institutions. Although the pious Maria Theresa insisted that Joseph receive rigorous instruction and training in the Roman Catholic religion, she neither alienated him from the Church nor turned him into a zealot. Joseph remained throughout his life a convinced, practicing Catholic.

To increase Austrian influence in Italy, Maria Theresa had her son marry Isabella of Parma in 1760. The marriage nevertheless became a love match. A slim, good-looking young man with remarkably blue eyes, Joseph was immediately attracted to the beautiful, intelligent, and well-educated young princess. Her early death after less than two years left Joseph despondent. The

death of their young daughter and a second, brief marriage with a Bavarian princess whom he detested further dulled his affections. Henceforth, he remained cool and aloof toward people, reserving his emotional energies for the affairs of state.

Active, restless, and headstrong, Joseph learned the art of governing more through travel and practical experience in public affairs than through reading or academic training. In 1761, he began attending meetings of the state council. Crowned king of the Romans in 1764, he ascended the imperial throne the following year upon the death of Francis Stephen. Joseph's new imperial responsibility was largely honorific, but it prompted Maria Theresa to give him the office of coregent and a share of her power.

LIFE'S WORK

As coregent, Joseph was not permitted to carry out the radical, sweeping reform that he wished. Mistrusting her son's judgment, Maria Theresa retained control of the government. Since he was expected to sign all state documents, however, he could sometimes insist successfully that his views be adopted. Convinced that the oppression of peasants by their lords was depriving the state of productive subjects, Joseph agitated with some success for reforms. In Bohemia, where the evils of serfdom brought the peasantry to the point of insurrection, Joseph was responsible for a law of 1775 reducing the peasants' forced labor to a maximum of three days per week.

During the last several years of the coregency, tension between Maria Theresa and Joseph was aggravated by the issue of religious toleration. Although the Austrian Habsburgs had vigorously restored Catholicism in their dynastic lands during the Counter-Reformation, they had failed to eradicate Protestantism. In the kingdom of Hungary, Protestants formed a strong, legalized minority. Moreover, in Bohemia and Moravia, thousands of crypto-Protestants were drawn out into the open during the peasant unrest of the 1770's. Joseph's opposition to his mother's decision to force these dissenters back into the Catholic Church caused an impasse that remained unresolved, until he became the sole ruler of the monarchy.

In military and foreign affairs, Joseph was active but usually unsuccessful. His model, as well as his chief opponent, was Frederick the Great of Prussia. Endowed with modest military talents, Joseph attempted to Prussianize the Austrian army. His improvements, however,

544

fell far short of giving Austria an advantage over Prussia. When Joseph's scheme to annex Bavaria provoked a brief war with Prussia in 1788, his army was unable to prevent the Prussians from occupying much of Bohemia. Pushing Joseph aside, Maria Theresa negotiated peace with Frederick in 1779, thereby restoring the prewar boundaries except for a small part of Bavarian territory that was given to Austria.

With Maria Theresa's death on November 29, 1780, Joseph became the sole ruler of the Habsburg monarchy. He began his administration with uncharacteristic patience and good sense. He retained her chancellor, Wenzel Anton von Kaunitz, to advise him on key foreign and domestic issues. He also kept his mother's system of government virtually intact, but he tried to make it work more efficiently.

During his first year in charge, Joseph issued the Edict of Toleration, one of the most lasting reforms of his reign. Lutherans, Calvinists, and Greek Orthodox Christians were allowed to form congregations, worship together, own property, enter the professions, and hold public office. About 150,000 persons in Bohemia, Moravia, and Austria declared themselves Protestant, many more than had been expected, prompting strong protests from the Catholic hierarchy. Convinced that Catholicism should continue as the state's religion, Joseph, in 1783, made leaving the Catholic Church more difficult. He also denied recognition to radical Protestant sects. The express purpose of the edict was to enable non-Catholics to become more useful subjects. A similar pragmatic concern moved Joseph to extend toleration to the Jews. Crafts and trades, including the army, were opened to Jewish subjects, and many obstacles to their assimilation into Austrian society were removed.

It seemed clear to Joseph's utilitarian mind that the monastic system was grossly inefficient. Closing about one-third of the convents and monasteries, he reduced the number of nuns and monks from sixty thousand to forty thousand. With the money realized from the sale of confiscated monastic property, he greatly improved the parish ministry of secular priests by reforming seminary education, building new churches where they were needed, and assigning the parish clergy a significant role in enlightening the people. He also carried out a rational realignment of diocesan boundaries. Although these reforms provoked protests from some members of the Catholic hierarchy and prompted Pope Pius VI to travel to Vienna, the emperor continued to bring the Church securely under the control of the state and to make it an effective instrument of social improvement.

As sole ruler, Joseph quickly attempted to free the peasantry from bondage and oppression and to make them productive citizens of the state. In 1781, he decreed the abolition of serfdom in Bohemia, Moravia, and the Austrian duchies. He devised a new system of taxation of land, based on Physiocratic principles (that is, the principles that governments should not interfere with natural economic laws and that all wealth had its ultimate source in the land). The new system shifted the heaviest tax burden from the peasants to the landowners who could afford to bear it. Joseph's scheme included commuting the peasantry's forced labor into cash payments. These remarkable measures, however, were frustrated by the resistance of the privileged classes and by financial pressures of war at the end of his reign.

Often thwarted by concerted domestic opposition, Joseph undermined his own reform program with several unsuccessful ventures into European power politics. In 1784, he tried in vain to force the Dutch to lift the blockade that had closed the port of Antwerp in the Austrian Netherlands. The next year, his plan to exchange the Austrian Netherlands for Bavaria was frustrated by the coalition of German princes organized by Frederick. These failures further alienated the population of the

Joseph II. (Library of Congress)

Austrian Netherlands, who were already disturbed by Joseph's ecclesiastical and administrative reforms. Joseph nevertheless joined Catherine the Great of Russia in a plan to dismember the Ottoman Empire. The war that broke out in August of 1787 went badly for Austria at first. Joseph, who personally commanded the army, was blamed for its humiliating defeat.

During the last two years of his reign, Joseph had to acknowledge the failure of much of his program of reform. The revolt in the Austrian Netherlands ended his rule there. The Hungarian nobility forced him to revoke all the reforms except the abolition of serfdom and the Edict of Toleration. Ravaged by tuberculosis, Joseph died disillusioned and alone, his life's work apparently in ruins.

SIGNIFICANCE

Joseph II is generally regarded as the enlightened despot who most consistently attempted to apply reason and humanity to the administration of a major European state. His reforms were so sweeping as to be justly considered a revolution from above. They might have failed in any case, since he underestimated the resistance of the vested interests that they upset. He also lacked the well-trained, disciplined bureaucracy that was needed to carry out the reforms. Their failure was ensured by the breakdown of Joseph's health and by the severe economic repercussions of his unfortunate war with the Turks.

Not all was lost, however. Begun by his mother and extended by Joseph, the public educational system survived. Moreover, his eclectic economic policies contributed to the rapid growth of industry in Austria and Bohemia. His religious toleration led to the establishment of two Protestant denominations in the western parts of the monarchy and the gradual assimilation of a large Jewish minority. As limited as it was, Joseph's toleration was remarkably enlightened by contemporary standards. While some of his reforms of the Catholic Church, such as the state-controlled seminaries, were revoked, the improved parish ministry survived. In time, as the shortcomings of the man receded from public consciousness, a mythical Joseph II, "The People's Emperor," took hold in the popular imagination and influenced the growth of liberalism in Austrian politics in the nineteenth century.

—*Charles H. O'Brien*

FURTHER READING

Beales, Derek. *In the Shadow of Maria Theresa, 1741-1780.* Vol. 3 in *Joseph II.* New York: Cambridge University Press, 1987. General study of Joseph's life and work up to 1780. A second volume in preparation will complete the study. A serious scholarly work, it is the first major interpretation of Joseph to appear in English. Contains a bibliographical essay, abundant footnotes discussing documentary sources and secondary literature, and a bibliography listing Beales's archival and printed sources. Beales's aim is to redraw the conventional picture of the coregency.

Bernard, Paul P. *Joseph II.* New York: Twayne, 1968. Brief but dependable survey of the monarch's life. He is represented as an autocrat whose primary concern was to centralize the state and make it run more efficiently. Contains a short selected bibliography.

Blanning, T. C. W. *Joseph II.* London: Longman, 1994. In his second book on Joseph, Blanning focuses on the emperor's struggles to transform his multinational empire into a unified state.

_____. *Joseph II and Enlightened Despotism.* New York: Longman, 1970. Contains an analysis of the monarch's reign, a representative selection of documentary material, and a comprehensive bibliography. Presents Joseph as a pragmatic despot who was Catholic as well as enlightened.

Ingrao, Charles W. *The Habsburg Monarchy, 1618-1815.* 2d ed. New York: Cambridge University Press, 2000. Examines the social, political, economic, and cultural forces that enabled the Habsburg empire to become a major military and cultural power in the eighteenth century. Includes genealogical tables and bibliography.

O'Brien, Charles H. *Ideas of Religious Toleration at the Time of Joseph II: A Study of the Enlightenment Among Catholics in Austria.* Philadelphia: American Philosophical Society, 1969. Devoted to the sources and the principal features of Joseph's policy of religious toleration. Contends that Joseph viewed the Edict of Toleration as a genuine reform of the Catholic church as well as a measure making Protestants more useful to the state. Analyzes Joseph's policies toward Jews and radical Protestant sects.

Padover, Saul K. *The Revolutionary Emperor: Joseph II of Austria.* Reprint. London: Jonathan Cape, 1967. The most popular biography of the monarch in English, it has strongly influenced subsequent biographies. Its main point is that Joseph is an outstanding product of the Enlightenment. Draws evidence and illustrations uncritically from the numerous contemporary fables about Joseph.

Temperley, Harold. *Frederic the Great and Kaiser Joseph: An Episode of War and Diplomacy in the Eighteenth Century.* 2d ed. London: Frank Cass, 1968. Valuable study contrasting the personalities, achievements, and significance of the two German monarchs. Focuses particularly on their conflicts over Bavaria. Includes bibliographical notes.

Wangermann, Ernst. *The Austrian Achievement, 1700-1800.* New York: Harcourt Brace Jovanovich, 1973. An excellent brief description of Josephism, the concept of government which was embodied in the monarch's reforms, especially those dealing with the relationship between church and state. Pays particular attention to social and economic forces that influenced political changes in the monarchy.

See also: Catherine the Great; Charles VI; Frederick the Great; Maria Theresa.

Related articles in *Great Events from History: The Eighteenth Century, 1701-1800:* May 31, 1740: Accession of Frederick the Great; October 20, 1740: Maria Theresa Succeeds to the Austrian Throne; December 16, 1740-November 7, 1748: War of the Austrian Succession; October, 1768-January 9, 1792: Ottoman Wars with Russia; 1775-1790: Joseph II's Reforms.

IMMANUEL KANT
German philosopher

Kant is considered by many to represent the culmination of modern philosophy and is the crucial transition figure between the Enlightenment and the nineteenth century. His career was spent seeking an answer to the question, How can humans be a part of deterministic physical reality and yet have free will?

Born: April 22, 1724; Königsberg, Prussia (now Kaliningrad, Russia)
Died: February 12, 1804; Königsberg, Prussia
Area of achievement: Philosophy

EARLY LIFE

Immanuel Kant (ih-MAHN-ew-ehl KAHNT) was the son of a harness maker and the grandson of a Scottish emigrant. As a child, Kant was especially close to his mother, a serene woman who possessed an incisive curiosity about the natural world and a great native intelligence. As one of nine children in a devout Lutheran Pietist family, Kant was reared to respect inner tranquillity, industry, truthfulness, godliness, and order as the highest goods in human life. Kant's mother died when he was thirteen, but he remembered her throughout his life with deep devotion; he told his friends that she had planted and nurtured the first seed of good in him and that her teachings had both opened his mind and provided a healing influence on his life.

Perhaps the most remarkable feature of Kant's life, especially in the light of his profound and pervasive influence on the history of Western thought, is his provinciality. Kant never left the environs of the town of Königsberg in which he was born. He was educated in the local high school, the Collegium Fredericianum, and later at the University of Königsberg. After completing his baccalaureate studies in 1746, he worked as a tutor for a number of local families. He was able to maintain his studies while working as a tutor and so was able to take his master's degree at Königsberg in 1755. That same year, he was appointed to the post of *privatdocent* (private lecturer) in the university. He gave regular courses of lectures, which continued through his 1770 appointment to the professorship of logic and metaphysics. Kant's early lectures and writings covered diverse topics, including physical geography, anthropology, mathematics, and theoretical physics, as well as logic, metaphysics, and moral philosophy.

LIFE'S WORK

Kant did his most original and important work quite late in his life. His project of critical philosophy began with *Kritik der reinen Vernunft* (1781; *The Critique of Pure Reason*, 1838), on which he worked between 1775 and 1781. This work aimed to resolve the disputes of all contemporary and traditional metaphysics by reinterpreting the conditions for human knowledge. Kant viewed the whole history of metaphysical inquiry as a series of failures to establish conclusive truths of first principles concerning God, human freedom, and immortality. In particular, he observed that rational cosmology (that is, metaphysical speculation concerning the nature of the world and its origin) was prone toward generating conflicting demonstrations that appeared to be equally valid. Kant named these conflicting arguments "antinomies," and he found them to be in a sense inherent in reason itself. In Kant's view, the preponderance of antinomies in the history of thought cast doubt on the whole enterprise of metaphysics.

Juxtaposed to his preoccupation with the self-contradictory nature and uncertainty of metaphysics were Kant's deep convictions about the value and trustworthiness of Sir Isaac Newton's mathematical science. Mathematics and natural science yielded genuine knowledge. Kant took this as a clue to the sort of reformation that was called for in metaphysics. By inquiring into what made mathematical science possible, Kant hoped to uncover the conditions under which true metaphysical knowledge is possible.

Here is Kant's seminal discovery: What makes knowledge possible in mathematics or physics is an individual's possession of necessarily true propositions that are universally recognized as correct without any reference to experience. An example of such a proposition in mathematics is "The sum of the angles in a triangle are equal to two right angles." The possession of such truths proves that an individual's cognition of the world is not necessarily a product of experience or the functioning of his or her senses. From one's senses one obtains raw intuitions, but these intuitions do not constitute authentic cognitions. Raw intuitions become substantive cognitions only when they are processed actively by the mind. The mind organizes and synthesizes the raw intuitions according to innate rules. Without the raw intuitions given by the senses, a person could not be aware of any object, but without the active participation of the mind, that person could form no conception of any object.

Kant reasoned that the certainty of science rested on the purity of its truths, that is, their independence of sensation. Nothing that was given to sense experience from the outside could be guaranteed even by science, for an additional observation might reveal an alternate sequence that would prove the scientist's first conclusion to be neither always nor inevitably true—neither universal nor necessary. If observational science was to be certain, it needed to proceed from propositions that were pure of sensation, that were a priori, or "present from the very first."

From this discovery, Kant devolved a new, chastened metaphysics, free of the liabilities of all previous metaphysical inquiry. He had determined that the mind actively supplied certain concepts to intuition or sensation before that raw material was perceived and subsequently cognized, prior to its being registered as experience at all. Accordingly, it was also clear that humans are not immediately in touch with things as they are in themselves. It is as if one views the world through a particular set of rose-colored glasses, glasses that one can never remove. Thus, according to Kant, previous metaphysicians had been misguided in their aspirations to know about the ultimate nature of things. What one can know, or make certain claims about, is one's experience of things (the appearances of things), not things in themselves. Kant said that one must take for granted that the thing-in-itself (*Ding-an-sich*) is real per se, but that it is not directly known. Rather, one knows appearances of things, as mediated through one's perceptual and cognitive apparatus. What one has no experience of, including the nature and existence of God and the fate of the soul, one can access only by faith, not speculative knowledge. Thus, the new Kantian metaphysics confined itself to determining the necessary features of all objects of possible experience and to determining the structures of the mind that themselves impart to all objects of possible experience the features that they of necessity have.

This strict limitation on objects of knowledge, this restriction on the valid application of pure human reason, did not end in pure skepticism for Kant. Kant claimed that he found it necessary to deny knowledge in order to make room for faith. With the elimination of dogmatic metaphysics, he had silenced those who made knowledge claims or arguments on either side of speculative metaphysical issues. It was of no use, for example, to argue for or against God's existence, or to try to prove that humans have or do not have free will. Such issues were beyond the ken of human understanding. Objections to morality and religion therefore carried no weight, since they mistook what was beyond the limits of human experience to be legitimate objects of human understanding. This engendered the other substantial phase of the Kantian philosophy, the writings on ethics and religion.

Although Kant set limits on speculative reason, he granted a practical employment of reason that articulated postulates, articles of faith, in matters where discursive knowledge was impossible. Kant saw that humans as a matter of fact made moral commitments and acted as if they had free will. This did not involve an illegitimate metaphysical knowledge claim but rather a postulate born of practical necessity. Kant's *Grundlegung zur Metaphysik der Sitten* (1785; *Foundations of the Metaphysics of Morals*, 1950) and his *Kritik der praktischen Vernunft* (1788; *The Critique of Practical Reason*, 1873) were devoted to working out such rational principles of morality.

Kant's analysis of morality revealed that an agent's goodness was not some quality of his or her behavior, nor a quality of his or her desire to cause some particular state

Immanuel Kant. (Library of Congress)

of affairs. Goodness involved doing one's duty solely for the sake of so doing. Duty was what conformed with the moral law that Kant called the categorical imperative. This stipulated that an action was moral if and only if one could will that it should become a universal law. The categorical imperative thus enunciated a purely formal, logical criterion for morality whose hallmark was a demand for complete impartiality.

The next ten years of Kant's life were spent in vigorous productivity. Among the twenty or so books and treatises composed during this time were enormously influential works on aesthetics, *Kritik der Urteilskraft* (1790; *The Critique of Judgment*, 1892), on rational theology and ethics, *Die Religion innerhalb der Grenzen der blossen Vernunft* (1793; *Religion Within the Boundaries of Pure Reason*, 1838); and on political theory, the fa-

mous essay *Zum ewigen Frieden* (1795; *Perpetual Peace*, 1796), in which Kant proposed the creation of a federation or league of nations as an antidote to international conflict. Kant's powers began to fail in his last years. He gave up lecturing in 1799, and as he lost his eyesight and intellectual clarity, he slowly faded away. Almost all of Königsberg and many persons from all over Germany attended his funeral.

SIGNIFICANCE

Immanuel Kant said that his project could be codified in the following three questions: What can I know? What ought I to do? For what may I hope? These are the questions that have occupied every philosopher in the history of Western thought, but Kant's answers to them dramatically altered how they were approached by his successors. No one before Kant had regarded human minds as actively operative organisms that drew their material from the senses while shaping this material autonomously, according to their own laws. His discovery that the mind forms its cognitions itself supplanted all previous epistemological theories and quickly became a philosophical commonplace. Since Kant, no one has been able to neglect the transforming and intrusive influence of the observer's cognizing process upon the object of observation. This insight spawned the whole twentieth century analytic movement in philosophy, which emphasizes logic and theory of knowledge and rejects metaphysics. It also gave rise to anti-Kantian theories of human experience offered by philosophers G. W. F. Hegel, Edmund Husserl, John Dewey, and Alfred North Whitehead.

The influence of Kant's deontological, antinaturalistic moral views was also very strong, especially among later ethical intuitionists. Yet it is a mistake to separate Kant's ethical thought from his overall system. The richest meaning of the moral doctrines emerges when they are seen as the central focus of his overall systematic approach to philosophy. The whole system yields a doctrine of wisdom concerning the human condition: What humans can know is ex-

---

KANT'S CATEGORIES

At the heart of Immanuel Kant's philosophy of mind are the Categories, the twelve fundamental filters for processing perceptions that are hardwired into the human mind and upon which all other perceptual filters (which Kant calls "concepts") are based. Reproduced here is Kant's table of the Categories he believed structure all human understanding.

TABLE OF CATEGORIES
I
Of Quantity
Unity
Plurality
Totality
II
Of Quality
Reality
Negation (substantia et accidens)
Limitation
III
Of Relation
Of Inherence and Subsistence
Of Causality and Dependence (cause and effect)
Of Community (reciprocity between agent and patient)
IV
Of Modality
Possibility—Impossibility
Existence—Non-existence
Necessity—Contingency
This then is the list of all original pure concepts of synthesis that the understanding contains within itself *a priori*.

Source: Immanuel Kant, *The Critique of Pure Reason.* Translated by Norman Kemp Smith (New York: Humanities Press, 1929), p. 113.

tremely limited, but this fact need not be regarded as regrettable or disappointing, for it testifies to the wise adaptation of a person's cognitive faculties to his or her practical vocation. If humans had a clearer vision of the true natures of things, they would always do what they ought, but then individuals would not be acting out of a pure motive to do their duty. Humans would be acting rather out of fear or hope of reward. Thus individuals would lose the opportunity to manifest goodwill, which Kant called the only thing in the world (or even out of this world) which can be taken as good without qualification.

—*Patricia Cook*

FURTHER READING

Broad, C. D. *Kant: An Introduction*. New York: Cambridge University Press, 1978. Broad provides a close textual commentary of Kant's three critiques. The book's fifteen-page general introduction is most helpful for newcomers to Kantian philosophy; the rest of the book is an invaluable companion for one attempting to read Kantian texts for the first time.

Cassirer, Ernst. *Kant's Life and Thought*. Translated by James Hayden. New Haven, Conn.: Yale University Press, 1981. Cassirer was an influential neo-Kantian and offers here an eminently readable intellectual biography of Kant. This substantial work is well indexed.

Guyer, Paul, ed. *The Cambridge Companion to Kant*. New York: Cambridge University Press, 1992. Collection of essays analyzing various aspects of Kant's philosophical thought. Aimed at readers with some previous knowledge of Kant's work.

Hartnack, Justus. *Immanuel Kant: An Explanation of His Theory of Knowledge and Moral Philosophy*. Atlantic Highlands, N.J.: Humanities Press, 1974. A concise exposition of these two main aspects of Kant's thought.

Hendel, Charles W., ed. *The Philosophy of Kant and Our Modern World*. New York: Liberal Arts Press, 1957. This is a series of lectures given at Yale University, focusing on the twentieth century legacy of Kantian thought. Contains a helpful bibliography of Kantian scholarship, including many classical sources.

Kemp, John. *The Philosophy of Kant*. New York: Oxford University Press, 1968. This book offers an exposition of Kant's epistemology, practical philosophy, and aesthetics in less than one hundred pages. It is very well indexed and contains an annotated bibliography.

Körner, Stephan. *Kant*. Baltimore: Penguin Books, 1955. This overview of Kant's thought is concise, though quite technical. It would serve to help an advanced student interpret some of the nuances of Kant's system. It is well indexed and includes a short bibliography.

Kuehn, Manfred. *Kant: A Biography*. New York: Cambridge University Press, 2001. Kuehn examines Kant's philosophical works, describing their origin and meaning. He also refutes the image of Kant as a pure thinker living an uneventful life in an isolated Prussian town. Kuehn's Kant leads an active social life and is a witty conversationalist and an elegant dresser.

Scruton, Roger. *Kant: A Very Short Introduction*. Rev. ed. New York: Oxford University Press, 2001. A concise overview of Kant's philosophy, written for readers with no previous knowledge of his work. One in a series of books providing short introductions to major philosophers.

See also: Johann Gottlieb Fichte; Johann Wolfgang von Goethe; Jean-Jacques Rousseau; Friedrich Schiller.

Related articles in *Great Events from History: The Eighteenth Century, 1701-1800*: October, 1725: Vico Publishes *The New Science*; 1739-1740: Hume Publishes *A Treatise of Human Nature*; April, 1762: Rousseau Publishes *The Social Contract*; July, 1764: Voltaire Publishes *A Philosophical Dictionary for the Pocket*; 1770: Publication of Holbach's *The System of Nature*; 1781: Kant Publishes *Critique of Pure Reason*; 1784-1791: Herder Publishes His Philosophy of History; 1792-1793: Fichte Advocates Free Speech.

KARĪM KHĀN ZAND
Vakil of Persia (r. 1751-1759)

The vakil, *or regent, of Persia under the infant Shah Esmā'īl III, Karīm founded the short-lived Zand Dynasty. His regency brought a period of peace to Persia after four decades of war and developed commerce, handicrafts, and architecture. He established Shīrāz as his capital city and enriched it particularly with magnificent architecture.*

Born: c. 1705; Khorāsān, Persia (now in Iran)
Died: March, 1779; Shīrāz, Persia (now in Iran)
Also known as: Karīm Khān Zand Muḥammad; Muḥammad Karīm Beg; Tushmal Karīm
Areas of achievement: Government and politics, warfare and conquest

EARLY LIFE

Among the men who ruled Persia between the sixteenth and early twentieth centuries, Karīm Khān Zand (kah-REEM khahn ZAHND) was the only one not of Turkish origin. He was a member of the Zand, an indigenous pastoral tribe that was part of the Aryan tribe of Lak in southern Persia. Karīm Khān, known then as Muḥammad Karīm, was reared while the Zand were in exile in northern Khorāsān. The Zand had been deported from their home territory in the course of punitive raids on several Zagros tribes launched by Nādir Shāh in 1732. Enlisted as a common soldier in Nādir Shāh's army, the young Muḥammad Karīm marked himself as a great fighter in clashes with neighboring chieftains. Soon his abilities rendered him a leader. After Nādir Shāh's death in 1747, he succeeded in leading the Zand out of exile to the village of Piriya (modern Pari), a short distance from Malavir, where the clan had settlements prior to their exile.

At the time of Nādir Shāh's assassination, there were multiple rivals for his throne. Two of the most prominent were members of groups that returned from exiles imposed by Nādir Shāh in the wake of his death. 'Ali Mardan Khān led the Bakhtiari tribe back to their homeland, just as Muḥammad Karīm guided the Zand to theirs. As Nādir Shāh's Afshar successors proved unable to maintain hegemony over the former Ṣafavid capital of Eṣfahān, a power vacuum emerged. The two chieftains, Karīm and 'Ali, moved in to occupy the city in 1750. To enhance their legitimacy, they soon placed an eight-year-old Ṣafavid prince on the throne in Eṣfahān and pronounced him Esmā'īl III.

LIFE'S WORK

Nominally in the service of Esmā'īl III, Karīm held the office of commander in chief, while 'Ali Mardan Khān held the office of *vakil*, or guardian of the sovereign. 'Ali made a bid for exclusive power but was defeated in battle. Karīm captured Eṣfahān, set 'Ali Mardan Khān aflight, and assumed the title of *vakil* himself. Later, in 1764, his rival would be assassinated. In the meantime, Karīm Khān found himself defending the cities of Eṣfahān and Shīrāz against new claimants to the throne, who included the Kajar Muḥammad ḥasan Khān, the Afshar Fath 'Ali, and the Afghan Azad Khān. After a fierce struggle in which Muḥammad ḥasan was assassinated in 1759, Fath 'Ali and Azad Khān joined forces with Karīm in 1763 and 1765 respectively.

Emerging as the undisputed ruler of Persia, Karīm sought peace in the land. He left Khorāsān in the hands of Nādir Shāh's descendants and succeeded in suppressing local revolts among tribes in Khūzestān, Kohkīlūyeh Kermān, Fārs, Astarabad, Māzandarān, and the Gulf region. Meanwhile, Esmā'īl III had deserted Karīm in 1752, only to return seven years later, at which point the nominal shāh (king) was deposed as incompetent. Esmā'īl was held in honored captivity, while Karīm forged ahead as de facto ruler. He had no claim to the title of shāh, and he did not abandon his official title of *vakil*. Instead, he altered its meaning to define his role as regent for the people and turned his attention to the establishment of trade and domestic development.

Karīm Khān established new commerce, local crafts, and agriculture by removing some of the heavy burdens of taxation from the agricultural classes. He granted commercial privileges to European companies in the Persian Gulf in return for their agreement to police the coasts. In 1763, he opened Persia itself to foreign influence by allowing the British East India Company to establish a trading post in the Persian Gulf port of Būshehr. To further advance his trade policy, in 1775-1776 he attacked and captured Basra, the Ottoman port at the mouth of the Persian Gulf, which had previously diverted much of the trade with India away from Persian ports.

Karīm Khān is perhaps best known for his patronage of the arts. He established a new capital city at Shīrāz, where he instigated an urban renewal on par with the reconstruction of Eṣfahān under Ṣafavid ruler Shāh 'Abbās. He reinforced the city walls and oversaw the construction of a palace citadel, a covered bazaar, mosques, shrines, and numerous gardens. He also drew poets and artists into residence in the capital, expanding its reputation as a premier cultural center.

The ruler's last years were wrought with personal losses. He mourned the loss of a young son and a beloved wife and endured a series of illnesses, to which he finally succumbed in March of 1779. Karīm Khān was buried in the capital city of Shīrāz, which he had worked tirelessly to embellish. Members of the Kajar Dynasty, eager to extinguish his popularity, transferred the ruler's remains to Tehran and later to Najaf. His death was followed by internal dissentions and a series of disputes over the succession. Between the years 1779 and 1789, five Zand shāhs ruled for short periods of time. In 1789, Lutf ʿAli Khān proclaimed himself the new Zand shāh and attempted to put down a rebellion led by the Kajar Agha Muḥammad Khān. Outnumbered by the Kajar forces, Lutf ʿAli Khān was finally defeated and captured at Kermān in 1794, marking the end of the Zand Dynasty.

SIGNIFICANCE

Karīm Khān Zand reorganized Persia's fiscal system, expanded its foreign trade, and decreased taxation of the agricultural classes. His rule, a paternal monarchy based on tribal traditions, was marked by unprecedented peace and good will. His only foreign expedition was an attack on Basra, driven by specific commercial motivations rather than a quest for territorial gain as an end in itself. The peaceful interregnum he created allowed for the development of the capital city of Shīrāz and for achievement in the arts of literature and painting. His many impressive qualities—including his military skills, physical strength, sense of humor, and benevolence—have been commemorated in Persian folktales.

—*Anna Sloan*

FURTHER READING

Amīn, ʿAbd al-Amīr Muhammad. *British Interests in the Persian Gulf, 1747-1780*. Leiden, the Netherlands: E. J. Brill, 1967. Explores the role of trade and foreign policies under Karīm Khān.

Avery, Peter, Gavin Hambly, and Charles Melville, eds. *From Nadir Shah to the Islamic Republic*. Vol. 7 in *The Cambridge History of Iran*. New York: Cambridge University Press, 1991. The most comprehensive source on political developments between the fall of the Safavid Dynasty and the rise of the Kajar Dynasty. Contains plates, maps, illustrations, genealogical tables, and a rich bibliography.

Clarke, John I. *The Iranian City of Shiraz*. Durham, England: Department of Geography, University of Durham, 1963. A monograph on Shīrāz under Karīm Khān.

Daniel, Elton L. *The History of Iran*. Westport, Conn.: Greenwood Press, 2001. A general survey that locates Karīm Khān's rule in the broader scope of Persia's history. Contains maps, a glossary of terms, and a bibliographical essay.

Lockhart, Laurence. *The Fall of the Safavid Dynasty and the Afghan Occupation of Persia*. Cambridge, England: Cambridge University Press, 1958. The primary study that laid out the historical framework of the late Safavid period, this source still offers unsurpassed information on the end of Safavid hegemony and the period leading up to Karīm Khān's rule. Contains illustrations, maps, a genealogical table of the Safavid Dynasty, and a bibliography listing primary sources, including European travelers' accounts.

_____. *Nadir Shah: A Critical Study Based Mainly upon Contemporary Sources*. London: Luzac, 1938. The principal monograph on the period preceding Karīm Khān's rule. This study, which contains material from difficult-to-access primary sources, is yet to be surpassed. Contains a genealogical table, maps, and a bibliography of primary sources.

Perry, John R. *Karim Khan Zand: A History of Iran, 1747-1779*. Chicago: University of Chicago Press, 1979. The single best source on the ruler. Incorporates the chief Persian histories and contains a comprehensive bibliography of primary and secondary sources from both premodern and modern eras. Contains maps and illustrations.

Zarrinkoob, A. H. "Karim Khan Zand." In *The Encyclopedia of Islam*, edited by H. A. R. Gibb. Rev. ed. Vol. 4. Leiden, the Netherlands: E. J. Brill, 1960-2004. Comprehensive synopsis of scholarship on Karīm Khān Zand's life and accomplishments. Includes a thorough bibliography complete with sources published in both Persian and English.

See also: Nādir Shāh; Vaḥīd Bihbahānī.

Related articles in *Great Events from History: The Eighteenth Century, 1701-1800*: 1709-1747: Persian-Afghan Wars; 1725-November, 1794: Persian Civil Wars.

ANGELICA KAUFFMANN
Swiss painter

Refusing to accept the traditional role for the woman artist as a painter of portraits or still lifes, Kauffmann instead became a history painter. An early exponent of neoclassicism, she produced some of the finest works in this style, which helped to popularize the movement throughout Europe.

Born: October 30, 1741; Chur, Swiss Confederation (now in Switzerland)
Died: November 5, 1807; Rome, Papal States (now in Italy)
Also known as: Maria Anna Catharina Angelica Kauffmann (full name)
Area of achievement: Art

EARLY LIFE

Angelica Kauffmann (ahng-GAY-lee-kah KOWF-mahn) was born in a small village in Switzerland in 1741, the daughter of a minor portraitist and painter of religious murals. She was a child prodigy who received her first commission at age eleven for a portrait of the bishop of Como. Recognizing their daughter's talents, her parents made certain that she received a sound education in poetry, history, religion, languages, and the visual arts. She was also an accomplished musician with a remarkably good voice; indeed, while still very young, she was faced with a choice between a career in opera or one in art. Later, Kauffmann emphasized the importance of this difficult decision in a painting entitled *The Artist Hesitating Between the Arts of Music and Painting* (1794), in which she appears between two allegorical female figures representing Music and Painting. Using gesture to indicate her choice, she looks with longing and regret at Music and squeezes her hand in farewell while making an openhanded sign of acceptance toward Painting.

Johann Kauffmann took his family to Milan in 1754 to further Angelica's artistic training in the city's many excellent galleries. There, she encountered for the first time the prejudice against women in the art world. Generally, women were allowed to work in the galleries only under the patronage of some important man. Legend has it that Kauffmann, lacking such a sponsor, copied in the galleries disguised in boy's clothing until her work attracted the attention of the duke of Modena, who gave her several portrait commissions and introduced her into Milanese society. Thus, Kauffmann realized the necessity of acquiring important patrons early in her career. Later, in the Florentine galleries, she obtained studio space by us-

ing letters of introduction from her Milanese patrons to circumvent opposition from male students who resented her presence there.

After Kauffmann's mother died in 1757, she and her father traveled through northern Italy—where she studied the works of Correggio, the Carracci, and Guido Reni—arriving finally in Florence in 1762. It was there that she first encountered the newly emerging style of neoclassicism, primarily in the works of the young American painter Benjamin West. Going on to Rome the following year, she found herself at the center of the new style and became part of a sophisticated circle that included Johann Joachim Winckelmann, the principal theoretician of neoclassicism, as well as artists such as Gavin Hamilton, Raphael Mengs, Pompeo Batoni, and Nathaniel Dance.

This was a busy, productive period for Kauffmann, as she studied classical art and literature, architecture, and perspective. Acknowledgment of her success came in 1765, when she was elected to membership in the prestigious Roman Academy of St. Luke. Also during this period, the first of her neoclassical works appeared.

LIFE'S WORK

In October of 1765, the Kauffmanns went to Venice, where Angelica studied the great colorists Titian, Tintoretto, and Paolo Veronese, combining what she learned from them with the exalted language of the neoclassicists and the sensuality of Correggio. She was well on her way to formulating her own style of neoclassicism, which was witty, sophisticated, and elegant. In Venice, Kauffmann met Lady Wentworth, wife of the British ambassador, and was invited to return with her to London as her houseguest. Tempted by promises of commissions and fees exceeding what she could hope to get in Italy, Kauffmann accepted, but—as the invitation had been extended to her alone—she found herself separated from her father for the first time in her life.

Arriving in London in 1766, Kauffmann was reunited with her friends West and Dance. She also met Sir Joshua Reynolds, the principal exponent of painting in the grand manner, who was so impressed with her work that he asked to exchange portraits with her. The friendship and patronage of people such as Lady Wentworth and Sir Reynolds undoubtedly launched Kauffmann into a wealthy and aristocratic London society, but it was entirely through her own efforts that she succeeded there.

Realizing that appearances were important in this society, she soon transformed herself into a fashionable lady and took a small apartment in a suitable neighborhood where she could receive her clients. Kauffmann was an attractive woman of great personal charm. Friends described her as talented, unpretentious, thoughtful, and modest, yet ambitious and industrious. A year after her arrival in London, she had saved enough money to send for her father and to acquire a comfortable house.

Kauffmann's studio became one of the most popular salons of the day, frequented by serious patrons drawn there by her work, as well as many fashionable young men and women who came to socialize. Although Kauffmann had many suitors, including the artists Henri Fuseli and Nathaniel Dance, it was not until 1767 that she made a brief and unfortunate marriage of which she soon repented.

When the Royal Academy was formed in London in 1768, Kauffmann was among the forty original members. The only other woman in this group was the popular English still-life painter, Mary Moser. It was unusual for two women to be included as founders of the Royal Academy and still more remarkable that Kauffmann had attained a position of such prominence in English society after having been in the country for only two years.

Although it was her Romantic portrait style that first attracted the British, she had now introduced neoclassicism into the country and it was becoming the fashion. In the Royal Academy's first annual exhibition, Kauffman showed four paintings with subjects drawn from classical antiquity, one of which, *The Parting of Hector and Andromache*, was praised as having been among the most original and popular works in the exhibition. It is interesting to note that only Kauffmann and West sent history pictures to this exhibition—even Reynolds exhibited portraits.

Kauffmann continued to paint classical subjects throughout her London years, but she and others, such as West and Fuseli, who wanted to raise history painting to the prominence it had in France, never fully succeeded in winning the British audience away from its first love, portraiture. Thus, Kauffmann's subject pictures were always more highly regarded in Europe. Since Kauffmann earned most of her income in London with portraiture, she looked for ways to bring it closer to history painting. Primarily, she accomplished this goal by painting portraits as allegories; for example, the Marchioness Townshend and her son appeared as Venus and Cupid, Sir John Webb and Lady Webb and their children staged *An Offering to Ceres*, and Frances Hoare offered sacrifice to a statue of Minerva. Kauffmann also worked with some of the most fashionable architects in England, decorating the interiors of neoclassical homes. She also contributed four allegorical paintings for the lecture hall ceiling in the new quarters of the Royal Academy.

Kauffmann's London period ended in 1781, when she married the painter Antonio Zucci and returned to Europe. In Venice, Kauffmann met Grand Duke Paul of Russia, the first of the large numbers of European nobility who gave her their patronage in the next years. Then, during a brief stay in Naples, she was offered the position of royal painter to King Ferdinand IV (also known as Ferdinand I of the Two Sicilies), which she declined. In 1782, Kauffmann and Zucci settled permanently in Rome, where, during the next fifteen years, she produced some of her finest works. Many of these were sent to England, where she was still highly esteemed. In Rome, she was honored as the most famous and successful living painter, with her home and studio attracting many distinguished visitors. She worked at a slower pace after Zucci's death in 1795, although she continued to be at the center of artistic and literary circles and was considered the head of the Roman school of painting. When she died in 1807, at age sixty-six, her funeral procession was lavish, in the manner of Renaissance masters such as Raphael, and included all the academicians of St. Luke, as well as representatives from academies throughout Europe.

SIGNIFICANCE

Angelica Kauffmann's neoclassical style was witty, sophisticated, and painterly. Her compositions were elegant. As a colorist, she was the equal of any painter of her day. She also had a greater influence upon her contemporaries than was understood by her early critics. Artists such as Gavin Hamilton emulated her, and many landscape painters of the later nineteenth century were influenced by her interpretations of the English light and countryside. Even Reynolds, from whom she herself learned much, gained a broader range of color and emotion from her example.

Kauffmann was a talented and serious artist who paid a high price for her success: the loss of her privacy and the impugning of her moral character. Such a price was paid, to some extent, by most successful women artists in the eighteenth and nineteenth centuries, but in Kauffmann's case, the slander was particularly vicious, vindictive, and totally absurd. It all began with her arrival in London, coinciding with her first successes as a history painter. Some of the attempts to defame her resulted from simple envy and jealousy. Beyond that, in the art world of Kauffmann's day, a woman might be tolerated only if she contented herself with a career as a still-life painter or minor portraitist. Any woman who aspired to go beyond those limits, as Kauffmann did, left herself open to personal as well as professional criticism. The private life of such a woman artist became public property, and, if she happened to be young and pretty, she would almost certainly be accused of using her feminine charms to further her career. Kauffmann was ambitious, but she also had the talent to succeed without resorting to tactics of that kind. It is very much to her credit that, having the courage of her own artistic convictions, she refused to allow anything to deter her from the goals she had set for herself and for her art.

—*LouAnn Faris Culley*

FURTHER READING

Clement, Clara Erskine. *Women in the Fine Arts, from the Seventh Century B.C. to the Twentieth Century A.D.* New York: Hacker, 1974. Originally published in 1904, this was an early attempt to assess the contributions made by women artists throughout history. Arranged alphabetically, the biographies are brief but fairly accurate in terms of basic facts. Affords the reader a handy and reliable way to compare and contrast the career of a particular artist with those of her peers.

Greer, Germaine. *The Obstacle Race: The Fortunes of Women Painters and Their Work.* New York: Farrar, Straus & Giroux, 1979. A perceptive and often witty analysis of the struggles and achievements of women artists in general. Contains a lengthy discussion of Kauffmann's personality and works, with a much-deserved indictment of those writers who, while largely ignoring her contributions, have perpetuated "the foolish prattle about her love life."

Harris, Ann Sutherland, and Linda Nochlin. *Women Artists, 1550-1950.* Los Angeles: Los Angeles County Museum of Art, 1976. The catalog of one of the first exhibitions to concentrate solely on women artists. Contains an essay summarizing the complicated and varied highlights of Kauffmann's career, emphasizing her major achievements and contributions. Also analyzes several of her most significant neoclassical compositions.

Manners, Victoria, and G. C. Williamson. *Angelica Kauffmann, R. A.: Her Life and Her Works.* New York: Hacker, 1976. A reprint of a biography first published in 1924, which was based on a manuscript discovered in London's Royal Academy Library. Includes listings of Kauffmann's works, arranged alphabetically by owners, by country, and by sale at auction. Contains a catalog of the engravings made after her works, with the names of the engravers.

Mayer, Dorothy. *Angelica Kauffmann, R. A., 1741-1807.* Gerrards Cross, England: Colin Smythe, 1972. This biography of Kauffmann updates the material found in Manners and Williamson. Also discusses the fluctuation of her reputation in the art world since her own time, pointing out that her work has regained some of its original prominence as a result of a revival of interest in the neoclassical era.

Mellor, Anne K. "British Romanticism, Gender, and Three Women Artists." In *The Consumption of Culture, 1600-1800: Image, Object, Text,* edited by Ann Bermingham and John Brewer. New York: Routledge, 1995. Explores the relationship of eighteenth century British romantic writing to the work of Kauffmann and two other contemporary women artists, Mary Moser and Maria Hadfield Cosway.

Roworth, Wendy Wassyng, ed. *Angelica Kauffmann: A Continental Artist in Georgian England.* London: Reaktion Books, 1992. Collection of essays, published to accompany an exhibition of Kauffmann's work at the Royal Pavilion, Art Gallery and Museums. Contributors examine Kauffmann's life, her career, and why she has not received due credit by art historians. Concentrates on the work Kauffmann created during her fifteen years in England and the work she produced in Italy for British clients.

See also: Sir Joshua Reynolds; Benjamin West; Johann Joachim Winckelmann.

Related articles in *Great Events from History: The Eighteenth Century, 1701-1800*: 1762: *The Antiquities of Athens* Prompts Architectural Neoclassicism; December 10, 1768: Britain's Royal Academy of Arts Is Founded; 1787: David Paints *The Death of Socrates.*

WENZEL ANTON VON KAUNITZ
Austrian state chancellor (1753-1792)

Wenzel Anton von Kaunitz served Austrian empress Maria Theresa in various diplomatic and governmental posts from 1740 until 1780, when she was succeeded by her son, Joseph II, with whom Kaunitz often had strained relations. He continued to serve the government under Emperor Leopold II and Emperor Francis II before retiring in 1792.

Born: February 2, 1711; Vienna, Austria
Died: June 27, 1794; Vienna, Austria
Also known as: Prince of Kaunitz-Reitberg
Areas of achievement: Government and politics, diplomacy

EARLY LIFE

Wenzel Anton von Kaunitz (VEHNT-suhl AHN-tohn fawn KOW-nihts) was the son of a family that for generations had held political posts in Moravia. His father, Maximilian Ulrich von Kaunitz (1679-1746), carried out several diplomatic missions for the government and, from 1720 until the year of his death, served as governor of Moravia. He was an authoritarian leader who saw to it that Moravia functioned as an orderly police state.

Wenzel was Maximilian's sixth child and second son, born into a family that produced a total of sixteen children, eleven of whom survived infancy. Wenzel, however, was the only son to live a normal life span. Maximilian appreciated Wenzel's intelligence and admired the self-discipline that made him a fine student. The boy was educated according to Protestant pedagogical theories that emphasized hard work directed at well-defined goals and suppression of one's emotions.

Because the Kaunitz family was hard pressed financially, young Wenzel learned frugality. Maximilian discouraged maternal—indeed, any female—influences in the raising of his sons. In order to alleviate the family's economic woes, Maximilian directed his sons toward ecclesiastical careers, in which their sinecures, called prebends, would assure their futures.

Before Wenzel turned fourteen, the age recognized by the church as the age of consent, he was granted a prebend in the cathedral chapter of Münster. Although the boy showed little inclination toward religion, the prebend, once granted, became the property of one's family, so Wenzel, if he wished, could pass it on to one of his brothers. Thus, he felt that he could not refuse the prebend so long as his brothers lacked financial security. When all of his brothers died before reaching maturity,

however, this consideration disappeared, and Wenzel renounced the position of canon.

For the next decade, Wenzel pursued a secular vocation. In 1731 and 1732, he attended the University of Leipzig, accompanied by his erstwhile tutor, Johann Friedrich Schwanau, who directed his curriculum in German grammar, German history, rhetoric, Latin, music, classics, and, most important, public and private law. Kaunitz subsequently traveled extensively in Europe then returned to Vienna, where he was presented at court. On April 22, 1736, he married Maria Ernestine Starhemburg, who produced seven children. After holding minor posts in local government, in 1740, at age twenty-nine, Kaunitz joined the Austrian foreign service. In 1742, he became Austria's minister to Sardinia.

LIFE'S WORK

Through his association with Sardinia's king, Charles Emmanuel III, Kaunitz quickly learned about diplomacy and about corruption in both Sardinia and Turin. His talents had already come to the attention of Empress Maria Theresa in 1740, when she had sent him to Turin and Rome as a special envoy. It was his great success as special envoy that led the empress to appoint him as minister to Sardinia in 1742. Unable to finance a move to Sardinia, Kaunitz initially declined the appointment, but Maria Theresa finally made it possible for him to accept it by granting him a generous loan. This marked the beginning of an illustrious career for Kaunitz in the service of the Habsburgs.

Kaunitz was sent to the Netherlands as chief minister to Charles of Lorraine and Maria Anne, the empress's sister. His next diplomatic foray was as a representative of Austria at the Aachen Peace Congress of 1748. At this meeting, because of his dislike of Prussia, he implemented plans to negate Europe's established system of alliances. He sought to nullify Austria's alliances with England and the United Provinces because they favored Prussia. He wished to ally the Habsburg Dynasty with France and Russia instead.

Maria Theresa sent Kaunitz to France as the Austrian ambassador, but he failed to bring about the kind of alliance most desirable for Austria. Nevertheless, he returned to Vienna and, in 1753, was appointed head of the Austrian State Chancery. In this position, he tried to implement the kind of alliance he had proposed earlier. In 1756, Austria and France signed a treaty at Versailles,

Wenzel Anton von Kaunitz. (The Granger Collection, New York)

With the death of Maria Theresa's husband, Francis I, in 1765, Kaunitz became increasingly important to the empress, who sought his guidance in reaching important political decisions. In 1772, he helped to bring about the first partition of Poland. Facing the harsh reality of Prussia's strength, he tried to overcome his earlier reservations and worked toward achieving diplomatic solutions to Austria's problems with Prussia.

Maria Theresa's son, Joseph II, served with her as coregent until 1780, when Joseph II was crowned emperor. The son was much more an aggressive activist than his mother. The two often disagreed, and Kaunitz frequently served as mediator between them. His relationship with Joseph was difficult, and Joseph severely curtailed Kaunitz's ministerial powers. The aging minister, feeling humiliated and unappreciated, continued nevertheless to serve.

The French Revolution destroyed the system of alliances for which Kaunitz was largely responsible. Emperor Leopold II, whom Kaunitz also served, responded by moving toward closer ties with Prussia, much to Kaunitz's distress. Finally, while serving under Emperor Francis II, a disenchanted Kaunitz resigned from public office on August 9, 1792. He died less than two years afterward.

SIGNIFICANCE

Wenzel Anton von Kaunitz was an accomplished statesman. Even when his diplomatic missions failed, he refocused on the tasks ahead and worked productively toward achieving them. Kaunitz was never a "team player." He was a hard-working eccentric who set goals and worked tirelessly to achieve them. He was vain, although when he had the full support of Maria Theresa, his vanity presented no problems for him.

After her husband's death, when Maria Theresa most needed a confidante with whom she could openly discuss delicate matters of state, she turned to Kaunitz, realizing that confidences she shared with him would remain confidential. As a major representative of the Habsburgs, Kauntiz was able to form alliances that strengthened Europe, although not all of them survived the turbulent years of the Seven Years' War and the French Revolution.

The term "enlightened absolutist" has been applied quite aptly to Kaunitz. He was certainly an enlightened, well-educated man, schooled at the University of Leip-

which the Russians entered into in 1757. This marked Kaunitz's greatest diplomatic victory. The treaty succeeded in cutting Prussia off from the rest of Europe and in enhancing Austria's position in European politics. It was not enough, however, to forestall the Seven Years' War waged by Prussia's King Frederick the Great.

Kaunitz began to involve himself in domestic affairs, while maintaining his foreign affairs portfolio as well. In 1760, he reorganized and consolidated the activities of many Habsburg governmental agencies. In 1763, he entered into the Treaty of Paris, thereby ending the Seven Years' War in a way that best saved face for Austria and its allies. The following year, partly in recognition of his contributions to Austrian security, Maria Theresa named him Fürst (prince) von Kaunitz-Rietberg, the highest honor the Habsburgs could bestow.

zig, which was probably the best university for legal studies in Germany. He was intelligent and assiduous in his work and study habits. On the other hand, Kaunitz was raised in an absolutist atmosphere by a father who encouraged him to quash his emotions and proceed diligently on an undeviating course. Kaunitz's absolutism sometimes worked to his advantage and was considered resoluteness, but in his diplomatic ventures, he could be perceived as unbending and difficult to deal with.

When Maria Theresa's reign ended, her successors found Kaunitz's absolutism untenable and simply pushed this once-venerated diplomat into the background. Kaunitz, following a productive life, died a broken man.

—*R. Baird Shuman*

FURTHER READING

Beales, Derek. *Joseph II: In the Shadow of Maria Theresa, 1741-1780*. New York: Cambridge University Press, 1987. Beales presents a wealth of material about Joseph's relationship with Kaunitz, demonstrating how the seeds of dissension between the two were sown early.

Blanning, T. C. W. *Joseph II*. New York: Longman, 1994. This slim volume delves into the Joseph-Kaunitz relationship in the years after Joseph became emperor in 1780. Shows how Joseph's attempts at censorship often ran counter to Kaunitz's beliefs.

Kann, Robert A. *A History of the Hapsburg Empire, 1526-1918*. New York: Barnes and Noble Books, 1992. Kann offers insights into how Joseph II disliked the Jesuits and used Kaunitz to work behind the scenes against them.

Roider, Karl A., ed. *Maria Theresa*. Englewood Cliffs, N.J.: Prentice-Hall, 1973. Chapter 3 on foreign affairs provides interesting insights into the empress's relationship with Kaunitz and into his role in the partition of Poland. Other information about Kaunitz pervades the book.

Szabo, Franz A. J. *Kaunitz and Enlightened Absolutism, 1753-1780*. New York: Cambridge University Press, 1994. This well-researched book is the most important resource in print on the life and political activities of this influential Austrian. The material is well presented and insightful.

See also: Frederick the Great; Joseph II; Maria Theresa.

Related articles in *Great Events from History: The Eighteenth Century, 1701-1800*: May 31, 1740: Accession of Frederick the Great; October 20, 1740: Maria Theresa Succeeds to the Austrian Throne; December 16, 1740-November 7, 1748: War of the Austrian Succession; January, 1756-February 15, 1763: Seven Years' War; February 10, 1763: Peace of Paris; August 5, 1772-October 24, 1795: Partitioning of Poland; 1775-1790: Joseph II's Reforms; April 20, 1792-October, 1797: Early Wars of the French Revolution; September 20, 1792: Battle of Valmy.

JOHN KAY
English inventor

Kay invented the flying shuttle that helped mechanize the process of weaving, contributing to the beginnings of the Industrial Revolution.

Born: July 16, 1704; Park, Walmersley, near Bury, Lancashire, England
Died: c. 1780-1781; France
Area of achievement: Science and technology

EARLY LIFE

The early life of John Kay is obscure. According to documented evidence, he was born the youngest of the five children of Robert Kay of Park and Ellin Entwisle of Quarlton. John Kay's father was a yeoman farmer, rather than a woolen manufacturer as claimed by some biographies, who died a few months before his son was born.

The father provided a modest inheritance for all of his children and a small amount for their education. Reared by his mother and her brother, William Entwisle, John Kay was close to his older brothers. Some biographies claim that Kay was educated on the Continent, but there is little to support that contention, for the provisions of his father's will were not sufficient to send any of the children abroad.

Kay was apprenticed to learn the trade of a reed maker. Reeds were used in the process of weaving thread into cloth, which was an important industry in Lancashire. In the horizontal hand loom, which had become standard in Great Britain, a series of threads, called the warp, were drawn out parallel to one another with alternate threads being lifted vertically by a pair of heddles to form a triangular open area called the shed. Another thread, called the weft, was then passed through the shed from one side to the other. In the next step, the warp threads that the weft had passed over were now raised and the alternate threads lowered, resulting in the weft thread being woven through the warp. In such looms, a reed, or comb, came between the warp threads and was used to press, or beat, the weft threads close together to make the cloth firm and tight.

Kay was a self-confident, some say arrogant, youth with a great mechanical aptitude. Before the age of twenty-one, he was established as a reed maker in his hometown of Park and had begun to invent improvements for the loom. While producing traditional reeds out of cane, Kay began to improve the reeds by making them out of thin polished blades of iron. Although he did not have enough money to patent his idea, his longer-lasting metal reeds soon were in great demand. On June 29, 1735, with his career as a reed maker assured, Kay married Anne Holte, the daughter of a neighbor, John Holte of Bury, and established a home in Park. The marriage would produce twelve children. Although he made trips to Colchester and Leeds to sell his reeds, Kay continued to reside in Park until 1753.

LIFE'S WORK

John Kay's most significant invention came in 1733, when he patented his flying or fly shuttle (or wheeled shuttle). Before his invention, weavers attached the weft thread to a piece of wood, called a shuttle, and had to pass it back and forth through the warp by hand. After each pass, the weaver had to change hand positions to beat the weft with a reed. Weaving broadcloth required two workers to throw the shuttle to each other. Because of this, weaving was both slow and expensive.

Kay's improvement for the loom consisted of a shuttle on wheels, which could run along a race-board attached to the reed. The shuttle was propelled from side to side by devices called dummy-hands, or pickers, at each side of the loom. These pickers could be controlled by the weaver using one hand to pull on a single cord at the center of the loom. With Kay's invention, a weaver could double his or her output because one hand could control the shuttle while the other hand could beat the weft. Also, a weaver could weave broadcloth without the help of an extra worker. Because of the speed with which weaving could be done, the invention came to be known as a flying shuttle.

Although the flying shuttle became quite popular among textile manufacturers, its invention brought Kay

neither fame nor fortune. Many manufacturers secretly installed the devices on their looms so that they would not have to pay Kay royalties. Other manufacturers became much more open in their defiance of Kay's patent. Between 1738 and 1745, several woolen manufacturers in Yorkshire organized what they called the Shuttle Club to defray the cost of lawsuits brought against them by Kay for infringement of his patent. Kay petitioned the government several times for help in enforcing his patent but received no response. During 1744-1745, he became involved in several lawsuits in Leeds over the use of his flying shuttle. The cost of these lawsuits nearly ruined Kay financially.

Other problems grew for Kay. While the flying shuttle had become popular with woolen manufacturers, the workers were strongly opposed to the new invention. Because a single weaver using a flying shuttle could produce as much cloth as two weavers using the old hand shuttle, the workers believed that Kay's invention would lead to unemployment for as much as half of the work force. Some workers using the flying shuttle loitered and spoiled their work so that the manufacturers would not realize the advantage of the invention. In other areas, mobs of workers seized and burned the new shuttles. In 1753, a mob from Bury marched on Kay's house with the intention of killing him. Kay narrowly escaped with his life, but the contents of his house were destroyed.

In 1764, Kay wrote a letter to the Society of Arts and Manufactures stating that he had many more ideas for inventions but that he would not make them public because of the bad treatment he had received in England. In the same year, his son Robert wrote to the society in an attempt to get some reward for his father, but he was also turned down. Because of his treatment in England, Kay moved to France in 1765, where he assisted the French in adapting recently smuggled English machinery to the textile industry. A year later Kay returned to England, encouraged by the British ambassador to Paris, in the hope of receiving some financial reward from the British government for his invention, but again he was ignored and again he left for France, where he lived the rest of his life, accompanied only by his daughter Ann. There is no record of his death or burial place, only some evidence that he died during the winter of 1780-1781.

Kay's son Robert carried on the reed and shuttle business in Bury and improved the use of the flying shuttle by inventing the drop box, which allowed several different shuttles, each with different colors or different types of weft, to be used on a single loom.

SIGNIFICANCE

John Kay's invention of the flying shuttle made a significant contribution to the mechanization of the textile industry and helped that industry play a fundamental role in the Industrial Revolution. The transformation of the textile industry from a decentralized cottage system based on hand-powered looms and spinning wheels to a centralized factory system based on water-powered machinery became a model for manufacturers in other areas of the economy.

The flying shuttle allowed weavers to produce greater quantities of cloth, increasing the demand for yarn and thread. That is, a technological imbalance was created that put pressure on the spinners to develop new machinery to keep pace with the weavers. James Hargreaves's spinning jenny in 1764 was one result, followed by Sir Richard Arkwright's water-frame in 1769 and Samuel Crompton's spinning mule in 1779. These inventions mechanized the spinning of thread and in turn put new pressure on manufacturers to develop a water-powered loom. The essential problem of mechanizing weaving had been solved by Kay's flying shuttle, but it took several years before a workable power loom was perfected. Edmund Cartwright's steam-powered loom, patented in 1785, was eventually perfected by Richard Roberts in 1822.

The flying shuttle helped to set into motion a series of events that transformed the textile industry. Not only did John Kay's invention lead to the mechanization of the production of textiles, but, as foreseen by the textile workers in Kay's own time, it also had widespread and long-lasting social effects, none of which had been anticipated by Kay.

—David F. Channell

FURTHER READING

Addy, John. *The Textile Revolution*. London: Longmans, Green, 1976. Discusses Kay's role in terms of the changes taking place in the textile industry. Includes an analysis of the social effects of Kay's invention. Contains a useful set of historical documents relating to the textile revolution.

Berg, Maxine. *The Age of Manufactures: Industry, Innovation, and Work in Britain, 1700-1820*. 2d ed. New York: Routledge, 1994. Excellent survey of eighteenth century British industry. Although it includes only a mention of Kay, it features two chapters on the country's textile industry during Kay's lifetime.

Cardwell, D. S. L. *Turning Points in Western Technology*. New York: Science History, 1972. Analyzes the technological significance of Kay's invention and discusses the role of the textile industry in the Industrial Revolution.

Hills, Richard L. *Power in the Industrial Revolution*. New York: August M. Kelley, 1970. Provides an analysis of the application of power to the textile industry and includes a discussion of Kay's contributions.

Lord, John. *Memoir of John Kay of Bury*. Rochdale, England: James Clegg, 1903. Gives a detailed and documented account of the known facts of Kay's life. Disproves several myths concerning Kay and contains genealogical records concerning Kay and his family.

Usher, Abbot Payson. "The Textile Industry, 1750-1830." In *Technology in Western Civilization*, edited by Melvin Kranzberg and Carroll Pursell, Jr. Vol. 1. New York: Oxford University Press, 1967. Provides a good overview of the industrialization of the textile industry and Kay's role in its transformation from a domestic system to a factory system.

See also: Sir Richard Arkwright; James Hargreaves; Thomas Newcomen; James Watt; Eli Whitney.

Related articles in *Great Events from History: The Eighteenth Century, 1701-1800:* 1701: Plumier Publishes *L'Art de tourner*; 1705-1712: Newcomen Develops the Steam Engine; 1733: Kay Invents the Flying Shuttle; 1764: Invention of the Spinning Jenny; 1765-1769: Watt Develops a More Effective Steam Engine; 1767-1771: Invention of the Water Frame; 1779: Crompton Invents the Spinning Mule; April, 1785: Cartwright Patents the Steam-Powered Loom; February 14, 1788: Meikle Demonstrates His Drum Thresher; 1790: First Steam Rolling Mill; December 20, 1790: Slater's Spinning Mill; 1793: Whitney Invents the Cotton Gin; 1795: Invention of the Flax Spinner.

FRIEDRICH GOTTLIEB KLOPSTOCK
German poet

Klopstock's writings mark the transition from the classical ideas and practices of the early eighteenth century in Germany to those of the Sturm und Drang and Romantic movements at century's end.

Born: July 2, 1724; Quedlinburg, Saxony (now in Germany)
Died: March 14, 1803; Hamburg (now in Germany)
Area of achievement: Literature

EARLY LIFE

Friedrich Gottlieb Klopstock (FREE-drihkh GAWT-leep KLAWP-shtawk) was the eldest of the seventeen children of Gottlieb Heinrich Klopstock, a lawyer and government official, and his wife, Anna Maria Schmidt. Although his father was always mired in serious financial difficulties, Klopstock was able to receive an excellent education that stressed classical languages and religion at the Prince's School, Schulpforta, between 1739 and 1745. He proceeded to the University of Jena to study theology but was soon occupied with plans for an epic titled *Der Messias* (1748-1773; *The Messiah*, 1776), modeled on John Milton's *Paradise Lost* (1667, 1674). He began writing a prose version of the epic's first three cantos.

The next year, 1746, Klopstock moved to the University of Leipzig. There, he joined a group of young writers who called themselves the Bremer Beiträger (Bremen contributors), after the name of a literary periodical, the *Bremer Beitrag*. While in Leipzig, Klopstock garnered high praise for the first three cantos of his epic, published anonymously in the *Bremer Beitrag*. It was in Leipzig as well that he began to turn against the rule-bound classicism of Johann Christoph Gottsched in favor of the freer, subjective, and emotional forms of expression evident in the first of his odes.

LIFE'S WORK

After a year as a private tutor in a noble household in Langensalza, Klopstock traveled to Switzerland. He proposed to complete *The Messiah* while he was a houseguest of the Swiss poet Jakob Bodmer, who had translated *Paradise Lost* into German. A quarrel with Bodmer, who found him too worldly, shortened his stay. However, this event coincided with a fortuitous offer from King Frederick V of Denmark that gave Klopstock a refuge and a pension. During a stop in Hamburg on his way to Copenhagen, Klopstock met Margarethe Moller,

herself a gifted poet and letter writer, who became first the "Cidli" of his odes and in 1754 his wife. Their happy life together lasted only four years. In 1758, Margarethe Klopstock, together with her infant, died in childbirth. Klopstock tried to console himself by collecting her literary remains, which he published in 1759.

Except for a few trips to Germany, Klopstock remained in Denmark among his devoted Danish and German literary friends for twenty years. He continued work on *The Messiah*, publishing cantos 1 to 10 in unrhymed hexameter to great acclaim in 1755. His writing also appeared in a literary periodical called *Der nördlichen Aufseher* (the northern overseer). A biblical drama, *Der Tod Adams* (pb. 1757; *The Death of Adam*, 1763), followed. Klopstock did not abandon his favorite subjects, love, nature, friendship, and religion, but during the late 1750's and 1760's, influenced by his friend Heinrich Wilhelm von Gerstenberg and by James Macpherson's Ossian poems—*Fingal* (1762) and *Temora* (1763), collected as *The Works of Ossian, the Son of Fingal* (1765)—he developed an intense interest in early German poetry and in the Germanic past. This patriotic enthusiasm bore fruit in the first of his three bardic dramas, *Hermanns Schlacht* (pb. 1769; Herman's battle).

In 1770, when Klopstock's patron, count von Bernstorff, was dismissed from his post at the Danish court, Klopstock followed him to Hamburg. He remained there for the rest of his life, managing to continue to draw his Danish pension. In Hamburg, too, he was surrounded by friends and admirers. They encouraged him to bring out an authorized edition of his odes in 1771 to replace two unauthorized editions that had been printed a short time before. The next year, Klopstock published another biblical drama, *David* (pb. 1772).

Klopstock's *Die deutsche Gelehrtenrepublik* (1774; the German literary republic) put forward a plan that had originated in Klopstock's literary circle in Denmark for a German learned society inspired by the French Academy and the English Royal Society. In this work, Klopstock proposed a utopian community composed of practitioners of the arts and sciences, who would devote themselves to discovering, forming, and giving life to whatever was beautiful and useful. The book received a mixed reception. However, the young adherents of the Sturm und Drang (storm and stress) movement, Johann Wolfgang von Goethe among them, welcomed the work.

Die deutsche Gelehrtenrepublik also made a great impression on Margrave Karl Friedrich of Baden. Karl Friedrich invited Klopstock to visit and also bestowed on him the title of *Hofrat* (privy councillor) and a pension, which the poet collected in addition to his Danish pension for the rest of his life. On a side trip from Baden to Frankfurt, Klopstock met Goethe. Their brief friendship lasted until 1776, when Klopstock broke with Goethe because of the latter's alleged immoral conduct.

Back in Hamburg, Klopstock's interest in his own and others' poetry began to wane. However, he cultivated an interest in poetic diction, verse patterns, and language. He published several critical essays on these subjects in 1778 and 1779 and made two more forays into patriotic drama, *Hermann und die Fürsten* (pb. 1784; Hermann and the princes) and *Hermanns Tod* (pb. 1787; Hermann's death).

In 1791, at the age of sixty-seven, Klopstock married for a second time. His bride was Johanna Elisabeth von Winthem, a niece of his first wife. The union seems to have been a happy one. In the last decade of his life, Klopstock's literary production continued to diminish, both in quantity and in quality. In the early 1790's, he turned from poetry to philological studies, publishing *Grammatische Gespräche* (1794; grammatical conversations). However, admirers of his work, especially of his early writings, continued to increase among young German poets and even among literary people from foreign countries.

Klopstock's enthusiasm for liberty, equality, and fraternity brought him to the attention of the duke de la Rochefoucault, one of the early leaders of the French Revolution. In 1792, the French national assembly named Klopstock an honorary citizen. However, the Reign of Terror, which began the following year, filled him with disappointment and disgust and led him to reject the designation. In 1802, however, he accepted another honor from France, an invitation to be a foreign correspondent to the French National Institute.

Klopstock died in Hamburg on March 14, 1803. He was buried with much pomp and honor next to his first wife in the churchyard in suburban Ottensen.

SIGNIFICANCE

Although *The Messiah,* which occupied Klopstock for more than twenty-eight years, is his best-known work, his odes and other lyric poems written before 1780 are an important part of his place in German literature. In these poems, he turned away from the traditional subject matter, attitude, and form of German neoclassical poetry. Instead, he wrote on love, friendship, nature, and religious feeling. Rather than providing impersonal imitations of the classics, his poems concern the heartfelt experiences of an individual who is obviously often Klopstock himself. Expressing strong natural emotion in simple lively words was something new to German literature in the eighteenth century, as was Klopstock's insistence that thought, feeling, and language were inseparable. In the interests of authentic expression, Klopstock also experimented with various verse forms, among them free verse; in this, he greatly influenced the practice of German poets of the late eighteenth and early nineteenth centuries.

Klopstock was indebted to several English poets, among them Milton; Edward Young, whose *The Complaint: Or, Night Thoughts* (1742-1745) he much admired; and James MacPherson, whose *The Works of Ossian* was the inspiration for the Hermann trilogy and his bardic poems. Klopstock, in turn, was revered and imitated by young poets and writers of his own time, among them Johann Gottfried Herder, Friedrich Hölderlin, and Goethe, who praised his intensity, energy, openendedness, and imagination. His influence is still perceptible in the work of twentieth century poets who wrote in German, such as Rainer Maria Rilke and Stefan George.

—*Margaret Duggan*

Friedrich Gottlieb Klopstock. (Library of Congress)

FURTHER READING

Hilliard, Kevin. *Philosophy, Letters, and the Fine Arts in Klopstock's Thought*. London: Institute of Germanic Studies, University of London, 1987. Revision of Oxford University doctoral thesis on the influence of culture upon Klopstock. Bibliography.

Hilliard, Kevin, and Katrin Kohl, eds. *Klopstock an der Grenze der Epochen*. New York: W. de Gruyter, 1995. Essays on various aspects of Klopstock's work. Includes a bibliography of works written between 1972 and 1992, compiled by Helmut Riege.

Hurlebusch, Klaus. *Friedrich Gottlieb Klopstock*. Foreword by Helmut Schmidt. Hamburg: Ellert & Richter, 2003. Brief biography. Illustrated. Bibliographical references.

_____. *Klopstock, Hamann, und Herder als Wegbereiter autorzentrischen Schreibens*. Tübingen: Max Niemeyer Verlag, 2001. Concerned with Klopstock's contribution to literary modernity and, very briefly, with oral recitation or declamation of his poetry. Includes bibliography.

Klopstock, Friedrich Gottlieb. *Werke und Briefe: Historisch-kritische Ausgabe*. Edited by Adolf Beck et al. New York: W. de Gruyter, 1974- . Multivolume standard edition of Klopstock's works and letters. Each volume is accompanied by separate volume of commentary.

Kohl, Katrin. *Friedrich Gottlieb Klopstock*. Weimar: J. B. Metzler, 2000. Reviews recent criticism and research. Includes bibliography and index.

Kommerell, Max. *Der Dichter als Führer in der deutschen Klassik*. 3d ed. Preface by Eckhard Heftrich. Frankfurt, Germany: Vittorio Klostermann, 1982. First published in Berlin in 1928. Historical and critical treatment of Klopstock, Herder, Goethe, Schiller, Jean Paul, and Hölderlin. Lively and insightful.

Pape, Helmut. *Klopstock, Die "Sprache des Herzens" neu entdeckt*. Frankfurt, Germany: Peter Lang, 1998. Life-and-works approach. Claims that Klopstock freed the reader from emotional immaturity. Quotes texts to show Klopstock's influence on the language of his time and on new concepts of the nature of poetry and of poets. Bibliography.

See also: Johann Wolfgang von Goethe; Johann Gottfried Herder; Sophie von La Roche; Gotthold Ephraim Lessing; Friedrich Schiller.

Related articles in *Great Events from History: The Eighteenth Century, 1701-1800*: 1773: Goethe Inaugurates the Sturm und Drang Movement; 1784-1791: Herder Publishes His Philosophy of History.

TADEUSZ KOŚCIUSZKO
Polish military leader and engineer

Kościuszko played a major role in supporting the Continental army in its struggle with British forces during the American Revolution. His efforts led to the establishment of fortifications that allowed the Americans to withstand the British invasion. In Poland, he led a legendary albeit abortive uprising against Russian forces.

Born: February 4, 1746; Mereczowszczyzna, Poland (now in Belarus)

Died: October 15, 1817; Solothurn, Switzerland

Also known as: Tadeusz Andrzej Bonawentura Kościuszko (full name)

Areas of achievement: Military, warfare and conquest, government and politics

EARLY LIFE

Tadeusz Kościuszko (tah-DEH-ewsh kawsh-CHEWSH-kaw), second son of a minor Polish nobleman, was born on the family estate near Novorudok in 1746. Like most children of families of stature, he was educated at home before being sent to study with the Piarist fathers at Lubieszów. His father died in 1758, leaving an already impoverished estate open to plunder. His mother managed to hold things together for a decade before she died in 1768; the estate then passed to Kościuszko's elder brother, and for decades the two brothers had to ward off a series of creditors.

Shortly before his mother died, Kościuszko had managed to gain an appointment to the newly created Royal Military Academy in Warsaw, joining its inaugural class in 1765. There, he learned the military arts, including principles of engineering that would later allow him to achieve distinction in two countries. Upon graduation, he was commissioned a second lieutenant and assigned to the teach at the academy; shortly thereafter, he was promoted to captain and sent to France in 1769 for further study. At the French Academy of Painting and Sculpture, he improved his knowledge of art and drafting; at the same time, he sought private tutoring in mathematics, military science, and engineering.

When Kościuszko returned to Poland four years later, he discovered he had no future in a Polish uniform. The major powers that had traditionally dominated Polish affairs—France, Russia, Prussia, and Austria—had made it impossible for the Polish military to function effectively. Frustrated, he found work as a tutor, but in 1775 he decided to leave Poland. He went first to France and Germany, but in 1776 decided to go to America to seek a commission in the newly organized Continental army.

LIFE'S WORK

Kościuszko landed in America in the summer of 1776 to find a country badly in need of his engineering skills. Commissioned a colonel of engineers shortly after arriving, he quickly established a reputation as a skilled engineer by assisting the militia in Philadelphia to construct defenses for the city. There he worked briefly for General Horatio Gates, a key figure in the Continental army; the two struck up a lifelong friendship.

Kościuszko's first posting with the regular army was in the Northern Command at Fort Ticonderoga. His work on the defenses of this outpost led to criticism from officers who shared the ideas of French engineers regarding defensive fortifications. Throughout the War for American Independence, Kościuszko found himself at odds with French engineers, who had been sought by the Continental Congress to fill a void in the American army's expertise. Since the Congress found itself beholden to the French, the Polish officer was frequently passed over for promotion or preferential assignment in favor of the cadre of officers led by Louis du Portail, who was eventually promoted to brigadier general and made chief of engineers.

When the British drove the Americans from Ticonderoga, Kościuszko was reunited with his mentor General Gates, and he was instrumental in designing fortifications at Bemis Hill that led to the American victory at Saratoga in October, 1777. Following this victory, Kościuszko joined American troops assigned to fortify a spot on the Hudson River where they could control ship traffic and deny the British easy access through New York. For the next eighteen months, the Pole worked on a series of fortifications above the river at a strategic spot known as West Point. To maintain control of the river, he devised a series of connected outposts on the heights and stretched a great chain across the Hudson to prevent ships from passing either way. Although he applied on more than one occasion for transfer from this garrison

Tadeusz Kościuszko. (The Granger Collection, New York)

duty for assignment with troops in the field, General George Washington himself determined that Kościuszko's expertise was vital to operations at West Point and kept him there until 1780. He was released only by special request from General Gates, newly appointed to head the Continental army's Southern Command, who asked that Kościuszko be assigned as his chief engineer.

Although Gates did not remain in the south for long after the Americans' disastrous defeat at Camden, Kościuszko stayed on for two years, helping to fortify American positions and to design plans for storming British fortifications. For a brief time, he served with line troops, commanding several squadrons of cavalry on reconnaissance missions and raids. He was present at the Siege of Charleston, South Carolina, and was among the first to enter the city when the British evacuated.

Sadly for Kościuszko, the country that depended heavily on his services in war was not so quick to settle its debts with him when peace ensued. For two years, he remained in America attempting to get the back pay owed to him. In 1784, armed with an IOU for a portion of what was due him, he returned to Europe, making his way to Poland via Paris.

Kościuszko's homeland was once again in turmoil. The stirrings of democratic feeling among the populace were viewed with great skepticism by the outside nations that had for some time controlled events in Poland. When the Polish government was granted permission to reestablish a national army in 1789, Kościuszko was offered a commission as a major general. Relying on his experiences in America, he attempted to organize the army into a small standing force of professionals augmented by a civilian militia.

In 1791, emboldened by popular sentiment, the Poles adopted a constitution that promoted democracy and provided individual rights. Russian empress Catherine the Great objected, and, in 1792, she sent 100,000 Russian troops to quash what was in her view rebellious behavior. Under Kościuszko, the Polish army held the Russians at bay for some time. Eventually, however, Russia and her ally Prussia prevailed and further divided the country into spheres of influence that reduced independent Poland to a small area around Warsaw.

Kościuszko was forced to flee Poland; he spent the next two years in exile, plotting a return and rebellion that eventually came to fruition in early 1794. Unfortunately, Kościuszko found the tasks of leading an army in the field and simultaneously establishing a new government too much to handle. Although his personal bravery assisted the Poles in winning an important battle at Racławice in the spring of 1794, eventually his forces were defeated at Maciejowice in October of that year. To punish the Poles, Russia and Prussia partitioned the country even further, virtually wiping it off the map.

Kościuszko was wounded seriously at Maciejowice, taken prisoner, and sent to Russia, where he was imprisoned for two years. Paroled by the czar on the promise that he would lead no more rebellions, Kościuszko spent most of the remainder of his life in exile from Poland, eventually taking up residence in Solothurn, Switzerland, where he died of influenza in 1817.

SIGNIFICANCE

Tadeusz Kościuszko's work with the Continental army and his leadership in Poland near the end of the century earned him a place in the annals of both countries. His engineering prowess not only provided significant assistance to the Continental army but also established for the United States a fortress on the Hudson River that would one day become home to the world's foremost military academy. In Poland, his selfless service to the nation and his fierce commitment to individual liberty and democ-

racy inspired his people even when their efforts to achieve independence failed. The memory of his ill-fated revolt passed into the lore of the Polish people and was used over the next two hundred years as a rallying cry by groups struggling against foreign powers to gain independence for the nation.

—Laurence W. Mazzeno

FURTHER READING

Gardner, Monica M. *Kosciuszko: A Biography*. Rev. ed. New York: W. W. Norton, 1943. The first modern scholarly study of Kościuszko, Gardner's brief biographical sketch is a good introduction to the major events of his life; Gardner also offers insight into his contributions to the United States and Poland.

Haiman, Miecislaus. *Kosciuszko in the American Revolution*. New York: Polish Institute of the Arts and Sciences in America, 1943. Although somewhat biased in favor of his subject, Haiman examines the role Kościuszko played in assisting colonial forces in defeating the British in both the Northern and Southern theaters of operations during the American Revolution.

_____. *Kosciuszko: Leader and Exile*. New York: Polish Institute of the Arts and Sciences in America, 1946. In the second volume of his biography of the Polish soldier, Haiman describes his role in the 1794 uprising in Poland and his life in exile following the defeat of the rebels.

Lukowski, Jerry, and Hubert Zawadski. *A Concise History of Poland*. New York: Cambridge University Press, 2001. The authors place the story of the 1794 rebellion in which Kościuszko played a significant role in the larger context of Polish history.

Pula, James S. *Thaddeus Koskiuszko: The Purest Son of Liberty*. New York: Hippocrene Books, 1999. Pula offers a thoroughly researched account of Kościuszko's life, detailing his contributions to both the American colonies' struggle for freedom and the ill-fated 1794 rebellion in his native Poland.

See also: Catherine the Great; George Washington.

IGNACY KRASICKI
Polish writer and cleric

Poland's foremost Enlightenment author, Krasicki wrote an impressive range of works, including the first Polish novel, that introduced Western European neoclassical influences into his country and added to the Age of Reason's debates on such fundamental issues as education, public duty, and utopian society.

Born: February 3, 1735; Dubiecko, Poland
Died: March 14, 1801; Potsdam, Prussia (now in Germany)
Also known as: Ignatius Krasicki
Areas of achievement: Literature, religion and theology

EARLY LIFE

Born into a family of landed gentry with no wealth but with impressive social connections, Ignacy Krasicki (eeg-NAHT-sih krah-SEETS-kee) grew up on an estate in southern Poland. He early chose a life in the Church over the only other profession then considered acceptable for a gentleman—the army. At the age of eight, therefore, Krasicki entered the Jesuit College in Lvov, where he studied until 1750. The next stage in his training was three years at the Catholic Seminary in Warsaw. In 1751, he was ordained. He rounded out his theological studies with a sojourn in Rome and Vienna from 1759 to 1761.

LIFE'S WORK

Krasicki was remarkable not only in combining a brilliant career in the clergy with success as a writer but also in enjoying the patronage of both Stanisław II Augustus Poniatowski (r. 1764-1795), the Polish king, and Frederick the Great, the king of Prussia, whose country joined Russia and Austria in partitioning Poland as spoils in 1772. It was Stanisław II who paved the way for Krasicki's achievements in both literature and the Church. In 1764, after being elected to the throne, he invited Krasicki to edit a recently established literary journal modeled on Addison and Steele's *Tatler* and *Spectator* (1709-1711). *The Monitor*, which Stanisław hoped to use as a vehicle for his projected reforms, was Krasicki's first public venue for his urbane moralizing about society's ills.

The young priest also became Stanisław's chaplain and adviser and served on his commission for national education. Krasicki supported Stanisław's efforts to create a flourishing national theater by writing drama criti-

cism, as well as eight comedies heavily indebted to Molière. Two years later, Krasicki, then only thirty-two, was made bishop of Warmia (Ermeland), a northeastern region near the Prussian border that had long been colonized by both Poles and Prussians. In 1768, he gave up his long-distance editorship of *The Monitor* but continued to contribute translations and essays—so much so that in 1772, the year of the partition, the entire journal was devoted to his writings. Despite such commitment to the publication, however, Krasicki became a Prussian subject after the partition and did not return to Poland for almost a decade.

Krasicki's first major original work was a mock-heroic epic called *Myszeis* (1775; the mouseiad), in which wit, linguistic skill, and old Polish legends about a king eaten by mice combined with neoclassical lucidity and proportion to excellent effect. His second mock-epic poem elicited stronger and more negative responses: *Monachomachia* (1778; the war of the monks) was a gently Horatian satire of superstition, institutional tyranny, and the ignorance, drunkenness, and other failings of monks in a small town. Already provocative as an anticlerical work by a bishop, *Monachomachia* also offended Polish patriots as a literary tribute to the Prussian king (whom Krasicki served as an adviser, considered a friend, and praised in personal letters). Eventually, Krasicki replied to his critics by writing *Antimonachomachia* (1780; the antiwar of the monks 1780), although this was more a sequel than a retraction.

Krasicki followed up the *Monachomachia* with *Satyry* (1779; satires), focusing his criticisms on the wealthy and the powerful. He continued his attack on such follies as drunkenness, hypocrisy, and cruelty to underlings, but he added the innovation of using far more irony than any of his literary predecessors. It is *Bajki i przypowieści* (1779; fables and parables; partial translation in *Polish Fables*, 1997), however, that most regard as his crowning achievement in poetry—perhaps because this collection proved the truth of his claim, "Witty fables are the most perfect aim of poetry." While drawing on Aesop, Jean de La Fontaine, and even some eastern fables for material, Krasicki managed to give an original Polish flavor to his poems relaying wisdom through familiar subjects. He depicted a rather harsh world—where the strong and wise survive, while the weak and foolish perish—in impeccably concise, simple prose that is simultaneously dramatic and elegant.

567

Although his contemporaries dubbed him Prince of Poets, Krasicki likewise left his mark on Polish prose. Indeed, he produced what is essentially the first Polish novel, *Mikołaja Doświadczyńskiego przypadki* (1776; *The Adventures of Mr. Nicsholas Wisdom*, 1992). This picaresque tale of a youth's wanderings and visit to a utopian island was clearly indebted to such Western models as Daniel Defoe's *Robinson Crusoe* (1719), Jonathan Swift's *Gulliver's Travels* (1726), Voltaire's philosophical tales, and Jean-Jacques Rousseau's *Émile: Ou, De l'éducation* (1762; *Emilius and Sophia: Or, A New System of Education*, 1762-1763) and *Du contrat social: Ou, Principes du droit politique* (1762; *A Treatise on the Social Contract: Or, The Principles of Politic Law*, 1764).

More obviously Swiftian was Krasicki's *Historia* (1779; story), in which a narrator called Grumdypp—after a Luggnagg immortal from *Gulliver's Travels*—recounts his travels to past civilizations, always reserving his highest praise not for their rulers and soldiers but for their educators, philosophers, scientists, and lawmakers. Between these two novels came *Pan Podstoli* (1778-1784; Mr. Pantler), a work loosely structured around conversations on such ethical and social issues as education, farming, and civic duties. A valuable historical resource, *Pan Podstoli* is encyclopedic in its descriptions of late eighteenth century life among the gentry.

Over the years, alongside the prestige he gained as cleric, writer, and friend of kings, Krasicki enjoyed the humbler pleasures of collecting rare books, gardening, and sampling fancy jams and wines. In 1794, the various honors Frederick the Great had conferred on him—including the Orders of the White Eagle and of Saint Stanisław—culminated in the archbishopric of Gniezno (Gnesen). Krasicki died at the age of sixty-six in Potsdam, near Berlin, in 1801. His *Bajki nowe* (1803; new fables; partial translation in *Polish Fables*, 1997) was published posthumously in 1803.

SIGNIFICANCE

Poland's foremost eighteenth century poet, the learned and cosmopolitan Ignacy Krasicki was an exemplar of Enlightenment reason and moderation in his life as well as in his works. The same detachment, good will, and humor that characterized his writings kept him from patriotic fervor and made him as valuable a courtier to Frederick as to Stanisław II. Similarly, although he used his writings to urge the gentry into taking moral responsibility for improving their peasants' lives, Krasicki never questioned the institution of serfdom itself or advocated radical reform.

By emulating such towering predecessors as Voltaire, Molière, Swift, and Alexander Pope in the many genres that he tackled—critical essays, satire, mock-heroic verse, history, comic plays, fables, novels—Krasicki almost single-handedly enabled Poland to catch up with the West's high literary achievements in the Age of Reason. Although his moralizing accorded well with his religious vocation, his didacticism certainly sprang as much from his neoclassical devotion to improving humankind through reason and mockery as from his own clerical identity. Less acerbic than Voltaire, he nevertheless shared the French author's belief that the writer should "teach with a smile."

Like his Western counterparts of the same century, Krasicki displaced the Baroque era's linguistic intricacy with vigorous and elegant simplicity, especially in his poetry and most of all in *Bajki i przypowieści*. He continued to demonstrate that he was a consummate stylist in his best-known prose work, *The Adventures of Mr. Nicholas Wisdom*, which is a testimony to the Enlightenment's love of symmetry, concentrated but pellucid language, and confident plainness in the service of moral instruction.

—*Margaret Bozenna Goscilo*

FURTHER READING

Goscilo, Helena. "Introduction." *The Adventures of Mr. Nicholas Wisdom*, by Ignacy Krasicki. Translated by Thomas H. Hoisington. Evanston, Ill.: Northwestern University Press, 1992. A comprehensive introduction, relating Krasicki's novel to Enlightenment values and to a range of Western counterparts, which manages despite its brevity to pinpoint neatly the first Polish novel's place in European literature.

Krzyżanowski, Julian. "Bishop of Warmia." In *A History of Polish Literature*, translated by Doris Ronowicz. Warsaw: PWN-Polish Scientific, 1978. A balanced appraisal of Krasicki's literary output that considers the author's temperament as well as his genial literary persona.

Miłosz, Czesław. "Ignacy Krasicki." In *The History of Polish Literature*. Los Angeles: University of California Press, 1983. Focuses on Krasicki's success in stamping traditional forms with a distinctly Polish identity and credits him with introducing the novel of customs and manners into his national literature.

Welsh, David J. *Ignacy Krasicki*. New York: Twayne, 1969. Still the only full-length study in English, this monograph offers a detailed analysis of Krasicki's complete writings, with separate chapters not just on each major work but also on such lesser publications as his personal letters, his Horatian *Epistles,* and his now-unperformed comedies. Welsh discusses Krasicki's oeuvre within the framework of Western traditions while also linking it to the achievements of his Polish contemporaries and successors.

See also: Joseph Addison; Daniel Defoe; Frederick the Great; Alexander Pope; Jean-Jacques Rousseau; Richard Steele; Jonathan Swift; Voltaire.

Related articles in *Great Events from History: The Eighteenth Century, 1701-1800*: March 1, 1711: Addison and Steele Establish *The Spectator*; April 25, 1719: Defoe Publishes the First Novel; 1726: Swift Satirizes English Rule of Ireland in *Gulliver's Travels*; 1740-1741: Richardson's *Pamela* Establishes the Modern Novel; May 31, 1740: Accession of Frederick the Great; 1742: Fielding's *Joseph Andrews* Satirizes English Society; January, 1759: Voltaire Satirizes Optimism in *Candide*; April, 1762: Rousseau Publishes *The Social Contract*; August 5, 1772-October 24, 1795: Partitioning of Poland.

MIKHAIL ILLARIONOVICH KUTUZOV
Russian military leader

An innovative Russian military commander, Kutuzov is best known for defeating Napoleon during the French invasion of Russia in 1812 after having lost to him at Austerlitz in 1805.

Born: September 16, 1745; St. Petersburg, Russia
Died: April 28, 1813; Bunzlau, Silesia (now Bolesławiec, Poland)
Also known as: Mikhail Illarionovich Golenishchev-Kutuzov (birth name)
Areas of achievement: Warfare and conquest, military

EARLY LIFE
Born in St. Petersburg, Russia's capital and "Window on the West," Mikhail Illarionovich Kutuzov (myihkh-uh-EEL ihl-uhr-YAWN-uhv-yihch kew-TEW-zuhf) was the son of Illarion Matveevich Kutuzov, a lieutenant general of the army corps of engineers who had married well and enjoyed the Empress Elizabeth Petrovna's patronage. Following his mother's early death, young Mikhail was raised in the country by his maternal grandmother but eventually spent time at his father's house in the capital, where he acquired the social graces necessary to function among the high nobility.

At age twelve, Kutuzov was sent to military engineering school, where he compiled a stellar academic record. By 1761, he attained the rank of ensign and entered military service. Promoted to captain in 1762, he was posted to Astrakhan, serving under Colonel Aleksandr Vasilyevich Suvorov, who would become Russia's most revered military leader. Later the same year, Kutuzov was transferred to Reval to serve as aide-de-camp to the Estonian military governor. An accomplished horseman, Kutuzov first saw action in cavalry sorties against Polish patriots in 1768.

In 1770, Kutuzov, now a major, moved south to serve with Count Pyotr Rumyantsev's army against the Turks near Bucharest. Although he distinguished himself in battle and earned a position on the count's staff, he was transferred in disgrace in 1772 for mimicking his commander. Thereafter, Kutuzov would be less open and trusting and more prone to suspicion and keeping his own counsel. His subsequent service with the Second Army in the Crimea introduced him to operational service with the Cossacks. Nearly fatally wounded near the eye during an assault on Alushta in 1773, he returned to St. Petersburg for convalescence. (After sustaining a nearly identical wound years later, he would retain his sight but suffer recurring bouts of pain and display a disfiguring scar for the rest of his life.) In 1774, Kutuzov began a tour of Western Europe in search of medical help. Over the following two years, he traveled in Prussia, Holland, Britain, Austria, and Italy. In London, he developed an interest in the American Revolution, especially George Washington's later leadership of the Continental army.

In 1776, Kutuzov returned to the Crimea, once again serving under Suvorov. From Rumyantsev, he had learned the importance of maneuvering his army to avoid unfavorable conditions for battle and of even being willing to retreat to gain an advantage. From Suvorov, he would gain a deep respect for the bravery and endurance of the Russian soldier, learn the necessity of leading by example, and cultivate a commonsense approach to training and managing his army. During his decade in the Crimea, Kutuzov was promoted to brigadier general (1782) and married Ekaterina Il'inichna Bibikova, with whom he had five daughters and one son who died prematurely. Renewed hostilities took his unit to the Turkish border in 1787. In 1790, Kutuzov won commendations and a promotion to lieutenant general following his heroism in the storming of the stronghold of Ismail, of which Suvorov appointed him commandant.

Between 1792 and 1802, Kutuzov served Russia as a diplomat or administrator in Poland, Istanbul, Berlin (where he acquired an appreciation of the superiority of the new French battle tactics and of the backwardness of the Prussian military), Vilna (where he served as governor-general), and St. Petersburg (also as governor-general). In this last post, he was implicated in the assassination of Paul III, the "Mad Czar," and exiled from the capital by the new czar, Alexander I. After three years on his estates, Alexander recalled Kutuzov to assume command of the Russian forces in the War of the Third Coalition (August, 1805).

LIFE'S WORK

Despite a notable career to 1805, the world knows Kutuzov as the opponent of Napoleon I. The highly influential Prussian military theorist Carl von Clausewitz, an observer in Kutuzov's army, declared that "the wily Kutuzov was [Napoleon's] most dangerous adversary." In their two main encounters, Kutuzov was able to utilize the lessons learned from Rumyantsev and Suvorov to good effect, always concentrating on maneuvering and preserving his army rather than rashly committing it to possible destruction.

During the 1805 campaign, the Russians and Austrians combined forces near the Danube River for an assault on the Rhine region as the southern arm of a giant pincer designed to wrest Germany from French control. Napoleon, having concentrated the French Grand Army in Boulogne, France, in preparation for an invasion of England, was supposed to be caught off guard. The Austrians under Baron Karl Mack von Leiberich proceeded westward too rapidly, however, and the Russians never caught up. Napoleon discovered the plan and, with fabled speed, caught the Austrians in a trap near Ulm on the Danube River and forced their surrender.

Kutuzov now stood between Napoleon and Vienna, awaiting reinforcements from Russia. Despite political pressure to shield Vienna, he maneuvered his army north and eastward away from it, using tributaries of the Danube River as obstacles to the pursuing French vanguard. Though Kutuzov knew that this would doom Vienna, it would also overextend French supply and communication lines and increase the likelihood of Russian reinforcement. He feigned a stand at St. Polten and gained

additional time by making the French commander believe an armistice had been signed. Enraged at the ruse, General Joachim Murat furiously attacked the Russian rear at Schöngraben, but Kutuzov's strategic withdrawal continued. Finally, the Austrian and Russian emperors intervened and forced Kutuzov to engage Napoleon near Austerlitz.

Both overall command and the plan of battle were Austrian, however, and Kutuzov, in his customary plain gray tunic and battered peaked hat, commanded only the center. Rankling at the subordination, he nonetheless chose to stay with his troops for the sake of morale; he often referred to them as his "children" and never shirked his responsibility to them. In the ensuing battle on December 2, 1805, the French annihilated the allied army of ninety-five thousand men, inflicting thirty thousand casualties. Perhaps Kutuzov's principal achievement was his management of the orderly withdrawal of the Russian units under his command.

Understandably, if not justifiably, Kutuzov was passed over for the Russian command during the Prussian-French War and remained in Kiev until the spring of 1807. He then returned to garrison duty along the Turkish front, serving under the unstable and extremely suspicious Prince Prozorovski. Suspected of intrigue, Kutuzov was removed to Vilna in 1809 to serve as the military governor of the Lithuanian province. Meanwhile, the French stepped up operations in the east, and the Turks once again became restive, while Alexander strengthened his western armies.

Kutuzov returned to the Turkish frontier in March, 1811, with orders to strike a swift and decisive blow. He gathered scattered garrison units into an army at Rustchuk and countered a Turkish attack. Waiting until the Turks split their forces while crossing the Danube in late September, Kutuzov surrounded and besieged their army of fifty thousand men. Despite demands for action by Alexander, Kutuzov refused to attack and only lifted the siege in May with the signing of the Treaty of Bucharest. Although rewarded with the title "most illustrious Prince," Kutuzov had incurred Alexander's displeasure and was sent to Vilna, a fine vantage point from which to view the growing French menace to the Russian frontier.

On June 23, 1812, France's army crossed the Nieman River, headed for Smolensk and Moscow. Mikhail Barclay de Tolly commanded the Russian army while Kutuzov recruited and trained men for the campaign. Barclay proved indecisive and ineffective, but Alexander's disdain for Kutuzov delayed his appointment as Barclay's replacement until Napoleon had captured

Smolensk in mid-August. Although Kutuzov suffered from rheumatism, corpulence, and severe headaches, he was extremely popular with both civilians and the military. The army's morale, if not its fortunes, soon rose, and leaders now expected a fight. Under Barclay, the first and second armies had lost one-quarter of their men, and Kutuzov had received only fifteen thousand of a requested eighty-thousand-man reserve when he began to deploy near Borodino on September 3, 1812.

Napoleon faced the Russian army of 128,000 men and 640 cannon with 130,000 men and 587 guns of his own. Initial clashes on September 5 cost each side five thousand casualties. Napoleon used September 6 to prepare for his assault on the Russian redoubts—well-chosen and heavily fortified positions from which the Russians could inflict heavy losses. Typically pragmatic, Kutuzov's idea of preparation for battle was a good night's rest for all. The next day, as the French assault slowly forced the Russian lines back, both commanders seemed detached and lost in their own thoughts; Kutuzov was accused of lethargy and apathy by his enemies. Whatever his mental state, he refused to abandon the field of battle and at day's end dressed his line where his baggage train had been posted earlier. He declared victory and prepared to fight again, a ploy that heightened his men's morale and convinced them of their success.

His declaration also encouraged the Muscovites. At the council of war (September 13) held at Fili on the outskirts of Moscow, however, Kutuzov decided to abandon the capital: "The loss of Moscow is not the loss of Russia. My first obligation is to preserve the army." He would retreat through Moscow to draw the French forces into the city, then withdraw to the southeast toward Ryazan. Though neither "scorched earth" nor the burning of Moscow were Kutuzov's ideas, his armies benefited from both, which deprived Napoleon of badly needed supplies.

The Russian withdrawal to the southeast turned abruptly westward after reaching Bronniski, south of the Pakra River. Murat's pursuing cavalry, however, was shielded from this maneuver and led farther south, while Kutuzov headed west and then southwest to Tarutino, fifty miles southwest of Moscow. This strategic point allowed him to block French movement to southern supply depots in Kaluga and Tula and placed him in a position to intercept or harry a French retreat westward. He was also able to consolidate and augment his forces (from 85,000 to 120,000) and organize partisan detachments that would prove brutally effective.

On October 18, Kutuzov attacked Murat at Chernishna, west of Tarutino, which brought the French

Grand Army out of Moscow. Napoleon decided to strike toward Kaluga, a potential gateway to Russia's southwestern agricultural heartland, but was checked in a furious battle at Maloyaroslavets on October 24. The next day he decided to abandon his invasion and retreat westward along the Moscow-Smolensk road. Kutuzov had his army shadow the French along their horrific winter exodus. Though he planned several major attacks on the bedraggled columns, only minor actions resulted.

Kutuzov continued into Prussia on January 9, 1813, and was named commander of the Russian-Prussian coalition army at a meeting at Kalisch. Soon attacked by cold and fever, he died in Bunzlau on April 28 and was interred in St. Petersburg's Kazan Cathedral.

Significance

Mikhail Illarionovich Kutuzov was considered by Russian poet Alexander Pushkin to have been the "Savior of Russia," and many Russians would agree. Though he enjoyed high company, he eschewed military glory, preferring patience to rashness and striking when he held the advantage. Though Czar Alexander disdained him, Kutuzov's men knew that he understood them, and they proved fiercely loyal. Such loyalty was vital in the aftermaths of Austerlitz and Borodino and during the abandonment of Moscow. "General Winter" indeed battered the remnants of the Grand Army, but only because Kutuzov's Tarutino maneuver cut it off from the resources of the south. Kutuzov always considered retention of the integrity of his army more important than victory in battle, a philosophy that served him well in the Patriotic War of 1812.

—Joseph P. Byrne

Further Reading

Austin, Paul Britten. *1812: Napoleon in Moscow*. Mechanicsburg, Pa.: Stackpole Books, 1995. Scholarly, well-researched account of Napoleon's Russian campaign, including information about Kutuzov. Austin has written two other books about Napoleon's military experiences in Russia: *1812: The Great Retreat* (1996) and *1815: The Return of Napoleon* (2002).

Duffy, Christopher. *Austerlitz 1805*. London: Seeley Service, 1977. Detailed military history of the Austerlitz campaign with maps and illustrations.

_____. *Borodino: Napoleon Against Russia, 1812*. London: Seeley Service, 1972. Excellent account of the battle, including aftermath. Nicely illustrated.

Palmer, Alan. *Napoleon in Russia*. New York: Simon and Schuster, 1967. Standard military history of the

1812 campaign that balances French and Russian viewpoints. Includes excellent notes on sources.

Parkinson, Roger. *The Fox of the North: The Life of Kutuzov, General of War and Peace*. Abingdon, England: Purnell, 1976. The only critical full biography in English of Kutuzov, it places him firmly in the context of his time while giving him the benefit of every doubt.

Tolstoy, Leo. *War and Peace*. New York: Penguin Classics, 1996. This great novel is the only introduction most have to Kutuzov; a portrayal firmly grounded in reality and colored by Tolstoy's admiration.

Zamoyski, Adam. *1812: Napoleon's Fatal March on Moscow*. London: HarperCollins, 2004. A detailed, well-balanced, and thoroughly researched account of Napoleon's Russian campaign. Chapter 12, "Kutuzov," focuses on the Russian military commander, but there is information about Kutuzov throughout the book.

See also: Elizabeth Petrovna; Aleksandr Vasilyevich Suvorov; George Washington.

Related articles in *Great Events from History: The Eighteenth Century, 1701-1800*: October, 1768-January 9, 1792: Ottoman Wars with Russia; 1788-September, 1809: Russo-Swedish Wars; November 9-10, 1799: Napoleon Rises to Power in France.

JOSEPH-LOUIS LAGRANGE
French mathematician

One of the most brilliant mathematicians of the mid- to late eighteenth century, Lagrange accomplished astonishing syntheses of the mathematical innovations of his predecessors, especially in the systems underlying classic physics. Almost as remarkable for his winning personality as for his incisive intellect, Lagrange created the mathematical basis of modern mechanics.

Born: January 25, 1736; Turin, Sardinia (now in Italy)
Died: April 10, 1813; Paris, France
Also known as: Giuseppe Luigi Lagrangia (birth name); Comte de l'Empire
Area of achievement: Mathematics

EARLY LIFE

Born in what was then the kingdom of Sardinia of mixed French and Italian though predominantly French descent, Joseph-Louis Lagrange (zhoh-zehf-lwee lah-grahnzh) was the first son in an influential and wealthy family. His father, however, once a highly placed cabinet official, burned with the speculative fevers of the early eighteenth century and ended by losing everything. Typically, Lagrange took that in stride, remarking later that losing his inheritance forced him to find a profession; he chose wisely. Although early in his formal education he found mathematics boring, probably because it began with geometry, at age fourteen he chanced on an essay by the astronomer Edmond Halley, which changed his mind, and his life. In this essay, Halley, one of Isaac Newton's disciples, proclaimed the superiority of the new analytical methods of calculus to the old synthetic geometry. From that moment, Lagrange devoted as much time as he could to the new science, becoming a professor of mathematics at the Royal Artillery School in Turin before the age of eighteen.

From the beginning, Lagrange specialized in analysis, starting the trend toward specialization that has since characterized the study of mathematics. His concentration on analytical methods also liberated the discipline for the first time from its dependence on Greek geometry. In fact, of his major work, *Mécanique analytique* (analytical mechanics), first conceived when he was nineteen but not published until 1788, he boasted that it contained not a single diagram. He then stated offhandedly that in the future the physics of mechanics might be approached as a geometry of four dimensions, the three familar Cartesian coordinates combined with a time coordinate; in such a system, a moving particle could be de-fined in time and space simultaneously. This system of analyzing mechanics reemerged in 1916, when Albert Einstein employed it to explain his general theory of relativity.

From the ages of nineteen to twenty-three, Lagrange continued as a professor at Turin, producing a number of revolutionary studies in the calculus of variations, analysis of mechanics, theory of sound, celestial mechanics, and probability theory, for which he won a number of international prizes and honors. In 1766, he succeeded Leonhard Euler as court mathematician to Frederick the Great in the Berlin Academy, the most prestigious position of the time. There, freed from lecturing duties, he continued to produce epochal studies in celestial mechanics, number theory, Diophantine analysis, and numerical and literal equations. He also found it possible to marry a younger cousin; the marriage was successful, and Lagrange was later devastated when his wife died of a wasting disease. Characteristically, he tried to overcome his grief by losing himself in his work.

LIFE'S WORK

For most of Lagrange's life, overwork was a habit. Yet it enabled him to achieve much at an early age. At twenty-three, Lagrange wrote an article on the calculus of variations, in which he foreshadowed his later unifying theory on the whole of mechanics, both solids and fluids. This integrated general mechanics in much the same way that Newton's law of gravitation unified celestial motion. Lagrange's theory proceeds from the disarmingly simple observation that all physical force is identical, whether operating in the solid or liquid state, whether aural, visual, or mechanical. It thus integrates a diverse array of physical phenomena, simplifying their study. In the same work, Lagrange applied differential calculus to the theory of probability. He also surpassed Newton by absorbing the mathematical theory of sound into the theory of elastic physical particles, becoming the first to understand sound transmission as straight-line projection through adjacent particles. Furthermore, he put to rest a controversy over the proper mathematical description of a vibrating string, laying the basis of the more general theory of vibrations as a whole. At this early age, Lagrange already ranked with the giants of his age, Euler and the Bernoulli family.

The next problems Lagrange attacked at Turin were those involved in the libration of the Moon in celestial mechanics: Why does the Moon present the same surface to the Earth at every point in its revolution? He deduced the answer to this special instance of the three-body problem, a classic in mechanics, from Newton's law of universal gravitation. For solving this problem, Lagrange won the Grand Prix of the French Academy in 1764. The academy followed by proposing a four-body problem; Lagrange solved this, winning the prize again in 1766. The academy then proposed a six-body problem involving calculating the relative position of the Sun, Jupiter, and its four then-known satellites. This problem was not completely solvable by modern methods before the development of computers. Nevertheless, Lagrange developed methods of approximation that were superseded only in the twentieth century. After his move to Berlin, for further work on similar problems— the general three-body problem, the motion of the Moon, and cometary disturbances—Lagrange won further awards.

His career in Berlin lasted twenty years; during this career, he distinguished himself by unfailing courtesy, generosity to other mathematicians, and diplomacy in difficult situations—he was a stranger in a strange court, but he thrived. In addition to working on celestial me-

Joseph-Louis Lagrange. (Library of Congress)

chanics there, he diverted himself by investigations into number theory, the humble matter of what his age considered higher arithmetic. Quadratic forms and Diophantine analysis—exponential equations—particularly interested him: He first solved the problem of determining for which square numbers x^2, $nx^2 + 1$ is also a square, when n is a nonsquare, for example, $n = 3$, $x = 4$. This problem was an ancient one; Lagrange's paper is a classic, couched in his elegant language and supported by his equally elegant reasoning. He followed this by offering the first successful proofs of some of Pierre de Fermat's theorems and the one of John Wilson that states that only prime numbers are factors of the sum of the factorial series of the next lowest number plus one—that is, p divides $(p - 1)(p - 2)\cdots3 \cdot 2 \cdot 1 + 1$ only if it is prime. His most famous proof in number theory shows that every positive integer can be represented as a sum of four integral squares—a theorem that has had extensive applications in many scientific fields. He later did great work— which proved preliminary—on quadratic equations in two unknowns.

Perhaps the most important work of the Berlin period, however, relates to Lagrange's work in modern algebra. In a memoir of 1767 and in later sequels, he investigated the theoretical bases for solving various algebraic equations. Though once again he fell short of providing definitive answers, his work became an invaluable source for the nineteenth century algebraists who succeeded in finding them. The essential principles—that both necessary and sufficient conditions be established before solution—eluded him, but his work contained the clue.

Eventually, Lagrange's propensity for work broke both his body and his spirit. By 1783, he had sunk into a profound depression, in the grip of which he found further work in mathematics impossible. When Frederick died in 1786 and Lagrange fell out of favor in Berlin, he willingly accepted a position with the French Academy. Still, a change of scene brought no renewal of his interest in mathematics. When his monumental *Mécanique analytique* was published in 1788, Lagrange took no notice of it, leaving a copy unopened on his desk for more than two years. Instead, he turned his attention to various other sciences and the humanities.

It took the French Revolution to reawaken Lagrange's interest in mathematics. Although he could have fled, as many aristocratic scholars did, he did not. The atrocities of the Terror appalled Lagrange, and he had little sympathy with the destructive practices of revolutionary zealots. Yet when appointed to the faculties of the new schools—the École Normale and the École Poly-technique—intended to replace the abolished universities and academies, Lagrange took up his professional duties enthusiastically. Because he became aware of the difficulties his basically unprepared students had with the theoretical bases of calculus, he reformulated the theory to make it independent of concepts of infinitesimals and limits. His attempt was unsuccessful, but he prepared the foundation on which modern theories are built.

Part of his duties at the École Polytechnique required Lagrange to supervise the development of the metric system of weights and measures. Fortunately, he insisted that the base 10 be adopted. Radical reformers lobbied for base 12, alleging superior factorability; it is still occasionally proposed as more "rational," and for centuries it played an infernal role in the British monetary system. To suppress the reformers, Lagrange argued ironically for the advantages of a system with base 11, or any prime, since then all fractions would have the same denominator. A small amount of practice convinced the radicals that 10 was more functional.

Teaching and supervision alone, however, did not suffice to relieve Lagrange's besetting melancholy. He was saved from despair at the age of fifty-six, by the intervention of a young woman, the daughter of his friend the astronomer Pierre-Charles Lemonnier. She insisted on marrying him despite their disparity in age, and, contrary to all expectations, the marriage proved a brilliant success. For the following twenty years, Lagrange could not bear to have her out of his sight, and she proved to be a faithful companion, adept at drawing him out of his shell. At the end of his life, he worked on a second edition of his masterpiece, *Mécanique analytique*, adding many profound insights. He was still improving it when death came, gradually and almost imperceptibly, on April 10, 1813.

SIGNIFICANCE

Joseph-Louis Lagrange ranks with the outstanding mathematicians of all time; in his prime, he was widely recognized as the greatest living mathematician, and he is certainly the most significant figure between Euler and Carl Friedrich Gauss. Beyond the quality of his work, he was noted equally for the brilliance of his demonstrations and for his accessibility and personal charm. He is particularly celebrated as one of the classic stylists of mathematical writing, almost the incarnation of mathematical elegance. His composition combines exceptional clarity of description and development with remarkable beauty of phrasing. His language is supple, never stilted or contorted; he somehow seems to ease the effort of strenuous thought. Lagrange once remarked that chemistry was as easy as algebra; in his writing, he is able to make things seem transparent, especially those which seemed particularly dense before reading him.

Perhaps because of this ease of expression, Lagrange is more important for the stimulus he provided for others than for his own original work. Time after time, his contemporaries and descendants found inspiration in him. He made his foundations so complete that others were able to apply them to other cases. In some instances, he was simply ahead of his time; his ideas have had to wait for the ground to be prepared. At any rate, Lagrange's work proved to be extraordinarily rich for those who labored after him.

Lagrange's most important contributions lie in mechanics and the calculus of variations. In fact, the latter is the centerpiece on which all of his achievements depend, the insight he used to integrate the theory of mechanics. This calculus derives from the ancient principle of least action or least time, which concerns the determination of the path a beam of light will follow when passing through or refracting off layers of varying densities. Hero of Alexandria began the inquiry by determining that a beam reflected from a series of mirrors reaches its object by following the shortest possible route; that is, it is the minimum of a function. René Descartes elaborated on the theory by experimenting with the effects of various lenses on a ray of light, showing that refraction also produced minima. Lagrange then proceeded to demonstrate that the general postulates for matter and motion established by Newton, which did not seem to harmonize, also fit this scheme of minima. Thus, he used a principle of economy in nature—that physical mechanics also tended to minimal extremes—to unify the principles of particles in motion. This not only was revolutionary in his time but also gave rise to the further integrating work of William Rowan Hamilton and James Clerk Maxwell, and eventually blossomed in Einstein's general theory of relativity.

—James Livingston

FURTHER READING

Bell, Eric T. *Men of Mathematics*. New York: Simon & Schuster, 1937. Bell's work is famous for three features: readability, accessibility to the general reader, and general historical background. This is the preferred reference work, though Bell does not provide the technical detail of other sources.

Burton, David M. *The History of Mathematics: An Introduction*. Newton, Mass.: Allyn & Bacon, 1985. Burton's book has some very attractive features, especially the examples and practical exercises in real mathematics. However, readers should be aware that his focus is on major developments and broad concepts, so his treatment of Lagrange, while in one sense admirably concise, is also somewhat cursory.

Fraser, Craig G. *Calculus and Analytical Mechanics in the Age of Enlightenment*. Brookfield, Vt.: Variorum, 1997. This collection of essays written between 1981 and 1994 includes studies of Lagrange's early contributions to the principles and methods of mechanics, and his problems in the calculus of variations.

Grabiner, Judith V. *The Calculus of Algebra: J-L Lagrange, 1736-1813*. New York: Garland, 1990. Grabiner describes Lagrange's work in calculus.

Kline, Morris. *Mathematical Thought from Ancient to Modern Times*. New York: Oxford University Press, 1972. Kline offers a more thorough and more rigorously theoretical treatment than Burton (see above), but he requires considerable mathematical sophistication. Still, the book is not aimed at specialists, and Kline explains thoroughly, emphasizing the coherent evolution of mathematical thought. He highlights Lagrange's consistency admirably.

Porter, Thomas Isaac. "A History of the Classical Isoperimetric Problem." In *University of Chicago Contributions to the Calculus of Variations*. Vol. 3. Chicago: University of Chicago Press, 1933. Porter's article is a study for professionals and scholars, with much detail and requiring knowledge of advanced mathematics. It does, however, contain the most extensive account of Lagrange's most important work in the calculus of variations, with incidental reference to his other achievements.

Smith, David Eugene, comp. *A Source Book in Mathematics*. Reprint. Mineola, N.Y.: Dover, 1959. Smith's work is for historians of mathematics, but his selections of extracts from Lagrange's works are representative and reveal Lagrange's clarity of exposition, making them quite accessible.

Struik, D. J., ed. *A Source Book in Mathematics, 1200-1800*. Cambridge, Mass.: Harvard University Press, 1969. This is an anthology of extracts from the original works, such as David Eugene Smith's, but it is more extensive and representative of the entire body of Lagrange's work. The introductions and notes are useful and thorough, and particularly good in helping the reader reach an appreciation of Lagrange's accomplishments.

See also: Leonhard Euler; Frederick the Great.

Related articles in *Great Events from History: The Eighteenth Century, 1701-1800*: 1704: Newton Publishes *Optics*; 1718: Bernoulli Publishes His Calculus of Variations; 1733: De Moivre Describes the Bell-Shaped Curve; 1738: Bernoulli Proposes the Kinetic Theory of Gases; 1740: Maclaurin's Gravitational Theory; 1743-1744: D'Alembert Develops His Axioms of Motion; 1748: Agnesi Publishes *Analytical Institutions*; 1748: Euler Develops the Concept of Function; 1763: Bayes Advances Probability Theory; 1784: Legendre Introduces Polynomials; c. 1794-1799: Proust Establishes the Law of Definite Proportions; 1796: Laplace Articulates His Nebular Hypothesis.

SOPHIE VON LA ROCHE
German novelist

La Roche was the first woman to write a German novel and one of the first novelists to use letters as the key means of constructing her narrative. She also translated into German the works of British feminists and intellectuals known as the Bluestockings, thus sharing British feminist ideas with German readers.

Born: December 6, 1731; Kaufbeuren, Bavaria (now in Germany)
Died: February 18, 1807; Offenbach, Hesse (now in Germany)
Also known as: Sophie Gutermann (birth name)
Area of achievement: Literature

EARLY LIFE

Sophie von La Roche (lah-ROHSH) was the first child of a well-educated and cultured German physician. She had thirteen brothers and sisters, and like many children of her class, Sophie was educated at home, largely by her mother and in her father's large library. In 1743, Sophie was engaged to an Italian doctor who did not speak German, so she learned Italian.

Her life changed dramatically in 1748 when her mother died, her engagement ended, and she went to live with her cousins, the Wielands. There she met poet and writer Christoph Martin Wieland (1733-1813), who became her lifelong friend and literary patron. He was a successful novelist himself. Between 1750 and 1753, Sophie was engaged to Wieland, but following her father's wishes, she broke off with him to marry a well-placed German government adviser, Georg Michael von La Roche.

Sophie moved to Mainz with her husband, where she assisted in hosting literary evenings that exposed her to the latest in literary, philosophical, and political ideas. Georg encouraged Sophie to read widely and to use her self-taught skills in Italian, French, and English to converse with their guests. In 1768, Georg's father and patron, Count Stadion, died, and the La Roches were no longer prominent in Mainz society, temporarily. The couple's two daughters, Maximiliana and Luise, were being educated away from home, so Sophie felt a sense of loss with no children to raise or parties to host. She described herself to friends as lonely, and soon she was being encouraged to take up writing to help her pass her time. This was not an unusual activity for women in the eighteenth century, as writing was considered a good way to spend time and to make money as long as the pub-

lications were not scandalous and they fit the time's ideal of womanhood.

In 1771, Sophie published the first part of her novel in letters, *Geschichte des Fräuleins von Sternheim* (*The History of Lady Sophia Sternheim*; best known as *Sternheim*), followed in 1772 by a second, shorter part. In 1772, she met the young writer Johann Wolfgang von Goethe (1749-1832), whom she is reputed to have encouraged to write his first epistolary novel, *Die Leiden des jungen Werthers* (1774; *The Sorrows of Young Werther*, 1779), based on a story he told Sophie about unrequited love and death. Just as Sophie was becoming famous, her husband was returned to the Mainz court as an adviser in 1774. She then arranged for her daughter, Maximiliana, to marry a much older and prosperous businessman, Peter Bretano, and the couple had two children, Clemens and Bettina (von Arnim), who were to become prominent writers themselves.

LIFE'S WORK

When Sophie von La Roche published *Sternheim*, she was capitalizing on the enormous popularity of novels with the German reading public, notably the imitations of the novels of British writer Samuel Richardson. His *Pamela: Or, Virtue Rewarded* (1740-1741) and *Clarissa: Or, The History of a Young Lady* (1747-1748) used correspondence to advance the narrative and were seen to offer role models for women readers that parents and pastors could admire. In Richardson's story, the character Pamela Andrews raises herself from servitude to marriage and motherhood without sacrificing her honor. The character Clarissa stubbornly refuses to accept the marriage her father arranges for her and is severely punished by rape and abandonment; Clarissa then chooses death over further dishonoring her family. For her novel, La Roche borrowed the popular epistolary narrative and some of the sensational elements of *Clarissa* (including the rape) to balance the overall virtue of her heroine, Lady Sophia, modeled on Pamela.

In *Sternheim*, the first letters Lady Sophia sends her friend Emilia suggest precise borrowing from Richardson and from La Roche's own life: Lady Sophia experiences family deaths that change the course of her life, she is admired by both men and women, she has several aggressive suitors, and she speaks and teaches English to her friends. Lady Sophia's charmingly awkward behavior in mixed company anticipates the success of Fanny

Burney (1752-1840), whose heroine in her epistolary novel *Evelina: Or, The History of a Young Lady's Entrance into the World* (1778) has to find her way in London society in a journey not without some peril. La Roche balances a number of correspondents, both male and female, and uses her novel to state some bold truths about the social position of women, especially regarding marriage. For instance, Lord Derby writes that while he is attracted to Lady Sophia, he knows he cannot marry her, because her uncle is arranging a marriage for her that will help her uncle win a lawsuit. She also openly portrays male and female friendship, as a tribute to her own with Wieland, who helped her publish the novel anonymously.

Critics have argued that La Roche's ambition in *The History of Lady Sternheim* does not wholly match her abilities as a novelist. The critics point out that elements of *The History of Lady Sternheim*'s plot are unevenly handled, with excessive reliance on circumstances to move the story along; that characters are not fully developed; and that major and minor characters are not always clearly distinguished in their importance to the story. The character of Lady Sophia has been deemed successful, however, because she learns from her mistakes and absorbs information around her that improves her judgment, making her a good role model.

By 1783, with *The History of Lady Sternheim* in its eighth edition and her success proven, La Roche used her reputation to launch a periodical called *Pomona für Teutschlands Tochter* (fruits for Germany's daughter). The periodical title's spelling of "Teutschlands," meaning "Germany," reflects her regional dialect. For the periodical she wrote essays and translated poetry and prose by women writers, especially her much-loved British women writers, to whom Wieland had introduced her in the 1750's, when they read English books together (including *Pamela*). *Pomona* gave La Roche the opportunity to make German readers—mainly women—aware of the conversations British women writers were having in poetry and prose about literature, education, and women's duties in society—subjects not openly discussed in the 1780's. As a translator of Bluestocking writings, La Roche protected her reputation, as the words and ideas belonged to others: She merely rendered them into German.

Considering herself an Anglophile, La Roche visited London in 1786. She was delighted to attend the theater and to visit the numerous cultural attractions, including the city's bookstores. She met Fanny Burney, and in her conversations with British women, she keenly felt that German women, while having physically accomplished a great deal as wives and mothers, were behind their British counterparts intellectually. Indeed, German women's writing was considered *Trivialliteratur* (trivial literature) and women's novels were called *Frauenromane* (women's novels), implying that they had little in the way of intellectual or literary merit. However, nearly four thousand women were writing and publishing in the eighteenth and nineteenth centuries across Germany.

SIGNIFICANCE

Sophie von La Roche earned her place in literary history with *The History of Lady Sternheim* and in feminist thought with her translations and essays published in *Pomona für Teutschlands Tochter* (1783-1784). Her appreciation of English culture and her comments on English society in her letters, diaries, and travel journals reveal how continental Europeans perceived the English in the eighteenth century. At a time when German women were discouraged from writing, La Roche took advantage of her husband's position in the Mainz court and Wieland's position in literary circles to break new ground in German fiction and to publish quality translations of feminist poetry and prose.

—*Beverly Schneller*

FURTHER READING

Brewer, John. *The Pleasures of the Imagination.* New York: Farrar, Straus, and Giroux, 1997. Discusses La Roche's visit to London in 1768 and uses excerpts from her letters and diaries as evidence of what she valued in English culture.

Brown, Hilary. "The Reception of the Bluestockings by Eighteenth Century German Women Writers." *Women in German Yearbook* (2002): 110-132. Convincingly argues that La Roche shared the feminist ideas of the Bluestockings in her translations for *Pomona.*

Cocalis, Susan L. "'Around 1800': Reassessing the Role of German Women Writers in Literary Production of the Late Eighteenth and Early Nineteenth Centuries." *Women in German Yearbook* (1992): 159-177. A review essay that describes the devaluation of German women as writers and explains the historical challenges women faced in bringing their work to press.

Fronius, Helen. "Der Reiche Man und die Arme Frau (The Powerful Man and the Poor Woman): German Women Writers and the Eighteenth-Century Literary Marketplace." *German Life and Letters* 56, no. 1 (January, 2003): 1-19. Uses two sets of publishers' correspondence to trace how women writers navigated the male-dominated publishing world and provides new evidence on the number of women publishing in Germany.

Joeres, Ruth-Ellen Boetcher. *Respectability and Deviance*: *Nineteenth-Century German Women Writers and the Ambiguity of Representation*. Chicago: University of Chicago Press, 1998. Establishes how *The History of Lady Sternheim* allowed La Roche to discuss gender issues and how she influenced other women writers.

La Roche, Sophie von. *The History of Lady Sophia Sternheim*. Translated by Christina Baguss Britt. Albany: State University of New York Press, 1991. An English translation of La Roche's novel, with useful notes, a historical introduction, and a bibliography.

See also: Abigail Adams; Anna Barbauld; Fanny Burney; Hester Chapone; Aagje Deken; Johann Wolfgang von Goethe; Mary Wortley Montagu; Samuel Richardson; Mary Wollstonecraft.

Related articles in *Great Events from History: The Eighteenth Century, 1701-1800:* April 25, 1719: Defoe Publishes the First Novel; 1740-1741: Richardson's *Pamela* Establishes the Modern Novel; 1792: Wollstonecraft Publishes *A Vindication of the Rights of Woman.*

ANTOINE-LAURENT LAVOISIER
French chemist

In addition to making important contributions to eighteenth century geology, physics, cartography, and economic reform (particularly in agriculture and manufacturing), Lavoisier, by discrediting the phlogiston theory and proving the law of the conservation of matter, founded modern chemistry. He also discovered and named gases, namely oxygen and nitrogen.

Born: August 26, 1743; Paris, France
Died: May 8, 1794; Paris, France
Areas of achievement: Chemistry, cartography, science and technology, business, economics

EARLY LIFE

Antoine-Laurent Lavoisier (ahn-twahn-law-rah lahv-wahz-yay) was born into an eminent bourgeois family. Over the preceding century, his family had risen gradually from humble origins. His father, who had inherited considerable wealth from an uncle as well as his position as attorney to the Paris parliament, was a lawyer. Émilie Punctis, Antoine's mother, was equally well positioned socially, being the daughter of a parliamentary advocate. The Lavoisiers lived in Paris, and Antoine remained in his parents' home until he married.

Lavoisier's schooling, which probably began in 1754, seems principally to have been in Paris's small but exclusive Collège Mazarin. Guided by tradition, he studied law, receiving his bachelor's degree in 1763 and his licentiate the following year. Not really engaged by his profession, Lavoisier began scientific studies with four of France's most eminent scientists: Abbé Nicolas-Louis de Lacaille, an astronomer and mathematician; Bernard de Jussieu, a botanist; Jean-Étienne Guettard, a geologist and mineralogist; and Guillaume Rouelle, a chemist. Each of these men was a cynosure of Parisian intellectual circles who closely interacted with leading figures in Europe's scientific communities: individuals exceptional in an eighteenth century context for the breadth of their curiosities.

Three such superficially unrelated curiosities marked Lavoisier's earliest research. First, his inquiries into the properties of minerals, gypsum in particular, led to his invention in 1764 of plaster of Paris, a feat that produced his first published work by the Academy of Sciences. In 1765, he was encouraged by an academy-sponsored prize competition for development of the best night lighting for large towns. He won both the prize and a medal awarded by the king. Concomitantly, pursuing geological and cartological work with France's premier geologist, Lavoisier collaborated in the production of an official geological atlas of France. Reward was swift: Considered for nomination as an academician in 1766, he was elected in 1768, a vacancy having opened with the death of a renowned chemist, Théodore Baron. Remarkable vigor characterized his academy work, which ranged over hundreds of projects, such as the adulteration of cider, theories of color, and mesmerism.

LIFE'S WORK

Lavoisier's scientific milieu, as had been true for two millennia, essentially accepted that all natural phenomena were the result of various mutations of earth, air, fire, and water. The general belief was that these "elements" were inexplicable, hence the long-standing interest in alchemy—the transformation of something base into something precious or valuable to the prolongation of life, invariably accompanied by often indecipherable language explaining alchemists' experimentation. Some alchemical philosophizing had been eroded by several of Lavoisier's predecessors, such as Robert Boyle, and contemporaries such as Joseph Priestley. Boyle, for example, had demonstrated that combustion (fire) cannot occur in an airless vessel, nor could many other processes, including life. In the mid-1600's, however, German chemists, notably Johann Joachim Becher and Georg Ernst Stahl, contrived a theory that combustion required no air, only an "oily earth" dubbed phlogiston. Armed with this dictum, followers of the phlogiston theory could also explain numerous other chemical processes.

Anxieties about the purity of the Parisian water supply brought Lavoisier into conflict with such traditional assumptions and methods. No standards existed then to ascertain water's purity; indeed, common scientific opinions held that evaporating water was transformed into earth. Lavoisier, having reviewed the endeavors of his predecessors, went directly to the fundamentals of

Antoine-Laurent Lavoisier. (Library of Congress)

the water problem; namely, whether matter was transmutable. After a series of exquisite experiments, he demonstrated that the earth produced in distilling and evaporating water, in fact, came from abrasive actions of water on the glass. Thus, two thousand years of belief in the transmutability of matter was refuted.

Both Lavoisier's public responsibilities and his science were made less burdensome by his happy marriage in 1771 to Marie Paulze, a woman of wealth and important family connections, but, more significant, a person intellectually drawn to her husband's work. She not only translated scientific materials for him but also aided him in the niceties of his experiments and made excellent scientific sketches.

Air and fire preoccupied Lavoisier during the late 1760's and the early 1770's; that is, he was absorbed by the phlogiston question. During the 1760's, Priestley experimented with the properties of gases and discovered new ones, such as ammonia and sulfur dioxide. Heating the calx of mercury (a compound resulting from heating a substance below its melting point), Priestley produced a special "air," one in which candles burned vigorously and mice lived longer than in ordinary air. Yet Priestley, a believer in phlogiston, simply described this as dephlogisticated air.

Lavoisier launched an intricate series of experiments on combustion: Was the destruction of a diamond by heating merely an evaporation, or was it combustion? Was the same true of phosphorus, or of sulfur? By 1774, his answers appeared in his *Opuscules physiques et chymiques* (*Essays, Physical and Chemical*, 1776). Burning sulfur or phosphorus, instead of expelling something, actually absorbed air. Further reduction of the calx of lead unleashed air (now known as carbon dioxide) that sustained neither combustion nor life; in sum, reduction of the calx of metals expelled rather than absorbed something. By 1778 and 1779, continuing such investigations, Lavoisier reported that air consisted of two distinct gases: The first, which he named oxygen, sustained life and combustion and made up one-quarter of the volume, and the other, not respirable, made up the other three-quarters of the volume and is now identified as nitrogen. The phlogiston theory had been overthrown, and the foundations of modern chemistry emplaced, with his publication in 1786 of *Réflexions sur la phlogistique* (*Reflections on Phlogiston*, 1788). Lavoisier in 1787 then published his *Méthode de nomenclature chimique* (*Method of Chemical Nomenclature*, 1788), identifying a table of thirty-one chemical elements, adding heat and light as materials without mass. In full vigor, he proceeded conclusively to

A COMPOUND CALLED WATER

Until the late eighteenth century, water was considered to be a chemical element rather than a compound. This 1783 report, excerpted below, prepared for the Royal Academy relates how Antoine-Laurent Lavoisier advanced Henry Cavendish's experiments to identify water as a compound of hydrogen and oxyen.

M. Cavendish . . . observed that if one operates in dry vessels a discernible quantity of moisture is deposited on the inner walls. Since the verification of this fact was of great significance to chemical theory, M. Lavoisier and M. de la Place proposed to confirm it in a large-scale experiment. . . . The quantity of inflammable air burned in this experiment was about thirty pints [pintes] and that of dephlogisticated air from fifteen to eighteen.

As soon as the two airs had been lit, the wall of the vessel in which the combustion took place visibly darkened and became covered by a large number of droplets of water. Little by little the drops grew in volume. Many coalesced together and collected in the bottom of the apparatus, where they formed a layer on the surface of the mercury.

After the experiment, nearly all the water was collected by means of a funnel, and its weight was found to be about 5 gros, which corresponded fairly closely to the weight of the two airs combined. This water was as pure as distilled water.

A short time later, M. Monge addressed to the Academy the result of a similar combustion . . . which was perhaps more accurate. He determined with great care the weight of the two airs, and he likewise found that in burning large quantities of inflammable air and dephlogisticated air one obtains very pure water and that its weight very nearly approximates the weight of the two airs used. Finally . . . M. Cavendish recently repeated the same experiment by different means and that when the quantity of the two airs had been well proportioned, he consistently obtained the same result.

It is difficult to refuse to recognize that in this experiment, water is made artificially and from scratch, and consequently that the constituent parts of this fluid are inflammable air and dephlogisticated air, less the portion of fire which is released during the combustion.

Source: Antoine-Laurent Lavoisier, "Report of a Memoir Read by M. Lavoisier . . . , on the Nature of Water and on Experiments Which Appear to Prove That This Substance Is Not Strictly Speaking an Element but That It Is Susceptible of Decomposition and Recomposition." *Observations sur la Physique* 23 (1783): 452-455. Translated by Carmen Giunta.

David portrait. Both an original experimenter and a superb scientific synthesizer, Lavoisier, aside from his establishment of modern chemistry, made immense contributions as a responsible, innovative public official. Though independently wealthy, Lavoisier had become a tax farmer to ensure his fortune. As a tax farmer, he relieved Jews from payment of the outrageous "cloven-hoof" tax; he sought relief for the poor from unjust taxation and instituted waste-cutting administrative reforms; he tried to protect honest Parisian merchants from smugglers who slipped by the *octrois* (a local import tax); he reformed the system and improved the quality of France's gunpowder production and generated a number of studies on the manufacture of saltpeter; like his brilliant successor, Alexis de Tocqueville, he sought the reformation of France's penal system; and his elaborate calculations of French agricultural conditions entitle him to front rank as a political economist. These are only partial indications of Lavoisier's genius beyond the bounds of chemistry.

As is so often the case, he died for his mistakes and for misinterpretations of his intentions. During the Reign of Terror during the French Revolution, he was imprisoned, charged with counterrevolutionary conspiracy against France, and executed in Paris on May 8, 1794. One French notable remarked to another in respect of Lavoisier: "Only a moment to cut off a head and a hundred years may not give us another like it." The remark, like Lavoisier's achievements, remains a tribute to eighteenth century French culture.

SIGNIFICANCE

Antoine-Laurent Lavoisier, though a man of many talents that would have qualified him for eminence in half a dozen scientific disciplines or fields of public service, was the founder of modern chemistry not only in an ab-

expound his oxygen theory, his new chemical nomenclature, and his statement of the law of the conservation of matter with publication in 1789 of a work rivaling any in the history of science: *Traité élémentaire de chimie (Elements of Chemistry, in a New Systematic Order, Containing All the Modern Discoveries*, 1790).

Genuine goodness and breadth of mind characterized both Lavoisier and his wife. Fine featured, delicate, and keenly intellectual, they look to each other lovingly, but with a hint of amused embarrassment, in a Jacques-Louis stract or theoretical dimension but also in immediately practical ways. His intellections and experimentation banished the phlogiston theory that had led and entranced many fine minds for centuries. In the tradition of Carolus Linnaeus, he sought only the facts, then classified them as they were verifiable through critical experimentation; he identified thirty-six chemical elements, not the least oxygen, and defined their characteristics and roles. He wrote the first precise texts, from which subsequent chemistry sprang, destined to be of incalculable benefit to humankind. Some of his work was entirely original; some was derivative; and, inevitably for great minds, some was magnificently synthetic. His official services to France ran a gamut that was encyclopedic and generally pragmatic, practical, and useful. He was preeminently the son of what then was Europe's greatest nation-state as well as its greatest center of mischief, intellection, and high culture.

—Clifton K. Yearley

FURTHER READING

Donovan, Arthur. *Antoine Lavoisier: Science, Administration, and Revolution.* Cambridge, Mass.: Blackwell, 1993. A biography examining both Lavoisier's scientific discoveries and his work as a public administrator before and during the French Revolution.

French, Sidney J. *Torch and Crucible: The Life and Death of Antoine Lavoisier.* Princeton, N.J.: Princeton University Press, 1931. A readable and adequate survey of Lavoisier's life. The general context within which Lavoisier worked and the specifics of his experiments are not fully treated. There are a small number of illustrations and only a modest bibliography, which, through no fault of the author, needs updating.

Hall, Alfred R. *The Scientific Revolution, 1500-1800: The Formation of the Modern Scientific Attitude.* 2d ed. Boston: Beacon Press, 1966. This now classic work, written for general readers, does an outstanding job of placing Lavoisier and his work in context. The study is amply footnoted and has three appendices, along with brief but excellent bibliographical notes at the end of each chapter.

Holmes, Frederic Lawrence. *Antoine Lavoisier, the Next Crucial Year, or The Sources of His Quantitative Method in Chemistry.* Princeton, N.J.: Princeton University Press, 1998. Recounts Lavoisier's daily laboratory work during several months in 1773, when he was studying his oxygen theory of combustion. Holmes argues these experiments were the first step toward Lavoisier's eventual development of quantitative experimental methods.

McKie, Douglas. *Antoine Lavoisier: Scientist, Economist, Social Reformer.* New York: Henry Schuman, 1952. The most expert and best-written coverage of Lavoisier's life and work, this book is essential reading. It covers, with the simplicity that only a skilled scholar can manage, an amazing array of Lavoisier's activities. Includes many helpful illustrations, a select but good bibliography, and a minimal index.

Poirier, Jean-Pierre. *Lavoisier, Chemist, Biologist, Economist.* Translated by Rebecca Balinski. Philadelphia: University of Pennsylvania Press, 1996. Biography of Lavoisier describing his many activities, ranging from his scientific discoveries to his work in politics and economics.

Westfall, Richard S. *The Construction of Modern Science: Mechanisms and Mechanics.* New York: John Wiley & Sons, 1971. This scholarly work is chiefly about seventeenth century science, but chapter 11 is essential background for an understanding of Lavoisier. While authoritative, this work is for university undergraduates. Contains many illuminating illustrations, a fine critical bibliography, and a solid double-columned index.

See also: Carolus Linnaeus; Joseph Priestley; Georg Ernst Stahl.

Related articles in *Great Events from History: The Eighteenth Century, 1701-1800*: 1714: Fahrenheit Develops the Mercury Thermometer; 1718: Geoffroy Issues the *Table of Reactivities*; 1722: Réaumur Discovers Carbon's Role in Hardening Steel; 1723: Stahl Postulates the Phlogiston Theory; 1738: Bernoulli Proposes the Kinetic Theory of Gases; 1745: Lomonosov Issues the First Catalog of Minerals; 1748: Nollet Discovers Osmosis; June 5, 1755: Black Identifies Carbon Dioxide; 1771: Woulfe Discovers Picric Acid; August 1, 1774: Priestley Discovers Oxygen; 1779: Ingenhousz Discovers Photosynthesis; 1781-1784: Cavendish Discovers the Composition of Water; 1786-1787: Lavoisier Devises the Modern System of Chemical Nomenclature; 1789: Leblanc Develops Soda Production; c. 1794-1799: Proust Establishes the Law of Definite Proportions.

THOMAS LAWRENCE
English painter

The foremost portrait painter of his day, Lawrence enhanced the reputation of English art. As a collector and adviser to patrons and government, he established and enriched a number of museums.

Born: April 13, 1769; Bristol, Gloucestershire, England
Died: January 7, 1830; London, England
Areas of achievement: Art, patronage of the arts

EARLY LIFE

In his *Miscellanies* (1781), Davies Barrington included the following observation:

> I here cannot pass unnoticed a Master Lawrence, son of an innkeeper at Devizes, in Wiltshire. This boy is now nearly ten years old, but at the age of nine, without the most distant instruction given by anyone, he was capable of copying historical pictures in a masterly style, and also succeeded amazingly in compositions of his own. . . . In about seven minutes, he scarcely ever failed of drawing a strong likeness of any person present, which had generally much freedom and grace, if the subject permitted.

Thomas Lawrence would later in life joke about his precociousness. On a pastel he gave to Mrs. Edward Forster he wrote, "Done when three weeks old, I believe." Yet Lawrence was clearly born to paint, exhibiting his extensive talents at an early age.

It was fortunate for the Lawrence family that he did so, for the elder Thomas Lawrence was well educated but impecunious. Trained as a lawyer, he held the post of supervisor of the excise at the busy port of Bristol when his namesake was born. Indolent by nature, though, he shortly afterward gave up this office to manage the White Lion Inn and American Coffee House. The hostelry failed to provide sufficient income to support the large family—Lawrence was the youngest of fourteen children—nor would Mrs. Lawrence's parents help. The former Lucy Read was the daughter of a prosperous clergyman, but she had been disinherited when she eloped with the elder Lawrence.

In 1773, Thomas Lawrence, Sr., moved the family to Devizes to become proprietor of the Black Bear Inn, on the Great West Road leading to the resort town of Bath. By the time Lawrence was five, his father was introducing him to guests by asking, "Will you have him recite from the poets or take your portraits?" At Devizes, Lawrence received his only formal education, which ended when the boy was eight. In 1779, the Black Bear failed, and the family left Devizes.

Already, though, Lawrence had established a regional reputation. Traveling through Oxford and Weymouth, he began his role as his family's chief supporter by painting portraits of all the leading figures in these towns. When the family settled in Bath, the twelve-year-old Lawrence set up a studio at 2 Alfred Street; the address soon became the resort of the most fashionable people of the town.

Not only did people flock to Lawrence to have their portraits painted, giving the youth an income of more than £500 a year, but they also wanted to paint him. All of his life he was to be popular because of his graceful manners and elegant looks, the one coming to him as naturally as the other. In 1780, Fanny Burney wrote in her diary, "I was equally struck with the boy and his works." Sarah Thackeray remembered that at sixteen Lawrence "was remarkably handsome . . .; and his hair, which was beautiful, was so redundant, that its rich, dark curls almost obscured his face when he stooped to draw." William Hoare, a member of the Royal Academy, painted Lawrence about 1780 and was so taken with the youth that he offered to send him to Italy to study the masters. The elder Lawrence, fearing the loss of income that would result, replied that his son's talents were in need of no cultivation.

Others besides Hoare were enchanted by the young prodigy. Mary Hartley, another local artist, gave him instruction. Thomas Barker, a landscape painter, showed him how to use oils. Sir Henry Harpur and his wife, Lady Frances, wanted to adopt him, and a local collector, Mr. Hamilton, opened his private gallery to the boy. Lawrence took advantage of this opportunity by copying a number of old masters, among them Raphael's *Transfiguration*. In 1784, two years after he had reproduced the work, he submitted his version to the Royal Academy's annual competition. Because it had not been painted within the year, it was not eligible for the first prize, a gold palette, but the academy was so impressed that it ordered the second prize, a silver palette, completely gilded, and added an award of five guineas "as a token of the Society's approbation of his abilities."

LIFE'S WORK

Aided by Edward Poore of Salisbury and the Reverend Henry Kent, Lawrence moved to London in 1786. Lawrence was living at 4 Leicester Square, close to Sir Joshua Reynolds, president of the Royal Academy and dean of English art. Reynolds was as captivated by Lawrence as everyone else; Lawrence became a frequent guest, and Reynolds observed, "This young man has begun at a point of excellence where I left off." Lawrence was only slightly less confident of his abilities, writing to his mother in September, 1786, "Excepting Sir Joshua, for the painting of a head, I would risk my reputation with any painter in London."

Impartial observers agreed. One critic of the 1789 exhibition of the Royal Academy, to which Lawrence submitted thirteen pieces, called him "the Sir Joshua of futurity not far off," and another reviewer said that the portrait of Charlotte Lennox might "easily be mistaken for one of the President's best heads." Among the portraits Lawrence exhibited in 1789 was one of Lady Cremorne. Together with the painting of Lennox it earned for him an introduction to the royal family and a commission to paint Queen Caroline and her daughter, Princess Amelia.

An artist's sketch of Sir Thomas Lawrence in 1789. (Library of Congress)

The promise of the 1789 showing seemed fulfilled the next year, when Lawrence exhibited two of his finest works. His portrait of actor Elizabeth Farren was the highlight of the Royal Academy show. The picture ensured Lawrence's reputation. He became the highest-paid artist in London; for the rest of his career his income ranged between £10,000 and £20,000 a year.

As impressive as *Portrait of an Actress* was Lawrence's rendition of Queen Charlotte and her daughter. Because of Lawrence's early work in pastels, he remained an indifferent colorist all of his life, yet in this painting, the limited range of blue-green, white, and gray shows a harmonious variation that prevents monotony. Behind the figures is a rich landscape of Windsor, showing a prospect of Eton College.

Such an individualized background was typical of Lawrence's early work. The 1794 portrait of Richard Payne Knight includes a volume of architectural drawings and an antique urn, reflecting Payne's interest in classical art. Lady Suffield's pose in her portrait imitates that of a figure on the garden urn behind her. Later, under pressure to produce paintings rapidly, Lawrence would rely on more generalized backgrounds.

Following the triumph of the 1790 exhibition, Lawrence was nominated by George III to become an associate of the Royal Academy. In a fit of independence, the academy rejected him, but on November 10, 1791, he

was elected. Early the next year, Sir Joshua Reynolds died, and on February 26, 1792, George III named Lawrence Painter-in-Ordinary in Reynolds's place. The Dilettanti Society also chose Lawrence as Reynolds's successor, waiving its long-standing rule of admitting no one who had not visited Italy. Two years later, as soon as he was old enough to be eligible, he was granted full membership in the Royal Academy.

Although Lawrence's portraits were earning high praise and high prices, he hoped to make his reputation as a historical painter. Generalized scenes were still regarded as the highest form of art in the late eighteenth century, and as early as 1787, Lawrence was exhibiting these along with his portraits at the Royal Academy. In 1797, he submitted *Satan Summoning up His Legions*, which he was perversely to claim as his greatest work. No one else shared that view. It never sold in Lawrence's lifetime, and even his friend and admirer Henry Fuseli called it "a damned thing certainly, but not the devil." Antony Pasquin was still less flattering, claiming that Satan resembled "a mad sugar-baker dancing naked in a conflagration of his own treacle." However much Lawrence defended the picture, he never again attempted a purely historical painting, though he would introduce elements of the grand manner in such works as *The Princess of Wales and Princess Charlotte* (1800-1801), in which he depicted Princess Caroline as an inspired harpist. He also enjoyed painting the actor John Philip Kemble in various guises, such as Coriolanus, Hamlet, and Cato.

Kemble's is also the face of the archfiend in Lawrence's 1797 *Satan*, for at that time, Kemble was interfering with the artist's pursuit of his niece Sally, the older daughter of Sarah Siddons. Sarah herself also appears in the painting as one of the devils. Lawrence's romance with the members of the Siddons family reveals his less attractive side, not only in the vindictiveness exhibited in his picture but also in the fickleness of his affections. After being engaged to Sally, he transferred his love to her sister, Maria, and became engaged to her instead. Then he deserted her and returned to Sally. Neither girl was physically strong, but Lawrence's behavior was blamed for hastening Maria's death in 1798. As she lay dying, she made Sally promise not to marry Lawrence; Sally was to die unwed five years later, in April, 1803. Lawrence would die a bachelor, and after Sally's death, he always wore black and sealed his letters with dark wax.

Despite troubles in his personal life, Lawrence's professional reputation continued to grow. In typical Hanoverian fashion, the prince of Wales rejected the king's choice of artist, patronizing John Hoppner. When Hoppner died in 1810, though, even the prince regent recognized that no one else approached Lawrence's talent. In 1814, he commissioned Lawrence to provide a series of portraits for Windsor Castle to depict all the Allied leaders who had participated in the defeat of Napoleon. In the course of this commission, which required six years to complete and which took the painter to France, Vienna, and Rome, Lawrence created some of his finest work, particularly the picture of Pope Pius VII (1819), which demonstrates the weariness and resignation of a spiritually strong man.

Already in 1815, the prince regent had knighted Lawrence for enhancing the reputation of English art. Upon Lawrence's return from the Continent in 1820, the prince, now George IV, named him president of the Royal Academy and reappointed him Painter-in-Ordinary, thus completing Lawrence's inheritance of Reynolds's honors. Awards continued to pour in: Oxford presented him with a doctorate of civil letters on June 14, 1820; the academies of Bologna, Venice, Vienna, Turin, and Copenhagen sent him diplomas; and Charles X of France made him a Chevalier de l'Ordre Royal de la Légion d'Honneur in 1825.

Lawrence was enriching British art not only with his brush but also with his advice and his purse. His testimony before Parliament in 1816 was instrumental in convincing the country to purchase the Elgin Marbles at a time when a number of reputable artists and critics failed to appreciate their value. Lawrence was a close friend and artistic counselor to John Julius Angerstein; after Angerstein's death, Lawrence convinced the col-

lector's son to sell his father's extensive art collection to the nation at a substantial discount. On May 10, 1824, the National Gallery opened with Angerstein's pictures. Fittingly, Lawrence was named a trustee. Meanwhile, Lawrence himself was assembling England's largest collection of drawings by the old masters. Among the five thousand works were one hundred by Albrecht Dürer, almost two hundred Raphaels, and seventy-five that were attributed to Leonardo da Vinci. Lawrence had hoped to keep the collection together and make it public by offering it in his will to George IV for £18,000, about a quarter of its value. Because Lawrence died in debt, the pictures were dispersed to satisfy his creditors. Still, Oxford University's Ashmolean Museum and the Malcolm Collection of the British Museum were able to secure important pieces that remain national treasures.

At the peak of his reputation, Lawrence died suddenly on January 7, 1830, probably from excessive bleeding by his physician. His body lay in state at the Royal Academy's Somerset House, and he was buried near the grave of Reynolds in St. Paul's on January 21, 1830.

SIGNIFICANCE

On the day after Sir Thomas Lawrence's death, Charles Greville expressed the general opinion of Lawrence's achievements:

> He was *longè primus* of all living Painters, and has left no one fit to succeed him in the chair of the Royal Academy.... He is an irreparable loss; since Sir Joshua there has been no painter like him; his Portraits as pictures I think are not nearly so fine as Sir Joshua's, but as likenesses many of them are quite perfect.

Lawrence himself was less certain of his status, commenting, "I do not for a moment suppose that my reputation will ever stand as high after my death as it has in my lifetime."

Lawrence's prediction proved accurate. Writing some eighty years after Lawrence's death, Sir Walter Armstrong rated him lowest of the six major artists of the late eighteenth century, beneath Thomas Gainsborough, Reynolds, Henry Raeburn, George Romney, and Hoppner. Yet Armstrong's judgment seems as misguided as that of Lawrence's contemporaries who ranked him with Titian. Lawrence was a fine draftsman, and throughout his career, he demonstrated his capacity for capturing the spirit as well as the physical likeness of an individual.

Too often Lawrence was rushed. Whereas Reynolds attempted only seventy to eighty portraits a year after

1769, Lawrence throughout his career accepted hundreds of commissions, starting as many as four portraits in a day. Many of these naturally remained unfinished. Even the excellent painting of his good friend Mrs. Jens Wolff, completed in 1815, took him twelve years, and visitors to his house at 65 Russell Square commented on the large number of unfinished canvases in evidence. Under financial pressure to churn out portraits, he relied on his extensive technical genius to produce exact likenesses that lacked spirit. Even his admirer and defender Kenneth Garlick concedes that his "great powers . . . often went unexpressed."

When he did exhibit those great powers, Lawrence united classical composition with Romantic intensity to produce some of the finest portraits of his, or any, age. He also recognized talent in others, such as William Blake, John James Audubon, and the young J. M. W. Turner, encouraging them with praise and money. Blake's *The Wise and Foolish Virgins*, now hanging in the Tate Gallery, London, was Lawrence's, purchased for fifteen guineas in 1822 when scarcely anyone appreciated the arch-Romantic. Other museums, too, have benefited from his collecting, and without his efforts neither the National Gallery nor the Royal Hibernian Society would have been established as early as it was.

As an artist, collector, adviser, and patron, he raised the English School to a new level of excellence. What has been said of Augustus Caesar and Rome may with equal justice be applied to Lawrence and English art: He found it brick, and he left it marble.

—*Joseph Rosenblum*

FURTHER READING

Armstrong, Sir Walter. *Lawrence*. London: Methuen, 1913. Reflecting the sentiment of the day, Armstrong did not rate Lawrence highly. Yet this was a pioneering study that called attention to the artist and led to more careful study than Lawrence had previously received.

Garlick, Kenneth. *Sir Thomas Lawrence*. London: Routledge and Kegan Paul, 1954. In nineteen pages of text, Garlick offers a sound critical assessment of Lawrence's achievement, which he then demonstrates in more than one hundred carefully chosen reproductions.

_____. *Sir Thomas Lawrence: Portraits of an Age, 1790-1830*. Alexandria, Va.: Art Services International, 1993. Garlick wrote the text for this catalog, which accompanied an exhibition of Lawrence's portraits. Includes reproductions of the paintings.

_____, ed. *A Catalogue of the Paintings, Drawings, and Pastels of Sir Thomas Lawrence*. Glasgow, Scotland: Walpole Society, 1964. An indispensable listing of the works of Lawrence, noting the provenance of each and the fee that Lawrence charged. The pictures are briefly described but none is reproduced.

Goldring, Douglas. *Regency Portrait Painter: The Life of Sir Thomas Lawrence, P. R. A.* London: MacDonald, 1951. A sympathetic, detailed biography with little critical evaluation of the works. Devotes much space to defending Lawrence's relationship with the Siddons family.

Mayoux, Jean Jacques. *English Painting*. New York: St. Martin's Press, 1975. A survey of British art from the mid-1700's to the mid-1800's. Puts Lawrence within the context of his period.

Redgrave, Richard, and Samuel Redgrave. *Century of English Painters*. London: Phaidon, 1947. Covers the same period as Mayoux's book but devotes an entire chapter to Lawrence.

Vaughan, William. *British Painting: The Golden Age from Hogarth to Turner*. New York: Thames and Hudson, 1999. Examines British painting from 1730 through 1851, including Lawrence's innovations in portraiture. Analyzes the class structure and political climate in the eighteenth and early nineteenth centuries that created a distinctive British painting style.

Wark, Robert R. *The Blue Boy [and] Pinkie*. San Marino, Calif.: Huntington Library Press, 1998. Wark, a former curator of art collections at the Huntington, provides a history of the Huntington's best-known paintings: *Pinkie* by Lawrence, and *The Blue Boy* by Thomas Gainsborough. Discusses the identity of the two children and why the artists chose to paint them.

Young, Mahonri Sharp. "Sir Thomas Lawrence, R. A.: Millionaire Collector." *Art News* 54 (October, 1955): 24-27. Emphasizes the important role that Lawrence played as a collector of old masters and explores the artist's perennially troubled finances.

See also: Fanny Burney; Caroline; Queen Charlotte; John Singleton Copley; Thomas Gainsborough; Charlotte Lennox; Sir Joshua Reynolds; Sarah Siddons; Benjamin West.

Related articles in *Great Events from History: The Eighteenth Century, 1701-1800:* 1737: Revival of the Paris Salon; December 10, 1768: Britain's Royal Academy of Arts Is Founded; 1787: David Paints *The Death of Socrates*.

NICOLAS LEBLANC
French chemist

Leblanc, an amateur chemist, developed a process for making soda from salt that now bears his name. The use of limestone to cause this conversion was at the core of his process, which played a fundamental role in creating the modern chemical industry.

Born: December 6, 1742; Ivoy-le-Pré, France
Died: January 16, 1806; Saint-Denis, France
Area of achievement: Chemistry

EARLY LIFE

Tragedy haunted Nicolas Leblanc's (nee-kaw-lah luh-blahnk) life, but scholars do not agree about whether his numerous misfortunes were self-generated or the result of historical circumstances. His troubles began when his mother died not long after his birth in 1742 at Ivoy-le-Pré, a small town about 125 miles south of Paris. His father, an official in an ironworks, died in 1751, and Nicolas was sent to Bourges, about twenty miles northeast of his hometown, where he came under the care and influence of his father's good friend, Dr. Bien. From him, Nicolas absorbed an interest in medicine, and, when his guardian died in 1759, Nicolas went to Paris to study medicine at the École de Chirugie. While studying to become a doctor, Leblanc became very interested in chemistry and began attending the lectures of prominent chemists and befriending them.

After obtaining his master's degree in surgery, Leblanc began to practice medicine, but he continued to be interested in chemistry. After attending the popular lectures of the chemist Jean Darcet, Leblanc became a pupil of Darcet and through him met such chemists as Claude-Louis Berthollet, Louis-Nicolas Vauquelin, Antoine-François de Fourcroy, and Réné-Just Haüy.

Leblanc married in 1775, and his first child was born in 1779. His education had consumed the money left to him by his father, and his family responsibilities necessitated a greater income than he was obtaining from the fees paid by his patients. Consequently, in 1780 he became the private physician of Louis-Philippe-Joseph, the future duc d'Orléans. The patronage of the Orléans family also gave Leblanc the opportunity for chemical research. The duke was interested in chemistry, and he encouraged Leblanc's work.

LIFE'S WORK

Since his means were limited, Leblanc initially chose to study crystallization, a subject that required few sup-plies. The work that he did on crystal growth so impressed the French Academy of Sciences that a reviewing committee recommended the academy's support for a project in which Leblanc would study methods of obtaining complete crystals of a wide variety of substances. Yet before its recommendation could become a reality, the French Revolution resulted in the academy's dissolution, and it was not until 1802 that Leblanc was able to publish his work on crystallization.

Through his contact with the academy, Leblanc became aware of a prize that Louis XVI had established for a practical process for making soda (sodium carbonate) from common salt. During the late eighteenth century, the shortage of soda was becoming an acute problem. Much of French soda was manufactured from barilla, a plant growing along the coast of Spain. This meant that France was forced to pay large amounts of money annually to the Spaniards, and during times of war, which were frequent in the eighteenth century, soda supplies would become scarce and expensive. A need clearly existed for a locally produced artificial soda. While working for the duc d'Orléans, Leblanc became interested in applying chemistry to industrial problems. Most of his time was devoted to the synthesis of soda—a goal which, as he knew, other researchers were also pursuing.

According to his patent application, Leblanc began research on soda in 1784, but some scholars are skeptical of this early date because of the lack of specific records. Leblanc once stated that he got the idea for his process by reading Jean-Claude de la Métherie's account of his visit to England and Scotland in 1788 to study British industry. In de la Métherie's account, an erroneous soda-producing process is discussed directly after a section on iron industry, and some scholars believe that this juxtaposition gave Leblanc the crucial idea for his discovery: the use of limestone in helping to transform common salt into soda.

Leblanc's method was straightforward. He first treated common salt with sulfuric acid to produce "salt-cake" (sodium sulfate), which he then mixed with coal and ground limestone. He heated this mixture in a furnace, and the resulting black ash was leached to obtain the soda. Leblanc probably prepared soda crystals by this process in the latter half of 1789, for he and his assistant J. J. Dizé went to England in October, 1789, to confer with the duke about the commercial development of the process. The duke, Leblanc, Dizé, and Henri Shée (the duke's agent) then signed an agreement on February 12, 1790, the major provisions of which were that Leblanc would patent his process for making soda and the duke would furnish 200,000 livres to enable Leblanc and Dizé to carry out its commercial exploitation. In another agreement, signed about a year later, the duke, Leblanc, Dizé, and Shée stated the shares of future profits that each would receive.

The French Revolution delayed the implementation of these agreements. During this period, the duke abandoned his title, changed his name to Philippe Égalité, turned republican, and voted for the death of the king. These actions did not erase the Republic's difficulties with the duke's aristocratic background, but they permitted Leblanc to obtain a secret patent on September 25, 1791, which meant that he did not have to make a public disclosure of his method and that he obtained the exclusive right to exploit his process in whatever way he saw fit for a period of fifteen years. Between 1791 and 1793, with capital provided by Égalité, Leblanc oversaw the construction of a small factory at Saint-Denis, a town four miles north of Paris. This plant began to make soda.

Because of France's war with Spain, the price of barilla rose dramatically, and the shareholders of the Saint-Denis factory reaped huge profits from their manufacture of artificial soda. Unfortunately, the initial success of the plant was short-lived, and, in July, 1793, the impossibility of obtaining sulfuric acid forced Leblanc to close the plant. He was unable to resume operations so long as stocks of sulfur and saltpeter were needed by the munitions industry.

The reopening of the plant was complicated further when Égalité, its principal owner, was tried and guillotined in November, 1793. Leblanc was compelled to leave the idle factory in Shée's care and return to Paris, where he took a post in the Gunpowder Agency and became involved in various political activities. On January 28, 1794, the plant and its associated property were formally confiscated by the Republic. The political authorities, in their revolutionary exuberance, believed that they could use the plant to enhance the industrial power of the Republic. On the very day that local authorities placed the Saint-Denis plant under sequestration, the Committee of Public Safety adopted a decree on the manufacture of artificial soda and appointed Darcet and other scientists to collect and publish all available information on the process. The committee hoped that the free flow of information would help resolve the shortage of soda. Perhaps through patriotism, perhaps through fear, Leblanc divulged the secrets of his process to the Com-

mittee of Public Safety. Some scholars see the committee's action as a great injustice to Leblanc, whereas others think that the committee showed Leblanc unusual consideration.

In either event, the publication of the Leblanc process did the war effort little good, and the report of Darcet's group, which was published in June, 1794, concluded that the procedure for making soda devised by a Benedictine father named Malherbe was more economical than Leblanc's. At the time that the Saint-Denis plant was nationalized, Leblanc had not yet been able to show the superiority of his method over all others. Nevertheless, he had expected to be employed by the Republic to direct the soda works for the good of the people. Instead, he was notified that his government salary would end after April 1, 1794.

Within a short time, Leblanc's life was in disorder. Instead of running a profitable business, he found himself without a salary to support his ailing wife and their four children and severed from the discovery and factory on which he had planned his future. From this time until his death, his life became a dispiriting struggle against poverty.

Following the Reign of Terror, authorities sought to revive industrial enterprises, especially mining, and in June, 1795, the Committee of Public Safety sent Leblanc on a mission to the departments of Tarn and Aveyron in the south of France. His job was to resurrect the manufacture of alum, a substance widely used by dyers, paper makers, goldsmiths, and doctors. His salary and expenses were supposed to be paid by some of the people he was helping, but he received nothing; after thirteen months, he returned to Paris more impoverished and embittered than before. His proclivity for blaming his troubles on the authorities deepened.

Throughout these years of frustration, Leblanc continued the vain struggle to secure recompense for his soda process. His despair deepened when one of his young daughters died suddenly. Leblanc's luck seemed to change in 1801, however, when the minister of finance finally ordered the works at Saint-Denis to be given to Leblanc and his associates, although the state continued to own a substantial portion of the enterprise. The remnant of Leblanc's family returned to their former house on the factory grounds, and Leblanc tried to resume the production of soda but encountered insuperable difficulties. The plant had been abandoned for seven years, and both the government and vandals had removed much of the best equipment and supplies. Leblanc also found himself competing with manufacturers whose plants had not suffered the misfortunes of Saint-Denis. He tried in vain to attract investors and to diversify his factory's products, but each of these ventures consumed more of his time, energy, and money without enhancing his position.

Finally, on November 8, 1805, some of his claims, which had been in the courts for years, were recognized, and a board of arbitrators decided that, though most of Égalité's business belonged to the state, Leblanc's share was worth a sum equal to about $10,000. When even this inadequate sum was never paid, Leblanc became despondent. He had no income, his plant had failed, he was deeply in debt, and his wife was ill. His fortunes had reached bottom, and he increasingly withdrew into himself. Broken in spirit, he shot himself in the head on January 16, 1806.

Some scholars have suggested that Leblanc hoped that his suicide would shock the authorities into granting his family what they had previously denied him, but this did not happen. His death attracted little attention. In 1855, his achievements received belated recognition when Napoleon III made Leblanc's heirs a payment in lieu of the prize for his discovery of the soda process. In 1887, a monument was erected in his honor in Paris that depicts him as a somber man with downcast eyes: His clean-shaven face and classical head would have been appropriate on the shoulders of an ancient tragic hero.

SIGNIFICANCE

Nineteenth century industrial chemistry is largely the story of the rise and fall of the soda-making process of Nicolas Leblanc. In the middle of the century, the great English chemical manufacturer James Muspratt wrote that the Leblanc process had a greater impact on social life, commerce, and chemical technology than any other discovery. Though most twentieth century historians would not go as far as Muspratt, they too recognize the great importance of Leblanc's method of producing soda in initiating the large-scale chemical industry. It is difficult to find an industry that was not influenced by the Leblanc process. For example, since the first step in the process depended on sulfuric acid, the expansion of Leblanc soda works was directly responsible for the growth of the sulfuric acid industry.

Unfortunately, Leblanc did not live to see the triumph of his method. Although he introduced his process in 1791, it did not become a significant producer of soda until two decades into the nineteenth century. By the time of Leblanc's discovery, scientists knew more than a dozen processes for converting salt into soda, at least seven of which had been tested on a large scale; five establishments were actually manufacturing artificial soda, mostly in association with more profitable chemical products. None of these processes, however, could compete with natural soda, which France continued to import from Spain. Though Leblanc's process was not completely novel, it was superior to these other methods, and it eventually came to be generally adopted. Leblanc himself did not really understand the detailed chemistry of the process he had discovered. In fact, the reactions of the Leblanc process were not precisely understood until the end of the nineteenth century, when the process itself began to go out of use.

During the 1820's, the Leblanc process began its triumphant spread to other countries. James Muspratt built his first major soda plant in Liverpool in 1823. A few years later, Charles Tennant built a soda factory in Glasgow, and it quickly became the largest in Europe, covering 100 acres and employing more than one thousand workers. As these and other factories prospered, they encountered problems, because the Leblanc process, besides producing soda, produced poisonous fumes and large quantities of solid toxic wastes. Despite its obvious drawbacks, the Leblanc process dominated the industrial production of soda for nearly a century. It did not have a serious competitor until the end of the nineteenth century, when the process of a Belgian chemist, Ernest Solvay, proved its superiority. The Leblanc process continued to hold onto a significant proportion of the soda market until World War I, but its inevitable end came in 1923, when the last Leblanc soda works was scrapped.

The discovery, development, and decline of the Leblanc process are now part of the history of technology. Despite his deficiencies as a scientist and entrepreneur, Leblanc showed how soda, so vital to the glass, soap, dye, and textile industries, could be made cheaply from common salt. His process also led to the foundation of the first chemical industries to be operated on a massive scale, which forced technicians to develop new mechanical equipment to handle large amounts of material more efficiently. The disadvantages connected with the process also forced scientists to find ways to use or control the harmful by-products produced by the process. In this way the Leblanc process became the paradigm of not only nineteenth century chemical industry but also its twentieth century counterparts. Thus, Leblanc, a man who considered his life a dismal failure, became a posthumous success.

—Robert J. Paradowski

FURTHER READING

Brock, William H. *The Chemical Tree: A History of Chemistry.* New York: Norton, 2000. Chapter 9, "Chemistry Applied to Arts and Manufactures," contains information on the alkali industry, including an account of Leblanc's discovery and process.

Clark, Ronald W. *Works of Man: A History of Invention and Engineering from the Pyramids to the Space Shuttle.* New York: Viking Press, 1985. Clark offers an anecdotal history of technology from the invention of the wheel to the miniaturization of the electronic computer. He briefly discusses Leblanc's work in connection with the development of man-made materials in the eighteenth and nineteenth centuries. Intended for general audiences and profusely illustrated with color and black-and-white photographs.

Daumas, Maurice, ed. *The First Stages of Mechanization.* Vol. 2 in *A History of Technology and Invention: Progress Through the Ages.* New York: Crown, 1969. This volume has chapters written by distinguished experts and represents original work rather than a synthesis of secondary sources. Lavishly illustrated with hundreds of photographs, drawings, and diagrams, this book provides a chronicle of industrial civilization told largely through the creative technical ideas of Leblanc and other inventors.

Gillispie, Charles C. "The Discovery of the Leblanc Process." *Isis* 48 (1957): 152-170. Offers a revisionist view, attacking the so-called legend of Leblanc, the chemist whose discovery of the artificial soda process should have garnered him rewards but instead made him a victim of the revolution. Gillispie believes this legend rests on very shaky information, almost all of which comes from a memoir published in 1884 by Leblanc's grandson, and that Leblanc was more the victim of his own difficult personality than of the accidents of history.

Haber, L. F. *The Chemical Industry During the Nineteenth Century: A Study of the Economic Aspect of Applied Chemistry in Europe and North America.* Oxford, England: Clarendon Press, 1958. This history of chemical technology, with an emphasis on economics, centers on the inorganic chemical industries and especially on four materials that governed the rate of expansion in the industry as a whole: sulfuric acid, soda ash, caustic soda, and bleaching powder. The changing role of the Leblanc process is studied in some detail. The technical and economic factors causing the rise and decline of Leblanc soda works in different countries and at different times form a major theme of this book.

Oesper, Ralph E. "Nicolas Leblanc (1742-1806)." *Journal of Chemical Education* 19/20 (1942/1943): 567-572. A major source for Leblanc's life and work in English. Presents a fairly detailed account of Leblanc's life, the genesis of his process, his efforts to obtain recompense for his discovery, and his tragic end. In contrast to the Gillispie article (see above), Oesper blames circumstances rather than Leblanc for Leblanc's misfortunes.

Partington, J. R. *A History of Chemistry.* Vol. 3. New York: Macmillan, 1962. Contains information on the origins of some important chemical industries, including a detailed account of Leblanc's work. Partington bases his text almost entirely on original sources, and he gives many quotations from these sources. His approach is encyclopedic rather than analytic, but this is a reliable source for those without the time or language skills to prospect through the original material.

See also: Louis XVI; Duc d'Orléans.

Related articles in *Great Events from History: The Eighteenth Century, 1701-1800*: 1714: Fahrenheit Develops the Mercury Thermometer; 1718: Geoffroy Issues the *Table of Reactivities*; 1722: Réaumur Discovers Carbon's Role in Hardening Steel; 1723: Stahl Postulates the Phlogiston Theory; 1738: Bernoulli Proposes the Kinetic Theory of Gases; 1745: Lomonosov Issues the First Catalog of Minerals; 1748: Nollet Discovers Osmosis; June 5, 1755: Black Identifies Carbon Dioxide; 1771: Woulfe Discovers Picric Acid; August 1, 1774: Priestley Discovers Oxygen; 1781-1784: Cavendish Discovers the Composition of Water; 1786-1787: Lavoisier Devises the Modern System of Chemical Nomenclature; 1789: Leblanc Develops Soda Production.

ANN LEE

English-born American religious leader

Lee was the founder of the United Society of Believers in Christ's Second Coming, a religious sect commonly known as the Shakers. Members of the sect believed Lee to be the female embodiment of Christ and the maternal component of the Father/Mother God.

Born: February 29, 1736; Manchester, England
Died: September 8, 1784; Niskeyuna (now Watervliet), New York
Also known as: Mother Ann
Area of achievement: Religion and theology

EARLY LIFE

Information about Ann Lee's childhood is scarce. According to Shaker tradition, she was born in the slums of Manchester, a manufacturing town in northwestern England. Cathedral records indicate that she was baptized in the Anglican Church on June 1, 1742. Apparently, she was the second of eight children, five boys and three girls, in the John Lee household. Her father was a blacksmith. Little is known about her mother, whose name is unknown, except that she was a pious woman in the Anglican Church.

Like most eighteenth century girls born into English working-class families, Ann Lee received no formal education and remained illiterate throughout her life, but she was industrious from her youth. As a teenager, she worked in the textile mills; at age twenty, she became a cook in a public infirmary. A turning point in Lee's life occurred in 1758, when she joined a society of religious dissenters led by Jane and James Wardley.

The Wardley group, called the Shaking Quakers by their critics, called people to repent and to be prepared for the imminent reappearance of Christ, who would sweep away all anti-Christian denominations and establish a millennial kingdom on earth. Worship at the Wardleys' was informal and spirited. Believers gathered, sat briefly in silent meditation, and then responded to the impulses of the spirit. The services included ecstatic utterances, prophecies concerning the end of the world, physical manifestations such as falling and jerking, and personal testimonies of supernatural assistance.

In 1762, Lee was persuaded by her parents to marry Abraham Standerin, an illiterate blacksmith who may have worked for Lee's father. Historians have speculated that this marriage was arranged to wean Lee from her association with the Wardley sect. The marriage, which Lee apparently never desired, resulted in the birth of four children, all of whom died in infancy. The delivery of her last child was especially difficult. Forceps were used, and Lee lost much blood and almost her life. When the infant died in October of 1766, the physically weak and emotionally dispirited mother sought divine consolation. In the midst of her anguish, Lee became convinced that sexual cohabitation was the source not only of her travails but also of all evil. For Lee and for her future religious followers, salvation from sin demanded public confession and holy, celibate living after the pattern of Jesus.

LIFE'S WORK

After the death of her fourth child, Ann Lee assumed a more vocal and prominent role in the Wardley society. By the early 1770's, this religious sect was engaging in confrontational tactics designed to attract attention to its teachings. On several occasions, for example, the Shakers invaded the sanctuaries of congregations gathered for worship to disrupt the church services and proclaim their message of apocalyptic judgment. For these actions, they were prosecuted for assault, the destruction of property, and the breaching of the Sabbath. Among those fined and imprisoned was Ann Lee Standerin. While in prison, Lee received a "grand vision." In this vision, Christ appeared to Lee and told her she was to be his special instrument. As the "Mother of the New Creation" she would teach confession as the door to regeneration and celibacy as its "rule and cross."

Like many other groups of religious dissenters throughout history, the Shakers thrived on opposition, which united them against the "wicked world." Persecution, however, also brought much unpleasantness. Neighbors, disliking the noise, speaking in tongues, and dark prophecies of the Shaker meetings, verbally abused the members of the sect, charged them with heresy and witchcraft, and even threatened mob violence. Local authorities permitted the sect to worship together in private, but no street preaching or disruptive intrusions into other public services of worship were allowed. Although the sect won a few converts, such as John Lee, Ann's father, and William Lee, her brother, under these difficult circumstances, the prospects for evangelical success in England were limited.

In the spring of 1774, Lee received another vision informing her that a harvest of souls awaited her ministry in America. Shortly thereafter, eight members of the sect, plus Abraham Standerin, who never joined the group, left England for New York. The immigrants did not include the Wardleys, who by now disagreed with some of the teachings of Mother Ann. After a three-month voyage across the Atlantic Ocean aboard the ship *Mariah*, the group arrived in New York City on August 6. Financial problems forced the scattering of the small Shaker band. Several members sought work in upper New York State, near Albany. Lee remained in Manhattan, finding employment as a domestic worker. At this time, Lee still lived in a platonic relationship with her husband. Within a few years, however, the couple formally separated. Unlike Lee, Abraham Standerin refused to accept the Shaker commitment to celibacy.

In 1779, the Shakers purchased an isolated piece of land in Niskeyuna, near Albany. The dozen disciples of Mother Ann constructed a small building that served as both their communal quarters and meetinghouse. In April of 1780, two travelers stumbled upon the Shaker site. After receiving food, shelter, and religious instruction, the men promised to tell others in the New Light Baptist Church, where they were members, about the witness of Mother Ann. On May 19, 1780, the Shakers held their first worship service open to the general public. According to Shaker tradition, on this "Dark Day in New England" the Sun did not shine, a phenomenon that may have been caused by smoke from burning farmland. In the excitement of the meeting, several visitors experienced religious conversion. News about the spiritual quickenings at Niskeyuna spread throughout the towns of New Lebanon and Albany, and soon the Shaker site was deluged with curious and spiritually hungry guests.

Upstate New York, like other areas in the British colonies at this time, was bitterly divided between the American patriots who supported independence and the Loyalists (or Tories) who opposed independence from England. When a born-again Shaker convert was found by American patriots bringing some sheep to the commune at Niskeyuna, the anti-Tory forces became suspicious. Believing the Shaker sect to be a front organization for the British crown, the American authorities issued a warrant for Lee's arrest. To secure her release, William Lee, Ann's brother, asked General James Clinton of Albany to write a letter about the situation to the New York governor. The American general agreed, and with his assistance, Mother Ann was freed on December 4.

Publicity surrounding the arrest and release of Mother Ann aroused public sympathy from many New Yorkers who questioned why the authorities, who were allegedly fighting for freedom and personal liberty, would harass and imprison a religious pacifist who caused no harm to anyone. Buoyed by this positive response from the public, Mother Ann, William Lee, and James Whittaker, another Shaker elder who had come with the group from England, decided to begin a missionary tour into the neighboring states. Between May of 1781 and September of 1783, the three itinerant English Evangelists traveled throughout Massachusetts and Connecticut spreading the tenets of the Shaker faith.

In New England, as in England, Shaker success and opposition went hand in hand. In community after community, Mother Ann's simple message, regeneration through confession and perfection through celibacy, provoked a great response. On several occasions, opponents stormed the meetings and quarters of the itinerant preachers, insulting, threatening, and even stoning and beating them nearly to death. In Harvard, Massachusetts, for example, when rumors circulated that the Shakers refused to support the American revolutionary cause, local officials called the militia to drive the Shaker leaders out of town. After a three-week stay in Stonington, Connecticut, the Shaker ambassadors were warned by members of the local Baptist society to leave town within twenty-four hours or face brutal beatings. In Petersham, Massachusetts, an angry mob attacked Mother Ann, dragged her down a flight of stairs feet first, and ripped off her garments. Despite, or perhaps in some cases because of, the fierce opposition, the saintly female pacifist committed new converts to the Shaker faith in nearly every town she entered. Her evangelistic successes during this twenty-eight-month missionary tour laid the foundation for the establishment of future Shaker communities in Harvard, Shirley, and Hancock, Massachusetts, and in Enfield, Connecticut.

In September of 1783, the weary itinerants returned to their home in New York. Shortly after their arrival, the elders at Niskeyuna began the economic experiment in joint ownership for which later Shaker communities would become well known. The resulting form of Shaker communism, established so "that the poor might have an equal privilege of the gospel with the rich," rested on the common understanding that whatever was gained by individual industry would be used for the benefit and good of the whole society. The Shaker edict "Give all members of the Church an equal privilege, according to their abilities, to do good, as well as an equal privilege to receive according to their needs" became a central tenet of Shaker culture for the next two centuries.

Despite the tenacious spirit of the English immigrants, the years of toil, travel, persecution, and poverty took their toll on the Lee family. On July 21, 1784, William Lee died. According to Shaker tradition, he did not "appear to die by any natural infirmity; but he seemed to give up his life in sufferings." The death of Ann Lee's brother and spiritual comrade saddened the founder of the faith. The ailing leader, harassed in both body and spirit from her youth, yearned to be freed from her earthly travails. Less than two months after William's death, early in the morning of September 8, 1784, Mother Ann exclaimed her final words, "I see Brother William coming, in a golden chariot, to take me home."

News of the passing of the "Mother of Zion" shocked many of Ann Lee's followers, who believed, in spite of her rejection of the doctrine, that her earthly ministry would last one thousand years. Although many followers lost faith and fell away from the church, the United Society of Believers in Christ's Second Coming under the leadership of James Whittaker—the sole remaining member of the Shaker triumvirate—survived this time of crisis. Notwithstanding its twentieth century demise, the Shaker movement exhibited an inner vitality and strength that enabled it to outlive all subsequent utopian experiments in New World socialism.

SIGNIFICANCE

The daughter of an illiterate blacksmith from Manchester, England, Ann Lee lived most of her life in dire poverty. She never attended school and never read a book. None of her children survived infancy. She suffered through a difficult marriage and divorce. Yet Lee was revered as the female embodiment of God by thousands of American men and women who called her Mother Ann, who pledged all their belongings to her cause, and who, in time, attempted to recall and publish for future generations every word she uttered.

As the charismatic leader of a millennialist movement, Mother Ann possessed an extraordinary power over people. For her followers, her saintly life was proof enough of the truth of her teachings. Although she never attempted to develop a systematic theology, her thoughts on the importance of public confession, celibate living, and the need to share one's worldly possessions inspired many people to strive for human perfection. Moreover, her understanding of God as a feminine as well as a masculine deity provided future generations of Shakers with a theological basis for promoting equal rights for women.

—*Terry D. Bilhartz*

FURTHER READING

Andrews, Edward Deming. *The People Called Shakers: A Search for the Perfect Society.* Oxford, England: Oxford University Press, 1953. Until the publication of Stephen Stein's 1992 text, this was the definitive work on the Shaker movement. Although dated, this sympathetic treatment remains an excellent introduction to the study of Shaker origins.

Bencini, Robert F. *Ms. Inventor: Circular Saws, Flat Brooms, and Clothes Pins: The Remarkable Inventions of Ann Lee.* San Francisco, Calif.: Robert D. Reed, 2001. This work focuses on Lee's inventions, including an early computer, the rocking chair, and clothespins. Bencini describes how Lee and other Shakers were innovative inventors but were too humble to take credit for their discoveries.

Brewer, Priscilla J. *Shaker Communities, Shaker Lives.* Hanover, N.H.: University Press of New England, 1986. A scholarly yet sympathetic treatment of the origins of, and developments within, Shakerism to 1904.

Campion, Nardi Reeder. *Mother Ann Lee: Morning Star of the Shakers.* Hanover, N.H.: University Press of New England, 1990. Perhaps the best biography of Ann Lee, this volume is a revised edition of Campion's 1976 book *Ann the Word.* Includes bibliographic references.

Francis, Richard. *Ann, the Word: The Story of Ann Lee, Female Messiah, Mother of the Shakers, the Woman Clothed with the Sun.* New York: Arcade, 2001. An updated biography by a novelist and professor, recounting Lee's life and the early, radical history of the Shaker movement.

Humez, Jean M., ed. *Mother's First-Born Daughters: Early Shaker Writings on Women and Religion.* Bloomington: Indiana University Press, 1993. Although Mother Ann never wrote a book, reminiscences of her life and many of her sayings were later compiled and published by her followers. Chapter 1 of this volume includes a number of testimonies about the beloved Shaker founder.

Joy, Arthur F. *The Queen of the Shakers.* Minneapolis, Minn.: Denison, 1960. A biography of Ann Lee drawn largely from uncritical Shaker sources.

Stein, Stephen J. *The Shaker Experience in America: A History of the United Society of Believers.* New Haven, Conn.: Yale University Press, 1992. The best single-volume textbook to survey the history of the Shaker church from its origins to its twentieth century demise.

See also: Isaac Backus; Charles Carroll; Jonathan Edwards; Cotton Mather; Increase Mather; Samuel

Sewall; Charles Wesley; John Wesley; George Whitefield.

Related articles in *Great Events from History: The Eighteenth Century, 1701-1800:* 1739-1742: First Great Awakening; October 30, 1768: Methodist Church Is Established in Colonial America; 1773-

1788: African American Baptist Church Is Founded; January 16, 1786: Virginia Statute of Religious Liberty; July 28-October 16, 1789: Episcopal Church Is Established; 1790's-1830's: Second Great Awakening.

CHARLOTTE LENNOX
English novelist and scholar

Lennox's novels, which could be described as sentimentally romantic, include her second novel, The Female Quixote, *which enjoyed both popular and critical acclaim in its own day and endures as one of the period's better fictional works. Lennox was the first to examine Shakespeare's use of his sources in her work of criticism, and her French translations introduced Anglophones to significant French works of the period.*

Born: c. 1729; probably Gibraltar
Died: January 4, 1804; Westminster, England
Also known as: Charlotte Ramsay (birth name); Barbara Ramsay
Areas of achievement: Literature, theater

EARLY LIFE
The details of Charlotte Lennox's early life are uncertain, in part because she distorted her biography in appealing to the Royal Literary Fund. To win greater sympathy, she claimed to be about ten years older than she was, and she claimed that her father had been a colonel instead of an infantry captain and then claimed he was lieutenant-governor of New York. Also to blame for the ambiguity surrounding her life is the desire of readers to turn her first novel, *The Life of Harriot Stuart* (1750), into fictionalized autobiography.

Charlotte apparently was born about 1729, probably in Gibraltar, where her father, James Ramsay, was serving in an infantry regiment. In late 1738, Ramsay was posted to Albany, New York, where Charlotte absorbed details of the landscape and its indigenous peoples that would figure in her first and last novels. When her father died in 1743, Charlotte returned to England without her mother, Catherine Tisdale Ramsay. Catherine died in America in 1765.

In London, Lennox, like her heroine Harriot Stuart, was befriended by two aristocratic women, Lady Isabella Finch and her sister, the countess of Rockingham. Lennox dedicated her first book, *Poems on Several Oc-*

casions (1747), to Lady Isabella, but *The Life of Harriot Stuart* satirizes Lady Cecelia (a thinly disguised version of Lady Isabella), indicating that Lennox was disappointed in her expectations of her patron.

A month before the appearance of Lennox's book of poems, she married Alexander Lennox (October 6, 1747). Her husband was to prove a financial and emotional drain on Charlotte. His chief contributions to her life consisted of providing the model for the disreputable husband in Lennox's last novel, *Euphemia* (1790) and of introducing her to Samuel Johnson. (Alexander had worked for a time with Johnson's printer, William Strahan.) Johnson proved to be Lennox's greatest supporter, and he introduced her to other important London literary figures, including the novelist and printer Samuel Richardson, the publisher Andrew Millar, and John Boyle, the earl of Orrery. Lennox tried unsuccessfully to earn a living as an actor; Horace Walpole described her as "deplorable," in a letter to George Montagu (1748). Lennox then turned to writing to earn a living.

LIFE'S WORK
In 1750, Charlotte Lennox published a quasi-epistolary novel called *The Life of Harriot Stuart, Written by Herself.* The book received mostly favorable reviews, though the *Monthly Review* (December, 1750) noted a lack of interesting characters or memorable events. Lennox's next book and by far her best was *The Female Quixote: Or, The Adventures of Arabella* (1752). The heroine Arabella devours seventeenth century French romances, and her reading has affected her perception of reality. Thus, she believes an "under-gardener" to be a prince in disguise and a prostitute to be a damsel in distress. She frequently thinks she is about to be ravished. Late in the novel, fleeing from imagined pursuers, she leaps into the Thames River and nearly dies. During her convalescence, a minister disabuses her of her romantic notions, and she later marries her long-suffering cousin.

The chapter with the minister shows Johnson's influence and may have been written by him. Johnson and Richardson persuaded Millar to publish the book, after Johnson and novelist Henry Fielding touted the book in their reviews. The novel went through multiple editions in English and was translated into German (1754), French (1773), and Spanish (1808). George Colman's comedy *Polly Honeycombe* (1760) is based on Lennox's novel. Jane Austen read the book at least twice and used it as a model for *Northanger Abbey* (1818).

In 1753, Lennox published *Shakespear Illustrated*. The project was suggested by Johnson, who was preparing to edit the playwright's works and intended to discuss Shakespeare's debts to his sources. Lennox thus could help him and herself. Lennox already knew French; to deal with Italian works she studied the language with Giuseppe Baretti, whom she then introduced to Johnson. The two men became lifelong friends. In her three volumes, Lennox presents the sources of twenty-two plays, the first such study of the subject. Lennox's neoclassical views led her to condemn Shakespeare's adaptations. Of *Measure for Measure*, she wrote, "What he has altered from *Cinthio*, is altered greatly for the worse." Elsewhere she stated that, "Wherever Shakespeare has altered or invented, his *Winter's Tale* is greatly inferior to the old paltry Story that furnished him with the Subject of it." She also objected to Shakespeare's treatment of his heroines, blaming him for making them weak and silly.

Throughout her life Lennox needed money. In the 1750's she undertook a series of translations from the French. She also found time to write another novel, *The History of Henrietta* (1758), based on Pierre Carlet de Chamblain de Marivaux's *La vie de Marianne* (1731-1741). The second edition of *The History of Henrietta* (1761) is dedicated to the duchess of Newcastle, who had provided financial assistance when the struggling author was ill in 1760. The novel shows that for women, wealth is more important than virtue, beauty, and birth in securing a good marriage.

In the 1760's, Lennox launched the short-lived magazine *The Lady's Museum* (March, 1760-January, 1761), in which she serialized her next novel, published separately as *Sophia* (1762). The serious heroine of the novel, Sophia, and her worldly sister, Harriot, anticipate Elinor and Marianne in Jane Austen's *Sense and Sensibility* (1811). To eke out a living, Lennox served as governess to the daughters of Saunders Welch, a London police magistrate, and, in 1765, Lennox gave birth to a daughter, Harriot Holles Lennox (d. 1783 or 1784). In 1771, she had a son named George Louis.

Lennox was unable to have her dramatic pastoral *Philander* (1757) staged, and *The Sister* (1769), based on *The History of Henrietta*, closed after just one performance. She enjoyed more success with *Old City Manners* (1775), which she adapted from Ben Jonson, George Chapman, and John Marston's *Eastward Hoe!* (1605) at the urging of David Garrick, who produced her comedy at his Drury Lane Theatre in London on November 9, 1775. The play was performed six times that month and once more in January, 1776.

Lennox's last novel, *Euphemia*, appeared in 1790. Like *Harriot Stuart*, this work draws on Lennox's years in New York and incorporates her unhappy experiences with her husband, from whom she had separated sometime after 1782. Lennox spent her last years in poverty, dependent on grants from the Royal Literary Society (established in 1790. She died in Dean's Yard, Westminster, on January 4, 1804, and was buried in an unmarked grave.

SIGNIFICANCE

Charlotte Lennox's reputation rests on *The Female Quixote*, though her *Shakespear Illustrated* also is an important landmark in the study of Shakespeare's use of his sources. Her greatest significance as a writer lies in her influence on her successors, especially Jane Austen, who admired Lennox's writings. Feminist critics of the late twentieth century and the twenty-first century find in Lennox's work an exploration of the difficulties women faced in a patriarchal society. For example, *The Female Quixote*'s Arabella is led astray by her faulty education, and *The History of Henrietta* examines the plight of a woman without money.

Lennox's life reveals the same difficulties. Although aristocratic patronage for writers was fading in the late eighteenth century, it was being supplanted by another kind of patronage: support from private individuals. Johnson, Richardson, and Fielding helped Lennox get published, and Garrick and Colman tried to promote her plays. Without their assistance, Lennox would not have been noticed and thereby would not have enjoyed any success. Also, the writing life in the eighteenth century, and into the nineteenth century, remained more difficult for women than for men. Lennox's younger contemporary, Charlotte Smith, also struggled to earn a living by her pen, and Austen's six novels combined earned her less than £200.

—*Joseph Rosenblum*

FURTHER READING

Berg, Temma F. "Getting the Mother's Story Right: Charlotte Lennox and the New World." *Papers on*

Language and Literature 32 (Fall, 1996): 369-398. Examines how women are presented in Lennox's two "American" novels (*Harriot Stuart* and *Euphemia*).

Hanley, Brian. "Henry Fielding, Samuel Johnson, Samuel Richardson, and the Reception of Charlotte Lennox's *The Female Quixote*." *ANQ* 13 (Summer, 2000): 27-32. Discusses how Fielding, Johnson, and Richardson promoted the publication and then sale of Lennox's most popular novel.

Howard, Susan Kubica, ed. *The Life of Harriot Stuart, Written by Herself.* Madison, N.J.: Fairleigh Dickinson University Press, 1995. Howard's introduction supplements and corrects earlier biographical studies. It also provides a good critical introduction to Lennox's novel.

Small, Miriam Rossiter. *Charlotte Ramsay Lennox: An Eighteenth Century Lady of Letters.* New Haven,

Conn.: Yale University Press, 1935. Still the standard biography, though some information is out of date. Includes good discussions of Lennox's writings.

Spender, Dale. *Mothers of the Novel: One Hundred Good Women Writers Before Jane Austen.* London: Pandora, 1986. Offers a feminist perspective on Lennox's career.

See also: Hannah Cowley; Daniel Defoe; Henry Fielding; David Garrick; Samuel Johnson; Thomas Lawrence; Hannah More; Samuel Richardson.

Related articles in *Great Events from History: The Eighteenth Century, 1701-1800:* December 7, 1732: Covent Garden Theatre Opens in London; 1742: Fielding's *Joseph Andrews* Satirizes English Society.

ALAIN-RENÉ LESAGE
French playwright, novelist, and satirist

Lesage's Gil Blas de Santillane *brought the Spanish picaresque form of the novel to France. Moreover, his versatility as a playwright enabled him to write successful plays for both the middle- and working-class Théâtre de la Foire and the upper-class Comédie-Française, thereby entertaining the entire Parisian theatergoing public.*

Born: May 8, 1668; Sarzeau, Brittany, France
Died: November 17, 1747; Boulogne, France
Also known as: Alain-René LeSage; Alain-René Le Sage
Areas of achievement: Literature, theater

EARLY LIFE

Alain-René Lesage (ah-la-ruh-nay lay-sahzh) was the son of a royal notary; his mother belonged to the provincial bourgeoisie. The family was economically comfortable. On September 11, 1677, at the age of nine, Lesage lost his mother. Then, just five years later, on December 24, 1682, his father died, leaving him an orphan at the age of fourteen. Lesage remained in Brittany under the tutelage of his uncle. He studied at the Jesuit school at Vannes. Although his father had left him an adequate fortune, he was soon ruined by his uncle.

In 1690, Lesage went to Paris, where he studied law and philosophy. In 1692, he obtained his degree and was placed on the list of lawyers at the Palais de Justice. Dur-

ing this time, he may or may not have had a brief liaison with an older woman of the nobility. While in Paris, he met and courted Marie-Élisabeth Huyard. In spite of the fact that neither had an adequate fortune, they married on September 28, 1694. Few details are known of this period of his life. It is believed that he spent some time in the provinces working for a tax collector. Lesage was far more attracted to a literary life than to that of a lawyer, however. In 1695, he translated the *Epistolai Erōtikai* (pb. 1566; love letters) of Aristaenetus (fl. fifth century) and published them as *Les Lettres galantes d'Aristénète*.

LIFE'S WORK

In 1698, Lesage returned to Paris; the abbot of Lyon was providing him with a modest allowance. Soon, though, in order to support himself, Marie-Élisabeth, and their children, he was working in the book trade. Because Spain was very fashionable to Parisians at the time and because he knew the Spanish language, Lesage translated works from Spain's Golden Age into French. In 1707, he published *Théâtre espagnol: Ou, Les Meilleures comédies des plus fameux auteurs espagnols, traduites en français* (Spanish theater: or, the best comedies of the most famous Spanish authors, translated into French), which contained translations of Spanish plays including works by Francisco de Rojas Zorilla and Lope de Vega.

In 1707, Lesage enjoyed his first success as an author. On March 15, 1707, two of his plays were performed at the Comédie-Française. *Don César Ursin* (pr. 1707) failed to appeal to the audience, but the other play, *Crispin rival de son maître* (pr., pb. 1707; *Crispin, Rival of His Master*, 1766), was extremely well received. The play treated on the then-popular theme of thwarted marriage. This theme usually dealt with young people hoping to get married over the objections of the girl's parents. The couple's problems would then be solved by the clever efforts of a trusted family valet. Lesage's play was innovative in that his hero, the valet Crispin, was working to arrange his own marriage. This same year, Lesage's novel *Le Diable boiteux* (1707; *The Devil upon Two Sticks*, 1708, 1726) met with great success among the reading public. An imitation of a Spanish novel, the work permitted the reader to spy on the various characters as the devil lifted the roofs of houses. The work was actually a satire of contemporary French society.

In 1709, Lesage tried to get his play *Les Étrennes* (New Year's gifts) performed. The actors refused. Lesage then rewrote the play and named it *Turcaret: Comédie en cinq actes* (pr., pb. 1709; English translation, 1923). This comedy of manners attacked unscrupulous financiers. The opposition to its performance by the community of financiers in Paris was phenomenal. Some of them even tried to prevent its performance by bribing Lesage. On February 14, 1709, the play was performed by order of the Crown.

After the scandal caused by *Turcaret*, Lesage shied away from the Comédie-Française; he turned his attention to the Théâtre de la Foire. He wrote almost one hundred comic operas for this theater. Between 1712 and 1737, he prepared a collection of comic opera scripts for publication as *Le Théâtre de la Foire: Ou, L'Opéra comique* (pr. 1712-1738, pb. 1721-1737; 10 volumes; with d'Orneval, Louis Fuzelier, and others). These scripts differed from those actually used at the Théâtre de la Foire, however. In the original scripts, the actors had opportunities to improvise. They told bawdy jokes and provided other crass forms of entertainment. The scripts published by Lesage contained none of this. Whether Lesage was actually trying to elevate the comic opera by purging it of grossness or whether he was preparing scripts that would be approved by the censors and appeal to upper-class readers remains an unanswered question. Lesage did, however, spend almost twenty-five years working with this theater.

In 1715, Lesage published the first six books of his masterpiece, *Histoire de Gil Blas de Santillane* (1715-1735, 4 volumes; *The History of Gil Blas of Santillane*, 1716, 1735; better known as *Gil Blas*, 1749, 1962). In

Alain-René Lesage. (The Granger Collection, New York)

1724, books seven through nine appeared. In 1735, books ten through twelve were published. Lesage was once again borrowing from Spanish literature, this time in the form that he used for his novel. *Gil Blas* is a picaresque novel. The hero is a young adventurer of the peasant class who sets off to see the world. The novel recounts his adventures and those of the people he meets along the way. During this period, Lesage continued to produce translations and adaptations of Spanish works. His final work, *Le Bachelier de Salamanque* (*The Bachelor of Salamanca*, 1737-1739), appeared in 1736.

Lesage spent the last years of his life with his second son at Boulogne. The death of his oldest son, the actor Montménil, in 1743 had seriously affected him. He spent his time reworking and correcting *Gil Blas*. A new edition appeared in 1747. On November 17, 1747, Lesage died at Boulogne-sur-Mer.

SIGNIFICANCE

The eighteenth century was the period in which the French novel was perfected and developed into a literary genre. With the publication of *Gil Blas*, Alain-René Lesage introduced a new form into French fiction, the picaresque, and gave the genre a new hero, a naïve young man of common class who, by recounting his adventures, presented contemporary society to the reader. The novel also depicted the man's rise in society and a certain moral improvement in his character. This hero appeared again as Jacob in Marivaux's *Le Paysan parvenu* (1734-1735; *The Fortunate Peasant*, 1735).

Through the end of the seventeenth century, French novels had been historical, recounting happenings and adventures set in the past. In his novels, Lesage depicted contemporary French society. It was often lightly concealed under a Spanish veil, but it was contemporary French society. The depiction of contemporary society became an essential element of the novel as the century progressed. In both his plays, especially *Turcaret*, and his novels, Lesage recorded the manners, morals, and foibles of his time.

—Shawncey Webb

FURTHER READING

Benoit, Annick, and Guy Fontaine. "The Picaresque Novel." In *History of European Literature*, edited by Annick Benoit-Dusausoy and Guy Fontaine. New York: Routledge, 2000. Discusses the genre Lesage introduced into France, and its Spanish origins.

Lesage, Alain-René. *Le Diable boiteux: Or, The Devil upon Two Sticks*. New York: Garland, 1972. English translation of Lesage's first novel imitating the Spanish novel.

_____. *The History and Adventure of Gil Blas de Santillane*. New York: Garland, 1972. English translation of Lesage's masterpiece.

Longhurst, Jennifer. "Lesage and the Spanish Tradition: *Gil Blas* as a Picaresque Novel." In *Studies in Eighteenth Century Literature*, edited by J. H. Fox, M. H. Waddicor, and D. A. Watts. Exeter, Devon, England: University of Exeter Press, 1975. Discusses the picaresque form and how it was modified and used by Lesage.

Runte, Roseann. "Parallels Between Lesage's Theater and His Novels." In *Enlightenment Studies in Honor of Lester G. Crocker*, edited by Alfred Bingham and Virgil W. Topazio. Oxford, England: Voltaire Foundation, 1979. Looks at Lesage's work in both genres; identifies his main themes and style.

Rush, Jane. "The Pricking of Balloons in Lesage's Le Théatre de la Foire." *Eighteenth Century Life* 19, no. 3 (November, 1995): 70-85. Examines Lesage and popular theater, and his lesser-known work.

See also: Pierre-Augustin Caron de Beaumarchais; Marquis de Sade; Madame de Staël; Marquis de Vauvenargues; Voltaire.

Related articles in *Great Events from History: The Eighteenth Century, 1701-1800*: April 25, 1719: Defoe Publishes the First Novel; 1721-1750: Early Enlightenment in France; 1740-1741: Richardson's *Pamela* Establishes the Modern Novel; 1742: Fielding's *Joseph Andrews* Satirizes English Society; January, 1759: Voltaire Satirizes Optimism in *Candide*.

GOTTHOLD EPHRAIM LESSING
German playwright and critic

In addition to being a major literary critic and dramatist, Lessing helped bring the ideas of the European Enlightenment to Germany and founded the discipline of philosophy of religion.

Born: January 22, 1729; Kamenz, Saxony (now in Germany)
Died: February 15, 1781; Braunschweig, Brunswick (now in Germany)
Areas of achievement: Literature, theater, philosophy

EARLY LIFE

Born the son of a Protestant minister, Gotthold Ephraim Lessing (GAWT-hawlt AY-frah-ihm LEHS-ihng) enrolled as a student of theology at the University of Leipzig in 1746, but he was soon attracted by literature and

the theater. He wrote his first play, *Der junge Gelehrte* (the young scholar), a comedy that was performed with great success by the local company in 1748. Other comedies were to follow, and soon it became apparent that Lessing had embarked on a literary rather than a theological career. Lessing's early comedies were comparatively trivial, following the model advocated by Johann Christoph Gottsched, who dominated literary life in Germany until approximately 1750. Although Lessing followed Gottsched, he did write two problem plays, which show his departure from the Gottschedian model: *Die Juden* (wr. 1749, pb. 1754; *The Jews*, 1801) and *Die Freigeist* (wr. 1749, pb. 1755; *The Freethinker*, 1838). In the first comedy, Lessing attacked anti-Semitic prejudices, while in the second, he neither glorified nor criti-

Gotthold Ephraim Lessing. (Library of Congress)

cized his protagonist but tried to provide his character with a larger degree of realism. While *The Jews* is a forerunner of *Nathan der Weise* (1779; *Nathan the Wise*, 1781) in terms of its topicality, *The Freethinker* is an anticipation of contemporary realist comedy, as represented by Lessing's *Minna von Barnhelm: Oder, Das Soldatenglück* (1767; *Minna von Barnhelm: Or, The Soldier's Fortune*, 1786).

In 1748, Lessing went to Berlin, where he stayed until 1755. Lessing was one of the first free-lance writers in German literature, trying to live by the work of his pen. He failed in the end and had to take a civil service position, as did the majority of intellectuals in eighteenth century Germany, such as Johann Wolfgang von Goethe and Friedrich Schiller; Lessing's endeavors, nevertheless, were an inspiration to subsequent generations of writers. Beginning his career as a journalist, Lessing also published a number of scholarly articles and was active as a translator, editor, and literary critic. In 1751-1752, he briefly attended the University of Wittenberg to obtain a master's degree but returned to Berlin in November, 1752.

One of the most important events of Lessing's life in Berlin was the beginning of his lifelong friendship with

Moses Mendelssohn. Mendelssohn had made the transition from the protected existence within the Jewish community, which had lived in the physical and intellectual isolation of the ghettos since the Middle Ages, to participation in the surrounding German and European life of commerce and intellect. Mendelssohn met with much prejudice, but Lessing accepted him on equal terms. Indeed, Lessing's support of Mendelssohn paved the way for Jewish emancipation in Germany. The Lessing-Mendelssohn friendship was perceived as a symbol of a successful German-Jewish symbiosis. While this symbol was rendered totally invalid by the Holocaust of World War II, it was, nevertheless, true for the eighteenth century. Lessing modeled Nathan the Wise, the noble Jewish protagonist of his last drama, after Mendelssohn.

Lessing's first successful tragedy, *Miss Sara Sampson* (English translation, 1789), was written, performed, and published in 1755. Lessing introduced domestic, or bourgeois, tragedy to the German stage. The introduction of middle-class characters and their family problems into tragedy constituted his break with Gottsched, who had reserved tragedy for affairs of state and the fate of princes. Because of its sentimental appeal and audience identification with the protagonists, the performance was a great success. The middle-class audience saw characters of its class onstage and witnessed their struggle with ethical norms and their ensuing tragic failures.

In 1756, Lessing planned to embark on a three-year Grand Tour of Europe as traveling companion to a wealthy young man, but they had to abandon their travel plans when the Seven Years' War broke out in Europe. After a short stay in Leipzig, Lessing returned to Berlin in 1758. There, he edited and published, together with Mendelssohn and Christoph Friedrich Nicolai, *Briefe, die neueste Literatur betreffend* (1759-1760; letters on current literature), a journal that employed the fiction of letters, reporting on recent publications to a friend. The criteria developed by Lessing and his friends in their literary criticism provided new standards of excellence for German literature, which was still in its beginnings at this time. One of Lessing's most famous contributions was the seventeenth letter of February, 1759, attacking Gottsched and his hold on German literature and recommending William Shakespeare instead of the French classicists as a model for German drama. Lessing praised Shakespeare as a far greater tragic poet than Pierre Corneille and suggested the Faust theme as appropriate for German drama in the Shakespearean tradition.

Lessing's journeyman years were over when he became a secretary to the Prussian commanding general in Breslau, Silesia, in 1760. This interlude from 1760 to 1765 marks the transition from Lessing's early years to the major works of his life.

LIFE'S WORK

Lessing's treatise *Laokoon: Oder, Über die Grenzen der Mahlerei und Poesie* (1766; *Laocoön: An Essay on the Limits of Painting and Poetry*, 1836) and his comedy *Minna von Barnhelm* were the major results of the productive pause of his Breslau years. With his treatise *Laocoön,* Lessing settled a problem that had plagued writers for generations, namely, that literature should paint with words. Lessing showed that literature cannot be judged by the same criteria as painting and sculpture; the various arts proceed according to their differing materials and methods, and their subjects are presented according to these differences.

Minna von Barnhelm is the first modern German comedy. Against the backdrop of the Seven Years' War, the comedy confronts the problem of honor and love. Uniting subjects of former enemy states (Prussia and Saxony) in marriage injected an element of a new German national consciousness into the play. The new realism made *Minna von Barnhelm* one of Lessing's masterpieces.

After resigning from his position in Breslau in 1765, Lessing went for a short stay in Berlin. In 1767, he accepted the position as official critic of the German National Theater. As such, he was to write weekly commentaries on the current productions, reviewing the plays and analyzing the performance of the actors. When the project of a national theater at Hamburg was abandoned, Lessing lost his position. His reviews were published in book form under the title *Hamburgische Dramaturgie* (1767-1769; *Hamburg Dramaturgy*, 1889). In these weekly commentaries, Lessing developed his own theory of drama, based on a reinterpretation of Aristotle's poetics. Rejecting French classical drama, Lessing embraced Shakespearean tragedy, which did not follow Aristotle's rules yet always achieved, according to Lessing, the effects of tragedy. Lessing interpreted Aristotle's concept of catharsis as purification of the passions of pity and fear aroused in the spectators. The goal of tragedy was the "transformation of the passions into virtuous faculties."

After the collapse of the national theater enterprise in Hamburg, Lessing accepted a position as court librarian at the ducal library in Wolfenbüttel, where the dukes of Braunschweig-Lüneburg had assembled one of Europe's largest libraries. During his years in Wolfenbüttel, Lessing was very productive as a scholar, playwright, and theologian. In 1772, he

---

A SOLDIER'S FORTUNE

Gotthold Ephraim Lessing's play Minna von Barnhelm *was written in the wake of the Seven Years' War, which involved every major European power. Lessing used the war as a backdrop for his love story between a soldier and his now-married love. In the scene excerpted here, the main characters, Major von Tellheim and Minna von Barnhelm, have just found themselves together in an inn. It is the first time they have seen each other since Minna's marriage.*

MIN. Well, are we still both mistaken?

MAJ. T. Would to heaven it were so!—But there is only one Minna, and you are that one.

MIN. What ceremony! The world might hear what we have to say to one another.

MAJ. T. You here? What do you want here, Madam?

MIN. Nothing now (going to him with open arms). I have found all that I wanted.

MAJ. T. (drawing back). You seek a prosperous man, and one worthy of your love; and you find—a wretched one.

MIN. Then do you love me no longer? Do you love another?

MAJ. T. Ah! he never loved you, who could love another afterwards.

MIN. You draw but one dagger from my breast; for if I have lost your heart, what matters whether indifference or more powerful charms than mine have robbed me of it? You love me no longer; neither do you love another? Wretched man indeed, if you love nothing!

MAJ. T. Right; the wretched must love nothing. He merits his misfortunes, if he cannot achieve this victory over himself—if he can allow the woman he loves to take part in his misfortune . . . Oh! how difficult is this victory! . . . Since reason and necessity have commanded me to forget Minna von Barnhelm, what pains have I taken! I was just beginning to hope that my trouble would not for ever be in vain—and you appear.

Source: Gotthold Ephraim Lessing, Minna von Barnhelm: Or, The Soldier's Fortune. *Translated by Ernest Bell (New York: P. F. Collier, 1909-1914), act 2, scene 9, lines 1-10.*

authored the tragedy *Emilia Galotti* (English translation, 1786). Its subject is a middle-class woman named Virginia who lacks the political elements of the Roman Virginia, who was killed by her father to protect her honor from a tyrannical ruler. This sacrifice caused a revolt that abolished the tyranny in Rome around 450 B.C.E. Lessing may have wanted his audience to draw its own conclusions, but it took more than ten years before the political content of his tragedy was realized.

As a scholar, Lessing made available in print excerpts from a manuscript of his late friend Hermann Samuel Reimarus, who had advocated Deism, a denial of revelation in Christian religion. Such views were so controversial in Germany that Lessing published these excerpts from 1774 to 1778 under the fictitious claim of anonymous manuscripts, *Fragmente . . . aus den Papieren eines Ungenannten* (fragments . . . from the papers of an unknown [author]), found in the Wolfenbüttel library. Even this fiction, however, did not protect Lessing from attacks by the Protestant clergy. He had to defend himself in numerous pamphlets against his adversaries, but finally the duke of Braunschweig-Lüneburg imposed strict censorship on Lessing's theological writings. Lessing then turned to the stage, since literature was not subject to censorship, and presented his theological thoughts in the form of a drama, *Nathan the Wise*. The place of action is Jerusalem, where representatives of the three revealed religions, Judaism, Christianity, and Islam, meet during the Crusades to engage in a controversy that may end in tragic death. The main representatives are Sultan Saladin, a historical figure; Nathan the Wise, a noble Jew; and a Christian Knight Templar. The drama poses the question: Which of the three great religions is the true one? Nathan answers by telling the parable of the three rings. The moral of the parable advises the three principal characters of the play that verification of the true religion is as impossible as the identification of the original ring in the parable. The revelations of the major religions must rely on faith and tradition. Their representatives are enjoined to exercise tolerance and to strive for ethical superiority.

While Lessing's treatise *Ernst und Falk: Gespräche für Freimaurer* (*Masonic Dialogues*, 1927) of 1778 is considered a statement of his political philosophy, his tract *Die Erziehung des Menschengeschlechts* (*The Education of the Human Race*, 1858) of 1780 is called his religious testament. Lessing regarded Freemasonry as a means to counterbalance the inevitable evils of the absolutist state. The goal of Freemasonry was to unite men regardless of nationality, religion, and class. Lessing did not advocate revolution but expected changes to bring about a republican form of government. In *The Education of the Human Race,* Lessing presented his religious convictions within the framework of a philosophy of history. He conceived history as the process of the immanent revelation of God, which leads humankind toward independence and self-determination. This work may be considered the seminal document of the modern philosophy of religion.

SIGNIFICANCE

Gotthold Ephraim Lessing has been declared "the founder of German literature" by H. B. Garland. In 1750, when Lessing began his career, German literature was provincial and practically unknown in Europe. By 1781, when Lessing died, German literature had achieved world acclaim. As a theologian, Lessing defended religion against mysticism as well as rationalism. He became the most prominent spokesman and practitioner of religious and racial tolerance of his age. As the founder of the philosophy of religion, Lessing's ideas contributed toward the concept of the death of God long before Friedrich Nietzsche.

The most characteristic elements of Lessing's personality were his independence of mind, common sense, and integrity. These qualities made him, according to Garland, "the most admirable figure in the history of German thought and literature between Martin Luther and Nietzsche."

—Ehrhard Bahr

FURTHER READING

Allison, Henry E. *Lessing and the Enlightenment: His Philosophy of Religion and Its Relation to Eighteenth-Century Thought.* Ann Arbor: University of Michigan Press, 1966. An intellectual history of the philosophies of John Locke, Pierre Bayle, Baruch Spinoza, and Gottfried Leibniz and their impact on Lessing. Includes notes and index.

Batley, Edward M. *Catalyst of Enlightenment, Gotthold Ephraim Lessing: Productive Criticism of Eighteenth-Century Germany.* New York: P. Lang, 1990. Examines Lessing's efforts to advance the ideas of the Enlightenment, placing his efforts within the social, cultural, and political climate of eighteenth century Germany. Recounts his life and explains how his work reflected his concern for humankind and belief in the right to free speech and thought.

Brown, F. Andrew. *Gotthold Ephraim Lessing*. New York: Twayne, 1971. This biography discusses Lessing's works with references to scholarly works. Includes a selected bibliography, with annotations for individual titles, and an index.

Fisher, Barbara, and Thomas C. Fox, eds. *A Companion to the Works of Gotthold Ephraim Lessing.* Columbia, S.C.: Camden House, 2005. Collection of essays designed for graduate students and scholars. The essays analyze Lessing's life, the full range of his work, his contribution to Jewish emancipation, and his reception by twentieth century critics.

Garland, H. B. *Lessing: The Founder of German Literature.* 2d ed. London: Macmillan, 1962. Best summary before Brown's biography appeared. Includes a one-page bibliographical note and an index.

Lamport, F. J. *Lessing and the Drama.* Oxford, England: Clarendon Press, 1981. A study of Lessing's practice and theory of dramatic writing. Includes a bibliography and an index.

Metzger, Michael M. *Lessing and the Language of Comedy.* The Hague, the Netherlands: Mouton, 1966. A study of Lessing's theory of comedy and discussion of individual works. Includes a bibliography of sources consulted and an index.

Robertson, J. G. *Lessing's Dramatic Theory: Being an Introduction to and Commentary on His "Hamburgische Dramaturgie."* Edited by Edna Purdie. Cambridge, England: Cambridge University Press, 1939. Exhaustive study of Lessing's predecessors and sources.

Ugrinsky, Alexej, ed. *Lessing and the Enlightenment.* New York: Greenwood Press, 1986. Scholarly essays on current trends in Lessing studies. Numerous bibliographical notes, including an index of names.

See also: Johann Wolfgang von Goethe; Moses Mendelssohn; Friedrich Schiller.

Related articles in *Great Events from History: The Eighteenth Century, 1701-1800*: 1742: Fielding's *Joseph Andrews* Satirizes English Society; 1751-1772: Diderot Publishes the *Encyclopedia*; July 27, 1758: Helvétius Publishes *De l'esprit*; January, 1759: Voltaire Satirizes Optimism in *Candide*; August, 1763-April, 1765: David Garrick's European Tour; July, 1764: Voltaire Publishes *A Philosophical Dictionary for the Pocket*; 1773: Goethe Inaugurates the Sturm und Drang Movement; 1781: Kant Publishes *Critique of Pure Reason*; 1782-1798: Publication of Rousseau's *Confessions*; April 27, 1784: First Performance of *The Marriage of Figaro*.

LEVNI
Turkish painter

A court painter for the Ottoman sultan, Levni was responsible for illustrating the Surname-i Vehbi, *a manuscript produced around 1720 to record royal circumcision festivities. The more than one hundred illustrations he produced for the work are a crowning achievement of late Ottoman painting.*

Born: Unknown; Edirne, Ottoman Empire (now in Turkey)

Died: 1732; Constantinople, Ottoman Empire (now Istanbul, Turkey)

Also known as: Abdulcelil Celebi (birth name); Abdulcelil Levni; Ressam Levni

Areas of achievement: Art, patronage of the arts

EARLY LIFE

Born Abdulcelil Celebi, the artist known as Levni (lehv-NIH) was born and raised in Edirne, which was the second Ottoman capital and the preferred residence of the sultans during the late seventeenth and early eighteenth centuries. Little is known about Levni's early life and education. The only contemporary account appears in a history published in 1734-1735 by Demetrius Cantemir, a resident at the Ottoman court between 1701 and 1710. A later account is found in the *Mecmua-i Tevarih* (1765-1787; compendium of histories) by Hafiz Huseyin Ayvansarayi.

The Ottoman sultan Mustafa II (r. 1695-1703) was most likely Levni's first patron. However, Levni's career is more closely associated with Mustafa's brother, Ahmed III, whose reign between the years 1703 and 1730 is known as the Tulip Period in reference to his preoccupation with the flower. Ahmed III brought Levni with him when he moved the royal court to Constantinople in 1718. Upon his arrival, Levni entered the Ottoman *nakkashane*, or royal design workshop, where he began to work as an apprentice. According to Ayvansarayi, Levni excelled initially at the classical art of *saz*, a decorative style comprising abstract foliage and fantastic creatures. He later became interested in more representational and realistic forms of painting when he aspired to become a portraitist.

Sometime between 1700 and 1710, Levni left his signature on a portrait of Mustafa II in the *Silsilename* of Seyyid Muhammed, and in the following decade he signed twenty-two of the images in a well-preserved *murakka*, or album of figurative paintings. The compositional schemes and figural types in both of these early works are highly conservative. Levni achieved his mature style, however, in a series of paintings made for a manuscript of the *Surname-i Vehbi*, a festival book produced around 1720 to commemorate the circumcision of the sons of Amhed III. This, his crowning achievement, set a new standard for Ottoman painting in the eighteenth century. Levni's virtuoso technique, his ability to create dramatic movement on the two-dimensional surface, and the clarity of his scenes remained unsurpassed in paintings by his contemporaries.

LIFE'S WORK

Levni's patron, Ahmed III, was a sensitive ruler with a cultivated artistic sense. Like many of his predecessors, he composed poetry and practiced calligraphy. Under his leadership, Constantinople underwent a cultural renaissance in the early eighteenth century, and the revival of painting under Levni may be seen as one component of a broader revitalization that also included such arts as ceramics, metalwork, textiles, and horticulture. Levni's singular achievement halted the decline of illustrated manuscripts that had become notable after 1650 and stimulated what is frequently described as a second classical age of painting at the Ottoman court.

Levni appears to have held an elevated status in Ahmed's court, for his title Celebi is an honorific given to gentlemen, scholars, and princes. In addition, the artist portrayed himself as a participant in the festival, riding in close proximity to the officials of the Enderun (the inner service of the palace) during the circumcision parade. Verses written by Levni have been preserved in the Topkapi Palace Museum, corroborating Ayvansarayi's statement that he was a poet as well as a painter and suggesting that the artist belonged to the class of literati.

The subject of Levni's visual masterpiece is a festival that took place over fifteen days and nights. While the entire program of the event was recorded by the poet Vehbi in the *Surname-i Vehbi*, it is clear that Levni's illustrations reflect the artist's own firsthand account of the ceremonies. His paintings capture the colors and bustling activity of the proceedings and detail their chief protagonists and architectural settings. Moreover, the illustrations leave an invaluable record of Istanbul at the beginning of the eighteenth century. They provide a rare sociological account of ceremonial practices under Ahmed III, when the Ottoman court was caught up in the prevailing trend for elaborate festivals. Among its many descriptive images of contemporary architecture, Levni's *Surname-i Vehbi* contains the only extant visual record of the painting workshop, from which the sultan is shown watching the circumcision procession. The workshop is shown as a two-storied structure with shuttered windows and a tiled revetment on its lower facade.

With one exception, the paintings in the *Surname-i Vehbi* are spread over double folios. Each figure in the illustrations is presented individually and identified, yet the compositions successfully reconstruct the progression of events during the festival. Unlike Levni's earlier works, which presented single figures, the *Surname-i Vehbi* maintains a narrative structure, in which an abundance of figures move through space and time in distinct relationship to one another.

Although in many cases Levni followed pictorial formulae established during the sixteenth century, his work bears an individual quality that renders it distinct from that of earlier or contemporary artists. He employed a variety of narrative techniques within the manuscript. In some cases, he used wide-angle compositions, and in others he chose close-up views. By alternating unique compositions with more repetitive units, Levni invigorated the progression of scenes in the book, and he devised an innovative technique for re-creating the continuous movement of parades. In a handful of double folios, Levni extended his narrative not only across two facing pages but also onto the following spread. In addition, by breaking groups of figures at one page's edge, Levni sought to maintain continuity as his viewers turned the book's folios.

Levni's accomplishments extend to his virtuoso brushwork and unique use of color. His brush strokes not only delineate forms but also create texture, shading, and volume. By comparison with the bright primary colors that typify earlier Ottoman painting, Levni's palette is subdued, incorporating olive greens, golden browns, rust, and beige. The subtlety of his palette and his use of metallic pigments to create shimmering highlights contribute an expressive style that was unprecedented in Ottoman painting. Unfortunately, Levni's *Surname-i Vehbi* does not have a colophon, and as a result the exact date of its completion and presentation to the sultan are not known. Levni died in 1732 and was buried in the neighborhood of the Ortakcilar Mosque in Constantinople. His manuscripts were originally housed in the library built by Ahmed III in 1718 in the third court of the Topkapi

Sarayi. Later, when the Topkapi Sarayi became a museum, they were moved to the Mosque of the Agas, near the palace's harem.

SIGNIFICANCE

Under the patronage of Sultan Ahmed III in Constantinople, Levni revived the *nakkashane* and stimulated a second classical age of manuscript painting at the Ottoman court—an era that extended into the middle of the eighteenth century. His influence is witnessed in a second copy of the *Surname-i Vehbi* made by the members of his studio several years later. Although they display a cruder manner of execution, the paintings in the later book mimic the compositional schemes, figurative groupings, and pictorial movements invented by Levni.

Levni's version of the *Surname-i Vehbi* stands out not only as a masterpiece of Ottoman painting but also as the last great illustrated Ottoman manuscript. By the mid-eighteenth century, as Ottoman ambassadors were sent to Paris and Vienna, royal painting would begin to be infused with elements drawn from Western European art, bringing to an end the second classical age of Ottoman painting.

—*Anna Sloan*

FURTHER READING

Atasoy, Nurhan, and Filiz Cagman. *Turkish Miniature Painting*. Istanbul: R. C. D. Cultural Institute, 1974. Good general survey of painting's development under the Ottoman sultans. Contains information on the royal library and workshop. Illustrated.

Atil, Esin. *Levni and the "Surname": The Story of an Eighteenth-Century Ottoman Festival*. Istanbul: Koçbank, 1999. The premier source on the artist and his manuscript. Provides reproductions of the *Surname-i Vehbi*'s illustrated folios alongside detailed descriptions of their content.

_____, ed. *Turkish Art*. Washington, D.C.: Smithsonian Institution Press, 1980. A good introduction to art of the Ottoman period, with a concise essay on the arts of book illustration.

Blair, Sheila S., and Jonathan Bloom. *The Art and Architecture of Islam, 1250-1800*. New Haven, Conn.: Yale University Press, 1994. Detailed survey of Islamic arts and architecture, with a chapter on Ottoman book arts. Contains illustrations and a complete list of bibliographic sources.

Hillenbrand, Robert. *Islamic Art and Architecture*. London: Thames and Hudson, 1999. Survey of Islamic art forms, with a chapter on the Ottomans and relevant bibliography.

Unver, Suheyl. *Levni*. Istanbul: Turkish Press, 1951. A concise monograph on the artist, with biographical detail and illustrations.

See also: Ahmed III; Mahmud I.

Related articles in *Great Events from History: The Eighteenth Century, 1701-1800*: 1718-1730: Tulip Age; December 10, 1768: Britain's Royal Academy of Arts Is Founded; 1787: David Paints *The Death of Socrates*.

CAROLUS LINNAEUS
Swedish botanist

Linnaeus created a new classification system for all of nature, establishing in the process the modern binomial system of nomenclature for organisms.

Born: May 23, 1707; Råshult, Småland, Sweden
Died: January 10, 1778; Uppsala, Sweden
Also known as: Carl Linnaeus; Carl von Linné
Areas of achievement: Biology, science and technology

EARLY LIFE

The father of Carolus Linnaeus (KAR-uh-luhs luh-NEE-uhs) adopted the name Linné and the Latin form, Linnaeus, while studying for the ministry. Ordained in 1704 at the age of thirty, the minister married Christina Brodersonia, the daughter of the vicar of Stenbrohult. In addition to his pastoral duties, Nils Linné was an enthusiastic gardener and was particularly knowledgeable about herbs. Carolus Linnaeus, his eldest son, was born on May 23, 1707, and soon exhibited an avid interest in botany. As a young child, Linnaeus enjoyed taking nature walks with his father and developed a firsthand knowledge and appreciation of plant and animal life.

School, however, was not enjoyable for the younger Linnaeus, and his only successes came in the physical and mathematical subjects. He had tremendous powers of observation, and in his four autobiographies he often commented on his own "brown, quick, sharp eyes." His physics teacher, Johan Rothman, recognizing Linnaeus's penchant for empiricism, encouraged him by giving him Hermann Boerhaave's and Joseph Pitton de Tournefort's works to read. At Rothman's urging, Linnaeus's parents agreed to send him to medical school. In 1727, at the age of twenty, he went to southern Sweden and entered the University of Lund, but he transferred the following year to the University of Uppsala, which not only was nearer his home but also had a reputation for higher standards. His knowledge of botany and understanding of nature soon brought him to the attention of Olof Celsius, a theology professor and dean, who took him into his home.

While still an undergraduate, Linnaeus conducted research on the reproductive structures of plants, gave lectures on botany (attracting large audiences), and received travel grants to collect materials for research on both natural materials and human customs and habits. During one of these trips, he met his future wife, Sara Elisabeth Moraea, the daughter of the wealthy town physician of Falun. Linnaeus was granted permission to marry her (and thus have access to her father's wealth) on the condition that he go to the Netherlands to obtain the degree of doctor of medicine, a degree not then available in Sweden. Linnaeus went to the small and not-too-rigorous university in Harderwijk, where he took his doctor's degree in a few weeks. He then went to Amsterdam and Leiden, where he met a number of noted scientists, and through these contacts was able to secure the patronage necessary to continue his research. During the three years he spent in the Netherlands, he published the work for which he is best known, *Systema naturae* (1735; *A General System of Nature: Through the Three Grand Kingdoms of Animals, Vegetables, and Minerals*, 1800-1801).

Linnaeus returned to Sweden, married Sara, tried to establish a medical practice in Stockholm, and became increasingly disillusioned with medicine as a career. Finally, in 1741, he was named professor of botany at Uppsala. His fame spread, and he attracted students from many countries to join him in identifying new species and classifying them. The period of the late 1740's to the 1750's was the apogee of his career.

LIFE'S WORK

Linnaeus was interested in a wide range of topics in natural history, but his primary interest was classification. His goal was to produce a system by which one could correctly identify organisms, and his method was to use the common Aristotelian technique of downward classification. This method involved taking a class of objects, dividing it into two groups (for example, the class of

living organisms can be divided into animals and non-animals), and continuing the process of dichotomous divisions until only the lowest set, the species, which could not be further divided, remained. Such a system was highly artificial, since the basis for many of the divisions was arbitrary. Based on his philosophical and theological commitment to the argument from design, however, Linnaeus believed that if the correct character was chosen as the basis of division, natural relationships would be revealed. In his characteristically arrogant manner, he claimed to have discovered that correct trait and built his system around it. He called it his "sexual system."

Linnaeus first presented his ideas in *A General System of Nature*. In its first edition, the book contained only about a dozen pages and presented what Linnaeus referred to as a natural system. His only taxonomic groupings at this stage were class, genus, and species. In this work, he accepted the ideas of earlier taxonomists that species, which he took as the starting point for his system, were immutable and that each one had been created at the beginning of time. Moreover, he believed that every species must be strictly intermediate between two other species in order to maintain the plenitude of the chain of being.

Carolus Linnaeus. (Library of Congress)

Plants were assigned to a particular species based on the number and position of their reproductive parts (hence the term "sexual system"). Four elementary criteria were used to classify a plant: number, shape, proportion, and situation. Thus, to assign a plant to a particular species, one counted the number of stamens (the pollen-bearing male organs) and pistils (the female organs), examined them to see if they were separated or fused, compared relative size, determined their position vis-à-vis each other and the other flower parts, and found out whether both male and female elements were on the same flower. Species that had obvious similarities were brought together into a higher-level grouping labeled "genus"; similar genera were grouped into classes. Linnaeus believed that only the first two categories—species and genus—were natural ones, with higher division existing only as an artificial aid for the ordering of nature.

Since the primary purpose of a classification system, as far as Linnaeus was concerned, was to allow one to know the plants, that is, to be able to name them quickly and accurately, it did not matter if the system mixed natural and artificial categories. The value of the Linnaean system was that any botanist who learned a few parts of a flower and fruit could come to the same decision as to its name that Linnaeus did. This value was quickly recognized and greatly appreciated given the state of plant taxonomy at that time. It is estimated that in 1600, a total of approximately six thousand plants had been recognized; by 1700, an additional twelve thousand plants had been discovered. It was therefore crucial to know what a plant was and to what group of plants it belonged. Linnaeus immediately became famous for the way in which he solved these problems. His victory was complete when Bernard de Jussieu, the leader of French botany, declared in 1739 that the Linnaean system was preferable to that of the Frenchman Tournefort.

Linnaeus was not content with his first attempt. He published *Fundamenta botanica* (1736; foundation of botany) the following year and *Classes plantarum* (1738; classes of plants) two years later. Including *A General System of Nature,* which went through ten revisions by 1758, these works contain the basis of all the essential changes that Linnaeus would bring to systematics. By the tenth edition of *A General System of Nature,* which had grown to two volumes and 1,384 pages, Linnaeus had added the category "order" above class, and he recognized twenty-four classes of plants. The number of pistils determined the order to which the plant was assigned, while the number of stamens determined the class. Moreover, he had begun to use the only two

natural categories—genus and species—as the basis for naming plants.

The contribution for which he is best known, the binomial system of nomenclature, was first articulated in *Species plantarum* (1753; species of plants), in which Linnaeus himself classified more than eight thousand plants from all over the world. Yet Linnaeus viewed the binomial system as only a minor modification and outgrowth of his sexual system. Having assigned an organism to a particular genus and species as a result of the characteristics of the reproductive organs, he suggested using the Latinized names of the genus and species together to identify a specific plant. This reform is currently viewed as his most lasting contribution to biology, for it could be retained even when the specific Linnaean system of classification was rejected in favor of one acknowledging phylogenetic relationships.

During his later years, Linnaeus was increasingly plagued by poor health. He suffered from migraine headaches, rheumatism, fevers, and bouts of depression. In 1761, he was ennobled and appointed a member of the Swedish House of Lords. In 1774, he suffered the first of a series of stroke-like attacks, which he called his "message of death." A second attack in 1778 left him totally incapacitated, and he died in the early winter of that year. A family quarrel between his widow and daughters, on one side, and his son, on the other, over possession of his library, herbarium, and papers was finally settled in favor of his son, who died shortly after the arrangements were completed. Linnaeus's widow then sold the collection to a London physician, J. E. Smith, who, along with two friends, founded the Linnean Society, the organization that would become famous for first receiving the papers of Alfred Russell Wallace and Charles Darwin on their theory of evolution by natural selection.

SIGNIFICANCE

Peter J. Bowler described Linnaeus's goal for his work very well when he wrote:

> If the species were created by God, one could assume that a rational Creator would have formed the world according to a meaningful order that man himself could hope to understand. Linnaeus believed that he had been privileged to see the outline of the Creator's plan and his efforts to represent it would become the basis of a new biology.

In fact, his "new biology" was more adapted to botany than to zoology. With his system, he was personally able to classify more than eighteen thousand species of plants.

His attempts to classify animals, however, created duplications and confusion, primarily because he could not find a characteristic that would work for animals the way reproductive structures did for plants. His inclination to classify everything can also be seen in his attempts to classify diseases, humans, and even botanists.

Linnaeus should not be regarded as merely a taxonomist. His essays and lectures provide evidence that he was exploring ideas that would now be considered basic to ecology and biogeography. He sought to develop, within both a theological and biological context, a concept of the harmony of nature. Finally, he tried not to allow his philosophical or theological positions to blind him to his data. As a result of his evidence, he revised his views on fixity of species to allow for a kind of evolution—formation of new species by hybridization—below the genus level.

—*Sara Joan Miles*

FURTHER READING

Blunt, Wilfrid. *The Compleat Naturalist: A Life of Linnaeus.* New ed. Princeton, N.J.: Princeton University Press, 2001. Originally published in 1971, some critics consider this the definitive biography. Blunt recounts Linnaeus's life and work, quoting from Linnaeus's writings and placing his botanical discoveries within the context of eighteenth century Enlightenment thought. Contains an appendix describing Linnaean classification, and two hundred illustrations, including some eighteenth century botanical drawings.

Bowler, Peter J. *Evolution: The History of an Idea.* Berkeley: University of California Press, 1984. Bowler traces the interactions of philosophy, natural history, and taxonomic systems to show their effects on the concepts of species and species change. He furnishes an excellent context for Linnaeus and shows the effect of his work on future evolutionary ideas.

Fara, Patricia. *Sex, Botany, and Empire: The Story of Carl Linnaeus and Joseph Banks.* New York: Columbia University Press, 2004. Despite its title, the book focuses more on Banks and Linnaeus than on sex and botany, describing how Linnaeus developed a system to classify organisms and how Banks, who never met Linnaeus, popularized the classification system.

Frängsmyr, Tore, ed. *Linnaeus: The Man and His Work.* Berkeley: University of California Press, 1983. This edited collection of works by Swedish scholars describes the personality of Linnaeus and examines his contributions to botany, geology, and human anthro-

pology. It also looks at him as a Swedish national hero, trying to understand the difference between the man and his works, and the myth which has developed.

Gardner, Eldon J. *History of Biology.* 3d ed. Minneapolis, Minn.: Burgess, 1972. The chapter "Systematizers of Plants and Animals" describes the various pre-Linnaean systems of classification, the contributions of Linnaeus (including a minimum amount of biographical material), and the post-Linnaean strategies with respect to taxonomy. There are helpful chronological and reference sections at the end of the chapter.

Gilbert, Bil. "The Obscure Fame of Carl Linnaeus." *Audubon* 86 (September, 1984): 102-114. This relatively short article gives personal glimpses of Linnaeus while discussing his many scientific contributions. It does not analyze the strengths and weaknesses of his works, but it does create a good introduction to his ideas and the intellectual environment in which he worked.

Hankins, Thomas. *Science and the Enlightenment.* New York: Cambridge University Press, 1985. The last third of chapter 5 is an excellent introduction to the philosophical commitments underlying eighteenth century taxonomy, showing how Linnaeus was both a product of his time and an innovator. The bibliography for the chapter provides the serious reader with several references dealing with specific issues concerning Linnaeus's system.

Mayr, Ernst. *The Growth of Biological Thought: Diversity, Evolution, and Inheritance.* Cambridge, Mass.: Harvard University Press, 1982. Mayr's treatment of Linnaeus places his work within the context of other naturalists, making clear the extent to which Linnaeus depended on other ideas and the degree to which his work was original.

Weinstock, John, ed. *Contemporary Perspectives on Linnaeus.* Lanham, Md.: University Press of America, 1985. This series of essays covers a number of aspects of Linnaeus's work, including his relationship to Scholasticism, his impact on the development of evolutionary theory and the impact of evolutionary ideas on Linnaean taxonomy, the connection between Linnaeus's theology and his understanding of ecological relationships and the problem of extinction, his anthropology, and his status as a Swedish folk hero.

See also: Sir Joseph Banks; Comte de Buffon; Lazzaro Spallanzani.

Related articles in *Great Events from History: The Eighteenth Century, 1701-1800*: 1714: Fahrenheit Develops the Mercury Thermometer; Beginning 1735: Linnaeus Creates the Binomial System of Classification; 1742: Celsius Proposes an International Fixed Temperature Scale; 1745: Lomonosov Issues the First Catalog of Minerals; 1749-1789: First Comprehensive Examination of the Natural World; 1751: Maupertuis Provides Evidence of "Hereditary Particles"; 1786-1787: Lavoisier Devises the Modern System of Chemical Nomenclature.

ANTÔNIO FRANCISCO LISBOA
Brazilian artist and architect

Lisboa, noted for his skilled technique, his harmonizing aesthetic, and the singular sensitivity and expressiveness of his work, was a preeminent Brazilian High Baroque sculptor for and designer of churches and their interiors. At around age thirty, Lisboa began suffering from a disease—possibly leprosy—that severely limited his movements and then partially paralyzed him, but his pain and disability did not stop him from producing his most intense and expressive artwork.

Born: c. 1738; Vila Rica (now Ouro Preto), Brazil
Died: November 18, 1814; Vila Rica, Brazil
Also known as: Aleijadinho
Areas of achievement: Art, architecture

EARLY LIFE

Antônio Francisco Lisboa (lees-BOH-ah) was the son of a Portuguese-born architect, Manuel Francisco da Costa Lisboa, and an African slave named Isabel. At baptism he received his father's surname and was manumitted, which allowed him to become a free laborer. However, manumission did not allow him to inherit his father's property.

Lisboa developed his style while obliquely aware of European techniques, adapting these to Brazilian materials and conditions. Of mixed race, typical for colonial artisans, Lisboa received his apprenticeship from his European-trained father, who was among the noted architects of the region. Like so many other skilled Portuguese artisans, his father had emigrated to wealthy provinces of Brazil to advance his career. Lisboa learned drawing and carving from artists who collaborated with his father.

LIFE'S WORK

The life and work of Antônio Francisco Lisboa are often divided into two phases. The start of the first phase began with the appearance in 1777 of the symptoms of a disabling disease, which may have been leprosy. After 1777 his deformities and pain increased, together with the singularly expressive nature of his artistic work. The date also marks a transformation in his personality, from an effulgent, bohemian character to one that was ever more introverted and morose. His productivity, nonetheless, was intense and resolute. As his disease progressed, he lost the use of his extremities, so he had to be carried about by his slaves, who also secured sculpting instruments to his hands. His sobriquet, Aleijadinho, which came from this period, means "little cripple," from the Portuguese word *aleijado* for "crippled" with the diminutive suffix *inho*.

Lisboa worked primarily and initially in Vila Rica, the capital of the captaincy of Minas Gerais. The name of the city changed to Ouro Preto after Brazil's independence in 1822. As Lisboa's fame grew, he and his staff were called to surrounding towns. He worked mainly in wood, principally cedar, and soapstone (*pedra de sabão*). He was sensitive to the unattractiveness of his deformities and to his status as someone of illegitimate birth and mixed race. However, his talent was frankly admitted and keenly sought by his contemporaries.

It is sometimes difficult to authenticate his works because others copied him as his fame spread. Moreover, Lisboa worked in teams with others artists, and the works were not individually signed. (Billing receipts are a common way of authenticating works.) As his physical disabilities increased, he trained his slaves to carve for him, following his instructions.

Of the hundreds of statues, altars, pulpits, fonts, communion rails, and choral balustrades that Lisboa produced, he is most noted for his work on the church of São Francisco de Assis in Ouro Preto and the pilgrimage complex in a neighboring town, Congonhas do Campo. His work at the former, an icon of the Brazilian Baroque, occurred in various stages from the late 1760's until the early 1790's. He carved the wooden ceiling vault and stone pulpits, designed the main entrance, and later carved the sanctuary backdrop. His work at Congonhas occurred in two stages. From 1795 to 1799, working in wood, he produced six sanctuaries or chapels with scenes of the Way of the Cross (Via Sacra). From 1800 to 1805, working in stone, he produced statues of twelve prophets. Virtually all his work can be found in places designated as world heritage sites by the United Nations Educational, Scientific, and Cultural Organization (UNESCO).

His church interiors possess a unity of composition and refinement of detail that convey the triumph and glory of faith and devotion. They hold a sense of robust and serene assurance. The arches and overhead sculpture of the main doorways are elaborate. However, they are contrasted and balanced by an immediate surrounding area that is bare and simple. This counterpoint of rich and spare produces a feeling of stark benevolence and dignified authority.

The stone and wooden statuary at the architectural complex at the basilica of Bom Jesus de Matosinhos in Congonhas do Campo are Lisboa masterworks and are expressive testaments to his acute suffering and austere spirituality. The basilica complex followed a pattern typical of similar pilgrimage sites in Catholic Europe. Entering the complex, pilgrims followed an ascending path, often on their knees, to the terrace of the church, as if accompanying Jesus on the path of his crucifixion on Mount Calvary. Along the path were six chapels holding life-size painted figures carved in cedar wood that portrayed the Way of the Cross.

The statues were extraordinarily natural and became increasingly moving as individuals progressed along the route. Lisboa absorbingly conveyed numerous details, such as the veins of a hand, the muscles of a leg, or the drape of a robe. The first chapel contained a scene of the Last Supper, with Christ and the twelve apostles. Later scenes showed the flagellation of Jesus and his crowning with thorns, his suffering borne with subdued dignity (flagellation was well known in slave societies). The climactic scene was the Crucifixion, mounted in the sanctuary of the church above.

Completing the Via Sacra and ascending the steps to the church terrace, a pilgrim encountered stone statues of twelve prophets. The statues rose on pedestals along the sidewalls of the steps. Nearing these figures individually and observing their distinct faces and gestures, stark against the arching sky, a pilgrim was struck by their power: The serene firmness of their eyes and mouths,

and the steady urgency of their gestures. Their clothing presented a curious hybrid. They were dressed in boots, having come from afar with their messages, and wore Old Testament robes that hung like contemporary frocks, their heads crowned with imperious turbans. Each prophet declaimed with a charging intimacy. The head and all the body were forces behind a voice announcing the immediacy of God's word, echoed through these human instruments from the heavens above. The veracity of their word could not to be doubted because the messiah and savior of whom they had foretold, the pilgrim had just witnessed in the preceding scenes.

Lisboa's suffering in his later life is conveyed in his final works. He had only one son, whom he trained along with his slaves, to help him. In bed for the last two years of his life, he was nursed by his daughter-in-law, a midwife and the primary source of (oral) information about his life. Lisboa died on November 18, 1814, and is buried in one of the principal churches of Ouro Preto, which also houses the Aleijadinho Museum. The city itself is a still-living monument of his work.

SIGNIFICANCE

Antônio Francisco Lisboa represents the culmination of Baroque artistic activity in Brazil. In Brazil this movement lasted throughout the colonial period, from the sixteenth century to the eighteenth century. The height of the phenomenon occurred in the gold and diamond mining province of Minas Gerais (general mines) during the eighteenth century. The movement was essentially a "counter-reformation"; that is, the Brazilian Baroque sought to intensify Catholic devotion. Therefore, the intense cultural activity of Minas Gerais in music, poetry, architecture, painting, and sculpting occurred within a religious, though nonetheless quite worldly, environment. The building of richly decorated churches asserted social status. Moreover, it helped to expiate for sins committed in the libertine frontier environment.

—Edward A. Riedinger

FURTHER READING

Hogan, James. "Antônio Francisco Lisboa, 'O Aleijadinho': An Annotated Bibliography." *Latin American Research Review* 2, no. 2 (1974): 83-94. A review of the literature on Lisboa, with nine pages of entries preceded by a brief essay.

_____. "The Contemporaries of Antônio Francisco Lisboa: An Annotated Bibliography." *Latin American Research Review* 16, no. 3 (1981): 138-145. Six pages of entries on the background period to Lisboa's work and the artists and craftsmen who collaborated with him; includes brief essays.

King, Catherine. *Views of Difference: Different Views of Art.* New Haven, Conn.: Yale University Press, 1999. A collection of articles on masterpieces of world art that includes an essay on Lisboa, examining his production both as sculptor and as architect and offering astute observations on his techniques and aesthetics.

Lukas, Gabriel. "Antonio Francisco Lisboa (O Aleijadinho), 1783-1814." Master's thesis, Columbia University, 1961. This unpublished master's thesis examines the later works of Lisboa as his art intensified because of his personal suffering.

Manguel, Alberto. *Reading Pictures: What We Think About When We Look at Art.* New York: Random House, 2002. Manguel examines the psychological aspects of various examples of narrative art, with one chapter focusing on "Aleijadinho: The Image as Subversion."

Mann, Graciela. *The Twelve Prophets of Aleijadinho.* Austin: University of Texas Press, 1967. A profusely illustrated publication with photographs, by Hans Mann, of Lisboa's works. One of the earliest books to introduce Lisboa to readers of English.

Sullivan, Edward J. *Brazil: Body and Soul.* New York: Harry N. Abrams, 2001. A richly illustrated catalog of a monumental exhibition of Brazilian art held at the Guggenheim Museum in New York City, highlighting the Baroque and modernist periods, framing Lisboa within the totality of Brazilian cultural history.

See also: Germain Boffrand; Francisco de Goya; Nicholas Hawksmoor; Giovanni Battista Tiepolo; Sir John Vanbrugh.

Related articles in *Great Events from History: The Eighteenth Century, 1701-1800:* 1715-1737: Building of the Karlskirche; 1726-1729: Voltaire Advances Enlightenment Thought in Europe; 1748: Excavation of Pompeii; 1748-1755: Construction of Istanbul's Nur-u Osmaniye Complex; 1762: *The Antiquities of Athens* Prompts Architectural Neoclassicism.

LITTLE TURTLE
American Indian military leader

Little Turtle united a coalition of American Indians in the Ohio Country to defeat the U.S. Army in a 1791 battle. Little Turtle's twelve hundred warriors, aided by the element of surprise, killed nearly one thousand U.S. soldiers and many of their wives, marking the largest single battlefield victory by an American Indian force in history.

Born: c. 1752; near Fort Wayne, Indiana
Died: July 14, 1812; Fort Wayne, Indiana
Also known as: Michikinikwa
Areas of achievement: Warfare and conquest, military

EARLY LIFE

Very little is known of Little Turtle's early life. It is likely, although not without contention, that he was born in present-day Whitley County, in northeastern Indiana. The name of Little Turtle's mother is unknown, but she was probably part Mohican. Little Turtle's father, Michikinikwa (the name Little Turtle inherited after his father's death), was a renowned war chief among the Miamis who played a major role in organizing his people in battles against the Iroquois to the east and the Sioux to the west during the eighteenth century.

Some accounts say that Little Turtle inherited from his father a network of alliances that covered much of Indiana and western Ohio. (Indeed, it was the elder Michikinikwa who was the first Miami to meet with European immigrants when he traveled in 1748 to Lancaster, Pennsylvania, to attend a treaty council.) Little Turtle would become a war chief of the Miamis—with alliances—because of his extraordinary personal abilities; under ordinary circumstances, the matriarchal nature of the culture would have prohibited a leadership role for him because his mother was not Miami.

LIFE'S WORK

In 1787, the hunting grounds that the Miamis and their allies had been guaranteed "in perpetuity" by the U.S. Congress were being invaded by Euro-American settlers. Little Turtle and his principal allies, the Shawnee Blue Jacket and the Delaware Buckongahelos, centered a military alliance in an attempt to stall the settlers' advance. This alliance first defeated a one-thousand-man force under Josiah Harmer during October, 1790. Harmer dispatched an advance force of 180 soldiers, which was drawn into a trap and annihilated. Harmer then dispatched 360 more men in an attempt to punish the American Indians. This force was drawn into a similar trap, in which about one hundred of them were killed. The remainder of Harmer's force then retreated to Fort Washington, on the present-day site of Cincinnati.

Harmer's defeat stunned the Army, whose commanders knew that the Old Northwest would remain closed to legal settlement as long as Little Turtle's alliance held. General Arthur St. Clair, who had served briefly as president of the Continental Congress during the middle 1780's, gathered an army of two thousand soldiers during the summer of 1791 and marched into the Ohio Country. About a quarter of the men deserted en route. To keep the others happy, St. Clair permitted about two hundred soldiers' wives to travel with them.

St. Clair's army was plagued by problems from the start, including the low quality of recruits (many of them were local militia and untrained volunteers), shoddy equipment, and other problems, including roughly nine hundred desertions and consistently wet weather. Tecumseh and other American Indian scouts spotted St. Clair's force long before the U.S. forces spotted the American Indians. Little Turtle's forces obtained support from several other indigenous nations in the area and were well supplied by British traders. Impatient with St. Clair's progress, on October 28, 1791, the American Indians broke camp and moved south to meet St. Clair's force in battle.

On November 4, 1791, Little Turtle and his allies lured St. Clair's forces into the same sort of trap that had defeated Harmer's smaller army near St. Mary's Creek, a tributary of the Wabash River. A total of 38 officers and 598 men died in the battle; 242 others were wounded, many of whom later died. Fifty-six women—soldiers' wives—also were killed, bringing the death toll to about 950, the largest defeat of a U.S. Army force during a single battle in all American Indian wars and a death toll higher, for example, than any inflicted on the United States by the British during the American Revolution. After the battle, St. Clair resigned his commission in disgrace.

Little Turtle was a military tactician of superior talents and intuition. He also was a sensitive man and a gentleman. He was revolted by the slaughter of St. Clair's forces and sought a negotiated peace after the battle, reasoning that the immigrant Americans would eventually overpower the Miamis and their allies because of their larger numbers and advantages in war-making technology. Little Turtle advocated negotiation from strength, but the majority of the Miamis whom he was leading dis-

agreed with him. Instead of negotiating, members of the alliance forced Little Turtle to resign; Blue Jacket assumed the primary leadership role. Those who supported Blue Jacket refused to cede land.

In 1794, "Mad" Anthony Wayne was dispatched with a fresh army, visiting the scene of St. Clair's debacle. According to Wayne, about five hundred skull bones lay in a space of 350 yards. The woods were strewn with skeletons, knapsacks, and other debris for five miles, artifacts of St. Clair's forces' pell-mell retreat. Little Turtle had more respect for Wayne than Harmer or St. Clair, calling him the chief who never sleeps. On August 29, 1794, Wayne's forces defeated the indigenous alliance at Fallen Timbers. On August 3, 1795, the American Indians gave up most of their land west of the Ohio River following the defeat by signing the Treaty of Greenville.

For almost two centuries, local historians placed the site of the Battle of Fallen Timbers along the Maumee River flood plain adjacent to what is now U.S. Highway 24 near Toledo, Ohio. A monument was erected at the site, even as American Indians contended that the battle had occurred a mile away in what is today a soybean field. In 1995, to settle the issue, G. Michael Pratt, an anthropology professor at Heidelberg College in Tiffin, Ohio, organized an archaeological dig in the soybean field. He organized teams that included as many as 150 people who excavated the site, which yielded large numbers of battlefield artifacts, indicating conclusively that the American Indian account of the site was correct.

Little Turtle spent the last years of his life in a house built for him by the U.S. government near the Eel River trading post. He died on July 14, 1812, at the Fort Wayne home of William Wells, near the junction of the St. Joseph River and St. Mary Creek. Little Turtle was buried with full military honors by Army officers, who knew his genius. William Henry Harrison, later a U.S. president and who had been an aide to Wayne and had later defeated Tecumseh, was among several nonindigenous speakers at Little Turtle's tribute.

SIGNIFICANCE

As Euro-American immigration began to explode across the Appalachians into the Ohio Valley and Great Lakes region around 1790, American Indian resistance expressed itself in attempts at confederation along lines of mutual interest. A confederation that included elements of the Shawnees, Delawares, Wyandots, Miamis, and Ottawas told representatives of the United States in 1790 that settlers were not to transgress beyond the Ohio River. Thousands of settlers were surging into the area, ignoring governmental edicts. The settlers, who were squatters in the eyes of the indigenous, sought military help after members of the American Indian confederacy began attacking their settlements.

For seventy-five years, from the "conspiracy" of Pontiac during the early 1760's to the defeat of Black Hawk during the 1830's, American Indians in the Old Northwest (roughly, the Ohio Valley northward and westward to the Great Lakes) formed confederations to protect their land against the rising tide of Euro-American immigration. The best-known alliance-builder was Tecumseh, who maintained that American Indian land was occupied and therefore "owned" in common and could not be sold or traded by individuals. Tecumseh assembled his alliance after the defeat of Little Turtle's alliance. After much suffering and struggle, both Little Turtle and Tecumseh were forced to surrender and sign away much of the Ohio Valley.

—*Bruce E. Johansen*

FURTHER READING

Carter, Harvey Lewis. *The Life and Times of Little Turtle: First Sagamore of the Wabash.* Urbana: University of Illinois Press, 1987. This biography of Little Turtle presents what is perhaps the most comprehensive portrait of his life.

Edel, Wilbur. *Kekionga!: The Worst Defeat in the History of the U.S. Army.* Westport, Conn.: Praeger, 1997. Edel considers the battles of Little Turtle and other American Indians in the context of the history of armed conflict between American Indians and the U.S. military, before, during, and after the revolutionary period. Chapter 2, "Native Americans Versus Settlers: A Continuing Confrontation," is an especially apt examination of this history.

Johansen, Bruce E. *Shapers of the Great Debate on Native Americans: Land, Spirit, and Power.* Westport, Conn.: Greenwood Press, 2000. Johansen examines the issue of American land "ownership," alliances between American Indian nations to ensure indigenous land sovereignty, and the ties between place and culture. Includes illustrations, bibliographical references, and an index.

Porter, C. Fayne. *Our Indian Heritage: Profiles of Twelve Great Leaders.* Philadelphia: Chilton, 1964. The profiles in this work place Little Turtle's life in the context of other notable American Indian leaders, including those, such as Tecumseh, who were influenced by his life.

Van Tine, Warren, and Michael Pierce, eds. *Builders of Ohio: A Biographical History.* Columbus: Ohio State University Press, 2003. A history of Ohio with a chapter on Little Turtle and Blue Jacket. Includes illustrations, bibliographical references, and an index.

Winger, Otho. *Last of the Miamis: Little Turtle.* Indianapolis, Ind.: Lawrence W. Shultz, 1935. A notable early biography of Little Turtle, which provided a foundation for the later work by Harvey Lewis Carter.

See also: Joseph Brant; Alexander McGillivray; Pontiac; Thanadelthur; Anthony Wayne.

Related articles in *Great Events from History: The Eighteenth Century, 1701-1800:* May 28, 1754-February 10, 1763: French and Indian War; October 5, 1759-November 19, 1761: Cherokee War; May 8, 1763-July 24, 1766: Pontiac's Resistance; May 24 and June 11, 1776: Indian Delegation Meets with Congress; October 22, 1784: Fort Stanwix Treaty; May 20, 1785: Ordinance of 1785; October 18, 1790-July, 1794: Little Turtle's War; August 20, 1794: Battle of Fallen Timbers; 1799: Code of Handsome Lake.